Rick Steves

BEST OF

EUROPE

Contents

Introduction

Big Ben, the Eiffel Tower, and the Roman Colosseum. Yodeling in the Alps, biking down cobblestone paths, and taking a canal ride under the stars. Michelangelo's *David* and "Mad" King Ludwig's castles. Sunny Riviera beaches, medieval German towns, and Spanish streets teeming with people after dark. Europe offers a rich smorgasbord of cultures: pasta and tapas, strudel and scones, Dutch pancakes and Swiss fondue, Parisian crêpes and Tuscan grapes.... Follow your tastes and sample a little of everything for an unforgettable trip.

To wrestle Europe down to a manageable size, this selective book features its top destinations—from powerhouse cities to sleepy towns and cliff-hanging villages.

To help you assemble your dream trip, I've included advice on what to see and do in each destination, plus how to connect destinations by car or train. Whether you have a week or a month for your trip, this book will show you the best that Europe has to offer.

England

London, a thriving metropolis, teems with world-class museums, monuments, churches, parks, palaces, markets, theaters, pubs, and double-decker buses.

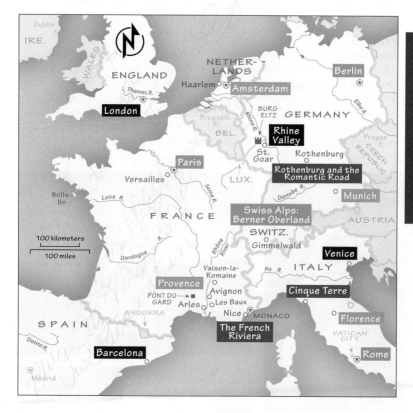

Spain

Barcelona is the center of Catalan culture, enlivened by people-friendly zones, a fun-to-explore old town, sandy beaches, and colorful works by native sons Gaudí, Picasso, and Miró.

France

Paris, the stylish world capital of food and culture, features the Eiffel Tower, grand boulevards, cutting-edge architecture, corner cafés, chic boutiques, and incomparable art at the Louvre and Orsay.

Provence is home to Arles (with Van Gogh sights and a Roman Arena), Avignon (with the famous bridge and brooding Palace of the Popes), the ancient Roman aqueduct of Pont du Gard, and the beautiful Côtes du Rhone wine road.

The French Riviera, a tempting stretch of sun-washed resorts, stars the elegant city of Nice, with its relaxed vibe, delicious seafood, and inviting beaches.

Italy

Rome is truly the Eternal City, studded with Roman remnants (Forum, Colosseum, Pantheon), floodlit-fountain squares, and the Vatican's Sistine Chapel.

Florence, the cradle of the Renaissance, offers the masterpiece-strewn Uffizi Gallery, Brunelleschi's dome-topped Duomo, Michelangelo's *David,* and Italy's best gelato.

The Cinque Terre consists of five idyllic Riviera hamlets along a rugged coastline, connected by hiking trails and dotted with vineyards and beaches.

Venice is a romantic island city, powerful in medieval times and famous for St. Mark's Basilica, the Grand Canal, and singing gondoliers.

Germany

Munich is a bustling city with a traffic-free center, excellent museums, Baroque palaces, stately churches, rowdy beer halls, and the beautiful English Garden.

Rothenburg, a medieval, half-timbered town encircled by a walkable wall, is the highlight of the Romantic Road route, linking time-passed towns in the lovely countryside.

The Rhine Valley stars a mighty river steeped in legend, lined with storybook villages and imposing castles.

Berlin has thought-provoking museums, gleaming architecture, and trendy nightlife, plus evocative sections of the Wall that once divided the city and country.

Switzerland

The **Swiss Alps'** best chunk is the **Berner Oberland,** featuring sky-high mountains, cliff-hanging villages, thundering waterfalls, scenic hikes, soaring lifts, and cogwheel train rides.

The Netherlands

Amsterdam is a progressive world capital with magnificent museums, dreamy canals, Golden-Age architecture, and the eye-opening Red Light District. Nearby Haarlem is a cozy, small-town home base alternative to big-city Amsterdam.

TRAVEL SMART

Approach Europe like a veteran traveler, even if it's your first trip. Design your itinerary, get a handle on your budget, make advance arrangements, and follow my travel strategies on the road. For advice on money, accommodations, transportation, and staying connected, see the Practicalities chapter. For cuisine tips, see each country's introduction.

Designing an Itinerary

Decide when to go. Peak season in much of Europe is June through September. For Spain and Italy, the best travel months are May, June, September, and October, which combine the convenience of peak season with pleasant weather (July and August can be sweltering along the Mediterranean). During peak season, it's best to reserve rooms well in advance, particularly in big cities. Throughout Europe, spring and fall generally have decent weather and lighter crowds. Winter can be cold and dreary, though big cities stay lively year-round.

As a general rule any time of year, the climate north of the Alps is mild (like Seattle), while south of the Alps it's like Arizona. If you wilt in the hot sun, avoid the Mediterranean in summer. If you want blue skies in the Swiss Alps and Britain, travel during the height of summer. (For climate specifics, see Wunderground.com.)

Choose your top destinations. The cosmopolitan cities of London and Paris are a must for anyone (and could merit a week apiece, if you've the time). Histori-

ans revel in Rome and romantics linger in Venice. If you'd like to storm some castles, explore the Rhine Valley. Art lovers are drawn to Florence's Renaissance treasures, and foodies savor France. Munich wins the award for the best beerhalls and oompah bands. For a mix of art, tapas, and irrepressible nightlife, experience Barcelona. Hikers make tracks to the Swiss Alps and Italy's Cinque Terre. To feel the pulse of 21st-century Germany, head to Berlin. Amsterdam, featuring Rembrandt, Anne Frank history, Van Gogh, and marijuana cafés, has something of interest for everyone. If medieval towns are your passion, walk the walls around Rothenburg. Beach baskers unroll their towels in the Cinque Terre, Barcelona, and the French Riviera. Photographers want to go everywhere.

Draft a rough itinerary. Figure out how many destinations you can comfortably fit in the time you have. Don't overdo it—few travelers wish they'd hurried more. Allow sufficient time per place. As a rough guideline, figure about three days for most major destinations and two days for smaller ones (take more time if you want to relax or explore). Any four or five of my recommended destinations (for example, London, Paris, the Rhine Valley, Swiss Alps, and Venice) would make a wonderful two-week trip. To reduce culture shock, start in London.

Staying in a home base—such as Arles, Munich, or Florence—and making day trips can be more time-efficient than changing locations and hotels. Minimize one-night stands, especially consecutive ones; it can be worth taking a late-afternoon drive or train ride to get settled into a town for two nights.

Connect the dots. Link your destinations into a logical route. Determine which cities in Europe you'll fly into and out of. Begin your search for flights at Kayak.com. Even if you fly into a cheap flight hub like Frankfurt, you don't need to begin your trip there (there's a handy train station at the airport). For a gentler

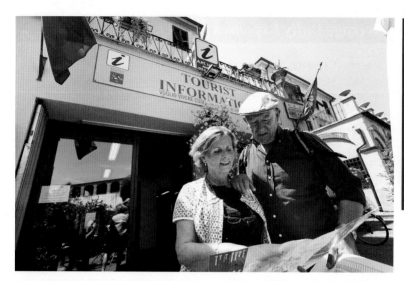

start to your trip, you could take a train to a nearby, smaller town for your first stop (such as a Rhine village).

Decide if you'll be traveling through Europe by car, public transportation, or a combination. Trains connect big cities easily and frequently. Regions that are rewarding to explore by car (such as Provence) have options for nondrivers, such as minibus tours, public transit, or taxis. A car is useless in cities.

Budget flights link many destinations. If your dream trip features Amsterdam, Rome, Berlin, and Barcelona, take planes instead of trains. To search for budget flights within Europe, try Skyscanner.com.

If you're on a tight budget, consider long-distance buses, which connect countries cheaply and slowly; Eurolines is one of several international companies.

Regardless of how you travel, allow at least a half-day to get between destinations. To determine the approximate length of train journeys, see the train chart in the Practicalities chapter (also check schedules at Bahn.com). For driving distances, try ViaMichelin.com.

Plan your days. Fine-tune your trip; write out a day-by-day plan of where you'll be and what you want to see. To help you make the most of your time, I've suggested day plans for destinations. But check the opening hours of sights; avoid visiting a town on the one day a week that your must-see sight is closed. Research whether any holidays or festivals will fall during your trip—these attract crowds and can close sights. For the latest, visit each country's national tourism website: VisitBritain.com, Us.France.fr, Germany. travel.com, Italia.it, Holland.com, Spain. info.com, and MySwitzerland.com.

Give yourself some slack. Nonstop sightseeing can turn a vacation into a blur. Every trip, and every traveler, needs downtime for doing laundry, picnic shopping, relaxing, people-watching, and so on. Pace yourself. Assume you will return.

Ready, set... You've designed the perfect itinerary for the trip of a lifetime.

Trip Costs per Person

Run a reality check on your dream trip. You'll have major transportation costs in addition to daily expenses.

Airfare: A basic round-trip flight from the US to Europe can cost about $1,000 to $2,000 total, depending on where you fly from and when (cheaper in winter). Save time in Europe by flying into one city

Average Daily Expenses Per Person: $160

Cost	Category	Notes
$45	Meals	$15 for lunch, $30 for dinner
$75	Lodging	Based on two people splitting the cost of a $150 double room that includes breakfast
$30	Sights and Entertainment	This daily average works for most people.
$10	City Transit	Buses or Metro
$160	Total	Allow about $200 for London, Paris, and the Swiss Alps.

and out of another (e.g., into London and out of Rome).

Car Rental: Figure on a minimum of $250 per week, not including tolls, gas, parking, and insurance. Weekly rentals are cheapest if arranged from the US. Note that some cities—especially in Italy—restrict or prohibit driving in the center. Italy and Spain technically require drivers to carry an International Driving Permit ($20 at AAA.com).

Public Transportation: Depending on your itinerary, it can be worthwhile to buy a rail pass to save money. For a Europe-wide trip, a Eurail pass is generally a good choice. Rail passes normally must be purchased outside of Europe; exceptions are German and Swiss passes, which can be purchased on site.

Keep in mind that many fast trains (such as France's TGV, and the Eurostar linking London, Paris, and Amsterdam) require seat assignments, and advance booking is strongly recommended (doable through RickSteves.com/rail).

Budget Tips: Cut your daily expenses by taking advantage of the deals you'll find throughout Europe and mentioned in this book.

Buying a city transit pass (for multiple rides or all-day use) lessens your cost per ride.

Avid sightseers get combo-tickets

or sightseeing passes (such as the Paris Museum Pass) that cover multiple museums. Or ask at sights if you're eligible for a discount, often available for youths (up to age 18), students (with proper I.D. cards, www.isic.org), families, and seniors, though some discounts apply only to citizens of the European Union.

Some businesses—especially hotels and walking-tour companies—offer discounts to my readers (look for the RS% symbol in the listings in this book).

Book your rooms directly with the hotel. Some hotels offer a discount if you pay in cash and/or stay three or more nights; check online or ask. And even seniors can sleep inexpensively in hostels (and some have double rooms). Or check Airbnb-type sites for deals.

It's easy to eat cheap in Europe. You can get tasty, affordable meals at cafeterias, local chain restaurants, and ethnic eateries.

Groceries are everywhere; cultivate the art of picnicking in atmospheric settings.

When you splurge, choose an experience you'll always remember, such as a concert, gondola ride, or alpine lift. Minimize souvenir shopping. Focus instead on collecting vivid memories, wonderful stories, and new friends.

Before You Go

You'll have a smoother trip if you tackle a few things ahead of time. For more information on these topics, see the Practicalities chapter, and check RickSteves.com for more travel tips and helpful travel talks.

Make sure your passport is valid. If it's due to expire within six months of your ticketed date of return, you need to renew it. Allow up to six weeks to renew or get a passport (www.travel.state.gov).

Arrange your transportation. Book your international flights. Figure out your main form of transportation within Europe. Consider whether to get a rail pass, order train tickets for longer trips (to get advance-purchase discounts), rent a car, or book cheap European flights. (You can wing it once you're there, but it may cost more.)

Book rooms well in advance, particularly if your trip falls during peak season or any major holidays or festivals.

Make reservations for major sights to avoid wasting time in lines. For example, you can reserve in advance for the Eiffel Tower in Paris, Florence's Uffizi Gallery, Barcelona's Sagrada Família, Amsterdam's Anne Frank House, and more (specifics are included in this book). Some sights require reservations, such as the Borghese Gallery in Rome.

Consider travel insurance. Compare the cost of the insurance to the cost of your potential loss. Check whether your existing insurance (health, homeowners, or renters) covers you and your possessions overseas.

Call your bank. Alert your bank that you'll be using your debit and credit cards in Europe. Ask about transaction fees, and get the PIN number for your credit card. You won't need to bring along any European cash for your trip; instead, withdraw the local currency from cash machines as you travel.

Use your smartphone smartly. Sign up for an international service plan to reduce your costs, or rely on Wi-Fi in Europe instead. Download any apps you'll want on the road, such as maps, transit schedules, translation, and Rick Steves Audio Europe (see sidebar).

Pack light. You'll walk with your luggage more than you think. Bring a single carry-on bag and a daypack. Use the packing checklist on page 1007 as a guide.

Travel Strategies on the Road

If you have a positive attitude, equip yourself with good information (this book), and expect to travel smart, you will.

∩ Stick This Guidebook in Your Ear!

My free Rick Steves Audio Europe app makes it easy for you to download my audio tours of many of Europe's top attractions and listen to them offline during your travels. For this book, my audio tours cover major sights in London, Paris, Berlin, Munich, the Rhine, Rothenburg, Rome, Venice, Florence, and Amsterdam. Sights covered by my audio tours are marked with this symbol: ∩. The app also offers insightful travel interviews from my public radio show with experts from Europe and around the globe. It's all free! You can download the app via Apple's App Store, Google Play, or Amazon's Appstore. For more info, see www.ricksteves.com/audioeurope.

Read—and reread—this book. To have an "A" trip, be an "A" student. Note the opening hours of sights, closed days, crowd-beating tips, and whether reservations are required or advisable. Check for any changes at RickSteves.com/update.

Be your own tour guide. As you travel, get up-to-date info on sights, reserve tickets and tours, reconfirm hotels and travel arrangements, and check transit connections. Find out the latest from tourist-information offices (TIs), your hoteliers, by checking online, or by phoning ahead. Upon arrival in a new town, lay the groundwork for a smooth departure; confirm the train, bus, or road you'll take when you leave.

Give local tours a spin. Your appreciation of a city or region and its history can increase dramatically if you take a walking tour in any big city or at a museum (some offer live or audio tours), or even hire a private guide (some will drive you around). If you want to learn more about any aspect of Europe, you're in the right place with experts happy to teach you.

Outsmart thieves. Pickpockets abound in crowded places where tourists congregate. Treat commotions as smokescreens for theft. Keep your cash, credit cards, and passport secure in a money belt tucked under your clothes; carry only a day's spending money in your front pocket. Don't set valuable items down on counters or café tabletops where they can be quickly stolen or easily forgotten.

To minimize potential loss, keep expensive gear to a minimum. Bring photocopies or take photos of important documents (passport and cards) to aid in replacement if they're lost or stolen.

Guard your time and energy. Taking a taxi can be a good value if it saves you a long wait for a cheap bus or an exhausting walk across town. To avoid long lines, take advantage of the crowd-beating tips in this book, such as visiting sights early or late, or reserving tickets in advance when possible.

Be flexible. Even if you have a well-planned itinerary, expect changes, closures, sore feet, drizzly days, and so on. Your Plan B could turn out to be even better. And when problems arise (a bad meal or a noisy hotel room), keep things in perspective. You're on vacation in Europe.

Connect with the culture. Interacting with locals carbonates your experience. Enjoy the friendliness of the European people. Ask questions—many locals are as interested in you as you are in them. Set up your own quest for the best dessert, grandest viewpoint, funniest sign, or the perfect sidewalk café. Slow down, step out of your comfort zone, and be open to unexpected experiences. When an interesting opportunity pops up, say "Yes!"

Hear the Swiss cowbells? Taste the beer-hall pretzel? Feel the magic of Venice? See the lights of the Eiffel Tower sparkling at night?

Your next stop. . .Europe!

Welcome to Rick Steves' Europe

Travel is intensified living—maximum thrills per minute and one of the last great sources of legal adventure. Travel is freedom. It's recess, and we need it.

I discovered a passion for European travel as a teen and have been sharing it ever since—through tours, my public television and radio shows, and travel guidebooks. Over the years, I've taught thousands of travelers how to best enjoy Europe's blockbuster sights—and experience "Back Door" discoveries that most tourists miss.

This book offers a balanced mix of the best of Europe's exciting cities and small-town getaways. It's selective: There are dozens of walled towns in Europe, but I've chosen only the most delightful: Rothenburg. And it's in-depth: My self-guided walks give insight into each city's vibrant history and today's living, breathing culture.

I advocate traveling simply and smartly. Take advantage of my money- and time-saving tips on sightseeing, transportation, and more. Try local, characteristic alternatives to expensive hotels and restaurants. In many ways, spending more money only builds a thicker wall between you and what you traveled so far to see.

We visit Europe to experience it—to become temporary locals. Thoughtful travel engages us with the world, as we learn to appreciate other cultures and new ways to measure quality of life.

Judging from the positive feedback I receive from my readers, this book will help you enjoy a fun, affordable, and rewarding vacation—whether it's your first trip or your tenth.

Happy travels!

Rick Steves

England

Hilly England occupies the lower two-thirds of the island of Great Britain (with Scotland in the north). England is the size of Louisiana (about 50,000 square miles), with a population of just over 55 million. England's ethnic diversity sets it apart from the rest of the United Kingdom: Nearly one in three citizens is not associated with the Christian faith. The cradle of the Industrial Revolution, today's Britain has little heavy industry—its economic drivers are banking, insurance, and business services, plus energy production and agriculture.

London is England's—and Great Britain's—cosmopolitan capital. For the tourist, London offers a little of everything associated with Britain: castles, cathedrals, royalty, theater, and tea.

CUISINE SCENE AT A GLANCE

British cooking embraces international influences and good-quality ingredients. It's easy to eat well here. Even in London, plenty of inexpensive choices are available.

Pub grub is the most atmospheric budget option. You'll usually get reasonably priced (£8-15), hearty lunches and dinners under ancient timbers. Meals are usually served 12:00-14:00 and 18:00-20:00—with a break in the middle. There's generally no table service. Order at the bar, then take a seat. Either they'll bring the food when it's ready, or you'll pick it up at the bar. Pay at the bar (sometimes when you order, sometimes after you eat). Don't tip unless it's a place with full table service. If you're on a tight budget, it's OK to share a meal.

Classier restaurants have some affordable deals. Lunch is usually cheaper than dinner; a top-end, £25-for-dinner restaurant often serves the same quality two courses as lunch deals for about half the price. Many restaurants have early-bird or pre-theater specials of two or three courses, often for significant savings, if you eat before 18:30 or 19:00; these deals may be offered daily or only on weekdays.

Ethnic restaurants add spice to England's cuisine. At Indian restaurants, an easy way to taste a variety of dishes is to order a *thali*—a sampler plate, generally served on a metal tray, with small servings of various specialties. Many Chinese and Thai places serve £6 meals and offer even cheaper takeaway boxes. Middle Eastern stands sell gyro sandwiches, falafel, and *shwarmas* (grilled meat in pita bread).

Chain restaurants abound, serving a variety of good-value meals, from sandwiches and salads (Pret à Manger, Le Pain Quotidien) and burgers (Byron) to sushi (Yo!, Wasabi, and Itsu), Indian (Masala Zone), Thai (Thai Square, Busaba Eathai), and more (Wagamama, Côte Brasserie, Ask, Pizza Express, Eat, and Loch Fyne Fish).

At **tearooms,** popular choices are a "cream tea," which consists of tea and a scone or two, or the pricier "afternoon tea," which comes with pastries and finger foods such as small, crust-less sandwiches. Two people can order one afternoon tea and one cream tea and share the afternoon tea's goodies.

Tipping: At pubs and places where you order at the counter, you don't have to tip. At restaurants and fancy pubs with waitstaff, tip about 10-12.5 percent. Most restaurants in London now add a 12.5 percent "optional" tip onto the bill. Tip only what you think the service warrants (if it isn't already added to your bill), and be careful not to tip double.

Other Budget Options: Fish-and-chips are a British classic; a takeaway box of fish-and-chips costs about £5-7. Grocery stores have inviting delis with good takeout food and sometimes sit-down eating. Good bets are the Marks & Spencer department stores, M&S Simply Food, and Sainsbury's Local.

London

A longtime tourist destination, London seems perpetually at your service, with an impressive slate of sights and entertainment. Blow through this urban jungle on the open deck of a double-decker bus and take a pinch-me-I'm-here walk through the West End. Hear the chimes of Big Ben and ogle the crown jewels at the Tower of London. Cruise the Thames River and take a spin on the London Eye. Hobnob with poets' tombstones in Westminster Abbey and rummage through civilization's attic at the British Museum.

London is also more than its museums and landmarks, it's a living, breathing, thriving organism...a coral reef of humanity. The city has changed dramatically in recent years: Many visitors are surprised to find how diverse and cosmopolitan it is. Chinese takeouts outnumber fish-and-chips shops. Eastern Europeans pull pints in British pubs, and Italians express your espresso. Outlying suburbs are home to huge communities of Indians and Pakistanis. This city of eight million separate dreams is learning—sometimes fitfully—to live as a microcosm of its formerly vast empire.

LONDON IN 4 DAYS

Day 1: Get oriented by taking my Westminster Walk from Big Ben to Trafalgar Square (stop in Westminster Abbey and the Churchill War Rooms on the way). Grab lunch near Trafalgar Square (maybe at the café at St. Martin-in-the-Fields Church), then visit the nearby National Gallery or National Portrait Gallery.

On any evening: Have an early-bird dinner and take in a play in the West End or at Shakespeare's Globe. Choose from a concert, walking tour, or nighttime bus tour. Extend your sightseeing into the evening hours; some attractions stay open late. Settle in at a pub, or do some shopping at any of London's elegant department stores (generally open until 21:00). Stroll any of the main squares, fine parks, or the Jubilee Walkway for people-watching. Ride the London Eye Ferris wheel for grand city views.

Day 2: Early in the morning, take a double-decker hop-on, hop-off sightseeing bus tour from Victoria Station, and hop off for the Changing of the Guard at Buckingham Palace. After lunch, tour the British Museum and/or the nearby British Library.

Day 3: At the Tower of London, see the crown jewels and take the Beefeater tour. Then grab a picnic, catch a boat at Tower Pier, and have lunch on the Thames while cruising to Blackfriars Pier.

Tour St. Paul's Cathedral and climb

London's Neighborhoods

The Tube's Circle Line

Regent's Park

NORTH LONDON

BRITISH MUSEUM

BAYSWATER   BLOOMSBURY

NOTTING HILL

Hyde Park

SOHO

EAST END

MAYFAIR   WEST END   TRAFALGAR SQ.

THE CITY

TOWER OF LONDON

KNIGHTSBRIDGE

WEST LONDON   VICTORIA   CENTRAL LONDON   ST. PAUL'S

BELGRAVIA

SOUTH KENSINGTON   PIMLICO   WEST-MINSTER

Thames River

BIG BEN

SOUTH BANK

To the Docklands

CHELSEA

LONDON EYE

To Greenwich

Not to Scale

THE CROWN JEWELS

its dome for views, then walk across Millennium Bridge to the South Bank to visit the Tate Modern, tour Shakespeare's Globe, or stroll the Jubilee Walkway.

Day 4: Take your pick of the Victoria and Albert Museum, Tate Britain, Imperial War Museum, or Houses of Parliament. Hit one of London's many lively open-air markets. Or cruise to Greenwich or Kew Gardens.

ORIENTATION

To grasp London more comfortably, see it as the old town in the city center without the modern, congested sprawl.

The River Thames (pronounced "tems") runs roughly west to east through the city, with most of the visitor's sights on the North Bank. Mentally, maybe even physically, trim down your map to include only the area between the Tower of London (to the east), Hyde Park (west), Regent's Park (north), and the South Bank (south). This is roughly the area bordered by the Tube's Circle Line. This four-mile stretch between the Tower and Hyde Park (about a 1.5-hour walk) looks like a milk bottle on its side (see map), and holds most of the sights mentioned in this chapter.

The sprawling city becomes much more manageable if you think of it as a collection of neighborhoods.

Central London contains **Westminster,** the location of Big Ben, Parliament, Westminster Abbey, Buckingham Palace, and Trafalgar Square, with its many major museums. It also includes the **West End,** the center of London's cultural life, where

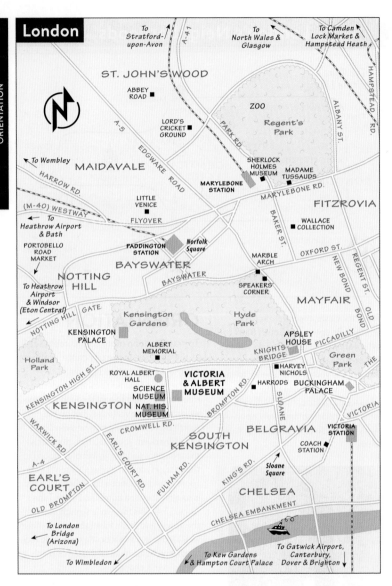

bustling Piccadilly Circus and Leicester Square host cinemas, tourist traps, and nighttime glitz. Soho and Covent Garden are thriving people zones with theaters, restaurants, pubs, and boutiques. And Regent and Oxford streets are the city's main shopping zones.

North London and its neighborhoods— including Bloomsbury, Fitzrovia, and Marylebone—contain such major sights as the British Museum and the overhyped Madame Tussauds Waxworks. Nearby, along busy Euston Road, is the British Library.

"The City," which is today's modern financial district, was a walled town in

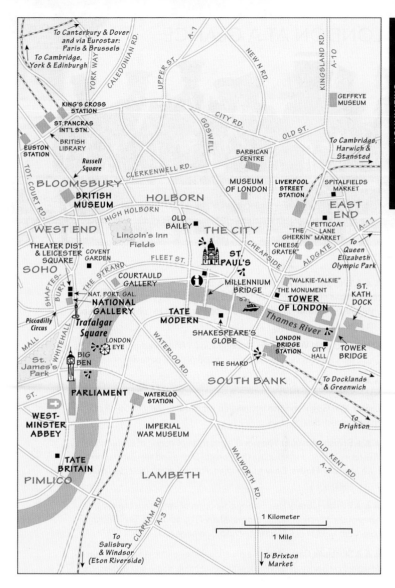

To Canterbury & Dover
and via Eurostar:
Paris & Brussels

To Cambridge,
York & Edinburgh

YORK WAY
CALEDONIAN RD.
UPPER ST.
A-1
NEW N RD.
KINGSLAND RD.
A-10

KING'S CROSS
STATION

ST. PANCRAS
INT'L STN.

EUSTON
STATION

BRITISH
LIBRARY

Russell
Square

CITY RD.
GOSWELL
OLD ST.

GEFFRYE
MUSEUM

To Cambridge,
Harwich &
Stansted

CLERKENWELL RD.

BARBICAN
CENTRE

BLOOMSBURY

TOT. COURT RD.

BRITISH
MUSEUM

HOLBORN

HIGH HOLBORN

MUSEUM
OF LONDON

LIVERPOOL
STREET
STATION

SPITALFIELDS
MARKET

EAST
END

A-11

WEST END

Lincoln's Inn
Fields

OLD
BAILEY

THE CITY

PETTICOAT
LANE
MARKET

"THE
GHERKIN"

"CHEESE
GRATER"

To
Queen
Elizabeth
Olympic Park

THEATER DIST.
& LEICESTER
SQUARE

SOHO

COVENT
GARDEN

FLEET ST.

CHEAPSIDE

ST.
PAUL'S

ALDGATE

ST.
KATH.
DOCK

COURTAULD
GALLERY

THE STRAND

SHAFTES.BURY

NAT. PORT. GAL.

NATIONAL
GALLERY

MILLENNIUM
BRIDGE

"WALKIE-TALKIE"

THE MONUMENT

TOWER
OF LONDON

Thames River

Piccadilly
Circus

Trafalgar
Square

MALL

WHITEHALL

LONDON
EYE

BIG
BEN

TATE
MODERN

SHAKESPEARE'S
GLOBE

WATERLOO RD.

THE SHARD

LONDON
BRIDGE
STATION

CITY
HALL

TOWER
BRIDGE

St.
James's
Park

SOUTH BANK

To Docklands
& Greenwich

PARLIAMENT

ST.

WATERLOO
STATION

WEST-
MINSTER
ABBEY

IMPERIAL
WAR MUSEUM

To
Brighton

OLD KENT RD.

A-2

TATE
BRITAIN

PIMLICO

LAMBETH

WALWORTH RD.

CLAPHAM RD.

A-3

To
Salisbury
& Windsor
(Eton Riverside)

To Brixton
Market

1 Kilometer

1 Mile

Roman times. Gleaming skyscrapers are interspersed with historical landmarks such as St. Paul's Cathedral and the Museum of London. The Tower of London and Tower Bridge lie at The City's eastern border.

The East End is the increasingly gentrified former stomping ground of Cockney ragamuffins and Jack the Ripper.

The South Bank of the Thames River offers major sights—Tate Modern, Shakespeare's Globe, and the London Eye— linked by a riverside walkway. Within this area, Southwark (SUTH-uck) stretches from the Tate Modern to London Bridge. Pedestrian bridges connect the South Bank with The City and Trafalgar Square.

LONDON AT A GLANCE

▲▲▲**Westminster Abbey** Britain's finest church and the site of royal coronations and burials since 1066. **Hours:** Mon-Fri 9:30-16:30, Wed until 19:00, Sat until 14:30, closed Sun to sightseers except for worship. See page 37.

▲▲▲**Churchill War Rooms** Underground WWII headquarters of Churchill's war effort. **Hours:** Daily 9:30-18:00. See page 45.

▲▲▲**National Gallery** Remarkable collection of European paintings (1250-1900), including Leonardo, Botticelli, Velázquez, Rembrandt, Turner, Van Gogh, and the Impressionists. **Hours:** Daily 10:00-18:00, Fri until 21:00. See page 46.

▲▲▲**British Museum** The world's greatest collection of artifacts of Western civilization, including the Rosetta Stone and the Parthenon's Elgin Marbles. **Hours:** Daily 10:00-17:30, Fri until 20:30 (selected galleries only). See page 57.

▲▲▲**British Library** Fascinating collection of important literary treasures of the Western world. **Hours:** Mon-Fri 9:30-18:00, Tue-Thu until 20:00, Sat until 17:00, Sun 11:00-17:00. See page 62.

▲▲▲**St. Paul's Cathedral** The main cathedral of the Anglican Church, designed by Christopher Wren, with a climbable dome and daily evensong services. **Hours:** Mon-Sat 8:30-16:30, closed Sun except for worship. See page 66.

▲▲▲**Tower of London** Historic castle, palace, and prison housing the crown jewels and a witty band of Beefeaters. **Hours:** Tue-Sat 9:00-17:30, Sun-Mon from 10:00; Nov-Feb closes one hour earlier. See page 72.

▲▲▲**Victoria and Albert Museum** The best collection of decorative arts anywhere. **Hours:** Daily 10:00-17:45, Fri until 22:00 (selected galleries only). See page 85.

▲▲**Houses of Parliament** London landmark famous for Big Ben and occupied by the Houses of Lords and Commons. **Hours:** When Parliament is in session, generally open Oct-late July Mon-Thu, closed Fri-Sun and during recess late July-Sept. Guided tours offered year-round on Sat and most weekdays during recess. See page 41.

▲▲**Trafalgar Square** The heart of London, where Westminster, The City, and the West End meet. See page 46.

▲▲**National Portrait Gallery** A *Who's Who* of British history, featuring portraits of this nation's most important historical figures. **Hours:** Daily 10:00-18:00, Fri until 21:00, first and second floors open Mon at 11:00. See page 51.

▲▲**Covent Garden** Vibrant people-watching zone with shops, cafés, street musicians, and an iron-and-glass arcade that once hosted a produce market. See page 54.

▲▲**Changing of the Guard at Buckingham Palace** Hour-long spectacle at Britain's royal residence. **Hours:** May-July daily at 11:00, Aug-April on Sun, Mon, Wed, and Fri. See page 54.

▲▲**London Eye** Enormous observation wheel, dominating—and offering commanding views over—London's skyline. **Hours:** Daily June-Aug 10:00-20:30 or later, Sept-May 11:00-18:00. See page 77.

▲▲**Imperial War Museum** Exhibits examining military conflicts from the early 20th century to today. **Hours:** Daily 10:00-18:00. See page 78.

▲▲**Tate Modern** Works by Monet, Matisse, Dalí, Picasso, and Warhol displayed in a converted powerhouse complex. **Hours:** Daily 10:00-18:00, Fri-Sat until 22:00. See page 80.

▲▲**Shakespeare's Globe** Timbered, thatched-roof reconstruction of the Bard's original "wooden O." **Hours:** Theater complex, museum, and actor-led tours generally daily 9:00-17:30; April-Oct generally morning theater tours only. Plays are also staged here. See page 81.

▲▲**Tate Britain** Collection of British painting from the 16th century through modern times, including works by William Blake, the Pre-Raphael-ites, and J. M. W. Turner. **Hours:** Daily 10:00-18:00. See page 82.

West London contains neighborhoods such as Mayfair, Belgravia, Pimlico, Chelsea, South Kensington, and Notting Hill. It's home to London's wealthy and has many trendy shops and enticing restaurants. Here you'll find the Victoria and Albert Museum, Tate Britain, and more museums, lively Victoria Station, and the vast green expanses of Hyde Park and Kensington Gardens.

Rick's Tip: *Through an initiative called Legible London, the city has erected pedestrian-focused maps around town—especially handy when exiting Tube stations. In this sprawling city—where predictable grid-planned streets are relatively rare—it's also smart to buy and use a good map.*

Tourist Information

It's hard to find unbiased sightseeing information and advice in London. You'll see "Tourist Information" offices advertised everywhere, but most are private agencies that make a big profit selling tours and advance sightseeing and/or theater tickets.

The **City of London Information Centre** next to St. Paul's Cathedral (just outside the church entrance) is the city's only publicly funded—and impartial—"real" TI. It sells Oyster cards, London Passes, and advance "Fast Track" sightseeing tickets. It also stocks various free publications: *London Planner* (a free monthly that lists all the sights, events, and hours), some walking-tour brochures, the *Official London Theatre Guide,* a free Tube and bus map (also see Tube map in "Transportation," later), and the *Guide to River Thames Boat Services.* The TI gives out a free map of The City and sells several city-wide maps; ask if they have yet another free map with various coupons for discounts on sights (Mon-Sat 9:30-17:30, Sun 10:00-16:00; Tube: St. Paul's, tel. 020/7332-1456, www.visitthecity.co.uk).

Visit London, which serves the greater London area, doesn't have an office you can visit in person—but does have an info-packed website (www.visitlondon.com).

Sightseeing Passes and Advance Tickets

To skip the ticket-buying queues at certain London sights, you can buy **Fast Track tickets** (sometimes called "priority pass" tickets) in advance—and they can be cheaper than tickets sold right at the sight. They're smart for the Tower of London, the London Eye, and Madame Tussauds Waxworks, which get busy in high season. They're available through various sales outlets (including the City of London TI, souvenir stands, and faux-TIs scattered throughout touristy areas).

The **London Pass** covers many big sights and lets you skip some lines. It's expensive but potentially worth the investment for extremely busy sightseers (£62/1 day, multi-day options available; sold at City of London TI, major train stations, and airports, www.londonpass.com).

Rick's Tip: *The Artful Dodger is alive and well in London.* **Beware of pickpockets,** *particularly on public transportation, among tourist crowds, and at street markets.*

Tours

To sightsee on your own, download my free Rick Steves Audio Europe app with **audio tours** of London's top sights and neighborhoods (see page 17 for details).

▲▲▲HOP-ON, HOP-OFF DOUBLE-DECKER BUS TOURS

London is full of hop-on, hop-off bus companies competing for your tourist pound. I've focused on the two companies I like the most: **Original** and **Big Bus.** Both offer essentially the same two tours of the city's sightseeing highlights.

Rick's Tip: *For an efficient intro to London, catch an 8:30 departure of a* **hop-on, hop-off overview bus tour,** *riding most of the loop (which takes about 1.5 hours, depending on traffic—lightest on Sunday morning). Hop off just before 10:00 at Trafalgar Square (Cockspur Street, stop "S"), then walk briskly to Buckingham Palace to find a spot to watch the* **Changing of the Guard ceremony** *at 11:00.*

Each company offers at least one route with live guides, and a second (sometimes slightly different route) with recorded narration. Buses run daily about every 10-15 minutes in summer and every 10-20 minutes in winter, starting at about 8:30. The last full loop usually leaves Victoria Station at about 20:00 in summer, and at about 17:00 in winter.

You can buy tickets online in advance, or from drivers or from staff at street kiosks (credit cards accepted at kiosks at major stops such as Victoria Station, ticket valid 24 hours in summer, 48 hours in winter).

Original: £32, £6 less with this book, limit four discounts per book, they'll rip off the corner of this page—raise bloody hell if the staff or driver won't honor this discount; also online deals, info center at 17 Cockspur Street; tel. 020/7389-5040, www.theoriginaltour.com.

Big Bus: £35, discount available online; tel. 020/7808-6753, www.bigbustours. com.

NIGHT BUS TOURS

Various companies offer a lower-priced, after-hours sightseeing circuit (1-2 hours). **Golden Tours** buses depart at 19:00 and 20:00 from their offices on Buckingham Palace Road (tel. 020/7630-2028; www.goldentours.com). **See London By Night** buses offer live English guides and frequent evening departures—starting from at 19:30—from Green Park (next to the Ritz Hotel); October-March at 19:30 and 21:20 only (tel. 020/7183-4744, www. seelondonbynight.com).

Rick's Tip: *If you're taking a bus tour mainly to get oriented,* **save time and money by taking a night tour.** *You can munch a memorable picnic dinner while riding on the top deck.*

▲▲WALKING TOURS

Top-notch local guides lead (sometimes big) groups on walking tours through specific slices of London's past. **London Walks** lists its daily schedule online, as well as in a beefy brochure available at hotels and in racks all over town. Their two-hour walks are led by top-quality professional guides (£10 cash only, private tours for groups-£140, tel. 020/7624-3978 for a live person, tel. 020/7624-9255 for a recording of today's or tomorrow's walks and the Tube station they depart from, www.walks.com).

London Walks also offers day trips into the countryside (£18 plus £36-64 for transportation and admission costs, cash only: Stonehenge/Salisbury, Oxford/Cotswolds, Bath, and so on).

PRIVATE GUIDES AND DRIVERS

Rates for London's registered Blue Badge guides are standard (about £160-200 for four hours; £260 or more for nine hours). I know and like five fine local guides: **Sean Kelleher** (tel. 020/8673-1624, mobile 07764-612-770, sean@seanlondonguide. com); **Britt Lonsdale** (£250/half-day, £350/day, tel. 020/7386-9907, mobile 07813-278-077, brittl@btinternet.com); **Joel Reid** (mobile 07887-955-720, joelyreid@gmail. com); and two others who work in London when they're not on the road leading my Britain tours: **Tom Hooper** (mobile 07986-048-047, tomh@ricksteves.net), and **Gillian Chadwick** (mobile 07889-976-598, gillychad@hotmail.co.uk). If you have a particular interest, London Walks (listed earlier) can book a guide for your exact focus (£180/half-day).

These guides have cars or a minibus for day trips, and also do walking-only tours: **Janine Barton** (£390/half-day, £560/day, tel. 020/7402-4600, http:// seeitinstyle.synthasite.com, jbsiis@aol. com); cousins **Hugh Dickson** and **Mike Dickson** (£345/half-day, £535/day; Hugh's mobile 07771/602-069, hughdickson@ hotmail.com; Mike's mobile 07769/905-811, michael.dickson5@btinternet.

com); and **David Stubbs** (£225/half-day, £330/day, about £50 more for groups of 4-6 people, mobile 07775-888-534, www.londoncountrytours.co.uk, info@ londoncountrytours.co.uk).

▲▲CRUISE BOAT TOURS

London offers many made-for-tourist cruises, most on slow-moving, open-top boats accompanied by entertaining commentary. Take a **short city center cruise** by riding a boat 30 minutes from Westminster Pier to Tower Pier (particularly handy if you're interested in visiting the Tower of London anyway), or choose a **longer cruise** that includes a peek at the East End, riding from Westminster all the way to Greenwich (save time by taking the Tube back).

Each company runs cruises daily, about twice hourly, from morning until dark; many reduce frequency off-season. Boats come and go from various docks in the city center (see sidebar). The most popular places to embark are Westminster Pier (at the base of Westminster Bridge across the street from Big Ben) and London Eye Pier (also known as Waterloo Pier, across the river on the South Bank).

A one-way trip within the city center costs about £10. A transit card (Travelcard

Thames Boat Piers

While Westminster Pier is the most popular, it's not the only dock in town. Consider all the options (listed from west to east, as the Thames flows).

Millbank Pier (North Bank): At the Tate Britain Museum, used primarily by the Tate Boat ferry service (express connection to Tate Modern at Bankside Pier).

Westminster Pier (North Bank): Near the base of Big Ben, offers round-trip sightseeing cruises and lots of departures in both directions (though the Thames Clippers boats don't stop here). Nearby sights include Parliament and Westminster Abbey.

London Eye Pier (a.k.a. **Waterloo Pier,** South Bank): At the base of the London Eye; good, less-crowded alternative to Westminster, with many of the same cruise options (Waterloo Station is nearby).

Embankment Pier (North Bank): Near Covent Garden, Trafalgar Square, and Cleopatra's Needle (the obelisk on the Thames). This pier is used mostly for special boat trips, such as some RIB (rigid inflatable boats) and lunch and dinner cruises.

Festival Pier (South Bank): Next to the Royal Festival Hall, just downstream from the London Eye.

Blackfriars Pier (North Bank): In The City, not far from St. Paul's.

Bankside Pier (South Bank): Directly in front of the Tate Modern and Shakespeare's Globe.

London Bridge Pier (a.k.a. **London Bridge City Pier,** South Bank): Near the HMS *Belfast*.

Tower Pier (North Bank): At the Tower of London, at the east edge of The City and near the East End.

St. Katharine's Pier (North Bank): Just downstream from the Tower of London.

or Oyster card) can snare you a discount on some cruises (see page 30).

The three dominant companies are **City Cruises** (handy 45-minute cruise from Westminster Pier to Tower Pier; www.citycruises.com), **Thames River Services** (fewer stops, classic boats, friendlier and more old-fashioned feel; www.thamesriverservices.co.uk), and **Circular Cruise** (full cruise takes about an hour, operated by Crown River Services, www.circularcruise.london).

Cruising Downstream, to Greenwich: Both **City Cruises** and **Thames River Services** head from Westminster Pier to Greenwich. To maximize both efficiency and sightseeing, take a narrated cruise to Greenwich one way, and go the other way on the DLR (Docklands Light Railway).

Cruising Upstream, to Kew Gardens: **Thames River Boats** leave for Kew Gardens from Westminster Pier (£13 one-way, £20 round-trip, cash only, discounts with Travelcard, 2-4/day depending on season, 1.5 hours, boats sail April-Oct, about half the trip is narrated, www.wpsa.co.uk).

Rick's Tip: *Zipping through London every 20-30 minutes, the* **Thames Clippers are designed for commuters.** *With no open deck and no commentary, they're* **not the best option for sightseeing.**

Helpful Hints

Wi-Fi: Besides your hotel, many major museums, sights, and even entire neighborhoods offer free Wi-Fi. For easy access everywhere, sign up for a free account with **The Cloud,** a Wi-Fi service found in many convenient spots around London (www.skywifi.cloud, you'll be asked to enter a street address and postal code—use your hotel's, or the Queen's: Buckingham Palace, SW1A 1AA).

Useful Apps: Mapway's free **Tube Map London Underground** and **Bus Times London** (www.mapway.com) apps show the easiest way to connect Tube stations and provide bus stops and route information. The handy **Citymapper** app for London covers every mode of public transit in the city. **City Maps 2Go** lets you download searchable offline maps; their London version is quite good. And **Time Out London**'s free app has reviews and listings for theater, museums, and movies (download the "Make Your City Amazing" version—it's updated weekly—not the boilerplate "Travel Guide" version).

Baggage Storage: Train stations have replaced lockers with more secure left-luggage counters. Each bag must go

through a scanner (just like at the airport). Expect long waits in the morning to check in (up to 45 minutes) and in the afternoon to pick up (most stations daily 7:00-23:00). You can also store bags at the airports (www.left-baggage.co.uk).

WESTMINSTER WALK

Just about every visitor to London strolls along historic Whitehall from Big Ben to Trafalgar Square. This walk gives you a whirlwind tour as well as a practical orientation to London. Most of the sights you'll see are described in more detail later in this chapter. ∩ You can download a free, extended audio version of this walk; see page 17.

Rick's Tip: Cars drive on the left side of the road—*confusing for foreign pedestrians and for foreign drivers. Always look right, look left, then look right again just to be sure.* **Jaywalking is treacherous** *when you're disoriented about which direction traffic is coming from.*

❷ Self-Guided Walk

Start halfway across ❶ **Westminster Bridge** for that "Wow, I'm really in London!" feeling. Get a close-up view of the **Houses of Parliament** and **Big Ben.** Downstream you'll see the **London Eye,** the city's giant Ferris wheel. Down the stairs to Westminster Pier are boats to the Tower of London and Greenwich (downstream) or Kew Gardens (upstream).

En route to Parliament Square, you'll pass a ❷ **statue of Boadicea,** the Celtic queen who unsuccessfully resisted Roman invaders in A.D. 60. Julius Caesar was the first Roman general to cross the Channel, but even he was weirded out by the island's strange inhabitants, who worshipped trees, sacrificed virgins, and went to war painted blue. Later, Romans subdued and civilized them, building

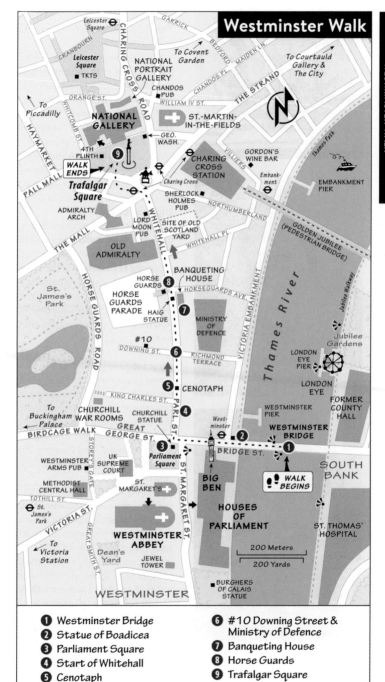

Westminster Walk

Leicester Square

CRANBOURN

To Covent Garden

To Courtauld Gallery & The City

GARRICK

BEDFORD

MAIDEN LN.

CHARING CROSS ROAD

NATIONAL PORTRAIT GALLERY

CHANDOS PL.

THE STRAND

To Piccadilly

WHITCOMB ST.

ORANGE ST.

CHANDOS PUB

WILLIAM IV ST.

ST-MARTIN-IN-THE-FIELDS

Thames Park

NATIONAL GALLERY

GEO. WASH.

VILLIERS ST.

GORDON'S WINE BAR

HAYMARKET

4TH PLINTH

9

CHARING CROSS STATION

Embankment

EMBANKMENT PIER

WALK ENDS

Trafalgar Square

Charing Cross

PALL MALL

ADMIRALTY ARCH

SHERLOCK HOLMES PUB

NORTHUMBERLAND

GOLDEN JUBILEE (PEDESTRIAN BRIDGE)

THE MALL

LORD MOON PUB

WHITEHALL

SITE OF OLD SCOTLAND YARD

WHITEHALL PL.

OLD ADMIRALTY

VICTORIA EMBANKMENT

Thames River

Jubilee Walkway

St. James's Park

HORSE GUARDS ROAD

BANQUETING HOUSE

HORSE GUARDS **8**

HORSEGUARDS AVE.

7

Jubilee Gardens

HORSE GUARDS PARADE

HAIG STATUE

MINISTRY OF DEFENCE

LONDON EYE PIER

#10

DOWNING ST.

6

RICHMOND TERRACE

LONDON EYE

5

CENOTAPH

FORMER COUNTY HALL

KING CHARLES ST.

WESTMINSTER PIER

To Buckingham Palace

CHURCHILL WAR ROOMS

CHURCHILL STATUE

4

West-minster

WESTMINSTER BRIDGE

BIRDCAGE WALK

GREAT GEORGE ST.

2

1

WESTMINSTER ARMS PUB

STOREY'S GATE

UK SUPREME COURT

3 *Parliament Square*

BRIDGE ST.

SOUTH BANK

METHODIST CENTRAL HALL

ST. MARGARET'S

ST. MARGARET ST.

BIG BEN

WALK BEGINS

TOTHILL ST.

St. James's Park

VICTORIA ST.

GREAT SMITH ST.

HOUSES OF PARLIAMENT

ST. THOMAS' HOSPITAL

To Victoria Station

Dean's Yard

WESTMINSTER ABBEY

JEWEL TOWER

200 Meters

200 Yards

WESTMINSTER

BURGHERS OF CALAIS STATUE

1 Westminster Bridge
2 Statue of Boadicea
3 Parliament Square
4 Start of Whitehall
5 Cenotaph

6 #10 Downing Street & Ministry of Defence
7 Banqueting House
8 Horse Guards
9 Trafalgar Square

Ⓐ *Boadicea statue*
Ⓑ *Churchill statue in Parliament Square*
Ⓒ *Horse Guards*

roads and making this spot on the Thames—"Londinium"—a major urban center.

You'll find four red phone booths lining the north side of **❸ Parliament Square** along Great George Street—great for a phone-box-and-Big-Ben photo op.

Wave hello to Winston Churchill and Nelson Mandela in Parliament Square. To Churchill's right is the historic **Westminster Abbey,** with its two stubby, elegant towers. The white building (flying the Union Jack) at the far end of the square houses Britain's **Supreme Court.**

Head north up Parliament Street, which turns into **❹ Whitehall,** and walk toward Trafalgar Square. You'll see the thought-provoking **❺ Cenotaph** in the middle of the boulevard, reminding passersby of the many Brits who died in the last century's world wars. To visit the **Churchill War Rooms,** take a left before the Cenotaph, on King Charles Street.

Continuing on Whitehall, stop at the barricaded and guarded **❻ #10 Downing Street** to see the British "White House," the traditional home of the prime minister since the position was created in the early 18th century. Break the bobby's boredom and ask him a question. The huge building across Whitehall from Downing Street is the **Ministry of Defence** (MOD), the "British Pentagon."

Nearing Trafalgar Square, look for the 17th-century **❼ Banqueting House** across the street, which is just about all that remains of what was once the biggest palace in Europe—Whitehall Palace. If you visit, you can enjoy its ceiling paintings by Peter Paul Rubens, and the exquisite hall itself. Also take a look at the **❽ Horse Guards** behind the gated fence. For 200 years, soldiers in cavalry uniforms have guarded this arched entrance that leads to Buckingham Palace. These elite troops constitute the Queen's personal bodyguard.

The column topped by Lord Nelson marks **❾ Trafalgar Square,** London's

Trafalgar Square and St. Martin-in-the-Fields

central meeting point. The stately domed building on the far side of the square is the **National Gallery,** which is filled with the national collection of European paintings, and has a classy café in the Sainsbury wing. To the right of the National Gallery is the 1722 **St. Martin-in-the-Fields Church** and its Café in the Crypt.

• *Our Westminster walk is over. But if you want to keep going, walk up Cockspur Street to Haymarket, then take a short left on Coventry Street to colorful Piccadilly Circus. Near here, you'll find several theaters and Leicester Square, with its half-price "TKTS" booth for plays (see page 93) Walk through trendy Soho (north of Shaftesbury Avenue) for its fun pubs.*

SIGHTS

Central London
Westminster

These sights are listed in roughly geographical order from Westminster Abbey to Trafalgar Square, and are linked in my self-guided Westminster Walk, earlier, and the 🎧 free Westminster Walk audio tour (see page 17 for details).

▲▲▲WESTMINSTER ABBEY

The greatest church in the English-speaking world, Westminster Abbey is where the nation's royalty has been wedded, crowned, and buried since 1066. Indeed, the histories of Westminster Abbey and England are almost the same. A thousand years of English history—3,000 tombs, the remains of 29 kings and queens, and hundreds of memorials to poets, politicians, scientists, and warriors—lie within its stained-glass splendor and under its stone slabs.

Cost and Hours: £22, £44 family ticket (covers 2 adults and 1 child), includes cloister and audioguide; Mon-Fri 9:30-16:30, Wed until 19:00 (main church only), Sat until 14:30, last entry one hour before closing, closed Sun to sightseers but open for services, guided tours available; cloister—daily 8:00-18:00; Tube: Westminster or St. James's Park, tel. 020/7222-5152, www.westminster-abbey.org.

Rick's Tip: *Westminster Abbey is most crowded at midmorning and all day Saturdays and Mondays.* **Visit early, during lunch, or late.** *Weekdays after 14:30—especially Wednesday—are less congested; come late and stay for the 17:00 evensong. Skip the line by booking tickets in advance via the Abbey's website at www.westminster-abbey.org.*

Church Services and Music: Mon-Fri at 7:30 (prayer), 8:00 (communion), 12:30 (communion), 17:00 evensong (except on Wed, when the evening service is generally spoken—not sung); **Sat** at 8:00 (communion), 9:00 (prayer), 15:00 (evensong; May-Aug it's at 17:00); **Sun** services generally come with more music: at 8:00 (communion), 10:00 (sung Matins), 11:15 (sung Eucharist), 15:00 (evensong), 18:30 (evening service). Services are free to anyone, though visitors who haven't paid church admission aren't allowed to linger afterward. Free **organ recitals** are usually held Sun at 17:45 (30 minutes).

Westminster Abbey Tour

To Little Cloister & College Garden

CAFÉ & WC

DEAN'S YARD

PYX

11

CHAPTER HOUSE

GREAT CLOISTER

ENTER (CLOISTERS & CAFÉ ONLY)

HIGH ALTAR

TOWER

10

9

GIFT SHOP

8

HENRY VII

7

6

CHAPEL

4

3

2

CHOIR

NAVE

1

12

← EXIT (WEST DOOR)

5

SIDE CHAPELS

"SCIENTISTS' CORNER"

To WC →

To Parliament Square & Whitehall ↓

ENTER (NORTH DOOR)

30 Meters

30 Yards

1. Nave
2. Choir
3. Coronation Spot
4. Shrine of Edward the Confessor
5. Tomb of Elizabeth I & Mary I
6. Chapel of King Henry VII
7. Royal Air Force Chapel
8. Tomb of Mary, Queen of Scots
9. Queen's Diamond Jubilee Galleries
10. Poets' Corner
11. Great Cloister
12. Coronation Chair

The west facade of Westminster Abbey

Tours: The included **audioguide** is excellent. The Westminster Abbey Official Tour **app** includes an audio tour narrated by Jeremy Irons. To add to the experience, you can take an entertaining **guided tour** from a verger—the church equivalent of a museum docent (£5, schedule posted both outside and inside entry, up to 6/day in summer, 2-4/day in winter, 1.5 hours).

⊙ SELF-GUIDED TOUR

You'll have no choice but to follow the steady flow of tourists through the church, along the route laid out for the audioguide. My tour covers the Abbey's top stops.

• *Walk straight through the north transept. Follow the crowd flow to the right and enter the spacious...*

❶ **Nave:** The Abbey's 10-story nave is the tallest in England. With saints in stained glass, heroes in carved stone, and the bodies of England's greatest citizens under the floor stones, Westminster Abbey is the religious heart of England.

The king who built the Abbey was Edward the Confessor. Find him in the stained-glass windows on the left side of the nave (as you face the altar). He's in the third bay from the end (marked *S: Edwardus rex...*), with his crown, scepter, and ring.

On the floor near the west entrance of the Abbey is the flower-lined Grave of the Unknown Warrior, one ordinary WWI soldier buried in soil from France with lettering made from melted-down weapons from that war. Contemplate the million-man army from the British Empire and all those who gave their lives. Their memory is so revered that when Kate Middleton walked up the aisle on her wedding day, by tradition she had to step around the tomb (and her wedding bouquet was later placed atop this tomb, also in accordance with tradition).

• *Walk up the nave toward the altar. This is the same route every future monarch walks on the way to being crowned. Midway up the nave, you pass through the colorful screen of an enclosure known as the...*

❷ **Choir:** These elaborately carved wood and gilded seats are where monks once chanted their services in the "quire"—as it's known in British churchspeak. Today, it's where the Abbey boys' choir sings the evensong. You're approaching the center of a cross-shaped church. The "high" (main) altar (which usually has a cross and candlesticks atop it) sits on the platform up the five stairs in front of you.

• *It's on this platform that the monarch is crowned.*

❸ **Coronation Spot:** The area immediately before the high altar is where every English coronation since 1066 has taken place. Royalty are also given funerals here. Princess Diana's coffin was carried to this spot for her funeral service in 1997. The "Queen Mum" (mother of Elizabeth II) had her funeral here in 2002. This is also where most of the last century's royal weddings have taken place, including the unions of Queen Elizabeth II and Prince Philip (1947), Prince Andrew and Sarah Ferguson (1986), and Prince William and Kate Middleton (2011).

• *Veer left and follow the crowd. Pause at the wooden staircase on your right.*

❹ **Shrine of Edward the Confessor:** Step back and peek over the dark coffin of Edward I to see the tippy-top of the green-and-gold wedding-cake tomb of King Edward the Confessor—the man who built Westminster Abbey.

God had told pious Edward to visit St. Peter's Basilica in Rome. But with the Normans thinking conquest, it was too dangerous for him to leave England. Instead, he built this grand church and dedicated it to St. Peter. It was finished just in time to bury Edward and to crown his foreign successor, William the Conqueror, in 1066. After Edward's death, people prayed at his tomb, and, after getting good results, Pope Alexander III canonized him. This elevated, central tomb—which lost some of its luster when Henry VIII melted down the gold coffin-case—is surrounded by the tombs of eight kings and queens.

• At the top of the stone staircase, veer left into the private burial chapel of Queen Elizabeth I.

 ❺ Tomb of Queens Elizabeth I and Mary I: Although only one effigy is on the tomb (Elizabeth's), there are actually two queens buried beneath it, both daughters of Henry VIII (by different mothers). Bloody Mary—meek, pious, sickly, and Catholic—enforced Catholicism during her short reign (1553-1558) by burning "heretics" at the stake.

Elizabeth—strong, clever, and Protestant—steered England on an Anglican course. She holds a royal orb symbolizing that she's queen of the whole globe. When 26-year-old Elizabeth was crowned in the Abbey, her right to rule was questioned (especially by her Catholic subjects) because she was considered the bastard seed of Henry

Tomb of Elizabeth I (and Mary I)

VIII's unsanctioned marriage to Anne Boleyn. But Elizabeth's long reign (1559-1603) was one of the greatest in English history, a time when England ruled the seas and Shakespeare explored human emotions. When she died, thousands turned out for her funeral in the Abbey. Elizabeth's face on the tomb, modeled after her death mask, is considered a very accurate take on this hook-nosed, imperious "Virgin Queen" (she never married).

• Continue into the ornate, flag-draped room up a few more stairs, directly behind the main altar.

 ❻ Chapel of King Henry VII (The Lady Chapel): The light from the stained-glass windows; the colorful banners overhead; and the elaborate tracery in stone, wood, and glass give this room the festive air of a medieval tournament. The prestigious Knights of the Bath meet here, under the magnificent ceiling studded with gold pendants. The ceiling—of carved stone, not plaster (1519)—is the finest English Perpendicular Gothic and fan vaulting you'll see (unless you're going to King's College Chapel in Cambridge). The ceiling was sculpted on the floor in pieces, then jigsaw-puzzled into place. It capped the Gothic period and signaled the vitality of the coming Renaissance.

• Go to the far end of the chapel and stand at the banister in front of the modern set of stained-glass windows.

 ❼ Royal Air Force Chapel: Saints in robes and halos mingle with pilots in parachutes and bomber jackets. This tribute to WWII flyers is for those who earned their angel wings in the Battle of Britain (July-Oct 1940). A bit of bomb damage has been preserved—look for the little glassed-over hole in the wall below the windows in the lower left-hand corner.

• Exit the Chapel of Henry VII. Turn left into a side chapel with the tomb (the central one of three in the chapel).

 ❽ Tomb of Mary, Queen of Scots: The beautiful, French-educated queen

(1542-1587) was held under house arrest for 19 years by Queen Elizabeth I, who considered her a threat to her sovereignty. Elizabeth got wind of an assassination plot, suspected Mary was behind it, and had her first cousin (once removed) beheaded. When Elizabeth died childless, Mary's son—James VI, King of Scots—also became King James I of England and Ireland. James buried his mum here (with her head sewn back on) in the Abbey's most sumptuous tomb.

• *Exit Mary's chapel. Continue on, until you emerge in the south transept. Look for the doorway that leads to a stairway and elevator to the...*

❾ Queen's Diamond Jubilee Galleries: In the summer of 2018, the Abbey will open a space that has been closed off for 700 years—an internal gallery 70 feet above the main floor known as the triforium. This balcony will house the new Queen's Diamond Jubilee Galleries, a small museum where you'll see exhibits covering royal coronations, funerals, and much more from the Abbey's 1,000-year history. There will also be stunning views of the nave straight down to the Great West Door. Because of limited access to the galleries, it's likely visitors will need a timed-entry ticket (see the Abbey website for details).

• *After touring the Queen's Galleries, return to the main floor. You're in...*

❿ Poets' Corner: England's greatest artistic contributions are in the written word. Here the masters of arguably the world's most complex and expressive language are remembered: Geoffrey Chaucer (*Canterbury Tales*), Lord Byron, Dylan Thomas, W. H. Auden, Lewis Carroll (*Alice's Adventures in Wonderland*), T. S. Eliot (*The Waste Land*), Alfred Tennyson, Robert Browning, and Charles Dickens. Many writers are honored with plaques and monuments; relatively few are actually buried here. Shakespeare is commemorated by a fine statue that stands near the end of the transept,

Poets' Corner

overlooking the others.

• *Exit the church (temporarily) at the south door, which leads to the...*

⓫ Great Cloister: The buildings that adjoin the church housed the monks. Cloistered courtyards gave them a place to meditate on God's creations.

• *Go back into the church for the last stop.*

⓬ Coronation Chair: A gold-painted oak chair waits here under a regal canopy for the next coronation. For every English coronation since 1308 (except two), it's been moved to its spot before the high altar to receive the royal buttocks. The chair's legs rest on lions, England's symbol.

▲▲HOUSES OF PARLIAMENT (PALACE OF WESTMINSTER)

This Neo-Gothic icon of London, the site of the royal residence from 1042 to 1547, is now the meeting place of the legislative branch of government. Like the US Capitol in Washington, DC, the complex is open to visitors. You can view parliamentary sessions in either the bickering House of Commons or the sleepy House of Lords. Or you can simply wander on your own (through a few closely monitored rooms) to appreciate the historic building itself.

The Palace of Westminster has been the center of political power in England for nearly a thousand years. In 1834, a horrendous fire gutted the Palace. It was rebuilt in a retro, Neo-Gothic style that recalled England's medieval Christian roots—pointed arches, stained-glass

Houses of Parliament

To Whitehall &
Trafalgar Square

PARL. ST.

PARLIAMENT
SHOP

PORTCULLIS HOUSE

VICTORIA EMBANKMENT

WESTMINSTER
PIER

STATUE OF
BOADICEA

STAIRS DOWN
TO RIVERSIDE

Westminster

BRIDGE ST.

CHURCHILL
STATUE

FENCE

BIG
BEN

Speaker's
Green

WESTMINSTER
BRIDGE

Parliament
Square

CARRIAGE
GATES

New
Palace
Yard

SPEAKER'S
HOUSE

BROAD SANCTUARY

SECURITY
FENCE

ST.
MARGARET'S

CAFÉ,
SHOP &
WC

Cromwell
Green

❷

PLAQUES

CROMWELL
STATUE

❻

❶

WESTMINSTER
ABBEY

STAINED
GLASS

BARRIER

Old
Palace
Yard

❸

❹

THE TERRACE

Thames
River

HOUSES OF
PARLIAMENT

CHAPTER
HOUSE

ST. MARGARET STREET

❺

JEWEL
TOWER

ABINGDON STREET

VICTORIA
TOWER

❶ Visitors Entrance
❷ Westminster Hall
❸ St. Stephen's Hall
❹ Central Lobby
❺ House of Lords
❻ House of Commons
❼ Portcullis House
   Ticket Office

Victoria
Tower
Gardens

BURGHERS
OF CALAIS
STATUE

N

50 Meters

50 Yards

windows, spires, and saint-like statues. At the same time, Britain was also retooling its government. Democracy was on the rise, the queen became a constitutional monarch, and Parliament emerged as the nation's ruling body. The Palace of Westminster became a kind of cathedral of democracy.

Cost and Hours: Free when Parliament is in session, otherwise must visit with a paid tour (see next); hours for nonticketed entry to House of Commons—Oct-late July Mon 14:30-22:30, Tue-Wed 11:30-19:30, Thu 9:30-17:30; for House of Lords—Oct-late July Mon-Tue 14:30-22:00, Wed 15:00-22:00, Thu 11:00-19:30;

last entry depends on debates; exact schedule at www.parliament.uk.

Tours: Audioguide—£18.50, guided tour—£25.50, Sat year-round 9:00-16:30 and most weekdays during recess (late July-Sept), 1.5 hours. Confirm the tour schedule and book ahead at www. parliament.uk or by calling 020/7219-4114. The ticket office also sells tour tickets, but there's no guarantee same-day spaces will be available (ticket office open Mon-Fri 10:00-16:00, Sat 9:00-16:30, closed Sun, located in Portcullis House next to Westminster Tube Station, entrance on Victoria Embankment).

Choosing a House: The House of Lords is less important politically, but they meet in a more ornate room, and the wait time is shorter (likely less than 30 minutes). The House of Commons is where major policy is made, but the room is sparse, and wait times are longer (30-60 minutes or more).

The history of the Houses of Parliament spans more than 900 years.

Rick's Tip: *For the* **public galleries** *in either House,* **lines are longest** *at the start of each session, particularly on Wednesdays. For the shortest wait, try to show up* **later in the afternoon** *(but don't push it, as things sometimes close down early).*

● SELF-GUIDED TOUR

Enter midway along the west side of the building (across the street from Westminster Abbey), where a tourist ramp leads to the ❶ **visitors entrance.** Line up for the airport-style security check. You'll be given a visitor badge. If you have questions, the attendants are extremely helpful.

• *First, take in the cavernous...*

❷ **Westminster Hall:** This vast hall—covering 16,000 square feet—survived the 1834 fire, and is one of the oldest and most important buildings in England. England's vaunted legal system was invented in this hall, as this was the major court of the land for 700 years. King Charles I was tried and sentenced to death here. Guy Fawkes

The history of the Houses of Parliament spans more than 900 years.

Affording London's Sights

London is one of Europe's most expensive cities, with the dubious distinction of having some of the world's steepest admission prices. But with its many free museums and affordable plays, this cosmopolitan, cultured city offers days of sightseeing thrills without requiring you to pinch your pennies (or your pounds).

Free Museums: Free sights include the British Museum, British Library, National Gallery, National Portrait Gallery, Tate Britain, Tate Modern, Imperial War Museum, Victoria and Albert Museum, Natural History Museum, and the Museum of London. Some museums request a donation of a few pounds, but whether you contribute is up to you.

Free Churches: Smaller churches let worshippers (and tourists) in free, although they may ask for a donation. The big sightseeing churches—Westminster Abbey and St. Paul's—charge higher admission fees, but offer free evensong services nearly daily (though you can't stick around afterward to sightsee). Westminster Abbey also offers free organ recitals most Sundays.

Other Freebies: London has plenty of free performances, such as lunch concerts at St. Martin-in-the-Fields. For other freebies, check out www.whatsfreeinlondon.co.uk. There's no charge to enjoy the pageantry of the Changing of the Guard, rants at Speakers' Corner in Hyde Park (on Sun afternoon), displays at Harrods, the people-watching scene at Covent Garden, and the colorful streets of the East End. It's free to view the legislature at work in the Houses of Parliament. You can get into the chapel at the Tower of London by attending Sunday services. And Greenwich is an inexpensive outing.

Good-Value Tours: The London Walks tours with professional guides (£10) are one of the best deals going. Hop-on, hop-off big-bus tours, while expensive (around £30), provide a great overview and include free boat tours as well as city walks. (Or, for the price of a transit ticket, you could get similar views from the top of a double-decker public bus.) A one-hour Thames ride to Greenwich costs about £12 one-way, but most boats come with entertaining commentary.

Theater: Compared with Broadway's prices, London's theater can be a bargain. Seek out the freestanding TKTS booth at Leicester Square to get discounts from 25 to 50 percent on good seats. And a £5 "groundling" ticket for a play at Shakespeare's Globe is the best theater deal in town.

was condemned for plotting to blow up the Halls of Parliament in 1605.

• *Continue up the stairs, and enter...*

❸ St. Stephen's Hall: This long, beautifully lit room was the original House of Commons. Members of Parliament (MPs) sat in church pews on either side of the hall—the ruling faction on one side, the opposition on the other

• *Next you reach the...*

❹ Central Lobby: This ornate, octagonal, high-vaulted room is often called the "heart of British government," because it sits midway between the House of Commons (to the left) and the House of Lords (right). Video monitors list the schedule of meetings and events in this 1,100-room governmental hive. This is the best place to admire the Palace's carved wood, chandeliers, statues, and floor tiles.

• *This lobby marks the end of the public space where you can wander freely. To see the House of Lords or House of Commons, you must wait in line and check your belongings.*

❺ **House of Lords:** When you're called, you'll walk to the Lords Chamber by way of the long Peers' Corridor—referring to the House's 800 unelected members, called "Peers." Paintings on the corridor walls depict the antiauthoritarian spirit brewing under the reign of Charles I. When you reach the House of Lords Chamber, you'll watch the proceedings from the upper-level visitors gallery. Debate may occur among the few Lords who show up at any given time, but these days, the Peers' role is largely advisory—they have no real power to pass laws on their own.

The Lords Chamber is church-like and impressive, with stained glass and intricately carved walls. At the far end is the Queen's gilded throne, where she sits once a year to give a speech to open Parliament. In front of the throne sits the woolsack—a cushion stuffed with wool. Here the Lord Speaker presides, with a ceremonial mace behind the backrest. To the Lord Speaker's right are the members of the ruling party (a.k.a. "government") and to his left are the members of the opposition (the Labour Party). Unaffiliated Crossbenchers sit in between.

❻ **House of Commons:** The Commons Chamber may be much less grandiose than the Lords', but this is where the sausage gets made. The House of Commons is as powerful as the Lords, prime minister, and Queen combined.

When the prime minister visits, her ministers (or cabinet) join her on the front bench, while lesser MPs (the "backbenchers") sit behind. It's often a fiery spectacle, as the prime minister defends her policies, while the opposition grumbles and harrumphs in displeasure. It's not unheard-of for MPs to get out of line and be escorted out by the Serjeant at Arms.

Big Ben

Nearby: Across the street from the Parliament building's St. Stephen's Gate, the **Jewel Tower** is a rare remnant of the old Palace of Westminster, used by kings until Henry VIII. The crude stone tower (1365-1366) was a guard tower in the palace wall, overlooking a moat. It contains a fine exhibit on the medieval Westminster Palace and the tower (£5.20, daily 10:00-18:00, Oct until 17:00; Nov-March Sat-Sun until 16:00, closed Mon-Fri; tel. 020/7222-2219). Next to the tower (and free) is a quiet courtyard with picnic-friendly benches.

Big Ben, the 315-foot-high clock tower at the north end of the Palace of Westminster, is named for its 13-ton bell, Ben. The light above the clock is lit when Parliament is in session. The face of the clock is huge—you can actually see the minute hand moving. For a good view of it, walk halfway over Westminster Bridge.

▲▲▲**CHURCHILL WAR ROOMS**
Take a fascinating walk through the underground headquarters of the British

government's WWII fight against the Nazis. It has two parts: the war rooms themselves, and a top-notch museum dedicated to Winston Churchill, who steered the war from here. Pick up the excellent audioguide at the entry, and dive in. The museum's gift shop is great for anyone nostalgic for the 1940s.

Cost and Hours: £19, includes audioguide, daily 9:30-18:00, last entry one hour before closing; café on site; on King Charles Street, 200 yards off Whitehall—follow signs, Tube: Westminster; tel. 020/7930-6961, www.iwm.org.uk/churchill-war-rooms.

Avoiding Lines: You can buy timed-entry tickets online to skip the long ticket-buying queue, but you may still need to wait in the security line.

Visiting the War Rooms and Museum: The 27 **War Rooms,** the heavily fortified nerve center of the British war effort, were used from 1939 to 1945. Churchill's room, the map room, and other rooms are just as they were in 1945. As you follow the one-way route, take advantage of the audioguide, which explains each room and offers first-person accounts of wartime happenings here. Be patient—it's well worth it. While the rooms are spartan, you'll learn how British gentility survived even as the city was bombarded.

The **Churchill Museum,** which occupies a large hall amid the war rooms, dissects every aspect of the man behind the famous cigar, bowler hat, and V-for-victory sign. Artifacts, quotes, political cartoons, clear explanations, and interactive exhibits to bring the colorful statesman to life. Many of the items on display—such as a European map divvied up in permanent marker, which Churchill brought to England from the postwar Potsdam Conference—drive home the remarkable span of history this man influenced.

Rick's Tip: *Some sights automatically add a* **"voluntary donation" of about 10 percent** *to their admission fees (those are the prices I quote), and some free museums request donations. All such contributions are completely optional.*

On Trafalgar Square

Trafalgar Square, London's central square (worth ▲▲), is at the intersection of Westminster, The City, and the West End. It's the climax of most marches and demonstrations, and is a thrilling place to simply hang out. At the top of Trafalgar Square (north) sits the domed National Gallery with its grand staircase, and to the right, the steeple of St. Martin-in-the-Fields, built in 1722. In the center of the square, Lord Nelson stands atop his 185-foot-tall fluted granite column, gazing out toward Trafalgar, where he lost his life but defeated the French fleet. Part of this 1842 memorial is made from his victims' melted-down cannons. He's surrounded by spraying fountains, giant lions, and hordes of people (Tube: Charing Cross).

▲▲▲NATIONAL GALLERY

Displaying an unsurpassed collection of European paintings from 1250 to 1900—including works by Leonardo, Botticelli, Velázquez, Rembrandt, Turner, Van Gogh, and the Impressionists—this is one of Europe's great galleries.

Cost and Hours: Free, £5 suggested donation, special exhibits extra, daily 10:00-18:00, Fri until 21:00, last entry to special exhibits 45 minutes before closing, on Trafalgar Square, Tube: Charing Cross or Leicester Square.

Churchill War Rooms

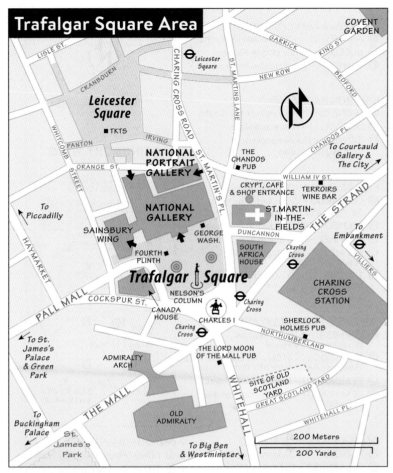

Trafalgar Square Area

COVENT
GARDEN

LISLE ST.

CRANBOURN

GARRICK

KING ST.

NEW ROW

BEDFORD

Leicester
Square

CHARING CROSS ROAD

ST. MARTIN'S LANE

Leicester
Square

WHITCOMB STREET

TKTS

PANTON

IRVING

ORANGE ST.

NATIONAL
PORTRAIT
GALLERY

NATIONAL
GALLERY

ST. MARTIN'S PL.

THE
CHANDOS
PUB

CRYPT, CAFÉ
& SHOP ENTRANCE

WILLIAM IV ST.

CHANDOS PL.

To Courtauld
Gallery &
The City

TERROIRS
WINE BAR

THE STRAND

To
Piccadilly

SAINSBURY
WING

FOURTH
PLINTH

HAYMARKET

GEORGE
WASH.

DUNCANNON

ST. MARTIN-
IN-THE-
FIELDS

To
Embankment

VILLIERS

SOUTH
AFRICA
HOUSE

Charing
Cross

Charing
Cross

CHARING
CROSS
STATION

Trafalgar Square

NELSON'S
COLUMN

CHARLES I

Charing
Cross

PALL MALL

COCKSPUR ST.

CANADA
HOUSE

Charing
Cross

SHERLOCK
HOLMES PUB

NORTHUMBERLAND

To St.
James's
Palace
& Green
Park

ADMIRALTY
ARCH

THE LORD MOON
OF THE MALL PUB

WHITEHALL

SITE OF OLD
SCOTLAND
YARD

GREAT SCOTLAND YARD

WHITEHALL PL.

THE MALL

To
Buckingham
Palace

St.
James's
Park

OLD
ADMIRALTY

To Big Ben
& Westminster

200 Meters

200 Yards

The massive National Gallery is one of the world's great art museums.

MEDIEVAL & EARLY RENAISSANCE

1 ANONYMOUS – The Wilton Diptych
2 UCCELLO – Battle of San Romano
3 VAN EYCK – The Arnolfini Portrait

ITALIAN RENAISSANCE

4 LEONARDO – The Virgin of the Rocks
5 BOTTICELLI – Venus and Mars
6 CRIVELLI – The Annunciation, with Saint Emidius

HIGH RENAISSANCE & MANNERISM

7 LEONARDO – Virgin and Child with St. Anne and St. John the Baptist
8 MICHELANGELO – The Entombment
9 RAPHAEL – Pope Julius II
10 BRONZINO – An Allegory with Venus and Cupid
11 TINTORETTO – The Origin of the Milky Way

NORTHERN PROTESTANT ART

12 VERMEER – A Young Woman Standing at a Virginal
13 VAN HOOGSTRATEN – A Peepshow with Views of the Interior of a Dutch House
14 REMBRANDT – Belshazzar's Feast
15 REMBRANDT – Self-Portrait at the Age of 63

BAROQUE & FRENCH ROCOCO

16 RUBENS – The Judgment of Paris
17 VELÁZQUEZ – The Rokeby Venus
18 VAN DYCK – Equestrian Portrait of Charles I
19 CARAVAGGIO –The Supper at Emmaus
20 BOUCHER – Pan and Syrinx

BRITISH ROMANTIC ART

21 CONSTABLE – The Hay Wain
22 TURNER – The Fighting Téméraire

To Leicester Square (5 min. walk)

SAINSBURY WING

ENTRANCE ON LEVEL 0

SELF-GUIDED TOUR STARTS ON LEVEL 2

TOUR BEGINS

SAINSBURY ENTRANCE

Information: Helpful £1 floor plan available from information desk; free one-hour overview tours leave from Sainsbury Wing info desk daily at 11:30 and 14:30, plus Fri at 19:00; excellent £4 audioguides—choose from one-hour highlights tour, several theme tours, or an option that lets you dial up info on any painting in the museum; tel. 020/7747-2885, www.nationalgallery.org.uk.

Eating: Consider splitting afternoon tea at the excellent-but-pricey National Dining Rooms, on the first floor of the Sainsbury Wing. The National Café, located near the Getty Entrance, has a table-service restaurant and a café. Seek out the Espresso Bar, near the Portico and Getty entrances, for sandwiches, pastries, and soft couches.

National Gallery

ORANGE ST. ENTRANCE

Not to Scale

⊠ Elevator/Lift

30 Meters
30 Yards

21   22
20 18   23 **15**
19   **14** 24 25 **13**
26 27 28
17 15   **16** 31 **18**
12   29   30
16
WOHL ROOM   14   SUNLEY ROOM   **19** 32   33 **20**
9
LINK   13 CENTRAL HALL 39 38 36 35 34 **21**
10 11 12   37   **22**
5   SHOP
10 **9** **11** 4 2   40
8   **29** **23** **24**
8 6   45 **25** 41
7   46   **28**   **26**
42   **27**

GETTY ENTRANCE (LEVEL 0)   STAIRS DOWN TO NAT'L CAFÉ & WC

PORTICO ENTRANCE

Trafalgar Square   NELSON'S COLUMN

To Charing Cross ⊖ (2 min. walk) →

IMPRESSIONISM & BEYOND
23 MONET – Gare St. Lazare
24 MONET – The Water-Lily Pond
25 MANET – Corner of a Café-Concert
26 SEURAT – Bathers at Asnières

27 RENOIR – The Skiff
28 VAN GOGH – Sunflowers
29 CÉZANNE – Bathers

Visiting the Museum: Enter through the Sainsbury Entrance (in the smaller building to the left of the main entrance), and approach the collection chronologically.

Medieval and Early Renaissance: In the first rooms, you see shiny paintings of saints, angels, Madonnas, and crucifixions floating in an ethereal gold never-never land. Art in the Middle Ages was religious, dominated by the Church. The illiterate faithful could meditate on an altarpiece and visualize heaven. It's as though they couldn't imagine saints and angels inhabiting the dreary world of rocks, trees, and sky they lived in.

After leaving this gold-leaf peace, you'll stumble into Uccello's *Battle of San Romano* and Van Eyck's *The Arnolfini Portrait,* called by some "The Shotgun

Wedding." This painting—a masterpiece of down-to-earth details—was once thought to depict a wedding ceremony forced by the lady's swelling belly. Today it's understood as a portrait of a solemn, well-dressed, well-heeled couple, the Arnolfinis of Bruges, Belgium (she likely was not pregnant—the fashion of the day was to gather up the folds of one's extremely full-skirted dress).

Italian Renaissance: In painting, the Renaissance meant realism. Artists rediscovered the beauty of nature and the human body, expressing the optimism and confidence of this new age. Look for Botticelli's *Venus and Mars*, Michelangelo's *The Entombment*, and Raphael's *Pope Julius II*.

In Leonardo's *The Virgin of the Rocks*, Mary plays with her son Jesus and little Johnny the Baptist (with cross, at left) while an androgynous angel looks on. Leonardo brings this holy scene right down to earth by setting it among rocks, stalactites, water, and flowering plants. But looking closer, we see that Leonardo has deliberately posed his people into a pyramid shape, with Mary's head at the peak, creating an oasis of maternal stability and serenity amid the hard rock of the earth.

In *The Origin of the Milky Way* by Venetian Renaissance painter Tintoretto, the god Jupiter places his illegitimate son, baby Hercules, at his wife's breast. Juno says, "Wait a minute. That's not my baby!" Her milk spurts upward, becoming the Milky Way.

Northern Protestant: While Italy had wealthy aristocrats and the powerful Catholic Church to purchase art, the North's patrons were middle-class, hardworking, Protestant merchants. They wanted simple, cheap, no-nonsense pictures to decorate their homes and offices. Greek gods and Virgin Marys are out, and hometown folks and hometown places are in.

Highlights include Vermeer's *A Young Woman Standing at a Virginal* and Rembrandt's *Belshazzar's Feast*. Rembrandt painted his *Self-Portrait at the Age of 63* in

the year he would die. He throws the light of truth on...himself. He was bankrupt, his mistress had just passed away, and he had also buried several of his children. We see a disillusioned, well-worn, but proud old genius.

Baroque: While artists in Protestant and democratic Europe painted simple scenes, those in Catholic and aristocratic countries turned to the style called Baroque—taking what was flashy in Venetian art and making it flashier, what was gaudy and making it gaudier, what was dramatic and making it shocking.

The museum's outstanding Baroque collection includes Van Dyck's *Equestrian Portrait of Charles I* and Caravaggio's *The Supper at Emmaus*. In Velázquez's *The Rokeby Venus*, Venus lounges diagonally across the canvas, admiring herself, with flaring red, white, and gray fabrics to highlight her rosy white skin and inflame our passion. This work by the king's personal court painter is a rare Spanish nude from that ultra-Catholic country.

British: The reserved British were more comfortable cavorting with nature than with the lofty gods, as seen in Constable's *The Hay Wain*. But Constable's landscape was about to be paved over by the Indus-

Van Eyck, The Arnolfini Portrait

trial Revolution, as Turner's *The Fighting Téméraire* shows. Machines began to replace humans, factories belched smoke over Constable's hay cart, and cloud-gazers had to punch the clock. But alas, here a modern steamboat symbolically drags a famous but obsolete sailing battleship off into the sunset to be destroyed. Turner's messy, colorful style influenced the Impressionists and gives us our first glimpse into the modern art world.

Impressionism: At the end of the 19th century, a new breed of artists burst out of the stuffy confines of the studio. They donned scarves and berets and set up their canvases in farmers' fields or carried their notebooks into crowded cafés, dashing off quick sketches in order to catch a momentary...impression. Check out Impressionist and Post-Impressionist masterpieces such as Monet's *Gare St. Lazare* and *The Water-Lily Pond,* Renoir's *The Skiff,* Seurat's *Bathers at Asnières,* and Van Gogh's *Sunflowers.*

Cézanne's *Bathers* are arranged in strict triangles. Cézanne uses the Impressionist technique of building a figure with dabs of paint (though his "dabs" are often larger-sized "cube" shapes) to make solid, 3-D geometrical figures in the style of the Renaissance. In the process, his cube shapes helped inspire a radical new style—Cubism—bringing art into the 20th century.

▲▲NATIONAL PORTRAIT GALLERY

Put off by halls of 19th-century characters who meant nothing to me, I used to call this museum "as interesting as someone else's yearbook." But a selective walk through this 500-year-long *Who's Who* of British history is quick and free, and puts faces on the story of England. The collection is well-described, not huge, and in historical sequence, from the 16th century on the second floor to today's royal family, usually housed on the ground floor. Highlights include Henry VIII and wives; portraits of the "Virgin Queen" Elizabeth I, Sir Francis Drake, and Sir Walter Raleigh; the only real-life portrait of William Shakespeare; Oliver Cromwell and Charles I with his head on; portraits by Gainsborough and Reynolds; the Romantics (William Blake, Lord Byron, William Wordsworth, and company); Queen Victoria and her era; and the present royal family, including the late Princess Diana and the current Duchess of Cambridge—Kate.

Cost and Hours: Free, £5 suggested donation, special exhibits extra; daily 10:00-18:00, Fri until 21:00, first and second floors open Mon at 11:00, last entry to special exhibits one hour before closing; excellent audioguide-£3, floor plan-£1; entry 100 yards off Trafalgar Square (around the corner from National Gallery, opposite Church of St. Martin-in-the-Fields), Tube: Charing Cross or Leicester Square, tel. 020/7306-0055, recorded info tel. 020/7312-2463, www.npg.org.uk.

▲ST. MARTIN-IN-THE-FIELDS

The church, built in the 1720s with a Gothic spire atop a Greek-type temple, is an oasis of peace on wild and noisy Trafalgar Square. St. Martin cared for the poor. "In the fields" was where the first church stood on this spot (in the 13th century), between Westminster and The City. Stepping inside, you

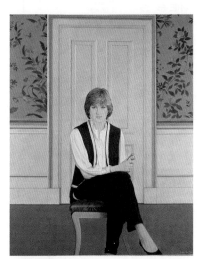

Princess Diana's portrait at the National Portrait Gallery

West End & Nearby

FITZROVIA

Cavendish Square

MARGARET ST.

GREAT PORTLAND ST.

REGENT ST.

BERNERS ST.

NEWMAN ST.

OXFORD STREET

Oxford Circus

DEAN ST.

POLAND ST.

BERWICK ST.

WARDOUR ST.

PRINCES ST.

SOHO

Hanover Square

HANOVER ST.

GREAT MARLBOROUGH ST.

LIBERTY DEPT STORE

BROADWICK ST.

BOURCH.

NEW BOND ST.

S. MOLTON ST.

ST. GEORGE ST.

MADDOX ST.

CARNABY ST.

MARSHALL ST.

LEXINGTON ST.

HOPKINS ST.

TISBURY CT.

BROOK ST.

HAMLEYS

KINGLY ST.

HANDEL & HENDRIX MUSEUM

GROSVENOR ST.

SOTHEBY'S AUCTION HOUSE

CONDUIT ST.

REGENT STREET

WARWICK ST.

PEAK ST.

BRIDLE LN.

G. PULTENEY ST.

JAMES ST.

BREWER ST.

SHAFTESBURY AVE.

RUPERT

Golden Square

SAVILE ROW

OLD BURLINGTON ST.

CLIFFORD ST.

SHERWOOD ST.

DEN-MAN

GLASSHOUSE ST.

COVENTRY

MAYFAIR

BRUTON ST.

OLD BOND ST.

BURLINGTON GARDENS

VIGO ST.

REGENT ST.

Piccadilly Circus

Piccadilly Circus

Berkeley Square

ALBEMARLE ST.

BURLINGTON ARCADE

SACKVILLE ST.

EROS STATUE

DOVER ST.

ROYAL ACADEMY OF ARTS

ST. JAMES

BERKELEY ST.

PICCADILLY

JERMYN ST.

LOWER REGENT ST.

CURZON ST.

BOLTON ST.

Green Park

FORTNUM & MASON

DUKE OF YORK ST.

ST. JAMES'S

St. James's Square

RITZ HOTEL

ST. JAMES ST.

CHRISTIE'S AUCTION HOUSE

KING ST.

PALL MALL

PICCADILLY

Green Park

200 Meters

200 Yards

MARLBOROUGH RD.

ST. JAMES'S PALACE

THE MALL

still feel a compassion for the needs of the people in this neighborhood—the church serves the homeless and houses a Chinese community center. The modern east window—with grillwork bent into the shape of a warped cross—was installed in 2008 to replace one damaged in World War II.

A freestanding glass pavilion to the left of the church serves as the entrance to the church's underground areas. There you'll find the concert ticket office, a gift shop, brass-rubbing center, and the recommended support-the-church Café in the Crypt.

Cost and Hours: Free, donations welcome; hours vary but generally Mon-Fri 8:30-13:00 & 14:00-18:00, Sat 9:30-18:00, Sun 15:30-17:00; services listed at entrance; Tube: Charing Cross, tel. 020/7766-1100, www.stmartin-in-the-fields.org.

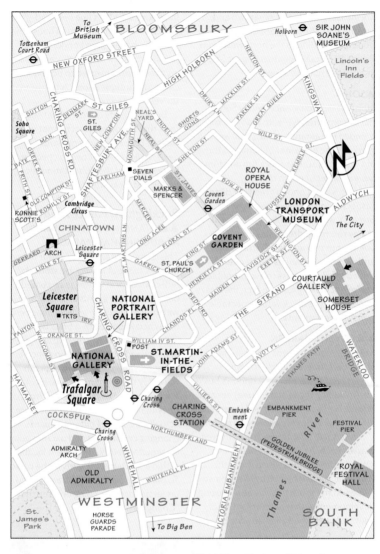

Rick's Tip: St. Martin-in-the-Fields
is famous for its **concerts**. *Consider a
free lunchtime concert (£3.50 suggested
donation; Mon, Tue, and Fri at 13:00), an
evening concert (£9-28, several nights a
week at 19:30), or Wednesday night jazz
(£8-15, at 20:00). See www.stmartin-in-the-
fields.org for the schedule.*

The West End and Nearby

▲PICCADILLY CIRCUS

Although this square is slathered with
neon billboards and tacky attractions
(think of it as the Times Square of London), the surrounding streets are packed
with great shopping opportunities. Nearby
Shaftesbury Avenue and Leicester Square
teem with fun-seekers, theaters, Chinese
restaurants, and street singers. To the

northeast is London's Chinatown and, beyond that, the funky Soho neighborhood. And curling to the northwest from Piccadilly Circus is genteel Regent Street, lined with exclusive shops.

▲SOHO

North of Piccadilly, once-seedy Soho has become trendy—with many recommended restaurants—and is well worth a gawk. It's the epicenter of London's thriving, colorful youth scene, a fun and funky *Sesame Street* of urban diversity.

Soho is also London's red light district (especially near Brewer and Berwick Streets), where "friendly models" wait in tiny rooms up dreary stairways, voluptuous con artists sell strip shows, and eager male tourists are frequently ripped off. But it's easy to avoid trouble if you're not looking for it. In fact, the sleazy joints share the block with respectable pubs and restaurants.

▲▲COVENT GARDEN

This large square teems with people and street performers—jugglers, sword swallowers, and guitar players. London's buskers (including those in the Tube) are auditioned, licensed, and assigned times and places where they are allowed to perform.

The square's centerpiece is a covered marketplace. A market has been here since medieval times, when it was the "convent" garden owned by Westminster Abbey. In the 1600s, it became a housing development with this courtyard as its center, done in the Palladian style by Inigo Jones. Today's fine iron-and-glass structure was built in 1830 to house the stalls of what became London's chief produce market. In 1973, its venerable arcades were converted to boutiques, cafés, and antique shops. A tourist market thrives here today.

Browse trendy crafts, market stalls, and food that's good for you (but not your wallet). For better Covent Garden lunch deals, walk a block or two to check out the places north of the Tube station, along Endell and Neal Streets.

Buckingham Palace Area
▲▲CHANGING OF THE GUARD AT BUCKINGHAM PALACE

This is the spectacle every visitor to London has to see at least once: stone-faced, red-coated (or in winter, gray-coated), bearskin-hatted guards changing posts with much fanfare, in an hour-long ceremony accompanied by a brass band.

Most tourists just show up and get lost in the crowds, but those who anticipate the action and know where to perch will enjoy the event more. The most famous part takes place right in front of Buckingham Palace at 11:00. But there actually are several different guard-changing ceremonies and parades going on simultaneously, at different locations within a few hundred yards of the palace. To plan your sightseeing strategy (and understand what's going on), see the "Changing of the Guard Timeline."

Piccadilly Circus

Covent Garden

Changing of the Guard Timeline

10:00	Arrive now for a spot front and center by the ❶ fence outside Buckingham Palace.
10:30-10:45	❷ Victoria Memorial gets crowded. "New Guard" gathers for inspection at ❸ Wellington Barracks. "Old Guard" gathers at ❹ St. James's Palace.
10:30 (9:30 Sun)	Changing of the Horse Guard at ❺, farther away, along Whitehall.
10:43-11:00	Tired St. James's Palace guards march down ❻ the Mall toward Buckingham Palace. Replacement troops head from Wellington Barracks down ❼ Spur Road to the palace. All guards gradually converge around the Victoria Memorial.
11:00-11:30	Changing of the Guard ceremony takes place inside ❽ the palace courtyard.

Rick's Tip: *Want to go inside* **Buckingham Palace?** *It's* **open to the public only in August and September,** *when the Queen is out of town (£23 for State Rooms; Aug-Sept daily from 9:30, last admission 17:15 in Aug and 16:15 in Sept; book timed-entry ticket in advance by phone, tel. 0303/123-7300, or online, www.royalcollection.org.uk).*

Cost and Hours: Free, May-July daily at 11:00, Aug-April Sun, Mon, Wed, and Fri; no ceremony in very wet weather; exact schedule can change—call 020/7766-7300 for the day's plan, or check www.householddivision.org.uk (search "Changing the Guard"); Buckingham Palace, Tube: Victoria, St. James's Park, or Green Park.

Sightseeing Strategies: The action takes place in stages over the course of an hour, at multiple locations; see the map. Here are a few options to consider:

Watch near the Palace: The main event is in the forecourt right in front of Buckingham Palace (between the palace and the fence) from 11:00 to 11:30. Arrive as close to 10:00 as possible to get a place front and center, next to the fence or on some raised surface to stand or sit on—a balustrade or a curb—so you can see over people's heads.

Watch near the Victoria Memorial: The high ground on the circular Victoria Memorial provides good (if more distant) views of the palace as well as the arriving and departing parades along The Mall and Spur Road. Come before 10:30 to get a place.

Watch near St. James's Palace: If you don't feel like jostling for a view, stroll down to St. James's Palace and wait near the corner for a great photo-op. At about 11:45, the parade marches up The Mall to the palace and performs a smaller changing ceremony—with almost no crowds.

Follow the Procession: You won't get the closest views, but you'll get something even better—the thrill of participating in the action. Start with the "Old Guard" mobilizing in the courtyard of St. James's Palace (10:30). Arrive early, and grab a spot just across the road (otherwise you'll be asked to move when the inspection begins). Just before they prepare to leave

The Changing of the Guard is all about pomp and ceremony.

(at 10:43), march ahead of them down Marlborough Street to The Mall. Pause here to watch them parade past, band and all, on their way to the Buckingham Palace, then cut through the park and head to the Wellington Barracks—where the "New Guard" is getting ready to leave for Buckingham (10:57). March along with full military band and fresh guards from the barracks to the palace. At 11:00 the two guard groups meet in the courtyard, the band plays a few songs, and soldiers parade and finally exchange compliments before returning to Wellington Barracks and St. James's Palace (11:40). Use this time to snap a few photos of the guards—and the crowds—before making your way across the Mall to Clarence House (on Stable Yard Road), where you'll see the "New Guard" pass one last time on their way to St. James's Palace. On their way, the final piece of ceremony takes place—one member of the "Old Guard" and one member of the first-relief "New Guard" change places here.

Join a Tour: Local tour companies such as **Fun London Tours** more or less follow the self-guided route above but add in history and facts about the guards, bands, and royal family to their already entertaining march (£17, Changing of the Guard tour starts at Piccadilly Circus at 9:40, must book online in advance, www.funlondontours.com).

North London

▲▲▲BRITISH MUSEUM

Simply put, this is the greatest chronicle of civilization...anywhere. A visit here is like taking a long hike through *Encyclopedia Britannica* National Park. The vast British Museum wraps around its Great Court (the huge entrance hall), with the most popular sections filling the ground floor: Egyptian, Assyrian, and ancient Greek, with the famous frieze sculptures from the Parthenon in Athens. The museum's stately Reading Room sometimes hosts special exhibits.

Cost and Hours: Free, £5 donation requested, special exhibits usually extra (and with timed ticket); daily 10:00-17:30, Fri until 20:30 (selected galleries only),

British Museum

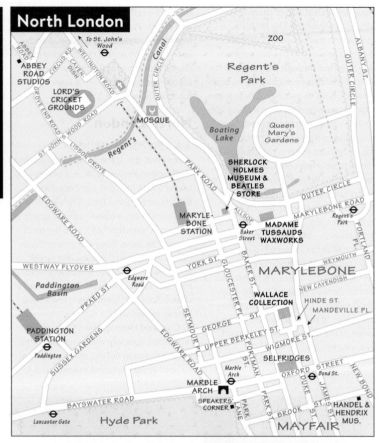

North London

To St. John's Wood

ABBEY ROAD STUDIOS

LORD'S CRICKET GROUNDS

MOSQUE

Regent's

ZOO

Regent's Park

Boating Lake

Queen Mary's Gardens

OUTER CIRCLE

ALBANY ST.

SHERLOCK HOLMES MUSEUM & BEATLES STORE

MARYLE-BONE STATION

MADAME TUSSAUDS WAXWORKS

Baker Street

OUTER CIRCLE

MARYLEBONE ROAD

Regent's Park

PORTLAND PL.

EDGWARE ROAD

ST. JOHN'S WOOD ROAD

LISSON GROVE

PARK ROAD

ALLSOP

WESTWAY FLYOVER

Edgware Road

Paddington Basin

PRAED ST.

YORK ST.

GLOUCESTER PL.

BAKER ST.

MARYLEBONE

WEYMOUTH

NEW CAVENDISH

WALLACE COLLECTION

HINDE ST.

MANDEVILLE PL.

PADDINGTON STATION

Paddington

SUSSEX GARDENS

SEYMOUR PL.

EDGWARE ROAD

GEORGE ST.

UPPER BERKELEY ST.

PORTMAN ST.

WIGMORE ST.

SELFRIDGES

OXFORD STREET

Bond St.

NEW BOND

Marble Arch

MARBLE ARCH

SPEAKERS' CORNER

BAYSWATER ROAD

Lancaster Gate

Hyde Park

PARK LANE

PARK ST.

BROOK ST.

DUKE ST.

JAMES ST.

HANDEL & HENDRIX MUS.

MAYFAIR

least crowded late on weekday afternoons, especially Fri; Great Russell Street, Tube: Tottenham Court Road, ticket desk tel. 020/7323-8181, www.britishmuseum.org.

Tours: Free 30- to 40-minute **Eye-Opener tours** are led by volunteers, who focus on select rooms (daily 11:00-15:45, generally every 15 minutes). Free 45-minute **gallery talks** on specific subjects are offered Tue-Sat at 13:15; a free 20-minute **spotlight** tour runs on Friday evenings. The £6 **multimedia guide** offers dial-up audio commentary and video on 200 objects, as well as several theme tours (must leave photo ID). There's also a fun family multimedia guide (£5). Or 🎧 download my free audio tour.

A mummy case

⊙ SELF-GUIDED TOUR

From the Great Court, doorways lead to all wings. To the left are the exhibits on Egypt, Assyria, and Greece—the highlights of your visit.

EGYPT

Egypt was one of the world's first civilizations. The Egypt we think of—pyramids, mummies, pharaohs, and guys who walk funny—lasted from 3000 to 1000 B.C. with hardly any change in the government, religion, or arts.

The first thing you'll see in the Egypt section is the **Rosetta Stone.** When this rock was unearthed in the Egyptian desert in 1799, it was a sensation in Europe. This black slab, dating from 196 B.C., caused a quantum leap in the study of ancient history. Finally, Egyptian writing could be decoded.

Next, wander past the many **statues,** including a seven-ton Ramesses, with the traditional features of a pharaoh (goatee, cloth headdress, and cobra diadem on his forehead). When Moses told the king of Egypt, "Let my people go!" this was the stony-faced look he got. You'll also see the Egyptian gods as animals—these include Amun, king of the gods, as a ram, and Horus, the god of the living, as a falcon.

At the end of the hall, climb the stairs or take the elevator to **mummy** land. To mummify a body is much like following a recipe. First, disembowel it (but leave the heart inside), then pack the cavities

British Museum Overview

MONTAGUE PLACE

MONTAGUE PLACE
ENTRANCE

Russell
Square

To Fitzrovia &
Charlotte Place
Eateries

UP TO
MUMMIES

CAFÉ

CAFÉ

E
G
Y
P
T

A
S
S
Y
R
I
A

ROSETTA
STONE

READING
ROOM
& SHOP

THE
KING'S
GALLERY

PARTHENON
GALLERIES

G
R
E
E
C
E

WC **THE** WC
GREAT COURT

WINGED
LIONS

INFO

INFO

BLOOMSBURY ST.

MONTAGUE ST.

BOUTIQUE

CLOAK-
ROOM

BOOK-
SHOP

PIZZERIA

COLUMNS

Not to Scale

**MAIN
ENTRANCE**

GREAT RUSSELL STREET

To Tottenham
Court Road ⊖ (10 min. walk)

To Holborn ⊖
(10 min. walk)

with pitch, and dry it with natron, a natural form of sodium carbonate (and, I believe, the active ingredient in Twinkies). Then carefully bandage it head to toe with hundreds of yards of linen strips. Let it sit 2,000 years, and...*voilà!* The mummy was placed in a wooden coffin, which was put in a stone coffin, which was placed in a tomb. The result is that we now have Egyptian bodies that are as well preserved as Larry King. Many of the mummies here are from the time of the Roman occupation, when fine memorial portraits painted in wax became popular. X-ray photos in the display cases tell us more about these people. Don't miss the animal mummies. Cats were popular pets. They were also considered incarnations of the cat-headed goddess Bastet. Worshipped in life as the sun god's allies, preserved in death, and memorialized with statues, cats were given the adulation they've come to expect ever since.

ASSYRIA

The British Museum's valuable collection of Assyrian artifacts has become even more priceless since the recent destruction of ancient sites in the Middle East by ISIS terrorists. Long before Saddam Hussein, Iraq was home to other palace-building, iron-fisted rulers—the Assyrians, who conquered their southern neighbors and dominated the Middle East for 300 years (c. 900-600 B.C.). Their strength came from a superb army (chariots, mounted cavalry, and siege engines), a policy of terrorism against enemies ("I tied their heads to tree trunks all around the city," reads a royal inscription), ethnic cleansing and mass deportations of the vanquished, and efficient administration (roads and express postal service).

Standing guard over the Assyrian exhibit halls are two human-headed **winged lions.** These stone lions guarded

Assyrian human-headed lions

A reconstructed Greek temple

an Assyrian palace (11th-8th century B.C.). With the strength of a lion, the wings of an eagle, the brain of a man, and the beard of ZZ Top, they protected the king from evil spirits and scared the heck out of foreign ambassadors and left-wing newspaper reporters. (What has five legs and flies? Take a close look. These winged quintupeds, which appear complete from both the front and the side, could guard both directions at once.)

Carved into the stone between the bearded lions' loins, you can see one of civilization's most impressive achievements—writing. This wedge-shaped **(cuneiform)** script is the world's first written language, invented 5,000 years ago by the Sumerians (of southern Iraq) and passed down to their less-civilized descendants, the Assyrians.

The **Nimrud Gallery** is a mini version of the throne room and royal apartments of King Ashurnasirpal II's Northwest Palace at Nimrud (9th century B.C.). It's filled with royal propaganda reliefs, 30-ton marble bulls, and panels depicting wounded lions (lion-hunting was Assyria's sport of kings).

GREECE

During their civilization's Golden Age (500-430 B.C.), the ancient Greeks set the tone for all of Western civilization to follow. Democracy, theater, literature, mathematics, philosophy, science, gyros, art, and architecture as we know them, were virtually all invented by a single generation of Greeks in a small town of maybe 80,000 citizens.

Your walk through Greek art history starts with pottery, usually painted red and black, and a popular export product for the sea-trading Greeks. The earliest featured geometric patterns (eighth century B.C.), then a painted black silhouette on the natural orange clay, then a red figure on a black background. Later, painted vases show a culture really into partying.

The highlight is the **Parthenon Sculptures**—taken from the temple dedicated to Athena—the crowning glory of an enormous urban-renewal plan during Greece's Golden Age. While the building itself remains in Athens, many of the Parthenon's best sculptures are right here in the British Museum. The sculptures are also called the Elgin Marbles, named for the shrewd British ambassador who had his men hammer, chisel, and saw them off the Parthenon in the early 1800s. Though the Greek government complains about losing its marbles, the Brits feel they rescued and preserved the sculptures. These much-wrangled-over bits of the Parthenon (from about 450 B.C.) are indeed impressive. The marble panels you see lining the walls of this large hall are part of the frieze that originally ran around the exterior of the Parthenon, under the eaves. The statues at either end of the hall once filled the Parthenon's triangular-shaped pediments and showed the birth of Athena. The relief panels known as metopes tell the story of the struggle between the forces of human civilization and animal-like barbarism.

THE REST OF THE MUSEUM

Venture upstairs to see artifacts from **Roman Britain** that surpass anything at Hadrian's Wall or elsewhere in the country. Also look for the Sutton Hoo Ship Burial artifacts from a seventh-century royal burial on the east coast of England (Room 41). A rare Michelangelo cartoon (preliminary sketch) is in Room 90 (level 4).

▲▲▲BRITISH LIBRARY

Here, in just two rooms, are the literary treasures of Western civilization, from early Bibles to Shakespeare's *Hamlet* to Lewis Carroll's *Alice's Adventures in Wonderland* to the *Magna Carta*. You'll see the Lindisfarne Gospels transcribed on an illuminated manuscript, Beatles lyrics scrawled on the back of a greeting card, and Leonardo da Vinci's genius sketched into his notebooks. The British Empire built its greatest monuments out of paper.

Cost and Hours: Free, £5 suggested donation, admission charged for special exhibits; Mon-Fri 9:30-18:00, Tue-Thu until 20:00, Sat until 17:00, Sun 11:00-17:00; 96 Euston Road, Tube: King's Cross St. Pancras or Euston, tel. 019/3754-6060 or 020/7412-7676, www.bl.uk.

The British Library is filled with treasures ranging from the Magna Carta to The Beatles' song sheets.

Tours: There are no guided tours or audioguides for the permanent collection, but you can 🎧 download my free British Library **audio tour.** Touch-screen computers in the permanent collection let you page virtually through some of the rare books.

➲ SELF-GUIDED TOUR

Everything that matters for your visit is in a tiny but exciting area variously called "The Sir John Ritblat Gallery," "Treasures of the British Library," or just "The Treasures." We'll concentrate on a handful of documents—literary and historical—that changed the course of history. Note that exhibits change often, and many of the museum's old, fragile manuscripts need to "rest" periodically in order to stay well-preserved.

Upon entering the Ritblat Gallery, start at the far side of the room with the display case of historic ❶ **maps** showing how humans' perspective of the world expanded over the centuries. Next, move into the area dedicated to ❷ **sacred texts and early Bibles** from several cultures, including the Codex Sinaiticus. This early bound book from around A.D. 350 is one of the oldest complete Bibles in existence. In the display cases called ❸ **Art of the Book,** you'll find beautifully illustrated, or "illuminated," Bibles from the early medieval period, including the Lindisfarne Gospels (A.D. 698). Look out for some Early English Bibles—the King James Version, the Wycliffe Bible, or others—dating from the 15th, 16th, and 17th centuries.

In the glass cases featuring early ❹ **printing,** you'll see the Gutenberg Bible, the first book printed in Europe using movable type (c. 1455)—a revolutionary document. Suddenly, the Bible was available for anyone to read, fueling the Protestant Reformation.

Through a nearby doorway is a small room that holds versions of the ❺ **Magna Carta,** assuming they're not "resting" when you visit (though historians talk about *the* Magna Carta, several different versions of the document exist). The basis for England's constitutional system of Government, this "Great Charter" listing rules about mundane administrative issues was radical because of the simple fact that the king had agreed to abide by them as law.

Return to the main room to find display cases featuring trailblazing ❻ **art and science** documents by early scientists such as Galileo, Isaac Newton, and many more. Pages from Leonardo da Vinci's notebook show his powerful curiosity, his genius for invention, and his famous backward and inside-out handwriting. Nearby are many more ❼ **historical documents.** The displays change frequently, but you may see letters by Henry VIII, Queen Elizabeth I, Darwin, Freud, Gandhi, and others.

Next, trace the evolution of ❽ **English literature.** Check out the A.D. 1000 manuscript of *Beowulf,* the first English literary masterpiece, and the *The Canterbury Tales* (c. 1410), Geoffrey Chaucer's bawdy collection of stories.

The only known manuscript of the epic saga Beowulf

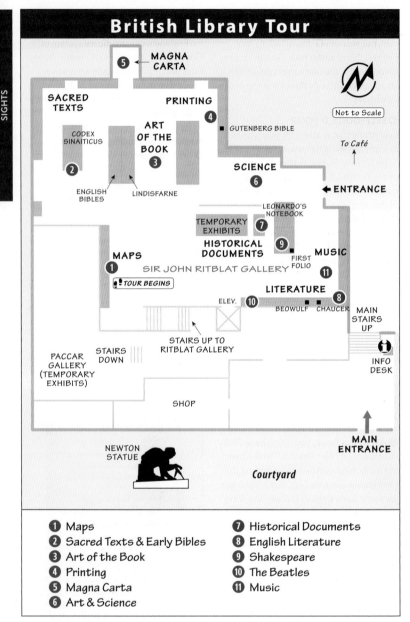

British Library Tour

MAGNA CARTA

SACRED TEXTS

CODEX SINAITICUS

ENGLISH BIBLES

LINDISFARNE

PRINTING

ART OF THE BOOK

GUTENBERG BIBLE

SCIENCE

Not to Scale

To Café

ENTRANCE

LEONARDO'S NOTEBOOK

TEMPORARY EXHIBITS

HISTORICAL DOCUMENTS

MAPS

SIR JOHN RITBLAT GALLERY

FIRST FOLIO

MUSIC

TOUR BEGINS

LITERATURE

ELEV.

BEOWULF   CHAUCER

MAIN STAIRS UP

STAIRS UP TO RITBLAT GALLERY

PACCAR GALLERY (TEMPORARY EXHIBITS)

STAIRS DOWN

INFO DESK

SHOP

NEWTON STATUE

Courtyard

MAIN ENTRANCE

1 Maps
2 Sacred Texts & Early Bibles
3 Art of the Book
4 Printing
5 Magna Carta
6 Art & Science

7 Historical Documents
8 English Literature
9 Shakespeare
10 The Beatles
11 Music

Lewis Carroll's manuscript for Alice's Adventures in Wonderland

The Literature wall is often a greatest-hits sampling of literature in English, from Brontë to Kipling to Woolf to Joyce to Dickens. The original *Alice's Adventures in Wonderland* by Lewis Carroll created a fantasy world, where grown-up rules and logic were turned upside down. The most famous of England's writers— **❾ Shakespeare**—generally gets his own display case. Look for the First Folio—one of the 750 copies of the first complete collection of his plays, published in 1623.

Now fast-forward a few centuries to **❿ The Beatles.** Look for photos of John Lennon, Paul McCartney, George Harrison, and Ringo Starr before and after their fame, as well as manuscripts of song lyrics written by Lennon and McCartney. In the **⓫ music** section, there are manuscripts by Mozart, Beethoven, Schubert, and others (kind of an anticlimax after the Fab Four, I know). George Frideric Handel's famous oratorio, the *Messiah* (1741), is often on display and marks the end of our tour. Hallelujah.

▲ MADAME TUSSAUDS WAXWORKS

This waxtravaganza is gimmicky, crass, and crazily expensive, but dang fun...a hit with the kind of tourists who skip the British Museum. The original Madame Tussaud did wax casts of heads lopped off during the French Revolution (such as Marie-Antoinette's). She took her show on the road and ended up in London in 1835. Now it's all about singing with Lady Gaga, partying with Benedict Cumberbatch, and hanging with the Beatles. In addition to posing with all the eerily realistic wax dummies—from the Queen and Will and Kate to the Beckhams—you'll have the chance to learn how they created this waxy army; hop on a people-mover and cruise through a kid-pleasing "Spirit of London" time trip; and visit with Spider-Man, the Hulk, and other Marvel superheroes. A nine-minute "4-D" show features a 3-D movie heightened by wind, "back ticklers," and other special effects.

Rick's Tip: *To* **skip Madame Tussauds' ticket-buying line** *(which can be an hour or more), purchase a Fast Track ticket in advance (available from souvenir shops or at the TI), or consider getting the pricey* **Priority Entrance** *ticket and reserving a time slot at least a day in advance. The place is less crowded if you arrive after 15:00.*

Cost: £35, kids-£30 (free for kids under 5), up to 25 percent discount and shorter lines if you buy tickets in advance on their website; combo-deal with the London Eye.

Hours: Roughly July-Aug and school holidays daily 8:30-18:00, Sept-June Mon-Fri 10:00-16:00, Sat-Sun 9:00-17:00, these are last entry times—it stays open roughly two hours later; check website for the latest times as hours vary widely depending on season, Marylebone Road, Tube: Baker Street, tel. 0871-894-3000, www.madametussauds.com.

The Beatles at Madame Tussauds

The City

When Londoners say "The City," they mean the one-square-mile business center in East London that 2,000 years ago was Roman Londinium. The outline of the Roman city walls can still be seen in the arc of roads from Blackfriars Bridge to Tower Bridge. It's a fascinating district to wander on weekdays, but since almost nobody actually lives there, it's dull in the evening and on Saturday and Sunday.

You can 🎧 download my free audio tour of The City, which peels back the many layers of history in this oldest part of London.

▲▲▲ST. PAUL'S CATHEDRAL

Sir Christopher Wren's most famous church is the great St. Paul's, its elaborate interior capped by a 365-foot dome. There's been a church on this spot since 604. After the Great Fire of 1666 destroyed the old cathedral, Wren created this Baroque masterpiece. And since World War II, St. Paul's has been Britain's symbol of resilience. Despite 57 nights of bombing, the Nazis failed to destroy the cathedral, thanks to St. Paul's volunteer fire watchmen, who stayed on the dome.

Even now, as skyscrapers encroach, the 365-foot-high dome of St. Paul's rises majestically above the rooftops of the neighborhood. The tall dome is set on classical columns, capped with a lantern, topped by a six-foot ball, and iced with a cross. As the first Anglican cathedral built in London after the Reformation, it is Baroque: St. Peter's in Rome filtered through clear-eyed English reason. Though often the site of historic funerals (Queen Victoria and Winston Churchill), St. Paul's most famous ceremony was a wedding—when Prince Charles married Lady Diana Spencer in 1981.

Cost and Hours: £18, £16 in advance online, includes church entry, dome climb, crypt, tour, and audio/videoguide; Mon-Sat 8:30-16:30 (dome opens at 9:30), closed Sun except for worship; book ahead online to skip the line, 15-30-minute wait at busy times; Tube: St. Paul's; recorded info tel. 020/7246-8348, reception tel. 020/7246-8350, www.stpauls.co.uk.

Music and Church Services: Worship times are available on the church's website. Communion is generally Mon-Sat

St. Paul's Cathedral

ENTRANCE TO CRYPT
CAFÉ & WC

ENTER

STAIRS

DOME

NAVE

CHOIR

HIGH ALTAR

BISHOP'S CHAIR

To
St. Paul's ⊖

To →
One New Change
Terrace View

30 Meters
30 Yards

To
Millennium
Bridge

1 Nave
2 Wellington Monument
3 Dome
4 Choir & High Altar
5 HUNT–The Light of the World
6 MOORE–Mother and Child
7 American Memorial (Jesus Chapel)
8 John Donne Statue
9 Nelson & Cornwallis Monuments
10 Climb the Dome (2 entrances)
11 Crypt Entrance (2 entrances)

Majestic St. Paul's Cathedral is one of London's most iconic buildings.

The City, The Tower & East London

200 Meters
200 Yards

Farringdon

Barbican

BEECH ST.

GRAY'S INN RD.
HATTON GDN.
LEATHER LN.
GREVILLE ST.
COWCROSS ST.
CHARTERHOUSE ST.
LONG LN.
ALDERSGATE ST.

Gray's Inn Gdns.

HOLBORN

BARBICAN

HIGH HOLBORN
W. SMITHFIELD

MUSEUM OF LONDON

LONDON

CHANCERY LN.
FARRINGDON RD.
NEWGATE ST.
ANGEL ST.
GRESHAM ST.

THE

THE OLD BANK OF ENGLAND PUB
YE OLDE CHESHIRE CHEESE PUB
OLD BAILEY
ST. MARTIN
Paternoster Square
St. Paul's
ONE NEW CHANGE
ST. MARY LE BOW

CAREY ST.
FETTER LN.
ST. DUNSTAN
FLEET STREET
LUDGATE HILL
NEW CHANGE
BREAD ST.
BOW LANE

ROYAL COURTS OF JUSTICE

ST. CLEM. DANES
TEMPLE CHURCH
ST. BRIDE
ST. BRIDE

ST. PAUL'S

PETER'S HILL
WATLING
CANNON ST.

To Trafalgar Square
THE TEMPLE
MITRE CT.
TUDOR ST.
THE BLACK FRIAR PUB
Blackfriars
QUEEN VICTORIA ST.
Mansion House

TEMPLE PL.
VICTORIA EMBANKMENT
UPPER THAMES ST.

Temple

BLACKFRIARS PIER

Thames
NEW BRIDGE ST.
BLACKFRIARS BRIDGE
River

MILLENNIUM PEDESTRIAN BRIDGE

Thames Path

SOUTHWARK BRIDGE

Jubilee Walkway

OXO TOWER

BANKSIDE PIER

ROYAL NATIONAL THEATRE
SOUTH BANK
BANKSIDE

TATE MODERN
GLOBE

UPPER GROUND
STAMFORD ST.
HATFIELDS
HOPTON ST.
SOUTHWARK ST.
SUMNER ST.
PARK ST.

SOUTHWARK

at 8:00 and 12:30. On Sunday, services are held at 8:00, 10:15 (Matins), 11:30 (sung Eucharist), 15:15 (evensong), and 18:00. The rest of the week, evensong is at 17:00 (Mon is spoken—not sung). On some Sundays, there's a free organ recital at 16:45.

Rick's Tip: *If you come to St. Paul's 20 minutes **early for evensong worship** (under the dome), you may be able to grab a big wooden stall in the choir, next to the singers.*

Tours: Admission includes an **audio-guide** (with video clips), as well as a 1.5-hour guided **tour** (Mon-Sat at 10:00, 11:00, 13:00, and 14:00; call 020/7246-8357 to confirm or ask at church). Free 20-minute **introductory talks** are offered throughout the day. You can also ⌂ download my free St. Paul's Cathedral **audio tour.**

⊙ SELF-GUIDED TOUR

Enter, buy your ticket, pick up the free visitor's map, and stand at the far back of the ❶ **nave,** behind the font. This big church feels big. At 515 feet long and 250 feet wide, it's Europe's fourth largest, after

To Geffrye
Museum

QUAKER ST. BUXTON ST.

FORMER
TRUMAN
BREWERY

CHISWELL ST.

SUN ST.

SILK ST.

MOORE LN.

MOORFIELDS

MOORGATE

ELDON ST.

SHOREDITCH

COMMERCIAL

LAMB ST.

HANBURY ST.

GREAT
MOSQUE

SPITALFIELDS
MARKET

BRUSHFIELD ST.

FOURN.

CHRIST
CHURCH

FASHION ST.

BRICK LANE

LIVERPOOL
STREET
STATION

Liverpool
Street

WHITE'S
ROW

WIDEGATE

FINSBURY

Moorgate

FINSBURY
CIRCUS

LIVERPOOL ST.

PETTICOAT
LANE
MARKET

WENTWORTH ST.

WALL

BISHOPSGATE

MIDDLESEX STREET

EAST
END

Aldgate
East

THE
GUILDHALL

BARTHOLOMEW
LN.

TOWER
42

OLD BROAD

COULSTONE RD.

WHITECHAPEL HIGH

BRAHAM ST.

LEMAN ST.

CITY

THREADNEEDLE

LEADENHALL
BLDG.
"CHEESE
GRATER"

ST. MARY AXE

DUKES PL.

30 ST. MARY AXE
("THE GHERKIN")

Aldgate

ALDGATE

WHITE-
CHAPEL

BANK OF
ENGLAND

ROYAL EXCHANGE

CORNHILL

LEADENHALL ST.

CHEAPSIDE

Bank

THE COUNTING
HOUSE PUB

THE
SCALPEL

MOTEL
ONE

PRESCOT ST.

MANSION
HOUSE

KING WILLIAM ST.

LOMBARD

GRACECHURCH

LEADEN-
HALL
MARKET

FENCHURCH

MINORIES ST.

MANSELL

PREMIER INN
LONDON CITY
TOWER HILL

STREET

Cannon
Street

EASTCHEAP

20 FENCHURCH
("WALKIE-TALKIE")

MARK LN.

COOPERS ROW

Tower
Hill

ROMAN
WALL

Monument

THE
MONUMENT

Tower
Hill

LOWER

THAMES STREET

BYWARD ST.

ALL
HALLOWS

LOWER THAMES

TOWER HILL

CANNON
STREET
BRIDGE

LONDON BRIDGE

TOWER OF
LONDON

ST.
KATHARINE
DOCK

GOLDEN
HINDE
REPLICA

LONDON BRIDGE
PIER

TOWER
PIER

HMS
BELFAST

SOUTHWARK
CATHEDRAL

London
Bridge

LONDON BRIDGE
STATION

TOWER
BRIDGE

ST.
KATHARINE'S PIER

CHISWELL ST.

WALL

CITY

BANK OF
ENGLAND

CHEAPSIDE

MANSION
HOUSE

STREET

Cannon
Street

LOWER

those in Rome (St. Peter's), Sevilla, and Milan. The spaciousness is accentuated by the relative lack of decoration. The simple, cream-colored ceiling and the clear glass in the windows light everything evenly. Wren wanted this: a simple, open church with nothing to hide. Unfortunately, only this entrance area keeps his original vision—the rest was encrusted with 19th-century Victorian ornamentation.

Ahead and on the left is the towering, black-and-white ❷ **Wellington Monument.** Wren would have been appalled, but his church has become so central to England's soul that many national heroes are buried here (in the basement crypt).

The ❸ **dome** you see from here, painted with scenes from the life of St. Paul, is only the innermost of three. From the painted interior of the first dome, look up through the opening to see the light-filled lantern of the second dome. Finally, the whole thing is covered on the outside by the third and final dome, the shell of lead-covered wood that you see from the street. Wren's ingenious three-in-one design was psychological as well as functional—he wanted a low, shallow inner dome so worshippers wouldn't feel diminished. The ❹ **choir** area blocks your way, but you can see the altar at the far end under a golden canopy.

Do a quick clockwise spin around the church. In the north transept (to your left as you face the altar), find the big painting ❺ *The Light of the World* (1904), by the Pre-Raphaelite William Holman Hunt. Inspired by Hunt's own experience of finding Christ during a moment of spiritual crisis, the crowd-pleasing work was criticized by art highbrows for being "syrupy" and "simple"—even as it became the most famous painting in Victorian England.

Along the left side of the choir is the modern statue ❻ *Mother and Child,* by the great modern sculptor Henry Moore. Typical of Moore's work, this Mary and Baby Jesus—inspired by the sight of British moms nursing babies in WWII bomb shelters—renders a traditional subject in an abstract, minimalist way.

The area behind the altar, with three bright and modern stained-glass windows, is the ❼ **American Memorial Chapel**— honoring the Americans who sacrificed their lives to save Britain in World War II. In colored panes that arch around the big windows, spot the American eagle (center window, to the left of Christ), George Washington (right window, upper-right corner), and symbols of all 50 states (find your state seal). In the carved wood beneath the windows, you'll see

birds and foliage native to the US. The Roll of Honor (a 500-page book under glass immediately behind the altar) lists the names of 28,000 US servicemen and women based in Britain who gave their lives during the war.

Around the other side of the choir is a shrouded statue honoring ❽ **John Donne** (1621–1631), a passionate preacher in old St. Paul's, as well as a great poet ("never wonder for whom the bell tolls—it tolls for thee"). In the south transept are monuments to military greats ❾ **Horatio Nelson,** who fought Napoleon, and **Charles Cornwallis,** who was finished off by George Washington at Yorktown.

❿ **Climbing the Dome:** You can climb 528 steps to reach the dome and great city views. Along the way, have some fun in the **Whispering Gallery** (257 steps up). Whisper sweet nothings into the wall, and your partner (and anyone else) standing far away can hear you. For best effects, try whispering (not talking) with your mouth close to the wall, while your partner stands a few dozen yards away with his or her ear to the wall.

⓫ **Visiting the Crypt:** The crypt is a world of historic bones and interesting cathedral models. Many legends are buried here—Horatio Nelson, who wore down Napoleon; the Duke of Wellington, who finished Napoleon off; and even Wren himself. Wren's actual tomb is marked by a simple black slab with no statue, though he considered this church

The cathedral's interior is dazzling.

Views from St. Paul's dome are worth the climb.

London's Best Views

For some viewpoints, you need to pay admission. At the bars or restaurants, you'll need to buy a drink. The only truly free spots are Primrose Hill, One New Change Rooftop Terrace, and the Sky Garden at 20 Fenchurch.

London Eye: Ride the giant Ferris wheel for stunning London views. See page 77.

St. Paul's Dome: You'll earn a striking, unobstructed view by climbing hundreds of steps to the cramped balcony of the church's cupola.

One New Change Rooftop Terrace: Get fine, free views of St. Paul's Cathedral and surroundings—nearly as good as those from St. Paul's Dome—from the rooftop terrace of the One New Change shopping mall just behind and east of the church.

Tate Modern: Take in a classic vista across the Thames from the restaurant/bar on the museum's sixth level and from the new Blavatnik Building (a.k.a. the Switch House). See page 80.

20 Fenchurch (a.k.a. "The Walkie-Talkie"): Get 360-degree views of London from the mostly enclosed Sky Garden. It's free, but you'll need to make reservations in advance and bring photo ID (Mon-Fri 10:00-18:00, Sat-Sun 11:00-21:00, 20 Fenchurch Street, Tube: Monument, www.skygarden.london).

National Portrait Gallery: A mod top-floor restaurant peers over Trafalgar Square and the Westminster neighborhood.

Waterstones Bookstore: Its hip, low-key, top-floor café/bar has reasonable prices and sweeping views of the London Eye, Big Ben, and the Houses of Parliament (Mon-Sat 9:00-22:00, Sun 12:00-18:30, café closes hour earlier on Sun, 203 Piccadilly, www.5thview.co.uk).

The Shard: The observation decks that cap this 1,020-foot-tall skyscraper offer London's most commanding views in clear weather, but at a steep price (£31, less if booked online at least a day in advance; daily 10:00-22:00, shorter hours Oct-March; Tube: London Bridge—use London Bridge exit and follow signs, www.theviewfromtheshard.com).

to be his legacy. Back up in the nave, on the floor directly under the dome, is Christopher Wren's name and epitaph (written in Latin): "Reader, if you seek his monument, look around you."

▲MUSEUM OF LONDON

This museum tells the fascinating story of London, taking you on a walk from its pre-Roman beginnings to the present. It features London's distinguished citizens through history—from Neanderthals, to Romans, to Elizabethans, to Victorians, to Mods, to today. The displays are chronological, spacious, and informative without being overwhelming. Scale models and costumes help you visualize everyday life in the city at different periods. There are enough whiz-bang multimedia displays (including the Plague and the Great Fire) to spice up otherwise humdrum artifacts. This regular stop for the local school kids gives the best overview of London history in town.

Cost and Hours: Free, daily 10:00-18:00, last entry one hour before closing, see the day's events board for special talks and tours, café, baggage lockers, 150 London Wall at Aldersgate Street, Tube: Barbican or St. Paul's plus a 5-minute walk, tel. 020/7001-9844, www.museumoflondon.org.uk.

THE MONUMENT

Wren's recently restored 202-foot-tall tribute to London's 1666 Great Fire is at the junction of Monument Street and Fish Street Hill. Climb the 311 steps inside the column for a monumental view of The City (£4.50, £11 combo-ticket with Tower Bridge, cash only, daily 9:30-18:00, until 17:30 Oct-March, Tube: Monument).

▲▲▲TOWER OF LONDON

The Tower has served as a castle in wartime, a king's residence in peacetime, and, most notoriously, as the prison and execution site of rebels. You can see the crown jewels, take a witty Beefeater tour, and ponder the executioner's block

Tower of London

that dispensed with Anne Boleyn, Sir Thomas More, and troublesome heirs to the throne.

Cost and Hours: £28, family-£70, entry fee includes Beefeater tour (described later), Tue-Sat 9:00-17:30, Sun-Mon from 10:00, Nov-Feb until 16:30, skippable audioguide-£4; Tube: Tower Hill, tel. 0844-482-7788, www.hrp.org.uk.

Advance Tickets: To avoid the long ticket-buying lines, and save a few pounds off the gate price, buy a **voucher** in advance. You can purchase vouchers at the Trader's Gate gift shop, located down the steps from the Tower Hill Tube stop (pick it up on your way to the Tower; vouchers here can be used any day), or on the Tower website (£24, family-£59, vouchers purchased online are valid only on the date you select).

All vouchers, regardless of where purchased, must be exchanged for tickets at the Tower's group ticket office (see map). You can also try buying tickets, with credit card only, at the Tower Welcome Centre to the left of the normal ticket lines—though on busy days they may turn you away. Tickets are also sold by phone (tel. 0844-482-7788 within UK or tel. 011-44-20-3166-6000 from the US; £2 fee, pick up your tickets at the Tower's group ticket office).

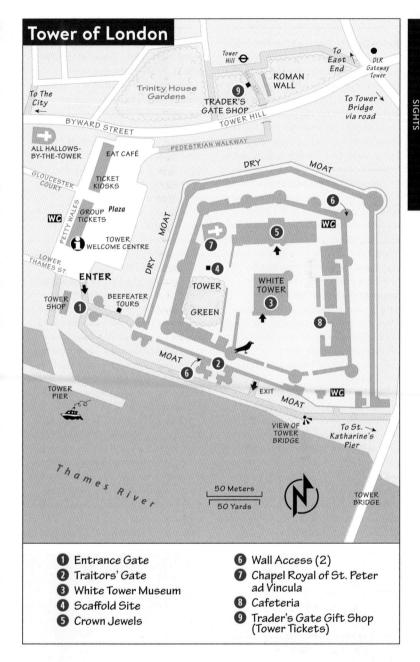

Tower of London

To East End

DLR Gateway Tower

Tower Hill

ROMAN WALL

Trinity House Gardens

To Tower Bridge via road

TRADER'S GATE SHOP

To The City

TOWER HILL

BYWARD STREET

PEDESTRIAN WALKWAY

ALL HALLOWS-BY-THE-TOWER

EAT CAFÉ

GLOUCESTER COURT

TICKET KIOSKS

DRY MOAT

WC

GROUP TICKETS

Plaza

PETTY WALES

TOWER WELCOME CENTRE

DRY MOAT

WC

LOWER THAMES ST.

ENTER

TOWER SHOP

BEEFEATER TOURS

TOWER GREEN

WHITE TOWER

MOAT

EXIT

TOWER PIER

WC

VIEW OF TOWER BRIDGE

To St. Katharine's Pier

Thames River

50 Meters

50 Yards

N

TOWER BRIDGE

1 Entrance Gate
2 Traitors' Gate
3 White Tower Museum
4 Scaffold Site
5 Crown Jewels

6 Wall Access (2)
7 Chapel Royal of St. Peter ad Vincula
8 Cafeteria
9 Trader's Gate Gift Shop (Tower Tickets)

Rick's Tip: *The* **Tower of London** *is most crowded in summer, on weekends (especially Sundays), and during school holidays. The line for the crown jewels can be just as long as the line for tickets.* **Arrive before 10:00 and go straight for the jewels.** *Alternatively, arrive in the afternoon, tour the rest of the Tower first, and see the jewels an hour before closing time, when crowds die down.*

Yeoman Warder (Beefeater) Tours: Today, while the Tower's military purpose is history, it's still home to the Beefeaters—the 35 Yeoman Warders and their families. (The original duty of the Yeoman Warders was to guard the Tower, its prisoners, and the jewels.) Free, worthwhile, one-hour Beefeater tours leave every 30 minutes from just inside the entrance gate (first tour Tue-Sat at 10:00, Sun-Mon at 10:30, last one at 15:30—or 14:30 in Nov-Feb). The boisterous Beefeaters are great entertainers, whose historical talks include lots of bloody anecdotes and corny jokes.

Sunday Worship: For a refreshingly different Tower experience, come on Sunday morning, when visitors are welcome on the grounds for free to worship in the Chapel Royal of St. Peter ad Vincula. You get in without the lines, but you can only see the chapel—no sightseeing (9:15 Communion or 11:00 service with fine choral music, meet at west gate 30 minutes early, dress for church, may be closed for ceremonies—call ahead).

Rick's Tip: *To scenically—though circuitously—connect the* **Tower of London with St. Paul's Cathedral,** *detour through Southwark on the South Bank (and stop by Borough Market for the fun food scene).*

Visiting the Tower: William the Conqueror, still getting used to his new title, built the stone "White Tower" (1077-1097) to keep the Londoners in line, a gleaming reminder of the monarch's absolute power. You could be feasting on roast boar in the banqueting hall one night and chained to the walls of the prison the next. The Tower also served as an effective lookout for seeing invaders coming up the Thames.

This square, 90-foot-tall tower was the original structure that gave this castle complex of 20 towers its name. William's successors enlarged the complex to its present 18-acre size. Because of the security it provided, the Tower of London served over the centuries as a royal residence, the Royal Mint, the Royal Jewel House, and, most famously, as a prison and execution site.

You'll find more bloody history per square inch in this original tower of power than anywhere else in Britain. Inside the White Tower is a **museum** with exhibits re-creating medieval life and chronicling the torture and executions that took place here. In the Royal Armory, you'll see some suits of armor of Henry VIII—slender in his youth (c. 1515), heavyset by

A Beefeater on duty   *Execution ax and block*

Henry VIII (1491-1547)

The notorious king who single-handedly transformed England was a true Renaissance Man—six feet tall, handsome, charismatic, well-educated, and brilliant. He spoke English, Latin, French, and Spanish. A legendary athlete, he hunted, played tennis, and jousted with knights and kings. When 17-year-old Henry, the second monarch of the House of Tudor, was crowned king in Westminster Abbey, all of England rejoiced.

Henry left affairs of state to others, and filled his days with sports, war, dice, women, and the arts. But in 1529, Henry changed the course of history. He wanted a divorce: His wife had become too old to bear him a son, and he'd fallen in love with Anne Boleyn. Henry begged the pope for an annulment, but—for political reasons—the pope refused. Henry divorced his wife anyway, and he was excommunicated.

Henry's rejection of papal authority sparked the English Reformation. He forced monasteries to close, sold off some church land, and confiscated everything else for himself and the Crown. Within a decade, monastic institutions that had operated for centuries were left empty and gutted. Meanwhile, the Catholic Church was reorganized into the (Anglican) Church of England, with Henry as its head. Though Henry himself basically adhered to Catholic doctrine, he discouraged the veneration of saints and relics, and commissioned an English translation of the Bible.

Henry famously had six wives. The issue was not his love life (which could have been satisfied by his numerous mistresses), but the politics of royal succession. To guarantee the Tudor family's dominance, he needed a male heir born by a recognized queen. Henry's first marriage, to Catherine of Aragon, had been arranged to cement an alliance with her parents, Ferdinand and Isabel of Spain. Catherine bore Henry a daughter, but no sons. Next came Anne Boleyn, who also gave birth to a daughter. After a turbulent few years with Anne and several miscarriages, a frustrated Henry had her beheaded. His next wife, Jane Seymour, finally had a son (but Jane died soon after giving birth). A blind-marriage with Anne of Cleves ended quickly when she proved to be both politically useless and ugly. Next, teen bride Catherine Howard ended up cheating on Henry, so she was executed. Henry finally found comfort—but no children—in his later years with his final wife, Catherine Parr.

Henry's last years were marked by paranoia, sudden rages, and despotism. He gave his perceived enemies the pink slip in his signature way—charged with treason and beheaded. Once-wealthy England was becoming depleted, thanks to Henry's expensive habits, which included making war on France, building and acquiring 50 palaces, and collecting fine tapestries and archery bows.

Henry forged a large legacy. He expanded the power of the monarchy, making himself the focus of a rising, modern nation-state. Simultaneously, he strengthened Parliament—largely because it agreed with his policies. He annexed Wales, and imposed English rule on Ireland (provoking centuries of resentment). He expanded the navy, paving the way for Britannia to soon rule the waves. And—thanks to Henry's marital woes—England would forever be a Protestant nation.

1540—with his bigger-is-better codpiece. On the top floor, see the Tower's actual execution ax and chopping block. The **scaffold site,** however, in the middle of Tower Green, looks pleasant enough today. Henry VIII axed a couple of his ex-wives here, including Anne Boleyn and Catherine Howard.

Across from the White Tower is the entrance to the **crown jewels.** The Sovereign's Scepter is encrusted with the world's largest cut diamond—the 530-carat Star of Africa, beefy as a quarter-pounder. The Crown of the Queen Mother (Elizabeth II's famous mum, who died in 2002) has the 106-carat Koh-I-Noor diamond glittering on the front (considered unlucky for male rulers, it only adorns the crown of the king's wife). The Imperial State Crown is what the Queen wears for official functions such as the State Opening of Parliament. Among its 3,733 jewels are Queen Elizabeth I's former earrings (the hanging pearls, top center), a stunning 13th-century ruby look-alike in the center, and Edward the Confessor's ring (the blue sapphire on top, in the center of the Maltese cross of diamonds).

At the far end of the Tower Green is the **Bloody Tower,** and beyond that, the **Medieval Palace.** From the medieval palace's throne room you can continue up the stairs to **walk the walls.** The Tower was defended by state-of-the-art walls and fortifications in the 13th century. Walking along them offers a good look at the walls, along with a fine view of the famous Tower Bridge, with its twin towers and blue spans.

TOWER BRIDGE

The iconic Tower Bridge (often mistakenly called London Bridge) was built in 1894 to accommodate the growing East End. While fully modern and hydraulically powered, the drawbridge was designed with a retro Neo-Gothic look. The bridge is most interesting when the drawbridge lifts to let ships pass, as it does a thousand times a year (best viewed from the Tower side of the Thames). For the bridge-lifting schedule, check the website or call.

You can tour the bridge at the **Tower Bridge Exhibition,** with a history display

The Tower Bridge has spanned the Thames since 1894.

and a peek at the Victorian-era engine room that lifts the span. Included in your entrance is the chance to cross the bridge—138 feet above the road along a partially see-through glass walkway. As an exhibit, it's overpriced, though the adrenaline rush and spectacular city views from the walkway may help justify the cost.

Cost and Hours: £9, £11 combo-ticket with The Monument, daily 10:00-18:00 in summer, 9:30-17:30 in winter, enter at northwest tower, Tube: Tower Hill, tel. 020/7403-3761, www.towerbridge.org.uk.

On the South Bank

The South Bank of the Thames is a thriving arts and cultural center, tied together by the riverfront Jubilee Walkway. For fun lunch options in this area, consider one of the nearby street food markets.

▲JUBILEE WALKWAY

This riverside path is a popular pub-crawling pedestrian promenade that stretches all along the South Bank, offering grand views of the Houses of Parliament and St. Paul's. On a sunny day, this is the place to see Londoners out strolling. The Walkway hugs the river except just east of London Bridge, where it cuts inland for a couple of blocks. It has been expanded into a 60-mile "Greenway" circling the city, including the 2012 Olympics site.

Rick's Tip: *If you're visiting London in summer,* **visit the South Bank after hours.** *Take a trip around the* **London Eye** *at sunset (the wheel spins until late—last ascent at 20:30, later in July-Aug). Then cap your night with a stroll along the* **Jubilee Walkway.**

▲▲LONDON EYE

This giant Ferris wheel, towering above London opposite Big Ben, is one of the world's highest observational wheels and London's answer to the Eiffel Tower. Riding it is a memorable experience, even though London doesn't have much of a skyline, and the price is borderline outrageous. Whether you ride or not, the wheel is a sight to behold.

Twenty-eight people ride in each of its

The London Eye adds whimsical fun to London's stately skyline.

The South Bank

32 air-conditioned capsules (representing the boroughs of London) for the 30-minute rotation (you go around only once). From the top of this 443-foot-high wheel—the second-highest public viewpoint in the city—even Big Ben looks small.

Cost: £24.95, about 10 percent cheaper if bought online. Combo-tickets save money if you plan on visiting Madame Tussauds. Buy tickets in advance at www.londoneye.com or try in person at the box office (in the corner of the County Hall building nearest the Eye), though day-of tickets are often sold out.

Hours: Daily June-Aug 10:00-20:30 or later, Sept-May generally 11:00-18:00, check website for latest schedule, these are last-ascent times, closed Dec 25 and a few days in Jan for maintenance, Tube: Waterloo or Westminster. Thames boats come and go from London Eye Pier at the foot of the wheel.

Rick's Tip: *The* **London Eye** *is busiest between 11:00 and 17:00, especially on weekends year-round and every day in July and August.* **Go online to book your ticket,** *then print it at home, retrieve it from an onsite ticket machine (bring your payment card and confirmation code), or stand in the "Ticket Collection" line. Even if you buy in advance, you may wait a bit to board the wheel (but it's not worth paying extra for a Fast Track ticket).*

▲▲IMPERIAL WAR MUSEUM

This impressive museum covers the wars of the 20th and 21st centuries—from World War I biplanes, to the rise of fascism, the Cold War, the Cuban Missile Crisis, the Troubles in Northern Ireland, the wars in Iraq and Afghanistan, and terrorism. Rather than glorify war, the museum encourages an understanding of the history of modern warfare and the wartime experience, including the effect it has on the everyday lives of people back home. The museum's coverage never neglects the human side of one of civilization's more uncivilized, persistent traits.

Allow plenty of time, as this powerful museum—with lots of artifacts and video clips—can be engrossing. War wonks love

Imperial War Museum

the place, as do general history buffs who enjoy patiently reading displays. For the rest, there are enough interactive experiences and multimedia exhibits and submarines for the kids to climb in to keep it interesting.

Cost and Hours: Free, £5 suggested donation, special exhibits extra, daily 10:00-18:00, last entry one hour before closing, Tube: Lambeth North or Elephant and Castle; buses #3, #12, and #159 from Westminster area; tel. 020/7416-5000, www.iwm.org.uk.

◗ SELF-GUIDED TOUR

Start with the atrium to grasp the massive scale of warfare as you wander among and under notable battle machines, then head directly for the museum's recently renovated **WWI galleries.** Here firsthand accounts connect the blunt reality of a brutal war with the contributions, heartache, and efforts of a nation.

How different this museum would be if the war to end all wars had lived up to its name. Instead, the museum, much like history, builds on itself. Ascending to the first floor, you'll find the permanent **Turning Points** galleries progressing up to and through World War II, including sections explaining the Blitzkrieg and its effects (see an actual Nazi parachute bomb like the ones that devastated London). The **Family in Wartime** exhibit shows London through the eyes of an ordinary family.

The second floor houses the **Secret War** exhibit, which peeks into the intrigues of espionage in World Wars I and II through present-day security. You'll learn about MI5 (Britain's domestic spy corps), MI6 (their international spies—like the CIA), and the Special Operations Executive (SOE), who led espionage efforts during World War II.

The third floor houses various (and often rotating) temporary art and film exhibits speckled with military-themed works including (when not on its own tour of duty) **John Singer Sargent**'s *Gassed* (1919), showing besieged troops in World War I.

The fourth-floor section on the **Holocaust,** one of the best on the subject anywhere, tells the story with powerful videos, artifacts, and fine explanations.

Crowning the museum on the fifth floor is the Lord Ashcroft Gallery and the **Extraordinary Heroes** display. Here, more than 250 stories celebrate Britain's

highest military award for bravery with the world's largest collection of Victoria Cross medals. Civilians who earned the George Cross medal for bravery are also honored.

▲▲TATE MODERN

Dedicated in the spring of 2000, the striking museum fills a derelict old power station across the river from St. Paul's—it opened the new century with art from the previous one. Its powerhouse collection includes Dalí, Picasso, Warhol, and much more.

Cost and Hours: Free, £4 donation appreciated, fee for special exhibits; open daily 10:00-18:00, Fri-Sat until 22:00, last entry to special exhibits 45 minutes before closing, especially crowded on weekend days (crowds thin out Fri and Sat evenings); view restaurant on top floor; tel. 020/7887-8888, www.tate.org.uk.

Tours: Multimedia guide-£4.75, free 45-minute guided tours at 11:00, 12:00, 14:00, and 15:00.

Getting There: Cross the Millennium Bridge from St. Paul's; take the Tube to Southwark, London Bridge, St. Paul's, Mansion House, or Blackfriars and walk 10-15 minutes; or catch Thames Clippers' Tate Boat ferry from the Tate Britain (Millbank Pier) for a 15-minute crossing (£8 one-way, every 40 minutes Mon-Fri 10:00-16:00, Sat-Sun 9:15-18:40, www.tate.org.uk/visit/tate-boat).

Visiting the Museum: The permanent collection is generally arranged according to theme—such as "Poetry and Dream"—not chronologically or by artist. Paintings by Picasso, for example, are scattered all

Imperial War Museum atrium

Tate Modern

over the building. Don't just come to see the Old Masters of modernism. Push your mental envelope with more recent works by Miró, Bacon, Picabia, Beuys, Twombly, and others.

Temporary exhibits are cutting-edge. Each year, the main hall features a different monumental installation by a prominent artist. The Tate recently opened a new wing to the south: This new Blavatnik Building (Switch House) gave the Tate an extra quarter-million square feet of display space. Besides showing off more of the Tate's impressive collection, the space hosts changing themed exhibitions, performance art, experimental film, and interactive sculpture incorporating light and sound.

▲MILLENNIUM BRIDGE

The pedestrian bridge links St. Paul's Cathedral and the Tate Modern across the Thames. This is London's first new bridge in a century, nicknamed the "blade of light" for its sleek minimalist design (370 yards long, four yards wide, stainless steel with teak planks). Its clever aerodynamic handrails deflect wind over the heads of pedestrians.

▲▲SHAKESPEARE'S GLOBE

This replica of the original Globe Theatre was built as it was in Shakespeare's time, half-timbered and thatched (in fact, with the first thatched roof constructed in London since they were outlawed after the Great Fire of 1666.) The original Globe opened in 1599, with its debut play, Shake-speare's *Julius Caesar*.) It accommodated 2,200 seated and another 1,000 standing. Today's Globe, leaving space for reasonable aisles, is slightly smaller, holding 800 seated and 600 groundlings. The working theater hosts authentic performances of Shakespeare's plays with actors in period costumes, modern interpretations of his works, and some works by other playwrights. For details on attending a play, see page 95.

The Globe complex has four parts: the Globe theater itself, the box office, a museum (called the Exhibition), and the Sam Wanamaker Playhouse (an indoor Jacobean theater around back). The Playhouse, which hosts performances through the winter, is horseshoe-shaped, intimate (seating fewer than 350), and sometimes uses authentic candle-lighting for period performances. The repertoire focuses less on Shakespeare and more on the work of his contemporaries (Jonson, Marlow, Fletcher), as well as concerts.

Cost: £16 for adults, £9 for kids 5-15, free for kids 5 and under, family ticket available; ticket includes Exhibition, audioguide, and 40-minute tour of the Globe; when theater is in use, you can tour the Exhibition only for £6.

Hours: The complex is open daily 9:00-17:30. Tours start every 30 minutes; during Globe theater season (late April-mid-Oct), last tour Mon at 17:00, Tue-Sat at 12:30, Sun at 11:30—it's safest to arrive for a tour before noon. Located on the South Bank over the Millennium Bridge

Millennium Bridge

Shakespeare's Globe

from St. Paul's, Tube: Mansion House or London Bridge plus a 10-minute walk; tel. 020/7902-1400, box office tel. 020/7401-9919, www.shakespearesglobe.com.

Visiting the Globe: You browse on your own in the **Exhibition** (with the included audioguide) through displays of Elizabethan-era costumes and makeup, music, script-printing, and special effects (the displays change). There are early folios and objects that were dug up on site. Videos and scale models help put Shakespearean theater within the context of the times. You'll also learn how they built the replica in modern times, using Elizabethan materials and techniques.

You must **tour the theater** at the time stamped on your ticket, but you can come back to the Exhibition museum afterward. A guide (usually an actor) leads you into the theater to see the stage and the various seating areas for the different classes of people. Learn how the new Globe is similar to the old Globe (open-air performances, standing-room by the stage, no curtain) and how it's different (female actors today, lights for night performances, concrete floor). It's not a

backstage tour, but the guides bring the Elizabethan period to life.

Eating: The **$$$$ Swan at the Globe** café offers a sit-down restaurant (for lunch and dinner, reservations recommended, tel. 020/7928-9444), a drinks-and-plates bar, and a sandwich-and-coffee cart (Mon-Fri 8:00-closing, depends on performance times, Sat-Sun from 10:00).

West London
▲▲TATE BRITAIN

One of Europe's great art houses, the Tate Britain specializes in British painting from the 16th century through modern times. This is people's art, with realistic paintings rooted in the individuals, landscape, and stories of the British Isles. The Tate shows off Hogarth's stage sets, Gainsborough's ladies, Blake's angels, Constable's clouds, Turner's tempests, the naturalistic realism of the Pre-Raphaelites, and the camera-eye portraits of Hockney and Freud.

Cost and Hours: Free, £4 donation suggested, admission fee for special exhibits; daily 10:00-18:00, last entry 45 minutes before closing, map-£1 suggested donation; free tours generally daily at

11:00, 12:00, 14:00, and 15:00, or download the Tate's handy app for a room-by-room guide; café and restaurant, tel. 020/7887-8888, www.tate.org.uk.

Getting There: It's on the River Thames, south of Big Ben and north of Vauxhall Bridge. Tube to Pimlico, then walk seven minutes. Or hop on the Tate Boat museum ferry from Tate Modern.

❍ SELF-GUIDED TOUR

Works from the early centuries are located in the west half of the building, 20th-century art is in the east half, the works of J. M. W. Turner and John Constable are in an adjacent wing (the Clore Gallery), and William Blake's work is upstairs. The Tate's great strength is championing contemporary British art in special exhibitions. There are generally two exhibition spaces: one in the east half of the main floor (often free), and another downstairs (usually requiring separate admission).

• *From the main Millbank entrance, walk through the bright, white rotunda and down the long central hall. Near the far end, enter the rooms on the left, labeled Walk Through British Art, where you'll find the beginnings of British painting (as you enter each room, you'll see the year etched into the floor).*

1700s—Art Blossoms: With peace at home (under three King Georges), a strong overseas economy, and a growing urban center in London, England's artistic life began to bloom. As the English grew more sophisticated, so did their portraits. Painters branched out into other subjects, capturing slices of everyday life (find William Hogarth, with his unflinchingly honest portraits, and Thomas Gainsborough's elegant, educated women).

1800-1850—The Industrial Revolution: Newfangled inventions were everywhere. Many artists rebelled against "progress" and the modern world. They escaped the dirty cities to commune with nature (Constable and the Romantics). Or they found a new spirituality in intense human emotions (dramatic scenes from history or literature). Or

they left the modern world altogether. William Blake, whose work hangs in a darkened room upstairs to protect his watercolors from deterioration, painted angels, not the dull material world. He turned his gaze inward, illustrating the glorious visions of the soul. His pen and watercolor sketches glow with an unearthly aura. In visions of the Christian heaven or Dante's hell, his figures have superhero musculature. The colors are almost translucent.

1837-1901—The Victorian Era: In the world's wealthiest nation, the prosperous middle class dictated taste in art. They admired paintings that were realistic (showcasing the artist's talent and work ethic), depicting Norman Rockwell-style slices of everyday life. Some paintings tug at the heartstrings, with scenes of parting couples, the grief of death, or the joy of families reuniting.

Overdosed with the gushy sentimentality of their day, a band of 20-year-old artists—including Sir John Everett Millais, Dante Gabriel Rossetti, and William Holman Hunt—said "Enough!" and dedicated themselves to creating less saccharine art (the Pre-Raphaelites). Like the Impressionists who followed them, they donned their scarves, barged out of the stuffy studio, and set up outdoors, painting trees, streams, and people, like scientists on a field trip. Still, they often captured nature with such a close-up clarity that it's downright unnatural.

Victorian-era Lady of Shalott

British Impressionism: Realistic British art stood apart from the modernist trends in France, but some influences drifted across the Channel (Rooms 1890 and 1900). John Singer Sargent (American-born) studied with Parisian Impressionists, learning the thick, messy brushwork and play of light at twilight. James Tissot used Degas' snapshot technique to capture a crowded scene from an odd angle. And James McNeill Whistler (born in America, trained in Paris, lived in London) composed his paintings like music—see some of his paintings' titles.

1900-1950—World Wars: As two world wars whittled down the powerful British Empire, it still remained a major cultural force. British art mirrored many of the trends and "-isms" pioneered in Paris (room marked 1930). You'll see Cubism like Picasso's, abstract art like Mondrian's, and so on. But British artists also continued the British tradition of realistic paintings of people and landscapes. Henry Moore's statues—mostly female, mostly reclining—catch the primitive power of carved stone. He captured the human body in a few simple curves, with minimal changes to the rock itself.

With a stiff upper lip, Britain survived the Blitz, World War II, and the loss of hundreds of thousands of men—but at war's end, the bottled-up horror came rushing out. Francis Bacon's deformed half-humans/half-animals express the existential human predicament of being caught in a world not of your making, isolated and helpless to change it.

1950-2000—Modern World: No longer a world power, Britain in the Swinging '60s became a major exporter of pop culture. British art's traditional strengths—realism, portraits, landscapes, and slice-of-life scenes—were redone in the modern style. Look for works by David Hockney, Lucian Freud, Bridget Riley, and Gilbert and George.

The Turner Collection: Walking through J. M. W. Turner's life's work, you can trace his progression from a painter of realistic historical scenes, through his wandering years, to Impressionist paintings of color-and-light patterns. You'll also see how Turner dabbled in different subjects: landscapes, seascapes, Roman ruins, snapshots of Venice, and so on. The corner room of the Clore Gallery is dedicated to Turner's great rival and contemporary, John Constable, who brought painting back into the real world. He painted the English landscape as it was—realistically, without idealizing it.

▲HYDE PARK AND SPEAKERS' CORNER

London's "Central Park," originally Henry VIII's hunting grounds, has more than 600 acres of lush greenery, Santander Cycles rental stations, the huge man-made Serpentine Lake (with rental boats and a lakeside swimming pool), the royal Kensington Palace (described next), and the ornate Neo-Gothic Albert Memorial across from the Royal Albert Hall. The western half of the park is known as Kensington Gardens. The park is huge—study a Tube map to choose the stop nearest to your destination (for more about the park, see www.royalparks.org.uk/parks/hyde-park).

On Sundays, from just after noon until early evening, **Speakers' Corner** offers soapbox oratory at its best (northeast corner of the park, Tube: Marble Arch). Characters climb their stepladders, wave their flags, pound emphatically on their sandwich boards, and share what they are

Hyde Park

convinced is their wisdom. Regulars have resident hecklers who know their lines and are always ready with a verbal jab or barb. "The grass roots of democracy" is actually a holdover from when the gallows stood here and the criminal was allowed to say just about anything he wanted to before he swung. I dare you to raise your voice and gather a crowd—it's easy to do.

The **Princess Diana Memorial Fountain** honors the "People's Princess," who once lived in nearby Kensington Palace. The low-key circular stream, great for cooling off your feet on a hot day, is in the south-central part of the park, near the Albert Memorial and Serpentine Gallery (Tube: Knightsbridge). A similarly named but different sight, the Diana, Princess of Wales Memorial Playground, in the park's northwest corner, is loads of fun for kids (Tube: Queensway).

KENSINGTON PALACE

For nearly 150 years (1689-1837), Kensington was the royal residence, before Buckingham Palace became the official home of the monarch. Sitting primly on its pleasant parkside grounds, the palace gives a barren yet regal glimpse into royal life—particularly that of Queen Victoria, who was born and raised here.

After Queen Victoria moved the monarchy to Buckingham Palace, lesser royals bedded down at Kensington. Princess Diana lived here both during and after her marriage to Prince Charles (1981-1997). More recently, Will and Kate moved here. However—as many disappointed visitors

discover—none of these more recent apartments are open to the public. To see what's on during your visit, check online.

Cost and Hours: £19, daily 10:00-18:00, Nov-Feb until 16:00; a long 10-minute stroll through Kensington Gardens from either High Street Kensington or Queensway Tube stations, tel. 0844-482-7788, www.hrp.org.uk.

Nearby: Garden enthusiasts enjoy popping into the secluded Sunken Garden, 50 yards from the exit. The nearby Orangery, once it reopens in 2020 after renovation, will again serve a fine yet pricey afternoon tea.

▲▲▲VICTORIA AND ALBERT MUSEUM

You could spend days wandering "the V&A," which encompasses 2,000 years of art and design (ceramics, stained glass, fine furniture, clothing, jewelry, carpets, and more). There's much to see, including Raphael's tapestry cartoons, a cast of Trajan's Column that depicts the emperor's conquests, one of Leonardo da Vinci's notebooks, ladies' underwear through the ages, a life-size *David* with detachable fig leaf, and Mick Jagger's sequined jumpsuit.

Cost and Hours: Free, £5 donation requested, extra for some special exhibits, daily 10:00-17:45, some galleries open Fri until 22:00, £1 suggested donation for much-needed museum map, free tours daily, on Cromwell Road in South Kensington, Tube: South Kensington, from the Tube station a long tunnel leads directly to museum, tel. 020/7942-2000, www.vam.ac.uk.

Rick's Tip: *The* **Victoria and Albert Museum** *is huge and tricky to navigate. Spend £1 for the* **museum map** *available from the info desk. It tells you how to find the museum's must-see objects.*

Visiting the Museum: In the Grand Entrance lobby, look up to see the colorful **chandelier/sculpture** by American glass artist Dale Chihuly. This elaborate

Kensington Palace

Victoria and Albert Museum

Greenwich

piece epitomizes the spirit of the V&A's collection—beautiful manufactured objects that demonstrate technical skill and innovation, wedding the old with the new, and blurring the line between arts and crafts.

The V&A has (arguably) the best collection of **Italian Renaissance sculpture** outside Italy. One prime example is *Samson Slaying a Philistine*, by Giambologna (c. 1562), carved from a single block of marble, which shows the testy Israelite warrior preparing to decapitate a man who'd insulted him. The statue's spiral-shaped pose is reminiscent of works by Michelangelo.

The museum's **Islamic art** reflects both religious influences and sophisticated secular culture. Notice floral patterns (twining vines, flowers, arabesques) and geometric designs (stars, diamonds). But the most common pattern is calligraphy—elaborate lettering of an inscription in Arabic, the language of the Quran. The **British Galleries** sweep chronologically through 400 years of British high-class living (1500-1900). Look for rare miniature portraits—a popular item of Queen Elizabeth I's day—including Hilliard's oft-reproduced *Young Man Among Roses* miniature. A room dedicated to Henry VIII has a portrait of him, his writing box (with quill pens, ink, and sealing wax), and a whole roomful of the fancy furniture, tapestries, jewelry, and dinnerware.

Greater London
▲▲ Greenwich

This borough of London—an easy boat trip or DLR (light rail) journey from downtown—combines majestic, picnic-perfect parks; the stately trappings of Britain's proud nautical heritage; and the Royal Observatory Greenwich, with a fine museum on the evolution of seafaring and a chance to straddle the eastern and western hemispheres at the prime meridian.

Getting There: Ride a boat to Greenwich for the scenery and commentary, and take the Docklands Light Rail (DLR) back. Various **tour boats** with commentary and open-deck seating (2/hour, 30-75 minutes), as well as faster Thames Clippers (departs every 20-30 minutes, 20-45 minutes, though these lack open decks) leave from several piers in central London.

By DLR, ride from Bank-Monument Station in central London to Cutty Sark Station in central Greenwich; it's one stop before the main—but less central—Greenwich Station (departs at least every 10 minutes, 20 minutes, all in Zone 2). Alternately, catch bus #188 from Russell Square near the British Museum (about 45 minutes to Greenwich).

Eating in Greenwich: Greenwich's parks are picnic-friendly, especially around the National Maritime Museum and Royal Observatory. Greenwich has almost 100 pubs, with some boasting that they're mere milliseconds from the prime

Greenwich

To Canary Wharf & The Docklands

WEST FERRY RD.

Island Gardens (DLR)

Island Gardens

ISLE OF DOGS

PRIME MERIDIAN

200 Meters
200 Yards

Thames River

PEDESTRIAN TUNNEL

To London

Riverside Stroll

WALK

CRANE ST.

TRINITY HOSPITAL

OLD WOOLWICH RD.

To O2 Arena

GREENWICH PIER

FIVE FOOT

PARK ROW

TRAFALGAR ROAD

TUNNEL ENTRANCE

DISCOVER GREENWICH

OLD ROYAL NAVAL COLLEGE

CHAPEL

CUTTY SARK

❸

ℹ ❷

WC

PAINTED HALL

TOUR BEGINS

CREEK RD.

❹

COLLEGE APPROACH

GREENWICH UNIVERSITY

ROMNEY ROAD

COLONNADES

Cutty Sark (DLR)

❶

CHURCH ST.

KING WILLIAM WALK

NATIONAL MARITIME MUSEUM

QUEEN'S HOUSE

ST. ALFEGE'S CHURCH

NELSON RD.

ROAN ST.

STOCKWELL ST.

Greenwich Park

PRIME MERIDIAN

GREENWICH STATION

GREENWICH HIGH RD.

CLOCK-TOWER MARKET

BURNEY ST.

CROOMS HILL

To London

THE AVENUE

TOUR ENDS

FLAMSTEED HOUSE

ROYAL OBSERVATORY GREENWICH

BLACKHEATH

KING GEORGE ST.

PETER HARRISON PLANETARIUM

WELLER ASTRONOMY GALLERIES

Eating
❶ Greenwich Market
❷ The Old Brewery
❸ Even Keel Café
❹ Marks & Spencer Simply Food

- - - Recommended Walking Route

meridian. **$$$ The Old Brewery,** in the Discover Greenwich center, is a gastropub decorated with all things beer. From Yorkshire pudding to paella to Thai cuisine, food stalls at the Greenwich Market (described next) offer an international variety of tasty options.

Markets: Thanks to its markets, Greenwich throbs with browsing Londoners on weekends. The **Greenwich Market** is an entertaining mini Covent Garden, located in the middle of the block between the Cutty Sark DLR station and the Old Royal Naval College (farmers market, arts and crafts, and food stands; daily 10:00-17:30; antiques Mon, Tue, Thu, and Fri, www.greenwichmarketlondon.com).

▲▲CUTTY SARK

When first launched in 1869, the Scottish-built *Cutty Sark* was the last of the great China tea clippers and the queen of the seas. She was among the fastest clippers ever built, the culmination of centuries of ship design. With 32,000 square feet of sail—and favorable winds—she could travel 300 miles in a day. But as a new century dawned, steamers began to outmatch sailing ships for speed, and by the mid-1920s the *Cutty Sark* was the world's last operating clipper ship.

In 2012, the ship was restored and reopened with a spectacular new glass-walled display space (though one critic groused that the ship now "looks like it has run aground in a giant greenhouse"). Displays explore the *Cutty Sark*'s 140-year history and the cargo she carried—everything from tea to wool to gunpowder—as she raced between London and ports all around the world.

Cost and Hours: £13.50, £7 for kids 5-15, free for kids under age 5, family tickets available, combo-ticket with Royal Observatory-£18.50, kids combo-ticket-£8.50; daily 10:00-17:00; reserve ahead online or by phone for school holidays and weekends, or just try showing up around 13:00; good Even Keel café open to the public; unnecessary £5 guidebook, reservation tel. 020/8312-6608, www.rmg.co.uk.

▲OLD ROYAL NAVAL COLLEGE— PAINTED HALL AND CHAPEL

These grand structures were built (1692) as a veterans' hospital to house disabled and retired sailors who'd served their country. King William III and Queen Mary II spared no expense. They donated land from the former royal palace and hired the great Christopher Wren to design the complex (though other architects completed it). Wren created a virtual temple to seamen. The honored pensioners ate in the Painted Hall and prayed in the Chapel of Sts. Peter and Paul.

In 1873, the hospital was transformed into one of the world's most prestigious universities for training naval officers.

Cost and Hours: Both the Painted Hall and Chapel are free (£3 suggested donation), daily 10:00-17:00, sometimes closed for private events, service Sun at 11:00 in chapel—all are welcome, www.ornc.org.

▲NATIONAL MARITIME MUSEUM

A big glass roof tops three levels of slick, modern, kid-friendly exhibits about all things seafaring. Great for anyone interested in the sea, this museum holds everything from a giant working paddlewheel to the uniform Admiral Horatio Nelson wore when he was killed at Trafalgar (look for the bullet hole, in the left shoulder).

Cost and Hours: Free, daily 10:00-17:00, tel. 020/8858-4422, www.rmg.co.uk. The museum hosts frequent family-oriented events; ask at the desk.

Cutty Sark

Old Royal Naval College

▲▲ROYAL OBSERVATORY GREENWICH

Located on the prime meridian (0° longitude), this observatory is famous as the point from which all time and distances on earth are measured. A visit here gives you a taste of the sciences of astronomy, timekeeping, and seafaring—and how they all meld together—along with great views over Greenwich and the distant London skyline. Outside, you can snap a selfie straddling the famous prime meridian line in the pavement. Within, there's the original 1600s-era **observatory,** the **Weller Astronomy Galleries,** and the state-of-the-art **Peter Harrison Planetarium.**

Cost and Hours: Observatory—£9.50, includes audioguide, combo-ticket with *Cutty Sark*-£18.50, combo-ticket with planetarium-£12.50, daily 10:00-17:00, until later in summer; astronomy galleries—free, daily 10:00-17:00; planetarium—£7.50; 30-minute shows generally run every hour (Mon-Fri 13:00-16:00, Sat-Sun 11:00-16:00, fewer in winter, confirm times in advance and consider calling ahead to order tickets; tel. 020/8858-4422, reservations tel. 020/8312-6608, www.rmg.co.uk).

▲▲KEW GARDENS

This fine riverside park and a palatial greenhouse are every botanist's favorite escape. Wander among 33,000 different types of plants, spread across 300 acres. For a quick visit, spend a fragrant hour wandering through three buildings: the Palm House, a humid Victorian world of iron, glass, and tropical plants that was built in 1844; a Waterlily House that Monet would swim for; and the Princess of Wales Conservatory, a meandering modern greenhouse with many different climate zones. With extra time, check out the Xstrata Treetop Walkway, a 200-yard-long scenic steel walkway that puts you high in the canopy 60 feet above the ground. Young kids will love the Climbers and Creepers indoor/outdoor playground and little zip line, and a slow and easy ride on the hop-on, hop-off Kew Explorer tram.

Cost and Hours: £16.50, June-Aug £11 after 16:00, £3.50 for kids 4-16, free for kids under 4; April-Aug Mon-Thu 10:00-18:30, Fri-Sun 10:00-19:30, closes earlier Sept-March—check schedule online, glasshouses close at 17:30 in high season—earlier off-season, free one-hour walking tours daily at 11:00 and 13:30, tel. 020/8332-5000, recorded info tel. 020/8332-5655, www.kew.org.

Getting There: If taking the Tube, ride to Kew Gardens; from the Tube station, cross the footbridge over the tracks, which drops you in a little community of plant-and-herb shops, a two-block walk from Victoria Gate (the main garden entrance). Another option is to take a boat, which runs April-Oct between Kew Gardens and Westminster Pier.

Eating: For a sun-dappled lunch or snack, walk 10 minutes from the Palm House to the **$$ Orangery Cafeteria**

Royal Observatory

Kew Gardens

(Mon-Thu 10:00-17:30, Fri-Sun until 18:30, daily until 15:15 in winter, closes early for events).

EXPERIENCES

Shopping

Most stores are open Monday through Saturday from roughly 9:00 or 10:00 until 17:00 or 18:00, with a late night on Wednesday or Thursday (usually until 19:00 or 20:00). Many close on Sundays. Large department stores stay open later during the week (until about 21:00 Mon-Sat) with shorter hours on Sundays. If you're looking for bargains, visit one of the city's many street markets.

Shopping Streets

London is famous for its shopping. The best and most convenient shopping streets are in the West End and West London (roughly between Soho and Hyde Park). You'll find midrange shops along **Oxford Street** (running east from

Tube: Marble Arch), and fancier shops along **Regent Street** (stretching south from Tube: Oxford Circus to Piccadilly Circus) and **Knightsbridge** (where you'll find Harrods and Harvey Nichols; Tube: Knightsbridge). Other streets are more specialized, such as **Jermyn Street** for old-fashioned men's clothing (just south of Piccadilly Street) and **Charing Cross Road** for books. **Floral Street,** connecting Leicester Square to Covent Garden, is lined with fashion boutiques.

Department Stores

Harrods is London's most famous and touristy department store, with more than four acres of retail space covering seven floors (Mon-Sat 10:00-21:00, Sun 11:30-18:00; Brompton Road, Tube: Knightsbridge, tel. 020/7730-1234, www.harrods.com).

Harvey Nichols, once Princess Diana's favorite, remains the department store *du jour* (Mon-Sat 10:00-20:00, Sun 11:30-18:00, near Harrods, 109 Knightsbridge, Tube: Knightsbridge, tel. 020/7235-5000, www.harveynichols.com).

Rick's Tip: *The fifth floor at* **Harvey Nichols** *is a* **veritable food fest,** *with a gourmet grocery store, a fancy restaurant, a sushi bar, and a café. Get takeaway food for a* **picnic in the Hyde Park rose garden,** *two blocks away.*

Fortnum & Mason, the official department store of the Queen, embodies old-fashioned, British upper-class taste, with a storybook atmosphere (Mon-Sat 10:00-21:00, Sun 11:30-18:00, 181 Piccadilly, Tube: Green Park, tel. 020/7734-8040, www.fortnumandmason.com). Elegant tea is served in their Diamond Jubilee Tea Salon.

Liberty is a still-thriving 19th-century institution known for its artful displays and castle-like interior (Mon-Sat 10:00-20:00, Sun 12:00-18:00, Great Marlborough Street, Tube: Oxford Circus, tel. 020/7734-1234, www.liberty.co.uk).

Street Markets

Antique buffs and people-watchers love London's street markets. The best markets—which combine lively stalls and a colorful neighborhood with cute and characteristic shops of their own—are Portobello Road and Camden Lock Market. Hagglers will enjoy the no-holds-barred bargaining encouraged in London's street markets.

IN NOTTING HILL

Portobello Road stretches for several blocks through the delightful, colorful, funky-yet-quaint Notting Hill neighborhood. Already-charming streets lined with pastel-painted houses and offbeat antique shops are enlivened on Fridays and Saturdays with 2,000 additional stalls (9:00-19:00), plus food, live music, and more (Tube: Notting Hill Gate, near recommended accommodations, tel. 020/7727-7684, www.portobelloroad. co.uk).

Rick's Tip: *Browse* **Portabello Road on Friday.** *Most stalls are open, with half the crowds of Saturday.*

IN CAMDEN TOWN

Camden Lock Market is a huge, trendy arts-and-crafts festival divided into three areas, each with its own vibe. The main market, set alongside the picturesque canal, features a mix of shops and stalls selling boutique crafts and artisanal foods. The market on the opposite side of Chalk Farm Road has ethnic food stalls, lots of canalside seating, and punk crafts. The Stables, a sprawling, incense-scented complex, is squeezed into tunnels under the old rail bridge just behind the main market (daily 10:00-19:00, busiest on weekends, tel. 020/3763-9999, www. camdenmarket.com).

IN THE EAST END

Spitalfields Market combines old brick buildings and sleek modern ones, all covered by a giant glass roof. The shops, stalls, and a rainbow of restaurants are open every day (Mon-Fri 10:00-17:00, Sat from 11:00, Sun from 9:00, Tube: Liverpool Street; from the Tube stop, take Bishopsgate East exit, turn left, walk to Brushfield Street, and turn right; www.spitalfields.co.uk).

Petticoat Lane Market, just a block from Spitalfields Market, sits on the otherwise dull Middlesex Street; adjoining Wentworth Street is grungier and more characteristic (Sun 9:00-14:00, sometimes later; smaller market Mon-Fri on Wentworth Street only; Middlesex Street and Wentworth Street, Tube: Liverpool Street).

The **Truman Markets,** housed in the former Truman Brewery on Brick Lane, are gritty and avant-garde, selling handmade clothes, home decor and ethnic street food in the heart of the "Bangla-town" Bangladeshi community. The markets are in full swing on Sundays (roughly 10:00-17:00), though you'll see some action on Saturdays (11:00-18:00). Surrounding shops and eateries are open all week (Tube: Liverpool Street or Aldgate East, tel. 020/7770-6028, www. bricklanemarket.com).

Brick Lane is lined with Sunday market stalls all the way up to Bethnal Green

Road, about a 10-minute walk (leading north out of the Truman Markets). Continuing straight (north) about five more minutes takes you to Columbia Road, a colorful shopping street made even more so on Sunday by the **Columbia Road Flower Market** (Sun 8:00-15:00, http://columbiaroad.info). Halfway up Columbia Road, be sure to loop left up little Ezra Street, with characteristic eateries, boutiques, and antique vendors.

IN THE WEST END

The iron-and-glass **Covent Garden Market,** originally the garden for Westminster Abbey, is a mix of fun shops, eateries, and markets. Mondays are for antiques, while arts and crafts dominate the rest of the week. Produce stalls are open daily (10:30-18:00), and on Thursdays, a food market brightens up the square (Tube: Covent Garden, tel. 020/7395-1350, www.coventgardenlondonuk.com).

Jubilee Hall Market, on the south side of Covent Garden, features antiques on Mondays (5:00-17:00); a general market Tuesday through Friday (10:30-19:00); and arts and crafts on Saturdays and Sundays (10:00-18:00). It's located on the south side of Covent Garden (tel. 020/7379-4242, www.jubileemarket.co.uk).

IN SOUTH LONDON

Borough Market has been serving the Southwark community for more than 800 years. These days there are as many people taking photos as buying fruit, cheese, and beautiful breads, but it's still a fun carnival atmosphere with fantastic stall food. For maximum market and minimum crowds, join the locals on Thursdays (full market open Wed-Sat 10:00-17:00, Fri until 18:00, surrounding food stalls open daily; south of London Bridge, where Southwark Street meets Borough High Street; Tube: London Bridge, tel. 020/7407-1002, www.boroughmarket.org.uk).

Theater (a.k.a. Theatre)

London's theater scene rivals Broadway's in quality and sometimes beats it in price. Choose from 200 offerings—Shakespeare, musicals, comedies, thrillers, sex farces, cutting-edge fringe, revivals starring movie celebs, and more. London does it all well.

Rick's Tip: *For the best list of what's happening and a look at the* **latest London scene,** *check www.timeout.com/london.*

West End Shows

Nearly all big-name shows are hosted in the theaters of the West End, clustering around Soho (especially along Shaftesbury Avenue) between Piccadilly and Covent Garden. With a centuries-old tradition of pleasing the masses, they present London theater at its grandest.

I prefer big, glitzy musicals over serious fare because London can deliver the multimedia spectacle I rarely get back home. If that's not to your taste, you might prefer revivals of classics to cutting-edge works by the hottest young playwrights. London is a magnet for movie stars who want to stretch their acting chops.

The free *Official London Theatre Guide,* updated weekly, is a handy tool (find it at hotels, box offices, the City of London TI, and online at www.officiallondontheatre.co.uk).

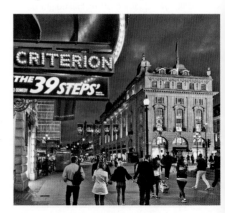

Most performances are nightly except Sunday, usually with two or three matinees a week. The few shows that run on Sundays are mostly family fare (such as *The Lion King*). Tickets range from about £25 to £120 for the best seats at big shows. Matinees are generally cheaper and rarely sell out.

Rick's Tip: *Just like at home, London's* **theaters sell seats in a range of levels**— *but the Brits use* **different terms:** *stalls (ground floor), dress circle (first balcony), upper circle (second balcony), balcony (sky-high third balcony), and slips (cheap seats on the fringes). Discounted tickets are called "concessions" (abbreviated as "conc" or "s").*

TICKETS

Most shows have tickets available on short notice—likely at a discount. If your time in London is limited or you have your heart set on a particular show that's likely to sell out, you can buy peace of mind by booking your tickets from home. For floor plans of the various theaters, see www. theatremonkey.com.

Advance Tickets: Buy your tickets directly from the theater, either through its website or by calling the theater box office. Often, a theater will reroute you to a third-party ticket vendor such as Ticketmaster. You'll pay with a credit card, and generally be charged a per-ticket booking fee (around £3). You can have your tickets

emailed to you or pick them up before show time at the theater's Will Call window. Many third-party websites sell London theater tickets, but these generally charge higher prices and fees.

Discount Tickets: The **TKTS Booth** at Leicester Square sells discounted tickets (25-50 percent off) for many shows, though they may not have the hottest shows in town. You must buy in person at the kiosk, and the best deals are same-day only (£3/ ticket service charge included, open Mon-Sat 10:00-19:00, Sun 11:00-16:30).

The list of shows and prices is posted outside the booth and on their constantly refreshed website (www.tkts.co.uk). Come early in the day—the line starts forming even before the booth opens, but moves quickly. Have a second-choice show in mind, in case your first choice is sold out. If TKTS runs out of its ticket allotment for a certain show, it doesn't necessarily mean the show is sold out— you can still try the theater's box office.

Rick's Tip: *The* **real TKTS booth** *(with its prominent sign) is a freestanding kiosk at the south edge of Leicester Square. Several dishonest outfits nearby advertise "official half-price tickets"—avoid these, where you'll pay closer to full price.*

Theater Box Office: Even if a show is "sold out," there's usually a way to get a seat. Many theaters offer various discounts or "concessions": same-day tickets, cheap returned tickets, standing-room, matinee, senior or student standby deals, and more. Start by checking the show's website, call the box office, or simply drop by (many theaters are right in the tourist zone).

Same-day tickets (called "day seats") are generally available only in person at the box office starting at 10:00 (people start lining up well before then). These tickets (£20 or less) tend to be either in the nosebleed rows or have a restricted

Evensong

One of my favorite experiences in Britain is to attend evensong at a great church. Evensong is an evening worship service that is typically sung rather than said (though some parts—including scripture readings, a few prayers, and a homily—are spoken). It follows the traditional Anglican service in the Book of Common Prayer, including prayers, scripture readings, canticles (sung responses), and hymns that are appropriate for the early evening—traditionally the end of the working day and before the evening meal. In major churches with resident choirs, a singing or chanting priest leads the service, and a choir—usually made up of both men's and boys—sings the responses. The choir usually sings a cappella, or is accompanied by an organ. Visitors are welcome and are given an order of service or a prayer book to help them follow along. (If you're not familiar with the order of service, watch the congregation to know when to stand, sit, and kneel.)

Impressive places for evensong in London include Westminster Abbey and St. Paul's. Evensong typically takes place in the small choir area, which is far more intimate than the main nave. It generally occurs daily between 17:00 and 18:00 (often two hours earlier on Sundays); check with individual churches for specifics. At smaller churches, evensong is sometimes spoken, not sung.

Note that evensong is not a performance—it's a worship service. If you enjoy worshipping in different churches, attending evensong can be a highlight. But if church services aren't your thing, consider an organ or choral concert—look for posted schedules or ask at the information desk or gift shop.

view (behind a pillar or extremely far to one side).

Another strategy is to show up at the box office shortly before show time (best on weekdays) and—before paying full price—ask about any cheaper options. Last-minute return tickets are often sold at great prices as curtain time approaches.

For a helpful guide to "day seats," consult www.theatremonkey.com/dayseatfinder.htm; for tips on getting cheap and last-minute tickets, visit www.londontheatretickets.org and www.timeout.com/london/theatre.

Other Agencies: Although booking through a middleman such as your hotel or a ticket agency is quick and easy, prices are greatly inflated. Ticket agencies and third-party websites are often just scalpers with an address. If you do buy from an agency, choose one who is a member of the Society of Ticket Agents and Retailers (look for the STAR logo—short for "secure tickets from authorized retailers"). These legitimate resellers normally add a maximum 25 percent booking fee to tickets.

Scalpers (or "Touts"): As at any event, you'll find scalpers hawking tickets outside theaters. And, just like at home, those people may either be honest folk whose date just happened to cancel at the last minute...or they may be unscrupulous thieves selling forgeries. London has many of the latter.

Beyond the West End

Tickets for lesser-known shows tend to be cheaper (figure £15-30), in part because most of the smaller theaters are government-subsidized. Remember that plays don't need a familiar title or famous actor to be a worthwhile experience—read up on the latest offerings online; Time Out's website is a great place to start.

MAJOR THEATERS

One particularly good venue is the **National Theatre,** which has a range of impressive options, often starring recognizable names. While the building is ugly on the outside, the acts that play out upon its stage are beautiful—as are the deeply discounted tickets it commonly offers (looming on the South Bank by Waterloo Bridge, Tube: Waterloo, www. nationaltheatre.org.uk).

The **Barbican Centre** puts on high-quality, often experimental work (right by the Museum of London, just north of The City, Tube: Barbican, www. barbican.org.uk), as does the **Royal Court Theatre,** which has £12 tickets for its Monday shows (west of the West End in Sloane Square, Tube: Sloane Square, www.royalcourttheatre.com).

Menier Chocolate Factory is a small theater in Southwark popular for its impressive productions and intimate setting. Check their website to see what's on—they tend to have a mix of plays, musicals, and even an occasional comedian (behind the Tate Modern at 53 Southwark Street, Tube: Southwark, www. menierchocolatefactory.com).

Royal Shakespeare Company performs at various theaters around London and in Stratford-upon-Avon year-round. To get a schedule, contact the RSC (Royal Shakespeare Theatre, Stratford-up-on-Avon, tel. 0844-800-1110, box office tel. 01789/403-493, www.rsc.org.uk).

SHAKESPEARE'S GLOBE

To see Shakespeare in a replica of the theater for which he wrote his plays, attend a play at the Globe. In this round, thatched-roof, open-air theater, the plays are performed much as Shakespeare intended—under the sky, with no amplification. I've never enjoyed Shakespeare as much as here, performed as it was meant to be in the "wooden O." If you can't get a ticket, take a guided tour of the theater and museum by day (see page 81).

The play's the thing from late April

A performance at Shakespeare's Globe

through early October (usually Tue-Sat 14:00 and 19:30, Sun either 13:00 and/ or 18:30, tickets can be sold out months in advance). You'll pay £5 to stand and £20-45 to sit, usually on a backless bench. Because only a few rows and the pricier Gentlemen's Rooms have seats with backs, £1 cushions and £3 add-on backrests are considered a good investment by many. Dress for the weather.

The £5 "groundling" tickets—which are open to rain—are most fun. Scurry in early to stake out a spot on the stage's edge, where the most interaction with the actors occurs. You're a crude peasant. You can lean your elbows on the stage, munch a picnic dinner (yes, you can bring in food), or walk around.

The indoor Sam Wanamaker Playhouse allows Shakespearean-era plays and early-music concerts to be performed through the winter. Many of the productions in this intimate venue are one-offs and can be quite pricey.

To reserve tickets for plays at the Globe or Sam Wanamaker, call or drop by the box office (Mon-Sat 10:00-18:00, Sun until 17:00, open one hour later on performance days, New Globe Walk entrance, no extra charge to book by phone, tel. 020/7401-9919). You can also reserve online (www. shakespearesglobe.com, £2.50 booking fee). If the tickets are sold out, don't despair; a few often free up at the last minute. Try calling around noon the day of the performance to see if the box office expects any returned tickets. If so, they'll advise you to show up a little more than an hour before the show, when these tickets are sold (first-come, first-served).

The theater is on the South Bank, directly across the Thames over the Millennium Bridge from St. Paul's Cathedral (Tube: Mansion House or London Bridge).

EATING

Eating out has become an essential part of the London experience. The sheer variety of foods—from every corner of Britain's former empire and beyond—is astonishing. But the thought of a £50 meal in Britain generally ruins my appetite, so my London dining is limited mostly to easygoing, fun, moderately priced alternatives. Pub grub and ethnic restaurants (especially Indian and Chinese) are good low-cost options.

Popular chain restaurants are a good bet, offering tasty food, reasonable prices, and branches throughout London and the UK (see page 21).

Of course, picnicking is the fastest and cheapest way to go. Good grocery stores and sandwich shops, fine park benches, and polite pigeons abound.

Central London
Soho
Foodies who want to eat well head to Soho. These restaurants are scattered throughout a chic, creative, and once-seedy zone that teems with hipsters, theatergoers, and London's gay community. Even if you plan to have dinner elsewhere, it's a treat just to wander around Soho.

On and near Wardour Street
$$ Princi is a vast, bright, efficient, wildly popular Italian deli/bakery with Milanese flair. Along one wall is a long counter with display cases offering a tempting array of *pizza rustica, panini* sandwiches, focaccia, pasta dishes, and desserts. Order your food at the counter, then find a space to share at a long table; or get it to go. They also have a classy restaurant section with reasonable prices if you'd rather have table service (daily 8:00-24:00, 135 Wardour Street, tel. 020/7478-8888).

$$$ The Gay Hussar, dressy and tight, squeezes several elegant tables into what the owners say is the only Hungarian restaurant in England. It's traditional Hungarian fare: cabbage, sauerkraut, sausage, paprika, and pork, as well as duck and chicken and, of course, Hungarian wine (Mon-Sat 12:15-14:30 & 17:30-22:45, closed Sun, 2 Greek Street, tel. 020/7437-0973).

$$$ Bocca di Lupo, a stylish and popular option, serves half and full portions of classic regional Italian food. Dressy but with a fun energy, it's a place where you're glad you made a reservation. The counter seating, on cushy stools with a view into the lively open kitchen, is particularly memorable, or you can take a table in the snug, casual back end (daily 12:30-15:00 & 17:15-23:00, 12 Archer Street, tel. 020/7734-2223, www.boccadilupo.com).

$$ Yalla Yalla is a bohemian-chic hole-in-the-wall serving up high-quality Beirut street food—hummus, baba ghanoush, tabbouleh, and *shawarmas.* It's tucked down a seedy alley across from a sex shop. Eat in the cramped and cozy interior or at one of the few outdoor tables (£4 sandwiches and *meze,* £8 mezes platter available until 17:00, daily 10:00-24:00, 1 Green's Court—just north of Brewer Street, tel. 020/7287-7663).

Gelato: Across the street from Bocca di Lupo (listed earlier) is its sister *gelateria,* **Gelupo,** with a wide array of ever-changing but always creative and delicious dessert favorites. Take away or enjoy their homey interior (daily 11:00-23:00, 7 Archer Street, tel. 020/7287-5555).

ON LEXINGTON STREET
$$$ Andrew Edmunds Restaurant is a tiny candlelit space where you'll want to hide your guidebook and not act like a tourist. This little place—with a jealous and loyal clientele—is the closest I've

found to Parisian quality in a cozy restaurant in London. The extensive wine list, modern European cooking, and creative seasonal menu are worth the splurge (daily 12:30-15:30 & 17:30-22:45, these are last-order times, come early or call ahead, request ground floor rather than basement, 46 Lexington Street, tel. 020/7437-5708, www.andrewedmunds.com).

$$ Mildred's Vegetarian Restaurant, across from Andrew Edmunds, has a creative, fun menu and a tight, high-energy interior filled with happy herbivores (Mon-Sat 12:00-23:00, closed Sun, vegan options, 45 Lexington Street, tel. 020/7494-1634).

Near Piccadilly

$$$$ The Wolseley is the grand 1920s showroom of a long-defunct British car. The last Wolseley drove out with the Great Depression, but today this old-time bistro bustles with formal waiters serving traditional Austrian and French dishes in an elegant black-marble-and-chandeliers setting fit for its location next to the Ritz. Although the food can be unexceptional, prices are reasonable considering the grand presentation and setting. Reservations are a must (cheaper soup, salad, and sandwich "café menu" available in all areas of restaurant, daily 7:00-24:00, 160 Piccadilly, tel. 020/7499-6996, www.thewolseley.com). They're popular for their fancy cream tea and afternoon tea.

$$$$ The Savini at the Criterion is a palatial dining hall offering an Italian menu in a dreamy neo-Byzantine setting from the 1870s. It's right on Piccadilly Circus but a world away from the punk junk, with fairly normal food served in an unforgettable Great Gatsby space. It's a deal for the visual experience during lunch or early (before 19:00) or late (after 22:00)—and if you order the £29-36 fixed-price meal or £16 cream tea (daily 12:00-23:30, 224 Piccadilly, tel. 020/7930-1459, www.saviniatcriterion.co.uk).

Covent Garden

$$$ Dishoom is London's hotspot for upscale Indian cuisine, with top-quality ingredients and carefully executed recipes. The dishes seem familiar, but the flavors are a revelation. People line up early (starting around 17:30) for a seat, either on the bright, rollicking, brasserie-like ground floor or in the less appealing basement. Reservations are possible only until 17:45 (daily 8:00-23:00, 12 Upper St. Martin's Lane, tel. 020/7420-9320). They also have locations near King's Cross Station, Carnaby Street, and in Shoreditch.

$$ Lamb and Flag Pub is a survivor—a spit-and-sawdust pub serving traditional grub (like meat pies) two blocks off Covent Garden, yet seemingly a world away. Here since 1772, this pub was a favorite of Charles Dickens and is now a hit with local workers. At lunch, it's all food. In the evening, the ground floor is for drinking and the food service is upstairs (long hours daily, 33 Rose Street, across from Stanfords bookstore entrance on Floral Street, tel. 020/7497-9504).

Near Trafalgar Square

$$ St. Martin-in-the-Fields Café in the Crypt is just right for a tasty meal on a monk's budget—maybe even on a monk's tomb. You'll dine sitting on somebody's gravestone in an ancient crypt. Their enticing buffet line is kept stocked all day, serving breakfast, lunch, and dinner (hearty traditional desserts, free jugs

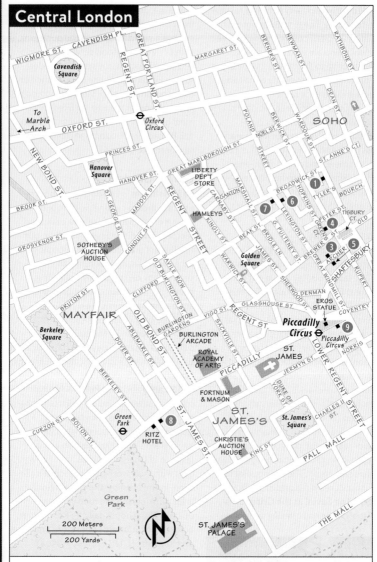

Central London

Eateries

1. Princi Italian Deli
2. The Gay Hussar
3. Bocca di Lupo
4. Yalla Yalla
5. Gelupo Gelato
6. Andrew Edmunds Restaurant
7. Mildred's Vegetarian Restaurant
8. The Wolseley
9. The Savini at the Criterion
10. Dishoom
11. Lamb & Flag Pub
12. St. Martin-in-the-Fields Café in the Crypt
13. The Chandos Pub's Opera Room

Taking Tea

Many London visitors partake in this most British of traditions. While some tearooms—such as the finicky Fortnum & Mason—still require a jacket and tie, most others happily welcome tourists in jeans and sneakers. Most tearooms are usually open for lunch and close about 17:00.

Popular choices are a "cream tea," which consists of tea and a scone or two, or the pricier "afternoon tea," which comes with pastries and finger foods such as small, crust-less sandwiches. Even at the fancier places, two people can order one afternoon tea and one cream tea and share the afternoon tea's goodies.

Many museum cafés offer a fine, inexpensive tea service; try the **$$ Victoria and Albert Museum** café (Sun 15:00-17:00, reserve by email at victoriantea@ benugo.com).

$$$ The Wolseley serves a good afternoon tea between their meal service (£13 cream tea, £30 afternoon tea, £40 champagne tea, generally served 15:00-18:30 daily).

$$$$ Fortnum & Mason department store offers tea at several different restaurants within its walls. You can "Take Tea in the Parlour" for £22 (including ice cream and scones; Mon-Sat 10:00-19:30, Sun 11:30-17:00). The pièce de resistance is their Diamond Jubilee Tea Salon, named in honor of the Queen's 60th year on the throne (and, no doubt, to remind visitors of Her Majesty's visit for tea here in 2012 with Camilla and Kate). At these royal prices, consider it dinner (£48, Mon-Sat 12:00-19:00, Sun until 18:00, dress up a bit—no shorts, "children must be behaved," 181 Piccadilly, smart to reserve at least a week in advance, tel. 020/7734-8040, www.fortnumandmason.com).

of water). They also serve a restful £10 afternoon tea (daily 12:00-18:00). You'll find the café directly under St. Martin-in-the-Fields, facing Trafalgar Square—enter through the glass pavilion next to the church (generally about 8:00-20:00 daily, profits go to the church, Tube: Charing Cross, tel. 020/7766-1158). On Wednesday evenings you can dine to the music of a live jazz band at 20:00 (£8-15 tickets). While here, check out the concert schedule for the busy church upstairs (or visit www.stmartin-in-the-fields.org).

$$ The Chandos Pub's Opera Room floats amazingly apart from the tacky crush of tourism around Trafalgar Square. Look for it opposite the National Portrait Gallery (corner of William IV Street and St. Martin's Lane) and climb the stairs—to the left or right of the pub entrance—to the Opera Room. This is a fine Trafalgar rendezvous point and a wonderfully local pub. They serve £7 sandwiches and a better-than-average range of traditional pub meals for £10—meat pies and fish-and-chips are their specialty. The ground-floor pub is stuffed with regulars and offers snugs (private booths) and more serious beer drinking. To eat on that level, you have to order upstairs and carry it down (kitchen open daily 11:30-21:00, Fri until 18:00, order and pay at the bar, 29 St. Martin's Lane, Tube: Leicester Square, tel. 020/7836-1401).

Near the British Museum and British Library

To avoid the touristy crush right around the British Museum, head a few blocks west to the Fitzrovia area. Here, tiny Charlotte Place is lined with small eateries (including the first two listed below); nearby, the much bigger Charlotte Street has several more good options. This area is a short walk from the Goodge Street Tube station.

$ Salumeria Dino serves up hearty £5 sandwiches, pasta, and Italian coffee. Dino, a native of Naples, has run his little shop for more than 30 years and has managed to create a classic-feeling Italian deli (cheap takeaway cappuccinos, Mon-Fri 9:00-18:00, closed Sat-Sun, 15 Charlotte Place, tel. 020/7580-3938).

$ Lantana OUT, next door to Salumeria Dino, is an Australian coffee shop that sells modern soups, sandwiches, and salads at their takeaway window (£8 daily hot dish). **Lantana IN** is an adjacent sit-down café that serves pricier meals (both open long hours daily, 13 Charlotte Place, tel. 020/7637-3347).

$$ Indian Food near the British Library: Drummond Street (running just west of Euston Station) is famous for cheap and good Indian vegetarian food. For a good, moderately priced *thali* (combo platter) consider **Chutneys** (124 Drummond, tel. 020/7388-0604) and **Ravi Shankar** (135 Drummond, tel. 020/7388-6458, both open long hours daily).

West London
Victoria Station Area

$$$ Grumbles brags it's been serving "good food and wine at non-scary prices since 1964." Offering a delicious mix of "modern eclectic French and traditional English," this unpretentious little place with cozy booths inside (on two levels) and a few nice sidewalk tables is the best spot to eat well in this otherwise workaday neighborhood. Their traditional dishes are their forte (early-bird specials, open daily 12:00-14:30 & 18:00-23:00, reservations wise, half a block north of Belgrave Road at 35 Churton Street, tel. 020/7834-0149, www.grumblesrestaurant.co.uk).

$$ Pimlico Fresh's breakfasts and lunches feature fresh, organic ingredients, served up with good coffee and/or fresh-squeezed juices. Choose from the dishes listed on the wall-sized chalkboard that lines the small eating area, then order at the counter. This place is heaven if you need a break from your hotel's bacon-eggs-beans routine (takeout lunches, plenty of vegetarian options; Mon-Fri 7:30-18:30, breakfast served until 15:00; Sat-Sun 9:00-18:00; 86 Wilton Road, tel. 020/7932-0030).

$$ Seafresh Fish Restaurant is the neighborhood place for plaice—and classic and creative fish-and-chips cuisine. You can either take out on the cheap or eat in, enjoying a white-fish ambience. Though Mario's father started this place in 1965, it feels like the chippy of the 21st century (Mon-Sat 12:00-15:00 & 17:00-22:30, closed Sun, 80 Wilton Road, tel. 020/7828-0747).

$$ The Jugged Hare, a 10-minute walk from Victoria Station, fills a lavish old bank building, with vaults replaced by kegs of beer and a kitchen. They have a traditional menu and a plush, vivid pub scene good for a meal or just a drink (food served Mon-Fri 11:00-21:00, Sat-Sun until 20:00, 172 Vauxhall Bridge Road, tel. 020/7828-1543).

$$ St. George's Tavern is the neighborhood's best pub for a full meal. They serve dinner from the same menu in three zones: on the sidewalk to catch the sun and enjoy some people-watching, in the ground-floor pub, and in a classier downstairs dining room with full table service.

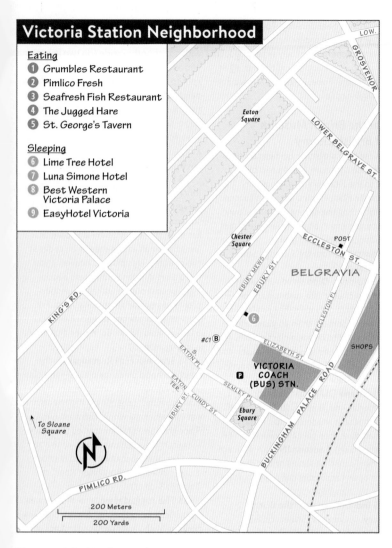

Victoria Station Neighborhood

Eating
1. Grumbles Restaurant
2. Pimlico Fresh
3. Seafresh Fish Restaurant
4. The Jugged Hare
5. St. George's Tavern

Sleeping
6. Lime Tree Hotel
7. Luna Simone Hotel
8. Best Western Victoria Palace
9. EasyHotel Victoria

LOW.

GROSVENOR

Eaton Square

LOWER BELGRAVE ST.

Chester Square

ECCLESTON ST.

POST

BELGRAVIA

EBURY MEWS

EBURY ST.

ECCLESTON PL.

KING'S RD.

6

#C1 Ⓑ

EATON PL.

ELIZABETH ST.

SHOPS

VICTORIA COACH (BUS) STN.

🅿

BUCKINGHAM PALACE ROAD

EATON TER.

SEMLEY PL.

CUNDY ST.

EBURY ST.

Ebury Square

To Sloane Square

🅝

PIMLICO RD.

200 Meters
200 Yards

The scene is inviting for just a beer, too (food served daily 12:00-22:00, corner of Hugh Street and Belgrave Road, tel. 020/7630-1116).

Bayswater and Notting Hill

$$$ Geales, which opened its doors in 1939 as a fish-and-chips shop, has been serving Notting Hill ever since. Today, while the menu is more varied, the emphasis is still on fish. The interior is casual, but the food is upscale. The crispy battered cod that put them on the map is still the best around (£10 two-course express lunch menu; Tue-Sun 12:00-15:00 & 18:00-22:00, closed Mon, reservations smart, 2 Farmer Street, just south of Notting Hill Gate Tube stop, tel. 020/7727-7528, www.geales.com).

$$ The Churchill Arms Pub and Thai Kitchen is a combo establishment that's a hit in the neighborhood. It offers good beer and a thriving old-English ambience in front and hearty £9 Thai plates in an enclosed patio in the back. Arrive by 18:00 or after 21:00 to avoid a line (food served daily 12:00-22:00, 119 Kensington Church Street, tel. 020/7727-4242 for the pub or 020/7792-1246 for restaurant, www. churchillarmskensington.co.uk).

$$$ Hereford Road is a cozy, mod eatery tucked away on Leinster Square. It's stylish but not pretentious, serving heavy, meaty English cuisine made with modern panache. Cozy two-person booths face the open kitchen up top; the main dining room is down below. There are also a few sidewalk tables (daily 12:00-15:00 & 18:00-22:00, reservations smart, 3 Hereford Road, tel. 020/7727-1144, www. herefordroad.org).

$$ The Prince Edward serves good grub in a comfy, family-friendly, upscale-pub setting and at its sidewalk tables (daily 10:30-22:30, 2 blocks north of Bayswater Road at the corner of Dawson Place and Hereford Road, 73 Prince's Square, tel. 020/7727-2221).

SLEEPING

London is an expensive city for lodging. Expect cheaper rooms to be relatively dumpy. I rank accommodations from **$** budget to **$$$$** splurge. To get the best deal, contact my family-run hotels directly by phone or email. Book your accommodations well in advance if you'll be traveling during peak season or if your trip coincides with a major holiday or festival.

Looking for Hotel Deals Online: Given London's high hotel prices, it's worth searching for a deal. For some travelers, short-term, Airbnb-type rentals can be a good alternative; search for places in my recommended hotel neighborhoods. You can also browse these accommodation discount sites: www.londontown.com (an informative site with a discount booking service), athomeinlondon.co.uk and www.londonbb.com (both list central B&Bs), www.lastminute.com, www.visitlondon.com, and www.eurocheapo.com.

Near Victoria Station

The safe, surprisingly tidy streets behind Victoria Station teem with little, moderately-priced-for-London B&Bs.

$$$$ Lime Tree Hotel, enthusiastically run by Charlotte and Matt, is a gem, with 28 spacious, stylish, comfortable, thoughtfully decorated rooms, a helpful staff, and a fun-loving breakfast room (small lounge opens onto quiet garden, 135 Ebury Street, tel. 020/7730-8191, www.limetreehotel.co.uk, info@limetreehotel.co.uk, Laura manages the office).

$$$ Luna Simone Hotel rents 36 fresh, spacious, remodeled rooms with modern bathrooms. It's a smartly managed place, run for more than 40 years by twins Peter and Bernard—and Bernard's son Mark—and they still seem to enjoy their work (RS%, family rooms, 47 Belgrave Road near the corner of Charlwood Street, handy bus #24 stops out front, tel. 020/7834-5897, www.lunasimonehotel.com, stay@lunasimonehotel.com).

$$ Best Western Victoria Palace offers modern business-class comfort compared with some of the other creaky old hotels listed here. Choose from the 43 rooms in the main building (elevator, at 60 Warwick Way), or pay about 20 percent less by booking a nearly identical room in one of the annexes, each a half-block away—an excellent value for this neighborhood if you skip breakfast (breakfast extra, air-con, no elevator, 17 Belgrave Road and 1 Warwick Way, reception at main building, tel. 020/7821-7113, www.bestwesternvictoriapalace.co.uk, info@bestwesternvictoriapalace.co.uk).

$ EasyHotel Victoria, at 34 Belgrave Road, is part of a budget chain.

North of Kensington Gardens

From the core of the tourist's London, the vast Hyde Park spreads west, eventually becoming Kensington Gardens. Bayswater anchors the area; it's bordered by Notting Hill to the west and Paddington to the east. This area has quick bus and Tube access to downtown and, for London, is very cozy.

Bayswater and Notting Hill

$$$ Vancouver Studios offers one of the best values in this neighborhood. Its 45 modern, tastefully furnished rooms come with fully equipped kitchenettes (utensils, stove, microwave, and fridge) rather than breakfast. It's nestled between Kensington Gardens Square and Prince's Square and has its own tranquil garden patio out back (30 Prince's Square, tel. 020/7243-1270, www.vancouverstudios.co.uk, info@vancouverstudios.co.uk).

$$$ Garden Court Hotel is understated, with 40 simple, homey-but-tasteful rooms (family rooms, includes continental breakfast, elevator, 30 Kensington Gardens Square, tel. 020/7229-2553, www.gardencourthotel.co.uk, info@gardencourthotel.co.uk).

$$$ Princes Square Guest Accommodation is a crisp (if impersonal) place renting 50 businesslike rooms with pleasant, modern decor. It's well located, practical, and a very good value, especially if you can score a good rate (elevator, 23 Prince's Square, tel. 020/7229-9876, www.princessquarehotel.co.uk, info@princessquarehotel.co.uk).

$$ London House Hotel has 103 spiffy, modern, cookie-cutter rooms on Kensington Gardens Square. Its rates are great considering the quality and fine location (family rooms, breakfast extra, elevator, 81 Kensington Gardens Square, tel. 020/7243-1810, www.londonhousehotels.com, reservations@londonhousehotels.com).

$$$$ Portobello Hotel is on a quiet residential street in the heart of Notting Hill. Its 21 rooms are funky yet elegant—both the style and location give it an urban-fresh feeling (elevator, 22 Stanley Gardens, tel. 020/7727-2777, www.portobellohotel.com, stay@portobellohotel.com).

Near Paddington Station

$$ Stylotel feels like the stylish, super-modern, aluminum-clad big sister of the EasyHotel chain. Their tidy 39 rooms come with hard surfaces—hardwood floors, prefab plastic bathrooms, and metallic walls. While rooms can be cramped, the beds have space for luggage underneath. You may feel like an astronaut in a retro science-fiction film, but if you don't need ye olde doilies, this place offers a good value (family rooms, elevator, 160 Sussex Gardens, tel. 020/7723-1026, www.stylotel.com, info@stylotel.com, well-run by Andreas). They have eight fancier, pricier, air-conditioned suites across the street with kitchenettes and no breakfast.

$$ Olympic House Hotel has clean public spaces and a no-nonsense welcome, but its 38 business-class rooms offer predictable comfort and fewer old-timey quirks than many hotels in this price range (air-con extra, elevator, pay Wi-Fi, 138 Sussex Gardens, tel. 020/7723-5935, www.olympichousehotel.co.uk, olympichousehotel@btinternet.com).

$ EasyHotel, a budget chain, has a branch at 10 Norfolk Place.

North London

$$$$ The Sumner Hotel rents 19 rooms in a 19th-century Georgian townhouse sporting large contemporary rooms and a lounge with fancy modern Italian furniture. This swanky place packs in all the amenities and is conveniently located north of Hyde Park and near Oxford Street, a busy shopping destination—close to Selfridges and a Marks & Spencer (RS%, air-con, elevator, 54 Upper Berkeley Street, a block and a half off Edgware Road, Tube: Marble Arch, tel. 020/7723-2244, www.thesumner.com, reservations@thesumner.com).

$$$ The 22 York Street B&B offers a casual alternative in the city center, with an inviting lounge and 10 traditional, hardwood, comfortable rooms, each named for a notable London landmark (near Marylebone/Baker Street: From Baker Street Tube station, walk 2 blocks down Baker Street and take a right to 22 York Street—no sign, just look for #22; tel. 020/7224-2990, www.22yorkstreet.co.uk, mc@22yorkstreet.co.uk, energetically run by Liz and Michael Callis).

Other Sleeping Options
Big, Good-Value, Modern Hotels

If you can score a double for £90-100 (or less—often possible with promotional rates) and don't mind a modern, impersonal, American-style hotel, one of these can be a decent value in pricey London. I've listed a few of the dominant chains, along with a quick rundown on their more

North of Kensington Gardens

Eating

1. Geales Restaurant
2. The Churchill Arms Pub & Thai Kitchen
3. Hereford Road Restaurant
4. The Prince Edward Pub
5. The Orangery (Afternoon Tea)

Sleeping

6. Vancouver Studios
7. Garden Court Hotel
8. Princes Square Guest Accommodation
9. London House Hotel
10. Portobello Hotel
11. Stylotel
12. Olympic House Hotel
13. EasyHotel

LONDON
SLEEPING

North London Neighborhood

Eating
1. Salumeria Dino Italian Deli & Lantana OUT and IN
2. Chutneys & Ravi Shankar

Sleeping
3. The Sumner Hotel
4. The 22 York Street B&B
5. London Central Youth Hostel
6. Generator Hostel

convenient London locations. Some of these branches sit on busy streets in dreary train-station neighborhoods, so use common sense after dark and wear a money belt.

$$ Motel One, the German chain that specializes in affordable style, has a branch at Tower Hill, a 10-minute walk north of the Tower of London (24 Minories, tel. 020/7481-6427, www.motel-one.com, london-towerhill@motel-one.com).

$$ Premier Inn has more than 70 hotels in greater London. Convenient locations include a branch inside **London County Hall** (next to the London Eye), at **Southwark/Borough Market** (near Shakespeare's Globe, 34 Park Street),

Southwark/Tate Modern (Great Suffolk Street), **Kensington/Earl's Court** (11 Knaresborough Place), **Victoria** (82 Eccleston Square), and **Leicester Square** (1 Leicester Place). In North London, the following branches cluster between King's Cross, St. Pancras, and the British Museum: **King's Cross St. Pancras, St. Pancras, Euston,** and **Brook House.** Avoid the **Tower Bridge** location, south of the bridge and a long walk from the Tube—but London City Tower Hill, north of the bridge on Prescot Street, works fine (www.premierinn.com, tel. 0871-527-9222; from North America, dial 011-44-1582-567-890).

$$ Travelodge has close to 70 locations in London, including at **King's Cross** (200 yards in front of King's Cross Station, Gray's Inn Road) and **Euston** (1 Grafton Place). Other handy locations include **King's Cross Royal Scot, Marylebone, Covent Garden, Liverpool Street, Southwark,** and **Farringdon;** www.travelodge. co.uk.

$$ Ibis, the budget branch of the AccorHotels group, has a few dozen options across the city, with a handful of locations convenient to London's center, including **Euston St. Pancras** (on a quiet street a block west of Euston Station, 3 Cardington Street), **London City Shoreditch** (5 Commercial Street),

and the more design-focused **Ibis Styles** branches at **Kensington** (15 Hogarth Road) and **Southwark,** with a theater theme (43 Southwark Bridge Road); www. ibishotel.com.

$ EasyHotel, with several branches in good neighborhoods, has a unique business model inspired by its parent company, the EasyJet budget airline. The generally tiny, super-efficient, no-frills rooms feel popped out of a plastic mold, down to the prefab ship's head-type "bathroom pod." Rates can be surprisingly low (with doubles as cheap as £30 if you book early enough)—but you'll pay à la carte for expensive add-ons, such as TV use, Wi-Fi, luggage storage, fresh towels, and daily cleaning (breakfast, if available, comes from a vending machine). If you go with the base rate, it's like hosteling with privacy—a hard-to-beat value. But you get what you pay for (thin walls, flimsy construction, noisy fellow guests, and so on). They're only a good deal if you book far enough ahead to get a good price and skip the many extras. Locations include **Victoria** (34 Belgrave Road—see map on page 102), **South Kensington** (14 Lexham Gardens), **Earl's Court** (44 West Cromwell Road), and **Paddington** (10 Norfolk Place); www.easyhotel.com.

Hostels

¢ **London Central Youth Hostel** is the flagship of London's hostels, with all the latest in security and comfortable efficiency. Families and travelers of any age will feel welcome in this wonderful facility. You'll pay the same price for any bed—so try to grab one with a bathroom (families welcome to book an entire room, book long in advance, between Oxford Circus and Great Portland Street Tube stations at 104 Bolsover Street, tel. 0845-371-9154, www.yha.org.uk, londoncentral@yha.org.uk).

¢ **Generator Hostel** is a brightly colored, hip hostel with a café and a DJ spinning the hits. It's in a renovated building tucked behind a busy street halfway between King's Cross and the British Museum (37 Tavistock Place, Tube: Russell Square, tel. 020/7388-7666, www.generatorhostels.com, london@generatorhostels.com).

TRANSPORTATION

Getting Around London

To travel smart in a city this size, you must get comfortable with public transportation. London's excellent taxis, buses, and subway (Tube) system can take you anywhere you need to go—a blessing for travelers' precious vacation time, not to mention their feet.

For more information about public transit (bus and Tube), the best single source is the helpful *Hello London* brochure, which includes both a Tube map and a handy schematic map of the best bus routes (available free at TIs, museums, hotels, and at www.tfl.gov.uk). For specific directions on how to get from point A to point B on London's transit, detailed bus maps, updated prices, and general information, check www.tfl.gov.uk or call the automated info line at 0843-222-1234.

Public Transit Tickets and Passes

While the transit system has six zones, almost all tourist sights are within Zones 1 and 2, so those are the prices I've listed. For more information, visit www.tfl.gov.uk/tickets. A few odd special passes are available, but for nearly every tourist, the answer is simple: Get the Oyster card and use it.

INDIVIDUAL TICKETS

Individual paper tickets for the Tube are ridiculously expensive (£5 per Tube ride). You can buy paper tickets at any Tube station from the easy-to-use self-service machines (select "Adult Single" from the options, then enter your destination). Tickets are valid only on the day of purchase. But unless you're literally taking only one Tube ride your entire visit, you'll save money (and time) with an Oyster card.

TRANSIT CARDS

Oyster Card: A pay-as-you-go Oyster card (a plastic card embedded with a microchip) allows you to ride the Tube, buses, Docklands Light Railway (DLR), and Overground (mostly suburban trains) for about half the rate of individual tickets. To use it, simply touch the card against the yellow card reader at the turnstile or entrance. It flashes green and the fare is automatically deducted. (You must also tap your card again to "touch out" as you exit.)

Buy the card at any Tube station self-service machine, or look for nearby shops displaying the Oyster logo, where you can purchase a card or add credit without the wait. You'll pay a £5 refundable deposit up front, then load it with as much credit as you'll need. One ride in Zones 1 and 2 during peak time costs £2.90; off peak is a little cheaper (£2.40/ride). The system comes with an automatic price cap that guarantees you'll never pay more than £6.80 in one day for rides within Zones 1 and 2. If you think you'll take more than two rides in a day, £6.80 of credit will cover you, but it's smart to add a little more if you expect to travel outside the city center. If you're staying five or more days, consider adding a 7-Day Travelcard to your Oyster card (details later).

Oyster cards are not shareable among companions taking the same ride; each traveler will need his or her own. If your balance gets low, simply add credit—or "top up"—at a ticket window, machine, or shop. You can always see how much credit remains on your card (along with a list of where you've traveled) by touching it to the pad at any ticket machine. Remember to turn in your Oyster card after your last ride (you'll get back the £5 deposit and unused balance up to £10) at a ticket window or by selecting "Pay as you go refund" on any ticket machine that gives change. This will deactivate your card. For balances of more than £10, you must go to a ticket window for your refund. If you don't deactivate your card, the credit never expires—you can use it again on your next trip.

PASSES AND DISCOUNTS

7-Day Travelcard: Various Tube passes and deals are available. Of these, the only option of note is the 7-Day Travelcard. This is the best choice if you're staying five or more days and plan to use public transit a lot (£34.10 for Zones 1-2; £62.30 for Zones 1-6). For most travelers, the Zone 1-2 pass works best. Heathrow Airport is in Zone 6, but there's no need to buy the Zones 1-6 version if that's the only ride outside the city center you plan to take—instead you can pay a small supplement to cover the difference. You can add the 7-Day Travelcard to your Oyster card or purchase the paper version at any National Rail train station.

Families: A paying adult can take up to four kids (10 and under) for free on the Tube, Docklands Light Railway (DLR), Overground, and buses. Kids 11-15 get a discount. Explore other child and student discounts at www.tfl.gov.uk/tickets or ask a clerk at a Tube ticket window which deal is best.

River Cruises: A Travelcard gives you a 33 percent discount on most Thames cruises. The Oyster card gives you roughly a 10 percent discount on Thames Clippers (including the Tate Boat museum ferry).

THE BOTTOM LINE

On a short visit (three days or fewer), I'd get an Oyster card and add £20-25 of credit (£6.60 daily cap times three days, plus a little extra for any rides outside Zones 1-2). If you'll be taking fewer rides, £15 will be enough (£2.90 per ride during peak time gets you 5 rides); if not, you can always top up. For a visit of five days or more, the 7-Day Travelcard—either the paper version or on an Oyster card—will likely pay for itself.

By Tube

London's subway system is called the Tube or Underground (but never "subway," which, in Britain, refers to a pedestrian underpass). The Tube is one of this

MAYOR OF LONDON

Correct at time of going to print

Reg. user No. 17/S/3254/P   Version B 12.2017   © Transport for London planet's great people-movers and usually the fastest long-distance transport in town (runs Mon-Sat about 5:00-24:00, Sun about 7:00-23:00; Central, Jubilee, Northern, Piccadilly, and Victoria lines also run Fri-Sat 24 hours). Two other commuter rail lines are tied into the network and use the same tickets: the Docklands Light Railway (called DLR) and the Overground.

Each line has a name (such as Circle, Northern, or Bakerloo) and two directions (indicated by the end-of-the-line stops). Find the line that will take you to your destination, and figure out roughly which direction (north, south, east, or west) you'll need to go to get there.

At the Tube station, there are two ways to pass through the turnstile. With an Oyster card, touch it flat against the turnstile's yellow card reader, both when you enter and exit the station. With a paper ticket or paper Travelcard, feed it into the turnstile, reclaim it, and hang on to it—you'll need it later.

Find your train by following signs to your line and the (general) direction it's headed (such as Central Line: east). Since some tracks are shared by several lines, double-check before boarding: Make sure your destination is one of the stops listed on the sign at the platform. Also, check the electronic signboards that announce which train is next, and make sure the destination (the end-of-the-line stop) is the direction you want. Some trains, particularly on the Circle and District lines, split off for other directions, but each train has its final destination marked above its windshield.

Trains run about every 3-10 minutes. A general rule of thumb is that it takes 30 minutes to travel six Tube stops (including walking time within stations), or roughly five minutes per stop.

When you leave the system, "touch out" with your Oyster card at the electronic reader on the turnstile, or feed your paper ticket into the turnstile (it will eat your now-expired ticket). With a paper Travelcard, it will spit out your still-valid card. Check maps and signs for the most convenient exit.

The system can be fraught with construction delays and breakdowns. Pay attention to signs and announcements explaining necessary detours. Rush hours (8:00-10:00 and 16:00-19:00) can be packed and sweaty. If one train is stuffed—and another is coming in three minutes—it may be worth a wait to avoid the sardine routine. If you get confused, ask for advice from a local, a blue-vested staffer, or at the information window located before the turnstile entry. Online, get help from the "Plan a Journey" feature at www.tfl.gov.uk, which is accessible (via free Wi-Fi) on any mobile device within most Tube stations before you go underground.

TUBE ETIQUETTE

- When your train arrives, stand off to the side and let riders exit before you board.
- When the car is jam-packed, avoid using the hinged seats near the doors of some trains—they take up valuable standing space.
- If you're blocking the door when the train stops, step out of the car and off to the side, let others off, then get back on.
- Talk softly in the cars. Listen to how quietly Londoners communicate and follow their lead.
- On escalators, stand on the right and pass on the left. But note that in some passageways or stairways, you might be directed to walk on the left (the direction Brits go when behind the wheel).
- Discreet eating and drinking are fine (nothing smelly); drinking alcohol and smoking are banned.
- Be zipped up to thwart thieves.
- Carefully check exit options before surfacing to street level. Signs point clearly to nearby sights—you'll save lots of walking by choosing the right exit.

By Bus

If you figure out the bus system, you'll swing like Tarzan through the urban jungle of London. Get in the habit of hopping buses for quick little straight shots, even just to get to a Tube stop. However, during bump-and-grind rush hours (8:00-10:00

and 16:00-19:00), you'll usually go faster by Tube.

You can't buy single-trip tickets for buses, and you can't use cash to pay when boarding. Instead, you must have an Oyster card, a paper Travelcard, or a one-day Bus & Tram Pass (£5, can buy on day of travel only—not beforehand, from ticket machine in any Tube station). If you're using your Oyster card, any bus ride in downtown London costs £1.50 (capped at £4.50/day).

When your bus approaches, it's wise to hold your arm out to let the driver know you want to get on. Hop on and confirm your destination with the driver (often friendly and helpful).

As you board, touch your Oyster card to the card reader, or show your paper Travelcard or Bus & Tram Pass to the driver. Unlike on the Tube, there's no need to show or tap your card when you hop off. On the older heritage "Routemaster" buses without card-readers (used on the #15 route), you simply take a seat, and the conductor comes around to check cards and passes.

To alert the driver that you want to get off, press one of the red buttons (on the poles between the seats) before your stop.

By Taxi

London is the best taxi town in Europe. Big, black, carefully regulated cabs are everywhere—there are about 25,000 of them.

Handy Bus Routes

Here are some of the most useful routes:

Route #9: High Street Kensington to Knightsbridge (Harrods) to Hyde Park Corner to Trafalgar Square to Somerset House.

Route #11: Victoria Station to Westminster Abbey to Trafalgar Square to St. Paul's and Liverpool Street Station and the East End.

Route #15: Trafalgar Square to St. Paul's to Tower of London (sometimes with heritage "Routemaster" old-style double-decker buses).

Routes #23 and #159: Paddington Station (#159 begins at Marble Arch) to Oxford Circus to Piccadilly Circus to Trafalgar Square; from there, #23 heads east to St. Paul's and Liverpool Street Station, while #159 heads to Westminster and the Imperial War Museum. In addition, several buses (including #6, #12, and #139) also make the corridor run between Marble Arch, Oxford Circus, Piccadilly Circus, and Trafalgar Square.

Route #24: Pimlico to Victoria Station to Westminster Abbey to Trafalgar Square to Euston Square, then all the way north to Camden Town (Camden Lock Market).

Route #38: Victoria Station to Hyde Park Corner to Piccadilly Circus to British Museum.

Route #88: Tate Britain to Westminster Abbey to Trafalgar Square to Piccadilly Circus to Oxford Circus to Great Portland Street Station (Regent's Park), then north to Camden Town.

Route #148: Westminster Abbey to Victoria Station to Notting Hill and Bayswater (by way of the east end of Hyde Park and Marble Arch).

Route #RV1 (a scenic South Bank joyride): Tower of London to Tower Bridge to Southwark Street (five-minute walk behind Tate Modern/Shakespeare's Globe) to London Eye/Waterloo Station, then over Waterloo Bridge to Somerset House and Covent Garden.

I've never met a crabby cabbie in London. They love to talk, and they know every nook and cranny in town. I ride in a taxi each day just to get my London questions answered. Drivers must pass a rigorous test on "The Knowledge" of London geography to earn their license.

If a cab's top light is on, just wave it down. Drivers flash lights when they see you wave. They have a tight turning radius, so you can hail cabs going in either direction. If waving doesn't work, ask someone where you can find a taxi stand. Telephoning a cab will get you one in a few minutes, but costs a little more (tel. 0871-871-8710).

Rates: Rides start at £2.60. The regular tariff #1 covers most of the day (Mon-Fri 5:00-20:00), tariff #2 is during "unsociable hours" (Mon-Fri 20:00-22:00 and Sat-Sun 5:00-22:00), and tariff #3 is for nighttime (22:00-5:00) and holidays. Rates go up about 40 percent with each higher tariff. Extra charges are explained in writing on the cab wall. All cabs accept credit and debit cards, including American cards. Tip a cabbie by rounding up (maximum 10 percent).

Connecting downtown sights is quick and easy, and will cost you about £8-10 (for example, St. Paul's to the Tower of London, or between the two Tate museums). For a short ride, three adults in a cab generally travel at close to Tube prices—and groups of four or five adults should taxi everywhere. All cabs can carry five passengers, and some take six, for the same cost as a single traveler.

Don't worry about meter cheating. Licensed British cab meters come with a sealed computer chip and clock that ensures you'll get the correct tariff. The only way a cabbie can cheat you is by taking a needlessly long route. One serious pitfall, however, is taking a cab when traffic is bad to a destination efficiently served by the Tube.

If you overdrink and ride in a taxi, be warned: Taxis charge £40 for "soiling" (a.k.a., pub puke). If you forget this book in a taxi, call the Lost Property office and hope for the best (tel. 0845-330-9882).

By Uber

Uber faces legal challenges in London and may not be operating when you visit. If Uber is running, it can be much cheaper than a taxi and is a handy alternative if there's a long line for a taxi or if no cabs are available. Uber drivers generally don't know the city as well as regular cabbies, and they don't have the access to some fast lanes that taxis do. Still, if you like using Uber, it can work great here.

By Boat

The sleek, 220-seat catamarans used by **Thames Clippers** are designed for commuters rather than sightseers. Think of the boats as express buses on the river—they zip through London every 20-30 minutes, stopping at most of the major docks en route. They're fast: roughly 20 minutes from Embankment to Tower, 10 more minutes to Docklands, and 15 more minutes to Greenwich. However, the only outside access is on a crowded deck at the exhaust-choked back of the boat, where you're jostling for space to take photos. Any one-way ride in Central London (roughly London Eye to Tower Pier) costs £8; a one-way ride to East London (Canary Wharf and Greenwich) is £8.70, and a River Roamer all-day ticket costs £18.50 (discounts with Travelcard and Oyster card, www.thamesclippers.com).

Thames Clippers also offers two express trips. The **Tate Boat** ferry service, which directly connects the Tate Britain (Millbank Pier) and the Tate Modern (Bankside Pier), is made for art lovers (£8 one-way, covered by River Roamer day ticket; buy ticket at kiosks or self-service machines before boarding or use Oyster Card; for frequency and times, see www.tate.org.uk/visit/tate-boat). The **O2 Express** runs only on nights when there are events at the O2 arena (departs from London Eye Pier).

By Bike

London operates a citywide bike-rental program similar to ones in other major European cities, and new bike lanes are still cropping up around town.

Still, London isn't (yet) ideal for biking. Its network of designated bike lanes is far from complete, and the city's many one-way streets (not to mention the need to bike on the "wrong" side) can make biking here a bit more challenging than it sounds.

Santander Cycles, intended for quick point-to-point trips, are fairly easy to rent. Approximately 700 bike-rental stations are scattered throughout the city (£2/day access fee; first 30 minutes free; £2 for every additional 30-minute period). When you're ready to ride, press "Hire a Cycle" and insert your credit card when prompted. You'll then get a ticket with a five-digit code. Take the ticket to any bike that doesn't have a red light (those are "taken") and punch in the number. After the yellow light blinks, a green light will appear: Now you can (firmly) pull the bike out of the slot. When your ride is over, find a station with an empty slot, then push your bike in until it locks and the green light flashes.

You can hire bikes as often as you like (which will start your free 30-minute period over again), as long as you wait five minutes between each use. Pick up a map of the docking stations at any major Tube station. The same map is also available online at www.tfl.gov.uk (click on "Santander Cycles") and as a free app (http://cyclehireapp.com).

By Car

If you have a car, stow it—you don't want to drive in London. An £11.50 **congestion charge** is levied on any private car entering the city center during peak hours (Mon-Fri 7:00-18:00, no charge Sat-Sun and holidays). You can pay the fee either online or by phone (www.cclondon.com, from within the UK call 0343/222-2222, from outside the UK call 011-44-20/7649-9122, phones answered Mon-Fri 8:00-22:00, Sat 9:00-15:00, be ready to give the vehicle registration number and country of registration). There are painfully stiff penalties for late payments.

Arriving and Departing
By Plane

London has six airports; I've focused my coverage on the two most widely used—Heathrow and Gatwick—with a few tips for using the others (Stansted, Luton, London City, and Southend).

HEATHROW AIRPORT

For Heathrow's airport, flight, and transfer information, call the switchboard at 0844-335-1801, or visit the helpful website www.heathrow.com (airport code: LHR).

Heathrow's terminals are numbered T-1 through T-5. Though T-1 is now closed for arrivals and departures, it still supports other terminals with baggage, and the newly renovated T-2 ("Queen's Terminal") will likely expand into the old T-1 digs eventually. Each terminal is served by different airlines and alliances; for example, T-5 is exclusively for British Air and Iberia Air flights, while T-2 serves mostly Star Alliance flights, such as United and Lufthansa. Screens posted throughout the airport identify which terminal each airline uses; this information should also be printed on your ticket or boarding pass.

You can walk between T-2 and T-3. From this central hub (called "Heathrow Central"), T-4 and T-5 split off in opposite directions (and are not walkable). The easiest way to travel between the T-2/T-3 cluster and either T-4 or T-5 is by Heathrow Express train (free to transfer between terminals, departs every 15-20 minutes). You can also take a shuttle bus (free, serves all terminals), or the Tube (requires a ticket, serves all terminals).

London's Airports

Luton ●
✈ Luton
✈ Stansted

Not to Scale

#157 & 41

Reading

ST. PANCRAS
PADDINGTON

LIVERPOOL STREET

Southend
✈ Southend ●

Windsor
#71 & 77
Rail Air Link
Tube →
✈ VICTORIA
D.L.R.

To Bath

Heathrow
VICTORIA COACH STN.

London City

London

Thames

Guildford

EUROSTAR

✈ *Gatwick*
Ashford ●

········· Rail
═══════ Eurostar Rail
─────── Tube & D.L.R.
- - - - - Bus

To Paris →

ALL BUSES ARE NATIONAL EXPRESS
UNLESS NOTED

↓ To Brighton

To Brighton

English Channel

If you're flying out of Heathrow, it's critical to confirm which terminal your flight will use (look at your ticket/boarding pass, check online, or call your airline in advance)—if it's T-4 or T-5, allow extra time. Taxi drivers generally know which terminal you'll need based on the airline, but bus drivers may not.

Services: Each terminal has an airport information desk (open long hours daily), car-rental agencies, exchange bureaus, ATMs, a pharmacy, a VAT refund desk (tel. 0845-872-7627, you must present the VAT claim form from the retailer here to get your tax rebate on purchased items), and baggage storage (£6/item up to 2 hours, £11/item for 2-24 hours, long hours daily, www.left-baggage.co.uk). Heathrow offers both free Wi-Fi and pay Internet access points (in each terminal, check map for locations). You'll find a post office on the first floor of T-3 (departures area). Each terminal also has cheap eateries.

Heathrow's small **"TI"** (tourist info shop), even though it's a for-profit business, is worth a visit if you're nearby and want to pick up free information, including the *London Planner* visitors guide (long hours daily, 5-minute walk from T-3 in Tube station, follow signs to Underground; bypass queue for transit info to reach window for London questions).

Getting Between Heathrow and Downtown London: You have several options for traveling the 14 miles between Heathrow Airport and downtown London: Tube, bus, express train (with connecting Tube or taxi), or taxi. The one that works best for you will depend on your arrival terminal, your destination in central London, and your budget.

By Tube (Subway): The Tube takes you from any Heathrow terminal to downtown London in 50-60 minutes on the Piccadilly Line (6/hour, buy ticket at Tube station ticket window or self-service machine). If you plan to use the Tube for transport in London, it makes sense to buy a pay-as-you-go Oyster card (possibly adding a 7-Day Travelcard) at the airport's Tube station ticket window. If you add a Travelcard that covers only Zones 1-2, you'll need to pay a small supplement for the initial trip from Heathrow (Zone 6) to downtown.

If you're taking the Tube from downtown London to the airport, note that Piccadilly Line trains don't stop at every terminal. Trains either stop at T-4, then T-2/T-3 (also called Heathrow Central), in that order; or T-2/T-3, then T-5. When leaving central London on the Tube, allow extra time if going to T-4 or T-5, and check the reader board in the station to make sure that the train goes to the right terminal.

By Bus: Most buses depart from the outdoor common area called the Central Bus Station, a five-minute walk from the T-2/T-3 complex. To connect between T-4 or T-5 and the Central Bus Station, ride the free Heathrow Express train or the shuttle buses.

National Express has regular service from Heathrow's Central Bus Station to Victoria Coach Station in downtown London, near several of my recommended hotels. While slow, the bus is affordable and convenient for those staying near Victoria Station (£8-10, 1-2/hour, less frequent from Victoria Station to Heathrow, 45-75 minutes depending on time of day, tel. 0871-781-8181, www.nationalexpress.com). A less-frequent National Express bus goes from T-5 directly to Victoria Coach Station.

By Train: A train runs between Heathrow Airport and London's Paddington Station, and will soon be competing with a new Tube line covering the same route. At Paddington Station, you're in the thick of the Tube system, with easy access to any of my recommended neighborhoods.

The **Heathrow Express train** is fast and runs frequently, but it's pricey (£22-25 one-way, price depends on time of day, £37 round-trip, £5 more if you buy your ticket on board, can also use Oyster card, covered by BritRail pass; 4/hour, daily 5:00-24:00, 15 minutes to downtown from Heathrow Central Station serving T-2/T-3, 21 minutes from T-5; for T-4 take free transfer to Heathrow Central, tel. 0345-600-1515, www.heathrowexpress.co.uk).

The new **Crossrail Elizabeth Tube line,** which may be completed by the time you visit, will provide a cheaper way to link Heathrow Airport with downtown London. It will connect Heathrow Central (a single station serving T-2/T-3) and T-4 with Paddington.

By Taxi: Taxis from the airport cost £45-75 to west and central London (one hour). For four people traveling together, this can be a reasonable option. Hotels can often line up a cab back to the airport for about £50. If running, Uber also offers London airport pickup and drop-off.

GATWICK AIRPORT

More and more flights land at Gatwick Airport, which is halfway between London and the south coast (airport code: LGW, tel. 0844-892-0322, www.gatwickairport. com). Gatwick has two terminals, North and South, which are easily connected by a free, two-minute monorail ride. Boarding passes say "Gatwick N" or "Gatwick S" to indicate your terminal. British Airways flights generally use Gatwick South. The Gatwick Express trains (described next) stop only at Gatwick South.

Getting Between Gatwick and Downtown London: The best way into London from this airport, Gatwick Express trains shuttle conveniently between Gatwick South and London's Victoria Station (£20 one-way, £35 round-trip, cheaper if purchased online, Oyster cards accepted, 4/hour, 30 minutes, runs 5:00-24:00 daily, a few trains as early as 3:30, tel. 0845-850-1530, www.gatwickexpress.com). When going to the airport, at Victoria Station note that Gatwick Express has its own ticket windows right by the platform (tracks 13 and 14).

A train also runs between Gatwick South and St. Pancras International Station (£10.40, 3-5/hour, 45-60 minutes, www.thetrainline.com)—useful for travelers taking the Eurostar train (to Paris, Brussels, or Amsterdam) or staying in the St. Pancras/King's Cross neighborhood.

While even slower, the **bus** is a cheap and handy option to the Victoria Station neighborhood. National Express runs a bus from Gatwick direct to Victoria Station (£9, at least hourly, 1.5 hours, tel. 0871-781-8181, www.nationalexpress.com).

LONDON'S OTHER AIRPORTS

Stansted Airport: Airport code: STN, tel. 0844-335-1803, www.stanstedairport. com. **Buses** run by National Express (£9-12, www.nationalexpress.com) and Ter-ravision (£4-10) connect the airport and London's Victoria Station neighborhood in about 1.5-2 hours. Or you can take the faster Stansted Express **train** (£19, www. stanstedexpress.com). Stansted is expensive by **cab**; figure £100-120 one-way from central London.

Luton Airport: Airport code: LTN, airport tel. 01582/405-100, www.london-luton.co.uk. The fastest way to go into London is by **train** to St. Pancras International Station (£10-14 one-way, 35-45 minutes, www.eastmidlandstrains.co.uk); catch the 10-minute shuttle bus from outside the terminal to the Luton Airport Parkway Station. The National Express **bus** A1 runs from Luton to Victoria Coach Station (£7-11 one-way, 1-1.5 hours, www. nationalexpress.com). The Green Line express **bus** #757 runs to Buckingham Palace Road, just south of Victoria Station, and stops en route near the Baker Street Tube station (£10 one-way, 1-1.5 hours, www.greenline.co.uk).

London City and Southend Airports: To get into the city center from London City Airport (airport code: LCY, tel. 020/7646-0088, www.londoncityairport. com). Take the Docklands Light Railway (DLR) to the Bank Tube station, which is one stop east of St. Paul's on the Central Line (£6, covered by Travelcard, a bit cheaper with an Oyster card, 20 minutes, www.tfl.gov.uk/dlr). Some EasyJet flights land farther out, at Southend Airport (airport code: SEN, tel. 01702/538-500, www.southendairport.com). Trains connect this airport to London's Liverpool Street Station (£16.20, 55 minutes, www. abelliogreateranglia.co.uk).

By Train

London, the country's major transportation hub, has a different train station for each region. There are nine main stations:

- **Euston:** Serves northwest England, North Wales, and Scotland.
- **St. Pancras International:** Serves north and south England, plus the Eurostar to Paris, Brussels, or Amsterdam.
- **King's Cross:** Serves northeast England and Scotland, including York and Edinburgh.
- **Liverpool Street:** Serves east England, including Essex and Harwich.
- **London Bridge:** Serves south England, including Brighton.
- **Waterloo:** Serves south England, including Salisbury and Southampton.
- **Victoria:** Serves Gatwick Airport, Canterbury, Dover, and Brighton.
- **Paddington:** Serves south and southwest England, including Heathrow Airport, Windsor, Bath, Oxford, South Wales, and the Cotswolds.
- **Marylebone:** Serves southwest and central England, including Stratford-upon-Avon.

Any train station has schedule information, can make reservations, and can sell tickets for any destination. Most stations offer a baggage-storage service; because of long security lines, it can take a while to check or pick up your bag (www.left-baggage.co.uk). For more details on the services available at each station, see www.nationalrail.co.uk/stations.

UK **train and bus info** is available at www.traveline.org.uk. For general info on tickets and rail passes, see page 1001.

TRAIN CONNECTIONS FROM LONDON

From Paddington Station to Points West: Windsor (Windsor & Eton Central Station, 2/hour, 35 minutes, easy change at Slough), **Bath** (2/hour, 1.5 hours), **Oxford** (4/hour direct, 1 hour, more with transfer), **Moreton-in-Marsh** (hourly, 1.5 hours).

From King's Cross Station to Points North: York (hourly, 2 hours), **Durham** (hourly, 3 hours), and **Edinburgh** (4.5 hours).

From Euston Station to Points North: Liverpool (at least hourly, 3 hours, more with transfer), **Keswick** (hourly, 4 hours, transfer to bus at Penrith).

London's Major Train Stations

To North Wales & Glasgow

To Luton

To Cambridge, York & Edinburgh

To Harwich & Stansted

To Stratford-upon-Avon

To Canterbury & Dover and via Eurostar: Paris, Brussels & Amsterdam

RAF MUSEUM LONDON

ST. PANCRAS INT'L

STRATFORD INT'L

To Heathrow Airport, Windsor (Eton Central), Bath, S. Wales, Cotswolds & Oxford

MARYLE-BONE

EUSTON

KING'S CROSS

LONDON CITY AIRPORT

PADDINGTON

TRAF. SQ.

LIVERPOOL STREET

DOCKLANDS

LONDON

WATER-LOO

VICTORIA

LONDON BRIDGE

O2 ARENA

CANARY WHARF ON ISLE OF DOGS

GREENWICH

Thames River

Kew Gardens

To Brighton

WIMBLEDON

☐ = Central London

HAMPTON COURT PALACE

To Gatwick Airport, Canterbury, Dover & Brighton▼

To Salisbury, Southampton & Windsor (Eton Riverside)

5 Kilometers

5 Miles

From London's Other Stations to:
Stratford-upon-Avon from Marylebone Station (1-2/hour with transfers, 2.5 hours hours), **Greenwich** from Bank or Monument Tube stop on the DLR—Docklands Light Railway (6/hour, 20 minutes).

By Bus

Buses are slower but considerably cheaper than trains for reaching destinations around Britain and beyond. Most depart from **Victoria Coach Station,** which is one long block south of Victoria Station (Tube: Victoria). Inside the station, you'll find basic eateries, kiosks, and a helpful information desk.

Ideally you'll buy your tickets online (www.nationalexpress.com, www.euro-lines.com, and www.megabus.com). But

if you must buy one at the station, try to arrive an hour before the bus departs, or drop by the day before. Ticketing machines are scattered around the station (separate machines for National Express/ Eurolines and Megabus; you can buy either for today or for tomorrow); there's also a ticket counter near gate 21. For UK train and bus info, check www.traveline. org.uk.

National Express buses go to: Bath (nearly hourly, 3 hours), **Oxford** (2/hour, 2.5 hours), **Stratford-upon-Avon** (3/day, 3.5 hours), **Liverpool** (8/day direct, 5.5 hours, overnight available), **York** (4/day direct, 5 hours), **Durham** (3/day direct, 7 hours, train is better), **Edinburgh,** Scotland (2/day direct, 10 hours, go by train instead).

Public Transportation near London

To North England & Scotland

To York & Scotland

King's Lynn

Norwich

Coventry

ENGLAND

Stratford-upon-Avon

Warwick

Long Buckby

Bedford

Hunt.

Ely

Worcester

Leam. Spa

Moreton

Banbury

Luton

Cambridge

Stansted

To Hoek van Holland

Stow

COTSWOLDS

Chelten-ham

Oxford

Blenheim

Swindon

Didcot

London City

Harwich

To Cardiff

Avebury

Reading

Slough

London

Southend

Bristol

Greenwich

Ramsgate

Bath

Bedwyn

Windsor

Heathrow

EUROSTAR

Canterbury

Dover

Wells

Stonehenge

Gatwick

Glaston-bury

Ashford

(CHUNNEL)

Calais

Salisbury

South-ampton

Brighton

Rye

Calais-Fréthun

To Cornwall

Poole

Bourne-mouth

Portsmouth

East-bourne

Hastings

To Paris

Weymouth

Isle of Wight

English Channel

FRANCE

- ····· **Rail**
- - - - **Bus**
- ········ **Boat**

Note:
Bus Lines Follow
Most Rail Lines

30 Kilometers

30 Miles
(approx. scale)

France

France is a place of gentle beauty. At 215,000 square miles (roughly 20 percent smaller than Texas), it is Western Europe's largest nation, with luxuriant forests, forever coastlines, and Europe's highest mountain ranges. You'll discover a dizzying array of artistic and architectural wonders—soaring cathedrals, chandeliered palaces, and museums filled with the cultural icons of the Western world.

Paris is the star of the show; Provence is small-town France at its best; and the French Riviera offers up beaches and an old-time elegance with a bit of glitz.

Wherever you visit in France, you'll enjoy *l'art de vivre*—the art of living. Experience the fine cuisine, velvety wines, and linger-long pastimes such as people-watching from sun-dappled cafés.

CUISINE SCENE AT A GLANCE

Know the terms for eating out: A menu is called *la carte* (which you use to order individual dishes á la carte). A *menu* is actually a multi-course, fixed-price meal. The daily special is a *plat du jour* (or just *plat*), a hearty, garnished hot plate for about €14-24. *Entrées* are appetizers. The main dish is the *plat principal*.

Cafés and brasseries are open long hours and serve food throughout the day. You're welcome to order just an omelet, salad, or bowl of soup, even for dinner. It's also fine to split starters and desserts, though not main courses.

Check the price list first, which by law must be posted prominently (if you don't see one, go elsewhere). There are two sets of prices: You'll pay more for the same drink if you're seated at a table (*salle*) than if you're seated or standing at the bar or counter (*comptoir*).

Restaurants open for dinner around 19:00. Last seating is about 21:00 (22:00 in cities and Riviera towns). The table is yours for the night.

If a restaurant serves lunch, it generally begins at 12:00, with last orders taken at about 14:00. Lunches at restaurants are cheaper than dinners; to save money, make lunch your main meal.

If you're hungry when restaurants are closed (late afternoon), or if you want a light meal, head for a café, brasserie, deli, or bakery.

At restaurants, two people can split an *entrée* or a big salad and then each get a *plat principal*. It's considered inappropriate for two diners to share one main course.

Fixed-price *menus*, which include two or three courses, are generally a good value. With a three-course *menu* you'll choose a starter of soup, appetizer, or salad; select from several main courses with vegetables; and then finish up with a cheese course or dessert.

To order inexpensive wine with your meal, ask for table wine in a carafe (*pichet*; pee-shay), though finer restaurants usually offer wine only by the glass or bottle.

Tipping: Your server, who doesn't want to rush you, will rarely bring you the bill unless you request it. At cafés and restaurants, a 12-15 percent service charge is always included in the price of what you order, but you won't see it listed on your bill. Most locals never tip. If you feel the service was good, you could tip up to 5 percent extra in cash (credit-card receipts don't even have space to add a tip). But don't feel guilty if you don't leave a tip.

Budget Options: Try takeout delis, food stands, *crêperies*, and *boulangeries* (bakeries selling sandwiches, quiches, and tiny pizzas). You can assemble a picnic at various small shops, a one-stop *super-marché*, or an open-air morning market.

Paris

Paris has been a beacon of culture for centuries. As a world capital of art, fashion, food, literature, and ideas, it stands as a symbol of all the fine things human civilization can achieve, with a splash of romance and joie de vivre.

Paris offers grand boulevards, chatty crêpe stands, chic boutiques, and world-class art galleries. Sip coffee at a sidewalk café near the Eiffel Tower, then step into an Impressionist painting in a tree-lined park. Rub shoulders with the gargoyles at Notre-Dame. Master the Louvre and Orsay museums. Explore the City of Light at night, when monuments are floodlit and Paris sparkles.

PARIS IN 3 DAYS

On your first day, follow my Historic Paris Walk, featuring Ile de la Cité, Notre-Dame, the Latin Quarter, and Sainte-Chapelle. In the afternoon, tour the Louvre. Late in the day, enjoy the Place du Trocadéro scene and a twilight ride up the Eiffel Tower.

On your second day, stroll the Champs-Elysées from the Arc de Triomphe (ascend for the view) to the Tuileries Garden, then tour the Orsay and Rodin museums.

On your third day, head to Versailles. Catch Train-C by 8:00 to arrive early. Tour the palace's interior, then either visit the vast gardens, or return to Paris for more sightseeing.

On any evening: Take a nighttime tour by cruise boat, taxi, or bus. Or enjoy dinner on Ile St. Louis, then a floodlit walk by Notre-Dame. For a free skyline view, head to the rooftop of the neighboring Galeries Lafayette or Printemps department stores.

With extra time: Choose from Montmartre (Sacré-Cœur Basilica), the Army Museum and Napoleon's Tomb, the Marais neighborhood (Picasso Museum and Pompidou Center), or the Opéra Garnier (near the department stores).

ORIENTATION

Central Paris is circled by a ring road and split in half by the Seine River, which runs east-west. If you were floating downstream, the Right Bank (Rive Droite) would be on your right, and the Left Bank (Rive Gauche) on your left. The bull's-eye on your map is Notre-Dame, on an island in the middle of the Seine.

Twenty arrondissements (administrative districts) spiral out from the center, like an escargot shell. If your hotel's zip code is 75007, you know (from the last two digits) that it's in the 7th arrondissement. The city is peppered with Métro stops, and most Parisians locate addresses by the closest stop. So in Parisian jargon, the Eiffel Tower is on *la Rive Gauche* (the Left Bank) in the *7ème* (7th arrondissement), zip code 75007, Mo: Trocadéro (the nearest Métro stop).

The major sights cluster in convenient

Paris Neighborhoods

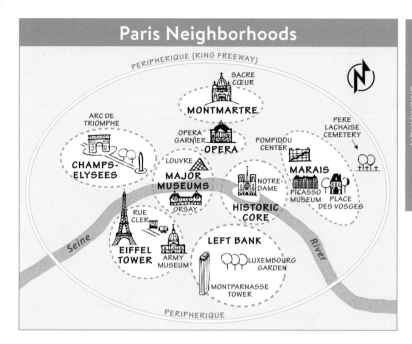

zones. Grouping your sightseeing, walks, dining, and shopping thoughtfully can save you lots of time and money.

Historic Core: This area centers on the Ile de la Cité ("Island of the City"), located in the middle of the Seine. On the Ile de la Cité, you'll find Paris' oldest sights, from Roman ruins to the medieval Notre-Dame and Sainte-Chapelle churches.

Major Museums Neighborhood: Located just west of the historic core, this is where you'll find the Louvre, Orsay, Orangerie, and Tuileries Garden.

Champs-Elysées: The greatest of the many grand, 19th-century boulevards on the Right Bank, the Champs-Elysées runs northwest from Place de la Concorde to the Arc de Triomphe.

Eiffel Tower Neighborhood: Dominated by the Eiffel Tower, this area also boasts the colorful Rue Cler, Army Museum and Napoleon's Tomb, and the Rodin Museum.

Opéra Neighborhood: Surrounding the Opéra Garnier, this area on the Right Bank is home to a series of grand boulevards and high-end shopping.

Left Bank: Anchored by the Luxembourg Garden, the Left Bank is the traditional neighborhood of Paris' intellectual, artistic, and café life.

Marais: Stretching eastward to Bastille along Rue de Rivoli/Rue St. Antoine, this neighborhood has lots of restaurants and hotels, shops, the delightful Place des Vosges, and artistic sights, such as the Pompidou Center and Picasso Museum.

Montmartre: This hill, topped by the bulbous white domes of Sacré-Cœur, hovers on the northern fringes of your Paris map.

Tourist Information

Paris' TIs can provide useful information but may have long lines (www.parisinfo.com). Most TIs sell Museum Passes and individual tickets to sights.

Paris has several TI locations, including **Pyramides** (daily May-Oct 9:00-19:00, Nov-April 10:00-19:00, 25 Rue des Pyramides—at Pyramides Métro stop), **Gare du Nord** (daily 8:00-18:00), **Gare de**

1e = Arrondissements (Districts)

D-111

D-909

RUE DU PRESIDENT WILSON

RUE VICTOR HUGO

BLVD. PERIPHERIQUE (RING FREEWAY)

BLVD. BERTHIER

RUE CHAMPIONNET

AVENUE DE CLICHY

AVENUE DE SAINT-OUEN

17e

MONT-

BLVD. PEREIRE

Montmartre
Cemetery

MOULIN
ROUGE

AVE. DE
VILLIERS

BLVD. MALESHERBES

BLVD. DE
BATIGNOLLES

RUE DE BLANCHE

BLVD. DE CLICHY

Blanche

BLVD. PEREIRE

RUE DE COURCELLES

RUE DE PRONY

RUE DE ROME

To La Défense,
La Grande Arche &
Louis Vuitton Foundation

BLVD. DE COURCELLES

Parc
Monceau

GARE
ST. LAZARE

GALERIES
LAFAYETTE

AVE. DE LE
GRANDE ARMEE

ARC DE
TRIOMPHE

JACQUEMART-
ANDRE MUSEUM

RUE ST. LAZARE

BLVD. HAUSSMANN

BLVD. HAUSSMANN

9e

AVE. KLEBER

AVENUE DES CHAMPS-ELYSEES

RUE LA BOETIE

8e

LA
MADELEINE

OPERA
GARNIER

To Bois de
Boulogne

16e

Place de
la Concorde

Place
Vendôme

RIGHT

To Marmottan
Museum

ARCHITECTURE &
MONUMENTS MUSEUM
& CAFE

GRAND
PALAIS

PETIT
PALAIS

Tuileries
Garden

PALAIS
ROYAL

Trocadero

RIVER
CRUISES

CAFE
CARLU

TROCADERO

RIVER
CRUISES

SEWER
TOUR

QUAI
D'ORSAY

ORANGERIE

QUAI DES TUILERIES

1e

RUE
DE

LOUVRE

QUAI
BRANLY
MUSEUM

Esplanade
des Invalides

MARITIME
MUSEUM

EIFFEL
TOWER

RUE ST. DOMINIQUE

Seine

ORSAY

LEFT

RUE DE SEINE

7e

RUE
CLER

ARMY MUSEUM
& NAPOLEON'S
TOMB

BLVD. ST. GERMAIN

Bir-
Hakeim

Parc du
Champ de
Mars

AVE. DE LA
MOTTE-PICQUET

RODIN
MUSEUM

DELACROIX
MUSEUM

AVE. DE TOURVILLE

BLVD. RASPAIL

ST. SULPICE

To
Versailles
via Train-C

ECOLE
MILITAIRE

AVE. DE SUFFREN

AVE. DE VILLARS

Rennes

Luxembourg
Garden

RUE DE RENNES

RUE D'ASSAS

BLVD. GARIBALDI

RUE DE SEYRES

MONTPARNASSE
TOWER

6e

15e

RUE DE VAUGIRARD

GARE
MONTPARNASSE

Montparnasse-
Bienvenüe

Montparnasse
Cemetery

Place
Denfert-
Rochereau

Denfert-
Rochereau

CATACOMBS

Only selected Metro stations are shown

MARCHE
AUX PUCES

To
De Gaulle Airport
& North

A-1

BLVD. PERIPHERIQUE   (RING FREEWAY)

BLVD. NEY

BLVD. MACDONALD

Porte de
la Villette

Porte de
Clignancourt

Parc
de la Villette

18e

CITE DES
SCIENCES
ET DE
L'INDUSTRIE

MARTRE

SACRE-
COEUR

BLVD. DE LA CHAPELLE

AVENUE JEAN JAURES

19e

BLVD. DE
ROCHECHOUART

Anvers

N

Pigalle

GARE DU
NORD

Gare du Nord

GARE DE
L'EST

Gare de l'Est

500 Meters

500 Yards

RUE LA FAYETTE

10e

RUE DE BELLEVILLE

BLVD. ST-DENIS

Place de la
République

20e

2e

BANK

FORUM
DES HALLES

JEWISH
MUSEUM

3e

PICASSO
MUSEUM

AVE. DE LA REPUBLIQUE

Père
Lachaise

Père
Lachaise
Cemetery

RIVOLI

POMPIDOU

MARAIS

RUE DE

CHEMIN VERT

River
Cruises

Place du
Châtelet

HOTEL
DE VILLE

CARNAVALET
MUSEUM

RUE DE LA ROQUETTE

SAINTE-
CHAPELLE

Ile de
la Cité

NOTRE-
DAME

RUE ST-ANTOINE

HOLOCAUST
MEMORIAL

Place
des Vosges

Place
de la
Bastille

11e

Philippe
Auguste

Ile St-Louis

4e

DEPORTATION
MEMORIAL

BLVD. ST GERMAIN

Bassin de
l'Arsenal

OPERA

CLUNY
MUSEUM

BANK

River

PROMENADE PLANTEE

Place de la
Nation

SORBONNE

PANTHEON

Monge

5e

BLVD. DIDEROT

AVE. DAUMESNIL

To Bois de
Vincennes

LATIN
QUARTER

Gare d'Austerlitz

Gare de Lyon

GARE DE
LYON

BLVD. DE
PORT-ROYAL

GARE
D'AUSTERLITZ

12e

BERCY

PARIS AT A GLANCE

▲▲▲**Notre-Dame Cathedral** Paris' most beloved church, with towers and gargoyles. **Hours:** Cathedral—daily 7:45-18:45, Sun until 19:15; Tower—daily April-Sept 10:00-18:30, Fri-Sat until 23:00 in July-Aug, Oct-March 10:00-17:30. See page 140.

▲▲▲**Sainte-Chapelle** Gothic cathedral with peerless stained glass. **Hours:** Daily April-Sept 9:00-19:00, Oct-March 9:00-17:00. See page 148.

▲▲▲**Louvre** Europe's oldest and greatest museum, starring *Mona Lisa* and *Venus de Milo.* **Hours:** Wed-Mon 9:00-18:00, Wed and Fri until 21:45, closed Tue. See page 153.

▲▲▲**Orsay Museum** Nineteenth-century art, including Europe's greatest Impressionist collection. **Hours:** Tue-Sun 9:30-18:00, Thu until 21:45, closed Mon. See page 160.

▲▲▲**Eiffel Tower** Paris' soaring exclamation point. **Hours:** Daily mid-June-Aug 9:00-24:45, Sept-mid-June 9:30-23:45. See page 167.

▲▲▲**Champs-Elysées** Paris' grand boulevard. **Hours:** Always open. See page 174.

▲▲▲**Versailles** The ultimate royal palace (Château), with a Hall of Mirrors, vast gardens, a grand canal, plus a queen's playground (Trianon Palaces and Domaine de Marie-Antoinette). **Hours:** Château—April-Oct Tue-Sun 9:00-18:30, Nov-March until 17:30; Trianon/Domaine—April-Oct Tue-Sun 12:00-18:30, Nov-March until 17:30; Gardens—generally April-Oct daily 8:00-20:30, Nov-March Tue-Sun 8:00-18:00; entire complex closed Mon year-round. See page 217.

▲▲**Orangerie Museum** Monet's water lilies and modernist classics in a lovely setting. **Hours:** Wed-Mon 9:00-18:00, closed Tue. See page 166.

▲▲**Army Museum and Napoleon's Tomb** The emperor's imposing tomb, flanked by museums of France's wars. **Hours:** Daily 10:00-18:00, Juiy-Aug until 19:00, Nov-March until 17:00; tomb plus WWI and WWII wings open Tue until 21:00 April-Sept; museum (except for tomb) closed first Mon of month Oct-June; Charles de Gaulle exhibit closed Mon year-round. See page 170.

▲▲**Rodin Museum** Works by the greatest sculptor since Michelangelo, with many statues in a peaceful garden. **Hours:** Tue-Sun 10:00-17:45, closed Mon. See page 171.

▲▲**Cluny Museum** Medieval art with unicorn tapestries. **Hours:** Wed-Mon 9:15-17:45, closed Tue. See page 172.

▲▲▲**Arc de Triomphe** Triumphal arch marking start of Champs-Elysées. **Hours:** Always viewable; interior—daily April-Sept 10:00-23:00, Oct-March until 22:30. See page 176.

▲▲**Picasso Museum** World's largest collection of Picasso's works. **Hours:** Daily Tue-Fri 10:30-18:00, Sat-Sun 9:30-18:00, closed Mon. See page 179.

▲▲**Pompidou Center** Modern art in colorful building with city views. **Hours:** Wed-Mon 11:00-21:00, closed Tue. See page 184.

▲▲**Sacré-Cœur** White basilica atop Montmartre with spectacular views. **Hours:** Daily 6:00-22:30; dome climb—daily May-Sept 9:30-19:00, Oct-April 9:30-17:00. See page 186.

▲**Opéra Garnier** Grand belle époque theater with a modern ceiling by Chagall. **Hours:** Generally daily 10:00-16:30, mid-July-Aug until 18:00. See page 176.

▲**Père Lachaise Cemetery** Final home of Paris' illustrious dead. **Hours:** Mon-Fri 8:00-18:00, Sat 8:30-18:00, Sun 9:00-18:00, until 17:30 in winter. See page 185.

Lyon (Mon-Sat 8:00-18:00, closed Sun), and **Gare de l'Est** (Mon-Sat 8:00-19:00, closed Sun).

In summer, TI kiosks may pop up in the squares in front of Notre-Dame and Hôtel de Ville.

Both city **airports** have handy TIs with long hours and short lines.

Event Listings: Several French-only but easy-to-decipher periodicals list the most up-to-date museum hours, art exhibits, concerts, festivals, plays, movies, and nightclubs. The best is the weekly magazine *L'Officiel des Spectacles* (available at any newsstand). The *Paris Voice*, with snappy English-language reviews of concerts, plays, and current events, is available online only at www.parisvoice.com.

Sightseeing Pass

In Paris there are two classes of sightseers—those with a **Paris Museum Pass,** and those who stand in line. The pass admits you to many of Paris' most popular sights, and it allows you to skip ticket-buying lines. You'll save time and money by getting this pass. Pertinent details about the pass are outlined here—for more info, visit www.parismuseumpass.com.

What the Pass Covers

Here's a list of key sights and their admission prices without the pass:
- Arc de Triomphe (€9.50)
- Army Museum (€9.50)
- Cluny Museum (€8)
- Conciergerie (€8.50)
- Louvre (€12)
- Notre-Dame Tower (€8.50)
- Orangerie Museum (€9)
- Orsay Museum (€11)
- Picasso Museum (€11)
- Pompidou Center (€14)
- Rodin Museum (€10)
- Sainte-Chapelle (€8.50)
- Versailles (€30)

Notable sights that are *not* covered by the pass include the Eiffel Tower, Opéra Garnier, Notre-Dame Treasury, and Sacré-Cœur's dome.

Buying the Pass

The pass pays for itself with four key admissions in two days (for example, the Louvre, Orsay, Sainte-Chapelle, and Versailles), and it lets you skip the ticket line at most sights (2 days-€42, 4 days-€56, 6 days-€69, no youth or senior discounts). It's sold at participating museums, monuments, and TIs (even at Paris' airports). Avoid buying the pass at a major museum (such as the Louvre), where the supply can be spotty and lines long. It's not worth the cost or hassle to buy the pass online.

Rick's Tip: **Don't buy the Museum Pass for kids,** *as most museums are free or discounted for those under age 18 (teenagers may need to show ID as proof of age). If parents have a Museum Pass, kids can usually skip the ticket lines as well. But a few places (Arc de Triomphe, Army Museum) require everyone—even passholders—to stand in line to collect free tickets for their children.*

Using the Pass

Plan carefully to make the most of your pass. Validate it only when you're ready to tackle the covered sights on consecutive days. Activating it is simple—just write the start date you want (and your name) on the pass. But first make sure the sights you want to visit will be open (many museums are closed Mon or Tue).

The pass provides the best value on days when sights close later, letting you extend your sightseeing day. Take advantage of late hours on selected evenings or times of year at the Arc de Triomphe, Pompidou Center, Notre-Dame Tower, Sainte-Chapelle, Louvre, Orsay, Rodin Museum, and Napoleon's Tomb. On days that you don't have pass coverage, plan to visit free sights and those not covered by the pass (see page 145 for a list of free sights).

To use your pass at sights, look for signs designating the entrance for reserved ticket holders. If it's not obvious, walk to the front of the ticket line, hold up your pass, and ask the ticket taker: *"Entrez, pass?"* (ahn-tray pahs). You'll either be allowed to enter at that point, or you'll be directed to a special entrance. For major sights, such as the Louvre and Orsay museums, I've identified passholder entrances on the maps in this book. Don't be shy—some places (the Orsay and the Arc de Triomphe, in particular) have long lines in which passholders wait needlessly. At a few sights with security lines (including the Louvre), passholders can skip to the front.

Avoiding Lines Without a Pass

If you don't purchase a Paris Museum Pass, or if a sight is not covered by the pass, there are other ways to avoid long waits in ticket-buying lines.

For some sights, you can reserve **timed-entry tickets** online. This is essential at the line-plagued Eiffel Tower, and it's a big advantage at the Picasso Museum.

You can buy **advance tickets** online for many other sights (including the Louvre, Orsay, Rodin Museum, and Monet's gardens at Giverny) as well as for activities and cultural events (Bateaux-Mouches cruises, Sainte-Chapelle concerts, and performances at the Opéra Garnier). Increasingly, other Paris sights are adding this timesaving service.

TIs, FNAC department stores, and travel-services companies sell individual *coupe-file* **tickets** (pronounced "koop feel") for some sights, which allow you to use the Museum Pass entrance (worth the trouble only for sights where lines are longest). TIs sell these tickets for no extra fee, but elsewhere you can expect a surcharge of 10-20 percent. FNAC stores are everywhere, even on the Champs-Elysées (ask your hotelier for the nearest one). Despite the surcharges and often-long lines to buy them, getting *coupe-file* tickets can still be a good idea.

Some sights, such as the Louvre, have **ticket-vending machines** that save time in line. These accept cash (usually no bills larger than €20) or chip-and-PIN cards

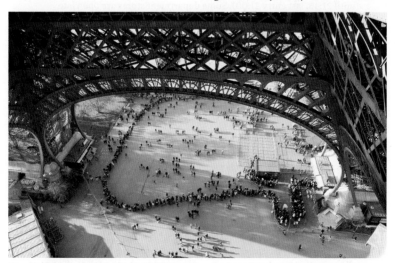

If you buy an advance ticket for the Eiffel Tower (or take the stairs), you can avoid this line.

Daily Reminder

SUNDAY: Many sights are free on the first Sunday of the month, including the Orsay, Rodin, Cluny, Pompidou, and Picasso museums. Several sights are free on the first Sunday, but only during winter, including the Louvre and Arc de Triomphe (both Oct-March) and all the sights at Versailles (Nov-March). These free days at popular sights attract hordes of visitors. Versailles is more crowded than usual on Sunday in any season, and the garden's fountains run (April-Oct).

Most of Paris' stores are closed on Sunday, but shoppers will find relief along the Champs-Elysées, at flea markets, and in the Marais neighborhood's lively Jewish Quarter, where many boutiques are open. Many recommended restaurants in the Rue Cler neighborhood are closed for dinner.

MONDAY: These sights are closed: Orsay, Rodin, Picasso, Victor Hugo's House at Place des Vosges, Deportation Memorial, and Versailles (but the gardens are open April-Oct). The Louvre is far more crowded because of these closings. From October through June, the Army Museum is closed the first Monday of the month, though Napoleon's Tomb remains open.

Market streets such as Rue Cler and Rue Mouffetard are dead today.

TUESDAY: Many sights are closed, including the Louvre, Orangerie, Cluny, and Pompidou museums. The Orsay and Versailles are crazy busy today. The fountains at Versailles run on Tuesdays from mid-May until late June; music (no fountains) fills the gardens April-mid-May and July-October. Napoleon's Tomb and the Army Museum's WWI and WWII wings are open until 21:00 (April-Sept).

WEDNESDAY: All sights are open, and some have late hours, including the Louvre (until 21:45, last entry 21:00).

THURSDAY: All sights are open. Some sights are open late, including the Orsay (until 21:45, last entry 21:00). Some department stores are open late.

FRIDAY: All sights are open. The Louvre is open until 21:45 (last entry 21:00) and Notre-Dame's tower is open until 23:00 (July-Aug). The Picasso Museum is open until 21:00 on the third Friday of every month.

SATURDAY: All sights are open. The fountains run at Versailles (April-Oct). Notre-Dame's tower is open until 23:00 (July-Aug).

(most American credit cards won't work). And at certain sights, including the Louvre and Orsay, **nearby shops** sell tickets, allowing you to avoid the main ticket lines (for details, see the Louvre and Orsay listings).

Tours

🎧 To sightsee on your own, download my **free audio tours** that illuminate some of Paris' top sights and neighborhoods, including the Historic Paris Walk, Louvre Museum, and Orsay Museum (see sidebar on page 145 for details).

Paris Walks offers a variety of thoughtful and entertaining two-hour walks, led by British and American guides (€12-20, generally 2/day, private tours available, family guides and Louvre tours are a specialty, tel. 01 48 09 21 40, www.paris-walks.com). Reservations aren't necessary for most tours, but specialty tours—such as the Louvre, fashion, or chocolate tours—require advance reservations and prepayment with credit card (deposits are nonrefundable).

Context Travel offers "intellectual by design" walking tours geared for serious learners. The tours are led by well-versed docents (historians, architects, and academics) and cover both museums and specific neighborhoods. It's best to book in advance—groups are limited to six participants and can fill up fast (€70-105/person, admission to sights extra, generally 3 hours, tel. 09 75 18 04 15, US tel. 800-691-6036, www.contexttravel.com). They also offer private tours and excursions outside Paris.

Bike About Tours offers easygoing tours with a focus on the eastern half of the city. Their four-hour tours run daily year-round at 10:00 (also at 15:00 May-Sept). You'll meet at the statue of Charlemagne in front of Notre-Dame, then walk nearby to get your bikes. Reserve online to guarantee a spot, or show up and take your chances (€30, ask about Rick Steves discount). Their private family tours of Paris include fun activities like scavenger hunts (€200 for 2 people, €25/person after that, complimentary boat-tour tickets—a €14 value).

For many, Paris merits hiring a Parisian as a personal guide. **Thierry Gauduchon** is a terrific guide and a gifted teacher (€230/half-day, €450/day, tel. 06 19 07 30 77, tgauduchon@gmail.com). **Sylvie Moreau** also leads good tours in Paris (€200 for 3 hours, €320 for 7 hours, tel. 01 74 30 27 46, mobile 06 87 02 80 67, sylvie.ja.moreau@gmail.com). **Elisabeth Van Hest** is another likable and very capable guide (€200/half-day, tel. 01 43 41 47 31, mobile 06 77 80 19 89, elisa.guide@gmail.com).

Helpful Hints

Theft Alert: Thieves thrive near famous monuments and on Métro and train lines that serve airports and high-profile tourist sights. Beware of pickpockets working busy lines (e.g., at ticket windows at train stations). Look out for groups of young girls who swarm around you (be very firm—even forceful—and walk away). Smartphones and tablets are thief magnets anytime, so be aware whenever you're using one or holding it up to take a picture.

It's smart to wear a money belt, put your wallet in your front pocket, loop your day bag over your shoulders, and keep a tight hold on your purse or shopping bag. When wearing a daypack, don't keep valuables in the outer pockets, and don't mark yourself as a tourist by wearing it on your front.

Muggings are rare, but they do occur. If you're out late, avoid the dark riverfront embankments and any place where the lighting is dim and pedestrian activity is minimal.

Tourist Scams: Be aware of the latest

You can explore Paris by bike.

Learn from an expert guide.

tricks, such as the "found ring" scam (a con artist pretends to find a "pure gold" ring on the ground and offers to sell it to you) or the "friendship bracelet" scam (a vendor asks you to help with a demo, makes a bracelet on your arm that you can't easily remove, and then asks you to pay for it).

Distractions by a stranger—often a "salesman," someone asking you to sign a petition, or someone posing as a deaf person to show you a small note to read—can all be tricks that function as a smokescreen for theft. As you try to wriggle away from the pushy stranger, an accomplice picks your pocket.

To all these scammers, simply say "no" firmly and step away purposefully. For reports from my readers on the latest scams, go to https://community.rick steves.com/travel-forum/tourist-scams.

Medical Help: There are a variety of English-speaking resources for medical help in Paris, including doctors who will visit your hotel. Try the **American Hospital** (tel. 01 46 41 25 25, www.american-hospital. org) or **SOS Médicins** (SOS Doctors, tel. 01 47 07 77 77, www.sosmedecins.fr).

Useful Apps: Gogo Paris is an intriguing app that reviews trendy places to eat, drink, relax, and sleep in Paris (www. gogocityguides.com/paris).

🎧 For free audio versions of some of the self-guided tours in this chapter, get the **Rick Steves Audio Europe** app (for details, see page 17).

Public WCs: Most public toilets are free. If it's a pay toilet, the price will be clearly indicated. If the toilet is free but there's an attendant, it's polite to leave a tip of €0.20-0.50. Bold travelers can walk into any sidewalk café like they own the place and find the toilet downstairs or in the back. Or do as the locals do—order a shot of espresso (un café) while standing at the café bar (then use the WC with a clear conscience). Keep tissues with you, as some WCs are poorly stocked.

Tobacco Stands (Tabacs): These little kiosks—usually just a counter inside a café—sell public-transit tickets, cards for parking meters, postage stamps (though not all sell international postage), and...oh yeah, cigarettes. Just look for a red, elongated diamond-shaped Tabac sign.

HISTORIC PARIS WALK

Paris has been the cultural capital of Europe for centuries. We'll start where the city did—on the Ile de la Cité—and make a foray onto the Left Bank. Along the way, we'll step into some of the city's greatest sights, including Notre-Dame and Sainte-Chapelle.

Getting There: The closest Métro stops are Cité, Hôtel de Ville, and St. Michel, each a short walk away.

Length of This Walk: Allow four hours to do justice to this three-mile self-guided walk, beginning at Notre-Dame Cathedral and ending at Pont Neuf; just follow the dotted line on the "Historic Paris Walk" map.

Tours: 🎧 Download my free Historic Paris Walk audio tour.

⊖ Self-Guided Walk

• *Begin in front of Notre-Dame Cathedral, the physical and historic bull's-eye of your Paris map.*

▲▲▲Notre-Dame Cathedral

The church is dedicated to "Our Lady" (Notre Dame), Mary, the mother of Jesus. There she is, cradling God, right in the heart of the facade, surrounded by the halo of the rose window. Though the church is massive and imposing, it has always stood for the grace and compassion of Mary, the "mother of God."

Imagine the faith of the people who built this cathedral. They broke ground in 1163 with the hope that someday their great-great-great-great-great-great grandchildren might attend the dedication Mass, which finally took place two centuries later, in 1345. Look up the 200-foot-tall bell towers and imagine a tiny medieval community mustering the money and energy for construction. Master masons supervised, but the people did much of the grunt work themselves for free—hauling the huge stones from distant quarries, digging a 30-foot-deep trench to lay the foundation, and treading like rats on a wheel designed to lift the stones up, one by one. This kind of backbreaking, arduous manual labor created the real hunchbacks of Notre-Dame.

Rick's Tip: *In summer,* **sound-and-light displays** *about the history of Notre-Dame generally run twice a week (free, usually Thu and Sat at 21:00—check cathedral website or call).*

Cost and Hours: Cathedral—free, daily 7:45-18:45, Sun until 19:15; audioguide—€5, free English tours—normally Mon-Tue and Sat at 14:30, Wed-Thu at 14:00.

The cathedral hosts **Masses** several times daily. Call or check the website for a full schedule (tel. 01 42 34 56 10, www.notredamedeparis.fr).

Tower Climb: Get a mandatory timed-entry reservation (even with a Museum Pass) from ticket machines on site (same-day only, starting at 7:30). The tower entrance is outside the cathedral, along the left side. You can hike to the top of the facade between the towers and then to the top of the south tower (400 steps total) for a gargoyle's-eye view of the cathedral, Seine, and city (€8.50, covered by Museum Pass; daily April-Sept 10:00-18:30, Fri-Sat until 23:00 in July-Aug, Oct-March 10:00-17:30, last entry 45 minutes before closing; tel. 01 53 40 60 80, www.notre-dame-de-paris.monuments-nationaux.fr).

Rick's Tip: *If you're* **claustrophobic or acrophobic, skip climbing Notre-Dame's tower.** *It's a tight, crowded space—and once you start up, you're expected to finish.*

The best view of Notre-Dame is from the Left Bank.

Historic Paris Walk

To Les Halles

LOUVRE

QUAI DU LOUVRE

RUE DU LOUVRE

RUE DE L'ARBRE-SEC

R. DES

RIGHT

Pont Neuf **M**

QUAI DE LA MEGISSERIE

10

Paris Plages
(summer)

PONT
NEUF

9

WALK
ENDS

PONT DES ARTS

To Orsay

QUAI DE CONTI

BOATS

Seine River

QUAI DE L'HORLOGE

MA SALLE
A MANGER

PONT AU CHANGE

INSTITUT
DE FRANCE

CAVEAU
DU PALAIS
REST.

*Place
Dauphine*

PALAIS
DE JUSTICE

6

CLOCK

8

RUE MAZARINE

PONT NEUF

5

EXIT

SAINTE-
CHAPELLE

RUE DAUPHINE

RUE DE L'ANC COMEDIE

PSG.

R. DES GRANDS-
AUGUSTINS

BLVD. DU PALAIS

L'ANNEXE
CAFE

Ile de

RUE DE SEINE

RUE ST. ANDRE-DES-ARTS

*Place
St. André-
des-Arts*

R. JARDINET

PONT ST. MICHEL

*Place
St. Michel*

St. Michel
M **t**

RUE DE LA HUCHETTE

PETIT PONT

To
St. Sulpice

M Odéon

R. DANTON

BOULEVARD ST. GERMAIN

BLVD. ST. MICHEL

RUE DE LA HARPE

R. DE LA HUCHETTE

R. STE
SEVERIN

RUE
ST. SULPICE

RUE DE TOURNON

RUE DE CONDE

LEFT

Cluny La
Sorbonne **M** **t**

4

ST.
SEVERIN

RUE ST. JACQUES

R. GALANDE

DANTE

*Place de
l'Odéon*

RUE RACINE

200 Meters

200 Yards

CLUNY
MUSEUM

BLVD. ST-MICHEL

SORBONNE

LUXEMBOURG
PALACE

*Luxembourg
Garden*

R. DE VAUGIRARD

To Panthéon

❶ Notre-Dame	❻ Palais de Justice
❷ Deportation Memorial	❼ Cité Métro Stop & Flower Market
❸ Ile St. Louis	❽ Conciergerie
❹ Latin Quarter	❾ Pont Neuf
❺ Sainte-Chapelle	❿ Paris Plages (2)

● SELF-GUIDED TOUR

On the square in front of the cathedral, stand far enough back to take in the whole **facade.** Look at the left doorway, and to the left of the door, to find the statue with his head in his hands. This is **St. Denis,** the city's first bishop and patron saint. He stands among statues of other early Christians who helped turn pagan Paris into Christian Paris. Denis proved so successful at winning converts that the Romans' pagan priests got worried. Denis was beheaded as a warning to those forsaking the Roman gods. But those early Christians were hard to keep down. Denis got up, tucked his head under his arm, headed north, paused at a fountain to wash it off, and continued until he found just the right place to meet his maker: Montmartre. The Parisians were convinced by this miracle, Christianity gained ground, and a church soon replaced the pagan temple.

Find the row of 28 statues, known as the **Kings of Judah,** above the arches. In the days of the French Revolution (1789-1799), these biblical kings were mistaken for the hated French kings, and Notre-Dame represented the oppressive Catholic hierarchy. The citizens stormed the church, crying, "Off with their heads!" Plop—they lopped off the crowned heads of these kings with glee, creating a row of St. Denises that weren't repaired for decades.

Rick's Tip: *Be careful—***pickpockets** *attend church here religiously.*

Notre-Dame Interior: Enter the church at the right doorway (the line moves quickly).

Notre-Dame has the typical basilica floor plan shared by so many Catholic churches: a long central nave lined with columns and flanked by side aisles. It's designed in the shape of a cross, with the altar placed where the crossbeam intersects. The church can hold up to 10,000 faithful, and it's probably buzzing with visitors now, just as it was 600 years ago. The quiet, deserted churches we see elsewhere are in stark contrast to the busy, center-of-life places they were in the Middle Ages.

Just past the altar is the choir, the area enclosed with carved-wood walls, where more intimate services can be held in

Headless St. Denis, Paris' patron saint

Pietà inside Notre-Dame

Affording Paris' Sights

Paris is an expensive city, with lots of pricey sights, but—fortunately—lots of free-bies, too. Smart travelers begin by buying and using the **Paris Museum Pass** (see page 136). Also consider these frugal sightseeing options.

Free (or Almost Free) Museums: Many of Paris' famous museums offer free entry on the first Sunday of the month year-round, including the Orsay, Rodin, Cluny, and Pompidou Center museums. Other sights are free on the first Sunday only in the off-season: the Louvre and Arc de Triomphe (both Oct-March) and Versailles (Nov-March). Expect big crowds on free days. You can usually visit the Orsay Museum for free right when the ticket booth stops selling tickets. For just €2, the Rodin Museum garden lets you enjoy many of his finest works in a lovely outdoor setting.

Other Freebies: There's no entry fee at Notre-Dame Cathedral, Père Lachaise Cemetery, Deportation Memorial, Paris *plages* (summers only), and Sacré-Cœur Basilica.

Reduced Prices: Several sights offer a discount if you enter later in the day, including the Orangerie and the Army Museum and Napoleon's Tomb. The Eiffel Tower costs less if you stick to the two lower levels—and even less if you use the stairs.

Free Concerts: Venues offering free or cheap (€6-8) concerts include the American Church, Army Museum, St. Sulpice Church, La Madeleine Church, and Notre-Dame Cathedral. For a listing of free concerts, check *L'Officiel des Spectacles* magazine (under the "Musique" section) and look for events marked *entrée libre*.

Good-Value Tours: At about €16, Paris Walks' tours are a good value. The €13-14 Seine River cruises, best after dark, are also worthwhile. The scenic bus route #69, which costs only the price of a transit ticket, could be the best deal of all.

Pricey...but worth it? Certain big-ticket items—primarily the top of the Eiffel Tower, the Louvre, and Versailles—are expensive and crowded, but offer once-in-a-lifetime experiences. All together they amount to less than the cost of a ticket to Disneyland—only these are real.

---

this spacious building. Looking past the altar to the far end of the choir (under the cross), you'll see a fine **17th-century pietà,** flanked by two kneeling kings: Louis XIII (1601-1643, not so famous) and his son, Louis XIV (1638-1715, very famous, also known as the Sun King).

In the right transept, a statue of **Joan of Arc** (Jeanne d'Arc, 1412-1431), dressed in armor and praying, honors the French teenager who rallied her country's soldiers to try to drive English invaders from Paris.

Join the statue in gazing up to the blue-and-purple, **rose-shaped window** in the opposite transept—with teeny green Mary and Baby Jesus in the center—the only one of the three rose windows still with its original medieval glass.

The back side of the choir walls feature scenes of the **resurrected Jesus** (c. 1350) appearing to his followers, starting with Mary Magdalene. Their starry robes still gleam, thanks to a 19th-century renovation. The niches below these carvings mark the tombs of centuries of archbishops.

Notre-Dame Side View: Back out-side, alongside the church, you'll notice many of the elements are Gothic: pointed arches, lacy stone tracery of the windows, pinnacles, statues on rooftops, a lead roof, and a pointed steeple covered with the prickly "flames" (Flamboyant Gothic) of the Holy Spirit. Most distinctive of all are the **flying buttresses.** These 50-foot stone "beams" that stick out of the church were the key to the complex Gothic architecture. The pointed arches we saw inside cause the weight of the roof to push outward rather than downward. The "flying" buttresses support the roof by pushing back inward.

Picture Quasimodo (the fictional hunchback) limping around along the railed balcony at the base of the roof among the **gargoyles.** These grotesque beasts sticking out from pillars and buttresses represent souls caught between heaven and earth. They also function as rainspouts (from the same French root word as "gargle") when there are no evil spirits to battle.

The Neo-Gothic 300-foot **spire** is a product of the 1860 reconstruction of the dilapidated old church. Victor Hugo's book *The Hunchback of Notre-Dame* (1831) inspired a young architecture student named Eugène-Emmanuel Viollet-le-Duc to dedicate his career to a major renovation in Gothic style. Find Viollet-le-Duc at the base of the spire among the green apostles and evangelists (visible as you approach the back end of the church). The apostles look outward, blessing the city, while the architect (at top) looks up the spire, marveling at his fine work.

• *Behind Notre-Dame, cross the street and enter through the iron gate into the park at the tip of the island. Look for the stairs and head down to reach the...*

▲Deportation Memorial (Mémorial de la Déportation)

This memorial to the 200,000 French victims of the Nazi concentration camps (1940-1945) draws you into their experience. France was quickly overrun by Nazi Germany, and Paris spent the war years under Nazi occupation. Jews and dissidents were rounded up and deported—many never returned.

Cost and Hours: Free, Tue-Sun 10:00-19:00, Oct-March until 17:00, closed Mon year-round; at the east tip of Ile de la Cité, behind Notre-Dame and near Ile St. Louis (Mo: Cité); www.cheminsdememoire. gouv.fr.

Visiting the Memorial: As you descend the steps, the city around you disappears. Surrounded by walls, you have become a prisoner. Your only freedom is your view of the sky and the tiny glimpse of the river below. Enter the dark, single-file chamber up ahead. Inside, the circular plaque in the floor reads, "They went to the end of the earth and did not return."

The hallway stretching in front of you is lined with 200,000 lighted crystals, one

Deportation Memorial

Shakespeare and Company bookstore

for each French citizen who died. Flickering at the far end is the eternal flame of hope. The tomb of the unknown deportee lies at your feet. Above, the inscription reads, "Dedicated to the living memory of the 200,000 French deportees shrouded by the night and the fog, exterminated in the Nazi concentration camps." The side rooms are filled with triangles—reminiscent of the identification patches inmates were forced to wear—each bearing the name of a concentration camp. Above the exit as you leave is the message you'll find at many other Holocaust sites: "Forgive, but never forget."

• Back on street level, look across the river (north) to the island called...

Ile St. Louis

If Ile de la Cité is a tugboat laden with the history of Paris, it's towing this classy little residential dinghy, laden only with high-rent apartments, boutiques, characteristic restaurants, and famous ice cream shops.

Ile St. Louis was developed in the 17th century, much later than Ile de la Cité. What was a swampy mess is now harmonious Parisian architecture and one of the city's most exclusive neighborhoods. If you won't have time to return here later, consider taking a brief detour across the pedestrian bridge, Pont St. Louis. It connects the two islands, leading right to Rue St. Louis-en-l'Ile. This spine of the island is lined with appealing shops, reasonably priced restaurants, and a handy grocery. A short stroll takes you to the famous Berthillon ice cream parlor at #31, which is still family-owned. The ice cream is famous not just because it's good, but because it's made right here on the island. Gelato lovers can comparison-shop by also sampling the (mass-produced-but-who's-complaining) Amorino Gelati at 47 Rue St. Louis-en-l'Ile. This walk is about as peaceful and romantic as Paris gets. When you're finished exploring, loop back to the pedestrian bridge along the parklike quays (walk north to the river and turn left).

• From the Deportation Memorial, cross the bridge to the Left Bank. Turn right and walk along the river toward the front end of Notre-Dame. Stairs detour down to the riverbank if you need a place to picnic. This side view of the church from across the river is one of Europe's great sights and is best from river level. At times, you may find barges housing restaurants with great cathedral views docked here.

After passing the Pont au Double (the bridge leading to the facade of Notre-Dame), watch on your left for **Shakespeare and Company,** an atmospheric reincarnation of the original 1920s bookshop (open long hours daily, 37 Rue de la Bûcherie, Mo: St. Michel, tel. 01 43 25 40 93). Before returning to the island, walk a block behind Shakespeare and Company, and take a spin through...

▲The Latin Quarter

This area's touristy fame relates to its intriguing, artsy, bohemian character. This was perhaps Europe's leading university district in the Middle Ages, when Latin was the language of higher education. The neighborhood's main boulevards (St. Michel and St. Germain) are lined with cafés—once the haunts of great poets and philosophers, now the hangouts of tired tourists. Though still youthful

The Latin Quarter

and artsy, much of this touristy area is filled with cheap North African eateries. Exploring a few blocks up or downriver from here gives you a better chance of feeling the pulse of what survives of Paris' classic Left Bank. For colorful wandering and café-sitting, afternoons and evenings are best.

Walking along Rue St. Séverin, you can still see the shadow of the medieval sewer system. The street slopes into a central channel of bricks. In the days before plumbing and toilets, when people still went to the river or neighborhood wells for their water, flushing meant throwing it out the window. At certain times of day, maids on the fourth floor would holler, *"Garde de l'eau!"* ("Watch out for the water!") and heave it into the streets, where it would eventually wash down into the Seine.

Consider a visit to the **Cluny Museum** for its medieval art and unicorn tapestries (see page 172). The **Sorbonne**—the University of Paris' humanities department—is also nearby; visitors can ogle at the famous dome, but they are not allowed to enter the building (two blocks south of the river on Boulevard St. Michel).

Don't miss **Place St. Michel.** This square (facing Pont St. Michel) is the traditional core of the Left Bank's district of artists, poets, philosophers, winos, and *baba* cools (neo-hippies). In less commercial times, Place St. Michel was a gathering point for the city's malcontents and misfits. In 1830, 1848, and again in 1871, the citizens took the streets from the government troops, set up barricades *Les Miz*-style, and fought against royalist oppression. During World War II, the locals rose up against their Nazi oppressors (read the plaques under the dragons at the foot of the St. Michel fountain). Even today, whenever there's a student demonstration, it starts here.

• *From Place St. Michel, look across the river and find the prickly steeple of the Sainte-Chapelle church. Head toward it.*

Cross the river on Pont St. Michel and continue north along the Boulevard du Palais. On your left, you'll see the doorway to Sainte-Chapelle (usually with a line of people).

▲▲▲ Sainte-Chapelle

This triumph of Gothic church architecture is a cathedral of glass like no other. It was speedily built between 1242 and 1248 for King Louis IX—the only French king who is now a saint—to house the supposed Crown of Thorns. Its architectural harmony is due to the fact that it was completed under the direction of one architect and in only six years—unheard of in Gothic times. In contrast, Notre-Dame took over 200 years.

Cost and Hours: €8.50, €13.50 combo-ticket with Conciergerie, free for those under age 18, covered by Museum Pass; daily April-Sept 9:00-19:00, Oct-March 9:00-17:00, audioguide-€4.50, 4 Boulevard du Palais, Mo: Cité, tel. 01 53 40 60 80, can buy tickets online at www.sainte-chapelle.fr. For information on upcoming church concerts, see page 192.

Getting In: Expect long lines to get in (shortest wait first thing in the mornings and on weekends; longest on Tue and any day around 13:00-14:00). First comes the security line (all sharp objects and glass are confiscated). Once past security, you'll encounter the ticket-buying line—those with combo-tickets or Museum Passes can skip this queue.

Visiting the Church: Though the inside is beautiful, the exterior is basically functional. The muscular buttresses hold up the stone roof, so the walls are essentially there to display stained glass. The lacy spire is Neo-Gothic—added in the 19th century. Inside, the layout clearly shows an *ancien régime* approach to worship. The low-ceilinged basement was for staff and other common folks—worshipping under a sky filled with painted fleurs-de-lis, a symbol of the king. Royal Christians worshipped upstairs. The

Sainte-Chapelle

To Cité Ⓜ & Notre-Dame

SOUVENIR SHOP & ANNEXE CAFÉ

To Notre-Dame & Latin Quarter

To Conciergerie

BLVD. DU PALAIS

ENTRANCE & SECURITY CHECK

EXIT

JESUS' PASSION SCENES

Sainte-Chapelle Courtyard

ALTAR

STAIRS

ST. LOUIS' PEEK-A-BOO WINDOW

CAMPAIGN OF HOLOFERNES

MORE MOSES

LIFE OF MOSES

BUTTRESSES

CAIN CLUBBING ABEL

SPIRAL STAIRCASES

HELENA IN JERUSALEM

ROSE WINDOW

PALAIS DE JUSTICE
(BUILDING SURROUNDS SAINTE-CHAPELLE)

CONCERT TICKETS

ENTRANCE (INTO LOWER CHAPEL)

■TICKETS

20 Meters
20 Yards

BUTTRESSES
STAINED GLASS

paint job, a 19th-century restoration, helps you imagine how grand this small, painted, jeweled chapel was. (Imagine Notre-Dame painted like this…) Each capital is playfully carved with a different plant's leaves.

Climb the spiral staircase to the Chapelle Haute. Fill the place with choral music, crank up the sunshine, face the top of the altar, and really believe that the Crown of Thorns is there, and this becomes one awesome space.

Fiat lux. "Let there be light." From the first page of the Bible, it's clear: Light is divine. Light shines through stained glass like God's grace shining down to earth.

Gothic architects used their new technology to turn dark stone buildings into lanterns of light. The glory of Gothic shines brighter here than in any other church.

There are 15 separate panels of **stained glass** (6,500 square feet—two thirds of it 13th-century original), with more than 1,100 different scenes, mostly from the Bible. These cover the entire Christian history of the world, from the Creation in Genesis (first window on the left, as you face the altar), to the coming of Christ (over the altar), to the end of the world (the round "rose"-shaped window at the rear of the church). Each individual scene is interesting, and the whole effect is overwhelming.

The **altar** was raised up high to better display the Crown of Thorns, which cost King Louis more than three times as much as this church. Today, the relic is kept in the treasury at Notre-Dame (though it's occasionally brought out for display).

• *Exit Sainte-Chapelle. Back outside, as you walk around the church exterior, look down to see the foundation and take note of how much Paris has risen in the 750 years since Sainte-Chapelle was built.*

Next door to Sainte-Chapelle is the...

Palais de Justice

Sainte-Chapelle sits within a huge complex of buildings that has housed the local government since ancient Roman times. It was the site of the original Gothic palace of the early kings of France. The only surviving medieval parts are Sainte-Chapelle and the Conciergerie prison.

Most of the site is now covered by the giant Palais de Justice, built in 1776, home of the French Supreme Court. The motto *Liberté, Egalité, Fraternité* over the doors is a reminder that this was also the headquarters of the Revolutionary government. Here they doled out justice, condemning many to imprisonment in the Conciergerie downstairs—or to the guillotine.

• *Now pass through the big iron gate to the noisy Boulevard du Palais. Cross the street to the wide, pedestrian-only Rue de Lutèce and walk about halfway down.*

Cité "Metropolitain" Métro Stop

Of the 141 original early-20th-century subway entrances, this is one of only a few survivors—now preserved as a national art treasure. (New York's Museum of Modern Art even exhibits one.) It marks Paris at

Sainte-Chapelle is a cathedral of stained glass like no other.

its peak in 1900—on the cutting edge of Modernism, but with an eye for beauty. The curvy, plantlike ironwork is a textbook example of Art Nouveau, the style that rebelled against the erector-set square-ness of the Industrial Age. Other similar Métro stations in Paris are Abbesses and Porte Dauphine.

The flower and plant market on Place Louis Lépine is a pleasant detour. On Sundays this square flutters with a busy bird market.

• *Pause here to admire the view.*

Sainte-Chapelle is a pearl in an ugly architectural oyster. Double back to the Palais de Justice, turn right onto Boulevard du Palais, and enter the Conciergerie. It's free with the Museum Pass; passholders can sidestep the bottleneck created by the ticket-buying line.

▲Conciergerie

Though pretty barren inside, this former prison echoes with history. Positioned next to the courthouse, the Conciergerie was the gloomy prison famous as the last stop for 2,780 victims of the guillotine, including France's last *ancien régime* queen, Marie-Antoinette. Before then, kings had used the building to torture and execute failed assassins. (One of its towers along the river was called "The Babbler," named for the pain-induced sounds that leaked from it.) When the Revolution (1789) toppled the king, the building kept its same function, but without torture.

The progressive Revolutionaries proudly unveiled a modern and more humane way to execute people—the guillotine. The Conciergerie was the epicenter of the Reign of Terror—the year-long period of the Revolution (1793-94) during which Revolutionary fervor spiraled out of control and thousands were killed. It was here at the Conciergerie that "enemies of the Revolution" were imprisoned, tried, sentenced, and marched off to Place de la Concorde for decapitation.

Cost and Hours: €8.50, €13.50 combo-ticket with Sainte-Chapelle, covered by Museum Pass, daily 9:30-18:00, 2 Boulevard du Palais, Mo: Cité, tel. 01 53 40 60 80, http://conciergerie.monuments-nationaux.fr.

Visiting the Conciergerie: Pick up a free map and breeze through the one-way circuit. See the spacious, low-ceilinged Hall of Men-at-Arms (Room 1), originally a guards' dining room, with four big fire-places (look up the chimneys). During the Reign of Terror, this large hall served as a holding tank for the poorest prisoners. Continue to the raised area at the far end of the room (Room 4, today's bookstore). In Revolutionary days, this was notorious as the walkway of the executioner, who was known affectionately as "Monsieur de Paris."

Upstairs is a memorial room with the names of the 2,780 citizens condemned to death by the guillotine, including ex-King Louis XVI, Charlotte Corday (who murdered the Revolutionary writer

Cité Métro entrance

Conciergerie prison

Jean-Paul Marat in his bathtub), and—oh, the irony—Maximilien de Robespierre, the head rabble-rouser of the Revolution, who himself sent so many to the guillotine.

Just past the courtyard is a re-creation of Marie-Antoinette's cell. On August 12, 1793, the queen was brought here to be tried for her supposed crimes against the people. Mannequins, period furniture, and the real cell wallpaper set the scene. In the glass display case, see her actual crucifix, rug, and small water pitcher. On October 16, 1793, the queen was awakened at 4:00 in the morning and led away. She walked the corridor, stepped onto the cart, and was slowly carried to Place de la Concorde, where she had a date with "Monsieur de Paris."

• *Back outside, turn left on Boulevard du Palais, then left again onto Quai de l'Horloge and walk along the river, past "The Babbler" tower.*

The bridge up ahead is the Pont Neuf, where we'll end this walk. At the first corner, veer left into a sleepy triangular square called **Place Dauphine.** *It's amazing to find such coziness in the heart of Paris. From the equestrian statue of Henry IV, turn right onto Pont Neuf. Pause at the little nook halfway across.*

Pont Neuf and the Seine

This "new bridge" is now Paris' oldest. Built during Henry IV's reign (about 1600), its arches span the widest part of the river. Unlike other bridges, this one never had houses or buildings growing on it. The turrets were originally for vendors and street entertainers. In the days of Henry IV, who promised his peasants "a chicken in every pot every Sunday," this would have been a lively scene. From the bridge, look downstream (west) to see the next bridge, the pedestrian-only Pont des Arts. Ahead on the Right Bank is the long Louvre museum. Beyond that, on the Left Bank, is the Orsay.

• *Our walk is finished. From here, you can tour the Seine by boat (the departure point for Seine River cruises offered by Vedettes du Pont Neuf is through the park at the end of the island—see page 187), continue to the Louvre, or (if it's summer) head to the...*

Pont Neuf crosses the widest part of the Seine.

▲Paris Plages (Paris Beaches)

The Riviera it's not, but this string of fanciful faux beaches—assembled in summer along a one-mile stretch of the Right Bank of the Seine—is a fun place to stroll, play, and people-watch on a sunny day. Each summer, the Paris city government closes the embankment's highway and trucks in potted palm trees, hammocks, and lounge chairs, conveying the fun feeling of an urban beach scene. You'll also find "beach cafés," climbing walls, prefab pools, trampolines, *boules*, a library, beach volleyball, badminton, and Frisbee areas.

Cost and Hours: Free, mid-July-mid-Aug daily 8:00-24:00, on Right Bank of Seine, just north of Ile de la Cité, between Pont des Arts and Pont de Sully; for information, go to www.quefaire.paris.fr/parisplages.

SIGHTS

Major Museums Neighborhood

Paris' grandest park, the Tuileries Garden, was once the private property of kings and queens. Today it links the Louvre, Orangerie, and Orsay museums, all of which are within pleasant strolling distance of one another.

▲▲▲LOUVRE (MUSEE DU LOUVRE)

This is Europe's oldest, biggest, greatest, and second-most-crowded museum (after the Vatican). Housed in a U-shaped, 16th-century palace (accentuated by a 20th-century glass pyramid), it's home to the *Mona Lisa, Venus de Milo,* and hall after hall of Greek and Roman masterpieces, medieval jewels,

Major Museums Neighborhood

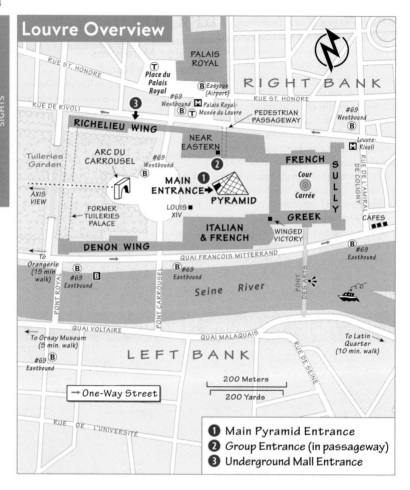

Louvre Overview

RUE ST. HONORE

PALAIS ROYAL

RIGHT BANK

Place du Palais Royal

(T)

(B) Easybus (Airport)

#69 Westbound

(M) Palais Royal-Musée du Louvre

(B)(T)

RUE ST. HONORE

PEDESTRIAN PASSAGEWAY

#69 Westbound

(B)

RUE DE RIVOLI

❸

Louvre-Rivoli (M)

RICHELIEU WING

NEAR EASTERN

FRENCH

S
U
L
L
Y

RUE DE L'AMIRAL DE COLIGNY

Tuileries Garden

ARC DU CARROUSEL

#69 Westbound

(B)

❷

MAIN ENTRANCE→

PYRAMID

Cour

Carrée ◎

❶

AXIS VIEW

FORMER TUILERIES PALACE

LOUIS ■ XIV

GREEK

CAFES ■■■

ITALIAN & FRENCH

WINGED VICTORY

DENON WING

QUAI FRANÇOIS MITTERRAND

(B) #69 Eastbound

To Orangerie (15 min walk)

(B)

(B) #69 Eastbound

(B) #69 Eastbound

PONT ROYAL

PONT CARROUSEL

Seine River

PONT DES ARTS

QUAI VOLTAIRE

To Orsay Museum (5 min. walk)

#69 (B) Eastbound

QUAI MALAQUAIS

LEFT BANK

RUE DE SEINE

To Latin Quarter (10 min. walk)

200 Meters

200 Yards

RUE DE L'UNIVERSITÉ

→ One-Way Street

❶ Main Pyramid Entrance
❷ Group Entrance (in passageway)
❸ Underground Mall Entrance

Michelangelo statues, and paintings by the greatest artists from the Renaissance to the Romantics.

Under the Louvre's pyramid entrance

Touring the Louvre can be overwhelming, so be selective. Focus on the Denon wing, with Greek sculptures, Italian paintings (by Raphael and Leonardo), and—of course—French paintings (Neoclassical and Romantic), and the adjoining Sully wing, with Egyptian artifacts and more French paintings. For extra credit, tackle the Richelieu wing, displaying works from ancient Mesopotamia, as well as French, Dutch, and Northern art.

Expect Changes: The sprawling Louvre is constantly shuffling its deck. Rooms close, and pieces can be on loan or in restoration.

Cost and Hours: €12, €15 includes special exhibits, free on first Sun of month Oct-March, covered by Museum Pass, tickets good all day, reentry allowed; open Wed-Mon 9:00-18:00, Wed and Fri until 21:45 (except on holidays), closed Tue, galleries start shutting 30 minutes before closing, last entry 45 minutes before closing; videoguide-€5, several cafés, tel. 01 40 20 53 17, recorded info tel. 01 40 20 51 51, www.louvre.fr.

When to Go: Crowds are bad on Sun, Mon (the worst day), Wed, and in the morning (arrive 30 minutes before opening to secure a good place in line). Evening visits are quieter, and the glass pyramid glows after dark.

Buying Tickets: Self-serve ticket machines located under the pyramid may be faster to use than the ticket windows (machines accept euro bills, coins, and chip-and-PIN Visa cards). A shop in the underground mall sells tickets to the Louvre, Orsay, and Versailles, plus Museum Passes, for no extra charge (cash only). To find it from the Carrousel du Louvre entrance off Rue de Rivoli, turn right after the last escalator down onto Allée de France, and follow *Museum Pass* signs.

Rick's Tip: *Anyone can **enter the Louvre from its less crowded underground entrance,** accessed through the Carrousel du Louvre shopping mall. Enter the mall at 99 Rue de Rivoli (the door with the red awning) or directly from the Métro stop Palais Royal-Musée du Louvre (stepping off the train, take the exit to Musée du Louvre-Le Carrousel du Louvre).*

Getting There: It's at the Palais Royal-Musée du Louvre Métro stop. (The old Louvre Métro stop, called Louvre-Rivoli, is farther from the entrance.) Bus #69 also runs past the Louvre.

Getting In: There is no grander entry than through the main entrance at the **pyramid** in the central courtyard, but lines (for security reasons) can be long. Pass-holders should look for a queue that puts them near the head of the security line.

Tours: Ninety-minute English-

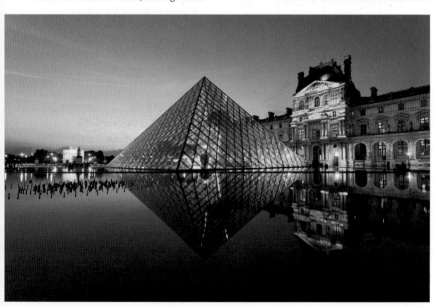

The Louvre and its pyramid glows at night.

language **guided tours** leave twice daily (except the first Sun of the month Oct–March) from the *Accueil des Groupes* area, under the pyramid (€12 plus admission, usually 11:15 and 14:00, tour tel. 01 40 20 52 63). **Videoguides** (€5) provide commentary on about 700 masterpieces.

🎧 Download my free Louvre Museum **audio tour.**

Baggage Check: The free *bagagerie* is under the pyramid, behind the Richelieu wing escalator (look for the *visiteurs individuels* sign).

❯ SELF-GUIDED TOUR

With more than 30,000 works of art, the Louvre is a full inventory of Western civilization. To cover it all in one visit is impossible. Let's focus on the Louvre's specialties—Greek sculpture, Italian painting, and French painting. If you don't find the artwork you're looking for, ask the nearest guard for its location.

• *We'll start in the Sully Wing, in Salle 16. To get there from the pyramid entrance, first enter the Denon Wing, ascend several flights of escalators, and follow the crowds—then get out your map or ask directions to the Venus de Milo.*

THE GREEKS

Venus de Milo (*Aphrodite,* late 2nd century B.C.): This goddess of love created

Venus de Milo

a sensation when she was discovered in 1820 on the Greek island of Melos. The Greeks pictured their gods in human form (meaning humans are godlike), telling us they had an optimistic view of the human race. *Venus'* well-proportioned body captures the balance and orderliness of the Greek universe. The twisting pose gives a balanced S-curve to her body (especially noticeable from the back view) that Golden Age Greeks and succeeding generations found beautiful. Most "Greek" statues are actually later Roman copies; this is a rare Greek original.

• *Now head to Salle 6, behind Venus de Milo.*

Parthenon Friezes (mid-5th century B.C.): These stone fragments once decorated the exterior of the greatest Athenian temple of the Greek Golden Age. The temple glorified the city's divine protector, Athena, and the superiority of the Athenians, who were feeling especially cocky, having just crushed their archrivals, the Persians. A model of the Parthenon shows where the panels might have hung.

• *About 50 yards away, find a grand staircase. Climb it to the first floor and the...*

Winged Victory of Samothrace (c. 190 B.C.): This woman with wings, poised on the prow of a ship, once stood on an island hilltop to commemorate a naval victory. Her clothes are windblown and sea-sprayed, clinging close enough to her body to win a wet T-shirt contest. Originally, her right arm was stretched high, celebrating the victory like a Super Bowl champion, waving a "we're number one" finger. This is the *Venus de Milo* gone Hellenistic, from the time after the culture of Athens was spread around the Mediterranean by Alexander the Great (c. 325 B.C.).

• *Facing Winged Victory, turn right (entering the Denon Wing), and proceed to the large Salle 3.*

THE MEDIEVAL WORLD, 1200-1500

Cimabue—*The Madonna and Child in Majesty Surrounded by Angels* (c. 1280): During the Age of Faith (1200s), almost every church in Europe had a painting like this one. Mary was a cult figure—even bigger than the late-20th-century Madonna—adored and prayed to by the faithful for bringing Baby Jesus into the world. These figures are laid flat on a gold background like cardboard cutouts, existing in a golden never-never land, as though the faithful couldn't imagine them as flesh-and-blood humans inhabiting our dark and sinful earth.

Giotto—*St. Francis of Assisi Receiving the Stigmata* (c. 1295-1300): Francis of Assisi (c. 1181-1226), a wandering Italian monk of renowned goodness, kneels on a rocky Italian hillside, pondering the pain of Christ's torture and execution. Suddenly, he looks up, startled, to see Christ himself, with six wings, hovering above. Christ shoots lasers from his wounds to the hands, feet, and side of the empathetic monk, marking him with the stigmata. Francis' humble love of man and nature inspired artists like Giotto to portray real human beings with real emotions, living in a physical world of beauty.

• *Room 3 spills into the long Grand Gallery. Find the following paintings in the Gallery, as you make your way to the* Mona Lisa *(midway down the gallery, in the adjoining Salle 6—just follow the signs and the people).*

ITALIAN RENAISSANCE, 1400-1600
Andrea Mantegna—*St. Sebastian* (c. 1480): Not the patron saint of acupuncture, St. Sebastian was a Christian martyr. Notice the *contrapposto* stance (all of his weight resting on one leg) and the Greek ruins scattered around him. His executioners look like ignorant medieval brutes bewildered by this enlightened Renaissance man. Italian artists were beginning to learn how to create human realism and earthly beauty on the canvas. Let the Renaissance begin.

Leonardo da Vinci—*The Virgin and Child with St. Anne* (c. 1510): Three generations—grandmother, mother, and child—are arranged in a pyramid, with Anne's face as the peak and the lamb as the lower right corner. It's as orderly as the

Ⓐ Winged Victory of Samothrace

Ⓑ *Giotto,* St. Francis Receiving the Stigmata

Ⓒ *Leonardo da Vinci,* Mona Lisa

geometrically perfect universe created by the Renaissance god. There's a psychological kidney punch in this happy painting: Jesus, the picture of childish joy, is innocently playing with a lamb—the symbol of his inevitable sacrificial death. The Louvre has the greatest collection of Leonardos in the world—five of them. Look for the neighboring *Virgin of the Rocks* and *John the Baptist*.

Raphael—*La Belle Jardinière* (c. 1507): Raphael perfected the style Leonardo pioneered. This configuration of Madonna, Child, and John the Baptist is also a balanced pyramid with hazy grace and beauty. The interplay of gestures and gazes gives the masterpiece both intimacy and cohesiveness, while Raphael's blended brushstrokes varnish the work with an iridescent smoothness. With Raphael, the Greek ideal of beauty— reborn in the Renaissance—reached its peak.

Leonardo da Vinci—*Mona Lisa* (1503-1519): When Leonardo moved to France late in life, he packed light, bringing only a few paintings with him. One was a portrait of Lisa del Giocondo, the wife of a wealthy Florentine merchant. *Mona* may disappoint you. She's smaller than you'd expect, darker, engulfed in a huge room, and hidden behind a glaring pane of glass. The famous smile attracts you first, but try as you might, you can never quite see the corners of her mouth. The overall mood is one of balance and serenity, but there's also an element of mystery. Mona's smile and long-distance beauty are subtle and elusive, tempting but always just out of reach. Mona doesn't knock your socks off, but she winks at the patient viewer.

Paolo Veronese—*The Marriage at Cana* (1563): Venetian artists like Veronese painted the good life of rich, happy-go-lucky Venetian merchants. In a spacious setting of Renaissance architecture, colorful lords and ladies, decked out in their fanciest duds, feast on a great spread of food and drink. But

Ⓐ *Raphael,* La Belle Jardinière
Ⓑ *Veronese,* The Marriage at Cana
Ⓒ *Ingres,* La Grande Odalisque
Ⓓ *Delacroix,* Liberty Leading the People

believe it or not, this is a religious work showing the wedding celebration in which Jesus turned water into wine. With true Renaissance optimism, Venetians pictured Christ as a party animal, someone who loved the created world as much as they did.

• *Exit behind* Mona *into the Salle Denon (Room 76). Turn right for French Neoclassicism (Salle Daru, David and Ingres); then backtrack through the Salle Denon for French Romanticism (Room 77, Géricault and Delacroix).*

FRENCH PAINTING, 1780-1850

Jacques-Louis David—*The Coronation of Emperor Napoleon* (1806-1807): Napoleon holds aloft an imperial crown. This common-born son of immigrants is about to be crowned emperor of a "New Rome." He has just made his wife, Josephine, the empress, and she kneels at his feet. Seated behind Napoleon is the pope, who journeyed from Rome to place the imperial crown on his head. But Napoleon feels that no one is worthy of the task. At the last moment, he shrugs the pope aside... and crowns himself.

Jean-Auguste-Dominique Ingres—*La Grande Odalisque* (1814): Take *Venus de Milo,* turn her around, lay her down, and stick a hash pipe next to her, and you have the *Grande Odalisque.* Using clean, polished, sculptural lines, Ingres exaggerates the S-curve of a standing Greek nude. As in the *Venus de Milo,* rough folds of cloth set off her smooth skin. Ingres gave the face, too, a touch of *Venus'* idealized features, taking nature and improving on it. Ingres preserves Venus' backside for posterior—I mean, posterity.

Théodore Géricault—*The Raft of the Medusa* (1819): Clinging to a raft is a tangle of bodies and lunatics sprawled over each other. The scene writhes with agitated, ominous motion—the ripple of muscles, churning clouds, and choppy seas. The bodies rise up in a pyramid of hope, culminating in a flag wave. They signal frantically, trying to catch the attention of the tiny ship on the horizon, their last desperate hope...which did finally save them. Géricault uses rippling movement and powerful colors to catch us up in the excitement. (This painting was based on the actual sinking of the ship *Medusa* off the coast of Africa in 1816.)

Eugène Delacroix—*Liberty Leading the People* (1831): The year is 1830. Parisians take to the streets to fight royalist oppressors. Leading them on through the smoke and over the dead and dying is the figure of Liberty, a strong woman waving the French flag. Does this symbol of victory look familiar? It's the *Winged Victory,* wingless and topless. To stir our emotions, Delacroix uses only three major colors—the red, white, and blue of the French flag. France is the symbol of modern democracy, and this painting has long stirred its citizens' passion for liberty.

• *Exit the room at the far end, go downstairs, where you'll bump into...*

MORE ITALIAN RENAISSANCE

Michelangelo—*Slaves* (1513-1515): These two statues by the earth's greatest sculptor are a bridge between the ancient and

Michelangelo's Slave *sculptures*

modern worlds. Michelangelo, like his fellow Renaissance artists, learned from the Greeks. The perfect anatomy, twisting poses, and idealized faces appear as if they could have been created 2,000 years earlier.

The *Dying Slave* twists listlessly against his T-shirt-like bonds, revealing his smooth skin. This is probably the most sensual nude that Michelangelo, the master of the male body, ever created. The *Rebellious Slave* fights against his bondage. His shoulders rotate one way, his head and leg turn the other. He even seems to be trying to release himself from the rock he's made of. Michelangelo said that his purpose was to carve away the marble to reveal the figures God put inside. This slave shows the agony of that process and the ecstasy of the result.

• *But, of course, there's so much more. After a break (or on a second visit), consider a stroll through a few rooms of the Richelieu wing, which contain some of the Louvre's most ancient pieces.*

Rick's Tip: *Across from the Louvre (to the north) are the lovely courtyards of the stately* Palais Royal *(always open and free, entrance off Rue de Rivoli). Bring a picnic and create your own* quiet break *amid flowers and surrounded by a serene arcade.*

▲▲▲ORSAY MUSEUM (MUSÉE D'ORSAY)

The Musée d'Orsay houses French art of the 1800s and early 1900s, picking up where the Louvre's art collection leaves off. For us, that means Impressionism, the art of sun-dappled fields, bright colors, and crowded Parisian cafés. The Orsay houses the best general collection anywhere of works by Manet, Monet, Renoir, Degas, Van Gogh, Cézanne, and Gauguin.

Cost and Hours: €11, €8.50 Tue-Wed and Fri-Sun after 16:30 and Thu after 18:15, free on first Sun of month and often right when the ticket booth stops selling tickets (Tue-Wed and Fri-Sun at 17:00, Thu at 21:00; they won't let you in much after that), covered by Museum Pass, tickets valid all day, combo-ticket with Orangerie Museum (€16) or Rodin Museum (€15) valid four days. Museum open Tue-Sun 9:30-18:00, Thu until 21:45, closed Mon, last entry one hour before closing; cafés and a restaurant, tel. 01 40 49 48 14, www.musee-orsay.fr.

Avoiding Lines: You can skip long ticket-buying lines by using a Museum Pass or purchasing tickets online in advance, both of which entitle you to use a separate entrance. You can buy tickets and Museum Passes (no mark-up; tickets valid 3 months) at the newspaper kiosk just outside the Orsay entrance (along Rue de la Légion d'Honneur).

Rick's Tip: *If you're planning to* get a combo-ticket for the Orsay Museum *with either the Orangerie or the Rodin Museum, start at one of those museums instead, as they have shorter lines.*

Getting There: The museum, at 1 Rue de la Légion d'Honneur, sits above the Train-C stop called Musée d'Orsay; the nearest Métro stop is Solférino. Bus #69 also stops at the Orsay.

Getting In: As you face the entrance, passholders and ticket holders enter on the right (Entrance C). Ticket purchasers enter on the left (Entrance A). Security checks slow down all entrances.

Tours: Audioguides cost €5. English **guided tours** usually run daily at 11:30 (€6/1.5 hours, none on Sun, tours may also run at 14:30—inquire when you arrive).

🎧 Download my free Orsay Museum **audio tour.**

❍ SELF-GUIDED TOUR

This former train station, the Gare d'Orsay, barely escaped the wrecking ball in the 1970s, when the French realized it'd be a great place to house the enormous collections of 19th-century art scattered throughout the city.

The ground floor (level 0) houses early 19th-century art, mainly conservative art of the Academy and Salon, plus Realism. On the top floor is the core of the collection—the Impressionist rooms. If you're pressed for time, go directly there. The museum rotates its large collection often, so find the latest arrangement on your current Orsay map, and be ready to go with the flow.

CONSERVATIVE ART

In the Orsay's first few ground-floor rooms, you're surrounded by visions of idealized beauty—nude women in languid poses, Greek mythological figures, and anatomically perfect statues. This was the art adored by 19th-century French academics and the middle-class (bourgeois) public.

Jean-Auguste-Dominique Ingres' *The Source* (1856) is virtually a Greek statue on canvas. Like the Louvre's *Venus de Milo*, she's a balance of opposite motions. Alexandre **Cabanel** lays Ingres' *Source* on her back. His *Birth of Venus* (1863) is a perfect fantasy, an orgasm of beauty.

REALISM

The French Realists rejected idealized classicism and began painting what they saw in the world around them. For Honoré **Daumier,** that meant looking at the stuffy bourgeois establishment that controlled the Academy and the Salon. In the 36 bustlets of *Celebrities of the Happy Medium* (1835), Daumier, trained as a political cartoonist, exaggerates each subject's most distinct characteristic to capture with vicious precision the pomposity and self-righteousness of these self-appointed arbiters of taste.

Jean-François Millet's *The Gleaners* (1867) shows us three poor women who pick up the meager leftovers after a field has been harvested for the wealthy. Here he captures the innate dignity of these stocky, tanned women who bend their backs quietly in a large field for their small reward. This is "Realism" in two senses. It's painted "realistically," not prettified. And it's the "real" world—not the fantasy world of Greek myth, but the harsh life of the working poor.

For a Realist's take on the traditional Venus, find Edouard Manet's *Olympia*

The Orsay Museum occupies an early-20th-century railway station.

A *Cabanel,*
Birth of Venus

B *Millet,*
The Gleaners

C *Manet,*
Olympia

D *Toulouse-*
Lautrec, Jane
Avril Dancing

(1863). Compare this uncompromising nude with Cabanel's idealized, pastel, Vaseline-on-the-lens beauty in the *Birth of Venus.* In *Olympia,* the sharp outlines and harsh, contrasting colors are new and shocking. Manet replaced soft-core porn with hard-core art.

Gustave Courbet's *The Painter's Studio* (1855) takes us backstage, showing us the gritty reality behind the creation of pretty pictures. We see Courbet himself in his studio, working diligently on a Realistic landscape, oblivious to the confusion around him. Milling around are ordinary citizens, not Greek heroes.

TOULOUSE-LAUTREC DETOUR

The Henri **Toulouse-Lautrec** paintings tucked away on the ground floor (Room 10) rightly belong with the Post-Impressionist works on level 2, but since you're already here, enjoy his paintings, which incarnate the artist's love of nightlife and show business. Every night, Toulouse-Lautrec put on his bowler hat and visited the Moulin Rouge to draw the crowds, the can-can dancers, and the backstage action. He worked quickly, creating sketches in paint that serve as snapshots of a golden era. In *Jane Avril Dancing* (1891), he depicts the slim, graceful, elegant, and melancholy dancer, who stood out above the rabble. Her legs keep dancing while her mind is far away.

IMPRESSIONISM

The Impressionist collection is scattered randomly through Rooms 29-36, on the top floor. Look for masterworks by these artists:

In Edouard Manet's *Luncheon on the Grass* (1863), you can see that a new revolutionary movement was starting to bud—Impressionism. Notice the background: the messy brushwork of trees and leaves, the play of light on the pond, and the light that filters through the trees onto the woman who stoops in the haze. Also note the strong contrast of colors (white skin, black clothes, green grass). Let the

Orsay Museum—Ground Floor

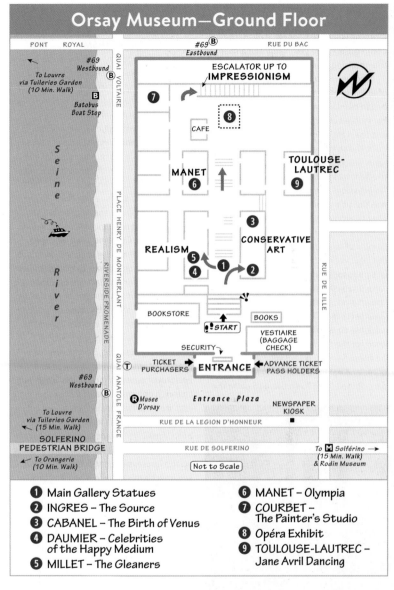

1. Main Gallery Statues
2. INGRES – The Source
3. CABANEL – The Birth of Venus
4. DAUMIER – Celebrities of the Happy Medium
5. MILLET – The Gleaners
6. MANET – Olympia
7. COURBET – The Painter's Studio
8. Opéra Exhibit
9. TOULOUSE-LAUTREC – Jane Avril Dancing

Impressionist revolution begin!

Edgar **Degas** blends classical lines and Realist subjects with Impressionist color, spontaneity, and everyday scenes from urban Paris. He loved the unposed "snapshot" effect, catching his models off guard. Dance students, women at work, and café scenes are approached from odd angles that aren't always ideal but make the scenes seem more real. He gives us the backstage view of life. For instance, a dance rehearsal let Degas capture a behind-the-scenes look at bored, tired, restless dancers (*The Dance Class*, c.

1873-1875). In the painting *In a Café* (1875-1876), a weary lady of the evening meets morning with a last, lonely, nail-in-the-coffin drink in the glaring light of a four-in-the-morning café.

Next up is Claude **Monet,** the father of Impressionism. In the 1860s, Monet began painting landscapes in the open air. He studied optics and pigments to know just the right colors he needed to reproduce the shimmering quality of reflected light. The key was to work quickly, when the light was just right, creating a fleeting "impression" of the scene. In fact, that was the title of one of Monet's canvases; it gave the movement its name.

Pierre-Auguste **Renoir** started out as a painter of landscapes, along with Monet, but later veered from the Impressionist's philosophy and painted images that were unabashedly "pretty." His best-known work is *Dance at the Moulin de la Galette* (1876). On Sunday afternoons, working-class folk would dress up and head for the fields on Butte Montmartre (near Sacré-Cœur Basilica) to dance, drink, and eat little crêpes (galettes) until dark. Renoir liked to go there to paint the common Parisians living and loving in the afternoon sun.

POST-IMPRESSIONISM

Post-Impressionism—the style that employs Impressionism's bright colors while branching out in new directions—is scattered all around the museum. You'll get a taste of the style with Paul Cézanne, on the top floor, with much more on level 2.

Paul **Cézanne** brought Impressionism into the 20th century. After the color of Monet and warmth of Renoir, Cézanne's rather impersonal canvases can be difficult to appreciate (see *The Card Players,* 1890-1895). Where the Impressionists built a figure from a mosaic of individual brushstrokes, Cézanne used blocks of paint to create a more solid, geometrical shape. These chunks are like little "cubes." It's no coincidence that his experiments in reducing forms to their geometric basics inspired the Cubists. Because of his style (not the content), he is often called the first Modern painter.

Like Michelangelo, Beethoven, Rembrandt, Wayne Newton, and a select handful of others, Vincent **van Gogh** put so much of himself into his work that art and life became one. In the Orsay's collection of paintings (level 2), you'll see both Van Gogh's painting style and his life unfold, from his early days in Paris soaking up the Impressionist style (for example, see how he might build a bristling brown beard using thick strokes of red, yellow, and green side by side) to his richly creative but wildly unstable stint in the south of France (*Van Gogh's Room at Arles,* 1889). Don't miss his final self-portrait (1889), showing a man engulfed in a confused background of brushstrokes that swirl and rave. Perhaps his troubled eyes know that in only a few months he would take a pistol and put a bullet through his chest.

Nearby are the paintings of Paul **Gauguin,** who got the travel bug early and grew up wanting to be a sailor. Instead,

Degas, The Dance Class

he became a stockbroker. At the age of 35, he got fed up with it all, quit his job, abandoned his wife (her stern portrait bust may be nearby) and family, and took refuge in his art.

Gauguin traveled to the South Seas in search of the exotic, finally settling on Tahiti. Gauguin's best-known works capture an idyllic Tahitian landscape peopled by exotic women engaged in simple tasks and making music (*Arearea*, 1892). The style is intentionally "primitive," collapsing the three-dimensional landscape into a two-dimensional pattern of bright colors. Gauguin wanted to communicate to his "civilized" colleagues back home that he'd found the paradise he'd always envisioned.

A *Renoir,* Dance at the Moulin de la Galette
B *Cézanne,* The Card Players
C *Van Gogh,* Van Gogh's Room at Arles
D *Gauguin,* Arearea

FRENCH SCULPTURE

The open-air mezzanine of level 2 is lined with statues. Stroll the mezzanine, enjoying the work of great French sculptors, including Auguste **Rodin.**

Born of working-class roots and largely self-taught, Rodin combined classical solidity with Impressionist surfaces to become the greatest sculptor since Michelangelo. Like his statue *The Walking Man* (c. 1900), Rodin had one foot in the past, while the other stepped into the future. This muscular, forcefully striding man could be a symbol of Renaissance Man with his classical power. With no mouth or hands, he speaks with his body. But get close and look at the statue's surface. This rough, "unfinished" look reflects light in the same way the rough Impressionist brushwork does, making the statue come alive, never quite at rest in the viewer's eye. Rodin created this statue in a flash of inspiration. He took two unfinished statues—torso and legs—and plunked them together at the waist. You can still see the seam. Rodin's sculptures capture the groundbreaking spirit of much of the art in the Orsay Museum. With a stable base of 19th-century stone, he launched art into the 20th century.

▲▲ORANGERIE MUSEUM (MUSEE DE L'ORANGERIE)

This Impressionist museum is as lovely as a water lily. Step out of the tree-lined, sun-dappled Impressionist painting that is the Tuileries Garden and into the Orangerie (oh-rahn-zhuh-ree), a bijou of select works by Monet, Renoir, Matisse, Picasso, and others.

Cost and Hours: €9, €6.50 after 17:00, €16 combo-ticket with Orsay Museum, covered by Museum Pass; Wed-Mon 9:00-18:00, closed Tue; audioguide-€5, English guided tours usually Mon and Thu at 14:30 and Sat at 11:00, located in Tuileries Garden near Place de la Concorde, Mo: Concorde or scenic bus #24, tel. 01 44 77 80 07, www.musee-orangerie.fr.

Visiting the Museum: On the main floor you'll find the main attraction, Monet's *Water Lilies (Nymphéas),* floating dreamily in oval rooms. These eight mammoth, curved panels immerse you in Monet's garden. We're looking at the pond in his garden at Giverny—dotted with water lilies, surrounded by foliage, and dappled by the reflections of the sky, clouds, and trees on the surface. But the true subject of these works is the play of reflected light off the surface of the pond.

Working at his home in Giverny, Monet built a special studio with skylights and wheeled easels to accommodate the canvases. For 12 years (1914-1926), Monet worked on these paintings obsessively. Monet completed all the planned canvases, but didn't live to see them installed here. In 1927, the year after his death, these rooms were completed and the canvases put in place. Some call this the first "art installation"—art displayed in a space specially designed for it in order to enhance the viewer's experience.

In the Orangerie's underground gallery are select works from the personal collection of Paris' trend-spotting art dealer of the 1920s, Paul Guillaume. These paintings—Impressionist, Fauvist, and Cubist—are a snapshot of what was hot in the world of art, circa 1920.

Monet's Water Lilies *at the Orangerie Museum*

Eiffel Tower & Nearby

Eiffel Tower and Nearby

▲▲▲ EIFFEL TOWER (LA TOUR EIFFEL)

It's crowded, expensive, and there are probably better views in Paris, but visiting this 1,000-foot-tall ornament is worth the trouble. Visitors to Paris may find the *Mona Lisa* to be less than expected, but the Eiffel Tower rarely disappoints, even in an era of skyscrapers. This is a once-in-a-lifetime, I've-been-there experience. Making the trip gives you membership in the exclusive society of the quarter of a billion other humans who have made the Eiffel Tower the most visited monument in the modern world.

Cost and Hours: €25 all the way to the top, €16 for just the two lower levels, €10 to climb the stairs to the first or second level, not covered by Museum Pass; daily mid-June-Aug 9:00-24:45, last ascent to top at 23:00 and to lower levels 23:00 (elevator or stairs); Sept-mid-June 9:30-23:45, last ascent to top at 22:30 and to lower levels at 23:00 (elevator or stairs); cafés and great view restaurants, Mo: Bir-Hakeim or Trocadéro, Train-C: Champ de Mars-Tour Eiffel.

Reservations: You'd be crazy to show up without a reservation. At www.toureiffel.paris, you can book an entry date and time, and skip the initial entry line (the longest)—at no extra cost.

Time slots fill up months in advance (especially from April through September). Online ticket sales open up about three months before any given date (at 8:30 Paris time)—and can sell out for that day within hours. Reservations are non-refundable. When you "Choose a ticket," make sure you select "Lift entrance ticket with access to the summit" to go all the way to the top. You must create an account, with a 10-digit mobile phone number as your log-in.

If no reservation slots are available, buy a "Lift entrance ticket with access to 2nd floor only"—but you can't upgrade to the summit once inside. Or, try the website again about a week before your visit—last-minute spots can open up.

When to Go: For the best of all worlds, arrive with enough light to see the views, then stay as it gets dark to see the lights. The views are grand whether you ascend or not. At the top of the hour, a five-minute display features thousands of sparkling lights (best viewed from Place du Trocadéro or the grassy park below).

Rick's Tip: **No reservation for the Eiffel Tower?** *Get in line 30 minutes before it opens. Going late is the next-best bet (after 19:00 May-Aug). You can bypass some (but not all) lines if you have a tower restaurant reservation (at Le Jules Verne or 58 Tour Eiffel) or take a Fat Tire Tour (www.fattiretours.com).*

Getting In: If you have a reservation, arrive at the tower 10 minutes before your entry time, and look for either of the two entrances marked *Visiteurs avec Reservation* (Visitors with Reservation),

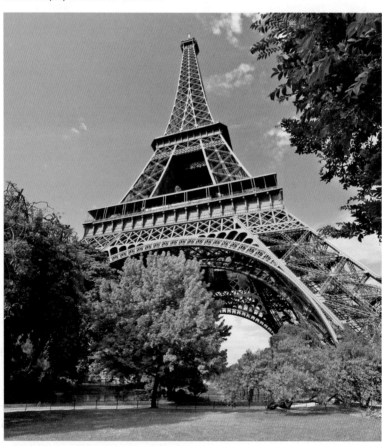

The Eiffel Tower stands more than 1,000 feet tall.

where attendants scan your ticket and put you on the first available elevator. If you don't have a reservation, follow signs for *Individuels* or *Visiteurs sans Tickets* (avoid lines selling tickets only for *Groupes*). The stairs entrance (usually a shorter line) is at the south pillar (next to Le Jules Verne restaurant entrance). When you buy tickets on-site, all members of your party must be with you. To get reduced fares for kids, bring ID.

Security Check: Bags larger than 19″ × 8″ × 12″ inches are not allowed, but there is no baggage check. All bags are subject to a security search. No knives, glass bottles, or cans are permitted.

Rick's Tip: *Tourists in crowded elevators are like fish in a barrel for* **pickpockets.** *Beware. Thieves plunder awestruck visitors gawking below the tower. A* **police station** *is at the Jules Verne pillar.*

Background: The first visitor to the Paris World's Fair in 1889 walked beneath the "arch" formed by the newly built Eiffel Tower and entered the fairgrounds. This event celebrated both the centennial of the French Revolution and France's position as a global superpower. Bridge builder Gustave Eiffel (1832-1923) won the contest to build the fair's centerpiece by beating out rival proposals such as a giant guillotine. The tower was nothing but a showpiece, with no functional purpose except to demonstrate to the world that France had the wealth, knowledge, and can-do spirit. The original plan was to dismantle the tower as quickly as it was built after the celebration ended, but it was kept by popular demand.

The tower, including its antenna, stands 1,063 feet tall, or slightly higher than the 77-story Chrysler Building in New York. Its four support pillars straddle an area of 3.5 acres. Despite the tower's 7,300 tons of metal and 60 tons of paint, it is so well-engineered that it weighs no

Open-Air Markets

Several traffic-free street markets overflow with flowers, bakeries, produce, fish vendors, and butchers, illustrating how most Parisians shopped before there were supermarkets. Shops are open daily except Sunday afternoons, Monday, and lunchtime throughout the week. You can shop for a picnic or grab a seat at a sidewalk café to watch the action.

Rue Cler—a wonderful place to sleep and dine as well as shop—is like a refined street market, serving an upscale neighborhood near the Eiffel Tower (Mo: Ecole Militaire).

Rue Daguerre, near the Catacombs and off Avenue du Général Leclerc, is the least touristy of the street markets listed here, mixing food shops with cafés along a traffic-free street (Mo: Denfert-Rochereau).

Rue Mouffetard, on the Left Bank, is a happening market street by day and does double-duty as restaurant row at night. Hiding several blocks behind the Panthéon, it starts at Place Contrescarpe and ends below at St. Médard Church (Mo: Censier Daubenton). The upper stretch is touristic; the bottom stretch is purely Parisian.

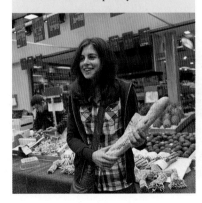

more per square inch at its base than a linebacker on tiptoes.

VISITING THE TOWER

There are three observation platforms, at roughly 200, 400, and 900 feet. If you want to see the entire tower, from top to bottom, then see it...from top to bottom.

There isn't a single elevator straight to the top (le sommet). To get there, you'll first ride an elevator to the second level. (For the hardy, there are 360 stairs to the first level and another 360 to the second.) Once on the second level, immediately line up for the next elevator, to the top. Enjoy the views, then ride back down to the second level (which has the best views). When you're ready, head to the first level via the stairs (no line and can take as little as 5 minutes) or take the elevator down (ask if it will stop on the first level—some don't). Explore the shops and exhibits on the first level and have a snack. To leave, you can line up for the elevator, but it's quickest and most memorable to take the stairs back down to earth.

For a final look at the tower, stroll

Army Museum and Napoleon's Tomb

across the river to Place du Trocadéro or to the end of the Champ de Mars and look back for great views. However impressive it may be by day, the tower is an awesome thing to see at twilight, when it becomes filled with light, and virile Paris lies back and lets night be on top. When darkness fully envelops the city, the tower seems to climax with a spectacular light show at the top of each hour...for five minutes.

Near the Eiffel Tower
▲▲ARMY MUSEUM AND NAPOLEON'S TOMB (MUSEE DE L'ARMEE)

The Hôtel des Invalides—a former veterans' hospital topped by a golden dome—houses Napoleon's over-the-top-ornate tomb, as well as Europe's greatest military museum. Visiting the Army Museum's different sections, you can watch the art of war unfold from stone axes to Axis powers.

Cost and Hours: €9.50, €7.50 after 17:00, free for military personnel in uniform, free for kids but they must wait in line for ticket, covered by Museum Pass, special exhibits are extra; daily 10:00-18:00, July-Aug until 19:00, Nov-March until 17:00, tomb plus WWI and WWII wings open Tue until 21:00 April-Sept, museum (except for tomb) closed first Mon of month Oct-June, Charles de Gaulle exhibit closed Mon year-round; videoguide-€6, cafeteria, tel. 08 10 11 33 99, www.musee-armee.fr.

Getting There: The Hôtel des Invalides is at 129 Rue de Grenelle, a 10-minute walk from Rue Cler (Mo: La Tour Maubourg, Varenne, or Invalides). You can also take bus #69 (from the Marais and Rue Cler) or bus #87 (from Rue Cler and Luxembourg Garden area).

Visiting the Museum: At the center of the complex, Napoleon Bonaparte lies majestically dead inside several coffins under a grand dome—a goose-bumping pilgrimage for historians. The dome overhead glitters with 26 pounds of thinly pounded gold leaf.

Your visit continues through an impressive range of museums filled with medieval armor, cannons and muskets, Louis XIV-era uniforms and weapons, and Napoleon's horse—stuffed and mounted.

The best section is dedicated to the two World Wars. Walk chronologically through displays on the trench warfare of World War I, the victory parades, France's horrendous losses, and the humiliating Treaty of Versailles that led to World War II.

The WWII rooms use black-and-white photos, maps, videos, and artifacts to trace Hitler's rise, the Blitzkrieg that overran France, America's entry into the war, D-Day, the concentration camps, the atomic bomb, the war in the Pacific, and the eventual Allied victory. There's special insight into France's role (the French Resistance), and how it was Charles de Gaulle that actually won the war.

▲▲RODIN MUSEUM (MUSEE RODIN)

This user-friendly museum is filled with passionate works by the greatest sculptor since Michelangelo. You'll see *The Kiss*, *The Thinker*, *The Gates of Hell*, and many more.

Cost and Hours: €10 (special exhibits cost extra), free on first Sun of the month Oct-March, €4 for garden only (many important works are on display there), €15 combo-ticket with Orsay Museum, museum and garden covered by Museum Pass; Tue-Sun 10:00-17:45, closed Mon; gardens close at 18:00, Oct-March at 17:00; audioguide-€6, slow security and baggage check, self-service café in garden, 79 Rue de Varenne, Mo: Varenne, tel. 01 44 18 61 10, www.musee-rodin.fr.

Visiting the Museum: Auguste Rodin (1840-1917) was a modern Michelangelo, sculpting human figures on an epic scale, revealing through their bodies his deepest thoughts and feelings. Like many of Michelangelo's unfinished works, Rodin's statues rise from the raw stone around them, driven by the life force. With missing limbs and scarred skin, these are prefab classics, making ugliness noble. Rodin's people are always moving restlessly. Even the famous *Thinker* is moving; while he's plopped down solidly, his mind is a million miles away.

Well-displayed in the mansion where the sculptor lived and worked, exhibits

Rodin's Burghers of Calais

trace Rodin's artistic development, explain how his bronze statues were cast, and show some of the studies he created to work up to his masterpiece, the unfinished *Gates of Hell*. Learn about Rodin's tumultuous relationship with his apprentice and lover, Camille Claudel. Mull over what makes his sculptures some of the most evocative since the Renaissance. And stroll the beautiful gardens, packed with many of his greatest works (including *The Thinker*, *Balzac*, the *Burghers of Calais*, and the *Gates of Hell*) and ideal for artistic reflection.

Left Bank

Opposite Notre-Dame, on the left bank of the Seine, is the Latin Quarter. (For more about this neighborhood, see my Historic Paris Walk, earlier.)

▲▲CLUNY MUSEUM (MUSEE NATIONAL DU MOYEN AGE)

The Cluny is a treasure trove of Middle Ages (Moyen Age) art. Located on the site of a Roman bathhouse, it offers close-up looks at stained glass, Notre-Dame carvings, fine goldsmithing and jewelry, and rooms of tapestries. The highlights are several original stained-glass windows from Sainte-Chapelle and the exquisite series of six Lady and the Unicorn tapestries: A delicate, as-medieval-as-can-be noble lady introduces a delighted unicorn to the senses of taste, hearing, sight, smell, and touch.

Cost and Hours: €8, includes audioguide, free on first Sun of month, covered by Museum Pass; Wed-Mon 9:15-17:45, closed Tue, ticket office closes at 17:15; near corner of Boulevards St. Michel and St. Germain at 6 Place Paul Painlevé; Mo: Cluny-La Sorbonne, St. Michel, or

Grands Cafés Near St. Germain-des-Prés

On the Left Bank, where Boulevard St. Germain meets Rue Bonaparte, you'll find several Parisian cafés that seem like monuments to another time (all open daily, Mo: St. Germain-des-Prés; for locations, see map on page 190). Before visiting, review my tips on cafés and brasseries on page 127.

$$$ Les Deux Magots offers prime outdoor seating and a warm interior. Once a favorite of Ernest Hemingway (in *The Sun Also Rises*, Jake met Brett here) and Jean-Paul Sartre (he and Simone de Beauvoir met here), today the café is filled with international tourists (6 Place St. Germain des Prés).

$$$ Le Café de Flore, next door, feels more literary—wear your black turtleneck. Pablo Picasso was a regular (172 Boulevard St. Germain).

$ Café Bonaparte, just a block away, offers scenic outdoor seating and the same delightful view for a bit less (42 Rue Bonaparte).

$$ Café le Procope, Paris' first and most famous (1686), was a *café célèbre*, drawing notables such as Voltaire, Rousseau, Honoré de Balzac, Emile Zola, Maximilien de Robespierre, Victor Hugo, and two Americans, Benjamin Franklin and Thomas Jefferson (13 Rue de l'Ancienne Comédie).

Odéon; tel. 01 53 73 78 16, www.musee-moyenage.fr.

ST. GERMAIN-DES-PRES

A church was first built on this site in A.D. 558. The church you see today was constructed in 1163 and is all that's left of a once sprawling and influential monastery. The colorful interior reminds us that medieval churches were originally painted in bright colors. The surrounding area hops at night with venerable cafés, fire-eaters, mimes, and scads of artists.

Cost and Hours: Free, daily 8:00-20:00, Mo: St. Germain-des-Prés.

▲LUXEMBOURG GARDEN (JARDIN DU LUXEMBOURG)

This lovely 60-acre garden is an Impressionist painting brought to life. Slip into a green chair pondside, enjoy the radiant flower beds, go jogging, play tennis or basketball, sail a toy sailboat, or take in a chess game or puppet show. Some of the park's prettiest (and quietest) sections lie around its perimeter.

Cost and Hours: Free, daily dawn until dusk, Mo: Odéon, Train-B: Luxembourg.

Cluny Museum's Lady and the Unicorn tapestry

Luxembourg Garden

Champs-Elysées and Nearby

▲▲▲CHAMPS-ELYSEES

This famous boulevard is Paris' backbone, with its greatest concentration of traffic. From the Arc de Triomphe down Avenue des Champs-Elysées, all of France seems to converge on Place de la Concorde, the city's largest square. And though the Champs-Elysées has become as international as it is Parisian, a walk down the two-mile boulevard is still a must.

In 1667, Louis XIV opened the first section of the street, and it soon became the place to cruise in your carriage. (It still is today.) By the 1920s, this boulevard was pure elegance—fancy residences, rich hotels, and cafés. Today it's home to big business, celebrity cafés, glitzy nightclubs, high-fashion shopping, and international people-watching. People gather here to

Looking down the Champs-Elysées from the Arc de Triomphe

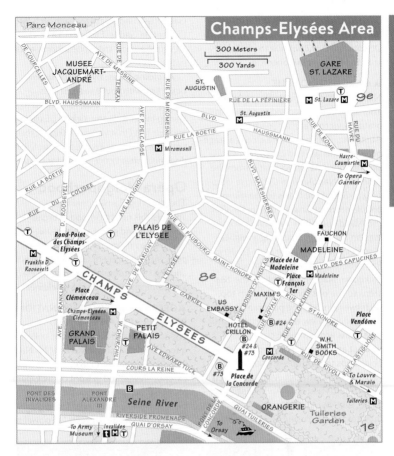

Champs-Elysées Area

300 Meters

300 Yards

Parc Monceau

MUSEE JACQUEMART-ANDRÉ

GARE ST. LAZARE

St. Lazare

9e

BLVD. HAUSSMANN

ST. AUGUSTIN

RUE DE LA PÉPINIÈRE

St. Augustin

Miromesnil

BLVD.

HAUSSMANN

RUE LA BOÉTIE

Havre-Caumartin

To Opera Garnier

Rond-Point des Champs-Elysées

PALAIS DE L'ELYSEE

FAUCHON

MADELEINE

Franklin D. Roosevelt

Place de la Madeleine

Place François 1er

Madeleine

BLVD. DES CAPUCINES

Place Clémenceau

CHAMPS

8e

MAXIM'S

US EMBASSY

Place Vendôme

Champs-Elysées Clémenceau

ELYSEES

#24

GRAND PALAIS

PETIT PALAIS

HOTEL CRILLON

#24 & #75

W.H. SMITH BOOKS

AVE. EDWARD TUCK

Concorde

To Louvre & Marais

COURS LA REINE

#75

Place de la Concorde

PONT DES INVALIDES

PONT ALEXANDRE III

Seine River

RIVERSIDE PROMENADE

ORANGERIE

Tuileries Garden

Tuileries

1e

To Army Museum

Invalides

QUAI D'ORSAY

To Orsay

celebrate Bastille Day (July 14), World Cup triumphs, and the finale of the Tour de France.

⊙ SELF-GUIDED WALK

Start at the Arc de Triomphe (Mo: Charles de Gaulle-Etoile; if you're planning to tour the Arc, do it before starting this walk) and head downhill on the left-hand side. The arrival of McDonald's (at #140) was an unthinkable horror, but these days dining chez MacDo has become typically Parisian, and this branch is the most profitable McDonald's in the world.

Fancy car showrooms abound, including Peugeot (#136) and Renault (#53). The Lido (#116) is Paris' largest burlesque-type cabaret (and a multiplex cinema). Across the boulevard is the flagship store of leather-bag makers Louis Vuitton (#101). Fouquet's café (#99) is a popular spot for French celebrities, especially movie stars—note the names in the sidewalk in front. Enter if you dare for an €8 espresso. Ladurée café (#75) is also classy but has a welcoming and affordable takeout bakery.

Continuing on, you pass international-brand stores, such as Sephora, Virgin, Disney, and the Gap. Car buffs should park themselves at the sleek café in the Renault store (#53, open until midnight). The car exhibits change regularly, but the great tables looking down onto the Champs-Elysées are permanent.

You can end your walk at the round Rond Point intersection (Mo: Franklin D. Roosevelt) or continue to obelisk-studded Place de la Concorde.

▲▲ARC DE TRIOMPHE

Napoleon had the magnificent Arc de Triomphe commissioned to commemorate his victory at the 1805 battle of Austerlitz. The foot of the arch is a stage on which the last two centuries of Parisian history have played out—from the funeral of Napoleon to the goose-stepping arrival of the Nazis to the triumphant return of Charles de Gaulle after the Allied liberation. Examine the carvings on the pillars, featuring a mighty Napoleon and excitable Lady Liberty. Pay your respects at the Tomb of the Unknown Soldier. Then climb the 284 steps to the observation deck up top, with sweeping skyline panoramas and a mesmerizing view down onto the traffic that swirls around the arch.

Cost and Hours: Free and always viewable; steps to rooftop—€9.50, free on first Sun of month Oct-March, covered by Museum Pass; daily April-Sept 10:00-23:00, Oct-March until 22:30, last entry 45 minutes before closing; Place Charles de Gaulle, use underpass to reach arch, Mo: Charles de Gaulle-Etoile, tel. 01 55 37 73 77, http://arc-de-triomphe.monuments-nationaux.fr.

Avoiding Lines: Bypass the *slooow* ticket line with your Museum Pass (though if you have kids, you'll need to line up to get their free tickets). Expect another line (that you can't skip) at the entrance to the stairway up the arch. Lines disappear after 17:00—come for sunset.

Opéra Neighborhood

The glittering Garnier opera house anchors this neighborhood of broad boulevards and grand architecture. This area is also nirvana for high-end shoppers, with the opulent Galeries Lafayette and the sumptuous shops that line Place Vendôme and Place de la Madeleine.

▲OPERA GARNIER (OPERA NATIONAL DE PARIS—PALAIS GARNIER)

A gleaming grand theater of the belle époque, the Palais Garnier was built for Napoleon III and finished in 1875. For the best exterior view, stand in front of the Opéra Métro stop. From Avenue de l'Opéra, once lined with Paris' most fashionable haunts, the facade suggests "all power to

Arc de Triomphe

the wealthy." And a shimmering Apollo, holding his lyre high above the building, seems to declare, "This is a temple of the highest arts."

But the elitism of this place prompted former President François Mitterrand to have an opera house built for the people in the 1980s, situated symbolically on Place de la Bastille, where the French Revolution started in 1789. The smaller Opéra Garnier is now home to ballet, some opera, and other performances.

You have two choices for seeing the interior: Take a guided or self-guided tour of the public areas, or buy tickets to a performance. If you opt to tour the building, note that the auditorium is sometimes off-limits due to performances and rehearsals (you'll get your best look at the auditorium on the fully guided tour).

Cost and Hours: €11, not covered by Museum Pass, generally daily 10:00-16:30, mid-July-Aug until 18:00, 8 Rue Scribe, Mo: Opéra, Train-A: Auber, www.visitepalaisgarnier.fr.

Tours: The €5 audioguide gives a good self-guided tour. Guided tours in English run at 11:30 and 14:30 July-Aug daily, Sept-Jun Wed and Sat-Sun—call to confirm

schedule (€14.50, includes entry, 1.5 hours, tel. 01 40 01 17 89 or 08 25 05 44 05).

Visiting the Theater: You'll enter around the left side of the building (as you face the front), across from American Express on Rue Scribe. As you pass the bust of the architect, Monsieur Garnier, pay your respects and check out the bronze floor plan of the complex etched below. Notice how little space is given to seating.

Rick's Tip: *Across the street from the Opéra Garnier is the illustrious* **Café de la Paix** *(on Place de l'Opéra). It's been a meeting spot for the local glitterati for generations. If you can afford the coffee, this spot offers a delightful break.*

The building is huge—though the auditorium itself seats only 2,000. The building's massive foundations straddle an underground lake (inspiring the mysterious world of the *Phantom of the Opera*). The real show was before and after the performance, when the elite of Paris—out to see and be seen—strutted their elegant stuff in the extravagant lobbies. Think of the grand marble stairway as a theater. The upstairs foyer feels more like

Opéra Garnier

Baron Georges-Eugène Haussmann

The elegantly uniform streets that make Paris so Parisian are the work of Baron Haussmann (1809-1891), who oversaw the modernization of the city in the mid-19th century. He cleared out the cramped, higgledy-piggledy, unhygienic medieval cityscape and replaced it with broad, straight boulevards lined with stately buildings and linked by modern train stations.

The quintessential view of Haussmann's work is from the pedestrian island immediately in front of the Opéra Garnier. You're surrounded by Paris, circa 1870, when it was the capital of the world. Spin slowly and find the Louvre in one direction and Place Vendôme in another. Haussmann's uniform, cohesive buildings are all five stories tall, with angled, black slate roofs and formal facades. The balconies on the second and fifth floors match those of their neighbors, creating strong lines of perspective as the buildings stretch down the boulevard. Haussmann was so intent on putting the architecture at center stage that he insisted that no trees be planted along these streets.

Chagall ceiling at the Opéra Garnier

a ballroom at Versailles. As you wander the halls and gawk at the decor, imagine this place in its heyday, filled with beautiful people sharing gossip at the Salon du Glacier.

From the uppermost floor open to the public, visitors can peek from two boxes into the actual red-velvet performance hall. Admire Marc Chagall's colorful ceiling (1964), playfully dancing around the eight-ton chandelier. The box seats next to the stage are the most expensive in the house, with an obstructed view of the stage...but just right if you're here only to be seen. Snoop about to find the side library, information panels describing costume management, and a portrait gallery of famous ballerinas and guests.

Marais Neighborhood and Nearby

Naturally, when in Paris you want to see the big sights—but to experience the city, you also need to visit a vital neighborhood. The Marais fits the bill, with hip boutiques, busy cafés, trendy art galleries, narrow streets, leafy squares, Jewish bakeries, aristocratic châteaux, nightlife, and real Parisians. It's the perfect setting to appreciate the flair of this great city.

Place des Vosges and West
▲PLACE DES VOSGES

Henry IV (r. 1589-1610) built this centerpiece of the Marais in 1605 and called it "Place Royale." As he'd hoped, it turned the Marais into Paris' most exclusive neighborhood. Walk to the center, where Louis XIII, on horseback, gestures, "Look at this wonderful square my dad built." He's surrounded by locals enjoying their community park. You'll see children frolicking in the sandbox, lovers warming benches, and pigeons guarding their fountains while trees shade this escape from the glare of the big city.

Study the architecture: nine pavilions (houses) per side. The two highest—at the front and back—were for the king and queen (but were never used). Warm red brickwork—some real, some fake—is topped with sloped slate roofs, chimneys, and another quaint relic of a bygone era: TV antennas.

The insightful writer Victor Hugo lived at #6 from 1832 to 1848. (It's at the southeast corner of the square, marked by the French flag.) This was when he wrote much of his most important work, including his biggest hit, *Les Misérables*. Inside **Victor Hugo's House,** you'll wander through eight plush rooms, enjoy a fine view of the square, and find good WCs (€8, Tue-Sun 10:00-18:00, closed Mon, http://maisonsvictorhugo.paris.fr).

Sample the upscale art galleries ringing the square (the best ones are behind Louis). Consider a daring new piece for that blank wall at home. Or consider a pleasant break at one of the eateries on the square.

▲▲PICASSO MUSEUM (MUSEE PICASSO)

Whatever you think about Picasso the man, as an artist he was unmatched in the 20th century for his daring and productivity. The Picasso Museum has the world's largest collection of his work—some 400 paintings, sculptures, sketches, and ceramics—spread across this mansion in the Marais. A visit here walks you through the full range of this complex man's life and art.

Cost and Hours: €11, covered by Museum Pass, free on first Sun of month; open Tue–Fri 10:30–18:00, Sat–Sun 9:30–18:00, closed Mon, last entry 45 minutes before closing; videoguide-€4, timed-entry tickets available via museum website; 5 Rue de Thorigny, Mo: St-Paul or Chemin Vert, tel. 01 42 71 25 21, www. musee-picasso.fr.

⊘ SELF-GUIDED TOUR

The core of the museum is organized chronologically. Use this overview to trace Picasso's life and some of the themes in his work.

Early Years and Early Cubism (Floor 0): In 1900, Picasso set out from Barcelona to make his mark in Paris. The brash Spaniard quickly became a poor, homesick foreigner, absorbing the styles of many painters while searching for his own artist's voice. When his best friend committed suicide (*Death of Casagemas*, 1901), Picasso plunged into a "Blue Period," painting emaciated beggars,

Relaxing at the Place des Vosges

Marais Neighborhood & Nearby

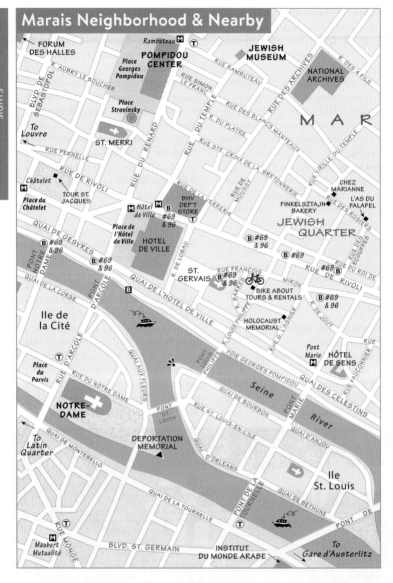

FORUM
DES HALLES

Rambuteau Ⓜ Ⓣ

POMPIDOU
CENTER

Place
Georges
Pompidou

JEWISH
MUSEUM

RUE RAMBUTEAU

R. DES 4 FILS

RUE DES ARCHIVES

NATIONAL
ARCHIVES

RUE SIMON
LE FRANC

BLVD. DE SEBASTOPOL

R. AUBRY LE BOUCHER

Place
Stravinsky

RUE DES BLANCS MANTEAUX

RUE DU TEMPLE

R. DU PLATRE

M A R

To
Louvre

ST. MERRI

RUE DU RENARD

RUE STE. CROIX DE LA BRETONNERIE

RUE PERNELLE

RUE VIEILLE DU TEMPLE

Châtelet

RUE DE RIVOLI

RUE DE LA VERRERIE

RUE DE MOUSSY

CHEZ
MARIANNE

L'AS DU
FALAFEL

TOUR ST.
JACQUES

RUE DE LA VERRERIE

FINKELSZTAJN
BAKERY

Ⓜ
Place du
Châtelet

Hôtel
de Ville Ⓜ

BHV
DEP'T
STORE

RUE DES ROSIERS

JEWISH
QUARTER

#69
& 96

Ⓣ

Ⓑ #69
& 96

Place de
l'Hôtel
de Ville

HOTEL
DE VILLE

R. DE LOBAU

Ⓑ #69
& 96

Ⓑ #69

RUE DE RIVOLI

RUE DU ROI DE

RUE DES ECOUFFES

QUAI DE GESVRES

Ⓑ #69
& 96

ST.
GERVAIS

RUE FRANÇOIS

Ⓑ #69
& 96

MIRON

Ⓑ #69

PONT NOTRE DAME

Ⓑ #69
& 96

RUE DE JOUY

QUAI DE LA CORSE

PONT D'ARCOLE

Ⓑ

QUAI DE L'HÔTEL DE VILLE

RUE DES BARRES

BIKE ABOUT
TOURS & RENTALS

RUE R. LASNIER

R. DE JOUY

Ile de
la Cité

RUE LOUIS PHILIPPE

HOLOCAUST
MEMORIAL

Pont
Marie

HÔTEL
DE SENS

RUE

Place
du
Parvis

Ⓣ RUE D'ARCOLE

RUE DU NOTRE DAME

RUE AUX FLEURS

PONT LOUIS PHILIPPE

VOIE GEORGES POMPIDOU

QUAI DES CELESTINS

RUE FAUCONNIER

NOTRE-
DAME

Seine

QUAI DE BOURBON

PONT MARIE

River

To
Latin
Quarter

QUAI DE MONTEBELLO

DEPORTATION
MEMORIAL

PONT
ST.
LOUIS

RUE ST. LOUIS-EN-L'ILE

QUAI D'ORLEANS

QUAI D'ANJOU

Ile
St. Louis

QUAI DE LA TOURNELLE

PONT DE LA TOURNELLE

QUAI DE BETHUNE

PONT DE

Ⓣ
Maubert
Mutualité

RUE MONGE

BLVD. ST. GERMAIN

INSTITUT
DU MONDE ARABE

To
Gare d'Austerlitz

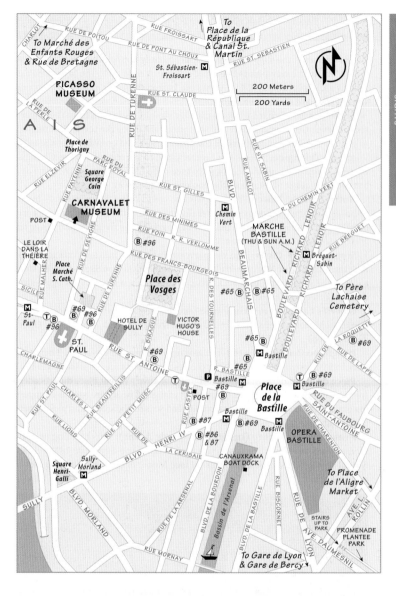

To Place de la
République
& Canal St.
Martin

RUE DE POITOU

RUE FROISSART

CHARLOT

RUE DE PONT AU CHOUX

To Marché des
Enfants Rouges
& Rue de Bretagne

St. Sébastien-
Froissart

RUE ST. SEBASTIEN

St. Sébastien-Froissart

PICASSO
MUSEUM

RUE ST. CLAUDE

200 Meters

200 Yards

RUE DE
LA PERLE

RUE DE TURENNE

A I S

Place de
Thorigny

RUE DU
PARC ROYAL

RUE ELZEVIR

Square
George
Cain

RUE PAYENNE

RUE ST. GILLES

BLVD.

RUE ST. SABIN

R. DU CHEMIN VERT

RICHARD LENOIR

CARNAVALET
MUSEUM

RUE DE SEVIGNE

RUE DES MINIMES

RUE AMELOT

RUE BRÉGUET

POST

RUE FOIN

R. R. VERLOMME

Chemin
Vert

MARCHE
BASTILLE
(THU & SUN A.M.)

RICHARD LENOIR

LE LOIR
DANS LA
THÉIÈRE

RUE MALHER

#96

RUE DES FRANCS-BOURGEOIS

Bréguet-
Sabin

SICILE

Place
Marché
S. Cath.

RUE DE TURENNE

Place des
Vosges

R. DES TOURNELLES

BEAUMARCHAIS

#65 #65

To Père
Lachaise
Cemetery

M
St-
Paul

T B
#96

#69
#96

HOTEL DE
SULLY

R. BIRAGUE

VICTOR
HUGO'S
HOUSE

#65

LA ROQUETTE

#69

ST.
PAUL

RUE ST. ANTOINE

R. #69

Bastille

RUE DE

RUE DE LAPPE

CHARLEMAGNE

RUE ST. PAUL

CHARLES V

RUE BEAUTREILLIS

RUE DU PETIT MUSC

R. #69

R. BASTILLE
#65
Bastille
#69

P
POST

T B #69

Bastille

RUE DU FAUBOURG
SAINT-ANTOINE

RUE LIONS

RUE DE

RUE CASTEX

Bastille

#87

Place
de la
Bastille

Bastille

RUE DE CHARENTON

#86
& 87

B #69

OPERA
BASTILLE

Square
Henri-
Galli

Sully-
Morland

BLVD. HENRI IV

LA CERISAIE

CANAUXRAMA
BOAT DOCK

RUE BISCORNET

To Place
de l'Aligre
Market

SULLY

BLVD. MORLAND

RUE DE L'ARSENAL

BLVD. DE LA BOURDON

Bassin de l'Arsenal

BLVD. DE LA BASTILLE

RUE DE LYON

AVE. DAUMESNIL

STAIRS
UP TO
PARK

AVE. L.
ROLLIN

PROMENADE
PLANTEE
PARK

RUE MORNAY

To Gare de Lyon
& Gare de Bercy

Best Views over the City of Light

The brilliance of the City of Light can only be fully appreciated by rising above it all. Many of the viewpoints I've listed are free or covered by the Museum Pass; otherwise, expect to pay €8-15. Views are best in the early morning or around sunset. Here are some prime locations:

Eiffel Tower: It's hard to find a grander view of Paris than from the tower's second level. Go around sunset and stay after dark to see the tower illuminated; or go in the early morning to avoid the midday haze and crowds (see page 167).

Arc de Triomphe: This is the perfect place to see the glamorous Champs-Elysées, if you don't mind the 284 steps (see page 176). It's great during the day, but even greater at night, when the boulevard glitters.

Notre-Dame's Tower: This viewpoint couldn't be more central—but it requires climbing 400 steps and is usually crowded with long lines (arrive early or late). You'll get an unobstructed view of gargoyles, the river, the Latin Quarter, and the Ile de la Cité (see page 141).

Steps of Sacré-Cœur: Join the party on Paris' only hilltop. Walk uphill, or take the funicular or Montmartrobus, then hunker down on Sacré-Cœur's steps to enjoy the sunset. Stay in Montmartre for dinner, then see the view again after dark (free, see page 186).

Galeries Lafayette or Printemps: Take the escalator to the top floor of either department store (they sit side by side) for a stunning overlook of the old Opéra district (free).

Pompidou Center: Take the escalator up to admire the cityscape. There may be better views over Paris, but this is the best one from a museum (see page 184).

Place du Trocadéro: Start or end your Eiffel Tower visit at Place du Trocadéro for dramatic views of the tower, particularly at night. The square itself is a happening place, with street performers, souvenir vendors, skateboarders, and pickpockets. Gawk with caution.

Arab World Institute (Institut du Monde Arabe): This building near Ile St. Louis has free views from its terrific roof terrace (Tue-Sun 10:00-18:00, closed Mon, 1 Rue des Fossés Saint-Bernard, Place Mohammed V, Mo: Jussieu, www.imarabe.org).

hard-eyed pimps, and himself, bundled up against the cold, with eyes all cried out (*Autoportrait*, 1901).

In 1904, Picasso got a steady girlfriend, and suddenly saw the world through rose-colored glasses (the Rose Period). With his next-door neighbor, Georges Braque, Picasso invented Cubism, a fragmented, "cube"-shaped style. He'd fracture a figure (such as the musician in *Man with a Mandolin*, 1911) into a barely recognizable jumble of facets. Picasso sketched reality from every angle, then pasted it all together, a composite of different views.

Cubist Experiments and *Guernica* (Floor 1): Modern art was being born. The first stage had been so-called Analytic Cubism: breaking the world down into small facets, to "analyze" the subject from every angle. Now it was time to "synthesize" it back together with the real world (Synthetic Cubism). Picasso created "constructions" that were essentially still-life paintings (a 2-D illusion) augmented with glued-on, real-life materials—wood, paper, rope, or chair caning (the real 3-D world). In a few short years, Picasso had turned painting in the direction it would go for the next 50 years.

Meanwhile, Europe was gearing up for war. From Paris, Picasso watched as his homeland of Spain erupted in a brutal civil war (1936-1939). Many canvases from this period are gray and gloomy. The most famous one—*Guernica* (1937)—captured the chaos of a Spanish village caught in an air raid (painted in Paris, but now hanging in Madrid). In 1940, Nazi tanks rolled into Paris. Picasso decided to stay for the duration and live under gray skies and gray uniforms.

The South of France and Last Years (Floor 2): At war's end, Picasso left Paris, finding fun in the sun in the south of France. Sixty-five-year-old Pablo Picasso was reborn, enjoying worldwide fame. Picasso's Riviera works set the tone for the rest of his life—sunny, light-hearted, childlike, experimenting in new media, and using motifs of the sea, Greek mythology (fauns, centaurs), and animals (birds, goats, and pregnant baboons). Picasso was fertile to the end, still painting with bright thick colors at age 91.

RUE DES ROSIERS: PARIS' JEWISH QUARTER

The intersection of Rue des Rosiers and Rue des Ecouffes marks the heart of the small neighborhood that Jews call the Pletzl ("little square"). Once the largest in Western Europe, Paris' Jewish Quarter is much smaller today but still colorful. Rue des Rosiers (named for the roses that once covered the city wall) has become the epicenter of Marais hipness and fashion. But it still features kosher (*cascher*) restaurants and fast-food places selling falafel, *shawarma, kefta,* and other Mediterranean dishes. Bakeries specialize in braided challah, bagels, and strudels. Delis offer gefilte fish, piroshkis, and blintzes.

Picasso Museum

The Jewish Quarter's Rue des Rosiers

Art galleries exhibit Jewish-themed works, and store windows post flyers for community events.

▲▲POMPIDOU CENTER (CENTRE POMPIDOU)

One of Europe's greatest collections of far-out modern art is housed in the Musée National d'Art Moderne, on the fourth and fifth floors of this colorful exoskeletal building. Created ahead of its time, the modern and contemporary art in this collection is still waiting for the world to catch up.

The Pompidou Center and the square that fronts it are lively, with lots of people, street theater, and activity inside and out—a perpetual street fair. Kids of any age enjoy the fun, colorful fountain (called *Homage to Stravinsky*) next to the Pompidou Center.

Cost and Hours: €14, free on first Sun of month, Museum Pass covers permanent collection and escalators to sixth-floor panoramic views (but not special exhibits); Wed-Mon 11:00-21:00, closed Tue, ticket counters close at 20:00, café and pricey view restaurant, Mo: Rambuteau or Hôtel de Ville, tel. 01 44 78 12 33, www.centrepompidou.fr.

Visiting the Museum: Buy your ticket on the ground floor, then ride up the escalator (or run up the down escalator to get in the proper mood). When you see the view, your opinion of the Pompidou's exterior should improve a good 15 percent.

The Pompidou's "permanent" collection...isn't. It changes so often that a painting-by-painting tour is impossible. Generally, art from 1905 to 1980 is on the fifth floor, while the fourth floor contains more recent art. Use the museum's floor plans (posted on the wall) to find select artists. See the classics—Picasso, Matisse, Chagall, Braque, Dalí, Warhol—and leave time to browse the work of more recent artists.

As you tour, remember that most of the artists, including foreigners, spent their

Ⓐ *Pompidou Center*

Ⓑ *Otto Dix,* Portrait of Journalist Sylvia von Harden

Ⓒ *Joan Miró,* Le Catalan

formative years in Paris. In the 1910s, funky Montmartre was the mecca of Modernism—the era of Picasso, Braque, and Matisse. In the 1920s the center shifted to the grand cafés of Montparnasse, where painters mingled with American expats such as Ernest Hemingway and Gertrude Stein. During World War II, it was Jean-Paul Sartre's Existentialist scene around St. Germain-des-Prés. After World War II, the global art focus moved to New York, but by the late 20th century, Paris had reemerged as a cultural touchstone for the world of Modern art.

Rick's Tip: *The sixth floor of the* **Pompidou** *has* **stunning views of the Paris cityscape.** *Your Pompidou ticket or Museum Pass gets you there, or you can buy the €3 View of Paris ticket (doesn't include museum entry).*

East of Place des Vosges

PROMENADE PLANTEE PARK (VIADUC DES ARTS)

This elevated viaduct, once used for train tracks, is now a two-mile-long, narrow garden walk and a pleasing place for a refreshing stroll or run. Botanists appreciate the well-maintained and varying vegetation.

Cost and Hours: Free, opens Mon-Fri at 8:00, Sat-Sun at 9:00, closes at sunset (17:30 in winter, 20:30 in summer). It runs from Place de la Bastille (Mo: Bastille) along Avenue Daumesnil to St. Mandé (Mo: Michel Bizot) or Porte Dorée, passing within a block of Gare de Lyon.

Getting There: To get to the park from Place de la Bastille (exit the Métro following *Sortie Rue de Lyon* signs), walk a looooong block down Rue de Lyon, hugging the Opéra on your left. Find the low-key entry and steps up the red-brick wall a block after the Opéra.

▲PERE LACHAISE CEMETERY (CIMETIERE DU PERE LACHAISE)

Lined with the tombstones of many of the city's most illustrious dead, this is your best one-stop look at Paris' fascinating, permanent residents.

Cost and Hours: Free, Mon-Fri 8:00-18:00, Sat 8:30-18:00, Sun 9:00-18:00, until 17:30 in winter; two blocks from Mo: Gambetta (do not go to Mo: Père Lachaise) and two blocks from bus #69's last stop; tel. 01 55 25 82 10, searchable map available at unofficial website: www.pere-lachaise.com.

Visiting the Cemetery: Enclosed by a massive wall and lined with 5,000 trees, the peaceful, car-free lanes and dirt paths of Père Lachaise cemetery encourage parklike meandering. Named for Father (*Père*) La Chaise, whose job was listening to Louis XIV's sins, the cemetery is relatively new, having opened in 1804 to accommodate Paris' expansion. Today, this city of the dead (pop. 70,000) still accepts new residents, but real estate prices are sky high (a 21-square-foot plot costs more than €11,000).

The 100-acre cemetery is big and confusing, with thousands of graves and tombs crammed every which way, and only a few pedestrian pathways to help you navigate. The maps available from street vendors can help guide your way. I recommend taking a one-way tour between two convenient Métro/bus stops (Gambetta and Père Lachaise),

Père Lachaise Cemetery

connecting a handful of graves from some of this necropolis' best-known residents, including Frédéric Chopin, Molière, Edith Piaf, Oscar Wilde, Gertrude Stein, Jim Morrison, Héloïse and Abélard, and more.

Rick's Tip: *To* **beat the crowds at Montmartre,** *come on a weekday or early on weekend mornings.*

Montmartre

Paris' highest hill, topped by Sacré-Cœur Basilica, is best known as the home of cabaret nightlife and bohemian artists. Struggling painters, poets, dreamers, and drunkards came here for cheap rent, untaxed booze, rustic landscapes, and the high-kicking cancan girls at the Moulin Rouge. These days, the hill is equal parts charm and kitsch—still vaguely village-like but mobbed with tourists and pickpockets on sunny weekends. Come for a bit of history, a getaway from Paris' noisy boulevards, and the view.

▲▲SACRE-CŒUR

You'll spot Sacré-Cœur, the Byzantine-looking white basilica atop Montmartre, from most viewpoints in Paris. Though only 130 years old, it's impressive and iconic, with a climbable dome.

Cost and Hours: Church—free, daily 6:00-22:30; dome—€6, not covered by Museum Pass, daily May-Sept 9:30-19:00, Oct-April 9:30-17:00; tel. 01 53 41 89 00, www.sacre-coeur-montmartre.com.

Getting There: For the location of the church, see the map on page 133. You can take the Métro to the Anvers stop (to avoid the stairs up to Sacré-Cœur, buy one more Métro ticket and ride up on the funicular). Alternatively, from Place Pigalle, you can take the "Montmartrobus," a city bus that drops you right by Sacré-Cœur (Funiculaire stop, costs one Métro ticket, 4/hour). A taxi from the Seine or the Bastille saves time and avoids sweat (about €15, €20 at night).

Visiting the Church: The Sacré-Cœur (Sacred Heart) Basilica's exterior, with its onion domes and bleached-bone pallor, looks ancient, but was finished only a century ago by Parisians humiliated by German invaders. Otto von Bismarck's Prussian army laid siege to Paris for more than four months in 1870. Things got so bad for residents that urban hunting for dinner (to cook up dogs, cats, and finally rats) became accepted behavior. Convinced they were being punished for the country's liberal sins, France's Catholics raised money to build the church as a "praise the Lord anyway" gesture.

The five-domed, Roman-Byzantine-looking basilica took 44 years to build (1875-1919). It stands on a foundation of 83 pillars sunk 130 feet deep, necessary because the ground beneath was honeycombed with gypsum mines. The exterior is laced with gypsum, which whitens with age.

Take a clockwise spin around the crowded interior to see impressive mosaics, a statue of St. Thérèse, a scale model of the church, and three stained-glass

Sacré-Cœur

windows dedicated to Joan of Arc. Pause near the Stations of the Cross mosaic to give St. Peter's bronze foot a rub. For an unobstructed panoramic view of Paris, climb 260 feet (300 steps) up the tight spiral stairs to the top of the dome.

EXPERIENCES

Seine Cruises

Several companies run boat cruises on the Seine. For the best experience, cruise at twilight or after dark. Another option is a longer dinner cruise, featuring multicourse meals and music (€100 and up, reservations required).

The companies listed below run daily one-hour sightseeing tours year-round (April-Oct 10:00-22:30, 2-3/hour; Nov-March shorter hours). On dinner cruises, proper dress is required—no denim, shorts, or sport shoes.

Bateaux-Mouches, the oldest boat company in Paris, departs from Pont de l'Alma's right bank and has the biggest open-top, double-decker boats (higher up means better views). The boats are often jammed and noisy (€13.50, kids 4-12-€5.50, Train-C: Pont de l'Alma, tel. 01 42 25 96 10, www.bateaux-mouches. fr). Dinner cruises include violin and piano music (jacket and tie required for men).

Bateaux Parisiens has smaller covered boats with handheld audioguides, fewer crowds, and only one deck. The boats leave from right in front of the Eiffel Tower (€14, kids 3-12-€5, tel. 01 76 64 14 45, www.bateauxparisiens.com). Dinner cruises feature a lively atmosphere with a singer, band, and dance floor.

Vedettes du Pont Neuf cruises start and end at Pont Neuf. The boats feature a live guide whose delivery (in English and French) is as stiff as a recorded narration—and as hard to understand, given the quality of their sound system (€14, ask about Rick Steves discount, tip requested, tel. 01 46 33 98 38, www. vedettesdupontneuf.com).

Shopping

Wandering among elegant boutiques provides a break from the heavy halls of the Louvre, and, if you approach it right, a little cultural enlightenment. Even if you don't intend to buy anything, do some window shopping, or as the French call it: *faire du lèche-vitrines* ("window licking").

Before you enter a Parisian store, remember the following points:

In small stores, always say, "*Bonjour, Madame* or *Mademoiselle* or *Monsieur*" when entering and "*Au revoir, Madame* or *Mademoiselle* or *Monsieur*" when leaving.

The customer is not always right. In fact, figure the clerk is doing you a favor by waiting on you.

Except in department stores, it's not normal for the customer to handle clothing. Ask first before you pick up an item: "*Je peux?*" (zhuh puh), meaning, "Can I?" Don't feel obliged to buy. If a shopkeeper offers assistance, just say, "*Je regarde, merci.*"

Saturday afternoons are *très* busy and not for the faint of heart.

Stores are generally closed on Sunday. Exceptions include the Carrousel du Louvre (underground shopping mall at the Louvre with a Printemps department store) and some shops near Sèvres-Babylone, along the Champs-Elysées, and in the Marais (for eclectic, avant-garde boutiques in the Marais neighborhood, peruse the artsy shops between Place des Vosges and the Pompidou Center).

Department Stores (Les Grands Magasins)

Parisian department stores begin with their showy perfume sections, almost always central on the ground floor. Information desks are usually located at the main entrances near the perfume section (with floor plans in English). Stores generally have affordable restaurants (some with view terraces) and a good selection of fairly priced souvenirs and toys. Shop at **Galeries Lafayette** (Mo: Chaussée d'Antin–La Fayette, Havre-Caumartin, or Opéra), **Printemps** (next door to Galeries Lafayette), and **Bon Marché** (Mo: Sèvres-Babylone). Opening hours are customarily Monday through Saturday from 10:00 to 19:00, with some open later on Thursdays. All are jammed on Saturdays and closed on Sundays (except in December, and except for the Printemps store in the Carrousel du Louvre, which is open daily year-round).

Boutique Strolls

Two very different areas to lick some windows are Place de la Madeleine to Place de l'Opéra, and Sèvres-Babylone to St. Sulpice.

⬥ LA MADELEINE TO L'OPERA

The ritzy streets connecting several high-priced squares—Place de la Madeleine, Place de la Concorde, Place Vendôme, and Place de l'Opéra—form a miracle mile of gourmet food shops, glittering jewelry stores, five-star hotels, exclusive clothing boutiques, and people who spend more on clothes in one day than I do all year.

Start at Place de la Madeleine (Mo: Madeleine). In the northeast corner at #24 is the black-and-white awning of **Fauchon**. Founded on this location in 1886, this bastion of over-the-top edibles became famous around the world, catering to the refined tastes of the rich and famous. **Hédiard** (#21, northwest corner of the square) is older than Fauchon, and

Sampling perfume

it's weathered the tourist mobs better. Wafting the aroma of tea and coffee, it showcases handsomely displayed produce and wines. Hédiard's small red containers—of mustards, jams, coffee, candies, and tea—make great souvenirs.

Step inside tiny **La Maison des Truffe** (#19) to get a whiff of the product—truffles, those prized edible mushrooms. Check out the tiny jars in the display case. The venerable **Mariage Frères** (#17) shop demonstrates how good tea can smell and how beautifully it can be displayed. At **Caviar Kaspia** (#16), you can add Iranian caviar, eel, and vodka to your truffle collection.

Continue along, past **Marquise de Sévigné chocolates** (#11) to the intersection with **Boulevard Malesherbes.** When the street officially opened in 1863, it ushered in the Golden Age of this neighborhood. Cross the three crosswalks traversing Boulevard Malesherbes. Straight ahead is **Patrick Roger Chocolates** (#3), famous for its chocolates, and even more so for M. Roger's huge, whimsical, 150-pound chocolate sculptures of animals and fanciful creatures.

Turn right down broad **Rue Royale.** There's Dior, Chanel, and Gucci. At Rue St. Honoré, turn left and cross Rue Royale, pausing in the middle for a great view both ways. Check out **Ladurée** (#16) for an out-of-this-world pastry break in the busy 19th-century tea salon or to just pick up some world-famous macarons. Continue east for three long blocks down **Rue St. Honoré.** The street is a parade of chic boutiques—L'Oréal cosmetics, Jimmy Choo shoes, Valentino...Looking for a €10,000 handbag? This is your spot.

Turn left on Rue de Castiglione to reach **Place Vendôme.** This octagonal square is *très* elegant—enclosed by symmetrical Mansart buildings around a 150-foot column. On the left side is the original Hôtel Ritz, opened in 1898. The square is also known for its upper-crust jewelry and designer stores—Van Cleef & Arpels, Dior,

La Madeleine to L'Opéra Walk

200 Meters
200 Yards

To Musée Jacquemart-André & Parc Monceau

BD. HAUSSMANN   PRINTEMPS   RUE DE PROVENCE

GALERIES LAFAYETTE

Havre Caumartin Ⓜ Ⓣ

RUE DE LA CHAUSSÉE

RUE LA FAYETTE

R. GLUCK

Chaussée d'Antin La Fayette Ⓜ

RUE DES MATHURINS   RUE AUBER

BD. D'ANJOU

BD. MALESHERBES

R. CHAUVEAU LAGARDE

R. DE SURENE

R. PASQUIER

RUE TRONCHET

RUE VIGNON

RUE GODOT DE MAUROY

OPERA GARNIER

RUE SCRIBE

RUE HALÉVY

FRAGONARD PERFUME MUSEUM

CAFE DE LA PAIX   Place de l'Opéra

Place de la Madeleine

LA MADELEINE   Madeleine Ⓜ

RUE DE SEZE

R. DES CAPUCINES

BD. DES Ⓣ   Opéra Ⓜ   Opéra

CAPUCINES

RUE DU 4 SEPT

Quatre Septembre Ⓜ

RUE ST. AUGUSTIN

R. BOISSY D'ANGLAS

R. DE SURENE

RUE ST. FLORENTIN

RUE DUPHOT

RUE CAMBON

RUE DANOU

RUE DE LA PAIX

RUE LE GRAND

AVE. DE L'ANTIN

RUE DE L'OPERA

PASSAGE STE. ANNE

PASSAGE CHOISEUL

HOTEL RITZ

Place Vendôme Ⓣ

RUE DES PETITS CHAMPS

HOTEL CRILLON Ⓜ Concorde

RUE ST.

RUE ST. HONORE

RUE DE LA SOURDIERE

RUE ST. ROCH

Pyramides Ⓜ

RUE ST. ANNE

Place de la Concorde

JEU DE PAUME

RUE DE RIVOLI

RUE DU MARCHE

RUE DES PYRAMIDES

RUE 29 JUILLET

Jardin des Tuileries

Chanel, Cartier, and others (if you have to ask how much...).

Leave Place Vendôme by continuing straight, up **Rue de la Paix**—strolling by still more jewelry, high-priced watches, and crystal—and enter **Place de l'Opéra.** Here you'll find the Opéra Garnier (described on page 176). If you're not shopped out yet, the Galeries Lafayette and Printemps department stores are located a block or two north, up Rue Halévy.

❹ SEVRES-BABYLONE TO ST. SULPICE

This Left Bank shopping stroll lets you sample smart clothing boutiques and clever window displays while enjoying one of Paris' more attractive neighborhoods. Start at the Sèvres-Babylone Métro stop (take the Métro or bus #87). You'll find

the **Bon Marché** (Mo: Sèvres-Babylone), Paris' oldest department store.

From the Bon Marché, follow Rue de Sèvres, where you'll find **La Maison du Chocolat** at #19. Their mouthwatering window display will draw you helplessly inside. The shop sells handmade chocolates in exquisitely wrapped boxes and delicious ice-cream cones in season.

Lick the chocolate off your fingers before entering **Hermès** (a few doors down, at #17), famous for pricey silk scarves. Don't let the doorman intimidate you: Everyone's welcome here. This store, opened in 2011, is housed in the original Art Deco swimming pool of Hôtel Lutetia, built in 1935.

Across the street sits the old-school **Au Sauvignon Café** (open daily, 10 Rue de Sèvres). It's well situated for watching

Sèvres-Babylone to St. Sulpice Walk

1. Bon Marché
2. La Maison du Chocolat & Hermès
3. Au Sauvignon Café
4. Poilâne
5. Comtesse du Barry
6. Théâtre du Vieux-Colombier & Longchamp
7. Victoire
8. Vilebrequin
9. Aubade & Hervé Chapelier
10. Café de la Mairie

smartly coiffed shoppers glide by. Continue a block farther down Rue de Sèvres to Place Michel Debré, a six-way intersection, where a *Centaur* statue stands guard. From here, boutique-lined streets fan out like spokes on a wheel.

Make a short detour up Rue du Cherche-Midi (follow the horse's fanny). This street offers an ever-changing but always chic selection of shoe, purse, and clothing stores. Find Paris' most celebrated bread—beautiful round loaves with designer crust—at the low-key **Poilâne** (#8). Return to the *Centaur* in

Place Michel Debré. Check out the **Comtesse du Barry** pâté store, which sells small gift packs. Then turn right and head down Rue du Vieux Colombier, passing the (#6) **Théâtre du Vieux-Colombier** (1913), one of three key venues for La Comédie Française, a historic state-run troupe. At **Longchamp** (#21), you can hunt for a stylish French handbag in any color, and **Victoire** offers items for the gentleman.

Cross busy Rue de Rennes and continue down Rue du Vieux Colombier. Here you'll find more specialty boutiques.

There's **Vilebrequin** (#5) for men's swimwear, **Aubade** (#4) for lingerie, and **Hervé Chapelier** (#1) for travel totes and handbags. Spill into Place St. Sulpice, with its big, twin-tower church. **Café de la Mairie** is a great spot to sip a *café crème*, admire the lovely square, and consider your next move.

Nightlife

Paris is brilliant after dark. Save energy to experience the City of Light lit. Whether it's a concert at Sainte-Chapelle, a cruise on the Seine, a walk in Montmartre, a hike up the Arc de Triomphe, or a late-night café, you'll see Paris at its best.

Jazz and Blues Clubs

With a lively mix of American, French, and international musicians, Paris has been an internationally acclaimed jazz capital since World War II. You'll pay €12-25 to enter a jazz club (may include one drink; if not, expect to pay €5-10 per drink; beer is cheapest). See *L'Officiel des Spectacles* under "Musique" for listings, or, even better, the *Paris Voice* website. You can also check each club's website (all have English versions), or drop by the clubs to check out the calendars posted on their front doors. Music starts after 21:00 in most clubs. Some offer dinner concerts from about 20:30 on. Here are several good bets:

Caveau de la Huchette fills an ancient Latin Quarter cellar with live jazz and frenzied dancing every night (admission about €13 on weekdays, €15 on weekends, €6-8 drinks, daily 21:30-2:30 in the morning or later, no reservations needed, buy tickets at the door, 5 Rue de la Huchette, Mo: St. Michel, tel. 01 43 26 65 05, www.caveaudelahuchette.fr).

Autour de Midi et Minuit is an Old World bistro that sits at the foot of Montmartre, above a *cave à jazz*. Eat upstairs if you like, then make your way down to the basement to find bubbling jam sessions Tuesday through Thursday and concerts on Friday and Saturday nights (no cover,

€5 minimum drink order Tue-Thu; €18 cover Fri-Sat includes one drink; jam sessions at 21:30, concerts usually at 22:00; no music Sun-Mon; 11 Rue Lepic, Mo: Blanche or Abbesses, tel. 01 55 79 16 48, www.autourdemidi.fr).

For a spot teeming with late-night activity and jazz, go to the two-block-long **Rue des Lombards,** at Boulevard Sébastopol, midway between the river and the Pompidou Center (Mo: Châtelet). **Au Duc des Lombards** is one of the most popular and respected jazz clubs in Paris, with concerts nightly in a plush, 110-seat theater (admission €25-40, €50-80 with dinner, buy online and arrive early for best seats, cheap drinks, shows at 20:00 and 22:00, 42 Rue des Lombards, tel. 01 42 33 22 88, www.ducdeslombards.fr). **Le Sunside,** just a block away, offers two stages: "le Sunset" on the ground floor for contemporary world jazz; and "le Sunside" downstairs for more traditional and acoustic jazz (concerts range from free to €25, check their website; 60 Rue des Lombards, tel. 01 40 26 46 60, www.sunset-sunside.com).

Old-Time Parisian Cabaret

Au Lapin Agile, a historic little cabaret on Montmartre, tries its best to maintain the atmosphere of the heady days when bohemians would gather here to enjoy wine, song, and sexy jokes. Today, you'll mix in with a few locals and many tourists for a drink and as many as 10 different performers—mostly singers with a piano. Though tourists are welcome, there's no accommodation for English speakers (except on their website), so non-French speakers will be lost. The soirée covers traditional French standards, love ballads, sea chanteys, and more (€28, €8 drinks, Tue-Sun 21:00-2:00 in the morning, closed Mon, best to reserve ahead, 22 Rue des Saules, tel. 01 46 06 85 87, www.au-lapin-agile.com).

Classical Concerts

For classical music on any night, consult *L'Officiel des Spectacles* magazine (check "Concerts Classiques" under "Musique" for listings), and look for posters at tourist-oriented churches. From March through November, these churches regularly host concerts: St. Sulpice, St. Germain-des-Prés, La Madeleine, St. Eustache, St. Julien-le-Pauvre, and Sainte-Chapelle.

At **Sainte-Chapelle,** enjoy the pleasure of hearing Mozart, Bach, or Vivaldi, surrounded by 800 years of stained glass. The acoustical quality is surprisingly good. There are usually two concerts per evening, at 19:00 and 20:30; specify which one you want when you buy or reserve your ticket. VIP tickets get you a seat in rows 3-10 (€40), Prestige tickets cover the next 15 rows (€30), and Normal tickets are the last 5 rows (€25). Seats are unassigned within each section, so arrive at least 30 minutes early to get through the security line and snare a good view. It's unheated—bring a sweater.

Book tickets at the box office, by phone, or online. Two different companies present concerts, but the schedule will tell you which one to contact for a particular performance. The small box office (with schedules and tickets) is to the left of the chapel entrance gate (8 Boulevard du Palais, Mo: Cité), or call 01 42 77 65 65 or 06 67 30 65 65 for schedules and reservations. You can leave your message in English—just speak clearly and spell your name. You can check schedules and buy your ticket at www.euromusicproductions.fr (ask about Rick Steves discount on Euromusic events—cash only at box office close to concert time).

Philharmonie de Paris, a dazzling, 2,400-seat concert hall situated in the Parc de la Villette complex, hosts world-class artists, from legends of rock and roll to string quartets to international opera stars (221 Avenue Jean-Jaurès, Mo: Porte de Pantin, tel. 01 44 84 44 84, www.philharmoniedeparis.fr).

You can also enjoy live classical **Concerts on the Seine** while cruising past Paris' iconic monuments (€30-40, summer months only, board at Vedettes du Pont Neuf, Square du Vert Galant, tel. 01 42 77 65 65, http://vedettesdupontneuf.com/concerts-en-seine). Also look for concerts in parks, such as the Luxembourg Garden, or even the Galeries Lafayette department store. Many are free *(entrée libre)*, such as the Sunday atelier concert sponsored by the American Church (generally Sept-June at 17:00 but not every week and not in Dec, 65 Quai d'Orsay, Mo: Invalides, Train-C: Pont de l'Alma, tel. 01 40 62 05 00, www.acparis.org). The Army Museum offers inexpensive afternoon and evening classical music concerts year-round (for programs—in French only—see www.musee-armee.fr/programmation).

Paris churches host frequent concerts.

Extend your sightseeing into the night.

Night Walks

Go for one of these ▲ ▲ ▲ evening walks to best appreciate the City of Light. Break for ice cream, pause at a café, and enjoy the sidewalk entertainers as you participate in the post-dinner Parisian parade. Remember to exercise normal big-city caution when exploring Paris at night; avoid poorly lit areas and stick to main thoroughfares.

○ TROCADERO AND EIFFEL TOWER

This stroll delivers one of Paris' most spectacular views at night. Take the Métro to the Trocadéro stop and join the party on Place du Trocadéro for a magnificent view of the glowing Eiffel Tower. It's a festival of hawkers, gawkers, drummers, and entertainers.

Walk down the stairs, passing the fountains and rollerbladers, then cross the river to the base of the tower, well worth the effort even if you don't go up. From the Eiffel Tower you can stroll through the Champ de Mars park past tourists and romantic couples, and take the Métro home (Ecole Militaire stop, across Avenue de la Motte-Picquet from far southeast corner of park). Or there's a handy suburban train stop (Champ de Mars-Tour Eiffel) two blocks west of the Eiffel Tower on the river.

○ CHAMPS-ELYSEES AND THE ARC DE TRIOMPHE

The Avenue des Champs-Elysées glows after dark. Start at the Arc de Triomphe, then stroll down Paris' lively grand promenade. A right turn on Avenue George V leads to the Bateaux-Mouches river cruises. A movie on the Champs-Elysées is a fun experience (weekly listings in *L'Officiel des Spectacles* under "Cinéma"), and a drink or snack at Renault's futuristic car café is a kick (at #53).

EATING

Entire books (and lives) are dedicated to eating in Paris. Though it lacks a style of its own (only French onion soup is truly Parisian; otherwise, there is no "Parisian cuisine" to speak of), it draws from the best of France.

My recommendations center on the same great neighborhoods as my hotel listings. Serious eaters looking for even more suggestions should consult the always appetizing www.parisbymouth.com, an eating-and-drinking guide.

To save piles of euros, go to a bakery for takeout, or stop at a café for lunch. Cafés and brasseries are happy to serve a *plat du jour* (garnished plate of the day, about €12-20) or a chef-like salad (about

€10-14) day or night. To save even more, consider picnics (tasty takeout dishes available at charcuteries).

Linger longer over dinner—restaurants expect you to enjoy a full meal. Most restaurants I've listed have set-price *menus* between €20 and €38. In most cases, the few extra euros you pay are well spent and open up a variety of better choices. A service charge is included in the prices (so little or no tipping is expected).

Rue Cler Area
Close to the Eiffel Tower
(Mo: Ecole Militaire)

$$$ Le Florimond is fun for a special occasion. The setting is warm and welcoming. Locals come for classic French cuisine at fair prices. Friendly English-speaking Laurent, whose playful ties change daily, gracefully serves one small room of tables and loves to give suggestions. The stuffed cabbage and the *confit de canard* are particularly tasty, and the house wine is excellent (closed Sun and first and third Sat of month, reservations encouraged, 19 Avenue de la Motte-Picquet, tel. 01 45 55 40 38, www.leflorimond.com).

$$$ Bistrot Belhara, named for a legendary 35-foot wave and surfing spot off the Basque coast, is a true French dining experience. Watch as chef Thierry peers from his kitchen window to ensure that all is well. He bases his cuisine on what's in season, but the foie gras and *riz au lait de mémé*—his grandma's rice pudding—are delicious any time of year. If you don't know French, the charming Frédéric

will translate—and help you choose the perfect wine (closed Sun-Mon, reservations smart, a block off Rue Cler at 23 Rue Duvivier, tel. 01 45 51 41 77, www.bistrotbelhara.com).

$$$ La Terrasse du 7ème is a sprawling, happening café with grand outdoor seating and a living-room-like interior with comfy love seats. Located on a corner, it overlooks a busy intersection with a constant parade of people. Chairs are set up facing the street, so a meal here is like dinner theater—and the show is slice-of-life Paris (€20-25 *plats*, good €13 *salade niçoise* or Caesar salad, €8 French onion soup, tasty foie gras, no fixed-price *menu*, daily until at least 24:00, at Ecole Militaire Métro stop, tel. 01 45 55 00 02).

Between Rue de Grenelle and the River
(Mo: Ecole Militaire)

$$$$ L'Ami Jean offers authentic Basque specialties in a snug-but-fun atmosphere with red peppers and Basque stuff hanging from the ceiling. It's not cheap, but the portions are hearty and delicious, and the whole menu changes every two weeks. Parisians detour long distances to savor the gregarious chef's special cuisine and convivial atmosphere. For dinner, arrive by 19:30 or reserve ahead (€20 starters, €35 plats, €78 eight-course dinner menu, a more accessible lunch menu for €35, closed Sun-Mon, 27 Rue Malar, Mo: La Tour-Maubourg, tel. 01 47 05 86 89, www.lamijean.fr).

$$$$ La Fontaine de Mars, a longtime favorite and neighborhood institution, draws Parisians who want to be seen. It's charmingly situated on a tiny, jumbled square with tables jammed together for the serious business of eating. Reserve in advance for a table on the ground floor or on the square, and enjoy the same meal Barack Obama did. Street-level seats come with the best ambience (€20-30 plats du jour, daily, superb foie gras, superb

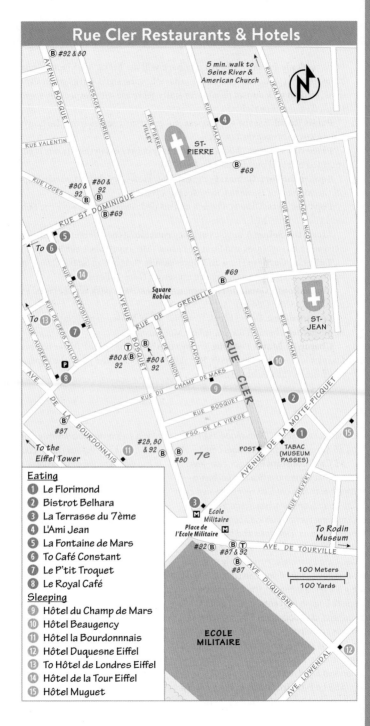

Rue Cler Restaurants & Hotels

5 min. walk to
Seine River &
American Church

AVENUE BOSQUET

PASSAGE LANDRIEU

RUE VALENTIN

RUE PIERRE VILLEY

RUE MALAR

RUE JEAN NICOT

B #92 & 80

B #69

ST-
PIERRE

RUE LOGES

#80 & 92 **B**

#80 & 92 **B**

RUE ST. DOMINIQUE

B #69

RUE CLER

RUE DE L'EXPOSITION

AVENUE BOSQUET

Square
Robiac

RUE DE GRENELLE

RUE VALADON

PSG DE L'UNION

RUE DUVIVIER

RUE PSICHARI

RUE AMELIE

PASSAGE J. NICOT

#69

B #69

ST-
JEAN

To **6**

5

14

To **13**

RUE DE GROS CAILLOU

RUE AUGEREAU

7

P

8

T **B**
#80 & 92

B
#80 & 92

RUE DU CHAMP DE MARS

RUE DE BOSQUET

RUE BOSQUET

PSG. DE LA VIERGE

10

2

9

RUE CLER

AVENUE DE LA MOTTE-PICQUET

1

15

B
#87

AVE. DE LA BOURDONNAIS

To the
Eiffel Tower

11

#28, 80
& 92

B
#80

7e

POST

TABAC
(MUSEUM
PASSES)

RUE CHEVERT

To Rodin
Museum

3

M

Ecole
Militaire

Place de
l'Ecole Militaire

M

#92 **B**

B **T**
#87 & 92

AVE. DE TOURVILLE

B
#87

100 Meters

100 Yards

ECOLE
MILITAIRE

AVE. DUQUESNE

AVE. LOWENDAL

12

Eating
1 Le Florimond
2 Bistrot Belhara
3 La Terrasse du 7ème
4 L'Ami Jean
5 La Fontaine de Mars
6 To Café Constant
7 Le P'tit Troquet
8 Le Royal Café

Sleeping
9 Hôtel du Champ de Mars
10 Hôtel Beaugency
11 Hôtel la Bourdonnnais
12 Hôtel Duquesne Eiffel
13 To Hôtel de Londres Eiffel
14 Hôtel de la Tour Eiffel
15 Hôtel Muguet

Good Picnic Spots

Paris is picnic-friendly. Almost any park will do. Many have benches or grassy areas, though some lawns are off-limits—obey the signs. Parks generally close at dusk, so plan your sunset picnics carefully. Here are some especially scenic areas located near major sights:

Palais Royal: Escape to this peaceful courtyard across from the Louvre (Mo: Palais Royal-Musée du Louvre).

Place des Vosges: This exquisite grassy courtyard in the Marais is surrounded by royal buildings (Mo: Bastille).

Square du Vert-Galant: For great river views, try this little triangular park on the west tip of Ile de la Cité (Mo: Pont Neuf).

Pont des Arts: Dine at a bench on this pedestrian bridge over the Seine, near the Louvre (Mo: Pont Neuf).

Along the Seine: A grassy parkway runs along the left bank of the Seine between Les Invalides and Pont de l'Alma (Mo: Invalides, near Rue Cler).

Tuileries Garden: Have an Impressionist "Luncheon on the Grass" nestled between the Orsay and Orangerie museums (Mo: Tuileries).

Luxembourg Garden: This expansive Left Bank park is the classic Paris picnic spot (Mo: Odéon).

Les Invalides: Take a break from the Army Museum and Napoleon's Tomb in the gardens behind the complex (Mo: Varenne).

Champ de Mars: The long grassy strip below the Eiffel Tower has breathtaking views of this Paris icon. Eat along the sides of the park; the central lawn is off-limits (Mo: Ecole Militaire).

---

desserts, 129 Rue St. Dominique, tel. 01 47 05 46 44, www.fontainedemars.com).

$$ Café Constant is a cool, two-level place that feels more like a small bistro-wine bar than a café. Its owner, famed chef Christian Constant, has made a career of making French cuisine accessible to people like us. Delicious and fairly priced dishes are served in a snug setting to a dedicated clientele. Arrive early to get a table downstairs if you can (upstairs seating is a good fallback); the friendly staff speak English (€11 *entrées*, €16 *plats*, €7 desserts, daily, opens at 7:00 for breakfast, meals served nonstop 12:00-23:00, no reservations taken, corner of Rue Augereau and Rue St. Dominique, next to Hôtel de Londres Eiffel, tel. 01 47 53 73 34).

$$$ Le P'tit Troquet is a petite eatery taking you back to the Paris of the 1920s.

Marie welcomes you warmly, and chef José cooks a delicious three-course €35 *menu* with a range of traditional choices prepared creatively. The homey charm and gourmet quality make this restaurant a favorite of connoisseurs (the same three-course *menu* is available for €25 at lunch, dinner service from 18:30, closed Sun, reservations smart, 28 Rue de l'Exposition, tel. 01 47 05 80 39).

$ Le Royal is a tiny, humble, time-warp place, with prices and decor from another era, that offers the cheapest meals in the neighborhood. Parisians dine here because "it's like eating at home." Gentle Guillaume is a fine host (€6 omelets, €9-12 *plats*, €14 for filling three-course *menu*, daily, 212 Rue de Grenelle, tel. 01 47 53 92 90).

In the Marais
On Romantic Place des Vosges
(Mo: Bastille or St-Paul)

$$$ **La Place Royale** has a fine location on the square with good seating inside or out. Expect a warm welcome and patient waiters, as owner Arnaud prides himself on service. The cuisine is traditional, priced well, and served nonstop all day, and the exceptional wine list is reasonable (try the Sancerre white). The €42 *menu* comes with a kir, three courses, a half-bottle of wine per person, and coffee—plenty of food to allow you to savor the setting (€26-42 *menus*, €17 lunch special, daily, 2 bis Place des Vosges, tel. 01 42 78 58 16).

$$$ **Chez Janou,** a Provençal bistro, tumbles out of its corner building and fills its broad sidewalk with happy eaters. Don't let the trendy and youthful crowd intimidate you: It's relaxed and charming, with helpful and calm service. The curbside tables are inviting, but I'd sit inside (with very tight seating) to immerse myself in the happy commotion. The style is French Mediterranean, with an emphasis on vegetables (daily—book ahead or arrive when it opens, 2 blocks beyond Place des Vosges at 2 Rue Roger Verlomme, tel. 01 42 72 28 41, www.chezjanou.com). They're proud of their 81 varieties of *pastis* (licorice-flavored liqueur, €4.80 each, browse the list above the bar).

$$ **Café des Musées** is an unspoiled bistro serving traditional meaty dishes with little fanfare. They offer a great €17 lunch special. The place is just far enough away to be overlooked by tourists, but it's packed with locals, so arrive early or book ahead (€19-26 *plats*, daily, 49 Rue de Turenne, tel. 01 42 72 96 17, www.lecafedesmusees.fr).

Near the Place de la Bastille
(Mo: Bastille)

$$ **Au Temps des Cerises** serves wines by the glass and meals with a smile. The woody 1950s atmosphere has tight seating and wads of character. Come for a glass of wine at the small zinc bar and say *bonjour* to Ben (try their Viognier), or stay for a tasty dinner (€11 starters, €20 *plats*, good cheap wine, daily, at the corner of Rue du Petit Musc and Rue de la Cerisaie, tel. 01 42 72 08 63).

In the Heart of the Marais
(Mo: St-Paul)

$ **Breizh (Brittany) Café** is worth the walk. It's a simple Breton joint serving organic crêpes and small rolls made for dipping in rich sauces and salted butter. The crêpes are the best in Paris and run the gamut from traditional ham-cheese-and-egg to Asian fusion. They also serve oysters, have a fantastic list of sweet crêpes, and talk about cider like a sommelier would talk about wine. Try a sparkling cider, a Breton cola, or my favorite—*lait ribot*, a buttermilk-like drink (€7-13 dinner crêpes, serves nonstop from 11:30 to late, closed Mon-Tue, reservations recommended for lunch and dinner, 109 Rue du Vieille du Temple, tel. 01 42 72 13 77).

$$ **Chez Marianne** is a Jewish Quarter fixture that blends delicious Jewish cuisine with Parisian *élan* and wonderful atmosphere. Choose from several indoor zones with a cluttered wine shop/deli feeling, or sit outside. You'll select from two dozen *Zakouski* elements to assemble your €14-18 *plat*. For takeout, pay inside first and get a ticket before you order outside. Vegetarians will find great options (€12 falafel sandwich—half that if you order it to go, long hours daily, corner of Rue des Rosiers and Rue des Hospitalières-St-Gervais, tel. 01 42 72 18 86).

$$$ **Au Bourguignon du Marais** is a handsome wine bar/bistro for Burgundy lovers, where excellent Burgundian wines blend with a good selection of well-designed dishes and efficient service. The *œufs en meurette* are mouthwatering, and the *bœuf bourguignon* could feed two (€11-14 starters, €20-30 *plats*, closed Sun-Mon,

pleasing indoor and outdoor seating, 52 Rue François Miron, tel. 01 48 87 15 40).

On Ile St. Louis
(Mo: Pont Marie)
$$$ L'Orangerie is an inviting eatery with soft lighting and comfortable seating where diners speak in hushed voices so that everyone can appreciate the delicious cuisine and tasteful setting. Patient owner Monika speaks fluent English, and her *gratin d'aubergines* is sinfully good (€27-35 *menus*, closed Mon, 28 Rue St. Louis-en-l'Ile, tel. 01 46 33 93 98).

$ Café Med, near the pedestrian bridge to Notre-Dame, is a tiny, cheery *crêperie* with good-value salads, crêpes, and €11 *plats* (€14 and €20 *menus*, daily, 77 Rue St. Louis-en-l'Ile, tel. 01 43 29 73 17). Two similar *crêperies* are just across the street.

On the Left Bank
Near the Odéon Theater
(Mo: Odéon or Cluny-La Sorbonne)
$$$ La Méditerranée is all about seafood from the south served in a pastel and dressy setting...with similar clientele. The scene and the cuisine are sophisticated yet accessible, and the view of the Odéon is *formidable*. The sky-blue tablecloths and the lovingly presented dishes add to the romance (€29 two-course *menus*, €36 three-course *menus*, daily, reservations smart, facing the Odéon at 2 Place de l'Odéon, tel. 01 43 26 02 30, www.la-mediterranee.com).

$ L'Avant Comptoir, a stand-up-only hors d'oeuvres bar serving a delightful array of French-Basque tapas for €3-6 on a sleek zinc counter, was created to give people a sample of the cuisine from the *très* trendy Le Comptoir Restaurant next door, where the reservation wait time is four months. The menu is fun and accessible, it has a good list of wines by the glass, and crêpes are made fresh to go (daily 12:00-23:00, 9 Carrefour de l'Odéon, tel. 01 44 27 07 97).

$ Restaurant Polidor, a bare-bones neighborhood fixture since 1845, is much loved for its unpretentious quality cooking, fun old-Paris atmosphere, and fair value. Step inside to find noisy, happy diners sitting tightly at shared tables, savoring classic bourgeois *plats* from every corner of France (€12-17 *plats*, €25-35 three-course *menus*, daily 12:00-14:30 & 19:00-23:00, cash only, no reservations, 41 Rue Monsieur-le-Prince, tel. 01 43 26 95 34). Next door is the restaurant's wine shop, **Les Caves du Polidor,** where you can sip wine and nibble on cheese-and-meat plates (daily, wine and snacks served 18:00-20:00, opens earlier when weather or owner is feeling sunny).

Between the Panthéon and the Cluny Museum
(Mo: Cluny-La Sorbonne, Train-B: Luxembourg)
$$$ At Les Papilles you just eat what's offered—and you won't complain. It's a foodie's dream come true—one *menu*, no choices, and no regrets. Choose your wine from the shelf or ask for advice from the burly, rugby-playing owner, then relax and let the food arrive. Book this place ahead (€35 four-course *menu*, €20 daily *marmite du marché*—a.k.a. market stew, bigger and cheaper selection at lunch, closed Sun-Mon, 30 Rue Gay Lussac, tel. 01 43 25 20 79, www.lespapillesparis.fr).

$$ Le Pré Verre, a block from the Cluny Museum, is a chic wine bistro—a refreshing alternative in a part of the Latin Quarter mostly known for low-quality, tourist-trapping eateries. Offering imaginative, modern cuisine at fair prices and a good wine list, the place is packed. The astonishing bargain lunch *menu* includes a starter, main course, glass of wine, and coffee for €15. The three-course dinner *menu* at €32 is worth every *centime* (closed Sun-Mon, 8 Rue Thénard, reservations necessary, tel. 01 43 54 59 47, www.lepreverre.com).

The Paris Food Scene

To dig deeper into the food scene in Paris, take a culinary tour, cooking class, or a wine-tasting class.

Food Tours

Rosa Jackson designs personalized **"Edible Paris"** itineraries based on your interests and three-hour "food-guru" tours (unguided from €125, guided from €300, tel. 06 81 67 41 22, www.edible-paris.com).

Paris by Mouth offers more casual and frequent small group tours, with a maximum of seven foodies per group. Tours are organized by location or flavor and led by local food writers (€95/3 hours, includes tastings, www.parisbymouth.com). Sit-down cheese and wine workshops include seven wines and 14 cheeses (€95/3 hours). Given that there are 350 different types of cheese in France, you may need to take this class more than once.

Cooking Classes

At **Les Secrets Gourmands de Noémie,** Noémie shares her culinary secrets in 2.5 hours of hands-on fun in the kitchen. Thursday classes, designed for English speakers, focus on sweets; classes on other days are in French, English, or both, depending on the participants, and tackle savory dishes with the possibility of a market tour (€75-105, 92 Rue Nollet, Mo: La Fourche, tel. 06 64 17 93 32, www.lessecretsgourmandsdenoemie.com).

Cook'n with Class gets rave reviews for its convivial cooking and wine and cheese classes with a maximum of six students; tasting courses offered as well (6 Rue Baudelique, Mo: Jules Joffrin or Simplon, tel. 06 31 73 62 77, www.cooknwithclass.com).

La Cuisine Paris has a variety of classes in English, reasonable prices, and a beautiful space in central Paris (2- or 3-hour classes-€65-95, 80 Quai de l'Hôtel de Ville, tel. 01 40 51 78 18, www.lacuisineparis.com).

Susan Herrmann Loomis, an acclaimed chef and author, offers cooking courses in Paris or at her home in Normandy. Your travel buddy can skip the class but should come for the meal at a reduced "guest eater" price (www.onruetatin.com).

If you're looking for a pricey demonstration course, you'll find it at **Le Cordon Bleu** (tel. 01 53 68 22 50, www.lcbparis.com) or **Ritz Escoffier Ecole de Gastronomie** (tel. 01 43 16 30 50, www.ritzparis.com).

Wine Tasting

Olivier Magny and his team of sommeliers teach fun wine-tasting classes at the **Ô Château** wine school/bar, in the 17th-century residence of Madame de Pompadour, King Louis XV's favorite mistress. Olivier's goal is to "take the snob out of wine." Learn the basics of wine regions, the techniques of tasting, and how to read a label (68 Rue Jean-Jacques Rousseau, Mo: Louvre-Rivoli or Etienne Marcel, tel. 01 44 73 97 80, www.o-chateau.com).

Marais Restaurants & Hotels

Eating
1. La Place Royale
2. Chez Janou
3. Café des Musées
4. Au Temps des Cerises
5. Breizh Café
6. Chez Marianne
7. Au Bourguignon du Marais
8. L'Orangerie
9. Café Med

Sleeping
10. Hôtel le Pavillon de la Reine
11. Hôtel St. Louis Marais
12. Hôtel Jeanne d'Arc
13. Hôtel de la Bretonnerie
14. Hôtel Beaubourg
15. Hôtel du Jeu de Paume
16. Hôtel Saint-Louis

SLEEPING

I've focused my recommendations on three safe, handy, and colorful neighborhoods: the village-like Rue Cler (near the Eiffel Tower); the artsy and trendy Marais (near Place de la Bastille); and the historic island of Ile St. Louis (next door to Notre-Dame).

In the Rue Cler Neighborhood

(7th arrond., Mo: Ecole Militaire, La Tour Maubourg, or Invalides)

Rue Cler is so French that when I step out of my hotel in the morning, I feel like I must have been a poodle in a previous life. This is a neighborhood of wide, tree-lined boulevards, stately apartment buildings, and lots of Americans. Hotels here are a fair value, considering the elegance of the neighborhood. And you're within walking distance of the Eiffel Tower, Army Museum, Seine River, Champs-Elysées, and Orsay and Rodin museums.

In the Heart of Rue Cler

Many of my readers stay in the Rue Cler neighborhood. If you want to disappear into Paris, choose a hotel elsewhere. The following hotels are within Camembert-smelling distance of Rue Cler.

$$ Hôtel du Champ de Mars*** is a top choice, brilliantly located barely 10 steps off Rue Cler. This plush little hotel has a small-town feel from top to bottom. The adorable rooms are snug but lovingly kept by hands-on owners Françoise and Stéphane, and single rooms can work as tiny doubles. It's popular, so book well ahead (Sb-€150, Db-€170, no air-con, 30 yards off Rue Cler at 7 Rue du Champ de Mars, tel. 01 45 51 52 30, www. hotelduchampdemars.com, reservation@ hotelduchampdemars.com).

$$ Hôtel Beaugency***, a fair value on a quieter street a short block off Rue Cler, has 30 smallish rooms and a lobby

that you can stretch out in (Sb-€109-193, Db-€129-213, occasional discounts for Rick Steves readers—ask when you book, breakfast-€9.50, 21 Rue Duvivier, tel. 01 47 05 01 63, www.hotel-beaugency.com, infos@hotel-beaugency.com).

Close to Ecole Militaire Métro

$$$$ Hôtel la Bourdonnais****, near the Champs de Mars park, is upscale and tastefully designed, with comfy public spaces and rooms that blend modern and traditional accents. It's run well with American-style service (Db-€230-350, elaborate breakfast-€17 but free for Rick Steves readers, 113 Avenue de la Bourdonnais, tel. 01 47 05 45 42, www. hotellabourdonnais.fr, labourdonnais@ inwood-hotels.com).

$$$$ Hôtel Duquesne Eiffel***, a few blocks farther from the action, is calm, hospitable, and very comfortable. It features handsome rooms (some with terrific Eiffel Tower views) and a welcoming lobby (Db-€249-300, Tb-€279-339, big, hot breakfast-€13 but free for Rick Steves readers, 23 Avenue Duquesne, tel. 01 44 42 09 09, www.hde.fr, contact@hde.fr).

Closer to Rue St. Dominique

$$$ Hôtel de Londres Eiffel*** is my closest listing to the Eiffel Tower and the Champ de Mars park. Here you get immaculate, warmly decorated rooms (several are connecting, for families), snazzy public spaces, and a service-oriented staff. Some rooms are pretty small—request a bigger room. It's less convenient to the Métro (10-minute walk), but very handy to buses #69, #80, #87, and #92, and to Train-C: Pont de l'Alma (Sb-€185, small Db-€235, bigger Db-€260, Db with Eiffel Tower view-€380, Tb-€360, 1 Rue Augereau, tel. 01 45 51 63 02, www.hotel-paris-londres-eiffel.com, info@londres-eiffel.com, helpful Cédric and Arnaud).

$$ Hôtel de la Tour Eiffel** is a solid two-star value on a quiet street near several of my favorite restaurants. The rooms are well-designed, well-kept, and comfortable, but they don't have air-conditioning and some have thin walls. The six sets of connecting rooms are ideal for families (snug Db-€115, bigger Db-€135-155, 17 Rue de l'Exposition, tel. 01 47 05 14 75, www.hotel-toureiffel.com, hte7@wanadoo.fr).

Near La Tour Maubourg Métro

$$$ Hôtel Muguet*** has had a full face-lift. I thought the hotel was terrific before the renovation—it's still quiet, well-located, and well-run (Db-€150-235—more with view, Tb-€235-275, strict cancellation policy, 11 Rue Chevert, tel. 01 47 05 05 93, www.hotelparismuguet.com, muguet@wanadoo.fr).

In the Marais Neighborhood

Those interested in a more central, diverse, and lively urban locale should make the Marais their Parisian home. Running from the Pompidou Center east to the Bastille (a 15-minute walk), the Marais is jumbled, medieval Paris at its finest. Classy stone mansions sit alongside trendy bars, antique shops, and fashion-conscious boutiques. The streets are an intriguing parade of art-ists, students, tourists, immigrants, and baguette-munching babies in strollers. The Marais is also known as a hub of the Parisian gay and lesbian scene. This area is *sans* doubt livelier and edgier than the Rue Cler area.

Near Place des Vosges
(3rd and 4th arrond., Mo: Bastille, St-Paul, or Sully-Morland)

$$$$ Hôtel le Pavillon de la Reine*****, 15 steps off the beautiful Place des Vosges, merits its stars with top service and comfort and exquisite attention to detail, from its melt-in-your-couch lobby to its luxurious rooms (Db-€350-1,000, buffet breakfast-€35, free access to spa and fitness room, free loaner bikes and parking, 28 Place des Vosges, tel. 01 40 29 19 19, www.pavillon-de-la-reine.com, contact@pavillon-de-la-reine.com).

$$$ Hôtel St. Louis Marais***, an intimate and sharp little hotel, lies on a quiet street a few blocks from the river. The handsome rooms come with character, spacious bathrooms, and reasonable rates (Db-€175-230, Tb-€245, Qb-€265, buffet breakfast-€13, 1 Rue Charles V, Mo: Sully-Morland, tel. 01 48 87 87 04, www.saintlouismarais.com, marais@saintlouis-hotels.com).

$ Hôtel Jeanne d'Arc**, a lovely small hotel with thoughtfully appointed rooms, is ideally located for (and very popular with) connoisseurs of the Marais. It's an exceptional value and worth booking way ahead. Corner rooms are wonderfully

Apartment Rentals

Intrepid travelers are accustomed to using Airbnb and VRBO when it comes to renting a vacation apartment. In Paris, you have many additional options among rental agencies; I've found the following to be the most reliable. Their websites are essential to understanding your choices. Read the rental conditions very carefully.

Paris Perfect has offices in Paris with English-speaking staff who seek the "perfect apartment" for their clients. Many units have Eiffel Tower views, and most have air-conditioning and washers and dryers (discount off regular rates for Rick Steves readers, US toll-free tel. 888-520-2087, www.parisperfect.com).

Adrian Leeds Group offers apartments owned by North Americans and is ideal for travelers looking for all the comforts, conveniences, and amenities of home (tel. 877-880-0265, ext. 701, www.adrianleeds.com).

Home Rental Service offers a big selection of apartments throughout Paris with no agency fees (120 Champs-Elysées, tel. 01 42 25 65 40, www.homerental.fr).

Haven in Paris offers exactly that—well-appointed, stylish havens for travelers looking for a temporary home. Also check out their fun blog, *Hip Paris* (tel. 617/395-4243, www.haveninparis.com).

Paris Home offers two little studios, both located on Rue Amélie in the heart of the Rue Cler area. Each has modern furnishings and laundry facilities. Friendly Slim, the owner, is the best part (no minimum stay, special rates for longer stays, free maid service, airport/train station transfers possible, mobile 06 19 03 17 55, www.parishome2000.com).

Cobblestone Paris Rentals is a small, North American-run outfit offering furnished rentals in central neighborhoods. Apartments come stocked with English-language DVDs about Paris, coffee, tea, cooking spices, basic bathroom amenities, and an English-speaking greeter who will give you the lay of the land (two free river cruises for Rick Steves readers who stay five nights or more, www.cobblestoneparis.com).

Paris for Rent, a San Francisco-based group, has been renting top-end apartments in Paris for more than a decade (US tel. 866-437-2623, www.parisforrent.com).

Cross-Pollinate is a reputable online booking agency representing B&Bs and apartments throughout Paris. Minimum stays vary from one to seven nights (US tel. 800-270-1190, France tel. 09 75 18 11 10, www.cross-pollinate.com).

---

bright in the City of Light but have twin beds only. Rooms on the street can be noisy until the bars close (Sb-€72-98, Db-€120, larger twin Db-€150, family rooms available, continental breakfast-€8, no air-con, 3 Rue de Jarente, Mo: St-Paul, tel. 01 48 87 62 11, www.hoteljeannedarc.com, information@hoteljeannedarc.com).

Near the Pompidou Center
(4th arrond., Mo: St-Paul, Hôtel de Ville, or Rambuteau)

$$ Hôtel de la Bretonnerie*, three blocks from Hôtel de Ville, makes a fine Marais home. It has a warm, welcoming lobby, helpful staff, and 29 well-appointed, good-value rooms with an antique, open-beam warmth (standard "classic" Db-€180, bigger "charming" Db-€220, Db suite-€250, Tb/Qb-€245, buffet breakfast-€10, no air-con, between Rue Vieille du Temple and Rue des Archives at 22 Rue Ste. Croix de la Bretonnerie, tel. 01 48 87 77 63, www.bretonnerie. com, hotel@bretonnerie.com).

$$ **Hôtel Beaubourg***** is a terrific three-star value on a small street in the shadow of the Pompidou Center. The lounge is inviting, and the 28 plush and traditional rooms are quiet and thoughtfully appointed (standard Db-€135-165, bigger twin or king-size Db-€145-175 and worth the extra cost, Db suite with private patio-€190-230, continental breakfast-€9.50, 11 Rue Simon Le Franc, Mo: Rambuteau, tel. 01 42 74 34 24, www. hotelbeaubourg.com, reservation@ hotelbeaubourg.com).

On Ile St. Louis
(4th arrond., Mo: Pont Marie or Sully-Morland)
The peaceful, residential character of this river-wrapped island, with its brilliant location and homemade ice cream, has drawn Americans for decades. There are no budget deals here—all the hotels are three-star or more—though prices are fair considering the level of comfort and killer location.

$$$$ **Hôtel du Jeu de Paume******, occupying a 17th-century tennis center, is among the most expensive hotels I list in Paris. When you enter its magnificent lobby, you'll understand why. Greet Scoop, *le chien*, then take a spin in the glass elevator for a half-timbered-tree-house experience. The 30 rooms are carefully designed and tasteful, though not particularly spacious (you're paying for the location and public areas). Most rooms face a small garden; all are pin-drop peaceful (Sb-€195-255, standard Db-€295-360, suite Db-€450-560, apartment for up to 6-€620-900, breakfast-€18, 54 Rue St. Louis-en-l'Ile, tel. 01

43 26 14 18, www.jeudepaumehotel.com, info@jeudepaumehotel.com).

$$$ **Hôtel Saint-Louis***** blends character with modern comforts. The well-maintained rooms come with cool stone floors and exposed beams. Rates are reasonable...for the location (Db-€185-225, top-floor Db with micro-balcony-€255, Tb-€295, buffet breakfast-€13, 75 Rue St. Louis-en-l'Ile, tel. 01 46 34 04 80, www.saintlouisenlisle.com, info@saintlouisenlisle.com).

TRANSPORTATION

Getting Around Paris
Paris is easy to navigate. Your basic choices are Métro (in-city subway), train (suburban rapid transit tied into the Métro system), public bus, and taxi.

You can buy tickets and passes at Métro stations and at many *tabacs*. Staffed ticket windows in stations are being phased out, so expect some stations to have only machines and an information desk. Machines accept coins, small bills of €20 or less, and chip-and-PIN cards (no American magnetic-stripe or chip-and-signature cards).

Rick's Tip: *Sometime in 2019,* **Métro tickets will be replaced with travel cards: Navigo Easy** *(better for travelers, can be shared and topped up)* and **Navigo Liberté** *(better for residents). Check www.ratp.fr for the latest.*

Public-Transit Tickets: The Métro, suburban trains (lines A-K), trams, and buses all work on the same tickets. You can make as many transfers as you need on a single ticket, except between the Métro/suburban train and the bus or tram systems (additional ticket required). A single ticket costs €1.80. To save money, buy a *carnet* (kar-nay) of 10 tickets for €14.10. *Carnets* can be shared among travelers. Kids under four ride free.

Passe Navigo: This chip-embedded card costs a one-time €5 fee (plus another €5 for the required photo; photo booths are in major Métro stations). The weekly unlimited pass (Navigo Semaine) costs €21.25 (plus the fees listed above) and covers all forms of transit from Monday to Sunday (expiring on Sunday, even if you buy it on, say, a Thursday). The pass is good for all zones in the Paris region, which means that you can travel anywhere within the city center, out to Versailles, and to Charles de Gaulle and Orly airports. To use the Navigo, touch the card to the purple pad, wait for the green validation light and the "ding," and you're on your way. You can buy your Passe Navigo at any Métro station in Paris (for more details, visit www.ratp.fr).

Navigo or *Carnet*? The Navigo covers a far greater area than *carnet* tickets, but cannot be shared, and is most worthwhile for visitors who use it for regional trips, stay a full week, and start their trip early in the week. Two 10-packs of *carnets*—enough for most travelers staying a week—cost €28.20, are shareable, don't expire, but are only valid in the center of Paris.

Other Passes: A handy one-day bus/Métro pass (called **Mobilis**) is available for €7. If you are under 26 and in Paris on a Saturday or Sunday, you can buy an unlimited daily transit pass called **Ticket Jeunes Week-end** for the unbeatable price of €3.85.

Métro ticket machines

By Métro

In Paris, you're never more than a 10-minute walk from a Métro station. Europe's best subway system allows you to hop from sight to sight quickly and cheaply (runs Sun-Thu 5:30-24:30, Fri-Sat 5:30-2:00 in the morning, www.ratp.fr).

Using the Métro System: To get to your destination, determine the closest "Mo" stop and which line or lines will get you there. The lines are color-coded and numbered, and you can tell their direction by the end-of-the-line stops. For example, the La Défense/Château de Vincennes line, also known as line 1 (yellow), runs between La Défense, on its west end, and Vincennes on its east end. Once in the Métro station, you'll see the color-coded line numbers and/or blue-and-white signs directing you to the train going in your direction (e.g., *direction: La Défense*). Insert your ticket in the automatic turnstile, reclaim your ticket, pass through, and keep it until you exit the system (some stations require you to pass your ticket through a turnstile to exit). Be warned that fare inspectors regularly check for cheaters, accept absolutely no excuses, and have portable credit-card machines to fine you on the spot: Keep that ticket or pay a minimum fine of €45.

Transfers are free and can be made wherever lines cross, provided you do so within 1.5 hours.

When you reach your destination, look for the blue-and-white *sortie* signs pointing you to the exit. Before leaving the station, check the helpful *plan du quartier* (map of the neighborhood) to get your bearings.

After you finish the entire ride and exit onto the street, toss or tear your used ticket so you don't confuse it with unused tickets.

Métro Resources: Métro maps are free at Métro stations. Several good online tools can also help you navigate the public-transit system. The website Metro.paris provides an interactive map of Paris'

Transit Basics

- The same tickets are good on the Métro, suburban trains (within the city), and city buses.
- Save money by buying a *carnet* of 10 discounted tickets or a Passe Navigo.
- Beware of pickpockets, and don't buy tickets from men roaming the stations.
- Find your train by its end-of-the-line stop.
- Insert your ticket into the turnstile, retrieve it, and keep it until the end of your journey.
- Safeguard your belongings; avoid standing near the train doors with luggage.
- At a stop, if the door doesn't open automatically, either push a square button (green or black) or lift a metal latch.
- Transfers (*correspondances*) between the Métro and suburban train system are free (but not between Métro/suburban train and bus).
- Trash or tear used tickets after you complete your ride and leave the station (not before) to avoid confusing them with fresh ones.

sights and Métro lines (www.metro.paris). The free RATP mobile app (in English, download at www.ratp.fr) and the more user-friendly Kemtro app (www.kemtro.com) can estimate Métro travel times, help you locate the best station exit, and tell you when the next bus will arrive, among other things.

By Suburban Train

The suburban train, formerly called the RER, is an arm of the Métro, serving outlying destinations such as Versailles and the airports. These routes are identified on Métro maps by the letters A-K.

Within the city center, the train works like the Métro and can be speedier if it serves your destination directly, because it makes fewer stops. Métro tickets are good on the suburban train when traveling in the city center. You can transfer between the Métro and suburban train systems with the same ticket. But to travel outside the city (to Versailles or the airport, for example), you'll need a separate, more expensive ticket (unless you're using a Passe Navigo). Unlike the Métro, not every train stops at every station along the way; check the sign over the platform to see if your destination is listed as a stop ("*toutes les gares*" means it makes all stops along the way), or confirm with a local before you board. For suburban trains, you may need to insert your ticket in a turnstile to exit the system.

By City Bus

Paris' excellent bus system is worth figuring out (www.ratp.fr). Bus stops are everywhere, and every stop comes with all the information you need: a good city bus map, route maps showing exactly where each bus goes that uses the stop, a frequency chart and schedule, a *plan du quartier* map of the immediate neighborhood, and a *soirées* map explaining night service, if available. Bus-system maps are also available in any Métro station (and in the *Paris Pratique* map book sold at newsstands).

Using the Bus System: Buses use the same tickets and passes as the Métro and suburban train. One ticket buys you a bus ride anywhere in central Paris within the freeway ring road (*le périphérique*). Use your Métro ticket or buy one on board for €0.20 more, though note that tickets bought on board are *sans correspondance*, which means you can't use them to transfer to another bus.

Paris bus stops are getting a face-lift, and they are looking sharp; at some locations, you can charge your phone while you wait. Board your bus through the front door. Validate your ticket in the machine and reclaim it. With a Passe Navigo, scan it on the purple touchpad. Keep track of which stop is coming up next by following the onboard diagram or listening to recorded announcements. When you're ready to get off, push the red button to signal you want a stop, then exit through the central or rear door.

More Bus Tips: *Carnet* ticket holders—but not those buying individual tickets on the bus—can transfer from one bus to another on the same ticket (within 1.5 hours, revalidate ticket on next bus), but you can't do a round-trip or hop on and off on the same line. You can use the same ticket to transfer between buses and tramlines, but you can't transfer between the bus and Métro/RER systems.

By Taxi

Parisian taxis are reasonable, especially for couples and families. Fares and supplements (described in English on the rear windows) are straightforward and tightly regulated.

A taxi can fit three people comfortably. Cabbies are legally required to accept four passengers, though they don't always like it. Beyond three passengers, expect to pay €3 extra per person.

Rates: All Parisian taxis start with €2.60 on the meter and have a minimum charge of €7. A 20-minute ride (e.g., Bastille to the Eiffel Tower) costs about €25. Drivers charge higher rates at rush hour, at night, all day Sunday, for extra passengers, and to the airport. To tip, round up to the next euro (at least €0.50).

The A, B, or C lights on a taxi's rooftop sign correspond to hourly rates, which vary with the time of day and day of the week (for example, the A rate of €32.50/hour applies Mon-Sat 10:00-17:00). Tired travelers need not bother with these mostly subtle differences in fares—if you need a cab, take it.

Scenic Buses for Tourists

These scenic bus routes provide a great, cheap, and convenient introduction to the city.

Bus #69 runs east-west between the Eiffel Tower and Père Lachaise Cemetery by way of Rue Cler, Quai d'Orsay, the Louvre, and the Marais.

Bus #87 links the Marais and Rue Cler areas, but stays mostly on the Left Bank, connecting the Eiffel Tower, St. Sulpice Church, Luxembourg Garden, St. Germain-des-Prés, the Latin Quarter, the Bastille, and Gare de Lyon.

Bus #24 runs east-west along the Seine riverbank from Gare St. Lazare to Madeleine, Place de la Concorde, Orsay Museum, the Louvre, St. Michel, Notre-Dame, and Jardin des Plantes.

Bus #63 is another good east-west route, connecting Trocadéro (Eiffel Tower), Pont de l'Alma, Orsay Museum, St. Sulpice, Luxembourg Garden, Latin Quarter/Panthéon, and Gare de Lyon.

Bus #73 is one of Paris' most scenic lines, starting at the Orsay Museum and running westbound around Place de la Concorde, then up the Champs-Elysées, around the Arc de Triomphe, and down Avenue Charles de Gaulle to the La Défense business district.

How to Catch *un Taxi*: You can try waving down a taxi, but it's often easier to ask someone for the nearest taxi stand (*"Où est une station de taxi?"*; oo ay ewn stah-see-ohn duh tahk-see). Taxi stands are indicated by a circled "T" on good city maps and on many maps in this book. To order a taxi in English, call the reservation line for the G7 cab company (tel. 01 41 27 66 99), or ask your hotelier or waiter to call for you. When you summon a taxi by phone, a €4 surcharge is added to the fare (€7 if you schedule a timed pickup).

To download a taxi app, search for either "Taxi G7" or "Taxis Bleus" (the two major companies, both available in English).

If you need to catch a train or flight early in the morning, book a taxi the day before (especially for weekday departures). Some taxi companies require a €5 reservation fee by credit card for weekday morning rush-hour departures (7:00-10:00).

By Bike

Paris is surprisingly easy by bicycle. The city is flat, and riders have access to more than 370 miles of bike lanes and many of the priority lanes for buses and taxis (be careful on these). You can rent from a bike-rental shop or use the city-operated Vélib' bikes (details later). All bike-rental shops have good route suggestions. I biked along the river from Notre-Dame to the Eiffel Tower in 15 wonderfully scenic minutes. The riverside promenade between the Orsay Museum and Pont de l'Alma is magnificent for biking.

The TIs have a helpful "Paris à Vélo" map, which shows all the dedicated bike paths. Many other versions are available for sale at newsstand kiosks, some bookstores, and department stores.

Rental Bikes: Bike About Tours is your best bet for rental, with good information and kid-friendly solutions such as baby seats, tandem attachments, and kid-sized bikes (bike rental—€15/day during office hours, €20/24 hours, includes lock and helmet; mid-Feb-Nov Thu-Tue 9:30-17:30, closed Wed; closed Dec-mid-Feb; shop/café—called the Yellow Jersey Café—at 17 Rue du Pont Louis Philippe, Mo: Hôtel de Ville, mobile 06 18 80 84 92, www.bikeabouttours.com).

Vélib' Bikes: The city's Vélib' program (from *vélo* + *libre* = "bike freedom" or "free bike") gives residents and foreigners alike access to more than 20,000 bikes at nearly 1,500 stations scattered around the city. While the curbside stations only accept American Express or chip-and-PIN credit cards, any kind of credit card will work if you buy a subscription in advance online at www.velib-metropole.fr. The subscription process is easy to follow; select the "Short-Term Subscription" to create a PIN, pay, and get an ID number. To pick up a bike, go to any bike rack, enter your ID number and PIN at the machine (all have English instructions), and away you go! Make sure to pick a bike in working order; if a bike has a problem,

Bike tours can be fun and informative.

locals will turn the seat backward (€1.70/1 day, €8/7 days, tel. 01 30 79 79 30).

Arriving and Departing

Whether you're aiming to catch a train or plane, budget plenty of time to reach your departure point. Paris is a big, crowded city, and getting across town on time is a goal you'll share with millions of other harried people. Factor in traffic delays and walking time through huge stations and vast terminals.

By Plane

CHARLES DE GAULLE AIRPORT

Paris' main airport (airport code: CDG) has three terminals: T-1, T-2, and T-3. Most flights from the US use T-1 or T-2 (check your ticket). You can travel between terminals on the free CDGVAL shuttle train (departs every 5 minutes, 24/7, 30 minutes).

When leaving Paris, make sure you know which terminal you are departing from (if it's T-2, you'll also need to know which hall you're leaving from—they're labeled A through F). For flight info, visit www.adp.fr.

Car-rental offices, TIs, post offices, pharmacies, and ATMs are all well-signed. All terminals have shops, cafés, and bars. T-2 has a **train station,** with suburban trains into Paris (described later), as well as longer-distance trains to the rest of France (including high-speed TGV trains).

Getting between Charles de Gaulle and Paris: Buses, airport vans, commuter trains, and taxis link the airport's terminals with central Paris. Total travel time to your hotel should be around 1.5 hours by bus and Métro, one hour by train and Métro, or 50 minutes by taxi.

By RoissyBus: The RoissyBus drops you off at the Opéra Métro stop in central Paris (€11.50, runs 6:00-23:00, 3-4/hour, 50 minutes, buy ticket at airport Paris Tourisme desk, ticket machine, or on bus, tel. 3246, www.ratp.fr/en).

Rick's Tip: When deciding how to get from Charles de Gaulle airport into Paris, keep in mind that **using buses and taxis requires shorter walks than taking suburban trains.** *Also remember that transfers to Métro lines often involve stairs.*

By Le Bus Direct: Several bus routes drop travelers at convenient points in and near the city (€17 one-way, €30 round-trip, runs 5:45-22:30, 2/hour, Wi-Fi and power outlets, toll tel. 08 92 35 08 20, www.lebusdirect.com). **Bus #2** goes to Porte Maillot (with connections to Beauvais Airport), the Arc de Triomphe (Etoile stop, 1 Avenue Carnot, 50 minutes), the Trocadéro (10 Place du Trocadéro, near Avenue d'Eylau), and ends near the Eiffel Tower at 20 Avenue de Suffren (1.25 hours). **Bus #4** runs to Gare de Lyon (45 minutes) and the Montparnasse Tower/train station (1.25 hours). **Bus #3** goes to Orly Airport (€21, 1.25 hours). You can book tickets online (must print out and bring with you), ticket machines at stops, or pay driver (cash only, see www.lebusdirect.com for round-trip and group discount details). Le Bus Direct stops are marked with an airplane icon.

From **Paris to the airport,** catch Le Bus Direct coaches at any of these locations: on Avenue de Suffren near the Eiffel Tower, on Place du Trocadéro, Arc de Triomphe/Etoile (on Avenue Mac Mahon—the non-Champs-Elysées side), Porte Maillot (on Boulevard Gouvion St-Cyr—east side of the Palais des Congrès), Gare Montparnasse (on Rue du Commandant René Mouchotte—facing the station with the tower behind you, it's around the left side), or Gare de Lyon (look for *Navette-Aéroport* signs, and find the stop on Boulevard Diderot across from Café Les Deux Savoies).

By Suburban Train (formerly called RER): Paris' Train-B is the fastest public-transit option for getting between the airport and the city center (€9.75, runs

5:00-24:00, 4/hour, about 35 minutes). It runs directly to well-located Train-B/Métro stations, including Gare du Nord, Châtelet-Les Halles, St. Michel, and Luxembourg. The train is handy and cheap, but it can require walking with your luggage through big, crowded stations and may include stairs. If you've been to Paris before, these trains used to be called the RER; you may see maps or websites still using the old name. For step-by-step instructions on taking the train into Paris, see www.parisbytrain.com (under "CDG Airport to Paris RER Trains").

To **return to the airport by suburban train** from central Paris, allow plenty of time to get to your departure gate. Your Métro or bus ticket is not valid on Train-B to the airport (but a Passe Navigo is); buy the ticket at any Métro or suburban train station from a clerk or the machines (bills of €20 or less, some American credit cards also work). When you catch your train, make sure the sign over the platform shows *Aéroport Roissy-Charles de Gaulle* as a stop served. (The line splits, so not every Train-B serves the airport.) If you're not clear, ask another rider, *"Air-o-por sharl duh gaul?"*

By Airport Van: Shuttle vans work best for trips from your hotel to the airport, and can be a good value for single travelers and big families (about €32 for one person, €46 for two, €58 for three; have hotelier book at least a day in advance).

By Taxi or Uber: The 50-minute trip costs about €50-65. **Taxis** are less appealing on weekday mornings as traffic into Paris can be bad—in that case, the train is likely a better option. Don't take an unau-

thorized taxi from cabbies greeting you on arrival. Official taxi stands are well-signed.

For trips from Paris to the airport, have your hotel arrange it. Specify that you want a real taxi (*un taxi normal*), not a more expensive limo service. For weekday morning departures (7:00-10:00), reserve at least a day ahead (€7 reservation fee payable by credit card). For more on taxis in Paris, see page 210.

Uber offers Paris airport pickup and drop-off for the same rates as taxis, but since they can't use the bus-only lanes (normal taxis can), expect some added time.

By Private Car Service: **Paris Webservices** will meet you inside the terminal and wait if you're late (€85 one-way for up to two people, about €120-225 round-trip for up to four people, tel. 01 45 56 91 67 or 09 52 06 02 59, www.pariswebservices.com).

Car Rental: Car-rental desks are well-signed from the arrival halls. Be prepared for a maze of ramps as you drive away from the lot—get directions from the rental clerks when you do the paperwork.

When **returning your car,** allow ample time to reach the drop-off lots. There are separate rental return lots depending on your T-2 departure hall—and imperfect signage can make the return lots especially confusing to navigate.

ORLY AIRPORT

This easy-to-navigate airport (airport code: ORY) feels small, but has all the services you'd expect at a major airport (www.adp.fr). Orly is good for rental-car pickup and drop-off, as it's closer to Paris and far easier to navigate than Charles de Gaulle Airport. Orly has two terminals: Ouest (west) and Sud (south). You can connect the two terminals with the free Orlyval shuttle train (well-signed) or with any of the shuttle buses that also travel into downtown Paris.

Getting between Orly and Paris: Shuttle buses (*navettes*), suburban trains, taxis, and airport vans connect Paris with either terminal.

By Bus: Bus bays are found in the Sud terminal outside exits L and G, and in the Ouest terminal outside exit D.

Le Bus Direct route #1 runs to Gare Montparnasse, Invalides, and Etoile Métro stops. For Rue Cler hotels, take Le Bus Direct to the Eiffel Tower stop, then walk 15 minutes across the Champ de Mars park to your hotel. Buses depart from the arrivals level—Ouest exit B-C or Sud exit L—look for signs to *navettes* (€12 one-way, €20 round-trip, 4/hour, 40 minutes to the Eiffel Tower, buy ticket from driver or book online, store the ticket on your smartphone or print it out and bring your ticket with you). See www.lebusdirect.com for details on round-trip and group discounts.

For the cheapest access to the Marais area, take **tram line 7** from outside the Sud terminal (direction: Villejuif-Louis Aragon) to the Villejuif Métro station (€3.40—plus one Métro ticket, 4/hour, 45 minutes).

The next two bus options take you to the **Train-B,** with access to the Luxembourg Garden area, Notre-Dame Cathedral, handy Métro line 1 at the Châtelet stop, Gare du Nord, and Charles de Gaulle Airport. The **Orlybus** goes directly to the Denfert-Rochereau Métro and Train-B stations (€8, 3/hour, 30 minutes). The **Orlyval shuttle train** takes you to the Antony Train-B station (€12.05, 6/hour, 40 minutes, buy ticket to Paris—not just to Antony—before boarding, smart to purchase your 10-ticket *carnet* for the Métro here too). The Orlyval train leaves from the departure level at both terminals. Take Train-B in direction Mitry-Claye or Aéroport Charles de Gaulle to reach central Paris stops.

For access to Left Bank neighborhoods via **Train-C,** take the bus marked *Go Paris* to the Pont de Rungis station, then catch Train-C (direction: Versailles Château Rive Gauche or Pontoise) to St. Michel, Musée d'Orsay, Invalides, or Pont de l'Alma (€1.90 shuttle only, €6.25 combo-ticket includes Train-C, 4/hour, 35 minutes).

By Taxi: Taxis are outside the Ouest terminal exit B, and to the far right as you leave the Sud terminal at exit M. Allow 30 minutes for a taxi ride into central Paris (fixed fare of €30 for Left Bank, €35 for Right Bank).

BEAUVAIS AIRPORT

Budget airlines such as Ryanair use this small airport, offering cheap airfares but leaving you 50 miles north of Paris. Still, this airport has direct buses to Paris and is handy for travelers heading to Normandy or Belgium (car rental available). The airport is basic, waiting areas are crowded, and services are sparse (airport code: BVA, airport tel. 08 92 68 20 66, www.aeroportbeauvais.com).

Getting Between Beauvais and Paris: You can take a bus (1.5 hours), train (at least 2 hours), or taxi (1.5 hours).

By Bus: Buses depart from the airport when they're full (about 20 minutes after flights arrive) and take 1.5 hours to reach Paris. Buy your ticket (€17 one-way, €16 online) at the little kiosk to the right as you exit the airport. Buses arrive at Porte Maillot on the west edge of Paris (on Métro line 1 and Train-C).

Buses heading to Beauvais Airport leave from Porte Maillot about 3.5 hours before scheduled flight departures. Catch the bus in the parking lot on Boulevard Pershing next to the Hyatt Regency. Arrive with enough time to purchase your bus ticket before boarding or buy online at http://tickets.aeroportbeauvais.com.

By Train: Trains connect Beauvais' city center and Paris' Gare du Nord (20/day, 1.5 hours). To reach Beauvais' train station, take the Hôtel/Aéroport Navette shuttle or local bus #12 (each hourly, 25 minutes).

By Taxi: Taxis run from Beauvais Airport to Beauvais' train station or city center (€20), or to central Paris (allow €150 and 1.5 hours).

Eurostar Routes

ENGLAND   **Amsterdam**

London   North
⊗ .·Ebbsfleet   Sea   NETH.

Ashford

Calais-
Fréthun   **Brussels**
English   Lille-
Channel   Europe   BELG.

FRANCE

Paris⊗

Not to Scale   - - - - Eurostar
·········· Channel Tunnel

By Train

Paris is Europe's rail hub, with six major stations and one minor one:

- Gare du Nord (northbound trains)
- Gare Montparnasse (west- and southwest-bound trains)
- Gare de Lyon (southeast-bound trains)
- Gare de l'Est (eastbound trains)
- Gare St. Lazare (northwest-bound trains)
- Gare d'Austerlitz (southwest-bound trains)
- Gare de Bercy (smaller station with non-TGV southbound trains)

The main train stations have free Wi-Fi, banks or currency exchanges, ATMs, train information desks, cafés, newsstands, and clever pickpockets (pay attention in ticket lines—keep your bag firmly gripped in front of you). You'll find TIs at Gare du Nord and Gare de Lyon. Because of security concerns, not all have baggage checks. Any train station has schedule information, can make reservations, and can sell tickets for any destination.

Each station offers two types of rail service: long distance to other cities, called **Grandes Lignes** (major lines, TGV—also called "InOui"—or TER trains); and commuter service to nearby areas, called Banlieue, Transilien, or suburban trains (lines A-K, formerly called RER). When arriving by Métro, follow signs for *Grandes*

Lignes-SNCF to find the main tracks. Métro and suburban train lines A-K, as well as buses and taxis, are well-marked at every station.

For clear communication at ticket/info windows, it helps to write down the date and ticket you want. For instance: "28/05 Paris-Nord→Lyon dep. 18:30." All stations have helpful information booths *(accueil);* the bigger stations have roving helpers, usually wearing red or blue vests.

GARE DU NORD

The granddaddy of Paris' train stations serves cities in northern France and international destinations north of Paris, including Copenhagen, Amsterdam, and London via the Eurostar (for more on the Eurostar, see www.ricksteves.com/eurostar).

From Gare du Nord to: Charles de Gaulle Airport (via Train-B, 4/hour, 35 minutes, track 41-44).

GARE MONTPARNASSE

This big, modern station covers three floors, serves lower Normandy and Brittany, and has TGV service to the Loire Valley and southwestern France, as well as suburban service to Chartres.

From Gare Montparnasse to: Chartres (14/day, 1 hour), **Amboise** (8/day in 1.5 hours with change in St-Pierre-des-Corps, requires TGV reservation; non-TGV trains leave from Gare d'Austerlitz), **Pontorson/Mont St-Michel** (5/day, 5.5 hours, via Rennes or Caen), and **Sarlat** (4/day, 6-6.5 hours, change in Libourne or Bordeaux).

GARE DE LYON

This huge, bewildering station offers TGV and regular service to southeastern France, Italy, Switzerland, and other international destinations. **Le Bus Direct** coaches—to Gare Montparnasse (easy transfer to Orly Airport) and direct to Charles de Gaulle Airport—stop outside the station's main entrance. They are signed *Navette-Aéroport.*

From Gare de Lyon to: Beaune (roughly hourly at rush hour but few midday, 2.5 hours, most require change in Dijon; direct trains from Paris' Bercy station take an hour longer), **Chamonix** (7/day, 5.5-7 hours, some change in Switzerland), **Avignon** (10/day direct, 2.5 hours to Avignon TGV Station, 5/day in 3.5 hours to Avignon Centre-Ville Station, more connections with change—3-4 hours), **Arles** (11/day, 2 direct TGVs—4 hours, 9 with change in Avignon—5 hours), **Nice** (hourly, 6 hours, may require change, 11.5-hour night train possible out of Gare d'Austerlitz), and **Carcassonne** (8/day, 7-8 hours, 1 change, night trains leave from Gare d'Austerlitz).

GARE DE L'EST

This two-floor station (with underground Métro) serves northeastern France and international destinations east of Paris.

From Gare de l'Est to: Colmar (12/day with TGV, 3.5 hours, change in Strasbourg) and **Reims** Centre Station (12/day with TGV, 50 minutes).

GARE ST. LAZARE

This compact station serves upper Normandy, including Rouen and Giverny.

From Gare St. Lazare to: Giverny (train to Vernon, 8/day Mon-Sat, 6/day Sun, 45 minutes), **Honfleur** (13/day, 2-3.5 hours, via Lisieux, Deauville, or Le Havre, then bus), **Bayeux** (9/day, 2.5 hours, some change in Caen), and **Pontorson/Mont St-Michel** (2/day, 4-5.5 hours, via Caen; more trains from Gare Montparnasse).

GARE D'AUSTERLITZ

This small station currently provides non-TGV service to the Loire Valley, southwestern France, and Spain.

From Gare d'Austerlitz to: Versailles (via Train-C, 4/hour, 35 minutes), **Amboise** (3/day direct in 2 hours, 5/day with transfer in Blois or Les Aubrais-Orléans; faster TGV connection from Gare Montparnasse), and **Sarlat** (1/day, 6.5 hours, requires change to bus in Souillac, 3 more/day via Gare Montparnasse).

GARE DE BERCY

This smaller station mostly handles southbound non-TGV trains, but some TGV trains do stop here in peak season (Mo: Bercy).

By Bus

Buses generally provide the cheapest—if less comfortable and more time-consuming—transportation to major European cities. The bus is also the cheapest way to cross the English Channel; book at least two days in advance for the best fares. Eurolines is the old stand-by; two relative newcomers (Ouibus and Flixbus) are cutting prices drastically for travelers and amping up onboard comfort with snacks you can purchase, Wi-Fi, and easy, online booking. These companies provide service usually between train stations and airports within France and to many international destinations.

OuiBus has routes mostly within France but serves some European cities as well (central Paris stop is at Gare de Bercy, Mo: Bercy, toll tel. 08 92 68 00 68, www.ouibus.com). **FlixBus** connects key cities within France and throughout Europe, often from secondary airports and train stations (central Paris stop is near Porte Maillot at 16 Boulevard Pershing, Mo: Porte Maillot, handy eticket system and smartphone app, tel. 01 76 36 04 12, www.flixbus.com). **Eurolines'** buses depart from Paris' Gare Routière du Paris-Gallieni in the suburb of Bagnolet (28 Avenue du Général de Gaulle, Mo: Gallieni, toll tel. 08 92 89 90 91; from the US, dial 011 33 1 41 86 24 21, www.eurolines.com).

By Car

A car is nothing but a headache in Paris: Park it and use public transportation. Street parking is generally free at night (20:00-9:00) and all day Sunday. To pay for streetside parking, you can use your credit card or go to a *tabac* shop and buy a parking card (*une carte de stationnement*), sold in €10 and €30 denominations (figure €4/hour in central Paris). Insert the card into the meter (chip-side in) and punch the desired amount of time, then take the receipt and display it in your windshield. Meters limit street parking to a maximum of two hours.

Underground garages are plentiful. You'll find them under Ecole Militaire, St. Sulpice Church, Les Invalides, the Bastille, and the Panthéon; all charge about €35-50/day (€66/3 days, €10/day more after that, for locations see www.vincipark.com). Some hotels offer parking for less—ask your hotelier.

For a longer stay, park for less at an airport (about €15/day) and take public transport or a taxi into the city. Orly is closer and easier for drivers to navigate than Charles de Gaulle.

NEAR PARIS

Day-trippers looking for a refreshing change from urban Paris can choose among these fascinating destinations. I've listed them in order of importance. If you have time for only one sight, visit Versailles.

The palace at Versailles, fit for a king and queen, is Europe's best. Chartres Cathedral is a Gothic masterpiece with magnificent stained glass. The city of Reims has a knockout cathedral and Champagne *caves*, too. For art lovers, Monet's flowery Giverny gardens are an Impressionist dream.

The Neptune fountain at Versailles

Versailles

Every king's dream, Versailles (vehr-"sigh") was the residence of French monarchs and the cultural heartbeat of Europe for about 100 years—until the Revolution of 1789 changed all that.

Versailles offers three ▲▲▲ blockbuster sights: The main attraction is the palace itself, the **Château,** where you'll walk through dozens of lavish, chandeliered rooms once inhabited by the Sun King Louis XIV and his successors. Next come the expansive **Gardens,** a landscaped wonderland dotted with statues and fountains. The pastoral **Trianon Palaces and Domaine de Marie-Antoinette,** designed for frolicking blue bloods and featuring several small palaces, are perfect for getting away from the mobs at the Château.

Getting There

To reach Versailles, 10 miles west of Paris, take the **Train-C** "Versailles Château Rive Gauche" (abbreviated "Versailles Chât" or "Versailles RG") from any of these Paris train stops: Gare d'Austerlitz, St. Michel, Musée d'Orsay, Invalides, Pont de l'Alma, or Champ de Mars (€7.10 round-trip, 4/hour). You can also buy train tickets at any Métro ticket window in Paris (includes connection from that Métro stop to the suburban train).

Versailles

Petit | *Canal*

Grand Canal

GRAND TRIANON
EXIT

WC

TRIANON TOUR BEGINS

T

ALLEE DE LA REINE

AVE. DE TRIANON

WC | RESTAURANT & SNACKS

T

ALLEE ST. ANTOINE

BIKE & GOLF CART RENTAL

B

ALLEE DES MATELOTS

BOAT RENTAL

ROUTE DE ST. CYR

(N-10)

ALLEE D'APOLLON

Apollo Basin

WC

KING'S GARDEN

G A R D E N S

COLONNADE

OBELISK GROVE

ROYAL DRIVE

MIRROR FOUNTAIN

STAR GROVE

AVE. DE TRIANON

WC & SNACK KIOSK

WC

Latona Basin

APOLLO'S BATHS GROVE

QUEEN'S GROVE

PORTE DE LA REINE

B

Pièce d'Eau des Suisses

GARDENS TOUR BEGINS

Neptune Basin

ORANGERIE

EXIT CHATEAU

GOLF-CART RENTAL

ENTRANCE "A"

T

PETIT TRAIN

ENTRANCE "H"

CHATEAU

TICKET SALES

See detail map

CHATEAU TOUR BEGINS

KING'S VEGETABLE GARDEN

GUIDED TOURS

RUE CARNOT

RUE DE LA PAROISSE

NOTRE DAME

Place d'Armes

Place Hoche

RUE DE SATORY

P

ST. LOUIS

AVENUE DE SCEAUX

DE PARIS

AVENUE

AVENUE DE ST-CLOUD

STABLES

STABLES

AVE. DU GENERAL DE GAULLE

B

L'EUROPE

Place du Marché

TRAIN STATION
(VERSAILLES CHATEAU RIVE GAUCHE)

AVENUE DE

↓ To Paris

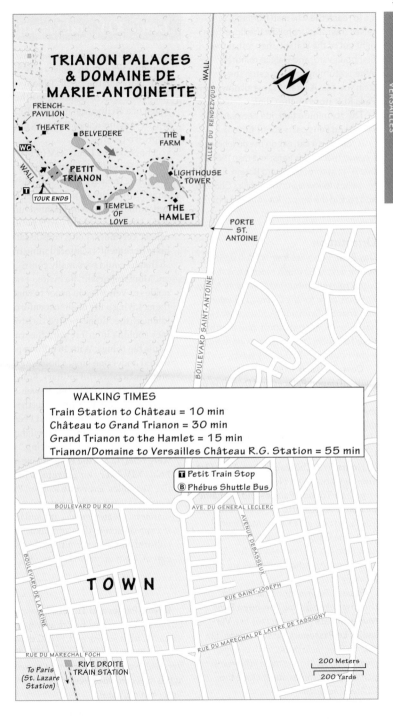

TRIANON PALACES
& DOMAINE DE
MARIE-ANTOINETTE

FRENCH
PAVILION
THEATER
BELVEDERE
THE
FARM
WC
PETIT
TRIANON
LIGHTHOUSE
TOWER
TOUR ENDS
TEMPLE
OF
LOVE
THE
HAMLET

WALL
ALLÉE DU RENDEZVOUS
WALL

PORTE
ST.
ANTOINE

BOULEVARD SAINT-ANTOINE

WALKING TIMES
Train Station to Château = 10 min
Château to Grand Trianon = 30 min
Grand Trianon to the Hamlet = 15 min
Trianon/Domaine to Versailles Château R.G. Station = 55 min

T Petit Train Stop
B Phébus Shuttle Bus

BOULEVARD DU ROI
AVE. DU GÉNÉRAL LECLERC

AVENUE DE BASSEUX

BOULEVARD DE LA REINE

RUE SAINT-JOSEPH

T O W N

RUE DU MARÉCHAL DE LATTRE DE TASSIGNY

RUE DU MARÉCHAL FOCH

To Paris
(St. Lazare
Station)
RIVE DROITE
TRAIN STATION

200 Meters
200 Yards

To reach the Château from the Versailles train station, follow the flow: Turn right out of the station, then left at the first boulevard, and walk 10 minutes. When returning to Paris, catch the first train you see: All trains serve all downtown Paris RER stops on the C line.

The 30-minute **taxi** ride between Versailles and Paris costs about €60.

If you have a **car,** get on the *périphérique* freeway that circles Paris, and take the toll-free A-13 autoroute toward Rouen. Exit at Versailles, follow signs to *Versailles Château*, and park in the big pay lot at the foot of the Château on Place d'Armes.

Orientation

Day Plan: Versailles merits a full sightseeing day and is much more enjoyable with a relaxed, unhurried approach. Allow 1.5 hours each for the Château, Gardens, and Trianon/Domaine. Add another two hours for round-trip transit, plus another hour for lunch, and you're looking at an eight-hour day—at the very least.

Cost: Château-€18 (includes audioguide); **Trianon Palaces and Domaine de Marie-Antoinette**-€12; **Gardens**-free, except on Spectacle days, when the fountains are on and admission is €9 (weekends April-Oct plus many Tue; see "Spectacles in the Gardens," later).

Hours: The **Château** is open April-Oct Tue-Sun 9:00-18:30, Nov-March until 17:30. The **Trianon Palaces and Domaine de Marie-Antoinette** are open April-Oct Tue-Sun 12:00-18:30, Nov-March until 17:30. The **Gardens** are open April-Oct daily 8:00-20:30; Nov-March Tue-Sun 8:00-18:00. All palace buildings are closed Monday year-round.

Passes: To save money and avoid the long ticket-buying line, buy a **Paris Museum Pass** (see page 136) or a **Versailles Le Passeport Pass** (€20/one day, €27 on Spectacle days), both of which give you access to the most important parts of the complex and include the Château audioguide.

Louis XIV and Versailles

Versailles is the architectural embodiment of a time when society was divided into rulers and the ruled. To some it's the pinnacle of civilization; to others, it's a sign of a civilization in decay. Either way, it remains one of Europe's most impressive sights.

The Sun King Louis XIV (r. 1643-1715) created Versailles, spending freely from the public treasury to turn his dad's hunting lodge into a palace fit for the gods (among whom he counted himself). His reasons were partly political—at Versailles, Louis consolidated his government's scattered ministries so that he could personally control policy. More important, he invited France's nobles to Versailles in order to control them. Living a life of almost enforced idleness, the "domesticated" aristocracy couldn't interfere with the way Louis ran things. With 18 million people united under one king, a booming economy, and a powerful military, France was Europe's number-one power.

Around 1700, Versailles was the cultural heartbeat of Europe, and French culture was at its zenith. Throughout Europe, when you said "the king," you were referring to the French king— Louis XIV. Every king wanted a palace like Versailles. Everyone learned French. French taste in clothes, hairstyles, table manners, theater, music, art, and kissing spread across the Continent. That cultural dominance continued, to some extent, right up to modern times.

Buying Passes and Tickets: Ideally, buy your ticket or pass before arriving at Versailles from any Paris TI, FNAC department store, or www.chateauversailles.fr. In Versailles, you can buy tickets or passes at the rarely crowded Versailles TI (see "Information," later).

Versailles Château—
Ground Floor & Entrances

To Trianon Palaces & Domaine de Marie-Antoinette via Apollo Basin

GARDENS

Water Parterre

GARDENS TOUR BEGINS

South Parterre

5

STATE APARTMENTS

North Parterre

6 T

Marble Court

WC

3

4

To Gardens

ENTRANCE FOR TOUR

To Stairs Up to First Floor

Prince's Court

INFO DESK

WC

Royal

Courtyard

WC

ROYAL CHAPEL

GRAND CAFE D'ORLEANS

DIRECT ACCESS TO GARDENS

ROYAL GATE

TICKET SALES

WC

1

ENTRANCE STRUCTURE & SECURITY CHECK

CHATEAU ENTRANCE (ENTRANCE A)

WC

GUIDED TOURS **2**

Not to Scale

To Train Station

- - - Self-Guided Tour

1 Château Ticket & Pass Sales
2 Guided-Tour Reservations
3 Exit from State Apartments
4 Fountain Spectacle Tickets
5 Golf-Cart Rental
6 Petit Train (Tram)

Crowd-Beating Tips: Versailles is packed May-Sept 10:00-13:00, so come early or late. Consider seeing the Gardens during midmorning and the Château in the afternoon, when crowds die down. Avoid Sundays, Tuesdays, and Saturdays (in that order), when the place is jammed from open to close.

To skip ticket-buying lines, buy tickets or passes in advance (see earlier), or book a guided tour (covered below). Unfortunately, all ticket holders—including those with advance tickets and passes—must go through the often-slow security checkpoint at the Château's Royal Gate entrance (longest lines 10:00-12:00). Only by booking a tour can you skip the security line.

Information: Tel. 01 30 83 78 00, www. chateauversailles.fr. You'll pass the city TI on your walk from the train station to the palace—it's just past the Pullman Hôtel (daily 9:00-19:00, Sun until 18:00, shorter hours in winter, tel. 01 39 24 88 88). The on-site information office is to the left of the Château.

Tours: Taking the 1.5-hour English **guided tour** lets you bypass the long security check line (€22 includes palace entry; ignore the tours hawked near the train station). Book a tour in advance on the palace website, or reserve immediately upon arrival at the guided-tours office (to the right of the Château—look for yellow *Visites Conferences* signs).

🎧 Download my free Versailles **audio tour.**

Eating: The Grand Café d'Orléans, to the left of the Château's Royal Gate entrance, offers good-value self-service meals; the sandwiches are great for picnicking in the Gardens. In the Gardens, near the Latona Fountain and clustered at the Grand Canal, you'll find several cafés and snack stands with fair prices.

Spectacles in the Gardens: The fountains at Versailles come alive at selected times; check the website for current hours and prices. **Les Grandes Eaux Musicales**

has 55 fountains gushing to classical music (April-Oct Sat-Sun, plus mid-May-June Tue). On some summer weekends, **Les Grandes Eaux Nocturnes** adds a fireworks show to the music-and-fountains display (mid-June-mid-Sept).

❍ *Self-Guided Tour*

On this tour, you'll see the Château (the State Apartments of the king and queen as well as the Hall of Mirrors), the landscaped Gardens in the "backyard," and the Trianon Palaces and Domaine de Marie-Antoinette, located at the far end of the Gardens. If your time is limited, skip the Trianon/Domaine, which is a 30-minute hike from the Château.

THE CHATEAU

• *Stand in the huge courtyard and face the palace. The golden Royal Gate in the center—nearly 260 feet long and decorated with 100,000 gold leaves—is a replica of the original.*

The section of the palace with the clock is the original château, where little Louis XIV spent his happiest boyhood years. Naturally, the Sun King's private bedroom (the three arched windows beneath the clock) faced the rising sun. The palace and grounds are laid out on an east-west axis.

• *Enter the Château. Continue into the reception area (bag check and WCs), where you can pick up a free map and audioguide. Follow the crowds across the courtyard to pick up an audioguide.*

On the way to the stairs up to the first floor (and our first stop), you'll pass through a dozen ground-floor rooms (the route and displays change often). Once you climb the stairs, you reach a palatial golden-brown room, with a doorway that overlooks the...

Royal Chapel: Dut-dutta-dah! Every morning at 10:00, the organist and musicians struck up the music, these big golden doors opened, and Louis XIV and his family stepped onto the balcony

Louis XIV attended Mass in Versailles' Royal Chapel.

to attend Mass. While Louis looked down on the golden altar, the lowly nobles on the ground floor knelt with their backs to the altar and looked up—worshipping Louis worshipping God.

• *Enter the next room, with a colorful painting on the ceiling.*

Hercules Drawing Room: Pleasure ruled. The main suppers, balls, and receptions were held in this room. Picture elegant partygoers in fine silks, wigs, rouge, lipstick, and fake moles (and that's just the men) as they danced to the strains of a string quartet.

• *From here on, it's a one-way tour—getting lost is not allowed.*

The King's Wing: The names of the rooms generally come from the paintings on the ceilings. For instance, the Venus room was the royal make-out space, where couples would cavort beneath the goddess of love, floating on the ceiling. In the **Diana Room,** Louis and his men played pool on a table that stood in the center of the room, while ladies sat surrounding them on Persian-carpet cushions, and music wafted in from next door.

Also known as the Guard Room (as it was the room for Louis' Swiss bodyguards),

the red **Mars Room** is decorated with a military flair. The **Mercury Room** may have served as Louis' official (not actual) bedroom, where the Sun King would ritually rise each morning to warm his subjects.

The **Apollo Room** was the grand throne room. Louis held court from a 10-foot-tall, silver-and-gold, canopied throne on a raised platform placed in the center of the room. Even when the king was away, passing courtiers had to bow to the empty throne.

The final room of the King's Wing is the **War Room,** depicting Louis' victories—in marble, gilding, stucco, and paint.

• *Next you'll visit the magnificent...*

Hall of Mirrors: No one had ever seen anything like this hall when it was opened. Mirrors were still a great luxury at the time, and the number and size of these monsters were astounding. The hall is nearly 250 feet long. There are 17 arched mirrors, matched by 17 windows letting in that breathtaking view of the Gardens.

In another age altogether, this is where Germany and the Allies signed the Treaty of Versailles, ending World War I (and, some say, starting World War II).

• *Next up: the queen's half of the palace.*

The vast painted ceiling of the Hercules Drawing Room

A *Hall of Mirrors*

B *A royal bedchamber*

C *Louis XIV, the Sun King*

D *Domaine de Marie-Antoinette*

Getting Around the Gardens

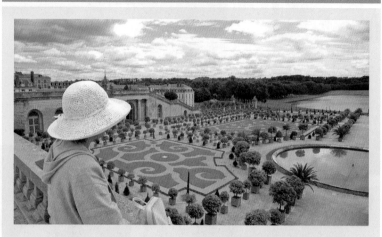

On Foot: It's a 45-minute walk from the palace and down the Grand Canal to the far end of Domaine de Marie-Antoinette. Allow more time for stops.

By Bike: You can bike through the gardens, but not inside the grounds of the Trianon/Domaine (about €7/hour or €16/half-day).

By *Petit Train*: The slow-moving tram leaves from behind the Château (north side) and makes a one-way loop, stopping at the Petit and Grand Trianons (entry points to Domaine de Marie-Antoinette), and then the Grand Canal before returning to the Château (€7.50, round-trip only, free under age 11, 4/hour, runs 10:00-18:00, 11:00-17:00 in winter). You can hop on or off the train at stops.

By Golf Cart: A cart makes for a fun drive, though it's not allowed off its circuit or in the Trianon/Domaine. Late fees are steep. To go out to the Hamlet, sightsee quickly, and return within your allotted hour, you'll need to rent a cart at the Grand Canal and put the pedal to the metal (€32/hour, €8/15 minutes after that, 4-person limit per cart, rent down by canal or just behind Château, near *petit train* stop).

By Shuttle Bus: Phébus runs an hourly TRI line shuttle bus between the Versailles Château Rive Gauche train station and the Trianon/Domaine (but doesn't stop at the Château). It works well for the end of your Versailles visit, if you want to go directly from the Trianon/Domaine to the train station (€2 or one Métro ticket, mid-April-Oct only, check schedule for "Ligne TRI" at www.phebus.tm.fr or at small Phébus office across from Versailles Château Rive Gauche train station, near McDonald's).

The Queen's Wing: The King's Wing was mostly ceremonial and used as a series of reception rooms; the Queen's Wing is more intimate.

The **Queen's Bedchamber** was where the queen rendezvoused with her husband. Two queens died here, and this is where 19 princes were born. Louis XIV made a point of sleeping with the queen as often as possible, regardless of whose tiara he tickled earlier in the evening. This room looks just like it did in the days of the last queen, Marie-Antoinette, who substantially redecorated the entire wing. That's her bust over the fireplace, and the double eagle of her native Austria in the corners.

THE GARDENS

Louis XIV was a divine-right ruler. One way he proved it was by controlling nature like a god. These lavish grounds—elaborately planned, pruned, and decorated—showed everyone that Louis was in total command. Louis loved his gardens and, until his last days, presided over their care. He personally led VIPs through them and threw his biggest parties here.

Rick's Tip: *It's fun pedaling around the greatest royal park in all of Europe. A* **bike-rental station** *is by the Grand Canal, with kid-size bikes and tandems available.*

TRIANON PALACES AND DOMAINE DE MARIE-ANTOINETTE

Versailles began as an escape from the pressures of kingship. But in a short time, the Château had become as busy as Paris ever was. Louis XIV needed an escape from his escape and built a smaller palace out in the boonies. Delicate, pink, and set amid gardens, the **Grand Trianon** was the perfect summer getaway. Nearby is the fantasy world of palaces, ponds, pavilions, and pleasure gardens called the **Domaine de Marie-Antoinette.**

Provence

This magnificent region is shaped like a giant wedge of quiche. From its sunburned crust, fanning out along the Mediterranean coast, it stretches north along the Rhône Valley. The splendid recipe *provençale* mixes pastel hills, appealing cities, bountiful vineyards, and sweet, hilltop villages.

The Romans were here in force and left many ruins—some of the best anywhere. Over the centuries, they were followed by seven popes, who resided in a formidable palace in Avignon, and artist Vincent van Gogh, whose work celebrates Provence's sunflowers and starry nights.

A tour of Provence villages is best on your own by car. Public transit is good between cities and decent to some towns, but marginal at best to the smaller towns. For those traveling *sans* car, a variety of minivan tours can help fill in the gaps.

PROVENCE IN 2 DAYS

Make Arles or Avignon your sightseeing base—particularly if you have no car. While Francophiles usually pick urban Avignon, Italophiles prefer smaller Arles.

You'll want one day for sightseeing in Arles and Les Baux. Spend most of the day in Arles—try to time your arrival for Wednesday or Saturday, to enjoy the market. Then visit Les Baux in the late afternoon or early evening. On the second day, allow a half-day for Avignon and a half-day for Pont du Gard.

With another day, measure the pulse of rural Provence and spend at least one night in a smaller town, such as Vaison-la-Romaine. Exploring the Côtes du Rhône wine country takes about a half-day, but you may want to linger.

Provence

To Lyon & Burgundy

Grignan

To Chamonix & Alps

Ardèche

Ardèches Gorges

Valréas

Bollène

Nyons

Buis-les-Baronnies

St. Cécile

Rasteau

Vaison-la-Romaine

Rhône

Sablet

Séguret

Dentelles de Montmirail

Orange

Gigondas

Suzette

Malaucène

Vacqueyras

Beaumes de Venise

Uzès

Gard

Châteauneuf-du-Pape

CÔTES DU RHÔNE

Mont Ventoux

To Gorges du Tarn

PONT DU GARD

Remoulins

Avignon

Isle-sur-la-Sorgue

Nîmes

Durance

Gordes

Joucas

Roussillon

Beaucaire

Tarascon

Oppède

Apt

Les Baux

St-Rémy

Cavaillon

LUBERON

Petit Rhône

Fontvieille

Alpilles

Lourmarin

Arles

Pertuis

Aigues-Mortes

CAMARGUE

Rhône

To Gorges du Verdon

Saintes-Maries-de-la-Mer

Aix-en-Provence

Palette

Martigues

To Nice & Côte d'Azur

Paris

FRANCE

Marseille

Aubagne

Mediterranean Sea

Les Calanques

Cassis

100 Miles

20 Kilometers

20 Miles

PROVENCE AT A GLANCE

Arles

▲▲**Roman Arena** A big amphitheater, once used by gladiators, that hosts summer "bullgames" and occasional bullfights. **Hours:** Daily May-Sept 9:00-19:00, shorter hours off-season. See page 240.

▲▲**St. Trophime Church** Church with exquisite Romanesque entrance. **Hours:** Daily 9:00-12:00 & 14:00-18:30, until 17:00 Oct-March. See page 244.

▲▲**Ancient History Museum** Filled with models and sculptures, taking you back to Arles' Roman days. **Hours:** Wed-Mon 10:00-18:00, closed Tue. See page 248.

▲**Fondation Van Gogh** Small gallery with works by major contemporary artists paying homage to Van Gogh. **Hours:** Generally daily 11:00-19:00, likely closed Mon off-season. See page 246.

Avignon

▲▲**Palace of the Popes** Fourteenth-century Gothic palace built by the popes who made Avignon their home. **Hours:** Daily March-Oct 9:00-19:00, July-Aug until 20:00, Nov-Feb 9:30-17:45. See page 262.

▲**St. Bénezet Bridge** The "Pont d'Avignon" of nursery-rhyme fame, once connecting the pope's territory to France. **Hours:** Daily March-Oct 9:00-19:00, July-Aug until 20:00, Nov-Feb 9:30-17:45. See page 261.

▲**Jardin du Rochers des Doms** View park overlooking the Rhône River Valley and Avignon's famous broken bridge. **Hours:** Daily from 7:30 until dark. See page 261.

Nearby

▲▲▲**Pont du Gard** Part bridge and part aqueduct, a huge stone structure heralding the greatness of Rome. **Hours:** Aqueduct—daily until 24:00; museum—daily May-Sept 9:00-19:00, until 20:00 July-Aug, until 17:00 Oct-April, closed two weeks in Jan. See page 267.

▲▲▲**Les Baux** Rock-top village sitting in the shadow of its ruined medieval citadel. **Hours:** Village always open; castle—daily Easter-June and Sept 9:00-19:15, July-Aug 9:00-20:15, March and Oct 9:30-18:30, Nov-Feb 10:00-17:00. See page 269.

▲▲▲**Côtes du Rhône Wine Road** A drive through picturesque villages and vineyards, unfurling along a scenic wine-tasting route. See page 276.

Vaison-la-Romaine History-rich town atop a 2,000-year-old Roman site. See page 272.

ARLES

In Roman times, Arles (pronounced "arl") was an important port city. With the first bridge over the Rhône River, it was a key stop on the Roman road from Italy to Spain, the Via Domitia. After reigning as the seat of an important archbishop and a trading center for centuries, the city became a sleepy backwater of little importance in the 1700s. Vincent van Gogh settled here in the late 1800s, but left only a chunk of his ear (now long gone). American bombers destroyed much of Arles in World War II as the townsfolk hid out in its underground Roman galleries. But today Arles thrives again, with its evocative Roman ruins, an eclectic assortment of museums, made-for-ice-cream pedestrian zones, and squares that play hide-and-seek with visitors.

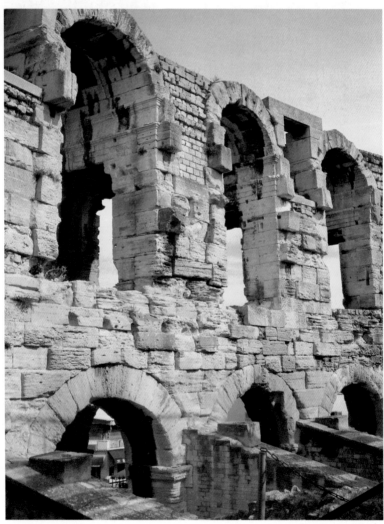

Roman Arena

Workaday Arles is not a wealthy city and, compared to its neighbor Avignon, it feels unpolished and even a little dirty. But to me, that's part of its charm.

Orientation

Though the town is built along the Rhône, it largely ignores the river. Landmarks hide in Arles' medieval tangle of narrow, winding streets. Hotels have good, free city maps, and helpful street-corner signs point you toward sights and hotels.

Tourist Information: The TI is on the ring road Boulevard des Lices, at Esplanade Charles de Gaulle (April-Sept daily 9:00-18:45; Oct-March Mon-Sat 9:00-16:45, Sun 10:00-13:00; tel. 04 90 18 41 20, www.arlestourisme.com).

Sightseeing Pass: A good-value €11 combo-ticket—the **Liberty Passport** (Le Passeport Liberté)—covers any four monuments and the Ancient History Museum (but not the Fondation Van Gogh gallery). Buy the pass at the TI or any included sight. While only the Ancient History Museum is essential, the pass makes the city fun to explore, as you can pop into any sight, even for just a couple of minutes.

***

Rick's Tip: *In Arles, the* **ancient monuments**—*Roman Arena, Classical Theater, Cryptoporticos, and St. Trophime Cloisters—* **all have the same hours** *(daily May-Sept 9:00-19:00, April and Oct 9:00-18:00, Nov-March 10:00-17:00).*

***

Baggage Storage and Bike Rental: Hôtel Régence will store your bags for a small fee (daily, closed in winter, 5 Rue Marius Jouveau). They also rent bikes (reserve ahead for electric bikes, one-way rentals within Provence possible).

Car Rental: Avis is at the train station (tel. 04 90 96 82 42). Downtown you'll find **Europcar** (61 Avenue de Stalingrad, tel. 04 90 93 23 24) and **Hertz** (10 Boulevard Emile Combes, nearer Place Voltaire, tel. 04 90 96 75 23).

Local Guide: Charming **Agnes Barrier** offers tours covering Van Gogh and Roman history (€130/3 hours, mobile 06 11 23 03 73, agnes.barrier@hotmail.fr).

Minivan Excursions: Provence Reservation runs day tours to nearby sights (such as Pont du Gard) from Arles, Avignon, and other cities. While the tours provide introductory commentary, there's no guiding at the actual sights. They use eight-seat, air-conditioned minivans (about €60-80/half-day, €100-120/day). Ask about their cheaper big-bus excursions, or consider hiring a van and driver for your private use (plan on €220/half-day, €490/day, tel. 04 90 14 70 00, www.provence-reservation.com).

Arles City Walk

The joy of Arles is how its compact core mixes ancient sights, Van Gogh memories, and a raw and real contemporary scene that can be delightfully covered on foot. All the dimensions of the city come together in this self-guided walk. While workable in the evening, taking this walk during business hours allows you to pop into the sights and shops that give the city its unique character.

Much of the walk focuses on the story of Van Gogh in Arles. We'll also visit ancient sites, including the Roman Arena, Classical Theater, Cryptoporticos, and the cloisters at St. Trophime Church (all covered by the Liberty Passport), along with some of Arles' most characteristic streets and squares.

At the Café Van Gogh

Arles

RUE GEORGES GUYNEMER

RUE DES CAPUCINS

RUE DE LA VERRIERE

RUE ROBESPIERRE

RUE CAMARGUE

TRINQUETAILLE

RUE

QUAI ST. PIERRE

Rhône

TRINQUETAILLE BRIDGE

QUAI MARX DORMOY

PROMENADE

R DE LA TOUR DU FABRE

R. DORMOY

R. DR. FANTON

R. TRUCHET

B Envia Bus Stops

RUE A. FRANCE

R. JOUVENE

14

15

LIBERTE

QUAI DE LA ROQUETTE

ARLATEN FOLK MUSEUM
(REOPENS IN 2018)

Place Paul Doumier

R. DES PORCELETS

RUE DE LA RÉPUBLIQUE

RUE DE LA ROQUETTE

RUE GAMBETTA

12

RUE CROIX ROUGE

13

ESPACE VAN GOGH

R. PRES. WILSON

To Ancient History Museum

LA ROQUETTE

RUE DE CHARTROUSE

RUE JEAN GRANAUD

RUE MOLIERE

Place Genive

RUE MOLIERE

RUE FLEURY PRUDHON

To Nimes via A-84

RUE RAILLON

BLVD. G CLEMENCEAU

B

RUE PARMENTIER

To Ancient History Museum

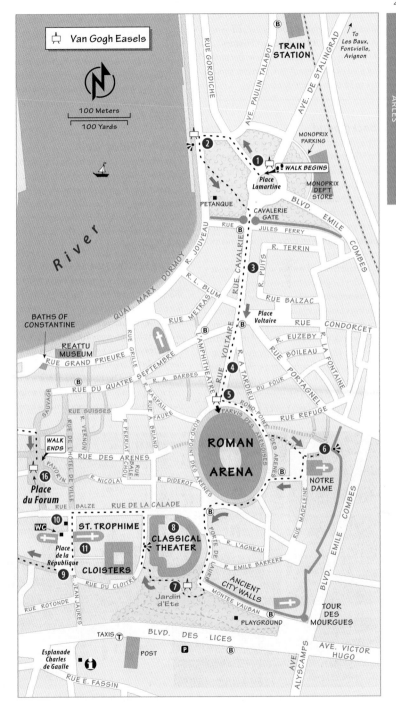

Rick's Tip: *Before following my self-guided Arles walk,* **visit the Ancient History Museum** *for a helpful overview. Because it's located at the edge of town, drivers should try to stop on their way into Arles.*

Background

The life and artistic times of Dutch artist **Vincent van Gogh** form a big part of Arles' draw, and the city does a fine job of highlighting its Van Gogh connection: Throughout town, about a dozen steel-and-concrete "easels," with photos of the final paintings and the actual view of that painting's subject, provide then-and-now comparisons.

In the dead of winter in 1888, 35-year-old Van Gogh left big-city Paris for Provence, hoping to jump-start his floundering career and social life. He was as inspired as he was lonely. Coming from the gray skies and flat lands of the north, Vincent was bowled over by everything Provençal—the sun, bright colors, rugged landscape, and down-to-earth people. For the next two years he painted furiously, cranking out a masterpiece every few days.

Only a few of the 200-plus paintings that Van Gogh did in the south can be found today in the city that so moved him (you can see a few at the Fondation Van Gogh gallery, which we'll visit on this stroll). But here you can walk the same streets he knew and see the places he painted.

⊙ Self-Guided Walk

• *Start at the north gate of the city, just outside the medieval wall in Place Lamartine (100 yards in front of the medieval gate, with the big Monoprix store across the street to the right, just beyond the roundabout). A four-foot-tall metal panel (or "easel") shows Van Gogh's painting.*

❶ THE YELLOW HOUSE EASEL

Vincent arrived in Arles on February 20, 1888, to a foot of snow. He rented a small house on the north side of Place Lamartine. The house was destroyed in 1944 by an errant bridge-seeking bomb, but the four-story building behind it—where you see the brasserie—still stands (find it in the painting). The house had four rooms, including a small studio and the cramped trapezoid-shaped bedroom made famous

Van Gogh "easels" throughout Arles pair the artist's paintings with actual views.

The Rules of Boules

The game of *boules*—also called *pétanque*—is the horseshoes of France. Invented here in the early 1900s, it's a social yet serious sport, and endlessly entertaining to watch—even more so if you understand the rules.

The game is played with heavy metal balls and a small wooden target ball called a *cochonnet* (piglet). Whoever gets his *boule* closest to the *cochonnet* is awarded points. Teams commonly have specialist players: a *pointeur* and a *tireur*. The pointeur's goal is to lob his balls as close to the target as he can. The tireur's job is to blast away opponents' *boules*.

In teams of two, each player gets three *boules*. The starting team traces a small circle in the dirt (in which players must stand when launching their *boules*), and tosses the *cochonnet* about 30 feet to establish the target. The *boule* must be thrown underhand, and can be rolled, launched sky-high, or rocketed at its target. The first *pointeur* shoots, then the opposing *pointeur* shoots until his *boule* gets closer. Once the second team lands a *boule* nearer the *cochonnet*, the first team goes again. If the other team's *boule* is near the *cochonnet*, the *tireur* will likely attempt to knock it away.

Once all *boules* have been launched, the tally is taken. The team with a *boule* closest to the *cochonnet* wins the round, and they receive a point for each *boule* closer to the target than their opponents' nearest *boule*. The first team to get to 13 points wins. A regulation *boules* field is 10 feet by 43 feet, but the game is played everywhere—just scratch a throwing circle in the sand, toss the *cochonnet*, and you're off.

in paintings. It was painted yellow inside and out, and Vincent named it..."The Yellow House." In the distance, the painting shows the same bridges you see today.

• *Walk directly to the river. You'll pass a monument in honor of two WWII American pilots killed in action during the liberation of Arles, a post celebrating Arles' many sister cities (left), and a big concrete high school (right).*

At the river, find the easel in the wall where ramps lead down.

❷ STARRY NIGHT OVER THE RHONE EASEL

One night, Vincent set up shop along the river and painted the stars boiling above the city skyline. Vincent looked to the night sky for the divine and was the first to paint outside after dark, adapting his straw hat to hold candles (which must have blown the minds of locals back then). The lone couple in the painting pops up again and again in his work. (This painting is not the *Starry Night* you're thinking of—that one was painted later, in another town.)

To his sister Wilhelmina, Vincent wrote, "At present I absolutely want to paint a starry sky. It often seems to me that night is still more richly colored than the day; having hues of the most intense violets, blues, and greens. If only you pay attention to it, you will see that certain stars are lemon yellow, others pink or a green, blue, and forget-me-not brilliance." Vincent painted this scene on his last night in Arles.

• *With your back to the river, angle right through the small park of sycamore trees. Continue into town through the park (past a WC) and through the stumpy 14th-century stone towers where the city gates once stood.*

❸ RUE DE LA CAVALERIE

Van Gogh walked into town the same way. Arles' 19th-century red light district was just east of Rue de la Cavalerie, and the far-from-home Dutchman spent many lonely nights in its bars and brothels. The street still has a certain edgy local color. Belly up to the bar in the down-and-dirty café at Hôtel de Paris for a taste. It's a friendly watering hole with fun paintings of football and bull fighting.

• *Continuing uphill, you'll come to an ornately decorated fountain from 1887: two columns with a mosaic celebrating the high culture of Provence (she's the winged woman who obviously loves music and reading).*

Stay left and keep walking uphill to Place Voltaire, a center of this working-class neighborhood (you'll see the local Communist Party headquarters across on the left).

❹ OLD TOWN

You've left the bombed-out part of town and entered the old town, with buildings predating World War II. The stony white arches of the ancient Roman Arena ahead mark your destination. As you hike up Rue Voltaire, notice the shutters, which contribute to Arles' character. The old town is strictly preserved: These traditional shutters come in a variety of styles but cannot be changed.

• *Keep straight up Rue Voltaire, climb to the Roman Arena, and find the Arena easel at the top of the stairs, to the right.*

❺ *ARENA EASEL*

All summer long, fueled by sun and alcohol, Vincent painted the town. He loved the bullfights in the arena and sketched the colorful surge of the crowds, spending more time studying the people than watching the bullfights (notice how the bull is barely visible). Vincent had little interest in Arles' antiquity—it was people and nature that fascinated him.

• *Now, let's visit the actual...*

ROMAN ARENA (AMPHITHEATRE)

This well-preserved arena is worth ▲▲ and is still in use today. Nearly 2,000 years ago, gladiators fought wild animals here to the delight of 20,000 screaming fans. Now local daredevils still fight wild animals here—"bullgame" posters around the arena advertise upcoming spectacles (see page 250).

Cost and Hours: €8 combo-ticket with Classical Theater, covered by Liberty Passport; open daily May-Sept 9:00-19:00, April and Oct 9:00-18:00, Nov-March 10:00-17:00, Rond-point des Arènes, tel. 04 90 49 36 86, www.arenes-arles.com.

Visiting the Arena: After passing the ticket kiosk, find the helpful English infor-

A look at Arles' old town

Inside the Roman Arena

mation display that describes the arena's history and renovation, then take a seat in the upper deck. In Roman times, games were free (sponsored by city bigwigs), and fans were seated by social class. More than 30 rows of stone bleachers extended all the way to the top of those vacant arches that circle the arena. All arches were numbered to help distracted fans find their seats. The many passageways you'll see (called vomitoires) allowed for rapid dispersal after the games—fights would break out among frenzied fans if they couldn't leave quickly. During medieval times and until the early 1800s, the arches were bricked up and the stadium became a fortified town—with 200 humble homes crammed within its circular defenses. Parts of three of the medieval towers survive (the one above the ticket booth is open and rewards those who climb it with terrific views).

• Leaving the arena, walk clockwise around its perimeter, marveling at the ancient stonework. A quarter of the way around, go up the cute stepped lane (Rue Renan, next to Volubilis Restaurant). Take three steps and turn around to study the arena.

The big stones are Roman. Notice the little medieval stones—more like rubble—filling two upper-level archways. These serve as a reminder of how the arena encircled a jumble of makeshift houses through the Middle Ages. You can even see rooflines and beam holes where the

Roman structure provided a solid foundation to lean on.

• Hike up the pretty lane and continue past the stark and stony church to the highest point in Arles. Take in the view.

❻ ALPILLES MOUNTAINS VIEW

This view pretty much matches what Vincent, an avid walker, would have seen. Imagine him hauling his easel into those fields under intense sun, leaning against a ferocious wind, struggling to keep his hat on.

Vincent carried his easel as far as the medieval Abbey of Montmajour, that bulky structure three miles straight ahead on the hill. The St. Paul Hospital, where he was eventually treated in St-Rémy, is on the other side of the Alpilles mountains, several miles beyond Montmajour.

• Continue circling the Roman Arena. At the high point, turn left and walk out Rue de Porte de Laure. (You'll pass the Classical Theater on your right, which we'll see later.) After a couple of blocks, just after the street turns left, go right, down the curved staircase into the park. At bottom of the stairs take the second right (through the gate and into the park) and find the...

❼ JARDIN D'ETE EASEL

Vincent spent many a sunny day painting the leafy Jardin d'Eté. In another letter to his sister, Vincent wrote, "I don't know whether you can understand that one may make a poem by arranging colors... In a similar manner, the bizarre lines, purposely selected and multiplied, meandering all through the picture may not present a literal image of the garden, but they may present it to our minds as if in a dream."

• Hike uphill through the park toward the three-story surviving tower of the ancient Roman Theater. At the tower, follow the white metal fence to the left along "the garden of stone"—a collection of ancient carved bits of a once grand Roman theater. Go up four steps and around to the right for a fine view of the...

The well-preserved arena

How About Them Romans?

Many scholars claim the best-preserved ancient Roman buildings are not in Italy, but in France. These ancient stones will compose an important part of your sightseeing agenda.

Classical Rome endured from about 500 B.C. through A.D. 500—spending about 500 years growing, 200 years peaking, and 300 years declining. Julius Caesar conquered Gaul—which included Provence—during the Gallic Wars (58-51 B.C.), then crossed the Rubicon River in 49 B.C. to incite civil war within the Roman Republic. He erected a temple to Jupiter on the future site of Paris' Notre-Dame Cathedral.

The concept of one-man rule lived on with his grandnephew, Octavian (whom he had also adopted as his son). Octavian took the title "Augustus" and became the first in a line of emperors who would control Rome for the next 500 years. Rome morphed from a Republic into an Empire: a collection of many diverse territories ruled by a single man. At its peak (c. A.D. 117), the Roman Empire had 54 million people; "Rome" didn't just refer to the city, but to all of Western civilization.

Provence, with its strategic location, benefited greatly from Rome's global economy and grew to become an important part of its worldwide empire. After Julius Caesar conquered Gaul, Emperor Augustus Romanized it, building and renovating cities in the image of Rome.

When it came to construction, the Romans' magic building ingredient was concrete. Easier to work than stone, and longer-lasting than wood, concrete served as flooring, roofing, filler, glue, and support. Builders would start with a foundation of brick, then fill it in with poured concrete. They would then cover important structures, such as basilicas, in sheets of expensive marble (held on with nails), or decorate floors and walls with mosaics.

Most cities had a theater, baths, and aqueducts; the most important cities had sports arenas. A typical Roman city (such as Arles) was a garrison town, laid out on a grid plan with two main roads: one running north-south (the *cardus*), the other east-west (the *decumanus*). Approaching the city on your chariot, you'd pass by the cemetery, which was located outside town for hygienic reasons. You'd enter the main gate and speed past warehouses and apartment houses to the

town square (forum). Facing the square were the most important temples, dedicated to the patron gods of the city. Nearby, you'd find bathhouses; like today's fitness clubs, these served the almost sacred dedication to personal vigor. Also close by were businesses that catered to the citizens' needs: the marketplace, bakeries, banks, and brothels. Aqueducts brought fresh water for drinking, filling the baths, and delighting the citizens with bubbling fountains.

Some cities in Provence were more urban 2,000 years ago than they are today. For instance, Roman Arles had a population of 100,000—double today's size.

❽ CLASSICAL THEATER (THEATRE ANTIQUE)

This elegant, three-level, first-century B.C. Roman theater once seated 10,000. There was no hillside to provide structural support, so the builders created 27 buttress arches, which radiate out behind the seats. From the outside, it looked much like the adjacent arena.

Cost and Hours: €8 combo-ticket with Roman Arena, covered by Liberty Passport, same hours as Arena.

Visiting the Theater: Start with the 10-minute video outside, which provides helpful background and images that make it easier to put the scattered stones back in place. A large information panel nearby on the grass adds more context.

Walk into the theater and pull up a stone seat in a center aisle. Imagine that for 500 years, ancient Romans gathered here for entertainment. The original structure was much higher, with 33 rows of seats covering three levels to accommodate demand. During the Middle Ages, the old theater became a convenient town quarry—much of St. Trophime Church was built from theater rubble. Precious little of the original theater survives—though it still is used for events, with seating for 2,000 spectators.

• *From the theater, walk downhill on Rue de la Calade. Take the first left into a big square.*

❾ REPUBLIC SQUARE (PLACE DE LA REPUBLIQUE)

This square was called "Place Royale"—until the French Revolution. The obelisk was once the centerpiece of Arles' Roman Circus. The lions at its base are the symbol of the city, whose slogan is (roughly) "the gentle lion." Observe the age-old scene: tourists, peasants, shoppers, pilgrims, children, and street musicians. The City Hall (Hôtel de Ville) has a French Baroque facade, built in the same generation as Versailles. Where there's a City Hall, there's always a free WC (if you win the Revolution, you can pee for free at the mayor's home). Notice the flags: The yellow-and-red of Provence is the same as the yellow-and-red of Catalunya, the region's linguistic cousin in Spain.

• *Today's City Hall sits upon an ancient city center. Inside you'll find the entrance to an ancient cryptoportico (foundation).*

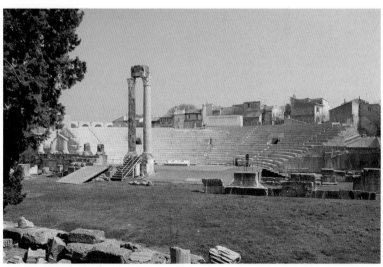

Classical Theater

⑩ CRYPTOPORTICOS (CRYPTOPORTIQUES)

This dark, drippy underworld of Roman arches was constructed to support the upper half of Forum Square. Two thousand years ago, most of this gallery of arches was at or above street level; modern Arles has buried about 20 feet of its history over the millennia. Through the tiny windows high up you would have seen the sandals of Romans on their way to the forum. Other than dark arches and broken bits of forum littering the dirt floor, there's not much down here beyond ancient memories (€3.50, covered by Liberty Passport, same hours as Arena).

• The highlight of Place de la République is St. Trophime Church. Enjoy its exquisitely carved facade.

⑪ ST. TROPHIME CHURCH

Named after a third-century bishop of Arles, this church, worth ▲▲, sports the finest Romanesque main entrance I've seen anywhere. The Romanesque and Gothic interior—with tapestries, relics, and a rare painting from the French Revolution when this was a "Temple of Reason"—is worth a visit.

Cost and Hours: Free, daily 9:00-12:00 & 14:00-18:30, until 17:00 Oct-March.

Exterior: Like a Roman triumphal arch, the church **facade** trumpets the promise of Judgment Day. The tympanum (the semicircular area above the door) is filled with Christian symbolism. Christ sits in majesty, surrounded by symbols of the four evangelists: Matthew (the winged man), Mark (the winged lion), Luke (the ox), and John (the eagle). The 12 apostles are lined up below Jesus. It's Judgment Day...some are saved and others aren't. Notice the condemned (on the right)—a chain gang doing a sad bunny-hop over the fires of hell. For them, the tune trumpeted by the three angels above Christ is not a happy one. Below the chain gang, St. Stephen is being stoned to death, with his soul leaving through his mouth and instantly being welcomed by angels. Study the exquisite detail. In an illiterate medieval world, this was colorfully painted, like a neon billboard over the town square. It's full of meaning, and a medieval pilgrim understood it all.

Interior: Just inside the door on the right, a chart locates the interior highlights and helps explain the carvings you just

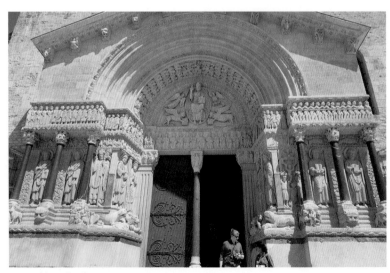

St. Trophime Church

saw on the tympanum. The tall 12th-century Romanesque nave is decorated by a set of tapestries (typical in the Middle Ages) showing scenes from the life of Mary (17th century, from the French town of Aubusson). Circle the church counterclockwise.

Step into the brightly lit **Chapel of Baptism** to view a statue of St. John Paul II under the window. Facing the window, look to the right wall where you'll see a faded painting from 1789. The French Revolution secularized the country and made churches "Temples of Reason." The painting of a triangle with a sunburst is the only example of church decor I've seen from this age.

Amble around the ambulatory toward the **Gothic apse.** Choose which chapel you need or want: If you have the plague or cholera, visit the chapel devoted to St. Roch—notice the testimonial plaques of gratitude on the wall. Some spaces are still available...if you hurry.

Two-thirds of the way around, find the **relic chapel** behind the ornate wrought iron gate, with its fine golden boxes that hold long-venerated bones of obscure saints. These relics generated lots of money for the church from pilgrims through the ages. Pop in a coin to share some light. The next chapel houses the skull of St. Anthony of the Desert.

Several chapels down, look for the early-Christian **sarcophagi** from Roman Arles (dated about A.D. 300). One sarcophagus shows Moses and the Israelites crossing the Red Sea. You'll see Christians wearing togas and praying like evangelicals do today—hands raised. The heads were likely lopped off during the French Revolution.

This church is a stop on the ancient pilgrimage route to Santiago de Compostela in northwest Spain. For 800 years pilgrims on their way to Santiago have paused here...and they still do today. Notice the modern-day pilgrimages advertised on the far right near the church's entry.

• *To reach the adjacent peaceful cloister, leave the church, turn left, then left again through a courtyard.*

ST. TROPHIME CLOISTERS

Worth seeing if you have the Liberty Passport (otherwise €4, same hours as Arena), the cloisters' many small columns were scavenged from the ancient Roman theater. Enjoy the sculpted capitals, the rounded Romanesque arches (12th century), and the pointed Gothic ones (14th century). The pretty vaulted hall exhibits 17th-century tapestries showing scenes from the First Crusade to the Holy Land. There's an instructive video at the base of the stairs. On the second floor, you'll walk along an angled rooftop designed to catch rainwater—notice the slanted gutter that channeled the water into a cistern and the heavy roof slabs covering the tapestry hall below.

• *From Place de la République, exit on the far corner (opposite the church and kitty-corner from where you entered) to stroll a delightful pedestrian street.*

⓬ RUE DE LA REPUBLIQUE

Rue da la République is Arles' primary shopping street. Walk downhill, enjoying the scene and popping into shops that catch your interest.

At the start is **Soulier Bakery.** Inside, you'll be tempted by *fougasse* (bread studded with herbs, olives, and bacon bits), *sablés Provençal* (cookies made with honey and almonds), *tarte lavande* (a sweet almond lavender tart), and big crispy meringues. A few doors down is **Restaurant L'Atelier** (with two prized Michelin stars), **L'Occitane en Provence** (local perfumes), **Puyricard Chocolate** (with enticing €1 treats and *calisson,* a sweet/bitter almond delight), as well as local design and antique shops. The fragile spiral columns on the right (just before the tourist-pleasing Lavender Boutique on the corner) show what 400 years of weather can do to decorative stonework.

• *Take the first left onto Rue Président*

*Wilson. Just after the butcher shop, turn right to find **Hôtel Dieu,** a hospital made famous by one of its patients: Vincent van Gogh.*

⑬ *ESPACE VAN GOGH EASEL*

In December 1888, shortly after his famous ear-cutting incident (see *Café at Night* easel, described later), Vincent was admitted into the local hospital—today's Espace Van Gogh cultural center (free, only the courtyard is open to the public). It surrounds a flowery courtyard that the artist loved and painted when he was being treated for blood loss, hallucinations, and severe depression that left him bedridden for a month. The citizens of Arles circulated a petition demanding that the mad Dutchman be kept under medical supervision. Félix Rey, Vincent's kind doctor, worked out a compromise: The artist could leave during the day so that he could continue painting, but he had to sleep at the hospital at night. Look through the postcards sold in the courtyard and find a painting of Vincent's ward showing nuns attending to patients in a gray hall *(Ward of Arles Hospital).*

• *Return to Rue de la République. Take a left and continue two blocks downhill. Take the second right up Rue Tour de Fabre and follow signs to Fondation Van Gogh. After a few steps, you'll pass **La Main Qui Pense** (The Hand That Thinks), a pottery workshop. A couple blocks farther, at the "no right turn" sign, turn right onto Rue du Docteur Fanton. On your immediate right is the...*

⑭ FONDATION VAN GOGH

This art foundation, worth ▲, delivers a refreshing stop for modern-art lovers and Van Gogh fans, with two temporary exhibits per year in which contemporary artists pay homage to Vincent through thought-provoking interpretations of his works. You'll also see at least one original work by Van Gogh (painted during his time in the region).

Cost and Hours: €9, daily 11:00-19:00 except closed between exhibits and likely Mon off-season—check website for current hours, audioguide-€3, Hôtel Leautaud de Donines, 35 Rue du Docteur Fanton, tel. 04 90 49 94 04, www. fondation-vincentvangogh-arles.org.

• *Continue down Rue du Docteur Fanton toward the river.*

⑮ RUE DU DOCTEUR FANTON

A string of recommended restaurants is on the left. On the right is **Crèche Municipale.** Open workdays, this is a free government-funded daycare where parents can drop off their infants up to two years old. The notion: No worker should face financial hardship in order to receive quality childcare. At the next corner is the recommended **Soleileis,** Arles' top ice cream shop.

At the strawberry-and-vanilla ice cream cone, turn right and step into **Bar El Paseo** at 4 Rue des Thermes. The main museum-like room is absolutely full of bull—including the mounted heads of three big ones who died in the local arena and a big black-and-white photo of Arles'

Fondation Van Gogh

A café on Forum Square

arena packed to capacity. Senora Leal—whose family is famous for its bullfighters—has wallpapered the place with photos and bullfighting memorabilia, and serves good Spanish Rioja wine and sangria.

• A few steps farther is...

⑯ FORUM SQUARE (PLACE DU FORUM)

Named for the Roman forum that once stood here, Forum Square, worth ▲, was the political and religious center of Roman Arles. Still lively, this café-crammed square is a local watering hole and popular for a *pastis* (anise-based aperitif). The bistros on the square can put together a passable salad or *plat du jour*—and when you sprinkle on the ambience, that's €14 well spent.

At the corner of Grand Hôtel Nord-Pinus, a plaque shows how the Romans built a foundation of galleries to level the main square and to compensate for Arles' slope down to the river. The two columns are all that survive from the upper story of the entry to the forum. Steps leading to the entrance are buried—the Roman street level was about 20 feet below you.

The statue on the square is of **Frédéric Mistral** (1830-1914). This popular poet, who wrote in the local dialect rather than in French, was a champion of Provençal culture. After receiving the Nobel Prize in Literature in 1904, Mistral used his prize money to preserve and display the folk identity of Provence. He founded a regional folk museum at a time when France was rapidly centralizing and regions like Provence were losing their unique identities. (The fierce, local mistral wind—literally "master"—has nothing to do with his name.)

• Nearby, facing the brightly painted yellow café, find your final Van Gogh easel.

CAFE AT NIGHT EASEL

In October 1888, lonely Vincent—who dreamed of making Arles a magnet for fellow artists—persuaded his friend Paul Gauguin to come south. He decorated Gauguin's room with several humble canvases of sunflowers (now some of the world's priciest paintings). Their plan was for Gauguin to be the "dean" of a new art school in Arles, and Vincent its instructor-in-chief. At first, the two got along well. They spent days side by side, rendering the same subject in their distinct styles. At night, they hit the bars and brothels. Van Gogh's well-known *Café at Night* captures the glow of an absinthe buzz at Café la Nuit on Place du Forum.

After two months together, the two artists clashed over art and personality differences (Vincent was a slob around the house, whereas Gauguin was meticulous). The night of December 23, they were drinking absinthe at the café when Vincent suddenly went ballistic. He threw his glass at Gauguin. Gauguin left. Walking through Place Victor Hugo, Gauguin heard footsteps behind him and turned to see Vincent coming at him, brandishing a razor. Gauguin quickly fled town. The local paper reported what happened next: "At 11:30 p.m., Vincent van Gogh, painter from Holland, appeared at the brothel at no. 1, asked for Rachel, and gave her his cut-off earlobe, saying, 'Treasure this precious object.' Then he vanished." He woke up the next morning at home with his head wrapped in a bloody towel and his earlobe missing. Was Vincent emulating a successful matador, whose prize is cutting off the bull's ear?

The **bright-yellow café**—called Café la Nuit—was the subject of one of Vincent van Gogh's most famous works in Arles. Although his painting showed the café in a brilliant yellow from the glow of gas lamps, the facade was bare limestone, just like the other cafés on this square. The café is now a tourist trap painted by its current owners to match Van Gogh's version...and to cash in on the Vincent-crazed hordes who pay too much to eat or drink here.

In spring 1889, the bipolar genius (a modern diagnosis) checked himself into the St. Paul Monastery and Hospital in St-Rémy-de-Provence. He spent a year there, thriving in the care of nurturing doctors and nuns. Painting was part of his therapy, so they gave him a studio to work in, and he produced more than 100 paintings. Alcohol-free and institutionalized, he did some of his wildest work. With thick, swirling brushstrokes and surreal colors, he made his placid surroundings throb with restless energy.

Eventually, Vincent's torment became unbearable. In the spring of 1890, he left Provence to be cared for by a sympathetic doctor in Auvers-sur-Oise, just north of Paris. On July 27, he wandered into a field and shot himself. He died two days later.

• With this walk, you have seen the best of Arles. It's time to enjoy a drink on the Place du Forum and savor the essence of Provence.

On the Outskirts
▲▲ANCIENT HISTORY MUSEUM (MUSEE DE L'ARLES ET DE LA PROVENCE ANTIQUES)

The Ancient History Museum provides valuable background on Arles' Roman history. Begin your town visit here before delving into the city's sights (drivers should stop on the way into town).

Located on the site of the Roman chariot racecourse (the arc of which is built into the parking lot), this air-conditioned, all-on-one-floor museum is just west of central Arles along the river. Models and original sculptures re-create the Roman city, making workaday life and culture easier to imagine.

Cost and Hours: €8, covered by Liberty Passport; open Wed-Mon 10:00-18:00, closed Tue; Presqu'île du Cirque Romain, tel. 04 13 31 51 03, www.arles-antique.cg13.fr.

Getting There: Drivers entering the city will see signs for the museum. If you're coming from the city center, take the free **Envia minibus** (stops at the train station and along Rue du 4 Septembre, then along the river—see map on page 255; 2/hour Mon-Sat, none Sun). If you're walking from the city center (allow 20 minutes), turn left at the river and take the scruffy riverside path under two bridges to the big, modern blue building. Approach-

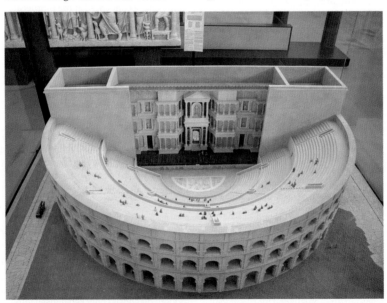

Model of Arles' Classical Theater

ing the museum, you'll pass the verdant Hortus Garden—designed to recall the Roman circus and chariot racecourse that were located here. A **taxi** ride costs €11.

Visiting the Museum: The permanent collection is housed in a large hall flooded with natural light. You'll tour it counter-clockwise: models of the ancient city and its major landmarks, a Roman boat (with a fine video in a tiny theater at the end of the hall), statues, mosaics, and sarcoph-agi. Read what English you can find, but—as much of the exhibit is in French only—here's a rundown on what you'll see.

A wall **map** of the region during the Roman era greets visitors and shows the geographic importance of Arles: Three important Roman trade routes—vias Domitia, Grippa, and Aurelia—all con-verged on or near Arles.

After a small exhibit on pre-Roman Arles you'll come to fascinating **models** of the Roman city and the impressive Roman structures in (and near) Arles. These breathe life into the buildings as they looked 2,000 years ago. Start with the model of Roman Arles and ponder the city's splendor over 2,000 years ago when Arles' population was double that of today. Find the forum—still the center of town today, though only two columns survive (the smaller section of the forum is where today's Place du Forum is built).

At the museum's center stands the original **statue** of Julius Caesar that once graced Arles' ancient theater stage wall. From there find individual models of the major buildings shown in the city model: the elaborately elegant forum; the floating wooden bridge that gave Arles a strategic advantage (over the widest, and therefore slowest, part of the river); the theater (with its magnificent stage wall); the arena (with its movable stadium cover to shelter spectators from sun or rain); and the hydraulic mill of Barbegal (with its 16 waterwheels powered by water cascading down a hillside).

Don't miss the large model of the **chariot racecourse.** Part of the original racecourse was just outside the windows, and though long gone, it likely resembled Rome's Circus Maximus.

A wing (to the right) is dedicated to the museum's newest and most excit-ing exhibit: a **Gallo-Roman vessel** and much of its cargo. This almost-100-foot-long Roman barge was hauled out of the Rhône in 2010, along with some 280 amphorae and 3,000 ceramic artifacts. It was typical of flat-bottomed barges used to shuttle goods between Arles and ports along the Mediterranean (vessels were manually towed upriver).

Continuing your counterclockwise cir-cle of the museum, you'll see displays of pottery, jewelry, metal, and glass artifacts, as well as well-crafted mosaic floors that illustrate how Roman Arles was a city of art and culture. The many **statues** are all original, except for the greatest—the *Venus of Arles,* which Louis XIV took a liking to and had moved to Versailles.

Experiences

▲▲MARKETS

Provençal market days offer France's most colorful and tantalizing outdoor shopping. On Wednesday and Saturday mornings, Arles' ring road erupts into an open-air festival of fish, flowers, produce...and everything Provençal. The main event is on Saturday, with vendors jamming the ring road from Boulevard Emile Combes to the east, along Boulevard des Lices

Wednesday and Saturday are market days.

near the TI (the heart of the market), and continuing down Boulevard Georges Clemenceau to the west. Wednesday's market runs only along Boulevard Emile Combes, between Place Lamartine and Avenue Victor Hugo; the segment nearest Place Lamartine is all about food, and the upper half features clothing, tablecloths, purses, and so on. On the first Wednesday of the month, a flea market doubles the size of the usual Wednesday market along Boulevard des Lices near the main TI. Both markets are open until about 12:30.

▲▲BULLGAMES (COURSES CAMARGUAISES)

The nonviolent *courses camarguaises* (bullgames) held in Arles are more sporting than bloody bullfights (though traditional Spanish-style bullfights still take place on occasion). Spectators occupy the same seats that fans have used for nearly 2,000 years. The bulls of Arles (who, locals insist, "die of old age") are promoted in posters even more boldly than their human foes. In the bullgame, a ribbon (*cocarde*) is laced between the bull's horns. The *razeteur,* with a special hook, has 15 minutes to snare the ribbon. Local businessmen encourage a *razeteur* (dressed in white, with a red cummer-

bund) by shouting out how much money they'll pay for the *cocarde*. If the bull pulls a good stunt, the band plays the famous "Toreador" song from *Carmen*. The following day, newspapers report on the games, including how many *Carmens* the bull earned.

Three classes of bullgames—determined by the experience of the *razeteurs*—are advertised in posters: The *course de protection* is for rookies. The *trophée de l'Avenir* comes with more experience. And the *trophée des As* features top professionals. During Easter (*Féria du Pâques*) and the fall rice-harvest festival (*Féria du Riz),* the arena hosts traditional Spanish bullfights (look for *corrida*) with outfits, swords, spikes, and the whole gory shebang. (Nearby villages also stage *courses camarguaises* in small wooden bullrings nearly every weekend; TIs have the latest schedule.)

Cost and Hours: Arles' bullgame tickets usually run €7-20; bullfights are pricier (€36-100). Schedules for bullgames vary (usually July-Aug on Wed and Fri)—ask at the TI or check online at www.arenes-arles.com.

DOMINIC ARIZONA

Bulls are not harmed in Provençal-style "bullgames," but humans may be!

Provence's Cuisine Scene

The extravagant use of garlic, olive oil, herbs, and tomatoes makes Provence's cuisine France's liveliest. To sample it, order anything *à la provençale*. Among the area's specialties are **ratatouille** (a mixture of vegetables in a thick, herb-flavored tomato sauce), **aioli** (a rich, garlicky mayonnaise spread over vegetables, potatoes, fish, or whatever), **tapenade** (a paste of pureed olives, capers, anchovies, herbs, and sometimes tuna), *soupe au pistou* (thin yet flavorful vegetable soup with a sauce of basil, garlic, and cheese), and *soupe à l'ail* (garlic soup, called *aigo bouido* in the local dialect). Look for *riz de Camargue* (reddish, chewy, nutty-tasting rice) and *taureau* (bull's meat). The native goat cheeses are **Banon de Banon** or **Banon à la Feuille** (wrapped in chestnut leaves) and spicy **Picodon**. Don't miss the region's prized **Cavaillon melons** (cantaloupes) or its delicious cherries and apricots, which are often turned into jams and candied fruits.

Wines of Provence: Provence produces some of France's great wines at relatively reasonable prices. Look for wines from **Gigondas, Rasteau, Cairanne, Beaumes-de-Venise, Vacqueyras,** and **Châteauneuf-du-Pape.** For the cheapest but still tasty wines, look for labels showing **Côtes du Rhône Villages** or **Côtes de Provence.** If you like rosé, you'll be in heaven. **Rosés from Tavel** are considered among the best in Provence. For reds, splurge for Châteauneuf-du-Pape or Gigondas, and for a fine aperitif wine or a dessert wine, try the **Muscat** from **Beaumes-de-Venise.**

Eating

You can dine well in Arles on a modest budget (most of my listings have *menus* for under €25). Sunday is a quiet night for restaurants, though eateries on Place du Forum are open. For groceries, consider the big, Monoprix supermarket/department store on Place Lamartine (closed Sun).

Rick's Tip: *Cafés on the Place du Forum deliver great atmosphere and fair prices, but mediocre food.* **Avoid the garish yellow tourist trap Café la Nuit.** *For serious cuisine, wander away from the square.*

On Rue du Docteur Fanton

$$ Les Filles du 16 is a warm, affordable place to enjoy a fresh salad (€11), or a fine two- or three-course dinner (€21-27). The choices are limited, so check the selection before sitting down. The *taureau* (bull's meat) in a tasty sauce is a good choice (closed Sat-Sun, 16 Rue du Docteur Fanton, tel. 04 90 93 77 36).

$$ Le Plaza buzzes with happy diners and is run by a young couple (Stéphane cooks while Graziela serves). It features delicious Provençal cuisine at good prices (€23 *menus*, closed Wed Oct-March, 28 Rue du Docteur Fanton, tel. 04 90 96 33 15).

$$$ Le Galoubet is a popular local spot,

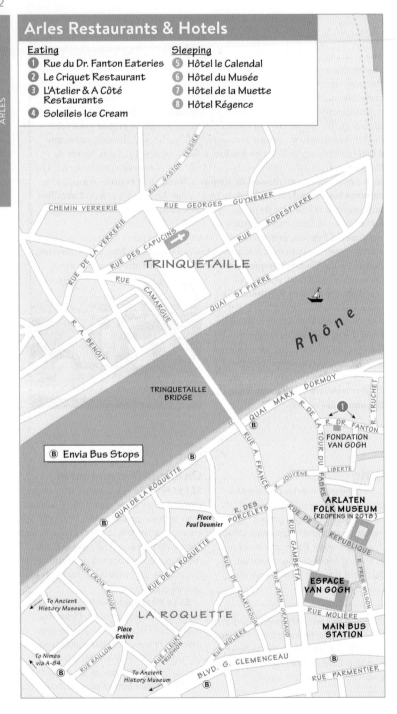

Arles Restaurants & Hotels

Eating

1. Rue du Dr. Fanton Eateries
2. Le Criquet Restaurant
3. L'Atelier & A Côté Restaurants
4. Soleileis Ice Cream

Sleeping

5. Hôtel le Calendal
6. Hôtel du Musée
7. Hôtel de la Muette
8. Hôtel Régence

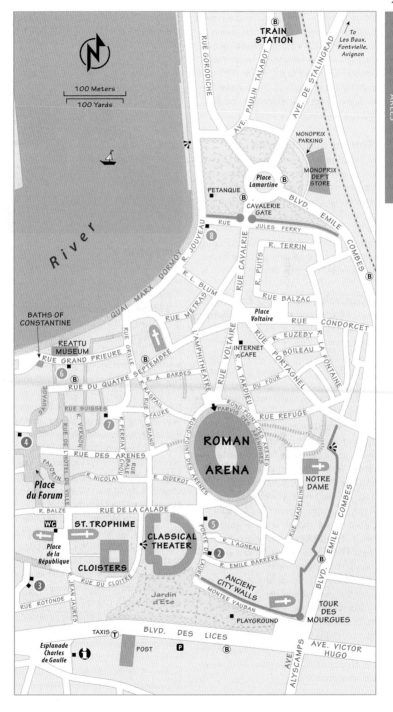

Map labels:

N — 100 Meters / 100 Yards

B TRAIN STATION

To Les Baux, Fontvieille, Avignon

RUE GORODICHE

AVE. PAULIN TALABOT

AVE. DE STALINGRAD

MONOPRIX PARKING

MONOPRIX DEP'T STORE

B Place Lamartine

PETANQUE **B**

CAVALERIE GATE

BLVD. EMILE COMBES

RUE JULES FERRY

RUE CAVALRIE

R. TERRIN

R. PUITS

8

RUE L. BLUM

RUE BALZAC

QUAI MARX DORMOY R. JOUVEAU

RUE METRASI

Place Voltaire

RUE CONDORCET

R. EUZEBY

BATHS OF CONSTANTINE

REATTU MUSEUM

6 **B**

RUE GRAND PRIEURE

RUE GRILLE

RUE DU QUATRE SEPTEMBRE

L'AMPHITHEATRE

RUE VOLTAIRE

RUE VOLTAIRE

RUE BOILEAU

PORTAGNEL

LA FONTAINE

INTERNET CAFE

A. TARDIEU

DU FOUR

R. A. BARBES

RUE SUISSES

R. VERNON

7

R. RASPAIL

R. PERRIAT

CHOU

RUE BRIAND

R. FAURE

ROND-POINT DES ARENES

RUE REFUGE

SAUVAGE

4

RUE DE L'HOTEL DE VILLE

RUE DES ARENES

BALZE

R. NICOLAI

R. DIDEROT

ROND-POINT DES ARENES

PARVIS DES ARENES

ROMAN ARENA

NOTRE DAME

RUE MADELEINE

BLVD. EMILE COMBES

FAVORIN

Place du Forum

Place de la République

WG

ST. TROPHIME

R. BALZE

RUE DE LA CALADE

5

PORTE DE LAURE

R. L'AGNEAU

R. EMILE BARRERE

B

CLASSICAL THEATER

2

CLOISTERS

RUE DU CLOITRE

3

R. JEAN JAURES

RUE ROTONDE

Jardin d'Ete

MONTEE VAUBAN

ANCIENT CITY WALLS

TOUR DES MOURGUES

PLAYGROUND

TAXIS **T**

POST **P**

BLVD. DES LICES

B

AVE. ALYSCAMPS

AVE. VICTOR HUGO

Esplanade Charles de Gaulle **i**

blending a warm interior, traditional French cuisine, and service with a smile, thanks to owner Frank. It's the most expensive of the places I list on this street and the least flexible, serving a €32 *menu* only. If it's cold, a roaring fire keeps you toasty (closed Sun-Mon, great fries and desserts, 18 Rue du Docteur Fanton, tel. 04 90 93 18 11).

Near the Roman Arena

$$ Le Criquet, a sweet little eatery two blocks above the arena, serves Provençal classics with joy at good prices. If you're really hungry, try the €25 *bourride*—a creamy fish soup thickened with aioli and garlic and stuffed with mussels, clams, calamari, and more (good €24-28 *menus*, indoor and outdoor dining, 21 Rue Porte de Laure, tel. 04 90 96 80 51).

A Gastronomic Dining Experience

One of France's most recognized chefs, Jean-Luc Rabanel, runs two different places 50 yards from Place de la République (at 7 Rue des Carmes). They sit side by side, both offering indoor and terrace seating.

$$$$ L'Atelier, a destination restaurant with two Michelin stars, attracts people from great distances to happily pay €125 for dinner and €65 for lunch. There is no menu, just a parade of delicious taste sensations served in artsy dishes. Don't plan on a quick dinner, and don't come for a traditional setting: Everything is enthusiastically contemporary. You'll probably see or hear the famous chef with his long salt-and-pepper hair and a deep voice. Friendly servers will hold your hand through this palate-widening experience (closed Mon-Tue, book ahead, tel. 04 90 91 07 69, www.rabanel.com).

$$$ A Côté, next door, offers a wine bar/bistro ambience and the chef's top-quality cuisine for much less money. There is a limited selection of wines by the glass (open daily, tel. 04 90 47 61 13, www.bistro-acote.com).

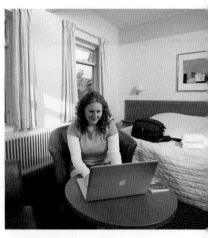

Sleeping

Hotels are a great value here. Many are air-conditioned, though few have elevators.

$$ Hôtel le Calendal*** is a thoughtfully managed place ideally located between the Roman Arena and Classical Theater. The hotel opens to the street with airy lounges and a lovely palm-shaded courtyard, providing an enjoyable refuge. The rooms sport Provençal decor and come in random shapes and sizes (standard Db-€119, larger or balcony Db-€139-159, family rooms available, breakfast buffet-€12, air-con, reserve ahead for parking-€8/day, café/sandwich bar open daily, just above arena at 5 Rue Porte de Laure, tel. 04 90 96 11 89, www.lecalendal.com, contact@lecalendal.com).

$ Hôtel du Musée** is a quiet, affordable manor-home hideaway tucked deep in Arles (if driving, ask for access code to street barrier so you can drop off your bags). This delightful place comes with 28 wood-floored rooms, a flowery courtyard, and comfortable lounges. Light-hearted Claude and English-speaking Laurence are good hosts (Sb-€65, Db-€70-90, family rooms available, buffet breakfast-€8.50, no elevator, garage parking-€10/day, follow signs to *Réattu Museum* to 11 Rue du Grand Prieuré, tel.

04 90 93 88 88, www.hoteldumusee.com, contact@hoteldumusee.com).

$ Hôtel de la Muette**, run by Brigitte and Alain, is located in a quiet corner of Arles. Rooms come with stone walls, tiled floors, and pebble showers (Db-€81, family rooms available, direct booking discount for Rick Steves readers, buffet breakfast-€9, no elevator, private garage-€10/day, 15 Rue des Suisses, tel. 04 90 96 15 39, www.hotel-muette.com, hotel.muette@wanadoo.fr).

Rick's Tip: *An international photo event* **jams hotels in Arles the second weekend of July,** *while the twice-yearly Féria* **draws crowds over Easter and in mid-September.**

$ Hôtel Régence**, a top budget deal, has a riverfront location, comfortable Provençal rooms, safe parking, and a location near the train station. Gentle Valérie and Eric speak English (Db-€60-75, family rooms available, choose river-view or quieter courtyard rooms, good buffet breakfast-€6, no elevator but only two floors, garage parking-€7/day; from Place Lamartine, turn right after passing between towers to reach 5 Rue Marius Jouveau; tel. 04 90 96 39 85, www.hotel-regence.com, contact@hotel-regence.com).

Transportation
Getting Around Arles

In this flat city, everything's within **walking** distance. Only the Ancient History Museum requires a healthy walk (20 minutes). The elevated riverside promenade provides Rhône views and a direct route to the Ancient History Museum (to the southwest) and the train station (to the northeast). Keep your head up for *Starry Night* memories, but eyes down for doggie droppings.

Arles' **taxis** charge a set fee of about €11, but nothing except the Ancient History Museum is worth a taxi ride. To call a cab, dial 04 90 96 52 76 or 04 90 96 90 03.

The free **Envia minibus** circles the town, useful for access to the train station, hotels, and the Ancient History Museum (2/hour, Mon-Sat 7:00-19:00, none Sun).

Arriving and Departing

Compare train and bus schedules: For some nearby destinations the bus may be the better choice, and it's usually cheaper.

BY TRAIN

The train station is on the river, a 10-minute walk from the town center. There's no baggage storage at the station, but you can walk 10 minutes to stow it at Hôtel Régence (see "Orientation," earlier).

To reach the town center or Ancient History Museum from the train station, wait for the free **Envia minibus** at the glass shelter facing away from the station (cross the street and veer left, 2/hour Mon-Sat 7:00-19:00, none Sun). The bus makes a counterclockwise loop around Arles, stopping near most of my recommended hotels (see map on page 236 for stops). **Taxis** usually wait in front of the station.

Train Connections from Arles to: Paris (11/day, 2 direct TGVs—4 hours, 9 more with transfer in Avignon—5 hours), **Avignon Centre-Ville** (roughly hourly, 20 minutes; 5-minute shuttle train from Avignon Centre-Ville connects to Avignon TGV Station), **Carcassonne** (4/day direct, 2.5 hours, more with transfer in Narbonne, direct trains may require reservations), **Beaune** (10/day, 5 hours), **Nice** (11/day, 4 hours, most require transfer in Marseille).

BY BUS

Arles' bus station is on Boulevard Georges Clémenceau. Most buses to regional destinations depart from here and most cost only €1.50. Get schedules at the TI or from the bus company (tel. 08 10 00 13 26, www.lepilote.com).

Bus Connections from Arles Train Station to Avignon TGV Station: The direct SNCF bus is easier than the train (€9, 9/day, 1 hour, included with rail pass).

Bus Connections from Arles to Les Baux: Bus #57 connects Arles to Les Baux (6/day daily July-Aug, Sat-Sun only in May-June and Sept, none Oct-April; 35 minutes to Les Baux, then runs to Avignon).

BY CAR

For most hotels, first follow signs to *Centre-Ville*, then *Gare SNCF* (train station). You'll come to a big roundabout (Place Lamartine) with a Monoprix department store to the right. You can park along the city wall (except on Tue night when tow trucks clear things out for the Wed market); the hotels I list are no more than a 15-minute walk from here. Fearless drivers can plunge into the narrow streets between the two stumpy towers via Rue de la Calade, and follow signs to their hotel. Theft is a problem—leave nothing in your car, and trust your hotelier's advice on where to park.

Most hotels have metered parking nearby (free Mon-Sat 12:00-14:00 & 19:00-9:00, and all day Sun; some meters limited to 2.5 hours). If you can't find a space near your hotel, Parking des Lices (Arles' only parking garage), near the TI on Boulevard des Lices, is a good fallback.

AVIGNON

Famous for its nursery rhyme, medieval bridge, and brooding Palace of the Popes, contemporary Avignon (ah-veen-yohn) bustles and prospers behind its mighty walls. For nearly 100 years (1309-1403) Avignon was the capital of Christendom, home to seven popes. (And, for a difficult period after that—during the Great Schism when there were two competing popes—Avignon was "the other Rome.") During this time, it grew from a quiet village into a thriving city.

Today, with its large student population and fashionable shops, Avignon is an intriguing blend of medieval history, youthful energy, and urban sophistication. Street performers entertain the international throngs who fill Avignon's ubiquitous cafés and trendy boutiques. And each July the city goes crazy during its huge theater festival (with about 2,000 performances, big crowds, higher prices, and hotels booked up long in advance). Clean, lively, and popular with tourists, Avignon is more impressive for its outdoor ambience than for its museums and monuments.

Orientation

Cours Jean Jaurès, which turns into Rue de la République, runs straight from the Centre-Ville train station to Place de l'Horloge and the Palace of the Popes, splitting Avignon in two. The larger eastern half is where the action is. Climb to the Jardin du Rochers des Doms for the town's best view, tour the pope's immense palace, lose yourself in Avignon's back streets, and find a shady square to call home.

Tourist Information: The TI is helpful, with lots of information about the city and the region (April-Oct Mon-Sat 9:00-18:00, Sun 10:00-17:00, daily until 19:00 in July, shorter hours off-season; between the train station and the old town at 41 Cours Jean Jaurès, tel. 04 32 74 32 74, www.avignon-tourisme.com).

Sightseeing Pass: At the TI, pick up the free **Avignon Passion Pass** (for up to 5 family members). Get it stamped at your first sight to receive discounts at the others. The pass comes with the Avignon "Passion" map and guide, which includes several good (but tricky-to-follow) walking tours. The TI also has bike maps for good rides in the area, including the Ile de la Barthelasse.

Bike Rental: Rent pedal and electric bikes and scooters near the train station at **Provence Bike** (April-Oct 9:00-18:30, 7 Avenue St. Ruf, tel. 04 90 27 92 61, www.provence-bike.com). You'll enjoy riding on the Ile de la Barthelasse (the TI has bike maps).

Car Rental: The TGV Station has

counters for all the big companies; only Avis is at the Centre-Ville Station.

Local Guides: Imagine Tours focuses on cultural excursions adapted to your interests. Guides will meet you at your hotel or the departure point of your choice (€190/half-day, €315/day, prices for up to 4 people starting from near Avignon or Arles, mobile 06 89 22 19 87, www.imagine-tours.net, imagine.tours@gmail.com). The **Avignon Gourmet Walking Tour** is a wonderful experience if you like to eat; charming Aurelie meets small groups daily (except Sun and Mon) at the TI at 9:15 for a well-designed three-hour, eight-stop walk. Book in advance on her website (€55/person, 2-8 people per group, tel. 06 35 32 08 96, www.avignongourmetours.com).

Tourist Train: The little train leaves regularly from in front of the Palace of the Popes and offers a decent overview of the city, including the Jardin du Rochers des Doms and St. Bénezet Bridge (€7, 2/hour, 40 minutes, English commentary, mid-March-mid-Oct daily 10:00-18:00, July-Aug until 19:00).

Minivan Excursions: Provence Reservation offers day tours by minivan or bus

to nearby sights (such as lavender fields) from Avignon, Arles, and more. Tours from Avignon run year-round and cover a great variety of destinations; tours from other cities run April through September only and are more limited in scope. You'll get comfortable transportation but not guiding; you're on your own at the sights (about €60-80/half-day, €100-120/day for minivan tours, less for their big-bus tours, tel. 04 90 14 70 00, www.provence-reservation.com).

◉ Avignon Walk

This self-guided walk, worth ▲▲, offers a fine overview of the city and its major sights.

• *Start your tour where the Romans did, on Place de l'Horloge, in front of City Hall (Hôtel de Ville).*

PLACE DE L'HORLOGE

In ancient Roman times this was the forum, and in medieval times it was the market square. The square is named for the clock tower (now hiding behind the more recently built City Hall), which, in its day, was a humanist statement. In medieval France, the only bells in town rang

Place de l'Horloge

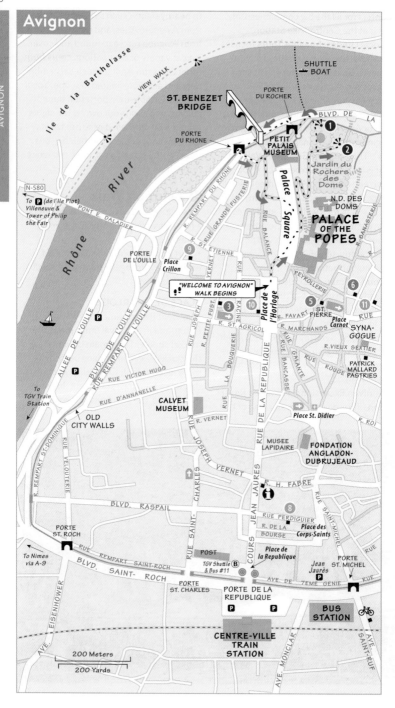

Avignon

Ile de la Barthelasse

VIEW WALK

SHUTTLE BOAT

ST. BENEZET BRIDGE

PORTE DU ROCHER

BLVD. DE LA

Rhône River

PORTE DU RHONE

PETIT PALAIS MUSEUM

Palace Square

Jardin du Rochers des Doms

N.D. DES DOMS

N-580

To P (de l'Ile Plot)
Villeneuve &
Tower of Philip
the Fair

PONT E. DALADIER

R. REMPART DU RHONE

R. STE GRANDE FUSTERIE

RUE BALANCE

PALACE OF THE POPES

PORTE DE L'OULLE

Place Crillon

R. ST. ETIENNE
VERNET

PEYROLLERIE

"WELCOME TO AVIGNON" WALK BEGINS

R. PETITE FUST.

R. ST. AGRICOL

RACINE

Place de l'Horloge

ST. PIERRE

Place Carnot

PEYROLLERIE

SYNA-GOGUE

R. FAVART

R. MARCHANDS

RUE

R. VIEUX SEXTIER

RUE ROUGE

PATRICK MALLARD PASTRIES

ALLEE DE L'OULLE

BLVD. DE L'OULLE

RUE REMPART DE L'OULLE

RUE JOSEPH

RUE LA BOUQUERIE

RUE DE LA REPUBLIQUE

RUE GALANTE

RUE BANCASSE

To TGV Train Station

RUE VICTOR HUGO

RUE D'ANNANELLE

CALVET MUSEUM

R. VERNET

RUE

Place St. Didier

R. ROI

OLD CITY WALLS

R. REMPART ST-DOMINIQUE

RUE VELOUTERIE

RUE JOSEPH VERNET

RUE SAINT- CHARLES

MUSEE LAPIDAIRE

FONDATION ANGLADON-DUBRUJEAUD

BLVD. RASPAIL

R. H. FABRE

RUE SAINT-MICHEL

PORTE ST. ROCH

RUE PERDIGUIER

R. DE LA BOURSE

Place des Corps-Saints

RUE

To Nimes via A-9

RUE REMPART SAINT-ROCH

BLVD. SAINT- ROCH

PORTE ST. CHARLES

COURS JEAN JAURES

POST

TGV Shuttle & Bus #11

Place de la Republique

Jean Jaures

PORTE ST. MICHEL

AVE. DE 7EME GENIE

AVE. EISENHOWER

PORTE DE LA REPUBLIQUE

BUS STATION

CENTRE-VILLE TRAIN STATION

AVE. MONCLAR

AVE. SAINT-RUF

200 Meters

200 Yards

1 2 9 3 10 5 6 11 8

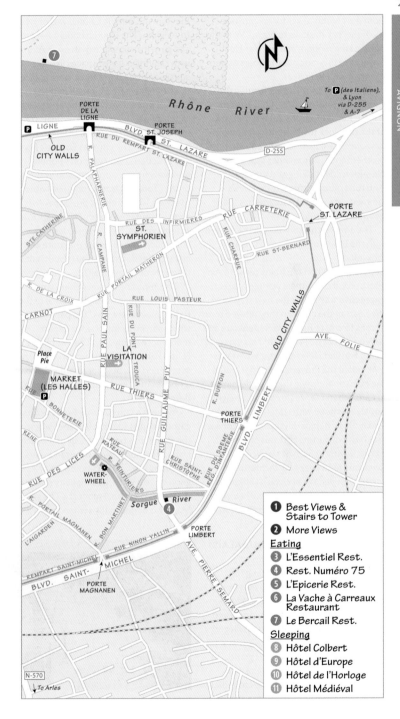

Rhône River

To **P** (des Italiens),
& Lyon
via D-255
& A-7

PORTE
DE LA
LIGNE

P LIGNE

BLVD. ST. JOSEPH

PORTE
ST. JOSEPH

OLD
CITY WALLS

RUE DU REMPART ST. LAZARE

ST. LAZARE

D-255

R. PALAPHARNERIE

STE. CATHERINE

RUE CAMPANE

RUE DES INFIRMIERES

RUE CARRETERIE

PORTE
ST. LAZARE

ST.
SYMPHORIEN

RUE CHARRUE

RUE ST-BERNARD

R. DE LA CROIX

RUE PORTAIL MATHERON

RUE LOUIS PASTEUR

CARNOT

RUE PAUL SAIN

RUE DU PONT TROUCA

OLD CITY WALLS

AVE. FOLIE

Place
Pie

LA
VISITATION

MARKET
(LES HALLES)

P

RUE THIERS

RUE GUILLAUME PUY

R. BUFFON

PORTE
THIERS

BLVD. LIMBERT

R. BONNETERIE

RENE

RUE DES LICES

RUE RATEAU

R. TEINTURIERS

RUE SAINT-CHRISTOPHE

RUE DU 5EME
RÉG. D'INFANTERIE

WATER-
WHEEL

Sorgue River

4

PORTE
LIMBERT

R. PORTAIL MAGNANEN

R. BON MARTINET

RUE NINON VALLIN

AVE. PIERRE SEMARD

L'AIGARDEN

REMPART SAINT-MICHEL

MICHEL

BLVD. SAINT-

PORTE
MAGNANEN

N-570

To Arles

1 Best Views &
Stairs to Tower

2 More Views

Eating

3 L'Essentiel Rest.

4 Rest. Numéro 75

5 L'Epicerie Rest.

6 La Vache à Carreaux
Restaurant

7 Le Bercail Rest.

Sleeping

8 Hôtel Colbert

9 Hôtel d'Europe

10 Hôtel de l'Horloge

11 Hôtel Médiéval

from the church tower to indicate not the hours but the calls to prayer. With the dawn of the modern age, secular clock towers like this rang out the hours as people organized their lives.

Taking humanism a step further, the City Hall (Hôtel de Ville), built after the French Revolution, obstructed the view of the old clock tower while celebrating a new era. The slogan "liberty, equality, and brotherhood" is a reminder that the people supersede the king and the church. And today, judging from the square's jammed cafés and restaurants, it's the people who do rule.

The square's present popularity arrived with the trains in 1854. Facing City Hall, look left down the main drag, Rue de la République. When the trains came to Avignon, proud city fathers wanted a direct, impressive way to link the new station to the heart of the city—so they plowed over homes to create Rue de la République and widened Place de l'Horloge. This main drag's Parisian feel is intentional—it was built not in the Provençal manner, but in the Haussmann style that is so dominant in Paris (characterized by broad, straight boulevards lined with stately buildings). Today, this Champs-Elysées of Avignon is lined with department stores and banks.
• *Walk slightly uphill past the Neo-Renaissance facade of the theater and the carousel (public WCs behind). Look back to see the late Gothic bell tower. Then veer right at the Hôtel des Palais des Papes and continue into...*

PALACE SQUARE (PLACE DU PALAIS)
Pull up a concrete stump just past the café. Nicknamed *bites* (slang for penis), these effectively keep cars from double-parking in areas designed for people. Many of the metal ones slide up and down by remote control to let privileged cars come and go.

Now take in the scene. This grand square is lined with the Palace of the Popes, the Petit Palais, and the cathedral. In the 1300s, the entire headquarters of

the Roman Catholic Church was moved to Avignon. The Church bought Avignon and gave it a complete makeover. Along with clearing out vast spaces like this square and building a three-acre palace, the Church erected more than three miles of protective wall (with 39 towers), "appropriate" housing for cardinals (read: mansions), and residences for its entire bureaucracy. The city was Europe's largest construction zone. Avignon's population grew from 6,000 to 25,000 in short order. (Today, 13,000 people live within the walls.) The limits of pre-papal Avignon are outlined on your city map: Rues Joseph Vernet, Henri Fabre, des Lices, and Philonarde all follow the route of the city's earlier defensive wall (about half the diameter of today's wall).

The imposing facade behind you, across the square from the Palace of the Popes' main entry, was "the papal mint," which served as the finance department for the Holy See. The Petit Palais (Little Palace) seals the uphill end of the square and was built for a cardinal; today it houses medieval paintings (museum described next).

Avignon's 12th-century Romanesque cathedral, just to the left of the Palace of the Popes, has been the seat of the local bishop for more than a thousand years. Predating the Church's purchase of Avignon by 200 years, its simplicity reflects Avignon's pre-papal modesty. The gilded Mary was added in 1854 when the Vatican

Palace Square

established the doctrine of her Immaculate Conception (born without the stain of original sin).

• *You can visit the massive **Palace of the Popes** (described on page 262) now, but it's better to visit it at the end of this walk.*

Now is a good time to take in the...

PETIT PALAIS MUSEUM (MUSEE DU PETIT PALAIS)

This former cardinal's palace now displays the Church's collection of (mostly) art. The information is only in French, but a visit here before going to the Palace of the Popes helps furnish and populate that otherwise barren building. You'll see bits of statues and tombs—an inventory of the destruction of exquisite Church art wrought by the French Revolution (which tackled established French society with Taliban-esque fervor). Then come many rooms filled with religious Italian paintings, organized in chronological order from early Gothic to late Renaissance.

Cost and Hours: €6, Wed-Mon 10:00-13:00 & 14:00-18:00, closed Tue, at north end of Palace Square, tel. 04 90 86 44 58, www.petit-palais.org.

• *From Palace Square, head up to the cathedral (enjoy the viewpoint overlooking the square), and zig-zag up the ramps to the top of a rocky hill where Avignon was first settled. Atop the hill is an inviting café and pond in a park—our next stop. At the far side is a viewpoint high above the river from where you can see Avignon's beloved broken bridge.*

Petit Palais Museum

▲JARDIN DU ROCHERS DES DOMS

Enjoy the view from this bluff. On a clear day, the tallest peak you see, with its white limestone cap, is Mont Ventoux ("Windy Mountain"). Below and just to the right, you'll spot free passenger ferries shuttling across the river to Ile de la Barthelasse, an island nature-preserve where Avignon can breathe. Tucked amid the trees on the island side of the river is a fun, recommended restaurant, Le Bercail, a local favorite. To the left in the distance is the TGV rail bridge.

The Rhône River marked the border of Vatican territory in medieval times. Fort St. André (across the river on the hill) was across the border, in the kingdom of France. The fort was built in 1360, shortly after the pope moved to Avignon, to counter the papal incursion into this part of Europe. Avignon's famous bridge was a key border crossing, with towers on either end—one was French, and the other was the pope's. The French one, across the river, is the Tower of Philip the Fair.

• *Take the walkway down to the left and find the stairs (closed at dusk) leading down to the tower. You'll catch glimpses of the...*

RAMPARTS

The only bit of the rampart you can walk on is accessed from St. Bénezet Bridge (pay to enter—see next). Just after the papacy took control of Avignon, the walls were extended to take in the convents and monasteries that had been outside the city. What you see today was partially restored in the 19th century.

• *When you leave the tower on street level, exit the walls, then turn left along the wall to the old bridge. Pass under the bridge to find its entrance shortly after.*

▲ST. BENEZET BRIDGE (PONT ST. BENEZET)

This bridge, whose construction and location were inspired by a shepherd's religious vision, is the "Pont d'Avignon" of nursery-rhyme fame. The ditty (which you've probably been humming all day) dates back to the 15th century: *Sur le Pont d'Avignon, on y danse, on y danse, sur le Pont d'Avignon, on y danse tous en rond* ("On the bridge of Avignon, we will dance, we will dance, on the bridge of Avignon, we will dance all in a circle").

And the bridge was a big deal even outside of its kiddie-tune fame. Built between 1171 and 1185, it was strategic—one of only three bridges crossing the mighty Rhône in the Middle Ages, important to pilgrims, merchants, and armies. It was damaged several times by floods and subsequently rebuilt. In 1668 most of it was knocked out for the last time by a disastrous icy flood. The townsfolk decided not to rebuild this time, and for more than a century, Avignon had no bridge across the Rhône. While only four arches survive today, the original bridge was huge: Imagine a 22-arch, 3,000-foot-long bridge extending from Vatican territory across the island to the lonely Tower of Philip the Fair, which marked the beginning of France (see displays of the bridge's original length).

Cost and Hours: €5, includes audioguide, €13.50 combo-ticket includes Palace of the Popes, daily March-Oct 9:00-19:00, July-Aug until 20:00, Nov-Feb 9:30-17:45, last entry one hour before closing; tel. 04 90 27 51 16.

• *To get to the Palace of the Popes from here, leave via the riverfront exit, turn left, then turn left again back into the walls. Walk to the end of the short street, then turn right following signs to Palais des Papes. Next, look for brown signs leading left under the passageway, then stay the course up the narrow steps to Palace Square.*

▲▲PALACE OF THE POPES (PALAIS DES PAPES)

In 1309 a French pope was elected (Pope Clément V). His Holiness decided that dangerous Italy was no place for a pope, so he moved the whole operation to Avignon for a secure rule under a supportive French king. The Catholic Church literally bought Avignon (then a two-bit town), and popes resided here until 1403. Meanwhile, Italians demanded a Roman pope, so from 1378 on, there were twin popes—one in Rome and one in Avignon—causing a schism in the Catholic Church that

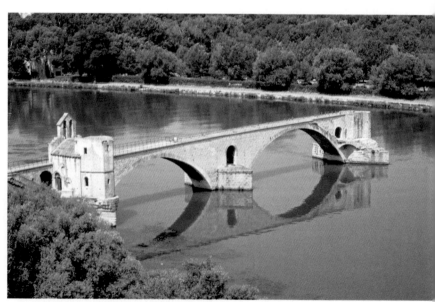

St. Bénezet Bridge

wasn't fully resolved until 1417.

Cost and Hours: €11, €13.50 combo-ticket includes St. Bénezet Bridge, daily March-Oct 9:00-19:00, July-Aug until 20:00, Nov-Feb 9:30-17:45, last entry one hour before closing; thorough and essential audioguide-€2; tel. 04 90 27 50 00, www.palais-des-papes.com.

Visiting the Palace: You'll follow a one-way route. A big room near the start functions as "the museum," with artifacts (such as cool 14th-century arrowheads) and a good intro video.

The palace was built stark and strong, before the popes knew how long they'd be staying (and before the affluence and fanciness of the Renaissance and Baroque ages). This was the most fortified palace of the time (remember, the pope left Rome to be more secure). With 10-foot-thick walls, it was a symbol of power. There are huge ceremonial rooms (rarely used) and more intimate living quarters. The bedroom comes with the original wall paintings, a decorated wooden ceiling, and fine tiled floor. And there's one big "chapel" (twice the size of the adjacent cathedral) that, while simple, is majestic in its pure French Gothic lines.

This largest surviving Gothic palace in Europe was built to accommodate 500 people as the administrative center of the Holy See and home of the pope. Seven popes ruled from here, making this the center of Christianity for nearly 100 years. The last pope checked out in 1403, but the Church owned Avignon until the French Revolution in 1791. During this interim period, the palace still housed Church authorities. Avignon residents, many of whom had come from Rome, spoke Italian for a century after the pope left, making the town a cultural oddity within France.

The palace is pretty empty today—nothing portable survived both the pope's return to Rome and the French Revolution. You can climb the tower (Tour de la Gâche) for grand views. The artillery room is now a gift shop, channeling all visitors on a full tour of knickknacks for sale.

• *You'll exit at the rear of the palace. To return to Palace Square, make two rights after exiting the palace.*

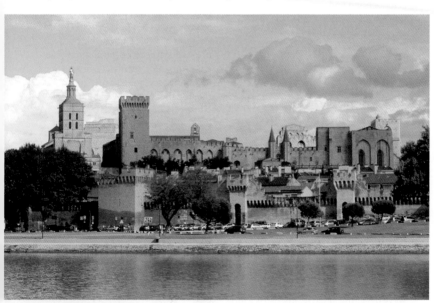

Palace of the Popes

Experiences

Ile de la Barthelasse Saunter

A free shuttle boat, the *Navette Fluviale*, plies back and forth across the Rhône River to Ile de la Barthelasse. This peaceful island offers grassy walks, bike rides, and the recommended riverside restaurant Le Bercail. For great views, walk the riverside path to Daladier Bridge, and then cross back over the bridge into town.

Cost and Hours: Free; 3 boats/hour depart from near St. Bénezet Bridge, daily April-June and Sept 10:00-12:30 & 14:00-18:00, July-Aug 11:00-21:00; Oct-March weekends and Wed afternoons only.

Rick's Tip: *If you stay on the island for dinner, check the schedule to make sure you* **don't miss the last return boat.**

Eating

Avignon offers a good range of restaurants and settings, from lively squares to atmospheric streets. Skip the overpriced, underwhelming restaurants on Place de l'Horloge and find a more intimate location for your dinner. At the finer places, reservations are generally smart (especially on weekends).

Fine Dining

$$$$ L'Essentiel is where locals go for a fine meal. The setting is classy-contemporary inside, the back terrace is romantic, the wine list is extensive, the cuisine is classic French, and gentle owner Dominique makes timid diners feel at ease (€31-45 *menus,* closed Sun-Mon, inside and outdoor seating, 2 Rue Petite Fusterie, tel. 04 90 85 87 12, www.restaurantlessentiel.com).

$$$ Restaurant Numéro 75 is worth the walk. It fills the Pernod mansion (of *pastis* liquor fame) with a romantic, chandeliered, Old World dining hall that extends to a leafy, gravelly courtyard. They serve delightful lunch salads, fish is a forte,

and the French cuisine is beautifully presented (€32 lunch *menu*, dinner *menus*: €29 two-course and €37 three-course, closed Sun, 75 Rue Guillaume Puy, tel. 04 90 27 16 00, www.numero75.com).

Dining on a Moderate Budget

$$$ L'Epicerie sits alone under green awnings on the romantic Place St-Pierre and is ideal for dinner outside (or in the small but cozy interior). The cuisine is as delicious as the setting (€10 starters, €24 *plats*, daily, 10 Place St-Pierre, tel. 04 90 82 74 22).

$$ La Vache à Carreaux venerates cheese and wine while offering a range of choices from its big chalkboard. It's a young, lively place, with colorful decor, easygoing service (thanks to owner Jean-Charles), and a reasonable wine list (€12 starters, €12-16 *plats*, €5 wines by the glass, daily, just off atmospheric Place des Châtaignes at 14 Rue de la Peyrolerie, tel. 04 90 80 09 05).

Across the Rhône

$$$ Le Bercail offers a fun opportunity to get out of town (barely) and take in *le fresh air* with a terrific riverfront view of Avignon, all while enjoying big portions of Provençal cooking (*menus* from €28, daily April-Oct, serves late, reservations recommended, tel. 04 90 82 20 22). Take the free shuttle boat (located near St.

Bénezet Bridge) to the Ile de la Barthelasse, turn right, and walk five minutes.
As the boat usually stops running at about
18:00 (except in July-Aug, when it runs
until 21:00), you can either taxi back or
walk 25 minutes along the pleasant riverside path and over Daladier Bridge.

Sleeping
Hotel values are better in Arles, though
I've found some pretty good deals in Avignon. Drivers should ask about parking
discounts through hotels.

Rick's Tip: *During the* **July theater festival,**
*rooms are few in Avignon—you must book
long ahead and pay inflated prices.*
It's better to stay in Arles.

Near Centre-Ville Station
$ Hôtel Colbert** is on a quiet lane, with
a dozen spacious rooms gathered on four
floors around a skinny spiral staircase (no
elevator). Patrice decorates each room
with a colorful (occasionally erotic) flair.
There are warm public spaces and a sweet
little patio (Sb-€74, small Db-€82, bigger
Db-€100, some tight bathrooms, rooms
off the patio can be musty, closed Nov-
mid-March, 7 Rue Agricol Perdiguier, tel.
04 90 86 20 20, www.lecolbert-hotel.com,
contact@avignon-hotel-colbert.com).

Near Place de l'Horloge
$$$ Hôtel d'Europe***,** with Avignon's
most prestigious address, lets peasants
sleep royally—but only if they land one
of the 13 reasonable "classique" rooms.
Enter through a shady courtyard, linger
in the lounges, and savor every comfort.
The hotel is located on the handsome
Place Crillon, near the river (standard
"classique" Db-€230, large Db-€390-590,
view suites-€1,100, breakfast-€22, garage
parking-€20/day, near Daladier Bridge at
12 Place Crillon, tel. 04 90 14 76 76, www.
heurope.com, reservations@heurope.
com).

$$ Hôtel de l'Horloge** is as central
as it gets—on Place de l'Horloge. It offers
66 unimaginative but comfortable rooms
at fair rates, some with terraces and views
of the city and the Palace of the Popes
(standard Db-€140-170, bigger Db with
terrace-€180-225, elaborate €18 buffet
breakfast/brunch, 1 Rue Félicien David,
tel. 04 90 16 42 00, www.hotel-avignon-
horloge.com, hotel.horloge@hotels-ocre-
azur.com).

$ Hôtel Médiéval,** burrowed deep a
few blocks from the Church of St. Pierre,
was built as a cardinal's home. This stone
mansion's grand staircase leads to 35
comfortable, pastel rooms (Sb-€65,
Db-€75-102, family rooms available, no
elevator, 5 blocks east of Place de l'Horloge, behind Church of St. Pierre at 15 Rue
Petite Saunerie, tel. 04 90 86 11 06, www.
hotelmedieval.com, hotel.medieval@
wanadoo.fr, run by helpful Régis).

Transportation
Getting Around Avignon
Avignon's walled city is compact, and all
the major sights can be visited on foot.
The streets are cobbled, so wear comfortable shoes.

Arriving and Departing
BY TRAIN
Avignon has two train stations: Centre-
Ville and TGV. While most TGV trains
serve only the TGV Station, some also
stop at Centre-Ville—check your ticket
and verify your station in advance.
    Centre-Ville Station *(Gare Avignon
Centre-Ville):* This station gets all non-
TGV trains and a few TGV trains. To reach
the town center, cross the busy street in
front of the station and walk through the
city walls onto Cours Jean Jaurès (the TI
is three blocks down).
    *Train Connections from Centre-Ville
Station to:* **Arles** (roughly hourly, 20
minutes, less frequent in the afternoon),
Carcassonne (8/day, 7 with transfer in
Narbonne or Nîmes, 3 hours).

TGV Station (*Gare TGV*): On the outskirts of town, this station has a summer-only TI (short hours), but no baggage storage. Car rental, buses, and taxis are outside the north exit (*sortie nord*). To reach the city center, take the **shuttle train** from platform A or B to Centre-Ville Station (€1.60, 2/hour, 5 minutes, buy ticket from machine on platform or at desk in main hall). A **taxi** ride between the TGV station and downtown Avignon costs about €15.

If you're connecting from the TGV Station to other points, you'll find **buses** to Arles' Centre-Ville train station at the second bus shelter (€9, 9/day, 1 hour, included with rail pass, schedule posted on shelter and available at info booths inside station). If you're **driving** a rental car directly to Arles or Les Baux, leave the station following signs to *Avignon Sud*, then *La Rocade*. You'll soon see exits to Arles (best for Les Baux, too).

Train Connections from TGV Station to: **Nice** (10/day, most by TGV, 4 hours, many require transfer in Marseille), Paris' Gare de Lyon (10/day direct, 2.5 hours; more connections with transfer, 3-4 hours), Paris' **Charles de Gaulle airport** (7/day, 3.25 hours).

BY BUS

The efficient bus station (*gare routière*) is 100 yards to the right as you leave the Centre-Ville train station, beyond and below Hôtel Ibis (info desk open Mon-Fri 8:00-19:30, Sat 10:00-12:30 & 13:30-18:00, closed Sun, tel. 04 90 82 07 35). Nearly all buses leave from this station (a few leave from the ring road outside the station—

ask, buy tickets on bus, small bills only). Service is reduced or nonexistent on Sundays and holidays. Make sure to verify your destination with the driver.

Bus Connections from Avignon to: **Pont du Gard** (3/day, 50 minutes, departs from bus station), **Arles** (9/day, 1 hour, leaves from TGV Station), **Vaison-la-Romaine** and **Séguret** (3-6/day during the school year—*période scolaire*, 3/day otherwise; 1/day from TGV Station; 1.5 hours, all buses pass through Orange—faster to take train to Orange, and transfer to bus there).

BY CAR

Drivers entering Avignon follow *Centre-Ville* and *Gare SNCF* (train station) signs. You'll find central pay lots in the garage next to the Centre-Ville train station and at the Parking Jean Jaurès under the ramparts across from the station (enter the old city through the Porte St-Michel gate). Hotels have advice for overnight parking, and some offer parking deals.

Two free parking lots have complimentary shuttle buses to the center except on Sunday (follow *P Gratuit* signs): **Parking de l'Île Piot** is across Daladier Bridge (Pont Daladier) on Île de la Barthelasse, with shuttles to Place Crillon; **Parking des Italiens** is along the river east of the Palace of the Popes, with shuttles to Place Carnot (allow 30 minutes to walk from either to the center). Street parking is free in the *bleu* zones 12:00-14:00 and 19:00-9:00. (Hint: If you put €2 in the meter anytime between 19:00 and 9:00, you're good until 14:00.)

No matter where you park, leave nothing of value in your car.

NEAR ARLES AND AVIGNON

It's a short hop from Arles or Avignon to splendid scenery, Roman sights, warm stone villages, and world-class wine. See the great Roman Pont du Gard aqueduct; explore the ghost town that is ancient Les Baux; and spend time in pleasant Vaison-la-Romaine, a handy hub for the sunny Côtes du Rhône wine road.

Pont du Gard

Throughout the ancient world, aqueducts were like flags of stone that heralded the greatness of Rome. A visit to ▲▲▲ Pont du Gard still works to proclaim the wonders of that age. This impressively preserved Roman aqueduct was built in about 19 B.C., and while most of it is on or below the ground, at Pont du Gard it spans a canyon on a massive bridge over the Gardon River—one of the most remarkable surviving Roman ruins anywhere. The 30-mile aqueduct supported a small canal that, by dropping one inch for every 350 feet, supplied nine million gallons of water per day (about 100 gallons per second) to Nîmes—one of ancient Europe's largest cities. Allow about four or five hours for visiting Pont du Gard (including transportation time from Avignon).

Cost and Hours: €18/car (regardless of number of passengers), otherwise €7/person; aqueduct—daily until 24:00; museum—daily May-Sept 9:00-19:00, until 20:00 July-Aug, until 17:00 Oct-April, closed two weeks in Jan.

After Hours: The aqueduct is illuminated on summer evenings, and after the museum closes, you'll pay only €10 per carload to enter.

Getting There: The aqueduct is a 30-minute **drive** due west of Avignon (via N-100), and 45 minutes northwest of Arles (via Tarascon on D-6113). It's also reachable from Avignon by **bus** (3/day, 50 minutes), **taxi** (about €60), or **minivan tour** (Provence Reservation, also runs tours from Arles; see page 235).

Information: Tel. 04 66 37 59 99, www.pontdugard.fr.

Tours: In July and August, six tours a day go through the water channel at the top of the aqueduct (€4, check times posted at the museum and entry, no reservations are taken—limited to 33 people).

Canoe Rental: Floating under Pont du Gard by canoe is an unforgettable experience. **Collias Canoes** will pick you up at Pont du Gard (or elsewhere, if pre-arranged) and shuttle you to the town of Collias. You'll float down the river to the nearby town of Remoulins, where they'll pick you up and take you back to Pont du Gard (€21/person, €12/child under 12, usually 2 hours, though you can take as long as you like, reserve the day before in July-Aug, tel. 04 66 22 85 54).

Rick's Tip: **Pont du Gard** *is perhaps best enjoyed on your back and in the water—* **bring a swimsuit and flip-flops** *for the rocks. The best Pont du Gard viewpoints are up steep hills with uneven footing—* **bring good shoes, too.**

Visiting the Aqueduct: There are two riversides to Pont du Gard—the Left Bank (Rive Gauche) and Right Bank (Rive Droite). Park on the Rive Gauche, where you'll find the ticket booth and TI. You'll see the aqueduct in two parts: first the

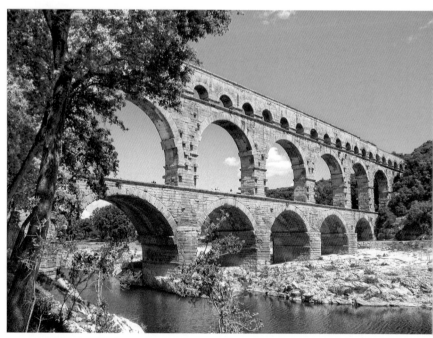

Pont du Gard

fine ▲ museum complex, then the actual river gorge spanned by the ancient bridge.

In the state-of-the-art **museum** (well-presented in English), you'll enter to the sound of water and understand the critical role fresh water played in the Roman "art of living." You'll see copies of lead pipes, faucets, and siphons; walk through a mock rock quarry; and learn how they moved those huge rocks into place and how those massive arches were made. A wooden model shows how Roman engineers determined the proper slope. While actual artifacts from the aqueduct are few, the exhibit shows the immensity of the undertaking as well as the payoff. Imagine the jubilation when this extravagant supply of water finally tumbled into Nîmes.

A parklike path leads to the **aqueduct.** Until a few years ago, this was an actual road—adjacent to the aqueduct—that had spanned the river since 1743. Before you cross the bridge, walk to the riverside viewpoint: Pass under the bridge and aqueduct and hike about 300 feet along the riverbank to the concrete steps leading down to a grand view of the world's second-highest standing Roman structure.

Ninety percent of the aqueduct is on or under the ground, but a few river canyons like this required bridges—and this was the biggest bridge in the whole 30-mile-long aqueduct. The arches are twice the width of standard aqueducts, and the main arch is the largest the Romans ever built—80 feet across (the width of the river). The bridge is about 160 feet high and was originally about 1,200 feet long.

A stone lid hides a four-foot-wide, six-foot-tall chamber lined with waterproof mortar that carried the stream for more than 400 years. For 150 years, this system provided Nîmes with good drinking water.

Hike over the bridge for a closer look and the best views. Steps lead up a high trail (marked *viewpoint/panorama*) to a superb vista (go right at the top;

best views are soon after the trail starts descending).

Les Baux

Tucked between Arles and Avignon, the hilltop town of Les Baux crowns the rugged Alpilles mountains. Many of the ancient walls of its striking castle still stand, a testament to the proud past of this village—now more a museum than a living town.

Orientation

Les Baux is actually two visits in one: castle ruins perched on an almost lunar landscape, and a medieval town below.

Day Plan: It's mobbed with tourists most of the day, but Les Baux rewards those who arrive by 9:00 or after 17:30. Savor the castle, then tour—or blitz—the lower streets on your way out. The lower town's polished-stone gauntlet of boutiques is a Provençal dream come true for shoppers.

Rick's Tip: *From Arles you can* **ride a rental bike to Les Baux** *(25 miles round-trip). It's a darn steep climb going into Les Baux, so consider busing up there (regional buses have bike racks) and gliding back.*

Getting There: Les Baux is a 20-minute **drive** from Arles: Follow signs for *Avignon,* then *Les Baux.* From Arles, Cartreize **bus #57** runs to Les Baux (daily July-Aug, Sat-Sun only in May-June and Sept, no service Oct-April, 6/day, 35 min-

A demonstration at Les Baux

Les Baux

Eating & Sleeping

1 Hostellerie de la Reine Jeanne
2 Le Mas d'Aigret Hôtel

100 Meters
100 Yards

To Views,
Carrières de Lumières
& St-Rémy
via most scenic route

D-27

To St-Rémy,
Maussane &
Le Paradou

D-27A

P

P

P

RUE PORTE MAGE

PORTE
MAGE

WC

DONJON

MUSEUM OF
SANTONS

Place
St-Louis
Jou

Uphill !

CASTLE
RUINS

GRAND RUE

LOWER

MANVILLE
MANSION
CITY HALL

CITADEL

EYGUIERES
GATE

TOWN

NEUVE

RENAISSANCE
WINDOW

YVES BRAYER
MUSEUM

FOURS

CHATEAU

R. L'ORINE

CHAPEL OF
PENITENTS

ST.
VINCENT

WC

TICKETS &
ENTRY TO
CASTLE RUINS

Cemetery

TRENCAT

ST. BLAISE
CHAPEL

Cliffs

D-27

Cliffs

To Arles &
Fontvielle

CHARLOUN-RIEU
MONUMENT

utes, www.lepilote.com). The best option for many is a **minivan tour** from Arles or Avignon; consider Provence Reservation tours (see page 235).

Arrival in Les Baux: Drivers will find pay lots near the entrance to the village. Or park for free at the Carrières de Lumières (described later) and walk along the road to Les Baux. The cobbled street into town and up the main drag leads directly to the castle—just keep going uphill (10-minute walk).

Tourist Information: The TI is immediately on the left as you enter the village (daily April-Oct, closed Sun off-season).

Sights
▲▲▲THE CASTLE RUINS (CHATEAU DES BAUX)
The sun-bleached ruins of the stone fortress of Les Baux are carved into, out of, and on top of a rock 650 feet above the valley floor. Here you can imagine the struggles of a strong community of people who lived a rough-and-tumble life—more interested in top-notch fortifications than dramatic views.

In the 11th century, Les Baux was a powerhouse in southern France, controlling about 80 towns. The lords of Baux fought the counts of Barcelona for control of Provence...and eventually lost. Later, Les Baux struggled with the French kings, who destroyed the fortress in 1483 and again in 1632. The once-powerful town of 4,000 was forever crushed.

Cost and Hours: €8, €10 if there's entertainment (see next), €15 combo-ticket with Carrières de Lumières (described later), includes excellent audioguide, daily Easter-June and Sept 9:00-19:15, July-Aug 9:00-20:15, March and Oct 9:30-18:30, Nov-Feb 10:00-17:00, tel. 04 90 54 55 56, www.chateau-baux-provence.com.

Rick's Tip: **Château des Baux** *closes at the end of the day, but once you're inside, you can* **stay as long as you like.** *You're welcome to bring a picnic (no food sold inside) and live out your medieval fantasies, all night long.*

View from the Château des Baux

Entertainment: Every day from April through September, the castle presents medieval pageantry, tournaments, demonstrations, and jousting matches. Pick up a schedule as you enter (or check online).

Visiting the Castle: As you walk on the windblown spur (*baux* in French), you'll pass kid-thrilling medieval siege weaponry (go ahead, try the battering ram). Good displays help reconstruct the place. Imagine 4,000 people living up here. Notice the water-catchment system (a slanted field that caught rainwater and drained it into cisterns—necessary during a siege) and find the reservoir cut into the rock below the castle's highest point. Look for post holes throughout the stone walls that reveal where beams once supported floors. For the most sensational views, climb to the blustery top of the citadel. Hang on. The mistral wind just might blow you away.

▲**LOWER TOWN**

After your castle visit, you can shop and eat your way back through the lower town. Or, escape some of the crowds by dropping in at these minor but worthwhile

sights as you descend. The 15th-century **City Hall** offers art exhibits under its cool vaults; the enjoyable Musée Yves Brayer lets you peruse three floors of Van Gogh-like Expressionist paintings; the 12th-century Romanesque **St. Vincent Church** was built short and wide to fit the terrain; and the free and fun **Museum of Santons** displays a collection of *santons* ("little saints"), popular folk figurines that decorate local Christmas mangers.

▲**CARRIERES DE LUMIERES (QUARRIES OF LIGHT)**

A 10-minute walk from Les Baux, this colossal quarry-cave with immense vertical walls offers a mesmerizing sound-and-slide experience. The show lasts 40 minutes and runs continuously. Dress warmly, as the cave is cool.

Cost and Hours: €11, €16 combo-ticket with Les Baux castle ruins, daily April-Sept 9:30-19:30, March and Oct-Dec 10:00-18:00, closed Jan-Feb, tel. 04 90 54 47 37, www.carrieres-lumieres.com.

Eating and Sleeping

In the **lower town,** you'll find quiet view cafés such as **$ Hostellerie de la Reine Jeanne****, which also offers **$** good-value rooms (just inside the town gate, www.la-reinejeanne.com). A plusher overnight option is **$$ Le Mas d'Aigret*****, a 10-minute walk east of Les Baux on D-27 (www.masdaigret.com).

Vaison-la-Romaine

With quick access to vineyards and villages, this lively little town of 6,000 sits north of Avignon and makes a good base for exploring the Côtes du Rhône wine region. You get two villages for the price of one: The "modern" lower city has Roman ruins and a bustling main square—café-lined Place Montfort. The car-free medieval hill town looms above, with meandering cobbled lanes and a ruined castle with a fine view.

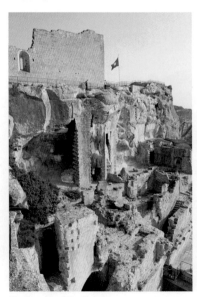

Castle ruins at Les Baux

Le Mistral

Provence lives with its vicious mistral winds, which blow 30 to 60 miles per hour, about 100 days of the year. The mistral clears people off the streets and turns lively cities into ghost towns. You'll likely spend a few hours or days taking refuge.

When the mistral blows, you can't escape. Author Peter Mayle said it could blow the ears off a donkey (I'd include the tail). According to the natives, it ruins crops, shutters, and roofs (look for stones holding tiles in place on many homes). They'll also tell you that this pernicious wind has driven many people crazy (including young Vincent van Gogh).

The mistral starts above the Alps and Massif Central mountains, then gathers steam as it heads south, funneling through the Rhône Valley before exhausting itself when it hits the Mediterranean. And though this wind rattles shutters everywhere in the Riviera and Provence, it's strongest over the Rhône Valley...so Avignon, Arles, and the Côtes du Rhône villages bear its brunt. While wiping the dust from your eyes, remember the good news: The mistral brings clear skies.

Orientation

The city is split in two by the Ouvèze River. The town's Roman Bridge connects the lower town (Ville-Basse) with the hill-capping upper town (Ville-Haute).

Getting There: Bus service connects Avignon and Vaison-la-Romaine, usually via Orange (3-6/day, 1.5 hour; 1 express bus/day, 1 hour). Vaison-la-Romaine is about a 40-minute **drive** from Avignon.

Arrival in Vaison-la-Romaine: If you're riding the bus, tell the driver you want to go to the *Office de Tourisme*. From the bus stop, walk five minutes down Avenue Général de Gaulle to reach the TI. Drivers should follow signs to *Centre-Ville,* then *Office de Tourisme;* parking is free across from the TI and at most places in town.

Tourist Information: The superb TI is in the lower city, between the two Roman ruin sites, at Place du Chanoine Sautel (daily but closed Sun off-season, tel. 04 90 36 02 11, www.vaison-ventoux-tourisme.com).

Private Guide: For historic town walks, try **Anna-Marie Melard** (tel. 04 90 36 50 48) or **Janet Henderson** (www.provencehistorytours.com).

Cooking Classes: Charming Barbara Schuerenberg offers reasonably priced cooking classes from her view home (€80, cash only, includes lunch, www.cuisinedeprovence.com).

Sights
ROMAN RUINS

Ancient Vaison-la-Romaine had a treaty that gave it a preferred "federated" relationship with Rome. This, along with a healthy farming economy (olives and vineyards), made it a prosperous place, as a close look at its sprawling ruins demonstrates.

Cost and Hours: €8; daily April-May 9:30-18:00, June-Sept until 18:30, shorter hours off-season, closed Jan-Feb; videoguide-€3 or download free app, tel. 04 90 36 50 48, www.vaison-la-romaine.com.

Visiting the Ruins: Vaison-la-Romaine's Roman ruins are split by a modern road into two sites: Puymin and La Villasse. Each is well-presented, thanks to the videoguide and information panels, offering a good look at life during the Roman Empire. What you can see is only a small fraction of the ancient town's extent—most is still buried under today's city.

Visit **Puymin** first. Nearest the entry are the scant but impressive ruins of a sprawling mansion. Find the faint remains of a colorful frescoed wall. Climb the hill

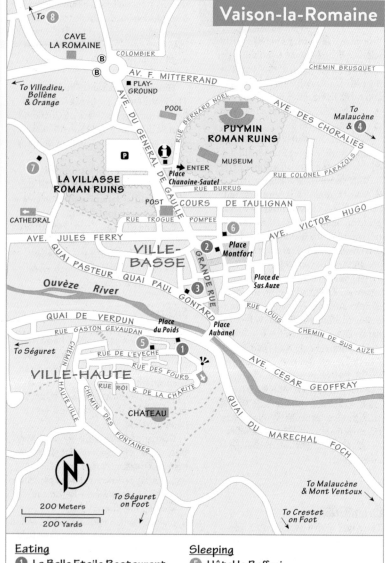

Vaison-la-Romaine

Eating
1 La Belle Etoile Restaurant
2 O'Natur'elles Restaurant
3 Le Patio
4 To Auberge d'Anaïs

Sleeping
5 Hôtel le Beffroi
6 Hôtel Burrhus
7 Les Tilleuls d'Elisée
8 To L'Ecole Buissonnière Chambres

to the good little **museum** (pick up your videoguide here). Be sure to see the **3-D film** that takes you inside the home of a wealthy Vaison resident and explores daily life some 2,000 years ago. Behind the museum is a still well-used, 6,000-seat theater, with just enough seats for the whole town (of yesterday and today).

Back across the modern road in **La Villasse,** you'll explore a "street of shops" and the foundations of more houses. You'll also see a few wells, used before Vaison's two aqueducts were built.

LOWER TOWN (VILLE-BASSE)

Vaison-la-Romaine's modern town centers on café-friendly Place Montfort. A 10-minute walk below Place Montfort, the stout **Notre-Dame de Nazareth Cathedral** is a good example of Provençal Romanesque dating from the 11th century, with an evocative cloister and fine stone carvings (free, daily, closed Oct-March). The pedestrian-only Grand Rue is a lively shopping street leading to the small river gorge and the **Roman Bridge,** a sturdy, no-nonsense

vault cut by the Romans into the canyon rock 2,000 years ago.

UPPER TOWN (VILLE-HAUTE)

Although there's nothing of particular importance to see in the fortified medieval old town atop the hill, the cobbled lanes and enchanting fountains make you want to break out a sketchpad. Vaison-la-Romaine was ruled by a prince-bishop starting in the fourth century. He came under attack by the Count of Toulouse in the 12th century. Anticipating a struggle, the prince-bishop abandoned the lower town and built a castle on this rocky outcrop (about 1195). Over time, the townspeople followed, vacating the lower town and building their homes at the base of the château behind the upper town's fortified wall.

To reach the upper town, hike up from the Roman Bridge through the medieval gate, under the lone tower crowned by an 18th-century wrought-iron bell cage. The château is closed, but a steep, uneven trail to its base rewards hikers with a sweeping view.

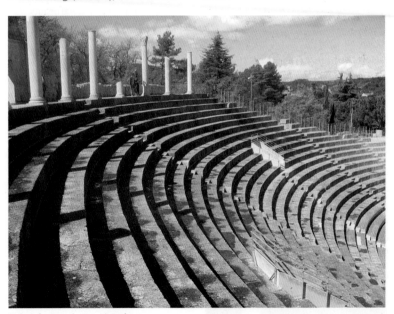

Vaison-la-Romaine's ancient theater

▲HIKING AND BIKING

The hills above Vaison-la-Romaine are picture-perfect for hikers and bikers. The TI has good information on your options, and can direct you to bike-rental shops. For destinations, consider the quiet hill town of Crestet, cute little Séguret, or delightful Villedieu.

Eating

$$ La Belle Etoile is where locals go for fresh, good-value meals (closed Thu, 5 Rue du Pont Romain). **$$ O'Natur'elles** is ideal for vegetarians; the all-organic dishes can be served with or without meat (reservations smart, closed Tue eve, tel. 04 90 65 81 67). Romantic **$$$ Le Patio** has soft lighting and good food (closed Wed eve and Sat lunch, 4 Rue du Ventoux). With a car, drive 10 minutes east from town to **$$ Auberge d'Anaïs** for a true Provençal experience—ask for a table *sur la terrasse* (closed Sun eve and Mon, on the road to St-Marcellin, tel. 04 90 36 20 06).

Sleeping

In the upper town, try the cozy **$$ Hôtel le Beffroi***** (www.le-beffroi.com); in the lower town, two good choices are **$ Hôtel Burrhus**** (1 Place Montfort,

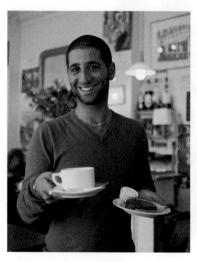

www.burrhus.com) and **$ Les Tilleuls d'Elisée** (1 Avenue Jules Mazen, www.vaisonchambres.info). Drivers will enjoy a stay at **$ L'Ecole Buissonnière Chambres,** a restored farmhouse 10 minutes north of town (cash only, between Villedieu and Buisson on D-75, www.buissonniere-provence.com).

Rick's Tip: Sleep in Vaison-la-Romaine on Monday night, and you'll wake to an amazing **Tuesday market,** *one of France's best. But be* **careful where you park:** *Avoid anyplace signed* Stationnement Interdit le Mardi *(parking forbidden on Tuesday), or you won't find your car where you left it.*

Côtes du Rhône Wine Road

To experience the best of the Côtes du Rhône vineyards and villages, take this half-day ▲▲▲ loop around the rugged Dentelles de Montmirail mountain peaks (figure about 40 miles total; see map on facing page). You'll experience the finest this region has to offer: natural beauty, glowing limestone villages, inviting wineries, and rolling hills of vineyards.

Start just south of Vaison-la-Romaine in little **Séguret.** This town is best for a visit early or late, when it's quieter. Explore the village (ideal for a morning coffee break), then drive up and up to the **Domaine de Mourchon** winery. From here, return to Vaison-la-Romaine and follow signs toward *Carpentras/Malaucène,* pass through Crestet, then follow signs leading up to *Le Village* (D-76).

After ambling the quiet village of **Crestet,** follow signs to *Malaucène* and turn right on D-90 (direction: Suzette) just before the gas station. The D-90 route is the scenic highlight of this loop, which follows the back side of the Dentelles de Montmirail past mountain views, remote villages, and beautifully situated wineries (**Domaine de Coyeux** is best).

Côtes du Rhône Driving Tour

Wine Tasting

18 MILE BIKE LOOP

To Ardèche Gorges

L'ECOLE BUISSONIERE CHAMBRES

Villedieu

Vaison-la-Romaine

BIKE LOOP BEGINS

Mirabel

Puyméras

11 MILE BIKE LOOP

Faucon

To Buis-les-Baronnies

Roaix

St-Romain

St-Marcellin

Cairanne   Rasteau

DRIVING TOUR BEGINS

② 🍷

PATH

③ Crestet

To Brantes (Drôme Provençale Loop Drive)

① Séguret

DOMAINE DE CABASSE

Entrechaux

Sablet

Dentelles de Montmirail

Gigondas ⑦ 🍷

HOTEL LES FLORETS

Suzette ⑤

④ LA FERME DEGOUTARD

Malaucène

To Mont Ventoux

⑥ 🍷

Vacqueyras

La Fare   La Roque Alric   Le Barroux

Bédoin

To Orange & A-7

Beaumes-de-Venise

To Mont Ventoux

5 Kilometers
5 Miles

Carpentras

To Avignon

To Isle-sur-la-Sorgue & Luberon

Paris
FRANCE

100 Miles

① Séguret
② Domaine de Mourchon Winery
③ Crestet
④ Col de la Chaîne Mountain Pass

⑤ Suzette
⑥ Domaine de Coyeux Winery
⑦ Gigondas

Take your time for this drive: You'll pass trailheads, scenic pullouts, and good picnic spots. Consider lunch along the way.

D-90 ends in Beaumes de Venise. Follow signs back toward *Vaison-la-Romaine* to **Gigondas** and explore this village.

⊙ Self-Guided Tour
❶ SEGURET

Séguret's name comes from the Latin word *securitas* (meaning "security"). The bulky entry arch came with a massive gate, which drilled in the message of the village's name. In the Middle Ages, Séguret was patrolled 24/7—they never took their *securitas* for granted. Walk through the arch. To appreciate how the homes' outer walls provided security in those days, drop down the first passage on your right (near the fountain). These exit passages, or *poternes*, were needed in periods of peace to allow the town to expand below. Wander deep. Rue Calade leads up to the unusual 12th-century St. Denis church for views (the circular village you see below is Sablet). Make your way down to the main drag and a café, and return to parking along Rue des Poternes.

❷ DOMAINE DE MOURCHON WINERY

This high-flying winery blends state-of-the-art technology with traditional winemaking methods (a shiny ring of stainless-steel vats holds grapes grown on land plowed by horses). Free and informative English tours of the vineyards are usually offered (wines–€8-33/bottle; winery open Mon-Sat 9:00-18:00, Sun by appointment only; from Easter-Sept, call to verify; tel. 04 90 46 70 30, www.domainedemourchon.com).

❸ CRESTET

This village—founded after the fall of the Roman Empire, when people banded together in high places like this for protection from marauding barbarians—followed the usual hill-town evolution. The outer walls of the village did double duty as ramparts and house walls. The castle above (from about A.D. 850) provided a final safe haven when the village was attacked.

Wander the peaceful lanes and appreciate the amount of work it took to put these stones in place. Notice the elaborate water channels. Crestet was served by 18 cisterns in the Middle Ages. The peaceful (usually closed) church has a beautiful stained-glass window behind the altar. Imagine hundreds of people living here and animals roaming everywhere. Get to the top of town. Signs from the top of the village lead to the footpath to Vaison-la-Romaine. The café-restaurant **Le Panoramic,** at the top of old **Crestet,** must have Provence's greatest view tables (closed Dec-March).

❹ COL DE LA CHAINE MOUNTAIN PASS

Get out of your car at the pass (elevation: about 1,500 feet) and enjoy the breezy views. Wander about. The peaks in the distance—thrusting up like the back of a stegosaurus or a bad haircut (you decide)—are the Dentelles de Montmirail, a small range running just nine miles basically north to south and reaching 2,400 feet in elevation.

Now turn around and face Mont Ventoux. Are there clouds on the horizon? You're looking into the eyes of the Alps (behind Ventoux), and those "foothills" help keep Provence sunny.

❺ SUZETTE

Tiny Suzette floats on its hilltop, with a small 12th-century chapel, one café, a handful of residents, and the gaggle of houses where they live. Park in Suzette's lot, below, then find the big orientation board above the lot. Look out to the broad shoulders of Mont Ventoux. At 6,000 feet, it always seems to have some clouds hanging around. If it's clear, the top looks like it's snow-covered; if you drive up there, you'll see it's actually white stone.

The village of Séguret

❻ DOMAINE DE COYEUX WINERY

A private road winds up and up to this impossibly beautiful setting, with the best views of the Dentelles I've found. Olive trees frame the final approach, and *Le Caveau* signs lead to a modern tasting room (you may need to ring the buzzer). This stop is for serious wine lovers—skip it if you only want a quick taste or are not interested in buying (wines–€8-16/bottle; winery generally open daily 10:00-12:00 & 14:00-18:00, except closed Sun off-season and no midday closure July-Aug; tel. 04 90 12 42 42, http://domainedecoyeux.com/en, some English spoken).

❼ GIGONDAS

This town produces some of the region's best reds and is ideally situated for hiking, mountain biking, and driving into the mountains. The **TI** has lists of wineries, rental bikes, and tips for good hikes or drives (Mon-Sat 10:00-12:30 & 14:00-18:00, closed Sun, Place du Portail, tel. 04 90 65 85 46, www.gigondas-dm.fr). Take a short walk through the village lanes above the TI—the church is an easy destination with good views over the heart of the Côtes du Rhône vineyards.

You'll find several good tasting opportunities on the main square; **Le Caveau de Gigondas** is the best (daily 10:00-12:00 & 14:00-18:30, near TI, www.caveaudugigondas.com). The restaurant at **Hôtel les Florets,** serving classic French cuisine with Provençal accents, is well worth it—particularly if you dine on the magnificent terrace (closed Wed, service can be slow).

❹ *Wine tasting in the Côtes du Rhône*
❺ *Vineyards of Domaine de Coyeux*
❻ *Côtes du Rhône vineyards*
❼ *Café in Suzette*

The French Riviera

A hundred years ago, celebrities from London to Moscow flocked to the French Riviera to socialize, gamble, and escape the dreary weather at home. Today, budget vacationers and heat-seeking Europeans fill belle époque resorts at France's most sought-after fun-in-the-sun destination.

Some of the Continent's most stunning scenery and intriguing museums lie along this strip of land—as do millions of sun-worshipping tourists. The Riviera's gateway is urban Nice, with world-class museums, a splendid beachfront promenade, a seductive old town, the best selection of hotels in all price ranges, and good nightlife options.

This sunny sliver of land is well-served by public transportation, making day trips by train or bus almost effortless. If you drive here, expect traffic—although you'll be rewarded with sensational views on the coastal routes. If you head east from Nice, you'll find little Villefranche-sur-Mer staring across the bay at exclusive Cap Ferrat. Farther along, Monaco offers a royal welcome and a fairytale past. To the west, Antibes has a thriving port and silky sand beaches. Wherever you choose to spend your days, evenings everywhere on the Riviera are radiant—made for a promenade and outdoor dining.

THE FRENCH RIVIERA IN 2 DAYS

My favorite home bases are Nice, Villefranche-sur-Mer, and Antibes. Nice, with convenient train and bus connections to most regional sights, is the most practical base for train travelers. Villefranche-sur-Mer is the romantic's choice, with a peaceful setting and small-town warmth, while midsize Antibes has the best beaches and works best for drivers.

Allow a full day for Nice: Spend your morning sifting through the old city (called Vieux Nice; take my Old Nice Walk) and ascend the elevator up Castle Hill for fine views. Devote the afternoon to the museums (Chagall is best, closed Tue) and strolling the Promenade des Anglais, taking my self-guided walk (best before or after dinner, but anytime is fine).

Save most of your second day for Monaco (tour Monaco-Ville, have lunch, and drop by the famous Monte Carlo casino), then consider a late afternoon or dinner in Villefranche-sur-Mer. With more time, explore Antibes' fine Picasso Museum and sandy old town. Or stop by lush Cap Ferrat, filled with mansions, gardens, and beaches.

THE FRENCH RIVIERA AT A GLANCE

Nice

▲▲▲**Promenade des Anglais Walk** Nice's sunstruck seafront promenade. **Hours:** Always open. See page 286.

▲▲▲**Chagall Museum** The world's largest collection of Marc Chagall's work, popular even with people who don't like modern art. **Hours:** May-Oct Wed-Mon 10:00-18:00, Nov-April until 17:00, closed Tue year-round. See page 294.

▲▲**Old Nice Walk** Exploring the enjoyable old city, with its charming French-Italian cultural blend. **Hours:** Always open. See page 291.

▲**Matisse Museum** Modest collection of Henri Matisse's paintings, sketches, and paper cutouts. **Hours:** Wed-Mon 10:00-18:00, closed Tue. See page 296.

▲**Russian Cathedral** Finest Orthodox church outside Russia. **Hours:** Mon 13:30-17:00, Tue-Sun 10:00-17:00. See page 297.

▲**Castle Hill** Site of an ancient fort boasting great views. **Hours:** Park closes at 20:00 in summer, earlier off-season. See page 297.

Nearby

▲▲▲**Villefranche-sur-Mer** Romantic Italianate beach town with a serene setting, yacht-filled harbor, and small-town ambience. See page 309.

▲▲▲**Monaco** Tiny independent municipality known for its classy casino and Grand Prix car race. See page 315.

▲▲**Cap Ferrat** Exclusive, woodsy peninsula with a family-friendly beach and tourable Rothschild mansion. See page 313.

▲▲**Antibes** Laid-back beach town with a medieval center, worthwhile Picasso Museum (closed Mon), sandy beaches, and view-strewn hikes. See page 321.

NICE

Nice (sounds like "niece"), with its spectacular Alps-to-Mediterranean surroundings, is the big-city highlight of the Riviera. Its traffic-free old town mixes Italian and French flavors to create a spicy Mediterranean dressing, while its big squares, broad seaside walkways, and long beaches invite lounging and people-watching. Nice may be nice, but it's hot and jammed in July and August—reserve ahead and get a room with air-conditioning.

Orientation

The main points of interest lie between the beach and the train tracks (about 15 blocks apart). The city revolves around its grand Place Masséna, where pedestrian-friendly Avenue Jean Médecin meets Vieux (Old) Nice and the Albert I parkway (with quick access to the beaches). It's a 20-minute walk (or about €12 by taxi) from the train station to the beach, and a 20-minute stroll along the promenade from the fancy Hôtel Negresco to the heart of Vieux Nice.

Everything you'll want to see in Nice is either within walking distance, or a short bike, bus, or tram ride away. A 10-minute ride on the smooth-as-silk tram through the center of the city connects the train station, Place Masséna, Vieux Nice, and the port (from nearby Place Garibaldi).

Tourist Information: Nice has several helpful TIs (tel. 08 92 70 74 07, www. nicetourisme.com), including branches at the **airport** (daily 9:00-18:00, April-Sept until 20:00), the **train station** (summer, daily 8:00-20:00, rest of year Mon-Sat 9:00-19:00, Sun 10:00-17:00), at 5 **Promenade des Anglais** (daily 9:00-18:00, July-Aug until 20:00), and on the north side of **Place Masséna** (May-mid-Sept only, daily 10:00-17:00). Ask for day-trip information, including details on boat excursions, and train and bus schedules.

Theft Alert: Nice has its share of pickpockets (especially at the train station, on the tram, and trolling the beach). Stick to main streets in Vieux Nice after dark.

SNCF Boutique: A French rail ticket office is a half-block west of Avenue Jean Médecin at 2 Rue de la Liberté (Mon-Fri 10:00-17:50, closed Sat-Sun).

Nice's historic Hôtel Negresco overlooks the Promenade des Anglais.

The French Riviera

Renting a Bike (and Other Wheels): Holiday Bikes has multiple locations, including one across from the train station, and they have electric bikes (www. loca-bike.fr). **Roller Station** is well-situated near the sea and rents bikes, rollerblades, skateboards, and Razor-style scooters (bikes–€5/hour, €10/half-day, €15/day, leave ID as deposit, open daily, next to yellow awnings of Pailin's Asian restaurant at 49 Quai des Etats-Unis, tel. 04 93 62 99 05).

Private Guide: Consider **Pascale Rucker,** an art-loving guide who teaches with the joy and wonder of a flower child (€160/half-day, €260/day, tel. 06 16 24 29 52, pascalerucker@gmail.com).

Minivan Tours: These two energetic and delightful women have comfortable minibuses and enjoy taking couples and small groups anywhere in the region: **Sylvie Di Cristo** (€600/day, €350/half-day for up to 8 people, mobile 06 09 88 83 83, www.frenchrivieraguides.net, dicristosylvie@gmail.com) and **Ingrid Schmucker** (€490/day for 4 people or €550/day for 5-7 people, €180/half-day or €285/day if you don't need transportation, tel. 06 14 83 03 33, www.kultours.fr, info@ kultours.fr). The TI and most hotels have information on more economic shared minivan excursions from Nice (roughly €50-70/person per half-day, €80-120/ person per day).

Nice City Walks
● *Promenade des Anglais Walk*

This leisurely, level self-guided walk, worth ▲▲▲, is a straight line along this much-strolled beachfront. It begins near the landmark Hôtel Negresco and ends just before Castle Hill. While this one-mile section is enjoyable at any time, the first half makes a great pre- or post-dinner stroll (perhaps with a dinner on the beach). If you plan to extend this stroll to Castle Hill, try to time it so you end up on top of the hill at sunset. Allow one hour at a promenade pace to reach the elevator up to Castle Hill.

Biking the Promenade: To rev up the pace of your promenade, rent a bike and glide along the coast in either or both directions (about 30 minutes each way; for rental info, see page 285). The path to the **west** stops just before the airport at perhaps the most scenic *boules* courts in France. If you take the path heading **east,** you'll round Castle Hill to the harbor of Nice, with a chance to survey some fancy yachts.

• *Start your walk at the pink-domed...*

HOTEL NEGRESCO

Nice's finest hotel is also a historic monument, offering up the city's most expensive beds and a museum-like interior. While the hotel is off-limits to nonguests, the doorman explained to me that shoppers and drinkers are "guests" as much as people actually sleeping there. So if you say you're going in for a drink (at their

Biking the promenade

pricey Le Bar du Negresco) or to shop, you may be allowed in.

The huge ballroom (walk straight until you see the big chandelier) is the **Salon Royal.** The chandelier hanging from its Eiffel-built dome is made of 16,000 pieces of crystal. It was built in France for the Russian czar's Moscow palace...but thanks to the Bolshevik Revolution in 1917, he couldn't take delivery. Bronze portrait busts of Czar Alexander III and his wife, Maria Feodorovna—who returned to her native Denmark after the revolution—are to the right, facing the shops. Circle the interior and then the perimeter to enjoy both historic and modern art. Fine portraits include Emperor Napoleon III and wife, Empress Eugénie (who acquired Nice for France from Italy in 1860), and Jeanne Augier (who owns the hotel).

If you wonder why such a grand hotel has such an understated entry, it's because today's front door was originally the back door. In the 19th century, elegant people stayed out of the sun, and any posh hotel that cared about its clientele would design its entry on the shady north side. If you walk around to the back you'll see a grand but unused front door.

• *Across the street from Hôtel Negresco is...*

VILLA MASSENA

When Nice became part of France, France invested heavily in what it expected to be the country's new high society retreat—an elite resort akin to Russia's Sochi on the Black Sea. The government built this fine palace for the military hero of the Napoleonic age, Jean-Andre Masséna and his family. Take a moment to stroll around the lovely garden (free, daily 10:00-18:00).

• *From Villa Masséna, head for the beach and begin your Promenade des Anglais stroll. But first, grab a blue chair and gaze out to the...*

BAY OF ANGELS (BAIE DES ANGES)

Face the water. The body of Nice's patron saint, Réparate, was supposedly escorted into this bay by angels in the fourth century. To your right is where you might have been escorted into France—Nice's airport, built on a massive landfill. The tip of land beyond the runway is Cap d'Antibes. Until 1860, Antibes and Nice were in different countries—Antibes was French, but Nice was a protectorate of the Italian kingdom of Savoy-Piedmont, a.k.a. the Kingdom of Sardinia. During that period, the Var River—just west of Nice—was the geographic border between these two peoples. In 1850 the people here spoke Italian and ate pasta. As Italy was uniting, the region was given a choice: Join the new country of Italy or join France (which was enjoying prosperous times under the rule of Napoleon III). The vast majority voted in 1860 to go French...and *voilà!* (In reality, the Italian king needed France's support in helping Italian regions controlled by Austria break away to join the emerging union of Italian states. Italy's price for France's support against Austria: Nice.)

The lower green hill to your left is Castle Hill. Farther left lie Villefranche-sur-Mer and Cap Ferrat (marked by the tower at land's end, and home to lots of millionaires), then Monaco (which you can't see, with more millionaires), then Italy. Behind you are the foothills of the Alps, which trap threatening clouds, ensuring that the Côte d'Azur enjoys sunshine more than 300 days each year.

• *With the sea on your right, begin strolling.*

THE PROMENADE

Nearby sit two fine belle époque establishments: the West End and Westminster hotels, both boasting English names to help those original guests feel at home (the West End is now part of the Best Western group...to help American guests feel at home). These hotels symbolize Nice's arrival as a tourist mecca in the 19th century, when the combination of leisure time and a stable economy allowed visitors to find the sun even in winter.

As you walk, be careful to avoid the green bike lane. You'll pass a number of separate rocky beaches. You can go local and rent gear—about €15 for a *chaise longue* (long chair) and a *transat* (mattress), €5 for an umbrella, and €4 for a towel. You'll also pass several beach restaurants. Some of these eateries serve breakfast, all serve lunch, some do dinner, and a few have beachy bars...tailor-made for a break from this walk. (Plage Beau

The Bay of Angels epitomizes the beauty of the French Riviera.

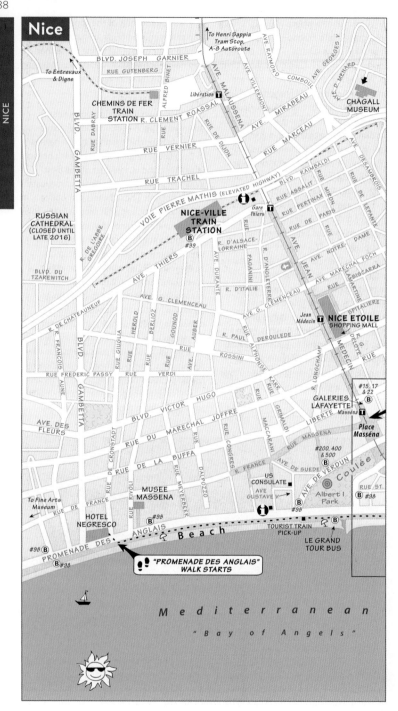

Nice

To Henri Sappia
Tram Stop,
A-8 Autoroute

BLVD. JOSEPH GARNIER
RUE GUTENBERG
To Entrevaux
& Digne

CHEMINS DE FER
TRAIN
STATION
R. CLEMENT ROASSAL

Libération 🚊

CHAGALL
MUSEUM

RUE VERNIER

RUE TRACHEL

RUSSIAN
CATHEDRAL
(CLOSED UNTIL
LATE 2016)

BLVD. DU
TZAREWITCH

VOIE PIERRE MATHIS (ELEVATED HIGHWAY)

NICE-VILLE
TRAIN
STATION
ⓑ #99

Gare
Thiers 🚊

AVE. THIERS

R. D'ALSACE-LORRAINE

AVE. G. CLEMENCEAU

R. D'ITALIE

AVE. G. CLEMENCEAU

Jean
Médecin 🚊 NICE ETOILE
SHOPPING MALL

RUE FREDERIC PASSY

BLVD. VICTOR HUGO

#15, 17
& 22
ⓑ

GALERIES
LAFAYETTE
LIBERTE Masséna 🚊

Place
Masséna

AVE. DES
FLEURS

RUE DU MARECHAL JOFFRE

RUE MASSENA

#200, 400
& 500
ⓑ

AVE. DE SUEDE

MUSEE
MASSENA

US
CONSULATE

AVE. DE VERDUN

Coulée

RUE ST.
ⓑ #98

To Fine Arts
Museum

AVE
GUSTAVE V →

Albert I
Park

HOTEL
NEGRESCO

🚻
ⓑ #98

#98

PROMENADE DES ANGLAIS

Beach

TOURIST TRAIN
PICK-UP

LE GRAND
TOUR BUS

ⓑ

#98 ⓑ

ⓑ #98

👣 "PROMENADE DES ANGLAIS"
WALK STARTS

M e d i t e r r a n e a n

"B a y   o f   A n g e l s"

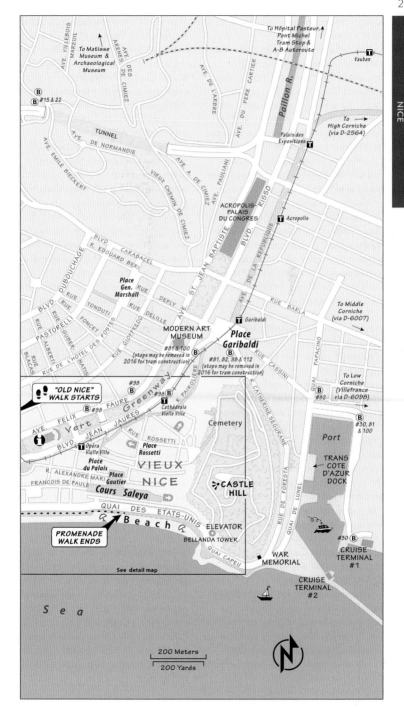

Rivage, farther along on Quai des Etats-Unis, is cool for a drink.)

Even a hundred years ago, there was sufficient tourism in Nice to justify building its first casino (a leisure activity imported from Venice). Part of an elegant casino, La Jetée Promenade stood on those white-covered pilings (with flags flapping) just offshore, until the Germans destroyed it during World War II. When La Jetée was thriving, it took gamblers two full days to get to the Riviera by train from Paris.

Although La Jetée Promenade is gone, you can still see the striking 1927 Art Nouveau facade of the **Palais de la Méditerranée,** a grand casino, hotel, and theater. It became one of the grandest casinos in Europe, and today it is one of France's most exclusive hotels, though the casino feels cheap and cheesy.

The unappealing Casino Ruhl (with the most detested facade on the strip) disfigures the next block. Anyone can drop in for some one-armed-bandit fun, but to play the tables at night, you'll need to dress up and bring your passport.

Albert I Park is named for the Belgian king who enjoyed wintering here—these were his private gardens. While the English came first, the Belgians and Russians were also big fans of 19th-century Nice. That tall statue at the edge of the park commemorates the 100-year anniversary of Nice's union with France. The happy statue features two beloved women embracing the idea of union (Marianne, the symbol of the Republic of France, and Catherine Ségurane, a 16th-century heroine who helped Nice against Saracen pirates).

The park is a long, winding greenbelt called the Promenade du Paillon. The Paillon River flows under the park on its way to the sea. This is the historical divide between Old Nice and the new town. Continue along, past the vintage belle époque carousel. You're now on Quai des Etats-Unis ("Quay of the United States"). This name was given as a tip-of-the-cap to the Americans for finally entering World War I in 1917. Check out the laid-back couches at the Plage Beau Rivage lounge. The big, blue chair statue celebrates the inviting symbol of this venerable walk and kicks off what I consider the best stretch of beach—quieter and with less traffic.

The tall, rusted **steel girders** reaching for the sky were erected in 2010 to celebrate the 150th anniversary of Nice's union with France. (The seven beams represent the seven valleys of the Nice region.) Designed by the same artist who created the popular Arc of the Riviera sculpture in the parkway near Place Masséna, this "art" infuriates many locals as an ugly waste of money.

The elegant back side of Nice's opera house faces the sea. In front of it, a tiny bronze Statue of Liberty reminds all that this stretch of seafront promenade is named for the USA.

The long, low building lining the walk on the left once served the city's fishermen. Behind its gates bustles the Cours Saleya Market—long the heart and soul of Old Nice.

Ahead, on the right, find the three-foot-tall white **metal winch.** It's a reminder that before tourism, hardworking fishing boats lined the beach rather than vacationing tourists. The boats were hauled in through the surf by winches like this and tied to the iron rings on either side.

• *Your walk is over. From here you have several great options: Continue 10 minutes along the coast to the* **port,** *around the foot of Castle Hill (fine views of the entire promenade and a monumental war memorial carved into the hillside); hike or ride the free elevator up to* **Castle Hill** *(see page 297); head into the* **old town** *(you can follow my "Old Nice Walk," next); or grab a blue chair or piece of* **beach** *and just be on vacation—Riviera style.*

● Old Nice Walk

This self-guided walk through Nice's old town, from Place Masséna to Place Rossetti, gives you a helpful introduction to the city's bicultural heritage and its most interesting neighborhoods. Allow about an hour at a leisurely pace for this level walk, rated ▲▲. It's best done in the morning (while the outdoor market thrives), and preferably not on a Sunday, when things are quiet. This ramble is also a joy at night, when fountains glow and pedestrians control the streets.

• *Start where Avenue Jean Médecin hits the people-friendly Place Masséna—the successful result of a long, expensive city upgrade and the new center of Nice.*

PLACE MASSENA

The grand Place Masséna is Nice's drawing room, where old meets new, and where the tramway bends between Vieux (Old) Nice and the train station. The square's black-and-white pavement feels like an elegant outdoor ballroom, with the sleek tram waltzing across its dance floor. While once congested with cars, the square today is frequented only by these trams, which swoosh silently by every couple of minutes. The men on pedestals sitting high above are modern-art additions that arrived with the tram. For a mood-altering experience, return after dark and watch the illuminated figures float yoga-like above. Place Masséna is at its sophisticated best after the sun goes down.

This vast square dates from 1848 and pays tribute to Jean-André Masséna, a French military leader during the Revolutionary and Napoleonic wars. Not just another pretty face in a long lineup of French military heroes, he's considered among the greatest commanders in history—anywhere, anytime. Napoleon called him "the greatest name of my military Empire."

Standing in the center of the square, face the sea and start a clockwise spin tour: The towering **modern swoosh sculpture** in the park is meant to represent the arc of the bay. To the right stretches modern Nice, born with the arrival of tourism in the 1800s. **Avenue Jean Médecin,** Nice's main street, cuts from here through the new town to the train station. In the distance you can see the tracks, the freeway, and the Alps beyond that. Once crammed with cars, buses, and delivery vehicles, Avenue Jean Médecin was turned into a walking and cycling nirvana in 2007. Businesses flourish in the welcoming environment of generous sidewalks and no traffic.

Appreciate the city's Italian heritage—it feels as much like Venice as Paris. The portico flanking Avenue Jean Médecin is Italian, not French. The rich colors of the buildings reflect the taste of previous Italian rulers.

Turn to your right and look east to see the **Promenade du Paillon,** a green parkway that stretches from the sea to Place Masséna. Notice the fountain—its surprise geysers delight children by day and its fine lighting enhances romance at night. Beyond the fountain stands a

Promenade du Paillon

292

THE FRENCH RIVIERA
NICE

bronze statue of the square's namesake, Masséna. And the hills beyond that separate Nice from Villefranche-sur-Mer.

Turn farther to the right to see the old town, with its jumbled facades below Castle Hill. The **statue of Apollo** holds a beach towel as if to say, "It's beer o'clock, let's go."

• *Walk past Apollo with the beach towel into the old town. After a block down Rue de l'Opéra, turn left onto Rue St. François de Paule (or you can detour right one block to the* **Molinard** *perfume shop at #20, which has a free one-room museum and offers create-your-own-perfume sessions for a price; see www.molinard.com).*

RUE ST. FRANÇOIS DE PAULE

This colorful street leads into the heart of Vieux Nice. On the left is Hôtel de Ville (City Hall). Peer into the **Alziari olive oil shop** (at #14 on the right). Dating from 1868, the shop produces top-quality stone-ground olive oil. The proud and charming owner, Gilles Piot, claims that stone wheels create less acidity, since metal grinding builds up heat (see photo in back over the door). Locals fill their own containers from the huge vats.

La Couqueto (at #8) is a colorful shop filled with Provençal handicrafts, including lovely folk characters (*santons*).

Across the street is Nice's grand **opera house.** Imagine this opulent jewel back in the 19th century. With all the fancy big-city folks wintering here, this rough-edged

town needed some high-class entertainment. And Victorians needed an alternative to those "devilish" gambling houses. (Queen Victoria, so disgusted at casinos, would actually close the drapes on her train window when passing Monte Carlo.) The four statues on top represent theater, dance, music, and party poopers.

On the left (at #7), **Pâtisserie Auer's** grand old storefront tempts you with chocolates and candied fruits. It's changed little over the centuries. The writing on the window says, "Since 1820 from father to son." The gold royal shields on the back wall remind shoppers that Queen Victoria indulged her sweet tooth here.

• *Continue on, sifting your way through a cluttered block of tacky souvenir shops to the big market square.*

COURS SALEYA

Named for its broad exposure to the sun (*soleil*), Cours Saleya is a commotion of color, sights, smells, and people. It's been Nice's main market square since the Middle Ages (flower market all day Tue-Sun, produce market Tue-Sun until 13:00, antiques on Mon). While you're greeted by the ugly mouth of an underground parking lot, much of this square itself was a parking lot until 1980, when the mayor of Nice had this solution dug.

The first section is devoted to the Riviera's largest flower market. In operation since the 19th century, this market offers

Cours Saleya Market

A movable art gallery

plants and flowers that grow effortlessly and ubiquitously in this climate, including these favorites: carnations, roses, and jasmine. Locals know the season by what's on sale (mimosas in February, violets in March, and so on). Until the recent rise in imported flowers, this region supplied all of France with flowers. Still, fresh flowers are cheap here, the best value in this notoriously expensive city. The Riviera's three big industries are tourism, flowers, and perfume (made from these flowers... take a whiff).

Rick's Tip: The **Cours Saleya** produce and flower market is replaced by antique stalls **on Mondays.**

The boisterous produce section trumpets the season with mushrooms, strawberries, white asparagus, zucchini flowers, and more—whatever's fresh gets top billing.

The market opens up at Place Pierre Gautier. It's also called Plassa dou Gouvernou—you'll see bilingual street signs here that include the old Niçois language, an Italian dialect. This is where farmers set up stalls to sell their produce and herbs directly.

Look up to the **hill** that dominates to the east. In the Middle Ages, a massive castle stood there with soldiers at the ready. Over time, the city grew down to where you are now. With the river guarding one side and the sea the other, this mountain fortress seemed strong—until Louis XIV leveled it in 1706. Nice's medieval seawall ran along the line of two-story buildings where you're standing.

Now, look across Place Pierre Gautier to the large "palace." The **Ducal Palace** was where the kings of Sardinia, the city's Italian rulers until 1860, resided when in Nice. (For centuries, Nice was under the rule of the Italian capital of Torino.) Today, the palace is the police headquarters. The land upon which the Cours Saleya sits was once the duke's gardens and didn't

become a market until Nice's union with France.

• *Continue down Cours Saleya. The fine golden building that seals the end of the square is where Henri Matisse spent 17 years. I imagine he was inspired by his view. The **Café les Ponchettes** is perfectly positioned for you to enjoy the view, too, if you want a coffee break. At the café, turn onto...*

RUE DE LA POISSONNERIE

Look up at the first floor of the first building on your right. **Adam and Eve** are squaring off, each holding a zucchini-like gourd. This scene represents the annual rapprochement in Nice to make up for the sin of too much fun during Carnival (Mardi Gras, the pre-Lenten festival). Residents of Nice have partied hard during Carnival for more than 700 years.

Next, check out the small **Baroque church** (Notre-Dame de l'Annonciation) dedicated to St. Rita, the patron saint of desperate causes and desperate people. She holds a special place in locals' hearts, making this the most popular church in Nice. Drop in for a peek at the dazzling Baroque interior. Inside, the first chapel on the right is dedicated to St. Erasmus, protector of mariners.

• *Turn right on the next street, where you'll pass Vieux Nice's most happening bar (**Distilleries Ideales**). Pause at the next corner and simply study the classic Old Nice scene. Now turn left on Rue Droite and enter an area that feels like Little Naples.*

RUE DROITE

In the Middle Ages, this straight, skinny street provided the most direct route from river to sea within the old walled town. Pass the recommended restaurant L'Acchiardo. Notice stepped lanes leading uphill to the castle. Stop at **Espuno's bakery** (at Place du Jésus) and say "*Bonjour*, what's cooking?" to Natalie from England and her husband Fabrice, who's from here. Notice the firewood stacked behind the oven. Try the house specialty, *tourte aux blettes*—a tart stuffed with

Swiss chard, apples, pine nuts, and raisins.

Pop into the Jesuit **Eglise St-Jacques** for an explosion of Baroque exuberance hidden behind that plain facade.

The balconies of the large mansion on the left mark the **Palais Lascaris** (c. 1647), home of one of Nice's most prestigious families. Today it is a museum with an impressive collection of antique musical instruments—harps, guitars, violins, and violas—along with elaborate tapestries and a few well-furnished rooms. The palace has four levels: The ground floor was used for storage, the first floor was devoted to reception rooms (and musical events), the owners lived a floor above that, and the servants lived at the top. Look up and make faces back at the guys under the balconies.

• *Turn left on the Rue de la Loge, then left again on Rue Benoît Bunico.*

In the 18th century, Rue Benoît served as a **ghetto** for Nice's Jews. At sunset, gates would seal the street at either end, locking people in until daylight. To identify Jews as non-Christians, the men were forced to wear yellow stars and the women wore yellow scarves. The white columns across from #19 mark what was the synagogue until 1848, when revolution ended the notion of ghettos in France.

• *Around the corner and downhill on Rue Benoît Bunico find...*

PLACE ROSSETTI

The most Italian of Nice's piazzas, Place Rossetti comes alive after dark—in part because of the **Fenocchio gelato shop,** popular for its many innovative flavors.

Check out the **Cathedral of St. Répa-rate**—an unassuming building for a big-city cathedral. It was relocated here in the 1500s, when Castle Hill was temporarily converted to military use. The name comes from Nice's patron saint, a teenage virgin named Réparate, whose martyred body floated to Nice in the fourth century accompanied by angels.

• *This is the end of our walk. From here you can hike up* **Castle Hill** *(from Place Rossetti, take Rue Rossetti uphill; see page 297). Or you can have ice cream and browse the colorful lanes of Old Nice. Or you can grab Apollo and hit the beach.*

Sights

Some of Nice's top attractions—the Promenade des Anglais, the beach, and the old town—are covered in my self-guided walks. But Nice offers other worthwhile sights as well.

The Chagall and Matisse museums are a long walk northeast of the city center. If you want to visit both, combine them in one trip, because they're in the same direction and served by the same bus line (#15 Mon-Sat, #22 Sun). From Place Masséna, the Chagall Museum is a 10-minute bus ride, and the Matisse Museum is a few stops beyond that.

▲▲▲CHAGALL MUSEUM (MUSEE NATIONAL MARC CHAGALL)

Even if you don't get modern art, this museum—with the world's largest collection of Marc Chagall's work in captivity—

Eglise St-Jacques

Place Rossetti

is a delight. After World War II, Chagall returned from the United States to settle in Vence, not far from Nice. Between 1954 and 1967 he painted a cycle of 17 large murals designed for, and donated to, this museum. These paintings, inspired by the biblical books of Genesis, Exodus, and the Song of Songs, make up the "nave," or core, of what Chagall called the "House of Brotherhood."

Rick's Tip: *Both the **Chagall** and **Matisse** museums* are **closed on Tuesdays.**

Cost and Hours: €8, €1-2 more with special exhibits, includes audioguide, May-Oct Wed-Mon 10:00-18:00, Nov-April until 17:00, closed Tue year-round, Avenue Docteur Ménard, tel. 04 93 53 87 20, http://en.musees-nationaux-alpesmaritimes.fr. An idyllic café awaits in the corner of the garden.

Getting There: Taxis to and from the city center cost €12. Buses connect the museum with downtown Nice and the train station. From downtown, catch bus #15 (6/hour, 10 minutes) from the east end of the Galeries Lafayette department store, near the Masséna tram stop, on Rue Sacha Guitry; on Sunday catch #22 from the same stop. Exit the bus at the stop called Musée Chagall on Boulevard de Cimiez.

Visiting the Museum: This small museum consists of six rooms: two rooms (the main hall and Song of Songs room) with the 17 murals, two rooms for special exhibits, an auditorium with stained-glass windows, and a mosaic-lined pond.

In the **main hall** you'll find the core of the collection (Genesis and Exodus scenes). Each painting is a lighter-than-air collage of images that draws from Chagall's Russian folk-village youth, his Jewish heritage, biblical themes, and his feeling that he existed somewhere between heaven and earth. He believed that the Bible was a synonym for nature, and that color and biblical themes were key for understanding God's love for his creation. Chagall's brilliant blues and reds celebrate nature, as do his spiritual and folk themes. Notice the focus on couples. To Chagall, humans loving each other mirrored God's love of creation.

The adjacent **octagonal room** houses five paintings inspired by the Old Testament Song of Songs. Chagall was one of the few "serious" 20th-century artists to portray unabashed love. Where the Bible uses the metaphor of earthly, physical, sexual love to describe God's love for humans, Chagall uses unearthly colors and a mystical ambience to celebrate human love. These red-toned canvases are hard to interpret on a literal level, but they capture the rosy spirit of a man in love with life.

The **auditorium** is worth a peaceful moment to enjoy three Chagall stained-glass windows depicting the seven days of creation. This is also where you'll find a wonderful film (52 minutes) on Chagall, which plays at the top of each hour.

Chagall Museum

Chagall, Song of Songs IV

The Riviera's Art Scene

The list of artists who have painted the Riviera reads like a *Who's Who* of 20th-century art. Henri Matisse, Marc Chagall, Georges Braque, Raoul Dufy, Fernand Léger, and Pablo Picasso all lived and worked here—and raved about the region's wonderful light. Their simple, semiabstract, and—most important—colorful works reflect the pleasurable atmosphere of the Riviera. You'll experience the same landscapes they painted in this bright, sun-drenched region, punctuated with views of the "azure sea." Try to imagine the Riviera with a fraction of the people and development you see today.

The Riviera's collection of museums allows art lovers to appreciate these masters' works while immersed in the same sun and culture that inspired them. The designs of many of the museums blend artworks with surrounding views, gardens, and fountains, thus highlighting that modern art is not only stimulating, but sometimes simply beautiful.

Leaving the Museum: From here, you can return to downtown Nice or the train-station area, or go to the Matisse Museum. For the bus back to downtown Nice, turn right out of the museum, then make another right down Boulevard de Cimiez, and ride bus #15 or #22 heading downhill. To continue on to the Matisse Museum, catch #15 or #22 using the uphill stop located across the street. To walk to the train-station area from the museum takes about 20 minutes.

▲MATISSE MUSEUM (MUSEE MATISSE)

This small and neglected little museum, which fills an old mansion in a park surrounded by scant Roman ruins, contains a sampling of works from the various periods of Henri Matisse's artistic career. The museum offers an introduction to the artist's many styles and materials, both shaped by Mediterranean light and by fellow Côte d'Azur artists Picasso and Renoir.

Matisse, the master of leaving things out, could suggest a woman's body with a single curvy line—letting the viewer's mind fill in the rest. Ignoring traditional 3-D perspective, he expressed his passion for life through simplified but recogniz-able scenes in which dark outlines and saturated, bright blocks of color create an overall decorative pattern. As you tour the museum, look for Matisse's favorite motifs—including fruit, flowers, wallpaper, and sunny rooms—often with a window opening onto a sparkling landscape. Another favorite subject is the *odalis-que* (harem concubine), usually shown

Matisse "cutout" painting

sprawled in a seductive pose and with a simplified, masklike face. You'll also see a few souvenirs from his foreign travels, which influenced much of his work.

Cost and Hours: €10, Wed-Mon 10:00-18:00, closed Tue, 164 Avenue des Arènes de Cimiez, tel. 04 93 81 08 08, www.musee-matisse-nice.org.

Getting There: Take a cab (€15 from Promenade des Anglais). Alternatively, hop bus #15 Mon-Sat or #22 on Sun (6/hour, 15 minutes, board from east end of Galeries Lafayette department store, near Masséna tram stop, on Rue Sacha Guitry—see map on page 288). Get off at the Arènes-Matisse bus stop (look for the crumbling Roman arena), then walk 50 yards into the park to find the pink villa.

Leaving the Museum: Turn left from the museum into the park, exiting at the Archaeological Museum. The bus stop across the street is for bus #20, which heads to the port. For buses #15 and #22 (frequent service to downtown and the Chagall Museum), turn right, passing the stop above, walk to the small roundabout, and find the shelter (facing downhill).

Russian Cathedral

▲RUSSIAN CATHEDRAL (CATHEDRALE RUSSE)

Nice's Russian Orthodox church—claimed by some to be the finest outside Russia—is worth a visit.

Five hundred rich Russian families wintered in Nice in the late 19th century, and they needed a worthy Orthodox house of worship. Czar Nicholas I's widow provided the land and Czar Nicholas II gave this church to the Russian community in 1912. (A few years later, Russian comrades who *didn't* winter on the Riviera assassinated him.) Here in the land of olives and anchovies, these proud onion domes seem odd. But, I imagine, so did those old Russians.

Pick up an English info sheet on your way in. The one-room interior is filled with icons and candles, and traditional Russian music adds to the ambience. The park around the church makes a fine setting for picnics.

Cost and Hours: Free; Mon 13:30-17:00, Tue-Sun 10:00-17:00; services Sat at 17:00, Sun at 10:00; no tourist visits during services, no shorts allowed, 17 Boulevard du Tzarewitch, tel. 04 93 96 88 02, www.sobor.fr.

▲CASTLE HILL (COLLINE DU CHATEAU)

This hill—in an otherwise flat city center—offers sensational views over Nice, the port (to the east, created for trade and military use in the 15th century), the foothills of the Alps, and the Mediterranean. The views are best early, at sunset, or whenever the weather's clear.

Nice was founded on this hill. Its residents were crammed onto the hilltop until the 12th century, as it was too risky to live in the flatlands below. Today you'll find a playground, a café, and a cemetery—but no castle—on Castle Hill.

Cost and Hours: Park is free and closes at 20:00 in summer, earlier off-season.

Getting There: You can get to the top

by foot or by elevator (free, daily 10:00-19:00, until 20:00 in summer, next to beachfront Hôtel Suisse).

See the Promenade des Anglais Walk on page 286 for a pleasant stroll that ends near Castle Hill.

Leaving Castle Hill: After enjoying the views and hilltop fun, you can walk via the cemetery directly down into Vieux Nice (just follow the signs), descend to the beach (via the elevator or a stepped lane next to it), or hike down the back side to Nice's port (departure point for boat trips and buses to Monaco and Villefranche-sur-Mer).

Experiences

Mediterranean Cruise

To see Nice from the water, hop aboard a one-hour ▲Trans Côte d'Azur cruise. You'll travel on a comfortable yacht-size vessel to Cap Ferrat and past Villefranche-sur-Mer, then return to Nice with a final lap along Promenade des Anglais.

Guides play Robin Leach (in French and English), pointing out mansions owned by famous people, including Elton John, Sean Connery, and Microsoft co-founder Paul Allen (€18; April-Oct Tue-Sun 2/day, usually at 11:00 and 15:00, no boats Mon or in off-season; verify schedule, arrive 30 minutes early to get best seats; boats leave from Nice's port—Bassin des Amiraux, tel. 04 92 98 71 30, www.trans-cote-azur.com).

The view from Castle Hill is worth the climb.

Nightlife

While you should choose your neighborhoods with caution, the city is a delight after dark. Promenade des Anglais, Cours Saleya, the old town, and Rue Masséna are all safe and worth an evening walk. Nice's bars play host to a happening late-night scene, filled with jazz, rock, and trolling singles.

Most activity focuses on Vieux Nice. Rue de la Préfecture and Place du Palais are ground zero for bar life, though Place Rossetti and Rue Droite are also good targets. **Distilleries Ideales** is a good place to start or end your evening, with a lively international crowd, a *Pirates of the Caribbean* interior, and a *Cheers* vibe (15 beers on tap, happy hour 18:00-21:00, where Rue de la Poissonnerie and Rue Barillerie meet). **Wayne's Bar** is a happening spot for the younger, English-speaking backpacker crowd (15 Rue Préfecture). Along the Promenade des Anglais, the plush bar at **Hôtel Negresco** is fancy-cigar old English.

Eating

For the most energy and variety, I'd eat in Vieux Nice. If Vieux Nice is too far, I've listed good places handier to your hotel. Promenade des Anglais is ideal for picnic dinners on warm, languid evenings or a meal at a beachside restaurant. For a more romantic (and expensive) meal, head for nearby Villefranche-sur-Mer (see page 309). Avoid the fun-to-peruse but terribly touristy eateries lining Rue Masséna.

In Vieux Nice

$$$ Le Safari is a fair option for Niçois cuisine and outdoor dining on Cours Saleya. The place, convivial and rustic with a mix of modern art inside, is packed with locals and tourists, and staffed with hurried waiters (€18-30 *plats*, open daily, 1 Cours Saleya, tel. 04 93 80 18 44, www.restaurantsafari.fr).

$$ L'Acchiardo is a homey eatery that mixes loyal clientele with hungry tourists.

The Riviera's Cuisine Scene

While many of the same dishes served in Provence are available throughout the Riviera (see page 298), there are differences, especially if you look for anything Italian or from the sea. When dining on the Riviera, I expect views and ambience more than top-quality cuisine.

La salade niçoise is where most Riviera meals start. A true specialty from Nice, the classic version is a base of green salad with boiled potatoes, tomatoes, anchovies, olives, hard-boiled eggs, and lots of tuna. This is my go-to salad for a tasty, healthy, and fast lunch. I like to spend a couple of extra euros and eat it in an elegant, atmospheric place with a view.

For lunch on the go, look for a *pan bagnat* (like a *salade niçoise* stuffed into a hollowed-out soft roll). Other tasty bread treats include *pissaladière* (bread dough topped with onions, olives, and anchovies), *fougasse* (a spindly, lace-like bread sometimes flavored with nuts, herbs, olives, or ham), and *socca* (a thin chickpea crêpe, seasoned with pepper and olive oil and often served in a paper cone by street vendors).

Bouillabaisse is the Riviera's most famous dish; you'll find it in any seafront village or city. It's a spicy fish stew based on recipes handed down from sailors in Marseille. This dish often requires a minimum order of two and can cost up to €40-60 per person.

Those on a budget can enjoy other seafood soups and stews. Far less pricey than bouillabaisse and worth trying is the local *soupe de poisson* (fish soup). It's a creamy soup flavored like bouillabaisse, with anise and orange, and served with croutons and *rouille* sauce (but has no chunks of fish).

The Riviera specializes in all sorts of fish and shellfish. Options include *fruits de mer,* or platters of seafood (including tiny shellfish, from which you get the edible part only by sucking really hard), herb-infused mussels, stuffed sardines, squid (slowly simmered with tomatoes and herbs), and tuna *(thon)*. The popular *loup flambé au fenouil* is grilled sea bass, flavored with fennel and torched with *pastis* prior to serving.

Do as everyone else does, and drink **wines** from Provence. **Bandol** (red) and **Cassis** (white) are popular and from a region nearly on the Riviera. The only wines made in the Riviera are **Bellet** rosé and white, the latter often found in fish-shaped bottles.

As soon as you sit down you know this is a treat. The simple, hearty Niçois cuisine is served by Monsieur Acchiardo and his good-looking sons. The small plaque under the menu outside says the restaurant has been run by father and son since 1927 (€9 starters, €16 *plats*, €7 desserts, closed Sat-Sun, indoor seating only, 38 Rue Droite, tel. 04 93 85 51 16).

$$ Bistrot D'Antoine has street appeal.

It's a warm, popular, vine-draped option with a menu that emphasizes Niçois cuisine and good grilled selections. The food is delicious and the prices are reasonable. Call a day ahead to reserve a table—the upstairs room is quieter (€10 starters, €17 *plats*, €7 desserts, closed Sun-Mon, 27 Rue de la Préfecture, tel. 04 93 85 29 57).

$$ La Merenda is a shoebox where you'll sit on small stools and dine on sim-

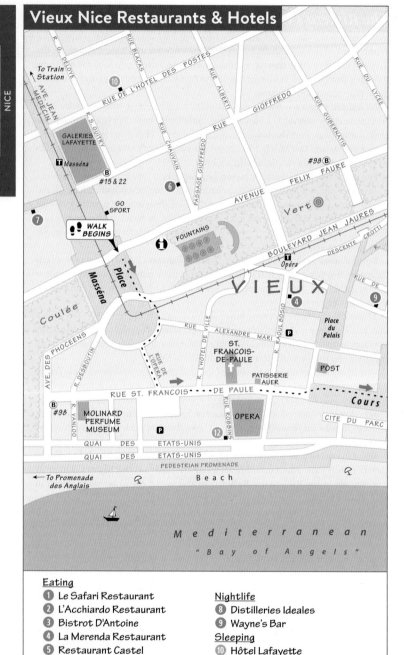

Vieux Nice Restaurants & Hotels

To Train Station

GALERIES LAFAYETTE

Masséna

#15 & 22

GO SPORT

WALK BEGINS

FOUNTAINS

Place Masséna

Coulée

V I E U X

Opéra

#98 B

Vert

BOULEVARD JEAN JAURES

DESCENTE CROTTI

RUE DE

RUE DE L'HOTEL DES POSTES

RUE BLACAS

RUE ALBERTI

RUE CHAUVAIN

PASSAGE GIOFFREDO

RUE GIOFFREDO

AVENUE FELIX FAURE

RUE GUBERNATIS

RUE DU LYCÉE

AVE JEAN MEDECIN

R G DELOYE

R S GUITRY

To Train Station

AVENUE

Place du Palais

RUE ALEXANDRE MARI

ST. FRANCOIS-DE-PAULE

R. L'HOTEL DE VILLE

RUE DE L'OPERA

RUE ST. FRANCOIS - - - DE PAULE

RAOUL BOSIO

POST

Cours

RUE DE

AVE. DES PHOCEENS

R. DESBOITIN

PATISSERIE AUER

#98 B

MOLINARD PERFUME MUSEUM

R. VANLOO

RUE ROBBINS

OPERA

CITE DU PARC

QUAI DES ETATS-UNIS

QUAI DES ETATS-UNIS

PEDESTRIAN PROMENADE

To Promenade des Anglais

B e a c h

M e d i t e r r a n e a n
" B a y   o f   A n g e l s "

Eating
1. Le Safari Restaurant
2. L'Acchiardo Restaurant
3. Bistrot D'Antoine
4. La Merenda Restaurant
5. Restaurant Castel
6. Le Luna Rossa Restaurant
7. La Maison de Marie Restaurant

Nightlife
8. Distilleries Ideales
9. Wayne's Bar

Sleeping
10. Hôtel Lafayette
11. Hôtel la Perouse
12. Hôtel Mercure Marché aux Fleurs

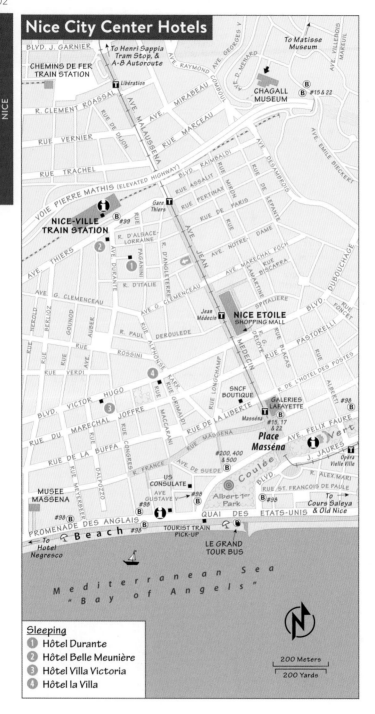

Nice City Center Hotels

BLVD. J. GARNIER
To Henri Sappia Tram Stop, & A-8 Autoroute
To Matisse Museum

CHEMINS DE FER TRAIN STATION
Libération
CHAGALL MUSEUM
#15 & 22

R. CLEMENT ROASSAL
AVE. MIRABEAU
AVE. MARCEAU
AVE. MALAUSSENA
AVE. RAYMOND COMBOUL
AVE. D. MENARD
AVE. GEORGES V
AVE. VILLEBOIS
MAREUIL
RUE DE DIJON

RUE VERNIER
RUE TRACHEL
AVE. EMILE BIECKERT
AVE. DESAMBROIS
AVE. DE LEVANTE
RUE DE

VOIE PIERRE MATHIS (ELEVATED HIGHWAY)
BLVD. RAIMBALDI
RUE ASSALIT
RUE PERTINAX
RUE MIRON
RUE DE PARIS

NICE-VILLE TRAIN STATION
Gare Thiers
#99
R. D'ALBACE-LORRAINE
PAGANINI
RUE D'ANGLETERRE
AVE. JEAN
AVE. NOTRE-DAME
AVE. MARECHAL FOCH
RUE LAMARTINE
RUE BISCARRA

AVE. THIERS
AVE. DURANTE
R. D'ITALIE
AVE. G. CLEMENCEAU
AVE. G. CLEMENCEAU
SPITALIERE
BLVD. DUBOUCHAGE
RUE FONCET

HEROLD
BERLIOZ
GOUNOD
AUBER
R. PAUL DEROULEDE
ROSSINI
RUE ALPHONSE KARR
RUE GRIMALDI
RUE LONGCHAMP
MEDECIN
R. G. DELOYE
RUE BLACAS
PASTORELLI

Jean Médecin
NICE ETOILE SHOPPING MALL

RUE VERDI
BLVD. VICTOR HUGO
RUE DU MARECHAL JOFFRE
RUE MACCARANI
RUE DE LA LIBERTE
RUE DE L'HOTEL DES POSTES
RUE ALBERTI

SNCF BOUTIQUE
GALERIES LAFAYETTE
Masséna
#15, 17 & 22
#98

RUE DE LA BUFFA
RUE DALPOZZO
R. FRANCE
AVE. DE SUEDE
RUE MASSENA
Place Masséna
AVE. FELIX FAURE
Opéra Vieille Ville
J. JAURES

MUSEE MASSENA
US CONSULATE
AVE GUSTAVE V
#98
#98
#200, 400 & 500
Coulée
Albert 1er Park
RUE ST. FRANCOIS DE PAULE
R. ALEX.MARI
To Cours Saleya & Old Nice
#98

PROMENADE DES ANGLAIS
#98
Beach
#98
QUAI DES ETATS-UNIS
BLVD.

To Hotel Negresco
TOURIST TRAIN PICK-UP
LE GRAND TOUR BUS

Mediterranean Sea
"Bay of Angels"

N

200 Meters
200 Yards

Sleeping
1 Hôtel Durante
2 Hôtel Belle Meunière
3 Hôtel Villa Victoria
4 Hôtel la Villa

ple, home-style dishes in a communal environment. The menu changes with the season, but the hardworking owner, Dominique, does not. This place fills fast, so arrive early, or better yet, drop by during the day to reserve—they have two seatings at 19:00 and 21:00 (€10 starters, €14 *plats*, €6 desserts, closed Sat-Sun, cash only, 4 Rue Raoul Bosio, no telephone, www.lamerenda.net).

On the Beach

$$$ Restaurant Castel is a fine eat-on-the-beach option, thanks to its location at the very east end of Nice, under Castle Hill. The city vanishes as you step down to the beach. The food is creative and nicely presented, and the tables feel classy, even at the edge of the sand. Arrive for the sunset and you'll have an unforgettable meal (€19 salads and pastas, €20-25 daily plates, open for dinner mid-May-Aug, lunch April-Sept, 8 Quai des Etats-Unis, tel. 04 93 85 22 66, www.castelplage.com). Sunbathers can rent beach chairs and have drinks and meals served literally on the beach (lounge chairs €16/half-day, €19/day).

In the City Center

For a more contemporary slice of France, try one of these spots around the Nice Etoile shopping mall.

Rick's Tip: Nice's **dinner scene converges on Cours Saleya,** *which is entertaining enough in itself to make the generally mediocre food a good deal. It's a fun spot to compare tans and mussels—and worth wandering through even if you eat elsewhere.*

$$ Le Luna Rossa is a small neighborhood eatery serving delicious French-Italian dishes. Owner Christine welcomes diners with attentive service and reasonable prices. Dine inside (classy tables) or outside on a sidewalk terrace (€10 starters, €14-27 *plats*, closed Sun-Mon, just north of parkway at 3 Rue Chauvain, tel. 04 93 85 55 66).

$$ La Maison de Marie is a surprisingly high-quality refuge off Nice's touristy restaurant row—Rue Masséna. The interior tables are as appealing as those in the courtyard, but expect some smokers outside. The €24 *menu* is a good value (€12-18

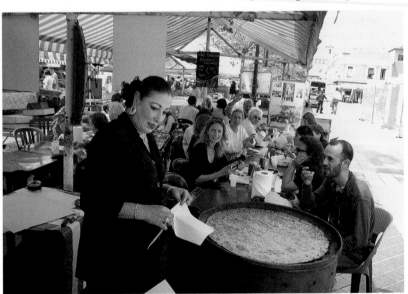

Pick an outdoor table in Nice and try the socca *(thin chickpea crêpe).*

starters, €20-30 plats, open daily, 5 Rue
Masséna, tel. 04 93 82 15 93).

Sleeping

Don't look for charm in Nice. I prefer to
stay in the new town—a 10-minute walk
from the Old Town—for modern, clean,
and air-conditioned rooms. For parking,
ask your hotelier, or see page 307.

In the City Center

The train station area offers Nice's cheapest sleeps, but the neighborhood can feel
seedy after dark. The cheapest places are
older, well-worn, and come with some
street noise. Places closer to Boulevard
Victor Hugo are more expensive and in a
more comfortable area.

Rick's Tip: *The Riviera is famous for staging
major* **events.** *Stay away unless you're actually participating, as you'll only experience
room shortages, higher prices, and traffic jams.
The three biggies are the* **Nice Carnival** *(Feb-
March, www.nicecarnaval.com),* **Cannes
Film Festival** *(mid-May, www.festival-
cannes.com), and* **Grand Prix of Monaco**
*(late May, www.acm.mc). To accommodate
the busy schedules of the rich and famous
(and really mess up a lot of normal people),
the film festival and car race often overlap.*

$ Hôtel Durante*** feels Medi-
terranean—a happy, orange building
with rooms wrapped around a flowery
courtyard. All but two of its quiet rooms
overlook the well-maintained patio. The
rooms are good enough (mostly modern
decor), the price is right enough, and the
parking is free—book well ahead (Sb-
€85-115, Db-€100-130, Tb-€155-185,
Qb-€190-220, breakfast-€10, 16 Avenue
Durante, tel. 04 93 88 84 40, www.hotel-
durante.com, info@hotel-durante.com).

$$ Hôtel Lafayette***, located a block
behind the Galeries Lafayette depart-
ment store, is a modest, homey place
with 17 mostly spacious and good-value

rooms (some with thin walls, some traffic
noise, all one floor up from the street). It's
family-run by Kiril and George (standard
Db-€105-130, spacious Db-€120-150,
Tb-€130-180, preferential direct booking
rates for Rick Steves readers, break-
fast-€12, no elevator, 32 Rue de l'Hôtel
des Postes—see map on page 300, tel. 04
93 85 17 84, www.hotellafayettenice.com,
info@hotellafayettenice.com).

$ Hôtel Belle Meunière*, in an old
mansion built for Napoleon III's mistress,
attracts budget-minded travelers of all
ages with cheap beds and private rooms
a block below the train station. Creaky
but well-kept, the place has adequate
rooms, thin mattresses, and charismatic
Mademoiselle Marie-Pierre presiding
with her perfect English (bunk in 4-bed
dorm-€28 with private bath, less with
shared bath; Db-€60-86, Tb-€86-100,
Qb-€118-135, breakfast-€6 or free if
you book direct, no air-con, no eleva-
tor, laundry service, limited parking-€9/
day, 21 Avenue Durante, tel. 04 93 88 66
15, www.bellemeuniere.com, hotel.belle.
meuniere@cegetel.net).

In or near Vieux Nice

These Vieux Nice hotels are either on the
sea or within an easy walk of it. For loca-
tions, see the map on page 300.

$$$$ Hôtel la Perouse****, built into the rock of Castle Hill at the east end of the bay, is a fine splurge. This refuge-hotel is top-to-bottom flawless in every detail—from its elegant rooms (satin curtains, velour headboards) and attentive staff to its rooftop terrace with hot tub, sleek pool, and lovely garden restaurant (€40 *menus*). Sleep here to be spoiled and escape the big city (garden-view Db-€300-400, seaview Db-€420-580, good family options and Web deals, 11 Quai Rauba Capeu, tel. 04 93 62 34 63, www.hotel-la-perouse.com, lp@hotel-la-perouse.com).

$$ Hôtel Mercure Marché aux Fleurs**** is ideally situated near the sea and Cours Saleya. Rooms are tastefully designed and prices can be reasonable—check their website for deals (standard Db-€180, superior Db-€225-260 and worth the extra euros, smaller seaview room-€50 extra, 91 Quai des Etats-Unis, tel. 04 93 85 74 19, www.hotelmercure.com, h0962@accor.com).

Near the Promenade des Anglais

These hotels are close to the beach (and mostly far from Vieux Nice).

$$$ Hôtel Villa Victoria**** is managed by cheery Marlena, who welcomes travelers into this spotless, classy old building that has an open, attractive lobby overlooking a sprawling garden-courtyard. Rooms are comfortable and well-kept, with space to stretch out (streetside Db-€170-200, gardenside Db-€175-225, Tb-€190-240, suites-€210, breakfast-€15, parking-€18/day, 33 Boulevard Victor Hugo, tel. 04 93 88 39 60, www.villa-victoria.com, contact@villa-victoria.com).

$$ Hôtel la Villa*** is a well-run hotel with 47 rooms, contemporary decor in its light-filled public spaces, and a small front terrace (standard Db-€100-160, larger Db-€200, good breakfast-€12, 19 bis Boulevard Victor Hugo, tel. 04 93 87 15 00, www.hotels-la-villa.com, contact@hotel-villa-nice-centre.com).

Transportation
Getting Around Nice
BY PUBLIC TRANSPORTATION

Although you can walk to most attractions, smart travelers make good use of the buses and tram.

Tickets: Both buses and trams are covered by the same €1.50 single-ride ticket, or you can pay €10 for a 10-ride ticket that can be shared (each use good for 74 minutes in one direction, including transfers between bus and tram). The €5 all-day pass is valid on city buses and trams, as well as buses to some nearby destinations (including Villefranche-sur-Mer and Cap Ferrat, but not buses to the airport). You must validate your ticket on every bus or tram trip. Buy single tickets from the bus driver or from the ticket machines on tram platforms (coins only—press the button twice at the end to get your ticket). Passes and 10-ride tickets are also available from machines at tram stops. Info: www.lignesdazur.com.

Buses: The bus is handy for reaching the Chagall and Matisse museums (for specifics, see museum listings under "Sights"), and the Russian Cathedral. Route diagrams inside the buses identify each stop. For more on riding buses in Nice and throughout the Riviera, see page 306.

Trams: Nice has a single modern and efficient L-shaped tram line. Trams run every few minutes along Avenue Jean Médecin and Boulevard Jean Jaurès, and connect the main train station with Place Masséna and Old Nice (Opéra stop), the port (Place Garibaldi stop),

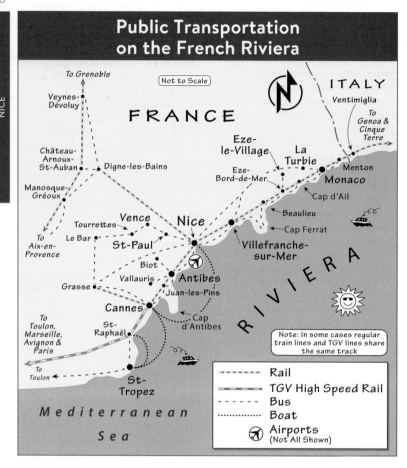

Public Transportation on the French Riviera

and buses east along the coast (Vauban stop). Boarding the tram in the direction of Hôpital Pasteur takes you toward the beach and Vieux Nice (direction: Henri Sappia goes the other way). Tram info: http://tramway.nice.fr.

BY TAXI

While pricey, cabs can be useful for getting to Nice's less-central sights. Cabbies normally pick up only at taxi stands (*tête de station*), or you can call 04 93 13 78 78.

Getting Around the Riviera from Nice

Nice is perfectly situated for exploring the Riviera. Trains and buses do a good job of linking towns along the coast, with bonus views along many routes. Have coins handy. Ticket machines don't take US credit cards or euro bills; smaller train stations may be unstaffed; and bus drivers can't make change for large bills.

BY BUS

Buses are an amazing deal in the Riviera, whether you're riding just within Nice or to Villefranche-sur-Mer, Cap Ferrat, Monaco, or Antibes. The €1.50 single-ride ticket allows transfers between the buses of the Lignes d'Azur (the region's main bus company, www.lignesdazur.com) and the TAM (Transports Alpes-Maritimes); if you board a TAM bus and need a transfer, ask for *un ticket correspondance*. The €5 all-day ticket good on Nice's city buses and tramway also covers buses serving Villefranche and Cap Ferrat. The maps throughout this chapter indicate the locations of the handiest bus stops.

Rick's Tip: *I follow this general rule of thumb when riding a Nice-area bus with an* **all-day bus pass:** *If the bus number has one or two digits, it's covered with the pass; with three digits, it's not.*

Bus Connections Heading East to: **Villefranche-sur-Mer** (#100, 3-4/hour, 20 minutes; or #81, 2-3/hour, 20 minutes), **St-Jean-Cap-Ferrat** (#81, 2-3/hour, 30 minutes), **Monaco** (#100, 3-4/hour, 45 minutes). Due to work on the tram system, eastbound buses may stop only at the port (Le Port stop) when you visit. Ask at the TI if a closer bus stop is now available.

Bus Connections Heading West to: Antibes (#200, 4/hour Mon-Sat, 2/hour Sun, 1.5 hours). Use the Albert I/Verdun stop on Avenue de Verdun, a 10-minute walk along the parkway west of Place Masséna.

BY TRAIN

Speedy trains link the Riviera's beach-front destinations. The train is a bit more expensive than the bus (Nice to Monaco by train is about €4), but there's no quicker way to move about the Riviera (http://en.voyages-sncf.com). Never board a train without a ticket or valid pass—fare inspectors accept no excuses. The minimum fine is €70. See later under "Arriving and Departing" for specific trip information.

BY CAR

This is France's most challenging region to drive in. Beautifully distracting vistas (natural and human), loads of Sunday-driver tourists, and every hour being lush-hour in the summer make for a dangerous combination. Parking can be exasperating. Bring lots of coins and patience.

Rick's Tip: *The Riviera is awash with* **scenic roads.** *To sample one of its most beautiful and thrilling drives, take the coastal* **Middle Corniche road** *from Nice to Monaco. You'll find breathtaking views over the Mediterranean and several scenic pullouts.*

BY BOAT

Trans Côte d'Azur offers boat service from Nice to Monaco seasonally (reservations required, tel. 04 92 98 71 30, www.trans-cote-azur.com). They also run one-hour round-trip cruises along the coast to Cap Ferrat (see page 313).

Arriving and Departing
BY TRAIN

All trains stop at Nice's main station, called Nice-Ville (you don't want the suburban Nice Riquier Station). The TI is straight out the main doors. Nice's single tram line zips you to the center in a few minutes (exit left as you leave the station, departs every few minutes, direction: Hôpital Pasteur). To walk to the beach, Promenade des Anglais, or many of my recommended hotels, cross Avenue Thiers in front of the station, go down the steps by Hôtel Interlaken, and continue down Avenue Durante.

Train Connections from Nice to: Antibes (2/hour, 20 minutes), **Villefranche-sur-Mer** (2/hour, 10 minutes), **Monaco** (2/hour, 20 minutes), **Arles** (11/day, 4 hours, most require transfer in Marseille or Avignon), **Avignon** (10/day, most by TGV, 4 hours, many require transfer in Marseille), **Paris'** Gare de Lyon (hourly, 6 hours, may require change; 11-hour night train goes to Paris' Gare d'Austerlitz), **Chamonix** (4/day, 10 hours, many change in St-Gervais and Lyon), **Beaune** (7/day, 7 hours, 1-2 transfers). Most long-distance train connections to other French cities require a change in Marseille.

BY CAR

To reach the city center on the autoroute from the west, take the first Nice exit (for the airport—called *Côte d'Azur, Central*) and follow signs for *Nice Centre* and *Promenade des Anglais*. Hoteliers know where to park (allow €18-30/day; some hotels offer deals but space is limited—book ahead). The parking garage at the Nice Etoile shopping center on Avenue Jean Médecin is near many recommended hotels (ticket booth on third floor, about €26/day, 18:00-8:00). Other centrally located garages have similar rates. All on-street parking is metered (9:00-18:00), but usually free on Sunday.

You can avoid driving in the center—and park for free during the day (no overnight parking)—by ditching your car at a parking lot at a remote tram or bus stop. Look for blue-on-white *Parcazur* signs (find locations at www.lignesdazur.com), and ride the bus or tram into town (must buy round-trip tram or bus ticket and keep it with you because you'll need it later to exit the parking lot; for details on riding the tram, see "Getting Around Nice," earlier). As lots are unguarded, don't leave anything in your car.

BY PLANE

Nice's easy-to-navigate airport (Aéroport de Nice Côte d'Azur, airport code: NCE) is literally on the Mediterranean, with landfill runways a 30-minute drive west of the city center. The two terminals are connected by shuttle buses (*navettes*). Both terminals have TIs, banks, ATMs, and buses to Nice (tel. 04 89 88 98 28, www.nice.aeroport.fr).

A **taxi into the city center** is expensive considering the short distance (figure €35 to Nice hotels, €60 to Villefranche-sur-Mer, €70 to Antibes, small fee for bags). Nice's airport taxis are notorious for overcharging. Before riding, confirm that your fare into town is roughly €35 (or €40 at night or on Sun). Don't pay much more.

It's always a good idea to ask for a receipt (*reçu*).

Airport shuttles work better for trips from your hotel to the airport, since they offer a fixed price (figure €30 for one person, and only a little more for additional people). Your hotel can arrange this. Try **Nice Airport Shuttle** (1-2 people-€32, additional person-€14, mobile 06 60 33 20 54, www.nice-airport-shuttle.com) or **Med-Tour** (tel. 04 93 82 92 58, mobile 06 73 82 04 10, www.med-tour.com).

Two **bus lines** connect the airport with the city center. **Bus #99** (airport express) runs to Nice's main train station (€6, 2/hour, 8:00-21:00, 30 minutes, drops you within a 10-minute walk of many recommended hotels). To take this bus *to* the airport, catch it right in front of the train station (departs on the half-hour). **Bus #98** runs along Promenade des Anglais and along the edge of Vieux Nice (€6, 3/hour, from the airport 6:00-23:00, to the airport until 21:00, 30 minutes).

For all buses, buy tickets from the driver. To reach the bus-information office and stops at Terminal 1, turn left after passing customs and exit the doors at the far end. Buses serving Terminal 2 stop across the street from the airport exit (info kiosk and ticket sales to the right as you exit).

Getting from the Airport to Nearby Destinations: To reach **Villefranche-sur-Mer**, take bus #98 (described above) to Place Garibaldi; from there, use the same ticket to transfer to bus #81 or #100 (you may need to walk to the port to catch eastbound buses in 2016, due to work on the tram system). To get to **Antibes**, take bus #250 from either terminal (about 2/hour, 40 minutes, €10). Express bus #110 runs from the airport directly to **Monaco** (2/hour, 50 minutes, €20).

NEAR NICE

Day-trip possibilities from Nice are easy and exciting. Villefranche-sur-Mer has a serene setting and small-town warmth. Woodsy Cap Ferrat boasts belle époque mansions and a family-friendly beach. Glitzy little Monaco offers a fancy casino and royal flair. Antibes has sandy beaches, a Picasso museum, and good walking trails. Quick and easy public transportation gets you where you want to go (see "Getting Around the Riviera from Nice" on page 306 for details).

Villefranche-sur-Mer

Villefranche-sur-Mer, just east of Nice, is a romantic's top Riviera choice. Come here for an upscale Mediterranean atmosphere, narrow cobbled streets tumbling into a mellow waterfront, and fancy yachts bobbing in the harbor. Pebbly beaches and a handful of interesting sights keep visitors just busy enough.

Orientation

Tiny and easy-to-cover, Villefranche-sur-Mer snuggles around its harbor.

Day Plan: My self-guided walk laces together everything of importance in town. Your biggest decision will be choosing between a beachfront dinner or an ice-cream-licking village stroll.

Getting There: From Nice, **trains** run to Villefranche twice an hour (10 minutes); **bus #81** or **#100** will also get you there (2-4/hour, 20 minutes). From Nice's port, **drivers** should follow signs for *Menton, Monaco,* and *Basse Corniche.*

Arrival in Villefranche: The train station is just above the beach, a short stroll from the old town. Bus riders can get off at the Octroi stop and walk downhill past the TI to town. Drivers will find pay lots just below the TI or on the water (at Parking Wilson).

Rick's Tip: Skip the useless white tourist train, *which goes nowhere interesting.*

Tourist Information: The main TI is off the road that runs between Nice and Monaco, located in a park—Jardin François Binon—below the Nice/Monaco

The beautiful deep-water bay at Villefranche-sur-Mer attracts every kind of boat.

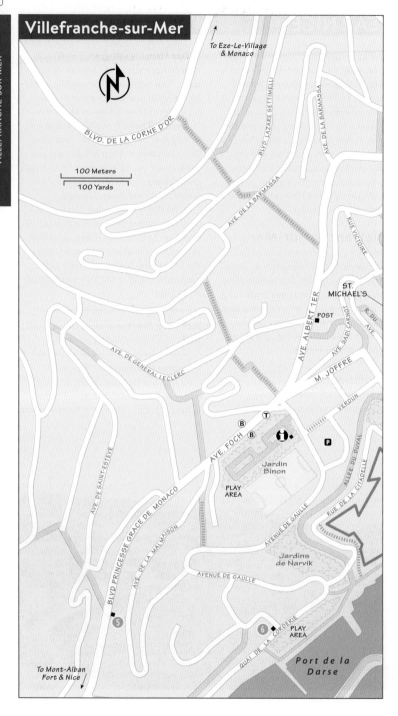

Villefranche-sur-Mer

To Eze-Le-Village & Monaco

100 Meters
100 Yards

BLVD. DE LA CORNE D'OR

BLVD. LAZARE SETTIMELLI

AVE. DE LA BARMASSA

AVE. DE LA BARMASSA

RUE VICTOIRE

ST. MICHAEL'S

AVE. ALBERT 1ER

POST

AVE. SADI CARNOT

R. DU

AVE.

AVE. DE GENERAL LECLERC

M. JOFFRE

VERDUN

AVE. DE SAINT-ESTEVE

AVE. FOCH

Ⓑ Ⓣ
Ⓑ

Ⓟ

ALLEE DU DUVAL

Jardin Binon

PLAY AREA

BLVD PRINCESSE GRACE DE MONACO

AVE. DE LA MALMAISON

AVENUE DE GAULLE

RUE DE LA CITADELLE

RUE DE LA

Jardins de Narvik

AVENUE DE GAULLE

⑤

⑥ ◆ PLAY AREA

QUAI DE LA CORDERIE

Port de la Darse

To Mont-Alban Fort & Nice

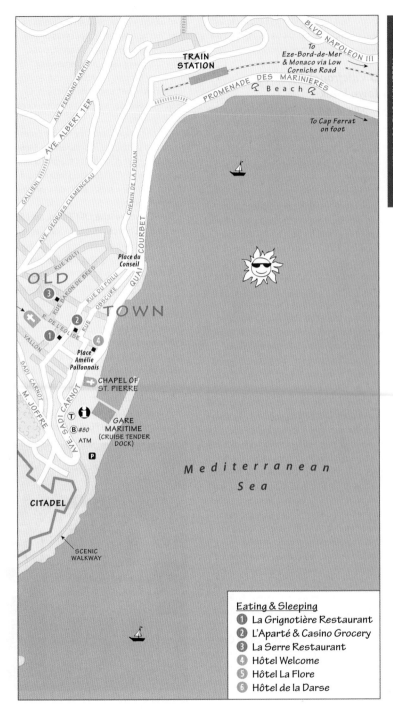

TRAIN STATION

To Eze-Bord-de-Mer & Monaco via Low Corniche Road

BLVD NAPOLEON III

PROMENADE DES MARINIERES

Beach

To Cap Ferrat on foot

AVE. FERNAND MARTIN

AVE. ALBERT 1ER

GALIENI

AVE. GEORGES CLEMENCEAU

CHEMIN DE LA FOUAN

QUAI COURBET

RUE VOLTI

RUE BARON DE BRES

Place du Conseil

OLD

RUE DU POILU

R. DE L'EGLISE

RUE OBSCURE

TOWN

VALLON

SADI-CARNOT

M. JOFFRE

AVE. SADI CARNOT

Place Amélie Pollonnais

CHAPEL OF ST. PIERRE

T
B #80
ATM
P

GARE MARITIME (CRUISE TENDER DOCK)

Mediterranean Sea

CITADEL

SCENIC WALKWAY

Eating & Sleeping

1 La Grignotière Restaurant
2 L'Aparté & Casino Grocery
3 La Serre Restaurant
4 Hôtel Welcome
5 Hôtel La Flore
6 Hôtel de la Darse

Octroi bus stop (daily in season, closed Sun off-season, tel. 04 93 01 73 68, www. villefranche-sur-mer.com).

⊙ Villefranche-sur-Mer Town Walk

This quick self-guided stroll starts at the waterfront and finishes at the citadel.

• *Go to the end of the little pier directly in front of Hôtel Welcome, where we'll start with a spin tour (spin to the right) to get oriented.*

The Harbor: At 2,000 feet, this is the deepest natural harbor on the Riviera and was the region's most important port until Nice built its own in the 18th century. Look out to sea. Cap Ferrat, the hill across the bay, is a landscaped paradise where the 1 percent of the 1 percent compete for the best view. Geologically, Cap Ferrat is the southern tip of the Alps. The range emerges from the sea here and arcs all across Europe, over 700 miles, to Vienna. The Rothschild's pink mansion, Villa Ephrussi (slightly left of center, hugging the top) is the most worthwhile sight to visit on the Cap (see page 314).

Up on the hill, the 16th-century citadel is marked by flags. The yellow fisherman's chapel (with the little-toe bell tower) has an interior painted by the writer/artist Jean Cocteau. Hôtel Welcome offers the balconies of dreams. Up the lane is the baroque facade of St. Michael's Church. The promenade, lined by fancy fish restaurants, leads to the town beach. Fifty yards above the beach stands the train station and above that, supported by arches, is the Low Corniche road, which leads to Monaco.

• *Walk left 30 yards past the last couple of boats surviving from the town's once important fishing community to a small bronze bust of Jean Cocteau. Step up to the little chapel he painted.*

Chapel of St. Pierre (Chapelle Cocteau): This chapel is the town's cultural highlight (open Wed-Mon 10:00–12:00 & 15:00–19:00, usually closed Tue). Cocteau, who decorated the place, was a Parisian

transplant who adored little Villefranche-sur-Mer and whose career was distinguished by his work as an artist, poet, novelist, playwright, and filmmaker. Influenced by his pals Marcel Proust, André Gide, Edith Piaf, and Pablo Picasso, Cocteau was a leader among the 20th-century avant-garde.

• *From the chapel, stroll the harbor promenade 100 yards past Restaurant La Mère Germaine. Just past the restaurant, a lane (signed Vieille Ville) leads up into the old town. Walk a few steps until you reach a long tunnel-like street.*

Rue Obscure, the Old Town, and St. Michael's Church: Here, under these 13th-century vaults, you're in another age. Before the long stepped lane (which we'll climb later), turn right and walk to the end of Rue Obscure (which means "dark street"). At the end, wind up to the sunlight past a tiny fountain at Place du Conseil, and a few steps beyond that to a viewpoint overlooking the beach. Then stroll back past the fountain and gently downhill. At Place des Deux Canons, turn right and climb the stepped lanes, and then take your first left (at a restaurant) to St. Michael's Church, facing a delightful square (Place de l'Eglise) with a single

Chapel of St. Pierre

magnolia tree. The church features an 18th-century organ, a particularly engaging crucifix at the high altar, and a fine statue of a recumbent Christ—carved, they say, from a fig tree by a galley slave in the 1600s.

• *Leaving St. Michael's, go downhill halfway to the water, where you hit the main commercial street. Go right on Rue du Poilu to Place de la République. Head through the square and angle left, up the hill to the...*

Citadel: The town's mammoth castle, with walls sloping thickly at the base, was built in the 1500s, the so-called "Age of Black Powder." With the advent of gunpowder, stout cannonball-deflecting walls became a necessity for any effective fortification.

• *That concludes our introductory walk.*

Experiences

BOAT RIDES (PROMENADES EN MER)

To view this beautiful coastline from the sea, take a quick sightseeing cruise (€12 for one-hour trip around Cap Ferrat, €20 for two-hour cruise as far as Monaco, departures from harbor across from Hôtel Welcome, June-Sept Wed and Sat, also Thu in July-Aug, no trips Oct-May, reservations a must, tel. 04 93 76 65 65, www. amv-sirenes.com).

HIKE TO MONT-ALBAN FORT

This fort, with a remarkable setting on the high ridge that separates Nice and Villefranche-sur-Mer, is a good destination for hikers (also accessible by car; info at TI). From the TI, walk on the main road toward

Nice about 200 yards past Hôtel Versailles. Look for wooden trail signs labeled *Escalier de Verre* and climb about 45 minutes as the trail makes long switchbacks through the woods up to the ridge. Find your way to Mont-Alban Fort (interior closed to tourists) and its view terrace.

MARKETS

A fun bric-a-brac market enlivens Villefranche-sur-Mer on Sundays (on Place Amélie Pollonnais by Hôtel Welcome, and in Jardin François Binon by the TI). On Saturday and Wednesday mornings, a small food market sets up in Jardin François Binon.

Eating and Sleeping

$$$ **La Grignotière** serves generous and tasty *plats* (closed Wed off-season, 3 Rue du Poilu). $$$ **L'Aparté** is where locals go for fresh cuisine and a special experience (closed Mon, 1 Rue Obscure). $ **La Serre** serves well-priced dinners (open evenings only, 16 Rue de May). Picnickers can raid the handy **Casino grocery** (closed Sun afternoon and all day Wed, 12 Rue du Poilu).

Overnighters will find seaview rooms at $$$ **Hôtel Welcome****** (3 Quai Amiral Courbet, www.welcomehotel. com); $$ **Hôtel La Flore***** (5 Boulevard Princesse Grace de Monaco, www.hotel-la-flore.fr), and $ **Hôtel de la Darse**** (32 Avenue du Général de Gaulle, www. hoteldeladarse.com).

Cap Ferrat

Exclusive Cap Ferrat is a peaceful eddy off the busy Nice-Monaco route. If you owned a house here, some of the richest people on the planet would be your neighbors. Take a leisurely tour of the Villa Ephrussi de Rothschild mansion and gardens, then enjoy the late afternoon on the beach at Plage de Passable.

Getting There: Take **Bus #81** (direction: *Le Port/Cap Ferrat*); for the Villa Ephrussi or the beach, get off at the

Waterfront tables line Villefranche's harbor.

Passable stop (the return bus is direction: *Nice*). **Warning:** Late-afternoon buses back to Villefranche-sur-Mer or Nice can be jammed (worse on weekends), potentially leaving passengers stranded at stops for long periods.

Cap Ferrat is quick by **car** (take the Low Corniche) or **taxi** (allow €25 one-way from Villefranche-sur-Mer, €50 from Nice).

Tourist Information: The main TI is near the Villa Ephrussi (Mon-Fri 9:00-16:00, closed Sat-Sun, 59 Avenue Denis Séméria, bus #81 stops here). A smaller TI is in the sleepy village of St-Jean-Cap-Ferrat (closed Sun, 5 Avenue Denis Séméria, tel. 04 93 76 08 90, office-tourisme@saintjeancapferrat.fr).

Rick's Tip: Cap Ferrat is perfect for a walk; you'll find **well-maintained, mostly level foot trails** *covering most of its length. The TIs in Villefranche-sur-Mer and on the Cap have maps with walking paths marked.*

Sights

▲ VILLA EPHRUSSI DE ROTHSCHILD

In what seems like the ultimate in Riviera extravagance, Venice, Versailles, and the Côte d'Azur come together in the pastel-pink Villa Ephrussi. Rising above Cap Ferrat, this 1905 mansion has views west to Villefranche-sur-Mer and east to Beaulieu-sur-Mer.

Cost and Hours: Palace and gardens-

Villa Ephrussi de Rothschild

€13, includes audioguide; mid-Feb-Oct daily 10:00-18:00, July-Aug until 19:00, shorter hours off-season; tel. 04 93 01 33 09, www.villa-ephrussi.com.

Visiting the Villa: Pick up the audioguide and garden map as you enter, then start with the well-furnished belle époque **interior.** Upstairs, an 18-minute film covers the life of rich and eccentric Beatrice, Baroness de Rothschild, the French banking heiress who built and furnished the place. Don't miss the view over the gardens from the terrace.

As you stroll through the rooms, you'll pass royal furnishings and personal possessions, including the baroness's porcelain collection and her bathroom case for cruises. An appropriately classy **garden-tearoom** serves drinks and lunches with a view (12:00-17:30).

Behind the mansion are literally ship-shape gardens, inspired by Beatrice's many ocean-liner trips. The seven lush gardens are re-created from locations all over the world. Highlights include the Jardin Exotique's wild cactus, the rose garden at the far end, and the view back to the house from the "Temple of Love" gazebo.

PLAGE DE PASSABLE

Located below the Villa Ephrussi is a pebbly little beach with great views, popular with families. One half is public (free, with snack bar, shower, and WC), and the other is run by a small restaurant (€22 includes changing locker, lounge chair, and shower; they have 260 "beds," but still reserve ahead in summer or on weekends as this is a prime spot, tel. 04 93 76 06 17). If you were ever to do the French Riviera rent-a-beach ritual, this would be the place.

Getting There: Bus #81 stops just above the beach (Passable stop). Drivers can park curbside or in a pay lot near the beach.

Eating: Plage de Passable is a great place for dinner. Arrive before sunset, then watch as darkness descends and lights flicker over Villefranche-sur-Mer's heavenly setting. **Restaurant de la Plage de Passable** is your chance to dine on the beach with romance and class while enjoying terrific views and the sounds of children still at play (€12-16 starters, €18-30 plats, open daily late May-early Sept, always make a reservation, tel. 04 93 76 06 17, www.plage-de-passable.com).

Monaco

The minuscule principality of Monaco (less than a square mile) is a special place—it's home to one of the world's most famous auto races and one of its fanciest casinos. The glamorous 1956 marriage of the American actress Grace Kelly to Prince Rainier added to Monaco's mystique. Don't look for anything too deep in this glittering little land of luxury; the majority of its 36,000 residents have relocated here mainly to avoid paying income tax. Yet despite high prices, wall-to-wall daytime tourists, and a Disney-esque atmosphere, Monaco is a Riviera must for many a traveler.

Orientation

All of Monaco's major sights except the casino are in Monaco-Ville, packed within a few cheerfully tidy blocks. The famous casino is in the Monte Carlo neighborhood.

Day Plan: The surgical-strike plan is to start with my self-guided walk in Monaco-Ville, and then finish by gambling away whatever you have left in the Monte Carlo Casino.

Getting There: Ride **bus #100** (3-4/hour) from Nice (45 minutes) or Villefranche-sur-Mer (20 minutes). Trains run twice an hour (20 minutes from Nice, 10 minutes from Villefranche). Monaco's traffic isn't worth the fight for drivers—leave the car behind and ride the train or bus into town.

Arrival in Monaco: Bus riders wanting to start with the self-guided walk should disembark at the Place d'Armes stop at the base of Monaco-Ville; casino-goers should

wait for the Monte Carlo-Casino stop.

From the train station, for Monaco-Ville, take the exit marked Sortie Fontvieille/Le Rocher, which leads through a long tunnel to Place d'Armes. For the casino, follow Sortie Port and Accès Port signs until you pop out at the port. From here, it's a 20-minute walk to the casino (up Avenue d'Ostende to your left), or a short trip via bus (#1 or #2, find stops across the busy street).

Getting Around Monaco: City buses #1 and #2 link all areas with frequent service (single ticket-€2, 6 tickets-€10, day pass-€5, pay driver or buy from curbside machines). You can split a six-ride ticket with your travel partners.

Tourist Information: The main TI is at the top of the park above the casino (Mon-Sat 9:00-19:00, Sun 11:00-13:00, 2 Boulevard des Moulins, tel. 00-377/92 16 61 16 or 00-377/92 16 61 66, www.visitmonaco.com). Another TI is at the train station (Tue-Sat 9:00-18:00, also open Sun-Mon in July-Aug, closed 12:00-14:00 off-season).

Rick's Tip: If you want an official memento of your Monaco visit, you can get your **passport stamped** at the main TI.

○ Monaco-Ville Walk

This self-guided walk connects many of the main sights with a tight little loop, starting from the palace square, Monaco-Ville's sightseeing center.
• If you're walking up from the Place d'Armes stop for bus #100, a well-marked lane leads directly to the palace.

PALACE SQUARE (PLACE DU PALAIS)

This square is the best place to get oriented to Monaco. Facing the palace, go to the right and look out over the city (er...principality). This rock gave birth to the little pastel Hong Kong look-alike in 1215, and it's managed to remain an independent country for most of its 800 years.

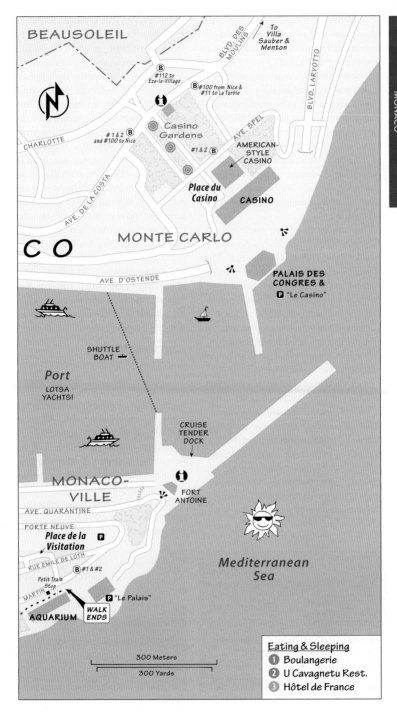

Looking beyond the glitzy port, notice the faded green roof above and to the right: It belongs to the casino that put Monaco on the map in the 1800s.

The modern buildings just past the casino mark the eastern limit of Monaco. The famous Grand Prix runs along the port and then up the ramp to the casino (at top speeds of 180 mph). Italy is so close, you can almost smell the pesto. Just beyond the casino is France again (which flanks Monaco on both sides)—you could walk one-way from France to France, passing through Monaco in about 60 minutes.

The odd statue of a woman with a fishing net is dedicated to the glorious reign of **Prince Albert I** (1889-1922). The son of Charles III (who built the casino), Albert I was a true Renaissance man. He had a Jacques Cousteau-like fascination with the sea (and built Monaco's famous aquarium) and was a determined pacifist who made many attempts to dissuade Germany's Kaiser Wilhelm II from becoming involved in World War I.

• *As you head toward the palace, you'll find a statue of a monk grasping a sword nearby.*

Meet **François Grimaldi,** a renegade Italian dressed as a monk, who captured Monaco in 1297 and began the dynasty that still rules the principality. The current ruler, Prince Albert, is his great-great-great...grandson, which gives Monaco's royal family the distinction of being the longest-lasting dynasty in Europe.

• *Now walk to the...*

PRINCE'S PALACE (PALAIS PRINCIER)

A medieval castle sat where the palace is today. Its strategic setting has had a lot to do with Monaco's ability to resist attackers. Today, Prince Albert and his wife live in the palace, while poor Princesses Stephanie and Caroline live down the street. The palace guards protect the prince 24/7 and still stage a **Changing of the Guard** ceremony with all the pageantry of an important nation (daily at 11:55, fun to watch but jam-packed, arrive by 11:30). Audioguide tours take you through part of the prince's lavish palace in 30 minutes. The rooms are well-furnished and impressive, but interesting only if you haven't seen a château lately (€8, includes audioguide, €19 combo-ticket also covers Oceanographic Museum and Aquarium; April-Oct daily 10:00-18:00, closed Nov-March, www.palais.mc).

• *Head to the west end of the palace square. Below the cannonballs is the district known as...*

FONTVIEILLE

Monaco's newest, reclaimed-from-the-sea area has seen much of Monaco's post-WWII growth (notice the lushly planted building tops). Prince Rainier continued—some say, was obsessed with—Monaco's economic growth, creating landfills (and topping them with apartments such as in Fontvieille), flashy ports, more beaches, a big sports stadium marked by tall arches, and a rail station.

• *With your back to the palace, leave the square through the arch at the far right (Rue Colonel Bellando de Castro) and find the...*

Monaco's classy port   Palace Square

CATHEDRAL OF MONACO (CATHEDRALE DE MONACO)

The somber but beautifully lit cathedral, rebuilt in 1878, shows that Monaco cared for more than just its new casino. It's where centuries of Grimaldis are buried, and where Princess Grace and Prince Rainier were married. Inside, circle slowly behind the altar (counterclockwise). The second tomb is that of Albert I, who did much to put Monaco on the world stage. The second-to-last tomb—inscribed "*Gratia Patricia, MCMLXXXII*"—is where Princess Grace was buried in 1982. Prince Rainier's tomb lies next to Princess Grace's (daily 8:30-19:15).

• As you leave the cathedral, find the 1956 wedding photo of Princess Grace and Prince Rainier, then dip into the immaculately maintained **Jardin Botanique**, with more fine views. In the gardens, turn left. Eventually you'll find the impressive building housing the...

Rick's Tip: If you're into **stamps,** drop by the **post office,** where postcard writers with panache can see—or buy—impressive Monegasque stamps (closed Sun, on Place de la Mairie, a few blocks from the Oceanographic Museum and Aquarium).

OCEANOGRAPHIC MUSEUM AND AQUARIUM (MUSEE OCEANOGRAPHIQUE)

Prince Albert I built this cliff-hanging aquarium in 1910 as a monument to his enthusiasm for things from the sea. The aquarium, which Jacques Cousteau captained for 32 years, has 2,000 different specimens, representing 250 species. You'll find Mediterranean fish and colorful tropical species. Rotating exhibits occupy the entry floor. Upstairs, the fancy Albert I Hall houses a museum that's filled with ship models, whale skeletons, and oceanographic instruments. Take the elevator to the rooftop terrace view café (€14, €19 combo-ticket includes Prince's Palace;

Ⓐ *Changing of the guard*
Ⓑ *Cathedral of Monaco*
Ⓒ *Fontvieille harbor*
Ⓓ *Oceanographic Museum*

daily April-Sept 10:00-19:00, July-Aug until 19:30, Oct-March until 18:00, www. oceano.mc).

• *Our walk is over. The red-brick steps across from the aquarium lead up to stops for buses #1 and #2, both of which run to the casino and the train station.*

Rick's Tip: *For a **cheap and scenic loop ride** through Monaco, ride bus #2 from one end to the other and back (25 minutes each way). You need two tickets (€2 each) and have to get off the bus at the last stop and then get on again.*

Experiences
▲ MONTE CARLO CASINO (CASINO DE MONTE-CARLO)

Monte Carlo, which means "Charles' Hill" in Spanish, is named for the prince who presided over Monaco's 19th-century makeover. In the mid-1800s, olive groves stood here. Then, with the construction of a casino and spas, and easy road and train access, one of Europe's poorest countries was on the Grand Tour map—*the* place for the vacationing aristocracy to play.

Today, Monaco has the world's highest per-capita income.

The Monte Carlo casino is intended to make you feel comfortable while losing your retirement nest egg. Charles Garnier designed the place (with an opera house inside) in 1878, in part to thank the prince for his financial help in completing Paris' Opéra Garnier (which the architect also designed).

The **first rooms** (Salle Renaissance, Salon de l'Europe, and Salle des Amériques) have European and English roulette, blackjack, craps, and slot machines. The more glamorous **private game rooms** (Salons Touzet, Salle Medecin, and Terrasse Salle Blanche) have those same games, plus Trente et Quarante, Ultimate Texas Hold 'Em poker, and Punto Banco—a version of baccarat.

Cost and Hours: Hours and entry fees are shuffled regularly. Plan on €10 to enter at any hour, whether you gamble or not. Public areas are open daily 9:00-12:30 (no gambling). Guided tours may be available, or take an English brochure and tour on your own. From 14:00 to very late the gaming rooms are open to appropriately

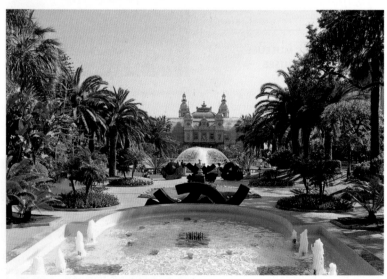

Lush gardens lead to Monte Carlo Casino.

attired humans over 18 (bring your passport as proof, www.montecarlocasinos.com).

Dress Code: Before 14:00, shorts are allowed in the atrium area, though you'll need decent attire to go any farther. After 14:00, shorts are off-limits everywhere, and tennis shoes are not permitted. Men should wear a jacket and slacks, and women should dress up a bit as well.

Take the Money and Run: The stop for buses returning to Nice and Villefranche-sur-Mer and for local buses #1 and #2 is on Avenue de la Costa, at the top of the park above the casino (at the small shopping mall). To reach the train station from the casino, take bus #1 or #2 from this stop, or walk about 15 minutes down Avenue d'Ostende toward the port, and follow signs to *Gare SNCF*.

Eating and Sleeping

In Monaco-Ville, you'll find massive *pan bagnat*, quiche, and sandwiches at the yellow-bannered **$ Boulangerie,** a block off Place du Palais (8 Rue Basse). At **$$ U Cavagnetu,** just a block from Albert's palace, you'll dine cheaply on specialties from Monaco (14 Rue Comte Félix Gastaldi).

Centrally located and comfortable, **$$ Hôtel de France**** is reasonably priced—for Monaco (6 Rue de la Turbie, www.monte-carlo.mc/france).

Antibes

Rising above the blue Mediterranean south and west of Nice, Antibes is charming in a sandy-sophisticated way. Besides offering wide, pleasant beaches, it's the launching point for several scenic hikes along the rocky coast.

Orientation

Day Plan: Visitors can browse Europe's biggest yacht harbor, snooze on a sandy beach, loiter through the charming old town, and hike along a sea-swept trail. The town's cultural claim to fame, the Picasso Museum, shows off its appealing collection in a fine old building.

Getting There: Trains and buses run from Nice to Antibes, but the train is the better choice—it's faster and won't get you stuck in traffic (2/hour, 20 minutes).

Arrival in Antibes: To walk from the train station to the port, the old town, and

Antibes' Plage de la Gravette

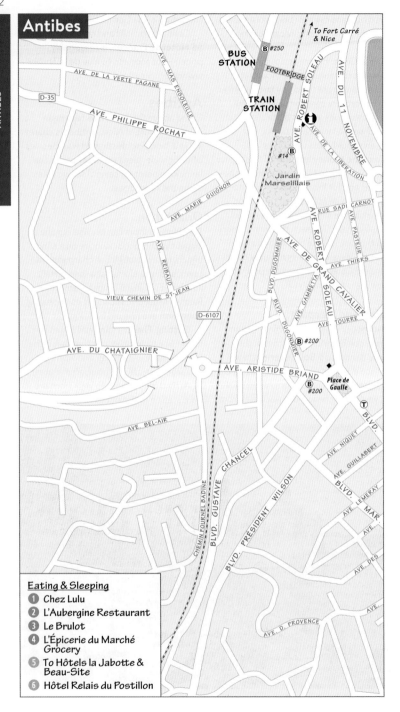

Antibes

To Fort Carré & Nice

BUS STATION

B #250

FOOTBRIDGE

TRAIN STATION

AVE. DE LA VERTE PAGANE

D-35

AVE. PHILIPPE ROCHAT

AVE. MAS ENSOLEILLE

AVE. ROBERT SOLEAU

AVE. DU 11 NOVEMBRE

AVE. DE LA LIBERATION

B #14

Jardin Marseillais

AVE. MARIE GUIGNON

AVE. REIBAUD

RUE SADI CARNOT

AVE. PASTEUR

AVE. ROBERT SOLEAU

AVE. THIERS

AVE. DE GRAND CAVALIER

VIEUX CHEMIN DE ST-JEAN

BLVD. DUGOMMIER

BLVD. DUGOMMIER

AVE. GAMBETTA

AVE. TOURRE

D-6107

AVE. DU CHATAIGNIER

B #200

AVE. ARISTIDE BRIAND

B #200

Place de Gaulle

T

BLVD.

AVE. BEL-AIR

AVE. NIQUET

AVE. GUILLABERT

BLVD.

AVE. LEMERAY

AVE. MAR.

AVE.

CHEMIN FOURNEL BADINE

BLVD. GUSTAVE CHANCEL

BLVD. PRÉSIDENT WILSON

AVE. DES

AVE. D. PROVENCE

AVE.

Eating & Sleeping

1. Chez Lulu
2. L'Aubergine Restaurant
3. Le Brulot
4. L'Épicerie du Marché Grocery
5. To Hôtels la Jabotte & Beau-Site
6. Hôtel Relais du Postillon

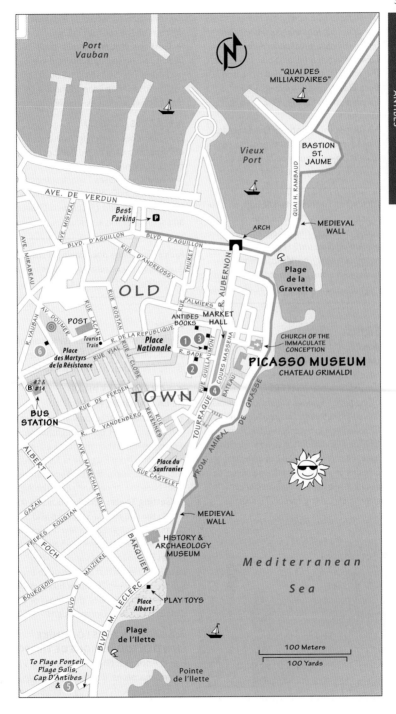

the Picasso Museum (15 minutes), cross the street in front of the station, skirting left of the café, and follow Avenue de la Libération downhill as it bends left. At the end of the street, head right along the port. Day-trippers arriving by car should follow signs to *Centre-Ville,* then *Port Vauban.*

Tourist Information: The TI is a few blocks from the train station at 42 Avenue Robert Soleau (open daily, tel. 04 22 10 60 10, www.antibesjuanlespins.com).

Rick's Tip: *Antibes'* **market hall,** *on Cours Masséna, bustling under a 19th-century canopy, changes throughout the day: flowers and produce until 13:30 (daily but closed Mon Sept-May), handicrafts most afternoons (Thu-Sun), and outdoor dining in the evenings.*

Sights
▲▲PICASSO MUSEUM (MUSEE PICASSO)

Sitting serenely where the old town meets the sea, this compact three-floor museum offers a manageable collection of Picasso's paintings, sketches, and ceramics. Picasso lived in this castle (the former Château Grimaldi) for several months in 1946, when he cranked out an amazing amount of art. Most of the paintings you'll see here are from this short but prolific stretch of his long career. The result-

Terrace at the Picasso Museum

ing collection (donated by Picasso) put Antibes on the tourist map.

Cost and Hours: €6; mid-June-mid-Sept Tue-Sun 10:00-18:00, mid-Sept-mid-June Tue-Sun 10:00-12:00 & 14:00-18:00, closed Mon year-round; tel. 04 92 90 54 20, www.antibes-juanlespins.com.

▲BEACHES (PLAGES)

Good beaches stretch from the south end of Antibes toward Cap d'Antibes. They're busy but manageable in summer and on weekends, with cheap snack stands and good views of the old town. The closest beach is at the port (Plage de la Gravette) and seems calm in any season.

Rick's Tip: *Locals* **don't swim in July and August,** *as the warming sea brings swarms of* **stinging jellyfish.** *Ask before you dip.*

Hikes

The two hikes below are easy to combine by bus, bike, or car. For bus schedules, ask at the TI or consult www.envibus.fr.

▲▲CHAPELLE ET PHARE DE LA GAROUPE HIKE

The exceptional territorial views—best in the morning—from this lighthouse viewpoint more than merit the 20-minute uphill climb from Plage de la Salis. An orientation table explains that you can see from Nice to Cannes and up to the Alps.

Getting There: Take Envibus bus #2 or #14 to the Plage de la Salis stop and find the trail a block ahead (a few blocks after Maupassant Apartments; where the road curves left, follow signs and the rough, cobbled Chemin du Calvaire up to the lighthouse tower). By car or bike, follow signs for *Cap d'Antibes,* then look for *Chapelle et Phare de la Garoupe* signs.

▲▲CAP D'ANTIBES LOOP HIKE (SENTIER TOURISTIQUE DE TIREPOIL)

Cap d'Antibes is filled with exclusive villas and mansions. Roads are just lanes, bounded on both sides by the high and greedy walls of some of the most expensive real estate in France. But all the money in the world can't buy you the beach in France, so a thin strip of rocky coastline forms a two-mile long, parklike zone with an extremely scenic, mostly paved but often rocky trail (Sentier Touristique de Tirepoil).

At a fast clip you can walk the entire circle in just over an hour. Don't do the hike without the tourist map (available at hotels or the TI). While you can do it in either direction (or in partial segments), I prefer a counterclockwise loop.

Rick's Tip: *You can tour star-shaped* **Fort Carré,** *on the headland overlooking the harbor, but there's little to see inside. It's only worth a visit for* **fantastic views** *over Antibes.*

Getting There: Ride Envibus bus #2 from Antibes for about 15 minutes to the La Fontaine stop at Rond-Point A. Meiland (next to Hôtel Beau-Site). By car or bike, follow signs to *Cap d'Antibes*, then to *Plage de la Garoupe*, and park there. The trail begins at the far-right end of Plage de la Garoupe.

Eating and Sleeping

$$ Chez Lulu is a fun family dining adventure (arrive early, opens at 19:00, closed Sun-Mon, 5 Rue Frédéric Isnard). Intimate **$$ L'Aubergine** delivers fine cuisine at fair prices (opens at 18:30, closed Wed, 7 Rue Sade). **$$ Le Brulot** is known for its meats cooked on an open fire (closed Sun, 2 Rue Frédéric Isnard). Romantics on a shoestring can drop by the handy **L'Épicerie du Marché** and assemble a picnic dinner to enjoy on the beach or ramparts (3 Cours Masséna).

$$ Hôtel la Jabotte** is a cozy boutique hotel (13 Avenue Max Maurey, www.jabotte.com). The comfortable **$$ Hôtel Beau-Site***** is a good-value option, a 10-minute drive from town (141 Boulevard Kennedy, www.hotelbeausite.net). **$ Hôtel Relais du Postillon**** has cute rooms at good rates (8 Rue Championnet, www.relaisdupostillon.com).

Cap d'Antibes' seaside walk

Spain

Spain (*España*) is in Europe, but not *of* Europe—it has a unique identity and history, thanks largely to the Pyrenees Mountains that physically isolate it from the rest of the continent. Spain's seclusion contributed to the creation of distinctive customs: bullfights, flamenco dancing, and a national obsession with ham.

Spain, with 46 million people (mostly Roman Catholic), is a little bigger than California. It's been ruled by Roman emperors, Muslim sultans, hard-core Christians, conquistadors, French dandies, and a Fascist dictator; all left their mark on Spain's art, architecture, and culture.

Your best stop in Spain is trend-setting Barcelona. Nursing a glass of wine at a sidewalk table on any square gets you a front-row seat to Spain's urban scene, the best show in town.

CUISINE SCENE AT A GLANCE

Spanish cuisine is hearty, and meals are served in big, inexpensive portions. You can eat well in restaurants for about €15-20—or even more cheaply with more variety if you graze on tapas (appetizers) in bars.

The Spanish eating schedule—lunch from 13:00 to 16:00, and dinner after 21:00—frustrates many visitors. Lunch, eaten around 14:00, is the major meal of the day for most Spaniards. Because many people work until 19:30, dinner is usually served at about 21:00 or 22:00.

To satisfy your hunger nearly any time of day, it's easy to get a quick, cheap meal (see "Budget Options" below), or go to a tapas bar to build a light meal out of appetizers. Tapas are small portions of seafood, salads, meat-filled pastries, and on and on, typically costing about €5-10 a plate.

Eating and drinking at a bar is usually cheapest if you sit or stand at the counter *(barra)*. You may pay a little more to eat sitting at a table *(mesa* or *salón)* and still more for an outdoor table *(terraza)*. Traditionally, tapas are served at the bar. It's bad form to order food at the bar, then take it to a table.

When you're ready to order, be assertive or you'll never be served. *Por favor* (please) grabs the guy's attention. You can often just point to what you want in the display case, and get your food. Don't worry about paying until you're ready to leave (he's keeping track of your tab).

Many bars push larger portions called *raciones* (dinner plate-sized). Ask for the smaller tapas portions or a *media-ración* (listed as ½ *ración* on a menu)—though some bars simply don't serve anything smaller than a *ración*.

Most **restaurants** (like bars) serve their dishes as *raciones* and *media-raciones*. Enjoy this as an opportunity to explore the regional cuisine. Two people can fill up on four *media-raciones*.

For a budget meal in a restaurant, try a *plato combinado* (combination plate), which usually includes portions of one or two main dishes, a vegetable, and bread. Another option is the *menú del día* (menu of the day, also known as *menú turístico*), a substantial three- to four-course meal that usually comes with a carafe of house wine.

Tipping: Most sit-down restaurants include a service charge in the bill *(servicio incluido)*. If you like to tip for good service, round up to about 5 percent. If service is not included *(servicio no incluido)*, tip up to 10 percent.

Budget Options: Fast-food sandwich shops such as Pans & Company serve fresh sandwiches and salads. Many bakeries sell sandwiches and *empanadas* (pastry turnovers filled with seasoned meat and veggies). For a hearty snack any time of day, drop by a bar for a *tortilla española*—a potato omelet cooked fresh every morning and sold in wedges. Pizza shops offer slices to go. The popular El Corte Inglés department stores have a cafeteria and supermarket.

Barcelona

Barcelona may be Spain's second city, but it's undoubtedly the first city of the proud and distinct region of Catalunya. Catalan flags wave side by side with Spanish flags, and locals—while fluent in both languages—insist on speaking Catalan first. Joining hands to dance the patriotic *sardana* is a tradition that's going strong. This lively culture is on an unstoppable roll in Spain's most cosmopolitan corner.

The city itself is a work of art. Catalan architects, including Antoni Gaudí, Lluís Domènech i Montaner, and Josep Puig i Cadafalch, forged the Modernista style and remade the city's skyline into a curvy fantasy—culminating in Gaudí's over-the-top Sagrada Família, a church still under construction. Pablo Picasso lived here as a teenager, right as he was on the verge of reinventing painting; his legacy is today's Picasso Museum.

Barcelona bubbles with life—in the narrow alleys of the Barri Gòtic, along the pedestrian boulevard called the Ramblas, in the funky bohemian quarter of El Born, along the bustling beach promenade, and throughout the chic Eixample. The cafés are filled by day, and people crowd the streets at night, popping into tapas bars for a drink and a perfectly composed bite of seafood.

If you surrender to any city's charms, let it be Barcelona.

BARCELONA IN 3 DAYS

Day 1: In the cool of the morning, follow my Barri Gòtic Walk, exploring the winding lanes, unique boutiques, and historic cathedral.

Then take my Ramblas Ramble, strolling down the grand pedestrian boulevard—a festival of people-watching, street performers, and pickpockets. On the Ramblas, duck into La Boqueria Market for fresh produce and unforgettable taste treats. In the afternoon, head to the trendy El Born district to tour the Picasso Museum or Palace of Catalan Music, or both.

On any evening: Have a tapa-hopping dinner in El Born, the Barri Gòtic, or the Eixample. Take in some music (flamenco, guitar, concerts). Zip up to the hilltop of Montjuïc for the sunset, then down to the Magic Fountains (illuminated on weekends). Or stroll the long, inviting beach promenade.

Day 2: Tour the city's fanciful Modernista architecture, championed by Antoni Gaudí. Marvel at the buildings on the

Barcelona Neighborhood Overview

Park Güell

GRÀCIA

EIXAMPLE

LA
PEDRERA

SAGRADA
FAMÍLIA

PASSEIG DE GRÀCIA

CASA
BATLLÓ

Citadel
Park

Plaça de
Catalunya

CITY

EL
BORN

CATHEDRAL

VIA LAIETANA

PICASSO
MUSEUM

OLD

BARRI
GÒTIC

SANTS
STATION

LAS RAMBLAS

EL
RAVAL

BARCELONETA

Plaça
d'Espanya

FUNDACIÓ
JOAN MIRÓ

Port
Vell

Not to Scale

MONTJUÏC

CRUISE
PORT

Mediterranean Sea

← To Airport

Block of Discord and the street's master-piece, La Pedrera. Tour Gaudí's soaring church, the Sagrada Família. Then head to Park Güell, with its colorful mosaics, fountains, and stunning city views.

Day 3: Tour the museums on Montjuïc: The Catalan Art Museum displays top medieval sculptures (reservation required), while Fundació Joan Miró features the hometown artist's whimsical work. The hilltop castle ramparts offers sweeping views. You could head back downtown (for museums, shopping, exploring) or take the slow, scenic cable-car from Montjuïc to the port. For a pleasant evening, stroll the beach along Barceloneta, collect another sunset, and find your favorite *chiringuito* (beach bar).

Day Trips: Allot an extra day for a side trip: the holy site of Montserrat, with its dramatic mountain scenery, or Figueres, with its mind-bending Salvador Dalí museum.

ORIENTATION

A large square, **Plaça de Catalunya** at the center of Barcelona, divides the older and newer parts of town. Below Plaça de Catalunya is the Old City, with the Ramblas boulevard running down to the harbor.

The **Old City (Ciutat Vella)** is the compact core of Barcelona—ideal for strolling, shopping, and people-watching. It's a labyrinth of narrow streets, once confined by medieval walls. The lively pedestrian drag called the **Ramblas** goes through the heart of the Old City from Plaça de Catalunya to the harbor. The Old City is divided into thirds by the Ramblas and another major thoroughfare (running roughly parallel to the Ramblas), **Via Laietana.** Between the Ramblas and Via Laietana is the character-istic **Barri Gòtic** (BAH-ree GOH-teek, Gothic Quarter), with the cathedral as its navel. Locals call it "El Gòtic" for short. To the east of Via Laietana is the **El Born** district (a.k.a. "La Ribera"), a shopping, dining, and nightlife mecca centered on the Picasso Museum and the Church of Santa Maria del Mar. To the west of the Ramblas is the **Raval** (rah-VAHL), with a modern-art museum and a university. The Raval is of least interest to tourists (some parts of it are dodgy and should be avoided).

The old harbor, **Port Vell,** gleams with landmark monuments and new devel-opments. A pedestrian bridge links the Ramblas with the modern Maremagnum entertainment complex. On the penin-sula across the quaint sailboat harbor is **Barceloneta,** a traditional fishing neigh-borhood with gritty charm and good sea-food restaurants. Beyond Barceloneta, a gorgeous man-made **beach** several miles long leads to the commercial and conven-tion district called the **Fòrum.**

Above the Old City, beyond the bus-tling hub of Plaça de Catalunya, is the elegant **Eixample** (eye-SHAM-plah) dis-trict, its grid plan softened by cutoff cor-ners. Much of Barcelona's Modernista architecture is here—especially along the swanky **Passeig de Gràcia,** an area called **Quadrat d'Or** ("Golden Quarter"). To the east is the **Sagrada Família;** to the north is the **Gràcia** district and Antoni Gaudí's **Park Güell.**

The large hill overlooking the city to the southwest is **Montjuïc** (mohn-jew-EEK), home to some excellent museums (Cata-lan Art, Joan Miró).

Tourist Information

Barcelona's TI has several branches (cen-tral tel. 932-853-834, www.barcelona turisme.cat). The primary one is beneath the main square, **Plaça de Catalunya** (daily 8:30-21:00, entrance across from El Corte Inglés department store—look for red sign and take stairs down, tel. 932-853-832); this TI offers a **Picasso walk** (€22, includes museum admission; Tue-Sat at 15:00; 2 hours including museum visit), as well as walks for **gourmets** (€22, Mon-Fri at 10:30, 2 hours) and fans of **Modernisme** (€16; April-Oct Mon, Wed, and Fri at 18:00; Nov-March Wed and Fri at 15:30; 2 hours).

The TI on **Plaça de Sant Jaume,** just south of the cathedral in the City Hall, offers great guided **Barri Gòtic walks** (€16, daily at 9:30, 2 hours, groups lim-ited to 35, buy your ticket 15 minutes early at the TI desk—not from the guide, in summer stop by the office a day ahead to reserve, Mon-Fri 8:30-20:30, Sat 9:00-19:00, Sun 9:00-14:00, Ciutat 2, tel. 932-853-832, www.barcelonaturisme.cat).

Other convenient branches include a kiosk near the top of the **Ramblas** (#115); near the **cathedral** in the Catalan College of Architects building; inside the base of the **Columbus Monument** at the harbor; at the **airport** (Terminals 1 and 2B); and at the **Sants Train Station.** Smaller kiosks are on **Plaça d'Espanya,** in the park across from the **Sagrada Família** entrance, and on **Plaça de Catalunya.**

At any TI, pick up the free city map (although the free El Corte Inglés map pro-vided by most hotels is better), the small Metro map, the monthly *Barcelona Plan-ning.com* guidebook (with tips on sight-seeing, shopping, events, and restaurants), and the quarterly *See Barcelona* guide (with practical information on museums and a neighborhood-by-neighborhood sightsee-ing rundown). The monthly *Time Out BCN Guide* offers a concise but thorough day-by-day list of events. The monthly *Bar-celona Metropolitan* magazine has timely,

Daily Reminder

SUNDAY: Most sights are open, but the Boqueria and Santa Caterina markets are closed. Some sights close early today, including the Fundació Joan Miró and the Catalan Art Museum (both close at 15:00). Informal performances of the *sardana* national dance take place in front of the cathedral at 11:15 (none in Aug). Some museums are free at certain times: Catalan Art Museum and Palau Güell (free on first Sun of month), and the Picasso Museum. The Magic Fountains come alive on summer evenings (May-Sept).

MONDAY: Many sights are closed, including the Picasso Museum, Catalan Art Museum, Palau Güell, and Fundació Joan Miró. Most major Modernista sights are open today, including the Sagrada Família, La Pedrera, Park Güell, Casa Batlló, and Casa Amatller.

TUESDAY/WEDNESDAY: All major sights are open.

THURSDAY: All major sights are open. Fundació Joan Miró and the Picasso Museum are open late year-round, and the Magic Fountains spout on summer evenings (May-Sept).

FRIDAY: All major sights are open. The Magic Fountains light up Montjuïc year-round.

SATURDAY: All major sights are open. Barcelonans occasionally dance the *sardana* on Saturdays at 18:00 in front of the cathedral, and in summer you're likely to see traditional folk activities there at 19:30. The Magic Fountains dance all year. The Catalan Art Museum is free after 15:00.

LATE-HOURS SIGHTSEEING: Sights with **year-round** evening hours (19:30 or later) include La Boqueria Market, Cathedral of Barcelona, Casa Batlló, and Church of Santa Maria del Mar.

Sights offering later hours only in **peak season** (roughly April-Sept) include the Sagrada Família, La Pedrera, Palau Güell, Park Güell, Fundació Joan Miró, Catalan Art Museum, and Gaudí House Museum.

---

substantial coverage of local topics and events. All are free.

Modernisme Route: A handy map showing all 116 Modernista buildings is available at the Institut Municipal del Paisatge Urbà, inside the Edificio Colón (Mon-Fri 9:00-14:00, closed Sat-Sun, Avinguda de les Drassanes 6, 21st floor, www.rutadelmodernisme.com). They also offer a sightseeing discount package (€12) with a great guidebook.

Regional Catalunya TI: The all-Catalunya TI can help with travel and sightseeing tips for the entire region. They also have a relaxing café and a space for tasting regional treats (daily 10:00-21:00, in Palau Moja, midway along the Ram-

blas, Portaferrisa 1, tel. 933-162-740, www.palaumoja.com).

Advance Tickets and Sightseeing Passes

To save time, it's smart to **buy tickets in advance online,** especially for the popular biggies—Picasso Museum, Sagrada Família, La Pedrera, and Park Güell's Monumental Zone—and even for the less-crowded Casa Batlló and Palau Güell.

Advance tickets are required to tour the Palace of Catalan Music.

Consider getting the **Articket BCN pass** if you plan to visit the Picasso Museum, Catalan Art Museum, and Fundació Joan Miró. The pass saves

BARCELONA AT A GLANCE

▲▲▲**Picasso Museum** Extensive collection offering insight into the brilliant Spanish artist's early years. **Hours:** Tue-Sun 9:00-19:00, Thu until 21:30, closed Mon. See page 364.

▲▲▲**Sagrada Família** Gaudí's remarkable, unfinished church—a masterpiece in progress. **Hours:** Mon-Sat 9:00-20:00, Sun from 10:30, Oct-March until 18:00. See page 379.

▲▲**The Ramblas** Barcelona's colorful, gritty, tourist-filled pedestrian thoroughfare. **Hours:** Always open. See page 359.

▲▲**Palace of Catalan Music** Best Modernista interior in Barcelona. **Hours:** 50-minute English tours daily every hour 10:00-15:00, plus frequent concerts. See page 371.

▲▲**La Pedrera** Barcelona's quintessential Modernista building and Gaudí creation. **Hours:** Daily March-Oct 9:00-20:00, Nov-Feb 9:00-18:30. See page 377.

▲▲**Park Güell** Colorful Gaudí-designed park overlooking the city. **Hours:** Paid Monumental Zone open daily 8:00-21:30, Nov-March 8:30-18:00. See page 387.

▲▲**Catalan Art Museum** World-class showcase of this region's art, including a substantial Romanesque collection. **Hours:** May-Sept Tue-Sat 10:00-20:00 (Oct-April until 18:00), Sun 10:00-15:00, closed Mon. See page 389.

▲**La Boqueria Market** Colorful but touristy produce market, just off the Ramblas. **Hours:** Mon-Sat 8:00-20:00, best mornings after 9:00, closed Sun. See page 359.

▲**Palau Güell** Exquisitely curvy Gaudí interior and fantasy rooftop. **Hours:** Tue-Sun 10:00-20:00, Nov-March until 17:30, closed Mon. See page 359.

▲**Cathedral of Barcelona** Colossal Gothic cathedral ringed by distinctive chapels. **Hours:** Generally open to visitors Mon-Fri 8:00-19:30, Sat-Sun 8:00-20:00. See page 362.

▲*Sardana* **Dances** Patriotic dance in which proud Catalans join hands in a circle, often held outdoors. **Hours:** Every Sun at 11:15, sometimes also Sat at 18:00, no dances in Aug. See page 364.

▲**Santa Caterina Market** Fine market hall built on the site of an old monastery and updated with a wavy Gaudí-inspired roof. **Hours:** Mon-Sat 7:30-15:30, Tue and Thu-Fri until 20:30, closed Sun. See page 372.

▲**Church of Santa Maria del Mar** Catalan Gothic church in El Born, built by wealthy medieval shippers. **Hours:** Generally open to visitors daily 9:00-20:30. See page 372.

▲**Casa Batlló** Gaudí-designed home topped with fanciful dragon-inspired roof. **Hours:** Daily 9:00-21:00. See page 373.

▲**Fundació Joan Miró** World's best collection of works by Catalan modern artist Joan Miró and his contemporaries. **Hours:** Tue-Sat 10:00-20:00 (Nov-March until 18:00), Thu until 21:00, Sun 10:00-15:00, closed Mon. See page 392.

▲**Magic Fountains** Lively fountain spectacle. **Hours:** April-May & Oct Thu-Sat 21:00-22:00, June-Sept Wed-Sun 21:30-22:30, Nov-Dec & March Thu-Sat 20:00-21:00, no shows Jan-Feb. See page 393.

▲**Barcelona's Beaches** Fun-filled, man-made beach reaching from the harbor to the Fòrum. **Hours:** Always open. See page 393.

"You're Not in Spain, You're in Catalunya!"

You may see this popular nationalistic refrain on T-shirts or stickers around town. Catalunya is *not* the land of bullfighting and flamenco that many visitors envision when they think of Spain (visit Madrid or Sevilla for those).

Catalunya, with Barcelona as its capital, has its own language, history, and culture. Its eight million people have a proud, independent spirit. Historically, Catalunya ("Cataluña" in Spanish, sometimes spelled "Catalonia" in English) has often been at odds with the central Spanish government in Madrid. The Catalan language and culture were discouraged or even outlawed at various times in history, as Catalunya often chose the wrong side in wars and rebellions against the kings in Madrid. In the Spanish Civil War (1936-1939), Catalunya was one of the last pockets of democratic resistance against the military coup of fascist dictator Francisco Franco, who punished the region with four decades of repression. During that time, the Catalan flag was banned—but locals vented their national spirit by flying their football team's flag instead.

Reminders of royal and Franco-era suppression live on in Barcelona's landmarks. Citadel Park (Parc de la Ciutadella) was originally a much-despised military citadel, constructed in the 18th century to keep locals in line. The Castle of Montjuïc has been the site of numerous political executions, including hundreds during the Franco era. Today, many Catalans favor breaking away from Spain, but the central government has vowed to block secession. Time will tell.

To see Catalan culture, look for the *sardana* dance or an exhibition of *castellers* (both described on page 363). The main symbol of Catalunya is the dragon, which was slain by St. George ("Jordi" in Catalan)—the region's patron saint. You'll find dragons all over Barcelona, along with the Catalan flag—called the Senyera—with four horizontal red stripes on a gold field.

After the end of the Franco era in the mid-1970s, the Catalan language made a huge comeback. Schools are now required by law to conduct classes in Catalan; most children learn Catalan first and Spanish second. While all Barcelonans still speak Spanish, nearly all understand Catalan, three-quarters speak Catalan, and half can write it.

you money and lets you skip the ticket lines (especially helpful at the Picasso Museum). It covers admission to six museums and their temporary exhibits. Just show your Articket BCN (to the ticket taker, at the info desk, or at a special Articket window), and you'll get your entry ticket (€30, valid for three months; sold at participating museums and the TIs at Plaça de Catalunya, Plaça de Sant Jaume, and Sants Station; www.articketbcn.org).

Skip the Barcelona Card and the Barcelona Card Express, which cover public transportation and include free admission to mostly minor sights, with only small discounts on some major sights (Barcelona Card—€45/3 days, €55/4 days, €60/5 days; Barcelona Card Express—€20/2 days; sold at TIs and El Corte Inglés department stores, www.barcelonaturisme.com).

Tours

The handy **hop-on, hop-off Tourist Bus** (Bus Turístic), which departs from Plaça de Catalunya, offers three multistop circuits in double-decker buses, all with

Here are the essential Catalan phrases:

English	Catalan	Pronounced
Hello	*Hola*	OH-lah
Please	*Si us plau*	see oos plow
Thank you	*Gracies*	GRAH-see-es
Goodbye	*Adéu*	ah-DAY-oo
Long live Catalunya!	*¡Visca Catalunya!*	BEE-skah kah-tah-LOON-yah

When finding your way, these words and place names will come in handy:

exit	*sortida*	sor-TEE-dah
square	*plaça*	PLAS-sah
street	*carrer*	kah-REHR
boulevard	*passeig*	PAH-sage
avenue	*avinguda*	ah-veen-GOO-dah

Here's how to pronounce the city's major landmarks:

Plaça de Catalunya	PLAS-sah duh kah-tah-LOON-yah
Eixample	eye-SHAM-plah
Passeig de Gràcia	PAH-sage duh grass-EE-ah
Catedral	KAH-tah-dral
Barri Gòtic	BAH-ree GOH-teek
Montjuïc	mohn-jew-EEK

headphone commentary. The two-hour blue route covers north Barcelona (most Gaudí sights, departs from El Corte Inglés). The two-hour red route covers south Barcelona (Barri Gòtic and Montjuïc, departs from the west—Ramblas—side of the square). A short 40-minute green route covers the beaches in summer (1 day-€27, 2 days-€38; buy on bus, from TI, or online; offers small discounts on major sights; daily 9:00-20:00 in summer, off-season until 19:00, buses run every 10-25 minutes, www.barcelonabusturistic.cat).

Reliable **Runner Bean Tours** offer 2.5-hour walks covering the Old City and Gaudí, as well as night tours, family walks, and more (tours depart from Plaça Reial daily at 11:00 year-round, plus daily at 16:30 in April-mid-Oct, mobile 636-108-776, www.runnerbeantours.com). **Discover Walks** leads similar tours focusing on Gaudí, the Ramblas, and Barri Gòtic, along with other offerings; see website for schedule (about €19, www.discoverwalks.com, tel. 931-816-810).

Food tours, lasting about three hours,

Greater Barcelona

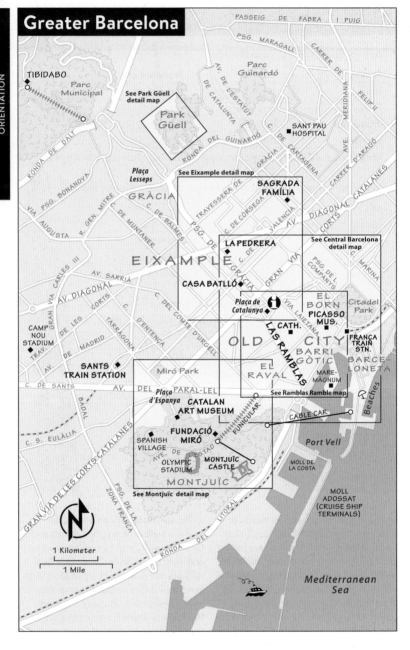

PASSEIG DE FABRA I PUIG

PSG. MARAGALL

TIBIDABO
Parc
Municipal

See Park Güell
detail map

Park
Güell

Parc
Guinardó

AV. DE L'ESTATUT DE CATALUNYA

C. DE CARTAGENA

SANT PAU
HOSPITAL

RONDA DEL GUINARDÓ

Plaça
Lesseps

See Eixample detail map

GRÀCIA

SAGRADA
FAMÍLIA

TRAVESSERA DE GRÀCIA

C. DE CÒRSEGA

VALÈNCIA AV.

DIAGONAL CATALANES

CORTS

CARRER D'ARAGÓ

VIA AUGUSTA

PSG. BONANOVA

VIA

R. GEN. MITRE

C. DE MUNTANER

C. DE BALMES

PSG. DE GRÀCIA

EIXAMPLE

LA PEDRERA

CASA BATLLÓ

See Central Barcelona
detail map

PSG. DE L. COMPANYS

C. MARINA

RONDA DE DALT

GRAN VIA CARLES III

AV. SARRIA

AV. DIAGONAL

C. DE LES CORTS

TARRAGONA

C. D'ENTENÇA

C. DEL COMTE D'URGELL

GRAN VIA

VIA LAIETANA

Plaça de
Catalunya

EL
BORN

PICASSO
MUS.

Citadel
Park

CAMP
NOU
STADIUM

C. DE MADRID

TRAV.

AV. DE MADRID

SANTS
TRAIN STATION

Miró Park

CATH.

OLD   CITY

BARRI
GÒTIC

LAS RAMBLAS

FRANÇA
TRAIN
STN.

BARCE-
LONETA

C. DE SANTS   AV.

DEL   PARAL-LEL

Plaça
d'Espanya

CATALAN
ART MUSEUM

EL
RAVAL

MARE-
MAGNUM

See Ramblas Ramble map

Beaches

BADAL

C. S. EULÀLIA

SPANISH
VILLAGE

FUNDACIÓ
MIRÓ

AV. DE L'ESTADI

OLYMPIC
STADIUM

MONTJUÏC
CASTLE

FUNICULAR

CABLE CAR

Port Vell

MOLL DE
LA COSTA

MOLL
ADOSSAT
(CRUISE SHIP
TERMINALS)

GRAN VIA DE LES CORTS CATALANES

PSG. DE LA ZONA FRANCA

MONTJUÏC

See Montjuïc detail map

RONDA DEL LITORAL

1 Kilometer

1 Mile

Mediterranean
Sea

make several informative, fun stops for tastings in a characteristic neighborhood. Consider **The Barcelona Taste** (€80/person, Tue-Sat, run by US expats, www.thebarcelonataste.com) or **Food Lovers Company** (€90/person Mon-Sat, www.foodloverscompany.com). **Cook & Taste** offers daily cooking classes (€65/person, www.cookandtaste.com).

The **Barcelona Guide Bureau** is a co-op with about 20 local guides. Tour options include day trips outside the city to Montserrat and Figures (customized tours-€102/person for 2, €53/person for 4, Via Laietana 54, tel. 932-682-422, www.barcelonaguidebureau.com).

Helpful Hints

Theft and Safety: You're more likely to be pickpocketed here—especially on the Ramblas—than about anywhere else in Europe. Most crime is nonviolent, but muggings do occur. Leave valuables in your hotel and wear a money belt.

Street scams are easy to avoid if you recognize them. Most common is the too-friendly local who tries to engage you in conversation by asking for the time or whether you speak English. If a friendly man acts drunk and wants to dance, he's a pickpocket. Beware of thieves posing as lost tourists who ask for your help. Don't fall for street-gambling shell games. Beware of groups of women aggressively selling carnations, people offering to clean off a stain from your shirt, and so on.

Some areas feel seedy and can be unsafe after dark. Avoid the southern part of the Barri Gòtic (basically the two or three blocks directly south and east of Plaça Reial—though the strip near the Carrer de la Mercè tapas bars is better). Don't venture too deep into the Raval (just west of the Ramblas).

Internet Access: The free city network, Barcelona Wi-Fi, has hundreds of hotspots around town; look for the blue diamond-shaped sign with a big "W" (see www.bcn.cat/barcelonawifi).

Baggage Storage: Locker Barcelona is located near Hotel Denit. Pay for the day and access your locker as many times as you want. You can also leave bags overnight (€3.50-11 depending on locker size, daily 9:00-21:00, Carrer Estruc 36, tel. 933-028-796, www.lockerbarcelona.com).

BARCELONA WALKS

My two self-guided walks will help you explore the old town—down the main boulevard ("The Ramblas Ramble") and through the cathedral neighborhood ("Barri Gòtic Walk").

🎧 My free Barcelona City Walk audio tour covers the Ramblas (in part) and the Barri Gòtic neighborhood.

The Ramblas Ramble

For more than a century, this walk down Barcelona's pedestrian-only boulevard has drawn locals and visitors alike for the best people-watching in town. Raft the river of Barcelonan life, passing a grand opera house, elegant cafés, flower stands, artists, street mimes, con men, prostitutes, people charging more for a shoeshine than what you paid for the shoes.

The Ramblas is a one-hour, level stroll that goes from Plaça de Catalunya to the waterfront, with an easy return by the Metro. The word "Ramblas" is plural; the street is actually a succession of five separately named segments. But street signs and addresses treat it as a single long street—"La Rambla," singular.

• *Start your ramble on Plaça de Catalunya, at the top of the Ramblas.*

❶ *Plaça de Catalunya*

Dotted with fountains, statues, and pigeons, and ringed by grand Art Deco buildings, this plaza is Barcelona's center.

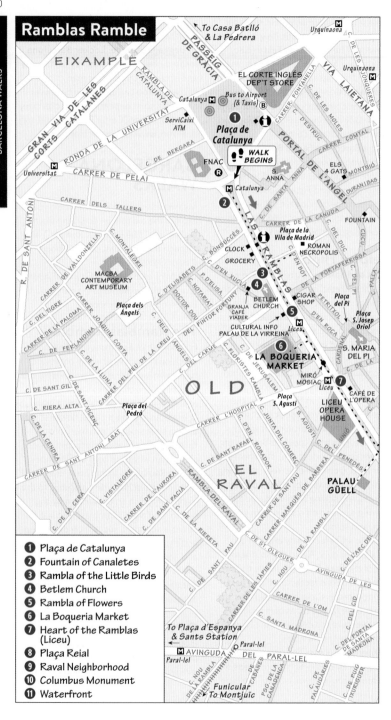

Ramblas Ramble

❶ Plaça de Catalunya
❷ Fountain of Canaletes
❸ Rambla of the Little Birds
❹ Betlem Church
❺ Rambla of Flowers
❻ La Boqueria Market
❼ Heart of the Ramblas (Liceu)
❽ Plaça Reial
❾ Raval Neighborhood
❿ Columbus Monument
⓫ Waterfront

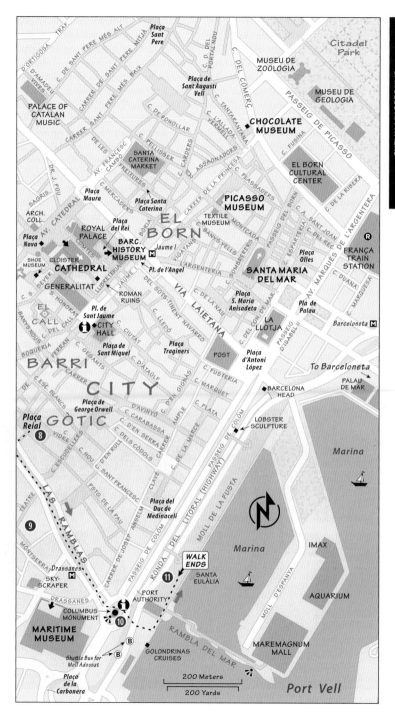

The square's straight lines are a reaction to the curves of Modernisme (which predominates in the Eixample district, just north of the square). Plaça de Catalunya is the hub for the Metro, bus, airport shuttle, and Tourist Bus. It's where Barcelona congregates to watch soccer matches on the big screen, to demonstrate, to celebrate, and to enjoy concerts and festivals. More than half of the eight million Catalans live in greater Barcelona; this is their Times Square.

The 12-acre square links the narrow streets of old Barcelona with the broad boulevards of the newer city. Four great thoroughfares radiate from here. The Ramblas is the popular pedestrian promenade. Passeig de Gràcia has fashionable shops and cafés (and traffic). Rambla de Catalunya is equally fashionable but cozier and more pedestrian-friendly. Shopper-friendly and traffic-free Avinguda del Portal de l'Angel leads to the Barri Gòtic.

At the Ramblas end of the square, the odd, inverted-staircase **monument** represents the shape of Catalunya and honors one of its former presidents, Francesc Macià i Llussà, who declared independence for the breakaway region in 1931. (It didn't stick.) Sculptor Josep Maria Subirachs, whose work you'll see at the Sagrada Família, designed it.

Venerable Café Zürich, just across the street from the monument, is a popular rendezvous spot. Homesick Americans might prefer the nearby Hard Rock Café. The giant El Corte Inglés department store (on the northeast side) has just about anything you might need.

• *Cross the street and head down the Ramblas. To get oriented, pause 20 yards down, at the ornate lamppost with a fountain as its base (on the right, near #129).*

❷ Fountain of Canaletes

The black-and-gold fountain has been a local favorite for more than a century. When Barcelona tore down its medieval wall and transformed the Ramblas into an elegant promenade, this fountain was one of its early attractions. Legend says that a drink from the fountain ensures that you'll come back to Barcelona one day. Watch

Plaça de Catalunya

tourists struggle with the awkwardly high water pressure. It's still a popular rendez-vous spot.

Get your bearings for our upcoming stroll. You'll see the following features here and all along the way:

The wavy **tile work** of the pavers underfoot represents the stream that once flowed here. *Rambla* means "stream" in Arabic. Look up to see the city's characteristic shallow **balconies.** The **plane trees** lining the boulevard are known for their hardiness in urban settings. These deciduous trees let in maximum sun in the winter and provide maximum shade in the summer.

Nearby, notice the **chairs** fixed to the sidewalk at jaunty angles. At one time, you'd pay to rent a chair for the view of passersby. Enjoy these chairs—you'll find virtually no public benches or other seating farther down the Ramblas, only cafés that serve beer and sangria in just one expensive size: *gigante.*

• Continue strolling.

All along the Ramblas are **24-hour newsstands.** Among their souvenirs,

you'll see soccer paraphernalia, especially the scarlet-and-blue of FC Barcelona (known as "Barça"). The team is owned by its more than 170,000 "members"—fans who buy season tickets, which come with a share of ownership. Their motto, "More than a club" (*Mes que un club),* suggests that Barça represents not only athletic prowess but the Catalan cultural identity. This comes to a head during a match nicknamed "El Clásico," in which they face their bitter rivals, Real Madrid (whom many fans view as stand-ins for Castilian cultural chauvinism).

Walk 100 yards farther to #115 and the venerable **Royal Academy of Science and Arts building** (now home to a theater). Look up: The clock high on the facade marks official Barcelona time—synchronize. The **TI** kiosk right on the Ramblas is a handy stop for any questions. The **Carrefour** supermarket just behind it (at #113) has cheap groceries (daily 10:00-22:00).

• *You're now standing at the...*

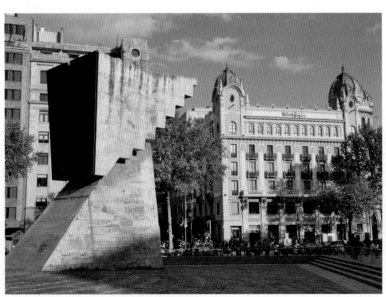

Subirachs sculpture on Plaça de Catalunya

❸ Rambla of the Little Birds

Traditionally, kids brought their parents here to buy pets, especially on Sundays. Today, only one of the traditional pet kiosks survives—there's not a bird in sight. You'll find bird-related pet supplies and recorded chirping.

• At #122 (the big, modern Citadines Hotel on the left, just behind the pet kiosk), take a 100-yard detour through a passageway marked Passatge de la Ramblas to a restored...

Roman Necropolis: Look down and imagine a 2,000-year-old tomb-lined road. Outside the walls of Roman cities, tombs typically lined the roads leading into town. Emperor Augustus spent time in modern-day Spain conquering new land, so the Romans incorporated Hispania into the empire's infrastructure. This road, Via Augusta, led into the Roman port of Barcino (today's highway to France still follows the route laid out by this Roman thoroughfare).

• Return to the Ramblas and continue 100 yards or so to the next street, Carrer de la Portaferrissa (across from the big church). Turn left a few steps and look right to see the **decorative tile** over a fountain still in use by locals. The scene shows the original city wall with the gate that once stood here. Now cross the boulevard to the front of the big church.

❹ Betlem Church

This church is dedicated to Bethlehem, and for centuries locals have flocked here at Christmastime to see Nativity scenes.

The church's sloping roofline, ball-topped pinnacles, corkscrew columns, and scrolls above the entrance all identify it as 17th-century Baroque. The Baroque style is unusual in Barcelona because it missed out on several centuries of architectural development. Barcelona enjoyed two heydays: during the medieval period (before the Renaissance) and during the turn of the 20th century (after Baroque). In between those periods, from about 1500 until 1850, the city's importance dropped—first, New World discoveries shifted lucrative trade to ports on the Atlantic, and then the Spanish crown kept unruly Catalunya on a short leash.

For a sweet treat, head around to the narrow lane on the far side of the church (running parallel to the Ramblas) to **Café Granja Viader,** which has specialized in baked and dairy delights since 1870. Step inside to see Viader family photos and early posters advertising Cacaolat—the local chocolate milk Barcelonans love. (For other sugary treats nearby, follow "A Short, Sweet Walk" on page 398.)

• Continue down the boulevard, through the stretch called the...

Canaletes fountain

Rambla of Flowers

❺ Rambla of Flowers

This colorful block is lined with flower stands. Besides admiring the blossoms on display, gardeners covet the seeds sold here for varieties of radishes, greens, peppers, and beans seldom seen in the US—including the iconic green Padrón pepper. (If you buy seeds, you're obligated to declare them at US customs when returning home.) On the left, at #100, **Gimeno** sells cigars. Step inside and appreciate the dying art of cigar boxes.

If you are interested in dance or musical events, tickets are available at the cultural center at Palau de la Virreina at Ramblas 99, on your right.

• *Continue to the Metro stop marked by the red M. At #91 (on the right) is the arcaded entrance to Barcelona's covered market, La Boqueria. If this main entry is choked with visitors (as it often is), you can skirt around to a side entrance, one block in either direction (look for the round arches that mark passages into the market colonnade).*

❻ La Boqueria Market

This lively market hall is an explosion of chicken legs, bags of live snails, stiff fish, delicious oranges, odd odors, and sleeping dogs. The best day for a visit is Saturday, when the market is thriving. It's closed on Sundays, and locals avoid it on Mondays, when it's open but (they believe) vendors are selling items that aren't necessarily fresh—especially seafood, since fishermen stay home on Sundays.

While tourists are drawn to the area around the main entry (below the colorful stained-glass sign), locals know that the stalls up front pay the highest rent—and therefore inflate their prices and cater to out-of-towners. For example, the juice bars along the main drag charge more than those a couple of aisles to the right.

Stop by the **Pinotxo Bar**—just inside the market, under the sign, and snap a photo of animated Juan giving a thumbs-up for your camera. Juan and his family are busy feeding shoppers. The stools nearby are a fine perch for enjoying both coffee and people-watching.

The market and lanes nearby are busy with tempting little eateries (see page 398). Drop by a café for an *espresso con leche* or *tortilla española* (potato omelet). Once you get past the initial gauntlet, do some exploring.

The produce stands show off seasonal fruits and vegetables. The fishmonger stalls could double as a marine biology lab. Fish is sold whole—local shoppers like to look their dinner in the eye to be sure it's fresh. At meat stands, full legs of *jamón* (ham)—some costing upwards of €200—tempt the Spaniards who so love this local delicacy. You'll see many types of *chorizo* (red spicy sausage). *Huevos del toro* are bull testicles—surprisingly inexpensive... and oh so good.

• *Head back out to the street and continue down the Ramblas.*

You're skirting the western boundary of the old Barri Gòtic. As you walk, glance to the left through a modern cutaway arch for a glimpse of the medieval church tower of **Santa Maria del Pi,** a popular venue for guitar concerts. This also marks Plaça del Pi and a great shopping street, Carrer Petritxol, which runs parallel to the Ramblas.

At the corner directly opposite the modern archway, find the **Escribà** bakery, with its fine Modernista facade and interior (look for the *Antigua Casa Figueras* sign over the doorway). Notice the mosaics of twining plants, the stained-glass peacock, and woodwork. In the sidewalk in front of the door, a plaque dates the building to 1902.

• *After another block, you reach the Liceu Metro station, marking the...*

❼ Heart of the Ramblas

At the Liceu Metro station's elevators, the Ramblas widens into a small, lively square (Plaça de la Boqueria). Liceu marks the midpoint of the Ramblas, half-

A *Chinese dragon ornament*

B *Joan Miró's mosaic*

C *Plaça Reial*

D *La Boqueria Market*

E *Columbus monument*

F *Palau Güell*

way between Plaça de Catalunya and the waterfront.

Underfoot in the center of the Ramblas, find the red-white-yellow-and-blue **mosaic** by homegrown abstract artist Joan Miró. The mosaic's black arrow represents an anchor, a reminder of the city's attachment to the sea. Miró's colorful designs are found all over the city, from murals to mobiles to the La Caixa bank logo. The best place in Barcelona to see his work is in the Fundació Joan Miró.

The surrounding buildings have playful ornamentation typical of the city. The **Chinese dragon** holding a lantern (at #82) decorates a former umbrella shop (notice the umbrella mosaics high up). The dragon is a symbol of Catalan pride for its connection to local patron saint, dragon-slayer St. George (Jordi).

Hungry? Swing around the back of the umbrella shop to **Taverna Basca Irati** (a block up Carrer del Cardenal Casanyes), one of many user-friendly tapas bars in town. Instead of ordering, just grab or point to what looks good on the display platters, then pay per piece.

Back on the Ramblas, a few steps down (on the right) is the **Liceu Opera House** (Gran Teatre del Liceu), which hosts world-class opera, dance, and theater (box office around the right side, open Mon-Fri 13:30-20:00). Opposite the opera house is Café de l'Opera (#74), an elegant stop for an expensive beverage. This bustling café, with Modernista decor and a historic atmosphere, has been open since 1929, even during the Spanish Civil War.

• *We've seen the best stretch of the Ramblas; to cut this walk short, you could catch the Metro back to Plaça de Catalunya. Otherwise, let's continue to the port. The wide, straight street that crosses the Ramblas in another 30 yards (Carrer de Ferran) leads left to Plaça de Sant Jaume, the government center.*

Head down the Ramblas another 50 yards (to #46), and turn left down an arcaded lane (Carrer de Colom) to the square called...

❽ *Plaça Reial*

Dotted with palm trees, surrounded by an arcade, and ringed by yellow buildings with white Neoclassical trim, this elegant square has a colonial ambience. It comes complete with old-fashioned taverns, modern bars with patio seating, and a Sunday coin-and-stamp market (10:00-14:00). Completing the picture are Gaudí's first public works—the two colorful helmeted lampposts. The square is a lively hangout by day or night (though the small streets stretching toward the water from the square can be sketchy). To just relax over a drink, the Ocaña cocktail bar is a good bet.

• *Head back out to the Ramblas.*

Across the boulevard, a half-block detour down Carrer Nou de la Rambla brings you to **Palau Güell** (on the left, at #3), the first of Antoni Gaudí's Modernista buildings, built 1886-1890. The two parabolic-arch doorways and elaborate wrought-iron work signal his emerging nonlinear style. Palau Güell offers an informative look at a Gaudí interior (see page 359).

• *Proceed along the Ramblas.*

❾ *Raval Neighborhood*

The neighborhood on the right-hand side of this stretch of the Ramblas is El Raval. In the last century, this was a rough neighborhood, frequented by sailors, prostitutes, and poor immigrants. Today, it's becoming gentrified, but the back streets can be edgy.

Along this part of the Ramblas, you'll often see surreal **human statues.** These performers—with creative and elaborate costumes—must audition and register with the city government; only 15 can work along the Ramblas at any one time. To enliven your Ramblas ramble, stroll with a pocketful of small change. As you wander downhill, drop coins into their cans (the money often kicks the statues into entertaining gear). But remember, wherever people stop to gawk, pickpockets are at work.

You're also likely to see some old-fashioned **shell games** in this part of town. Stand back and observe these nervous no-necks at work. They swish around their little boxes, making sure to show you the pea. Their shills play and win. Then, in hopes of making easy money, fools lose big time.

Near the bottom of the Ramblas, take note of the Drassanes Metro stop, which can take you back to Plaça de Catalunya when you're ready. The skyscraper to the right of the Ramblas is the Edificio Colón. Built in 1970, the 28-story structure was Barcelona's first high-rise. Near the skyscraper is the Maritime Museum, housed in what were the city's giant medieval shipyards.

• Up ahead is the...

❿ Columbus Monument

The 200-foot **column** honors Christopher Columbus, who came to Barcelona in 1493 after journeying to America. It was erected for the 1888 Universal Exposition, an international fair that helped vault a surging Barcelona onto the world stage.

It's ironic that Barcelona celebrates Columbus; his discoveries started 300 years of decline for the city, as Europe began to face West (the Atlantic and the New World) rather than East (the Mediterranean and the Orient). Within a few decades of Columbus, Barcelona had become a depressed backwater, and it didn't rebound until events like the 1888 Expo cemented its comeback.

A tiny elevator ascends to the top of the monument, lifting visitors to an observation area for fine panoramas over the city (€4.50, daily 8:30-20:30, last entry 30 minutes before closing, entrance/ticket desk in TI inside the base of the monument).

• Scoot across the busy traffic circle to survey the...

⓫ Waterfront

Stand on the boardwalk (between the modern bridge and the kiosks selling harbor cruises), and survey Barcelona's bustling maritime zone. Although the city is one of Europe's top 10 ports, with many busy industrial harbors and several cruise

Modernista port authority building and the Old Port

terminals, this low-impact stretch of seafront is clean, fresh, and people-friendly.

As you face the water, the frilly yellow building to your left is the fanciful Modernista-style port-authority building. The wooden pedestrian **bridge** jutting straight out into the harbor is a modern extension of the Ramblas. Called La Rambla de Mar ("Rambla of the Sea"), the bridge swings out to allow boat traffic into the marina; when closed, the footpath leads to an entertainment and shopping complex. Just to your right are the *golondrinas*—**harbor cruise boats,** (€7.20-15, daily on the hour 11:30-19:00, more in summer, fewer in winter, tel. 934-423-106, www. lasgolondrinas.com), which can be fun if you love to be out on the water (though the views from the harbor aren't great).

• *Turn left and walk 100 yards along the promenade between the port authority and the harbor.*

This delightful promenade is part of Barcelona's Old Port (Port Vell). The port's pleasant sailboat marina is completely enclosed by a modern complex with the Maremagnum shopping mall, an IMAX cinema, and a huge aquarium. Along the promenade is a moored historic schooner, the *Santa Eulália* (part of the Maritime Museum; €3 for entry without museum visit, Tue-Sun 10:00-20:30 except Sat when it opens at 14:00, Nov-March until 17:30, closed Mon). On a sunny day, it's fun to walk the length of the promenade to the iconic *Barcelona Head* sculpture (by American artist Roy Lichtenstein, not quite visible from here), which puts you right at the edge of El Born.

From here, you can also pick out some of Barcelona's more distant charms. The triangular spit of land across the harbor is **Barceloneta.** This densely populated community was custom-built to house fishermen and sailors whose traditional neighborhood in El Born was razed so Philip V could build a military citadel there in the 18th century. Today's Barceloneta is

popular for its easy access to a gorgeous stretch of sandy beaches (on the other side of the Barceloneta peninsula).

Looking back toward the Columbus Monument, you'll see in the distance the majestic, 570-foot bluff of **Montjuïc,** a parklike setting dotted with sights and museums (see page 388; to get there, ride the Metro from Drassanes one stop to the Paral-lel stop, then take the funicular up).

• *Your ramble is over. If it's a nice day, consider strolling the promenade and looping back around on La Rambla del Mar. Or maybe dip into El Born. If you're truly on vacation, walk through Barceloneta to the beach.*

To get to other points in town, your best bet is to backtrack to the Drassanes Metro stop, at the bottom of the Ramblas. Alternatively, you can catch buses #14 or #59 from along the top of the promenade back to Plaça de Catalunya.

Barri Gòtic Walk

The Barri Gòtic (Gothic Quarter) is a bustling world of shops, bars, and nightlife packed into narrow, winding lanes and undiscovered courtyards. This is Barcelona's birthplace—where the ancient Romans built a city, where medieval Christians built their cathedral, where Jews gathered together, and where Barcelonans lived within a ring of protective walls until the 1850s, when the city expanded.

Today "El Gòtic" is a grab bag of grand squares, Art Nouveau storefronts, Thursday flea markets, antique and junk shops, and street musicians. In the center of it all is the cathedral, surrounded by other legacy sights from the city's 2,000-year history. Use this walk to get the lay of the land, then explore the shopping streets nearby.

• *Start on Barcelona's grand main square,* **Plaça de Catalunya.** *From the northeast corner (between the giant El Corte Inglés department store and the Banco de España), head down the broad pedestrian boulevard called...*

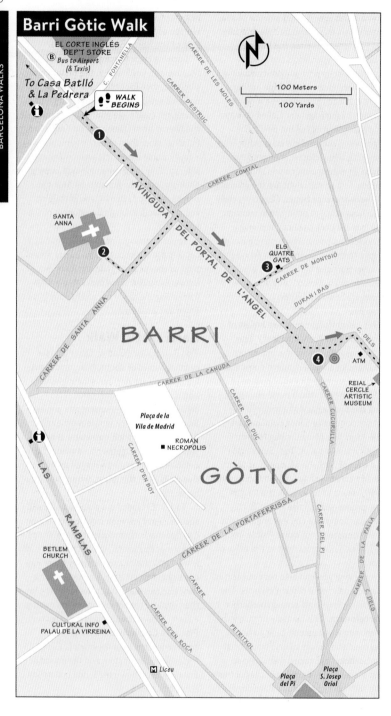

Barri Gòtic Walk

EL CORTE INGLÉS DEP'T STORE
Ⓑ Bus to Airport (& Taxis)

To Casa Batlló & La Pedrera

👣 **WALK BEGINS**

C. FONTANELLA

CARRER DE LES MOLES

CARRER D'ESTRUC

100 Meters

100 Yards

❶

CARRER COMTAL

AVINGUDA DEL PORTAL DE L'ANGEL

SANTA ANNA

❷

ELS QUATRE GATS

❸

CARRER DE MONTSIÓ

DURAN I BAS

BARRI

CARRER DE SANTA ANNA

CARRER DE LA CANUDA

❹ 🎯 ATM

C. DELS

REIAL CERCLE ARTISTIC MUSEUM

Plaça de la Vila de Madrid

CARRER DEL DUC

ROMAN ■ NECROPOLIS

CARRER D'EN BOT

CARRER CUCURULLA

GÒTIC

LAS RAMBLAS

CARRER DE LA PORTAFERRISSA

CARRER DEL PI

CARRER DE LA PALLA

C. DELS

BETLEM CHURCH

CARRER

CARRER DEL PI

PETRITXOL

CULTURAL INFO PALAU DE LA VIRREINA

CARRER D'EN ROCA

Ⓜ *Liceu*

Plaça del Pi

Plaça S. Josep Oriol

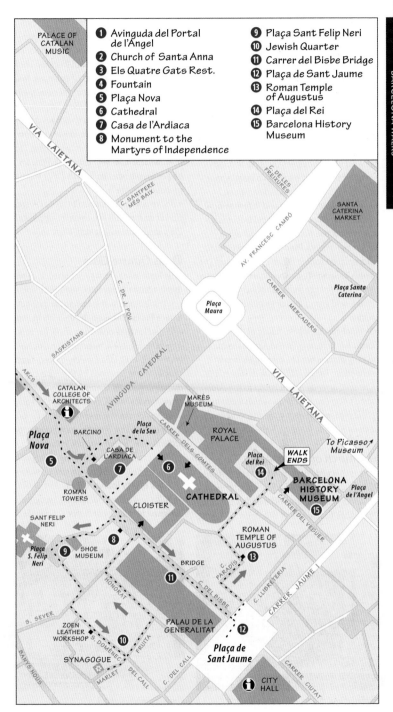

① Avinguda del Portal de l'Àngel
② Church of Santa Anna
③ Els Quatre Gats Rest.
④ Fountain
⑤ Plaça Nova
⑥ Cathedral
⑦ Casa de l'Ardiaca
⑧ Monument to the Martyrs of Independence
⑨ Plaça Sant Felip Neri
⑩ Jewish Quarter
⑪ Carrer del Bisbe Bridge
⑫ Plaça de Sant Jaume
⑬ Roman Temple of Augustus
⑭ Plaça del Rei
⑮ Barcelona History Museum

PALACE OF CATALAN MUSIC

VIA LAIETANA

C. SANTPERE MÉS BAIX

C. DR J. POU

AV. FRANCESC CAMBÓ

C. DE LES FREIXURES

SANTA CATERINA MARKET

Plaça Maura

CARRER MERCADERS

Plaça Santa Caterina

SAGRISTANS

VIA LAIETANA

ARCS

CATALAN COLLEGE OF ARCHITECTS

AVINGUDA CATEDRAL

MARÈS MUSEUM

ROYAL PALACE

Plaça Nova

BARCINO

Plaça de la Seu

CARRER DELS COMTES

⑤

CASA DE L'ARDIACA

⑦

⑥

Plaça del Rei

⑭

WALK ENDS

To Picasso Museum

ROMAN TOWERS

CLOISTER

CATHEDRAL

BARCELONA HISTORY MUSEUM

Plaça de l'Àngel

⑮

SANT FELIP NERI

Plaça S. Felip Neri

⑨

SHOE MUSEUM

⑧

ROMAN TEMPLE OF AUGUSTUS

⑬

C. PARADIS

CARRER DEL VEGUER

S. SEVER

HONORAT

BRIDGE

⑪

C. DEL BISBE

C. LLIBRETERIA

CARRER JAUME I

ZOEN LEATHER WORKSHOP

⑩

S. DOMÈNEC

FRUITA

PALAU DE LA GENERALITAT

⑫

BANYS NOUS

SYNAGOGUE

MARLET

DEL CALL

C. DEL CALL

Plaça de Sant Jaume

CARRER CIUTAT

CITY HALL

❶ Avinguda del Portal de l'Angel

For much of Barcelona's history, this was a major city gate. A medieval wall enclosed the city, and there was an entrance here—the "Gate of the Angel" that gives the street its name. It was thought that the angel statue atop the gate kept the city safe from plagues and bid voyagers safe journey as they left the city.

Today, the pedestrians-only street is choked with shoppers cruising through some of the most expensive retail space in town. It's globalized and sanitized, with high-end Spanish and international chains, but a handful of local businesses survive. At the first corner (at #21), a green sign marks **Planelles Donat**—long appreciated for ice cream, sweet *turró* (or *turrón* in Spanish, almond candy), refreshing *orxata* (or *horchata,* almond-flavored drink), and *granissat* (or *granizado,* ice slush).

• *A block farther down, pause at Carrer de Santa Anna to admire the Art Nouveau awning at another El Corte Inglés department store. Take a half-block detour to the right on Carrer de Santa Anna to the doorway at #29 (on the right), which leads into to the pleasant, flower-fragrant courtyard of the...*

❷ Church of Santa Anna

This 12th-century gem, which used to be part of a convent, has a fine cloister—an arcaded walkway around a leafy courtyard (viewable to the left of the church). Climb the modern stairs for views of the bell tower. Inside, you'll see a bare Romanesque interior and Greek-cross floor plan, topped with an octagonal wooden roof. The door at the far end of the nave leads to the cloister (€2, church generally open Mon-Fri 11:00-19:00, closed Sat-Sun).

As you head back to the main drag, you'll pass—a few doors down—a **condom shop** on your left. It advertises (to men with ample self-esteem): *Para los pequeños placeres de la vida* ("For the little pleasures in life").

• *Backtrack to Avinguda Portal de l'Angel. At Carrer de Montsió (on the left), opposite the Zara store, side-trip a half-block to...*

❸ Els Quatre Gats

This restaurant (at #3) is a historic monument, tourist attraction, nightspot, and eatery. It's famous as the bohemian hangout where Picasso nursed drinks with friends and had his first one-man show (in 1900). The building itself, by prominent architect Josep Puig i Cadafalch, is Neo-Gothic Modernisme, inspired by the Paris bohemian intellectual scene. While you can have a snack, meal, or drink here, if you just want to admire the menu cover art—originally painted by Picasso—and take a look around, ask *"Solo mirar, por favor?"*

• *Return to and continue down Avinguda del Portal de l'Angel. In a square on the left is a rack of* **city loaner bikes,** *part of the popular and successful "Bicing" program designed to reduce car traffic (available only*

Architectural details enliven the shopping street.

Fountain with tilework

to Barcelona residents). You'll soon reach a fork in the road and a building with a...

❹ Fountain

The blue-and-yellow tilework, a circa-1918 addition to this even older fountain, depicts ladies carrying jugs of water. In the 17th century, this was the last watering stop for horses before leaving town. As recently as 1940, about 10 percent of Barcelonans got their water from fountains like this.

• *You may feel the pull of wonderful little shops down the street to the right. But take the left fork, down Carrer dels Arcs.*

Pause after a few steps at the yellow La Caixa ATM (on the right, under the terrace). Touch the screen to see various languages pop up—in addition to English, French, and German, you'll see the **four languages of Spain** and their flags: Català (Catalan; thin red-and-gold stripes), Galego (Galicia, in northwest Spain; white with a diagonal blue slash), Castellano (Español or Spanish; broad red, yellow, and red bands), and Euskara (Basque; red, green, and white). Fiercely proud of its own customs and language, Catalunya is in solidarity with other small ethnic groups.

Just past the ATM, you'll pass the **Reial Cercle Artistic Museum,** a private collection of Dalí's work sculptures that's fun for fans of Surrealism. Don't miss the smaller rooms with additional artworks that are behind the red curtains inside (€10, daily 10:00-22:00).

• *Enter the large square called...*

❺ Plaça Nova

Two bold Roman towers flank the main street. These once guarded the entrance gate of the ancient Roman city of Barcino. The big stones that make up the base of the reconstructed towers are actually Roman. Near the base of the left tower, modern bronze letters spell out "BARCINO." The city's name may have come from Barca, one of Hannibal's generals, who is said to have passed through during Hannibal's roundabout invasion of Italy. At Barcino's peak, the Roman wall (see the section stretching to the left of the towers) was 25 feet high and a mile around, with 74 towers. It enclosed a population of 4,000.

One of the towers has a bit of reconstructed **Roman aqueduct** (notice the stream bed on top). In ancient times, bridges of stone carried fresh water from the distant hillsides into the walled city.

Opposite the towers is the modern **Catalan College of Architects** building (Collegi d'Arquitectes de Barcelona, TI inside), which is, ironically for a city with so much great architecture, quite ugly. The frieze was designed by Picasso (1962) in his distinctive simplified style, showing Catalan traditions: shipping, music, the *sardana* dance, bullfighting, and branch-waving kings and children celebrating a festival. Picasso spent his formative years (1895-1904, ages 14-23) here in the old town. He frequented brothels a few blocks from here on Carrer d'Avinyó ("Avignon")—which inspired his influential Cubist painting *Les Demoiselles d'Avignon.*

Picasso frieze on the Catalan College building

• *Immediately to the left as you face the Picasso frieze,* **Carrer de la Palla** *is an inviting shopping street (and the starting point of my "Barri Gòtic Shopping Stroll"; see page 394). But let's head left through Plaça Nova and take in the mighty facade of the...*

❻ Cathedral of Barcelona

While this location has been a center of Christian worship since the fourth century, what you see today dates mainly from the 14th century, with a 19th-century Neo-Gothic facade. The facade is a virtual catalog of Gothic motifs: a pointed arch over the entrance, robed statues, tracery in windows, gargoyles, and bell towers with winged angels. This Gothic variation is called French Flamboyant (meaning "flame-like"), and the roofline sports the prickly spires meant to give the impression of a church flickering with spiritual fires. The area in front of the cathedral is where Barcelonans dance the *sardana* (see page 364).

The cathedral's interior—with its vast size, peaceful cloister, and many ornate chapels—is worth a visit (see page 362). If you interrupt this tour and visit the cathedral now, you'll exit from the cloister a block down Carrer del Bisbe. From there you can circle back to the right to visit stop #7—or skip #7 and step directly into stop #8.

• *As you stand in the square facing the cathedral, look far to your left to see the multicolored, wavy canopy marking the roofline of the* **Santa Caterina Market.** *The busy street between here and the market—called Via Laietana—is the boundary between the Barri Gòtic and the funkier, edgier* **El Born** *neighborhood.*

For now, return to the Roman towers. Pass between the towers to head up Carrer del Bisbe, and take an immediate left, up the ramp to the entrance of...

❼ Casa de l'Ardiaca

It's free to enter this mansion, formerly the archdeacon's residence and now the city archives. The elaborate doorway is Renaissance. Enter a small courtyard with a fountain, then step inside the lobby (often featuring free temporary exhibits). Go through the archway at the left end of the lobby and look down into the stairwell at the back side of the ancient Roman wall. Back in the courtyard, climb the balcony for views of the cathedral steeple, gargoyles, and the small Romanesque chapel (on the right)—the only surviving 13th-century bit of the cathedral.

• *Return to Carrer del Bisbe and turn left. After a few steps, you reach a small square with a bronze statue ensemble.*

❽ Monument to the Martyrs of Independence

Five Barcelona patriots—including two priests—calmly receive their last rites before being strangled for resisting Napoleon's occupation of Spain in the early 19th century. They'd been outraged by French atrocities in Madrid (depicted in Goya's famous *Third of May* painting in Madrid's Prado Museum). According to the plaque marking their mortal remains, these martyrs gave their lives in 1809 *"por Dios, por la Patria, y por el Rey"*—for God, country, and king.

The plaza offers interesting views of the cathedral's towers. Opposite the square is the "back door" entrance to the cathedral (through the cloister; relatively uncrowded and open sporadically).

• *Exit the square down tiny Carrer de Montjuïc del Bisbe (to the right as you face the martyrs). This leads to the cute...*

❾ Plaça Sant Felip Neri

This square serves as the playground of an elementary school and is often bursting with energetic kids speaking Catalan (just a generation ago, this would have been illegal). The Church of Sant Felip Neri, which Gaudí attended, is still pockmarked with bomb damage from the Spanish Civil War. As a stronghold of democratic, anti-Franco forces, Barcelona

Cathedral of Barcelona

Ⓐ *Roman towers on Plaça Nova*

Ⓑ *Carrer del Bisbe Bridge*

Ⓒ *Church of Sant Felip Neri*

Ⓓ *Monument to the Martyrs of Independence*

Ⓔ *Architectural detail, Casa de l'Ardiaca*

saw a lot of fighting. A plaque on the wall (left of church door) honors the 42 killed—mostly children—in a 1938 aerial bombardment.

The buildings here were paid for by the craft guilds that powered the local economy (notice the decorative carved reliefs high above that represent their handiwork). To the right of the arch where you entered the square, look for shoe reliefs above the windows. This was the former home of the shoemakers' guild.

• Exit the square past the fun Sabater Hermanos artisanal soap shop, and head down Carrer de Sant Felip Neri. At the T-intersection, turn right onto Carrer de Sant Sever, then immediately left on Carrer de Sant Domènec del Call (look for the blue El Call sign). You've entered the...

⑩ Jewish Quarter (El Call)

In Catalan, a Jewish quarter goes by the name El Call—literally "narrow passage," for the tight lanes where medieval Jews were forced to live, under the watchful eye of the nearby cathedral. At the peak of Barcelona's El Call, some 4,000 Jews were crammed into just a few alleys in this neighborhood.

Walk down Carrer de Sant Domènec del Call, passing through the charming little square (a gap cleared by another civil war bomb) where you will find a rust-colored sign displaying a map of the Jewish Quarter. Take the next lane to the right (Carrer de Marlet). On the right (#5) is the low-profile entrance to what was likely Barcelona's **main synagogue** during the Middle Ages (Antigua Sinagoga Mayor, €2.50 entry includes a little tour by the attendant if you ask; Sun 10:30-15:00, Mon-Fri 10:30-18:30, closed Sat, shorter hours off-season, www.calldebarcelona.org). The sparse interior includes access to two small subterranean rooms with Roman walls topped by a medieval Catalan vault.

• At the synagogue, start back the way you came, continuing straight as the street becomes Carrer de la Fruita. At the T-intersection, turn left, then right, to find your way back to the Martyrs Statue. From here, turn right down Carrer del Bisbe to the...

⑪ Carrer del Bisbe Bridge

This structure connects the Catalan government building (on the right) with the Catalan president's ceremonial residence (on the left). Though the bridge looks medieval, it was constructed in the 1920s by Catalan architect Joan Rubió, who also carved the ornamentation on the buildings.

The delicate facade a few steps farther down on the right marks the 15th-century entry to the government palace.

• Continue along Carrer del Bisbe to...

⑫ Plaça de Sant Jaume

This stately central square of the Barri Gòtic takes its name from the Church of St. James (in Catalan: Jaume, JOW-mah) that once stood here.

Set at the intersection of ancient Barcino's main thoroughfares, this square was once a Roman forum. In that sense, it's been the seat of city government for 2,000 years. Today it's home to the two top governmental buildings in Catalunya: Palau de la Generalitat and, across from it, the Barcelona City Hall.

For more than six centuries, the **Palau de la Generalitat** (to your immediate right as you enter the square) has housed the offices of the autonomous government of Catalunya. It flies the Catalan flag next to the obligatory Spanish one. Above the doorway is Catalunya's patron saint—St. George (Jordi), slaying the dragon. From these balconies, the nation's leaders (and soccer heroes) greet the people on momentous days. The square is often the site of demonstrations, from a single aggrieved citizen with a megaphone to riotous thousands.

Look left and right down the main streets branching off the square; they're lined with ironwork streetlamps and balconies draped with plants. Carrer de Ferran, which leads to the Ramblas, is classic Barcelona.

• *Facing the Generalitat, exit the square going up the second street to the right of the building, on tiny Carrer del Paradís. Follow this street as it turns right. When it swings left, pause at #10, the entrance to the...*

⓭ *Roman Temple of Augustus*

You're standing at the summit of Mont Tàber, the Barri Gòtic's highest spot. A plaque on the wall reads: "Mont Tàber, 16.9 meters" (elevation 55 feet). A millstone inlaid in the pavement at the doorstep of #10 also marks the spot. Here the ancient Romans founded the town of Barcino around 15 B.C. They built a *castrum* (fort) on the hilltop, protecting the harbor.

Go inside for a peek at the last vestiges of the imposing **Roman Temple of Augustus** (free, daily 10:00-19:00 except Mon until 14:00, good English info on-site, Carrer del Paradís 10, tel. 933-152-311). All that's left now are four columns and some fragments of the transept and its plinth.

Roman Temple of Augustus

The huge columns are as old as Barcelona itself, dating from the late first century B.C. They were part of a temple dedicated to the Emperor Augustus, who was worshipped as a god. These Corinthian columns were the back corner of a 120-foot-long temple that extended from here to Barcino's forum.

• *Continue down Carrer del Paridís one block. When you bump into the back end of the cathedral, take a right, and go downhill a block (down Carrer de la Pietat/Baixada de Santa Clara) until you emerge into a square called...*

⓮ *Plaça del Rei*

The buildings enclosing this square exemplify Barcelona's medieval past. The central section (topped by a five-story addition) was the core of the **Royal Palace** (Palau Reial Major). A vast hall on its ground floor once served as the throne room and reception room. From the 13th to the 15th century, the Royal Palace housed Barcelona's counts as well as the resident kings of Aragon. In 1493, a triumphant Christopher Columbus, accompanied by six New World natives and several gold statues, entered the Royal Palace. King Ferdinand and Queen Isabel welcomed him home, honoring him with the title "Admiral of the Oceans." To the right is the palace's church, the 14th-century **Chapel of Saint Agatha,** which sits atop the foundations of a Roman wall.

• *From the square, go downhill onto Carrer del Veguer, where you'll find the entrance to the...*

⓯ *Barcelona History Museum*

This museum primarily contains objects from archaeological digs around Barcelona. But the real highlight is underground, where you can examine excavated Roman ruins (€7, free all day first Sun of month and other Sun from 15:00; open Tue-Sat 10:00-19:00, Sun 10:00-20:00, closed Mon; ticket includes English audioguide). For a peek at the Roman streets, look through the low windows lining the street.

• *Your walk is over. Get your bearings by backtracking to either Plaça de Sant Jaume or the cathedral. The Jaume I Metro stop is two blocks away (leave the square on Carrer del Veguer and turn left). Or simply wander and enjoy Barcelona at its Gothic best.*

SIGHTS

On or near the Ramblas

▲▲THE RAMBLAS

Rife with people-watching opportunities, Barcelona's most famous boulevard meanders through the heart of the Old City, from Plaça de Catalunya, past the core of the Barri Gòtic, to the harborfront Columbus Monument. Boasting a generous pedestrian strip down the middle, the Ramblas features vibrant flower vendors, costumed "human statues," and La Boqueria Market. For a self-guided walk, see page 339.

▲LA BOQUERIA MARKET

Housed in a cool glass-and-steel structure, La Boqueria features a wide variety of edibles that are priced at a premium. Its handy location in the heart of the Old City makes it well worth a visit. For more on the market, see page 345. For a less touristy market, consider Santa Caterina in El Born (page 372).

Cost and Hours: Free, Mon-Sat 8:00-20:00, best on mornings after 9:00, closed Sun, Rambla 91, tel. 933-192-584, www.boqueria.info.

▲PALAU GÜELL

This early mansion by Antoni Gaudí (completed in 1890) shows the architect taking his first tentative steps toward what would become his trademark curvy style. Dark and masculine, with its castle-like rooms, Palau Güell (pronounced "gway") was custom-built to house the Güell clan and gives an insight into Gaudí's artis-

tic genius. Despite the eye-catching roof (visible from the street), I'd skip touring the interior of Palau Güell if you plan to see the more interesting La Pedrera (see page 377).

Cost and Hours: €12, free first Sun of the month, open Tue-Sun 10:00-20:00, Nov-March until 17:30, closed Mon, last entry one hour before closing, includes audioguide, a half-block off the Ramblas at Carrer Nou de la Rambla 3, Metro: Liceu or Drassanes, tel. 934-725-775, www.palauguell.cat.

Tickets: As with any Gaudí sight, you may encounter lines. Each ticket has an entry time, so at busy times you may have to wait to enter. It's best to buy advance tickets for a set day and time of your choice, either on-site or online (though the predominantly Catalan website is tricky).

Visiting the House: The parabolic-arch **entryways** are the first clue that this is not a typical townhouse. For inspiration, Gaudí hung a chain to create a U-shape, then flipped it upside down. The wrought-iron doors were cleverly designed so that those inside could see out, and light from the outside could get in—but not vice versa.

Once inside, an engaging 24-stop audioguide, included with your admission, fills in the details. The Neo-Gothic **cellar,** with its mushroom pillars, was used as a stable—notice the big carriage doors in the back and the rings on some of the posts used to tie up the horses.

A grand staircase leads to the **living space.** The intricacy of Gaudí's design work evokes the complex patterns that decorate great Moorish palaces. Step onto the terrace out back to take a look at the elaborate (and unmistakably organic-looking) bay window.

The tall, atrium-like **central hall** fills several floors under a parabolic dome. Behind the gilded doors is a personal chapel, which made it easy to convert the

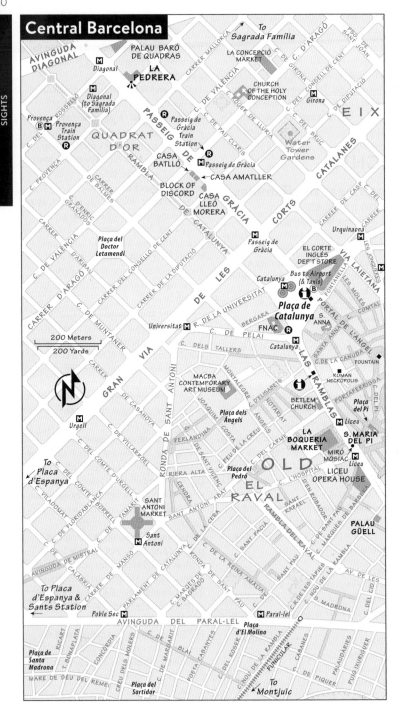

Central Barcelona

To Sagrada Família

AVINGUDA DIAGONAL

PALAU BARÓ DE QUADRAS

LA CONCEPCIÓ MARKET

Diagonal

LA PEDRERA

CHURCH OF THE HOLY CONCEPTION

Diagonal (to Sagrada Família)

Girona

EIX

Provença

Provença Train Station

Passeig de Gràcia Train Station

QUADRAT D'OR

CATALANES

Water Tower Gardens

CASA BATLLÓ

Passeig de Gràcia

CASA AMATLLER

BLOCK OF DISCORD

CASA LLEÓ MORERA

CORTS

Plaça del Doctor Letamendi

Passeig de Gràcia

EL CORTE INGLÉS DEP'T STORE

Urquinaona

VIA LAIETANA

Bus to Airport (& Taxis)

Catalunya

Plaça de Catalunya

S. ANNA

Universitat

LES

Bergara

FNAC

Catalunya

FOUNTAIN

C. DE LA CANUDA

200 Meters
200 Yards

ROMAN NECROPOLIS

MACBA CONTEMPORARY ART MUSEUM

BETLEM CHURCH

Plaça del Pi

Urgell

Plaça dels Àngels

LA BOQUERIA MARKET

S. MARIA DEL PI

Liceu

MIRÓ MOSAIC

Plaça del Pedró

OLD

Liceu

LICEU OPERA HOUSE

To Plaça d'Espanya

EL RAVAL

PALAU GÜELL

SANT ANTONI MARKET

Sant Antoni

To Plaça d'Espanya & Sants Station

Poble Sec

Paral·lel

AVINGUDA DEL PARAL·LEL

Plaça d'El Molino

Plaça de Santa Madrona

FUNICULAR

Plaça del Sortidor

To Montjuïc

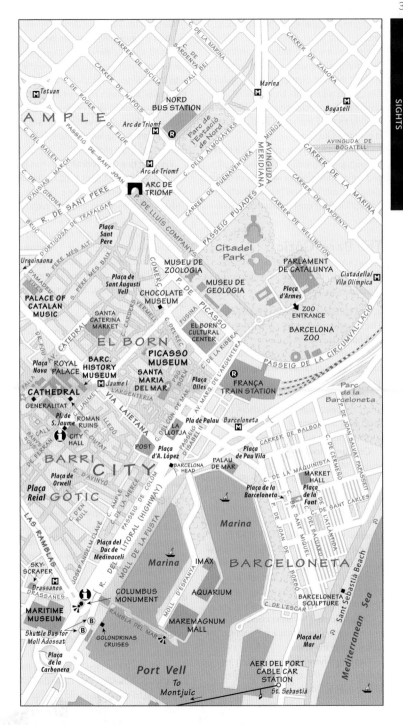

hall from a secular space to a religious one.

Upstairs are the Güells' his-and-hers bedrooms, along with a **film** telling the story of the two men behind this building: Gaudí and his patron, Eusebi Güell. At a time when most wealthy urbanites were moving to the Eixample, Güell decided to stay in the Old City.

The most dramatic space is the **rooftop.** Gaudí slathered the 20 chimneys and ventilation towers with bits of stained glass, ceramic tile, and marble to create a forest of giant upside-down ice-cream cones.

The Barri Gòtic

For an interesting route from Plaça de Catalunya to the cathedral neighborhood, see page 349.

▲CATHEDRAL OF BARCELONA

The city's 14th-century, Gothic-style cathedral (with a Neo-Gothic facade) has played a significant role in Barcelona's history—but as far as grand cathedrals go, this one is relatively unexciting. Still, it's worth a visit to see its richly decorated chapels, finely carved choir, tomb of St. Eulàlia, and restful cloister with gurgling fountains and resident geese.

Cost and Hours: Generally open to visitors Mon-Fri 8:00-19:30, Sat-Sun 8:00-20:00. Free to enter Mon-Sat before 12:45, Sun before 13:45, and daily after 17:15, but during free times you must pay to enter the cathedral's three minor sights (museum-€2, terrace-€3, choir-€3). The church is officially "closed" for a few hours each afternoon (Mon-Sat 13:00-17:00, Sun 14:00-17:00), but you can get in to see the interior sights by paying €7. Tel. 933-151-554, www.catedralbcn.org.

Dress Code: The dress code is strictly enforced; don't wear tank tops, shorts, or skirts above the knee.

Getting There: The huge, can't-miss-it cathedral is in the center of the Barri Gòtic on Plaça de la Seu (Metro: Jaume I).

Getting In: The front door is open most of the time. While it can be crowded, the line generally moves fast. Sometimes you can also enter directly into the cloister (through the door facing the Martyrs Statue on the small square along Carrer del Bisbe) or through the side door (facing Carrer dels Comtes).

Services: A tiny, semiprivate WC is in the center of the cloister.

Visiting the Cathedral: This has been Barcelona's holiest spot for 2,000 years, since the Romans built their Temple of Jupiter here. In A.D. 343, the pagan temple was replaced with a Christian cathedral, and in the 11th century, by a Romanesque-style church. The current Gothic structure was started in 1298 and finished in 1450, during the medieval glory days of the Catalan nation. The facade was humble, so in the 19th century the proud local bourgeoisie (enjoying a second Golden Age) renovated it in a more ornate, Neo-Gothic style. Construction was capped in 1913 with the central spire, 230 feet tall.

Inside, the nave is ringed with 28 **chapels.** These serve as interior buttresses supporting the roof (which is why the exterior walls are smooth, without the normal Gothic buttresses outside).

In the middle of the nave, the 15th-century choir (*coro*) features ornately carved stalls. During the standing parts of the Mass, the chairs were folded up, but VIPs still had those little wooden ledges to lean on. Each was creatively carved and—since you couldn't sit on sacred things—the artists were free to enjoy some secular and naughty fun here.

Look behind the high altar (beneath the crucifix) to find the bishop's chair, or cathedra. To the left of the altar is the organ and the elevator up to the terrace.

The steps beneath the altar lead to the **crypt,** featuring the marble-and-alabaster sarcophagus (1327-1339) containing the remains of St. Eulàlia. The cathedral is dedicated to the 13-year-old Eulàlia,

Circle Dances in Squares and Castles in the Air

From group circle dancing to human towers, Catalans have interesting, unique traditions. A memorable Barcelona experience is watching (or participating in) the patriotic **sardana** dances. Locals of all ages seem to spontaneously appear. For some it's a highly symbolic, politically charged action representing Catalan unity—but for most it's just a fun chance to kick up their heels. Participants gather in circles after putting their things in the center. All are welcome, even tourists cursed with two left feet. The dances are held in the square in front of the cathedral on Sundays at 11:15 (and occasionally on Saturdays at 18:00).

Holding hands, dancers raise their arms—slow-motion, *Zorba the Greek*-style—as they hop and sway gracefully to the music. The band (*cobla*) consists of a long flute, tenor and soprano oboes, strange-looking brass instruments, and a tiny bongo-like drum (*tambori*). During 36 years of Franco's dictatorship, the *sardana* was forbidden.

Another Catalan tradition is the **castell,** a tower erected solely of people. *Castells* pop up on special occasions, such as the Festa Major de Gràcia in mid-August and La Mercè festival in late September. Towers can be up to 10 humans high. Imagine balancing 50 or 60 feet in the air, with nothing but a pile of flesh and bone between you and the ground. The base is formed by burly supports called *baixos;* above them are the *manilles* ("handles"), which help haul up the people to the top. The *castell* is capped with a human steeple—usually a child—who extends four fingers into the air, representing the four red stripes of the Catalan flag. A scrum of spotters (called *pinyas*) cluster around the base in case anyone falls. *Castelleres* are judged both on how quickly they erect their human towers and how fast they can take them down. Besides during festivals, you can usually see this spectacle in front of the cathedral on spring and summer Saturdays at 19:30 (as part of the Festa Catalana).

One thing that these two traditions have in common is their communal nature. Perhaps it's no coincidence, as Catalunya is known for its community spirit, team building, and socialistic bent.

daughter of a prominent Barcelona family, who was martyred by the Romans for her faith in A.D. 304. Legends say she was subjected to 13 tortures.

Exit through the right transept and into the circa-1450 **cloister**—the arcaded walkway surrounding a lush courtyard. It's a tropical atmosphere of palm, orange, and magnolia trees; a fish pond; trickling fountains; and squawking geese. As you wander the cloister (clockwise), check out the coats of arms as well as the tombs in the pavement. These were rich merchants who paid to be buried as close to the altar as possible. Notice the symbols of their trades: scissors, shoes, bakers, and so on. The resident geese have been here for at least 500 years. There are always 13, in memory of Eulàlia's 13 years and 13 torments.

The little museum (at the far end of the cloister) has the six-foot-tall, 14th-century Great Monstrance, a ceremonial display case for the communion wafer that's paraded through the streets during the Corpus Christi festival in June. The next room, the Sala Capitular, has several altarpieces, including a pietá (a.k.a. *Desplà*) by Bartolomé Bermejo (1490).

▲SARDANA DANCES

If you're in town on a weekend, you can see the *sardana*, a patriotic dance in which Barcelonans link hands and dance in a circle (see sidebar).

Cost and Hours: Free, Sun at 12:00, sometimes also Sat at 18:00, no dances in Aug, event lasts 1-2 hours, in the square in front of the cathedral.

El Born

Despite being home to the top-notch Picasso Museum, El Born (also known as "La Ribera") feels wonderfully local, with a higher ratio of Barcelonans to tourists than most other city-center zones. Narrow lanes sprout from the neighborhood's main artery, Passeig del Born—the perfect springboard for exploring artsy boutiques, inviting cafés and restaurants, funky shops, and rollicking nightlife. For tips on shopping streets in El Born, see page 395. The most convenient Metro stop is Jaume I.

▲▲▲PICASSO MUSEUM (MUSEU PICASSO)

Pablo Picasso may have made his career in Paris, but the years he spent in Barcelona—from age 14 through 23—were among the most formative of his life. Here, young Pablo mastered the realistic painting style of his artistic forebears— and also first felt the freedom that would allow him to leave all that behind and explore his creative, experimental urges. When he left Barcelona, Picasso went to Paris...and revolutionized art forever.

The pieces in this museum capture the moment just before this bold young thinker changed the world. While you won't find Picasso's famous later Cubist works here, you will enjoy a representative sweep of his early years, from the careful crafting of art-school pieces to the gloomy hues of his Blue Period and the revitalized cheer of his Rose Period. You'll also see works from his twilight years, including dozens of wild improvisations inspired by Diego Velázquez's seminal *Las Meninas,* as well as works that reflect the exuberance of an old man playing like a child on the French Riviera. It's the top collection of Picassos in his native country, and the best anywhere of his early years.

Rick's Tip: *To avoid wasting time in ticket-buying lines, buy* **advance tickets** *for the* **Picasso Museum.**

Cost and Hours: €11 for timed-entry ticket to permanent collection, free Thu 18:00-21:30 and all day first Sun of month; open Tue-Sun 9:00-19:00, Thu until 21:30, closed Mon; audioguide-€5, tel. 932-563-000, www.museupicasso.bcn.cat.

Picasso Museum—First Floor

Not to Scale

ENTRANCE
(AT GROUND LEVEL)
CARRER DE MONTCADA

← To Santa Caterina Market
(5 min. walk)

To Church of Santa Maria del Mar →
(5 min. walk)

↙ To Jaume 1 Ⓜ (5 min. walk)
& Cathedral (10 min. walk)

❶ Portraits &
Art-School Work
❷ First Communion
❸ Science and Charity
❹ Velázquez Copy
❺ Horta de San Joan
❻ Cancan Dancer
❼ Still Life
❽ The Waiting (Margot)
❾ Motherhood
❿ Rooftops of Barcelona
⓫ Portrait of Bernadetta
Bianco
⓬ Woman with Mantilla
⓭ Gored Horse
⓮ Synthetic Cubism
⓯ Las Meninas Studies
⓰ Ceramics
⓱ French Riviera
⓲ Portraits of Jacqueline (2)

Crowd Control: There's almost always a line, sometimes with waits of more than an hour. During peak season, it's possible that tickets, which include an entry time, may sell out altogether. It's best to buy tickets online in advance, or get an **Articket BCN** (see page 333), which lets you go straight to the special Articket window near the main entrance (you'll be allowed in at the next timed-entry slot).

Advance tickets are sold via the

Pablo Picasso (1881-1973)

Pablo Picasso was the most famous and—OK, I'll say it—greatest artist of the 20th century. He became the master of many styles (Cubism, Surrealism, Expressionism) and many media (painting, sculpture, prints, ceramics, and assemblages). Still, anything he touched looked unmistakably like "a Picasso."

Born in Málaga, Spain, Picasso was the son of an art teacher. At a young age, he quickly advanced beyond his teachers. Picasso's teenage works are stunningly realistic and capture the inner complexities of the people he painted. As a youth in Barcelona, he fell in with a bohemian crowd that mixed wine, women, and art.

In 1904, Picasso moved to the City of Light to paint. When his best friend, Spanish artist Carlos Casagemas, committed suicide, Picasso plunged into a **Blue Period** (1901-1904)—the dominant color in these paintings matches their melancholy mood and subject matter (such as emaciated beggars, and hard-eyed pimps).

In 1904, Picasso got a steady girlfriend (Fernande Olivier) and suddenly saw the world through rose-colored glasses—his **Rose Period.** Picasso played with the "building blocks" of line and color to find new ways to reconstruct the real world on canvas. At his studio in Montmartre, Picasso and his neighbor Georges Braque worked together, in poverty so dire they often didn't know where their next bottle of wine was coming from.

Then, at the age of 25, Picasso reinvented painting. Fascinated by the primitive power of African and Iberian tribal masks, he sketched human faces with simple outlines and almond eyes. He sketched nudes from every angle, then experimented with showing several different views on the same canvas. Nine months and a hundred paintings later, Picasso gave birth to a monstrous canvas of five nude, fragmented prostitutes with mask-like faces—*Les Demoiselles d'Avignon* (1907).

This bold new style was called **Cubism.** With Cubism, Picasso shattered the Old World and put it back together in a new way. The subjects are somewhat recognizable (with the help of the titles), but they're built with geometric

museum website (no additional booking fee) and guarantee an entry time with no wait. Note that the ticketing part of the website can be temperamental; if you can't get it to work, try it on another device (such as your mobile phone).

To buy **same-day tickets,** go as early as possible. Upon arrival, check the screen near the ticket office for the day's available entry times (and how many spaces are open for each). Depending upon availability, you can either buy tickets for immediate entry, or purchase tickets to return later that day. You can also buy same-day tickets online, up to two hours before you want to go. Off-season, you can probably just line up for tickets and get right in.

Note that the museum's busiest times are mornings before 13:00, all day Tuesday, and during the free entry times on Sundays.

Getting There: It's at Carrer de Mont-shards ("cubes")—like viewing the world through a kaleidoscope of brown and gray.

In 1918, Picasso traveled to Rome and entered a **Classical Period** (the 1920s) of more realistic, full-bodied women and children, inspired by the three-dimensional sturdiness of ancient statues. While he flirted with abstraction, throughout his life, Picasso always kept a grip on "reality." His favorite subject was people. The anatomy might be jumbled, but it's all there.

Though he lived in France and Italy, Picasso remained a Spaniard at heart, incorporating Spanish motifs into his work. Unrepentantly macho, he loved bull-fights, seeing them as a metaphor for the timeless human interaction between the genders. To Picasso, the horse symbolizes the feminine, and the bull, the masculine. Spanish imagery—bulls, screaming horses, a Madonna—appears in Picasso's most famous work, *Guernica* (1937, on display in Madrid). The monumental canvas of a bombed village summed up the pain of Spain's brutal Civil War (1936-1939) and foreshadowed World War II.

At war's end, Picasso left Paris behind, finding fun in the sun in the **south of France** (1948-1954). Sixty-five-year-old Picasso was reborn, enjoying worldwide fame and the love of a beautiful 23-year-old painter named Françoise Gilot. Bursting with creativity, Picasso cranked out more than one painting a day. His Riviera works set the tone for the rest of his life—sunny, lighthearted, and uncomplicated, using motifs of the sea, Greek myths, and animals. His simple sketch of a dove holding an olive branch became an international symbol of peace.

Picasso also made collages, built "statues" out of wood, wire, ceramics, and papier-mâché, and turned everyday household objects into statues (like his famous bull's head made of a bicycle seat with handlebar horns). **Multimedia** works like these have become so standard today that we forget how revolutionary they were when Picasso invented them. His last works have the playfulness of someone much younger. It's said of Picasso, "When he was a child, he painted like a man. When he was old, he painted like a child."

cada 15; the ticket office is at #21. From the Jaume I Metro stop, it's a quick five-minute walk. Just head down Carrer de la Princesa (across the busy Via Laietana from the Barri Gòtic), turning right on Carrer de Montcada.

Services: The ground floor, which is free to enter, has a required bag check, as well as a handy array of other services (bookshop, WC, and cafeteria). For places to eat near the museum, see page 399.

◆ SELF-GUIDED TOUR

The Picasso Museum's collection of nearly 300 paintings is presented more or less chronologically. With the help of thoughtful English descriptions (and guards who don't let you stray), it's easy to follow the evolution of Picasso's work. This tour is arranged by the stages of his life and art. If you don't see a specific piece, it may be out for restoration, on tour, or "sleeping," as the museum guards say. The rooms might be rearranged every so often, but the themes and chronology of the museum remain constant.

• *Begin in Rooms 1 and 2.*

BOY WONDER

Pablo's earliest art (in the first room) is realistic and earnest. Childish pencil drawings from about 1890 quickly advance through a series of technically skilled **art-school works** (copies of plaster feet and arms), to oil paintings of impressive technique. Even at a young age, his **portraits** of grizzled peasants demonstrate surprising psychological insight. Because his father—himself a curator and artist—kept everything his son ever did, Picasso has the best-documented youth of any great painter.

• *In Room 2, you'll find more paintings relating to Pablo's...*

DEVELOPING TALENT

During a summer trip to Málaga in 1896, Picasso dabbles in a series of fresh, Impressionistic-style landscapes (rare in Spain at the time). As a 15-year-old, Pablo dutifully enters art-school competitions. His first big work, ***First Communion,*** features a prescribed religious subject, but Picasso makes it an excuse to paint his family. His sister Lola is the model for the communicant (notice her exquisitely painted veil), and the features of the man beside her belong to Picasso's father.

Picasso's relatives star in a number of portraits from this time. Find the **portrait of his mother** if it's on view (these portraits are among the works that are frequently rotated). The teenage Pablo is working on the fine details and gradients of white in her blouse and the expression in her cameo-like face. Notice the signature: Pablo Ruiz Picasso. Spaniards keep both parents' surnames, with the father's first, followed by the mother's.

• *Continue into Room 3.*

EARLY SUCCESS

Science and Charity (1897), which won second prize at a fine-arts exhibition, got Picasso the chance to study in Madrid. Now Picasso conveys real feeling. The doctor (modeled on Pablo's father) represents science. The nun represents charity and religion. From her hopeless face and lifeless hand, it seems that Picasso believes nothing will save this woman from death.

Picasso travels to Madrid for further study. He hangs out in the Prado Museum and learns by copying the masters. An example of his mimicry is at the end of this room. Notice young Picasso's nearly perfect copy of a **portrait of Philip IV** by an earlier Spanish master, Diego Velázquez.

• *Head to Room 4.*

BARCELONA FREEDOM

Art Nouveau is all the rage in Barcelona when Picasso returns there in 1900. He falls in with the bohemian crowd, who congregate daily at Els Quatre Gats ("The Four Cats," a popular restaurant to this day). Picasso even created the **menu cover** for this favorite hangout (it's sometimes on view here in Room 4). He paints **portraits** of his new friends, including one of Jaume Sabartés (who later became his personal assistant and donated the works to establish this museum). Still a teenager, Pablo puts on his first one-man show at Els Quatre Gats in 1900.

• *Continue through Room 5. The next few pieces are displayed in Rooms 6 and 7.*

PARIS

In 1900 Picasso makes his first trip to Paris, where he befriends poets, artists, and prostitutes. He paints **cancan dancers** like Toulouse-Lautrec, **still lifes** like Paul Cézanne, brightly colored Fauvist works like Henri Matisse, and Impressionist **landscapes** like Claude Monet. In ***The Waiting (Margot),*** the subject—with her bold outline and strong gaze—pops out from the vivid, mosaic-like background. It is Cézanne's technique of "building" a

1 *Picasso,* First Communion

2 *Picasso,* Science and Charity

3 *Picasso's menu design for Els Quatre Gats*

4 *Picasso,* La Mujer del Mechón

5 *Picasso,* Blanquita Suárez

6 *Picasso,* Las Meninas

figure with "cubes" of paint that will later inspire Picasso to invent Cubism.

• *Turn right into the hall, then—farther along—right again, to find Rooms 8 and 9.*

BLUE PERIOD

Picasso travels to Paris several times (settling there permanently in 1904). The suicide of his best friend, his own poverty, and the influence of new ideas linking color and mood lead Picasso to abandon jewel-bright color for his Blue Period (1901-1904). He cranks out stacks of blue art just to stay housed and fed. With blue backgrounds and depressing subjects, this period was revolutionary in art history. The artist is painting not what he sees, but what he feels.

Back home in Barcelona, Picasso paints his hometown at night from **rooftops** (in the main part of Room 8). The painting is still blue, but here we see proto-Cubism... five years before the first real Cubist painting.

• *In the left section of Room 8, we get a hint of Picasso's...*

ROSE PERIOD

Picasso is finally lifted out of his funk after meeting a new lady, Fernande Olivier, and moves into his happier Rose Period (1904-1907). For a fine example, see the portrait of a woman wearing a classic Spanish mantilla, **Portrait of Bernadetta Bianco.** Its soft pink and reddish tones are the colors of flesh and sensuality. (This is the only actual Rose Period painting in the museum, but don't be surprised if it is on loan.)

BARCELONA

Picasso spent six months back in Barcelona in 1917 (his girlfriend, a Russian ballet dancer, had a gig in town). The paintings in these rooms demonstrate the artist's irrepressible versatility: He's already developed Cubism (with his friend Georges Braque), but he also continues to play with other styles. In **Woman with Mantilla** (Room 9), we see a little Post-Impressionistic Pointillism in

a portrait as elegant as a classical statue. Nearby, **Gored Horse** has all the anguish and power of his iconic *Guernica* (painted years later).

CUBISM

Pablo's role in the invention of the revolutionary Cubist style is well-known—at least I hope so, since this museum has no true Cubist paintings. A Cubist work gives not only the basics of a subject—it shows every aspect of it simultaneously. The technique of "building" a subject with "cubes" of paint simmered in Picasso's artistic stew for years. In this museum, you'll see some so-called **Synthetic Cubist paintings** (Room 10)—a later variation that flattens the various angles, as opposed to the purer, original "Analytical Cubist" paintings, in which you can simultaneously see several 3-D facets of the subject.

• *Remember that this museum focuses on Picasso's early years. As a result, it has little from the most famous and prolific "middle" part of his career—basically, from Picasso's adoption of Cubism to his sunset years on the French Riviera. Skip ahead more than 30 years and into Rooms 12-14 (at the end of the main hallway, on the right).*

PICASSO AND VELÁZQUEZ

A series of Picasso's works relate to what many consider the greatest painting by anyone, ever: Diego Velázquez's *Las Meninas* (the 17th-century original is displayed in Madrid's Prado Museum). Heralded as the first completely realistic painting, *Las Meninas* became an obsession for Picasso centuries later.

Picasso, who had great respect for Velázquez, painted more than **40 interpretations** of this piece. Picasso seems to enjoy a relationship of equals with Velázquez. Like artistic soul mates, the two Spanish geniuses spar and tease. Picasso deconstructs Velázquez and then injects light, color, and perspective as he improvises on the earlier masterpiece. See the fun Picasso had playing paddleball with Velázquez's tour de force—filtering Velázquez's realism through the kaleidoscope of Cubism.

• *Head back down the hall and turn right, through the* ceramics *area (Room 16), to find a flock of carefree white birds in Room 15. Enjoy the palace decoration as it looked before the building became a museum.*

THE FRENCH RIVIERA (LAST YEARS)

Picasso spends the last 36 years of his life living simply in the south of France. He said many times that "Paintings are like windows open to the world." We see his sunny Riviera world: With simple black outlines and Crayola colors, Picasso paints sun-splashed nature, peaceful doves, and the joys of the beach. He dabbles in the timeless art of ceramics, shaping bowls and vases into fun animals decorated with simple, childlike designs. He's enjoying life with his second (and much younger) wife, Jacqueline Roque, whose portraits hang nearby.

Picasso died with brush in hand. Sadly, since he vowed never to set foot in a fascist, Franco-ruled Spain, the artist never returned to his homeland...and never saw this museum (his death came in 1973—two years before Franco's). Picasso con-

tinued exploring and loving life through his art to the end.

▲▲PALACE OF CATALAN MUSIC (PALAU DE LA MÚSICA CATALANA)

This concert hall, built in just three years and finished in 1908, features an unexceptional exterior but boasts my favorite Modernista interior in town (by Lluís Domènech i Montaner). Its inviting arches lead you into the 2,138-seat hall, which is accessible only with a tour (or by attending a concert). A kaleidoscopic skylight features a choir singing around the sun, while playful carvings and mosaics celebrate music and Catalan culture. If you're interested in Modernisme, taking this tour is one of the best in town—and helps balance the local fixation on Gaudí as "Mr. Modernisme."

Cost and Hours: €18, 50-minute tours in English run daily every hour 10:00-15:00, tour times may change based on performance schedule, about 6 blocks northeast of cathedral, Carrer Palau de la Música 4, Metro: Urquinaona, tel. 902-442-882, www.palaumusica.cat.

Tour Reservations: You must buy your ticket in advance to get a spot on an English guided tour (tickets available up

Palace of Catalan Music

to 4 months in advance—purchase yours at least 2 days before, though they're sometimes available the same day or day before—especially Oct-March). You can buy the ticket in person at the concert hall box office (open daily 9:30-15:30, less than a 10-minute walk from the cathedral or Picasso Museum); by phone with your credit card (for no extra charge, tel. 902-475-485); or online at the concert hall website (€1 fee).

Concerts: Another way to see the hall is by attending a concert (300 per year, €20-50 tickets, box office tel. 902-442-882, see website for details and online purchases).

▲SANTA CATERINA MARKET

This eye-catching market hall's colorful, rippling roof covers a delightful shopping zone that caters more to locals than tourists. Come for the outlandish architecture, but stay for a chance to shop for a picnic without the tourist logjam of La Boqueria Market on the Ramblas. Besides fresh produce, it has many inviting eateries.

Cost and Hours: Free, Mon-Sat 7:30-

15:30, Tue and Thu-Fri until 20:30, closed Sun, Avinguda de Francesc Cambó 16, www.mercatsantacaterina.cat.

▲CHURCH OF SANTA MARIA DEL MAR

This "Cathedral of the Sea" was built entirely with local funds and labor, in the heart of the El Born quarter (home to wealthy merchants). Proudly independent, the church features a purely Catalan Gothic interior that was forcibly uncluttered of its Baroque decor by civil war belligerents.

Cost and Hours: Free admission daily 9:00-13:00 & 17:00-20:30, also open 13:00-17:00 with €5 ticket; €8 guided rooftop tours in summer; English tours on the hour Mon-Fri 12:00-16:00, Sat-Sun 11:00-16:00, in summer tours run until 19:00; Plaça Santa Maria, Metro: Jaume I, tel. 933-102-390.

Visiting the Church: On the big front doors, notice the figures of workers who donated their time and sweat to build the church. The stone for the church was quarried at Montjuïc and carried across town on the backs of porters.

Step inside. The church features a purely Catalan Gothic interior. During the Spanish Civil War (1936-1939), Catalan patriots fighting Franco burned the ornate Baroque decoration (carbon still blackens the ceiling), leaving behind this unadorned Gothic. The colorful windows come with modern themes. The tree-like columns inspired Gaudí's work on Sagrada Família. Befitting a church "of the sea," sailors traditionally left models of ships at the altar to win Mary's protection—one remains today.

The Eixample

For many visitors, Modernista architecture is Barcelona's main draw. And at the heart of the Modernista movement was the Eixample, a carefully planned "new town," just beyond the Old City, with wide sidewalks, hardy shade trees, and a rigid

Church of Santa Maria del Mar

grid plan cropped at the corners to create space and lightness at each intersection. Conveniently, all of this new construction provided a generation of Modernista architects with a blank canvas for creating boldly experimental designs.

Block of Discord

At the center of the Eixample is the Block of Discord, where three colorful Modernista facades compete for your attention: Casa Batlló, Casa Amatller, and Casa Lleó Morera (all three are on Passeig de Gràcia—near the Metro stop of the same name—between Carrer del Consell de Cent and Carrer d'Aragó). All were built by well-known Modernista architects at the end of the 19th century. Because the mansions look as though they are trying to outdo each other in creative twists, locals nicknamed the noisy block the "Block of Discord." By the way, if you're tempted to snap photos from the middle of the street, be careful—Gaudí died after being struck by a streetcar.

▲CASA BATLLÓ

While the highlight of this Gaudí-designed residence is its roof, the interior is also interesting—and much more over-the-top than La Pedrera's. Paid for with textile industry money, the house features a funky mushroom-shaped fireplace nook on the main floor, a blue-and-white-ceramic-slathered atrium, and an attic (with parabolic arches). There's barely a straight line in the house. You can also get a close-up look at the dragon-inspired rooftop. Because preservation of the place is privately funded, the entrance fee is steep—but it includes a good (if long-winded) audioguide.

Cost and Hours: €21.50, daily 9:00-21:00, may close early for special events—closings posted in advance at entrance, €3 videoguide shows rooms as they may have been, Passeig de Gràcia 43, tel. 932-160-306, www.casabatllo.cat. Purchase a ticket online to avoid lines, which are especially fierce in the morning. Your eticket isn't a timed reservation (it's good any time within 3 months of purchase), but it will let you skip to the front of the queue.

CASA AMATLLER

The middle residence of the Block of Discord, Casa Amatller was designed by Josep Puig i Cadafalch in the late 19th century for the Amatller chocolate-making family. It is viewable via guided tour, allowing you to see the modernist interior design, including many original pieces.

Rick's Tip: *If you don't want to pay for a ticket, you can step inside* **Casa Amatller's foyer (free during opening hours)** *to see the Modernist stained-glass door and ceiling, and an elaborate staircase.*

Admire the home's Neo-Catalan Gothic facade, with tiles and *esgrafiado* decoration. Inside you'll see the Modernista foyer with an elaborate staircase and rooms for dining, billiards, and smoking, among others. There's also a chocolate shop, where you can taste Amatller hot chocolate with toast.

Cost and Hours: €17 for 1-hour English tour (ask about schedule), €14 for video-guide tour; open daily 10:00-18:00, advance tickets available online, Passeig de Gràcia 41, tel. 934-617-460, www.amatller.org.

▲CASA LLEÓ MORERA

This house designed by Lluís Domènech i Montaner was finished in 1906. The architect rebuilt the facade, embellishing it with galleries and balconies on the different floors. To create the sculptural ornamentation, he hired the city's best craftsmen. Look for the recurring references to mulberries in the decoration—an allusion to the family name (which means mulberry in Spanish). The house has one of the finest Modernista interiors in town—but it's closed indefinitely to visitors (check at the TI or www.casalleomorera.com for the latest).

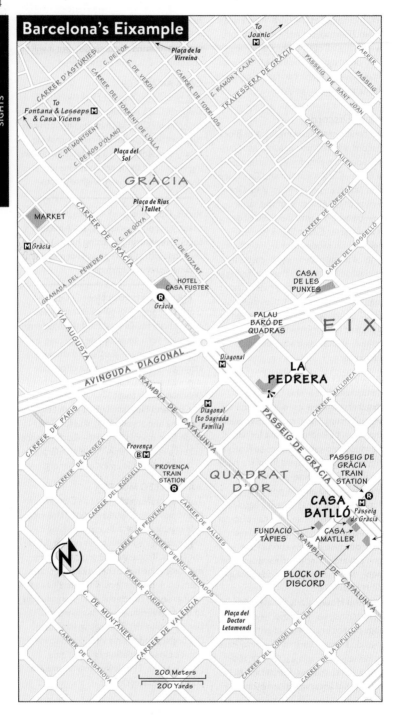

Barcelona's Eixample

To Joanic

Plaça de la Virreina

C. DE L'OR
C. DE VERDI
CARRER D'ASTÚRIES
CARRER DEL TORRENT DE L'OLLA
CARRER DE TORRIJOS
E. RAMÓN Y CAJAL
TRAVESSERA DE GRÀCIA
PASSEIG DE SANT JOAN
CARRER PASSEIG.

To Fontana & Lesseps & Casa Vicens

C. DE MONTSENY
C. DE ROS D'OLANO
CARRER DE BAILÈN

Plaça del Sol

GRÀCIA

Plaça de Rius i Tallet

MARKET

CARRER DE GRÀCIA
C. DE GOYA
C. DE MOZART
CARRER DE CÒRSEGA
CARRER DEL ROSSELLÓ

Gràcia

GRANADA DEL PENEDES

VIA AUGUSTA

HOTEL CASA FUSTER

Gràcia

CASA DE LES PUNXES

PALAU BARÓ DE QUADRAS

E I X

Diagonal

AVINGUDA DIAGONAL

RAMBLA DE CATALUNYA

LA PEDRERA

CARRER DE MALLORCA

Diagonal (to Sagrada Família)

CARRER DE PARIS

PASSEIG DE GRÀCIA

Provença

CARRER DE CÒRSEGA
CARRER DEL ROSSELLÓ

PROVENÇA TRAIN STATION

QUADRAT D'OR

PASSEIG DE GRÀCIA TRAIN STATION

CARRER DE PROVENÇA
CARRER DE BALMES

CASA BATLLÓ

Passeig de Gràcia

FUNDACIÓ TÀPIES

CASA AMATLLER

CARRER D'ENRIC GRANADOS

BLOCK OF DISCORD

RAMBLA DE CATALUNYA

C. DE MUNTANER
C. DE ARIBAU
CARRER DE VALÈNCIA

CARRER DEL CONSELL DE CENT

Plaça del Doctor Letamendi

CARRER DE CASANOVA

CARRER DE LA DIPUTACIÓ

200 Meters

200 Yards

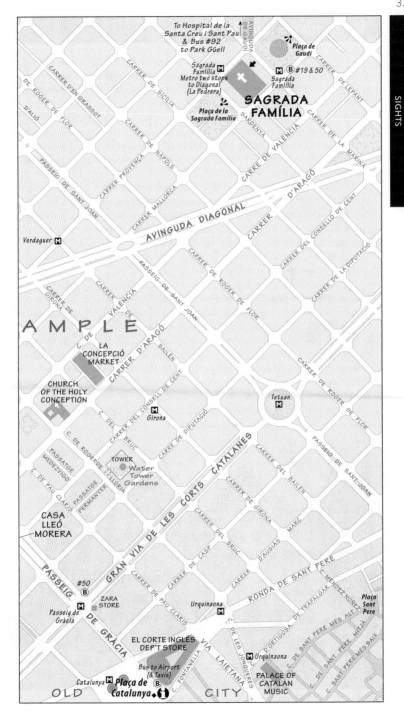

To Hospital de la
Santa Creu i Sant Pau
& Bus #92
to Park Güell

Plaça de
Gaudí

AVINGUDA DE GAUDÍ

CARRER DE SICÍLIA

CARRER D'EN GRASSOT

DE ROGER DE FLOR

D'ALIÓ

Sagrada
Família
Metro two stops
to Diagonal
(La Pedrera)

Plaça de la
Sagrada Família

SAGRADA
FAMÍLIA

CARRER DE LEPANT

#19 & 50
Sagrada
Família

CARRER DE LA MARINA

CARRER PROVENÇA

CARRER DE NÀPOLS

PASSEIG DE SANT JOAN

CARRER MALLORCA

CARRER DE VALÈNCIA

D'ARAGÓ

SARDENYA

CARRER DEL CONSELLO DE CENT

AVINGUDA DIAGONAL

CARRER

CARRER DE LA DIPUTACIÓ

Verdaguer

PASSEIG DE SANT JOAN

CARRER DE VALÈNCIA

CARRER DE ROGER DE FLOR

CARRER DE GIRONA

A M P L E

LA
CONCEPCIÓ
MARKET

C. DE

CARRER D'ARAGÓ

BAILÉN

CHURCH
OF THE HOLY
CONCEPTION

C. DEL CONSELL DE CENT

CARRER DE ROGER DE FLOR

Tetuan

CARRER DE BRUC

Girona

CARRER DE DIPUTACIÓ

PASSATGE
MEDEZVIGO

C. DE ROGER DE T. LLÚRIA

PASSATGE
PERMANYER

TOWER
Water
Tower
Gardens

CARRER DEL BAILÉN

CARRER DEL BRUC

CARRER DE GIRONA

PASSEIG DE SANT JOAN

C. DE PAU CLARIS

CASA
LLEÓ
MORERA

GRAN VIA DE LES CORTS CATALANES

CARRER DE CASP

D'AUSIAS
MARC

#50

PASSEIG

ZARA
STORE

Passeig de
Gràcia

DE GRÀCIA

CARRER DE PAU CLARIS

Urquinaona

RONDA DE SANT PERE

C. MÉNDEZ-NÚÑEZ

Plaça
Sant
Pere

EL CORTE INGLÉS
DEP'T STORE

Bus to Airport
(& Taxis)

VIA LAIETANA

C. DE LES JONQUERES

C. FONTANELLA

D'ORTIGOSA DE TRAFALGAR

C. DE SANT PERE MÉS ALT

C. DE SANT PERE MÉS BAIX

Urquinaona

Catalunya

Plaça de
Catalunya

PALACE OF
CATALAN
MUSIC

OLD   CITY

Modernisme and the Renaixença

Modernisme is Barcelona's unique contribution to the European Art Nouveau movement. Meaning "a taste for what is modern"—things like streetcars, electric lights, and big-wheeled bicycles—this free-flowing organic style lasted from 1888 to 1906.

The starting point for the style was a kind of Neo-Gothic, clearly inspired by medieval castles, towers, and symbols—logically, since architects wanted to recall Barcelona's glory days of the 1400s. From the Neo-Gothic look, Antoni Gaudí branched off on his own, adding the color and curves we most associate with Barcelona's Modernisme look.

The aim was to create objects that were both practical and decorative. Modernista architects experimented with new construction techniques, especially concrete, which they could use to make a hard stone building that curved and rippled like a wave. Then they sprinkled it with brightly colored glass and tile. The structure was fully modern, but the decoration was a clip-art collage of nature images, exotic Moorish or Chinese themes, and fanciful Gothic crosses and knights to celebrate Catalunya's medieval glory days.

It's ironic to think that Modernisme was a response to the Industrial Age—and that all those organic shapes were only made possible thanks to Eiffel Tower-like iron frames. The Eixample's fanciful facades and colorful, leafy ornamentation were built at the same time as the first skyscrapers.

Fueling Modernisme was the Catalan cultural revival called the Renaixença. As Europe was waking up to the modern age, downtrodden peoples across Europe—from the Basques to the Irish to the Hungarians to the Finns—were throwing off the cultural domination of other nations and celebrating what made their own cultures unique. Here in Catalunya, the Renaixença encouraged everyday people to get excited about all things Catalan: their language, patriotic dances, art—and their surprising architecture.

Casa Amatller, with stepped roofline, and Casa Batlló, to the right

▲▲LA PEDRERA (CASA MILÀ)

One of Gaudí's trademark works, this house—built between 1906 and 1912—is an icon of Modernisme. The wealthy industrialist Pere Milà i Camps commissioned it, and while some still call it Casa Milà, most call it La Pedrera (The Quarry) because of its jagged, rocky facade. While it's fun to ogle from the outside, it's also worth going inside, as it's arguably the purest Gaudí interior in town—executed at the height of his abilities (unlike his earlier Palau Güell)—and still contains original furnishings. While Casa Batlló has a Gaudí facade and rooftop, these were appended to an existing building; La Pedrera, on the other hand, was built from the ground up according to Gaudí's plans. Besides entry to the interior, a ticket also gets you access to the delightful rooftop, with its forest of colorful tiled chimneys.

Cost and Hours: €20.50, daily March-Oct 9:00-20:00, Nov-Feb 9:00-18:30, last entry 30 minutes before closing, good audioguide-€4, at the corner of Passeig de Gràcia and Provença (visitor entrance at Provença 261), Metro: Diagonal, info tel. 902-400-973, www.lapedrera.com.

Crowd Control: As lines can be long (up to a 1.5-hour wait to get in), it's best to reserve ahead at www.lapedrera.com (tickets come with an assigned entry time). If you come without a ticket, the best time to arrive is right when it opens.

Rick's Tip: To enter **La Pedrera without a wait,** buy a €29 premium ticket, which allows you to arrive whenever you wish (no assigned entry time) and skip all lines, including those for audioguides and the elevator to the apartment and roof (sometimes a 30-minute wait).

Nighttime Visits: The building hosts after-hour visits dubbed "The Secret Pedrera." On this pricey visit, you'll get a guided tour of the building with the lights

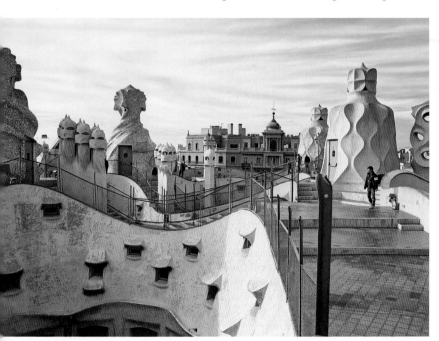

La Pedrera rooftop

Modernista Masters

Here's a summary of the major players who took part in the architectural revolution of Modernisme:

Antoni Gaudí (1852-1926), Barcelona's most famous Modernista artist, was descended from four generations of metalworkers—a lineage of which he was quite proud. He incorporated ironwork into his architecture and came up with novel approaches to architectural structure and space. His work strongly influenced his younger Catalan contemporary, Salvador Dalí. While Dalí was creating unlikely and shocking juxtapositions of photorealistic images, Gaudí did the same in architecture—using the spine of a reptile for a bannister or a turtle shell design on windows. His best work in Barcelona includes his great unfinished church, the Sagrada Família; several mansions in the town center,

including La Pedrera, Casa Batlló, and Palau Güell; and Park Güell, his ambitious and never-completed housing development.

Lluís Domènech i Montaner (1850-1923), a professor and politician, was responsible for some major civic buildings, including his masterwork, the Palace of Catalan Music (see page 371). He also designed Casa Lleó Morera on the Block of Discord. Although Gaudí is more famous, Domènech i Montaner's work is perhaps more purely representative of the Modernista style.

Josep Puig i Cadafalch (1867-1956) was a city planner who oversaw the opening up of Via Laietana through the middle of the Old City. He was instrumental in the redevelopment of Montjuïc for the 1929 World Expo. He designed Casa Amatller (see page 373). Perhaps most important, Puig i Cadafalch designed the building housing Els Quatre Gats (see page 352), a bar that became a cradle for the Modernista movement.

All architects worked with a team of people who, while not famous, made real contributions. For example, Gaudí's colleague **Josep Maria Jujol** (1879-1949) is primarily responsible for the broken-tile mosaic decorations (called *trencadís*) on Park Güell's benches and Casa Milà's chimneys—which became Gaudí's trademark.

Though not an artist, businessman **Eusebi Güell** (1846-1918) used his nearly $90 billion fortune to bankroll Gaudí and other Modernista masters. Güell's name still adorns two of Gaudí's most important works: Palau Güell (see page 359) and Park Güell (see page 387).

turned down low and a glass of *cava* (€30; English tour offered daily March-Oct at 21:15, but check changeable schedule and offerings online).

Concerts: On summer weekends, La Pedrera has an evening rooftop concert series, "Summer Nights at La Pedrera," featuring live jazz. In addition to the music, it gives you the chance to see the rooftop illuminated (€27, late June-early Sept Thu-Sat at 22:30, book advance tickets online or by phone, tel. 902-101-212, www.lapedrera.com).

Visiting the House: A visit covers three sections—the apartment, the attic, and the rooftop. Enter and head upstairs to the apartment. If it's near closing time, continue up to see the attic and rooftop first, to make sure you have enough time to enjoy Gaudí's works and the views (note that the roof may close when it rains).

The typical bourgeois **apartment** is decorated as it might have been when the building was first occupied by middle-class urbanites (a 7-minute video explains Barcelona society at the time). Notice Gaudí's clever use of the atrium to maximize daylight in all of the apartments.

The **attic** houses a sprawling multimedia exhibit tracing the history of the architect's career, with models, photos, and videos of his work. It's all displayed under distinctive parabola-shaped arches.

From the attic, a stairway leads to the undulating, jaw-dropping **rooftop,** where 30 chimneys and ventilation towers play volleyball with the clouds.

Back at the **ground level** of La Pedrera, poke into the dreamily painted original entrance courtyard.

▲▲▲SAGRADA FAMÍLIA (HOLY FAMILY CHURCH)

Antoni Gaudí's grand masterpiece sits unfinished in a residential Eixample neighborhood 1.5 miles north of Plaça de Catalunya. An icon of the city, the Sagrada Família boasts bold, wildly creative, unmistakably organic architecture and decor inside and out—from its melting Glory Facade to its skull-like Passion Facade to its rainforest-esque interior. Begun under Gaudí's careful watch in 1883, the project saw some setbacks in the mid-20th century, but lately the progress has been remarkable. The city has set a goal of finishing by 2026, the centennial of Gaudí's death. For now, visitors get a close-up view of the dramatic exterior flourishes, the chance to walk through the otherworldly interior, and access to a fine museum detailing the design and engineering behind this one-of-a-kind architectural marvel.

The main challenges for this massive undertaking today are to ensure that construction can withstand the vibrations caused by the speedy AVE trains rumbling underfoot, to construct the tallest church spire ever built, and to find a way to buy out the people who own the condos in front of the planned Glory Facade so that Gaudí's vision of a grand esplanade approaching the church can be realized.

Rick's Tip: *To avoid wasting time in ticket-buying lines, buy* **advance tickets** *for the* **Sagrada Família.**

Cost and Hours: Church-€15, tower elevators-€4.50 each, €18.50 combo-ticket includes church (no towers) and Gaudí House Museum at Park Güell (see page 387); Mon-Sat 9:00-20:00, Sun from 10:30, Oct-March until 18:00.

Advance Tickets: Reserve entry times and buy tickets in advance for both the church and the tower elevators (this is the best way to synch up the timing of your church visit and elevator ride). The easiest option is to book at www.sagrada familia.cat and print tickets at home.

Crowd Control: Waits can be up to 45 minutes at peak times—and occasionally stretch much longer (most crowded in the morning). To minimize waiting, arrive right at 9:00 (when the church opens) or after

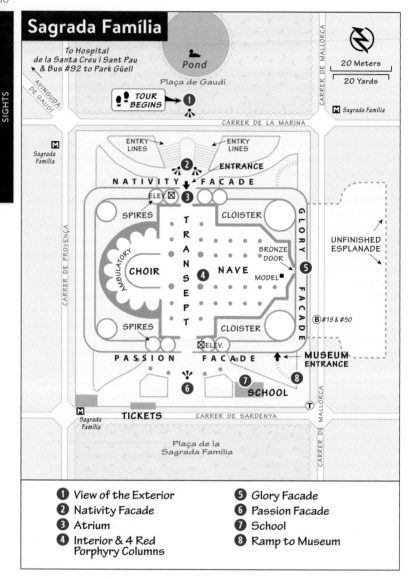

Sagrada Família

To Hospital
de la Santa Creu i Sant Pau
& Bus #92 to Park Güell

AVINGUDA DE GAUDÍ

CARRER DE MALLORCA

Pond

Plaça de Gaudí

20 Meters
20 Yards

Ⓜ Sagrada Família

TOUR BEGINS → ❶

CARRER DE LA MARINA

Ⓜ Sagrada Família

ENTRY LINES   ENTRY LINES

❷   ENTRANCE

N A T I V I T Y   F A C A D E

ELEV. ⊠ ❸

SPIRES   CLOISTER

CARRER DE PROVENÇA

T R A N S E P T

AMBULATORY

CHOIR   ❹   NAVE

BRONZE DOOR

MODEL ■ ❺

G L O R Y   F A C A D E

UNFINISHED ESPLANADE

Ⓑ #19 & #50

SPIRES   CLOISTER

⊠ELEV.

P A S S I O N   F A C A D E

MUSEUM ENTRANCE

❻   ❼ ❽

SCHOOL

Ⓣ

Ⓜ Sagrada Família

TICKETS   CARRER DE SARDENYA

CARRER DE MALLORCA

Plaça de la Sagrada Família

❶ View of the Exterior
❷ Nativity Facade
❸ Atrium
❹ Interior & 4 Red Porphyry Columns
❺ Glory Facade
❻ Passion Facade
❼ School
❽ Ramp to Museum

16:00. To skip the line, buy advance tickets, take a tour, or hire a private guide.

Getting There: The church address is Carrer de Mallorca 401. The Sagrada Família Metro stop puts you right on its doorstep.

Getting In: The ticket windows are on the west side of the church, at the Passion Facade (from the Metro, exit toward Plaça de la Sagrada Família). If you already have tickets, head straight for the Nativity Facade (in front of Plaça de Gaudí), where you'll find entry lines for individuals. Show your ticket to the guard, who will direct you to the right line.

Information: Good English information

is posted throughout. Tel. 932-073-031, www.sagradafamilia.cat.

Tours: The 50-minute **English tours** (€4.50) run daily at 11:00, 12:00, 13:00, and 15:00 (no 12:00 tour Mon-Fri in Nov-April; choose tour time when you buy ticket). Or rent the good 1.5-hour **audioguide** (€4.50).

Tower Elevators: Two different elevators take you (for a fee) partway up the towers for a great view of the city and a gargoyle's-eye perspective of the loopy church. Reserve an elevator time when you buy your church ticket.

The easier option is the **Passion Facade elevator,** which takes you 215 feet up and down. You can climb higher, but expect the spiral stairs to be tight, hot, and congested.

The **Nativity Facade elevator** is more exciting and demanding. You'll get the opportunity to cross the dizzying bridge between the towers, but you'll need to take the stairs all the way down.

➋ SELF-GUIDED TOUR

• Start outside the Nativity Facade (where the entry lines for individuals are located), on the eastern side of the church. Before heading to the entrance, take in the...

➊ View of the Exterior: Stand and imagine how grand this church will be when completed. The four 330-foot spires topped with crosses are just a fraction of this mega-church. When finished, the church will have 18 spires. Four will stand at each of the three entrances. Rising above those will be four taller towers, dedicated to the four Evangelists. A tower dedicated to Mary will rise still higher—400 feet. And in the center of the complex will stand the grand 560-foot Jesus tower, topped with a cross that will shine like a spiritual lighthouse, visible even from out at sea.

The Nativity Facade, where tourists enter today, is only a side entrance to the church. The grand main entrance will be around to the left. That means that the nine-story apartment building will eventually have to be torn down to accommodate it. The three facades—Nativity, Passion, and Glory—will chronicle Christ's life from birth to death to resurrection. Inside and out, a goal of the church is to bring the lessons of the Bible to the world. Despite his boldly modern architectural vision, Gaudí was fundamentally traditional and deeply religious. He designed

Sagrada Família

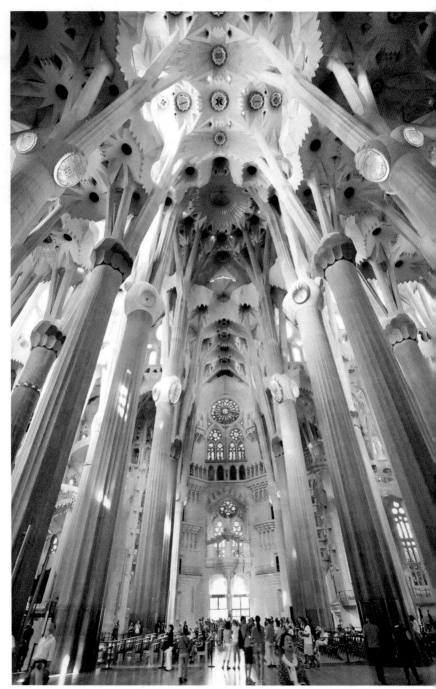

Sagrada Família nave

the Sagrada Família to be a bastion of solid Christian values in the midst of what was a humble workers' colony in a fast-changing city.

When Gaudí died, only one section (on the Nativity Facade) had been completed. The rest of the church has been inspired by Gaudí's long-range vision but designed and executed by others. This artistic freedom was amplified in 1936, when civil war shelling burned many of Gaudí's blueprints. Supporters of the ongoing work insist that Gaudí, who enjoyed saying, "My client [God] is not in a hurry," knew he wouldn't live to complete the church and recognized that later architects and artists would rely on their own muses for inspiration.

• Now approach the...

❷ **Nativity Facade:** This is the only part of the church essentially finished in Gaudí's lifetime. The four spires decorated with his unmistakably nonlinear sculpture mark this facade as part of his original design. Mixing Gothic-style symbolism, images from nature, and Modernista asymmetry, the Nativity Facade is the best example of Gaudí's original

Nativity Facade detail

vision, and it established the template for future architects who would work on the building.

The theme of this facade, which faces the rising sun, is Christ's birth. A statue above the doorway shows Mary, Joseph, and Baby Jesus in the manger, while curious cows peek in. It's the Holy Family—or "Sagrada Família"—to whom this church is dedicated. Flanking the doorway are the three Magi and adoring shepherds. Other statues show Jesus as a young carpenter and angels playing musical instruments. Higher up on the facade, in the arched niche, Jesus crowns Mary triumphantly.

The four **spires** are dedicated to apostles, and they repeatedly bear the word "Sanctus," or holy. Their colorful ceramic caps symbolize the miters (formal hats) of bishops. The shorter spires (to the left) symbolize the Eucharist (communion), alternating between a chalice with grapes and a communion host with wheat.

• Enter the church. As you pass through the
❸ **atrium,** look right to see one of the **elevators** up to the towers. For now, continue to the center of the church, near the altar, to survey the magnificent...

❹ **Interior:** Typical of even the most traditional Catalan and Spanish churches, the floor plan is in the shape of a Latin cross, 300 feet long and 200 feet wide. Ultimately, the church will encompass 48,000 square feet, accommodating 8,000 worshippers. The nave's roof is 150 feet high. The crisscross arches of the ceiling (the vaults) show off Gaudí's distinctive engineering. The church's roof and flooring were only completed in 2010—just in time for Pope Benedict XVI to arrive and consecrate the church.

Part of Gaudí's religious vision was a love for nature. He said, "Nothing is invented; it's written in nature." Like the trunks of trees, these **columns** (56 in all) blossom with life, complete with branches, leaves, and knot-like capitals. The columns are a variety of colors—

brown clay, gray granite, dark-gray basalt. The taller columns are 72 feet tall; the shorter ones are exactly half that.

Little **windows** let light filter in like the canopy of a rainforest, giving both privacy and an intimate connection with God. The clear glass is temporary and will gradually be replaced by stained glass. High up at the back half of the church, the U-shaped **choir**—suspended above the nave—can seat 1,000. The singers will eventually be backed by four organs (there's one now).

Work your way up the grand nave, walking through this forest of massive columns. At the center of the church stand four **red porphyry columns,** each marked with an Evangelist's symbol and name in Catalan: angel (Mateu), lion (Marc), bull (Luc), and eagle (Joan).

Stroll behind the altar through the **ambulatory** to reach a small chapel set aside for prayer and meditation. Look through windows down at the **crypt** (which holds the tomb of Gaudí). Peering down into that surprisingly traditional space, imagine how the church was started as a fairly conventional, 19th-century Neo-Gothic building until Gaudí was given the responsibility to finish it.

• Head to the far end of the church, to what will eventually be the main entrance. Just inside the door, find the **bronze model** *of the floor plan for the completed church. Facing the doors, look high up to see Subirachs' statue of one of Barcelona's patron saints,* **George (Jordi).** *While you can't see it, imagine that outside these doors will someday be the…*

❺ **Glory Facade:** Study the life-size image of the **bronze door,** emblazoned with the Lord's Prayer in Catalan, surrounded by "Give us this day our daily bread" in 50 languages. If you were able to walk through the actual door, you'd be face-to-face with…drab, doomed apartment blocks. In the 1950s, the mayor of Barcelona, figuring this day would never really come, sold the land destined for the church project. Now the city must buy back these buildings in order to complete Gaudí's vision: that of a grand esplanade leading to this main entry. Four towers will rise. The facade's sculpture will represent how the soul passes through death, faces the Last Judgment, avoids the pitfalls of hell, and finds its way to eternal glory with God. Gaudí purposely left the facade's design open for later architects—stay tuned.

• Head back up the nave, and exit through the left transept. Notice the second **elevator** *up to the towers. Once outside, back up to take in the…*

❻ **Passion Facade:** Judge for yourself how well Gaudí's original vision has been carried out by later artists. The Passion Facade's four spires were designed by Gaudí and completed (quite faithfully) in 1976. But the lower part was only inspired by Gaudí's designs. The stark sculptures were interpreted freely (and controversially) by Josep Maria Subirachs (1927-2014), who completed the work in 2005.

Subirachs tells the story of Christ's torture and execution. The various scenes—Last Supper, betrayal, whipping, and so on—zigzag up from bottom to top, culminating in Christ's crucifixion over the doorway. The style is severe and unadorned, quite different from Gaudí's signature playfulness. But the bone-like archways are closely based on Gaudí's original designs. And Gaudí had made it clear that this facade should be grim and terrifying.

• Now head into the small building outside the Passion Facade. This is the…

❼ **School:** Gaudí erected this school for the children of the workers building the church. Today it includes exhibits about the design and engineering of the church, along with a classroom and a replica of Gaudí's desk as it was the day he died.

• Back outside, head down the ramp, where you'll find WCs and the entrance to the…

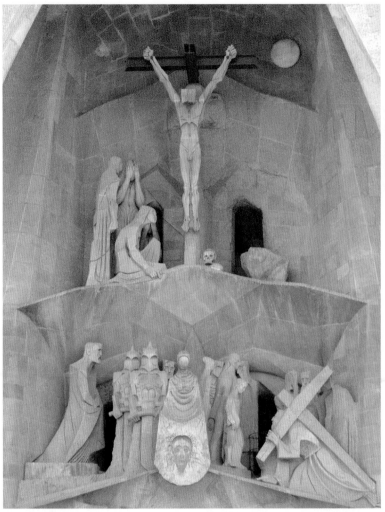

Sagrada Família Passion Facade

❸ Museum: Housed in what will someday be the church's crypt, the museum displays Gaudí's original models and drawings, and chronicles the progress of construction over the last 130-plus years.

Upon entering, you'll see **photos** (including one of the master himself) and a **timeline** illustrating how construction work has progressed from Gaudí's day to now. Before turning into the main hall, find **three different visions** for this church.

As you wander, notice how the **plaster models,** used for the church's construction, don't always match the finished product—these are ideas, not blueprints. The Passion Facade model shows Gaudí's original vision, with which Subirachs tinkered freely (see "Passion Facade," earlier). The models also make clear the influence of nature. The columns seem light, with branches springing forth and capitals that look like palm trees.

Turn right up the main hallway, walking under a huge **model of the nave,** and past some original **sculptures** from the different facades (on the left). Farther along, a small hallway on the left leads to some original Gaudí architectural **sketches** in a dimly lit room and a worthwhile 20-minute **movie** (continuously shown in Catalan with English subtitles).

From the end of this hall, you have another opportunity to look down into the crypt and at **Gaudí's tomb.** Gaudí lived on the site for more than a decade and is buried in the Neo-Gothic 19th-century crypt (also viewable from the apse). There's a move afoot to make Gaudí a saint. Gaudí prayer cards provide words of devotion to his beatification. Perhaps someday his tomb will be a place of pilgrimage.

On the right, you can peek into a busy **workshop** still used for making the

same kind of plaster models Gaudí used to envision the final product in three dimensions.

• *Our tour is over. From here, you could...*

Visit Park Güell: *The park is nearly two (uphill) miles to the northwest. The easiest way to get there is to spring for a taxi (around €10-12). Or you could reach the park by taking the Metro to the Joanic stop, then hopping on bus #116 (described next, under the "Park Güell" listing).*

Return to Central Barcelona: *You can either hop on the Metro or take one of two handy buses (both stop on Carrer de Mallorca, directly in front of the Glory Facade). Bus #19 takes you back to the* **Old City** *in 15 minutes, stopping near the cathedral and in the El Born district. Bus #50 goes from the Sagrada Família to the heart of the* **Eixample** *(corner of Gran Via de les Corts Catalanes and Passeig de Gràcia), then continues on to Plaça Espanya, where you can get off for* **Montjuïc.**

Beyond the Eixample
▲▲PARK GÜELL

Tucked in the foothills at the edge of Barcelona, this fanciful park—designed by Antoni Gaudí as part of an upscale housing development for early-20th-century urbanites—combines playful whimsy, inviting spaces, and a terrace offering sweeping views over the city.

To control crowds, the part of the park with the most popular sights has been declared the "Monumental Zone," which requires a time-entry admission fee to visit (the rest of the park is free). This fairly compact zone contains a pair of gingerbread-style houses, a grand staircase monitored by a colorful dragon, a forest of columns supporting a spectacular view terrace, and an undulating balcony slathered in tile shards. The park also contains the Gaudí House Museum, Calvary viewpoint, picnic area, and a pleasant network of nature trails.

Cost and Hours: Monumental Zone—€8 at the gate or €7 online, smart to reserve timed-entry tickets in advance, daily 8:00-21:30, Nov-March 8:30-18:15, www.parkguell.cat; Gaudí House Museum—€5.50, daily April-Sept 9:00-20:00, Oct-March 10:00-18:00, www.casamuseugaudi.org.

Getting There: Park Güell is about 2.5 miles from Plaça de Catalunya, in Barcelona's foothills. From downtown, a **taxi** will drop you at the main entrance for about €12. From Plaça de Catalunya, the blue **Tourist Bus** stops about four blocks downhill from the historical entrance, and **public bus #24** travels from Plaça de Catalunya to the park's side entrance. Or you can ride the **Metro** to Joanic, exit toward Carrer de l'Escorial, and find the bus stop in front of #20, where you can catch bus #116 to the park's historical entrance.

Getting In: The Monumental Zone has four entrances for ticket holders—two of which also sell tickets. If you arrive at the park's historical front entrance (currently an exit only), attendants will direct you to the entrances, ticket booths, and ticket machines at the far left or far right corners of the Monumental Zone.

If you arrive at the park's side entrance,

Park Güell's entry stairway

you'll find a ticket office near the bus stop. Follow the Rosary Pathway (to the left of the building) to one of two view-terrace entrances.

Hang on to your ticket; you'll need to show it at the exit when you leave.

Visiting the Park: Enjoy Gaudí's **historical front entrance** (now exit only) with its palm-frond gate and wrought-iron gas lamps (1900-1914). Gaudí's dad was a blacksmith, and he always enjoyed this medium. (If you arrive at the side entrance and already have your Monumental Zone ticket, walk along the path to the view-terrace entrance; then go down to the stairway to find the front entrance.)

Two Hansel-and-Gretel gingerbread lodges flank this former entrance. One of the buildings houses a bookshop; the other is home to the skippable La Casa del Guarda, a branch of the Barcelona History Museum (MUHBA).

Climb the grand **stairway,** past the famous ceramic dragon fountain. At the top, dip into the "Hall of 100 Columns," designed to house a produce market for the neighborhood's 60 mansions. The fun columns—each different, made from concrete and rebar, topped with colorful ceramic, and studded with broken bottles and bric-a-brac—add to the market's vitality.

As you continue up (on the left-hand staircase), look left, down the playful **"pathway of columns"** that supports a long arcade. Gaudí drew his inspiration from nature, and this arcade is like a surfer's perfect tube.

Once up top on the **terrace,** sit on a colorful bench—designed to fit your body ergonomically—and enjoy one of Barcelona's best views. Look for the Sagrada Família church in the distance. As a community development, Park Güell ultimately failed, but it was an idea a hundred years ahead of its time. Back then, high-society ladies didn't want to live so far from the cultural action. Today, the surrounding neighborhoods are some of the wealthiest in town.

Gaudí House Museum: This pink house with a steeple, standing in the middle of the park (near the side entrance), was Gaudí's home for 20 years (though he didn't design the actual house). It was originally built as a model home to attract prospective residents. His humble artifacts are mostly gone, but the house is now a museum with some quirky Gaudí furniture. Though small, it offers a good taste of what could have been if the envisioned housing development had prospered.

Montjuïc

Montjuïc (mohn-jew-EEK), overlooking Barcelona's hazy port, has always been a show-off. Ages ago, it was capped by an impressive castle. When the Spanish enforced their rule in the 18th century, they built the imposing fortress that you'll see the shell of today. Montjuïc was also prominent during the last century. In 1929, it hosted an international fair, from which many of today's sights originated. And in 1992, the Summer Olympics directed the world's attention to this pincushion of attractions once again.

For art lovers, the most worthwhile sights are the Fundació Joan Miró and Catalan Art Museum. The hilltop castle isn't worth entering, but offers great city views from its ramparts. It serves as a park, jogging destination, and host to a popular summer open-air cinema.

For evening fun, you could drop by the Magic Fountains, and any time of day, you can escalate up to the top of Las Arenas Mall for a view of Montjuïc.

Getting to Montjuïc: You have several choices. The simplest is to take a **taxi** directly to your destination (about €8 from downtown). If you want to visit only the Catalan Art Museum, you can just take the **Metro** to Plaça d'Espanya and ride the escalators up the hill (with some stairs as well).

Buses also take you up to Montjuïc. From Plaça de Catalunya, **bus #55** rides as far as Montjuïc's cable-car station/funicular. If you want to get higher (to the castle), ride the Metro to Plaça d'Espanya, then make the easy transfer to **bus #150** to ride all the way up the hill—then you can do the rest of your Montjuïc sightseeing going downhill. Alternatively, the red Tourist Bus will get you to the Montjuïc sights.

Another option is by **funicular** (covered by Metro ticket, runs every 10 minutes 9:00-22:00). To reach it, take the Metro to the Paral-lel stop, then follow signs for *Parc Montjuïc* and the little funicular icon—you can enter the funicular without using another ticket. From the top of the funicular, turn left and walk gently downhill 4 minutes to the Miró museum or 12 minutes to the Catalan Art Museum. If you're heading all the way up to the castle, you can catch a bus or cable car from the top of the funicular.

For a scenic (if slow) approach to Montjuïc, you could ride the fun, circa-1929 Aeri del Port **cable car** *(telefèric)* from the tip of the Barceloneta peninsula (across the harbor, near the beach) to the Miramar viewpoint park in Montjuïc.

Since the cable car is expensive, loads slowly, and goes between two relatively remote parts of town, it's only worthwhile for its sweeping views or if you'd like to cap off your Montjuïc day with some beach time near Barceloneta (€11 one-way, €16.50 round-trip, 3/hour, daily 11:00-17:30, June-Sept until 20:00, closed in high wind, tel. 934-414-820, www.telefericodebarcelona.com).

Getting Around Montjuïc: Up top, it's easy and fun to walk between the sights—especially downhill. You can also connect the sights using the red Tourist Bus or one of the public buses: Bus #150 does a loop around the hilltop and is the only bus that goes to the castle; on the way up, it stops at or passes the Catalan Art Museum, Fundació Joan Miró, the lower castle cable-car station/top of the funicular, and finally, the castle. On the downhill run, it loops by Miramar, the cable-car station for Barceloneta. Bus #55 connects only the fairgrounds, Fundació Joan Miró, and the Catalan Art Museum.

▲▲CATALAN ART MUSEUM (MUSEU NACIONAL D'ART DE CATALUNYA)

This wonderful museum showcases Catalan art from the 10th century through

Montjuïc's Magic Fountains

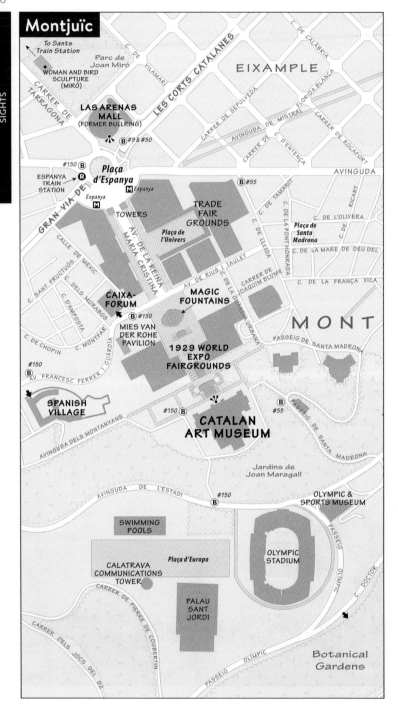

Montjuïc

To Sants Train Station

Parc de Joan Miró

WOMAN AND BIRD SCULPTURE (MIRÓ)

EIXAMPLE

C. DE VILAMARI

LES CORTS CATALANES

C. DE CALABRIA

CARRER DE TARRAGONA

LAS ARENAS MALL (FORMER BULLRING)

B #9 & #50

CARRER DE SEPULVEDA

AVINGUDA DE MISTRAL

FLORIDA BLANCA

CARRER DE BLANCA

CARRER DE ROCAFORT

CARRER DE C D'ENTENCA

#150 B

ESPANYA TRAIN STATION

R

Plaça d'Espanya

M Espanya

Espanya M

B #55

AVINGUDA

C. DE TAMARIT

C. DE RICART

G. DE L'OLIVERA

GRAN VIA DE

AV. DE LA REINA MARIA CRISTINA

TOWERS

TRADE FAIR GROUNDS

Plaça de l'Univers

C. DE LA FONT HONRADA

C. DE LLEIDA

Plaça de Santa Madrona

C. DE L'OLIVERA

C. DE LA MARE DE DÉU DEL

CALLE DE MÉXIC

C. SANT FRUCTUÓS

C. DELS MORABOS

C. D'AMPOSTA

CAIXA-FORUM

B #150

MIES VAN DER ROHE PAVILION

MAGIC FOUNTAINS

AV. DE RIUS I TAULET

CARRER DE JOAQUIM BLUME

CARRER DE LA GUARDIA URBANA

C. DE LA FRANÇA XICA

MONT

C. DE CHOPIN

C. MONTFAR

1929 WORLD EXPO FAIRGROUNDS

PASSEIG DE SANTA MADRONA

#150 B

AV. FRANCESC FERRER I GUARDIA

SPANISH VILLAGE

AVINGUDA DELS MONTANYANS

#150 B

CATALAN ART MUSEUM

B #55

PASSEIG DE SANTA MADRONA

Jardins de Joan Maragall

AVINGUDA DE L'ESTADI

#150 B

OLYMPIC & SPORTS MUSEUM

SWIMMING POOLS

Plaça d'Europa

CALATRAVA COMMUNICATIONS TOWER

OLYMPIC STADIUM

PASSEIG OLÍMPIC

C. DOCTOR

CARRER DE PIERRE DE COUBERTIN

PALAU SANT JORDI

CARRER DELS JOCS DEL 92

PASSEIG OLÍMPIC

Botanical Gardens

SANT ANTONI MARKET

Sant Antoni

CARRER DE TAMARIT

CARRER DE MANSO

CARRER DE LA CERA

C. PISTALEGRE

C. DE L'AURORA

RÀMBLA DEL RAVAL

C. DE SANT PACIÀ

C. DE LA RIERETA

C. DE SANT PAU

To Las Ramblas

CARRER DE LA REINA AMÀLIA

CARRETES

EL RAVAL

CARRER DEL CATALUNYA

RONDA DE SANT PAU

C. DEL PARLAMENT DE COMTE

C. DEL MARQÈS DE CAMPO SAGRADO

BORRELL

C. DE LES FLORS

C. DE

SANT PAU

CARRER DE LES TÀPIES

CARRER NOU DE LA RAMBLA

To Maritime Museum & Port

Poble Sec

DEL PARAL-LEL

Paral-lel

Paral-lel

C. DE LA CONCORDIA

C. DE RADAS

C. DE BLAI

C. DE BÈKAY

C. DE BLASCO DE GARAY

C. DE LA CREU DELS MOLERS

CARRER DE MARGARIT

CARRER DE TAPIOLES

CARRER DEL POETA CABANYES

CARRER DE SALVÀ

CARRER DEL ROSER

FONTRODONA

CARRER NOU DE LA RAMBLA

C. DE CABANES

PSG. DE LA CANADENCA

REMEI

Plaça del Sortidor

CARRER D'ELKANO

CARRER D'EN

CARRER D'ANNIBAL

CARRER DE MAGALHAES

C. DE VILA I VILÀ

C. DE PIQUER

C. DE MAJÀ

C. DE BLESA

PASSEIG DE MONTJUÏC

PASSEIG DE L'EXPOSICIÓ

JUÏC

Parc del Mirador del Poble-Sec

#150

Miramar

FUNICULAR

P. DE MIRAMAR

C. FONT TROBADA

AV. DE MIRAMAR

AV. DE MIRAMAR

AERI DEL PORT CABLE CAR STATION
(To Barceloneta)

Jardin de Laribal

DIVING POOLS

FUNDACIÓ JOAN MIRÓ

AVINGUDA DE MIRAMAR

#55 & #150

Parc de Montjuïc

CARRER

Plaça de Dante

Jardins Joan Brossa

CARRETERA DE MONTJUÏC

SARDANA SCULPTURE

#150

Jardin de Mossèn Costa i Llobera

#55 & #150

CABLE CAR

CARRER DELS TARONGERS

Jardins del Mirador de l'Alcalde

CABLE CAR

CARRETERA DE MIRAMAR

FONT I QUER

Jardin de Mossèn Cinto Verdaguer

C. DELS TARONGERS

C. DE CAN VALERO

PASSEIG DEL MIGDIA

AVINGUDA DEL CASTELL

CAMÍ DE LA CARTOIXA

#150

MONTJUÏC CASTLE

RONDA DEL LITORAL

N

200 Meters

200 Yards

To Airport & Sitges

B-10

the mid-20th century. Often called "the Prado of Romanesque art" (and "MNAC" for short), it also holds Europe's best collection of Romanesque frescoes. Art aficionados are sure to find something in this diverse collection to tickle their fancy. It's all housed in the grand Palau Nacional, an emblematic building from the 1929 World Expo, with magnificent views over Barcelona, especially from the building's rooftop terrace.

Cost and Hours: €12, includes temporary exhibits and rooftop terrace, rooftop access only-€3.50, museum free Sat from 15:00 and first Sun of month; open May-Sept Tue-Sat 10:00-20:00 (Oct-April until 18:00), Sun 10:00-15:00, closed Mon, last entry 30 minutes before closing; audioguide-€3.10; in massive National Palace building above Magic Fountains, near Plaça d'Espanya—take escalators up; tel. 936-220-376, www.museunacional. cat.

Getting to the Rooftop Terrace: To reach the terrace from the main entrance, walk past the bathrooms to the left and show your ticket to get on the elevator. You'll ride up nearly to the viewpoint, and from there hike up a couple of flights of stairs to the terrace. To take an elevator the whole way, go to the far end of the museum, through the huge dome room, to the far right corner.

Visiting the Museum: As you enter, pick up a map. The left wing is Romanesque, and the right wing is Gothic, exquisite Renaissance, and Baroque. Upstairs is more Baroque, plus modern art, photography, coins, and more.

The MNAC's rare, world-class collection of **Romanesque** (Romànic) art came mostly from remote Catalan village churches. A series of videos shows the process of extracting the frescoes from the churches. The Romanesque wing features a remarkable array of 11th- to 13th-century frescoes, painted wooden altar fronts, and ornate statuary. This classic Romanesque art—with flat 2-D scenes, each saint holding his symbol, and Jesus (easy to identify by the cross in his halo)—is impressively displayed on replicas of the original church ceilings and apses.

Across the way, in the Gothic wing, are vivid 14th-century wood-panel paintings of Bible stories. A roomful of paintings (Room 26) by the Catalan master Jaume Huguet (1412-1492) deserves a look, particularly his Consecration of St. Agustí Vell. Also on the ground floor is a selection of **Renaissance** works covering Spain's Golden Age (Zurbarán, heavy religious scenes, Spanish royals with their endearing underbites) and examples of Romanticism (dewy-eyed Catalan landscapes). In addition, you'll find minor works by major—if not necessarily Catalan—names (Velázquez, El Greco, Tintoretto, Rubens, and so on).

For a break, go to the right from the Gothic exit to glide under the huge **dome,** which once housed an ice-skating rink. This was the prime ceremony room and dance hall for the 1929 World Expo.

From the big ballroom, you can ride the glass elevator upstairs to the **Modern Art** section, which takes you on an enjoyable walk from the late 1800s to about 1950, offering a big chronological clockwise circle covering Symbolism, Modernisme, fin de siècle fun, Art Deco, and more. Find the early 20th-century paintings by Catalan artists Santiago Rusiñol and Ramon Casas, both of whom had a profound impact on a young Picasso (and, through him, on all of modern art). Crossing over to the "Modern 2" section, you'll find furniture (pieces that complement the empty spaces you likely saw in Gaudí's buildings—including a Gaudí wooden sofa), Impressionism, the shimmering landscapes of Joaquim Mir, and several distinctly Picasso portraits of women.

▲**FUNDACIÓ JOAN MIRÓ**

This museum has the best collection anywhere of work by Catalan artist Joan Miró (ZHOO-ahn mee-ROH, 1893-1983).

Born in Barcelona, Miró divided his time between Paris and Catalunya (including Barcelona and his favorite village, Montroig del Camp). This building—designed in 1975 by Josep Lluís Sert, a friend of Miró and a student of Le Corbusier—was purpose-built to show off Miró's art.

The museum displays an always-changing, loosely chronological overview of Miró's work (as well as generally excellent temporary exhibits of 20th- and 21st-century artists). Consider renting the wonderful audioguide, well worth the extra charge.

If you don't like abstract art, you'll leave here scratching your head. But those who love this place are not faking it...they understand the genius of Miró and the fun of abstraction. Children probably understand it the best. Eavesdrop on what they say about the art; you may learn something.

Cost and Hours: €11; Tue-Sat 10:00-20:00 (Nov-March until 18:00), Thu until 21:00, Sun 10:00-15:00, closed Mon; great audioguide-€5, 200 yards from top of funicular, Parc de Montjuïc, tel. 934-439-470, www.fundaciomiro-bcn.org. The museum has two cafés and a bookshop (all accessible without museum ticket).

▲MAGIC FOUNTAINS

These fountains, near the base of Montjuïc, make an artistic, colorful, and coordinated splash some summer evenings, accompanied by music (free 20-minute shows start on the half-hour; April-May & Oct Thu-Sat 21:00-22:00, June-Sept Wed-Sun 21:30-22:30, Nov-Dec & March Thu-Sat 20:00-21:00, no shows Jan-Feb, near Plaça d'Espanya).

LAS ARENAS MALL

This mall, on Plaça d'Espanya, was built inside a former bullring. It hosts the usual shops and a food-court basement. Worth ascending, the rooftop terrace offers fine views of Montjuïc (daily 10:00-22:00, small fee for exterior elevator to terrace, but interior escalators are free).

The Beaches and Nearby

▲BARCELONA'S BEACHES

Barcelona has created a summer tourist trade by building a huge stretch of beaches east of the town center. The overall scene is great for sunbathing and for an evening paseo before dinner. A bustling night scene keeps the harborfront busy until the wee hours.

This artificial peninsula, once the home of working-class sailors, is like a resort today—complete with lounge chairs, volleyball, showers, WCs, bike paths, and inviting beach bars called *chiringuitos*. Each beach segment has its own vibe: Sant Sebastià (closest, popular with older beachgoers and families), Barceloneta (with many seafood restaurants), Nova Icària (pleasant family beach), and Mar Bella (attracts a younger crowd, clothing-optional). As you wander the promenade, you'll see Frank Gehry's striking "fish" sculpture shining brightly in the sun.

Fundació Joan Miró

Nova Icària beach

Getting There: The Barceloneta Metro stop leaves you blocks from the sand. To get to the beaches without a hike, take the bus. From the Ramblas, bus #59 will get you as far as Barceloneta Park; bus #D20 leaves from the Columbus Monument and follows a similar route. Bus #V15 runs from Plaça de Catalunya to the tip of Barceloneta (near the W Hotel).

Rick's Tip: *Biking is a joy in Citadel Park and along the beachfront. To rent a bike on the beach, try* **Biciclot** *(€5/hour, €10/3 hours, €17/24 hours, daily in summer 10:00-20:00, shorter hours off-season, Passeig Maritim 33, tel. 932-219-778, www.biking inbarcelona.net).*

CITADEL PARK (PARC DE LA CIUTADELLA)

In 1888, Barcelona's biggest, greenest park, originally the site of a much-hated military citadel, was transformed for a Universal Exhibition (world's fair). The stately Triumphal Arch at the top of the park, celebrating the removal of the citadel, was built as the main entrance. Inside you'll find wide pathways, plenty of trees and grass, a zoo, and museums of geology and zoology. Barcelona, one of Europe's most densely populated cities, suffers from a lack of real green space. This park is a haven and is especially enjoyable on weekends, when it teems with happy families. Enjoy the ornamental fountain that the young Antoni Gaudí helped design, and consider a jaunt in a rental rowboat on the lake in the center of the park. Check out the tropical Umbracle greenhouse and the Hivernacle winter garden, which has a pleasant café-bar (Mon-Sat 10:00-14:00 & 17:00-20:30, Sun 10:30-14:00, shorter hours off-season).

Cost and Hours: Park—free, daily 10:00 until dusk, north of França train station, Metro: Arc de Triomf, Barceloneta, or Ciutadella-Vila Olímpica.

EXPERIENCES

Shopping

The streets of the Barri Gòtic and El Born are bursting with characteristic hole-in-the-wall shops, while the Eixample is the upscale "uptown" shopping district. Near Plaça de Catalunya, Avinguda Portal de l'Angel has a staggering array of department and chain stores.

Souvenir Items: In this artistic city, consider picking up art prints, posters, and books. Museum gift shops (Picasso Museum, La Pedrera, and more) offer a bonanza of classy souvenirs. Home-decor shops have Euro-style housewares unavailable back home. Decorative tile and pottery (popularized by Modernist architects) and Modernista jewelry are easy to pack. Foodies might bring back olive oil, wine, spices (such as saffron or sea salts), cheese, or the local nougat treat, *torró*. An *espadenya*—or *espadrille* in Spanish—is the trendy canvas-and-rope shoe that originated as humble Catalan peasant footwear. For a souvenir of Catalan culture, consider a Catalan flag, a dragon of St. Jordi, or a jersey or scarf from the wildly popular Barça soccer team.

Barri Gòtic Shopping Stroll

This route, from the cathedral to the Ramblas, takes you through interesting streets lined with little shops. Avoid the midafternoon siesta and Sundays, when many shops are closed.

Face the cathedral, turn 90 degrees right, and exit Plaça Nova (just to the left of the Bilbao Berria "BB" restaurant) on the tight lane called Carrer de la Palla. This street has a half-dozen antique shops crammed with mothballed treasures. Mixed in are a few art galleries, offbeat shops, and a motorcycle museum. When you reach the fork in the road (where the inviting Caelum café is), you have a choice. If you go left, explore Carrer dels Banys Nous, another great shopping street (with Artesania Catalunya, a city-run market space featuring hand-made items from Catalan artisans).

To carry on toward the Ramblas, take the right fork. You'll pass by the Oro Líquido shop ("Liquid Gold," high-quality olive oils) and soon reach the Church of Santa Maria del Pi, ringed by a charming, café-lined square, Plaça de Sant Josep Oriol. Skirt around the right side of the church to find Plaça del Pi, a delightful square, with Josep Roca, a genteel gentleman's shop. Head up the narrow street, Carrer Petritxol, immediately left of the Josep Roca shop. The street is a fun combination of art galleries, jewelry shops, and simple places for hot chocolate and churros (check out Granja La Pallaresa, just after #11).

You'll dead-end onto Carrer de la Portaferrissa, with its international teen clothing stores. From here, head one block left to reach the Ramblas.

El Born

Although the main streets—Carrer de la Princesa, the perpendicular Carrer de Montcada, and the diagonal Carrer de l'Argenteria—are disappointing for shop-pers, if you lose yourself in the smaller back lanes between those arteries, you'll discover a world of artsy, funky little boutiques. Stroll along Carrer dels Flassaders (behind the Picasso Museum), Carrer dels Banys Vells (between Montcada and l'Argenteria), and Carrer del Rec (just south of Passeig del Born)—and all of the little lanes crossing each of these streets.

Plaça de Catalunya and Avinguda Portal de l'Angel

Barcelona natives do most of their shopping at big department stores. You'll find the highest concentration of stores on Avinguda del Portal de l'Angel, which leads south from Plaça de Catalunya to the cathedral.

Plaça de Catalunya hosts the gigantic **El Corte Inglés,** the Spanish answer to one-stop shopping, with clothing, electronics, a travel agency, events box office, a basement supermarket, and a ninth-floor view café (Mon-Sat 10:00-22:00, closed Sun). Across the square is **FNAC**—a French department store that sells electronics, music, books, and tickets for major concerts and events (Mon-Sat

Open-air market in the Barri Gòtic

10:00-22:00, closed Sun).

Along Avinguda Portal de l'Angel, you'll see popular clothing chains such as **Zara,** the Barcelona-based **Mango, Desigual** (with boldly colorful designs), the teen-oriented French chain **Pimkie,** and the more sophisticated **Podivm** and **Blanco.**

The Eixample

This ritzy "uptown" district is home to some of the city's top-end shops. From Plaça de Catalunya, head north up Passeig de Gràcia, which starts out with lower-end international stores (like Zara) and ends up with top-end brands at the top (Gucci, Luis Vuitton, Escada, Chanel). Detour one block west to Rambla de Catalunya for more local (but still expensive) options for fashion, jewelry, perfume, home decor, and more.

Nightlife

For evening entertainment, Barcelonans stroll the streets, greet neighbors, pop into a bar for drinks and tapas, nurse a cocktail on a floodlit square, or enjoy a late meal. Dinnertime is around 22:00, and even families with children can be out well after midnight. If you're near Montjuïc, take in the hilltop view, Magic Fountains, or both.

Neighborhoods for Tapas and Drinks

These neighborhoods party late, but they're also lively for tapas and drinks in the early evening.

El Born: Passeig del Born, a broad park-like strip stretching from the Church of Santa Maria del Mar, is lined with inviting bars and nightspots. Wander the side streets for more options. Miramelindo (Passeig del Born 15) is a favorite for mojitos. La Vinya del Senyor is mellower, for tapas and wine on the square in front of Santa Maria del Mar.

Plaça Reial (in the Barri Gòtic): A block off the Ramblas, this palm-tree-graced square bustles with trendy eateries

charging inflated prices for pleasant outdoor tables—perfect for nursing a drink. Try the Ocaña Bar (€5-14 tapas, reasonable drinks, at #13).

Carrer de la Mercè: This Barri Gòtic street near the harbor is lined with salty tapas bars, with a few trendy ones mixed in.

Barceloneta: The broad beach is dotted with *chiringuitos*—shacks selling drinks and snacks, creating a fun, lively scene on a balmy summer evening.

Performing Arts

Barcelona always has a vast array of cultural events. Pick up the TI's free monthly English-language magazine, *In BCN Culture & Leisure.* Another good source of info is the Palau de la Virreina ticket office (daily 10:00-20:30, Ramblas 99, tel. 933-161-000, www.lavirreina.bcn.cat).

You can buy tickets directly from the venue's website, from box offices at El Corte Inglés or the FNAC store (both on Plaça de Catalunya), from Palau de Verreina, or at www.ticketmaster.es or www.telentrada.com.

The **Palace of Catalan Music,** with one of the finest Modernista interiors in town, offers everything from symphonic to Catalan folk songs to chamber music to flamenco (Palau de la Música Catalana, €20-50 tickets, purchase online or in person, box office open Mon-Sat 9:30-21:00, Sun 10:00-15:00, Carrer Palau de la Música 4, Metro: Urquinaona, tel. 902-442-882).

The **Liceu Opera House,** right in the heart of the Ramblas, is a sumptuous venue for opera, dance, and concerts (Gran Teatre del Liceu, tickets from €10, buy tickets online up to 1.5 hours before the show or in person, Ramblas 51, box office just around the corner at Carrer Sant Pau 1, Metro: Liceu, box office tel. 934-859-913, www.liceubarcelona.cat).

"Masters of Guitar" concerts are offered nearly nightly at 21:00 in the Barri Gòtic's **Church of Santa Maria del Pi** (€23 at the door, €4 less if you buy at least

3 hours ahead—look for ticket sellers in front of church and scattered throughout town, Plaça del Pi 7, or sometimes in Sant Jaume Church at Carrer de Ferran 28, tel. 647-514-513, www.maestrosdelaguitarra. com).

Though flamenco music is not typical of Barcelona (it's from Andalucía), **Tarantos** offers entertaining concerts nightly (€10, at 20:30, 21:30, and 22:30; Plaça Reial 17, tel. 933-191-789, www.masimas.com/en/tarantos). **La Pedrera** hosts "Summer Nights at La Pedrera" jazz concerts on its fanciful floodlit rooftop, weekends from June to September (book ahead at tel. 902-101-212 or www.lapedrera.com).

EATING

Barcelona, the capital of Catalan cuisine, offers a tremendous variety of colorful places to eat, ranging from workaday eateries to homey Catalan bistros (*cans*) to crowded tapas bars to avant-garde restaurants. Many eateries serve both stand-up tapas and sit-down meals, often starring seafood.

Basque-style tapas places are popular and user-friendly. Just scan the enticing buffets of bite-size tapas, grab what looks good, order a drink, and save your toothpicks (they'll count them up to tally your bill). I've listed my favorite tapas bars (Taverna Basca Irati, Xaloc, and Sagardi Euskal Taberna), though there are many others (look for *basca* or *euskal*; both mean "Basque").

Budget Meals: Sandwich shops are everywhere, serving made-to-order bocadillos. Choose between bright (mass-produced) chains such as **Bocatta** and **Pans & Company,** or colorful holes-in-the-wall. **Mucci's Pizza** has good, fresh, €2 pizza slices and empanadas (just off the Ramblas, at Bonsuccés 10 and Tallers 75), and **Wok to Walk** has takeaway noodle and rice dishes (€6-9, near the main door of the Boqueria Market). Kebab places are another standby for quick and tasty €3-4 meals. For a fast, affordable lunch with a view, the ninth-floor cafeteria at **El Corte Inglés department store** on Plaça de Catalunya can't be beat. Picnickers can buy groceries at the basement supermarket in El Corte Inglés, or at **La Boqueria Market** on the Ramblas.

The fun Pinotxo Bar at La Boqueria Market

Near the Ramblas

Do not eat or drink at the tourist traps on the Ramblas. Within a few steps of the Ramblas, you'll find handy lunch places, an inviting market hall, and some good vegetarian options.

$$ Taverna Basca Irati serves hot and cold Basque *pintxos* for €2 each. These small open-faced sandwiches are like sushi on bread. Muscle in through the hungry local crowd, get an empty plate from the waiter, and then help yourself. Every few minutes, waiters circulate with platters of new, still-warm munchies. Grab munchies as they pass by...it's addictive (you'll be charged by the number of toothpicks left on your plate). For drink options, look for the printed menu on the wall in the back. Wash down your food with €3 glasses of Rioja (full-bodied red wine), Txakolí (sprightly Basque white wine), or *sidra* (apple wine) poured from on high to add oxygen and bring out the flavor (daily 11:00-24:00, a block off the Ramblas, behind arcade at Carrer del Cardenal Casanyes 17, Metro: Liceu, tel. 933-023-084).

Family-run since 1870, **$$ Café Granja Viader** boasts about being the first dairy business to bottle and distribute milk in Spain. This quaint time capsule—specializing in baked and dairy treats, toasted sandwiches, and light meals—is ideal for a traditional breakfast. Or indulge your sweet tooth: Try a glass of *orxata* (or *horchata*—*chufa*-nut milk, summer only), *llet mallorquina* (Majorca-style milk with cinnamon, lemon, and sugar), *crema catalana* (crème brûlée, their specialty), or *suis* ("Swiss"—hot chocolate with a snow-cap of whipped cream). *Mel i mató* is fresh cheese with honey...very Catalan (Mon-Sat 9:00-13:00 & 17:00-21:00, closed Sun, a block off the Ramblas behind Betlem Church at Xuclà 4, Metro: Liceu, tel. 933-183-486).

$$ Biocenter, a soup-and-salad restaurant popular with local vegetarians, takes its cooking seriously (€8-10 week-

A Short, Sweet Walk

Here's a dessert walk in three stops—all within a three-minute walk of one another just off the Ramblas (Metro: Liceu). Start at the corner of Carrer de la Portaferrissa midway down the Ramblas. For the best atmosphere, begin your walk at about 18:00.

Torró: Walk down Carrer de la Portaferrissa to #8 (on the right). **Casa Colomina,** founded in 1908, specializes in homemade *torró* (*turrón* in Spanish)—nougat made with almond, honey, and sugar (€2.20 wrapped chunks on counter, daily 10:00-20:30). In summer, try the refreshing *orxata* drink (*horchata* in Spanish).

Churros con Chocolate: Continue down Carrer de la Portaferrissa, taking a right at Carrer Petritxol to #11 to the fun-loving **Granja La Pallaresa,** where you can dip greasy *churros* into cups of hot chocolate pudding for €4.50 (daily 9:00-13:00 & 16:00-21:00).

Chocolate: Continue down Carrer Petritxol to the square, Plaça del Pi, hook left through the two-part square, then left up Carrer del Pi to the corner of Carrer de la Portaferrissa. Founded in 1827, **Fargas,** a traditional chocolate shop, sells even little morsels by weight, so don't be shy (Mon-Sat 9:30-20:30, closed Sun).

day lunch specials include soup or salad and plate of the day, €15 dinner specials, otherwise €7-9 salads and €12-13 main dishes, Mon-Sat 13:00-23:00, Sun 13:00-16:00, 2 blocks off the Ramblas at Carrer del Pintor Fortuny 25, Metro: Liceu, tel. 933-014-583).

Try eating at **La Boqueria Market** at least once. It's ringed by colorful, good-value eateries and several good bars—many with enticing seafood options. Lots of stalls sell fun takeaway food—especially fruit salads and fresh-squeezed juices—ideal for **picnics** (Mon-Sat 8:00-20:00). Just to the right as you enter the market, **$$$ Pinotxo Bar** is a fun, if touristy, spot for coffee, breakfast (spinach *tortillas*), or tapas. Fun-loving Juan and his family are La Boqueria fixtures. Be careful—this place can get expensive (Mercat de la Boqueria 466, tel. 933-171-731, www.pinotxobar.com). **$$ Kiosko Universal** is popular for its great prices on wonderful fish dishes. As you enter the market from the Ramblas, it's all the way to the left. It's always packed, but less crowded before 12:30. If you see people waiting, go to the cashier to put your name on a list (€8-12 *platos del día* with different fresh-fish options, €8 mixed veggies, €10 mushroom stir-fries, tel. 933-178-286).

In the Barri Gòtic

In the atmospheric Gothic Quarter, you can choose between sit-down meals at restaurants or a string of tapas bars.

Restaurants

If you want to eat outdoors on a convivial, mellow square, **$$$ Café de l'Academia** is the place. They serve refined market-fresh Catalan cuisine. The candlelit, air-conditioned interior is rustic yet elegant, with soft jazz, flowers, and modern art. Reservations are smart (€10-15 first courses, €13-20 second courses, fixed-price lunch for €11.50 at the bar or €15 at a table, Mon-Fri 13:00-15:30 & 20:00-23:00, closed Sat-Sun, near the City Hall square, off Carrer de Jaume I, up Carrer de la Dagueria at Carrer dels Lledó 1, Metro: Jaume I, tel. 933-198-253).

$$$ Els Quatre Gats was once the haunt of the Modernista greats—including a teenaged Picasso, who first publicly displayed his art here, and architect Josep Puig i Cadafalch, who designed the building. Inspired by Paris' famous Le Chat Noir café/cabaret, Els Quatre Gats ("The Four Cats") celebrated all that was mod-

ern at the turn of the 20th century. You can snack or drink at the bar, or go into the back for a sit-down meal (€18 three-course lunch special Mon-Fri 13:00-16:00, €12-28 plates, daily 10:00-24:00, just steps off Avinguda del Portal de l'Angel at Carrer de Montsió 3, Metro: Catalunya, tel. 933-024-140).

$$$ Xaloc offers nicely presented gourmet tapas in a woody, modern, and spacious dining room, with fun energy, good service, and reasonable prices. The walls are covered with *Ibérica* hamhocks and wine bottles. They focus on home-style Catalan classics and serve only one top-quality ham. A gazpacho, plank of ham, *pa amb tomàquet,* and nice glass of wine make a terrific light meal (€3-8 tapas, €6-14 main dishes, open daily, drinks and cold tapas 11:00-23:00, kitchen open 13:00-17:00 & 19:00-23:00, a block toward the cathedral from Plaça de Sant Josep Oriol at Carrer de la Palla 13, Metro: Catalunya, tel. 933-011-990).

$$ Bar del Pi is a simple, hardworking bar serving good salads, sandwiches, and tapas. It has just a handful of tables on the most inviting little square in the Barri Gòtic (daily 9:00-23:00 except closed Tue in winter, Plaça de Sant Josep Oriol 1, Metro: Liceu, tel. 933-022-123).

$$$$ Restaurant Agut, around since 1924, features a comfortable, wood-paneled dining room that's modern and sophisticated, but still retains a slight bohemian air. The pictures lining the walls are by Catalan artists who are said to have exchanged their canvases for a meal. The menu includes tasty traditional Catalan food (€14 three-course weekday lunch special, €10-15 starters, €13-29 main dishes, Tue-Sat 13:30-16:00 & 20:30-23:30, Sun 13:30-16:00, closed Mon, just up from Carrer de la Mercè and the harbor at Carrer d'En Gignàs 16, Metro: Jaume I, tel. 933-151-709).

$$ La Crema Canela, a few steps above Plaça Reial, feels cozier than the restaurants on that atmospheric square,

Barcelona's Old City Restaurants

1. Taverna Basca Irati
2. Café Granja Viader
3. La Boqueria Market Eateries
4. Biocenter Veggie Restaurant
5. Café de l'Academia
6. Els Quatre Gats
7. Xaloc
8. Bar del Pi
9. Restaurant Agut
10. La Crema Canela
11. Carrer de la Mercè Tapas
12. Sagardi Euskal Taberna
13. El Xampanyet
14. Bar del Pla
15. Mercat Princesa Food Circus

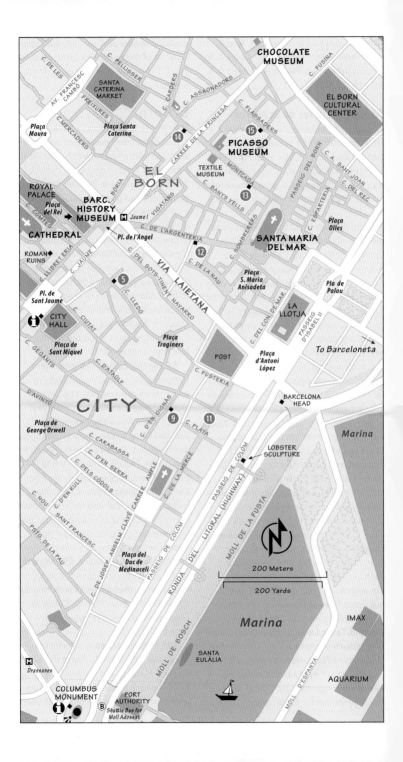

which are overrun with tourists. And it takes reservations (Mon-Thu 13:00-23:00, Fri-Sun until 23:30, Passatge de Madoz 6, tel. 933-182-744).

Tapas on Carrer de la Mercè

Carrer de la Mercè lets you experience a rare, unvarnished bit of old Barcelona with great *tascas*—colorful local $$ tapas bars. The neighborhood's dark, the regulars are rough-edged, and you'll get a glimpse of a crusty Barcelona from before the affluence hit.

From the bottom of the Ramblas (near the Columbus Monument, Metro: Drassanes), hike east along Carrer de Josep Anselm Clavé. When you reach Plaça de la Mercè, follow the small street (Carrer de la Mercè) that runs along the right side of the square's church. For a montage of edible memories, wander the next three or four blocks and consider these spots, stopping wherever looks most inviting. Most of these places close down around 23:00. For more refined bar-hopping, skip over to Carrer Ample and Carrer d'En Gignàs, inland streets parallel to Carrer de la Mercè.

Bar Celta (marked *la pulpería,* at #16) has less character than the others, but eases you into the scene with fried fish, octopus, and *patatas bravas,* all with Galician Ribeiro wine. Farther down at the corner (#28), **La Plata** keeps things wonderfully simple, serving extremely cheap plates of sardines (€3), little salads, and small glasses of keg wine (€1). **Tasca el Corral** (#17) serves mountain favorites from northern Spain by the half-*ración,* such as *queso de cabrales,* chorizo *al diablo,* and *cecina* (cured meat, like *jamón* but made from beef)—drink them with *sidra* (hard cider sold by the bottle-€6). **Sidrería Tasca La Socarrena** (#21) offers hard cider from Asturias in €6.50 bottles with *queso de cabrales* and chorizo. At the end of Carrer de la Mercè, **Cerveceria Vendimia** slings tasty clams and mussels (hearty *raciones* for €4-6 a plate). They don't do smaller portions, so order sparingly. Sit at the bar and point to what looks good. The house specialty, *pulpo* (octopus) is more expensive.

El Born

El Born (a.k.a. La Ribera) sparkles with eclectic and trendy as well as subdued and classy little restaurants hidden in the small lanes surrounding the Church of Santa Maria del Mar. Wander around for 15 minutes and pick the place that tickles your gastronomic fancy. Consider starting off your evening with a glass of fine wine at one of the *enotecas* on the square facing the Church of Santa Maria del Mar. Most of my picks are either on Carrer de l'Argenteria (stretching from the church to the cathedral area) or on or near Carrer de Montcada. Many restaurants and shops in this area are, like the nearby Picasso Museum, closed on Mondays. Use Metro: Jaume I.

$$ Sagardi Euskal Taberna offers tempting *pintxos* and *montaditos* (small open-faced sandwiches) at €2 each—along its huge bar. Ask for a plate and graze (just take whatever looks good). You can sit on the square with your plunder for about 20 percent extra. Wash it down with Txakolí, a Basque white wine poured from the spout of a huge wooden barrel into a glass as you watch. Study the two price lists—bar and terrace—posted at the bar (daily 12:00-24:00, Carrer de l'Argenteria 62-64, tel. 933-199-993). Hiding behind the tapas bar is the mod and minimalist restaurant, **$$$ Sagardi** (€11-24 first courses for two, €20-28 second courses, plan on €50 for dinner; daily 13:00-16:00 & 20:00-24:00, Carrer de l'Argenteria 62, tel. 933-199-993, www. sagardi.com).

$$$ El Xampanyet, a colorful family-run bar with a fun-loving staff (Juan Carlos, his mom, and the man who may be his father), specializes in tapas and anchovies. Don't be put off by the sea-

Catalan Cuisine

Like its culture and language, Catalan food is a fusion of styles and influences. Cod, hake, tuna, squid, and anchovies appear on many menus, and you'll see Catalan favorites such as *fideuà,* a thin, flavor-infused noodle served with seafood—a kind of Catalan paella—and *arròs negre,* black rice cooked in squid ink. *Pa amb tomàquet* is the classic Catalan way to eat your bread—toasted white bread with olive oil, tomato, and a pinch of salt. It's often served with tapas and used to make sandwiches. As everywhere in Spain, Catalan cooks love garlic and olive oil—many dishes are soaked in both.

Catalan cuisine can be heavy for Americans more accustomed to salads, fruits, and grains. A few perfectly good vegetarian and lighter options exist, but you'll have to seek them out. The secret to getting your veggies at restaurants is to order two courses, because the first course generally has a green option. Resist the cheese-and-ham appetizers and instead choose first-course menu items such as creamed vegetable soup, *parrillada de verduras* (sautéed vegetables), or *ensalada mixta.* (Spaniards rarely eat only a salad, so salads tend to be small and simple—just iceberg lettuce, tomatoes, and maybe olives and tuna.)

While the famous cured *jamón* (ham) is not as typically Catalan as it is Spanish, you'll still find lots of it in Catalunya. Another popular Spanish dish is the empanada—a pastry turnover filled with seasoned meat and vegetables. The cheapest meal is a simple *bocadillo de jamón* (ham sandwich on a baguette), sold virtually everywhere.

food from a tin: Catalans like it this way. A *sortido* (assorted plate) of *carne* (meat) or *pescado* (fish) with *pa amb tomàquet* makes for a fun meal. It's filled with tourists during the day, but is a local favorite after dark. The scene is great, but it can be tough without Spanish skills. Plan on spending €25 for a meal with wine (same price at bar or table, Tue-Sat 12:00-15:30 & 19:00-23:00, Sun 12:00-16:00, closed Mon, a half-block beyond the Picasso Museum at Carrer de Montcada 22, tel. 933-197-003).

Local favorite **$$$ Bar del Pla** is near the Picasso Museum but far enough away from the tourist crowds. Overlooking a tiny crossroads next to Barcelona's oldest church, this brightly lit, classic diner serves traditional Catalan dishes, *raciones,* and tapas. Crispy beef with foie gras (€6) is a highlight. The local IPA on tap is a change of pace from regular Spanish beer. Prices are the same at the bar or at a table, but eating at the bar puts you in the middle of a great scene (€6-15 tapas, Mon-Sat 12:00-23:00, closed Sun; with your back to the Picasso Museum, head right two blocks past Carrer de la Princesa to Carrer de Montcada 2; tel. 932-683-003, www.bardelpla.cat).

Corporate venture **$$ Mercat Princesa Food Circus** fills an old palace with a hive of trendy new bars and eateries sharing a central zone of tables. The energy is great, as is the variety: oysters, sushi, paella, and pizza. It's fun to simply explore, but at busy times, expect to wait in successive slow-moving lines (daily 12:30-24:00, behind the Picasso Museum, Carrer dels Flassaders 21, tel. 932-681-518, www.mercatprincesa.com).

In the Eixample

The people-packed boulevards of the Eixample are lined with appetizing eateries featuring breezy outdoor seating. For the best variety, walk down Rambla de Catalunya.

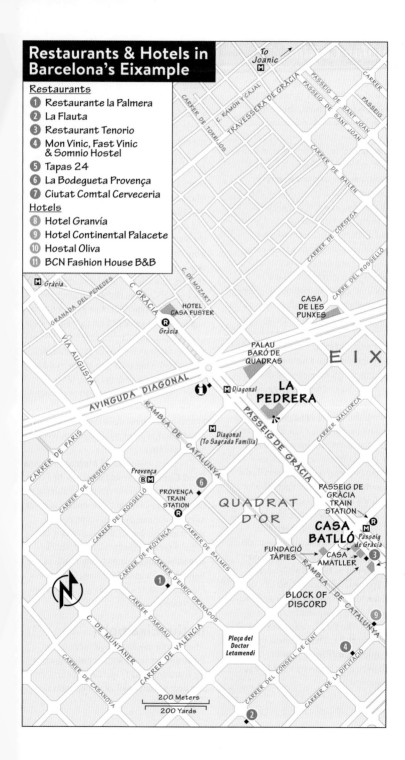

Restaurants & Hotels in Barcelona's Eixample

Restaurants
1. Restaurante la Palmera
2. La Flauta
3. Restaurant Tenorio
4. Mon Vinic, Fast Vinic & Somnio Hostel
5. Tapas 24
6. La Bodegueta Provença
7. Ciutat Comtal Cerveceria

Hotels
8. Hotel Granvía
9. Hotel Continental Palacete
10. Hostal Oliva
11. BCN Fashion House B&B

To Joanic

CARRER DE TORRIJOS

C. RAMÓN Y CAJAL

TRAVESSERA DE GRÀCIA

PASSEIG DE GRÀCIA

PASSEIG DE SANT JOAN

PASSEIG DE SANT JOAN

PASSEIG

CARRER

CARRER DE BAILEN

CARRER DE CÓRSEGA

CARRER DEL ROSSELLÓ

Gràcia

GRANADA DEL PENEDÉS

C. GRÀCIA

C. DE MOZART

CASA DE LES PUNXES

VIA AUGUSTA

HOTEL CASA FUSTER

Gràcia

PALAU BARÓ DE QUADRAS

EIX

AVINGUDA DIAGONAL

RAMBLA DE CATALUNYA

Diagonal

LA PEDRERA

PASSEIG DE GRÀCIA

CARRER DE PARÍS

Diagonal (To Sagrada Família)

CARRER MALLORCA

CARRER DE CÓRSEGA

Provença

CARRER DEL ROSSELLÓ

6

PROVENÇA TRAIN STATION

QUADRAT D'OR

PASSEIG DE GRÀCIA TRAIN STATION

CASA BATLLÓ

Passeig de Gràcia

CARRER DE PROVENÇA

CARRER DE BALMES

FUNDACIÓ TÀPIES

CASA AMATLLER

3

1

CARRER D'ENRIC GRANADOS

BLOCK OF DISCORD

RAMBLA DE CATALUNYA

9

C. DE MUNTANER

CARRER D'ARIBAU

CARRER DE VALÈNCIA

Plaça del Doctor Letamendi

CARRER DEL CONSELL DE CENT

4

CARRER DE CASANOVA

200 Meters

200 Yards

CARRER DE LA DIPUTACIÓ

2

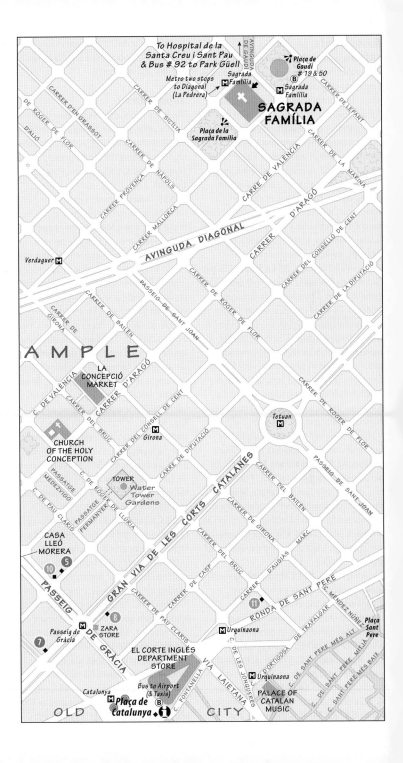

Restaurants

$$$ Restaurante la Palmera serves a mix of Catalan, Mediterranean, and French cuisine in an elegant room with bottle-lined walls. This untouristy place offers great food, service, and value. They have three zones: the classic main room, a more forgettable adjacent room, and a few outdoor tables. I like the classic room. Reservations are smart (€12-19 plates, creative €23 six-plate *degustation* lunch—also available during dinner Mon-Wed, open Mon-Sat 13:00-15:45 & 20:00-23:15, closed Sun, Carrer d'Enric Granados 57, at the corner with Carrer Mallorca, Metro: Provença, tel. 934-532-338, www.lapalmera.cat).

Fresh and modern, **$$ La Flauta** fills two floors with enthusiastic eaters (I prefer the ground floor). The fun, no-stress menu features €5 small plates, creative €5 *flauta* sandwiches, and a €13 three-course lunch deal including a drink. Consider the list of *tapas del día.* Order high on the menu for a satisfying, moderately priced meal (Mon-Sat 7:00-24:00, closed Sun, upbeat and helpful staff, no reservations, just off Carrer de la Diputació at Carrer d'Aribau 23, Metro: Universitat, tel. 933-237-038).

Hidden between the famous buildings and clamoring tourists in the Block of Discord, **$$ Restaurant Tenorio** is an actual restaurant (no tapas!). This modern, dressy, and spacious place serves a mix of international and Catalan dishes, concocted in the bustling open kitchen at the back (€10 salads, €15 plates, Passeig de Gràcia 37, Metro: Passeig de Gràcia, tel. 932-720-592).

Sleek, trendy **$$$$ Mon Vinic** is evangelical about local wines and offers an amazing eating experience. Their renowned chef creates made-to-order Mediterranean dishes to complement the wine (€12-18 starters—designed to share, €8 creative tapas, €25 main dishes with vegetables and potatoes, €20 fixed-price lunch, Diputació 249, Metro: Passeig de Gràcia, tel. 932-726-187, www.monvinic. com). **$$ Fast Vinic** is the associated fast-food and sandwich bar next door (Mon-Sat 12:00-24:00, closed Sun, Diputació 251, tel. 934-873-241).

Tapas Bars

Trendy and touristic tapas bars in the Eixample offer a cheery welcome. These are particularly handy to Plaça de Catalunya and the Passeig de Gràcia artery (closest Metro stops: Catalunya and Passeig de Gràcia).

$$$ Tapas 24 makes eating fun. This local favorite, with a few street tables, fills a spot a few steps below street level with happy energy, friendly service, funky decor (white counters and mirrors), and good yet pricey tapas. Along with daily specials, the menu has all the typical standbys and quirky inventions (such as the tiny McFoie burger—order it well-done if you don't want it to moo on your plate). The owner, Carles Abellan, is one of Barcelona's hot chefs; although his famous fare is pricey, you can enjoy it without going broke. Prices are the same whether you dine at the bar, a table, or outside. Figure about €50 for lunch for two with wine. Come early or wait; no reservations are taken (€4-14 tapas, €12-18 plates, Mon-Sat 9:00-24:00, closed Sun, just off Passeig de Gràcia at Carrer de la Diputació 269, tel. 934-880-977, www.carlesabellan.es/ restaurantes-tapas-24).

$$ Ciutat Comtal Cerveceria brags that it serves the best *montaditos* (€2-4 little open-faced sandwiches) and beers in Barcelona. It's an Eixample favorite, with an elegant bar and tables plus good seating for people-watching out on the Rambla de Catalunya. It's packed 21:00-23:00, when you'll need to put your name on a wait list. The list of tapas and *montaditos* is easy and fun, with great variety (including daily specials, most tapas around €4-10, daily 8:00-24:00, facing the intersection of Gran Via de les Corts Catalanes and Rambla de Catalunya at Rambla de Catalunya 18, tel. 933-181-997).

SLEEPING

Although Barcelona is Spain's most expensive city, it still has reasonably priced rooms. Book well in advance. Cheap places are more crowded in summer. Business-class hotels fill up in winter and offer discounts in summer (and on weekends)—when you can often get modern comfort in a centrally located business hotel for about the same price (€100) as you'll pay for ramshackle charm.

Near Plaça de Catalunya

These hotels are on big streets within two blocks of Barcelona's exuberant central square, where the Old City meets the Eixample. Expect shiny reception areas, modern bedrooms, and air-conditioning. As business-class hotels, they have hard-to-pin-down prices that fluctuate with demand. I've listed the average rate you'll pay. Most of these are located between two Metro stops: Catalunya and Universitat; if arriving by Aerobus, note that the bus stops at both places. For hotels on busy Carrer Pelai, request a quieter room in back.

$$$$ Hotel Catalonia Plaça Catalunya has four stars, an elegant old entryway with a modern reception area, splashy public

spaces, slick marble and hardwood floors, 140 comfortable but simple rooms, and a garden courtyard with a pool a world away from the big-city noise (Db-€200 but can swing much higher or lower with demand, extra bed-€38, breakfast-€19, air-con, elevator, a half-block off Plaça de Catalunya at Carrer de Bergara 11, Metro: Catalunya, tel. 933-015-151, www.hoteles-catalonia. com, catalunya@hoteles-catalonia.es).

$$ Hotel Denit is a small, stylish, 36-room hotel on a pedestrian street two blocks off Plaça de Catalunya. It's chic, minimalist, and fun: Guidebook tips decorate the halls, and the rooms are sized like T-shirts ("small" Sb-€79-109, "medium" Db-€99-119, "large" Db-€119-144, "XL" Db-€149-164, more on Fri-Sat, includes breakfast when you book directly with the hotel, air-con, elevator, Carrer d'Estruc 24, Metro: Catalunya, tel. 935-454-000, www. denit.com, info@denit.com).

$$$ Hotel Inglaterra has 60 rooms, a more traditional style, a rooftop terrace, and mini swimming pool (Sb-€119, Db-€139, higher rates Fri-Sat, €20-40 more for bigger "deluxe" rooms, breakfast €15, air-con, elevator, Carrer de Pelai 14, Metro: Universitat, tel. 935-051-100, www. hotel-inglaterra.com, reservas@hotel-inglaterra.com).

$$$ Hotel Reding, on a quiet street a 10-minute walk west of the Ramblas and Plaça de Catalunya action, is slick and sleek, renting 44 mod rooms at a reasonable price (Db-€130, €15-30 more for deluxe rooms, extra bed-€33, €15 breakfast, prices go up during trade fairs, air-con, elevator, Carrer de Gravina 5, Metro: Universitat, tel. 934-121-097, www. hotelreding.com, recepcion@hotelreding.com).

$$$ Hotel Lleó (YAH-oh) is well-run, with 92 big, bright, and comfortable rooms; a great breakfast room; a generous lounge; and a small rooftop pool (Db-€140 but varies with demand, extra bed-about €30, breakfast-€13, air-con, elevator, Carrer de Pelai 22, midway between

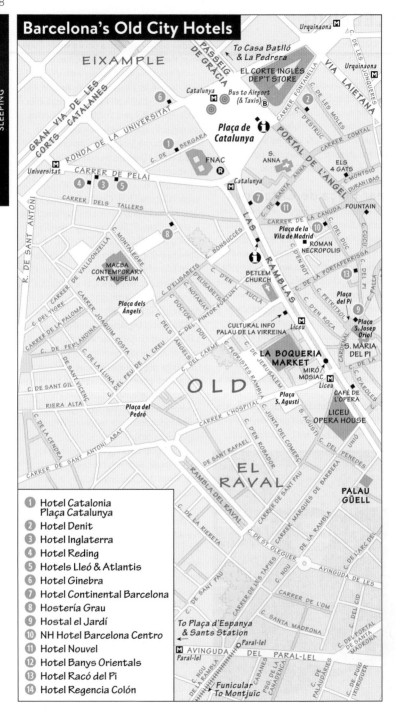

Barcelona's Old City Hotels

① Hotel Catalonia
   Plaça Catalunya
② Hotel Denit
③ Hotel Inglaterra
④ Hotel Reding
⑤ Hotels Lleó & Atlantis
⑥ Hotel Ginebra
⑦ Hotel Continental Barcelona
⑧ Hostería Grau
⑨ Hostal el Jardí
⑩ NH Hotel Barcelona Centro
⑪ Hotel Nouvel
⑫ Hotel Banys Orientals
⑬ Hotel Racó del Pi
⑭ Hotel Regencia Colón

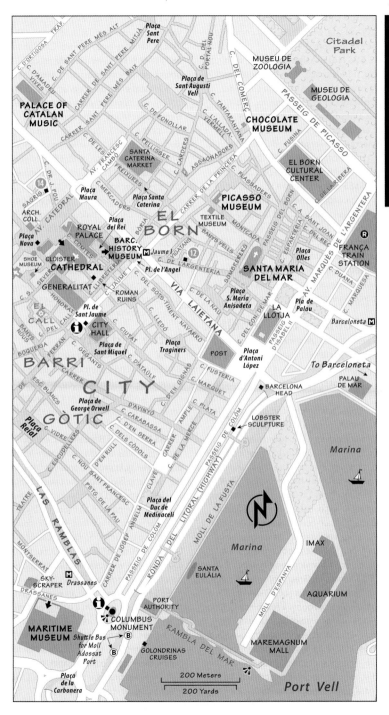

Citadel Park

MUSEU DE ZOOLOGIA

MUSEU DE GEOLOGIA

PASSEIG DE PICASSO

PALACE OF CATALAN MUSIC

Plaça Sant Pere

Plaça de Sant Agustí Vell

CHOCOLATE MUSEUM

SANTA CATERINA MARKET

EL BORN CULTURAL CENTER

Plaça Maura

Plaça Santa Caterina

EL BORN

PICASSO MUSEUM

TEXTILE MUSEUM

Plaça del Rei

ARCH. COLL.

ROYAL PALACE

BARC. HISTORY MUSEUM

Jaume I

SANTA MARIA DEL MAR

FRANÇA TRAIN STATION

Plaça Nova

Plaça Olles

SHOE MUSEUM

CLOISTER

CATHEDRAL

Pl. de l'Angel

GENERALITAT

ROMAN RUINS

VIA LAIETANA

Plaça S. Maria Anisadeta

LA LLOTJA

Pla de Palau

Barceloneta

EL CALL

Pl. de Sant Jaume

CITY HALL

Plaça de Sant Miquel

Plaça Traginers

POST

Plaça d'Antoni López

To Barceloneta

BARRI

CITY

GÒTIC

Plaça Retal

Plaça de George Orwell

BARCELONA HEAD

PALAU DE MAR

LOBSTER SCULPTURE

Marina

Plaça del Duc de Medinaceli

Marina

IMAX

LAS RAMBLAS

SANTA EULÀLIA

AQUARIUM

SKY-SCRAPER

Drassanes

PORT AUTHORITY

MARITIME MUSEUM

Shuttle Bus for Moll Adossat Port

COLUMBUS MONUMENT

GOLONDRINAS CRUISES

RAMBLA DEL MAR

MAREMAGNUM MALL

Plaça de la Carbonera

200 Meters
200 Yards

Port Vell

Metros: Universitat and Catalunya, tel. 933-181-312, www.hotel-lleo.com, info@hotel-lleo.com).

$$$ **Hotel Atlantis** is solid, with 50 big, nondescript, modern rooms and fair prices for the location (Sb-€80, Db-€160, check website for deals, includes breakfast, air-con, elevator, Carrer de Pelai 20, midway between Metros: Universitat and Catalunya, tel. 933-189-012, www.hotelatlantis-bcn.com, inf@hotelatlantis-bcn.com).

$$$$ **Hotel Ginebra** is a modern, fresh version of the old-school *pension* in a classic, well-located building at the corner of Plaça Catalunya (Sb-€50-120, Db-€180, breakfast-€8, laundry, air-con, elevator, Rambla de Catalunya 1, Metro: Catalunya, tel. 932-502-017, www.barcelonahotelginebra.com, info@barcelonahotelginebra.com).

On or near the Ramblas

These places are generally family-run, with ad-lib furnishings, more character, and lower prices.

$$$ **Hotel Continental Barcelona**, in a building overlooking the top of the Ramblas, has 40 comfortable but faded rooms that come with clashing carpets and wallpaper. Choose between your own little Ramblas-view balcony or a quieter back room. The free breakfast and all-day snack-and-drink bar are a plus (Sb-€110, Db-€130, twin Db-€140, Db with Ramblas balcony-€150, extra bed-€40/adult or €20/child, air-con, elevator, quiet terrace, Ramblas 138, Metro: Catalunya, tel. 933-012-570, www.hotelcontinental.com, barcelona@hotelcontinental.com).

$$ **Hostería Grau** is homey, family-run, and eco-conscious (LEED-certified). It has 24 cheery rooms a few blocks off the Ramblas in the colorful university district—but double-glazed windows keep it quiet (Db-€115-135, €20 more for superior Db, €50 more for family room, 5 percent discount for booking directly, breakfast extra, strict cancellation policy, air-con,

elevator, some rooms with balcony, 200 yards up Carrer dels Tallers from the Ramblas at Ramelleres 27, Metro: Catalunya, tel. 933-018-135, www.hostalgrau.com, bookgreen@hostalgrau.com, Monica).

$ **Hostal el Jardí** offers 40 tight, plain, comfy rooms on a breezy square in the Barri Gòtic. Many of the rooms come with petite balconies (for an extra charge) and enjoy an almost Parisian ambience. Book well in advance, as this family-run place has an avid following (small interior Db-€75, nicer interior Db-€90, outer Db with balcony or twin with window-€95, large outer Db with balcony or square-view terrace-€110, no charge for extra bed, breakfast-€6, air-con, elevator, some stairs, halfway between Ramblas and cathedral at Plaça Sant Josep Oriol 1, Metro: Liceu, tel. 933-015-900, www.eljardi-barcelona.com, reservations@eljardi-barcelona.com).

In the Old City

These accommodations are buried in Barcelona's Old City, mostly in the Barri Gòtic. The Catalunya, Liceu, and Jaume I Metro stops flank this tight tangle of lanes; I've noted which stops are best for each.

$$$ **NH Hotel Barcelona Centro**, with 156 rooms and tasteful chain-hotel predictability, is professional yet friendly, buried in the Barri Gòtic just three blocks off the Ramblas (Db-€160, but rates fluctuate with demand, €25 more for bigger superior rooms, breakfast-€15, air-con, elevator, pay guest computer, Carrer del Duc 15, Metro: Catalunya or Liceu, tel. 932-703-410, www.nh-hotels.com, barcelonacentro@nh-hotels.com).

$$$ **Hotel Nouvel**, in an elegant, Victorian-style building on a handy pedestrian street, offers more character than the others, boasting royal lounges and 78 comfy rooms (Sb-€75-100, Db-€110-165, online deals can be far cheaper, extra bed-€35, includes breakfast, €20 deposit for TV remote, air-con, elevator, pay Wi-Fi,

Carrer de Santa Anna 20, Metro: Catalunya, tel. 933-018-274, www.hotelnouvel.com, info@hotelnouvel.com).

$$$ Hotel Banys Orientals, a modern, boutique place, has refreshingly straightforward prices. Its 43 restful rooms are located in El Born on a pedestrianized street between the cathedral and Church of Santa Maria del Mar (Sb-€96, Db-€135, breakfast-€14, air-con, Carrer de l'Argenteria 37, 50 yards from Metro: Jaume I, tel. 932-688-460, www.hotelbanysorientals.com, reservas@hotelbanysorientals.com). They also run the adjacent, recommended El Senyor Parellada restaurant.

$$$$ Hotel Racó del Pi, part of the H10 hotel chain, is a quality, professional place with generous public spaces and 37 modern, bright, quiet rooms. It's located on a wonderful pedestrian street immersed in the Barri Gòtic (Db-often around €180, cheaper for booking "nonrefundable" online, breakfast-€16, air-con, around the corner from Plaça del Pi at Carrer del Pi 7, 3-minute walk from Metro: Liceu, tel. 933-426-190, www.h10hotels.com, h10.raco.delpi@h10.es).

$$ Hotel Regencia Colón, in a handy location one block in front of the cathedral, offers 50 slightly older but solid, classy, and well-priced rooms (Db-€120-155 but fluctuates with demand, extra bed-€37, breakfast-€13, air-con, elevator, Carrer dels Sagristans 13, Metro: Jaume I, tel. 933-189-858, www.hotelregenciacolon.com, info@hotelregenciacolon.com).

In the Eixample

For an uptown neighborhood, sleep in the Eixample, a 10-minute walk from the Ramblas action. Most of these places use the Passeig de Gràcia or Catalunya Metro stops. Because these stations are so huge—especially Passeig de Gràcia, which sprawls underground for a few blocks—study the maps posted in the station to establish which exit you want before surfacing.

$$$$ Hotel Granvía, filling a palatial, brightly renovated 1870s mansion, offers a large, peaceful sun patio, several comfortable common areas, and 58 spacious modern rooms (Sb-€75-185, Db-€90-180, superior Db-€105-225, family room-€150-260, breakfast €14, air-con, elevator, Gran Via de les Corts Catalanes 642, Metro: Passeig de Gràcia, tel. 933-181-900, www.hotelgranvia.com, hgranvia@nnhotels.com).

$$$$ Hotel Continental Palacete, with 22 small rooms, fills a 100-year-old chandeliered mansion. With flowery wallpaper and ornately gilded stucco, it's more gaudy than Gaudí, but it's also friendly, quiet, and well-located. Guests have unlimited access to the outdoor terrace and the fruit, veggie, and drink buffet (Sb-€114, Db-€170, €35-45 more for bigger and brighter view rooms, extra bed-€55/adult or €40/child, includes breakfast, air-con, 2 blocks northwest of Plaça de Catalunya at corner of Rambla de Catalunya and Carrer de la Diputació, Rambla de Catalunya 30, Metro: Passeig de Gràcia, tel. 934-457-657, www.hotelcontinental.com, palacete@hotelcontinental.com).

$$ Hostal Oliva, family-run with care, has 15 spartan but bright and high-ceilinged rooms and no breakfast or public spaces. It's on the fourth floor of a classic old Eixample building in a perfect location, just a couple of blocks above Plaça de Catalunya (S-€41, Sb-€55, D-€71, Db-€95, elevator, corner of Passeig de Gràcia and Carrer de la Diputació, Passeig de Gràcia 32, Metro: Passeig de Gràcia, tel. 934-880-162, www.hostaloliva.com, hostaloliva@lasguias.com).

$$ BCN Fashion House B&B has 10 basic rooms, a peaceful lounge, and a leafy backyard terrace on the first floor of a nondescript old building (S-€36-56, D-€56-83, bigger "veranda" D-€73-93, Db-€90-125, 2-night minimum, includes breakfast, between Carrer d'Ausiàs Marc and Ronda de Sant Pere at Carrer del Bruc

13, just steps from Metro: Urquinaona, mobile 637-904-044, www.bcnfashion house.com, info@bcnfashionhouse.com).

Hostels

$ Somnio Hostel, an innovative smaller place, has nine simple, clean rooms (S-€49-75, D-€57-84, Db-€65-99, air-con, self-service laundry, Carrer de la Diputació 251, second floor, Metro: Passeig de Gràcia, tel. 932-725-308, www. somniohostels.com, info@somniohostels. com). They have a second location that's five blocks farther out.

TRANSPORTATION

Getting Around Barcelona

Barcelona's Metro and bus system is run by **TMB**—Transports Metropolitans de Barcelona. Ask for TMB's excellent Metro/bus map at the TI, larger stations, or the TMB information counter in the Sants Train Station. Metro maps are often included on tourist maps as well (tel. 902-075-027, www.tmb.cat).

By Metro

The city's Metro, among Europe's best, connects just about every place you'll visit. A **single-ride ticket** (*bitllet senzill*) costs €2.15. The **T10 Card** is a great deal—€9.95 gives you 10 rides (cutting the per-ride cost by more than half). The card is shareable, even by companions traveling with you the entire ride (insert the card in the machine once per passenger). The back of your T10 Card will show how many trips were taken, with the time and date of each ride. One "ride" covers you for 1.25 hours of unlimited use on all Metro and local bus lines, as well as local rides on the RENFE and Rodalies de Catalunya train lines (including rides to the airport and train station) and the suburban FGC trains. Transfers made within your 1.25-hour limit are not counted as a new ride, but you still must revalidate your T10 Card whenever you transfer.

Multiday **"Hola BCN!" passes** are also available. Machines at the Metro entrance have English instructions and sell all types of tickets (€14/2 days, €20.50/3 days, €26.50/4 days, €32/5 days; most machines accept credit/debit cards as well as cash).

Enter the Metro by inserting your ticket into the turnstile (with the arrow pointing in), then reclaim it. Follow signs for your line and direction. On board, most trains have handy lighted displays that indicate upcoming stops. Because the lines cross one another multiple times, there can be several ways to make any one journey. (Keep a general map with you—especially if you're transferring.) Hang onto your ticket until you have exited the subway. You don't need the ticket to exit, but inspectors occasionally ask to see it. When riding the Metro, watch your valuables.

Barcelona has several color-coded lines. Most useful for tourists and pickpockets is the **L3 (green)** line, with handy city-center stops:

Sants Estació—Main train station

Espanya—Plaça d'Espanya, with access to the lower part of Montjuïc and trains to Montserrat

Paral-lel—Funicular to the top of Montjuïc

Drassanes—Bottom of the Ramblas, near Maritime Museum and Maremagnum mall

Liceu—Middle of the Ramblas, near the heart of the Barri Gòtic and cathedral

Plaça de Catalunya—Top of the Ramblas and main square with TI, airport bus, and lots of transportation connections

Passeig de Gràcia—Classy Eixample street at the Block of Discord; also connection to L2 (purple) line to Sagrada Família and L4 (yellow) line (described below)

Diagonal—Gaudí's La Pedrera

The **L4 (yellow)** line, which crosses the L3 (green) line at Passeig de Gràcia, is also useful. Helpful stops include **Joanic** (bus

#116 to Park Güell), **Jaume I** (between the Barri Gòtic/cathedral and El Born/Picasso Museum), and **Barceloneta** (at the south end of El Born, near the harbor action).

By Bus

Given the excellent Metro service, it's unlikely you'll spend much time on buses. Buses are useful for reaching Park Güell, connecting the sights on Montjuïc, and getting to the beach (also €2.15, covered by T10 Card, insert ticket in machine behind driver).

Also consider using the hop-on, hop-off Bus Turístic for transportation; it's far pricier than public transit, but it stops at the main sights (see page 336).

By Taxi

Barcelona is one of Europe's best taxi towns (and Uber is available). Taxis are plentiful and honest. The light on top shows which tariff they're charging; a **green light** on the roof indicates that a taxi is available. **Cab rates** are reasonable (€2.10 drop charge, about €1/kilometer, these "*Tarif 2*" rates are in effect 8:00-20:00, pay higher "*Tarif 1*" rates off-hours, €2.10 surcharge to/from train station, €3.10 surcharge for airport or cruise port). Figure €10 from Ramblas to Sants Station.

Arriving and Departing
By Plane

Most international flights arrive at **El Prat de Llobregat Airport,** eight miles southwest of town. Some budget airlines, including Ryanair, fly into **Girona-Costa Brava Airport,** 60 miles north of Barcelona near Girona.

EL PRAT DE LLOBREGAT AIRPORT

Barcelona's **El Prat de Llobregat Airport** is eight miles southwest of town (airport code: BCN, info tel. 913-211-000, www.aena-aeropuertos.es). Its two large terminals are linked by shuttle buses. **Terminal 1** serves Air France, Air Europa, American, British Airways, Delta, Iberia, Lufthansa,

United, US Airways, Vueling, and others. EasyJet and minor airlines use the older **Terminal 2,** which is divided into sections A, B, and C.

Terminal 1 and the bigger sections of Terminal 2 (A and B) each have a post office, a pharmacy, a left-luggage office, plenty of good cafeterias in the gate areas, and ATMs—use the bank-affiliated ATMs in the arrivals hall.

Getting Downtown: To reach central Barcelona cheaply and quickly, take the bus or train (about 30 minutes on either).

The **Aerobus** (#A1 and #A2, corresponding with Terminals 1 and 2) stops immediately outside the arrivals lobby of both terminals (and in each section of Terminal 2). In about 30 minutes, it takes you downtown, where it makes several stops, including Plaça d'Espanya and Plaça de Catalunya—near many of my recommended hotels (departs every 5 minutes, from airport 6:00-1:00 in the morning, from downtown 5:30-24:15, €5.90 one-way, €10.20 round-trip, buy ticket from machine or from driver, tel. 934-156-020, www.aerobusbcn.com).

The **RENFE train** (on the "R2 Nord" Rodalies line) leaves from Terminal 2 and involves more walking. Head up the escalators and down the long orange-roofed skybridge to reach the station (2/hour at about :08 and :38 past the hour, 20 minutes to Sants Station, 25 minutes to Passeig de Gràcia Station—near Plaça de Catalunya and many recommended hotels, 30 minutes to França Station; €4.10 or covered by T10 Card). If you are arriving or departing from Terminal 1, you will have to use the airport shuttle bus to connect with the train station, so leave extra time.

A **taxi** between the airport and downtown costs about €35 (including €3.10 airport supplement). For good service, you can round up to the next euro on the fare—but keep in mind that the Spanish don't tip cabbies.

Barcelona's Public Transportation

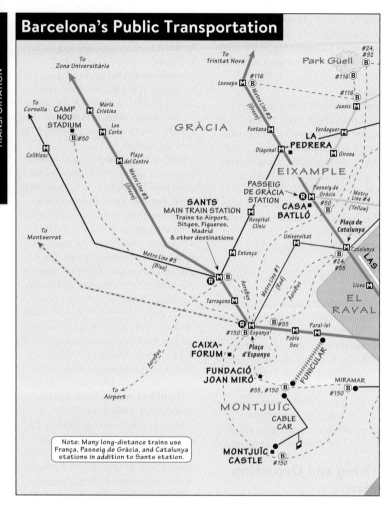

To Zona Universitària
To Trinitat Nova
Park Güell
#24, #92

Lesseps Ⓜ Ⓑ
#116 Ⓑ
#116 Ⓑ
Joanic Ⓜ

To Cornella
CAMP NOU STADIUM
Ⓑ#50
Maria Cristina Ⓜ
Les Corts
Fontana Ⓜ
LA PEDRERA
Verdaguer Ⓜ

GRÀCIA
Diagonal Ⓜ
Girona Ⓜ

Collblanc Ⓜ
Plaça del Centre Ⓜ
EIXAMPLE

To Montserrat
Metro Line #5 (Green)
PASSEIG DE GRÀCIA STATION
Passeig de Gràcia
Metro Line #4 (Yellow)

SANTS MAIN TRAIN STATION
Trains to Airport, Sitges, Figueres, Madrid & other destinations
CASA BATLLÓ
Ⓑ#50

Hospital Clínic Ⓜ
Plaça de Catalunya

Metro Line #5 (Blue)
Entença Ⓜ
Universitat Ⓜ
Catalunya Ⓜ
LAS

Ⓡ Ⓜ Ⓑ
AeroBus
Metro Line #1 (Red)
#24, #55

Tarragona Ⓜ
AeroBus
Liceu Ⓜ

EL RAVAL

Ⓡ Ⓜ Ⓑ #55
Paral·lel Ⓜ
#150 Ⓑ Espanya
Poble Sec

CAIXA-FORUM ■
Plaça d'Espanya

FUNICULAR

FUNDACIÓ JOAN MIRÓ ■
#55, #150 Ⓑ
MIRAMAR
#150 Ⓑ

To Airport
MONTJUÏC
CABLE CAR

Note: Many long-distance trains use França, Passeig de Gràcia, and Catalunya stations in addition to Sants station.

MONTJUÏC CASTLE ■ Ⓑ
#150

GIRONA-COSTA BRAVA AIRPORT

Some budget airlines, including Ryanair, use **Girona-Costa Brava Airport,** located 60 miles north of Barcelona near Girona (airport code: GRO, tel. 972-186-600, www.aena-aeropuertos.es). Ryanair runs a **bus,** operated by Sagalés, to the Barcelona Nord bus station (€16, departs airport about 20-25 minutes after each arriving flight, 1.5 hours, tel. 902-361-550, www.sagales.com). You can also take a Sagalés bus (hourly, 25 minutes, €2.75) or a taxi (€25) to the town of Girona, then catch a train to Barcelona (at least hourly, 1.5 hours, €15-20). A taxi between the Girona airport and Barcelona costs at least €120.

By Train

Virtually all trains arrive at Barcelona's Sants Train Station, west of the Old City. AVE trains from Madrid go only to Sants Station. But many trains also pass through other stations en route, such as França Station (between the El Born and Barceloneta neighborhoods), or the downtown Passeig de Gràcia or Plaça de Catalunya

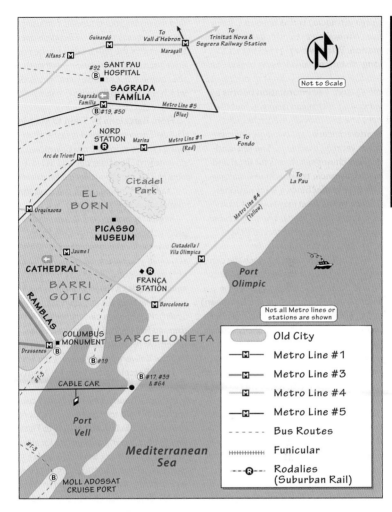

**Map labels:**

Guinardó · To Vall d'Hebron · To Trinitat Nova & Segrera Railway Station

Alfans X · Maragall

#92 SANT PAU HOSPITAL

Sagrada Família · SAGRADA FAMÍLIA

#19, #50 · Metro Line #5 (Blue)

Not to Scale

NORD STATION · Marina · Metro Line #1 (Red) · To Fondo

Arc de Triomf

Citadel Park

To La Pau

EL BORN · Urquinaona

Metro Line #4 (Yellow)

PICASSO MUSEUM

Jaume I · Ciutadella / Vila Olímpica

CATHEDRAL · FRANÇA STATION

BARRI GÒTIC · Port Olímpic

RAMBLAS · Barceloneta

COLUMBUS MONUMENT · BARCELONETA

Drassenes · #19

#T-3

CABLE CAR · #17, #39 & #64

Port Vell

Mediterranean Sea

#T-3

MOLL ADOSSAT CRUISE PORT

Not all Metro lines or stations are shown

Legend:
- Old City
- —Ⓜ— Metro Line #1
- —Ⓜ— Metro Line #3
- —Ⓜ— Metro Line #4
- —Ⓜ— Metro Line #5
- - - - - - Bus Routes
- ꟷꟷꟷꟷ Funicular
- ╍╍Ⓡ╍╍ Rodalies (Suburban Rail)

---

stations (which are also Metro stops—and close to most of my recommended hotels). Ask the conductor where your train stops and get off at the station most convenient to your hotel.

SANTS TRAIN STATION

Barcelona's main **Sants Train Station** is vast and sprawling, but manageable. In the large lobby area under the upper tracks, you'll find a TI, ATMs, handy shops and eateries, car-rental kiosks, and, in the side concourse, a classy, quiet Sala Club lounge for travelers with first-class reservations (TV, free drinks, coffee bar). Sants is the only Barcelona station with **luggage storage** (big bag-€5.20/day, requires security check, daily 5:30-23:00, follow signs to *consigna*, at far end of hallway from tracks 13-14).

In the vast main hall is a long wall of ticket windows. Figure out which one you need before you wait in line. Generally, **windows 1-7** (on the left) are for **local commuter** and *media distancia* trains, such as to Sitges. **Windows 8-21** handle advance tickets for **long-distance** (larga distancia) **trains** beyond Catalunya. **Windows 22-26** offer **general information. Windows 27-31** sell tickets for **long-distance trains** leaving today. These window assignments can shift during the off-season. The **information booths** by windows 1 and 21 can help you find the right line and provide train schedules. Scattered nearby are two types of train-ticket vending machines. The **red-and-gray machines** sell tickets for **local and** *media distancia* trains within Catalunya. The **purple machines** are for **national RENFE trains** (you may have difficulty using a US credit card). These machines can also print out prereserved tickets if you have a confirmation code.

Getting Downtown: To reach the center of Barcelona, take a train or the Metro. To ride the subway, follow signs for the **Metro (red M),** and hop on the **L3 (green)** or **L5 (blue)** line; both link to useful points in town. Purchase tickets for the Metro at touch-screen machines near the tracks.

To zip downtown in just five minutes, take any **Rodalies de Catalunya suburban train** from **track 8 (R1, R3, or R4)** to Plaça de Catalunya (departs at least every 10 minutes). Your long-distance RENFE train ticket comes with a complimentary ride on Rodalies, as long as you use it within three hours before or after your travels. Look for a code on your ticket labeled *Combinat Rodalies* or *Combinado Cercanías*. Go to the orange commuter ticket machines, touch *Combinat Rodalies,* type in your code, and the machine will print your ticket.

TRAIN CONNECTIONS

Unless otherwise noted, all of the following trains depart from Sants Station; however, remember that some trains also stop at other stations more convenient to the downtown tourist zone: França Station, Passeig de Gràcia, or Plaça de Catalunya. If your train stops at these stations, you can board there, saving yourself the trip to Sants.

If departing from the downtown Passeig de Gràcia Station, where three Metro lines converge with the rail line, you might find the underground tunnels confusing. You can't access the RENFE station directly from some of the entrances. Use the northern entrances to this station—rather than the southern "Consell de Cent" entrance, which is closest to Plaça de Catalunya (tel. 902-320-320, www.renfe.com).

From Barcelona by Train to Madrid: The AVE train to Madrid is faster than flying (you're zipping from downtown to downtown). The train departs at least hourly. The nonstop train is a bit pricier but faster (2.5 hours) than the train that makes a few stops (3 hours).

Regular reserved AVE tickets can be prepurchased (often with a discount) at www.renfe.com and picked up at the station. If you have a rail pass, you'll pay only a reservation fee of €23 for first class, which includes a meal on weekdays (€10 second class, buy at any train station in Spain). Passholders can't reserve online through RENFE but can make a more expensive reservation at www.raileurope.com for delivery before leaving the US.

From Barcelona by Train to: Montserrat (departs from Plaça d'Espanya—*not* from Sants, hourly, 1 hour, includes cable car or rack train to monastery); **Figueres** (hourly, 1 hour via AVE or Alvia to Figueres-Vilafant; hourly, 2 hours via local trains to Figueres Station); **Sevilla** (8-9/day, 5.5-6.5 hours); **Granada** (1/day, 7.5 hours via AVE and regional train, transfer in Antequera); **Salamanca** (8/day, 6-7.5 hours, change in Madrid from Atocha Station to Chamartín Station via Metro or *cercanías* train; also 1/day with a change in Valladolid, 8.5 hours); **San Sebastián** (2/day, 5.5-6 hours).

By Bus

Most buses depart from the Nord bus station at Metro: Arc de Triomf, but confirm when researching schedules (www.barcelonanord.com). Destinations served by Alsa buses (tel. 902-422-242, www.alsa.es) include **Madrid** and **Madrid's Barajas Airport** (nearly hourly, 8 hours), and **Sala-**

manca (2/day, 11 hours). Sarfa buses (tel. 902-302-025, www.sarfa.com) serve many **coastal resorts,** including **Cadaqués** (2-3/day, 3 hours).

The Mon-Bus leaves from the university and Plaça d'Espanya in downtown Barcelona to **Sitges** (4/day, 1 hour, www.monbus.cat). One bus departs daily for the **Montserrat** monastery, leaving from Carrer de Viriat near Sants Station.

By Car

You won't need a car in Barcelona because the taxis and public transportation are so good. Parking fees are outrageously expensive (the lot behind La Boqueria Market charges upwards of €25/day). If you want to rent a car, remember that it's smart to do it after you visit Madrid and Toledo.

Italy

Stretching 850 miles long and 150 miles wide, art-drenched Italy is the cradle of European civilization. Visitors here come face to face with some of the world's most iconic images: Michelangelo's *David* in Florence, Rome's ancient Colosseum, Venice's gondolas, and the colorful, coastal villages of the Cinque Terre—Italy's Riviera.

Italy's 62 million inhabitants are more social and communal than most other Europeans. Because they're so outgoing and their language is so fun, Italians are a pleasure to communicate with. This boot-shaped country has all the elements that make travel to Europe forever fresh and rewarding: visible history, enthusiastic locals, and plenty of pasta.

CUISINE SCENE AT A GLANCE

For Italians, lunch (between 13:00 and 15:00) is the largest meal of the day, and dinner is light and late (around 20:00-21:30). Most **restaurants** close between lunch and dinner; good restaurants don't reopen for dinner before 19:00. To bridge the gap, people drop into a bar in the late afternoon for a snack.

A full Italian meal consists of several courses—an appetizer (*antipasto*), a first course (*primo piatto*), and a second course (*secondo piatto*)—but no one is obliged to order all that food. To save money and avoid getting stuffed, order any two courses. For example, a couple could order and share two *antipasti* and two *primi*.

At restaurants with self-serve buffets, you can choose various cooked appetizers from a salad-type bar. Generally buffets are not all-you-can-eat; take a one-time moderate serving (watch locals and imitate).

Understand prices before ordering. Seafood and steak may be sold by weight, either priced by the kilo (1,000 grams, or just over two pounds) or by the *etto* (100 grams, about a quarter-pound). The abbreviation *s.q. (secondo quantità)* means an item is priced "according to quantity" (such as the size of a fish). Fish is usually served whole, with the head and tail. As for steak, restaurants may require a minimum order of four or five *etti* (which diners can share). Some special dishes come in big quantities for two people (shown as "X2" on the menu), though the price listed generally indicates the cost per person.

You can save money by getting a fixed-price, multicourse meal, such as a basic *menù turistico* or often tastier *menù del giorno* (menu of the day). While fixed-price meals are convenient, galloping gourmets prefer to order à la carte for more adventurous fare.

Cover and Tipping: Before you sit down, look at a menu to see the extra charges that are often tacked on: *coperto* and *servizio*. The *coperto* (or *pane e coperto*) is a cover charge, added onto your bill as a flat fee (€1-3.50 per person; the amount should be clearly noted on the menu). The *servizio* (service charge) of about 10 percent pays for the waitstaff. Usually the words *servizio incluso* are written on the menu or bill, which means the listed prices already include the fee. You don't need to tip further (many Italians don't), but if you want to tip more for good service, you could include €1-2 for each person in your party.

A few restaurants tack on a 10 percent *servizio* charge to your bill; in this case, the menu will read: *servizio 10%*.

Budget Options: Take advantage of bars—inexpensive cafés that quickly serve up sandwiches, mini-pizzas, salads, and more. Bars have a two- or three-tiered pricing system. If you order, say, a sandwich, it's cheapest if you eat it while standing at the bar, more if you sit at an indoor table, and the most at an outdoor table.

Self-serve cafeterias are easy. Pizzerias are affordable, and takeout shops sell pizza by the slice or by weight. Or assemble a delicious picnic at a grocery or a deli (*rosticceria*).

Rome

Rome is magnificent and brutal at the same time. It's a showcase of Western civilization, with truly ancient sights and a modern vibrance. But with the wrong attitude, you'll be frustrated by the kind of chaos that only an Italian can understand. On my last visit, a cabbie struggling with the traffic said, *"Roma chaos."* I responded, *"Bella chaos."* He agreed.

Over 2,000 years ago the word "Rome" meant civilization itself. Today, Rome is Italy's political capital, the capital of Catholicism, and the center of its ancient empire, littered with evocative remains. As you peel through its fascinating and jumbled layers, you'll find Rome's buildings, cats, laundry, traffic, and 2.8 million people endlessly entertaining.

Despite Rome's rough edges, you'll fall in love with it...if you pace yourself, if you're well-organized, if you protect yourself and your valuables with extra caution, if your hotel provides a comfortable refuge, and if you embrace the siesta. Rome is much easier to love if you can avoid the midsummer heat.

ROME IN 3 DAYS

Rome wasn't built in a day, and you can't hope to see it all in three. Pace yourself; never regret a siesta. If you miss something, add it to your list of excuses to return.

Day 1: The Colosseum is the best place to begin your tour of ancient Rome. Then continue to the Arch of Constantine, Roman Forum, Trajan's Column, and Pantheon. Have dinner on the atmospheric Campo de' Fiori. Then take this book's Heart of Rome Walk to the Trevi Fountain and Spanish Steps.

Day 2: See St. Peter's Basilica and climb its dome, then tour the Vatican Museums, featuring the divine Sistine Chapel (closed Sun, except first Sun of month; smart to reserve a museum entry time in advance).

With any remaining stamina, choose among these sights (or save for tomorrow afternoon): the Church of San Giovanni in Laterano (Holy Stairs), St. Peter-in-Chains (Michelangelo's *Moses*), and Capuchin Crypt (bone chapel).

Evening options: Do as the Romans do—join the Dolce Vita Stroll along the Via del Corso. Explore the Monti neighborhood; linger over dinner, or stop by an *enoteca* (wine bar) for a drink. Enjoy a classical concert or jazz.

Day 3: See the Borghese Gallery (reservations required, closed Mon; stroll through the park afterwards) and the Capitoline Museums. Zip up to the top of the nearby Victor Emmanuel Monument for a grand view of the Eternal City.

With extra time: Take a day trip to Ostia Antica (the remains of an ancient Roman town; closed Mon) or to the hill

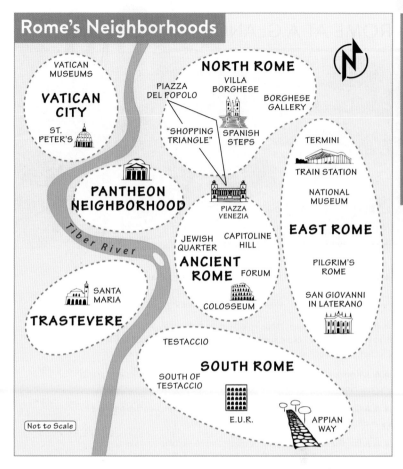

Rome's Neighborhoods

VATICAN MUSEUMS

VATICAN CITY

ST. PETER'S

NORTH ROME

PIAZZA DEL POPOLO

VILLA BORGHESE

BORGHESE GALLERY

"SHOPPING TRIANGLE"

SPANISH STEPS

TERMINI

TRAIN STATION

NATIONAL MUSEUM

PANTHEON NEIGHBORHOOD

PIAZZA VENEZIA

EAST ROME

JEWISH QUARTER

CAPITOLINE HILL

ANCIENT ROME

FORUM

PILGRIM'S ROME

SAN GIOVANNI IN LATERANO

Tiber River

SANTA MARIA

COLOSSEUM

TRASTEVERE

TESTACCIO

SOUTH ROME

SOUTH OF TESTACCIO

E.U.R.

APPIAN WAY

Not to Scale

town of Orvieto. Or visit Naples and Pompeii in a blitz day trip from Rome; take the early Rome-Naples express train (usually daily 7:35-8:45), see Naples, then Pompeii, and you'll be back in Rome before bedtime (but avoid this trip on Tue, when Naples' archaeological museum is closed).

Rick's Tip: *The* **siesta is the key to survival** *in summertime Rome. Lie down and contemplate the extraordinary power of gravity in the Eternal City. Drink lots of cold, refreshing water from Rome's many drinking fountains.*

ORIENTATION

Sprawling Rome actually feels manageable once you get to know it. The old core, with most of the tourist sights, sits in a diamond formed by Termini train station (in the east), the Vatican (west), Villa Borghese Gardens (north), and the Colosseum (south). The Tiber River runs through the diamond from north to south. In the center of the diamond sits Piazza Venezia, a busy square and traffic hub. It takes about an hour to walk from Termini Station to the Vatican. Think of Rome as a series of neighborhoods, huddling around major landmarks.

ROME AT A GLANCE

▲▲▲**Heart of Rome Walk** A stroll lacing the narrow lanes, intimate piazzas, fanciful fountains, and lively scenes of Rome's most colorful neighborhood. **Hours:** Any time, but best in evening. See page 431.

▲▲▲**Colosseum** Huge stadium where gladiators fought. **Hours:** Daily 8:30 until one hour before sunset: April-Aug until 19:15, Sept until 19:00, Oct until 18:30, off-season closes as early as 16:30. See page 442.

▲▲▲**Roman Forum** Ancient Rome's main square, with ruins and grand arches. **Hours:** Same hours as Colosseum. See page 447.

▲▲▲**Capitoline Museums** Ancient statues, mosaics, and expansive view of Forum. **Hours:** Daily 9:30-19:30. See page 457.

▲▲▲**Pantheon** The defining domed temple—2,000 years old. **Hours:** Mon-Sat 8:30-19:30, Sun 9:00-18:00, holidays 9:00-13:00, closed for Mass Sat at 17:00 and Sun at 10:30. See page 461.

▲▲▲**St. Peter's Basilica** Most impressive church on earth, with Michelangelo's *Pietà* and dome. **Hours:** Church—daily April-Sept 7:00-19:00, Oct-March 7:00-18:30, often closed Wed mornings; dome—daily April-Sept 8:00-18:00, Oct-March 8:00-17:00. See page 463.

▲▲▲**Vatican Museums** Four miles of the finest art of Western civilization, culminating in Michelangelo's glorious Sistine Chapel. **Hours:** Mon-Sat 9:00-18:00. Closed on religious holidays and Sun, except last Sun of the month (open 9:00-14:00). Open some Fri nights by online reservation only. See page 471.

▲▲▲**Borghese Gallery** Bernini sculptures and paintings by Caravaggio, Raphael, and Titian in a Baroque palazzo. Reservations mandatory. **Hours:** Tue-Sun 9:00-19:00, closed Mon. See page 477.

▲▲▲**National Museum of Rome** Greatest collection of Roman sculpture anywhere. **Hours:** Tue-Sun 9:00-19:45, closed Mon. See page 480.

▲▲**Palatine Hill** Ruins of emperors' palaces, Circus Maximus view, and museum. **Hours:** Same as Colosseum. See page 455.

▲▲**Trajan's Column** Tall ancient Roman column with narrative relief. See page 459.

▲▲**Museo dell'Ara Pacis** Shrine marking the beginning of Rome's Golden Age. **Hours:** Daily 9:30-19:30. See page 479.

▲▲**Dolce Vita Stroll** Evening *passeggiata,* where Romans strut their stuff. **Hours:** Roughly Mon-Sat 17:00-19:00 and Sun afternoons. See page 439.

▲▲**Church of San Giovanni in Laterano** Grandiose and historic "home church of the popes," with one-of-a-kind Holy Stairs across the street. **Hours:** Church—daily 7:00-18:30; Holy Stairs—generally same hours. See page 482.

▲**Arch of Constantine** Honors the emperor who legalized Christianity. See page 446.

▲**Monti Neighborhood** Lively fun-to-explore neighborhood with trendy eateries, workaday shops, and inviting lanes. See page 459.

▲**St. Peter-in-Chains Church** with Michelangelo's *Moses.* **Hours:** Daily 8:00-12:30 & 15:00-19:00, Oct-March until 18:00. See page 460.

▲**Piazza del Campidoglio** Square atop Capitoline Hill, designed by Michelangelo, with a museum, grand stairway, and Forum overlooks. See page 455.

▲**Victor Emmanuel Monument** Gigantic edifice celebrating Italian unity, with Rome from the Sky elevator ride up to 360-degree city view. **Hours:** Daily 9:00-17:30 (shorter in winter); elevator—until 19:30. See page 458.

▲**Spanish Steps** Popular hangout by day and night, particularly atmospheric when floodlit at night. See page 479.

▲**Trevi Fountain** Baroque hot spot into which tourists throw coins to ensure a return trip to Rome. See page 463.

▲**Baths of Diocletian/Basilica S. Maria degli Angeli** Once ancient Rome's immense public baths, now a Michelangelo church. **Hours:** Daily 7:30-18:30, closes later May-Sept and Sun year-round. See page 481.

Ancient Rome: In ancient times, this was home to the grandest buildings of a city of a million people. Today, the best of the classical sights stand in a line from the Colosseum to the Forum to the Pantheon. Just north of this area, between Via Nazionale and Via Cavour, is the atmospheric and trendy Monti district.

Pantheon Neighborhood: The Pantheon anchors the neighborhood I like to call the "Heart of Rome." It stretches eastward from the Tiber River through Campo de' Fiori and Piazza Navona, past the Pantheon to the Trevi Fountain.

Vatican City: Located west of the Tiber, it's a compact world of its own, with two great sights: St. Peter's Basilica and the Vatican Museums.

North Rome: With the Spanish Steps, Villa Borghese Gardens, and trendy shopping streets (Via Veneto and the "shopping triangle"—the area along Via del Corso and between the Spanish Steps, Piazza Venezia, and Piazza del Popolo), this is a more modern, classy area.

East Rome: This includes the area around Termini Station and Piazza della Repubblica, with many public-transportation connections.

South Rome: South of Vatican City is Trastevere, the colorful, wrong-side-of-the-river neighborhood that provides a look at village Rome. It's the city at its crustiest—and perhaps most "Roman."

Tourist Information

Rome has about a dozen small city-run tourist information offices scattered around town. The largest TIs are at Fiumicino Airport (daily 8:00-21:00, Terminal 3) and Termini train station (daily 8:00-18:45, exit by track 24 and walk 100 yards down along Via Giovanni Giolitti). Other TIs are directly across from the Forum entrance (on Via dei Fori Imperiali), at the Tiburtina train station, and at Ciampino Airport.

Info kiosks (generally open daily 9:30-19:00) are on Via Nazionale (at Palazzo delle Esposizioni), between the Trevi Fountain and Pantheon (at the corner of Via del Corso and Via Minghetti), near Piazza Navona (at Piazza delle Cinque Lune), and in Trastevere (at Piazza Sidney Sonnino).

The TI's website is www.turismoroma.it, but a better site for practical information is www.060608.it. That's also the number for Rome's **call center**—the best source of up-to-date tourist information, with English speakers on staff (answered daily 9:00-19:00, just dial 06-0608, and press 2 for English).

Two English-oriented **websites** provide insight into events and daily life in the city: www.inromenow.com (light tourist info on lots of topics); www.wantedinrome.com (events and accommodations).

Advance Tickets and Sightseeing Passes

Roma Pass: Rome offers several sight-seeing passes. The Roma Pass is the clear winner (www.romapass.it). Two versions are available: three-day and 48-hour.

The **three-day Roma Pass** costs €38.50, includes free admission to your first two sights, discounts on subsequent sights, and unlimited use of public transit for 72 hours (buses, trams, and Metro, plus the suburban train to Ostia, but not the airport train). Using the pass at the Colosseum/Roman Forum/Palatine Hill (considered a single sight) lets you go directly to the front of the regular line (be aggressive as you wave your pass to get there). Other covered sights include: Borghese Gallery (though a reservation is still required), Capitoline Museums, Ara Pacis, and Trajan's Market. The pass also covers the National Museum of Rome. The pass does not cover the Vatican Museums (which contain the Sistine Chapel).

If you'll be using public transit and visiting any two of the major sights in a three-day period, get the full pass. They are sold at participating sights, TIs, and many tobacco shops and newsstands all over town (look for a *Roma Pass* sign; all should charge the same price). Don't wait to buy it at a crowded sight like the Colosseum. There's no advantage in ordering a pass online—you still have to pick it up in Rome.

The pass is activated when you use it for the first time at a sight or on public transport. Once the pass is validated you can hop on any bus without showing it, but you'll need to swipe it to get through Metro turnstiles. At other sights, show it at the ticket office to get about 30 percent off.

Rick's Tip: *To get the most out of your* **Roma Pass, visit the two most expensive sights first**—*for example, the Colosseum/ Roman Forum/Palatine Hill (€12) and the Capitoline Museums (up to €15 with temporary exhibits).*

The **48-hour Roma Pass** costs €28 and includes free entry to one sight, discounts on additional ones, and unlimited use of public transit (for 48 hours after validation).

For families, only adults will need a Roma Pass. Since children under age 18 get into national museums and sights for free, and kids under 6 get into city museums (including Museo dell'Ara Pacis) for free, they can skip the lines alongside their pass-holding parents. Kids 10 and over need their own transit tickets or passes; those 9 and under ride free.

Colosseum, Forum, and Palatine Hill: These are covered by the Roma Pass and two different tickets (valid two consecutive days): The €12 combo-ticket allows one entry for the Colosseum (after 14:00) and one entry for the Forum/Palatine Hill complex. With the €18 SUPER ticket, you can enter the Colosseum anytime and visit the Forum/Palatine separately. To avoid lines, buy tickets ahead (www.coopculture.it) or at the lesser-used Forum entrance near Palatine Hill.

Museum Reservations: The Borghese Gallery requires reservations in advance (see page 477). You can also reserve online to avoid long lines at the Vatican Museums (see page 471).

Opening Hours: Rome's sights have notoriously variable hours from season to season. It's smart to check each sight's website in advance. On holidays, expect shorter hours or closures.

Churches: Many churches, which have divine art and free entry, open early (around 7:00-7:30), close for lunch (roughly 12:00-15:30), and close late (about 19:00). Visit churches before 9:00 or late in the day; if you're not resting during the siesta, see major sights that stay open all day (St. Peter's, Colosseum, Forum, Capitoline Museums, Pantheon, and National Museum of Rome). Dress modestly for church visits.

Tours

🎧 To sightsee on your own, download my **free audio tours** that illuminate some of Rome's top sights and neighborhoods, including tours of the Pantheon, Colosseum, Roman Forum, St. Peter's Basilica,

Spiral staircase at the Vatican Museums

Backstreet Rome

Rome

To Foro Italico &
Autostrada

To MAXXI &
Parco della
Musica

VIA FLAMINIA

CIRC. CLODIO

VIALE ANGELICO

VIALE DELLE MILIZIE

PONTE
MATTEOTTI

Flaminio

VIA GIULIO CESARE

Lepanto

S. MARIA
DEL POPOLO

VIA LEONE IV

VIA OTTAVIANO

VIA M.A. COLONNA

Piazza
del Popolo

Piazzale
degli Eroi

VIA ANDREA DORIA

VIA CANDIA

Ottaviano

VIA COLA DI RIENZO

PONTE
REG. MARG.

Cipro

V. PISANI

V. VATICANO

Piazza del
Risorgimento

MAUSOLEUM
OF AUGUSTUS

VIA CIPRO

VIA CRESCENZIO

ARA
PACIS

VATICAN
MUSEUMS

VIA BORGO PIO

Piazza
Cavour

PALACE OF
JUSTICE

PONTE
CAVOUR

VATICAN
CITY

CASTEL
SANT'
ANGELO

Piazza
Borg.

SISTINE
CHAPEL

ST.
PETER'S

St.
Peter's
Square

Piazza
Pio XII

VIA
CONCILIAZIONE

PONTE
S. ANGELO

PONTE
UMBERTO I

PONTE
VITTORIO
EMANUELE

VIA
CORONARI

VIA PORTA
CAVALLEGGERI

TUNNEL

PONTE
AMEDEO

CORSO VITTORIO

PANTHEON

To
Civitavecchia

V. GIULIA

Piazza
Navona

EMANUELE

SAN PIETRO
STATION

VIA MURA AURELIE

PONTE
MAZZINI

LUNGOTEVERE

V. MONSERRATO

Campo
de' Fiori

Tiber River

Largo
Argentina

To Termini Station
via Trastevere and
Ostiense Stations

ANITA
GARIBALDI
STATUE

VILLA
FARNESINA

PALAZZO
FARNESE

GHETTO

Parco
Gianicolense

PONTE
SISTO

Piazza
Trilussa

PONTE
GARIBALDI

Isola
Tiburina

Piazzale
Garibaldi

GIUSEPPE
GARIBALDI
STATUE

SAN PIETRO
IN MONTORIO
(TEMPIETTO)

VIA LUNGA

Piazza
Belli

PONTE
CESTIO

VIA AURELIA ANTICA

ACQUA
PAOLA
FOUNTAIN

SANTA MARIA
IN TRASTEVERE

TRASTEVERE

SAN
PANCRAZIO
GATE

ITALIAN
INDEPENDENCE
WAR
MEMORIAL

Villa
Doria
Pamphilj

OLD CITY
WALLS

PORTA
PORTESE

VIALE DI TRASTEVERE

PORTA
PORTESE
MARKET

VIA PORTUENSE

PONTE
SUBLICIO

VIA BRANCA

LUNG. TESTACCIO

500 Meters

500 Yards

Piazza
Testaccio

TESTAC

To Trastevere
Train Station

TESTACCIO
MARKET

Monte
Testaccio

Vatican Museums, Sistine Chapel, and Ostia Antica, and walks through the Heart of Rome, Jewish Ghetto, and Trastevere (for more on the audio tours, see page 17).

Rome's tour companies are highly competitive; I've listed several that are creative and well-established. Check their websites to learn about their various tours—there's always an introductory tour. Three-hour guided walks (always in English) generally cost €25-30 per person. It's sometimes required, and always smart, to book a spot in advance (easy to do online). Scheduling mishaps can occur. Make sure you know what you're booking, and when and where to meet.

Each of these companies offers a 10 percent discount with online bookings for Rick Steves travelers:

Enjoy Rome—Tel. 06-445-1843, www. enjoyrome.com, info@enjoyrome.com.

Europe Odyssey—Tel. 06-8854-2416, mobile 328-912-3720, www.europeodyssey. com, run by Rahul.

Through Eternity—For discount look for "Group Tours Rome" and enter "RICKSTEVES"; tel. 06-700-9336, www.througheternity.com, office@ througheternity.com, run by Rob.

Walks of Italy—For discount enter "10ricksteves"; US tel. 888/683-8670, tel. 06-9480-4888, www.walksofitaly.com, info@walksofitaly.com.

Helpful Hints

Sightseeing Tips: Those planning at least a couple of days of sightseeing can save money by buying the Roma Pass, available at TIs and participating sights. For the crowded Colosseum and Roman Forum/ Palatine Hill, use the Roma Pass or buy a combo-ticket online to shorten your wait in line. To sidestep the long Vatican Museums line, reserve an entry time online (see page 471). Reservations are required for the Borghese Gallery—make them at least a few days in advance (see page 477).

Theft and Safety: While violent crime is rare in the city center, petty theft is rampant. Pickpockets troll through the tourist crowds around the Colosseum, Forum, Vatican, and all train and Metro stations. Always use your money belt. Keep nothing important in your pockets. If you carry a backpack, never leave it unattended and try to keep it attached to your body in some way (even when you're seated for a meal). To report lost or stolen items, file a police report (at Termini Station, with polizia at track 11 or with Carabinieri at track 20; offices are also at Piazza Venezia and at the corner of Via Nazionale and Via Genova).

Medical Help: Embassies and hotels can recommend English-speaking doctors. Consider MEDline, a 24-hour home-medical service; doctors speak English and make calls at hotels for about €150 (tel. 06-808-0995, www.soccorso-medico. com). Anyone is entitled to emergency treatment at public hospitals. The hospital closest to Termini Station is Policlinico Umberto 1 (entrance for emergency treatment on Via Lancisi, Metro: Policlinico, translators available).

Emergency Numbers: Police—tel. 113. Ambulance—tel. 118.

Beggars: Throughout Rome, you may encounter downtrodden people asking for money. Know that social services are available to them, and give at your own discretion.

Traffic Safety: Use caution when crossing streets. Some streets have pedestrian-crossing signals (red means stop—or jaywalk carefully; green means go...also carefully; and yellow means go... extremely carefully, as cars may be whipping around the corner). Just as often, multilane streets have crosswalks with no signals at all. And even when there are traffic lights, they are provisional: Scooters don't need to stop at red lights, and even cars exercise what drivers call the "logical option" of not stopping if they see no oncoming traffic. As noisy, gasoline-powered scooters are replaced by electric ones, the streets get quieter (hooray) but more dangerous for pedestrians.

Follow locals like a shadow when you cross a street. Find a gap in the traffic and walk with confidence while making eye contact with approaching drivers—they won't hit you if they can tell where you intend to go.

Wi-Fi: All hotels in this book have Wi-Fi, but if yours doesn't, your hotelier can point you to a café that does.

Free Water: Carry a **water bottle** and refill it at Rome's many public drinking spouts.

WCs: Public restrooms are scarce. Use them when you can at museums, restaurants, and bars.

Laundry: Coin launderettes are common in Rome; ask your hotelier. The Wash & Dry Lavarapido chain has a branch near Piazza Barberini (Mon-Sat 9:00-21:00, closed Sun, Via degli Avignonesi 17, tel. 06-4201-3158).

Travel Agencies: You can get train tickets and rail-pass-related reservations and supplements at travel agencies (at little or no additional cost), instead of making a trip to a train station or purchasing online. Your hotelier will know of an agency nearby.

ROME WALKS

These two self-guided walks give you a moving picture of this ancient yet modern city.

❍ Heart of Rome Walk

Rated ▲▲▲, this walk through Rome's most colorful neighborhood takes you through squares lively with locals, small lanes sporting shops or chunks of Roman ruins, and playful fountains that are people-magnets. During the day, this walk shows off the Campo de' Fiori market and trendy fashion boutiques as it meanders past major monuments such as the Pantheon and the Spanish Steps.

But the sunset brings unexpected magic. A stroll in the cool of the evening offers the romance of the Eternal City at its best. Sit so close to a bubbling fountain that traffic noise evaporates. Jostle with kids to see the gelato flavors. Watch lovers straddling more than the bench. And marvel at the ramshackle elegance that softens this brutal city. These are the flavors of Rome, best enjoyed after dark.

This walk is equally pleasant in reverse order. You could ride the Metro to the Spanish Steps and finish at Campo de' Fiori, near my recommended restaurants.

🎧 Download my free Heart of Rome Walk audio tour via my Rick Steves Audio Europe app—see page 17.

• *Start this walk at Campo de' Fiori, my favorite outdoor dining room. It's a few blocks west of Largo Argentina, a major transportation hub. Buses #40, #64, and #492 stop at Largo Argentina and along Corso Vittorio Emanuele II (a long block northwest of Campo de' Fiori).*

❶ CAMPO DE' FIORI

This picturesque, bohemian piazza hosts a fruit and vegetable **market** in the morning, cafés in the evening, and pub-crawlers at night. In ancient times, the "Field of Flowers" was an open meadow. Later, Christian pilgrims passed through on their way to the Vatican, and a thriving market developed.

The square is watched over by a brooding statue of **Giordano Bruno,** an intellectual heretic who was burned on this spot in 1600. The pedestal shows scenes from Bruno's trial and execution, and reads, "And the flames rose up." When this statue honoring a heretic was erected in 1889, the Vatican protested, but they were overruled by angry Campo locals. The neighborhood is still known for its free spirit and anti-authoritarian demonstrations.

Campo de' Fiori is the product of centuries of unplanned urban development. At the east end of the square (behind Bruno), ramshackle apartments are built right into the outer wall of ancient Rome's mammoth Theater of Pompey. Julius Caesar was assassinated in the theater complex, where the Senate was renting space.

The square is surrounded by fun eateries, and is great for people-watching. Bruno faces the bustling **Forno** (in a corner of the square), where takeout *pizza bianca* ("white pizza," without red sauce) is sold hot from the oven. On weekend nights, when the Campo is packed with beer-drinking kids, the medieval square is transformed into a vast street party.

• *If Bruno did a hop, step, and jump forward, then turned left, in a block he'd reach...*

❷ PIAZZA FARNESE

While Campo de' Fiori feels free and easy, the 16th-century Renaissance Piazza Farnese, named for the family whose palace dominates it, stresses order. The nouveau riche Farnese family hired Michelangelo to help design their palace—which today houses the French embassy. The twin Roman tubs in the fountains decorating the square date from the third century and are from the Baths of Caracalla. They ended up here because the Farneses excavated the baths, giving them first dibs on the choicest finds.

• *Walk back to Campo de' Fiori, cross the square, and continue a couple of blocks down...*

❸ VIA DEI BAULLARI AND CORSO VITTORIO EMANUELE II

With a crush of cheap cafés, bars, and restaurants, the center of medieval Rome is now a playground for tourists, students, and suburban locals. High rents are driving families out and changing the character of this district. That's why the Campo de' Fiori market increasingly sells more gifty edibles than basic fruits and vegetables.

After a couple of blocks, you reach busy Corso Vittorio Emanuele II. In Rome, any road big enough to have city buses like this is post-unification: constructed after 1870. Look left and right down the street—the facades are mostly 19th-century Neo-Renaissance, built after this main thoroughfare sliced through the city. Traffic in much of central Rome is limited to city buses, taxis, motorbikes, "dark cars" (limos and town cars of VIPs), delivery vans, residents, and disabled people with permits (a.k.a. friends of politicians). This is one of the rare streets where any vehicle is welcome.

Campo de' Fiori

• *Cross Corso Vittorio Emanuele II, and enter a square with a statue of Marco Minghetti, an early Italian prime minister. Angle left at the statue, walking along the left side of the Museum of Rome, down Via di San Pantaleo. A block down, at the corner, you'll find a beat-up old statue.*

④ PASQUINO

A third-century B.C. statue that was discovered near here, Pasquino is one of Rome's "talking statues." For 500 years, this statue has served as a kind of community billboard, allowing people to complain anonymously when it might be dangerous to speak up. To this day, you'll see old Pasquino strewn with political posters, strike announcements, and grumbling graffiti. The statue looks literally worn down by centuries of complaining about bad government.

• *Facing Pasquino, veer to the left and head up Via di Pasquino to...*

⑤ PIAZZA NAVONA

Piazza Navona has been a center of Roman life since ancient times. By its shape you might guess that it started out as a racetrack, part of the training grounds built here by Emperor Domitian around A.D. 80. But much of what we see today came in the 1600s, when the whole place got a major renovation. At the time, the popes were trying to put some big scandals behind them, and beautification projects like this were a peace offering to the public.

Three Baroque fountains decorate the piazza. The first fountain, at the southern end, features a Moor wrestling with a dolphin. In the fountain at the northern end, Neptune slays a giant octopus.

The most famous fountain is in the center: the **Four Rivers Fountain** by Gian Lorenzo Bernini. Four burly river gods (representing the four quarters of the known world) support an Egyptian-style obelisk made in Rome.

Stroll around the fountain counterclockwise and admire the gods: The good-looking figure represents the Danube (for Europe). Next comes the Ganges (for Asia), holding an oar. After an exotic palm tree, you find the Nile (for Africa) with his head covered, since the river's source was unknown back then. Uruguay's Rio de la Plata, representing the Americas, tumbles backward in shock, wondering how he even made the top four. The

Piazza Navona with Bernini's Four Rivers fountain

Heart of Rome Walk

ARA PACIS

MAUSOLEUM OF AUGUSTUS

V. PONT.

Piazza Cavour

PONTE CAVOUR

VIA DI RIPETTA

Piazza Augusto Imperatore

PALACE OF JUSTICE

Tiber River

LUNGOTEVERE MARZIO

Piazza Borghese

CLEMENTINO

VIA DELLA SCROFA

PONTE UMBERTO

Piazza Ponte Umberto I

MONTE BRIANZO

PREFETTI

To Ponte Sant'Angelo

STELLETTA

VIA DEI CORONARI

UFFICI

CAMPO

GIOLITTI

VIEW INTO ANCIENT STADIUM

VOLPE

VIA DELLE COPPELLE

LA MADDE-LENA

Piazza Fico

TRE SCALINI

Piazza Navona

VIA IN AQUIRO

SAN LUIGI

SAN CRISPINO

SANT' AGNESE

SALVATORE

CARABINIERI

VIA GIUSTINIANI

Piazza della Rotonda

7

CHIESA NUOVA

V. DEL GOVERNO VECCHIO

FOUR RIVERS FOUNTAIN

ITALY'S SENATE

SANT' EUSTACHIO

MONTE-FORTE

6

PANTHEON

Piazza della Chiesa Nuova

PALAZZO PAMPHILJ

Piazza Pasquino

4

5

SANT' IVO

CORSO DEL RINASCIMENTO

CAFFÈ SANT' EUSTACHIO

Piazza Sant'Eustachio

To Vatican City & St. Peter's

CORSO VITTORIO

PANTALEO

CITY MUSEUM

B

3

MINGHETTI STATUE

EMANUELE II

ARGENTINA

VIA DE' CESTARI

SANT' ANDREA DELLA VALLE

VICE

Largo Argentina

WALK BEGINS

BRUNO STATUE

1

Campo de' Fiori

VIA D.BAULLARI

V. CHIAVARI

B T

LARGO ARGENTINA RUINS

PALAZZO FARNESE

Piazza Farnese

2

To Trastevere

VIA GIUBBONARI

Largo Pallaro

To Ghetto

1 Campo de' Fiori
2 Piazza Farnese
3 Via dei Baullari &
Corso Vittorio Emanuele II
4 Pasquino Statue
5 Piazza Navona
6 Pantheon
7 Caffè Tazza d'Oro
8 Piazza Capranica
9 Piazza di Montecitorio
10 Piazza Colonna & Via del Corso
11 Trevi Fountain
12 Palazzo di Propaganda Fide
13 Column of the Immaculate Conception
14 Spanish Steps

spilled coins represent the wealth of the New World. Bernini enlivens the fountain with horses plunging through rocks and the exotic flora and fauna of faraway lands.

Piazza Navona is Rome's most interesting night scene, with street music, artists, fire-eaters, local Casanovas, ice cream, and outdoor cafés worth the splurge for their front-row seats for people-watching.

• *Leave Piazza Navona directly across from* **Tre Scalini** *(famous for its rich chocolate gelato), and go east down Corsia Agonale, past rose peddlers and palm readers. Ahead of you (across the busy street) stands the stately Palazzo Madama, where the Italian Senate meets and the security is high. Jog left around this building, and follow the brown sign to the Pantheon, straight down Via del Salvatore.*

After a block, you'll pass (on your left) the **Church of San Luigi dei Francesi,** *with its très French decor and precious Caravaggio paintings. If it's open, pop in. Otherwise, continue along, following the crowd, as everyone seems to be heading for the…*

❻ PANTHEON

Sit for a while under the floodlit and moonlit portico of the Pantheon. The 40-foot, single-piece granite columns of the entrance show the scale of ancient Roman building. The columns support a triangular Greek-style roof with an inscription that says "M. Agrippa built this." In fact, the present structure was built *(fecit)* by Emperor Hadrian (A.D. 120), who gave credit to the builder of an earlier temple. This impressive entrance-way gives no clue that the greatest wonder of the building is inside—a domed room that inspired later domes, including Michelangelo's St. Peter's and Brunelleschi's Duomo in Florence.

• *With your back to the Pantheon, veer to the right, uphill toward the yellow sign on Via Orfani that reads Casa del Caffè— you've reached the…*

❼ CAFFÈ TAZZA D'ORO

This is one of Rome's top coffee shops, dating back to the days when this area was licensed to roast coffee beans. Locals come here for *granita di caffè con panna* (coffee and crushed ice with whipped cream).

• *From here, our walk continues past some interesting landmarks to the Trevi Fountain. But if you'd like to get to the fountain directly, take a* **shortcut** *by bearing right at the coffee shop onto Via de' Pastini, which leads through Piazza di Pietra, then across*

Pantheon

busy Via del Corso, where it becomes the pedestrianized Via delle Muratte and heads straight for the fountain.

To stick with me for the slightly longer version, bear left at the coffee shop and continue up Via degli Orfani to the next square...

❽ PIAZZA CAPRANICA

This square is home to the big, plain Florentine-Renaissance-style Palazzo Capranica (directly opposite as you enter the square). The six-story building to the left was once an apartment building for 17th-century Rome's middle class. Like so many of Rome's churches, Santa Maria in Aquiro, the church on the square, is older than the facade it was given during the Baroque period. Notice the little circular shrine on the street corner (between the palace and the apartment building).

• *Leave the piazza to the right of the palace, heading down Via in Aquiro. The street jogs to the left and into a square.*

❾ PIAZZA DI MONTECITORIO

The square is marked by a sixth-century B.C. **Egyptian obelisk,** taken as a trophy by Augustus after his victory in Egypt over Mark Antony and Cleopatra. The obelisk was originally set up as a sundial. Follow the zodiac markings to the well-guarded front door of Italy's **parliament building.**

• *One block to your right is Piazza Colonna, where we're heading next—unless you like gelato. A one-block detour to the left (past Albergo Nazionale) brings you a famous Roman gelateria, **Giolitti** (open daily until past midnight, Via Uffici del Vicario 40).*

❿ PIAZZA COLONNA AND VIA DEL CORSO

The centerpiece of **Piazza Colonna** is a huge second-century column. Its relief depicts the victories of Emperor Marcus Aurelius over the barbarians. Marcus once capped the column, but he was replaced by Paul, one of Rome's patron saints.

Beyond Piazza Colonna runs noisy **Via del Corso,** Rome's main north-south boulevard. It's named for the riderless horse races that took place here during Carnevale. Every evening, the pedestrian-only stretch of the Corso is packed with people on parade, taking to the streets for their *passeggiata.* It's an ideal venue for Romans to show off what they might have purchased from those classy shops (see the next walk, "Dolce Vita Stroll"). Before crossing the street, look left (to the obelisk marking Piazza del Popolo—the ancient north gate of the city) and right (to the Victor Emmanuel Monument).

• *Cross Via del Corso to enter a big palatial building with columns, the **Galleria Alberto Sordi** shopping mall. To the left are convenient toilets and ahead is Feltrinelli, the biggest Italian bookstore chain.*

Go to the right and exit out the back (if you're here after 21:00, when the mall is closed, circle around the right side of the Galleria on Via dei Sabini). At any time, be on guard for pickpockets, who thrive in the nearby Trevi Fountain crowds. Once out the back, the tourist kitsch builds as you head up Via de Crociferi to the roar of the water, lights, and people at the...

⓫ TREVI FOUNTAIN

This watery avalanche celebrates the abundance of pure water, which has been brought into the city since the days of ancient aqueducts. Oceanus rides across the waves in his chariot, pulled by horses and horn-blowing tritons, as he commands the flow of water. The illustrious Bernini sketched out the first designs. Nicola Salvi continued the project (c. 1740), using the palace behind the fountain as a theatrical backdrop.

The magic of the square is enhanced by the fact that no vehicular streets directly approach it. You can hear the excitement as you draw near, and then—bam!—you're there. The scene is always lively, with lucky Romeos clutching dates while unlucky ones clutch beers. Romantics toss a coin over their shoulder, thinking it will give them a wish and assure their return to Rome. It sounds silly, but every year I go through this tourist ritual...and so far it's working.

• *Facing the Trevi Fountain, walk along its right side up Via della Stamperia. Cross busy Via del Tritone. Continue about 30 yards up Via del Nazareno to #9, where you'll pass a fence on the left, with an exposed bit of the ancient Acqua Vergine aqueduct. Continue on to the T-intersection ahead, and turn right on Via Sant'Andrea delle Fratte. The street becomes Via di Propaganda. You'll pass alongside the...*

⑫ PALAZZO DI PROPAGANDA FIDE

At #1, on the right, the white-and-yellow entrance marks the palace from which the Catholic Church "propagated," or spread, its message to the world. Back in the 1600s, this "Propaganda Palace" was the headquarters of the Catholic Church's P.R. department—a priority after the Reformation. The building was designed by that dynamic Baroque duo, Bernini and Borromini (with his concave lines). It flies the yellow-and-white flag signifying that it is still owned by the Vatican.

Trevi Fountain

• *The street opens up into a long piazza. You're approaching the Spanish Steps. But first, pause at the...*

⑬ COLUMN OF THE IMMACULATE CONCEPTION

Atop a tall column stands a bronze statue of Mary. She wears a diadem of stars for a halo, and stands on a crescent moon atop a globe of the earth, which is crushing a satanic serpent.

The monument celebrates the Catholic doctrine of Immaculate Conception. This was the idea that, not only was Jesus born pure, but his mother Mary also was conceived without sin. The concept had been around since medieval times, but in 1854, Pope Pius IX finally proclaimed it official dogma and erected this statue in celebration. Every year on December 8, the feast day of the Immaculate Conception, this spot is the scene of a special celebration. The pope attends, the fire department places flowers on Mary's statue, and the Christmas season begins.

To Mary's immediate left stands the Spanish embassy to the Vatican. Rome has double the embassies of a normal capital because here countries need two: one to Italy and one to the Vatican. And because of this 300-year-old embassy, the square and its famous steps are called "Spanish."

• *Just 100 yards past Mary, you reach the climax of our walk, the...*

⑭ SPANISH STEPS

Piazza di Spagna, with the popular Spanish Steps, has been the hangout of many Romantics over the years (Keats, Wagner, Openshaw, Goethe, and others).

The British poet John Keats pondered his mortality, then died of tuberculosis at age 25 in the orange building on the right side of the steps. Fellow Romantic Lord Byron lived across the square at #66.

The 138 steps lead sharply up from Piazza di Spagna, forming a butterfly shape as they fan out around a central terrace. The design culminates in an obelisk framed between two Baroque church towers.

The **Sinking Boat Fountain** at the foot of the steps, built by Gian Lorenzo Bernini or his father, Pietro, is powered by an aqueduct (like all of Rome's fountains).

The main sight here is not the steps but the people who gather around them. By day, shoppers swarm the high-fashion boutiques at the base of the steps, along Via Condotti. At night, the area is alive with people enjoying—and creating—the ambience of Rome's piazzas.

• *Our walk is finished. To reach the top of the steps sweat-free, take the free elevator just inside the Spagna Metro stop (to the left, as you face the steps; elevator closes at 21:00). A pay WC is underground in the piazza near the Metro entrance, by the middle palm tree (10:00-19:30). A huge McDonald's (with a WC) is a block to the right of the steps. When you're ready to leave, zip home on the Metro or grab a taxi at either end of the piazza.*

⊙ Dolce Vita Stroll

This chic evening stroll, rated ▲▲, moves from Piazza del Popolo (Metro: Flaminio) down a traffic-free section of Via del Corso, and up Via Condotti to the Spanish Steps. You'll see people-watchers, flirts on the prowl, and shoppers browsing Rome's most fashionable stores (some are open roughly 16:00-19:30, after the siesta).

Although it's busy at any hour, crowds really come out from 17:00 to 19:00 (Fri and Sat are best), except on Sunday, when the stroll begins earlier in the afternoon. Leave before 18:00 if you plan to visit the Ara Pacis (Altar of Peace), which closes at 19:30 (last entry at 18:30). If you get hungry, see page 487 for a couple of restaurant listings.

To reach **Piazza del Popolo,** take Metro line A to Flaminio and walk south to the square. The car-free piazza is marked by an obelisk that was brought to Rome by Augustus after he conquered Egypt. It used to stand in the Circus Maximus.

If you're starting your stroll early enough, visit the Baroque church of **Santa Maria del Popolo,** next to the gate in the old wall on the north side of the square (Mon-Sat until 19:00, Sun until 19:30); look for Raphael's Chigi Chapel

Piazza del Popolo

Dolce Vita Stroll

Piazzale Flaminio M Flaminio
SANTA MARIA DEL POPOLO
V. L. SAVOIA
Piazza del Popolo
FERD. SAVOIA
• WALK BEGINS
SANTA MARIA DEI MIRACOLI
SANTA MARIA IN MONTESANTO
Villa Borghese
Galoppatoio
VIA DEL CORSO
VIA DI RIPETTA
LUNGOTEVERE IN AUGUSTA
V. FONT.
V. LAURINA
VIA MARGUTTA
VIA GESU E MARIA
VIA DEL BABUINO
VIA SAN GIACOMO
CANOVA
VIA DEI GRECI
FREZZA
PONTEFICI
VILLA MEDICI
M Spagna
Tiber River
ARA PACIS
VIA VITTORIA
RISTORANTE IL GABRIELLO
Spagna M
TRINITÀ DEI MONTI
ANTICA ENOTECA
Piazza di Spagna
WC
SPANISH STEPS
MAUSOLEUM OF AUGUSTUS
Piazza Imperatore
VIA CROCE
VIA CARROZZE
WALK ENDS FOR (WINDOW) SHOPPERS
PONTE CAVOUR
VIA CONDOTTI
VIA SISTINA
McDonald's
TOMACELLI
VIA BORGOGNONA
VIA FRATTINA
PROPA.
VIA DUE MACELLI
Piazza Borghese
VIA FONT. BORGHESE
Piazza S. Lorenzo
VIA VITE
POST
V. MERCEDE
To Barberini M
VIA DELLA SCROFA
PREFETTI
VALD.
CAMPO MARZO
Piazza Parlamento
V. CON.
TRITONE
DEL
T
Piazza Rotonda
PARLIAMENT
LARGO CHIGI
T
B
SABINA
TREVI FOUNTAIN
PALAZZO DEL QUIRINALE
Piazza di Montecitorio
Piazza Colonna
MURATTE
DATARIA
Piazza del Quirinale
Piazza di Pietra
CARAVITA
UMILTÀ
VIA DELLA SCROFA
PANTHEON
SANT' IGNAZIO
VIA DEL CORSO
L'ANTICA BIRRERIA PERONI
SANTA MARIA SOPRA MINERVA
Piazza del Collegio Romano
GALLERIA DORIA PAMPHILJ
CORSO VITT. EMANUELE II
BATT.
VIA 4 NOV.
VIA PLEBISCITO
Piazza Venezia
TRAJAN'S COLUMN
Largo Argentina
B
VIA MAG.
TRAJAN'S MARKET
SAN MARCO
VIA D'ARA COELI
B
VICTOR EMMANUEL MONUMENT
To Colosseum M
VIA DEI FORI IMPERIALI
CAPITOLINE HILL
N
200 Meters
200 Yards
GRAND STAIRCASE
Piazza del Campidoglio
WALK ENDS FOR HISTORIANS
FORUM

(second on left as you face main altar) and two paintings by Caravaggio (in Cerasi Chapel, left of altar).

From Piazza del Popolo, browse your way down **Via del Corso.** With the proliferation of shopping malls, many chain stores lining Via del Corso are losing customers and facing hard times. Still, this remains a fine place to feel the pulse of Rome at twilight.

History buffs should turn right down **Via Pontefici** to see the massive, round-brick **Mausoleum of Augustus,** topped with overgrown cypress trees. This neglected sight, honoring Rome's first emperor, is slated for restoration and redevelopment. Beyond it, next to the river, is Augustus' **Ara Pacis,** enclosed within a protective glass-walled museum (see page 480). From the mausoleum, walk down Via Tomacelli to return to Via del Corso and the 21st century.

From Via del Corso, window shoppers should take a left down **Via Condotti** to join the parade to the **Spanish Steps,** passing big-name boutiques. The streets that parallel Via Condotti to the south

(Borgognona and Frattina) are also filled with high-end shops. A few streets to the north hides the narrow Via Margutta, where Gregory Peck's *Roman Holiday* character lived (at #51). Today it's filled with pricey artisan and antique shops.

Historians should ignore Via Condotti and forget the Spanish Steps. Stay on Via del Corso and walk a half-mile down to the **Victor Emmanuel Monument.** Climb Michelangelo's stairway to his glorious square atop Capitoline Hill, floodlit at night. The mayor's palace is straight ahead. Stand on the balcony (to the right of the palace) overlooking the Forum. Enjoy one of the finest views in the city as the horizon reddens and cats prowl the unclaimed rubble of ancient Rome.

SIGHTS

I've clustered Rome's sights into walkable neighborhoods, some close together.

When you see a 🎧 in a listing, it means the sight is covered on a free audio tour (via my Rick Steves Audio Europe app—see page 17).

Spanish Steps

The best website for current opening hours is www.060608.it.

Rick's Tip: *Especially in this large city, make it a point to* **visit sights in a logical order.** *Needless backtracking wastes precious time and energy.*

Ancient Rome

The core of ancient Rome, where the grandest monuments were built, is between the Colosseum and Capitoline Hill. You can tour these sights in one great day: Start at the Colosseum, then it's a few minutes' walk to the Forum, then Capitoline Hill. From there, it's another 15-minute walk to the Pantheon. As a pleasant conclusion to your busy day, walk back south along the broad, parklike Via dei Fori Imperiali.

Ancient Core
▲▲▲COLOSSEUM (COLOSSEO)

This 2,000-year-old stadium is one of Europe's most recognizable landmarks—and a classic example of Roman engineering. Whether you're playing gladiator or simply marveling at the ancient design and construction, the Colosseum gets a unanimous thumbs-up.

Cost and Hours: €12 combo-ticket with Roman Forum/Palatine Hill (must see both on same visit) and allows entry to Colosseum after 14:00 only; €18 SUPER ticket allows you to see all three sights on separate visits and you can enter Colosseum anytime; also covered by Roma Pass; free for ages 17 and under with ID proof; free and crowded first Sun of the month, open daily 8:30 until one hour before sunset, last entry one hour before closing, audioguide-€5.50, Metro: Colosseo, tel. 06-3996-7700, www.coopculture.it.

Avoiding Lines: A line typically has already formed at 8:30 when the Colosseum opens. Lines shorter in the afternoon (especially after 16:00 in summer).

You'll save time if you...

1. Buy tickets online at www.coopculture.it (€2 booking fee; must pay fee even to obtain "free" youth ticket).

2. Buy a Roma Pass (see page 426), which you can use to cover your Colosseum and Forum admissions—and lets you skip the line and use the group

Colosseum

Ancient Rome

SANT' IGNAZIO
To Trevi Fountain
VIA DEL CORSO
VIA 4 NOVEMBRE
VIA NAZIONALE
To Termini Station
To Pantheon
PLEBISCITO
GESÙ
BATTISTI
Piazza Venezia
TRAJAN'S COLUMN & FORUM
Largo Magnanapoli
VIA DEI SERPENTI
VIA CAVOUR
S. MARCO
VIA D'ARACOELI
VICTOR EMMANUEL MONUMENT
MUSEUM OF IMPERIAL FORUMS & TRAJAN'S MARKET
MONTI
VIA BACCINA
V. LEONINA
Cavour
CAPITOLINE HILL
Piazza Camp.
MAMERTINE PRISON
VIA MADONNA
VIA CAVOUR
ANNIBALDI
VIA ALESSANDRINA
SANTI LUCA E MARTINA
ST. PETER-IN-CHAINS
VIA TEATRO MARCELLO
CAPITOLINE MUSEUMS
F & WC
EXIT ONLY
WC
VIA DEI FORI IMPERIALI
F & WC
WC
VIALE DEL MONTE OPPIO
TEATRO MARCELLO
WC
ROMAN FORUM
F
VIA TERME DI TITO
Parco del Colle Oppio
EXIT ONLY
B
M
Colosseo
VIA LABICANA
PONTE ROTTO
ACCESS BETWEEN FORUM & PALATINE HILL
ARCH OF TITUS
COLOSSEUM
F
PONTE PALATINO
BOCCA DELLA VERITÀ
VIA SAN TEODORO
WC
ARCH OF CONSTANTINE
T
Tiber River
S. MARIA IN COSMEDIN
PALATINE
WC HILL
VIA DEI CERCHI
VIA DI SAN GREGORIO
SANTI GIOVANNI E PAOLO
VIA CLAUDIA
CIRCUS MAXIMUS
WC
AVENTINO
VIA DEL CIRCO MASSIMO
Piazza Celimontana

F Food
● Water Fountain

200 Meters
200 Yards

Circo Massimo
M
To Baths of Caracalla
Villa Celimontana

---

entrance. The pass is sold at TIs, many tobacco shops and newsstands, at the green kiosk in front of the Colosseo Metro station, and at the Roman Forum information center on Via dei Fori Imperiali.

3. Buy tickets at a less-crowded place than the Colosseum. First check the Forum/Palatine Hill entrance facing the Colosseum (a 5-minute walk away). If that's crowded, try the Forum/Palatine Hill entrance 150 yards away, on Via di San Gregorio (facing the Forum, with the Colosseum at your back, go left).

4. Pay to join an official guided tour,

or rent an audioguide or videoguide (see "Tours," later). If the guard asks, say that you want to sign up for a tour, and they'll let you march right up to the guided visits (*Visite didattiche*) desk.

5. Hire a private guide. Guides linger outside the Colosseum, offering tours that allow you to bypass the line. Be aware that these private guides may try to mislead you into thinking the Colosseum lines are longer than they really are.

Getting There: The Colosseo Metro stop on line B is just across the street from the monument. Buses #51, #75, #85, #87,

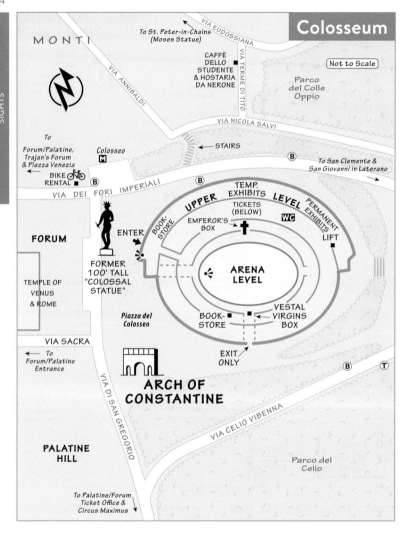

Colosseum

MONTI

VIA EUDOSSIANA

To St. Peter-in-Chains
(Moses Statue)

CAFFÈ
DELLO
STUDENTE
& HOSTARIA
DA NERONE

VIA TERME DI TITO

Not to Scale

Parco
del Colle
Oppio

VIA ANNIBALDI

VIA NICOLA SALVI

To
Forum/Palatine,
Trajan's Forum
& Piazza Venezia

Colosseo
M

STAIRS

B

To San Clemente &
San Giovanni in Laterano

BIKE
RENTAL

B

VIA DEI FORI IMPERIALI

B

UPPER LEVEL

TEMP.
EXHIBITS

TICKETS
(BELOW)

PERMANENT EXHIBITS

FORUM

ENTER

BOOK STORE

EMPEROR'S
BOX

WC

LIFT

FORMER
100' TALL
"COLOSSAL
STATUE"

ARENA
LEVEL

TEMPLE OF
VENUS
& ROME

Piazza del
Colosseo

BOOK-
STORE

VESTAL
VIRGINS
BOX

VIA SACRA

To
Forum/Palatine
Entrance

EXIT
ONLY

B

T

ARCH OF
CONSTANTINE

VIA DI SAN GREGORIO

VIA CELIO VIBENNA

PALATINE
HILL

Parco del
Celio

To Palatine/Forum
Ticket Office &
Circus Maximus

and #118, stop along Via dei Fori Imperiali near the Colosseum entrance, one of the Forum/Palatine Hill entrances, and Piazza Venezia. Tram #3 stops behind the Colosseum.

Getting In: Several lines lead to the turnstiles and into the Colosseum. Follow the signs to get into your correct line: 1) for ticket buyers; 2) for ticket holders (combo-ticket, SUPER ticket, Roma Pass, or those signing up for a tour); 3) for ticket pickup (for those who've reserved

but don't yet have a physical ticket). Farther beyond these lines, there's a group entrance (with a Roma Pass, you can likely use the group line—I did).

Tours: A fact-filled **audioguide** is available just past the turnstiles (€5.50). A handheld **videoguide** senses where you are in the site and plays related clips (€6).

🎧 Download my free Colosseum **audio tour.**

Official guided tours in English depart nearly hourly between 10:15 and 15:00, and last 45-60 minutes (€5 plus Colosseum ticket, purchase inside the Colosseum near the ticket booth marked *Visite didattiche*). A longer, interesting, but not essential 1.5-hour guided tour takes you through areas that are otherwise off-limits, including the top floor and underground passageways. Advance reservations are strongly advised, either by phone or online (no same-day reservations).

Private guides stand outside the Colosseum looking for business (€25-30/2-hour tour of the Colosseum, Forum, and Palatine Hill). Make sure that your tour will start right away and covers all three sights: the Colosseum, Forum, and Palatine Hill.

Services: A WC is inside the Colosseum.

Background: Built when the Roman Empire was at its peak in A.D. 80, the Colosseum represents Rome at its grandest. Known as the Flavian Amphitheater, it was an arena for gladiator contests and public spectacles. When killing became a spectator sport, the Romans wanted to share the fun with as many people as possible, so they stuck two semicircular theaters together to create a freestanding amphitheater. Towering 150 feet high, it could accommodate 50,000 roaring fans (100,000 thumbs). The outside (where slender cypress trees stand today) was decorated with a 100-foot-tall bronze statue of Nero that gleamed in the sunlight. In a later age, the colossal structure was nicknamed a "coloss-eum."

Rick's Tip: *Beware of the* **greedy, modern-day gladiators.** *They pose for photos with tourists and then attempt to intimidate them for lots of money. Don't be swindled. Also, look out for* **pickpockets.**

Exterior: The Romans were great engineers, not artists; the building is more functional than beautiful. (Ancient Romans visiting the US today might send home postcards of our greatest works of art—freeways.) While the essential structure is Roman, the four-story facade is decorated with mostly Greek columns—Tuscan columns on the ground level, Ionic on the second story, Corinthian on the next level, and at the top, half-columns with a mix of all three. Copies of Greek statues once stood in the arches of the middle two stories, adding sophistication to this arena of death.

Colosseum interior

Only a third of the original Colosseum remains. Earthquakes destroyed some of it, but most was carted off to build other buildings during the Middle Ages and Renaissance.

Interior: The games took place in the oval-shaped arena, 280 feet long by 165 feet wide. When you look down into the arena, you're seeing the underground passages beneath the playing surface (which can only be visited on a private tour). The arena was originally covered with a wooden floor, then sprinkled with sand (*arena* in Latin). The bit of reconstructed floor gives you a sense of the original arena level and the subterranean warren where animals and prisoners were held. The spectators ringed the playing area in bleacher seats that slanted up from the arena floor. Around you are the big brick masses that supported the tiers of seats.

The games began with a few warm-up acts—dogs bloodying themselves attacking porcupines, female gladiators fighting each other, or a one-legged man battling a dwarf. Then came the main event—the gladiators.

"Hail, Caesar! (*Ave, Caesar!*) We who are about to die salute you!" The gladiators would enter the arena from the west end, parade around to the sound of trumpets, acknowledge the Vestal Virgins (on the south side), then stop at the emperor's box (marked today by the cross that stands at the "50-yard line" on the north side—although no one knows for sure where it was). They would then raise their weapons, shout, and salute—and begin fighting. The fights pitted men against men, men against beasts, and beasts against beasts. Picture 50,000 screaming people around you (did gladiators get stage fright?), and imagine that they want to see you die.

▲ARCH OF CONSTANTINE

This well-preserved arch, which stands between the Colosseum and the Forum, commemorates a military coup and, more important, the acceptance of Christianity by the Roman Empire. The ambitious Emperor Constantine (who had a vision that he'd win under the sign of the cross) defeated his rival Maxentius in A.D. 312 to become sole emperor of the Roman Empire. He legalized Christianity soon after. The arch is free and always open.

🎧 It's covered in my free Colosseum audio tour.

Arch of Constantine

▲▲▲ROMAN FORUM (FORO ROMANO)

This is ancient Rome's birthplace and civic center, and the common ground between Rome's famous seven hills. As just about anything important that happened in ancient Rome happened here, it's arguably the most important piece of real estate in Western civilization. While only fragments of that glorious past remain, you'll find plenty to ignite your imagination amid the half-broken columns and arches.

Cost: €12 combo-ticket includes Palatine Hill on same visit, plus Colosseum (after 14:00 only); €18 SUPER ticket allows separate visits to Forum and Palatine, with no time restriction for Colosseum. Also covered by Roma Pass. Forum is free and crowded the first Sun of month.

Hours: The Roman Forum, Palatine Hill, and Colosseum are open daily 8:30 until one hour before sunset: April-Aug until 19:15, Sept until 19:00, Oct until 18:30, Nov-mid-Feb until 16:30, mid-Feb-mid-March until 17:00, mid-March-late March until 17:30; last entry one hour before closing.

Avoiding Lines: Buy your combo-ticket (or Roma Pass) at a less-crowded place or get a combo-ticket online; for specifics, see page 426. Or visit later in the day when crowds diminish.

Getting There: The closest Metro stop is Colosseo. Except on Sundays, buses #51, #75, #85, #87, and #118 stop along Via dei Fori Imperiali near the Colosseum, the Forum, and Piazza Venezia.

Getting In: There are three main entrances to the Forum/Palatine Hill sight: 1) from the Colosseum—nearest the Arch of Titus, where this chapter's guided walk starts; 2) from Via dei Fori Imperiali; and 3) from Via di San Gregorio—at the south end of Palatine Hill, which is least crowded. A fourth entry for those who already have their tickets is from the north (below Capitoline Hill).

Information: The free info center, located across from the Via dei Fori Imperiali entrance can sell you a Roma Pass and

has a bookshop, small café, and WCs (daily 9:30-19:00). Vendors outside sell a variety of colorful books with plastic overlays that restore the ruins (official price in bookstore for larger version with DVD is €20 and for smaller version is €10—don't pay more than these prices). Ticket info: Tel. 06-3996-7700, www.coopculture.it. General info: www.archeoroma.beniculturali.it/en.

Tours: An **audioguide** helps decipher the rubble (€5/2 hours, €7 version includes Palatine Hill and lasts 3 hours, must leave ID), but you have to return it to where you rented it.

🎧 Download my free Roman Forum **audio tour.**

Length of This Walk: Allow 1.5 hours. If you have less time, end the walk at the Arch of Septimius Severus. And don't miss the Basilica of Constantine hiding behind the trees.

Services: WCs are at the ticket entrances at Palatine Hill and at Via dei Fori Imperiali. Within the Forum itself, there's one near the Arch of Titus (in the "Soprintendenza" office), and another in the middle, near #7 on the map. Others are atop Palatine Hill.

Plan Ahead: The ancient paving at the Forum is uneven; wear sturdy shoes. I carry a water bottle and refill it at the Forum's public drinking fountains.

Improvise: Because of ongoing restoration, paths through the Forum are often rerouted. Use this tour as a starting point, but be prepared for a few detours and backtracking.

Nearby: Nighttime sound-and-light shows illuminate Caesar's Forum and the Forum of Augustus (part of the Imperial Forums). For details, see page 459.

❍ SELF-GUIDED TOUR

• Start at the Arch of Titus (Arco di Tito). It's the white triumphal arch that rises above the rubble on the east end of the Forum (closest to the Colosseum). Stand at the viewpoint alongside the arch and gaze over the valley known as the Forum.

Roman Forum

CAPITOLINE HILL

Not to Scale

GRAND STAIRCASE

VICTOR EMMANUEL MONUMENT

To Piazza Venezia

FORUM OF AUGUSTUS SOUND-AND-LIGHT SHOW SEATING

ENTRANCE ONLY WITH TICKETS

STEPS FROM CAPITOLINE HILL

15 TOUR ENDS

To Gaul

EXIT ONLY

UMBILICUS URBIS

14

13

16

9

FORUM SQUARE

12

11

F Food
• Water Fountain

WC

To Hollywood

8

10

7

5

ENTRANCE

6

4

WC TICKET OFFICE

(**F** & WC)

CIRCUS MAXIMUS

WC

PALATINE HILL

R O M A N

F O R U M

3

EXIT ONLY ACCESS

2

WC ACCESS BETWEEN FORUM & PALATINE HILL

TOUR BEGINS

S. FRAN. ROMANA

TO CLIMB PALATINE HILL

DIRECT TO FORUM

1

ENTRANCE

TEMPLE OF VENUS & ROME

ENTRANCE

WC

PALATINE HILL TICKET OFFICE

VIA DI SAN GREGORIO

To Carthage

ARCH OF CONSTANTINE

COLOSSEUM

F

B M Colosseo

TRAJAN'S FORUM

VIA CAVOUR

CAESARS FORUM

VIA SACRA

FORI IMPERIALI

VIA DEI

1 Arch of Titus
2 Basilica of Constantine
3 Via Sacra
4 Temple of Antoninus Pius & Faustina
5 Temple of Vesta
6 House of the Vestal Virgins
7 Caligula's Palace
8 Temple of Castor & Pollux

9 The Forum's Main Square
10 Temple of Julius Caesar
11 Basilica Aemilia
12 The Curia
13 Rostrum
14 Arch of Septimius Severus
15 Temple of Saturn
16 Column of Phocas

Viewing the Ruins: Try to see the Forum with "period eyes." We imagine the structures in ancient Rome as mostly white, but ornate buildings and monuments were originally more colorful. Through the ages, builders scavenged stone from the Forum; the colored marble was cannibalized first. The white stone is generally what was left. Statues were vividly painted, but the organic paint rotted away as they lay buried for centuries. Lettering was inset bronze and eyes were inset ivory. Even seemingly intact structures, like the Arch of Titus, have been reassembled. The columns are half smooth and half fluted. The fluted halves are original; the smooth parts are reconstructions.

❶ Arch of Titus (Arco di Tito): The Arch of Titus commemorated the Roman victory over the province of Judaea (Israel) in A.D. 70. The Romans had a reputation as benevolent conquerors who tolerated local customs and rulers. All they required was allegiance to the empire, shown by worshipping the emperor as a god. No problem for most conquered people, who already had half a dozen gods on their prayer lists anyway. But Israelites believed in only one god, and it wasn't the emperor. Israel revolted. After a short but bitter war, the Romans defeated the rebels, took Jerusalem, destroyed their temple (leaving only a fragment of one wall's foundation—today's revered "Wailing Wall"), and brought home 50,000 Jewish slaves...who were forced to build the Colosseum (and this arch).

Roman propaganda decorates the inside of the arch. A relief shows the emperor Titus in a chariot being crowned by the goddess Victory. The other side shows booty from the sacking of the temple in Jerusalem. Carved after Titus' death, the relief at the top of the ceiling shows him riding an eagle to heaven, where he'll become one of the gods.

• *Walk down Via Sacra into the Forum. The original basalt stones under your feet were walked on by Caesar Augustus 2,000 years ago. After about 50 yards, turn right and follow a path uphill to the three huge arches of the...*

❷ Basilica of Constantine (Basilica Maxentius): These arches represent only one-third of the original Basilica of Constantine, a mammoth hall of justice. There was a similar set along the Via Sacra side

Roman Forum

Rome's Rise and Fall (500 -   500)

Ancient Rome lasted for 1,000 years, from about 500 B.C. to A.D. 500. During that time, Rome expanded from a small tribe of barbarians to a vast empire, then dwindled slowly to city size again. For the first 500 years, when Rome's armies made her ruler of the Italian peninsula and beyond, Rome was a republic governed by elected senators. Over the next 500 years, a time of world conquest and eventual decline, Rome was an empire ruled by a military-backed dictator.

Julius Caesar bridged the gap between republic and empire. This ambitious, charismatic general and politician, popular because of his military victories, suspended the Roman constitution and assumed dictatorial powers in about 50 B.C. A few years later, he was assassinated by a conspiracy of senators. His adopted son, Augustus, succeeded him, and soon "Caesar" was not just a name but a title.

Emperor Augustus ushered in the Pax Romana, or Roman peace (A.D. 1-200), a time when Rome reached its peak, controlling an empire that stretched from England to Egypt, from Turkey to Morocco.

Then Rome fell into 300 years of gradual decay. Its fall had many causes, among them the barbarians who pecked away at Rome's borders. Christians blamed the fall on moral decay. Pagans blamed it on Christians. Socialists blamed it on a shallow economy based on the spoils of war. (Republicans blamed it on Democrats.) Whatever the reasons, the far-flung empire could no longer keep its grip on conquered lands. Barbarian tribes from Germany and Asia attacked the Italian peninsula, looting Rome itself in A.D. 410. In 476, when the last emperor checked out and switched off the lights, Europe plunged into centuries of ignorance and poverty—the Dark Ages.

But Rome lived on in the Catholic Church. Christianity was the state religion of Rome's last generations. Emperors became popes (both called themselves "Pontifex Maximus"), senators became bishops, orators became priests, and basilicas became churches. The glory of Rome remains eternal.

(only a few brick piers remain). Between them ran the central hall, spanned by a roof 130 feet high—about 55 feet higher than the side arches you see. (The stub of brick you see sticking up began an arch that once spanned the central hall.) The hall itself was as long as a football field, lavishly furnished with inlaid marble, a bronze ceiling, and statues. At the far (west) end was an enormous marble statue of Emperor Constantine on a throne. Pieces of this statue, including a hand the size of a man, are on display in Rome's Capitoline Museums.

• Now stroll deeper into the Forum, downhill along the...

❸ **Via Sacra:** Stroll through the trees, down this main drag of the ancient city. Imagine being an out-of-town visitor during Rome's heyday; nothing would have prepared you for the bustle of Rome—a city of a million people—by far the biggest city in Europe. This street would be swarming with tribunes, slaves, and courtesans. Chariots whizzed by. Wooden stalls lined the roads, where merchants peddled their goods.

On your right, you'll pass a building with a green door still swinging on its 17th-century hinges—the original bronze door to a temple that survived because it became a church shortly after the fall of

Rome. This ancient temple is still in use, sometimes hosting modern exhibits. No wonder they call Rome the Eternal City.

• *Just past the ancient temple, 10 huge columns stand in front of a much newer church. The colonnade was part of the...*

❹ **Temple of Antoninus Pius and Faustina:** This temple honors Emperor Antoninus Pius (A.D. 138-161) and his deified wife, Faustina. The 50-foot-tall Corinthian (leafy) columns were awe-inspiring to out-of-towners who grew up in thatched huts. Although the temple has been inhabited by a church, you can still see the basic layout—a staircase led to a shaded porch (the columns), which admitted you to the main building (now a church), where the statue of the god sat. Originally, these columns supported a triangular pediment decorated with sculptures.

Picture these columns supporting brightly painted statues in the pediment, with the whole building capped by a bronze roof. Today's gray rubble is a faded black-and-white photograph of a 3-D Technicolor era.

• *With your back to the colonnade, walk straight ahead—jogging a bit to the right to stay on the path—and head for the three short columns, all that's left of the...*

❺ **Temple of Vesta:** This was perhaps Rome's most sacred spot. Rome considered itself one big family, and this temple represented a circular hut, like the kind that Rome's first families lived in. Inside, a fire burned, just as in a Roman home. As long as the sacred flame burned, Rome would stand. The flame was tended by priestesses known as Vestal Virgins.

• *Backtrack a few steps up the path, behind the Temple of Vesta. You'll find a few stairs that lead up to a big, enclosed field with two rectangular brick pools (just below the hill). This was the courtyard of the...*

❻ **House of the Vestal Virgins:** The Vestal Virgins lived in a two-story building surrounding a long central courtyard with two pools at one end. This place was the model—both architecturally and sexually—for medieval convents and monasteries.

Chosen from noble families before they reached the age of 10, the six Vestal Virgins served a 30-year term. Honored and revered, the Vestals even had their own box opposite the emperor in the Colosseum. The statues that line the courtyard honor dutiful Vestals.

A Vestal took a vow of chastity. If she served her term faithfully—abstaining for 30 years—she was given a huge dowry and allowed to marry. But if they found any Virgin who wasn't, she was strapped to a funeral car, paraded through the streets of the Forum, taken to a crypt...and buried alive. Many suffered the latter fate.

• *Looming just beyond this field is Palatine Hill—the corner of which may have been...*

❼ **Caligula's Palace (Palace of Tiberius):** Emperor Caligula (ruled A.D. 37-41) had a huge palace on Palatine Hill overlooking the Forum. It actually sprawled down the hill into the Forum (some supporting arches remain in the hillside). Caligula tortured enemies, stole senators' wives, and parked his chariot in handicap spaces. He was not a nice person. But Rome's luxury-loving emperors only added to the glory of the Forum, with each one trying to make his mark on history.

• *Continue downhill, passing the three short columns of the Temple of Vesta, where you'll get a view of three very tall columns just beyond.*

Temple of Antoninus Pius and Faustina

❽ Temple of Castor and Pollux: These three columns are all that remain of a prestigious temple—one of the city's oldest, built in the fifth century B.C. It commemorated the Roman victory over the Tarquin, the notorious, oppressive Etruscan king. After the battle, the legendary twin brothers Castor and Pollux watered their horses here, at the Sacred Spring of Juturna (which was recently excavated nearby). As a symbol of Rome's self-governing republic, the temple was often used as a meeting place of senators; its front steps served as a podium for free speech.

• *The path spills into a flat, open area that stretches before you. This was the center of the ancient Forum.*

❾ Forum's Main Square: The original Forum, or main square, was this flat patch about the size of a football field, stretching to the foot of Capitoline Hill. Surrounding it were temples, law courts, government buildings, and triumphal arches.

Rome was born here. According to legend, twin brothers Romulus and Remus were orphaned in infancy and raised by a she-wolf on top of Palatine Hill. Growing up, they found it hard to get dates. So they and their cohorts attacked the nearby Sabine tribe and kidnapped their women. After they made peace, this marshy valley became the meeting place and then the trading center for the scattered tribes on the surrounding hillsides.

The square was the busiest—and often the seediest—section of town. Besides the senators, politicians, and currency exchangers, there were souvenir hawkers, pickpockets, fortune-tellers, gamblers, slave marketers, drunks, hookers, lawyers, and tour guides.

Ancient Rome's population exceeded one million, more than any city until London and Paris in the 19th century. All those Roman masses lived in tiny apartments as we would live in tents at a campsite, basically just to sleep. The Forum—today's piazza—is where they did their living. To this day, urban Italians spend a major part of their time outside, in the streets and squares.

The Forum is now rubble, but imagine it in its prime: brilliant marble buildings with 40-foot-high columns and shining metal roofs; rows of statues painted in realistic colors; processional chariots rattling down Via Sacra. Mentally replace tourists in T-shirts with tribunes in togas. Imagine people buzzing around you while an orator gives a rabble-rousing speech. If you still only see a pile of rocks, at least tell yourself, "Julius Caesar once leaned against these rocks."

• *At the near end of the main square (the end closest to the Colosseum) find the foundations of a temple now capped with a peaked wood-and-metal roof.*

❿ Temple of Julius Caesar (Tempio del Divo Giulio, or Ara di Cesare): On March 15, in 44 B.C., Julius Caesar was stabbed 23 times by political conspirators. After his assassination, Caesar's body was cremated on this spot (under the metal roof). Afterward, this temple was built to honor him. Peek behind the wall into

Temple of Castor and Pollux

the small apse area, where a mound of dirt usually has fresh flowers—given to remember the man who personified the greatness of Rome.

Caesar (100-44 B.C.) changed Rome—and the Forum—dramatically. He cleared out many of the wooden market stalls and began to ring the square with even grander buildings. Caesar's house was located behind the temple, near that clump of trees. He walked by here on the day he was assassinated ("Beware the Ides of March!" warned a street-corner Etruscan preacher).

Although he was popular with the masses, not everyone liked Caesar's urban design or his politics. When he assumed dictatorial powers, he was ambushed and stabbed to death by a conspiracy of senators, including his adopted son, Brutus ("*Et tu, Brute?*").

The funeral was held here, facing the main square. Mark Antony stood up to say (in Shakespeare's words), "Friends, Romans, countrymen, lend me your ears. I come to bury Caesar, not to praise him." When Caesar's body was burned, his adoring fans threw anything at hand on the fire, requiring the fire department to come put it out. Later, Emperor Augustus dedicated this temple in his name, making Caesar the first Roman to become a god.

• *Continue past the Temple of Julius Caesar, to the open area between the columns of the Temple of Antoninus Pius and Faustina (which we passed earlier) and the boxy brick building (the Curia). You can view these ruins of the Basilica Aemilia from a ramp next to the Temple of Antoninus Pius and Faustina, or (if the path is open) walk among them.*

❶ **Basilica Aemilia:** A basilica was a covered public forum, often serving as a hall of justice. In a society that was as legal-minded as America is today, you needed a lot of lawyers—and a big place to put them. Citizens came here to work out inheritances, file building permits, and sue each other.

It was a long, rectangular building. The row of stubby columns forms one long, central hall flanked by two side aisles. Medieval Christians required a larger meeting hall for their worship services than Roman temples provided, so they used the spacious Roman basilica as the model for their churches. Cathedrals from France to Spain to England, from Romanesque to Gothic to Renaissance, all have this same basic floor plan.

• *Now head for the big, well-preserved brick building with the triangular roof—the Curia. It's just to the right of the big triumphal arch at the foot of Capitoline Hill. While generally closed, the building is impressive even from outside.*

❷ **Curia (Senate House):** The Curia was the most important political building in the Forum. While the present building dates from A.D. 283, this was the site of Rome's official center of government since the birth of the republic. Three hundred senators, elected by the citizens of Rome, met here to debate and create the laws of the land. Their wooden seats once circled the building in three tiers; the Senate president's podium sat at the far end. The marble floor is from ancient times. Listen to the echoes in this vast room—the acoustics are great.

Rome prided itself on being a republic. Early in the city's history, its people threw out the king and established rule by elected representatives. Each Roman citizen was free to speak his mind and have a say in public policy. Even when emperors became the supreme authority, the Senate was a power to be reckoned with. The Curia building is well preserved, having been used as a church since early Christian times. In the 1930s, it was restored and opened to the public as a historic site. (Although Julius Caesar was assassinated in "the Senate," it wasn't here—the Senate was temporarily meeting across town.)

• *Go back down the Senate steps and find the 10-foot-high wall just to the left of the big arch, marked...*

⑬ Rostrum: Nowhere was Roman freedom of speech more apparent than at this "Speaker's Corner." The Rostrum was a raised platform, 10 feet high and 80 feet long, decorated with statues, columns, and the prows of ships.

On a stage like this, Rome's orators, great and small, tried to draw a crowd and sway public opinion. Mark Antony rose to offer Caesar the laurel-leaf crown of kingship, which Caesar publicly refused—while privately becoming a dictator. Men such as Cicero—a contemporary of Julius Caesar—railed against the corruption and decadence that came with the city's newfound wealth. (Cicero paid the price: he was executed, and his head and hands were nailed to the Rostrum.)

In front of the Rostrum are trees bearing fruits that were sacred to the ancient Romans: olives (provided food, oil for light, and preservatives), figs (tasty), and wine grapes (made a popular export product).

• *The big arch to the right of the Rostrum is the...*

⑭ Arch of Septimius Severus: In imperial times, the Rostrum's voices of democracy would have been dwarfed by images of the empire, such as the huge six-story-high Arch of Septimius Severus (A.D. 203). The reliefs commemorate the African-born emperor's battles in Mesopotamia. Near ground level, see soldiers marching captured barbarians back to Rome for the victory parade.

• *Our next stop is the Temple of Saturn. You can see it from here—it's the eight big columns just up the slope of Capitol Hill. Or you could make your way to it for a closer look.*

⑮ Temple of Saturn: These columns framed the entrance to the Forum's oldest temple (497 B.C.). Inside was a humble wooden statue of the god Saturn. But the statue's pedestal held the gold bars, coins, and jewels of Rome's state treasury, the booty collected by conquering generals.

Even older than the Temple of Saturn is the Umbilicus Urbis, which stands nearby (next to the Arch of Septimius Severus). A humble brick ruin marks this historic "Navel of the City." The spot was considered the center of the cosmos, and all distances in the empire were measured from here.

• *Now turn your attention from the Temple of Saturn, one of the Forum's first buildings, to one of its last monuments. Find a lone, tall column standing in the Forum in front of the Rostrum. It's fluted and topped with a leafy Corinthian capital. This is the...*

⑯ Column of Phocas: The Forum's last monument (A.D. 608) was a gift from the powerful Byzantine Empire to a fallen empire—Rome. Given to commemorate the pagan Pantheon's becoming a Christian church, it's like a symbolic last nail in ancient Rome's coffin. After Rome's 1,000-year reign, the city was looted by Vandals, the population of a million-plus shrank to about 10,000, and the once-grand Forum

Arch of Septimius Severus

Temple of Saturn

was abandoned, slowly covered by centuries of silt and dirt. In the 1700s, English historian Edward Gibbon overlooked this spot from Capitoline Hill, pondered the decline and fall of the Roman Empire, and thought, "Hmm, that's a catchy title..."

• *Your tour is over. If you want to see Palatine Hill, don't leave the Forum complex; you won't be allowed back in without a new ticket. To enter Palatine Hill, return to the Arch of Titus. If you'd rather exit the Forum, be aware that the exact ways in and out change from year to year. Refer to your map for possible exits.*

▲▲PALATINE HILL (MONTE PALATINO)

The hill overlooking the Forum is jam-packed with history—"the huts of Romulus," the huge Imperial Palace, a view of the Circus Maximus—but there's only the barest skeleton of rubble left to tell the story.

We get our word "palace" from this hill, where the emperors chose to live. It was once so filled with palaces that later emperors had to build out. (Looking up at it from the Forum, you see the substructure that supported these long-gone palaces.) The Palatine Museum contains statues and frescoes that help you imagine the luxury of the imperial Palatine. From the pleasant garden, you'll get an overview of the Forum. On the far side, unless excavations are blocking the viewpoint, look down into an emperor's private stadium and then beyond at the grassy Circus Maximus, once a chariot course.

While many tourists consider Palatine Hill extra credit after the Forum, it offers insight into the greatness of Rome. If you're visiting the Colosseum or Forum, you've already got a ticket.

Cost and Hours: €12 combo-ticket covers Forum on same visit, plus Colosseum (after 14:00 only); €18 SUPER ticket allows separate visits to all three sights, without time restriction for Colosseum. Also covered by Roma Pass. All three sights open daily 8:30 until one hour before sunset, last entry one hour before closing.

Getting In: The closest Metro stop is Colosseo. There are three entrances to the combined Palatine/Forum sight; see the map on page 448. The easiest for our tour is the entrance on Via di San Gregorio, 150 yards from the Colosseum. Upon entering, follow the path to the left as it winds to the top. Alternatively, if you sightsee the Forum first, to get to Palatine Hill you must walk up from the Arch of Titus.

Wherever you enter, our tour begins on the top of the hill at the one big building still standing—the museum. Remember, be sure to combine your visit with the Roman Forum; if you leave the complex, your ticket doesn't cover re-entry.

Services: WCs are at the ticket office when you enter, at the museum in the center of the site, and hiding among the orange trees in the Farnese Gardens.

Capitoline Hill

Of Rome's famous seven hills, this is the smallest, tallest, and most famous—home of the ancient Temple of Jupiter and the center of city government for 2,500 years. There are several ways to get to the top of Capitoline Hill. If you're coming from the north (from Piazza Venezia), take Michelangelo's impressive stairway to the right of the big, white Victor Emmanuel Monument. Coming from the southeast (the Forum), take the steep staircase near the Arch of Septimius Severus. From near Trajan's Forum along Via dei Fori Imperiali, take the winding road. All three converge at the top, in the square called Campidoglio (kahm-pee-DOHL-yoh).

▲PIAZZA DEL CAMPIDOGLIO

This square atop the hill, once the religious and political center of ancient Rome, is still the home of the city's government. In the 1530s, the pope called on Michelangelo to reestablish this square as a grand center. Michelangelo placed the ancient equestrian statue of Marcus Aurelius as its focal point. (The original statue is now in the adjacent museum.) The twin buildings

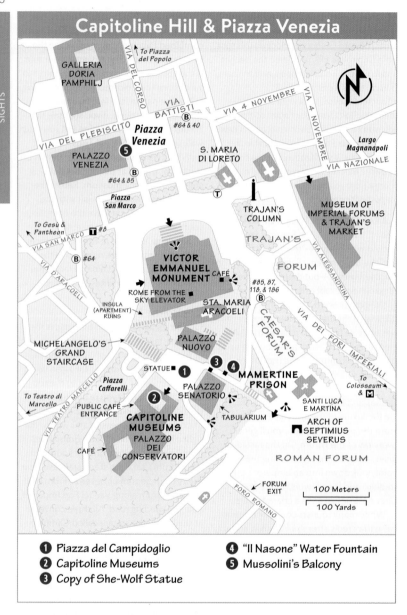

Capitoline Hill & Piazza Venezia

1 Piazza del Campidoglio
2 Capitoline Museums
3 Copy of She-Wolf Statue
4 "Il Nasone" Water Fountain
5 Mussolini's Balcony

on either side are the Capitoline Museums. Behind the replica of the statue is the mayor's palace (Palazzo Senatorio).

Michelangelo intended that people approach the square from his grand stairway off Piazza Venezia. From the top of

the stairway, you see the new Renaissance face of Rome, with its back to the Forum. Michelangelo gave the buildings the "giant order"—huge pilasters make the existing two-story buildings feel one-storied and more harmonious with the new square.

The statues atop these buildings welcome you and then draw you in.

The terraces just downhill (past either side of the mayor's palace) offer grand views of the Forum. To the left of the mayor's palace is a copy of the famous **she-wolf statue** on a column. Farther down is *Il Nasone* ("the big nose"), a refreshing water fountain. Block the spout with your fingers, and water spurts up for drinking. Romans joke that a cheap Roman boy takes his date out for a drink at *Il Nasone.*

▲▲▲CAPITOLINE MUSEUMS

Some of ancient Rome's most famous statues and art are housed in the two palaces (Palazzo dei Conservatori and Palazzo Nuovo) that flank the equestrian statue in the Campidoglio. They're connected by an underground passage that leads to the Tabularium, an ancient building with panoramic views of the Roman Forum.

Cost and Hours: €15, €11.50 if no special exhibits, daily 9:30-19:30, last entry one hour before closing, videoguide-€6, tel. 06-0608, www.museicapitolini.org.

Visiting the Museums: You'll enter at Palazzo dei Conservatori (on your right as you face the equestrian statue), then walk through a passageway underneath the square—stopping for a look at the Tabularium—to Palazzo Nuovo (on your left), where you'll exit.

With lavish rooms and several great statues, the worthwhile **Palazzo dei Conservatori** was founded in 1471 when a pope gave ancient statues to the citizens of Rome. Many of the museum's statues have become recognizable cultural icons, including the 13th-century *Capitoline She-Wolf* (the statues of Romulus and Remus were added in the Renaissance). Don't miss the *Boy Extracting a Thorn* and the *Commodus as Hercules.* Behind Commodus is a statue of his dad, Marcus Aurelius, on a horse. The greatest surviving equestrian statue of antiquity, it was the original centerpiece of the square (where a copy stands today). Christians in the Dark Ages thought that the statue's hand was raised in blessing, which probably led to their misidentifying him as Constantine, the first Christian emperor. While most pagan statues were destroyed by Christians, "Constantine" was spared.

The museum's second-floor café, **Caffè Capitolino,** has a patio offering city

Piazza del Campidoglio

views—lovely at sunset (public entrance for those without a museum ticket off Piazzale Caffarelli and through door #4).

The **Tabularium,** built in the first century B.C., once held the archives of ancient Rome. Its name comes from "tablet," on which Romans wrote their laws. You won't see any tablets, but you will see a stunning head-on view of the Forum from the windows. **Palazzo Nuovo** houses two must-see statues: the *Dying Gaul* and the *Capitoline Venus* (both on the first floor up).

Piazza Venezia

This vast square, dominated by the Victor Emmanuel Monument, is the focal point of modern Rome. With your back to the monument (you'll get the best views from the terrace by the guards and eternal flame), look down Via del Corso, the city's axis, surrounded by Rome's classiest shopping district. In the 1930s, fascist dictator Benito Mussolini whipped up Italy's nationalistic fervor from a balcony above the square (it's the less-grand building on the left) and created the boulevard Via dei Fori Imperiali (to your right, capped by Trajan's Column) to open up views of the Colosseum in the distance.

With your back still to the monument, circle around the left side. At the back end of the monument, look down into the ditch on your left to see the ruins of an ancient apartment building from the first century A.D.; part of it was transformed into a tiny church (faded frescoes and bell tower). Rome was built in layers—almost everywhere you go, there's an earlier version beneath your feet.

▲VICTOR EMMANUEL MONUMENT

This oversize monument to Italy's first king, built to celebrate the 50th anniversary of the country's initial unification in 1861, was part of Italy's attempt to create a national identity. The over-the-top monument is 200 feet high and 500 feet wide. The 43-foot-long statue of the king on his high horse is one of the biggest

equestrian statues in the world. The king's moustache forms an arc five feet long. A person could sit within the horse's hoof. At the base of this statue, Italy's Tomb of the Unknown Soldier is watched over by the goddess Roma (with the gold mosaic background).

Cost and Hours: Monument—free, daily 9:00-17:30 (shorter in winter), a few WCs scattered throughout, tel. 06-6920-2049. **Rome from the Sky elevator**—€7, daily until 19:30, ticket office closes 45 minutes earlier, WC at entrance, tel. 06-0608; follow *ascensori panoramici* signs inside the Victor Emmanuel Monument (no elevator access from street level).

Visiting the Monument: The "Vittoriano" (as locals call it) is open and free to the public. You can simply climb the front stairs, or go inside from one of several entrances: midway up the monument through doorways flanking the central statue, on either side at street level, and at the base of the colonnade (two-thirds of the way up). The little-visited **Museum of the Risorgimento** fills several floors with displays on the movement and war that led to the unification of Italy (€5 to enter museum, temporary exhibits around €14, tel. 06-679-3598, www.risorgimento.it).

Climb the stairs to the midway point for a decent view, keep climbing to the base of the colonnade for a better view, or, for the best view, ride the **Rome from the Sky** (Roma dal Cielo) **elevator,** which zips you from the top of the stair climb (at

Victor Emmanuel Monument

the back of the monument) to the rooftop for a 360-degree view of Rome that is even better than from the top of St. Peter's dome. Once on top, you stand on a terrace between the monument's two chariots. Look north up Via del Corso to Piazza del Popolo, west to the dome of St. Peter's Basilica, and south to the Roman Forum and Colosseum. Panoramic diagrams describe the skyline, with powerful binoculars available for zooming in. It's best in late afternoon, when it's beginning to cool off and Rome glows.

▲▲TRAJAN'S COLUMN

This 140-foot column is decorated with a spiral relief of 2,500 figures trumpeting the emperor's exploits. It has stood for centuries as a symbol of a cosmopolitan civilization. At one point, the ashes of Trajan and his wife were held in the base, and the sun glinted off a polished bronze statue of Trajan at the top. (Today, it's been replaced with St. Peter.) Built as a stack of 17 marble doughnuts, the column is hollow (note the small window slots) with a spiral staircase inside, leading up to the balcony.

The **relief** unfolds like a scroll, telling the story of Rome's last and greatest foreign conquest, Trajan's defeat of Dacia (modern-day Romania). Originally, the entire story was painted in bright colors. If you were to unwind the scroll, it would stretch over two football fields.

The column, just off Piazza Venezia, is free to see and always viewable.

SOUND-AND-LIGHT SHOWS

The Imperial Forums area hosts two atmospheric and inspirational sound-and-light shows that give you a chance to fantasize about the world of the Caesars—the Caesar's Forum Stroll and the Forum of Augustus Show. Consider one or both of the similar and adjacent evening experiences. During each of these "nighttime journeys through ancient Rome," you spend about an hour with a headphone dialed to English, listening to an artfully crafted narration synced with projections on ancient walls, columns, and porticos. The final effect is worth the price tag (€15, both for €25, they run nightly mid-April-mid-Nov, bring your warmest coat, tickets sold online and at the gate, shows can sell out on busy weekends, tel. 06-0608, www.viaggioneifori.it).

If you plan to see both, do Caesar first (runs every 20 minutes, last an hour, starting at Trajan's Column) and allow 80 minutes between starting times (Augustus showings offered on the hour, enter on Via dei Fori Imperiali just before Via Cavour—you'll see the bleachers).

North of Via dei Fori Imperiali
▲MONTI NEIGHBORHOOD: VILLAGE ROME

This quintessentially Roman district called Monti is one of the oldest corners of Rome...and newly trendy. Tucked behind Via dei Fori Imperiali, and squeezed between Via Nazionale and Via Cavour, this hilly tangle of lanes shows why Romans see their hometown not as a sprawling metropolis, but as a collection of villages. Neighbors hang out on

Trajan's Column

the square and chat. Funky boutiques share narrow streets with hole-in-the-wall hardware shops and grocery shops; and wisteria-strewn cobbled lanes beckon photographers.

To explore the Monti, head for its main square, **Piazza della Madonna dei Monti** (three blocks west of the Cavour Metro stop). To get oriented, face uphill, with the big fountain to your right.

From this hub, interesting streets branch off in every direction. I recommend strolling one long street with three names: **Via della Madonna dei Monti,** which leads from the ancient wall on the downhill side of the ancient forums, then to the central Piazza Madonna dei Monti, before continuing uphill as **Via Leonina** and then **Via Urbana.** Monti is an ideal place for a quick lunch or early dinner (see page 459).

▲ST. PETER-IN-CHAINS CHURCH (SAN PIETRO IN VINCOLI)

Built in the fifth century to house the chains that held St. Peter, this church is most famous for its Michelangelo statue of Moses, intended for the tomb of Pope Julius II (which was never built). Note that this church is not the famous St. Peter's Basilica, which is in Vatican City.

After viewing the much-venerated chains under the high altar, focus on mighty Moses. Pope Julius II commissioned Michelangelo to build a massive tomb, with 48 huge statues, topped with a grand statue of the egomaniacal pope himself. The pope had planned for his tomb to be in the center of St. Peter's Basilica. When Julius died, the work had barely started; no one had the money or necessary commitment to finish the project.

In 1542, remnants of the project were brought to St. Peter-in-Chains and pieced together by Michelangelo's assistants. Some of the best statues ended up elsewhere (*Prisoners* is in Florence and the *Slaves* is in the Louvre). *Moses* and the *Slaves* are the only statues Michelangelo personally completed for the project.

The statue of Moses is powerful. As he holds the Ten Commandments, his eyes show a man determined to win salvation for the people of Israel. Why the horns? Centuries ago, the Hebrew word for "rays" was mistranslated as "horns." Flanking *Moses* are the Old Testament sister-wives of Jacob, Leah (to our right) and Rachel, both begun by Michelangelo but probably finished by pupils.

Michelangelo, Moses

Pantheon Neighborhood

Cost and Hours: Free, daily April-Sept 8:00-12:20 & 15:00-19:00, until 18:00 in winter, modest dress required; the church is a 10-minute uphill walk from the Colosseum, or a shorter, simpler walk (but with more uphill steps) from the Cavour Metro stop; tel. 06-9784-4950.

Pantheon Neighborhood

The Pantheon area, despite its ancient sites and historic churches, has an urban-village feel. Exploring this neighborhood is especially good in the evening, when the restaurants bustle and the streets teem with pedestrians. Gather with the locals in squares marked by bubbling fountains.

Getting There: The Pantheon neighborhood is a 15-minute walk from Capitoline Hill. Taxis and buses stop at a chaotic square called Largo Argentina, a few blocks south of the Pantheon—from here you can walk north on either Via dei Cestari or Via di Torre Argentina to the Pantheon. Buses #40 and #64 run frequently between the Termini train station and Vatican City (#492 serves the same areas via a different route). Buses #85 and #87 connect to the Colosseum (stop: Corso/Minghetti).

▲▲▲PANTHEON

Built two millennia ago, this influential domed temple is perhaps the most influential building in art history, serving as the model for the Florence cathedral dome, which launched the Renaissance, and for Michelangelo's dome of St. Peter's, which capped it off. Its interior offers the greatest look at the splendor of Rome.

Cost and Hours: Often free but may cost €2, Mon-Sat 8:30-19:30, Sun 9:00-18:00, holidays 9:00-13:00, www.pantheonroma.com.

When to Go: Don't go at midday, when it's packed. To have it all to yourself, visit before 9:00.

Dress Code: No skimpy shorts or bare shoulders.

Tours: The Pantheon has a €6 audio-guide that lasts 30 minutes.

🎧 Download my free Pantheon audio tour.

Visiting the Pantheon: The Pantheon was a Roman temple dedicated to all (*pan*) of the gods (*theos*). The original temple was built in 27 B.C. by Augustus' son-in-law, Marcus Agrippa. The inscription below the triangular **pediment** proclaims in Latin, "Marcus Agrippa, son of Lucio, three times consul made this." But after two fires, the structure we see today was completely rebuilt by Emperor Hadrian around A.D. 120. After the fall of Rome, the Pantheon became a Christian church (from "all the gods" to "all the martyrs"), which saved it from architectural plunder and ensured its upkeep through the Dark Ages.

The **portico** is Greek in style, a visual reminder of the debt Roman culture owed to the Greeks. You cross this Greek space to enter a purely Roman space, the rotunda. The columns are huge and unadorned, made from 40-foot-high single pieces of red-gray granite. They were quarried in Egypt, then shipped down the Nile and across the Mediterranean to Rome.

The **dome,** which was the largest made until the Renaissance, is set on a circular base. The mathematical perfection of this design is a testament to Roman engineering. The dome is as high as it is wide—142 feet from floor to rooftop and from side to side. To picture it, imagine a basketball wedged inside a wastebasket so that it just touches bottom. It is made from concrete that gets lighter and thinner as it reaches the top. The base of the dome is

Inside the Pantheon

23 feet thick and made from heavy concrete mixed with travertine, while near the top, it's less than five feet thick and made with a lighter volcanic rock (pumice) mixed in.

At the top, the **oculus,** or eye-in-the-sky, is the building's only light source. It's completely open and almost 30 feet across. The 1,800-year-old floor—with 80 percent of its original stones surviving—has holes in it and slants toward the edges to let the rainwater drain. Though some of the floor's marble has been replaced, the design—alternating circles and squares—is original.

While its ancient statuary is long gone, the interior holds decorative statues and the tombs of famous people from more recent centuries. The artist **Raphael** lies to the left of the main altar. Facing each other across the base of the dome are the tombs of modern Italy's first two kings.

▲TREVI FOUNTAIN

The bubbly Baroque fountain is a minor sight to art scholars...but a major nighttime gathering spot for teens on the make and tourists tossing coins. For more on the fountain, see page 437.

Vatican City

Vatican City, the world's smallest country, contains St. Peter's Basilica (with Michelangelo's exquisite *Pietà*) and the Vatican Museums (with the Sistine Chapel). The entrances to St. Peter's and the Vatican Museums are a 15-minute walk apart (follow the outside of the Vatican wall, which links the two sights). The nearest Metro stop—Ottaviano—still involves a 10-minute walk to either sight.

▲▲▲ST. PETER'S BASILICA (BASILICA SAN PIETRO)

This is the richest and grandest church on earth. To call it vast is like calling Einstein smart. Plaques on the floor show you where other, smaller churches would end if they were placed inside. The ornamental cherubs would dwarf a large man. Birds roost inside, and thousands of people wander about, heads craned heavenward. Bernini's altar work and twisting, towering canopy are brilliant. Don't miss Michelangelo's

St. Peter's Square and Basilica

Hello from Vatican City

The Vatican is the religious capital of 1.2 billion Roman Catholics. If you're not a Catholic, become one for your visit. The pope is both the religious and secular leader of Vatican City. For centuries, the Vatican was the capital of the Papal States, and locals referred to the pontiff as "King Pope." Because of the Vatican's territorial ambitions, it didn't always have good relations with Italy. Even though modern Italy was created in 1870, the Holy See didn't recognize it as a country until 1929.

The tiny independent country of Vatican City is contained entirely within Rome. The Vatican has its own postal system, armed guards, a helipad, mini train station, and radio station (KPOP). Like every European country, Vatican City has its own versions of the euro coin (with a portrait of the pope). You're unlikely to find one in your pocket, though, as they're snatched up by collectors before falling into circulation.

Post Offices: The Vatican postal service is famous for its stamps, which you can get from offices on St. Peter's Square (one next to the TI, another between the columns just before the security checkpoint), in the Vatican Museums (closed Sun), or from a "post bus" that's often parked on St. Peter's Square (open Sun). To get a Vatican postmark, mail your cards from postboxes at the Vatican itself (although the stamps are good throughout Rome).

Pietà (behind bulletproof glass) to the right of the entrance. The huge square in front of the church is marked by an obelisk and bordered by Bernini's colonnade.

Cost: Free entry to basilica and crypt. Dome climb—€6 if you take the stairs all the way up, or €8 to ride an elevator part way (to the roof), then climb to the top of the dome (cash only). Treasury Museum—€7 (€3 audioguide).

Hours: The **church** is open daily April-Sept 7:00-19:00, Oct-March 7:00-18:30. It closes on Wednesday mornings during papal audiences, until roughly 13:00. The **dome** (*cupola*) is open to climbers daily from 8:00; if you're climbing the stairs all the way up, the last entry time is 17:00 (16:00 Oct-March); if you're riding the elevator, you can enter until 18:00 (17:00 Oct-March). The **Treasury Museum** is open daily 8:00-18:50, Oct-March until 17:50. The **crypt** (*grotte*) is open daily 9:00-16:00.

Information: Tel. 06-6988-3731, www.vaticanstate.va.

Avoiding Lines: To avoid the worst crowds, visit before 10:00. Going after 16:00 works, too, but the crypt will be closed, and the area around the altar is often roped off to prepare for Mass. There's no surefire way to avoid the long security lines; the checkpoint is typically on the right (north) side of the huge square in front of the church, but is sometimes closer to the church or tucked under the south colonnade.

St. Peter's is often accessible directly from the Sistine Chapel inside the Vatican Museums—a great time-saving trick, but unfortunately not a reliable one (for details, see page 472).

Dress Code: No shorts, above-the-knee skirts, or bare shoulders (this applies to men, women, and children). Attendants enforce this dress code, even in hot weather. Carry a cover-up, if necessary.

Getting There: Take the Metro to Ottaviano, then walk 10 minutes south on Via Ottaviano. The #40 express bus drops off at Piazza Pio, next to Castel Sant'Angelo (Hadrian's Tomb)—a 10-minute walk from St. Peter's. The more crowded bus #64 stops just outside St. Peter's Square to the south (get off the bus after it crosses the Tiber, at the first stop past the tunnel; backtrack toward the tunnel and turn left when you see the rows of columns; the return bus stop is adjacent to the tunnel). Bus #492 heads through the center of town, stopping at Largo Argentina, and gets you near Piazza Risorgimento (get off when you see the Vatican walls). Be alert for pickpockets on all public transit. A taxi from Termini train station to St. Peter's costs about €15.

Visitor Information: The Vatican TI, up close to the church on the left (south) side of the square is excellent (Mon-Sat 8:30-18:15, closed Sun, tel. 06-6988-1662).

Church Services: Mass is said daily, generally in Italian, usually in one of these three places: in the south (left) transept, the Blessed Sacrament Chapel (on the right side of the nave), or the apse. Typical schedule: Mon-Sat at 8:30, 10:00, 11:00, 12:00, 16:30, and 17:00 (in Latin, in the apse); and on Sun and holidays at 9:00, 10:30 (in Latin), 11:30, 12:15, 13:00, 16:00, 16:45 (vespers), and 17:30.

Tours: The Vatican TI conducts free 1.5-hour **tours of St. Peter's** (depart from TI Mon-Fri at 14:15, confirm schedule at TI). **Audioguides** can be rented near the checkroom (€5 plus ID, for church only, daily 9:00-17:00).

🎧 Download my free St. Peter's Basilica **audio tour.**

To see St. Peter's original grave, you can take a *Scavi* (excavations) tour into the **Necropolis** under the basilica (€13, 1.5 hours, ages 15 and older only). Book at least two months in advance by email (scavi@fsp.va) or fax (06-6987-3017), following the detailed instructions at www.vatican.va (search for "Excavations Office"); no response means they're booked.

Dome Climb: You can take the elevator (€8) or stairs (€6) to the roof (231 steps), then climb another 323 steps to the top of the dome. The entry to the elevator is just outside the north side of the basilica—look for signs to the *cupola.*

Length of This Tour: Allow one hour, plus another hour if you climb the dome (or a half-hour to the roof). With less time, you could stroll the nave, glance up at the dome, down at St. Peter's resting place, and adore the *Pietà* on your way out.

Vatican Museums Tickets: The Vatican TI at St. Peter's often has museum tickets (with same-day entry timed reservations) on sale for €20. There may also be a table for ticket sales in the narthex (portico) of St. Peter's (with a €5 service fee). See page 471 for other Vatican Museums ticketing options.

Baggage Check: The free bag check (mandatory for bags larger than a purse or daypack) is outside the basilica (to the right as you face the entrance), just inside the security checkpoint.

Services: WCs are to the right and left on St. Peter's Square (next to the Vatican post offices, with another near the baggage storage down the steps on the right side of the entrance) and on the roof.

❷ SELF-GUIDED TOUR

To sample the basilica's highlights, follow these points:

The narthex (portico) is itself bigger than most churches. The huge white columns on the portico date from the first church (fourth century). Five famous bronze doors lead into the church. The central door, made from the melted-down bronze of the original door of Old St. Peter's, was the first Renaissance work in Rome (c. 1450). It's only opened on special occasions. The far-right entrance is the ❶ **Holy Door,** opened only during Holy Years (and Jubilee years, designated by the pope). On Christmas Eve every 25 years, the pope knocks three times with a silver hammer and the door opens, welcoming pilgrims to pass through.

St. Peter's Basilica

Not to Scale

Vatican Gardens

APSE

MAIN ALTAR

DOME ENTRANCE

WINTER CRYPT ENTRANCE

VATICAN MUSEUMS (SHADED AREA)

TREASURY MUSEUM

SISTINE CHAPEL

EXIT FROM SISTINE CHAPEL (SOMETIMES CLOSED)

NAVE

Courtyard

EXIT   ENTRANCE

SWISS GUARD (POPE TICKETS)

STEPS

PLATFORM

AUDIOGUIDES, **WC** & BAGGAGE CHECK

- - - Route to church entrance

St. Peter's Square

1 Holy Door
2 Charlemagne's Coronation Site
3 Extent of Original "Greek Cross" Plan
4 St. Andrew Statue; View of Dome; Crypt Entrance
5 St. Peter Statue (with Kissable Toe)
6 Pope John XXIII
7 Main Altar (under Bernini's Canopy & over Peter's Tomb)

8 BERNINI – Dove Window & Throne of St. Peter
9 St. Peter's Crucifixion Site
10 RAPHAEL – Mosaic Copy of The Transfiguration
11 MICHELANGELO – Pietà
12 Tomb of St. Pope John Paul II
13 Blessed Sacrament Chapel
14 Treasury Museum
15 Dome Entrance
16 Vatican Museums Tickets

• *Enter the nave. On the floor near the central doorway, look for the round maroon pavement stone.*

❷ This is the spot where in A.D. 800 the king of the Franks, **Charlemagne,** was crowned Holy Roman Emperor. Look down the main hall—the golden window at the far end is two football fields away. The dove in the window has the wingspan of a 747 (OK, not quite, but it *is* big). The church covers six acres. The babies at the base of the pillars along the main hall are adult-size. The lettering in the gold band along the top of the pillars is seven feet high. The church has a capacity of 60,000 standing worshippers (or 1,200 tour groups).

• *Walk toward the altar.*

❸ Michelangelo was 71 years old when he took over the church project. He intended to put the dome over Donato Bramante's original **Greek-Cross** floor plan, with four equal arms. In the Renaissance, this symmetrical arrangement symbolized perfection—the orderliness of the created world and the goodness of man (created in God's image). But the Church, struggling against Protestants and its own corruption, opted for a plan designed to impress the world with its grandeur—the Latin cross of the Crucifixion, with its nave extended to accommodate the grand religious spectacles of the Baroque period.

❹ Park yourself in front of the **statue of St. Andrew** to the left of the altar, the guy holding an X-shaped cross. (The **crypt entrance,** described later, is usually here; in winter, it's by the dome entrance.) Like Andrew, gaze up into the dome and gasp. The dome soars higher than a football field on end, 448 feet from the floor of the cathedral to the top of the lantern. It glows with light from its windows, the blue-and-gold mosaics creating a cool, solemn atmosphere. In this majestic vision of heaven (not painted by Michelangelo), we see (above the windows) Jesus, Mary, and a ring of saints, rings of more angels above them, and, way up in the ozone, God the Father (a blur of blue and red, unless you have binoculars).

❺ Back in the nave sits a bronze **statue of Peter** under a canopy. This is one of a handful of pieces of art that were in the earlier church. In one hand he holds keys, the symbol of the authority given him by Christ, while with the other hand he blesses us. His big right **toe** has been worn smooth by the lips of pilgrims and foot fetishists. Stand in line to kiss it, or, to avoid foot-and-mouth disease, touch your hand to your lips, and then rub the toe. This is an act of reverence with no legend attached.

The nave of St. Peter's Basilica

• *Circle to the right around the statue of Peter to find the lighted glass niche.*

❻ The red-robed body was **Pope John XXIII,** whose papacy lasted from 1958 to 1963. He is best known for initiating the landmark Vatican II Council (1962-1965), bringing the Church into the modern age. In 2000, during the beatification process (a stop on the way to sainthood), Church authorities checked his body, and it was surprisingly fresh. So they moved it upstairs, put it behind glass, and now older Catholics who remember him fondly enjoy another stop on their St. Peter's visit. Pope John was canonized in 2014.

❼ Sitting over St. Peter's tomb, the **main altar** (the white marble slab with cross and candlesticks) is used only when the pope himself says Mass. He sometimes conducts the Sunday morning service when he's in town. The tiny altar would be lost in this enormous church if it weren't for Gian Lorenzo Bernini's seven-story **bronze canopy,** which "extends" the altar upward and reduces the perceived distance between floor and ceiling. The corkscrew columns echo the marble ones that surrounded the altar in Old St. Peter's.

❽ Bernini's **dove window** shines above the smaller front altar used for everyday services. The Holy Spirit, in the form of a six-foot-high dove, pours sunlight onto the faithful through the alabaster windows, turning into artificial rays of gold and reflecting off swirling gold clouds, angels, and winged babies. During a service, real sunlight passes through real clouds of incense, mingling with Bernini's sculpture. Beneath the dove is the centerpiece of this structure, the **Throne of St. Peter,** an oak chair built in medieval times for a king. Subsequently, it was encrusted with tradition and encased in bronze by Bernini as a symbol of papal authority.

• *In the south transept (left of main altar), find the dark "painting" of St. Peter crucified upside-down (far end, left side).*

❾ According to tradition, this is the exact spot of **Peter's crucifixion** 1,900 years ago. During the reign of Emperor Nero, he was arrested and brought to Nero's Circus so all of Rome could witness his execution. When the authorities told Peter he was to be crucified just like his Lord, Peter said, "I'm not worthy" and insisted they nail him on the cross upside down.

❿ Around the corner (heading back toward the central nave), pause at the mosaic copy of Raphael's epic painting of **The Transfiguration.** The original is now in

Michelangelo, Pietà

the Pinacoteca of the Vatican Museums. This and all the other "paintings" in the church are actually mosaic copies made from thousands of colored chips the size of a fingernail. Because smoke and humidity would damage real paintings, since about 1600 church officials have replaced the paintings with mosaics produced by the Vatican Mosaic Studio.

• *Back near the entrance of the church, in the far corner, behind bulletproof glass, is the sculpture everyone has come to see.*

⓫ Michelangelo was 24 years old when he completed this **pietà**—a representation of Mary with the body of Christ taken from the cross. It was his first major commission, for Holy Year 1500. Michelangelo, with his total mastery of the real world, captures the sadness of the moment. Mary cradles her crucified son in her lap. Christ's lifeless right arm drooping down lets us know how heavy this corpse is. Mary looks at her dead son with tenderness; her left hand turns upward, asking, "How could they do this to you?"

• *In the chapel to the left is a revered tomb.*

⓬ **John Paul II** (1920-2005) was one of the most beloved popes of recent times. During his papacy (1978-2005), he was the face of the Catholic Church. The first non-Italian pope in four centuries, he oversaw the fall of communism in his native Poland, survived an assassination attempt, and stoically endured Parkinson's disease. When he died in 2005, hundreds of thousands lined up outside, waiting up to 24 hours to pay their respects. He was sainted in April 2014, just nine years after his death. St. John Paul II lies beneath a painting of the steadfast St. Sebastian, his favorite saint.

⓭ Step into the next chapel through the metalwork gates. It's the **Blessed Sacrament Chapel,** an oasis of peace reserved for prayer and meditation.

⓮ The skippable **Treasury Museum,** located on the left side of the nave near the altar, contains the room-size tomb of Sixtus IV by Antonio Pollaiuolo, a big pair of Roman pincers used to torture Christians, an original corkscrew column from Old St. Peter's, and assorted jewels, papal robes, and golden reliquaries.

• *When you're finished viewing the church's interior, go down to the foundations of Old St. Peter's, to the* **crypt** (**grotte** *or* **tombe**) *containing tombs of popes and memorial chapels. Save the crypt for last because it exits outside the basilica.*

In summer, the **crypt entrance** is usually beside the ❹ statue of St. Andrew, to the left of the main altar; in winter, it's by the dome entrance. Stairs lead you down to the floor level of the previous church, where you'll pass the sepulcher of Peter. This lighted niche with an icon is not Peter's actual tomb, but part of a shrine that stands atop Peter's tomb. Next are the tombs of past popes. Finally, you can see a few column fragments from Old St. Peter's (a.k.a. "Basilica Costantiniana"). Continue your one-way visit until it spills you out, usually near the checkroom.

⓯ For one of the best views of Rome, go up to the **dome.** The entrance is along the right (north) side of the church, but the line begins to form out front, at

The view from atop St. Peter's

Seeing the Pope

Your best chances for a sighting are on Sunday or Wednesday. Most Sundays (though not always, especially in July or August), the pope gives a **blessing** at noon from the papal balcony (to the right as you face the basilica) on St. Peter's Square. You don't need a ticket—just show up. On most Wednesdays, the pope holds a **general audience** at 10:00 (tickets get you a closer-up spot but are not required; anyone can enjoy a look behind the fences via jumbo-screens). That's when he arrives in his Popemobile and gives a short sermon from a platform on the square. (In winter, it's sometimes held indoors at the Paolo VI Auditorium, next to St. Peter's Basilica, though Pope Francis prefers the square, even in cold weather.) Whenever the pope appears on the square, the basilica closes and crowds are substantial—so avoid these times if you just want to sightsee.

General Audience Tickets: For the Wednesday audience, a (free) ticket gets you closer to the papal action. You have several options:

• Reserve tickets a month or two in advance by sending a request by mail or fax (access the form at www.vatican.va, under "Prefecture of the Papal Household"—this path also shows his schedule). Pick up the tickets at St. Peter's Square before the audience (available Tue 15:00-19:00 and Wed 7:00-9:00; usually under Bernini's colonnade, to the left of the church).

• You can book tickets online through St. Patrick's Church, the American Catholic Church in Rome (free, but donations appreciated). Pick up your reserved tickets or check for last-minute availability at the church office the Tuesday before the audience between 16:30 and 18:30—some stay for the 18:00 English Mass (Via Boncompagni 31, Metro: Barberini, tel. 06-4201-4554, www.stpatricksamericanrome.org).

• Starting the Monday before the audience, Swiss Guards hand out tickets from their station near the basilica exit. There's no need to go through security— just march up, ask nicely, and say "*danke*." While this is perhaps the easiest way, it's best to reserve in advance.

Without a Ticket: If you just want to see the pope, get a long-distance photo, and don't mind standing, show up for the Wednesday audience at least by 9:30, and take your place behind the fences in the back of the square.

General Audience Tips: Dress appropriately (shoulders covered, no short shorts or tank tops; long pants or knee-length skirts are safest) and clear security (no big bags; lines move more quickly on the side of the square farthest from the Metro stop). To get a seat, get there a couple of hours early; there are far fewer seats than ticketholders. The service gets under way around 9:30 when the names of attending pilgrim groups are announced. Shortly thereafter, the Popemobile appears, winding through the adoring crowd (the best views are near the cloth-covered wooden fences that line the Popemobile route). Around 10:00, the Pope's multilingual message begins and lasts for about an hour (you can leave at any time).

the church's right door (as you face the church). Look for *cupola* signs. There are two levels: the rooftop of the church and the top of the dome. Climb (for €6) or take an elevator (€8) to the first level, on the church roof just above the facade. From the roof, you can also go inside the gallery ringing the interior of the dome and look down inside the church. To get to the top of the dome, you'll take a staircase that winds between the outer shell and the inner one. It's a sweaty, crowded, claustrophobic, 15-minute, 323-step climb, but the view from the summit is great, and the fresh air is even better. Admire the arms of Bernini's colonnade encircling St. Peter's Square. Find the Victor Emmanuel Monument and the Pantheon. The large rectangular building to the left of the obelisk is the Vatican Museums complex, stuffed with art. And down in the square are tiny pilgrims buzzing like electrons around the nucleus of Catholicism.

Rick's Tip: *If you're* **claustrophobic** *or* **acrophobic, skip climbing the dome.**

▲▲▲VATICAN MUSEUMS (MUSEI VATICANI)

The four miles of displays in this immense museum complex culminate in the Raphael Rooms and Michelangelo's glorious Sistine Chapel. This is one of Europe's top three or four houses of art. It can be exhausting, so plan your visit carefully, focusing on a few themes. Allow two hours for a quick visit, three or four hours for enough time to enjoy it.

Cost and Hours: €16, €4 online reservation fee, Mon-Sat 9:00-18:00, last entry at 16:00 (though the official closing time is 18:00, the staff starts ushering you out at 17:30), closed on religious holidays and Sun except last Sun of the month (when it's free, more crowded, and open 9:00-14:00, last entry at 12:30); may be open Fri night mid-April-Oct 19:00-23:00 (last entry at 21:30) by online reservation only—check the website. Hours are subject to constant change.

The museum closes frequently for holidays, including: Jan 1 (New Year's), Jan 6 (Epiphany), Feb 11 (Vatican City established), March 19 (St. Joseph's Day), Easter Sunday and Monday, May 1 (Labor Day), June 29 (Sts. Peter and Paul), Aug 15 (Assumption of the Virgin), Nov 1 (All Saints' Day), Dec 8 (Immaculate Conception), and Dec 25 and 26 (Christmas). Before you visit, check the current hours, holiday closures, and calendar at www.museivaticani.va. Info tel. 06-6988-4676.

Reservations: Expect waits of up to two hours to buy tickets. You're crazy to come without a reservation. Bypass the long ticket lines by reserving an entry time at www.museivaticani.va for €20 (€16 ticket plus €4 booking fee). Select the ticket called "Vatican Museums and Sistine Chapel," choose your day and time, then check your email for your confirmation and print out the voucher. At the Vatican Museums, you'll see three lines. Show your voucher to the guard and enter via the middle line. Inside, after the security check, go to any window on the left to show your voucher and pick up your ticket. With the actual ticket in hand, go up the steps and enter the museum.

When to Go: The museum is generally hot and crowded, except in winter. The worst days are Saturdays, the last Sunday of the month (when it's free), Mondays, rainy days, and any day before or after a holiday closure. Mornings are most crowded. It's best to visit on a weekday after 14:00—the later the better. Another good time is during the papal audience on Wednesday morning, when many tourists are at St. Peter's Square (the only drawback is that St. Peter's Basilica is closed until roughly 13:00, as is the exit to it from the Sistine Chapel—described later, under "Exit Strategies").

Avoiding Lines: Booking a **guided tour** (see "Tours," later) gets you right in—just show the guard your voucher. You can often buy **same-day timed-entry reservations** (for the same €20 online price) through the TI in St. Peter's Square (to the left, as you face the basilica). Also, the Opera Romana Pellegrinaggi (a.k.a., Roma Cristiana), a private pilgrimage tour company, sells same-day tickets for €30 (entrances almost hourly, office in front of St. Peter's Square, Piazza Pio XII 9, tel. 06-6980-6380, www.operaromanapellegrinaggi.org). If you're going to St. Peter's Basilica first, you can sometimes buy same-day Vatican Museums tickets in the narthex for €5 extra. Hawkers peddling skip-the-line access swarm the Vatican area, offering guided tours—but museum staff advise against accepting their offers (while legitimate, the tour caliber is often low).

Dress Code: Modest dress is required (no shorts, above-knee skirts, or bare shoulders).

Getting There: The Ottaviano Metro stop is a 10-minute walk from the entrance. Bus #49 from Piazza Cavour/Castel Sant'Angelo stops at Piazza Risorgimento and continues right to the entrance. Bus #492 heads from the city center past Piazza Risorgimento and the Vatican walls, and also stops on Via Leone IV. Bus #64 stops on the other side of St. Peter's Square, a 15- to 20-minute walk (facing the church from the obelisk, take a right through the colonnade and follow the Vatican Wall). A few other handy buses (see page 499) can get you close enough to snag a taxi for the final stretch. Or take a taxi from the city center—they are reasonable (hop in and say, "moo-ZAY-ee vah-tee-KAH-nee").

Getting In: Approaching the exterior entrance, you'll see three lines: individuals without reservations (far left), individuals with reservations (much shorter and faster, in the middle), and groups (on the right). Make sure you get in the correct entry line. All visitors must pass through a metal detector (no pocketknives allowed).

Tours: A €7 **audioguide** is available at the top of the spiral ramp/escalator, and can be prepaid when you book tickets online. A security ID is not required to rent an audioguide, and you can drop it off either where you rented it or after leaving the Sistine Chapel if taking the shortcut to St. Peter's (described later, under "Exit Strategies"). Confirm the drop-off location when renting.

🎧 Download my free Vatican Museums and Sistine Chapel **audio tours.**

The Vatican offers **guided tours** in English that are easy to book on their website (€32, includes admission). As with individual ticket reservations, present your confirmation voucher to a guard to the right of the entrance; then, once inside, go to the Guided Tours desk (in the lobby, up a few stairs).

For a list of **private tour** companies and guides, see page 427.

Length of This Tour: Until you expire, the museum closes, or 2.5 hours pass, whichever comes first. If you're short on time, see the octagonal courtyard (Laocoön), then follow the crowd flow directly to the Sistine Chapel, sightseeing along the way. From the Sistine Chapel, head straight to St. Peter's (see "Exit Strategies," next).

Exit Strategies: The museum has two exits. The **main exit** is near the entrance. Use this one if you're asked to return an audioguide there or if you plan on following this self-guided tour exactly as laid out, visiting the Pinacoteca at the end.

The other exit is a handy (but sometimes closed) **shortcut** that leads from the Sistine Chapel directly to St. Peter's Basilica (spilling out alongside the church). The shortcut saves you a 30-minute walk backtracking to the basilica's main entrance and lets you avoid the long security line for others entering the basilica. Officially, this exit is for Vatican guides and their groups only. However, it's often open to anyone (depending on how crowded the chapel is and how the guards feel). It's worth a shot (try blend-

Vatican Museums Overview

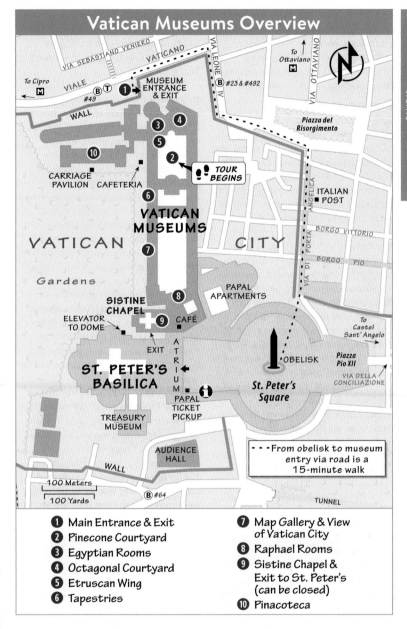

1 Main Entrance & Exit
2 Pinecone Courtyard
3 Egyptian Rooms
4 Octagonal Courtyard
5 Etruscan Wing
6 Tapestries
7 Map Gallery & View of Vatican City
8 Raphael Rooms
9 Sistine Chapel & Exit to St. Peter's (can be closed)
10 Pinacoteca

ing in with a group that's leaving), but be prepared for the possibility that you won't get through.

Baggage Check: The museum's "checkroom" (to the right after security) takes only bigger bags, not day bags.

⊙ SELF-GUIDED TOUR

Start, as civilization did, in **Egypt and Mesopotamia.** Decorating the museum's courtyard are some of the best **Greek and Roman statues** in captivity. The **Apollo Belvedere** is a Roman copy (4th century B.C.) of a Hellenistic original that followed the style of the Greek sculptor Praxiteles. It fully captures the beauty of the human form. Instead of standing at attention, face-forward with his arms at his sides (Egyptian-style), Apollo is on the move, coming to rest with his weight on one leg.

Laocoön was sculpted some four centuries after the Golden Age (5th-4th century B.C.), after the scales of "balance" had been tipped. *Apollo* is serene and graceful, while *Laocoön* is emotional and gritty. The figures (carved from four blocks of marble pieced together seamlessly) are powerful, with twisted poses that accentuate each rippling muscle and bulging vein.

The centerpiece of the next hall is the 2,000-year-old **Belvedere Torso,** which had a great impact on the art of Michelangelo. Finishing off the classical statuary are two fine fourth-century porphyry sarcophagi. These royal purple tombs were made for the Roman emperor Constantine's mother and daughter.

After long halls of tapestries, old maps, broken penises, and fig leaves, you'll come to what most people are looking for: the Raphael Rooms and Michelangelo's Sistine Chapel.

The highlight of the **Raphael Rooms,** frescoed by Raphael and his assistants, is the restored *School of Athens.* It is remarkable for its blatant pre-Christian classical orientation, especially considering it originally wallpapered the apartments of Pope Julius II. Raphael honors the great pre-Christian thinkers—Aristotle, Plato, and company—who are portrayed as the leading artists of Raphael's day. Leonardo da Vinci, whom Raphael worshipped, is in the role of Plato. Michelangelo, brooding in the foreground, was added later. When Raphael snuck a peek at the Sistine Chapel, he decided that his arch-competitor was so good that he put their differences aside and included him in this tribute. Today's St. Peter's was under construction as Raphael was working. In the *School of Athens,* he gives us a sneak preview of the unfinished church.

Next is the brilliantly restored **Sistine Chapel.** This is the pope's personal chapel and also the place where, upon the death of the ruling pope, a new pope is elected.

The Sistine Chapel is famous for Michelangelo's pictorial culmination of the Renaissance, showing the story of creation, with God weaving in and out of each scene through that busy first week. It's a stirring example of the artistic and

Laocoön

Raphael, School of Athens

Sistine Chapel

theological maturity of the 33-year-old Michelangelo, who spent four years on this work.

The ceiling shows the history of the world before the birth of Jesus. We see God creating the world, creating man and woman, destroying the earth by flood, and so on. God himself, in his purple robe, actually appears in the first five scenes. Along the sides (where the ceiling starts to curve), we see the Old Testament prophets and pagan Greek prophetesses who foretold the coming of Christ. Dividing these scenes and figures are fake niches (a painted 3-D illusion) decorated with nude figures with symbolic meaning.

In the central panel of the **Creation of Adam,** God and man take center stage in this Renaissance version of creation. Adam, newly formed in the image of God, lounges dreamily in perfect naked innocence. God, with his entourage, swoops in with a swirl of activity (which—with a little imagination—looks like a cross-section of a human brain...quite a strong humanist statement). Their reaching hands are the center of this work. Adam's is passive; God's is forceful, his finger twitching upward with energy. Here is the very moment of creation, as God passes the spark of life to man, the crowning work of his creation.

This is the spirit of the Renaissance. God is not reaching down to puny man from way on high. They are on an equal plane, divided only by the diagonal bit of sky. God's billowing robe and the patch of green that holds Adam balance each other. They are like the yin and yang symbols finally coming together—uniting, complementing each other, creating wholeness. God and man work together in the divine process of creation.

When the ceiling was finished and revealed to the public, it blew 'em away. It both caps the Renaissance and turns it in a new direction. The style is more dramatic and emotional than the balanced Renaissance works before it. This is a personal work—the Gospel according to Michelangelo—but its themes and subject matter are universal. Many art scholars contend that the Sistine ceiling is the single greatest work of art by any one human being.

Later, after the Reformation wars had begun and after the Catholic army of Spain had sacked the Vatican, the reeling Church began to fight back. As part of its Counter-Reformation, a much older Michelangelo was commissioned to paint the *Last Judgment* (behind the altar).

It's Judgment Day, and Christ—the powerful figure in the center, raising his arm to spank the wicked—has come to find out who's naughty and who's nice. Beneath him, a band of angels blows its trumpets Dizzy Gillespie-style: a wake-up call to the sleeping dead. The dead at lower left leave their graves and prepare to be judged. The righteous, on Christ's right hand (the left side of the picture), are carried up to heaven. The wicked on the other side are hurled into hell. Charon, from the underworld of Greek mythology, waits below to ferry the souls of the damned to hell.

When *The Last Judgment* was unveiled to the public in 1541, it caused a sensation. The pope dropped to his knees and cried, "Lord, charge me not with my sins when thou shalt come on the Day of Judgment."

And it changed the course of art. The complex composition, with more than 300 figures swirling around the figure of Christ, went far beyond traditional Renaissance balance. The twisted figures shown from every imaginable angle challenged other painters to try and top this master of 3-D illusion. The sheer terror and drama of the scene was a striking contrast to the placid optimism of, say, Raphael's *School of Athens*. Michelangelo had Baroque-en all the rules of the Renaissance, signaling a new era of art.

If you take the long march back, you'll find, along with the Pinacoteca, a cafeteria (long lines, uninspired food), the under-rated early-Christian art section, and the exit via the souvenir shop.

Rick's Tip: *A handy (but sometimes closed)* **shortcut leads from the Sistine Chapel directly to St. Peter's Basilica,** *saving a 30-minute walk backtracking to the basilica's main entrance and avoiding the security line there. Exit through the corner door labeled "for authorized guides and tour groups only." Try blending in, or pretend that your group has left you behind.*

North Rome

▲▲▲BORGHESE GALLERY (GALLERIA BORGHESE)

This plush museum, filling a cardinal's mansion in Rome's semiscruffy three-square-mile "Central Park," offers one of Europe's most sumptuous art experiences. Enjoy a collection of world-class Baroque sculpture, including Bernini's *David* and his excited statue of Apollo chasing Daphne, as well as paintings by Caravaggio, Raphael, Titian, and Rubens. The museum's mandatory reservation system keeps crowds to a manageable size.

Cost and Hours: €13, free and crowded first Sun of the month, Tue-Sun 9:00-19:00, closed Mon. Reservations are mandatory.

Information: Tel. 06-32810 (ticket service) or 06-841-3979 (museum), www.galleriaborghese.it.

Reservations: Reservations are mandatory and simple to get. Every two hours, 360 people are allowed to enter the museum. Entry times are 9:00, 11:00, 13:00, 15:00, and 17:00 (you'll get exactly two hours for your visit). The sooner you reserve, the better—at least several days in advance for a weekday visit, and at least a week ahead for weekends. (In winter, you may be able to get tickets on shorter notice.)

It's easiest to book online at www.tosc.it (€4/person booking fee; choose to pick up tickets at venue). You can also reserve with a real person over the telephone (€2/person booking fee, tel. 06-32810, press 2 for English, phones answered Mon-Fri 9:00-18:00, Sat 9:00-13:00, closed Sat in Aug and Sun year-round).

The museum recommends that you arrive at the gallery 30 minutes before your appointed time to pick up your ticket in the lobby on the lower level. Don't cut it close—arriving late can mean forfeiting your reservation.

You can use a Roma Pass for free or discounted entry, but you're still required to make a reservation (by phone only—not online; specify that you have the Roma Pass).

Getting There: The museum, at Piazzale del Museo Borghese 5, is set idyllically but inconveniently in the vast Villa Borghese Gardens. Bus #910 goes from Termini train station (and Piazza Repubblica) to the Via Pinciana stop, 100 yards from the museum. By Metro, from the Barberini Metro stop, walk 10 minutes up Via Veneto, enter the park, and turn right, following signs another 10 minutes to the Borghese Gallery.

Tours: Guided English tours are offered every day at 9:00 and 11:00, and occasionally on Thursdays at 13:00 (€6.50; reserve tours either online or by phone). The superb 1.5-hour audioguide tour (€5) covers more than my description.

Planning Your Time: Two hours is all you get...and you'll want every minute. Budget most of your time for the more interesting ground floor, but set aside 30 minutes for the paintings of the Pinacoteca upstairs (highlights are marked by the audioguide icons).

Services: Baggage check is free, mandatory, and strictly enforced.

Visiting the Museum: It's hard to believe that a family of cardinals and popes would display so many works with secular and sensual—even erotic—themes. But the Borgheses felt that all forms of human expression, including

Borghese Gallery—Ground Floor

Stairs up
to Pinacoteca

| ROOM VI | ROOM V | ROOM IV | ➡ ⑨ | ROOM III |

❻   ❹   ③

CHAPEL ⑤

ROOM II

❷

MAIN
ENTRY
HALL

ROOM VII

❼

ROOM VIII   START   ROOM I

❽   PORTICO   ❶

Not to Scale

To Basement
(Tickets, Info, Shop, WC)

❶ CANOVA – Pauline
Borghese as Venus

❷ BERNINI – David

❸ BERNINI – Apollo and
Daphne

❹ BERNINI – The Rape of
Proserpina

⑤ UNKNOWN – Diana the
Hunter; other marbles

❻ BERNINI – Aeneas and
Anchises

❼ "Theater of the Universe"

❽ CARAVAGGIO – Various

⑨ Stairs up to Pinacoteca

pagan myths and physical passion, glorified God.

The essence of the collection is the connection of the Renaissance with the classical world. As you enter, notice the second-century Roman reliefs with Michelangelo-designed panels above either end of the portico. The villa was built in the early 17th century by art collector Cardinal Scipione Borghese, to prove that the glories of ancient Rome were matched by the Renaissance.

In the main entry hall, high up on the wall, is a thrilling first-century Greek sculpture of a horse falling. The Renaissance-era rider was added by Pietro Bernini, father of the famous Gian Lorenzo Bernini.

Each room seems to feature a Baroque masterpiece. In Room I is *Pauline Borghese as Venus,* for which Napoleon's sister went the full monty for the sculptor Antonio Canova, scandalizing Europe. ("How could you have done such a thing?!" she was asked. She replied, "The room wasn't cold.") With the famous nose of her conqueror brother, she strikes the pose of Venus as conqueror of men's hearts. Her relaxed afterglow says she's already had her man.

In Room II, Gian Lorenzo Bernini's *David* twists around to put a big rock in his sling. He purses his lips, knits his brow, and winds his body like a spring as his eyes lock onto the target: Goliath, who's somewhere behind us, putting us right in the line of fire. Compared with Michelangelo's *David*, this is unvarnished realism—an unbalanced pose, bulging veins, unflattering face, and armpit hair. Michelangelo's *David* thinks, whereas Bernini's acts. Bernini slays the pretty-boy *David*s of the Renaissance and prepares to invent Baroque.

In Room III, Bernini's **Apollo and Daphne** is the perfect Baroque subject. Apollo—made stupid by Cupid's arrow of love—chases after Daphne, who has been turned off by the "arrow of disgust." Just as he's about to catch her, she calls to her father to save her. Magically, she transforms into a tree. Frustrated Apollo will end up with a handful of leaves.

In Room IV, Bernini's **The Rape of Proserpina** proves that even at the age of 24 the sculptor was the master of marble.

In Room VI, Bernini's **Aeneas and Anchises** reveals the then 20-year-old

sculptor's astonishing aptitude for portraying human flesh. In the same room, **Diana the Hunter** is a rare Greek original (second century B.C., sculptor unknown).

In Room VIII is a fabulous collection of paintings by **Caravaggio,** who brought Christian saints down to earth with gritty realism.

Upstairs, in the Pinacoteca (Painting Gallery), are busts and paintings by Bernini, as well as works by Raphael, Titian, Correggio, and Domenichino.

CAPUCHIN CRYPT

If you want to see artistically arranged bones, this is the place. The crypt is below the Church of Santa Maria della Immacolata Concezione on the tree-lined Via Veneto, just up from Piazza Barberini. The bones of about 4,000 friars who died in the 1700s are in the basement, all lined up in a series of six crypts to instruct wide-eyed visitors of the inevitability of mortality. Its macabre motto (in the first chapel) is: "What you are now, we used to be."

Cost and Hours: €8.50, daily 9:00-19:00, modest dress required, Via Veneto 27, Metro: Barberini, tel. 06-8880-3695.

▲SPANISH STEPS

The wide, curving staircase, culminating with an obelisk between two Baroque church towers, is one of Rome's iconic sights. Beyond that, it's a people-gathering place. By day, the area hosts shoppers looking for high-end fashions; on balmy evenings, it attracts young and old alike. For more about the steps, see page 438.

▲▲MUSEO DELL'ARA PACIS (MUSEUM OF THE ALTAR OF PEACE)

On January 30, 9 B.C., soon-to-be-emperor Augustus led a procession of priests up the steps and into this newly built "Altar of Peace." They sacrificed an animal on the altar and poured an offering of wine, thanking the gods for helping Augustus pacify barbarians abroad and rivals at home. This marked the dawn of the Pax Romana (c. A.D. 1-200), a Golden

Bernini, Apollo and Daphne

Age of good living, stability, dominance, and peace (*pax*). The Ara Pacis (AH-rah PAH-chees) hosted annual sacrifices by the emperor until the area was flooded by the Tiber River. For an idea of how high the water could get, find the measure (*idrometro*) scaling the right side of the church closest to the entrance. Buried under silt, it was abandoned and forgotten until the 16th century, when various parts were discovered and excavated. Mussolini had the altar's scattered parts reconstructed in a building here in 1938. Today, the Altar of Peace stands in a striking pavilion designed by American architect Richard Meier (opened 2006). It's about the only entirely new structure permitted in the old center of Rome since Mussolini's day. To see what the altar looked like in its day, consider the virtual reality show—a colorful 3D reconstruction of the altar.

Cost and Hours: €10.50 when no special exhibits, daily 9:30-19:30, last entry one hour before closing, videoguide-€6; virtual reality show-€12, daily April-Oct from 20:45, 45 minutes, reserve online; a long block west of Via del Corso on Via di Ara Pacis, on the east bank of the Tiber near Ponte Cavour, Metro: Spagna plus a 10-minute walk down Via dei Condotti; tel. 06-0608, www.arapacis.it.

Visiting the Museum: Start with the model in the museum's lobby. The Altar of Peace was originally located east of here, along today's Via del Corso. The model shows where it stood in relation to the Mausoleum of Augustus (now next door) and the Pantheon. Approach the Ara Pacis and look through the doorway to see the raised altar. This simple structure has just the basics of a Roman temple: an altar for sacrifices surrounded by cubicle walls that enclose a consecrated space. Climb the 10 steps and go inside. From here, the priest would climb the 8 altar steps to make sacrifices. The walls of the enclosure are decorated with the offerings to the gods: animals, garlands of fruit, and ceremonial platters. The reliefs on the north and south sides depict the parade of dignitaries who consecrated the altar, while the reliefs on the west side (near the altar's back door) celebrate peace (goddess Roma as a conquering Amazon, right side) and prosperity (fertility goddess surrounded by children, plants, and animals, left side).

East Rome

▲▲▲NATIONAL MUSEUM OF ROME

The National Museum's main branch houses the greatest collection of ancient Roman art anywhere, including busts of

Ara Pacis (Altar of Peace)

emperors and a Roman copy of the Greek *Discus Thrower*.

Cost and Hours: €7 combo-ticket valid for three days, also includes three other branches—all skippable, free and crowded first Sun of the month, Tue-Sun 9:00-19:45, closed Mon, last entry 45 minutes before closing, audioguide-€5.

Information: Tel. 06-3996-7700, www.museonazionaleromano.beniculturali.it.

Getting There: The museum is in Palazzo Massimo, situated between Piazza della Repubblica (Metro: Repubblica) and Termini Station (Metro: Termini). It's a few minutes' walk from either Metro stop. As you leave Termini, it's the sandstone-brick building on your left. Enter at the far end, at Largo di Villa Peretti.

Visiting the Museum: The museum is rectangular, with rooms and hallways built around a central courtyard. The ground-floor displays follow Rome's history as it changes from a republic to a dictatorial empire. The first-floor exhibits take Rome from its peak through its slow decline. The second floor houses rare frescoes and fine mosaics, and the basement presents coins and everyday objects.

On the first floor, along with statues and busts showing such emperors as Trajan and Hadrian, you'll see the best-preserved Roman copy of the Greek *Discus Thrower*. Statues of athletes like this commonly stood in the baths, where Romans cultivated healthy bodies, minds, and social skills, hoping to lead well-rounded lives. Other statues on this floor originally stood in the pleasure gardens of the Roman rich—surrounded by greenery with the splashing sound of fountains, all painted in bright, lifelike colors. Though created by Romans, the themes are mostly Greek, with godlike humans and human-looking gods.

The second floor contains frescoes and mosaics that once decorated the walls and floors of Roman villas. They feature everyday people, animals, flowery patterns, and geometrical designs. The Villa Farnesina frescoes—in black, red, yellow, and blue—are mostly architectural designs, with fake columns, friezes, and garlands. The Villa di Livia frescoes, owned by the wily wife of Augustus, immerse you in a leafy green garden full of birds and fruit trees, symbolizing the gods.

Finally, descend into the basement to see fine gold jewelry, an eight-year-old girl's mummy, and vault doors leading into the best coin collection in Europe, with fancy magnifying glasses maneuvering you through cases of coins from ancient Rome to modern times.

▲BATHS OF DIOCLETIAN/CHURCH OF SANTA MARIA DEGLI ANGELI

Of all the marvelous structures built by the Romans, their public baths were arguably the grandest, and the Baths of Diocletian were the granddaddy of them all. Built by Emperor Diocletian around A.D. 300 and sprawling over 30 acres—roughly five times the size of the Colosseum—these baths could cleanse 3,000 Romans at once. They functioned until A.D. 537, when barbarians attacked and the city's aqueducts fell into disuse, plunging Rome

Baths of Diocletian

Ostia Antica

1 Necropolis

2 Porta Romana

3 Republican Warehouses

4 Baths of Neptune

5 Theater

6 Square of the Guilds

7 Mill

8 Via Casa di Diana

9 Forum

10 Forum Baths

11 Ostia Museum

into a thousand years of poverty, darkness, and BO. Today, tourists can visit one grand section of the baths, the former main hall. This impressive remnant of the ancient complex was later transformed (with help from Michelangelo) into the Church of Santa Maria degli Angeli.

Cost and Hours: Free, daily 7:30-18:30, closes slightly later May-Sept and Sun year-round, entrance on Piazza della Repubblica (Metro: Repubblica), www. santamariadegliangeliroma.it.

▲▲CHURCH OF SAN GIOVANNI IN LATERANO

Built by Constantine, the first Christian emperor, this was Rome's most important church through medieval times. A building alongside the church houses the **Holy Stairs** (Scala Santa) said to have

Boxer at Rest (*National Museum of Rome*)

Pilgrims climbing the Holy Stairs

been walked up by Jesus, which today are ascended by pilgrims on their knees. You can join them.

Cost and Hours: Church and Holy Stairs—free, cloister—€5, chapel at Holy Stairs—€3.50 (€10 combo-ticket covers cloister, chapel, and audioguide); church open daily 7:00-18:30; Holy Stairs open Mon-Sat 6:30-19:00, Sun 7:00-19:00, Oct-March closes daily at 18:30. The church is on Piazza di San Giovanni in Laterano (east of the Colosseum and south of Termini train station, Metro: San Giovanni, or bus #87). Tel. 06-772-6641, www.vatican.va (search for "San Giovanni in Laterano"); for Holy Stairs, visit www.scala-santa.it.

Near Rome: Ostia Antica

For an exciting day trip, pop down to the Roman port of Ostia, which is similar to Pompeii but a lot closer and, in some ways, more interesting. Because Ostia was a working port town, it offers a more complete and gritty look at Roman life than wealthier Pompeii. Wandering around today, you'll see warehouses, apartment flats, mansions, shopping arcades, and baths that served a once-thriving port of 60,000 people. At its peak, Ostia was vital to the Roman Empire. Most of what the city of Rome consumed—and that was a lot by historical standards—came in through this port.

Today, with more than 70 peaceful acres to explore and relatively few crowds, it's a welcome break from the bustle of Rome. You can buy a map or follow the map on page 482 (which lists the major

stops) and explore the town, including the 2,000-year-old theater. Finish with the fine little museum.

Cost and Hours: €8 for the site and museum, €11 with special exhibits, April-Aug Tue-Sun 8:30-19:15, Sept until 19:00, Oct until 18:30, Nov-mid-Feb 8:30-16:30, shorter hours mid-Feb-March, closed Mon year-round, last entry one hour before closing. The small museum closes one hour before the site does.

Getting There: Getting from Rome to Ostia Antica is a 45-minute combination Metro/train ride (costs only one Metro ticket each way): Take Metro line B to the Piramide stop, which is part of the Roma Porta San Paolo train station. Exiting the Metro, follow signs to *Lido*—go up the escalator, turn left, and go down the steps into the Roma-Lido train station. All trains depart for the Lido, leave every 15 minutes, and stop at Ostia Antica. Hop on the next train, ride for about 30 minutes (no need to stamp your Metro ticket again, but keep it handy in case it's checked), and get off at Ostia Antica. Leaving the train station, walk over the blue skybridge, then head straight down Via della Stazione di Ostia Antica, continuing straight (through a small parking lot) to the large parking lot for the site (entrance on your left).

Information: A map of the site with suggested itineraries is available for €2 from the ticket office. Tel. 06-5635-0215. Helpful websites include www.ostiaantica.beniculturali.it and www.ostia-antica.org.

Tours: Audioguide-€5; choose between a short version (lasts 3 hours) or a longer one (7 hours). Or you can download my free Ostia Antica audio tour.

EXPERIENCES

Nightlife

The best after-dark activity is to grab a gelato and stroll the medieval lanes that connect the romantic, floodlit squares and fountains. Head for Piazza Navona, the

Ostia Antica Theater

Pantheon, Campo de' Fiori, Trevi Fountain, and the Spanish Steps; these marvelous sights are linked together in my self-guided "Heart of Rome" walk (page 431). Another great evening activity is my "Dolce Vita Stroll" along Via del Corso (page 439).

A fun neighborhood to explore at night is **Monti,** which is more like a lively village. Hang out at the fountain on Piazza della Madonna dei Monti, a popular gathering spot. Stop at the shop on the uphill side of the square, which sells cheap bottles of wine with plastic glasses, beer, fruit, and munchies. Or head to an actual bar, like **Fafiuché** (Via della Madonna dei Monti 28) or **Enoteca Cavour 313** (Via Cavour 313).

Performances

Get a copy of the entertainment guide *Evento* (free at TIs and many hotels) and check the listings of concerts, operas, dance, and films. For the most up-to-date events calendar, check these English-language websites: www.inromenow.com, www.wantedinrome.com, and www.angloinfo.com/rome.

The **Teatro dell'Opera** has an active schedule of opera and classical concerts. You'll see locals in all their finery, so pull your fanciest outfit from your backpack (Via Firenze 72, a block off Via Nazionale, Metro: Repubblica; box office takes phone reservations beginning 5 days prior at tel. 06-4816-0255, www.operaroma.it).

The Episcopal **Church of St. Paul's Within the Walls** offers musical events ranging from orchestral concerts (usually Tue and Fri at 20:30) to operatic performances (usually Sat at 20:30). Some Sunday evenings at 18:30, the church hosts hour-long candlelit "Luminaria" concerts. Check the church website (under "Music") to see what's on (€10-30, same-day tickets usually available, arrive 30-45 minutes early for best seat, Via Napoli 58 at corner of Via Nazionale, Metro: Repubblica, tel. 06-482-6296, www.stpaulsrome.it).

The venerable **Alexanderplatz** hosts jazz performances most evenings (Sun-Thu concerts at 21:45, Fri-Sat at 22:30, closed in summer, Via Ostia 9, Metro: Ottaviano, tel. 06-3972-1867, www.alexanderplatzjazzclub.it).

EATING

Romans take great pleasure in dining well, treating it as a lengthy social occasion. Embrace this passion over a multicourse meal at an outdoor table, watching a parade of passersby while you sip wine with loved ones.

Rome's fabled squares (most notably Piazza Navona, near the Pantheon, and Campo de' Fiori) are lined with the outdoor tables of touristy restaurants with enticing menus and formal-vested waiters. The atmosphere is super romantic. I, too, like the idea of dining under floodlit monuments, amid a constantly flowing parade of people. But you'll likely be surrounded by tourists and hawkers, and awkward interactions can kill the ambience...leaving you with just a forgettable and overpriced meal. Restaurants in these areas are notorious for surprise charges, bad service, and mediocre, microwaved food.

I enjoy the view by savoring just a drink or dessert on a famous square, but I dine with locals on nearby low-rent streets, where the proprietor needs to serve a good-value meal and nurture a local following to stay in business. If you're set on eating—or just drinking and snacking—on a famous piazza, you don't need a guidebook listing to choose a spot; enjoy the ritual of slowly circling the square, observing both the food and the people eating it, and sit where the view and menu appeal to you. (And pizza is probably your best value and least risky bet.)

I'm impressed by how small the price difference can be between a mediocre Roman restaurant and a fine one. You can pay about 20 percent more for double the quality. If I had $100 for three meals in Rome, I'd spend $50 for one and $25 each for the other two, rather than $33 on all three. For splurge meals, I'd consider Gabriello and Fortunato, in that order (details listed later).

Budget Eating: For a light budget meal, consider an *aperitivo* buffet. Bars all over town—especially in Monti—serve up an enticing buffet of small dishes, from about 18:00 to 21:00, and anyone buying a drink (generally €8-12) gets to eat "for free." Some places limit you to one plate; others allow refills.

For the cheapest meal, assemble a picnic and dine with Rome as your backdrop. Buy ingredients for your picnic at one of Rome's open-air produce markets (mornings only), an *alimentari* (corner grocery store), a *rosticcerie* (cheap food to go), or a *supermercato*, such as Conad or Coop. You'll find handy late-night supermarkets near the Pantheon (on Via Giustiniani), Spanish Steps (Via Vittoria), Trevi Fountain (Via del Bufalo), and Campo de' Fiori (Via di Monte della Farina).

Rome discourages people from picnicking or drinking at historic monuments (such as on the Spanish Steps) in the old center. Violators can be fined, though it rarely happens. You'll be OK if you eat *with* a view rather than *on* the view.

Pantheon Neighborhood

I've listed restaurants in this central area based on which landmark they're closest to: Piazza Navona, the Trevi Fountain, or the Pantheon.

Near Piazza Navona

Piazza Navona and the streets just to the west are jammed with an amazing array of restaurants. The places lining the piazza itself are traditional and touristy. Instead, survey the scene on the two streets heading west from the square.

$$ Ristorante and Bar del Fico is a sprawling, rustic-chic place with a split personality: The restaurant is a spacious, family-friendly, pizza-and-pasta type eatery, while the bar feels like a huge Italian saloon filled with young locals (3 blocks west of Piazza Navona at Via della Pace 34, tel. 06-688-91373).

$$ Ristorante Pizzeria "da Francesco," bustling and authentic, has a 50-year-old tradition, great indoor seating, and a few tables stretching along the quiet street. Their blackboard explains the daily specials (daily 12:00-15:30 & 19:00-24:00, requires reservations for evening seatings, Piazza del Fico 29, tel. 06-686-4009, www.dafrancesco.it).

$$ Vivi Bistrot is in the Museum of Rome building at the south end of Piazza Navona, with two delightful window tables overlooking the square. This cheery and modern little restaurant serves salads, pastas, and burger plates with a focus on organic ingredients (Tue-Sun 10:00-24:00, closed Mon, Piazza Navona 2, tel. 06-683-3779, www.vivibistrot.com).

$$ L'Insalata Ricca, specializing in filling salads alongside pastas and main courses, is handy and central (daily 12:00-24:00). They have a branch at Piazza Pasquino 72 (tel. 06-6830-7881) and a larger location a few blocks away, on a bigger square next to busy Corso Vittorio Emanuele (Largo dei Chiavari 85, tel. 06-6880-3656).

Near the Trevi Fountain

The streets surrounding the Trevi Fountain are littered with mediocre restaurants catering to tourists—try one of these instead.

$$$ Hostaria Romana is a busy bistro with a hustling, fun-loving gang of waiters.

Roman Cuisine

Simple, fresh, seasonal ingredients dominate Roman cuisine. It's robust, strongly flavored, and unpretentious—much like the people who've created it. Roman cooking didn't come out of emperors' or popes' kitchens, but from the *cucina povera*—the home cooking of the common people. That could explain why Romans have a fondness for meats known as the *quinto quarto* ("fifth quarter"), such as tripe (*trippa*), tail, brain, and pigs' feet.

Appetizers (*Antipasti*): Popular choices are *prosciutto e melone* (thin slices of ham wrapped around cantaloupe), *bruschetta* (toasted bread topped with chopped tomatoes), and *antipasto misto* (a plate of marinated or grilled vegetables, cheeses, cured meats, or seafood). *Fritti* are fried snacks that have been either battered or breaded, such as stuffed olives, potato croquettes, rice balls, and stuffed squash blossoms.

First Courses (*Primi*): A pasta dish born in Rome is *spaghetti alla carbonara,* with eggs, pancetta (Italian bacon), cheese, and pepper. Another traditional pasta is *bucatini all'amatriciana,* with tomato sauce, onions, pancetta, and cheese. *Gnocchi alla romana* are small, flattened dumplings from semolina (not potatoes), and baked with butter and cheese. If you like spaghetti with clams, try *spaghetti alle vongole veraci.*

Second Courses (*Secondi*): A very Roman dish is *saltimbocca alla romana* (thinly sliced, lightly fried veal layered with prosciutto). *Filetti di baccalà* is fried salt cod, like fish-and-chips minus the chips. Other choices are baby lamb chops (*abbacchio alla scottadito*), stewed baby eels (*anguillette in umid*), and braised oxtails (*coda alla vaccinara*). *Trippa alla romana* is braised tripe with onions and carrots.

Desserts (*Dolci*): Dessert can be a seasonal fruit, such as strawberries, peaches, or even cheese. *Bignè* are cream puff-like pastries filled with *zabaione* (egg yolks, sugar, and Marsala wine). *Tartufo* is a rich dark-chocolate gelato ball with a cherry inside, sometimes served *con panna* (with whipped cream). When you're out and about on a hot day, try a *grattachecca* (flavored, sweetened shaved ice) from a vendor's stand.

Local Wines (*Vini*): Frascati, probably the best-known wine of the region, is an inexpensive dry white. Others are Castelli Romani, Marino, Colli Albani, and Velletri. Torre Ercolana is a medium-bodied red made from the regional cesanese grape, as well as cabernet and merlot (known as the region's best-quality red, aged at least five years).

The upstairs is a glassed-in terrace, while the cellar has noisy walls graffitied by happy eaters. Try the traditional *saltimbocca alla romana* (veal) or the pasta dish, *bucatini all'amatriciana* (Mon-Sat 12:30-15:00 & 19:15-23:00, closed Sun and Aug, reservations smart, a block past the entrance to the big tunnel near the Trevi Fountain, corner of Via Rasella and Via del Boccaccio, tel. 06-474-5284, www.hostariaromana.it).

$$ L'Antica Birreria Peroni is Rome's answer to a German beer hall. Serving hearty mugs of Peroni beer and lots of beerhall food and Italian classics, the place is a hit with Romans for a cheap night out (Mon-Sat 12:00-24:00, closed Sun, midway between Trevi Fountain and Capitoline Hill, a block off Via del Corso at Via di San Marcello 19, tel. 06-679-5310).

Close to the Pantheon

Eating on the square facing the Pantheon is a temptation worth considering, but a block or two away, you'll get fewer views and better value.

$$$$ Ristorante da Fortunato is an Italian classic, with fresh flowers on the tables and white-coated waiters serving good meat and fish to dignitaries and tourists with good taste. On the walls, everyone from Muammar Gaddafi and Prince Charles to Bill Clinton are pictured with the late Signore Fortunato, who started this restaurant in 1975. For a dressy night out, this is a worthwhile splurge—reserve ahead (figure €50 per person, daily 12:30-23:30, a block in front of the Pantheon at Via del Pantheon 55, tel. 06-679-2788, www.ristorantefortunato.it).

$$ Enoteca Corsi is a wine shop that grew into a thriving lunch spot, serving traditional cuisine to an appreciative crowd of office workers. Kids do their homework at the family table in back. Enjoy pastas, main dishes, and fine wine at a third of the price of most restaurants—buy from their shop and pay a corking fee (Mon-Sat 12:00-15:30, Thu-Fri also 19:00-22:30, closed Sun, no reservations, a block toward the Pantheon from Gesù Church at Via del Gesù 87, tel. 06-679-0821).

$$$ Ristorante la Campana is an authentic slice of old Rome, claiming a history dating to 1518. It still serves appreciative locals typical Roman dishes and daily specials, plus a good self-service *antipasti* buffet (Tue-Sun 12:30-15:00 & 19:30-23:00, closed Mon, inside seating only, reserve for dinner, just off Via della Scrofa and Piazza Nicosia at Vicolo della Campana 18, tel. 06-687-5273, www.ristorantelacampana.com).

$$ Osteria delle Coppelle, a slapdash, trendy place, serves traditional dishes to a local crowd. It has a rustic interior, jumbled exterior seating, and a fun selection of €3 *cicchetti*. They also have a much classier dining section in the back (12:30-16:00 & 19:00-late, Piazza delle Coppelle 54, tel. 06-4550-2826).

$$ Miscellanea is run by much-loved Mikki, who's on a mission to keep foreign students well-fed with inexpensive, hearty food. It's a good value in a convenient location (daily 10:00-24:00, just behind the Pantheon at Via della Palombella 37, tel. 06-6813-5318).

North Rome
Near the Spanish Steps and Ara Pacis

These restaurants are located near the route of the "Dolce Vita Stroll" (see map on page 440).

$$$ Ristorante il Gabriello is inviting and small—modern under medieval arches—serving creative Roman cuisine using farm-fresh, organic products. Trust your waiter and say, "Bring it on." The atmosphere is fun and convivial. Invest €55—not including wine—in "Claudio's Extravaganza," created especially for my readers—it's not on the menu (dinner only, Mon-Sat 19:00-23:00, closed Sun, reservations smart, air-con, dress respectfully—no shorts, 3 blocks from Spanish Steps at Via Vittoria 51, tel. 06-6994-0810, www.ilgabriello.com).

Restaurants & Hotels in the Pantheon Neighborhood

Restaurants

1. Ristorante & Bar del Fico
2. Rist. Pizzeria "da Francesco"
3. Vivi Bistrot
4. L'Insalata Ricca
5. To Hostaria Romana
6. L'Antica Birreria Peroni
7. Ristorante da Fortunato
8. Enoteca Corsi
9. Ristorante la Campana
10. Osteria delle Coppelle
11. Miscellanea

To Piazza del Popolo

POST

To Spanish Steps

S. ANDREA

NAZARENO

To Barberini **M**

Piazza San Silvestro

Piazza del Parlamento

VIA DEL CORSO

VIA DEL TRITONE

T

VIA STAMPERIA

VIA MARONITI

VIA DELLA PANETTERIA

To **5**

CAMPO MARZIO

PARLIAMENT

VICARIO

T

GALLERIA ALBERTO SORDI

Piazza Colonna

TREVI FOUNTAIN

V. LAVATORE

PALAZZO DEL QUIRINALE

Piazza di Montecitorio

SABINI

MURATTE

SANTA MARIA IN VIA

VIA DELLA DATARIA

To Piazza del Quirinale

AQUIRO

Piazza di Pietra

PASTINI

Piazza Sant' Ignazio

VIA D. SEMINARIO

SANT' IGNAZIO

UMILTA

VIA DEL

Piazza Della Pilotta

SANTA MARIA SOPRA MINERVA

Piazza del Collegio Romano

S. APOST.

6

VIA SAN MARCELLO

N

100 Meters

100 Yards

ELEPHANT & OBELISK

MARMO

GALLERIA DORIA PAMPHILJ

CESTARI

8

VIA DEL GESÙ

VIA BATTISTI

VIA IV NOVEMBRE

B

VIA PLEBISCITO

Piazza Venezia

Piazza del Gesù

GESÙ

VIA D'ARACOELI

VIA D. BOTTEGHE OSCURE

Piazza San Marco

T #8

S. MARCO

B

T

To Termini

TRAJAN'S FORUM

VIA DEI FORI IMPERIALI

VICTOR EMMANUEL MONUMENT

STA. MARIA ARACOELI

To Colosseum & **M**

To Campidoglio

CAPITOLINE HILL

Hotels

⑫ Relais Teatro Argentina
⑬ Casa di Santa Brigida
⑭ Hotel Smeraldo
⑮ Dipendenza Smeraldo

⑯ Albergo Santa Chiara
⑰ Hotel Portoghesi
⑱ Hotel Due Torri

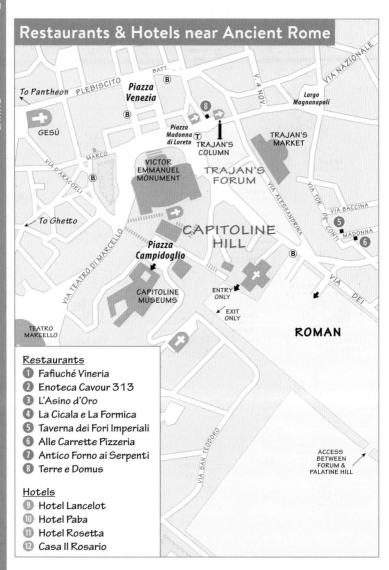

Restaurants & Hotels near Ancient Rome

Restaurants
1. Fafiuché Vineria
2. Enoteca Cavour 313
3. L'Asino d'Oro
4. La Cicala e La Formica
5. Taverna dei Fori Imperiali
6. Alle Carrette Pizzeria
7. Antico Forno ai Serpenti
8. Terre e Domus

Hotels
9. Hotel Lancelot
10. Hotel Paba
11. Hotel Rosetta
12. Casa Il Rosario

$$ Antica Enoteca is an upbeat, atmospheric 200-plus-year-old *enoteca*. For a light lunch, enjoy a glass of their best wine at the bar (listed on a big blackboard) and split their €22 *antipasti* plate of veggies, *salumi,* and cheese (daily 12:00-24:00, reserve for outdoor seating, Via della Croce 76B, tel. 06-679-0896).

Ancient Rome
Near the Colosseum and Forum

Within a block of the Colosseum and Forum, eateries cater to weary sightseers, offering neither memorable food nor good value. To get your money's worth, head to the Monti neighborhood. From the Forum, head up Via Cavour and then left on Via dei Serpenti; the action centers on Piazza della

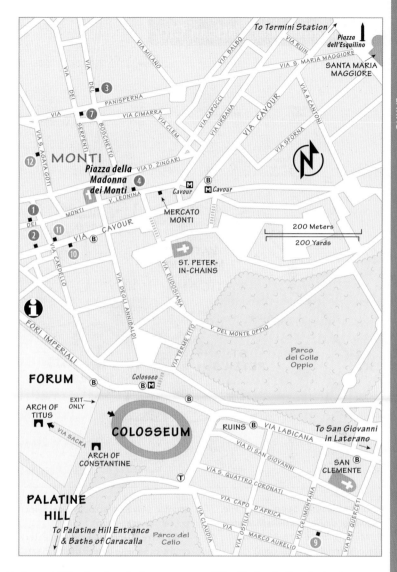

Madonna dei Monti and nearby lanes.

$$$ L'Asino d'Oro ("The Golden Donkey"), a top choice for foodies, serves Umbrian cuisine with a creative twist—mingling savory and sweet. The modern space is filled with savvy diners (Tue-Sat 12:30-14:30 & 19:30-23:00, closed Sun-Mon, reserve for dinner, Via del Boschetto 73, tel. 06-4891-3832).

$$ La Cicala e La Formica has its own nook on Via Leonina. While a bit tired, with a forgettable menu, it has an old-school coziness, and a terrace good for people-watching (daily 12:00-16:00 & 18:30-22:30, Via Leonina 17, tel. 06-481-7490).

$$ Taverna dei Fori Imperiali serves typical Roman cuisine in a snug interior that bustles with energy (Wed-Mon

Restaurants near Vatican City

12:30-15:00 & 19:30-23:00, closed Tue, reserve for dinner, Via della Madonna dei Monti 9, tel. 06-679-8643, www. latavernadeiforiimperiali.com).

$$ Alle Carrette Pizzeria—simple, rustic, and family-friendly—serves great wood-fired pizza in Monti (daily 19:00-24:00, Vicolo delle Carrette 14, tel. 06-679-2770).

$ Antico Forno ai Serpenti, a hip bakery with a few simple tables, puts out a small selection of *panini,* baked potatoes, and lasagna. They also bake good bread and pastries and do breakfasts (order at the counter, daily 8:00-20:00, Via dei Serpenti 122, tel. 06-4542-7920).

$$ Terre e Domus, a modern eatery on the otherwise unwelcoming Piazza Venezia, has a peaceful dining room and a menu that shows off local ingredients and cuisine (daily 9:00-23:00, Foro Traiano 82, immediately below Trajan's Column, tel. 06-6994-0273).

Near Vatican City

Eateries near the Vatican cater to exhausted tourists. Avoid the restaurant pushers handing out fliers: Their venues

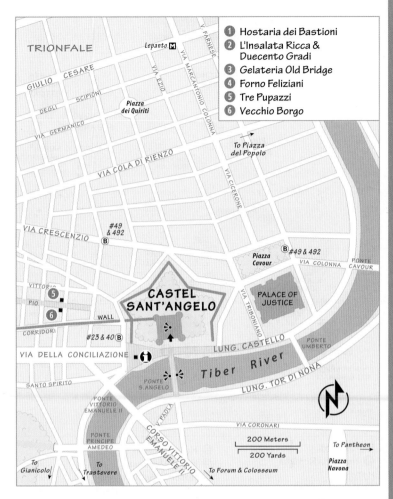

1 Hostaria dei Bastioni
2 L'Insalata Ricca & Duecento Gradi
3 Gelateria Old Bridge
4 Forno Feliziani
5 Tre Pupazzi
6 Vecchio Borgo

have bad food and expensive menu tricks. Tide yourself over with a slice of pizza or at any of these eateries and save your splurges for elsewhere.

These listings are mostly fast and cheap, a stone's throw from the Vatican wall, near Piazza Risorgimento: **$$ Hostaria dei Bastioni** has noisy streetside seating and a quiet interior (Mon-Sat 12:00-15:00 & 18:00-23:00, closed Sun, at corner of Vatican wall at Via Leone IV 29, tel. 06-3972-3034); **$ L'Insalata Ricca** serves hearty salads and pastas (daily 12:00-23:30, across from Vatican walls at Piazza Risorgimento

5, tel. 06-3973-0387); and **$ Duecento Gradi** is a good bet for fresh and creative, though a bit pricey, €5-8 sandwiches (daily 10:30-24:00, Piazza Risorgimento 3, tel. 06-3975-4239). For a treat, try **Gelateria Old Bridge,** which scoops up hearty portions of fresh gelato for tourists and nuns alike (just off Piazza Risorgimento across from Vatican walls at Viale dei Bastioni di Michelangelo 3).

$ Forno Feliziani serves nicely presented pizza by the slice and simple cafeteria-style dishes that you can eat in or take out (closed Sun, Via Candia 61).

Hotels near Termini Station

Restaurant
1. Hostaria Romana

Hotels
2. Residenza Cellini
3. Hotel Modigliani
4. IQ Hotel & Hotel Opera Roma
5. Hotel Rafaello
6. Hotel Aberdeen
7. Hotel Sonya
8. Hotels Oceania & Nardizzi Americana
9. Hotel Selene Roma
10. Hotel Italia Roma

The pedestrians-only **Borgo Pio**—a block from Piazza San Pietro near St. Peter's Basilica—has restaurants worth a look. Consider **$$ Tre Pupazzi** (Mon-Sat 12:00-15:00 & 19:00-23:00, closed Sun, at the corner of Via Tre Pupazzi and Borgo Pio) or **$ Vecchio Borgo,** across the street (daily 9:30-22:30, Borgo Pio 27a).

SLEEPING

Choosing the right neighborhood in Rome is as important as choosing the right hotel. All of my recommended accommodations are in safe, pleasant areas convenient to sightseeing.

Near Termini Train Station

The Termini train station neighborhood is handy for public transit and services. While

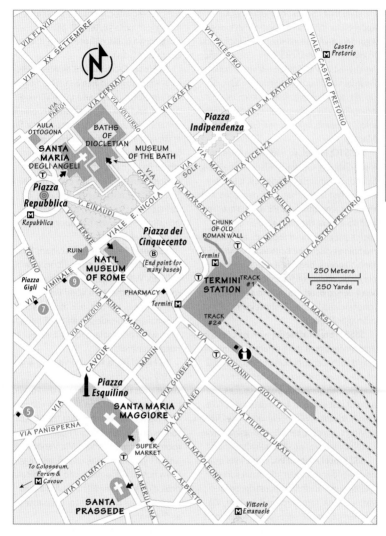

not as charming as other areas of Rome, the hotels near Termini train station are less expensive. The city's two main Metro lines intersect at the station, and most buses leave from here. Most of these hotels are a 10-minute walk west of the station, on or near Via Firenze, a safe, handy, central, and relatively quiet street. The Defense Ministry is nearby, so you've got heavily armed guards watching over you all night.

$$$$ Residenza Cellini feels like the guest wing of a gorgeous Neoclassical palace. It offers 11 rooms, "ortho/anti-allergy beds," four-star comforts and service, and a small, breezy terrace (RS%, air-con, elevator, Via Modena 5, third floor, tel. 06-4782-5204, www.residenzacellini.it, info@residenzacellini.it; Barbara, Gaetano, and Donato).

$$$$ Hotel Modigliani, a delightful 23-room place, is energetically run in a clean, bright, minimalist yet in-love-with-life style that its artist namesake would appreciate. It has a vast and plush lounge, a garden, and a newsletter introducing you to each of the staff (RS%, air-con, elevator; northwest of Via Firenze—from Tritone Fountain on Piazza Barberini, go 2 blocks up Via della Purificazione to #42; tel. 06-4281-5226, www.hotelmodigliani.com, info@hotelmodigliani.com, Giulia and Marco).

$$$$ IQ Hotel, in a modern blue building facing the Opera House, feels almost Scandinavian in its efficiency. It lacks charm, but more than compensates with modern amenities. Its 88 rooms are fresh and spacious, the roof garden comes with a play area and foosball, and vending machines dispense bottles of wine (RS%, family rooms, breakfast extra, air-con, elevator, cheap self-service laundry, gym, Via Firenze 8, tel. 06-488-0465, www. iqhotelroma.it, info@iqhotelroma.it, manager Diego).

$$$$ Hotel Raffaello, with its courteous and professional staff, offers 41 rooms in a grand 19th-century building on the edge of the Monti district. This formal hotel comes with generous public spaces and a breakfast room fit for aristocrats (RS%, family rooms, air-con, elevator, Via Urbana 3, Metro: Cavour, tel. 06-488-4342, www. hotelraffaello.it, info@hotelraffaello.it).

$$$ Hotel Aberdeen, combines quality and friendliness, with 36 comfy rooms (RS%—use "Rick Steves reader reservations" link, family rooms, air-con, Via Firenze 48, tel. 06-482-3920, www.hotel aberdeen.it, info@hotelaberdeen.it).

$$$ Hotel Opera Roma, with contemporary furnishings and marble accents, boasts 15 spacious, modern, and thoughtfully appointed rooms. It's quiet and just a stone's throw from the Opera House (air-con, elevator, Via Firenze 11, tel. 06-487-1787, www. hoteloperaroma.com, info@hoteloper-aroma.com, Reza, Litu, and Federica).

$$$ Hotel Sonya offers 40 well-equipped (if small) rooms, a hearty breakfast, and decent prices (family rooms, air-con, elevator, faces the Opera House at Via Viminale 58, tel. 06-481-9911, www. hotelsonya.it, info@hotelsonya.it, Francesca and Ivan).

$$ Hotel Oceania is a peaceful slice of air-conditioned heaven. The 24 rooms are spacious, quiet, and tastefully decorated, and the elegant sitting room has a manor-house feel. Stefano runs a fine staff, serves wonderful coffee, provides lots of thoughtful extra touches, and works hard to maintain a caring family atmosphere (RS%—use code "RICK-STEVES," family rooms, elevator, TV lounge, Via Firenze 38, third floor, tel. 06-482-4696, www.hoteloceania.it, info@hoteloceania.it).

$$ Hotel Selene Roma spreads its 40 stylish rooms out on a few floors of a big palazzo. With elegant furnishings and room to breathe, it's a good value (RS%, family rooms, air-con, elevator, Via del Viminale 8, reception at #10, tel. 06-474-4781, www.hotelseleneroma.it, reception@ hotelseleneroma.it).

$$ Hotel Italia Roma, in a busy and handy locale, is located safely on a quiet street next to the Ministry of the Interior. It has 35 modest but comfortable rooms plus four newer, more expensive "residenza" rooms on the third floor (RS%, family rooms, air-con, elevator, Via Venezia 18, just off Via Nazionale, tel. 06-482-8355, www.hotelitaliaroma.it, info@hotelitaliar-oma.it). They offer eight similar annex rooms across the street for the same price as the main hotel.

$$ Hotel Nardizzi Americana, with a small rooftop terrace, 40 standard rooms, and a laidback atmosphere, is a decent value (RS%—email reservation for discount, family rooms, air-con, elevator, Via Firenze 38, fourth floor, tel. 06-488-0035, www.hotelnardizzi.it, info@hotelnardizzi. it; friendly Stefano, Fabrizio, Mario, and Giancarlo).

Near Ancient Rome

Stretching from the Colosseum to Piazza Venezia, this area is central. Sightseers are a short walk from the Colosseum, Roman Forum, and Trajan's Column—as well as restaurants and shopping in the Monti district. All except Hotel Lancelot are within a 10-minute walk of the Cavour Metro stop.

$$$$ Hotel Lancelot is a comfortable refuge—a 60-room hotel with an elegant feel, fair price, and located in a pleasant residential neighborhood a 10-minute stroll from the Colosseum. It's quiet and safe, with a shady courtyard, restaurant, bar, and tiny communal sixth-floor terrace (family rooms, some view rooms, air-con, elevator, good €25 dinner, wheelchair-accessible, cheap parking, near San Clemente Church at Via Capo d'Africa 47, tel. 06-7045-0615, www.lancelothotel. com, info@lancelothotel.com). Faris and Lubna speak the Queen's English.

$$ Hotel Paba is cozy, with fresh, choc-olate-box-tidy rooms. It's just two blocks from the Forum. Even though some rooms overlook busy Via Cavour, it's quiet enough (RS%, email reservations pre-ferred, big beds, breakfast served in room, air-con, elevator, Via Cavour 266, second floor, tel. 06-4782-4902, www.hotelpaba. com, info@hotelpaba.com).

$$ Casa Il Rosario is a peaceful, well-run Dominican convent renting 40 rooms with monastic simplicity to both pilgrims and tourists in a steep but pleasant cor-ner of the Monti neighborhood. Doubles have two single beds that can be pushed together (cheaper single rooms with shared bath, reserve several months in advance, some rooms with air-con and others with fans, elevator, small garden and rooftop terrace, 23:00 curfew, near bottom of Via Nazionale at Via Sant'Agata dei Goti 10, bus #40 or #170 from Termini, tel. 06-679-2346, www.casailrosarioroma. it, irodopre@tin.it).

$ Hotel Rosetta, a homey and family-run *pensione,* rents 15 simple rooms. It's pretty minimal, with no lounge and no breakfast, but its great location makes it a fine budget option (air-con, up one flight of stairs, Via Cavour 295, tel. 06-4782-3069, www.rosettahotel.com, info@rosettahotel.com, Antonietta and Francesca).

Pantheon Neighborhood

The most romantic ambience is in neigh-borhoods near the Pantheon. Winding, narrow lanes are filled with foot traffic and lined with boutique shops and tiny trattorias...Rome at its best. Buses and taxis are the only practical way to connect with other destinations. The atmosphere doesn't come cheap, but this is where you want to be—especially at night.

This neighborhood has two main trans-portation hubs: Piazza delle Cinque Lune (just north of Piazza Navona) has a TI, a taxi stand, and (just around the corner) handy buses #81 and #87; Largo Argen-tina has buses to almost everywhere and a taxi stand.

Near Campo de' Fiori

You'll pay a premium (and endure a little extra night noise), but these places are set deep in the tangled back streets near idyl-lic Campo de' Fiori.

$$$$ Relais Teatro Argentina, a six-room gem, is steeped in tasteful old-Rome elegance, but has all the modern comforts. It's cozy and quiet like a B&B and couldn't be more centrally located (air-con, 3 flights of stairs, breakfast in room or on balcony, Via del Sudario 35, tel. 06-9893-1617, www. relaisteatroargentina.com, info@relaiste-atroargentina.com, kind Paolo).

$$$$ Casa di Santa Brigida overlooks the elegant Piazza Farnese. With soft-spoken sisters gliding down polished hallways and pearly gates instead of doors, this lavish 20-room convent makes exhaust-stained Roman tourists feel like they've died and gone to heaven. If you don't need a double bed or a TV in your room, it's worth the splurge—especially if you luxuriate in its ample public spaces or on its lovely roof terrace (book well in advance, air-con, elevator, tasty €25 dinners, roof garden, plush library, Via di Monserrato 54, tel. 06-6889-2596, www.brigidine.org, piazzafarnese@brigidine.org).

$$$ **Hotel Smeraldo,** with 66 rooms, is clean and a reasonable deal in a good location. Sixteen of the rooms are in an annex across the street, but everyone has breakfast in the main building (RS%—use code "ricksteves," air-con, elevator, flowery roof terrace, midway between Campo de' Fiori and Largo Argentina at Via dei Chiavari 20, tel. 06-687-5929, www.smeraldoroma.com, info@smeraldoroma.com; Massimo and Walter).

Close to the Pantheon

These places are buried in the pedestrian-friendly heart of ancient Rome, about a five-minute walk from the Pantheon. They're an easy walk from many sights, but are a bit distant from the major public transportation arteries.

$$$$ **Albergo Santa Chiara,** in the old center, is big and solid, with marbled elegance (but basic furniture) and all the hotel services. Its ample public lounges are dressy and professional, and its 97 rooms are quiet and spacious (RS%, family rooms, air-con, elevator, behind the Pantheon at Via di Santa Chiara 21, tel. 06-687-2979, www.albergosantachiara.com, info@albergosantachiara.com).

$$$$ **Hotel Portoghesi** is a classic hotel with 27 colorful rooms in the medieval heart of Rome. It's peaceful, quiet, and calmly run, and comes with a delightful roof terrace—though you pay for the location (family rooms, breakfast on roof, air-con, elevator, Via dei Portoghesi 1, tel. 06-686-4231, www.hotelportoghesiroma.it, info@hotelportoghesiroma.it).

$$$$ **Hotel Due Torri,** hiding out on a tiny quiet street, is beautifully located. It feels professional yet homey, with an accommodating staff, generous public spaces, and 26 rooms (the ones on upper floors are smaller but have views). While the location is great, the rooms are over-priced unless you score a discount (family rooms, air-con, elevator, a block off Via della Scrofa at Vicolo del Leonetto 23, tel. 06-6880-6956, www.hotelduetorriroma.com, info@hotelduetorriroma.com, Cinzia).

TRANSPORTATION

Getting Around Rome

The cheap, efficient public transportation system consists primarily of buses, a few trams, and three Metro lines. For information, visit www.atac.roma.it, which has a useful route planner in English, or call 06-57003. If you have a smartphone and an international data plan, consider downloading the free apps "Roma Bus" (by Movenda) or "Muoversi a Roma."

Buying Tickets

All public transportation uses the same ticket (€1.50), valid for one Metro ride—including transfers underground—plus unlimited city buses and trams during a 100-minute period. Passes good on buses and the Metro are sold in increments of 24 hours (€7), 48 hours (€12.50), 72 hours (€18), one week (€24, about the cost of three taxi rides), and one month (€35, plus €3 for the rechargeable card, valid for a calendar month).

You can purchase tickets and passes from machines at Metro stations and a few major bus stops (cash only), and from some newsstands and tobacco shops (*tabacchi,* marked by a black-and-white T sign). Tickets are not sold on board.

Validate your ticket at the Metro turnstile (magnetic-strip-side up, arrow-side first) or in the machine when you board the bus (magnetic-strip-side down, arrow-side first). It'll return with your expiration time printed on it. To get through a Metro turnstile with a transit pass or Roma Pass, press the card to the turnstile's electronic sensor pad. On buses and trams, you need to validate your pass only on your first time using it.

Rick's Tip: Stock up on Metro tickets early (or buy a Roma Pass) to avoid wasting time searching for an open tobacco shop that sells tickets.

By Metro

The Roman subway system ("Metro") is simple, clean, cheap, and fast. The two lines you need to know—A and B—intersect at Termini Station. The Metro runs from 5:30 to 23:30 (Fri-Sat until 1:30 in the morning). The partly finished C line serves only a suburb of little use to tourists.

Rick's Tip: Beware of pickpockets when boarding, while on board, and when leaving buses and subways. To experience less crowding and commotion—and less risk—wait for the end cars of a subway rather than boarding the middle cars.

By Bus

The Metro is handy, but it won't get you everywhere—take the bus (or tram). Bus routes are listed at each stop. Route and system maps aren't posted, but with some knowledge of major stops, you can wing it without one. (The ATAC website has a PDF bus map that you can download, bookstores sell paper transport maps, and the various ATAC journey planners are helpful.) Rome's few tram lines function nearly identically to buses.

Regular bus lines start running about 5:30, and during the day run every 10-15 minutes or so. After 23:30 (and sometimes earlier) and on Sundays, buses are less frequent. Night buses are marked with an N and an owl symbol on the bus-stop signs. The exact frequency of various bus routes is difficult to predict (and not printed at bus stops). At major stops, an electronic board shows the number of minutes until the next buses arrive.

Bus #64: Links Termini Station with the Vatican, stopping at Piazza della Repubblica (sights), Via Nazionale (recommended hotels), Piazza Venezia (near Forum), Largo Argentina (near Pantheon and Campo de' Fiori), St. Peter's Basilica (get off just past the tunnel), and San Pietro Station.

Bus #40: This express bus mostly follows the #64 route but has fewer stops and fewer crowds. It ends near Castel Sant'Angelo (Hadrian's Tomb, a 10-minute walk from St. Peter's) on the Vatican side of the river.

Rick's Tip: Buses #64 and #40 are popular with tourists and pickpockets. If one bus is packed, there's likely a second one on its tail with fewer crowds and thieves.

Other useful routes include:
Bus #16: Termini Station, Santa Maria Maggiore, and San Giovanni in Laterano.
Bus #49: Piazza Cavour/Castel Sant'Angelo, Piazza Risorgimento (Vatican), and Vatican Museums.
Bus #62: Tiburtina, Piazza Barberini, Piazza Venezia, Piazza Pia (near Castel Sant'Angelo).
Bus #81: San Giovanni in Laterano, Largo Argentina, and Piazza Risorgimento (Vatican).
Buses #85 and #87: Piazza Navona (#87 only), Pantheon, Via del Corso (#85 only), Piazza Venezia, Forum, Colos-

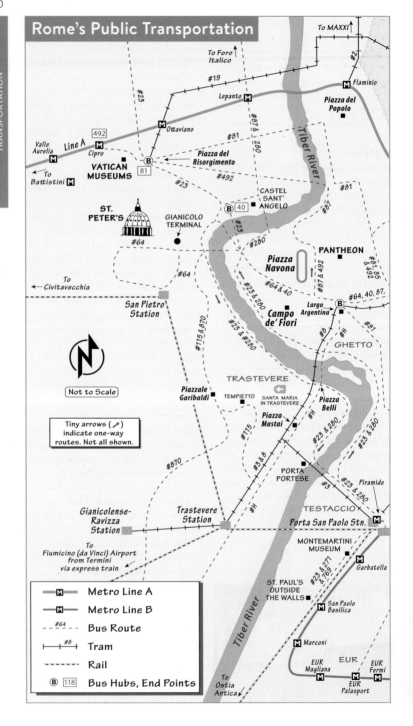

Rome's Public Transportation

To MAXXI↑

To Foro Italico

#19

#2

Flaminio

Lepanto

Piazza del Popolo

Ottaviano

#81

#87 & 280

Valle Aurelia

Line A

492

Cipro

Tiber River

VATICAN MUSEUMS

B

81

Piazza del Risorgimento

To Battistini

#25

#23

#492

#81

ST. PETER'S

GIANICOLO TERMINAL

B

40

CASTEL SANT' ANGELO

#87

#81

#23

#280

PANTHEON

#81, 85 & 492

#64

Piazza Navona

#87 & 492

To Civitavecchia

#64

San Pietro Station

#115 & 870

#23 & 280

#23 & 280

#64 & 40

Campo de' Fiori

Largo Argentina

B

#64, 40, 87,

#8

#81

GHETTO

TRASTEVERE

Piazzale Garibaldi

TEMPIETTO

SANTA MARIA IN TRASTEVERE

Piazza Belli

#115

Piazza Mastai

#23 & 280

#23 & 280

#23 & 280

Tiny arrows (↗) indicate one-way routes. Not all shown.

#870

#3 & 8

PORTA PORTESE

#3

#23 & 280

Piramide

Gianicolense-Ravizza Station

Trastevere Station

TESTACCIO

Porta San Paolo Stn.

To Fiumicino (da Vinci) Airport from Termini via express train

MONTEMARTINI MUSEUM

Garbatella

#23 & 271 & 769

ST. PAUL'S OUTSIDE THE WALLS

San Paolo Basilica

	Metro Line A
	Metro Line B
#64	Bus Route
#8	Tram
	Rail
B 118	Bus Hubs, End Points

Marconi

EUR Magliana

EUR

EUR Fermi

EUR Palasport

To Ostia Antica

Tiber River

Not to Scale

seum, San Clemente, and San Giovanni in Laterano.

Bus #492: Travels east-west across the city, connecting Tiburtina (train and bus stations), Largo Santa Susanna (near Piazza della Repubblica), Piazza Barberini, Piazza Venezia, Largo Argentina (near Pantheon and Campo de' Fiori), Piazza Cavour (Castel Sant'Angelo), and Piazza Risorgimento (St. Peter's Basilica and Vatican).

Bus #714: Termini Station, Santa Maria Maggiore, and San Giovanni in Laterano.

Tram #3: Zips from the Colosseum to San Giovanni (and onward to Valle Giulia) in one direction, and to Piramide/Testaccio (and onward to Trastevere) in the other.

Tram #19: Connects Piazza del Risorgimento and the Ottaviano Metro stop (by the Vatican Museums) to the Etruscan Museum and Villa Borghese.

By Taxi

Taxis in Rome are reasonable and useful for efficient sightseeing. Three or four companions with more money than time should taxi almost everywhere. Taxis start at €3, then charge about €1.50 per kilometer (surcharges: €1.50 on Sun, €3.50 for nighttime hours of 22:00-6:00, one regular suitcase or bag rides free, tip by rounding up—€1 or so). Sample fares: Termini area to Vatican-€15; Termini area to Colosseum-€7; Termini area to the Borghese Gallery-€9 (or look up your route at www.worldtaximeter.com).

You can always just hail a cab on the street. But Romans generally walk to the

nearest taxi stand (many are marked on this book's maps) or ask a passerby or a clerk in a shop, *"Dov'è una fermata dei taxi?"* (doh-VEH OO-nah fehr-MAH-tah DEH-ee TAHK-see). Easiest of all, have your hotelier or restaurateur call a taxi for you. The meter starts when the call is received. To call a cab on your own, dial 06-3570, 06-4994, or 06-6645, or use the official city taxi line, 06-0609; they'll ask for an Italian phone number (give them your mobile number or your hotel's).

The free MyTaxi app (www.mytaxi. com), popular with younger and tech-savvy Romans, lets you summon and pay for an official taxi using your smartphone. Uber works in Rome as it does in the US, but has been the focus of legal challenges.

Beware of corrupt taxis, including rip-off "express taxis" at the train station or airport. Only use official Rome taxis. They're white, with a taxi sign on the roof and a maroon logo on the door that reads *Roma Capitale*. When you get in, make sure the meter (*tassametro*) is turned on. If the meter isn't on, get out and hail another cab. Check that the meter is reset to the basic drop charge (should be around €3, or around €5 if you phoned for the taxi). You'll rarely pay more than €12 for a ride in town. Keep an eye on the fare on the meter as you near your destination; some cabbies turn the meter off instantly when they stop and tell you a higher price.

By law, every cab must display a multi-lingual official price chart—usually on the back of the seat in front of you. If the fare doesn't seem right, point to the chart and ask the cabbie to explain it.

Rick's Tip: A **common cabbie scam** *is to take your €20 note, drop it, and pick up a €5 note (similar color), claiming that's what you gave him. Pay in small bills; if you only have a large bill, show it to the cabbie as you state its face value.*

Arriving and Departing
Termini Train Station

Termini, Rome's main train station, is a buffet of tourist services. For security, entry to the train platforms themselves is restricted to ticketholders. Entrances are from the inner atrium and from the halls to the sides of the tracks. You may need to show your ticket, but there are no metal detectors and lines are generally short. In the hall along Via Giovanni Giolitti, on the southwest side of the station (near track 24), you'll find the **TI** (daily 8:00-18:45), a **car rental** desk, and **baggage storage** (*deposito bagagli*). A snack bar and a good selfservice **cafeteria** are perched one floor above the ticket windows in the outer atrium, accessible from the side closest to track 24.

Termini is a major transit hub. Local **Metro lines A and B** intersect downstairs at Termini Metro station. **Buses** leave from the square directly in front of the outer atrium. Buses to the airport leave from the streets on both sides of the station. The **Leonardo Express train** to Fiumicino Airport runs from track 23 or 24. **Taxis** queue in front and outside exits on both the north and south sides; if there's a long taxi line in front, try a side exit instead.

Rick's Tip: Shady characters *linger around the station, especially* **near ticket machines.** *Some offer help for a "tip"; others have official-looking business cards.* **Avoid anybody selling anything** *unless they're in a legitimate shop at the station. There are no official porters;* **carry your own bags.**

The banks of Trenitalia's user-friendly ticket machines (new ones are red, old ones are green-and-white; marked *Trenitalia/Biglietti*) are handy, but cover Italian destinations only. They take euros and credit cards (you may need to enter your PIN), display schedules, issue tickets, and even make reservations for railpass holders (found under the "Global Pass" ticket type).

TRAIN CONNECTIONS FROM TERMINI STATION

The customer service and ticket windows (in the outer, glassed-in atrium) can be jammed with travelers—find the small red kiosk, take a number, and wait. Whenever possible, use the ticket machines. Though most trains departing from Termini are operated by Italy's state rail company, Trenitalia, although a few Italo trains also use the station (for more on the privately run Italo, see page 559 and www.italotreno.it).

Rick's Tip: *Minimize your time in a train station—if you're not near a station,* **it's quicker to get tickets and train info from travel agencies or online.**

From Rome by Train to: Venice (Trenitalia: hourly, 4 hours, 1 direct night train, 7 hours; Italo: 4/day, 3-3.5 hours), **Florence** (Trenitalia: 2-3/hour, 1.5 hours; Italo: 2/hour, 1.5 hours), **Siena** (1-2/hour, 1 change, 3-4 hours), **Orvieto** (every 1-2 hours, 1.5 hours; regional trains are half the price and only slightly slower than Intercity trains), **Assisi** (4/day direct, 2 hours; more with change in Foligno), **Pisa** (1-2/hour, 3 hours, some change in Florence), **Milan** (Trenitalia: 1-3/hour, 3-3.5 hours; Italo: 11/day nonstop, 3 hours, more with stops), **Naples** (Trenitalia: 1-4/hour, 1 hour on Frecciarossa, 2 hours on Intercity, 2.5 hours and much cheaper on regional trains; Italo: hourly, 70 minutes).

Tiburtina Train Station

The smaller Tiburtina station is next to the Tiburtina Metro station in the city's northeast corner, and across the road from Rome's bus station. It's a pass-through station: Fast trains along the Milan-Naples line stop here and continue on quickly. A few of these fast trains now stop only at Tiburtina, but most stop at both Tiburtina and Termini. Use the station that's most convenient for you.

Autostazione Tiburtina, 200 yards from the Tiburtina train and Metro station, is a hub for bus service all across Italy. To reach the bus station from either Tiburtina station, don't follow the **Bus** signs, which lead to the city bus stop. Instead, exit the station, cross the street under the elevated freeway, and look for the fenced-in area with bus platforms. Ticket-window lines can be slow, so buy your ticket online in advance if possible.

Tiburtina is on **Metro line B,** with easy connections to Termini (a straight shot, four stops away) and the entire Metro system (when going to Tiburtina, Metro line B splits—you want a train signed *Rebibbia*). Or take **bus #492** from Tiburtina to various city-center stops (such as Piazza Barberini, Piazza Venezia, and Piazza Navona) and the Vatican neighborhood (as you emerge from the station, the city bus stop is to the left).

BUS CONNECTIONS FROM TRIBUTINA STATION

From Rome by Bus to: Assisi (2/day, 3 hours—the train makes more sense), **Siena** (9/day, 3 hours), **Sorrento** (1-2/day, 4 hours; this is a cheap and easy way to go straight to Sorrento, buy tickets at www.marozzivt.it—in Italian only, the Tiburtina ticket office, travel agencies, or on board for a €3.50 surcharge; tel. 080-579-0111).

By Plane

Rome has two airports: Fiumicino and the smaller Ciampino.

FIUMICINO AIRPORT

Rome's major airport, **Fiumicino** is manageable (a.k.a. Leonardo da Vinci, airport code: FCO, www.adr.it). Terminals T1, T2, and T3 are all under one roof—walkable end to end in 20 minutes. T5 is a separate building requiring a short shuttle trip. (T4 is still being built.) The T1-2-3 complex has a TI (daily 8:00-19:30, in T3), ATMs, banks, luggage storage, shops, and bars. For airport info, call 06-65951.

To get from the airport to downtown, take the direct **Leonardo Express train** to **Termini train station** (32 minutes for €14).

Trains run twice hourly in both directions from roughly 6:00 to 23:00. From the airport's arrival gate, follow signs to the train icon or *Stazione/Railway Station*. Buy your ticket from a Trenitalia machine, a ticket office *(biglietteria),* or a newsstand near the platform. Machines sell open tickets that can be used on any train. Board the train going to the central "Roma Termini" station, not "Roma Orte" or others.

Trains from Termini train station to the airport depart at about :05 and :35 past each hour, usually from track 23 or 24. Check the departure boards for "Fiumicino Aeroporto" and confirm with an official on the platform that the train is indeed going to the airport.

You can access most of the airport's terminals from the airport train station. If your flight leaves from terminal T5 (where most American air carriers flying direct to the US depart), catch the T5 shuttle bus *(navetta)* on the sidewalk in front of T3—it's too far to walk with luggage. Allow lots of time going to and from the airport; there's a fair amount of transportation involved. Flying to the US involves an extra level of security—plan on getting to the airport even earlier than normal (2.5 hours ahead of your flight).

Buses, including Terravision (www.terravision.eu), SIT (www.sitbusshuttle.com), Schiaffini (www.romeairportbus.com), and T.A.M. (www.tambus.it), connect Fiumicino and Termini train station, departing roughly every 40 minutes. While cheaper than the train (about €6 one-way), buses take twice as long (about an hour). The SIT bus also stops near the Vatican. At the airport, the companies' desks line up in T3, near the entrance to the train station.

Airport Shuttle vans can be economical for one or two people. Consider Rome Airport Shuttle (€25/1 person, extra people-€6 each, by reservation only, tel. 06-4201-4507, www.airportshuttle.it).

Your hotelier can arrange a taxi or private car service to the airport at any hour. A **taxi** between Fiumicino and downtown

Rome takes 45 minutes in normal traffic and costs €48. (Add a €2-5 tip for good service.) Cabbies based in Fiumicino are allowed to charge €60. It's best to use a white Rome city cab (with a maroon *Roma Capitale* logo on the door); the airport fare should be posted on the door. Confirm the price before you get in. If your Roman cabbie tries to overcharge you, state the correct price and say, *"È la legge"* (ay lah LEJ-jay; which means, "It's the law"), and they should back off.

CIAMPINO AIRPORT
Rome's smaller airport (airport code: CIA; tel. 06-6595-9515) handles charter flights and some budget airlines (including most Ryanair flights).

Various bus companies—including Terravision, Schiaffini, and SIT—run to Rome's Termini train station (about €5, 2/hour, 45 minutes). Atral runs a quick route (25 minutes, runs every 40 minutes) to the Anagnina Metro stop, where you can connect to a stop near your hotel. City bus #520 runs from Ciampino to the Subaugusta Metro stop for a single transit ticket.

The fixed price for any official **taxi** (with the maroon *"Roma Capitale"* logo on the door) is €30 to downtown (within the old city walls, including most of my recommended hotels).

Rick's Tip: *A car is a worthless headache in Rome. To save money and a pile of stress,* **park in the hill town of Orvieto** *at the huge, easy, and relatively safe lot behind the train station (follow P signs from autostrada) and catch the train to Rome (roughly hourly, 1.5 hours). Or, if Rome is the first stop of your trip,* **enjoy the city car-free,** *then take the train to Orvieto and rent a car there.*

By Car
I don't advise driving into or within Rome, but if you need to, here's how: Rome's ring road, the Grande Raccordo Anulare, encircles the city, with spokes that lead into the center. Entering from the north, leave the autostrada at the Settebagni exit. Following Via Salaria and black-and-white *Centro* signs, work your way doggedly into the Roman thick of things. This will take you along the Villa Borghese Gardens and dump you right on Via Veneto in downtown Rome. Avoid rush hour and drive defensively: Roman cars stay in their lanes like rocks in an avalanche.

Park your car in a safe place during your stay. Get advice from your hotelier or use Villa Borghese's handy underground garage (€18/day, Viale del Galoppatoio 33, www.sabait.it).

During most of the week, you need a special permit to drive in the old center of Rome. The restricted zone is roughly bounded by Piazza del Popolo, Termini Station, the Colosseum, and the river (for details, go to www.agenziamobilita.roma.it and search for "LTZ" in English). Without a permit, you'll be photographed and fined. Your hotel can help you get a permit if you absolutely must drive or park downtown.

Florence

Florence is the birthplace of the Renaissance and the modern world. It's geographically small but culturally rich—containing more artistic masterpieces per square mile than anyplace else. In a single day, you can look Michelangelo's *David* in the eyes, fall under the seductive sway of Botticelli's *Birth of Venus,* and climb the modern world's first dome, which still dominates the skyline.

A cosmopolitan vibe courses through the city's narrow lanes. You'll encounter children licking gelato, students riding Vespas, supermodels wearing Gucci fashions, and artisans sipping Chianti—Florence has long been perfecting the art of civilized living.

FLORENCE IN 2 DAYS

Compact Florence is packed with sights, but crowds and long lines can ruin your day's agenda. To maximize your time, either reserve the top two sights—Accademia (Michelangelo's *David*) and Uffizi Gallery (Renaissance paintings)—or get a pricey Firenze Card that allows you to skip the lines. Avoid both sights on Monday when they're closed, and on the first Sunday of the month, when they're free but impossibly crowded. Some sights such as the Bargello close early off-season and on Sundays or Mondays.

Day 1: In the cool of the morning, take my Renaissance Walk. Afterward, depending on your interests, choose among Florence's many sights: the Bargello (best statues), Medici Chapels (Michelangelo statues), Santa Maria Novella (Masaccio's 3-D painting), Palazzo Vecchio (Medici palace), Santa Croce Church (famous tombs), Galileo Science Museum, Pitti Palace (art), and Brancacci Chapel (more Masaccio). For lunch, grab a quick bite between sights; you have many options, including Mercato Centrale's upscale, upstairs food hall.

Around 16:30 when crowds die down, see the Uffizi Gallery's unforgettable paintings.

On any evening: Linger over dinner. Take a stroll, gelato in hand. Or take a taxi or bus to Piazzale Michelangelo for spectacular city views, and walk back into town for dinner. You can sightsee late at some sights, attend a concert at a church, or drop by a wine bar.

Day 2: See the Accademia (*David*) and visit the nearby Museum of San Marco (Fra Angelico's art). Then hit the street markets, wander, or do more museumgoing. Stroll to the river and cross the historic bridge, Ponte Vecchio, to the Oltrarno neighborhood for dinner.

With extra time: Fit in a day trip to Pisa (book ahead to climb the famous tower) or Siena (just 1.5 hours away by bus—and magic after dark.

ORIENTATION

Florence (pop. 360,000) can be intense. Prepare for scorching summer heat, crowded lanes and sidewalks, slick pickpockets, few WCs, steep prices, and long lines. The best of the city lies on the north bank of the Arno River. The main sights cluster around the dome of the cathedral (Duomo). Everything is within a 20-minute walk of the train station, cathedral, or Ponte Vecchio (Old Bridge). The less famous but more characteristic Oltrarno area (south bank) is just over the bridge. Here's a neighborhood-by-neighborhood rundown:

Historic Core: The Duomo—with its iconic, towering dome—is the visual, geographical, and historical center of Florence. A 10-minute walk away is the Palazzo Vecchio (City Hall), with its skyscraping medieval spire. Connecting these two landmarks is the north-south pedestrian street called Via de' Calzaiuoli. This central axis—Duomo to the Palazzo Vecchio to the Arno River—is the spine for Florentine sightseeing and the route of my self-guided Renaissance Walk. Via de' Calzaiuoli also links two central piazzas—Piazza della Repubblica and Piazza della Signoria (fronting the Uffizi Gallery). To the west of this axis is a glitzy shopping zone, and to the east is a characteristic web of narrow lanes.

Rick's Tip: **Don't drive into the city center.** *Don't even try it. Florence's traffic-reduction system is confusing even to locals. If you don't have a permit, you'll get a €100 traffic ticket in the mail. The no-go zone is confusing; several streets are classified ZTL ("limited traffic zone") at only certain times of day.*

Accademia/San Lorenzo (north of the Duomo): The area north of the Duomo is less atmospheric but has several crucial sights. From the Duomo, Via Cavour runs north, bisecting the neighborhood. To the east lies the Accademia

(Michelangelo's *David*) and the Museum of San Marco. The western part clusters around the Basilica of San Lorenzo, with its Medici Chapels. The area near San Lorenzo teems with tourists: There are the vendor stalls of San Lorenzo Market, the lively Mercato Centrale, and many hotels and trattorias.

Train Station/Santa Maria Novella (west of the Duomo): The area near the train station and Church of Santa Maria Novella is somewhat urban and dreary, but has inexpensive hotels and characteristic eateries. Closer to the river (near Palazzo Strozzi) is a posh shopping zone, with a more affordable mix of shops lining Via del Parione and Borgo Ognissanti.

Santa Croce (east of the Duomo): A 10-minute walk east from the Palazzo Vecchio leads to the neighborhood's main landmark, the Church of Santa Croce. Along the way is the Bargello sculpture museum. The area stretching north and west from Santa Croce is increasingly authentic and workaday, offering a glimpse at untouristy Florence.

Oltrarno (south of the river): Literally the "Other Side of the Arno River," this neighborhood reveals a Florence from a time before tourism. Many artisans still have workshops here, and open their doors to passing visitors. The Oltrarno starts just across Ponte Vecchio (jammed with tourists and tackiness) and stretches south to the giant Pitti Palace and surrounding gardens (Boboli and Bardini). To the west is the rough-but-bohemian Piazza di Santo Spirito and the lavishly frescoed Brancacci Chapel. To the east of Pitti Palace, perched high on the hill, is Piazzale Michelangelo, with Florence's most popular viewpoint. Tucked between there and the river is the funky little San Niccolò neighborhood, with lively bars and eateries.

Tourist Information

The city TI has several branches. The crowded main branch is across the square

FLORENCE AT A GLANCE

▲▲▲**Accademia** Michelangelo's *David* and powerful (unfinished) *Prisoners*. Reserve ahead or get a Firenze Card. **Hours:** Tue-Sun 8:15-18:50, possibly Tue until 22:00 June-Sept, closed Mon. See page 530.

▲▲▲**Uffizi Gallery** Greatest collection of Italian paintings anywhere. Reserve well in advance or get a Firenze Card. **Hours:** Tue-Sun 8:15-18:50, closed Mon. See page 532.

▲▲▲**Bargello** Underappreciated sculpture museum with Michelangelo, Donatello, and Medici treasures. **Hours:** Tue-Sat 8:15-17:00, until 13:50 Nov-March; also open second and fourth Mon and first, third, and fifth Sun of each month. See page 536.

▲▲▲**Duomo Museum** Underrated cathedral museum with sculptures. **Hours:** Daily 9:00-20:00, closed first Tue of each month. See page 525.

▲▲**Duomo** Gothic cathedral with colorful facade and the first dome built since ancient Roman times. **Hours:** Mon-Fri 10:00-17:00 (Thu until 16:30), Sat 10:00-16:45, Sun 13:30-16:45. See page 526.

▲▲**Museum of San Marco** Best collection anywhere of artwork by the early Renaissance master Fra Angelico. **Hours:** Tue-Fri 8:15-13:50, Sat 8:15-16:50; also open 8:15-13:50 on first, third, and fifth Mon and 8:15-16:50 on second and fourth Sun of each month. See page 531.

▲▲**Medici Chapels** Tombs of Florence's great ruling family, designed and carved by Michelangelo. **Hours:** Tue-Sat 8:15-17:00 except Nov-March until 13:50; also open second and fourth Mon and first, third, and fifth Sun of each month. See page 532.

▲▲**Palazzo Vecchio** Fortified palace, once the home of the Medici family, wallpapered with history. **Hours:** Museum and excavations open Fri-Wed 9:00-23:00 (Oct-March until 19:00), Thu 9:00-14:00; shorter hours for tower. See page 535.

▲▲**Galileo Science Museum** Fascinating old clocks, telescopes, maps, and three of Galileo's fingers. **Hours:** Wed-Mon 9:30-18:00, Tue until 13:00. See page 536.

▲▲**Santa Croce Church** Precious art, tombs of famous Florentines, and Brunelleschi's Pazzi Chapel in 14th-century church. **Hours:** Mon-Sat 9:30-17:30, Sun 14:00-17:30. See page 537.

▲▲**Church of Santa Maria Novella** Thirteenth-century Dominican church with Masaccio's famous 3-D painting. **Hours:** Mon-Thu 9:00-19:00 (Oct-March until 17:30), Fri 11:00-19:00 (Oct-March until 17:30), Sat 9:00-17:30, Sun 13:00-17:30. See page 538.

▲▲**Pitti Palace** Several museums in lavish palace plus sprawling Boboli and Bardini Gardens. **Hours:** Palatine Gallery, Royal Apartments, and Gallery of Modern Art—Tue-Sun 8:15-18:50, closed Mon; Boboli and Bardini Gardens, Costume Gallery, Argenti/Silverworks Museum, and Porcelain Museum—daily June-Aug 8:15-19:30, April-May and Sept until 18:30, March and Oct until 17:30, Nov-Feb until 16:30, closed first and last Mon of each month. See page 538.

▲▲**Brancacci Chapel** Works of Masaccio, early Renaissance master who reinvented perspective. **Hours:** Mon and Wed-Sat 10:00-17:00, Sun 13:00-17:00, closed Tue. Reservations required (unless you have a Firenze Card), though often available on the spot. See page 539.

▲▲**San Miniato Church** Sumptuous Renaissance chapel and sacristy showing scenes of St. Benedict. **Hours:** Mon-Sat 9:30-13:00 & 15:30-20:00, until 19:00 off-season, Sun 9:30-20:00, closed sporadically for special occasions. See page 542.

▲**Mercato Centrale** Bustling covered market with picnic fare on the ground floor and an upscale foodie court upstairs. **Hours:** Produce—Mon-Fri 7:00-14:00, Sat 7:00-17:00, closed Sun; food court—daily 10:00-24:00. See page 532.

▲**Ponte Vecchio** Famous, touristy bridge lined with gold and silver shops. **Hours:** Bridge always open. See page 525.

▲**Climbing the Duomo's Dome** Grand view into the cathedral, close-up of dome architecture, and, after 463 steps, a glorious city vista; reservations required. **Hours:** Mon-Fri 8:30-20:00, Sat 8:30-17:40, Sun 13:00-16:00. See page 526.

▲**Baptistery** Bronze doors fit to be the gates of paradise. **Hours:** Doors always viewable; interior open Mon-Sat 8:15-20:00, Sun 8:30-14:00. See page 527.

▲**Piazzale Michelangelo** Hilltop square with stunning view of Duomo and Florence. See page 540.

from the **train station** (Mon-Sat 9:00-19:00, Sun until 14:00; at the back corner of the Church of Santa Maria Novella at Piazza della Stazione 4; tel. 055-212-245, www.firenzeturismo.it). For help you'll need to take a number from the touch-screen computer by the door. Upstairs, the "Experience Florence" visitors center has big touch screens to help you virtually explore the city, and a well-produced 3-D movie of the big landmarks (free, 13 minutes, English subtitles).

A smaller branch is centrally located **next to the Duomo,** at the west corner of Via de' Calzaiuoli (inside the loggia, same hours as train station branch, tel. 055-288-496). Another TI is at the **airport.**

The least crowded and most helpful TI, which covers both the city and the greater province of Florence, can be less crowded and more helpful. It's a couple of blocks **north of the Duomo** (Mon-Fri 9:00-13:00, closed Sat-Sun, Via Cavour 1 red, tel. 055-290-832).

Sightseeing Pass, Advance Reservations, and Combo-Tickets
Firenze Card

The **Firenze Card** is pricey (€72) but convenient. This three-day sightseeing pass gives you admission to many of Florence's sights, including the Uffizi Gallery and Accademia. Just as important, it lets you skip the ticket-buying lines without needing to make reservations (except for the Duomo dome climb). Simply go to the entrance, find the Firenze Card priority line, show the card, and you'll be let in.

But even with the card, security bottlenecks may delay your entry. At some sights, you must first present your card at the ticket booth or info desk to get a physical ticket before proceeding to the entrance. For the Duomo sights, this means going to the ticket office across from the Baptistery (at #7), though there's a priority queue for cardholders.

Note that the Firenze Card does not let you skip the line for the Duomo dome climb—you must make a reservation for that—nor does it let you skip the line to enter the (free) Duomo.

Cost and Coverage: The Firenze Card costs €72 and is valid for 72 hours from when you validate it at your first museum (e.g., Tue at 15:00 until Fri at 15:00). Validate your card only when you're ready to tackle the covered sights on three consecutive days. Make sure the sights you want to visit will be open (some sights are closed Sun or Mon).

The Firenze Card covers the regular admission price as well as any special-exhibit surcharges, and is good for one visit per sight. (The €77 Firenze Card+ also includes free public transportation.)

To make the card pay for itself, you'd need to see all of these sights within three days: the Uffizi, Accademia, Bargello, Palazzo Vecchio, Medici Chapels, Duomo sights, and Pitti Palace's Palatine Gallery and Royal Apartments. But the real value of the card is that you can spend more time sightseeing rather than waiting in ticket-buying lines.

For a complete list of included sights, see www.firenzecard.it. Don't confuse this card with the lesser Firenze PASSport.

You can **buy the Firenze Card** at most TIs and most participating sights. The least-crowded sales point is the TI north of the Duomo (Via Cavour 1 red). The Palazzo Strozzi also has short lines and long hours. Other uncrowded, central sights covered by the card include the Bargello, the Bardini Museum, and the back ticket desk at the Church of Santa Maria Novella (on Piazza della Stazione, across from the train station). Buying the card at the Uffizi Gallery is surprisingly easy: Just enter door #2, passing to the left of the ticket-buying line.

You can also buy the card at more crowded places like the TI across from the train station and the airport TI, though not from the TI next to the Duomo. It's also sold at big sights like the Palazzo Vecchio and Pitti Palace.

Don't bother buying the card online, as you have to go to one of these desks to swap the voucher for the actual pass. The Firenze Card is not shareable, and there are no family or senior discounts.

If planning to climb the Duomo's dome, you must make a reservation in person when you present your Firenze Card at the Duomo ticket office—but in high season the chances of getting a time slot for the same day are slim (you're better off buying a Duomo combo-ticket online well in advance and booking your climb time then).

Children under 18 are allowed free into any state museum in Italy, and into any municipal museum in Florence. However, at the Uffizi and Accademia, if they want to skip the lines with their Firenze Card-holding parents, children still must (technically) pay the €4 "reservation fee." This can be paid on the spot—no need to reserve ahead. Enforcement of this policy varies.

Advance Reservations

If you only want to see the Accademia and Uffizi, you can skip the Firenze Card and instead make **reservations** for these two top sights, ideally as soon as you know when you'll be in town. Without a reservation at the Accademia and Uffizi, you can usually enter without significant lines from November through March after

16:00. But from April through October and on weekends, it can be crowded even late in the day. I'd reserve a spot any time of year. Reservations are not possible on the first Sunday of the month, when the museums are free and very busy.

Reservations are mandatory to climb the Duomo's dome. You can also make reservations for several other Florence sights—including the Bargello, Medici Chapels, and Pitti Palace—though they're unnecessary. The Brancacci Chapel officially requires a reservation (unless you have a Firenze Card, in which case you can walk right in), though it's usually possible to get a reservation on the spot at the chapel or in advance at the Palazzo Vecchio.

There are several ways to make reservations for the **Accademia** and **Uffizi:**

Online: Book and pay for your Accademia or Uffizi visit via the city's official site. You'll receive an order confirmation email, which is followed shortly by a voucher email. Bring your voucher to the ticket desk to swap for an actual ticket (€4/ticket reservation fee, www.firenzemusei.it—click on "B-ticket").

Pricey middleman sites—such as www.uffizi.com and www.tickitaly.com—are reliable and more user-friendly than the official site, but their booking fees run about €10 per ticket. (If ordering from a broker site, don't confuse Florence's Accademia with Venice's gallery of the same name.)

You can avoid waiting in line...

...if you make advance reservations.

By Phone: From a US phone, dial 011-39-055-294-883, or from an Italian phone call 055-294-883. When you get through, an English-speaking operator talks you through the process within a few minutes, and you'll end up with an entry time and a confirmation number. Present your confirmation number at the museum and pay for your ticket. You pay only for the tickets you pick up; for example, if you reserved two tickets but only use one, you'll pay for just one ticket (€4/ticket reservation fee; booking office open Mon-Fri 8:30-18:30, Sat until 12:30, closed Sun).

Through Your Hotel: Some hoteliers will make museum reservations (for a small fee) for guests who request this service when they book their room.

Private Tour: Various tour companies—including the ones listed in "Tours" in the next section—offer tours that include a reserved museum admission.

Last-Minute Strategies: If you arrive without a reservation, call the reservation number (tel. 055-294-883); ask your hotelier for help; or head to a booking window, either at Orsanmichele Church (daily 9:00-16:00, closed Sun off-season, along Via de' Calzaiuoli) or at Liberia My Accademia bookstore across from the Accademia's exit (Tue-Sun 8:15-17:30, closed Mon, Via Ricasoli 105 red). It's also possible to ask at the Uffizi's ticket office if they have any short-notice reservations available (ask the custodian at door #2 and ignore the long ticket-buying line). Any of these options will cost you the €4 reservation fee. Because both museums are closed on Mondays, the hardest day to snare last-minute, same-day reservations is Tuesday. If you've exhausted these options without success, remember you can buy a Firenze Card or take a private tour to see the sights.

Uffizi Combo-Ticket

Valid for three consecutive days, this combo-ticket offers a cost-saving, one-time priority (skip-the-line) admission to the Uffizi Gallery, Pitti Palace, and Boboli Gardens (€38 March-Oct, €18 Nov-Feb, not valid first Sun of the month when admission is free; www.uffizi.it).

Duomo Combo-Ticket

While the Duomo itself is free to enter, several related sights are all covered by a single €18 **combo-ticket** (valid for 48 hours): the Baptistery, dome climb (reservations required), Campanile, Duomo Museum, and Santa Reparata crypt. If you have a Firenze Card, you won't need the Duomo combo-ticket (both cover the same sights), unless you want to reserve your dome climb in advance (see page 526).

Tours

🎧 To sightsee on your own, download free audio tours via my free **Rick Steves Audio Europe** app (see page 17 for details).

Tour companies offer city tours as well as excursions in Tuscany (such as Siena, San Gimignano, Pisa, and the Chianti region for wine-tasting). Several offer Accademia and Uffizi tours, gaining you easy access to these popular sights. (And they often run cooking classes, too.)

Florencetown runs tours on foot or by bike. Their "Walk and Talk Florence" introductory tour includes the Oltrarno neighborhood (€25, 2.5 hours). My readers get a 10 percent discount, with an extra 10 percent off for second tours (if booking online, enter code "RICK-STEVES"; Via de Lamberti 1, facing Orsanmichele Church, tel. 055-281-103, www.florencetown.com).

Artviva offers a variety of tours (18 people maximum), including these popular overviews: "Original Florence" town walk (€29, 3 hours) and "Florence in One Glorious Day" (€104, 6 hours, adds Uffizi and Accademia tours). They offer a 10 percent discount at www.artviva.com/ricksteves (username "ricksteves," password "reader"; Via de' Sassetti 1, second floor, near Piazza della Repubblica, tel. 055-264-5033, www.artviva.com).

Good **private guides** for walking tours and countryside excursions include **Alessandra Marchetti,** a Florentine who has lived in the US (€60-75/hour, mobile 347-386-9839, www.tuscanydriverguide.com, alessandramarchettitours@gmail.com), and **Paola Migliorini** and her partners, who also offer cooking classes (€60/hour without car, €70/hour in a van for up to 8 people, mobile 347-657-2611, www.florencetour.com, info@florencetour.com).

Helpful Hints

Theft and Safety: Beware of the "slow count": Cashiers may count change back with odd pauses in hopes you'll gather up the money early and say *"Grazie."* Keep an eye out for slick pickpockets, especially near the train station, the station's underpass (particularly where the tunnel surfaces), and at major sights. Some thieves even dress like tourists to fool you. Any crowded bus likely holds at least one thief.

Medical Help: To reach a doctor who speaks English, call **Medical Service Firenze** at 055-475-411 (answered 24 hours a day); they can send a doctor to your hotel within an hour of your call, or you can go to their clinic when the doctor's in (Mon-Sat 11:00-12:00 & 13:00-15:00 plus Mon-Fri 17:00-18:00, closed Sun, no appointment necessary, Via Roma 4, between the Duomo and Piazza della Repubblica, www.medicalservice.firenze.it).

Visiting Churches: Modest dress is required at the Duomo, Santa Maria Novella, Santa Croce, Santa Maria del Carmine/Brancacci Chapel, and the Medici Chapels. Be respectful of worshippers and the paintings; don't use a flash. Churches usually close from 12:00 or 12:30 until 15:00 or 16:00.

Addresses: Florence has a ridiculously confusing system for street addresses. They use "red" numbers for businesses and "black" numbers for residences; in print, addresses are indicated with "r" (as in Via Cavour 2r) or "n" (for black—*nero,* as in Via Cavour 25n). Red and black numbers are interspersed on the same street; each set goes in roughly consecutive order, but their numbers bear no connection with each other.

Free Water: Carry a water bottle to refill at Florence's twist-the-handle public fountains (near the Duomo dome entrance, around the corner from the "Piglet" statue at Mercato Nuovo, or in front of Pitti Palace). Try the *fontanello* (dispenser of free cold water, *gassata* or *naturale*) on Piazza della Signoria, behind the statue of Neptune (on the left side of the Palazzo Vecchio).

Wi-Fi: The city's free Wi-Fi hotspot network ("Firenze WiFi," click on "Accedi") covers all of the main squares (no registration, good for two hours).

Useful App: For free audio versions of my Renaissance Walk and tours of the Uffizi, Bargello, Museum of San Marco, and Accademia Gallery, get the **Rick Steves Audio Europe** app (see page 17).

WCs: Public restrooms are scarce. Use them when you can, in any café or museum. Pay WCs are typically €1. Handy locations include one at the Baptistery ticket office (near the Duomo); just down the street from Piazza Santa Croce (at Borgo Santa Croce 29 red); up near Piazzale Michelangelo; and inside the train station (near track 5).

Laundry: The **Wash & Dry Lavarapido** chain offers long hours and efficient, self-service launderettes at several locations (generally daily 7:30-23:00). Locations are: near **David** (Via dei Servi 105 red); between the train station and river (Via del Sole 29 red and Via della Scala 52 red); near the Palazzo Vecchio (Via Ghibellina 143 red); and in the Oltrarno neighborhood (Via dei Serragli 87 red).

Getting Lost: The Duomo, the cathedral with the distinctive red dome, is the center of Florence. If you ever get lost, home's the dome.

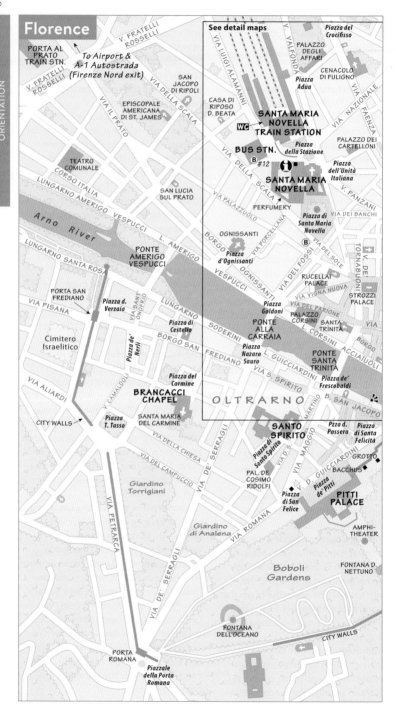

Florence

PORTA AL PRATO TRAIN STN.

To Airport & A-1 Autostrada (Firenze Nord exit)

V. FRATELLI ROSSELLI

V. FRATELLI ROSSELLI

V. IL PRATO

VIA DELLA SCALA

SAN JACOPO DI RIPOLI

EPISCOPALE AMERICANA DI ST. JAMES

TEATRO COMUNALE

CORSO ITALIA

LUNGARNO AMERIGO VESPUCCI

SAN LUCIA SUL PRATO

Arno River

LUNGARNO SANTA ROSA

PONTE AMERIGO VESPUCCI

L. AMERIGO

PORTA SAN FREDIANO

VIA PISANA

Piazza d. Verzaia

VIA SANT'ONOFRIO

LUNGARNO

VESPUCCI

Cimitero Israelitico

VIA ALIARDI

CITY WALLS

Piazza T. Tasso

V. CAMALDOLI

Piazza de' Nerli

Piazza di Cestello

BORGO SAN

Piazza del Carmine

BRANCACCI CHAPEL

SANTA MARIA DEL CARMINE

VIA DELLA CHIESA

VIA DEL CAMPUCCIO

VIA DE' SERRAGLI

VIA DE' SERRAGLI

VIA PETRARCA

Giardino Torrigiani

Giardino di Analena

VIA ROMANA

Boboli Gardens

FONTANA DELL'OCEANO

CITY WALLS

PORTA ROMANA

Piazzale della Porta Romana

See detail maps

V. VALFONDA

Piazza del Crocifisso

PALAZZO DEGLI AFFARI

CENACOLO DI FULIGNO

VIA LUIGI ALAMANNI

Piazza Adua

VIA NAZIONALE

VIA FAENZA

CASA DI RIPOSO D. BEATA

SANTA MARIA NOVELLA TRAIN STATION

WC

BUS STN.

VIA DELLA SCALA

Piazza della Stazione

B #12

PALAZZO DEI CARTELLONI

Piazza dell'Unità Italiana

SANTA MARIA NOVELLA

V. PANZANI

PERFUMERY

VIA PALAZZUOLO

Piazza di Santa Maria Novella

VIA DEI BANCHI

OGNISSANTI

BORGO OGNISSANTI

VIA PORCELLANA

B

VIA DEL FOSSI

VIA DEL SOLE

TORNABUONI

V. DE'

Piazza d'Ognissanti

RUCELLAI PALACE

VIA VIGNA NUOVA

STROZZI PALACE

OGNISSANTI

VESPUCCI

VIA DEL PARIONE

Piazza Goldoni

PALAZZO CORSINI

SANTA TRINITA

VIA

SODERINI

PONTE ALLA CARRAIA

L. CORSINI

BORGO

FREDIANO

Piazza Nazaro Sauro

L. GUICCIARDINI

VIA S. SPIRITO

PONTE SANTA TRINITA

ACCIAIUOLI

Piazza de' Frescobaldi

OLTRARNO

B. SAN JACOPO

SANTO SPIRITO

Pza d. Passera

Piazza di Santa Felicità

Piazza di Santo Spirito

VIA D. S.

VIA MAGGIO

V. D. GUICCIARDINI

GROTTO

BACCHUS

PAL. DE COSIMO RIDOLFI

Piazza di San Felice

V. D. GUICCIARDINI

Piazza de' Pitti

PITTI PALACE

AMPHI-THEATER

FONTANA D. NETTUNO

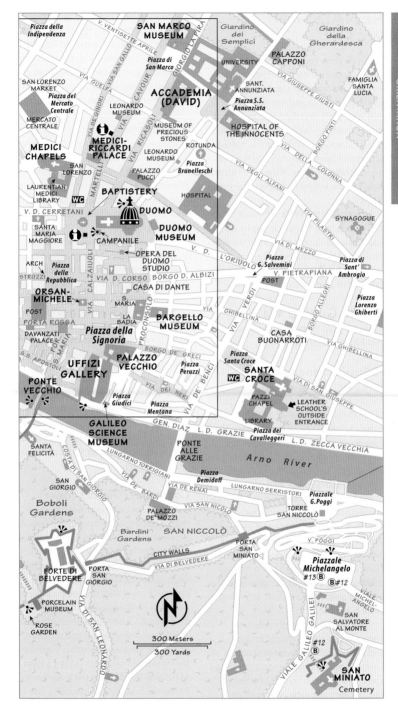

RENAISSANCE WALK

This walk gives you an overview of Florence's top sights. We'll start with the soaring church dome that stands as the proud symbol of the Renaissance spirit. Just opposite, you'll find the Baptistery doors that opened the Renaissance. Finally, we'll reach Florence's political center, dotted with monuments of that proud time. For more details on many of the sights on this walk, see the individual listings later in this chapter.

Length of This Walk: The walk is less than a mile long, but allow two hours if you add visits to the interiors of the Baptistery and Orsanmichele Church.

Tours: 🎧 Download my free Renaissance Walk audio tour.

⊙ Self-Guided Walk

• *Stand in front of the Duomo as you get your historical bearings.*

Florentine Renaissance

During the Dark Ages, it was obvious to the people of Italy—sitting on the rubble of the Roman Empire—that there had to be a brighter age on the horizon. The long-awaited rebirth, or Renaissance, began in Florence for good reasons: It was wealthy because of its cloth industry, trade, and banking, all powered by the Medici, the rich banking family who ruled Renaissance Florence. Locals were powered by a fierce city-state pride—they'd pee into the Arno with gusto, knowing rival city-state Pisa was downstream. And Florence was fertile with more than its share of artistic genius; imagine guys like Michelangelo and Leonardo attending the same high school.

The cultural explosion called the Renaissance—the "rebirth" of Greek and Roman culture that swept across Europe—started around 1400 and lasted about 150 years. In politics, the Renaissance meant democracy; in science, a renewed interest in exploring nature. Renaissance art was a return to the realism and balance of Greek and Roman sculpture. In architecture, domes and round arches replaced Gothic spires and pointed arches. The Duomo kicked off the architectural Renaissance in Florence.

The Duomo

Florence's massive cathedral is Florence's geographical and spiritual heart. Its dome, visible from all over the city, inspired Florentines to do great things. (Most recently, it inspired the city to make the area around the cathedral delightfully traffic-free.)

The church was begun in the 1296, in the Gothic style. After generations of work, it was still unfinished, lacking a roof. Its facade was little more than bare brick, and it stood that way until it was completed in 1870 in the "Neo"-Gothic style. Its "retro" look captures the feel of the original medieval facade, with green, white, and pink marble sheets that cover the brick construction. This over-the-top facade is adored by many, while others call it "the cathedral in pajamas."

We won't go inside the church on this tour. It has a cavernous, bare interior with a few noteworthy sights. Entry is free, but there's often a long wait (lines decrease late in the day).

Campanile (Giotto's Tower)

The 270-foot bell tower was begun in the 1300s by the great painter Giotto. As a forerunner of the Renaissance genius, Giotto excelled in many artistic fields, just as Michelangelo would do two centuries later. In his day, Giotto was called the ugliest man to ever walk the streets of Florence, but he designed what many call the most beautiful bell tower in all of Europe.

The bell tower served as a sculpture gallery for Renaissance artists. Find the four statues of prophets (about a third of the way up) done by the great Early Renaissance sculptor, Donatello. The most striking of them is bald-headed Habbakuk. Closer to ground level are several hexagonal panels that ring the Campanile. These reliefs depict Bible scenes. The realism of these groundbreaking works paved the way for Michelangelo and the High Renaissance generations later. (By the way, these are copies—the originals are at the excellent **Duomo Museum,** just behind the church.)

You can climb the Campanile for great views. It doesn't require a reservation, just a Duomo combo-ticket.

• *Now take in the Duomo's star attraction: the dome. The best viewing spot is just to the right of the facade, from the corner of the pedestrian-only Via de' Calzaiuoli.*

View of the Dome, by Brunelleschi

The dome rises 330 feet from ground level. It's made of red brick, held together

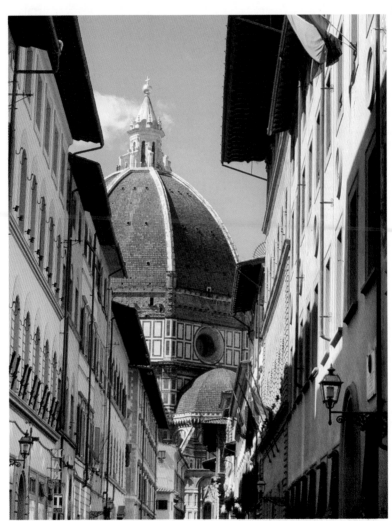

The Renaissance and Brunelleschi's dome live on in Florence.

Renaissance Walk

To Train Station

ZANNETTI

DUOMO TICKET OFFICE

WC

V. MART.

VIA RICASOLI

VIA DEL SERVI

To Accademia (David) & San Marco

VIA DE' CERRETANI

DUOMO INFO

❹

Piazza di San Giovanni

(MAIN ENTRANCE)

(DOME)

DUOMO MUSEUM

SANTA MARIA MAGGIORE

BAPTISTERY

❺

❶

DUOMO

VIA PECORI

WALK BEGINS

❷

EXIT

Piazza del Duomo

VIA DELL' ORIUOLO

❸

V. DE' VECCHIETTI

VIA CORSI

BRUNELLESCHI

MEDICI

CALZAIUOLI

❻

CANONICA

VIA DELL'OCHE

VIA DEL STUDIO

EDOARDO GELATO

BONIZZI

OPERA DEL DUOMO STUDIO

ARCH

Piazza della Repubblica

❼

SPEZIALI

S. MARIA DE' RICCI

VIA D. STROZZI

VIA DE'

VIA DEL CORSO

CERCHI

CASA DI DANTE

PRESTO

VIA DEL PROCONSOLO

V. D. ANSELMI

ST. GEORGE

SASSETTI

ORSAN-MICHELE

❽

VIA TAVOLINI

VIA D. ALIGHIERI

POST

V. PELLICCERIA

LAMBERTI

ST MARK

PERCHÉ NO! GELATO

CIMATORI

S. MARIA

LA BADIA

BARGELLO MUSEUM

VIA PORTA ROSSA

VIA CONDOTTA

DEL

VIA DELLE TERME

DAVANZATI PALACE

MERCATO NUOVO

ROMAN CITY PLAN

Piazza della Signoria

COSIMO I

VIA

V. DELL' ANGUILLARA

Piazza S. Firenze

To Santa Croce

B. S. APOSTOLI

VIA POR S. MARIA

ARMA

❾

❶❶

NEPTUNE

WC

GONDI

BORGO DE' GRECI

LOGGIA

PALAZZO VECCHIO

CORNO

LUNGARNO ACCIAIUOLI

Piazza de' Salt.

LAMB.

BARONCELLI

❶❷

❶⓪

LORENZO

Piazza del Grano

VIALEONI

VINEGRIA

S. STEFANO

UFFIZI GALLERY

MICHEL-ANGELO

EXIT

VIA DEI NERI

PONTE VECCHIO

❶❸

WALK ENDS

VASARI CORRIDOR

GALILEO

CASTELLO

100 Meters

100 Yards

To Pitti Palace

Arno River

GALILEO SCIENCE MUSEUM

LUNGARNO GEN. DIAZ

SAPONAI

Piazza Mentana

❶ The Duomo

❷ Campanile

❸ View of the Dome

❹ Baptistery – North Doors

❺ Baptistery – East Doors (Gates of Paradise)

❻ Via de' Calzaiuoli

❼ Piazza della Repubblica

❽ Orsanmichele Church

❾ Piazza della Signoria

❶⓪ Loggia dei Lanzi

❶❶ Savonarola Plaque

❶❷ Uffizi Courtyard Statues

❶❸ Ponte Vecchio

The Campanile

Ghiberti's bronze doors

with eight white ribs, and capped with a lantern.

Remember, although construction of the church had been begun in 1296, by the 1400s there still was no suitable roof. They'd intended to top it with a dome, but the technology to span the 140-foot-wide hole had yet to be invented. **Non c'è problema.** The brash Florentines knew that someday someone would come along who could handle the challenge. That man was Filippo Brunelleschi and he had a plan.

Brunelleschi built a dome within a dome. What you see is the outer shell, covered in terra-cotta tile. The inner dome is thicker and provides much of the structural support. The grand white skeletal ribs connect at the top, supporting each other in a way similar to a pointed arch. Hidden between them are interlocking bricks, laid in a herringbone pattern. Rather than being stacked horizontally, like traditional brickwork, the alternating vertical bricks act as "bookends." The dome grew upward like an igloo, supporting itself as it proceeded from the base.

When the ribs reached the top, Brunelleschi arched them in and fixed them in place with the lantern at the top. His dome, built in only 14 years, was the largest since ancient Rome's Pantheon.

When completed in 1436, Brunelleschi's dome was the wonder of the age. It became the model for many domes to follow, from St. Peter's to the US Capitol.

You can climb the dome for Florence's best views, but it requires a reservation, usually in advance (for details, see page 526).

• *Next up, the Baptistery. Step into the zone between the Duomo and the Baptistery that local tour guides call the "Piazza of Paradise."*

Baptistery and Ghiberti's Bronze Doors

The Baptistery's bronze doors bring us out of the Middle Ages and into the Renaissance. (These are copies; the originals are in the Duomo Museum.) Lorenzo Ghiberti beat out heavyweights such as Brunelleschi to design the **north doors,** which show scenes from the New Testament. (The original entries of Brunelleschi and Ghiberti are in the Bargello.) About the time Ghiberti completed the first set of doors, the Baptistery needed another set of doors for the entrance that faces the church. Ghiberti's Old Testament bronze panels for the **east doors** added a new dimension to art: depth. Here we see how the Renaissance masters merged art and science. Realism was in, and Renaissance artists used math, illusion, and dissection to create it. Ghiberti spent 27 years (1425-1452) working on these panels. That's him in the center of the doorframe, atop the second row of panels—the head on the left with the shiny male-pattern baldness.

The Baptistery **interior** features a fine example of pre-Renaissance mosaic art (1200s-1300s) in the Byzantine style (more on page 527).

• *Head south toward the river, taking the main pedestrian drag...*

Via de' Calzaiuoli

This street, Via de' Calzaiuoli (kahlts-ay-WOH-lee), has always been the main axis of the city; it was part of the ancient Roman grid plan that became Florence. Around the year 1400, as the Renaissance was blooming, this street connected the religious center (where we are now) with the political center (where we're heading), a five-minute walk away. In recent years this historic core has been transformed into a pleasant place to stroll, window-shop, lick your gelato cone, and wonder why American cities can't be more pedestrian-friendly.

Two blocks down from the Baptistery, look right on Via degli Speziali to see a triumphal arch that marks **Piazza della Repubblica.** The arch celebrates the unification of Italy in 1870 and stands as a reminder that, in ancient Roman times, this piazza was the city center. (Today the square hosts a carousel and the Rinascente department store, with a bar that has a rooftop terrace.)

• *A block farther, at the intersection with Via Orsanmichele, is the...*

Orsanmichele Church

Originally, this was an open loggia (covered porch) with a huge grain warehouse upstairs. The arches of the loggia were artfully filled in (14th century), and the building gained a new purpose—as a church. The 14 niches in the exterior walls feature replicas of the remarkable-in-their-day statues paid for by the city's rising middle class of merchants and their 21 guilds. The interior has a glorious Gothic tabernacle (1359) and a painted wooden panel that depicts *Madonna delle Grazie* (1346).

Head up Via Orsanmichele (to the right of the church) and circle the church exterior counterclockwise to enjoy the statues (these are all copies; the originals are in the museum on the church's top floor—open Mon only, and the most famous of the statues—St. George—is in the Bargello).

In the third niche is **Nanni di Banco's Quattro Santi Coronati** (c. 1415-1417). These four early Christians were sculp-

Donatello, St. George

Donatello, St. Mark

tors martyred by Roman emperor Diocletian because they refused to sculpt pagan gods. They seem to be contemplating the consequences of the fatal decision they're about to make. While Banco's saints are deep in the church's niche, the next statue, just to the right, feels ready to step out.

Donatello's **St. George** is alert, perched on the edge of his niche, scanning the horizon for dragons. He's anxious, but he's also self-assured. Comparing this Renaissance-style *St. George* to *Quattro Santi Coronati,* you can psychoanalyze the heady changes underway. This is humanism.

Continue counterclockwise around the church (bypassing the entrance), all the way to the opposite side. The first niche you come to features **Donatello's St. Mark** (1411-1413). The evangelist cradles his gospel in his strong, veined hand and gazes out, resting his weight on the right leg while bending the left. Though subtle, St. Mark's twisting *contrapposto* pose was the first seen since antiquity. Eighty years after young Donatello carved this statue, a teenage Michelangelo Buonarroti stood here and marveled at it.

The church hosts evening **concerts;** same-day tickets are sold from the door facing Via de' Calzaiuoli; you can also book tickets here for the Uffizi and Accademia (ticket window open daily 9:00-16:00, closed Sun off-season).

• *Continue down Via de' Calzaiuoli 50 more yards, to the huge and historic square.*

Piazza della Signoria

What a view! This piazza—the main civic center of Florence—is dominated by the massive stone facade of the Palazzo Vecchio, with a tower that reaches for the sky. The square is dotted with statues. The stately Uffizi Gallery is nearby, and the marble greatness of old Florence litters the cobbles. Piazza della Signoria still vibrates with the echoes of the city's past—executions, riots, and celebrations. There's even Roman history: Look for the **chart** showing the ancient city (on a freestanding display to your right as you enter the square, in front of Chanel). Today, it's a tourist's world with pigeons, selfie sticks, horse buggies, and tired tourists. For a sugar jolt, stop in at the **Rivoire** café to enjoy its fine desserts, pudding-thick hot chocolate, and the best view seats in town.

Piazza della Signoria

Before you towers the **Palazzo Vecchio,** the palatial Town Hall of the Medici—a fortress designed to contain riches and survive the many riots that went with local politics. The windows are just beyond the reach of angry stones, and the tower was a handy lookout post. Justice was doled out sternly on this square. Until 1873, Michelangelo's *David* stood where you see the replica today. The original was damaged in a 1527 riot (when a bench thrown from a palace window knocked its left arm off), but it remained here for several centuries, vulnerable to erosion and pollution, before being moved indoors for protection.

Step past the fake *David* through the front door into the Palazzo Vecchio's courtyard (free). This palace was Florence's symbol of civic power. You're surrounded by art for art's sake—a cherub frivolously marks the courtyard's center, and ornate stuccoes and frescoes decorate the walls and columns. Such luxury represented a big change 500 years ago. (For more on the palazzo and climbing its tower, see page 535.)

• *Back outside, check out the statue-filled...*

Loggia dei Lanzi

The loggia, a.k.a. **Loggia della Signoria,** was once a forum for public debate, perfect for a city that prided itself on its democratic traditions. But later, when the Medici figured that good art was more desirable than free speech, it was turned into an outdoor sculpture gallery. Notice the squirming Florentine themes—conquest, domination, rape, and decapitation. The statues lining the back are Roman originals brought back to Florence by a Medici when his villa in Rome was sold. Two statues in the front deserve a closer look: Giambologna's **The Rape of the Sabine Women** (c. 1583)—with its pulse-quickening rhythm of muscles—is from the restless Mannerist period, which followed the stately and confident Renaissance; Benvenuto Cellini's **Perseus** (1545-1553), the loggia's most noteworthy piece,

shows the Greek hero who decapitated the snake-headed Medusa.

• *Cross the square to the big* **fountain of Neptune** *by Bartolomeo Ammanati that Florentines (including Michelangelo) consider a huge waste of marble. The guy on the horse, to the left, is Cosimo I, one of the post-Renaissance Medici. Find the round marble plaque on the ground 10 steps in front of the fountain.*

Savonarola Plaque

The Medici family was briefly thrown from power by an austere monk named Savonarola, who made Florence a constitutional republic. He organized huge rallies lit by bonfires here on the square where he preached. While children sang hymns, the devout brought their rich "vanities" (such as paintings, musical instruments, and playing cards) and threw them into the flames. Encouraged by the pope, the Florentines fought back and arrested Savonarola. For two days, they tortured him, trying unsuccessfully to persuade him to see their side of things. Finally, on the very spot where Savonarola's followers had built bonfires of vanities, the monk was burned. The bronze plaque, engraved in Italian (*"Qui dove..."*), reads, "Here, Girolamo Savonarola and his Dominican brothers were hanged and burned" in the year "MCCCCXCVIII" (1498). Soon after, the Medici returned to power. The Renaissance picked up where it left off.

• *Stay cool, we have 200 yards to go. Follow the gaze of the fake* David *into the courtyard of the two-tone horseshoe-shaped building.*

Uffizi Courtyard Statues

The top floor of this building, known as the *uffizi* (offices) during Medici days, is filled with the greatest collection of Florentine painting anywhere. It's one of Europe's top art galleries (described on page 532). The courtyard, filled with souvenir stalls and hustling young artists, is watched over by 19th-century statues of the great figures of the Renaissance:

artists (Michelangelo, Giotto, Donatello, and Leonardo), philosophers (Niccolò Machiavelli), scientists (Galileo), writers (Dante), poets (Petrarch), cartographers (Amerigo Vespucci), and the great patron of so much Renaissance thinking, Lorenzo "the Magnificent" de' Medici. His support of Leonardo, Botticelli, and teenage Michelangelo helped Florence become Europe's most enlightened city.

After hours, talented street musicians take advantage of the space's superior acoustics.

• *Exiting at the far end of the courtyard, pause at the Arno River, overlooking...*

Ponte Vecchio

Ponte Vecchio (Old Bridge), rated ▲, has spanned this narrowest part of the Arno since Roman times. While Rome "fell," Florence never really did, remaining a bustling trade center along the river.

• *Hike to the center of the bridge.*

A famous goldsmith is honored with a fine bust at the central point of the bridge—the sculptor Cellini. This statue is a reminder that, in the 1500s, the Medici booted out the bridge's butchers and tanners and installed the gold- and silver-smiths who still tempt visitors to this day.

During World War II, the local German commander was instructed to blow up all of Florence's bridges to cover the Nazi retreat. But even some Nazis appreciate history: He blew up the other bridges, and left the Ponte Vecchio impassable

but intact. Look up to notice the protected and elevated passageway (called the Vasari Corridor) that led the Medici from the Palazzo Vecchio through the Uffizi, across Ponte Vecchio, and up to Pitti Palace, four blocks beyond the bridge.

• *Now that you've had a full meal of high culture, finish it off with a dessert of the world's finest gelato. Enjoy.*

SIGHTS

When you see a 🎧 in a listing, it means the sight is covered in an audio tour via my free **Rick Steves Audio Europe** app (see page 17).

The Duomo and Nearby Sights

A single **combo-ticket,** valid for 48 hours, covers all the paid Duomo sights: Baptistery, dome climb (which requires reservations), Campanile, Duomo Museum, and Santa Reparata crypt.

The main ticket office faces the Baptistery entrance (at #7 on the square) and has a staffed counter (credit cards or cash) as well as ticket machines (credit cards only, requires PIN); there's another office at the Duomo Museum. You can also buy tickets at the Santa Reparata crypt or at the Campanile, but they don't make reservations—which are mandatory—for the dome climb.

If you buy the €18 combo-ticket online in advance (www.museumflorence.com), you can make a dome-climb reservation at that time. Or you can reserve the climb in person at two of the Duomo ticket offices.

The **Firenze Card** also covers all the Duomo sights. Before entering any of the Duomo sights, you must present your Firenze Card at the ticket office opposite the Baptistery (look for a priority queue) to obtain a free combo-ticket and—with luck—reserve a time for the dome climb.

Ponte Vecchio

▲▲DUOMO

Florence's Gothic cathedral has the third-longest nave in Christendom. The church's noisy Neo-Gothic facade (from 1870) is covered with pink, green, and white Tuscan marble. The cathedral's claim to artistic fame is Brunelleschi's magnificent dome—the first Renaissance dome and the model for domes to follow. While viewing it from the outside is well worth ▲▲ (and it's described earlier on my Renaissance walk), the massive but empty-feeling interior is lucky to rate ▲— it doesn't justify the massive crowds that line up to get inside. Much of the church's great art is stored in the Duomo Museum behind the church.

Cost and Hours: Free; Mon-Fri 10:00-17:00 (Thu until 16:30); Sat 10:00-16:45, Sun 13:30-16:45; opening times sometimes change due to religious functions, modest dress code enforced, tel. 055-230-2885, www.operaduomo.firenze.it.

Tours: Themed tours (€30, which includes a combo-ticket you'll keep) cover the Duomo (daily at 10:30), Baptistery mosaics (Mon, Wed, and Fri at 16:30), and the still-active workshop where Michelangelo carved *David* (Mon, Wed, and Fri at 12:00). To reserve, call 055-282-226, email info@operaduomo.firenze. it, or go to the ticket office next to the Baptistery.

The Duomo is covered on my free Renaissance Walk audio tour.

Rick's Tip: Dome climb time slots can fill up, so it's smart to reserve well ahead (at www.museumflorence.com). Otherwise, try to reserve a time at the main Duomo ticket office (facing Baptistery entrance) or Duomo Museum (also has ticket machines).

▲CLIMBING THE DUOMO'S DOME

For a grand view into the cathedral from the base of the dome, a chance to see Brunelleschi's "dome-within-a-dome" construction, a glorious Florence view from the top, and the equivalent of 463 plunges on a StairMaster, climb the dome. The claustrophobic one-way route takes you up narrow, steep staircases and walkways to the top of the dome.

*Rick's Tip: If you're **claustrophobic** or **acrophobic**, skip climbing the dome. Once you start up the narrow staircase, there's no turning back until you reach the top. The slow climb to the top can feel like torture.*

As you're waiting in line, spend a few minutes studying the recently restored side entrance door, called the Porta della Mandorla ("Almond Door"): Just above the delicately carved door frame is a colorful Annunciation mosaic by Nanni di Banco, and above that, in a sculpted almond-shaped frame, the Madonna is borne heavenward by angels.

Cost: €18 combo-ticket covers all Duomo sights, covered by Firenze Card;

The Duomo with Brunelleschi's dome

with either, you must reserve a dome-climb time when obtaining your ticket—to ensure a climb it's best to buy a combo-ticket and reserve a time well ahead at www.museumflorence.com.

Hours: Mon-Fri 8:30-20:00, Sat 8:30-17:40, Sun 13:00-16:00, enter from outside church on north side. The dome is closed during rain.

▲CAMPANILE

The 270-foot bell tower has 50-some fewer steps than the Duomo's dome (but that's still 414 steps—no elevator); offers a faster, relatively less-crowded climb (with typically shorter lines); and has a view of that magnificent dome to boot. On the way up, there are several intermediate levels where you can catch your breath and enjoy ever-higher views. The stairs narrow as you go up, creating a mosh-pit bottleneck near the top—but the views are worth the hassle. While the various viewpoints are enclosed by cage-like bars, the gaps are big enough to let you snap great photos. Still, acrophobes and claustrophobes should beware!

Cost and Hours: €18 combo-ticket covers all Duomo sights, covered by Firenze Card, daily 8:30-20:00, last entry 40 minutes before closing.

▲BAPTISTERY

This is the octagonal building next to the Duomo. Check out the gleaming copies of Lorenzo Ghiberti's bronze doors facing the Duomo's facade (the originals are in the Duomo Museum); Michelangelo

Last Judgment *mosaic in the Baptistery*

said these doors were fit to be the gates of paradise. Making a breakthrough in perspective, Ghiberti used mathematical laws to create the illusion of receding distance on a basically flat surface. The doors on the north side of the building were designed by Ghiberti when he was young; he'd won the honor and opportunity by beating Brunelleschi in a competition (the rivals' original entries are in the Bargello).

Cost and Hours: €18 combo-ticket covers all Duomo sights, covered by Firenze Card, interior open Mon-Sat 8:15-20:00, Sun 8:30-14:00. The (facsimile) bronze doors are on the exterior, so they are always viewable and free.

Visiting the Baptistery: Workers from St. Mark's in Venice came here to make the remarkable ceiling mosaics (of Venetian glass) in the late 1200s. Sit and savor the ceiling, where it's always Judgment Day, giving us a glimpse of the medieval worldview. Life was a preparation for the afterlife, when you would be judged and saved, or judged and damned—with no in-between. Christ, peaceful and reassuring, blessed those at his right hand with heaven (thumbs-up) and sent those on his left to hell (the ultimate thumbs-down) to be tortured by demons.

The rest of the ceiling mosaics tell the history of the world, from Adam and Eve (over the north/entrance doors, top row) to Noah and the Flood (over south doors, top row), to the life of Christ (second row, all around), to the life, ministry, and eventual beheading of John the Baptist (bottom row, all around)—all bathed in the golden glow of pre-Renaissance heaven.

▲▲▲DUOMO MUSEUM

Brunelleschi's dome, Ghiberti's bronze doors, and Donatello's statues define the 1400s (the Quattrocento) in Florence, when the city blossomed and classical arts were reborn. While copies now decorate the exteriors of the cathedral, Baptistery, and Campanile, the originals are restored and displayed safely indoors, filling the Duomo Museum with some of

Heart of Florence

the best sculpture from the Renaissance. The museum also has two powerful statues by Florence's powerhouse sculptors—Donatello and Michelangelo. The museum has reopened after a remodel—expect changes.

Cost and Hours: €18 combo-ticket covers all Duomo sights, covered by Firenze Card. Daily 9:00-20:00, closed first Tue of each month, last entry one hour before closing, one of the few museums in Florence always open on Mon, free app available from iTunes and Google Play, Via del Proconsolo 9, tel. 055-282-226 or 055-230-7885, www.operaduomo.firenze.it.

Visiting the Duomo Museum: Start in Room 6, the big Sala del Paradiso (Hall of Paradise), which dominates the museum. This room re-creates the facades of the Duomo and the Baptistery, which were a showcase of the greatest art of Florence from roughly 1300 to 1600. The original statues, doors, and reliefs face each other as they once did on the buildings for which they were designed.

Facing the facade of the church, as they did in the Middle Ages, are the famous **bronze doors** of the Baptistery. The Renaissance began in 1401 with a citywide competition to build new doors for the Baptistery. Lorenzo Ghiberti (c. 1378-1455) won the job and built the doors for the north side of the building. Everyone loved them, so he was then hired to make another set of doors for the east entrance, facing the Duomo. These "Gates of Paradise" revolutionized the way Renaissance people saw the world around them. Each panel is bronze with a layer of gold on top. They tell several stories in one frame using perspective and realism as never before.

Also on the ground floor are rooms dedicated to the museum's most famous and evocative statues. Donatello's *Mary Magdalene (Maddalena, c. 1455)*, carved from white poplar and originally painted with realistic colors, is a Renaissance work of intense devotion. The aging Michelangelo (1475-1564) designed his own tomb, with a pietà (1547-1555) as the centerpiece. Three mourners tend the broken body of the crucified Christ. We see Mary, his mother; Mary Magdalene (on the left); and Nicodemus, the converted Pharisee, whose face is that of Michelangelo himself.

Upstairs, the first floor displays original **statues and panels** from the bell tower's third story, where copies stand today, two marble **choir lofts** *(cantorie;* by Lucca della Robbia and Donatello) that once sat above the sacristy doors of the Duomo, an exquisite half-ton **silver altar** honoring John the Baptist that once stood in the Baptistery, and **Brunelleschi's model** of the dome.

North of the Duomo
▲▲▲ACCADEMIA
This museum houses Michelangelo's *David,* the consummate Renaissance statue of the buff, biblical shepherd boy ready to take on the giant. When you look into the eyes of this magnificent sculpture, you're looking into the eyes of Renaissance Man.

Michelangelo, Pietà

Cost and Hours: €12.50 (€8 if there's no special exhibit), additional €4 for reservation, free and crowded on first Sun of the month, covered by Firenze Card; Tue-Sun 8:15-18:50, possibly Tue until 22:00 June-Sept, closed Mon; audioguide-€6, Via Ricasoli 60, reservation tel. 055-294-883, www.galleriaaccademiafirenze.beniculturali.it. To bypass long lines in peak season, get the Firenze Card (see page 512) or make reservations (see page 513).

🎧 Download my free Accademia audio tour.

Visiting the Accademia: In 1501, Michelangelo Buonarroti, a 26-year-old Florentine, was commissioned to carve a large-scale work. The figure comes from a Bible story. The Israelites are surrounded by barbarian warriors, who are led by a brutish giant named Goliath. When the giant challenges the Israelites to send out someone to fight him, a young shepherd boy steps forward. Armed only with a sling, David defeats the giant. This 17-foot-tall symbol of divine victory over evil represents a new century and a whole new Renaissance outlook.

Originally, *David* was meant to stand on the roofline of the Duomo, but was placed more prominently at the entrance of the Palazzo Vecchio (where a copy stands today). In the 19th century, *David* was moved indoors for his own protection; he stands under a Renaissance-style dome designed just for him.

Nearby are some of the master's other works, including his powerful (unfinished) *Prisoners, St. Matthew,* and a pietà (possibly by one of his disciples). Michelangelo Buonarroti believed that the sculptor was a tool of God, responsible only for chipping away at the stone until the intended sculpture emerged.

▲▲MUSEUM OF SAN MARCO (MUSEO DI SAN MARCO)

Located one block north of the Accademia, this 15th-century monastery houses the greatest collection of frescoes and paintings by Renaissance master Fra Angelico. Upstairs are 43 cells decorated by Fra Angelico and his assistants. Trained in the medieval style, he adopted Renaissance techniques to produce works that blended Christian symbols with realism. Be sure to see the cell of Savonarola, the charismatic monk who threw out the Medici, and sponsored "bonfires of the vanities."

Cost and Hours: €4, covered by Firenze Card, Tue-Fri 8:15-13:50, Sat 8:15-16:50; also open 8:15-13:50 on first, third, and fifth Mon and 8:15-16:50 on second and fourth Sun of each month; on Piazza San Marco, tel. 055-238-8608.

Michelangelo, David

Michelangelo sculptures, Medici Chapels

🎧 Download my free Museum of San Marco audio tour.

▲▲MEDICI CHAPELS

The burial site of the ruling Medici family in the Basilica of San Lorenzo includes the dusky crypt; the big, domed Chapel of Princes; and the magnificent New Sacristy, featuring architecture, tombs, and statues almost entirely by Michelangelo. The Medici made their money in textiles and banking, and patronized a dream team of Renaissance artists that put Florence on the cultural map. Michelangelo, who spent his teen years living with the Medici, was commissioned to create the family's final tribute.

Cost and Hours: €8, free and crowded on first Sun of month, covered by Firenze Card; Tue-Sat 8:15-17:00 (Nov-March until 13:50), last entry 40 minutes before closing; also open second and fourth Mon and first, third, and fifth Sun of each month; reservations possible but unnecessary (€3 fee), audioguide-€6, modest dress required, tel. 055-238-8602, www.bargellomusei.beniculturali.it.

▲MERCATO CENTRALE

Florence's giant iron-and-glass-covered central market is a wonderland of picturesque produce. While the San Lorenzo Market that fills the surrounding streets is only a step up from a flea market, Mercato Centrale retains its Florentine elegance.

Downstairs, you'll see parts of the cow (and bull) you'd never dream of eating

Mercato Centrale

(no, that's not a turkey neck), enjoy free samples, watch pasta being made, and have your pick of plenty of fun eateries sloshing out cheap and tasty pasta to locals (Mon-Fri 7:00-14:00, Sat until 17:00, closed Sun).

Upstairs, the meticulously restored glass roof and steel rafters soar over a sleek and modern food court, serving up a bounty of Tuscan cuisine (daily 10:00-24:00).

On and near Piazza della Signoria

▲▲▲UFFIZI GALLERY

This greatest collection of Italian paintings anywhere features works by Giotto, Leonardo, Raphael, Caravaggio, Titian, and Michelangelo, and a roomful of Botticellis, including the *Birth of Venus*. Start with Giotto's early stabs at Renaissance-style realism, then move on through the 3-D experimentation of the early 1400s to the real thing, rendered by the likes of Botticelli and Leonardo. Finish off with Michelangelo and Titian. Because only 600 visitors are allowed inside the building at any one time, there's generally a very long wait. The good news: no Vatican-style mob scenes inside. The museum is nowhere near as big as it is great. Few tourists spend more than two hours inside.

Cost and Hours: €20 (€10 if no special exhibit), extra €4 for reservation, €38 combo-ticket with Pitti Palace and Boboli Gardens gives you priority entry, admission is cheaper in winter, free and extremely crowded on first Sun of the month—don't visit on this day, covered by Firenze Card, Tue-Sun 8:15-18:50, closed Mon, audioguide-€6, reservation tel. 055-294-883, www.uffizi.it. To avoid the long ticket lines, get a Firenze Card (see page 512) or make reservations (see page 513).

🎧 Download my free Uffizi Gallery audio tour.

Getting In: There are several entrances; which one you use depends on whether you have a Firenze Card, a reservation, or neither.

Uffizi Gallery Overview

To Duomo

Piazza della Signoria

DAVID COPY

PALAZZO VECCHIO

Not to Scale

TERRACE (LOGGIA BELOW)

VIA DELLA NINNA

To Santa Croce

CAFÉ

STATUES OF FAMOUS FLORENTINES LINE THE COURTYARD

ELEVATOR

STAIRS UP FROM ENTRY & **WC**

STAIRS DOWN TO **WC** FIRST FLOOR & EXIT

CORRIDOR

TOUR BEGINS

EARLY ITALIAN

3 **1**

ENTRANCES

2

BOTTICELLI

MICHELANGELO

LEONARDO

Piazza degli Uffizi (Courtyard)

CORRIDOR

VENUS DE' MEDICI

VIA DI CASTELLANI

Piazza dei Giudici

GALILEO SCIENCE MUSEUM

VIEW OF PONTE VECCHIO

STATUES

UNDERPASS

To Ponte Vecchio

LUNGARNO A. M. L. DE'MEDICI

1 Reservation Entrance
2 Main Entrance & Same-Day Reservations
3 Reservation Ticket Office

Arno River

Firenze Card holders enter at door #1 (labeled *Reservation Entrance*). Read the signs carefully and get in the line for individuals—not groups—between door #1 and door #2.

People **buying a ticket on the spot** line up with everyone else at door #2, marked *Main Entrance*. An estimated wait time is posted.

To **buy a Firenze Card,** or to see if there are any same-day reservations available (€4 extra), enter door #2 to the left of the same-day ticket-buying line (marked *Booking Service and Today* or *Advance Sale*) to the left of the same-day ticket-buying line. Don't be shy: Ask the attendant to let you pass—and don't get into the long ticket-buying line. The doorway is kept open for same-day reservation buyers.

If you've **already made a reservation** and need to pick up your ticket, go to door #3 (labeled *Reservation Ticket Office,* across the courtyard from doors #1 and #2, under an archway and to the right). Tickets are available for pickup 10 minutes before your appointed time. If you booked online and have already prepaid, you'll exchange your voucher for a ticket. If you booked by phone, give them your confirmation number and pay for the ticket. Then walk briskly past the ticket-buying line. Get in the correct queue: groups to the left of door #1, individuals between doors #1 and #2.

Expect long waits even if you have a reservation or Firenze Card in hand. There may be a queue to pick up your reservation at door #3, another 30-minute wait to enter at door #1, and a slow shuffle through security.

Visiting the Uffizi: The Uffizi is U-shaped, running around the courtyard. The east wing contains Florentine paintings from medieval to Renaissance times. At the south end, you pass through a short hallway filled with sculpture. The west wing has later Florentine art (especially Michelangelo) and a café terrace facing the Duomo. Many more rooms of art are downstairs, showing how the Florentine Renaissance spread to Rome (Raphael) and Venice (Titian), and inspired the Baroque (Caravaggio). The gallery is nearing the end of a major, multiyear overhaul. Pieces frequently move, and new rooms open, so expect changes.

Medieval (1200-1400): Paintings by **Duccio, Cimabue,** and **Giotto** show the baby steps being made from the flat Byzantine style toward realism. In his *Madonna and Child with Angels,* Giotto created a "stage" and peopled it with real beings. The triumph here is Mary herself—big and monumental, like a Roman statue. Beneath her robe, she has knees and breasts that stick out at us. This three-dimensionality was revolutionary, a taste of the Renaissance a century before it began.

Early Renaissance (mid-1400s): Piero della Francesca's *Federico da Montefeltro and Battista Sforza* heralds the era of

Titian, Venus of Urbino

humanism and the new centrality of ordinary people in art. Fra Filippo Lippi's radiant Madonnas are light years away from the generic Marys of the medieval era.

Renaissance (1450-1500): The Botticelli room is filled with masterpieces and classical fleshiness (the famous *Birth of Venus* and *Spring*). Here is the Renaissance in its first bloom. This is a return to the pagan world of classical Greece, where things of the flesh are not sinful. Madonna is out; Venus is in.

Classical Sculpture: The foundation of the Renaissance was classical sculpture. Sculptors, painters, and poets turned for inspiration to ancient Greek and Roman works as the epitome of balance, 3-D perspective, human anatomy, and beauty.

In the Tribune Room, the highlight is the *Venus de' Medici,* a Roman copy of the lost original of the great Greek sculptor Praxiteles. Balanced, harmonious, and serene, this statue was considered the epitome of beauty and sexuality in Renaissance Florence.

The **sculpture hall** has 2,000-year-old copies of 2,500-year-old Greek originals...

and the best view in Florence of the Arno River and Ponte Vecchio through the window, dreamy at sunset.

High Renaissance (1500-1550): Don't miss Michelangelo's *Holy Family,* the only surviving completed easel painting by the greatest sculptor in history (in the Michelangelo Room).

After a break to enjoy Duomo views from the café terrace, head downstairs to find Raphael's *Madonna of the Goldfinch,* with Mary and the Baby Jesus brought down from heaven into the real world (Room 66), and Titian's voluptuous *Venus of Urbino* (Room 83).

More Art on the Lower Floor: On your way out, you'll see temporary exhibitions and works by foreign painters. It's worth pausing in Room 90 for works by Caravaggio.

Nearby: The statue-filled Uffizi courtyard and Loggia dei Lanzi are covered in the Renaissance Walk on page 524.

▲▲PALAZZO VECCHIO

This fortress with the 300-foot spire dominates Florence's main square. In Renaissance times, it was the Town Hall, where citizens pioneered the once-radical notion of self-rule. Its official name—Palazzo della Signoria—refers to the elected members of the city council. In 1540, the tyrant Cosimo I made the building his personal palace, redecorating the interior in lavish style. Today the building functions once again as the Town Hall.

Entry to the ground-floor courtyard is free, so even if you don't go upstairs to the museum, you can step inside and feel the essence of the Medici. Paying customers can see Cosimo's lavish royal apartments, decorated with paintings and statues by Michelangelo and Donatello. The highlight is the 13,000-square-foot Grand Hall (Salone dei Cinquecento), lined with frescoes and statues.

Underneath the Palazzo Vecchio are Roman-era excavations—the ruins of a 2,000-year-old theater from ancient Flo-

Palazzo Vecchio

rentia. Other than heavily restored brick-work and an interesting 10-minute video about the city's evolution over 22 centuries, there's little to see.

Cost and Hours: Courtyard-free, museum-€10, tower climb-€10 (418 steps), museum plus tower-€14, excavations-€4, combo-ticket for all three-€18, covered by Firenze Card (first pick up ticket at ground-floor info desk before entering museum). Museum and excavations open Fri-Wed 9:00-23:00 (Oct-March until 19:00), Thu 9:00-14:00 year-round; tower keeps shorter hours (last entry one hour before closing); last tickets for all sights sold one hour before closing; videoguide-€5, English tours available, Piazza della Signoria, tel. 055-276-8224, www.musefirenze.it.

▲▲GALILEO SCIENCE MUSEUM

When we think of the Renaissance, we think of visual arts: painting, mosaics, architecture, and sculpture. But when the visual arts declined in the 1600s (abused and co-opted by political powers), music and science flourished. Florence hosted many scientific breakthroughs, as you'll see in this collection of clocks, telescopes, maps, and ingenious gadgets. Trace the technical innovations as modern science emerges from 1000 to 1900. Exhibits include various tools for gauging the world, from a compass and thermometer to Galileo's telescopes. Some of the most talked about bottles in Florence are the ones here that contain Galileo's fingers. The museum is friendly, comfortably cool, never crowded, and just a block east of the Uffizi on the Arno River.

Cost and Hours: €9, €22 family ticket, covered by Firenze Card, Wed-Mon 9:30-18:00, Tue until 13:00, guided tours available, Piazza dei Giudici 1, tel. 055-265-311, www.museogalileo.it.

East of Piazza della Signoria

▲▲▲BARGELLO

The Renaissance began with sculpture—the great Florentine painters were "sculptors with brushes." You can see the birth of this revolution of 3-D in the Bargello (bar-JEL-oh), which boasts the best collection of Florentine sculpture. Housed

Celestial globe at Galileo Science Museum

Donatello, David

in a former police station, this small, uncrowded museum is a pleasure to visit.

Highlights include Donatello's influential, painfully beautiful *David* (the first male nude to be sculpted in a thousand years), multiple works by Michelangelo, and rooms of Medici treasures. Moody Donatello, who embraced realism with his lifelike statues, set the personal and artistic style for many Renaissance artists to follow. The best pieces are in the ground-floor room at the foot of the outdoor staircase (with fine works by Michelangelo, Cellini, and Giambologna) and in the "Donatello room" directly above (including his two different *David*s, plus Ghiberti and Brunelleschi's revolutionary dueling door panels and yet another *David* by Verrocchio).

Cost and Hours: €8, cash only, free and crowded on first Sun of the month, covered by Firenze Card; Tue-Sat 8:15-17:00 (later for special exhibits), Nov-March until 13:50; also open second and fourth Mon and the first, third, and fifth Sun of each month, last entry 40 minutes before closing; reservations possible but unnecessary, audioguide-€6 (€10/2 people), Via del Proconsolo 4, tel. 055-238-8606, www.bargellomusei.beniculturali.it.

🎧 Download my free Bargello audio tour.

▲▲SANTA CROCE CHURCH

This 14th-century Franciscan church, decorated with centuries of precious art, holds the tombs of great Florentines. The loud 19th-century Victorian Gothic facade faces a huge square ringed with tempting shops and littered with footsore tourists. Escape into the church and admire its sheer height and spaciousness.

Cost and Hours: €8, covered by Firenze Card, Mon-Sat 9:30-17:30, Sun 14:00-17:30, multimedia guide-€6 (€8/2 people), modest dress required, 10-minute walk east of the Palazzo Vecchio along Borgo de' Greci, tel. 055-246-6105, www.santacroceopera.it. The **leather school,** at the back of the church, is free and sells church tickets—handy when the church has a long line (daily 10:00-18:00, closed Sun Nov-March, has own entry behind church, plus an entry within church, www.scuoladelcuoio.com).

Santa Croce Church

Visiting the Church: On the left wall (as you face the altar) is the tomb of **Galileo Galilei** (1564-1642), the Pisan who lived his last years under house arrest near Florence. His crime? Defying the Church by saying that the earth revolved around the sun. His heretical remains were only allowed in the church long after his death.

Directly opposite (on the right wall) is the tomb of **Michelangelo Buonarroti** (1475-1564). Santa Croce was Michelangelo's childhood church, as he grew up a block west of here. Farther up the nave is the tomb of **Niccolò Machiavelli** (1469-1527), a champion of democratic Florence and author of *The Prince,* a how-to manual on hardball politics—which later Medici rulers found instructive.

The first chapel to the right of the main altar features the famous *Death of St. Francis* fresco by Giotto. With simple but eloquent gestures, Francis' brothers bid him a sad farewell. In the hallway near the bookstore, notice the photos of the devastating flood of 1966. Beyond that is the leather school (free entry).

Exit between the Rossini and Machiavelli tombs into the delightful cloister (peaceful open-air courtyard). On the left, enter Brunelleschi's Pazzi Chapel, which captures the Renaissance in miniature.

Near the Train Station
▲▲CHURCH OF SANTA MARIA NOVELLA

This 13th-century Dominican church is rich in art. Along with crucifixes by Giotto and Brunelleschi, it contains every textbook's example of the early Renaissance mastery of perspective: *The Trinity* by Masaccio. The exquisite chapels trace art in Florence from medieval times to early Baroque. The outside of the church features a dash of Romanesque (horizontal stripes), Gothic (pointed arches), Renaissance (geometric shapes), and Baroque (scrolls). Step in and look down the 330-foot nave for a 14th-century optical illusion.

Next to the church are the cloisters and the **museum,** located in the old Dominican convent of Santa Maria Novella. Its highlight is the breathtaking Spanish Chapel, with walls covered by a series of frescoes by Andrea di Bonaiuto.

Cost and Hours: Church and museum-€5, covered by Firenze Card; Mon-Thu 9:00-19:00 (Oct-March until 17:30), Fri 11:00-19:00 (Oct-March until 17:30), Sat 9:00-17:30, Sun 13:00-17:30, last entry 45 minutes before closing; multimedia guide-€3, modest dress required, main entrance on Piazza Santa Maria Novella, tel. 055-219-257, www.smn.it.

South of the Arno River
▲▲PITTI PALACE

Pitti Palace, several blocks southwest of Ponte Vecchio, offers many reasons for a visit: the palace itself, with its imposing exterior and lavish interior; the second-best collection of paintings in town; the statue-dotted Boboli Gardens; and a host of secondary museums. Focus on the highlights: the painting collection in the Palatine Gallery, plus the sumptuous rooms of the Royal Apartments. The paintings pick up where the Uffizi leaves off, at the High Renaissance. Lovers of Raphael's Madonnas and Titian's portraits will find some of the world's best here. If it's a nice day, take a stroll in the inviting Boboli Gardens, a rare patch of green space within old Florence.

Cost and Hours: The Palatine Gallery, Royal Apartments, and Gallery of Modern Art are covered by **ticket #1**—€16 (€8 if no special exhibits)—and are open Tue-Sun 8:15-18:50, closed Mon, last entry 45 minutes before closing. The Boboli and Bardini Gardens, Costume Gallery, Argenti/Silverworks Museum (the Medici treasures), and Porcelain Museum are covered by **ticket #2**—€10 (€7 if no special exhibits)—and are open daily June-Aug 8:15-19:30, April-May and Sept until 18:30, March and Oct until 17:30, Nov-Feb until 16:30, closed first and last

Pitti Palace

Silverworks Museum (ground and mezzanine floors; Medici treasures from jeweled crucifixes to gilded ostrich eggs), Costume Gallery, Porcelain Museum, and Boboli and Bardini gardens (behind the palace; enter from Pitti Palace courtyard—be prepared to climb uphill).

▲▲BRANCACCI CHAPEL

For the best look at works by Masaccio (one of the early Renaissance pioneers of perspective in painting), see his restored frescoes here. Instead of medieval religious symbols, Masaccio's paintings feature simple, strong human figures with facial expressions that reflect their emotions. The accompanying works of Masolino and Filippino Lippi provide illuminating contrasts.

Your ticket includes a 20-minute film (English subtitles) on the chapel, the frescoes, and Renaissance Florence; find it in the room next to the bookstore. The film's computer animation brings the paintings to 3-D life, while narration describes the events depicted in the panels. The film takes liberties with the art, but it's the best way to see the frescoes close up.

Cost and Hours: €6, cash only, covered by Firenze Card (which allows you to enter without a reservation); without a

Mon of each month, last entry one hour before closing. Reservations are possible but unnecessary. All palace sights are covered by the Firenze Card. The place is free and crowded on the first Sun of the month. The €8 audioguide (€13/2 people) explains the sprawling palace. Tel. 055-238-8614, www.uffizi.it.

Visiting Pitti Palace: In the Palatine Gallery you'll walk through one palatial room after another, walls sagging with masterpieces by 16th- and 17th-century masters, including Rubens, Titian, and Rembrandt. The Pitti's Raphael collection is the second-biggest anywhere—the Vatican beats it by one. Each room has some descriptions in English, though the paintings themselves have limited English labels.

The collection is all on one floor. To see the highlights, walk straight down the spine through a dozen or so rooms. Before you exit, consider a visit to the Royal Apartments. These 14 rooms (of which only a few are open at any one time) are where the Pitti's rulers lived in the 18th and 19th centuries. Each room features a different color and time period. Here, you get a real feel for the splendor of the dukes' world.

The rest of Pitti Palace is skippable, unless the various sights match your interests: the Gallery of Modern Art (second floor; Romantic, Neoclassical, and Impressionist works by 19th- and 20th-century Tuscan painters), Argenti/

Masaccio, Expulsion from the Garden of Eden

1. Signorvino
2. Golden View Open Bar
3. Gusta Osteria
4. Trattoria Casalinga
5. Il Santo Bevitore Ristorante & Enoteca Il Santino Gastronomia
6. Trattoria 4 Leoni
7. Olio & Convivium
8. Il Gelato di Filo
9. In Tavola Cooking School

Firenze Card, free and easy reservations are required, though it's usually possible to walk right in on weekdays and any day off-season, especially if you arrive before 15:30; Mon and Wed-Sat 10:00–17:00, Sun 13:00–17:00, closed Tue, last entry 45 minutes before closing; free 20-minute film, videoguide-€3, knees and shoulders must be covered; in Church of Santa Maria del Carmine, on Piazza del Carmine in Oltrarno neighborhood; reservations tel. 055-276-8224 or 055-276-8558, ticket

desk tel. 055-284-361, www.musefirenze.it.

Reservations: To reserve in advance, stop by the information desk in the Palazzo Vecchio or call the chapel a day ahead (tel. 055-276-8224 or 055-276-8558, English spoken, call center open Mon-Sat 9:30–13:00 & 14:00–17:00, Sun 9:30–12:30). You can also try reserving via email (info. muse@comune.fi.it).

▲PIAZZALE MICHELANGELO
Overlooking the city from across the river (look for the huge bronze statue of

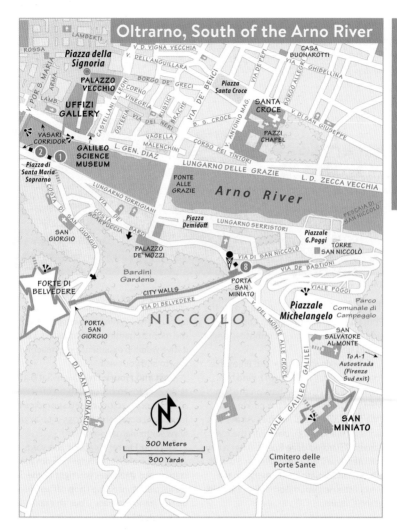

Oltrarno, South of the Arno River

David), this square has a superb view of Florence and the stunning dome of the Duomo. It's worth the 25-minute hike, taxi, or bus ride. When you're there, you can also visit the stark, beautiful, crowd-free, Romanesque San Miniato Church, about 200 yards beyond the square (see next listing).

At the square, the best cityscape photos are taken from the street immediately below the overlook (go around to the right and down a few steps). Nearby is an

inviting café (open seasonally) with great views. Off the west side of the piazza is a hidden terrace, excellent for a retreat from the mobs. After dark, the square is packed with school kids licking ice cream and each other. A WC is located just off the road, halfway between the two sights.

Getting There (and Back): It makes sense to take a taxi or ride the bus up and then enjoy the easy downhill walk back into town. Bus #12 takes you up (departs from train station, near Piazza

The view from Piazzale Michelangelo

di Santa Maria Novella, and just over the Ponte alla Carraia bridge on Oltrarno side of river; takes 20-30 minutes, longer in bad traffic).

The hike down is quick and enjoyable (or take bus #13 back down). Find the steps between the two bars on the San Miniato Church side of the parking lot (Via San Salvatore al Monte). At the first landing (marked #3), peek into the rose garden (Giardino delle Rose). After a few minutes, you'll walk through the old wall (Porta San Miniato) and emerge in the funky little neighborhood of San Niccolò in the Oltrarno.

▲▲SAN MINIATO CHURCH

According to legend, the martyred St. Minias—this church's namesake—was beheaded on the banks of the Arno in A.D. 250. He picked up his head and walked here (this was before the #12 bus), where he died and was buried in what became the first Christian cemetery in Florence. In the 11th century, this church was built to house Minias' remains. Imagine this fine church all alone—without any nearby buildings or fancy stairs—a quiet refuge where white-robed Benedictine monks could pray and work (their motto: *ora et labora*). The evening vesper service with the monks chanting in Latin offers a meditative worship experience—a peaceful way to end your visit.

Cost and Hours: Free, Mon-Sat 9:30-13:00 & 15:30-20:00, until 19:00 off-season, Sun 9:30-20:00, closed sporadically for special occasions, tel. 055-234-2731, www.sanminiatoalmonte.it.

Getting There: It's about 200 yards above Piazzale Michelangelo. From the station, bus #12 takes you right to the San Miniato al Monte stop (hop off and hike up the grand staircase); bus #13 takes you back down the hill.

San Miniato Church

EXPERIENCES

Shopping

One of Europe's best shopping towns, Florence has been known for its sense of style since the Medici days. Smaller stores are generally open about 9:00-13:00 and 15:30-19:30, usually closed on Sunday, often closed on Monday (or at least Monday morning), and sometimes closed for a couple of weeks around August 15. Bigger stores have similar hours, without the afternoon break.

Busy street scenes and markets abound. The vast open-air **San Lorenzo Market** sprawls in the streets ringing Mercato Centrale, between the Duomo and the train station (daily 9:00-19:00, closed Mon in winter). Originally a silk and straw market, **Mercato Nuovo** still functions as a rustic yet touristy market at the intersection of Via Calimala and Via Porta Rossa (daily 9:00-18:30). It's where you'll find *Il Porcellino* (a statue of a wild boar nicknamed "The Piglet"), which people rub and give coins to ensure their return to Florence. Other shopping areas can be found near Santa Croce and on Ponte Vecchio. At stalls or shops, prices are soft—don't be shy about bargaining, especially at San Lorenzo.

Leather jackets and handbags, perfume and cosmetics, edible goodies, and stationery are popular souvenirs. For authentic, locally produced wares, look for shops displaying the **Esercizi Storici Fiorentini** seal ("Historical Florentine Ventures"), with a picture of the Palazzo Vecchio's tower. You may pay a premium, but you can be assured of quality (for a list of shops, see www.esercizistorici.it).

The area between the Arno River and the cathedral is busy with fashion boutiques; browse along **Via della Vigna Nuova** (runs west from Via de' Tornabuoni) and **Via degli Strozzi** (runs east from Via de' Tornabuoni to Piazza della Repubblica). A tempting string of streets—**Borgo Santi Apostoli, Via del Parione,** and **Borgo Ognissanti**—runs parallel to the river one block inland, from near the Uffizi westward.

Across the river in the Oltrarno, known for its artisanal workshops, a short walk

San Lorenzo Market

Florence is a popular place to buy leather.

past the tourist crowds takes you to some less-discovered zones: near Pitti Palace, and the main street parallel to the river (**Borgo San Jacopo** to **Via di Santo Spirito**). Pick up the brochure "A Tour of Artisan Workshops" from the TI or at participating shops.

Nightlife

For me, nighttime is for dining, catching a concert, strolling through the old town with a gelato, or hitting one of the many pubs. Get the latest on nightlife from *The Florentine* magazine (free from TI, www. theflorentine.net) or *Firenze Spettacolo* (sold at newsstands, www.firenzespettacolo.it), or check www.firenzeturismo.it.

Strolling After Dark: Join the parade of locals on their evening *passeggiata*, strolling from the Duomo to the Arno on Via de' Calzaiuoli, enjoying cafés, gelato shops, great people-watching, and street performers. Pop into a wine bar (*enoteca*) to sample regional wines by the glass or a plate of meats and cheeses. (Psst. Near the Duomo, find La Congrega Lounge Bar—a tiny retreat on a tiny lane just off the main pedestrian drag, at Via Tosinghi 3/4 red.) End at the Arno, to stand atop

Ponte Vecchio and watch the sun set, the moon rise, and lovers kiss.

Lively squares include Piazzale Michelangelo's marvelous viewpoint, Piazza della Repubblica (with a carousel and street musicians), Piazza Santa Croce (with the popular, youthful Moyo bar nearby, at Via de' Benci 23 red), and Piazza di Santo Spirito (with trendy Volume and Pop Café on this Oltrarno square).

Live Music: Orsanmichele Church hosts chamber music under its Gothic arches (tickets sold on day of concert from door facing Via de' Calzaiuoli). **St. Mark's English Church** offers opera music several nights each week from February through October (Via Maggio 18, www.concertoclassico.info).

The recommended **Golden View Open Bar,** a river-view restaurant near Ponte Vecchio, has live jazz several nights a week at 21:00 (see page 202). **Boxoffice Toscana** sells tickets for rock concerts and more (Via delle Vecchie Carceri 1, tel. 055-210-804, www.boxofficetoscana.it).

Movies: Find English-language films at **Odeon Cinema** (near Piazza della Repubblica on Piazza Strozzi, tel. 055-214-068, www.odeonfirenze.com).

Ponte Vecchio after dark

EATING

Restaurants in Florence like to serve what's fresh. Seasonal ingredients are featured in the *piatti del giorno* (specials of the day) section on menus. Foodies should consider purchasing Elizabeth Minchilli's excellent app, Eat Florence (www.elizabethminchilliinrome.com).

Budget Eating: To save money and time, you can keep lunches fast and simple by eating at pizzerias, self-service cafeterias, or the countless sandwich shops and stands (though you may want to avoid the *trippa* carts selling tripe sandwiches—a prized local specialty).

Picnicking is easy. You can picnic your way through Mercato Centrale. You'll also find good *supermercati* throughout the city. I like the classy Sapori & Dintorni markets (run by Conad), which has branches near the Duomo (Borgo San Lorenzo 15 red) and just over Ponte Vecchio in the Oltrarno (Via de Bardi 45). Despar is another handy grocery chain (there's one around the corner from the Duomo Museum at Via dell'Oriuolo 66).

Mercato Centrale and Nearby

In Mercato Centrale

The Mercato Centrale (Central Market) is a foodie wonderland.

$ Ground Floor: The market zone, with lots of raw ingredients and a few humble

food counters, is open only through lunchtime (Mon-Fri 7:00-14:00, Sat 7:00-17:00, closed Sun). Buy a picnic of fresh mozzarella cheese, olives, fruit, and crunchy bread to munch on the steps of the nearby Basilica of San Lorenzo. The fancy deli, Perini, is famous for its quality (pricey) products and enticing display. For a simple sit-down meal, head for the venerable Nerbone in the Market. Join the shoppers and workers who crowd up to the bar to grab their inexpensive plates, and then find a stool at the cramped shared tables nearby. Of the several cheap market diners, this feels the most authentic (lunch menu served Mon-Sat 12:00-14:00, sandwiches available from 8:00 until the bread runs out, cash only, on the side closest to the Basilica of San Lorenzo). Its less-famous sisters, nearby, have better seating and fewer crowds.

$$ Upstairs: Under the old glass roof, the upper floor features a dozen upscale food counters open for lunch and dinner (daily 10:00-24:00). Grab what you want— pizza, pasta, fish, meat, *salumi, lampredotto,* wine, and so on—and pull up a stool at one of the food-court tables. Before choosing, do a full circuit around the scene to get to know your options.

Near Mercato Centrale

If you can't find what you want in the market itself, consider one of these alternatives on the surrounding streets. These eateries skew to an especially touristy clientele.

$$ Trattoria Mario's has been serving hearty lunches to market-goers since 1953 (Fabio and Romeo are the latest generation). Their simple formula: no-frills, bustling service, old-fashioned good value, and shared tables. It's *cucina casalinga*—home cooking *con brio*. Their best dishes (*ribollita,* bean soup, *amatriciana*) often sell out first, so go early. If there's a line, put your name on the list (cash only, Mon-Sat 12:00-15:30, closed Sun and Aug, no reservations, Via Rosina 2, tel. 055-218-550).

Gelato

The best ice cream in Italy—maybe the world—is in Florence. But beware of scams at touristy joints that turn a simple request for a cone into a €10 rip-off. Survey the options and specify the size you want—for example, *un cono da tre euro* (a €3 cone).

All of these places, a cut above, are open daily for long hours:

Near the Accademia: Gelateria Carabè is famous for *granite* (Italian ices made with fresh fruit). Try a *cremolata*: a *granita* with a dollop of gelato (Via Ricasoli 60 red; from the Accademia, it's a block toward the Duomo).

In the City Center: A favorite, **Edoardo** features organic ingredients and tasty handmade cones (facing the southwest corner of the Duomo at Piazza del Duomo 45 red). Creative **Perchè No!** is near Orsanmichele Church, just off busy Via de' Calzaiuoli (Via dei Tavolini 19). Mod **Carapina,** near Ponte Vecchio, has unusual flavors and seasonal ingredients (Via Lambertesca 18 red).

Near the Church of Santa Croce: Gelateria de' Neri has a wide array of enticing flavors (Via dei Neri 9 red).

In the Oltrarno: Tiny **Il Gelato di Filo** boasts some of Florence's best gelato (Via San Miniato 5 red).

$$ Pepò, a colorful and charmingly unpretentious space, is tucked just around the corner from the touristy Trattoria Zà-Zà glitz on Piazza del Mercato Centrale. The chef offers a short menu of simple but well-prepared Florentine classics such as *ribollita* and *pollo alla cacciatora*—chicken cacciatore (daily 12:00-14:30 & 19:00-22:30, Via Rosina 4 red, tel. 055-283-259).

$$ Trattoria Sergio Gozzi is your classic neighborhood lunch-only place, serving hearty, traditional Florentine fare to market-goers since 1915. The handwritten menu is limited and changes daily, and the service can be hectic, but it remains a local favorite (Mon-Sat 12:00-15:00, closed Sun, reservations smart, Piazza di San Lorenzo 8, tel. 055-281-941).

Around the Duomo

At lunchtime, my first listing is more of a sit-down place; the others are better for a fast meal.

$$ Enoteca Coquinarius—hip and welcoming—has a slow food ethic and great €15 salads and €10 pastas (open daily, a couple blocks south of the Duomo at Via delle Oche 11 red, tel. 055-230-2153).

$ Self-Service Ristorante Leonardo is an inexpensive, air-conditioned, quick, and handy cafeteria. While it's no-frills and old-school, the food is better than many table-service eateries in this part of town. It's a block from the Duomo, southwest of the Baptistery (lots of veggies, daily 11:45-14:45 & 18:45-21:45, upstairs at Via Pecori 11, tel. 055-284-446).

$$ Paszkowski Café is a venerable place on Piazza della Repubblica. While famously expensive as a restaurant, it serves up inexpensive, quick lunches. At the display case, order a salad or plate of pasta or cooked veggies (or half-and-half), pay the cashier, and find a seat upstairs or at one of the tables reserved for self-serve diners on the square (lunch served 12:00-15:00, Piazza della Repubblica 35 red—northwest corner, tel. 055-210-236).

$$ EATaly, a slick, modern space a half-block from the Duomo, is an outpost of a chain of foodie mini-malls located in big Italian cities. Along with a world of gifty edibles, it offers several food options under one roof, including an espresso counter, a soft-serve gelato counter and tempting pastry shop, a grocery store for top-end Italian ingredients and kitchen gadgets, and a bright, modern dining area serving pastas, pizzas, salads, and *secondi,* including daily specials (food shop open daily 10:00-22:30, restaurants open 12:00-15:00 and from 19:00, Via de' Martelli 22 red, tel. 055-015-3601).

Near Piazza della Signoria

Piazza della Signoria, the scenic square facing the Palazzo Vecchio, is ringed by beautifully situated yet touristy eateries serving overpriced and probably microwaved food. The following places offer better values off the square.

Dining

$$ Osteria Vini e Vecchi Sapori is a colorful eatery—tight and tiny, and with attitude. They serve Tuscan food—like pappardelle with duck—from a fun, accessible menu of delicious pastas and *secondi* (Mon-Sat 12:30-14:30 & 19:30-22:30, closed Sun, reservations smart, Via dei Magazzini 3 red, tel. 055-293-045, run by Mario while wife Rosanna cooks and son Tommaso serves).

$$$$ Frescobaldi Ristorante and Wine Bar, the showcase of Italy's aristocratic wine family, serves sophisticated dishes by candlelight under high-vaulted ceilings. They offer the same seasonal menu in their cozy interior, tight wine bar, and at a few outside tables. If coming for dinner, make a reservation and dress up (lighter wine-bar and good-value set menus at lunch, daily 12:00-14:30 & 19:00-22:30, air-con, Via dei Magazzini 2 red, tel. 055-284-724, www.deifrescobaldi.it).

Cheap, Simple Fare

$$ Cantinetta dei Verrazzano, a long-established bakery/café/wine bar, serves delightful sandwich plates in an old-time setting. Their *selezione Verrazzano* is a plate of four little crostini featuring different breads, cheeses, and meats from the Chianti region. The *tagliere di focacce,* a sampler plate of mini-focaccia sandwiches, is also fun. Office workers pop in for a quick lunch, and it's traditional to share tables. They also have benches and tiny tables for eating at takeout prices (Mon-Sat 8:00-21:00, Sun 10:00-16:30, no reservations taken, just off Via de' Calzaiuoli, at Via dei Tavolini 18 red, tel. 055-268-590).

$ I Fratellini is a hole-in-the-wall serving more than 30 kinds of sandwiches and a fine selection of wine at great prices (see list on wall) since 1875. Join the local crowd to order, then sit on a nearby curb to eat, placing your glass on the wall rack before you leave. It's worth ordering the most expensive wine they're selling by the glass (daily 9:00-19:30 or until the bread runs out, 20 yards in front of Orsanmichele Church on Via dei Cimatori, tel. 055-239-6096).

Café with a View

$$ Caffè La Terrazza is on the rooftop of La Rinascente department store overlooking Piazza della Repubblica. While fairly plain, it comes with commanding views of the Duomo, which looms gloriously on the horizon (€6 coffee drinks, daily 9:00-20:30).

The Oltrarno

Dining in the Oltrarno, south of the Arno River, offers a more authentic experience. While it's just a few minutes' walk from Ponte Vecchio, it sees far fewer tourists.

Dining or Drinking with a Ponte Vecchio View

$$ Signorvino is an *enoteca* (wine shop) with a simple restaurant that has a rare terrace literally over the Arno River. Fun-loving and unpretentious, this place has a passion for quality Italian ingredients, offering regional dishes and plates of fine meats and cheeses to pair with just the right wine from a wonderful array. If you're up for a bottle rather than a glass, their huge selection is available for the same fair prices at a table as in their wine store (shop open daily 9:30-24:00, food served 11:30-23:00, Via dei Bardi 46 red, tel. 055-286-258, www.signorvino.com, call to reserve, especially for terrace seating).

Cooking Classes

At cooking classes, you'll typically spend a couple of hours cooking, then sit down to a hard-earned meal. The options listed below represent only a few of your many choices. As this is a fast-changing scene, it's worth doing some homework online and booking well ahead.

In Tavola is a dedicated cooking school in the Oltrarno, featuring Italian, English-speaking chefs who quickly demonstrate each step before setting you loose. You'll work in a kitchen, then eat in the cozy wine cellar (€53-73/person, between Pitti Palace and Brancacci Chapel at Via dei Velluti 18 red, tel. 055-217-672, www.intavola.org, info@intavola.org, Fabrizio).

Both **Artviva** and **Florencetown** (listed under "Tours" on page 514) offer cooking classes and a 10 percent discount to my readers (Artviva: €53-68/person; Florencetown: €89/person for 5-hour class that includes shopping for the food you'll cook; €49/person for 3-hour pizza- and gelato-making class).

$$$ Golden View Open Bar is a modern, noisy, and touristy bistro, good for a salad, pizza, or pasta with fine wine and a fine view of Ponte Vecchio. Reservations for window tables are essential. They have three seating areas: a riverside pizza place, a classier restaurant, and a jazzy lounge. In the afternoon (12:00-18:00), they offer wine tastings (€9-15) that include three pours. Later (18:30 to 21:30), the wine bar serves a buffet of appetizers free with your €10 drink (daily 12:00-24:00, café opens at 7:30, jazz usually Mon, Fri, and Sat nights at 21:00, 50 yards east of Ponte Vecchio at Via dei Bardi 58, tel. 055-214-502, www.goldenviewopenbar.com, run by Antonio, Paolo, and Tommaso).

On or near Piazza di Santo Spirito

Piazza di Santo Spirito is a thriving neighborhood square with a collection of lively eateries and bars. Several bars offer *aperitivo* buffets with their drinks during happy hour. Late in the evening the area becomes a clubbing scene.

$$ Gusta Osteria, just around the corner from the piazza, serves big salads and predictable Tuscan fare at fun, cozy indoor seating or at outdoor tables (Tue-Sun 12:00-23:00, closed Mon, Via de' Michelozzi 13 red, tel. 055-285-033). For cheaper bites, try its sister restaurant **$ Gusta Panino,** a sandwich bar directly on the square.

At **$$ Trattoria Casalinga,** an inexpensive standby, Florentines (who enjoy the tripe and tongue) and tourists (who opt for easier to swallow Tuscan favorites) alike pack the place and leave full and happy (Mon-Sat 12:00-14:30 & 19:00-22:00, after 20:00 reserve or wait, closed Sun and Aug, just off Piazza di Santo Spirito, near the church at Via de' Michelozzi 9 red, tel. 055-218-624, www.trattorialacasalinga.it, Andrea and Paolo).

Dining Well

These are my favorite restaurants in the Oltrarno. Make reservations for dinner or come early.

$$$ Il Santo Bevitore Ristorante, lit like a Rembrandt painting and unusually spacious, serves creative modern Tuscan cuisine at dressy tables. They're enthusiastic about matching quality produce from the area with the right wine. This is a good break from the big, sloppy plates of pasta you'll get at many Florence eateries (good wine list by the glass or bottle, daily 12:30-14:30 & 19:30-23:00, closed Sun or Mon for lunch, reservations smart, three tables on the sidewalk, acoustics can make it noisy inside, Via di Santo Spirito 64 red, tel. 055-211-264, www.ilsantobevitore.com).

$$ Enoteca Il Santino Gastronomia, Il Santo Bevitore's smaller wine bar next door, feels like the perfect after-work hangout for foodies who'd like a glass of wine and a light bite. Tight, cozy, and atmospheric, the place has a prominent bar, where you can assemble an €8-12 *tagliere* of locally sourced cheeses and *salumi.* They also have a few affordable hot dishes (daily 12:30-23:00, Via di Santo Spirito 60 red, no reservations, tel. 055-230-2820).

$$$ Trattoria 4 Leoni creates the quintessential Oltrarno dinner scene, and is understandably popular with tourists. The Tuscan-style food is made with an innovative twist and an appreciation for vegetables. You'll enjoy the fun energy and characteristic seating, both outside on the colorful square and inside, where you'll dine in exposed-stone sophistication. While the wines by the glass are pricey, the house wine is good (daily 12:00-24:00, dinner reservations smart; midway between Ponte Vecchio and Piazza di Santo Spirito, on Piazza della Passera at Via dei Vellutini 1; tel. 055-218-562, www.4leoni.com).

$$$$ Olio & Convivium is primarily a catering company for top-end events. Their three intimate rooms are surrounded by fine *prosciutti,* cheeses, and wine shelves. Their list of €14-25 *gastronomia* plates offers an array of taste treats and fine wines by the glass. They also have €35-49 tasting menus and stylish €18 lunches with wine (Tue-Sun 12:00-14:30 & 19:00-22:30, closed Mon, Via di Santo Spirito 4, tel. 055-265-8198, www.oliorestaurant.it, Tommaso is the chef and owner).

Florence Restaurants

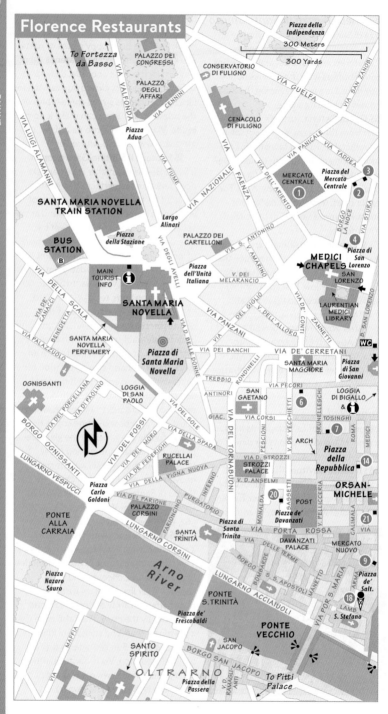

Piazza della Indipendenza

300 Meters

300 Yards

To Fortezza da Basso

PALAZZO DEI CONGRESSI

CONSERVATORIO DI FULIGNO

VIA VALFONDA

VIA GUELFA

VIA SAN ZANOBI

PALAZZO DEGLI AFFARI

VIA CENNINI

CENACOLO DI FULIGNO

Piazza Adua

VIA PANICALE

VIA TADDEA

VIA LUIGI ALAMANNI

VIA FIUME

VIA NAZIONALE

FAENZA

VIA DELL'ARIENTO

MERCATO CENTRALE ①

Piazza del Mercato Centrale ③

②

BORGO LA NOCE

VIA STURA

SANTA MARIA NOVELLA TRAIN STATION

Largo Alinari

PALAZZO DEI CARTELLONI

VIA S. ANTONINO

④

Piazza di San Lorenzo

BUS STATION Ⓑ

Piazza della Stazione

VIA DEGLI AVELLI

VIA S. AMARINO

MEDICI CHAPELS

SAN LORENZO

B. SAN LORENZO

MAIN TOURIST INFO ℹ

Piazza dell'Unità Italiana

V. DEI MELARANCIO

LAURENTIAN MEDICI LIBRARY

VIA DE' CANACCI

SANTA MARIA NOVELLA

VIA PANZANI

VIA DEL GIGLIO

V. DELL'ALLORO

VIA DE' CONTI

VIA ZANNETTI

WC

VIA DELLA SCALA

BENEDETTA

SANTA MARIA NOVELLA PERFUMERY

VIA D. BELLE DONNE

VIA DEI BANCHI

VIA DE' CERRETANI

Piazza di San Giovanni

VIA PALAZZUOLO

Piazza di Santa Maria Novella

SANTA MARIA MAGGIORE

RONDINELLI

OGNISSANTI

VIA DE PORCELLANA

VIA DI PAOLINO

LOGGIA DI SAN PAOLO

VIA DEL SOLE

TREBBIO

ANTINORI

VIA PECORI

LOGGIA DI BIGALLO & ℹ

VIA DEL FOSSI

SAN GAETANO ⑥

VIA CORSI

V. DE' VECCHIETTI

BRUNELLESCHI

TOSINGHI

BORGO OGNISSANTI

VIA DEL MORO

VIA DELLA SPADA

GIAC.

PESCIONI

ARCH ⑦

ROMA

MEDICI

N

VIA DI FEDERIGHI

RUCELLAI PALACE

VIA DELLA VIGNA NUOVA

VIA D. STROZZI

Piazza della Repubblica ⑭

LUNGARNO VESPUCCI

VIA DEL PARIONE

STROZZI PALACE

V. D. ANSELMI

ORSAN-MICHELE

Piazza Carlo Goldoni

PARIONCINO

PURGATORIO

INFERNO

MONALDA

SASSETTI

⑳

POST

PELLICCERIA

PONTE ALLA CARRAIA

PALAZZO CORSINI

SANTA TRINITA

Piazza de' Davanzati

CALIMALA

㉑

VIA

VIA PORTA ROSSA

Piazza di Santa Trinita

DAVANZATI PALACE

MERCATO NUOVO

LUNGARNO CORSINI

DELLE TERME

VIA

BORGO S. S. APOSTOLI

BOMBARDE

VIA POR S. MARIA

⑨

Piazza de' Salt.

Piazza Nazaro Sauro

Arno River

LUNGARNO ACCIAIUOLI

MANETTO

ARTE

⑱

PONTE S. TRINITA

Piazza de' Frescobaldi

S. Stefano

LAMB.

MAFFIA

SAN JACOPO

PONTE VECCHIO

SANTO SPIRITO

BORGO SAN JACOPO

V. D. RAMAGLIANTI

To Pitti Palace

OLTRARNO

Piazza della Passera

Gelateria

SAN MARCO MUSEUM

Piazza di San Marco

UNIVERSITY

ACCADEMIA (DAVID)

MUSEUM OF PRECIOUS STONES

LEONARDO MUSEUM

MEDICI-RICCARDI PALACE

Piazza Brunelleschi

LEONARDO MUSEUM

PALAZZO PUCCI

HOSPITAL

DUOMO SIGHTS TICKET OFFICE

BAPTISTERY

DUOMO

Piazza del Duomo

CAMPANILE

CANONICA

DUOMO MUSEUM

Piazza di Santa Maria Nuova

Piazza G. Salvemini

SANTA MARIA DE' RICCI

OPERA DEL DUOMO STUDIO

POST

CASA DI DANTE

S. MARIA LA BADIA

BARGELLO MUSEUM

Piazza della Signoria

Piazza S. Firenze

CASA BUONARROTI

LOGGIA

PALAZZO VECCHIO

WC

UFFIZI GALLERY

EXIT

Piazza Peruzzi

Piazza Santa Croce

SANTA CROCE

PAZZI CHAPEL

Piazza Giudici

Piazza Mentana

GALILEO SCIENCE MUSEUM

LIBRARY

1 Mercato Centrale Eateries, Perini & Nerbone in the Market
2 Trattoria Mario
3 Pepò
4 Trattoria Sergio Gozzi
5 Enoteca Coquinarius
6 Self-Service Rist. Leonardo
7 Paszkowski Café
8 EATaly
9 Rivoire Café
10 Osteria Vini e Vecchi Sapori
11 Frescobaldi Ristorante & Wine Bar
12 Cantinetta dei Verrazzano
13 I Fratellini
14 Caffè La Terrazza

Gelaterie
15 Gelateria Carabè
16 Edoardo
17 Perchè No!
18 Carapina
19 Gelateria de' Neri

Tour Companies
20 Artviva Tours & Cooking Classes
21 Florencetown Tours & Cooking Classes

SLEEPING

Most of my recommended hotels are grouped in central Florence, to either side of the River Arno. Around the big sights you'll find tourist-friendly options, just steps away from everything you came to Florence to see. And across the Arno in the Oltrarno area—between the Pitti Palace and Ponte Vecchio—good budget alternatives dot an area with a neighborly vibe. If arriving by train, you can either walk (usually around 10-20 minutes) or take a taxi (roughly €6-8) to reach most of my recommended accommodations.

Florence is notorious for its mosquitoes. If your hotel lacks air-conditioning, request a fan and don't open your windows, especially at night. Many hotels furnish a small plug-in bulb (*zanzariere*)—usually set in the ashtray—to keep the blood-suckers at bay. If not, you can purchase one cheaply at any pharmacy (*farmacia*).

Near the Duomo

While touristy—and expensive—this location puts just about everything at your doorstep.

$$$$ Hotel Duomo's 24 rooms are modern and comfortable enough, but you're paying for the location and the views—the Duomo looms like a monster outside the hotel's windows. If staying here, you might as well spring the extra €20 for a "superior" room with a view (RS%, air-con, historic elevator, Piazza del Duomo 1, fourth floor, tel. 055-219-922, www.hotelduomofirenze.it, info@hotelduomofirenze.it; Paolo, Gilvaneide, and Federico).

$$$ Residenza Giotto B&B offers a well-priced chance to stay on Florence's upscale shopping drag, Via Roma. Occupying the top floor of a 19th-century building, this place has six bright rooms (three with Duomo views) and a terrace with knockout views of the Duomo's tower. Reception is generally open Mon-Sat 9:00-17:00 and Sun 9:00-13:00; let

them know your arrival time in advance (RS%, air-con, elevator, Via Roma 6, tel. 055-214-593, www.residenzagiotto.it, info@residenzagiotto.it, Giorgio).

North of the Duomo
Near the Accademia

$$$ Hotel dei Macchiaioli offers 15 fresh and spacious rooms on one high-ceilinged, noble floor in a restored palazzo owned for generations by a well-to-do Florentine family. You'll eat breakfast under original frescoed ceilings while enjoying modern comforts (RS%, air-con, Via Cavour 21, tel. 055-213-154, www.hoteldeimacchiaioli.com, info@hoteldeimacchiaioli.com, helpful Francesca and Paolo).

$$$ Residenza dei Pucci rents 13 pleasant rooms (each one different) spread over three floors (with no elevator). The decor, a mix of soothing earth tones and aristocratic furniture, makes this place feel upscale for this price range (RS%—use code "RICK," family rooms, air-con, reception open 9:00-20:00, shorter hours off-season—let them know if you'll arrive late, Via dei Pucci 9, tel. 055-281-886, www.residenzadeipucci.com, info@residenzadeipucci.com, friendly Rossella and Marina).

$$$ Hotel Morandi alla Crocetta, a former convent, envelops you in a 16th-century cocoon. Located on a quiet street with 12 rooms, its period furnishings, squeaky clean parquet floors, and original frescoes take you back a few centuries and up a few social classes (family rooms, air-con, elevator, pay parking—reserve ahead, a block off Piazza S.S. Annunziata at Via Laura 50, tel. 055-234-4747, www.hotelmorandi.it, welcome@hotelmorandi.it, well-run by Maurizio, Rolando, and Cristiano).

$$$ Hotel Europa, family run since 1970, has a welcoming atmosphere fostered by cheery Miriam and Roberto. The breakfast room is large, and most of the 12 bright, simple rooms have views of the Duomo, including one with a terrace (RS%, family rooms, air-con, elevator, Via Cavour 14, tel. 055-239-6715, www.webhoteleuropa.com, firenze@webhoteleuropa.com).

Near the Medici Chapels

This touristy zone has lots of budget and midrange hotels, stacks of basic trattorias, and easy access to major sights. The mostly pedestrianized Via Faenza is the spine of this neighborhood, with lots of tourist services.

$$$$ Hotel Centrale is indeed central, just a short walk from the Duomo. The 35 spacious but overpriced rooms—with a tasteful mix of old and new decor—are over a businesslike conference center (RS%, air-con, elevator, Via dei Conti 3, check in at big front desk on ground floor, tel. 055-215-761, www.hotelcentralefirenze.it, info@hotelcentralefirenze.it, Margherita and Roberto).

$$$ Hotel Accademia has 21 newly renovated rooms in a well-located 14th-century mansion. Linger on its interior terrace or curl up with a book in its cozy reading room (air-con, nearby pay parking, Via Faenza 7, tel. 055-290-993, www.hotelaccademiafirenze.com, info@hotelaccademiafirenze, Tea).

East of the Duomo

While convenient to the sights and offering a good value, these places are located mostly along nondescript urban streets, lacking the grit, appeal, or glitz of other neighborhoods.

$$$ Residenza il Villino has 10 charming rooms and a picturesque, peaceful little courtyard. The owner, Neri, has turned part of the breakfast room into a museum-like tribute to his grandfather, a pioneer of early Italian fashion. As it's in a "little villa" (as the name implies) set back from the street, this is a quiet refuge from the bustle of Florence (RS%, family rooms, air-con, parking available, just north of Via degli Alfani at Via della Pergola 53, tel. 055-200-1116, www.ilvillino.it, info@ilvillino.it).

$$$ Panella's Residence, once a convent and today part of owner Graziella's extensive home, is a classy B&B, with five chic, romantic, and ample rooms, antique furnishings, and historic architectural touches (RS%, air-con, Via della Pergola 42, tel. 055-234-7202, mobile 345-972-1541, www.panellaresidence.com, panella_residence@yahoo.it).

$ Hotel Dalí has 10 cheery, worn rooms in a nice location for a great price.

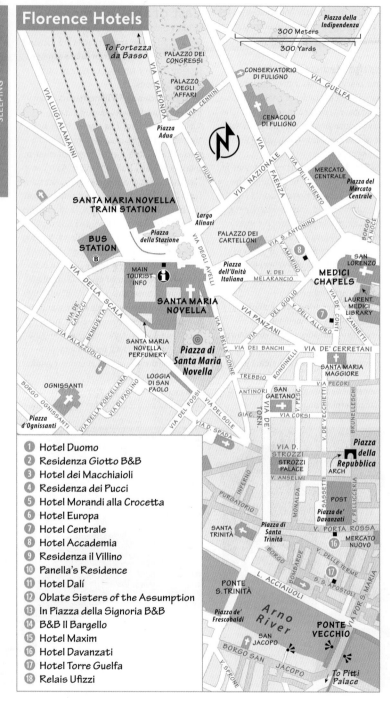

Florence Hotels

1 Hotel Duomo
2 Residenza Giotto B&B
3 Hotel dei Macchiaioli
4 Residenza dei Pucci
5 Hotel Morandi alla Crocetta
6 Hotel Europa
7 Hotel Centrale
8 Hotel Accademia
9 Residenza il Villino
10 Panella's Residence
11 Hotel Dalí
12 Oblate Sisters of the Assumption
13 In Piazza della Signoria B&B
14 B&B Il Bargello
15 Hotel Maxim
16 Hotel Davanzati
17 Hotel Torre Guelfa
18 Relais Ufizzi

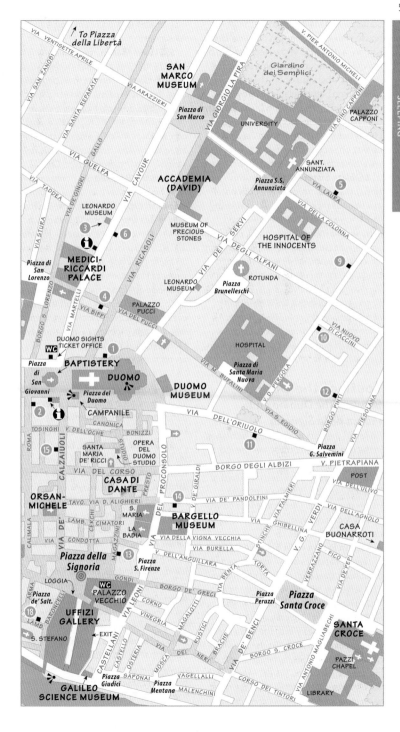

To Piazza della Libertà

V. PIER ANTONIO MICHELI

VIA VENTISETTE APRILE

VIA SAN ZANOBI

SAN MARCO MUSEUM

Giardino del Semplici

VIA ARAZZIERI

VIA GIORGIO LA PIRA

VIA GINO CAPPONI

PALAZZO CAPPONI

VIA SANTA REPARATA

Piazza di San Marco

UNIVERSITY

VIA GUELFA

VIA GALLO

VIA CAVOUR

VIA DEGINORI

VIA TADDEA

SANT. ANNUNZIATA

VIA LAURA

5

ACCADEMIA (DAVID)

Piazza S.S. Annunziata

VIA DELLA COLONNA

LEONARDO MUSEUM

VIA SIURA

3

6

MUSEUM OF PRECIOUS STONES

VIA DEI SERVI

VIA DEGLI ALFANI

HOSPITAL OF THE INNOCENTS

Piazza di San Lorenzo

MEDICI-RICCARDI PALACE

VIA RICASOLI

LEONARDO MUSEUM

Piazza Brunelleschi

ROTUNDA

9

BORGO S. LORENZO

VIA MARTELLI

4

VIA BIFFI

PALAZZO PUCCI

VIA DEL PUCCI

HOSPITAL

VIA NUOVO DI CACCINI

10

DUOMO SIGHTS TICKET OFFICE

WC

1

Piazza di Santa Maria Nuova

VIA M. BUFALINI

Piazza di San Giovanni

BAPTISTERY

DUOMO

Piazza del Duomo

DUOMO MUSEUM

VIA S. EGIDIO

V. DI PERGOLA

12

BORGO PINTI

VIA FIESOLANA

2

CAMPANILE

CANONICA

VIA DELL'ORIUOLO

TOSINGHI

V. DELL'OCHE

BONIZZI

CALZAIUOLI

ROMA

SANTA MARIA DE' RICCI

OPERA DEL DUOMO STUDIO

STUDIO

11

Piazza G. Salvemini

V. PIETRAPIANA

POST

VIA DELL'ULIVO

VIA DEL CORSO

CASA DI DANTE

BORGO DEGLI ALBIZI

ORSAN-MICHELE

TAYO. VIA D. ALIGHIERI

S. MARIA LA BADIA

VIA DE' GIRALDI

VIA DE' PANDOLFINI

VIA PALMIERI

VIA VERDI

VIA DELL'AGNOLO

CALIMALA

LAMB.

CERCHI

CIMATORI

14

BARGELLO MUSEUM

VIA GHIBELLINA

V. G.

CASA BUONARROTI

VIA CONDOTTA

MAGAZZINI

VIA DELLA VIGNA VECCHIA

VIA BURELLA

FICO

VIA DE' PEPI

Piazza della Signoria

13

Piazza S. Firenze

V. DELL'ANGUILLARA

STINCHE

TORTA

VERRAZZANO

LOGGIA

GONDI

BORGO DE' GRECI

Piazza Peruzzi

Piazza Santa Croce

PARMA

Piazza de' Salt.

WC

PALAZZO VECCHIO

VIA LEONI

CORNO

VINEGRIA

MAGALOTTI

RUSTICI

VIA DE' BENCI

SANTA CROCE

18

LAMB

BARONCELLI

UFFIZI GALLERY

EXIT

CASTELLANI

CASTELLO

OSTERIA

VIA

DEI

NERI

BRACHE

BORGO S. CROCE

VIA ANTONIO MAGLIABECHI

G. STEFANO

MOSCA

SAPONAI

PAZZI CHAPEL

GALILEO SCIENCE MUSEUM

Piazza Giudici

Piazza Mentana

VAGELLALLI

MALENCHINI

CORSO DEI TINTORI

LIBRARY

Samanta and Marco, who run this guest-house with a charming passion and idealism, are a delight to know (request one of the quiet and spacious rooms facing the courtyard when you book, cheaper rooms with shared bath available, nearby apartments sleep 2-6 people, no breakfast, fans but no air-con, elevator, free parking, 2 blocks behind the Duomo at Via dell'Oriuolo 17 on second floor, tel. 055-234-0706, www.hoteldali.com, hoteldali@tin.it).

$ Oblate Sisters of the Assumption run an institutional 30-room hotel in a Renaissance building with a dreamy garden, great public spaces, appropriately simple rooms, and a quiet, prayerful ambience (family rooms, single beds only, air-con, elevator, Wi-Fi with suggested donation, 23:30 curfew, limited pay parking—request when you book, Borgo Pinti 15, tel. 055-248-0582, www.bb-oblate. com, sroblateborgopinti@virgilio.it). As there's no night porter, it's best to time your arrival and departure to occur during typical business hours.

South of the Duomo
Between the Duomo and Piazza della Signoria

Buried in the narrow, characteristic lanes in the heart of town, these are the most central of my recommendations (and therefore a little overpriced). While this location can be worth the extra cost, nearly every hotel I recommend is conveniently located, given Florence's walkable, essentially traffic-free core.

$$$$ In Piazza della Signoria B&B, in a stellar location overlooking Piazza della Signoria, is peaceful, refined, and homey. The service is friendly, but the rates are high. The "partial view" rooms, while slightly larger, require craning your neck to see anything—not worth the extra euros. Guests enjoy socializing at the big, shared breakfast table (RS%, family apartments, air-con, tiny elevator, Via dei Magazzini 2, tel. 055-239-9546, mobile 348-321-0565, www.inpiazzadellasignoria.com, info@

inpiazzadellasignoria.com, Sonia and Alessandro).

$$$ Hotel Maxim, run by the Maoli family since 1981, has 26 straightforward rooms in a good location on the main pedestrian drag. Its narrow, painting-lined halls and cozy lounge have old Florentine charm (RS%—use code "RICK," family rooms, air-con, elevator, Via de' Calzaiuoli 11, tel. 055-217-474, www.hotelmaximfirenze.it, reservation@hotelmaximfirenze.it, Chiara).

$$ B&B Il Bargello is a home away from home, run by friendly and helpful Canadian expat Gabriella. Hike up three long flights (no elevator) to reach six smart, relaxing rooms, a cozy living room, and a communal kitchenette, along with an inviting rooftop terrace with close-up views of Florence's towers (RS%, fully equipped apartment across the hall sleeps up to six; air-con, 20 yards off Via Proconsolo at Via de' Pandolfini 33 black, tel. 055-215-330, mobile 339-175-3110, www. firenze-bedandbreakfast.it, info@firenze-bedandbreakfast.it).

Near Ponte Vecchio

This sleepy zone is handy to several sights and some fine shopping streets, though it lacks a neighborhood feel of its own.

$$$$ Hotel Davanzati, bright and shiny with artistic touches, has 25 cheerful rooms with all the comforts. It's a family affair, thoughtfully run by friendly Tommaso and father Fabrizio, who offer drinks and snacks each evening at their candlelit happy hour, plus lots of other extras (RS%, family rooms, free tablets in every room, air-con, 20 steep steps to the elevator, handy room fridges, next to Piazza Davanzati at Via Porta Rossa 5—easy to miss so watch for low-profile sign above the door, tel. 055-286-666, www.hoteldavanzati.it, info@hoteldavanzati.it).

$$$$ Hotel Torre Guelfa has grand public spaces and is topped by a fun medieval tower with a panoramic rooftop terrace (72 stairs take you up—and back 720 years). Its 31 pricey rooms vary wildly in size and furnishings, but most come with the noise of the city center. Room 315, with a private terrace, is worth reserving several months in advance (RS%, family rooms, air-con, elevator, a couple of blocks north-west of Ponte Vecchio, Borgo S.S. Apostoli 8, tel. 055-239-6338, www.hoteltorreguelfa.com, info@hoteltorreguelfa.com, Niccolo and Barbara).

$$$$ **Relais Uffizi** is a peaceful little gem, offering a friendly welcome and a tight maze of 15 classy rooms tucked away down a tiny alley off Piazza della Signoria. The lounge has a huge window overlooking the action in the square below (family rooms, air-con, elevator; official address is Chiasso del Buco 16—from the square, go down tiny Chiasso de Baroncelli lane—right of the loggia—and after 50 yards turn right through the arch and look for entrance on your right; tel. 055-267-6239, www.relaisuffizi.it, info@relaisuffizi.it, charming Alessandro and Elizabetta).

TRANSPORTATION

Getting Around Florence

I organize my sightseeing geographically and do it all on foot. Think of Florence as a Renaissance treadmill—it requires a lot of walking.

By Bus

The city's full-size buses don't cover the old center well (the whole area around the Duomo is off-limits to motorized traffic). To visit outlying sights, pick up a map of transit routes at the ATAF windows at the train station (TIs do not have them); you'll also find routes online (www.ataf.net). Of the many bus lines, I find these the most helpful:

Bus **#12** goes from the train station over the Carraia bridge to Porta Romana, then up to San Miniato Church and Piazzale Michelangelo. Bus #13 makes the return trip down the hill.

The train station and Piazza San Marco

are two major hubs near the city center; to get between these two, either walk (about 15 minutes) or take bus #1, #6, #14, #17, or #23.

Minibuses run every 10 minutes from 7:00 to 21:00 (less frequent on Sun), winding through the town center and up and down the river—just €1.20 gets you a 1.5-hour joyride. These buses also connect many major parking lots with the historic center (buy tickets from machines at lots).

Bus #C1 stops behind the Palazzo Vecchio and Piazza Santa Croce, then heads north, passing near the Accademia before ending up at Piazza Libertà.

Bus #C2 twists through the congested old center from the train station, passing near Piazza della Repubblica and Piazza della Signoria to Piazza Beccaria.

Bus #C3 goes up and down the Arno River, with stops near Piazza Santa Croce, Ponte Vecchio, the Carraia bridge to the Oltrarno (including Pitti Palace), and beyond.

Bus #D goes from the train station to Ponte Vecchio, cruises through the Oltrarno (passing Pitti Palace), and finishes in the San Niccolò neighborhood at Ponte San Niccolò.

Buying Bus Tickets: Buy bus tickets at tobacco shops (tabacchi), newsstands, or the ATAF ticket windows inside the train station. Validate your ticket in the machine on board (€1.20/90 minutes, €4.70/4 tickets, €5/24 hours, €12/3 days, €18/week, day passes aren't always available in tobacco shops, tel. 800-424-500, www.ataf.net). You can sometimes buy a ticket on board, but you'll pay more (€2) and you'll need exact change.

By Taxi

The minimum cost for a taxi ride is €5 (€8.30 after 22:00, €7 on Sun); rides in the center of town should be charged as tariff #1. A taxi ride from the train station to the Duomo costs about €8. Taxi fares and supplements (e.g., €2 extra to a cab rather than hail one) are clearly explained on signs in each taxi. Look for an official, regulated cab (white; marked with *Taxi/Comune di Firenze,* red fleur-de-lis, and one of the official phone numbers: 4390 or 4242). Before getting in a cab, mention your destination and ask for an approximate cost (*"Più o meno, quanto costa?"* pew oh MEH-noh, KWAHN-toh KOH-stah). If you can't get a straight answer or the price is outrageous, walk away. It can be hard to find a cab on the street; call 055-4390 or 055-4242 to summon one, or have your hotelier or restaurateur call for you. Uber does not operate in Florence.

Arriving and Departing

Florence is Tuscany's transportation hub, with fine train, bus, and plane connections to virtually anywhere in Italy.

By Train

Florence's main train station is called **Santa Maria Novella** (*Firenze S.M.N.* on schedules and signs). The city also has two suburban train stations: **Firenze Rifredi** and **Firenze Campo di Marte.** Note that some trains don't stop at the main station—before boarding, confirm that you're heading for S.M.N., or you may overshoot the city. (If this happens, don't panic; the other stations are a short taxi ride from the center.)

Rick's Tip: **Don't trust "porters"** *who want to help carry your bags (they're not official), and politely decline offers of help using the ticket machines by anyone other than uniformed staff.*

To orient yourself to Santa Maria Novella Station, stand with your back to the tracks. Look left to see the green cross of a 24-hour pharmacy (*farmacia*) and the exit to the taxi queue. **Baggage storage** (*deposito bagagli*) is also to the left, halfway down track 16 (long hours daily,

passport required). **Fast-food outlets** and a **bank** are also along track 16. Directly ahead of you is the main hall (*salone biglietti*), where you can buy train and bus tickets. **Pay WCs** are to the right, near the head of track 5.

To reach the **TI,** walk away from the tracks and exit the station; it's straight across the square, 100 yards away, by the stone church.

To buy **ATAF city bus tickets,** stop at windows #8-9 in the main hall—and ask for a transit map while you're there (TIs don't have them).

Getting to the Duomo and City Center: Orienting yourself with your back to the tracks, the Duomo and town center are to your left. Out the doorway to the left, you'll find city buses and the taxi stand. Taxis cost about €6-8 to the Duomo. If you'd rather walk (10-15 minutes), exit the station straight ahead through the main hall, and head straight across the square outside, toward the Church of Santa Maria Novella (and the TI). On the far side of the square, keep left and head down the main Via dei Panzani, which leads directly to the Duomo.

TRAIN CONNECTIONS

For travel within Italy, there's no reason to stand in line at a ticket window. It's quickest and easiest to buy tickets online; with a smartphone app, you can even purchase them minutes before the train departs. If you decide to buy tickets at the station, take advantage of the ticket (*biglietto*)

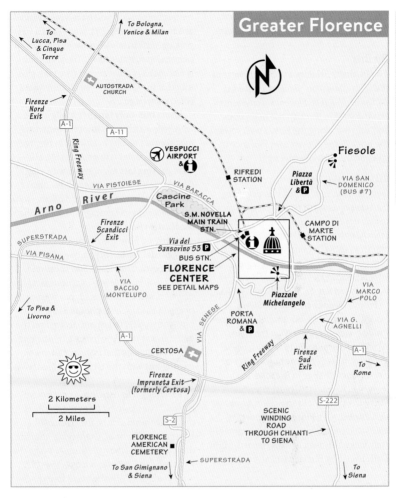

Greater Florence

To Bologna,
Venice & Milan

To Lucca, Pisa
& Cinque
Terre

AUTOSTRADA
CHURCH

Firenze
Nord
Exit

A-1

Ring Freeway

A-11

VESPUCCI
AIRPORT
&

Fiesole

RIFREDI
STATION

Piazza
Libertà
&

VIA SAN
DOMENICO
(BUS #7)

VIA PISTOIESE

VIA BARACCA

Cascine
Park

Arno River

Firenze
Scandicci
Exit

S.M. NOVELLA
MAIN TRAIN
STN.

CAMPO DI
MARTE
STATION

SUPERSTRADA

Via del
Sansovino 53

VIA PISANA

BUS STN.

FLORENCE
CENTER
SEE DETAIL MAPS

VIA
BACCIO
MONTELUPO

Piazzale
Michelangelo

VIA
MARCO
POLO

To Pisa &
Livorno

VIA SENESE

PORTA
ROMANA
&

VIA G.
AGNELLI

A-1

CERTOSA

Ring Freeway

Firenze
Sud
Exit

A-1

To
Rome

2 Kilometers

2 Miles

Firenze
Impruneta Exit
(formerly Certosa)

S-2

S-222

SCENIC
WINDING
ROAD
THROUGH CHIANTI
TO SIENA

FLORENCE
AMERICAN
CEMETERY

SUPERSTRADA

To San Gimignano
& Siena

To
Siena

machines that display schedules, issue tickets, and make reservations for rail-pass holders.

There are two train companies: **Trenitalia,** with most connections (toll tel. 892-021, www.trenitalia.it) and **Italo,** with high-speed routes (no rail passes accepted, tel. 06-0708, www.italotreno.it). Both companies have bright red self-service machines, so be sure you use the right one. For Trenitalia information, use window #18 or #19 (take a number). For Italo information, use window #10 or #11, or visit their main office, opposite track 5, near the exit.

From Florence by Train to: Pisa (2-3/hour, 45-75 minutes), **Lucca** (2/hour, 1.5 hours), **Siena** (direct trains hourly, 1.5-2 hours; bus is better because Siena's train station is far from the center), **Milan** (Trenitalia: hourly, 2 hours; Italo: 2/hour, 2 hours), **Venice** (Trenitalia: hourly, 2-3 hours, may transfer in Bologna; often crowded—reserve ahead; Italo: 4/day, 2 hours), **Assisi** (8/day direct, 2-3 hours), **Orvieto** (hourly, 2 hours, some with change in Campo di Marte or Rifredi Station), **Rome** (Trenitalia: 2-3/hour, 1.5 hours, most require seat reservations;

Italo: 2/hour, 1.5 hours), **Naples** (Trenitalia: hourly, 3 hours; Italo: hourly, 3 hours).

By Bus

The BusItalia Station is 100 yards west of the train station on Via Santa Caterina da Siena. To get to Florence's city center, exit the station through the main door, and turn left along the busy street toward the brick dome. Downtown Florence is straight ahead and to the right.

BUS CONNECTIONS

Generally it's best to buy bus tickets in the station, as you'll pay 30 percent more to buy tickets onboard. The bus posts schedules for regional trips, and video monitors show imminent departures. Bus service drops dramatically on Sunday. Bus info: tel. 800-373-760 (Mon-Fri 9:00-15:00, closed Sat-Sun), www.fsbusitalia.it.

From Florence by Bus to: Siena (roughly 2/hour, 1.5-hour *rapida/via super-strada* buses are faster than the train, avoid the slower *ordinaria* buses, www.sienamobilita.it), **Montepulciano** (1-2/day, 2 hours, change in Bettolle, LFI bus, www.lfi.it; or train to Chiusi, then Siena Mobilità bus to Montepulciano, www.sienamobilita.it), **Florence airport** (2/hour, 30 minutes, pay driver and immediately validate ticket, usually departs from platform 1, first bus departs at 5:30).

By Car

The autostrada has several exits for Florence. Get off at the Nord, Scandicci, Impruneta (formerly Certosa), or Sud exits and follow signs toward—but not into—the *Centro.*

Don't even attempt driving into the city center. Instead, park on the outskirts and take a bus, tram, or taxi in. Florence's traffic-reduction system is baffling even to locals. Every car passing into the "limited traffic zone" (*Zona Traffico Limitato,* or ZTL) is photographed; those who don't have a permit get a €100 ticket in the mail (with an "administrative" fee from the rental company). If you have a reservation at a hotel within the ZTL area—and it has parking—ask in advance if they can get you permission to enter town. The ZTL zone is Florence's historic center (the core plus much of the Oltrarno)—nearly anywhere you'd want to go.

Using **bus-only lanes** (usually marked with yellow stripes) is another expensive mistake that results in a ticket in the mail.

The city center is ringed with big, efficient **parking lots** (signposted with a big *P*). Check www.firenzeparcheggi.it for details on parking lots, availability, and prices. From the freeway, follow the signs to *Centro,* then *Stadio,* then *P.*

If arriving from the north, park at **Parcheggio del Parterre,** just beyond Piazza della Libertà. They have 600 spots and never fill up completely (€2/hour, €12/day, €70/week, automated, pay with cash or credit card, open 24 hours daily, tel. 055-500-1994). To get into town, find the taxi stand at the elevator exit, or ride one of the minibuses that connect all major parking lots with the city center (see www.ataf.net for routes).

Parcheggio Sansovino, a convenient lot for drivers coming from the south, is on the Oltrarno side of the river, right at a tram stop (€1/hour, €12/day, 24 hours daily, Via Sansovino 53—from A-1 take the Firenze Scandicci exit, tel. 055-363-362, www.scaf.fi.it). Park, then ride four quick stops to Santa Maria Novella Station.

By Plane

Amerigo Vespucci Airport, also called Peretola Airport, is about five miles northwest of the city (open 4:00-24:30, no overnighting allowed, has a TI, airport code: FLR, tel. 055-306-1830, www.aeroporto.firenze.it).

Shuttle buses (to the far right as you exit the arrivals hall) connect the airport with Florence's train and bus stations (2/hour until 22:00, then hourly until 00:30, 30 minutes, runs 5:00-00:30, €6—buy ticket on board and validate immediately).

If you're changing to a different intercity bus in Florence (for instance, one bound for Siena), stay on the bus through the first stop (at the train station); it will continue on to the bus station nearby. Allow about €25 and 30 minutes for a taxi.

The airport's **car rental** offices share one big parking lot just a three-minute drive away, but the streets around the airport are a dizzying maze, making it tricky to find the place to drop off your car. One option is to drive to the airport, wait for the rental-car shuttle bus to show up, then follow that bus to the lot.

By Private Car Service

For small groups with more money than time, hiring a private car service to zip comfortably to nearby towns can be a good value. Consider **Transfer Chauffeur Service** (tel. 338-862-3129, www.transfercs.com, marco.masala@transfercs.com, Marco) or **Prestige Rent** (office near Piazza della Signoria at Via Porta Rossa 6 red, tel. 055-398-6598, mobile 333-842-4047, www.prestigerent.com, usa@prestigerent.com, Saverio). Or you could simply hire a **taxi** after agreeing upon a rate (e.g., €120 from your Florence hotel to your Siena hotel).

The Cinque Terre

Along a six-mile stretch of the Riviera lies the Cinque Terre (CHINK-weh TAY-reh), gently carving a good life out of difficult terrain. With a traffic-free charm—a happy result of their natural isolation—these five *(cinque)* towns are the rugged alternative to the glitzy resorts nearby. With sun, sea, sand (well, pebbles), and wine, this is pure, unadulterated Italy.

Each addictively photogenic village fills a ravine with a lazy hive of human activity—calloused locals and sunburned travelers enjoying a unique mix of culture and nature. Enjoy swimming, hiking, and evening romance in one of God's great gifts to tourism. While the Cinque Terre is now discovered (and can be crowded midday, when tourist boats and cruise ships drop by), I've never seen happier, more relaxed tourists. Most of the crowds are day-trippers, so make a point to get the most out of those cool, relaxed, and quiet hours early in the day and in the evening.

I cover the five towns in order from north to south—from Monterosso to Riomaggiore. Vernazza is my top choice for a home base, while Monterosso, the most resorty of the five towns, is an excellent runner-up, offering more amenities and activities. Avoid visiting in winter, when tall, crashing waves batter the charm out of the Cinque Terre.

THE CINQUE TERRE IN 2 DAYS

This string of five villages dotting the Italian Riviera makes an idyllic escape from the obligatory museums of turnstile Italy. The ideal stay is two full days (or three days to really relax). It's easiest to arrive and depart by train. If you have a car, park it in one of the few lots, then catch a shuttle bus into town.

Within the Cinque Terre, you can connect the towns in three ways: by train, boat, or foot. Trains are cheap, boats are more scenic, and hiking lets you enjoy more pasta. Consider supplementing the often frustratingly late trains with the sometimes more convenient boats.

Study your options, and piece together your best visit, mixing hiking, swimming, trains, boat rides, and a search for the best focaccia.

You could spend one day hiking from town to town (or take a boat or train partway, or as the return trip). For the best light, coolest temperatures, and fewest crowds,

The Cinque Terre

To A-12 Autostrada
(Brugnato Exit)

To
Genoa

A-12

SP-1

To
La Spezia
& Pisa

To A-12 Autostrada
(Carrodano Exit)

SP-566

To
Sestri Levante,
Santa Margherita,
Genoa & Bonassola

2 Kilometers

2 Miles

Beverino

Pignone

SP-1

Pian di
Barca

SP-370

Levanto

To New Town
(Fegina)

To Monterosso's
Old Town

SP-38

SP-1

Monterosso
al Mare

SANDY
BEACH

SP-63

These roads may be closed.
Inquire locally.

To
La Spezia
& A-12

Vernazza

Punta
Mesco

Corniglia

SP-51

Volastra

CORNIGLIA STATION

Ligurian

Sea

Manarola

VIA DELL'AMORE ♥

Riomaggiore

VIA
LITORANEA

To
La Spezia
& A-12

SP-370

To Porto Venere

start your hike early in the morning (or late in the afternoon). Cool off at a beach. Spend a second day visiting each town, comparing main streets, beaches, and gelato. And fit in another hike, if you like.

In the evenings, linger at a restaurant, enjoy live music at a low-key club, stroll any of the towns, or take a glass of your favorite beverage out to the breakwater to watch the sun slip into the Mediterranean.

Helpful Hints for the Cinque Terre

Book in Advance: It's essential to reserve rooms well in advance for these busy times—May, June, September, October, all summer weekends, and holidays (including Easter and April 25). Many accommodations in the Cinque Terre (especially in Vernazza) are *affittacamere*, or private rooms for rent. You get a key and come and go as you like, rarely seeing your land-lord. Plan on paying cash. If you must cancel an *affittacamere* reservation, do it as early as possible. More formal places have strict cancellation policies.

Pickpocket Alert: At peak times, when the Cinque Terre is crowded, pickpockets (often female teens in groups of three or four) aggressively and expertly work the most congested areas. Be on guard, especially on train station platforms and while you're on trains and boats, particularly when getting on or off with a crush of people. Wear a money belt, and keep your things zipped up and buttoned down.

Money: You'll find banks and ATMs throughout the region.

Shuttle Buses: Each town has a helpful ATC shuttle bus route that generally runs through town and links the train station, nearest parking lot, and destinations farther up in the hills. Take a cheap joy-ride (€1.50 one-way, €2.50 from driver,

THE CINQUE TERRE AT A GLANCE

▲▲**Monterosso al Mare** Resorty, flat, and spread out, with a charming old town, a modern new town, and the region's best beaches, swimming, and nightlife. See page 570.

▲▲▲**Vernazza** The region's gem, crowned with a ruined castle above and a lively waterfront cradling a natural harbor below. See page 580.

▲**Corniglia** Quiet hilltop village known for its cooler temperatures (it's the only one of the five villages set above the water), fewer tourists, and tradition of fine wines. See page 591.

▲▲**Manarola** Waterfront village dotted with a picturesque mix of shops, houses, and vineyards. See page 593.

▲**Riomaggiore** The biggest and most workaday of the five villages. See page 598.

free with Cinque Terre park card required for coastal hikers—explained later). The buses don't connect Cinque Terre towns with each other.

Wi-Fi: All Cinque Terre train stations offer free Wi-Fi with a Cinque Terre park card.

Laundry: In Monterosso's new town, Wash and Dry Lavarapido offers full-service, same-day laundry at Via Molinelli 17 (also pickup/drop-off service, daily, mobile 339-484-0940). In Vernazza, a small self-serve launderette is at the top of town next to the post office (daily).

Baggage Storage: You can store bags at the bar that also functions as the *deposito bagagli* office at Riomaggiore's train station; at the gift shop in Vernazza's train station, and in Monterosso at the TI next to the station or at Wash and Dry Lavarapido. All are open daily in season; for details, see individual town listings.

Services: Every train station has a free WC, but it's smart to bring your own toilet paper. Otherwise, pop into a bar or restaurant.

Tours: Arbaspàa, which has an office in Manarola, can arrange wine tasting at a vineyard, cooking classes (6-person minimum), fishing trips, and active adventures (office at Via Discovolo 204, tel. 0187-920-783, www.arbaspaa.com).

HIKING IN THE CINQUE TERRE

All five towns are connected by good trails, marked with red-and-white paint, white arrows, and some signs. The region has several numbered trails, but most visitors stick to the main coastal trail that connects the villages—that's trail #592 (also called SVA or the Blue Trail). You'll need a Cinque Terre park card to hike the main coastal trail.

Trail Closures: Trails can be closed in bad weather or due to landslides. Usually one or two trails are closed at any given time. These two segments will probably be closed when you visit: the trail between Riomaggiore and Manarola (a.k.a. the Via dell'Amore), and the trail between Manarola and Corniglia. Official closures are noted on the national park website (www.parconazionale5terre.it) and are posted at the park-information desks in each town's train station.

Hiking Conditions: Most of the main coastal trail is narrow, steep, rocky, and comes with lots of challenging steps. Readers often say the trail was tougher than they expected. The rocks can be slippery in the rain (avoid the steep Monterosso-Vernazza stretch if it's wet). Don't venture up on these rocky cliffs without sun protection or water.

When to Go: The coastal trail can be crowded (and hot) at midday. For the best light, coolest temperatures, and fewest crowds, start your hike early or late. If you want to hike in the evening, find out when the sun will set, and leave yourself plenty of time to arrive at your destination (no lighting on trails).

Navigation: Maps aren't necessary for the basic coastal hikes. But for more serious hikes in the high country, pick up a good hiking map (about €5, sold locally).

Give a Hoot: To leave the park cleaner than you found it, bring a plastic bag and pick up trail trash along the way.

Rick's Tip: *The Cinque Terre national park recently* **renamed and renumbered** *many local hiking trails. But you'll hear people using the old names/numbers, and many maps haven't caught up with the new system. Prepare to be confused!*

Cinque Terre Park Cards

The Cinque Terre—villages and all—is a national park. Each town has a park information office, which generally serves as an all-purpose town TI as well (listed throughout this chapter). The park's website—with up-to-date information on park cards, trail closures, and more—is www.parconazionale5terre.it.

Visitors hiking on the mainline coastal trails must buy a park card (good for one or two days, with an option covering trains). Cards can be purchased online, at train stations, TIs, and trailheads—good for 24 or 48 hours after validation. Those under 18 or over 70 get a discount, as do families with kids under age 13. The configuration and pricing of these cards is often in flux—the following details may change.

The **Cinque Terre Trekking Card** costs €7.50 for one day of hiking or €14.50 for two days (covers trails and ATC shuttle buses plus a few other extras but does not cover trains).

The **Cinque Terre Treno Multi-Service Card** covers what the Cinque Terre Trekking Card does, plus local trains connecting all Cinque Terre towns, Levanto, and La Spezia (€16/24 hours, €29/48 hours, validate card at train station by punching it in the machine). Even if you're not planning to hike, this card can be worth the price to avoid waiting in train ticket lines.

The Coastal Trail

If all of the main trails between the towns are open, the entire seven-mile coastal hike (which is very hilly between Corniglia

and Monterosso) can be completed by fit hikers in about four hours; allow five or six for dawdling. Take it slow...smell the cactus flowers, notice the scurrying lizards, listen to birds singing in the olive groves, and enjoy vistas on all sides. You can tackle the hike in either direction, but remember that the coastal segments between Riomaggiore and Manarola and Corniglia are likely closed.

Of the hikes that are probably open: The trail from Corniglia to Vernazza is demanding, and the path from Vernazza to Monterosso is more challenging. Starting in Monterosso allows you to tackle the toughest section (with lots and lots of steep, narrow stairs) while you're fresh—and to enjoy some of the region's most dramatic scenery as you approach Vernazza.

Riomaggiore-Manarola (20 minutes): The popular, easy **Via dell'Amore** (Pathway of Love) was washed out by a landslide in 2012. If it's open, here's how to find the trailhead in Riomaggiore: Face the train station, go up the stairs to the right, following signs for *Via dell'Amore*. The photoworthy promenade winds along the coast to Manarola. A long tunnel and mega-nets protect hikers from

The trail views are worth the effort.

mean-spirited falling rocks. A recommended wine bar, Bar & Vini a Piè de Mà, is located at the Riomaggiore trailhead and offers light meals and awesome views. There's a picnic zone, a water fountain, and shade just above the Manarola station (and a WC at the station).

If the trail is closed, you can connect these towns by train, a scenic boat trip, or by taking the **alternative hiking route.** Trail #531 goes up and over the mountain between these two towns (1.5 hours). But be warned: It's essentially stairs all the way up, then all the way down—it's more intense and dizzying than other parts of the coastal trail.

Manarola-Corniglia (45 minutes): The walk from Manarola to Corniglia is closed indefinitely due to landslides. If open, it's a little longer, more rugged, and steeper than the Via dell'Amore. To avoid the last stretch (switchback stairs leading up to the hill-capping town of Corniglia), end your hike at Corniglia's train station and catch the shuttle bus to the town center (2/hour, usually timed to meet trains).

If the trail is closed, you can connect the towns by train or this **alternative hiking route:** Hike between Manarola and Corniglia via Volastra (2.5 hours).

The challenging trail leads from Manarola up to the village of Volastra, then north through high-altitude vineyard terraces, and steeply down through a forest to Corniglia (about four miles total). You can shave the two steepest miles off this route by taking the shuttle bus from Manarola up to Volastra (about hourly, 15 minutes).

Corniglia-Vernazza (1.5 hours): The scenic hike from Corniglia to Vernazza— the wildest and greenest section of the coast—is rewarding but hilly. From the Corniglia station and beach, zigzag up to the town (via the steep stairs, the longer road, or the shuttle bus). From Corniglia, you'll reach the trailhead on the main road, past Villa Cecio. You'll hike through vineyards and lots of fragrant and flowery vegetation. If you need a break before reaching Vernazza, stop by Bar la Torre, with a strip of shady tables perched high above the town.

Vernazza-Monterosso (1.5 hours): The trail from Vernazza to Monterosso is a challenging but scenic up-and-down-a-lot trek. Trails are narrow, steep, and crumbly, with a lot of steps, but easy to follow. The views just out of Vernazza, looking back at the town, are spectacular. From there you'll gradually ascend, passing little water-

Coastal trails are busiest at midday—hike early or late.

falls. As you approach Monterosso, you'll descend steeply—on tall, knee-testing stairs—through vineyards, eventually following a rivulet to the sea. The last stretch into Monterosso is along a pleasant, paved pathway clinging to the cliff. You'll end right at Monterosso's old town beach.

More Hikes

While the national park charges a fee to use the coastal trails, they also maintain a free, far more extensive network of trails higher in the hills to each town's sanctuary and beyond (no park card required). Shuttle buses make the going easier, connecting coastal villages with distant trailheads. Ask for pointers at a TI or park office. Manarola-based **Cinque Terre Trekking** is a good resource (see page 595).

One of many good options is the hike between **Monterosso and Levanto** (about 3 hours one-way, moderately strenuous, take the train to or from Levanto one-way).

MONTEROSSO AL MARE

Monterosso al Mare is a resort with lots of hotels, rentable beach umbrellas, crowds, and more late-night action than the neighboring towns. Even so, don't expect full-blown Riviera glitz. The small, crooked lanes of the old town cradle Old World charm. Strolling the waterfront promenade, you can pick out each of the Cinque Terre towns decorating the coast. After dark, they sparkle.

The only Cinque Terre town built on flat land, Monterosso has two parts: a new town (called Fegina) with a parking lot, train station, and TI; and an old town (Centro Storico). A pedestrian tunnel connects the old with the new, but you can take a small detour around the point for a nicer walk.

Orientation

Arrival in Monterosso: Trains arrive in the new town. For hotels in the new town, turn right out of the station. For the old town, turn left; it's a scenic, flat, 10-minute stroll.

Shuttle buses run along the waterfront between the old town (Piazza Garibaldi, just beyond the tunnel), the train station, and the parking lot at the end of Via Fegina (*Campo Sportivo* stop). The bus saves you a 10-minute schlep with your bags but only runs twice an hour (€1.50 one-way, €2.50 on board, free with Cinque Terre park card).

Taxis usually wait outside the train station, though you may have to call one (€10 from station to the old town, mobile 335-616-5842, 335-616-5845, or 335-628-0933).

For **drivers,** Monterosso is 30 minutes off the freeway (exit: Carrodano-Levanto); at the fork in the road, follow signs for Fegina to reach the new town (with a huge beachfront guarded lot, €25/24 hours), or for *Monterosso Centro Storico* to get to the old town (Loreto parking garage on Via Roma, 10-minute downhill walk into town, cheaper prices). Only locals are allowed to drive between the old and new towns.

Medical Help: English-speaking **Dr. Vitone** charges €50-100 for a simple visit (less for poor students, mobile 338-853-0949, vitonee@yahoo.it).

Tourist Information: The TI Proloco is next to the train station (daily 9:00-18:30, shorter hours off-season, exit station and go left a few doors, tel. 0187-817-506, www.prolocomonterosso.it). For national park tickets and information, head upstairs within the station to the ticket office near platform 1 (likely daily 8:00-20:00, shorter hours off-season).

Baggage Storage: The TI stores bags (€6/day—but confirm closing time) and so does the laundry (see next).

Laundry: Wash and Dry Lavarapido is two blocks from the train station (daily 8:00-19:00, also offers €5 bag-check service, Via Molinelli 17, mobile 339-484-0940).

◯ Monterosso Walk

This easy, self-guided walk begins at the breakwater. Part 1, focusing on the mostly level town center, takes about 30 minutes; for Part 2, summiting the adjacent hill, allow another hour or so.

PART 1: MONTEROSSO HARBOR AND TOWN CENTER

• *Hike out from the dock in the old town and stand at the edge of the concrete...*

Breakwater: If you're visiting by boat, you'll start here anyway. From this point you can survey Monterosso's old town (straight ahead) and new town (stretching to the left, with train station and parking lot).

Looking to the right, you can see all *cinque* of the *terre* from one spot: Vernazza, Corniglia (above the shore), Manarola, and a few buildings of Riomaggiore beyond that.

The partial breakwater (a row of giant rocks in the middle of the harbor) is

designed to save the beach from washing away, but sand erosion remains a major problem. While old-timers remember a vast beach, their grandchildren truck in sand each spring to give tourists something to lie on. (The Nazis liked the Cinque Terre, too—find two of their bomb-hardened bunkers, near left and far right.)

The four-star Hotel Porto Roca (pink building high on the hill, on the far right of the harbor) marks the trail to Vernazza. High above, you can see the roads that connect the Cinque Terre with the freeway over the hills.

Two prominent capes define the Cinque Terre. The farther cape is Punta di Montenero (to the right). The closer cape, Punta Mesco (to the left), marks a sea-life sanctuary, home to a rare grass that provides an ideal home for fish eggs. Buoys keep fishing boats away. The cape was once a quarry, providing employment to locals who chipped out the stones used to build the local towns (including

Monterosso al Mare

Monterosso al Mare

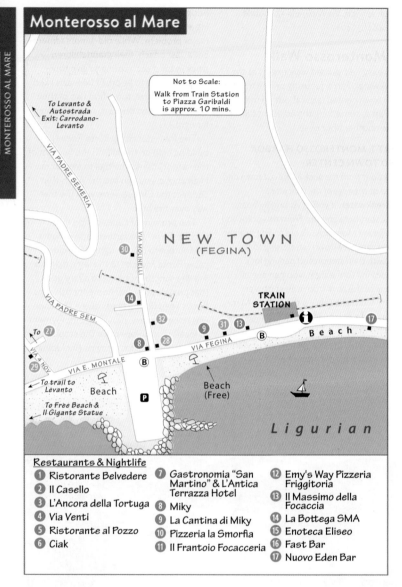

Not to Scale:

Walk from Train Station
to Piazza Garibaldi
is approx. 10 mins.

To Levanto &
Autostrada
Exit: Carrodano-
Levanto

VIA PADRE SEMERIA

VIA MOLINELLI

NEW TOWN
(FEGINA)

VIA PADRE SEM.

To 27

VIA 4 NOV.

VIA E. MONTALE

29

To trail to
Levanto   Beach

To Free Beach &
Il Gigante Statue

TRAIN
STATION

Beach

VIA FEGINA

Beach
(Free)

L i g u r i a n

Restaurants & Nightlife

1 Ristorante Belvedere
2 Il Casello
3 L'Ancora della Tortuga
4 Via Venti
5 Ristorante al Pozzo
6 Ciak

7 Gastronomia "San
Martino" & L'Antica
Terrazza Hotel
8 Miky
9 La Cantina di Miky
10 Pizzeria la Smorfia
11 Il Frantoio Focacceria

12 Emy's Way Pizzeria
Friggitoria
13 Il Massimo della
Focaccia
14 La Bottega SMA
15 Enoteca Eliseo
16 Fast Bar
17 Nuovo Eden Bar

the greenish stones making up part of the breakwater below you).

On the far end of the new town, marking the best free beach around, you can just see the statue named *Il Gigante* (hard to spot because it blends in with the gray rock). It's 45 feet tall and once held a tri-

dent. Made of reinforced concrete, it dates from the early 20th century, when it supported a dance terrace for a *fin de siècle* villa. A violent storm left the giant holding nothing but memories.

• *From the breakwater, walk toward the old town and under the train tracks. Then ven-*

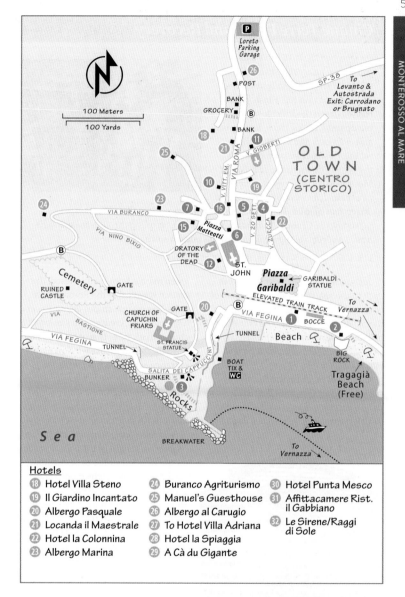

Hotels
- ⑱ Hotel Villa Steno
- ⑲ Il Giardino Incantato
- ⑳ Albergo Pasquale
- ㉑ Locanda il Maestrale
- ㉒ Hotel la Colonnina
- ㉓ Albergo Marina
- ㉔ Buranco Agriturismo
- ㉕ Manuel's Guesthouse
- ㉖ Albergo al Carugio
- ㉗ To Hotel Villa Adriana
- ㉘ Hotel la Spiaggia
- ㉙ A Cà du Gigante
- ㉚ Hotel Punta Mesco
- ㉛ Affittacamere Rist. il Gabbiano
- ㉜ Le Sirene/Raggi di Sole

ture right into the square and find the statue of a dandy holding what looks like a box cutter (near the big playground).

Piazza Garibaldi: The statue honors Giuseppe Garibaldi, the dashing firebrand who, in the 1860s, helped unite the people of Italy. Facing Garibaldi, with your back to the sea, you'll see (from right to left) the orange City Hall and a big home and recreation center for poor and homeless elderly. You'll also see A Ca' du Sciensa restaurant (with historic town photos inside and upstairs; you're welcome to pop in for a look).

Cinque Terre Flood and Recovery

On October 25, 2011, after a dry summer, a heavy rainstorm hit the Cinque Terre. Within four hours, 22 inches of rain fell. Flash floods rushed down the hillsides, picking up mud, rocks, trees, furniture, and even cars and buses in their raging, destructive path through the streets down to the sea. Part of Monterosso's old town and Vernazza's main drag were buried under a dozen feet of mud. Four villagers from Vernazza lost their lives.

Today, the Cinque Terre is back to normal. Strolling through these towns now, I appreciate the resilience of the human spirit.

Just under the bell tower (with your back to the sea, it's on your left), a set of covered arcades facing the sea is where the old-timers hang out. The crenellated bell tower marks the church.

• *Go to church (the entrance is on the inland side).*

Church of St. John the Baptist (Chiesa di San Giovanni Battista): Before entering, check out the facade. With white marble from Carrara and

Church of St. John the Baptist

green marble from Punta Mesco, this church is typical of the Romanesque style. The marble stripes get narrower the higher they go, creating the illusion of a church that's taller than it really is. Note the delicate stone rose window above the entrance, with 18 slender mullions.

Step inside for more Ligurian Gothic: original marble columns with pointed arches to match. The octagonal baptismal font (in the back of the church) was carved from Carrara marble in 1359. In the chapel to the right of the high altar, look for the wooden statue of St. Anthony, carved about 1400, which once graced a church that stood atop Punta Mesco. The church itself dates from 1307—see the proud inscription on the left-middle column: "MilloCCCVII." Outside the church, on the side facing the main street, find the high-water mark from an October 1966 flood. Nearly half a century later, the October 2011 flood hit Monterosso. But the church's statues survived, thanks to townspeople who carried them through raging waters to safety.

• *Leaving the church, immediately turn left and go to church again.*

Oratory of the Dead (Oratorio dei Neri): During the Counter-Reformation, the Catholic Church offset the rising influence of the Lutherans by creating brotherhoods of good works. These religious Rotary clubs were called "confraternities." Monterosso had two, nicknamed White and Black. This building is the oratory of the Black group, whose mission—as the macabre interior decor indicates—was to arrange for funerals and take care of widows, orphans, the shipwrecked, and the souls of those who ignore the request for a €1 donation. It dates from the 16th century; membership has passed from father to son for generations. Notice the fine carved choir stalls (c. 1700) just inside the door, and the haunted-house chandeliers. Look up at the ceiling to find the symbol of the confraternity: a skull-and-crossbones and an hourglass...death awaits us all.

• On that cheery note, if you're in a lazy mood, you can discreetly split off from our walking tour now to enjoy strolling, shopping, gelato, a day at the beach...or all of the above. If you're up for a hike, continue on to Part 2.

PART 2: CAPUCHIN CHURCH AND HILLTOP CEMETERY

• Return to the beach and find the brick steps that lead up to the hill-capping church (between the train tracks and the pedestrian tunnel, and passing in front of Albergo Pasquale). Approaching the bend in the path, watch for the stairs leading steeply and sharply to the right. This lane—Salita dei Cappuccini—is nicknamed Zii di Frati, or...

Switchbacks of the Friars: Follow the yellow brick road (OK, it's orange...but I couldn't help singing as I skipped skyward). Pause at the terrace above the seaside castle at a statue of St. Francis and a wolf. Enjoy another opportunity to see all five of the Cinque Terre towns. From here, backtrack 20 yards and continue uphill.

• When you reach a gate marked Convento e Chiesa Cappuccini, you have arrived at the...

Church of the Capuchin Friars: The former monastery is now staffed by a single caretaker. The church's striped Romanesque facade is all fake: not marble, just cheap 18th-century stucco. Go inside and sit in the rear pew. The high altarpiece painting of St. Francis can be rolled up to reveal a statue of Mary behind it. Look at the statue of St. Anthony to the right and smile (you're on convent camera). Wave at the security camera—they're nervous about the precious painting to your left.

This fine painting of the **Crucifixion** is attributed to Anthony van Dyck, the 17th-century Flemish master (though art historians suspect that it was painted by someone in the artist's workshop). Notice

View from the Capuchin Church

the eclipsed sun in the painting, just to the right of the cross. When Jesus died, the earth went dark.

• *Leave and turn left through another gate to hike 100 yards uphill to the cemetery that fills the ruined castle. Reaching the cemetery's gate, look back and enjoy the view over the town.*

Cemetery in the Ruined Castle: In the Dark Ages, the village huddled within this castle. You're looking at the oldest part of Monterosso, tucked behind the hill, out of view of 13th-century pirates. Explore the cemetery, keeping in mind that cemeteries are sacred places. *Q.R.P.* is *Qui Riposa in Pace* (a.k.a. R.I.P.). Climb to the summit—the castle's keep, or place of last refuge.

• *Your tour is over—any trail leads you back into town.*

Experiences
Beaches
Monterosso's **new town** has easily the Cinque Terre's best—and most crowded—beach (immediately in front of the train station). Most of the beach is private, where you'll pay €25 to rent two chairs and an umbrella for the day (prices get soft in the afternoon). Light lunches are served by beach cafés to sunbathers at their lounge chairs. Various outfits along here rent kayaks and stand-up paddle-boards (look for signs at the west end of the beach—near the parking lot—or ask around).

If there are no umbrellas on a stretch of beach, it's public, so you can spread out a towel anywhere. There's a free beach at the far-west end, near the Gigante statue.

The **old town** also has its own, predominantly private beach (rent umbrellas, chairs, kayaks, and paddleboats at the Beach Bar Alga, which is also a scenic spot for a drink). Tucked just beyond the private beach—under Il Casello restaurant at the east end of town—is the free public beach called Tragagià, which is gravelly and generally less crowded.

Boat Rides
In addition to the regularly scheduled boat service (see page 604), you can hire your own captain for transfers to other towns or for a full nautical tour. For example, Stefano has two six-person boats: the Matilde and the Babaah (about €100/hour, one hour is enough for a quick spin, two hours includes time for swimming stops; longer trips to Porto Venere and offshore islands possible; mobile 333-821-2007, www.matildenavigazione.com, info@matildenavigazione.com).

Wine Tasting
Buranco Agriturismo offers visits to their vineyard and cantina (reserve 2 days ahead). You'll taste some of their wines plus a grappa and a *limoncino,* along with home-cooked food (€20-30/person with snacks, English may be limited, follow Via Buranco uphill to path, 10 minutes above town, tel. 0187-817-677, www.buranco cinqueterre.it).

Nightlife
Enoteca da Eliseo, the best wine bar in town, comes with operatic ambience. Eliseo and his wife, Mary, love music as much as they love wine. Eliseo offers an education in *grappa,* stocking more than a hundred varieties (Wed-Mon 14:00-23:30, closed Tue, Piazza Matteotti 3, a block inland behind church, tel. 0187-817-308).

At **Fast Bar,** customers mix travel tales with cold beer. The crowd (and the rock 'n' roll) gets noisier as the night rolls on (cheap *panini* and salads usually served until midnight, Fri-Wed 9:30-late, closed Thu in winter; Via Roma in the old town).

La Cantina di Miky, in the new town just beyond the train station, is a trendy bar-restaurant with an extensive cocktail and *grappa* menu and occasional live music. They offer a fun "five villages" wine tasting with local meats and cheeses (€15/person for just wine, €20/person with food). It's the best place in

Cinque Terre Cuisine

Hanging out at a seaview restaurant while sampling local specialties could become one of your favorite memories.

The mainstay here is **anchovies** (*acciughe;* ah-CHOO-gay)—ideally served the day they're caught. Even if you've always hated American anchovies, try them fresh here. They can be prepared marinated, butterflied, and deep-fried (sometimes with a delicious garlic/vinegar sauce called *giada*). *Tegame alla vernazzana* is the most typical main course in Vernazza: a casserole-like dish of whole anchovies, fresh potatoes and tomatoes, white wine, oil, and herbs.

Antipasto here means *antipasti ai frutti di mare* (sometimes called simply *antipasti misti*), a plate of mixed "fruits of the sea." Splitting one of these and a pasta dish can be plenty for two people.

This region is the birthplace of **pesto.** Try it on *trenette* (the long, flat Ligurian noodle ruffled on one side) or *trofie* (short, dense twists made of flour with a bit of potato).

Pansotti are ravioli with ricotta and a mixture of greens, often served with a walnut sauce (*salsa di noci*).

Focaccia, the tasty pillowy bread, also originates here. Locals say the best focaccia is made between the Cinque Terre and Genoa. It comes plain or with onions, sage, or olives and is sold in rounds or slices by weight (a portion is about 100 grams, or *un etto*).

The ***vino delle Cinque Terre,*** while not one of Italy's top wines, flows cheap and easy throughout the region. It's white—great with seafood. ***Sciacchetrà*** dessert wine is worth the splurge (€4-12 per small glass).

town for top-end Italian beers (Thu-Tue until late, closed Wed, Via Fegina 90, tel. 0187-802-525).

Nuovo Eden Bar, overlooking the beach by the big rock just east of the train station, is a fine place to enjoy a cocktail or ice cream with a sea view (€6 cocktails, drinks come with a light snack, good ice cream, closed Mon off-season).

Eating
With a Sea View

$$ Ristorante Belvedere, big and sprawling, is *the* place for a good-value meal indoors or outdoors on the harborfront. Their €48 *anfora belvedere* (mixed seafood stew) can easily feed four and the *misto mare* plate (2-person minimum, €15/person) can be an entire meal (Wed-Mon 12:00-14:30 & 18:00-22:00, closed Tue

except Aug, on the harbor in the old town, tel. 0187-817-033).

$$ Il Casello, with outdoor tables on a rocky outcrop, is the only place for a fun meal overlooking the old town beach (daily April-Oct 12:00-22:00, closed Nov-March, mobile 333-492-7629).

$$$ L'Ancora della Tortuga is the top option in town for seaview elegance, with gorgeous outdoor seating high on a bluff and a lovely white-tablecloth-and-candles interior. The food doesn't quite live up to the fuss, and the service is uneven, but the setting is memorable (Tue-Sun 12:30-15:30 & 18:30-21:30, closed Mon, just outside the tunnel that connects the old and new town—or climb up the ramp in front of Albergo Pasquale, tel. 0187-800-065, mobile 333-240-7956).

In the Old Town

$$$ Via Venti is a quiet trattoria hidden in an alley deep in the heart of the Old Town. Imaginative seafood dishes use the day's catch and freshly made pasta. The outdoor tables are on a lane as nondescript as the humdrum interior—but you're here for the food (Fri-Wed 12:00-14:30 & 18:30-22:30, closed Thu, Via XX Settembre 32, tel. 0187-818-347).

$$$ Ristorante al Pozzo is a local favorite, with one of the best wine lists in town, homemade pasta, and wonderful seafood *antipasti misti* (Fri-Wed 12:00-15:00 & 18:30-22:30, closed Thu, Via Roma 24, tel. 0187-817-575).

$$$ Ciak is known for its huge, sizzling terra-cotta crock for two—crammed with the day's catch—and (sometimes) a bit of an attitude. Reservations are smart in summer (Thu-Tue 12:00-15:00 & 18:00-22:30, closed Wed, Piazza Don Minzoni 6, tel. 0187-817-014, www.ristoranteciak.net).

$ Gastronomia "San Martino" is a tiny, humble combination of takeaway and sit-down café with surprisingly affordable, quality dishes. Eat at one of the few tables—inside or out on a pleasant street—or find a driftwood log for a take-out feast to go (Tue-Sun 12:00-15:00 & 18:00-22:00, closed Mon, next to recommended L'Antica Terrazza hotel at Vicolo San Martino 3, mobile 346-109-7338).

In the New Town

$$$$ Miky is my Cinque Terre favorite, with well-dressed locals packed into a classy environment. Their elegantly presented, top-quality food celebrates local ingredients and traditions. Try their "pizza pasta"—finished in a bowl topped with a thin pizza crust and flambéed at your table. If I should want dessert, it would be their mixed sampler plate, *dolce misto* (Wed-Mon 12:00-15:00 & 19:00-23:00, closed Tue, reservations wise in summer, in the new town 100 yards from train station at Via Fegina 104, tel. 0187-817-608, www.ristorantemiky.it).

$$$ La Cantina di Miky, a few doors down toward the station, is more youthful and informal than Miky, yet serves artfully crafted Ligurian specialties in Miky's family tradition. Sit downstairs, in the garden, or overlooking the sea. They have creative desserts and large selection of Italian microbrews (Thu-Tue 12:00-24:00, closed Wed, Via Fegina 90, tel. 0187-802-525).

Light Meals, Takeout Food, and Breakfast

In the old town, shops and bakeries sell pizza and focaccia for an easy picnic.

$ Pizzeria la Smorfia is the local favorite (Fri-Wed 11:00-24:00, closed Thu, Via Vittorio Emanuele 73, tel. 0187-818-395). Other options are **$ Il Frantoio** (Fri-Wed 9:00-14:00 & 16:30-20:00, closed Thu, just off Via Roma at Via Gioberti 1) and **$ Emy's Way Pizzeria Friggitoria,** which also serves deep-fried seafood to go (daily 11:00-20:00, later in summer, along the skinny street next to the church).

$ Il Massimo della Focaccia, right at the train station, is a good bet for a light meal with a sea view (Thu-Tue 9:00-19:00, closed Wed except June-Aug, Via Fegina 50 at the entry to the station). **La Bottega SMA** is a smart minimart with fresh produce, *antipasti,* deli items, and sandwiches; pay by weight (daily 8:00-13:00 & 16:30-19:30—except closed Sun afternoon, shorter hours off-season, near Lavarapido at Vittoria Gianni 21).

For breakfast, try **Fast Bar** on Via Roma in the old town. They serve an American-style breakfast for €12, or cheaper à la carte (Fri-Wed 9:30-late, closed Thu in winter).

Sleeping

Rooms in Monterosso are a better value than similar rooms in crowded Vernazza. The TI Proloco just outside the train station can give you a list of rooms for rent.

In the Old Town

$$$$ Hotel Villa Steno features great

view balconies, panoramic gardens, and a roof terrace with sun beds, and air-conditioning. Of their 16 rooms, 14 have view balconies (RS%, family rooms, hearty buffet breakfast, elevator, laundry service, ask about pay parking when you reserve, hike up to the panoramic terrace, closed Nov-March, Via Roma 109, tel. 0187-817-028 or 0187-818-336, www.villasteno.com, steno@pasini.com). It's a 15-minute climb (or €8 taxi ride) from the train station to the top of the old town. Readers get a free Cinque Terre info packet and a glass of local wine when they check in—ask for it.

$$$$ **Il Giardino Incantato** ("The Enchanted Garden") is a charming and cozy four-room B&B with impressive attention to detail in a tastefully renovated 16th-century Ligurian home in the heart of the old town. Sip their homemade limoncino upon check-in, and have breakfast under lemon trees in a delightful hidden garden (RS%, air-con, free minibar and tea and coffee service, laundry service, Via Mazzini 18, tel. 0187-818-315, mobile 333-264-9252, www.ilgiardinoincantato.net, giardino_incantato@libero.it).

$$$$ **Albergo Pasquale,** modern and comfortable, has 15 seaview rooms. Located right on the harbor, it's just a few steps from the beach, boat dock, and tunnel entrance to the new town. While there is some train noise, the soundtrack is mostly a lullaby of waves. It has an elevator and offers easier access than most (RS%, family room, same welcome drink as Villa Steno, air-con, laundry service, Via Fegina 8, tel. 0187-817-550 or 0187-817-477, www.hotelpasquale.it, pasquale@pasini.com, Felicita and Marco).

$$$ **Locanda il Maestrale** rents six small, stylish rooms in a sophisticated and peaceful little inn. Although renovated with all the modern comforts, it retains centuries-old character under frescoed ceilings. Its peaceful sun terrace overlooking the Old Town and Via Roma action is a delight. Guests enjoy free drinks and snacks each afternoon (RS%, air-con, Via Roma 37, tel. 0187-817-013, mobile 338-4530-531, www.locandamaestrale.net, maestrale@monterossonet.com, Stefania).

$$$ **Hotel la Colonnina** has 21 big rooms, generous and meticulously cared-for public spaces, a cozy garden, and an inviting shared seaview terrace with sun beds. It's buried in the town's fragrant and sleepy back streets (family rooms, many rooms with private terraces, cash preferred, air-con, fridges, elevator, a block inland from the main square at Via Zuecca 6, tel. 0187-817-439, www.lacolonninacinque-terre.it, info@lacolonninacinqueterre.it, Cristina).

$$$ **Albergo Marina,** creatively run by enthusiastic husband-and-wife team Marina and Eraldo, has 23 pleasant rooms and a garden with lemon trees. With a free and filling buffet featuring local specialties each afternoon, they offer a fine value (RS%, family rooms, elevator, air-con, free kayak and snorkel equipment, Via Buranco 40, tel. 0187-817-613, www.hotelmarina-5terre.com, marina@hotelmarina5terre.com).

$$$ **Buranco Agriturismo,** a 10-minute hike above the Old Town, has wonderful gardens and views over the vine-covered valley. Its primary business is wine and olive-oil production, but they offer three apartments. It's a rare opportunity to stay in a farmhouse, but still be able to get to town on foot (air-con, €15 taxi from station, tel. 0187-817-677, mobile 349-434-8046, www.burancocinqueterre.it, info@buranco.it, informally run by Loredana, Mary, and Giulietta).

$$$ **Manuel's Guesthouse,** perched high above the town among terraces, is a garden getaway with six big, bright rooms and a grand view. After climbing the killer stairs from the town center, their killer terrace is hard to leave—especially after a few drinks (cash only, air-con, up about 100 steps behind church—you can ask them to carry your bags up the hill, Via San Martino 39, mobile 333-439-0809,

www.manuelsguesthouse.com, manuels-guesthouse@libero.it).

$$ L'Antica Terrazza rents five tight, classy rooms right in town. With a pretty terrace overlooking the pedestrian street and minimal stairs, Raffaella and John offer a good deal (RS%, cheaper room with private bath down the hall, air-con, Vicolo San Martino 1, mobile 380-138-0082 or 347-132-6213, www.anticaterrazza.com, post@anticaterrazza.com).

$ Albergo al Carugio is a practical nine-room place in a big apartment-style building at the top of the old town. It's quiet, comfy, and a fine value for those on a budget (RS%, no breakfast, air-con—but only during the daytime June-Sept, Via Roma 100, tel. 0187-817-453, www.alcarugio.it, info@alcarugio.it, conscientiously run by Andrea).

In the New Town

$$$$ Hotel Villa Adriana is a big, contemporary, bright hotel on a church-owned estate set in a peaceful garden with a pool, free parking, and a no-stress style. They rent 54 rooms—some with terraces and/or sea views—ask for one when you reserve, but no guarantees (family rooms, air-con, elevator, free loaner bikes, affordable dinners, Via IV Novembre 23, tel. 0187-818-109, www.villaadriana.info, info@villaadriana.info).

$$$$ Hotel la Spiaggia is a venerable old 19-room place facing the beach. Half the rooms come with sea views (cash only, air-con, elevator, free parking—reserve in advance, Via Lungomare 96, tel. 0187-817-567, www.laspiaggiahotel.com, hotellaspiaggia@libero.it).

$$$ A Cà du Gigante, despite its name, is a tiny yet chic refuge with nine rooms. About 100 yards from the beach (and surrounded by blocky apartments and big hotels on a modern street), the interior is tastefully done with upscale comfort in mind (RS%, air-con, limited free parking, Via IV Novembre 11, tel. 0187-817-401, www.ilgigantecinqueterre.it, gigante@ilgigantecinqueterre.it).

$$$ Hotel Punta Mesco is a tidy, well-run little haven renting 17 quiet, casual rooms at a good price. While none have views, 10 rooms have small terraces (RS%, family room, air-con, parking, Via Molinelli 35, tel. 0187-817-495, www.hotelpuntamesco.it, info@hotelpuntamesco.it).

$$ Affittacamere Ristorante il Gabbiano, a touristy restaurant right on the beach, rents five basic, dated, but affordable rooms upstairs. Three rooms face the sea, with small balconies; two overlook a little garden at the back. The Gabbiano family restaurant serves as your reception (family rooms, cash only, air-con, Via Fegina 84, tel. 0187-817-578, www.affittacamereristoranteilgabbiano.com, affittacamereilgabbiano@live.it).

$ Le Sirene/Raggi di Sole, with nine simple rooms in two humble buildings, is a decent budget choice in this pricey town. It's run from a hole-in-the-wall reception desk a block from the station, just off the water. I'd request the Le Sirene building, which has smaller bathrooms but no train noise, and is a bit more spacious and airy than Raggi di Sole (RS%, family rooms, fans, Via Molinelli 10, mobile 331-788-1088, www.sirenerooms.com, sirenerooms@gmail.com).

VERNAZZA

With a ruined castle and a stout stone church, Vernazza is the jewel of the Cinque Terre. Only the occasional noisy train reminds you of the modern world.

Proud of their Vernazzan heritage, the town's 500 residents like to brag: "Vernazza is locally owned. Portofino has sold out." Fearing change, keep-Vernazza-small proponents stopped the construction of a major road into the town and region. Families are tight and go back centuries; you'll notice certain surnames (such as Basso and Moggia) everywhere. Leisure time is devoted to taking part in the *passeggiata*—strolling lazily together up and down the main street. Learn—and live—the phrase *"la vita pigra di Vernazza"* (the lazy life of Vernazza).

The action is at the harbor, where you'll find outdoor restaurants, a bar hanging on the edge of the castle, and a breakwater with a promenade, corralled by a natural amphitheater of terraced hills. In the summer, the beach becomes a soccer field, with teams fielded by bars and restaurants providing late-night entertainment.

Orientation

Arrival in Vernazza: The town's **train station** is only about three train cars long, but the trains are much longer—so most of the cars come to a stop in a long, dark tunnel. Open the door, get out, and walk through the tunnel to the station. From there the main drag flows through town right to the harbor. The **boats** dock at the harborfront square, at the base of main street. If arriving by **car,** don't drive to Vernazza. Roads are in terrible shape and parking is limited. If you're coming from the north, park in Levanto. If arriving from the south, park your car in La Spezia. From either town, hop on the train.

Rick's Tip: *A steep 10-minute hike in either direction from Vernazza gives you a* **classic village photo op.** *For the best light, head toward Corniglia in the morning—best views are just before the ticket booth for the national park—and toward Monterosso in the evening—best views are after the ticket booth.*

Tourist Information: At the train station, you can get answers to basic questions at the gift shop (daily 8:00-20:00, closed in winter), or the train ticket desk/park office (likely daily 8:00-20:00, shorter hours off-season, tel. 0187-812-533). Public WCs are just behind. Locals run their own helpful tourist board/website, called VisitVernazza.org.

Baggage Storage: You can leave your bags at the train-station gift shop near track 1 (€1/hour, €10/day, daily 8:00-19:30, closed in winter). Friendly Francesco and his staff will happily take your luggage from the train station to your hotel—and back (€3/piece).

Market: On Tuesday mornings (8:00-13:00), cars and trucks pull into town for a tailgate market offering produce and more.

Vernazza

Vernazza

Trail to
Monterosso

Cliffs

Rocks

50 Meters

50 Yards

SUNNING &
SWIMMING

Harbor

ORATORY
(OPERA)

WALK
ENDS

SANTA
MARGHERITA
CHURCH

SUNNING

Breakwater

Beach

Piazza
Marconi

1

BOAT
DOCKS
HERE

5

14

4

15

VIA VISCONTI

3

7

6

TUNNEL

19

20

14

CASTLE

8

V. SAN GIOVANNI BATTISTA

Rocks and Cliffs

TUNNEL

Ligurian   Sea

Restaurants

1 Trattoria del Capitano &
   Martina Callo Rooms

2 Gianni Franzi
   Ristorante/Reception

3 Gambero Rosso

4 Ristorante Pizzeria Vulnetia &
   Nicolina Rooms Reception

5 Pizzeria Baia Saracena

6 Ristorante al Castello

7 Ristorante Belforte

8 Vernazza Wine Experience

9 Trattoria da Sandro

10 Antica Osteria il Baretto

11 Blue Marlin Bar

12 Il Pirata delle Cinque Terre Café

13 Forno Bakery

14 Gelaterias (3)

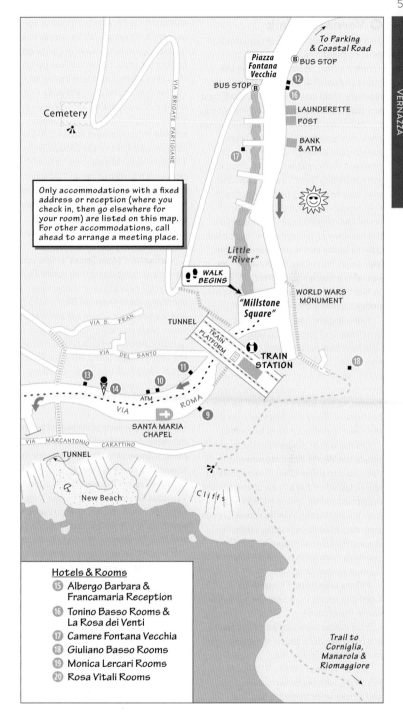

To Parking
& Coastal Road

ⓑ BUS STOP

Piazza Fontana Vecchia

BUS STOP ⓑ

⑫

⑯

LAUNDERETTE

POST

BANK
& ATM

Cemetery

VIA BRIGATE PARTIGIANE

⑰

Only accommodations with a fixed address or reception (where you check in, then go elsewhere for your room) are listed on this map. For other accommodations, call ahead to arrange a meeting place.

Little "River"

● WALK
   BEGINS

"Millstone Square"

WORLD WARS MONUMENT

VIA S. FRAN.

TUNNEL

TRAIN PLATFORM

VIA DEL SANTO

TRAIN STATION

⑬

⑪

⑱

⑭

⑩

ATM

VIA   ROMA

⑨

SANTA MARIA CHAPEL

VIA MARCANTONIO CARATTINO

TUNNEL

New Beach

Cliffs

Trail to Corniglia, Manarola & Riomaggiore

Hotels & Rooms

⑮ Albergo Barbara & Francamaria Reception

⑯ Tonino Basso Rooms & La Rosa dei Venti

⑰ Camere Fontana Vecchia

⑱ Giuliano Basso Rooms

⑲ Monica Lercari Rooms

⑳ Rosa Vitali Rooms

⊙ Vernazza Walk

This walk includes the town squares and ends on the scenic breakwater.

• *From the train station, walk under the tracks and uphill about 30 yards until you reach the sharp bend in the road. You'll see a tiny piazza with benches and big millstones.*

"Millstone Square": The big millstones are a reminder that the town stream (which goes underground here) once powered Vernazza's water mill. (You can still see its tiny "river" if you follow this road up a few steps.) Until the 1950s, the river ran openly through the center of town. Old-timers recall the days before the breakwater, when the river cascaded down and the surf sent waves rolling up Vernazza's main drag. (The name "Vernazza" is actually local dialect for "little Venice"—the town once had a string of bridges, evoking those in Venice.)

Corralling this stream under the modern street, and forcing it to take a hard right turn here, contributed to the damage caused by the 2011 flood. After the flood, alpine engineers were imported from Switzerland to redesign the drainage system, so any future floods will be less destructive. They also installed nets above the town to protect it from landslides.

On the wall at the bend in the road, notice the **World Wars Monument**—dedicated to those killed in World Wars I and II. Listed on the left are soldiers *morti in combattimento,* who died in World War I; on the right is the WWII section. Some were deported to *Germania;* others—labeled *Part* (for *partigiani,* or partisans, generally communists)—were killed while fighting against Mussolini.

Hikers take note: The **path to Corniglia** leaves from here (behind and above the plaque).

• *To see a more workaday part of Vernazza, you could wander a couple of minutes uphill from here, for a look at the...*

Top of Town: First you'll pass (on the left, at #7, with big brown garage doors and a *croce verde Vernazza* sign) the ambulance barn, where a group of volunteers is always on call for a dash to the hospital, 40 minutes away in La Spezia. Farther up, you'll come to a functional strip of modern apartment blocks facing the river. In this practical zone—the only place in town that allows cars—are a bank, the post office, a launderette, and the recommended tourist hub bar/café called Il Pirata delle Cinque Terre. The parking lot fills a square called Fontana Vecchia, named for an "old fountain" that's so old, it's long gone. Shuttle buses run from the post office to hamlets and sanctuaries in the hills above.

• *Whether or not you head up to the top of town, the next leg of our walk follows...*

Vernazza's "Main Street": Here you'll pass many locals doing their *vasche* (laps). Next you'll pass souvenir shops, wine shops, the recommended Blue Marlin Bar, and the tiny stone Chapel of Santa Marta, where Mass is celebrated only on special Sundays. Above and behind the chapel is the Vineria Santa Marta wine bar. Farther down, you'll walk by a *gelateria,* bakery, pharmacy, a grocery, and another *gelateria.* There are plenty of fun and cheap food-to-go options here.

• *On the left, in front of the second* gelateria, *a stone arch was blasted away by the 2011 flood. Scamper through the hole in the rock to reach Vernazza's shrinking...*

"New Beach": In the flood's aftermath, Vernazza's main drag and harbor were filled with mud and silt. Workers used the debris to fill in even more of this beach, and for several years Vernazza had a popular beach that felt a world away from the bustle of the main drag. But as time goes on, the erosion from the churning surf is taking it away.

• *Back on the main drag, continue downhill to the...*

Harbor Square (Piazza Marconi) and Breakwater: Vernazza, with the only natural harbor of the Cinque Terre, was established as the sole place boats could pick up the fine local wine. The two-foot-high square stone at the foot of the stairs (on the left) is marked *Sasso del Sego* (stone of tallow). Workers crushed animal flesh and fat in its basin to make tallow, which drained out of the tiny hole below. The tallow was then used to waterproof boats or wine barrels. Stonework is the soul of the region. Take some time to appreciate the impressive stonework of the restaurant interiors facing the harbor.

On the far side (behind the recommended Ristorante Pizzeria Vulnetia), peek into the tiny street with its commotion of arches. Vernazza's most characteristic side streets, called *carugi,* lead up from here. The narrow stairs mark the beginning of the trail that leads up to the quintessential view of Vernazza—and, eventually, on to Monterosso.

Located in front of the harborside church, the tiny piazza—decorated with a river-rock mosaic—is a popular hangout spot. The **church** is unusual for its strange entryway, which faces east (altar side), rather than the more typical western orientation. In the 16th century, the townspeople doubled the church in size, causing it to overtake a little piazza that once faced the west facade. From the square, use the "new" entry and climb the steps. Inside, the lighter pillars in the back mark the 16th-century extension. Three historic portable crosses hanging on the walls are replicas of crosses that (locals believe) Vernazza ships once carried on crusades.

• *Finish your town tour seated out on the breakwater. Face the town, and see...*

The Harbor: In a moderate storm, you'd be soaked, as waves routinely crash over the *molo* (breakwater, built in 1972). Waves can rearrange the huge rocks—depositing them onto the piazza and its benches. Freak waves have even washed away tourists. Enjoy the waterfront piazza—carefully.

The town's fishing fleet is down to just a few boats (with the net spools). Vernazzans are still more likely to own a boat than a car, and it's said that you stand a better chance of surviving if you mess with a local man's wife than with his boat. Boats are on buoys, except in winter or when the red storm flag (see the pole at the start of the breakwater) indicates bad seas. At these times, the boats are pulled up onto the square—which is usually reserved for restaurant tables.

The Castle (Castello Doria): On the far right, the castle, which is now a grassy park with great views (and nothing but stones), still guards the town (€1.50, not covered by Cinque Terre park card; daily 10:00-20:00, summer until 21:00, closed Nov-March; from harbor, take stairs by Trattoria Gianni and follow *Ristorante al Castello* signs, tower is a few steps beyond). This was the town's watchtower back in pirate days, and a Nazi lookout in World War II. The castle tower looks new because it was rebuilt after the British bombed it, chasing out the Germans.

Vernazza's harbor and breakwater

Sunbathing in Vernazza

The squat tower on the water (Ristorante Belforte) is a great spot for a glass of wine or a meal (from the breakwater, you can follow the rope to the restaurant and pop inside, past an actual submarine door; a photo of a major storm showing the entire tower under a wave—not uncommon in the winter—hangs near the bar).

The Town: Before the 12th century, pirates made the coast uninhabitable, so the first Vernazzans lived in the hills above (near the Reggio Sanctuary). The town itself—and its towers, fortified walls, and hillside terracing—are mostly from the 12th through the 15th centuries.

Vernazza has two halves. *Sciuiu* (Vernazzan dialect for "flowery") is the sunny side on the left, and *luvegu* (dank) is the shady side on the right. Houses below the castle were connected by an interior arcade. The square before you is locally famous for some of the area's finest restaurants. The big red central house—on the site where Genoan warships were built in the 12th century—used to be a guardhouse.

In the Middle Ages, there was no beach or square. The water went right up to the buildings, where boats would tie up, Venetian-style. Buildings had a water gate and a front door on the higher inland side. There was no pastel plaster—just fine stonework (traces survive above the Trattoria del Capitano).

Above the Town: The small, round tower above the red guardhouse reminds

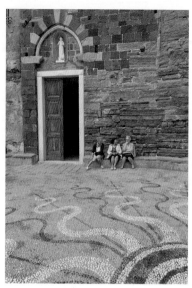

Santa Margherita Church

us of the town's importance in the Middle Ages. Back then, the enemies of key ally Genoa were Vernazza's enemies. Bar la Torre, just above and beyond the tower, welcomes hikers starting or finishing the Corniglia-Vernazza hike. That tower recalls a time when the entire town was fortified by a stone wall. Vineyards fill the mountainside beyond the town; notice the many terraces.

The Church, School, and City Hall: Vernazza's Ligurian Gothic church, built with black stones quarried from Punta Mesco (the distant point behind you), dates from 1318. The gray stone marks the church's 16th-century expansion. The gray-and-red house above the spire is the elementary school. Older students go to the "big city," La Spezia. The red building to the right of the schoolhouse, a former monastery, is the City Hall.

Finally, on the top of the hill is the town cemetery. It's only fair that hardworking Vernazzans—who spend their lives climbing up and down the hillsides—are rewarded with an eternal world-class view.

Castle at Vernazza

Experiences
Beaches
The harbor's sandy cove has sunning rocks and showers by the breakwater. A ladder on the breakwater allows deep-water access. The sunbathing lane directly under the church has a shower. Vernazza's other beach (the "new beach") can be accessed through a hole halfway along the town's main drag.

Wine Tasting
Vernazza Wine Experience, at the top of town just under the castle, is run by Alessandro, a sommelier who enjoys explaining wines and the various €15 small plates matched with them (like a meat-and-cheese plate served on a slab of olive tree). You'll pay €15 for three very different wines. While the bill can add up, the quality is excellent, the setting is romantic, and the view is unforgettable (cash only, daily 17:00-21:00, hike from harborfront and turn left before castle, Via S. Giovanni Battista 31, tel. 331-343-3801).

Vineria Santa Marta is simpler and mellower, with less scenery and pretense. At this wine shop/tasting bar with a stone terrace, brothers Wolfgang and Michael offer a basic tasting of three local wines plus light snacks for €9 per person (also serves salads and *bruschette,* daily 9:30-20:30, above the little chapel on Via Roma—the main drag, tel. 0187-882-1084).

A Little Taste of Opera
My favorite Cinque Terre evenings are spent at Vernazza's summer opera. A big-name maestro from Lucca brings talented singers to town twice weekly for performances in the small, beautiful oratory tucked behind the town's big church (find the steps up and around, next to Ananasso Bar). Performances begin at 19:00 and last just over an hour (€13 in advance, €15 at the door, April-Oct Wed and Fri at 19:00 but confirm times locally, book tickets at Cinque Terre Riviera office at #24

on main street, tel. 0187-812-123, info@ cinqueterreriviera.com).

"Voluntourism"
Save Vernazza, which began as a post-flood relief organization, has evolved into an advocacy group, emphasizing sustainable tourism. If you enjoy the Cinque Terre and would like to give something back, contact them to participate in a project designed to protect and promote Vernazza. "Voluntourism" activities, scheduled regularly through the high season, include rebuilding terrace walls and harvesting grapes (€29, reservations required, lunch and wine provided, generally 2/week late May-Oct 8:30-13:30, mobile 349-357-3572, www.savevernazza. com, workwithus@savevernazza.com).

Eating
Vernazza's restaurants take pride in their cooking. Wander around at about 20:00 and compare the ambience, but don't wait too long—many kitchens close at 22:00. To get an outdoor table on summer weekends, reserve ahead. Harborside restaurants and bars are easygoing. You're welcome to grab a cup of coffee or glass of wine and disappear somewhere on the **breakwater,** returning your glass when you're done.

Rick's Tip: *If you dine in Vernazza but are staying in Monterosso, be sure to* **check train schedules before sitting down to eat,** *as trains run less frequently in the evening.*

Harborside
$$$ Trattoria del Capitano serves a short menu of straightforward local dishes, including *spaghetti allo scoglio*—pasta entangled with seafood (Wed-Mon from 8:00 for breakfast, 12:00-22:00, closed Tue and Dec-Jan, tel. 0187-812-201).

$$$ Gianni Franzi is an old standby with well-prepared seafood and reliable, friendly service. While the outdoor seating is basic, the indoor seating is classy (check their *menù cucina tipica Vernazza,* Thu-Tue 12:00-15:00 & 19:00-22:00, closed Wed except in Aug, tel. 0187-812-228).

$$$$ Gambero Rosso is the priciest place on the square, but—ever since it was sold to a big-city restaurateur who runs it from afar—the quality can be hit-or-miss. Still, it has a fine interior and great outdoor tables (Fri-Wed 12:00-15:00 & 19:00-21:30, closed Thu and Dec-Feb, Piazza Marconi 7, tel. 0187-812-265).

$$$ Ristorante Pizzeria Vulnetia has a jovial atmosphere and serves regional specialties and affordable pizzas, making it a good choice for budget and family meals (Tue-Sun 12:00-22:00, closed Mon, Piazza Marconi 29, tel. 0187-821-193, Giuliano and Tullio).

$$ Pizzeria Baia Saracena ("Saracen Bay") is the budget option on the harbor, serving forgettable pizza and pastas out on the breakwater. Eat here not for high cuisine, but for a memorable atmosphere at reasonable prices (Sat-Thu 10:30-22:00, closed Fri, tel. 0187-812-113, Luca).

By the Castle

$$$ Ristorante al Castello is high above town, just below the castle, with commanding views. Reserve one of the dozen romantic cliff-side seaview tables for two, some of which snake around the castle, where you'll feel like you're eating all alone with the Mediterranean (Thu–Tue 12:00-15:00 & 19:00–22:00, closed Wed and Nov–April, tel. 0187-812-296).

$$$$ Ristorante Belforte serves a fine blend of traditional and creative cuisine, including a hearty *zuppa Michela* (a boatload of seafood), fishy *spaghetti alla Bruno, trofie al pesto* (hand-rolled noodles with pesto), and classic *antipasto misto di pesce.* Reserve ahead for tables on the view terrace (Wed-Mon 12:00-15:00 & 19:00-22:00, closed Tue and Nov-March, tel. 0187-812-222, Michela).

Rick's Tip: *After the restaurants close down, Vernazza is quiet except for a couple of* **nightspots: Blue Marlin Bar** *and* **Il Pirata delle Cinque Terre.** *All Vernazza bars must close by 24:00.*

On or near the Main Street

Several of Vernazza's inland eateries manage to compete without the harbor ambience, but with slightly cheaper prices.

$$ Trattoria da Sandro, on the main drag, mixes quality Genovese and Ligurian cuisine, including award-winning stuffed mussels, with friendly service (Wed-Mon 12:00-15:00 & 18:30-22:00, closed Tue, Via Roma 62, tel. 0187-812-223).

$$ Antica Osteria il Baretto is a solid bet for homey, reasonably priced traditional cuisine that's favored by locals (Tue-Sun 12:00-22:00, closed Mon, indoor and outdoor seating in summer, Via Roma 31, tel. 0187-812-381).

$$ Blue Marlin Bar, just below the train station, serves a short, creative menu of more casual dishes. It also serves breakfast and dominates the late-night scene with home-cooked food until 23:00, good drinks, and occasional piano jam sessions. If you're young and hip, hang out here (Thu-Tue 7:00-24:00, closed Wed). If you're awaiting a train any time of day, the Blue Marlin's outdoor seating beats the platform.

$$ Il Pirata delle Cinque Terre, behind and above the train station, is popular for breakfast and attracts many travelers for lunch and dinner. Don't come here for the cuisine, but for a memorable evening with the Cannoli twins, who entertain while they serve, and aim their menu squarely at American taste buds (daily 6:30-24:00, Via Gavino).

Other main-street eateries offer a fine range of quick meals. **Forno Bakery** has good focaccia and veggie tarts (at #5). **Pino's grocery store** makes inexpensive sandwiches to order (generally Mon-Sat 8:00-13:00 & 17:00-19:30, closed Sun).

Gelato

Gelateria Vernazza, near the top of the main street, takes gelato seriously. **Gelateria Amore Mio** (midtown) has great people-watching tables but the least exciting gelato. Out on the harbor, **Gelateria Il Porticciolo** is arguably the best, with fresh ingredients and intense flavors.

Sleeping

People recommended here are listed for their communication skills—they speak English, have email, and are reliable with bookings. Anywhere you stay here requires some climbing, but keep in mind that more climbing means better views. Most do not include breakfast. Cash is preferred or required almost everywhere. Night noise can be a problem if you're near the station. Rooms on the harbor come with church bells (but only between 7:00 and 22:00).

Guest Houses (Pensiones)

$$$ Gianni Franzi, a busy restaurant on the harbor square, runs the closest thing to a big hotel that Vernazza has got. Its 25 small rooms are scattered across three buildings that are one hundred tight, winding stairs above the harbor square. Some rooms (including a few cheaper ones with shared bathrooms) are funky and decorated à la shipwreck, with tiny balconies and grand sea views; the comfy, newer rooms lack views. All rooms have access to a super-scenic cliff-hanging guests' garden and the panoramic terrace (where breakfast is served in season). Check-in before 16:00 or call to explain when you're coming. Emanuele, Simona, Caterina, and the staff speak a little English (RS%, closed Jan-Feb, Piazza Marconi 1, tel. 0187-812-228, tel. 0187-821-003, mobile 393-9008-155, www.giannifranzi.it, info@giannifranzi.it). Pick up your keys at the Gianni Franzi restaurant on the harbor square (on Wed, when the restaurant is closed, call ahead to make other arrangements).

$ Albergo Barbara rents nine basic-but-tidy top-floor rooms overlooking the square. Only a few rooms have real views; most have small windows and small views. It's a good value in a nice location, run by Alessio and Alberto (cheaper rooms with shared bath are a good value, more for views, closed Dec-Feb, reserve online with credit card but pay cash, piles of stairs, Piazza Marconi 30, tel. 0187-812-398, www.albergobarbara.it, info@albergobarbara.it).

Rooms for Rent (Affittacamere)

Vernazza lacks any real hotels, and almost all of my listings are *affittacamere* (private rooms for rent). I favor hosts who rent multiple rooms, speak just enough English, have email, and are reliable. Most places accept only cash and don't include breakfast. Some have killer views; some come with lots of stairs.

While a few places have all their beds in one building, most have rooms scattered over town. Some have an informal "reception desk" (sometimes at a restaurant or other business) where you can check in. But many places have no reception at all. (On the Vernazza map, I've marked only places that have a fixed address or reception office; if I say "reception," you'll check in there, then continue on to your actual room.)

Because this can be confusing, clearly communicate your arrival time (by phone or email) and get instructions on where to meet the owner and pick up the keys. In some cases, they'll meet you at the train station—but only if they know when you're coming.

INLAND

$$ Camere Fontana Vecchia, run by Annamaria, has eight bright and cheery rooms overlooking the ravine and its rushing river (cheaper room with shared bath, more for terrace, Via Gavino 15, tel. 0187-821-130, mobile 333-454-9371, www. cinqueterrecamere.com, m.annamaria@ libero.it).

$$ Giuliano Basso's four carefully crafted, well-appointed rooms form a cozy little compound on the green hillside just above town, straddling a ravine among orange trees. Giuliano—the town's last stone-layer—proudly built the place himself (2 rooms have air-con, more train noise than others; follow the main road up above the station, take the ramp up toward Corniglia just before Pensione Sorriso, follow the path, and watch for a sharp left turn; mobile 333-341-4792, www. cameregiuliano.com, giuliano@cdh.it).

$$ Tonino Basso has four overpriced but colorful rooms in a drab, elevator-equipped, modern apartment block (air-con, Via Gavino 34, mobile 339-761-1651, www.toninobasso.com, Alessandra).

$ La Rosa dei Venti ("The Compass Rose"), run by Giuliana Basso, houses three airy, good-value rooms in her childhood home, on the third floor of an apartment building (call to arrange meeting time, air-con, Via Gavino 19, mobile 333-762-4679, www.larosadeiventi-vernazza. it, info@larosadeiventi-vernazza.it).

SCATTERED THROUGH TOWN AND THE HARBORSIDE

For the places not located on the map in this chapter, arrange a meeting time and/or ask for directions when you reserve.

$$$ La Malà is Vernazza's jet-setter pad. Four crisp, pristine white rooms boast fancy-hotel-type extras and a common seaview terrace. It's a climb—way up to the top of town—but they'll carry your bags to and from the station. Book early—this place fills up quickly (includes breakfast at a bar, family rooms, air-con, mobile 334-287-5718, www.lamala.it, info@lamala.it, charming Giamba and his mama, Amanda). They also rent the simpler **$ "Armanda's Room"** nearby—a great value, since you get Giamba's attention to detail and amenities without paying for a big view (includes simple breakfast, air-con).

$$$ Francamaria and her husband Andrea rent 10 sharp, comfortable, and creatively renovated rooms—all detailed on her website. Their reception desk is on the harbor square (on the ground floor at Piazza Marconi 30), but the rooms they manage are all over town (family rooms, some with air-con, spotty Wi-Fi, tel. 0187-812-002, mobile 328-711-9728, www.francamaria.com, info@francamaria.com).

$$$ Nicolina Rooms consists of seven units in three different buildings. Two cheaper rooms are in the center over the pharmacy, up a few steep steps; another, pricier studio with a terrace is on a twisty lane above the harbor; and four more rooms are in a building beyond the church, with great views and church bells (all include breakfast, Piazza Marconi 29—check in at Pizzeria Vulnetia, tel. 0187-821-193, mobile 333-842-6879, www.camerenicolina.it, camerenicolina.info@cdh.it).

$$ La Marina Rooms is run by hard-working Christian, who speaks English and happily meets guests at the station to carry bags. There are five well-tended (if slightly dated) units, most high above the main street: One single works as a (very) tight double, and three doubles share a fine oceanview terrace; they also have two **$$$** apartments—one with terrace and sea views, and the other on the harborfront square (mobile 338-476-7472, www. lamarinarooms.com, mapcri@yahoo.it).

\$\$ Martina Callo's four old-fashioned, spartan rooms overlook the harbor square; they're up plenty of steps near the silent-at-night church tower. While the rooms are simple, guests pay for and appreciate the views (family rooms, cheaper nonview room, air-con, ring bell at Piazza Marconi 26, tel. 0187-812-365, mobile 329-435-5344, www.roomartina.it, roomartina@roomartina.it).

\$\$ Rosa Vitali rents two four-person apartments across from the pharmacy overlooking the main street (and beyond the train noise). One has a terrace and fridge (top floor); the other has windows and a full kitchen (family rooms, ring bell at Via Visconti 10—just before the tobacco shop near Piazza Marconi, tel. 0187-821-181, mobile 340-267-5009, www. rosacamere.it, rosa.vitali@libero.it).

\$ Memo Rooms rents three clean and spacious rooms overlooking the main street, in what feels like a miniature hotel. Enrica will meet you if you call upon arrival (Via Roma 15, try Enrica's mobile first at 338-285-2385, otherwise tel. 0187-812-360, www.memorooms.com, info@memorooms.com).

\$ Monica Lercari rents several rooms with modern comforts, perched at the top of town (more for seaview terrace, includes breakfast, air-con, tel. 0187-812-296, mobile 320-025-4515, alcastellovernazza@yahoo.it). Monica and her husband, Massimo, run the Ristorante al Castello, in the old castle tower overlooking town.

CORNIGLIA

If you think of the Cinque Terre as The Beatles, Corniglia is Ringo. The only town of the Cinque Terre not on the water, Corniglia (pop. 240) is less visited and feels remote. It has cooler temperatures, a few restaurants, and a windy overlook on its promontory. Signs that say al mare or Marina lead from the town center steeply down to sunning rocks below the train station. The one-time beach has all been washed away.

According to legend, this tiny, sleepy town's ancient residents produced a wine so famous that vases found at Pompeii touted its virtues. Wine remains Corniglia's lifeblood today.

Orientation

Arrival in Corniglia: From the **train station,** located deep in a ravine, a footpath zigzags up 385 steps to town (allow at least 20 minutes). Thankfully, the shuttle bus—generally timed to meet arriving trains—connects the station with the hill town's Ciappà square (2/hour). **Drivers** can park on the main road into town, but check signs—spots closest to town are for residents only.

Rick's Tip: To avoid the steep hike to Corniglia and the long descent to the train station, **use the handy shuttle bus.** Upon arrival in town (where a schedule is posted at the bus stop), jot down the departure times for the bus and plan your time accordingly.

Tourist Information: A TI/park information office is down at the train station (likely daily 8:00-20:00, shorter hours off-season).

◉ Corniglia Walk

This self-guided walk might take up to 30 minutes...but only if you let yourself browse and lick a gelato cone.
• Begin near the shuttle bus stop, located at the...

Town Square: The gateway to this community is Ciappà square, with an ATM, phone booth, old wine press, and bus stop.
• Look for the arrow pointing to the **centro.** Stroll the spine of the town—Via Fieschi. In the fall, the smell of grapes becoming wine wafts from busy cellars. Along this main street, you'll see...

Enticing Shops: As you enter Via Fieschi, a trio of neighboring, fiercely competitive gelaterie jockey for your business. My favorite is **Alberto's Gelateria** (at #74).

Corniglia

Trail to Vernazza

To Vernazza

LOC. CANALE

VIA SERRA

LOC. CHIOSO

VIA ALLA STAZIONE

3

385 STEPS

B

VIA ALLA MARINA

VIA FIESCHI

VIA

VIA LARDARINA

Harbor

1 **2**

"CIAPPÀ" SQUARE & BUS STOP

To Manarola

B

SANTA MARIA BELVEDERE

LARGO TARAGIO & ORATORY

TRAIN STATION

SWIMMING

Ligurian Sea

Restaurants
1 Osteria Mananan
2 Enoteca il Pirùn
3 La Posada Ristorante

N

200 Meters
200 Yards

Before ordering, get a free taste of *miele di Corniglia,* made from local honey.

Farther along, on the left, **Enoteca il Pirùn**—named for an oddly shaped old-fashioned wine pitcher—is a cool cantina at Via Fieschi 115. Sample some local wines (small tastes generally free, or €3/glass). If you drink out of the *pirùn,* Mario will give you a bib. While this is a practical matter (rookies are known to dribble), it also makes a nice souvenir.

A bit farther along are two interesting shops—particularly for picnic shoppers. On the left (#151), Cinzia's shop **Kmo** ("kilometer zero") focuses on locally sourced wines, beers, meats, and cheeses (*panini,* smoothies; daily 10:00-22:00). Across the street, at **Butiega Gastromonia** (#142), Vincenzo and Veronica sell organic local specialties (€3 sandwiches and *antipasti misti* priced by the weight, daily 8:00-19:30). There are good places to picnic farther along on this walk.

• *Following Via Fieschi, you'll end up at the...*

Main Square: On Largo Taragio, tables from two bars and a trattoria spill around a WWI memorial and the town's old well. What looks like a church is the Oratory of Santa Caterina. Up the stairs behind the oratory, you'll find a clearing that children use as a soccer field. The stone benches and viewpoint make it a peaceful place for a picnic.

Hilltop Corniglia

• *From the square, continue up Via Fieschi to the...*

End-of-Town Viewpoint: The Santa Maria Belvedere, named for a church that once stood here, marks the scenic end of Corniglia and makes a super—but sometimes crowded—picnic spot. High to the west (right), the village and sanctuary of San Bernardino straddle a ridge. Below is the tortuous harbor, where locals hoist their boats onto the cruel rocks.

Eating

The typical array of pizzerias, *focaccerie,* and *alimentari* (grocery stores) line the narrow main drag. For a real meal, consider one of these options.

$$ Osteria Mananan—between the Ciappà bus stop and the main square—serves what many say is the best food in town in its stony, elegant interior (Tue-Sun 12:30-14:30 & 19:30-22:00, closed Mon, no outdoor seating, Via Fieschi 117, tel. 0187-821-166).

$$ Enoteca il Pirùn, next door on Via Fieschi, has a small restaurant above the wine bar that serves typical local fare

(daily 12:00-16:00 & 19:30-23:30, tel. 0187-812-315).

$$ La Posada Ristorante offers dinner in a garden under trees, overlooking the Ligurian Sea. To get here, stroll out of town to the top of the stairs that lead down to the station (daily 12:00-16:00 & 19:00-23:00, closed Nov-March, tel. 0187-821-174, mobile 338-232-5734).

MANAROLA

Mellow Manarola feels just right. Its hillsides are blanketed with vineyards and it provides the easiest access to the Cinque Terre's remarkable dry-stone terraces. The trail ringing the town's cemetery peninsula provides some of the most accessible and most striking sea views anywhere.

The town fills a ravine, bookended by its harbor to the west and a hilltop church square to the east. The touristy zone squeezed between the train tracks and the harbor can be congested, but just a few steps uphill, you can breathe again. The higher you go, the less crowded it

Manarola

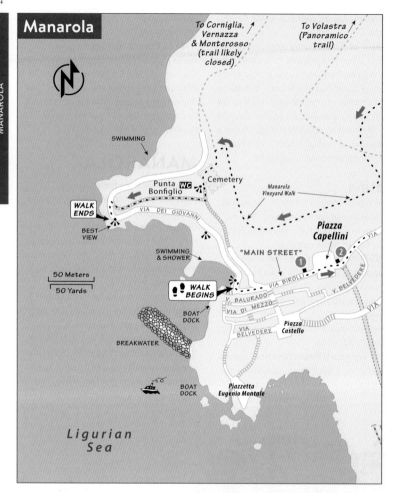

Manarola

To Corniglia,
Vernazza
& Monterosso
(trail likely
closed)

To Volastra
(Panoramico
trail)

SWIMMING

Punta **WC**
Bonfiglio

Cemetery

Manarola
Vineyard Walk

**WALK
ENDS**

BEST
VIEW

VIA DEI GIOVANNI

Manarola
Vineyard Walk

*Piazza
Capellini*

VIA

"MAIN STREET"

SWIMMING
& SHOWER

50 Meters

50 Yards

1

2

**WALK
BEGINS**

VIA BIROLLI

V. BELVEDERE

BOAT
DOCK

V. BALURADO

VIA DI MEZZO

VIA

BREAKWATER

VIA
BELVEDERE

*Piazza
Castello*

BOAT
DOCK

*Piazzetta
Eugenio Montale*

*Ligurian
Sea*

---

gets, culminating in the residential zone that clings to the ridge.

Orientation

Arrival in Manarola: The town is attached to its **train station** by a 200-yard-long tunnel. Walking through the tunnel, you'll reach Manarola's elevated square. To reach the hilltop church and vineyard strolls, turn right. Or, to reach the busy harbor, cross the square, then go down the other side. The **boat** docks near the base of the main street and the start of my self-guided walk.

Drivers can park in one of the two lots just before town (€2/hour), then walk down the road to the church; from there, the street twists down to the main piazza, train-station tunnel, and harbor.

Tourist Information: The TI/national park information office is in the train station (likely daily 7:30-19:30, shorter hours off-season).

Shuttle Bus: The ATC shuttle bus runs from near the post office (halfway up Manarola's main street), stopping first at the parking lots above town, and then going up to Volastra (about 2/hour).

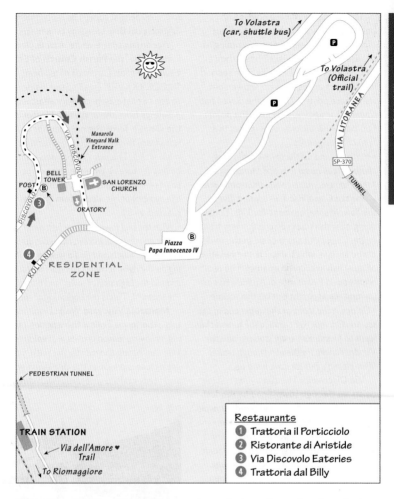

Restaurants
1 Trattoria il Porticciolo
2 Ristorante di Aristide
3 Via Discovolo Eateries
4 Trattoria dal Billy

Hiking Gear and Tips: Cinque Terre Trekking, near the top of the main street (halfway up to the church), fills its shop with hiking gear (boots, clothes, walking sticks, and more); they also sell hiking maps and offer free advice (daily 10:00-13:00 & 14:00-19:00, shorter hours off-season, Via Discovolo 136, tel. 0187-920-834, www.cinqueterretrekking.com).

◗ Manarola Walk

From the harbor, this 45-minute, self-guided circular walk shows you the town and surrounding vineyards and ends at a fantastic viewpoint, perfect for a picnic.

• *Start down at the waterfront. Belly up to the wooden banister overlooking the rocky harbor, between the two restaurants.*

The Harbor: Manarola is a picturesque tumble of buildings bunny-hopping down its ravine to the fun-loving waterfront. The breakwater was built just over a decade ago.

Facing the water, look up to the right, at the hillside Punta Bonfiglio cemetery and park. The trail running around the base of the point—where this walk ends—offers magnificent views.

The town's swimming hole is just below you. Manarola has no sand, but offers the best deep-water swimming in the area. The first "beach" has a shower, ladder, and wonderful rocks. The second has tougher access and no shower, but feels more pristine (follow the paved path toward Corniglia, just around the point). For many, the tricky access makes this "beach" dangerous.

• Hiking inland up the town's main drag, climb a steep ramp to reach Manarola's "new" square, which covers the train tracks.

Piazza Capellini: This square gives the town a safe, fun zone for kids. Locals living near the tracks also enjoy less train noise. Check out the mosaic in the middle of the square, which depicts the varieties of local fish in colorful enamel. The recommended Ristorante di Aristide has an inviting terrace right out on the square.

• Go down the stairs at the upper end of the square. On your right, notice the tunnel that leads to Manarola's train station (and the Via dell'Amore trailhead—though trail is likely closed). But for now, head up...

Via Discovolo: The sleepy main street twists up through town, lined by modest shops. Just before the road bends sharply right, watch (on the right) for a waterwheel. Mills like this once powered the local olive oil industry. Manarola's stream was covered over by a modern sewage system after World War II. Before then, romantic bridges arched over its ravine. You can peek below the concrete street in several places to see the stream surging below your feet.

Across the street from the waterwheel and a bit farther up, notice the helpful **Cinque Terre Trekking** shop (on your left).

• Keep switchbacking up until you come to the square at the...

Top of Manarola: The square is faced by a church, an oratory, and a bell tower which once served as a watchtower. Behind the church is a hostel, originally the church's schoolhouse. To the right of the oratory, a stepped lane leads to Mana-rola's residential zone. The recommended Trattoria dal Billy is nearby (see map).

According to the white marble plaque in its facade, the **Parish Church of St. Lawrence** (San Lorenzo) dates from "MCCCXXXVIII" (1338). Step inside to see two late-15th-century altarpiece paintings from the unnamed Master of the Cinque Terre, the only painter of any note from this region (left wall and above main altar). The humble painted stone ceiling features Lawrence, the patron saint of the Cinque Terre, with his grill, the symbol of his martyrdom (he was roasted on it).

• With the bell tower on your left, head about 20 yards back down the main street below the church and find a wooden railing on the right. It marks the start of a stroll around the high side of town, and back to the seafront. This is the beginning of the...

Manarola Vineyard Walk: Don't miss this experience. Follow the wooden railing, enjoying lemon groves and wild red valerian. Along the mostly flat path, you'll get a close-up look at the dry-stone walls and finely crafted vineyards (with dried-

Church of St. Lawrence

Vineyards above Manarola

Manarola's cemetery

heather thatches to protect the grapes from the southwest winds). Smell the rosemary and pick out the remains of an old fort. Notice the S-shape of the main road, which was once a riverbed. The town's roofs are made of locally quarried slate, rather than tile, and are held down by rocks during windstorms.

Halfway along the lip of the ravine, a path marked *Panoramico Volastra (Corniglia)* leads steeply up into the vineyards on the right. This path passes a variety of simple wooden religious scenes, the work of local resident Mario Andreoli. Before his father died, Mario promised him he'd replace the old cross on the family's vineyard—he's been adding figures ever since.

High above, a recent fire burned off the tree cover, revealing ancient terraces that line the terrain. This path also marks the start of the scenic route to Volastra (on the hilltop above), and eventually to Corniglia (see page 591).

• *Continue on the level trail around the base of the hill. Soon the harbor comes into view. Keep looping around the hill for even better views of town. Once you're facing the sea (after passing the cemetery peninsula below you), the trail takes a sharp left and heads down toward the water on concrete steps. When you're almost back to town, you'll see the entrance (on your right) to...*

The Cemetery: Ever since Napoleon—who was king of Italy in the early 1800s—decreed that cemeteries were health risks, Cinque Terre's burial spots have been

located outside the towns. The result: The dearly departed get first-class views. Each cemetery—with evocative yellowed photos and finely carved Carrara marble memorials—is worth a visit.

• *The Manarola cemetery is on...*

Punta Bonfiglio: This point offers commanding views of the entire region. For the best vantage point, take the stairs just below the cemetery (through the green gate), then walk farther out toward the water through a park. Your Manarola finale is the bench at the tip of the point. Pause and take in the view. The easiest way back to town is to take the stairs at the end of the point, which join the main walking path—offering more views on the way back to the harbor.

Eating

These restaurant options are listed from lowest to highest, in terms of elevation.

Touristy restaurants are concentrated in the tight zone between Piazza Capellini and the harbor. While these are mostly interchangeable, the Scorza family works hard at **$$ Trattoria il Porticciolo** (Thu-Tue 12:00-21:30, closed Wed, Via Birolli 92, tel. 0187-920-083).

$$ Ristorante di Aristide, right on Piazza Capellini, offers trendy atmosphere and a pleasant outdoor setting (Fri-Wed 12:00-22:30). Down the stairs, at the bottom of the main street, is their simpler **$ café** with indoor and streetside seating and breakfast options (Fri-Wed from 8:00, food served until restaurant opens for dinner, both closed Thu and Jan-Feb, Via Discovolo 290, tel. 0187-920-000).

Via Discovolo, the main street climbing up through town from Piazza Capellini to the church, is lined with simpler places, including some grocery stores and a *gelateria.*

Up at the top of town, in the residential zone above the church, **$$$ Trattoria dal Billy** offers both good food and impressive views over the valley. For black pasta with seafood and squid ink, mixed seafood starters, and homemade desserts, it's worth the climb. Across the street is an elegant dining room carved into the rock. Either setting is perfect for a romantic candlelight meal. Reservations are a must (Fri-Wed 12:00-15:00 & 18:00-22:00, closed Thu, Via Aldo Rollandi 122, tel. 0187-920-628, www.trattoriabilly.com).

RIOMAGGIORE

Riomaggiore is a laid-back, workaday town that feels more "real" than its touristy neighbors. The main drag through town, while traffic-free, feels more urban than "village," and surrounding the harbor is a fascinating tangle of pastel homes leaning on each other like drunken sailors.

Orientation

Arrival in Riomaggiore: The **train station** is separated from the town center by a steep hill. The easiest way to get into town is to take the pedestrian tunnel that begins by the big mural (and parallels the rail tunnel). You'll exit at the bottom of Via Colombo, the main street. Other options: You can take my self-guided walk into town; catch the shuttle bus at the bottom of Via Colombo and ride it partway up; or ride the elevator up from the pedestrian tunnel (€1/person, daily 7:00-18:00). The **boat** docks near the base of Via Colombo. **Drivers** can park at one of two pay-and-display lots above town (€3.50/hour, €23/day, best to pay in cash).

Tourist Information: The TI is in the train station at the ticket desk (daily 8:00-20:00, shorter hours off-season). If it's

Jumping for joy in Riomaggiore

crowded, you can buy your park card at the Cinque Terre park info/shop office next door (daily 8:00-20:00, shorter hours off-season).

Baggage Storage: You can check your bag at the casually run bar that also functions as the *deposito bagagli* office, which is straight ahead as you exit the station (€5/bag, daily 8:30-19:00, closed in winter).

◆ Riomaggiore Walk

This partly uphill but easy self-guided loop takes the long way from the station into town. Enjoy some fine views before strolling down the main street to the harbor.

• *Start at the train station. (If you arrive by boat, cross beneath the tracks and take a left, then hike through the tunnel along the tracks to reach the station.) You'll see some...*

Faded Murals: These murals, which may be removed due to their poor condition, glorify the nameless workers who constructed the nearly 300 million cubic feet of dry-stone walls that run through-

out the Cinque Terre. The walls, made without mortar, give the region its characteristic *muri a secco* terracing for vineyards and olive groves.

Looking left, notice the stairs climbing up just past the station building. These lead to the trail to Manarola, also known as the **Via dell'Amore** (likely closed for repairs).

• *. Facing the mural, turn left, then go right up the wide street just before the station café. Head up this street for about 100 yards, and watch for the stairs leading through the garden on your right to the upper switchback. Then, once on high ground, turn right (back toward the sea). Soon you'll pass the top of the concrete elevator tower and, a bit farther, arrive at a fine viewpoint.*

Top o' the Town: Here you're treated to spectacular sea views. Hook left around the bluff; once you round the bend, ignore the steps marked *Marina Seacoast* (which lead to the harbor) and continue another five minutes along level ground to the church (follow *salita castello* signs). You'll go by the City Hall, with murals celebrating the heroic grape-pickers and fishermen of

Riomaggiore's harbor

Restaurants
1. Bar Centrale
2. Trattoria la Grotta & Il Grottino Ristorante
3. Bar & Vini A Piè de Mà
4. Rio Bistrot
5. Enoteca & Ristorante Dau Cila
6. Primo Piatto
7. Il Pescato Cucinato
8. Tutti Fritti
9. Alimentari Franca

the region (also by Silvio Benedetto).
• *Before reaching the church, pause at the big terrace to enjoy the...*

Town View: The major river of this region once ran through this valley, as implied by the name Riomaggiore (local dialect for "river" and "major"). As in the other Cinque Terre towns, the river ravine is now paved over. The romantic arched bridges that once connected the two sides have been replaced by a practical modern road.

The church (established in 1340 and rebuilt in 1870) is dedicated to St. John the Baptist, the patron saint of Genoa, the maritime republic that once dominated the region.

• *Continue straight past the church and along the narrow lane, watching on the right for wide stairs leading down to Riomaggiore's main street...*

Via Colombo: Starting downhill, you'll pass (on the right, at #62) a good pizzeria/*focacceria*, facing the Co-op grocery store across the street (at #55). Below that is a delicious fresh pasta takeaway place (Primo Piatto, at #72). Farther along, the big covered terrace on the right belongs to Bar Centrale (at #144), the town's most popular hangout.

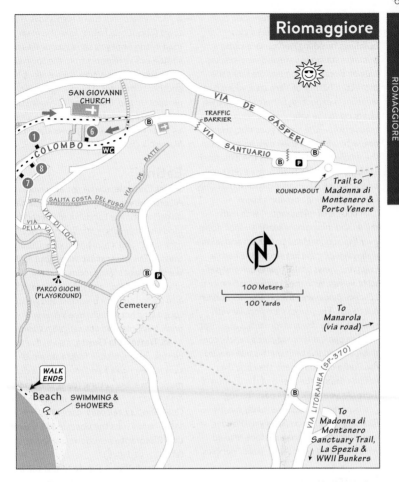

As you round the bend to the left, notice the old-time pharmacy just above (on the right). On your left, at #199, peek into the Il Pescato Cucinato shop, where Laura fries up her husband Edoardo's fresh catch; grab a paper cone of deep-fried seafood as a snack. Where the road bends sharply right, notice the bench on your left (just before La Zorza Café), probably occupied by the town's old-timers, who keep a running commentary on the steady flow of people. Straight ahead, you can already see where this street will dead-end. The last shop on the left, Alimentari Franca (at #251), is a well-stocked grocery where you can gather the makings for a picnic.

Where Via Colombo dead-ends, look right to see the tunnel leading back to the station. Look left to see two sets of stairs. The "up" stairs take you to a park like square built over the train tracks, which provides the children of the town level land on which to kick their soccer balls. The murals above celebrate the great-grandparents of these very children—the salt-of-the-earth locals who earned a humble living before the age of tourism.

• The "down" stairs take you to a pay WC and the...

Marina: This most picturesque corner of Riomaggiore features a cluster of buildings huddling nervously around a postage-stamp square and vest-pocket harbor. Because Riomaggiore lacks the protected harbor of Vernazza, when bad weather is expected, fishermen pull their boats up to the safety of the square. It's a team effort—the signal goes out, and anyone with a boat of their own helps move the whole fleet. Sometimes the fishermen are busy beaching their boats even on a bright, sunny day—an indication that they know something you don't know.

A couple of restaurants—with high prices and memorable seating—look down over the action. Head past them and up the walkway along the left side of the harbor. Enjoy the views of the town's colorful pastel buildings, with the craggy coastline just beyond. Below you, the breakwater curves out to sea. These rocks are popular with sunbathers by day and romantics at sunset.

For a peek at Riomaggiore's beach, continue around the bluff on this trail toward the Punta di Montenero, the cape that defines the southern end of the Cinque Terre. As you walk you'll pass the rugged boat landing and eventually run into Riomaggiore's beach (spiaggia). Ponder how Europeans manage to look relaxed when lounging on football-sized "pebbles."

Experiences

Riomaggiore's rugged **beach** (spiaggia) is rocky, but still peaceful and inviting. There's a shower here in the summer, and another closer to town by the boat landing—where many enjoy sunning on and jumping from the rocks.

The town has a **diving center** that rents scuba, snorkeling, and kayaking gear (daily May-Sept 9:00-18:00, open in good weather only—likely weekends only in shoulder season, office down the stairs and under the tracks on Via San Giacomo, tel. 0187-920-011, www.5terrediving.it).

A **hiking trail** rises scenically from Riomaggiore to the 14th-century Madonna di Montenero sanctuary, high above the town (about one hour). Take the main road inland until you see signs, or ride the shuttle bus 12 minutes from the town center to the sanctuary trail, then walk uphill another 15 minutes. There's a great picnic spot up top. If the Via dell'Amore trail to Manarola is closed, consider the steep 1.5-hour hike on trail #531 over the bluff to Manarola (see page 569).

Eating

$$ Bar Centrale, run by sociable Ivo and Alberto, serves Italian specialties (pasta dishes, anchovies) and American comfort food (hamburgers) with San Franciscan rock music and a fun-loving vibe. During the day, this popular expat hangout feels like the village's living room. At night, it offers lively action and great mojitos. It's also a good spot for breakfast and gelato (open long hours daily, free Wi-Fi with drink, Via Colombo 144, tel. 0187-920-208).

$$ Trattoria la Grotta, also in the town center, serves reliable food with a passion for anchovies and mussels in a dramatic, cave-like setting (daily 12:00-14:30 & 17:30-22:30, closed Wed in winter, Via Colombo 247, tel. 0187-920-187). The same family runs the upscale **$$$ Il Grottino Ristorante** next door (same hours, tel. 0187-920-938).

$$ Bar & Vini A Piè de Mà, at the Via dell'Amore trailhead on the Manarola end of town, has piles of charm. A meal or cocktail on its terrace offers striking, memorable views (daily 10:00-20:00, June-Sept until 24:00, free Wi-Fi, tel. 0187-921-037).

$$$$ Rio Bistrot, small and intimate at the top of the harbor, tries to jazz up its Ligurian cuisine with international influences. You can order à la carte but they tend to push their €39 tasting menu (simpler and cheaper lunch menu, daily 12:00-16:00 & 18:00-22:00, Via San Giacomo 46, tel. 0187-920-616).

$$$$ Enoteca & Ristorante Dau Cila (pronounced "dow CHEE-lah") is a mel-

Kayakers flock to Riomaggiore.

The catch of the day

low hideaway in a centuries-old boat shed on the harbor, with extra tables on a rustic deck. It's cool for cocktails, with a jazz-and-Brazilian-lounge ambience (daily 12:00-24:00, closed Feb, Via San Giacomo 65, tel. 0187-760-032).

Various eateries along the main drag, which you'll encounter on my self-guided walk, offer good lunches or snacks. At the top of town, **$ Primo Piatto** offers take-away handmade pastas and sauces—it's cheap and delicious (Wed-Mon 10:30-19:30 or later, closed Tue, Via Colombo 72, tel. 0187-920-038). For deep-fried seafood in a paper cone, try **$ Il Pescato Cucinato,** where the chalkboard out front explains what's fresh (11:20-20:30, Via Colombo 199, mobile 339-262-4815), or **$ Tutti Fritti,** a few doors away (daily 10:00-21:00, Via Colombo 161, mobile 347-826-1729).

For picnic supplies, head to handy **Alimentari Franca,** at the bottom of the main street, conveniently located right by the train-station tunnel and stairs down to the marina (daily 8:00-20:00, Via Colombo 251).

TRANSPORTATION

Getting Around the Cinque Terre

The five towns are close together and have good public transportation connections by train and boat (as well as hiking trails). Little shuttle buses provide local transport per town.

By Train

By train, the five towns are just a few minutes apart. Along the coast here, trains go in only two directions: northbound toward Genoa; or southbound toward La Spezia.

A train ride of any length between Cinque Terre towns costs a hefty €4 during peak times—whether you're hopping one town or four. You must buy a new ticket for every train ride, and tickets are valid only on the day of purchase. Purchase tickets online (at www.trenitalia.com), at station windows, Cinque Terre park desks, or self-service machines. The €16 **Cinque Terre Treno Multi-Service Card** can be worthwhile (even if you don't hike), because it provides the easiest way to train-hop, allowing you to catch trains at the last minute without ticket concerns. It pays for itself if you take four rides in one day, but its value comes more from its convenience than its economy.

Validate your ticket or card before you board by stamping it in the green-and-white machines on platforms and in station passages, but note these exceptions: Printed online tickets and smartphone e-tickets are prevalidated. Conductors levy stiff fines for riding with a ticket that hasn't been validated.

Rick's Tip: *If you have a* **Eurail Pass,** *don't spend one of your valuable travel days on the relatively cheap Cinque Terre.*

Trains run about twice hourly in each direction, connecting all five towns. Shops, hotels, and restaurants often post the current schedule, and may also hand out copies. Check the key on the printed schedules carefully: certain departures listed are for only weekdays, only Sundays, etc.

In the **station,** real-time **monitors** are the best, most current source of information. They show the departure times and directions of the next trains (and if they're late—*in ritardo; SOPP* means "cancelled"). Northbound trains are marked for *(per)* Levanto, Genoa *(Genova),* or Sestri Levante; southbound trains are marked for La Spezia. To be sure you get on the right train, know your train's number and final destination.

Important: Any train stopping at Vernazza, Corniglia, or Manarola is going to all the towns. Trains from Levanto, Monterosso, Riomaggiore, or La Spezia sometimes skip lesser stations, so confirm that the train will stop at the town you need.

Accept the unpredictability of Cinque Terre trains—they're often late. Relax while you wait—buy an ice cream or cup of coffee at a station bar. Scout the platform you need in advance, and then, when the train comes, hop on.

Know your stop. The train stations are small and the trains are long, so (especially in Vernazza and Monterosso) you might have to get off deep in a tunnel—if this happens to you, just head toward daylight. The door won't open automatically—push the green button, twist the black handle, or lift up the red one. If a door isn't working, go quickly to the next car to try another.

By Boat

From Easter through October, **daily boat service** connects Monterosso, Vernazza, Manarola, Riomaggiore, Porto Venere, and beyond. In peaceful weather, boats can be more reliable than trains, but if seas are rough, they don't run at all.

Boats depart Monterosso about hourly (10:30-18:00), stopping at the Cinque Terre towns (except for hilltop Corniglia) and ending up an hour later in nearby Porto Venere. (Porto Venere-Monterosso boats run 8:50-18:00.) The ticket price depends on the length of the boat ride (ranging from €6 for a short ride between towns, to €18 for a five-town, one-way ticket with stops; an all-day pass is €25, or €33 to include Porto Venere).

Buy **tickets** at stands at each town's harbor (tel. 0187-818-440). **Schedules** are posted at docks, harbor bars, Cinque Terre park offices, and hotels (www.navigazionegolfodeipoeti.it).

Rick's Tip: *In calm weather,* **boats connect the towns about as frequently as the trains,** *though at different times; if you're in a rush, take whichever form of transport is leaving first. In the unpredictable Cinque Terre, a departure now is worth two a little later.*

By Shuttle Bus

ATC shuttle buses (which locals call *pulmino*) connect each town with its closest parking lot and various points in the hills—but do not connect the towns with each other. The one you're most likely to use runs between Corniglia's sea-level train station and its hilltop town center. Most rides cost €1.50 one-way (€2.50 from driver, free with Cinque Terre park card). Ask about tickets and bus schedules at park info offices or TIs, or note the times posted at bus stops. Shuttle schedules change constantly; confirm the details carefully. Shuttles may not run from 12:30 to 15:00, when they break for lunch. As you board, tell the driver where you want to go. Departures often coordinate with train arrival times. Some shuttles go beyond the parking lots and high into the hills. To soak in the scenery, ride up and hike down, or just ride both ways (30-45 minutes covered by one ticket).

Arriving and Departing

By Train

Most big, fast trains from elsewhere in Italy speed right past the Cinque Terre, though some stop in Monterosso. Unless you're coming from a nearby town, you'll usually have to change trains at least once to reach Vernazza, Corniglia, or Manarola.

Generally, if you're coming from the north, you'll change trains at Genoa's Piazza Principe station, Sestri Levante, Levanto, or Monterosso. If you're coming from the south or east, you'll probably switch trains at La Spezia's Centrale station (not La Spezia Migliarina). Check your full schedule and route options in the train station before you leave (use the kiosks or ask at a ticket window).

TRAIN CONNECTIONS

The five towns of the Cinque Terre are on a milk-run line, with trains coming through about every 30 minutes (and connecting with La Spezia and Levanto). For points beyond the Cinque Terre (for example, Milan or Pisa), you'll usually have to change in La Spezia, Monterosso, Levanto, or Sestri Levante.

From Monterosso by Train to: Venice (5/day, 6 hours, change in Milan), **Milan** (8/day direct, otherwise hourly with change in Genoa, 3 hours), **Genoa** (hourly, 1.5 hours), **Pisa** (hourly, 1-1.5 hours), **Sestri Levante** (hourly, 30 minutes, most trains to Genoa stop here), **La Spezia** (2-3/hour, 15-30 minutes), **Levanto** (2-3/hour, 4 minutes), **Rome** (hourly, 4.5 hours, change in La Spezia).

From La Spezia Centrale by Train to:
Rome (8/day direct, more with transfers in Pisa, 3-4.5 hours), **Pisa** (about hourly, 1 hour), **Florence** (5/day direct, 2.5 hours, otherwise nearly hourly with change in Pisa), **Milan** (about hourly, 3 hours direct or with change in Genoa), **Venice** (about hourly, 5-6 hours, 1-3 changes).

By Taxi

Cinqueterre Taxi covers all five towns, providing transport to the nearest port or airport (mobile 334-776-1946 or 347-652-0837, www.cinqueterretaxi.com). The pricey **5 Terre Transfer** service can connect the five towns or beyond (Luciana mobile 339-130-1183; Marzio mobile 340-356-5268).

By Car

Given the narrow roads and lack of parking, bringing a car to the Cinque Terre is a bad idea. Consider parking in **Levanto** or **La Spezia** and riding the train into town. Or for simplicity, stay at a Cinque Terre hotel with parking; for this, **Monterosso** is your best bet (and it has parking lots in town). Each Cinque Terre town has a parking lot (handy for day-trippers) on its outskirts, with a shuttle bus into town. Try to arrive between 9:00 and 11:00, when overnight visitors are usually departing. But don't drive to **Vernazza,** where parking is particularly tight.

It's smart to have your hotel confirmation in hand during busy times—holidays, summer, and weekends—when police at the top of town may deny entry to cars without a hotel reservation. The rare street parking in the towns is best left for locals. Wherever you park, leave nothing of value in your car.

Venice

Venice is a world apart. Built on a hundred islands, its exotic-looking palaces are laced together by graceful bridges over sun-speckled canals. Romantics revel in the city's atmosphere of elegant decay, seeing the peeling plaster as a metaphor for beauty in decline. And first-time visitors are often stirred deeply, waking from their ordinary lives to a fantasy world unlike anything they've ever seen.

Those are strong reactions, considering that Venice today, frankly, can also be an overcrowded tourist trap. While there are about 270,000 people in greater Venice (counting the mainland, not counting tourists), the Old Town has a small-town feel. To see Venice away from the touristic flak, escape the Rialto-San Marco tourist zone and savor the town early and late. At night, when the hordes of day-trippers have gone, another Venice appears. Glide in a gondola through quiet canals. Dance across a floodlit square. Pretend it's Carnevale, don a mask—or just a clean shirt—and become someone else for a night.

VENICE IN 2 DAYS

Venice's greatest sight is the city itself, easily worth two days. It can be Europe's best medieval wander if you make time to stroll and explore.

Day 1: In the morning, take the slow vaporetto #1 from the train station down the Grand Canal to St. Mark's Square. Stop off midway at the Rialto market (Rialto Mercato) to grab an early lunch at the *cicchetti* (appetizer) bars nearby. Resume your ride down the Grand Canal to St. Mark's Square. Spend the afternoon on the square, visiting your choice of St. Mark's Basilica, Doge's Palace, Bridge of Sighs, the Correr Museum, and Campanile bell tower (open late in summer).

On any evening: Do a pub crawl for dinner (except on Sun, when most pubs are closed), or dine later at a restaurant. Enjoy a gondola ride (or, the budget version, a moonlit vaporetto, ideally one with open-air front seats). Catch a Vivaldi concert. Hum along with the dueling orchestras on St. Mark's Square, whether you get a drink or just stroll.

Day 2: Spend the morning shopping and exploring as you make your way over the Rialto Bridge to the Frari Church for the art. Afterward, head to the Dorsoduro neighborhood for lunch, then devote the afternoon to more art—select from the Accademia (Venetian art), Peggy Guggenheim Collection (modern art), and Ca' Rezzonico (18th-century palace).

Too many museums? Go on a photo safari through back streets and canals.

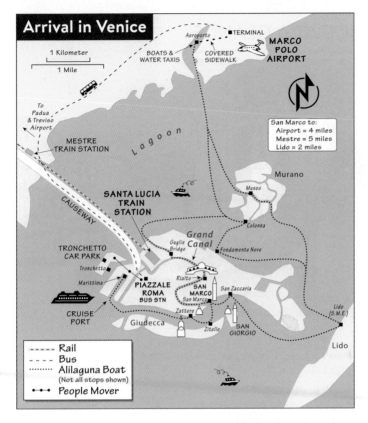

Arrival in Venice

Rail
Bus
Alilaguna Boat
(Not all stops shown)
People Mover

Or take a short vaporetto trip to the San Giorgio Maggiore island for a sublime skyline view of Venice.

With extra time: Visit the lagoon islands of Murano, Burano, and Torcello. For beach time, it's the Lido (across the lagoon via vaporetto). The nearby towns of Padua (with Giotto's frescoed Scrovegni Chapel—reserve ahead) and Verona (with a Roman amphitheater) make great day trips or stops to or from Venice.

Rick's Tip: *Venice is* **crowded with cruise-ship passengers and day-trippers** *daily from 10:00 to about 17:00. Major sights are busiest in the late morning, which makes that a delightful time to explore the back lanes. The sights that have crowd problems get even more packed when it rains.*

ORIENTATION

Venice is shaped like a fish. Its major thoroughfares are canals. The Grand Canal winds through the middle of the fish, starting at the mouth where all the people and food enter, passing under the Rialto Bridge, and ending at St. Mark's Square (Piazza San Marco). Park your 21st-century perspective at the mouth and let Venice swallow you whole.

Venice has six districts *(sestieri):* **San Marco** (from St. Mark's Square to the Accademia Bridge), **Castello** (the area east of St. Mark's Square), **Dorsoduro** (the "belly" of the fish, on the far side of the Accademia Bridge), **Cannaregio** (between the train station and the Rialto Bridge), **San Polo** (west of the Rialto Bridge), and **Santa Croce** (the "eye" of

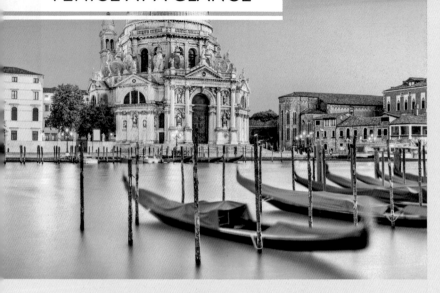

VENICE AT A GLANCE

▲▲▲**St. Mark's Square** Venice's grand main square. **Hours:** Always open. See page 628.

▲▲▲**St. Mark's Basilica** Cathedral with mosaics, saint's bones, treasury, museum, and viewpoint of square. **Hours:** Mon-Sat 9:45-17:00, Sun 14:00-17:00 (until 16:00 Nov-Easter). See page 628.

▲▲▲**Doge's Palace** Art-splashed palace of former rulers, with an attached prison. **Hours:** Daily April-Oct 8:30-19:00, Nov-March 8:30-17:30. See page 634.

▲▲▲**Rialto Bridge** Distinctive bridge spanning the Grand Canal, with a market nearby. **Hours:** Bridge—always open; market—souvenir stalls open daily, produce market closed Sun, fish market closed Sun-Mon. See page 639.

▲▲**Correr Museum** Venetian history and art. **Hours:** Daily April-Oct 10:00-19:00, Nov-March 10:00-17:00. See page 636.

▲▲**Accademia** Venice's top art museum. **Hours:** Mon 8:15-14:00, Tue-Sun 8:15-19:15. See page 637.

▲▲**Peggy Guggenheim Collection** Popular display of 20th-century art. **Hours:** Wed-Mon 10:00-18:00, closed Tue. See page 639.

▲▲**Frari Church** Franciscan church featuring Renaissance masters. **Hours:** Mon-Sat 9:00-18:00, Sun 13:00-18:00. See page 640.

▲▲**Scuola San Rocco** "Tintoretto's Sistine Chapel." **Hours:** Daily 9:30-17:30. See page 640.

▲**Campanile** Dramatic bell tower on St. Mark's Square with elevator to the top. **Hours:** Daily April-mid-Oct 8:30-21:00, mid-Oct-April 9:30-17:30. See page 636.

▲**Bridge of Sighs** Famous enclosed bridge, part of Doge's Palace, near St. Mark's Square. **Hours:** Always viewable. See page 637.

▲**La Salute Church** Striking church dedicated to the Virgin Mary. **Hours:** Daily 9:00-12:00 & 15:00-17:30. See page 639.

▲**Ca' Rezzonico** Posh Grand Canal palazzo with 18th-century Venetian art. **Hours:** Wed-Mon 10:00-18:00, Nov-March until 17:00, closed Tue year-round. See page 639.

Nearby Islands

▲▲**Burano** Sleepy island known for lacemaking and lace museum. **Hours:** Museum open Tue-Sun 10:00-18:00, Nov-March until 17:00, closed Mon year-round. See page 642.

▲**San Giorgio Maggiore** Island facing St. Mark's Square, featuring church with Palladio architecture, Tintoretto paintings, and fine views back on Venice. **Hours:** daily 9:00-19:00, Nov-March 8:30-18:00. See page 637.

▲**Murano** Island famous for glass factories and glassmaking museum. **Hours:** Glass Museum open daily 10:00-18:00, Nov-March until 17:00. See page 641.

▲**Torcello** Near-deserted island with old church, bell tower, and museum. **Hours:** Church—daily March-Oct 10:30-18:00, Nov-Feb 10:00-17:00; museum—closed Mon. See page 643.

▲**Lido** Family-friendly beach. See page 644.

San Michele Cemetery island on the lagoon. **Hours:** Daily 7:30-18:00, Oct-March until 16:30. See page 641.

the fish, across the canal from the train station).

The easiest way to navigate is by landmarks. Many street corners have a sign pointing you to (per) the nearest major landmark, such as San Marco, Accademia, Rialto, Ferrovia (train station), and Piazzale Roma (bus station). Determine whether your destination is in the direction of a major signposted landmark, then follow the signs through the maze. Obedient visitors stick to the main thoroughfares as directed by these signs...but miss the charm of back-street Venice.

Beyond the city's core lie several other islands, including San Giorgio Maggiore (with great views of Venice), San Michele (old cemetery), Murano (famous for glass), Burano (lacemaking), Torcello (old church), and the skinny Lido (with Venice's beach). The island that matters to drivers is Tronchetto, with the huge parking lot at the entrance to Venice.

Rick's Tip: *It's OK to* **get lost in Venice.** *Remind yourself, "I'm on an island, and I can't get off." When it comes time to find your way, just follow the arrows on building corners or simply ask a local,* **"Dov'è San Marco?"** *("Where is St. Mark's?") Most Venetians speak some English. If they don't, listen politely, watch where their hands point, say* **"Grazie,"** *and head in that direction. If you're lost, pop into a hotel and ask for their business card—it probably comes with a map and a prominent "You are here."*

Tourist Information

Venice's TIs are understaffed and don't have many free printed materials. Their websites, www.veneziaunica.it or www.turismovenezia.it, can be more helpful than an actual TI office. If you need to check or confirm something, try phoning the TI information line at 041-2424. Other useful websites are www.museicivicieveneziani.it (city-run museums in Venice), www.unospitedivenezia.it/en

(sights and events), www.veniceexplorer.net (detailed maps), www.veniceforvisitors.com (general travel advice), and www.venicelink.com (travel agent selling public and private transportation tickets).

If you must visit a TI, you'll find offices near **St. Mark's Square** (daily 9:00-19:00, in the far-left corner with your back to the basilica), at the **airport** (daily 9:00-20:00), next to the **bus station** (daily 7:30-19:30, inside the huge white Autorimessa Comunale parking garage), and at the **train station** (across from track 2, daily 7:00-21:00).

Rick's Tip: *Beware of* **travel agencies that masquerade as TIs** *but serve fancy hotels and tour companies. They're in the business of selling things you don't need.*

Maps: Venice demands a good map. Hotels give away freebies, but it's worth investing in a good one (around €5) that shows all the tiny alleys; they're sold at bookstores and newsstands. Also consider a mapping **app** for your smartphone. The **City Maps 2Go** and **Google Maps** apps have good maps that are searchable even when you're not online.

Sightseeing Passes

Venice offers an array of passes for sightseeing and transit. For most people, the best choice is the **Museum Pass,** which covers entry into the Doge's Palace, Correr Museum, Ca' Rezzonico (Museum of 18th-Century Venice), and sights on the islands: the Glass Museum on Murano, and the Lace Museum on Burano. At €24, this pass is the best value if you plan to see the Doge's Palace and Correr Museum and even just one of the other covered museums. Buy it at any TI, the participating museums, or their websites.

Note that some major sights are not covered on any pass, including the Accademia, Peggy Guggenheim Collection, Scuola San Rocco, and the Campanile, along with the three sights within St. Mark's Basilica that charge admission.

Light sightseers could get by with just a €20 **combo-ticket** that covers both the Doge's Palace and the Correr Museum. To bypass the long line at the palace, buy your combo-ticket at the never-crowded Correr or online (but not at TIs).

I'd skip the **Venice Card** (a.k.a. "city pass," covers 12 city-run museums and 16 churches) and the cheaper **San Marco Pack** (covers Doge's Palace and several sights). It's hard to make either of these passes pay off (valid for 7 days, www. veneziaunica.com).

Rolling Venice is a youth pass offering discounts at dozens of sights and shops, but its best deal is for transit. If you're under 30 and want to buy a 72-hour transit pass, it'll cost you just €22 with the pass—rather than €40 (€6 pass for ages 14-29, sold at TIs, vaporetto ticket offices, and VèneziaUnica shops, www. veneziaunica.com).

Tours

🎧 To sightsee on your own, download my **free audio tours** that illuminate some of Venice's top sights (see page 17).

Avventure Bellissime Venice Tours offers several two-hour walks, including a St. Mark's Square tour called the "Original Venice Walking Tour" (€25, includes church entry, most days at 11:00, Sun at 14:00); a 65-minute private boat tour of the Grand Canal (€48, daily at 16:00, 10 people maximum); and a Rialto Market-area food-and-wine tour (€69, in summer 3/week at 11:15; tel. 041-970-499, www.tours-italy.com, info@tours-italy. com). For a 10 percent Rick Steves discount, contact them before booking for a promo code.

Debonair guide **Alessandro Schezzini** organizes two-hour Venetian bar tours, including appetizers and wine at three pubs (€35/person, most nights at 18:00), plus a 1.5-hour Backstreets Tour that gets you into offbeat Venice (€20/person, most nights at 16:30). Tours depart nearly daily when six or more sign up

(book by email—alessandro@schezzini. it—or by phone, mobile 335-530-9024, www.schezzini.it). Meet 50 yards north of the Rialto Bridge under the big clock on Campo San Giacomo.

Artviva Tours offers many intro and themed tours (Grand Canal, Venice Walk, Doge's Palace, Gondola Tour), plus a private "Learn to Be a Gondolier" tour. Rick Steves readers get a 10 percent discount (at www.artviva.com/ricksteves, username "ricksteves" and password "reader").

Walks Inside Venice is enthusiastic about teaching in Venice and outlying destinations (€270/3 hours per group up to 6; or €62.50 for a 2.5-hour walking tour offered Mon-Sat at 14:30; Roberta: mobile 347-253-0560; Sara: mobile 335-522-9714; www.walksinsideitaly.com, info@walksinsidevenice.com). Ask about Rick Steves discounts.

Tour Leader Venice, a.k.a. Treviso Car Service, offers transfers (e.g., to/from airport) and tours outside of Venice, including the Dolomites (mobile 348-900-0700; www.trevisocarservice.com, tvcarservice@ gmail.com).

Helpful Hints

Theft and Safety: The dark, late-night streets of Venice are generally safe. Even so, pickpockets (often well dressed) work the crowded main streets, docks, and **vaporetti.** Your biggest risk is inside St. Mark's Basilica, near the Accademia and Rialto bridges (especially if you're preoccupied with snapping photos), or on a tightly packed vaporetto.

A handy *polizia* station is on the right side of St. Mark's Square as you face the basilica (at #63, near Caffè Florian). To call the police, dial 113. The Venice TI handles complaints—which must be submitted in writing—about crooks, including gondoliers, restaurants, and hotel rip-offs (fax 041-523-0399, complaint.apt@ turismovenezia.it).

It's illegal for street vendors to sell knockoff handbags, and it's also illegal for

Venice

GHETTO

Campo de
Gheto Novo

CANNA

Canale de Cannaregio

To Mestre &
Mainland

GUGLIE
BRIDGE

SAN LEONARDO

SAN
GEREMIA

SAN
MARCUOLA

Grand Canal

SANTA
LUCIA
STATION
(FERROVIA)

SCALZI

LISTA DI SPAGNA

SAN ZAN
DEGOLA

BEMBO

To
Tronchetto
& Mainland

SCALZI
BRIDGE

SAN SIMEONE
GRANDE

SAN
GIACOMO

Campo
S.Giacomo
de l'Orio

SAN SIMEONE
PICCOLO

SANTA CROCE

SAN

CALATRAVA
BRIDGE

P
GARAGE

PEOPLE MOVER

Piazzale
Roma

CA' AMAI

Campo
San Stin

SAN
POLO

To Stazione
Marittima
(Cruise Port)
& Tronchetto
(Parking)

BUS
STATION

SAN NICOLO
DA TOLENTINO

TINTORETTO

SAN
ROCCO

FRARI

Campo
dei Frari

RIO TERA DEI PENSIERI

FOND. DEL RIO NOVO

SCUOLA
SAN ROCCO

Campo
San Rocco

SAN
PANTALON

LARGA

SAN
TOMA

NOMBOLI

SAONERI

T

SANTA
MARGARITA

C. LARGA
FOSCARI

FONDAMENTA FOSCARINI

Campo
Santa
Margarita

CA'
FOSCARI

CA'
REZZONICO

PALAZZO
GRASSI

C. CAR. S. SAM.

SAL. S. SAM.

SANTA MARIA
DEI CARMINI

RIO TERA
CANAL

FOND. S. SEBASTIAN

AVOGARIA

C. LUNGA S. BARNABA

Campo
San Barnaba

SAN
BARNABA

Grand

SAN
SEBASTIAN

SALIZADA SAN BASEGIO

OGNISANTI

TOLETTA

CORFU

ACCADEMIA
BRIDGE

Campo
San Basegio

SAN
TROVASO

ACCADEMIA
GALLERY

AGNESE

RIO TERA
FOSCARINI

N

FONDAMENTA ZATTERE AL PONTE LONGO

DORSO

200 Meters
200 Yards

Giudecca Canal

you to buy them; both you and the vendor can get big fines.

Medical Help: A first-aid station staffed by English-speaking doctors is on St. Mark's Square (at #63, same address as the **polizia** station, daily 8:00-20:00). Venice's **Santi Giovanni e Paolo hospital** (tel. 118) is a 10-minute walk from both the Rialto and San Marco neighborhoods, located behind the big church of the same name on Fondamenta dei Mendicanti (toward Fondamente Nove). You can take vaporetto #4.1 from San Zaccaria, or #5.2 from the train station or Piazzale Roma, to the Ospedale stop.

Sightseeing Tips: To avoid the worst of the crowds at **St. Mark's Basilica,** go early or late, or reserve a time online. You can usually bypass the line if you have a large bag to check (see page 629). At the **Doge's Palace,** purchase your ticket at the never-crowded Correr Museum across St. Mark's Square, or visit later in the day. For the **Campanile,** ascend first thing in the morning or go late (it's open until 21:00 July-Sept), or skip it entirely if you're going to the similar San Giorgio Maggiore bell tower.

Wi-Fi: Almost all hotels have Wi-Fi, many have a computer that guests can use, and most provide these services for free. A few shops with pricey Internet access can be found on back streets (€5/hour, marked with an @ sign).

Laundry: The full-service Lavanderia Gabriella is a few streets north of St. Mark's Square (closed Sat-Sun, on Rio Terà de le Colonne, San Marco 985, tel. 041-522-1758, Elisabetta).

Water: Carry a water bottle to refill at public fountains fed by pure, safe water piped in from the foothills of the Alps.

Public Toilets: Public pay WCs are near major landmarks, including St. Mark's Square (behind the Correr Museum and at the waterfront park, Giardinetti Reali), Rialto, and the Accademia Bridge. Use free toilets in any museum or any café you're eating in, or get a drink at a bar and use their WC for free.

Travel Agencies: Agenzie 365, in the train station's main lobby, sells vaporetto and train tickets and has shorter lines than the ticket windows (9 percent surcharge on train tickets, daily 8:00-19:30, tel. 041-275-9412).

GRAND CANAL CRUISE

Take a joyride and introduce yourself to Venice by boat, an experience worth ▲▲▲. Cruise the Grand Canal all the way to St. Mark's Square, starting at the train station (Ferrovia) or the bus station (Piazzale Roma).

If it's your first trip down the Grand Canal, you might want to stow this book and just take it all in—Venice is a barrage on the senses that hardly needs narration. But these notes give the cruise a little meaning and help orient you to this great city.

You can break up the tour by hopping on and off at various sights described in greater depth later in the chapter. Just remember: a single-fare vaporetto ticket is good for just 75 minutes; passes let you hop on and off all day.

I've organized this tour by boat stop. I'll point out both what you can see from the current stop, and what to look forward to as you cruise to the next stop.

Orientation

Length of This Tour: Allow 45 minutes.

Cost: €7.50 for a 75-minute vaporetto ticket, or covered by a transit pass—the best choice if you want to hop on and off.

Getting There: This tour starts at the Ferrovia vaporetto stop (at Santa Lucia train station). If you want to board upstream at the less-crowded Piazzale Roma, it's a five-minute walk over the Calatrava Bridge from the Ferrovia stop.

Catching Your Boat: This tour is designed for **slow boat #1** (which takes about 45 minutes). The **express boat #2** travels the same route, but it skips some

Grand Canal

stops and takes 25 minutes, making it hard to sightsee. Also, early and late in the day, the vaporetto #2 terminates at Rialto; you'll have to get off and switch to #1 to do the whole tour.

Where to Sit: You're more likely to find an empty seat if you catch the vaporetto at Piazzale Roma. Try to snag a seat in the bow—in front of the captain's bridge—for the perfect vantage point for spotting sights left, right, and forward. Not all boats have seats in the bow, but some of the older vaporetti do. Otherwise, your options are sitting inside (and viewing the passing sights through windows); standing in the open middle deck (where you can move from side to side if the boat's not crowded—especially easy after dark); or sitting outside in the back (where you'll miss the wonderful forward views). The left side of the boat has a slight edge, with more sights and the best light late in the day.

Stops to Consider: Some interesting stops are Rialto Mercato (fish market and famous bridge), Ca' Rezzonico (Museum of 18th-Century Venice), Accademia (art museum and the nearby Peggy Guggen-

heim Collection), and Salute (huge art-filled church).

Audio Tour: 🎧 If you download my free audio tour (see page 17), you won't even have to look at the book. Because it's hard to see everything in one go, you may want to do this tour twice (perhaps once in either direction).

Overview

The Grand Canal is Venice's "Main Street." At more than two miles long, nearly 150 feet wide, and nearly 15 feet deep, it's the city's largest canal, lined with its most impressive palaces. It's the remnant of a river that once spilled from the mainland into the Adriatic. The sediment it carried formed barrier islands that cut Venice off from the sea, forming a lagoon.

Venice was built on the marshy islands of the former delta, sitting on wood pilings driven nearly 15 feet into the clay (alder was the preferred wood). About 25 miles of canals drain the city, dumping like streams into the Grand Canal. Technically, Venice has only three canals: Grand, Giudecca, and Cannaregio. The 45 small waterways that dump into the

Grand Canal are referred to as rivers (e.g., Rio Novo).

Venice is a city of palaces, dating from the days when the city was the world's richest. The most lavish palaces formed a grand architectural cancan along the Grand Canal. Once frescoed in reds and blues, with black-and-white borders and gold-leaf trim, they made Venice a city of dazzling color. This cruise is the only way to truly appreciate the palaces, approaching them at water level, where their main entrances were located. Today, strict laws prohibit any changes in these buildings. So while landowners gnash their teeth, we can enjoy Europe's best-preserved medieval/Renaissance city—slowly rotting. Many of the grand buildings are now vacant. Others harbor chandeliered elegance above mossy, empty, often flooded ground floors.

◉ Self-Guided Cruise

Start reading the tour when your vaporetto reaches Ferrovia.

❶ Ferrovia

The **Santa Lucia train station,** one of the few modern buildings in town, was built in 1954. It's been the gateway into Venice since 1860, when the first station was built. "F.S." stands for "Ferrovie dello Stato," the Italian state railway system.

More than 20,000 people a day commute in from the mainland, making this the busiest part of Venice during rush hour. The **Calatrava Bridge,** just upstream, was built in 2008 to alleviate some of the congestion.

❷ Riva de Biasio

Venice's main thoroughfare is busy with all kinds of boats: taxis, police boats, garbage boats, ambulances, construction cranes, and even brown-and-white UPS boats. Somehow they all manage to share the canal in relative peace.

About 25 yards past the Riva de Biasio stop, look left down the broad **Cannaregio Canal** to see what was the **Jewish Ghetto.** The twin, pale-pink, six-story "skyscrapers"—the tallest buildings you'll see at this end of the canal—are reminders of how densely populated the community was. Founded in 1516 near a copper foundry (a *geto*), this segregated community gave us our word "ghetto."

❸ San Marcuola

At this stop, facing a tiny square just ahead, stands the unfinished Church of San Marcuola, one of only five churches fronting the Grand Canal. Centuries ago, this canal was a commercial drag of expensive real estate in high demand by wealthy merchants. About 20 yards ahead on the right (across the Grand Canal) stands the stately gray **Turkish Exchange (Fondaco dei Turchi),** one of the oldest houses in Venice. Its horseshoe arches and roofline of triangles are reminders of its Byzantine heritage. Turbaned Turkish

Ferrovia vaporetto stop

Calatrava Bridge

traders docked here, unloaded their goods into the warehouse on the bottom story, then went upstairs for a home-style meal and a place to sleep. Venice in the 1500s was cosmopolitan, welcoming every religion and ethnicity—so long as they carried cash. (Today the building contains the city's Museum of Natural History—and Venice's only dinosaur skeleton.)

Just 100 yards ahead on the left, Venice's **Casinò** is housed in the palace where German composer Richard Wagner (*The Ring*) died in 1883. See his distinct, strong-jawed profile in the white plaque on the brick wall. In the 1700s, Venice was Europe's Vegas, with casinos and prostitutes everywhere. *Casinòs* ("little houses" in Venetian dialect) have long provided Italians with a handy escape from daily life. Today, they're run by the state to keep Mafia influence at bay. Notice the fancy front porch, which greets high rollers arriving by taxi or hotel boat.

❹ San Stae

The San Stae Church sports a delightful Baroque facade. Opposite the San Stae stop is a little canal opening. On the second building to the right of that opening, look for the peeling plaster that once made up **frescoes** (you can barely distinguish the scant remains of little angels on the lower floors). Imagine the facades of the Grand Canal at their finest. Most of them would have been covered in fres-

coes by the best artists of the day. As colorful as the city is today, it's still only a faded, sepia-toned remnant of a long-gone era, a time of lavishly decorated, brilliantly colored palaces.

Just ahead, on the right with blue posts, is the ornate white facade of **Ca' Pesaro,** which houses the International Gallery of Modern Art. "*Ca'*" is short for *casa* (house).

In this city of masks, notice how the rich marble facades along the Grand Canal mask what are generally just simple, no-nonsense brick buildings. Most merchants enjoyed showing off. However, being smart businessmen, they only decorated the side of the buildings that would be seen and appreciated. But look back as you pass Ca' Pesaro. It's the only building you'll see with a fine side facade. Ahead, on the left (just before the next stop), is Ca' d'Oro with its glorious triple-decker medieval arcade.

❺ Ca' d'Oro

The lacy **Ca' d'Oro** (House of Gold) is the best example of Venetian Gothic architecture on the canal. Its three stories offer different variations on balcony design, topped with a spiny white roofline. Venetian Gothic mixes traditional Gothic (pointed arches and round medallions stamped with a four-leaf clover) with Byzantine styles (tall, narrow arches atop thin columns), filled in with Islamic

All kinds of boats ply the canal.

A classic canal view

Grand Canal

To Jewish Ghetto

STRADA

GUGLIE BRIDGE

Canale de Cannaregio

SAN MARCUOLA

PALAZZO CORRER CONTARINI

Canal

CASINÒ

PALAZZO GRITTI

PALAZZO VENDRAMIN CALERGI

LISTA DI SPAGNA

SAN GEREMIA

Grand

PALAZZO FLANGINI

PALAZZO GIOVANELLI

TURKISH EXCHANGE

SCALZI

PALAZZO CALBO-CROTTA

PALAZZO MARCELLO

SANTA LUCIA TRAIN STATION (FERROVIA)

SCALZI BRIDGE

PAL. GRITTI

PALAZZO DONA BALBI

SAN ZAN DEGOLÀ

PALAZZO CA' TRON

SAN SIMEONE PICCOLO

SANTA CROCE

CALATRAVA BRIDGE

SAN

PIAZZALE ROMA
& PEOPLE MOVER
TO STAZIONE MARITTIMA
& TRONCHETTO

FRARI

PALAZZO CAPPELLO-LAYARD

SAN TOMÀ

PALAZZO BARBARIGO

PALAZZO GIUSTINIANI

T

A

9

PALAZZO BALBI

10

FIRE STATION

CA' FOSCARI

PALAZZO MOCENIGO

PALAZZO VECCHIA

PALAZZO MORO LIN

PALAZZO GIUSTINIAN

PALAZZO GRASSI

CA' REZZONICO

11

PALAZZO MALIPIERO-CAPPELLO

PALAZZO LOREDAN

PALAZZO FALIER

PALAZZO CONTARINI DEGLI SCRIGNI

PALAZZO QUERINI

PALAZZO GIUSTINIAN LOLIN

12

ACCADEMIA BRIDGE & GALLERY

PALAZZO BARBARO

PALAZZO BARBARIGO

FONDAMENTA ZATTERE AL PONTE LONGO

DORSODURO

Giudecca Canal

To Zattere

Vaporetto Stops

1 Ferrovia
2 Riva de Biasio
3 San Marcuola
4 San Stae
5 Ca' d'Oro
6 Mercato Rialto
7 Rialto
8 San Silvestro
9 Sant'Angelo
10 San Tomà
11 Ca' Rezzonico
12 Accademia
13 Santa Maria del Giglio
14 Salute
15 San Marco
16 San Zaccaria

Lagoon

FONDAMENTE NOVE

NOVA

200 Meters
200 Yards

PALAZZO
MARCELLO

PALAZZO
MOLIN
PALAZZO
ZULLAN

CANNAREGIO

4

SAN
STAE

PALAZZO
BARBARIGO
PALAZZO
FONTANA

PALAZZO
GIUSTI

PALAZZO
SAGREDO

STRADA NOVA

CA'
PESARO

PALAZZO
DONÀ
PALAZZO
FAVRETTO

CA'
D'ORO

PALAZZO
MICHIEL
COLONNE

5

PALAZZO
CORNER
DELLA REGINA
PALAZZO
BRANDOLIN

T

PALAZZO
VALMARANA

PALAZZO
CA' DA MOSTO

FISH
MARKET

6

PRODUCE
MARKET

PALAZZO
CIVRAN

POLO

FONDACO DEI
TEDESCHI
(FORMER GERMAN
EXCHANGE)

RIALTO
BRIDGE

A

SAL. S. LIO

S. MARIA
FORMOSA

7

PALAZZO
DOLFIN-
MANIN

PALAZZO
PAPADOPOLI
PALAZZO
BARZIZZA

PALAZZO
BEMBO

MERCERIE

CASTELLO

PALAZZO
DONÀ
PALAZZO
CORNER-
CONTARINI

8

PALAZZO
BERNARDO

PALAZZO
FARSETTI-
DANDOLO

PALAZZO
BENZON
PALAZZO
MARTINENGO

PALAZZO
GRIMANI

MERCERIE

PALAZZO
CORNER-
SPINELLI

FABBRI

ST.
MARK'S
BASILICA

CAMPANILE

BRIDGE
OF SIGHS

SAN
MARCO

DOGE'S
PALACE

SAN MARCO

16

SAN MARCO &
SAN THEODORE
COLUMNS

CALLE LARGA
XXII MARZO

HARRY'S
AMERICAN
BAR

A

To
Lido

GRITTI
PALACE
HOTEL

15

CA'
GRANDE

PALAZZO
FLANGINI

St. Mark's
Basin

Canal

13

T

14

LA
SALUTE
CHURCH

Grand

PALAZZO
DARIO
PALAZZO
GENOVESE

PUNTA DELLA
DOGANA MUSEUM

PEGGY
GUGGENHEIM
COLLECTION

To
San Giorgio
Maggiore &
Giudecca

frills. Like all the palaces, this was origi-nally painted and gilded to make it even more glorious than it is now. Today the Ca' d'Oro is an art gallery.

Look at the Venetian chorus line of palaces in front of the boat. On the right is the arcade of the covered **fish market,** with the open-air **produce market** just beyond (closed Sun). It bustles in the morning but is quiet the rest of the day. This is a great scene to wander through—even though European Union hygiene standards have made it cleaner but less colorful than it once was.

Find the *traghetto* gondola ferrying shoppers—standing like Washington crossing the Delaware—back and forth. There are three *traghetto* crossings along the Grand Canal, each one marked by a classy low-key green-and-black sign. Piloting a *traghetto* isn't these gondoliers' normal day jobs. As a public service, all gondoliers are obliged to row a *traghetto* a few days a month. Make a point to use them. At €2 a ride, *traghetti* offer the cheapest gondola rides in Venice (but at this price, don't expect them to sing to you).

❻ *Mercato Rialto*

Boats stop here to serve the busy market. The long and officious-looking build-ing at this stop is the Venice courthouse. Straight ahead in the distance, rising above the roofline, is the tip of the Cam-

panile (bell tower), crowned by its golden angel at St. Mark's Square, where this tour will end. The **Fondaco dei Tedeschi** (former German Exchange, a building just beyond, on the left) was the trading cen-ter for German metal merchants in the early 1500s. Today it's a shopping center with great views from its small rooftop terrace (free).

You'll cruise by some trendy and beau-tifully situated wine bars on the right, but look ahead as you round the corner and see the impressive Rialto Bridge come into view.

A major landmark of Venice, the **Rialto Bridge** is lined with shops and tourists. Constructed in 1588, it's the third bridge built on this spot. Until the 1850s, this was the only bridge crossing the Grand Canal. With a span of 160 feet and foundations stretching 650 feet on either side, the Rialto was a massive engineering feat in its day. Earlier Rialto Bridges could open to let big ships in, but not this one. When this new bridge was completed, much of the Grand Canal was closed to shipping and became a canal of palaces.

When gondoliers pass under the fat arch of the Rialto Bridge, they take full advantage of its acoustics: *"Volare, oh, oh..."*

❼ *Rialto*

Rialto, a separate town in the early days of Venice, has always been the commer-cial district, while San Marco was the reli-

Ca' d'Oro—the House of Gold

Mercato Rialto

gious and governmental center. Today, a winding street called the Mercerie connects the two, providing travelers with human traffic jams and a mesmerizing gauntlet of shopping temptations. This is the only stretch of the historic Grand Canal with landings upon which you can walk. They unloaded the city's basic necessities here: oil, wine, charcoal, iron. Today, the quay is lined with tourist-trap restaurants.

Venice's sleek, black, graceful **gondolas** are a symbol of the city. With about 500 gondoliers joyriding amid the churning **vaporetti,** there's a lot of congestion on the Grand Canal. Pay attention—this is where most of the gondola and vaporetto accidents take place. While the Rialto is the highlight of many gondola rides, gondoliers understandably prefer the quieter small canals. Watch your vaporetto driver curse the better-paid gondoliers.

❽ *San Silvestro*

We now enter a long stretch of important *merchants' palaces,* each with proud and different facades. Because ships couldn't navigate beyond the Rialto Bridge, the biggest palaces—with the major shipping needs—line this last stretch of the navigable Grand Canal.

Palaces like these were multifunctional: ground floor for the warehouse, offices and showrooms upstairs, and the living quarters above the offices on the "noble floors" (with big windows designed to let in maximum light). Servants lived and worked on the top floors (with the smallest windows). For fire-safety reasons, the kitchens were also located on the top floors. Peek into the noble floors to catch a glimpse of their still-glorious chandeliers of Murano glass.

The **Palazzo Grimani** (across from the San Silvestro dock) sports a heavy white Roman-style facade—a reminder that the Grimani family included a cardinal and had strong Roman connections.

The **Palazzo Papadopoli,** with the two obelisks on its roof (50 yards beyond the San Silvestro stop on the right, with the blue posts), is the very fancy Aman Hotel where George and Amal Clooney were married in 2014.

❾ *Sant'Angelo*

Notice how many buildings have a foundation of waterproof white stone (*pietra d'Istria*) upon which the bricks sit high and

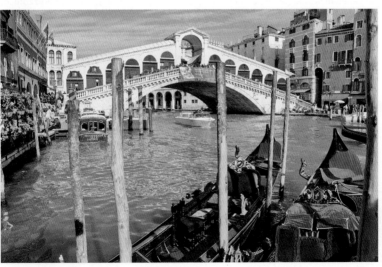

Rialto Bridge

dry. Many canal-level floors are abandoned as the rising water level takes its toll.

The **posts**—historically painted gaily with the equivalent of family coats of arms—don't rot underwater. But the wood at the waterline, where it's exposed to oxygen, does. On the smallest canals, little blue gondola signs indicate that these docks are for gondolas only (no motorized craft).

❿ San Tomà

Fifty yards ahead, on the right side (with twin obelisks on the rooftop) stands **Palazzo Balbi,** the palace of an early-17th-century captain general of the sea. This palace, like so many in the city, flies three flags: Italy (green-white-red), the European Union (blue with ring of stars), and Venice (a lion on a field of red and gold).

Just past the admiral's palace, look immediately to the right, down a side canal. On the right side of that canal, before the bridge, see the traffic light and the **fire station** (the 1930s Mussolini-era building with four arches hiding fireboats parked and ready to go).

The impressive **Ca' Foscari,** with a classic Venetian facade (on the corner, across from the fire station), dominates the bend in the canal. This is the main building of the University of Venice, which has about 25,000 students. Notice the elegant lamp on the corner—needed in the old days to light this intersection.

Best Views in Venice

- A slow vaporetto ride down the **Grand Canal**—ideally very early or just before sunset—is a shutterbug's delight.
- On St. Mark's Square, enjoy views from the soaring **Campanile** or the balcony of St. Mark's Basilica (both require admission).
- The **Rialto** and **Accademia Bridges** provide free, expansive views of the Grand Canal, along with a cooling breeze.
- The luxury "mall" **Fondaco dei Tedeschi,** just north of the Rialto bridge, has great views—but as the space is small and free, it can be crowded, especially near sunset.
- Get off the main island for a view of the Venetian skyline: Ascend **San Giorgio Maggiore's bell tower,** or venture to **Giudecca Island** to visit the swanky bar of the Molino Stucky Hilton Hotel (the free-to-"customers" shuttle boat leaves from near the San Zaccaria-B vaporetto dock).

The grand, heavy, white **Ca' Rezzonico,** just before the stop of the same name, houses the Museum of 18th-Century Venice (see page 639). Across the canal is the cleaner and leaner **Palazzo Grassi,** the last major palace built on the canal, erected in the late 1700s. It was purchased

Navigational posts

Ca' Foscari

by a French tycoon and now displays a contemporary art collection.

⑪ Ca' Rezzonico

Up ahead, the Accademia Bridge leads over the Grand Canal to the **Accademia Gallery** (right side), filled with the best Venetian paintings (see page 637). The bridge was put up in 1934 as a temporary structure. Locals liked it, so it stayed. It was rebuilt in 1984 in the original style.

⑫ Accademia

From here, look through the graceful bridge and way ahead to enjoy a classic view of **La Salute Church,** topped by a crown-shaped dome supported by scrolls. This Church of Saint Mary of Good Health was built to thank God for delivering Venetians from the devastating plague of 1630 (which had killed about a third of the city's population).

The low, white building among greenery (100 yards ahead, on the right, between the Accademia Bridge and the church) is the **Peggy Guggenheim Collection.** The American heiress "retired" here, sprucing up a palace that had been abandoned mid-construction. Peggy willed the city her fine collection of modern art (see page 639).

As you approach the next stop, notice on the right how the line of higgledy-piggledy palaces evokes old-time Venice. Two doors past the Guggenheim, Palazzo Dario has a great set of characteristic **funnel-shaped chimneys.** These forced embers through a loop-the-loop channel until they were dead—required in the days when stone palaces were surrounded by humble, wooden buildings, and a live spark could make a merchant's workforce homeless. Three doors farther is the **Salviati building,** which once served as a glassworks. Its Art Nouveau mosaic, done in the early 20th century, features Venice as a queen being appreciated by the big shots of society.

⑬ Santa Maria del Giglio

Back on the left stands the fancy **Gritti Palace hotel.** Hemingway and Woody Allen both stayed here (but not together).

Take a deep whiff of Venice. What's all this nonsense about stinky canals? All I smell is my shirt.

⑭ Salute

The huge **La Salute Church** towers overhead as if squirted from a can of Catholic Reddi-wip.

As the Grand Canal opens up into the lagoon, the last building on the right with the golden ball is the 17th-century **Customs House,** which now houses the Punta della Dogana contemporary art museum. Its two bronze Atlases hold a statue of Fortune riding the ball. Arriving ships used to stop here to pay their tolls.

⑮ San Marco

Up ahead on the left, the green pointed tip of the Campanile marks **St. Mark's Square,** the political and religious center of Venice... and the final destination of this tour. You could get off at the San Marco stop and go straight to St. Mark's Square (and you'll

La Salute Church

Is Venice Sinking?

Venice has battled rising water levels since the fifth century. Several factors, both natural and artificially-constructed, cause Venice to flood about 100 times a year—usually from October until late winter—a phenomenon called the *acqua alta*.

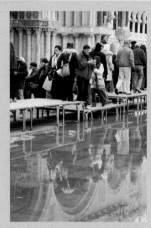

Venice sits atop sediments deposited at the ancient mouth of the Po River, which are still settling. Early industrial projects, such as offshore piers and the bridge to the mainland, affected the sea floor and tidal cycles, making the city more vulnerable to flooding. Twentieth-century industry pumped massive amounts of groundwater out of the aquifer beneath the lagoon for nearly 50 years before the government stopped the practice in the 1970s. In the last century, Venice has sunk by about nine inches.

Meanwhile, the waters around Venice are rising, especially in winter. The notorious *acqua alta* happens when an unusually high tide combines with strong winds and a storm. When a storm—an area of low pressure—travels over a body of water, it pulls the surface of the water up into a dome. As strong sirocco winds from Africa blow storms north up the Adriatic, they push this high water ahead of the front, causing a surging tide. Add the worldwide sea-level rise that's resulted from climate change, and the high sea gets that much higher.

During the *acqua alta*, the first puddles appear in the center of paved squares, pooling around the limestone grates. These grates cover cisterns that long held Venice's only source of drinking water. Surrounded by the lagoon and beset by constant flooding, this city had no natural source of fresh water. For centuries, residents carried water from the mainland. In the ninth century, they devised a way to collect rainwater by using paved, cleverly sloped squares as catchment systems, with limestone filters covering underground clay tubs. Venice's population grew markedly once citizens could access fresh water from these "wells." Several thousand cisterns provided the city with drinking water up until 1884, when an aqueduct was built. Now the wells are capped, and rain drains from squares into the lagoon—or up from it, as the case may be.

In 2003, a consortium of engineering firms began construction on the MOSE Project. Named for the acronym of its Italian name, *Modulo Sperimentale Elettromeccanico,* it's also a nod to Moses and his (albeit temporary) mastery over the sea. Underwater gates are being installed on the floor of the sea at the three inlets where it enters Venice's lagoon. When the seawater rises above a certain level, air will be pumped into the gates, causing them to rise and shut out the Adriatic. The first gates are already installed, but, in good Italian fashion, corruption and scandal have surrounded the project. Combined with technical challenges, the completion date continues to get pushed into the future—the latest estimate is 2021. You can learn more about the project at www.mosevenezia.eu.

have to if you're on vaporetto #2, which terminates here). But I'm staying on the #1 boat for one more stop, just past St. Mark's Square (it's a quick walk back).

Survey the lagoon. Opposite St. Mark's Square, across the water, the ghostly white church with the pointy bell tower is **San Giorgio Maggiore,** with superb views of Venice's skyline (see page 637). Next to it is the residential island Giudecca, stretching from close to San Giorgio Maggiore to the Hilton Hotel (good nighttime view, far-right end of island).

Still on board? If you are, as we leave the San Marco stop, look left and prepare for a drive-by view of St. Mark's Square. First comes the bold white facade of the old mint (marked by a tiny cupola, where Venice's golden ducat, the "dollar" of the Venetian Republic, was made) and the library facade. Then come the twin columns, topped by St. Theodore and St. Mark, who have welcomed visitors since the 15th century. Between the columns, catch a glimpse of two giant figures atop the **Clock Tower**—they've been whacking their clappers every hour since 1499.

The domes of **St. Mark's Basilica** are soon eclipsed by the lacy facade of the **Doge's Palace.** Next you'll see many gondolas with their green breakwater buoys, the **Bridge of Sighs** (leading from the palace to the prison—check out the maximum-security bars), and then the grand harborside promenade—the **Riva.**

Follow the Riva with your eye, past elegant hotels to the green area in the distance. This is the largest of Venice's few **parks,** which hosts the now-annual Biennale festival. Much farther in the distance is the **Lido,** the island with Venice's beach. Its sand and casinos are tempting, though its car traffic disrupts the medieval charm of Venice.

⓰ *San Zaccaria*

OK, you're at your last stop. Quick—muscle your way off this boat! (If you don't, you'll eventually end up at the Lido.)

At San Zaccaria, you're right in the thick of the action. A number of other vaporetti depart from here (see page 666). Otherwise, it's a short walk back along the Riva to St. Mark's Square. Ahoy!

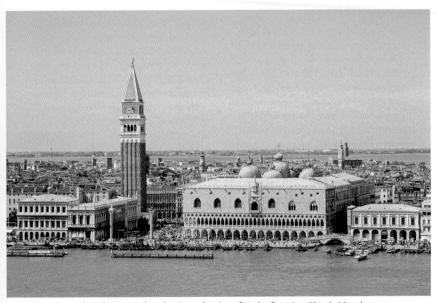

The Campanile and Doge's Palace dominate the view of Venice from San Giorgio Maggiore.

SIGHTS

Venice's city museums offer youth and senior discounts to Americans and other non-EU citizens. Also, when you see a 🎧 in a listing, it means the sight is covered in a free audio tour (via my Rick Steves Audio Europe app—see page 17).

San Marco District

▲▲▲ST. MARK'S SQUARE (PIAZZA SAN MARCO)

This grand square is surrounded by splashy, historic buildings and sights: St. Mark's Basilica, Doge's Palace, the Campanile bell tower, and Correr Museum. The square is filled with music, lovers, tourists, and pigeons by day. It's your private rendezvous with the Venetian past late at night, when it becomes Europe's most romantic dance floor.

St. Mark's Basilica dominates the square with its Eastern-style onion domes and glowing mosaics. Mark Twain said it looked like "a vast warty bug taking a meditative walk."

With your back to the church, survey one of Europe's great urban spaces, and the only square in Venice to merit the title "Piazza." Nearly two football fields long, it's surrounded by the offices of the republic. On your right are the "old offices" (16th-century Renaissance). On your left are the "new offices" (17th-century High Renaissance). Napoleon called the piazza "the most beautiful drawing room in Europe," and added to the intimacy by building the final wing, opposite the basilica.

🎧 For a detailed explanation of St. Mark's Square, download my free **audio tour.**

Rick's Tip: *If you're* **bombed by a pigeon,** *resist the initial response to wipe it off immediately—it'll just smear into your hair. Wait until it dries, and it should flake off cleanly. But if the poop splatters on your clothes, wipe it off immediately to avoid a stain.*

▲▲▲ST. MARK'S BASILICA (BASILICA DI SAN MARCO)

Built in the 11th century, this basilica's distinctly Eastern-style architecture underlines Venice's connection with Byzantium (which protected it from the ambition of Charlemagne and his Holy Roman Empire). It's decorated with booty from returning sea captains—a Venetian trophy chest. The interior glows mysteriously with gold mosaics and colored marble. Since about A.D. 830, the saint's bones have been housed on this site. The San Marco Museum within holds the original bronze horses (copies of these overlook the square), and a balcony offering a remarkable view over St. Mark's Square.

Rick's Tip: *To* **avoid crowds** *at* **St. Mark's Basilica,** *go early or late or book a time online.*

Cost: Basilica entry is free, but you can pay €2 for an online reservation that lets you skip the line (well worth it).

Three separate exhibits within the church charge admission: the **Treasury** (€3, includes audioguide); **Golden Altarpiece** (€2); and **San Marco Museum** (€5). The San Marco Museum has the original bronze horses (copies of these overlook the square), a balcony offering a remarkable view over St. Mark's Square, and various works related to the church.

Hours: Church open Mon-Sat 9:45-17:00, Sun 14:00-17:00 (Sun until 16:00 Nov-mid-June), interior brilliantly lit daily 11:30-12:45; museum open daily 9:45-16:45, including on Sunday mornings when the church itself is closed; if considering a Sunday visit, note that the museum has a balcony that provides a fine view down to the church's interior. The treasury and the Golden Altarpiece are both open Mon-Sat 9:45-17:00, Sun 14:00-17:00; Nov-mid-June Mon-Sat 9:45-16:30, Sun 14:00-16:30. On St. Mark's Square, vaporetto: San Marco or San Zaccaria, tel. 041-270-8311, www.basilicasanmarco.it.

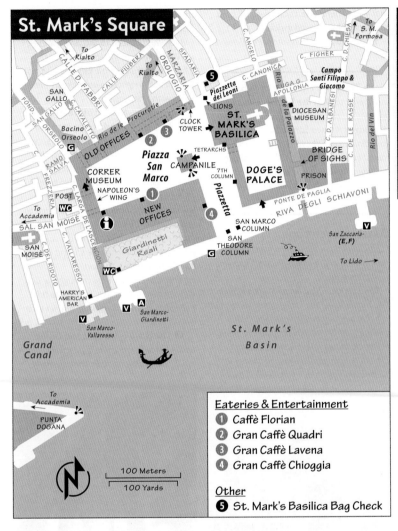

St. Mark's Square

Eateries & Entertainment
1 Caffè Florian
2 Gran Caffè Quadri
3 Gran Caffè Lavena
4 Gran Caffè Chioggia

Other
5 St. Mark's Basilica Bag Check

Theft Alert: St. Mark's Basilica is the most notorious place in Venice for pickpocketing—inside, it's always a crowded jostle.

Dress Code: Modest dress (no bare knees or bare shoulders) is strictly enforced for men, women, and even kids. Shorts are OK if they cover the knees.

Tours: Free, hour-long English **tours** (heavy on the mosaics' religious symbolism) are offered many days at 11:30 (meet in atrium, schedule varies, see schedule board just inside entrance).

🎧 Download my free St. Mark's Basilica **audio tour.**

Bag Check: Small purses and shoulder bags are usually allowed inside, but larger bags and backpacks are not. Check them for free for up to one hour at the nearby church called Ateneo San Basso, 30 yards to the left of the basilica, down narrow Calle San Basso (daily 9:30-17:00). Note that you generally can't check small bags that would be allowed inside.

Photography: No photos are allowed inside.

Rick's Tip: Those **checking large bags** *usually get to* **skip the line,** *as do their companions (at the guard's discretion). Leave your bag at Ateneo San Basso and pick up your claim tag. Take your tag to the basilica's tourist entrance. Keep to the left of the railing where the line forms and show your tag to the gatekeeper. He'll generally let you in ahead of the line.*

◑ SELF-GUIDED TOUR

• *Start outside in the square, far enough back to take in the whole facade. Then zero in on the details.*

❶ Exterior—Mosaic of Mark's Relics: The mosaic over the far left door shows two men (in the center, with crooked staffs) bearing a coffin with the body of St. Mark. Seven centuries after his death, his holy Christian body was in Muslim-occupied Alexandria, Egypt. In A.D. 828, two visiting

merchants of Venice "rescued" the body from the "infidels," hid it in a pork barrel (which was unclean to Muslims), and spirited it away to Venice.

• *Enter the atrium of the basilica, and look up and to the right into an archway decorated with fine mosaics.*

❷ Atrium—Mosaic of Noah's Ark and the Great Flood: In the scene to the right of the entry door, Noah and sons are sawing logs to build a boat. Below that are three scenes of Noah putting all species of animals into the ark, two by two. Across the arch, the flood drowns the wicked. Noah sends out a dove twice to see whether there's any dry land where he can dock. He finds it, leaves the ark with a gorgeous rainbow overhead, and offers a sacrifice of thanks to God.

• *Climb seven steps, pass through the doorway, and enter the nave. Just inside the door, step to the far left, stop, and let your eyes adjust.*

❸ The Nave—Mosaics and Greek-Cross Floor Plan: These golden mosaics are in the Byzantine style, though many

St. Mark's Basilica

Gold mosaics cover every surface of St. Mark's interior.

St. Mark's Basilica

To San Zaccaria

CALLE DE LA CANONICA

Not to Scale

11 MAIN ALTAR (MARK'S BONES BENEATH)

8

6

7

5 CENTRAL DOME

NORTH TRANSEPT

SOUTH TRANSEPT

9

C. RIZZA

ENTRY (WORSHIP ONLY)

4

BAG CHECK

SAN BASSO

Piazzetta dei Leoni

NARTHEX

NAVE **3**

BAPTISTERY

TREASURY **10**

To Rialto

MARZARIA OROLOGIO

LIONS

1

12

2

ATRIUM

TOUR BEGINS

ENTRANCE

To Doge's Palace

CLOCK TOWER

Piazza San Marco

To Campanile

1 Mosaic of Mark's Relics
2 Atrium Mosaic of Noah's Ark & the Great Flood
3 Nave Mosaics & Greek-Cross Floor Plan
4 Pentecost Mosaic
5 Central Dome Ascension Mosaic

6 Rood Screen
7 Doge's Pulpit
8 Nicopeia Icon
9 Discovery of Mark Mosaic
10 Treasury
11 Golden Altarpiece
12 Stairs up to Museum

were designed by artists from the Italian Renaissance and later. The often-overlooked lower walls are covered with colorful marble slabs, cut to expose the grain, and laid out in geometric patterns. Even the floor is mosaic, with mostly geometrical designs. It rolls like the sea. Venice is sinking and shifting, creating these cresting waves of stone. The church is laid out with four equal arms, topped with domes, radiating from the center to form a Greek cross (+).

• *Find the chandelier near the entrance doorway (in the shape of a Greek cross cathedral space station), and run your eyes up the support chain to the dome above.*

❹ Pentecost Mosaic: In a golden heaven, the dove of the Holy Spirit shoots out a pinwheel of spiritual lasers, igniting tongues of fire on the heads of the 12 apostles below, giving them the ability to speak other languages without a Rick Steves phrase book. One of the oldest mosaics in the church (c. 1125), it has distinct "Byzantine" features: a gold background and apostles with halos, solemn faces, almond eyes, delicate hands, and rumpled robes, all facing forward.

• *Shuffle along with the crowds up to the central dome.*

❺ Central Dome—Ascension Mosaic: Gape upward to the very heart of the church. Christ—having lived his miraculous life and having been crucified for man's sins—ascends into the starry sky on a rainbow. In Byzantine churches, the window-lit dome represented heaven, while the dark church below represented earth.

Under the Ascension Dome: Look around at the church's furniture and imagine a service here. The ❻ rood screen, topped with 14 saints, separates the congregation from the high altar, heightening the "mystery" of the Mass. The ❼ pulpit on the right was reserved for the doge, who led prayers and made important announcements.

North Transept: In the north transept (to the left of the altar), today's Venetians pray to a painted wooden icon of Mary

and Baby Jesus known as ❽ Nicopeia, or "Our Lady of Victory" (it's a small painting crusted over with a big stone canopy). In its day, this was the ultimate trophy—the actual icon used to protect the Byzantine army in war, looted by the Crusaders.

• *In the south transept (right of the main altar), find the dim mosaic high up on the three-windowed wall above the entrance to the treasury.*

❾ Discovery of Mark Mosaic: This mosaic isn't a biblical scene; it depicts the miraculous event that capped the construction of the present church. (It's high up and hard to read.)

It's 1094, the church is nearly complete (see the domes shown in cutaway fashion), and they're all set to re-inter Mark's bones under the new altar. There's just one problem: During the decades of construction, they forgot where they'd stored his body!

So (on the left), all of Venice gathers inside the church to bow down and pray for help finding the bones. The doge (from the Latin *dux*, meaning leader) leads them. Soon after (the right half),

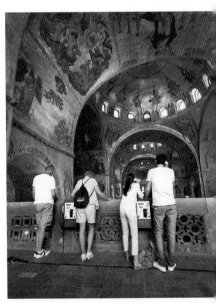

San Marco Museum offers close-up views of mosaics.

A *The altar and tomb of St. Mark*

B *Mosaic showing St. Mark's body being carried into the church*

C *Noah's Ark mosaic*

D *Central dome and the Ascension mosaic*

the patriarch (far right) is inspired to look inside a hollow column where he finds the relics. Everyone turns and applauds, including the womenfolk, who stream in from the upper-floor galleries. The relics were soon placed under the altar in a ceremony that inaugurated the current structure.

Additional Sights: The ❿ **Treasury** (Tesoro; ask for the included and informative audioguide when you buy your ticket) and ⓫ **Golden Altarpiece** (Pala d'Oro) give you the easiest way outside of Istanbul or Ravenna to see the glories of the Byzantine Empire. Venetian crusaders looted the Christian city of Constantinople and brought home piles of lavish loot (perhaps the lowest point in Christian history until the advent of TV evangelism). Much of this plunder is stored in the Treasury of San Marco. Most of these treasures were made in about A.D. 500, while Western Europe was stuck in the Dark Ages. Beneath the high altar lies the body of St. Mark ("Marce") and the Golden Altarpiece, made of 250 blue-backed enamels with religious scenes, all set in a gold frame and studded with 15 hefty rubies, 300 emeralds, 1,500 pearls, and assorted sapphires, amethysts, and topaz (c. 1100).

In the ⓬ **San Marco Museum** (Museo di San Marco) upstairs, you can see an up-close mosaic exhibition, a fine view of the church interior, a view of the square from the balcony with bronze horses, and (inside, in their own room) the original horses, which were stolen from Constantinople during the notorious Fourth Crusade. The staircase up to the museum is in the atrium, near the basilica's main entrance, marked by a sign in English.

▲▲▲DOGE'S PALACE (PALAZZO DUCALE)

The seat of the Venetian government and home of its ruling duke, or doge, this was the most powerful half-acre in Europe for 400 years. The Doge's Palace was built to show off the power and wealth of the Republic. The doge lived with his family on the first floor up, near the halls of power. From his once-lavish (now sparse) quarters, you'll follow the one-way tour through the public rooms of the top floor, finishing with the Bridge of Sighs and the prison. The place is wallpapered with masterpieces by Veronese and Tintoretto.

Cost and Hours: €20 combo-ticket includes Correr Museum, also covered by Museum Pass—see page 612, daily April-Oct 8:30-19:00, Nov-March until 17:30, last entry one hour before closing, café, photos allowed without flash, next to St. Mark's Basilica, just off St. Mark's Square, vaporetto stops: San Marco or San Zaccaria, tel. 041-271-5911, http://palazzoducale.visitmuve.it.

Rick's Tip: *To* **avoid long lines at the Doge's Palace,** *buy your combo-ticket at the* **Correr Museum** *across the square; then go straight to the Doge's Palace turnstile, skirting along to the right, entering at the "prepaid tickets" entrance. It's also possible to* **buy advance tickets online**—*at least 48 hours in advance—on the museum website (€0.50 fee). Or go later—crowds tend to diminish after 15:00.*

Tours: The **audioguide** tour is dry but informative (€5, 1.5 hours, need ID for deposit). For a 1.25-hour live **guided tour,** consider the Secret Itineraries Tour, which takes you into palace rooms otherwise not open to the public (€20, includes Doge's Palace admission but not Correr Museum admission; €14 with combo-ticket; three English-language tours each morning). Though the tour skips the palace's main hall, you're welcome to visit the hall afterward on your own. Reserve ahead for this tour in peak season—it can fill up as much as a month in advance. Book online (http://palazzoducale.visitmuve.it, €0.50 fee), or reserve by phone (tel. 848-082-000, from the US dial 011-39-041-4273-0892), or you can try just showing up at the info desk. Don't confuse this with the

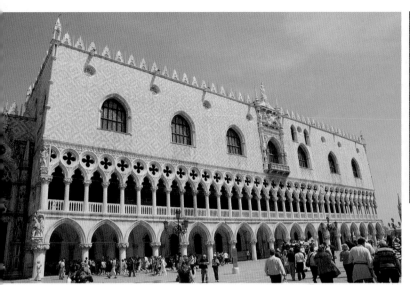

Doge's Palace

Doge's Hidden Treasures Tour—it reveals little that would be considered a "treasure" and is a waste of money.

Visiting the Doge's Palace: You'll see the restored facades from the **courtyard.** Notice a grand staircase (with nearly naked Moses and Paul Newman at the top). Even the most powerful visitors climbed this to meet the doge. This was the beginning of an architectural power trip.

In the **Senate Hall,** the 120 senators met, debated, and passed laws. Tintoretto's large *Triumph of Venice* on the ceiling (central painting, best viewed from the top) shows the city in all its glory. Lady Venice is up in heaven with the Greek gods, while barbaric lesser nations swirl up to give her gifts and tribute.

The **Armory**—a dazzling display originally assembled to intimidate potential adversaries—shows remnants of the military might that the empire employed to keep the East-West trade lines open (and the Venetian economy booming).

The giant **Hall of the Grand Council** (175 feet by 80 feet, capacity 2,600) is where the entire nobility met to elect the senate

and doge. It took a room this size to contain the grandeur of the Most Serene Republic. Ringing the top of the room are portraits of the first 76 doges (in chronological order). The one at the far end that's blacked out (in the left corner) is the notorious Doge Marin Falier, who opposed the will of the Grand Council in 1355. He was tried for treason, beheaded, and airbrushed from history.

On the wall over the doge's throne is Tintoretto's monsterpiece, *Paradise,* the largest oil painting in the world. Christ and Mary are surrounded by a heavenly

Tintoretto, Triumph of Venice

host of 500 saints. The painting leaves you feeling that you get to heaven not by being a good Christian, but by being a good Venetian.

Cross the covered **Bridge of Sighs** over the canal to the **prisons.** Circle the cells. Notice the carvings made by prisoners—from olden days up until 1930—on some of the stone windowsills of the cells, especially in the far corner of the building.

Cross back over the Bridge of Sighs, pausing to look through the marble-trellised windows at all of the tourists.

More Sights on the Square
▲▲CORRER MUSEUM (MUSEO CORRER)

This uncrowded museum gives you a good, easy-to-manage overview of Venetian history and art. The doge memorabilia, armor, banners, statues (by Canova), and paintings (by the Bellini family and others) re-create the festive days of the Venetian Republic. And it's all accompa-

Canova, Daedalus and Icarus

nied by English descriptions and breathtaking views of St. Mark's Square. The Correr Museum is a quiet refuge—a place to rise above St. Mark's Square when the piazza is too hot, too rainy, or too crowded.

Cost and Hours: €20 combo-ticket also includes the Doge's Palace; for €12 you can see the Correr Museum and tour the Clock Tower on St. Mark's Square, but this ticket doesn't include the Doge's Palace; daily April-Oct 10:00-19:00, Nov-March 10:00-17:00, last entry one hour before closing; bag check free and mandatory for bags bigger than a large purse, no photos, elegant café; enter at far end of square directly opposite basilica, tel. 041-240-5211, http://correr.visitmuve.it.

▲CAMPANILE (CAMPANILE DI SAN MARCO)

This dramatic bell tower replaced a shorter tower, part of the original fortress that guarded the entry of the Grand Canal. That tower crumbled into a pile of bricks in 1902, a thousand years after it was built. Ride the elevator 325 feet to the top for the best view in Venice (especially at sunset). For an ear-shattering experience, be on top when the bells ring. The golden archangel Gabriel at the top always faces into the wind. Avoid the crowds and enjoy the crisp morning air at 9:00 or the cool evening breeze at 18:00.

Rick's Tip: Beat the crowds *at the Campanile by going early or going late (it's open until 21:00 from spring through fall). Or head to the similar* **San Giorgio Maggiore bell tower** *across the lagoon. The lines are shorter and the view is just as good.*

Cost and Hours: €8, daily April-mid-Oct 8:30-21:00, mid-Oct-April 9:30-17:30, last entry 45 minutes before closing, may close during thunderstorms, audioguide-€3, tel. 041-522-4064, www.basilicasanmarco.it.

CLOCK TOWER
(TORRE DELL'OROLOGIO)

The clock tower, built during the Renaissance in 1496, marks the entry to the main shopping drag, called the Mercerie (or "Marzarie," in Venetian dialect), which connects St. Mark's Square with the Rialto Bridge. From the square, you can see the bronze men (Moors) swing their huge clappers at the top of each hour. In the 17th century, one of them knocked an unsuspecting worker off the top and to his death—probably the first-ever killing by a robot. Notice one of the world's first "digital" clocks on the tower facing the square (the time flips every five minutes). You can go inside the clock tower with a prebooked guided tour that takes you close to the clock's innards and out to a terrace with good views over the square.

Cost and Hours: €12 combo-ticket includes Correr Museum—where the tour starts—but doesn't cover Doge's Palace; €7 for the tour if you already have a Museum Pass or Correr/Doge's Palace combo-ticket; tours in English Mon-Wed at 10:00 and 11:00, Thu-Sun at 14:00 and 15:00; no kids under age 6.

Reservations: The mandatory tour requires reservations; call 848-082-000 or book online at http://torreorologio.visitmuve.it. You can also try dropping by the Correr Museum for same-day reservations.

Behind St. Mark's Basilica
▲BRIDGE OF SIGHS

This much-photographed bridge connects the Doge's Palace with the prison. Supposedly, a condemned man would be led over this bridge on his way to the prison, take one last look at the glory of Venice, and sigh—a notion popularized in the Romantic 19th century. Though overhyped, it's undeniably tingle-worthy—especially after dark, when the crowds have dispersed and it's just you and floodlit Venice.

Getting There: The Bridge of Sighs is around the corner from the Doge's Palace. From the palace, walk toward the waterfront, turn left along the water, and look up the first canal on your left. You can walk across the bridge (from the inside) by visiting the Doge's Palace. During the middle of the day, however, being immersed in the pandemonium of global tourism (and selfie sticks) can be a fascinating experience in itself.

Across the Lagoon from St. Mark's Square
▲SAN GIORGIO MAGGIORE

This is the dreamy church-topped island you can see from the waterfront by St. Mark's Square. The striking church, designed by Palladio, features art by Tintoretto, a bell tower, and good views of Venice.

Cost and Hours: Free entry to church; daily 9:00-19:00, Nov-March 8:30-18:00. The bell tower costs €6 and is accessible by elevator (runs until 20 minutes before the church closes but is not accessible Sun during services).

Getting There: To reach the island from St. Mark's Square, take the one-stop, five-minute ride on vaporetto #2 from San Zaccaria (single ticket-€5, 6/hour; direction: Tronchetto).

Dorsoduro District
▲▲ACCADEMIA
(GALLERIA DELL'ACCADEMIA)

Venice's top art museum, packed with highlights of the Venetian Renaissance, features paintings by the Bellini family, Titian, Tintoretto, Veronese, Tiepolo, Giorgione, Canaletto, and Testosterone. It's just over the wooden Accademia Bridge from the San Marco action.

Cost and Hours: €15, free first Sun of the month, Mon 8:15-14:00, Tue-Sun 8:15-19:15, last entry one hour before closing, dull audioguide-€6, no flash photos allowed. At Accademia Bridge, vaporetto: Accademia, tel. 041-522-2247, www.gallerieaccademia.org.

Rick's Tip: *Just 400 people are allowed into the* **Accademia** *gallery at one time. It's most crowded on Tuesday mornings and whenever it rains;* **it's least crowded Wednesday, Thursday, and Sunday mornings** *(before 10:00) and late afternoons (after 17:00). It's possible to book tickets in advance (€1.50/ ticket surcharge; online at www.gallerieaccademia.org or call 041-520-0345), but it's unnecessary if you avoid the busiest times.*

Renovation: The museum is nearing the end of a major, multiyear expansion and renovation. As a result, paintings come and go, and the actual locations of the pieces are hard to pin down. Still, the museum contains the best art in Venice. If you don't find a particular piece you'd like to see, check Room 23, which seems to be the holding pen for displaced art.

Visiting the Accademia: The Accademia is the greatest museum anywhere for Venetian Renaissance art and a good overview of painters whose works you'll see all over town. Venetian art is underrated and misunderstood. It's nowhere near as famous today as the work of the Florentine Renaissance, but it's livelier, more colorful, and simply more fun, with historical slices of Venice, ravishing nudes, and very human Madonnas. The Venetian love of luxury shines through in this collection, which starts in the Middle Ages and runs to the 1700s. Look for grand canvases of colorful, spacious settings, peopled with happy locals in extravagant clothes having a great time.

Medieval highlights include elaborate altarpieces and golden-haloed Madonnas, all painted at a time when realism, depth of field, and emotion were considered beside the point. Medieval Venetians, with their close ties to the East, borrowed techniques such as gold-leafing, frontal poses, and "iconic" faces from the religious icons of Constantinople (modern-day Istanbul).

Among early masterpieces of the Renaissance are Mantegna's studly *St. George* and Giorgione's mysterious *Tempest*. As the Renaissance reaches its heights, so do the paintings, such as Titian's magnificent *Presentation of the Virgin*. It's a religious scene, yes, but it's really just an excuse to display secular splendor (Titian was the most famous painter of his day—perhaps even more famous than Michelangelo). Veronese's sumptuous *Feast in the House of Levi* also has an ostensibly religious theme (in the middle, find Jesus eating his final

Bridge of Sighs

San Giorgio Maggiore

meal)—but it's outdone by the luxury and optimism of Renaissance Venice. Life was a good thing and beauty was to be enjoyed. (Veronese was hauled before the Inquisition for painting such a bawdy Last Supper...so he fine-tuned the title.) End your tour with Guardi's and Canaletto's painted "postcards" of the city—landscapes for visitors who lost their hearts to the romance of Venice.

▲▲PEGGY GUGGENHEIM COLLECTION

The popular museum of far-out art, housed in the American heiress' former retirement palazzo, offers one of Europe's best reviews of the art of the first half of the 20th century. Stroll through styles represented by artists whom Peggy knew personally—Cubism (Picasso, Braque), Surrealism (Dalí, Ernst), Futurism (Boccioni), American Abstract Expressionism (Pollock), and a sprinkling of Klee, Calder, and Chagall.

Cost and Hours: €15, usually includes temporary exhibits, Wed-Mon 10:00-18:00, closed Tue, audioguide-€7, pricey café, 5-minute walk from Accademia Bridge, vaporetto: Accademia or Salute, tel. 041-240-5411, www.guggenheim-venice.it.

▲LA SALUTE CHURCH (SANTA MARIA DELLA SALUTE)

This impressive church with a crown-shaped dome was built and dedicated to the Virgin Mary by grateful survivors of the 1630 plague.

Cost and Hours: Free entry to church, €4 to enter sacristy; daily 9:00-12:00 & 15:00-17:30, 10-minute walk from Accademia Bridge, vaporetto: La Salute, tel. 041-274-3928.

▲CA' REZZONICO (MUSEUM OF 18TH-CENTURY VENICE)

This Grand Canal palazzo offers the most insightful look at the life of Venice's rich and famous in the 1700s. Wander under ceilings by Tiepolo, among furnishings from that most decadent century, enjoying views of the canal and paintings by Guardi, Canaletto, and Longhi.

Cost and Hours: €10, Wed-Mon 10:00-18:00, Nov-March until 17:00, closed Tue year-round, audioguide-€4; last entry one hour before closing, no flash photography, café, vaporetto: Ca' Rezzonico, tel. 041-241-0100, http://carezzonico.visitmuve.it.

San Polo District
▲▲▲RIALTO BRIDGE

One of the world's most famous bridges, this distinctive and dramatic stone structure crosses the Grand Canal with a single confident span. The arcades along the top of the bridge help reinforce the structure... and offer some enjoyable shopping diversions, as does the **market** surrounding the bridge (produce market closed Sun, fish market closed Sun-Mon).

Veronese, Feast in the House of Levi

FONDACO DEI TEDESCHI (GERMAN EXCHANGE)

This luxury "mall," with fantastic views from its roof terrace, occupies a block-long building that was once the long-ago home to Germanic traders (*tedeschi*) in the city, and more recently the main post office. The ground floor features gourmet food shops, ritzy cafés, classy Venetian souvenirs, and free WCs.

Cost and Hours: Free, daily 10:00-20:00, longer hours in summer, less crowded in the morning, most crowded near sunset, north side of Rialto Bridge, www.tfondaco.com.

▲▲FRARI CHURCH (BASILICA DI SANTA MARIA GLORIOSA DEI FRARI)

My favorite art experience in Venice is seeing art in the setting for which it was designed—as it is at the Frari Church. The Franciscan "Church of the Brothers" and the art that decorates it are warmed by the spirit of St. Francis. It features the work of three great Renaissance masters: Donatello, Giovanni Bellini, and Titian— each showing worshippers the glory of God in human terms.

Cost and Hours: €3, Mon-Sat 9:00-18:00, Sun 13:00-18:00, modest dress recommended, no flash photos, on Campo dei Frari, near San Tomà vaporetto and *traghetto* stops, tel. 041-272-8618, www.basilicadeifrari.it.

Tours: You can rent an **audioguide** for €2, or 🎧 download my free Frari Church **audio tour.**

Visiting the Frari Church: In Donatello's wood statue of *St. John the Baptist* (just to the right of the high altar), the prophet of the desert—dressed in animal skins and nearly starving from his diet of bugs 'n' honey—announces the coming of the Messiah. Donatello was a Florentine working at the dawn of the Renaissance.

Bellini's *Madonna and Child with Saints and Angels* painting (in the sacristy farther to the right) came later, done by a Venetian in a more Venetian style—soft focus without Donatello's harsh realism. While Renaissance humanism demanded Madonnas and saints that were accessible and human, Bellini places them in a physical setting so beautiful that it creates its own mood of serene holiness. The genius of Bellini, perhaps the greatest Venetian painter, is obvious in the pristine clarity, rich colors (notice Mary's clothing), believable depth, and reassuring calm of this three-paneled altarpiece.

Finally, glowing red and gold like a stained-glass window over the high altar, **Titian's *Assumption of the Virgin*** sets the tone of exuberant beauty found in the otherwise sparse church. Titian the Venetian—a student of Bellini—painted steadily for 60 years...you'll see a lot of his art. As stunned apostles look up past the swirl of arms and legs, the complex composition of this painting draws you right to the radiant face of the once-dying, now-triumphant Mary as she joins God in heaven.

For many, these three pieces of art make a visit to the Accademia Gallery unnecessary (though they may whet your appetite for more). Before leaving, check out the Neoclassical pyramid-shaped Canova monument flanking the nave just inside the main entrance and (opposite that) the grandiose tomb of Titian. Compare the carved marble *Assumption* behind Titian's tombstone portrait with the painted original above the high altar.

▲▲SCUOLA SAN ROCCO

Sometimes called "Tintoretto's Sistine Chapel," this lavish meeting hall has some 50 large, colorful Tintoretto paintings plastered to the walls and ceilings. The best paintings are upstairs, especially the *Crucifixion* in the smaller room. View the neck-breaking splendor with the mirrors available in the Grand Hall.

Cost and Hours: €10, daily 9:30-17:30, no flash photography, next to the Frari Church, tel. 041-523-4864, www.scuola-grandesanrocco.it.

Venice's Lagoon

The island of Venice sits in a lagoon—a calm section of the Adriatic protected from wind and waves by the natural break-water of the Lido. The Lido is Venice's beach—nice for a break on a sunny day.

Beyond the church-topped island of San Giorgio Maggiore (directly in front of St. Mark's Square), four interesting islands hide out in the lagoon: San Michele, Murano, Burano, and Torcello. These islands make a good, varied, and long day trip.

Getting to the Lagoon: You can travel to any of the islands by vaporetto. Because single vaporetto tickets (€7.50) expire after 75 minutes, getting a vaporetto pass (€20/24 hours) for a lagoon excursion makes more sense.

For a route that takes you to all four islands, start at the **Fondamente Nove** vaporetto stop on the north shore of Venice (the "back" of the fish). Lines #4.1 and #4.2 converge here before heading out to Murano. Catch either one (every 10 minutes); you'll first cross to San Michele (which has a stop called Cimitero) in six minutes, then continue another three min-

utes to Murano-Colonna. Stroll through Murano, then leave that island from a different stop: Murano-Faro, where you can board vaporetto #12 for the 30-minute trip to Burano. From Burano, you can side-trip to Torcello on vaporetto #12 (5-minute trip each way, make sure it stops at Torcello). To make a quick return to Venice from Burano, hop vaporetto #12 (some of these skip Torcello), which returns you to Fondamente Nove (45 minutes).

SAN MICHELE (A.K.A. CIMITERO)

This is the cemetery island—and the final resting place of a few foreign VIPs, from poet Ezra Pound to composer Igor Stravinsky. The stopover is easy, since **vaporetti** come every 10 minutes. If you enjoy wandering through old cemeteries, you'll dig this one—it's full of flowers, trees, and birdsong, and has an intriguing chapel (cemetery open daily 7:30-18:00, Oct-March until 16:30; reception to the left as you enter, free WC to the right).

▲MURANO

Murano is famous for its glassmaking. From the Colonna vaporetto stop, skip

Frari Church

Titian, Assumption of the Virgin

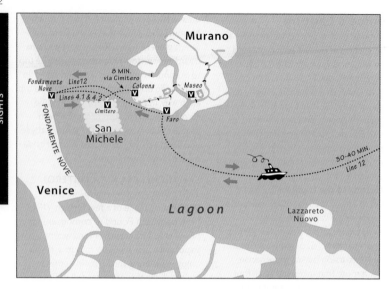

the glass shops in front of you, walk to the right, and wander up the street along the canal, **Fondamenta dei Vetrai** (Glassmakers' Embankment). The Faro district of Murano, on the other side of the canal, is packed with factories (*fabriche*) and their furnaces (*fornaci*). You'll pass dozens of **glass shops.** Early along this promenade, at #47, is the venerable **Venini** shop, with glass a cut above the rest, and with an interior showing off the ultimate in modern Venetian glass design (Mon-Sat 9:30-18:00, closed Sun).

Murano's **Glass Museum** (Museo Vetrario) traces the history of this delicate art (€10, daily 10:00-18:00, Nov-March

until 17:00, last entry one hour before closing, tel. 041-739-586, http://museovetro. visitmuve.it).

———————————————

Rick's Tip: *Venetian glass blowers claim that much of the cheap glass you'll see in Venice is imported from China.* **Genuine Venetian glass** *comes with the Murano seal.*

———————————————

▲▲BURANO

Known for lacemaking, Burano offers a delightful, vibrantly colorful village alternative to big, bustling Venice. The tight **main drag** is packed with tourists and lined with shops, selling lace or Burano's locally pro-

Murano's Fondamenta dei Vetrai

Firing up the glass furnace on Murano

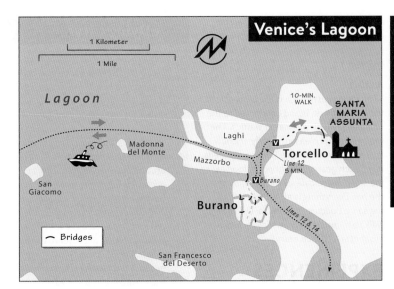

Venice's Lagoon

duced white wine. Wander to the far side of the island, and the mood shifts. Explore to the right of the leaning tower for a peaceful yet intensely colorful, small-town lagoon world. Benches line a little promenade at the water's edge—a pretty picnic spot.

Burano's **Lace Museum** (Museo del Merletto di Burano) shows the island's lace heritage (€5, Tue-Sun 10:00-18:00, Nov-March until 17:00, closed Mon year-round, tel. 041-730-034, http://museomerletto.visitmuve.it).

▲TORCELLO

This is the birthplace of Venice, where some of the first mainland refugees set-

tled, escaping the barbarian hordes. Today, it's marshy and shrub-covered, the least-developed island (pop. 20). There's little to see except the church (a 10-minute walk from the dock; the oldest in Venice, and still sporting some impressive mosaics), a climbable bell tower, and a modest museum of Roman sculpture and medieval sculpture and manuscripts (€12 combo-ticket covers museum, church, and bell tower; €9 combo-ticket covers church and bell tower; both combo-tickets include audioguide; museum only—€3; church and bell tower—€5 each; church open daily March-Oct 10:30-18:00, Nov-Feb 10:00-17:00, museum

Colorful Burano

Burano lace is prized.

and campanile close 30 minutes earlier and museum closed Mon year-round; museum tel. 041-730-761, church tel. 041-730-119).

▲LIDO

Venice's nearest beach is the Lido, across the lagoon on an island connected to the mainland (which means car traffic). The sandy beach is pleasant, family-friendly, and good for swimming. Rent an umbrella, buy beach gear at the shop, get food at the self-service café, or have a drink at the bar. Everything is affordable and in the same building (vaporetto: Lido S.M.E., walk 10 minutes on Gran Viale S. Maria Elisabetta to beach entry).

EXPERIENCES

Gondola Rides

Riding a gondola is simple, expensive, and one of the great experiences in Europe. Gondoliers hanging out all over town are eager to have you hop in for a ride. It's a rip-off for cynics, but a must for romantics.

The price for a gondola starts at €80 for a 35-minute ride during the day. You can divide the cost—and the romance—among up to six people per boat, but only two get the love seat. Prices jump to €100 after 19:00—when it's most romantic and relaxing. Adding a singer and an accordionist will cost an additional €120. If you value budget over romance, save money by recruiting fellow travelers to split a

A gondola station

A Dying City?

Venice's population (fewer than 55,000 in the historic city) is half what it was just 30 years ago, and people are leaving at a rate of a thousand a year. Of those who stay, 25 percent are 65 or older.

Sad, yes, but imagine raising a family here: Apartments are small, high up, and expensive. Humidity and occasional flooding make basic maintenance a pain. Home-improvement projects require navigating miles of red tape, and you must follow regulations intended to preserve the historical ambience. Everything is expensive because it has to be shipped in from the mainland. You can easily get glass and tourist trinkets, but it's hard to find groceries or get your shoes fixed. Running basic errands involves lots of walking and stairs—imagine crossing over arched bridges while pushing a child in a stroller and carrying a day's worth of groceries.

With millions of visitors a year (150,000 a day at peak times), on any given day Venetians are likely outnumbered by tourists. Despite government efforts to subsidize rents and build cheap housing, the city is losing its residents. The economy itself is thriving, thanks to tourist dollars and rich foreigners buying second homes. But the culture is dying. Even the most hopeful city planners worry that in a few decades Venice will not be a city at all, but a museum, a cultural theme park, a decaying Disneyland for adults.

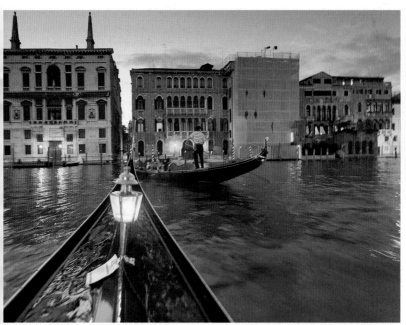

A gondola ride at night is worth the price.

gondola. Prices are standard and listed on the gondoliers' association website (go to www.gondolavenezia.it, click on "Using the Gondola," and look under "charterage").

Rick's Tip: *For* **cheap gondola thrills** *during the day, stick to the €2 one-minute ferry ride on a Grand Canal* traghetto. *At night, vaporetti are nearly empty, and it's a great time to cruise the Grand Canal on slow boat #1.*

Dozens of gondola stations (*servizio gondole*) are set up along canals all over town. Because your gondolier may offer narration or conversation during your ride, talk with several and choose one you like. Review the map and discuss the route; it's a good way to see if you enjoy the gondolier's personality and language skills. Establish the price, route, and duration of the trip before boarding, enjoy your ride, and pay only when you're finished. While prices are pretty firm, you might find them softer during the day. Most gondoliers

honor the official prices, but a few might try for some extra euros, particularly by insisting on a tip. (While not required or even expected, if your gondolier does the full 35 minutes and entertains you en route, a 5-10 percent tip is appreciated; if he's surly or rushes through the trip, skip it.) While gondoliers can be extremely charming, locals say that anyone who falls for one of these Venetian Romeos "has slices of ham over her eyes."

If you've hired musicians and want to hear a Venetian song (*un canto Veneziano*), try requesting *"Venezia La Luna e Tu."* Asking to hear *"O Sole Mio"* (which comes from Naples) is like asking a Chicago lounge singer to sing "Swanee River."

It's worth the extra cost to experience a gondola ride at night. The moon sails past otherwise unseen buildings and silhouettes gaze down from bridges while window glitter spills onto the black water. Put the camera down and make time for you and your partner to enjoy a threesome with Venice.

Festivals

Venice's most famous festival is **Carnevale,** the celebration Americans know as Mardi Gras (usually late Jan to early Feb, www.carnevale.venezia.it). Carnevale, which means "farewell to meat," originated as a wild, two-month-long party leading up to the austerity of Lent. In its heyday—the 1600s and 1700s—you could do pretty much anything with anybody from any social class if you were wearing a mask. These days it's a tamer 18-day celebration, culminating in a huge dance lit with fireworks on St. Mark's Square. Some Venetians don masks and join in the fun; others skip town.

Every year, the city hosts the world-class **Venice Biennale International Art Exhibition,** alternating between art in odd years (the main event) and architecture in even years (much smaller). The exhibition spreads over the Arsenale and Giardini park (take vaporetto #1 or #2 to Giardini-Biennale; for details and an events calendar, see www.labiennale.org). The actual exhibition usually runs from June through November, but other loosely connected events—film, dance, theater—are held throughout the year (as early as February) in various venues.

Nightlife

You must experience Venice after dark. The city is quiet at night, as many tour groups (not mine) stay on the mainland and day-trippers return to their beach resorts and cruise ships. Gondolas cost more, but are worth it.

Check at the TI or the TI's website (www.turismovenezia.it) for listings of entertainment and events, including church concerts. The free monthly Un Ospite di Venezia lists all the latest events in English (free at fancy hotels, or check www.unospitedivenezia.it/en).

St. Mark's Square

Streetlamp halos, floodlit history, and a ceiling of stars make St. Mark's Square magic at midnight. After dark, **dueling café orchestras** entertain. They feature similar food, prices, and a three- to five-

Carnevale is a masked extravaganza.

The evening café scene on St. Mark's Square

piece combo playing a selection of classical and pop hits. You can hang out for free behind the tables (allowing you to move on easily to the next orchestra when the musicians take a break). Dancing on the square is free—and encouraged.

If you spring for a seat to enjoy a concert, expect to pay €15 and up (for a drink and the cover charge for music)—money well spent. It's acceptable to nurse a drink for an hour—you're paying for the music with the cover charge. To save money (but forego proximity to the music), you can sip your coffee at the bar, because the law limits the charge for coffee at a bar.

Caffè Florian (on the right as you face the church) is the most famous Venetian café and was one of the first places in Europe to serve coffee. The outside tables are the main action, but walk inside through the richly decorated rooms where Casanova, Lord Byron, Charles Dickens, and Woody Allen have all paid too much for a drink (an espresso—your cheapest option—costs €12.50: €6.50 for the coffee and a €6 cover charge when the orchestra is playing, daily 10:00-24:00, shorter hours in winter, www.caffeflorian.com).

Gran Caffè Quadri, opposite the Florian, has equally illustrious clientele, including the writers Stendhal and Dumas, and composer Richard Wagner.

The scene at **Gran Caffè Lavena,** near the Clock Tower, can be great, despite its politically incorrect but dazzling chandelier.

Gran Caffè Chioggia, on the Piazzetta facing the Doge's Palace, charges no cover and has a few musicians playing—including a pianist—and a wider variety of tunes (no inside ambience, slightly cheaper than the others if you just want to sit on the square).

Rick's Tip: *You'll hear about the famous* **Harry's American Bar,** *which sells overpriced food and cocktails, but* **it's a tourist trap***...and the last place Hemingway would drink today. It's cheaper to get a drink at any of the hole-in-the-wall bars just off St. Mark's Square.*

Concerts

Venice is a city of the Baroque era. For about €25, you can take your pick of traditional Vivaldi concerts in churches throughout town. You'll find young, frilly-costumed Vivaldis hawking concert tickets on many corners. Most shows start at 20:30 and generally last 1.5 hours. Hotels sell tickets at face-value.

Tickets can usually be bought the same day as the concert, so don't bother with websites that sell tickets with a surcharge. Musicians in wigs and tights offer better spectacle; musicians in black-and-white suits are better performers.

The **Interpreti Veneziani orchestra,** considered the best group in town, generally performs 1.5-hour concerts nightly at 21:00 inside the sumptuous San Vidal Church (€29, church ticket booth open daily 9:30-21:00, north end of Accademia Bridge, tel. 041-277-0561, www.interpretiveneziani.com).

Musica a Palazzo is an evening of opera at a Venetian palace on the Grand Canal. You'll spend about 45 delightful minutes each in three sumptuous rooms as eight musicians—usually four instruments and four singers—perform (about 2.25 hours total). They generally present three different operas on successive nights. With these surroundings,

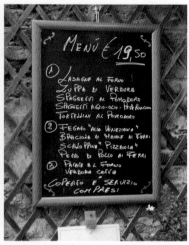

under Tiepolo frescoes, you'll be glad you dressed up. There are only 70 seats, so book in advance by phone or online (€85, nightly at 20:30, Palazzo Barbarigo Minotto, Fondamenta Duodo o Barbarigo, vaporetto: Santa Maria del Giglio, San Marco 2504, mobile 340-971-7272, www. musicapalazzo.com).

EATING

While touristy restaurants are the scourge of Venice, my recommended places are popular with locals and respect the tourists who happen by.

First trick: Walk away from triple-language menus or laminated pictures of food. Second trick: Eat fish. Many seafood dishes are the catch-of-the-day. Note that seafood (and steak) may be sold by weight—per 100 grams or *etto*—rather than a set price; be savvy or be surprised. Third trick: Eat later. A place that feels touristy at 19:00 can be filled with locals at 21:00.

Budget Eating: Unique to Venice, *cicchetti* bars specialize in small appetizers that can combine to make a quick, tasty meal (see "The Stand-Up Progressive Venetian Pub-Crawl Dinner" later in this section).

Takeout pizza is one of the cheapest ways to eat in Venice. Small hole-in-the-wall shops in every neighborhood sell takeout pizza—round, by the slice, or by weight. Takeout prices increase dramatically as you near the Rialto and St. Mark's Square.

The Rialto open-air market is great for picnic gatherers (closed Sun), though any respectable grocery (*alimentari*) will do. As for supermarkets, a handy **Co-op** is between St. Mark's and Campo Santa Maria Formosa (daily 8:30-22:00, on the corner of Salizada San Lio and Calle del Mondo Novo at Castello 5817). A **Conad** supermarket is in Dorsoduro (daily 8:00-23:00, vaporetto: San Basilio).

Gelato: Venice isn't known for its quality gelato but you'll still find good *gelaterie* in every Venetian neighborhood. Several cafés on St. Mark's Square have gelato counters in summer, including **Gran Caffè Lavena** (at #134) and **Todaro** (on the corner of the Piazzetta at #5, near the water and across from the Doge's Palace). **Gelatoteca Suso** serves delectable flavors on the San Marco side of the Rialto Bridge (next to recommended Rosticceria San Bartolomeo, on Calle de la Bissa). **Il Doge** also sells Sicilian-style granita, slushy ice with fresh fruit (on bustling Campo Santa Margarita).

Near the Rialto Bridge
North of the Bridge

These restaurants and wine bars are located beyond Campo Santi Apostoli, on or near the Strada Nova, the main drag going from Rialto toward the train station.

$$$ Trattoria da Bepi, bright and alpine-paneled, feels like a classic, where Loris carries on his mother's passion for good, traditional Venetian cuisine. Ask for the seasonal specialties: The seafood appetizer plate and crab dishes are excellent. There's good seating inside and out. If you trust Loris, you'll walk away with a wonderful dining memory (Fri-Wed 12:00-14:30 & 19:00-22:00, closed Thu, reservations recommended, half a block

Venetian Cuisine

Venetian cuisine relies heavily on fish, shellfish, risotto, and polenta.

Antipasti: Popular choices include *antipasto di mare* (a marinated mix of fish and shellfish served chilled) and *sarde in saor* (sardines marinated with onions). *Cicchetti* are Venetian tapas, the finger-food appetizers served in some pubs.

First courses (primi): Venice's favorite dish is risotto, a short-grain rice simmered in broth and often flavored with seafood (*risotto nero* is risotto made with squid and its ink; *risotto ai porcini* contains porcini mushrooms). Other first courses are *risi e bisi* (rice and peas), *pasta e fagioli* (pasta and bean soup), and *bigoli in salsa* (fat whole-wheat noodles with anchovy sauce). Pasta is commonly served *alla buzzara* (with a rich seafood-tomato sauce). You'll also see plenty of polenta—boiled cornmeal served soft or cut into firm slabs and grilled.

Second courses (secondi): It's mostly *frutti di mare* (seafood). The most common fish are farmed, not wild—such as *branzino* (sea bass), *orata* (sea bream), *salmone* (salmon), and *rombo* (turbot, a flounder-like flatfish). The weirder the animal (eel, octopus, frogfish), the more local it is. *Baccalà* is dried Atlantic salt cod that's rehydrated and often served with polenta. Other choices are calamari, *cozze* (mussels, often steamed in broth), *gamberi* (shrimp), *moleche col pien* (fried soft-shell crabs), *pesce spada* (swordfish), *rospo* (frogfish, a small marine fish), *seppia* (cuttlefish, a squid-like

Pasta with shellfish is a favorite.

creature; can be served in its own ink, often over spaghetti); *sogliola* (sole, served poached or oven-roasted), *vitello di mare* ("sea veal," like swordfish—firm, pink, mild, and grilled), and *vongole* (small clams, often steamed with herbs and wine). *Fritto misto di pesce* is assorted deep-fried seafood (often calamari and prawns). *Zuppa di pesce* is seafood stew.

Cocktails: The most popular *aperitivo* (pre-dinner drink) is *spritz,* which mixes white wine, soda or prosecco, and ice with either Campari (bitter) or Aperol (sweeter), garnished with an olive or skewer of fruit. Other options include the *bellini* (prosecco and white-peach puree) and *tiziano* (grape juice and prosecco). A popular *digestivo* (after-dinner drink) is *sgroppino:* squeezed lemon juice, lemon gelato, and vodka.

off Campo Santi Apostoli on Salizada Pistor, Cannaregio 4550, tel. 041-528-5031, www.dabepi.it).

$$$$ Vini da Gigio, a more expensive option, has a traditional Venetian menu and a classy but unsnooty setting that's a pleasant mix of traditional and contemporary (Wed-Sun 12:00-14:30 & 19:00-22:30, closed Mon-Tue, 4 blocks from Ca' d'Oro vaporetto stop on Fondamenta San Felice, behind the church on Campo San Felice, Cannaregio 3628a, tel. 041-528-5140, www.vinidagigio.com).

East of the Rialto Bridge

The next few places hide away in the

twisty lanes between the Rialto Bridge and Campo Santa Maria Formosa. Osteria da Alberto is a tad farther north of the others, in Cannaregio.

$ Rosticceria Gislon is a cheap—if confusing—self-service diner. This throw-back budget eatery—kind of an Italian Mel's Diner—has a surly staff: Don't take it personally. Notice that the different counters serve up different types of food—pastas, *secondi,* fried goodies, and so on. You can get it to go, grab one of the few tiny tables, or munch at the bar—but I'd skip their upper-floor restaurant option (prices listed on wall behind counter, cheap glasses of wine, no cover and no service charge, daily 9:00-21:30, San Marco 5424, tel. 041-522-3569). To find it, imagine the statue on Campo San Bartolomeo walks backward 20 yards, turns left, and goes under a passageway. Follow him.

$$ Osteria al Portego is a small and popular neighborhood eatery near Campo San Lio. Carlo serves good meals, bar-gain-priced house wine, and excellent €1-3 *cicchetti* appetizers—best enjoyed early, around 18:00. The *cicchetti* here can make a great meal, but consider sitting down for a dinner from their menu. From 12:00-14:30 & 17:30-21:30, their six tables are reserved for those ordering from the menu; the *cicchetti* are picked over by 21:00. Reserve ahead if you want a table (daily 11:30-15:00 & 17:30-22:00, on Calle de la Malvasia, Castello 6015, tel. 041-522-9038, www.osteriaalportego.it, Federica).

$$ Osteria da Alberto, up near Campo Santa Maria Novo, is one of my stand-bys. They offer up excellent daily specials: seafood dishes, pastas, and a good house wine in a woody and characteristic interior. It's smart to reserve at night—I'd request a table in front (daily 12:00-15:00 & 18:30-22:30; on Calle Larga Giacinto Gallina, midway between Campo Santi Apostoli and Campo San Zanipolo/Santi Giovanni e Paolo, and next to Ponte de la Panada bridge, Cannaregio 5401; tel. 041-

523-8153, www.osteriadaalberto.it, run by Graziano and Giovanni).

Rialto Market Area

The north end of the Rialto Bridge is great for menu browsing, bar-hopping, drinks, and snacks, as well as sit-down restaurants. You'll find lots of hardworking hole-in-the-walls catering to locals needing a quick, affordable, tasty bite. It's crowded by day, nearly empty early in the evening, and packed with Venetian hipsters later.

My listings below include a stretch of dark and rustic pubs serving *cicchetti* (Venetian tapas), a strip of trendy places fronting the Grand Canal, and several places at the market and nearby. All but the last eatery **(Osteria al Ponte Storto)** are within 200 yards of the market and each other.

Cicchetti Bars: The 100-yard-long "*Cicchetti* Strip," which starts two blocks inland from the Rialto Market (along Sotoportego dei Do Mori and Calle de le Do Spade), is beloved for its conviviality and tasty bar snacks. These four $ places (listed in the order you'll reach them, if coming from the Rialto Bridge) serve food all day, but the spread is best around noon (generally open daily 12:00-15:00 & 18:00-20:00 or 21:00, but the first two are closed Sun). Scout these places in advance to see which ambience appeals most to you. At each place, look for the list of snacks (around €1.50-2) and wine by the glass (about €1-3) at the bar or on the wall. **Bar all'Arco,** a bustling one-room joint, is particularly enjoyable for its tiny open-face sandwiches (closed Sun, San Polo 436; Francesco, Anna, Matteo). **Cantina Do Mori** has been famous with locals (since 1462) and savvy travelers (since 1982) for its fine wine and *francobolli,* a spicy selection of 20 tiny, mayo-soaked sandwiches nicknamed "stamps." Go here to be abused in a fine atmosphere—the frowns are part of the shtick. Be aware that prices add up quickly (closed Sun, can be shoulder-to-shoulder, San Polo 430). **Osteria ai Storti** is more

The Stand-Up Progressive Venetian Pub-Crawl Dinner

My favorite Venetian dinner is a pub crawl (*giro d'ombra*)—a tradition unique to Venice, where no cars means easy crawling. (*Giro* means stroll, and *ombra*—slang for a glass of wine—means shade, from the old days when a portable wine bar scooted with the shadow of the Campanile bell tower across St. Mark's Square.)

Venice's residential back streets hide characteristic bars (*bacari*) with countless trays of interesting toothpick munchies (*cicchetti*) and blackboards listing wines served by the glass. The *cicchetti* selection is best early, so start your evening by 18:00. Most bars are closed on Sunday. For a stress-free pub crawl, take a tour with Alessandro Schezzini (see page 613).

Cicchetti bars have a social stand-up zone and cozy tables where you can sit down with your *cicchetti* or order from a simple menu. Food generally costs the same price whether you stand or sit. Crowds sometimes happily spill into the street.

While you can order a plate, Venetians prefer going one-by-one...sipping their wine and trying this...then give me one of those...and so on. Try deep-fried mozzarella cheese, gorgonzola, calamari, artichoke hearts, and anything ugly on a toothpick. *Crostini* (small toasted bread with a topping) are popular, as are marinated seafood, olives, and prosciutto with melon. Meat and fish (*pesce;* PESH-ay) can be expensive; veggies (*verdure*) are cheap, at about €3 for a meal-sized plate. In many places, there's a set price per food item (e.g., €1.50). To get a plate of assorted appetizers for €8, ask for "*Un piatto classico di cicchetti misti da €8*" (oon pee-AH-toh KLAH-see-koh dee cheh-KET-tee MEE-stee dah OH-toh eh-OO-roh). Bread sticks (*grissini*) are free.

Bar-hopping Venetians enjoy an *aperitivo*—a before-dinner drink. Boldly order a bellini, a *spritz con Aperol,* or a prosecco, and draw approving looks from the natives. A small glass of house red or white wine (*ombra rosso* or *ombra bianco*) or a small beer (*birrino*) costs about €1. *Vin bon,* Venetian for fine wine, is €2-6 per little glass. A good last drink is *fragolino,* the local sweet wine—*bianco* or *rosso.* It often comes with a little cookie (*biscotto*) for dipping.

of a sit-down place (tables inside and on street). It's run by Alessandro, who speaks English and enjoys helping educate travelers (daily, around corner from Cantina Do Mori on Calle San Matio, San Polo 819). **Cantina Do Spade** is expertly run by Francesco and is also good for sit-down meals (30 yards down Calle de le Do Spade from Osteria ai Storti at San Polo 860, tel. 041-521-0583).

Canalside Seating: What I call the "Bancogiro Stretch," just past the Rialto Bridge, between Campo San Giacomo and the Grand Canal, has some of Venice's best canalside seating. Unless otherwise noted, all are open daily and serve drinks, *cicchetti,* and inventive, somewhat pricey sit-down meals. While you can get a drink anytime, dinner is typically served only after 19:00 or 19:30. During meals, they charge more and limit table seating to those ordering full lunches or dinners; but between mealtimes you can enjoy a drink or a snack at fine prices. After dinner, this stretch—especially in the surrounding alleys that house low-rent bars—becomes a trendy nightspot. I list them in the order you'll reach them from the Rialto Bridge. **$$$ Bar Naranzaria** serves Italian dishes with a few Japanese options. **$$ Caffè Vergnano** is your cheapest option (vegan dishes and a busy microwave oven). **$$$ Osteria al Pesador** has a friendly staff and serves local specialties. **$$$ Osteria Bancogiro** has the best reputation for dinner, a passion for the best cheese, and good *cicchetti* options at the bar (nice €17 cheese plate, closed Mon, tel. 041-523-2061, www.osteriabancogiro.it). The more modern **$$ Bar Ancòra** has a live piano player crooning lounge music during busy times (*cicchetti* at the bar).

At the Market: $ Al Mercà ("At the Market"), a few steps away and off the canal, is a lively little nook with a happy crowd. The price list is clear, and the youthful crowd seems to enjoy connecting with curious tourists (stand at bar or in square—there are no tables and no interior, Mon-Sat 10:00-14:30 & 18:00-21:00, closed Sun, on Campo Cesare Battisti, San Polo 213).

$$$$ Ristorante Vini da Pinto is a tourist-friendly eatery facing the fish market, with a large menu and relaxing outdoor seating (make sure you're sitting at the right restaurant and not their neighbors). Enjoy the lunch-only fixed-price, three-course seafood meal for €17. Rick Steves readers receive a welcoming prosecco and a farewell *limoncello* and homemade biscotti (daily 11:30-23:00, Campo de le Becarie, San Polo 367a, tel. 041-522-4599).

Farther Inland, off Campo San Aponal: $$ Osteria al Ponte Storto, on a quiet canalside corner a block off the main drag, is worth seeking out for its good-value main dishes, daily specials, and peaceful location (Tue-Sun 12:00-15:00 & 18:00-21:45, closed Mon, down Calle Bianca from San Aponal church, San Polo 1278, tel. 041-528-2144).

Near St. Mark's Square

At **$$$$ Ristorante Antica Sacrestia,** Pino greets you personally. His staff serves

Romantic Canalside Settings

If you want a meal with a canal view, it generally comes with lower quality and/or a higher price. But if you're determined to take home a canalside memory, these places can be great.

Near the Rialto Bridge: The "Bancogiro Stretch" offers fine places to enjoy a drink or a snack.

You'll also see tourist-trap eateries lining the Grand Canal just south of the Rialto Bridge. These places usually offer lousy food and aggressive "service." If you really want to eat here, ask if there's a minimum charge before you sit down (most places have one). The budget ideal would be to get a simple pizza or pasta and a drink for €15, and savor the ambience without getting ripped off. But few restaurants will allow you to get off that easy. To avoid a dispute over the bill, ask if there's a minimum charge before you sit down (most places have one).

In the Dorsoduro Neighborhood: $$ Bar Foscarini, next to the Accademia Bridge, offers decent pizzas overlooking the canal with no cover or service charge. **$$$ Terrazza dei Nobili,** overlooking the wide Giudecca Canal, is nice just before sunset. Both are listed under "In Dorsoduro" eateries.

creative fixed-price meals (€35, €55, or €80), a humdrum *menù del giorno,* and wonderful pizzas. (Be warned: Order carefully. Pizza is your only budget escape. And there's no wine by the glass.) You can also order à la carte; their €22 antipasto spread looks like a lagoon aquarium spread out on a plate. My readers are welcome to a free *sgroppino* (lemon vodka after-dinner drink) upon request (Tue-Sun 11:30-15:00 & 18:00-23:00, closed Mon, behind San Zaninovo/Giovanni Novo Church on Calle

Corona, Castello 4463, tel. 041-523-0749, www.anticasacrestia.it).

For a quick meal just steps away from St. Mark's Square, try **"Sandwich Row"**—Calle de le Rasse. The lane is lined with places to get a decent sandwich at an affordable price with a place to sit (most places open daily 7:00-24:00, about €1 extra per item to sit; from the Bridge of Sighs, head down the Riva and take the second lane on the left). **$ Birreria Forst** serves busy local workers a selection of meaty €3 sandwiches (daily 9:30-23:00, air-con, Castello 4540, tel. 041-523-0557). **$ Bar Verde** is a more modern sandwich bar (also splittable salads, fresh pastries, at the end of Calle de le Rasse facing Campo Santi Filippo e Giacomo, Castello 4526). **$$ Ristorante alla Basilica,** just one street behind St. Mark's Basilica, serves a solid €16 fixed-price lunch, often amid noisy school groups (Wed-Mon 12:00-15:00, closed Tue, air-con, Calle dei Albanesi, Castello 4255, tel. 041-522-0524).

Rick's Tip: *Though* **you can't legally picnic on St. Mark's Square,** *you're allowed to munch your meal at nearby* **Giardinetti Reali,** *the small park along the waterfront, west of the Piazzetta.*

North of St. Mark's Square

For a marginally less touristy scene, walk a few blocks north to inviting Campo Santa Maria Formosa.

$$$$ Osteria alle Testiere is my top dining splurge in Venice. Hugely respected, Luca and his staff are dedicated to quality, serving up creative, artfully presented market-fresh seafood (there's no meat on the menu), homemade pastas, and fine wine. They have daily specials, 10 wines by the glass, and one agenda: a great dining experience. They're open for lunch (12:00-15:00), and reservations are a must (taken only by email) well in advance for their two dinner seatings: 19:00 and 21:30 (plan on €50 for dinner, closed Sun-Mon, on Calle del Mondo Novo, just off Campo Santa Maria Formosa, Castello 5801, tel. 041-522-7220, www.osterialletestiere.it, info@osterialletestiere.it).

$$$ Osteria al Mascaron is a rustic little bar-turned-restaurant where Gigi, Momi, and their food-loving band of ruffians dish up rustic-yet-sumptuous pastas with steamy seafood. The €16 *antipasto misto* plate and two glasses of wine make a terrific light meal (Mon-Sat 12:00-15:00 & 19:00-23:00, closed Sun, reservations smart Fri-Sat; on Calle Lunga Santa Maria Formosa, a block past Campo Santa Maria Formosa, Castello 5225; tel. 041-522-5995, www.osteriamascaron.it). While they advertise pastas only for two, you are welcome to have a half-order for half-price—still plenty big.

In Dorsoduro

All of these recommendations are within a 10-minute walk of the Accademia Bridge and well worth the walk.

Near the Accademia Bridge

$$ Bar Foscarini, next to the Accademia Bridge and Galleria, offers decent pizzas and *panini* in a memorable Grand Canal-view setting. The food is forgettable and drinks are pricey. But you're paying a premium for this premium location. They also serve breakfast (daily 8:00-23:00, until 20:30 Nov-April, on Rio Terà A. Foscarini, Dorsoduro 878c, tel. 041-522-7281, Paolo and Simone).

$ Al Vecio Marangon is tucked away from the frenzy of Venice, about 100 yards west of the Accademia. This stylishly rustic bar serves *cicchetti*-style dishes and pastas within its tight and picturesque interior or at a line of outdoor tables. Consider their splittable *piatto di cicchetti misti.* As they take no reservations, arrive early or be prepared to wait (daily 12:00-22:00, on Calle de la Toletta, Dorsoduro 1210, tel. 041-277-8554).

Restaurants & Hotels near the Rialto Bridge

100 Meters
100 Yards

To Vaporetto Dock

C. VENIER
C. NUOVA
I'Acqua Dolce
C. DEL FORNO
C. DE LA MADONA
C. PROVERBI
PRETI

FONDAMENTE NOVE

CANNAREGIO

FONDAMENTA DEI MENDICANTI
Rio dei Mendicanti
Rio de la Panada
CALLA DE LA TESTA

HOSPITAL

SANTI APOSTOLI
Campo de la Cason
C. MAL
SAN CANZIAN
C. WIDMANN
Rio dei Santi Apostoli
Campo San Canzian
Campo Santa Maria Novo
5
CALLE LARGA GALLINA
Campo Corner
MAGAZEN
RIO TERA SAN CANZIAN
SALIZADA SAN CANZIAN
BOLDU
MIRACOLI
BAGATAN
SANTA MARIA DEI MIRACOLI
Campo dei Santi Giovanni e Paolo
COLLEONI STATUE
SANTI GIOVANNI E PAOLO (SAN ZANIPOLO)
SALIZADA S. ZANIPOLO
Rio de San Gio Grisostomo
SAN GIO. GRIS.
MARCO POLO BOOKSHOP
C. CASTELI
C. DE LA ERBE
F. DANDOLO
SAN GRISOSTOMO
ASEO
COIN DEP'T STORE
C. SCALETA
4
Campo Santa Marina
FRUTARIOL
C. PIOMBO
LARGA
MARCELLO
Rio de Santa Marina
Rio del piombo
14
C. BRESSANA
S. MADONA
F. FELZI
OSPEALETO

CASTELLO

ACQUA ALTA BOOKSHOP & PAPIER MACHÉ MASK SHOP
PISA
WC
Campo S. Bartolomeo
PONTE S ANTONIO
C. CARMINATI
Rio de la FAVA
SAN LIO
C. DE LA NAVE
SALIZADA SAN LIO
C. FAVA
C. DEL DOSE
Rio d. Pestrin
Campo Santa Maria Formosa
C. LUNGA S. MARIA FORMOSA
12
C. DEI ORBI
Rio de S. Ma Formosa
C. DE L'AQUILA NERA
C. DEI STAGNERI
Campo de la Fava
SANTA MARIA FAVA
DEL PARADISO
VENIERA
R. MALVASIA
SAN ANTONIO
MONDO NOVO
11
SANTA MARIA FORMOSA
RUGA GIUFFA
C. MEZO
S. SALV.
POST
13
C. DE LE BANDE
C. PIETRO MAGAZEN
MARZ. CAPITELLO
DE LE ACQUE
C. DE MEZO
S. ZUL

SAN   MARCO

CALLE QUERINI
F. D REMEDIO
To San Marco
To San Marco

Hotels

10 Osteria al Ponte Storto
11 Osteria alle Testiere
12 Osteria al Mascaron
13 Co-op Supermarket

14 Locanda la Corte
15 Hotel al Ponte Antico
16 Pensione Guerrato
17 To Hotel al Ponte Mocenigo

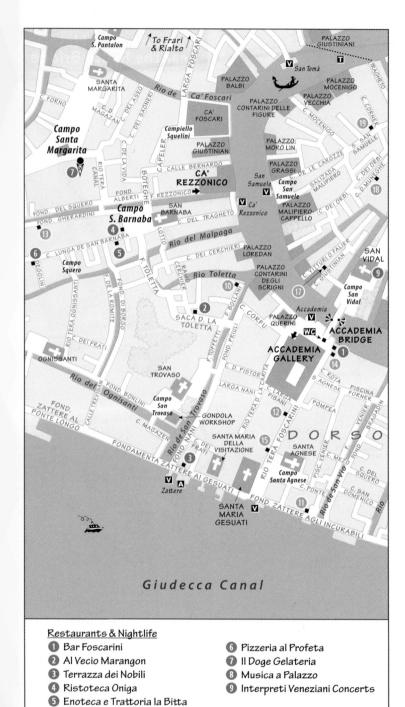

Restaurants & Nightlife

1 Bar Foscarini
2 Al Vecio Marangon
3 Terrazza dei Nobili
4 Ristoteca Oniga
5 Enoteca e Trattoria la Bitta

6 Pizzeria al Profeta
7 Il Doge Gelateria
8 Musica a Palazzo
9 Interpreti Veneziani Concerts

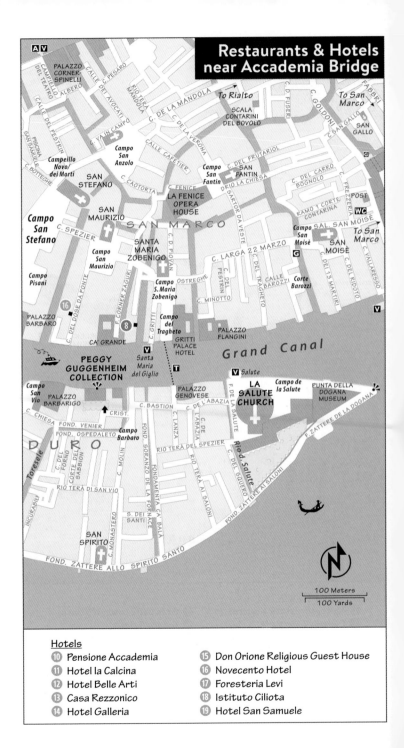

Restaurants & Hotels near Accademia Bridge

Hotels
- ⑩ Pensione Accademia
- ⑪ Hotel la Calcina
- ⑫ Hotel Belle Arti
- ⑬ Casa Rezzonico
- ⑭ Hotel Galleria
- ⑮ Don Orione Religious Guest House
- ⑯ Novecento Hotel
- ⑰ Foresteria Levi
- ⑱ Istituto Ciliota
- ⑲ Hotel San Samuele

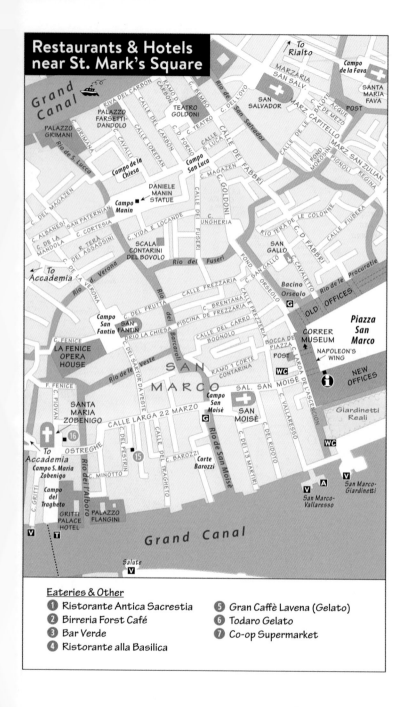

Restaurants & Hotels near St. Mark's Square

To Rialto

Grand Canal

Campo de la Fava

SANTA MARIA FAVÀ

POST

MARZARIA SAN SALV.

SAN SALVADOR

MARZ. CAPITELLO

C. DE L'OVO

C. DE LE ACQUE

C. BEMBO

C. DE MEZO

RIVA DEL CARBON

RAMO CARBON

CALLE DEL CARBON

CALLE TOREDAN

C. TEATRO

C. D. FORNO

C. DEL LOVO

C. SAN Salvador

PALAZZO FARSETTI-DANDOLO

TEATRO GOLDONI

CALLE DE LE

FOND. MOROSINI PIGNOLI REGINA

MARZ. SAN ZULIAN

PALAZZO GRIMANI

C. GRIMANA

C. CAVALLI

Campo de la Chiesa

Campo San Luca

C. LUCA

C. MAGAZEN

CALLE DEI FABBRI

Rio de S. Lucca

C. DEL MAGAZEN

DANIELE MANIN STATUE

Campo Manin

C. MAGAZEN

CALLE DEL FUSERI

CALLE GOLDONI

C. UNGHERIA

SAN PATERNIAN

SAN GALLO

CALLE FIUBERA

C. ALBANESI

C. CORTESIA

C. VIDA E LOCANDE

RIO TERA DE LE COLONNE

C. D FABBRI

C. DE LA MANDOLA

R. TERA ASSASSINI

SCALA CONTARINI DEL BOVOLO

Rio del Fuseri

C. DEI ASSASSINI

To Accademia

Rio d. Verona

CALLE FREZZARIA

FOND. SAN GALLO

C. CAVALETTO

Rio de le Procuratie

Bacino Orseolo

OLD OFFICES

Piazza San Marco

Campo San Fantin

C. DEL FRUTTA

Rio dei

C. BRENTANA

PISCINA DE FREZZARIA

CALLE DEL CARRO

CALLE FREZZARIA

BOGNOLO

BOCCA DE PIAZZA

CORRER MUSEUM

C. FENICE

LA FENICE OPERA HOUSE

DRIO LA CHIESA

CALLE DEL SARTOR DA VESTE

Rio de le Veste

Barcaroli

RAMO 1 CORTE CONTARINA

POST

NAPOLEON'S WING

NEW OFFICES

F. FENICE

SAN

MARCO

WC

SAL. SAN MOISÈ

Giardinetti Reali

C. PIOVAN

SANTA MARIA ZOBENIGO

CALLE LARGA 22 MARZO

Campo San Moisè

SAN MOISÈ

C. LARGA DE L'ASCENSION

C. VALLARESSO

To Accademia

Campo S. Maria Zobenigo

C. GRITTI

Campo del Tragheto

OSTREGHE

C. DEL PESTRIN

C. BAROZZI

Corte Barozzi

Rio de San Moisè

C. DEL 13 MARTIRI

C. DEL RIDOTO

WC

San Marco-Giardinetti

C. MINOTTO

CALLE DEL TRAGHETO

San Marco-Vallaresso

GRITTI PALACE HOTEL

PALAZZO FLANGINI

Rio dell'Alboro

Grand Canal

Salute

Eateries & Other

1. Ristorante Antica Sacrestia
2. Birreria Forst Café
3. Bar Verde
4. Ristorante alla Basilica
5. Gran Caffè Lavena (Gelato)
6. Todaro Gelato
7. Co-op Supermarket

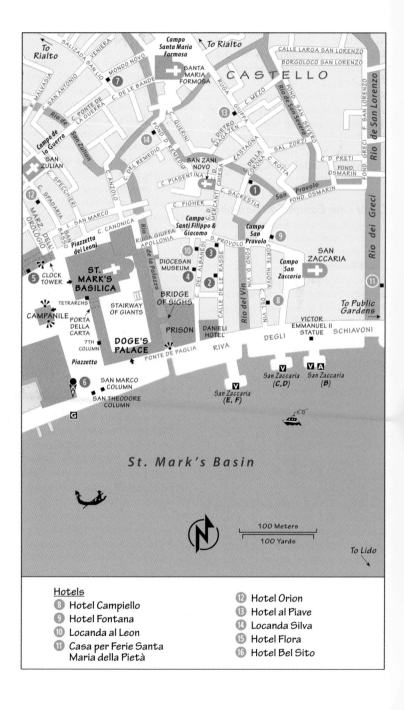

In Zattere

$$$ Terrazza dei Nobili takes full advantage of the warm, romantic evening sun. They serve regional specialties, along with pizza, at tolerable prices. The breezy and beautiful seaside seating comes with the rumble of vaporetti from the nearby stop. The interior is bright and hip (daily 12:00-24:00; from Zattere vaporetto stop, turn left to Dorsoduro 924; tel. 041-520-6895).

On or near Campo San Barnaba

This small square is a delight—especially for dinner. Make reservations to dine later in the evening.

$$$ Ristoteca Oniga has an eclectic yet cozy interior, great tables on the square, and is run by the enthusiastic Raffaele. The menu has a few vegetarian and meat dishes, but focuses on fresh fish and other sea creatures (daily 12:00-14:30 & 19:00-22:30, closed Tue in winter, reservations smart, Campo San Barnaba, Dorsoduro 2852, tel. 041-522-4410, www.oniga.it).

$$ Pizzeria al Profeta is a casual place popular for great pizza and steak. Its sprawling interior seems to stoke conviviality, as does its leafy garden out back (Wed-Mon 12:00-14:30 & 19:00-23:30, closed Tue; from Campo San Barnaba, a long walk down Calle Lunga San Barnaba to #2671, tel. 041-523-7466).

$$$ Enoteca e Trattoria la Bitta is dark and woody, with a soft-jazz bistro feel, tight seating, and a small back patio. They serve beautifully presented, traditional Venetian food with a "slow food" ethic. They do two dinner seatings (19:00 and 21:00) and require reservations (dinner only, Mon-Sat 19:00-23:00, closed Sun, cash only, just off Campo San Barnaba on Calle Lunga San Barnaba, Dorsoduro 2753a, tel. 041-523-0531, Debora and Marcellino).

SLEEPING

I've listed rooms in several neighborhoods: St. Mark's bustle, the Rialto action, and the quiet Dorsoduro area behind the Accademia. Note that hotel websites are particularly valuable for Venice, because they often include detailed directions that can help you get to your rooms with a minimum of wrong turns in this navigationally challenging city.

Prices can spike during festivals. Almost all places drop prices in July and August, and again from November through March (except during Christmas and Carnevale).

Near St. Mark's Square

To get here from the train station or Piazzale Roma bus station, ride the slow vaporetto #1 to San Zaccaria or the fast #2 (which also leaves from Tronchetto parking lot) to San Marco.

East of St. Mark's Square

Located near the Bridge of Sighs, just off the Riva degli Schiavoni waterfront promenade, these places rub drainpipes with Venice's most palatial five-star hotels.

$$$$ Hotel Campiello, lacy and bright, was once part of a 19th-century convent. Ideally located 50 yards off the waterfront on a tiny square, its 16 rooms offer a tranquil, friendly refuge for travelers who appreciate comfort and professional service (RS%, air-con, elevator, just steps from the San Zaccaria vaporetto stop, Castello 4647; tel. 041-520-5764, www.hcampiello.it, campiello@hcampiello.it; family-run for four generations, currently by Thomas, Nicoletta, and Monica). They also rent three modern family apartments, under rustic timbers just steps away.

$$$$ Hotel Fontana, two bridges behind St. Mark's Square, is a pleasant family-run place with 15 sparse but classic-feeling rooms overlooking a lively square (RS%, several rooms with terraces, family rooms, air-con, elevator, Wi-Fi in common areas, on Campo San Provolo at Castello 4701, tel. 041-522-0579, www. hotelfontana.it, info@hotelfontana.it, cousins Diego and Gabriele).

$$$$ Locanda al Leon, which feels a little like a medieval tower house, is conscientiously run and rents 12 rooms just off Campo Santi Filippo e Giacomo (RS%, some view rooms, family rooms, air-con, 2 apartments with kitchens, Campo Santi Filippo e Giacomo, Castello 4270, tel. 041-277-0393, www.hotelalleon.com, leon@hotelalleon.com, Giuliano and Marcella). Their annex down the street, B&B Marcella, has three newer, classy, and spacious rooms for the same rates (check in at main hotel).

$ Casa per Ferie Santa Maria della Pietà is a wonderful facility renting 53 beds in 15 rooms just a block off the Riva, with a fabulous lagoon-view roof terrace that could rival those at the most luxurious hotels in town. Institutional, with generous public spaces and dorm-style comfort, there are no sinks, toilets, or showers in any of its rooms, but there's plenty of plumbing down the hall (cash only, 2-night minimum on weekends in peak season, only twin beds, private rooms available, air-con, 100 yards from San Zaccaria-Pietà vaporetto dock, down Calle de la Pietà from La Pietà Church at Castello 3701, take elevator to third floor, tel. 041-244-3639, www.bedandvenice.it, info@bedandvenice.it).

North of St. Mark's Square

$$$$ Hotel Orion rents 21 simple, welcoming rooms in the center of the action. Steep stairs (there's no elevator) take you from the touristy street into a peaceful world high above (RS%—use code "RSTEVES," air-con, 2 minutes inland from St. Mark's Square, 10 steps toward St. Mark's from San Zulian Church at Calle Spadaria 700a, tel. 041-522-3053, www. hotelorion.it, info@hotelorion.it).

$$$ Hotel al Piave, with 27 rooms above a bright, tight lobby and breakfast room, is comfortable and cheery, and you'll enjoy the neighborhood (RS%, family rooms, lots of narrow stairs, air-con, on Ruga Giuffa at Castello 4838, tel. 041-528-5174, www. hotelalpiave.com, info@hotelalpiave.com; Mirella, Paolo, Ilaria, and Federico).

$$$ Locanda Silva is a well-located hotel with a functional 1960s feel and a peaceful terrace. It rents 23 simple rooms that are particularly worth considering if you're willing to share a bathroom to save some money (RS%, closed Dec-Jan, family rooms, air-con, lots of stairs, on Fondamenta del Remedio at Castello 4423, tel. 041-522-7643, www.locandasilva.it, info@locandasilva.it; Sandra, Katia, and Massimo).

Near Campo Santa Maria Formosa

Farther north, the quiet Castello area lies beyond inviting Campo Santa Maria Formosa.

$$$ Locanda la Corte is perfumed with elegance without being snooty. Its 14 attractive, high-ceilinged, wood-beamed rooms—Venetian-style, done in earthy pastels—circle a small, sun-drenched courtyard and a ground-level restaurant (RS%, family rooms, air-con, on Calle Bressana at Castello 6317, tel. 041-241-1300, www.locandalacorte.it, info@locandalacorte.it).

West of St. Mark's Square

These more expensive hotels are solid choices in a more elegant neighborhood.

$$$$ Hotel Flora sits buried in a sea of fancy designer boutiques and elegant hotels almost on the Grand Canal. It's formal, with uniformed staff and grand public spaces, yet the 40 rooms have a homey warmth and the garden oasis is a sanctuary for well-heeled, foot-weary guests (RS%, air-con, elevator, family apartment, on Calle Bergamaschi at San Marco 2283a, tel. 041-520-5844, www.hotelflora.it, info@hotelflora.it).

$$$$ Hotel Bel Sito offers pleasing Old World character, 34 smallish rooms, generous public spaces, a peaceful court-yard, and a picturesque location—facing a church on a small square between St. Mark's Square and the Accademia (RS%, some view rooms, air-con, elevator; near Santa Maria del Giglio vaporetto stop—line #1, on Campo Santa Maria Zobenigo/del Giglio at San Marco 2517, tel. 041-522-3365, www.hotelbelsitovenezia.it, info@hotelbelsitovenezia.it, graceful Rossella).

Near the Rialto Bridge

These places are on opposite sides of the Grand Canal, within a short walk of the Rialto Bridge. Express vaporetto #2 brings you to the Rialto quickly from the train station, the Piazzale Roma bus station, and the parking-lot island of Tronchetto, but you'll need to take the "local" vaporetto #1 to reach the minor stops closer to the last two listings (or take #2 and walk over Rialto Bridge to reach them).

$$$$ **Hotel al Ponte Antico** is exquisite, professional, and small. With nine plush rooms, a velvety royal living/breakfast room, and its own dock for water taxi arrivals, it's perfect for a romantic anniversary. Because its wonderful terrace overlooks the Grand Canal, Rialto Bridge, and market action, its rooms without a canal view may be a better value (air-con, 100 yards from Rialto Bridge at Cannaregio 5768, use Rialto vaporetto stop, tel. 041-241-1944, www.alponteantico.com, info@alponteantico.com, Matteo makes you feel like royalty).

$$$ **Pensione Guerrato,** right above the colorful Rialto produce market and just two minutes from the Rialto Bridge, is run by friendly, creative, and hardworking Roberto and Piero. Their 800-year-old building—with 22 spacious, charming rooms—is simple, airy, and wonderfully characteristic (RS%, cheaper rooms with shared bath, family rooms, air-con, on Calle drio la Scimia at San Polo 240a, take vaporetto #1 to Rialto Mercato stop to save walk over bridge, tel. 041-528-5927, www.hotelguerrato.com, info@hotelguer-rato.com, Monica and Rosanna). My tour groups book this place for 90 nights each year. Sorry. The Guerrato also rents family apartments in the old center (great for groups of 4-8) for around €60 per person.

$$$ **Hotel al Ponte Mocenigo** is off the beaten path—a 10-minute walk northwest of the Rialto Bridge—but it's a great value. This 16th-century Venetian palazzo has a garden terrace and 15 comfy, beautifully appointed, and tranquil rooms (RS%, air-con, Santa Croce 1985, tel. 041-524-4797, www.alpontemocenigo.com, info@alpontemocenigo.com, Sandro and Valter). Take vaporetto #1 to the San Stae stop and head inland along the right side of the church.

Near the Accademia Bridge

As you step over the Accademia Bridge, touristy Venice is replaced by a sleepy village laced with canals. This quiet area is a 15-minute walk from the Rialto or St. Mark's Square. The fast vaporetto #2 to the Accademia stop is the typical way to get here from the train station, Piazzale Roma bus station, Tronchetto parking lot, or St. Mark's Square (early and late, #2 terminates at the Rialto stop, where you change to #1). For hotels near the Zattere stop, good options are vaporetto #5.1 or the Alilaguna speedboat from the airport.

South of the Accademia Bridge, in Dorsoduro

$$$$ **Pensione Accademia** fills the 17th-century Villa Maravege like a Bellini painting. Its 27 comfortable, elegant rooms gild the lily. You'll feel aristocratic gliding through its grand public spaces and lounging in its wistful, breezy gardens (family rooms, must pay first night in advance, air-con, no elevator but most rooms on ground floor or one floor up, on Fondamenta Bollani at Dorsoduro 1058, tel. 041-521-0188, www.pensioneaccademia.it, info@pensioneaccademia.it).

$$$$ **Hotel la Calcina,** the home of English writer John Ruskin in 1876, maintains a 19th-century formality. It comes with three-star comforts in a professional yet intimate package. Its 26 nautical-feeling rooms are squeaky clean, with nice wood furniture, hardwood floors, and a peaceful waterside setting facing Giudecca Island (some view rooms, air-con, no elevator and lots of stairs, rooftop terrace, buffet breakfast outdoors in good weather on platform over lagoon, near Zattere vaporetto stop at south end of Rio de San Vio at Dorsoduro 780, tel. 041-520-6466, www.lacalcina.com, info@lacalcina.com).

$$$$ **Hotel Belle Arti,** with a stiff, serious staff, is pricey and lacks personality but has an inviting garden terrace and 67 heavily decorated rooms (air-con, elevator, 100 yards behind Accademia art museum on Rio Terà A. Foscarini at Dorsoduro 912a, tel. 041-522-6230, www.hotelbellearti.com, info@hotelbellearti.com).

$$$$ **Casa Rezzonico,** a tranquil getaway far from the crowds, rents seven inviting, nicely appointed rooms with a grassy private garden terrace. All the rooms overlook either the canal or the garden (RS%, family rooms, air-con, near Ca' Rezzonico vaporetto stop—line #1, a few blocks past Campo San Barnaba on Fondamenta Gherardini at Dorsoduro 2813, tel. 041-277-0653, www.casarezzonico.it, info@casarezzonico.it, brothers Matteo and Mattia).

$$$$ **Hotel Galleria** has nine tight, old-fashioned, velvety rooms, most with views of the Grand Canal. Some rooms are quite narrow. It's run with a family feel by Lucio (breakfast in room, ceiling fans, 30 yards from Accademia art museum, next to recommended Foscarini pizzeria at Dorsoduro 878a, tel. 041-523-2489, www.hotelgalleria.it, info@hotelgalleria.it).

$$$$ **Don Orione Religious Guest House** is a big cultural center dedicated to the work of a local man who became a saint in modern times. With 80 rooms filling an old monastery, it feels cookie-cutter-institutional (like a modern retreat center), but is also classy, clean, peaceful, and strictly run. It's beautifully located, comfortable, and a good value supporting a fine cause: Profits go to mission work in the developing world (family rooms, groups welcome, air-con, elevator, on Rio Terà A. Foscarini, Dorsoduro 909a, tel. 041-522-4077, www.donorione-venezia.it, info@donorione-venezia.it).

North of the Accademia Bridge

These places are between the Accademia Bridge and St. Mark's Square.

$$$$ **Novecento Hotel** rents nine plush rooms on three floors, complemented by a big, welcoming lounge, an elegant living room, and a small breakfast garden. This boutique hotel is nicely located and has a tasteful sense of style, mingling Art Deco with North African and Turkish decor (air-con, lots of stairs, on Calle del Dose, off Campo San Maurizio at San Marco 2683, tel. 041-241-3765, www.novecento.biz, info@novecento.biz).

$$$ **Foresteria Levi,** run by a foundation that promotes research on Venetian music, offers 32 quiet, institutional yet comfortable and spacious rooms—some are loft quads, a good deal for families (RS%, air-con, elevator, on Calle Giustinian at San Marco 2893, tel. 041-277-0542, www.foresterialevi.it, info@foresterialevi.it).

$$$ **Istituto Ciliota** (a.k.a. Domus Ciliota) is a big, efficient, and sparkling-clean place—well-run, well-located, church-owned, and plainly furnished—with 30 dorm-like rooms and a peaceful courtyard. If you want industrial-strength comfort with no stress and little character, this is a fine value (air-con, elevator, on Calle de le Muneghe just off Campo San Stefano, San Marco 2976, tel. 041-520-4888, www.ciliota.it, info@ciliota.it).

$$$ **Hotel San Samuele** rents 10 rooms in an old palazzo near Campo San Stefano. It's in a great locale, and the rooms with shared bath can be a good deal (no

breakfast, fans, some stairs, on Salizada San Samuele at San Marco 3358, tel. 041-520-5165, www.hotelsansamuele.com, info@hotelsansamuele.com, Judith).

TRANSPORTATION

Getting Around Venice

Narrow pedestrian walkways connect Venice's docks, squares, bridges, and courtyards. To navigate on foot, look for yellow signs on street corners pointing you to (per) the nearest major landmark (such as Per Rialto). Determine whether your destination is in the direction of a major signposted landmark, then follow the signs through the maze.

Some helpful street terminology: *Campo* means square, a *campiello* is a small square, *calle* (pronounced "KAH-lay" with an "L" sound) means "street," and a *ponte* is a bridge. A *fondamenta* is the embankment along a canal or the lagoon. A *rio terà* is a street that was once a canal and has been filled in. A *sotoportego* is a covered passageway. *Sal-izzada* literally means a paved area (usually a wide street). The abbreviations S. and S.S. mean "saint" and "saints," respectively. Don't get hung up on the exact spelling of street and square names, which may sometimes appear in Venetian dialect (which uses *de la, novo,* and *vechio*) and other times in standard Italian (which uses *della, nuovo,* and *vecchio*).

Every building in Venice has a house number. The numbers relate to the district (each with about 6,000 address numbers), not the street. If you need to find a specific address, it helps to know its district, street, house number, and nearby landmarks.

By Vaporetto

These motorized bus-boats run by the public transit system (ACTV) work like city buses except that they never get a flat, the stops are docks, and if you get off between stops, you might drown. You can purchase tickets and passes at docks and from ACTV affiliate VèneziaUnica

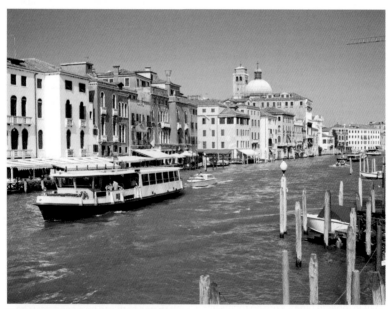

Vaporetto on the Grand Canal

Handy Vaporetti from San Zaccaria, near St. Mark's Square

Several vaporetti leave from the San Zaccaria docks, located 150 yards east of St. Mark's Square. There are four separate San Zaccaria docks spaced about 70 yards apart, with a total of six different berths, lettered A to F. While this may sound confusing, in practice it's simple: Check the big electronic board (next to the C/D dock), which indicates the departure time, line number, destination, and berth letter of upcoming vaporetti. Once you've figured out which boat you want, go to that letter berth and hop on. They're all within about a five-minute stroll of each other.

- **Line #1** goes up the Grand Canal, making all the stops, including San Marco, Rialto, Ferrovia (train station), and Piazzale Roma (but it does not go as far as Tronchetto). In the other direction, it goes from San Zaccaria to Arsenale and Giardini before ending on the Lido.
- **Line #2** zips over to San Giorgio Maggiore, the island church across from St. Mark's Square (5 minutes, €5 ride). From there, it continues on to stops on the island of Giudecca, the parking lot at Tronchetto, and then down the Grand Canal (dock B). Note: You cannot ride the #2 up the Grand Canal (for example, to Rialto or the train station) directly from this stop—you'll need to walk five minutes along the waterfront, past St. Mark's Square, to the San Marco-Giardinetti dock and hop on the #2 there.
- **Line #4.1** goes to San Michele and Murano in 45 minutes (dock D).
- **Line #7** is the summertime express boat to Murano (25 minutes, dock D).
- The **Molino Stucky shuttle boat** takes even nonguests to the Hilton Hotel, with its popular view bar (20-minute ride, 3/hour, from its own dock near the San Zaccaria dock B).
- **Lines #5.1** and **#5.2** are the *circulare* (cheer-koo-LAH-ray), making a loop around the perimeter of the island, with a stop at the Lido—perfect if you just like riding boats. Line #5.1 goes counterclockwise, and #5.2 goes clockwise. Both run less frequently in the evenings (#5.1 leaves from dock D, #5.2 from dock C).
- The **Alilaguna** shuttle to and from the airport stops here as well (dock D).

(ACTV—tel. 041-2424, www.actv.it; VèneziaUnica—www.veneziaunica.com).

TICKETS AND PASSES
Individual Vaporetto Tickets: A single ticket costs €7.50 (kids under 6 travel free). Tickets are good for 75 minutes in one direction; you can hop on and off at stops and change boats during that time. Your ticket (a plastic card embedded with a chip) is refillable; put more money on it at the automated kiosks to avoid wait- ing in line at the ticket window. The fare is reduced to €5 for a few one-stop runs *(corsa semplice)* that are hard to do by foot, including from San Zaccaria to the island of San Giorgio Maggiore.

Vaporetto Passes: Because a sin- gle ticket costs €7.50, an unlimited-use vaporetti pass pays for itself quickly (€20/24 hours, €30/48 hours, €40/72 hours, €60/7-day pass). For example, the 48-hour pass pays for itself after just five rides (for example: to your hotel on your arrival, on a Grand Canal joyride, into the lagoon and back, and to the train station). Smaller and/or outlying stops, such as Sant'Elena and Biennale, are unstaffed—another good reason to buy a pass. It's fun to be able to hop on and off spontaneously, and avoid long ticket lines. On the other hand, many tourists just walk through Venice and rarely use a boat.

Passes are also valid on some of ACTV's mainland buses, including bus #2 to Mestre (but not the #5 to the airport or the airport buses run by ATVO, a separate company). Passholders get a discounted fare for all ACTV buses that originate or terminate at Marco Polo Airport (€6 one-way, €12 round-trip, must be purchased at the same time as the pass; otherwise, the airport shuttle costs €8 one-way, €15 round-trip).

Travelers between ages 14 and 29 can get a 72-hour pass for €22 if they also buy a **Rolling Venice** discount pass for €6 (offers discounts at sights and shops, too; www.veneziaunica.com).

Buying and Validating Tickets and Passes: Purchase tickets and passes from machines at most stops, from ticket windows at larger stops, or from the VèneziaUnica offices at the train station, bus station, and Tronchetto parking lot (Rolling Venice youth passes also sold at TIs).

Before you board, validate your ticket or pass at the small white machine on the dock. If you're unable to purchase a ticket before boarding, seek out the conductor immediately to buy a single ticket (or risk a big fine).

IMPORTANT VAPORETTO LINES

For most travelers, only two vaporetto lines matter: line #1 and line #2, which leave every 10 minutes or so and go up and down the Grand Canal, between the "mouth" of the fish at one end and St. Mark's Square at the other. **Line #1** is the slow boat, taking 45 minutes and making every stop along the way. **Line #2** takes 25 minutes, stopping only at Tronchetto (parking lot), Piazzale Roma (bus station), Ferrovia (train station), Rialto Bridge, San Tomà (Frari Church), San Samuele (opposite Ca' Rezzonico), Accademia Bridge, and San Marco (west end of St. Mark's Square, end of the line).

Sorting out the different directions of travel can be confusing. Some boats run on circular routes, in one direction only (for example, lines #5.1 and #5.2, plus the non-Murano sections of lines #4.1 and #4.2). Line #2 runs in both directions and is almost, but not quite, a full loop. The #2 boat leaving from the San Marco stop goes in one direction (up the Grand Canal), while from the San Zaccaria stop—just a five-minute walk away—it goes in the opposite direction (around the tail of the "fish"). Make sure you use the correct stop to avoid taking the long way around to your destination.

To clear up any confusion, ask a ticket-seller or conductor on the dock for help. Get a copy of the most current ACTV map and timetable (in English and Italian, can be downloaded from www. actv.it, theoretically free at ticket booths but often unavailable). System maps are posted at stops, but it's helpful to print out your own copy of the map from the ACTV website before your trip.

BOARDING AND RIDING VAPORETTI

Many stops have two boarding platforms, and large stops—such as San Marco, San Zaccaria, Rialto, Ferrovia (train station), and Piazzale Roma—have multiple platforms. At these larger stops, electronic boards display which boats are coming next, when, and from which platform they leave; each platform is assigned a letter (clearly marked above the gangway). At smaller stops without electronic displays, signs on each platform show the vaporetto lines that stop there and the direction they are headed. As you board, confirm your destination by looking for an electronic sign on the boat or just asking the conductor.

You may notice some vaporetti sporting a *corsa bis* sign, indicating that they're running a shortened or altered route, and that riders may have to hop off partway (at Rialto, for example) and wait for the next boat. If you see a *corsa bis* sign, ask the conductor before you board if the boat is going to your desired destination (e.g., "San Marco?").

By Traghetto

Only four bridges cross the Grand Canal, but *traghetti* (shuttle gondolas) ferry locals and in-the-know tourists across the Grand Canal at three additional locations. Just step in, hand the gondolier €2, and enjoy the ride—standing or sitting. Some *traghetti* are seasonal, some stop running as early as 12:30, and all stop by 18:00. *Traghetti* are not covered by any transit pass.

By Water Taxi

Venetian taxis, like speedboat limos, hang out at busy points along the Grand Canal. Prices are regulated: €15 for pickup, then €2 per minute; €5 per person for more than four passengers; and €10 between

22:00 and 6:00. If you have more bags than passengers, the extra ones cost €3 apiece. Despite regulation, prices can be soft; negotiate and settle on the price or rate before stepping in. For travelers with lots of luggage or small groups who can split the cost, taxi boat rides can be a time-saving convenience—and a cool indulgence. For a little more than €100 an hour, you can have a private, unguided taxi-boat tour. You may find more competitive rates if you book through the Consorzio Motoscafi water taxi association (tel. 041-522-2303, www.motoscafivenezia.it).

Transport	Speed	Cost
Alilaguna boat	Slow	Moderate
Water taxi	Fast	Expensive
Airport bus to Piazzale Roma	Medium	Cheap
Land taxi to Piazzale Roma	Medium	Moderate

A traghetto *crossing*

Arriving and Departing

A two-mile-long causeway (with highway and train lines) connects the island to Mestre, the sprawling mainland section of Venice. Don't stop in Mestre unless you're changing trains or parking your car.

Marco Polo Airport

Venice's small, modern airport is on the mainland shore of the lagoon, six miles north of the city (airport code: VCE). There's one sleek terminal, with a TI (daily 9:00-20:00), car-rental agencies, ATMs, a bank, and a few shops and eateries. For flight info, call 041-260-9260, visit www.veniceairport.com, or ask your hotelier.

Treviso Airport, the next-closest airport, is described later.

GETTING BETWEEN MARCO POLO AIRPORT AND VENICE

There are several good options (including by boat) to get from the airport to Venice.

An advantage of the Alilaguna boats and water taxis is that you can reach my recommended hotels very simply, with no changes. Both kinds of boats leave from the airport's boat dock, an eight-minute walk from the terminal. Exit the arrivals hall and turn left, following signs along a paved, level, covered sidewalk.

When flying out of Venice, plan to arrive at the airport two hours before your flight, and remember that just getting there can easily take up to two hours. Water transport can be slow, and small Alilaguna boats fill up quickly. In an emergency, hop in a water taxi and get to the airport in 30 minutes.

ALILAGUNA AIRPORT BOATS

These boats make the slow, scenic journey across the lagoon, shuttling passengers between the airport and the island of Venice (€15, €27 round-trip, €1 surcharge if bought on boat, discount if bought online, includes 1 suitcase and 1 piece of hand luggage, additional bags–€3 each,

roughly 2/hour, 1-1.5-hour trip depending on destination). Alilaguna boats are not part of the ACTV vaporetto system, so they aren't covered by city transit passes. But they do use the same docks and ticket windows as the regular **vaporetti**. You can buy tickets for Alilaguna online at www.alilaguna.it or www.venicelink.com.

There are three key Alilaguna lines for reaching St. Mark's Square. From the airport, the **blue line** *(linea blu)* heads first to Fondamente Nove (40 minutes), then loops around to San Zaccaria and San Marco (about 1.5 hours) before continuing on to Zattere and the cruise terminal (almost 2 hours). The **orange line** *(linea arancio)* runs down the Grand Canal, reaching Guglie (45 minutes), Rialto (1 hour), and San Marco (1.5 hours). In high season, the red line *(linea rossa)* runs to St. Mark's in just over an hour. It circumnavigates Murano and then runs parallel to the blue line, ending at Giudecca Zitelle. For a full schedule, visit the TI, see the website (www.alilaguna.it), call 041-240-1701, ask your hotelier, or scan the schedules posted at the docks.

From the Airport to Venice: You can buy Alilaguna tickets at the airport's TI, the ticket desk in the terminal, and at the ticket booth at the dock. Any ticket seller can tell you which line you need. Blue- and orange-line boats from the airport run roughly twice an hour; red goes once an hour (blue line from 6:15, orange line from 7:45, red line from 9:40; blue and orange lines run until about midnight, the red line makes its last run at 18:40).

From Venice to the Airport: Ask your hotelier which dock and which line is best. Blue line boats leave Venice as early as 3:50 in the morning for passengers with early flights. Scope out the dock and buy tickets in advance to avoid last-minute stress.

WATER TAXIS

Luxury taxi speedboats zip directly between the airport and the closest dock to your hotel, getting you to within steps of your final destination in about

30 minutes. The official price is €110 for up to four people; add €10 for every extra person (10-passenger limit). You may get a higher quote—politely talk it down. A taxi can be a smart investment for small groups and those with an early departure.

From the airport, arrange your ride at the water-taxi desk or with the boat captains lounging at the dock. From Venice, book your taxi trip the day before you leave. Your hotel will help (since they get a commission), or you can book directly with the Consorzio Motoscafi water taxi association (tel. 041-522-2303, www. motoscafivenezia.it).

AIRPORT SHUTTLE BUSES
Buses between the airport and Venice are fast, frequent, and cheap. They drop you at Venice's bus station, at a square called Piazzale Roma. From there, you can catch a vaporetto down the Grand Canal—convenient for hotels near the Rialto Bridge and St. Mark's Square.

Two bus companies serve this route: ACTV and ATVO. ATVO buses go nonstop and take 20 minutes. ACTV buses make a few stops en route and take 30 minutes, but you get a discount if you buy a Venice vaporetto pass at the same time (see "By Vaporetto," earlier). The service is equally good (either bus: €8 one-way, €15 round-trip, ACTV bus with transit-pass discount: €6 one-way, €12 round-trip; runs about 5:00-24:00, 2/hour, drops to 1/hour early and late, check schedules at www.atvo.it or www.actv.it).

From the Airport to Venice: Both buses leave from just outside the arrivals terminal. Buy tickets from the TI, the ticket desk in the terminal, the kiosk near baggage claim, or ticket machines. ATVO tickets are not valid on ACTV buses and vice versa. Double-check the destination; you want Piazzale Roma. If taking ACTV, you want bus #5.

From Venice to the Airport: At Piazzale Roma, buy your ticket from the ACTV windows (in the building by the bridge) or the

ATVO office (at #497g) before heading out to the platforms (although sometimes there's an attendant selling tickets near the buses). The newsstand in the center of the lot also sells tickets.

LAND TAXI OR PRIVATE MINIVAN
It takes about 20 minutes to drive from the airport to Piazzale Roma or the cruise port. A **land taxi** can do the trip for about €50. To reserve a private minivan, contact **Treviso Car Service** (minivan-€55, seats up to 8; car-€50, seats up to 3; mobile 338-204-4390 or 333-411-2840, www.trevisocarservice.com).

Treviso Airport
Several budget airlines, such as Ryanair and Wizz Air, use Treviso Airport, 12 miles northwest of Venice (airport code: TSF, tel. 042-231-5111, www.trevisoairport.it). The fastest option into Venice takes 40 minutes on the **Barzi express bus** to the Tronchetto parking lot—convenient if you'll be taking vaporetto #2 (€12, buy tickets on board, every 1-2 hours, www. barziservice.com). From Tronchetto, hop on a vaporetto, or take the People Mover monorail to Piazzale Roma for €1.50. **ATVO buses** are more frequent and drop you right at Piazzale Roma (saving you the People Mover ride), but take nearly twice as long (€12 one-way, €22 round-trip, about 2/hour, 70 minutes, buy tickets at ATVO desk in airport and stamp them on bus, www.atvo.it). **Treviso Car Service** offers minivan service to Piazzale Roma (minivan-€75, seats up to 8; car-€65, seats up to 3; mobile 338-204-4390 or 333-411-2840, www.trevisocarservice.com).

By Train
All trains to "Venice" stop at Venezia Mestre (on the mainland). Most continue on to **Santa Lucia Station** (a.k.a. Venezia S.L.) on the island of Venice itself. If your train happens to terminate at Mestre, you'll need to buy a Mestre-Santa Lucia ticket at a machine for €1.25 and validate

it before hopping any nonexpress, regional train (with an R or RV prefix) for the ride across the causeway to Venice (6/hour, 10 minutes).

Santa Lucia train station is right on the Grand Canal, an easy vaporetto ride or fascinating 45-minute walk (with a number of bridges and steps) to St. Mark's Square. The station has a **baggage check** (daily 6:00-23:00, no lockers, along track 1). Pay **WCs** are at track 1. You'll find the **TI** across from track 2.

Before heading into town, confirm your departure plan (use the ticket machines or study the *partenze*/departures posters on walls). Minimize your time in the station—the banks of user-friendly ticket machines take euros and credit cards, display schedules, and issue tickets. There are two train companies and both have red ticket machines: **Trenitalia** has the most connections (toll tel. 892-021, www.trenitalia.it); the other is the high-speed **Italo** service (no rail passes accepted, cheaper in advance, tel. 06-0708, www.italotreno.it). **Ticket offices** for both Trenitalia and Italo are in the corner, near track 14. If you need international tickets or live help, head to the ticket windows (Trenitalia open 6:00-21:00; Italo open 8:30-20:00). Or take care of these tasks online or at a travel agency (extra ticket fee).

Getting from the Train Station to Downtown: Walk straight out of the station to the canal. You'll see vaporetto docks and ticket booths on both sides. The electronic signs show which boats are leaving when and from which platform. The slow boat down the Grand Canal is #1. The fast boat is #2; make sure that "Rialto" is among the destinations listed. If you're staying in the Dorsoduro neighborhood near the Zattere stop, take vaporetto #5.1. A water taxi from the train station to central Venice costs about €60-80 (the taxi dock is straight ahead).

TRAIN CONNECTIONS

Note that the departures listed below are operated by Trenitalia; a competing private rail company called Italo offers additional high-speed connections to major Italian cities including **Milan, Florence, and Rome,** but doesn't accept rail passes. When taking the train to nearby cities such as Padua and Verona, prices and journey times can vary greatly, depending on whether the train is express or regional.

From Venice by Train to: Padua (2/hour, 25-50 minutes); **Verona** (2/hour, 1.5-2.5 hours); **Bolzano/Dolomites** (to Bolzano about hourly, 3-3.5 hours, transfer in Verona; catch bus from Bolzano into mountains); **Milan** (2/hour, most direct on high-speed ES trains, 2.5 hours); **Cinque Terre/Monterosso** (5/day, 6 hours, change in Milan); **Florence** (hourly, 2-3 hours, often crowded so make reservations); **Rome** (hourly, 4 hours); **Naples** (almost hourly, 5.5 hours, some change in Bologna or Rome).

By Bus

Venice's "bus station" is actually an open-air parking lot called **Piazzale Roma.** The square itself is a jumble of different operators, platforms, and crosswalks over busy lanes of traffic, but bus stops are well-signed. The ticket windows for ACTV (local public buses, including #5 to Marco Polo Airport) are in a building between the bridge and vaporetto stop. The ATVO ticket office—for express buses to Marco Polo and Treviso airports and to Padua—is at #497g in the big white building, on the right side of the square as you face away from the canal (daily 6:45-19:30).

Piazzale Roma also has two big **parking garages** and the **People Mover monorail** (€1.50, links to cruise port and then the parking-lot island of Tronchetto). **Baggage storage** is next to the monorail at #497m (daily 6:00-20:00).

Getting from the Bus Station to Downtown: Find the vaporetto docks (just left of the modern bridge) and take #1 or the faster #2 down the Grand Canal to reach stops for the Rialto, Accademia, and San Marco (St. Mark's Square).

By Car

The freeway (monitored by speed cameras) dead-ends after crossing the causeway to Venice. At the end of the road you have two parking choices: garages at Tronchetto or Piazzale Roma. As you drive into the city, signboards with green and red lights indicate which lots are full.

The **Tronchetto garage** is much bigger, farther out, cheaper, and well-connected by vaporetto (€3-5/hour, €21/24 hours, discounts for longer stays, tel. 041-520-7555, www.veniceparking.it). After parking, cross the street to the brick building. While you can head left for a long walk to the People Mover monorail, it's easier to go right to the vaporetto dock (not well-signed, look for *ACTV*).

At the dock, catch vaporetto #2 in one of two directions: via the Grand Canal (more scenic, stops at Rialto, 40 minutes to San Marco), or via Giudecca (around the city, faster, no Rialto stop, 30 minutes to San Marco).

Don't be waylaid by **aggressive water taxi boatmen.** They charge €100 to take you where the vaporetto will take you for €7.50. Also **avoid the travel agencies masquerading as TIs;** deal only with the ticket booth at the vaporetto dock or the VèneziaUnica public transport office. If you're going to buy a local transport pass, do it now—to get maximum use out of it.

The two **Piazzale Roma garages** are closer in and more convenient—but more expensive and likelier to be full. Both face the busy square where the road ends. The big white building on your right is a 2,200-space public parking garage, **Autorimessa Comunale** (€26/24 hours, TI office in payment lobby open daily 7:30-19:30, tel. 041-272-7211, www.avmspa.it). In a back corner of the square is the private **Garage San Marco** (€32/24 hours, tel. 041-523-2213, www.garagesanmarco.it). At either of these, you'll have to give up your keys. Near Garage San Marco, avoid Parcheggio Sant'Andrea, which charges much higher rates.

Switzerland

Mountainous, efficient Switzerland is one of Europe's most appealing destinations. A tiny country (about twice the size of New Jersey), it's wedged neatly between Germany, Austria, France, and Italy.

Switzerland melds the best of all worlds—and adds a healthy dose of chocolate, cowbells, and cable cars. Fiercely independent and decidedly high-tech, the Swiss (at 8 million strong) stubbornly hold on to their quaint traditions, too. Join cheesemakers in a high valley, try to call the shepherds on an alphorn, and hike through some of the world's most stunning mountain scenery to find the perfect perch for a picnic.

CUISINE SCENE AT A GLANCE

The Swiss eat when we do and enjoy a straightforward, no-nonsense cuisine. Specialties include delicious fondue, a melted cheese dish called raclette, *Rösti* (hash browns), and 100 varieties of cheese.

The exorbitant prices at Swiss restaurants are up to double what you'd pay in neighboring Germany. If you're on a budget, think of restaurants as a luxury for special occasions, and self-service cafeterias and supermarkets as everyday options.

At **restaurants,** the cheapest main courses start at just under 20 CHF—typically starchy dishes topped with meat or cheese (pasta, pizza, and potato dishes) or sausages with kraut or potato salad. Meat courses (served with a starch and vegetable) will run you from 25-45 CHF at an average restaurant. Many, but not all, restaurants offer a daily special—a main course for about 20 CHF (at least Mon-Fri at lunch, sometimes weekends and evenings, too). High-priced drinks quickly run up the cost of a meal.

Different kinds of restaurants offer different experiences. Hotels often serve fine food. A *Gaststätte* is a simple, less expensive restaurant. A *Weinstübli* (wine bar) or *Bierstübli* (tavern) usually serves food.

Most restaurants tack a menu onto their door for browsers and have an English menu inside. If you're not too hungry, order from the *kleine Hunger* (small hunger) section of the menu. Many restaurants offer half-portions, which is a great relief on your budget (although two people save even more by sharing one full portion).

Tipping: If you buy your food at a counter, don't tip. Service is included at restaurants with table service, but it's customary to round up the bill (no more than 5-10 percent; for a 19-CHF meal, pay 20 CHF). Give the tip directly to your server. Rather than leaving coins on the table, the Swiss usually pay with paper, saying how much they'd like the bill to be (for example, for an 8.10-CHF meal, give a 20-CHF bill and say *"Neun Franken"*—"Nine francs"—to get 11 CHF change). Rounding up isn't required, though, and no one will come running after you if you don't.

Budget Options: Grocery stores, such as the midrange Migros and Co-op, are the hungry hiker's best budget bet. The larger stores have a great selection of prepared foods and picnic fixings. These include a variety of salads (green, potato, pasta, or meat), hard-boiled eggs, sandwiches, cheese, single portions of cake and ice cream, chocolate bars, and sometimes a hot-meal counter. By law, most supermarkets are required to close on Sunday, with a few exceptions, such as stores in train stations.

Self-service cafeterias have good food at much lower prices than restaurants. You'll find them in bigger cities, usually at downtown branches of Co-op, Migros, and Manor supermarkets. While cafeteria food may not be inventive, it is typical, fresh, and high-quality.

Tempting bakeries sell sandwiches, quiches, and pastries—enough to make a filling meal.

Swiss Alps:
The Berner Oberland

Head into the Alps to hike high above the clouds and the stress of the real world. This is just the place to recharge your touristic batteries and take a vacation from your busy vacation. The crunchy footsteps of happy hikers, the whistle of marmots, the clang of cowbells, and the fluff of down comforters are the dominant sounds.

Your gateway to the rugged Berner Oberland is the grand old resort town of Interlaken, a transportation hub. Use it as a springboard for alpine thrills.

Head deep into the heart of the Alps by train and cable car, riding to stops just this side of heaven—the villages in the Lauterbrunnen Valley. The cliff-hangers are Gimmelwald and Mürren, while Lauterbrunnen is on the valley floor. Use any of these as a base to explore alpine whitecaps at higher elevations, including the 9,748-foot Schilthorn peak.

What are you waiting for? The sun's coming out and the Alps beckon.

THE SWISS ALPS IN 2 DAYS

If the weather's decent, explore the two areas that tower above either side of the Lauterbrunnen Valley: On one side is the summit of Jungfrau (and beneath it, the tiny settlement of Kleine Scheidegg and touristy Wengen). On the other side is the summit of the Schilthorn, overlooking the villages of petite Gimmelwald and resorty Mürren.

Ideally, spend three nights in the region, with a day exploring each side of the valley. On one day, you could zip up to the Schilthorn in the morning for panoramic views, then tackle a hike or two (on the Schilthorn side) in the afternoon. On the other day, explore the Jungfrau

side. My favorite hike is the gentle downhill trail from Männlichen to Kleine Scheidegg, facing a panoramic mountain view the entire way if the weather's good. From there, you could take a pricey train up up up to the Jungfraujoch (for the highest viewpoint in the region), or simply train (or hike) down to Wengen (which is connected by train to Lauterbrunnen).

With another day, you could take more hikes, explore all the towns, or even relax. For a summary of the wildly scenic activities this region has to offer—from cogwheel train rides and sky-high lifts to spectacular hikes—read "Exploring the Alps," later.

Home Bases: Figuring out what you want to do will help you choose the best home base. For accommodations without the expense and headache of mountain lifts, consider the valley-floor village of Lauterbrunnen. But for alpine wonder, stay on a scenic ridge high above the valley. The rustic hamlet of Gimmelwald and the resort town of Mürren are both on the cable-car route to the Schilthorn. To base high on the Jungfrau side, consider Wengen, which has the lift to Männlichen, the trailhead for the hike to Kleine Scheidegg.

No matter where you stay, good hiking opportunities abound, but keep in mind that higher-altitude trails (such as Männlichen to Kleine Scheidegg) are best from June through October, and can be covered with snow off-season.

Rick's Tip: *In* **bad weather,** *take a low-altitude hike (see "Hiking," later), hang out at Mürren's Sportzentrum (sauna, steam bath, pool), visit the Lauterbrunnen Valley Folk Museum, or tour the Swiss Open-Air Museum at Ballenberg.*

Weather: Let your plans flex with the weather. The highest-altitude lifts are very expensive, and it only makes sense to splurge if you have a good chance of seeing an alpine panorama (usually clearest early in the morning) instead of fog or clouds. If the weather is good—go! Ask at your hotel or the TI for the latest info or check www.jungfrau.ch, www.schilthorn.ch, or www.meteo.search.ch. Webcams showing live video from the famous (and most expensive-to-reach) peaks play just about wherever you go in the area.

Rustic Gimmelwald

INTERLAKEN

When the 19th-century Romantics redefined mountains as something more than cold and troublesome obstacles, Interlaken became the original alpine resort. Ever since, tourists have flocked to the Alps "because they're there." Interlaken's glory days are over, its elegant old hotels eclipsed by newer, swankier alpine resorts. Today, it's an alpine gateway (rated ▲), with shops filled with chocolate bars, Swiss Army knives, and sunburned backpackers.

Interlaken (pop. 5,500) is a good administrative and shopping center. Take care of business, give the town a quick look, and view the webcam coverage (at the TI) of the weather higher up...then head for the hills.

Orientation

Interlaken straddles a river that connects two alpine lakes: Lake Brienz and Lake Thun. The part of town with the most services and both train stations is on the river's left bank.

Tourist Information: A small **TI** operates at the **Interlaken Ost train station** in summer and is convenient if you're arriving there (June-Sept daily 8:30-18:30, though hours may vary; closed Oct-May).

Otherwise, visit the **main TI,** located by the post office at Marktgasse 1 (May-June and Sept Mon-Fri 8:00-18:00, Sat 9:00-16:00, closed Sun; July-Aug Mon-Fri 8:00-19:00, Sat 9:00-17:00, Sun 10:00-16:00; shorter hours and closed Sun Oct-April; tel. 033-826-5300, www.interlaken.ch). Pick up the timetable and the hiking guide published by the Jungfraubahn mountain railway (both include a good map of the area); and the *Here & Now* monthly entertainment guide. The TI also sells tickets for the Swiss rail system and books adventure sports. If you're planning to visit Kleine Scheidegg, the Jungfraujoch, or other destinations served by the Jungfraubahn, you can buy tickets for those at the TI, too.

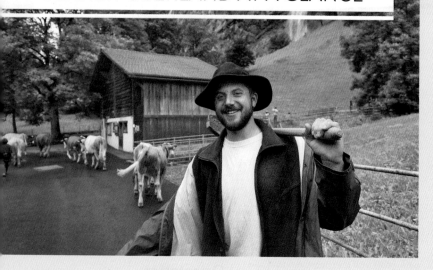

Towns, Villages, and Resorts

▲▲▲**Gimmelwald** Wonderfully rustic time-warp, cliff-hanging village—and fine home base—overlooking the Lauterbrunnen Valley from the Schilthorn side. See page 691.

▲▲**Mürren** Pleasant resort town near Gimmelwald, midway up the Schilthorn cable-car line; a good high-mountain home base for those who want more amenities than little Gimmelwald offers. See page 697.

▲▲**Kleine Scheidegg** Small resort area with breathtaking views of Eiger, Mönch, and Jungfrau peaks, plus train station for pricey ride to the high-altitude Jungfraujoch. See page 715.

▲**Lauterbrunnen** Small town and transit hub in the middle of the Lauterbrunnen Valley. From here, a cable car goes up to Grütschalp (with connections to Mürren and Gimmelwald), a cogwheel train runs up to Wengen and Kleine Scheidegg, and the PostBus goes to Stechelberg (near the Schilthornbahn lift). See page 686.

▲**Interlaken** Big town between Lake Brienz and Lake Thun, serving as the gateway to the Berner Oberland. See page 677.

Wengen Touristy, cliff-hanging resort town, with lift up to Männlichen for views and hikes; on the train route from Lauterbrunnen to Kleine Scheidegg. See page 715.

Top Lifts and Trains

▲▲▲**Schilthornbahn** Cable car soaring from Stechelberg in the Lauterbrunnen Valley to the 9,748-foot Schilthorn peak, with Piz Gloria revolving restaurant, James Bond exhibit, and stupendous views. Stops at Gimmelwald, Mürren, and Birg along the way. See page 703.

▲▲▲**Jungfraubahn** Train running from Kleine Scheidegg station and through tunnel inside Eiger and Mönch mountainsides to 11,333-foot Jungfraujoch saddle, with observation deck, restaurants, tip-top views, and snow activities. See page 705.

Walks and Hikes

▲▲▲**Männlichen to Kleine Scheidegg** Easy, mostly downhill ridge hike from cable-car station at Männlichen to Kleine Scheidegg, with spectacular views of Eiger and more. See page 712.

▲▲**Cloudy-Day Lauterbrunnen Valley Walks** Pleasant, level, easy walk along valley floor, plus short trail to Staubbach Falls at upper end of town—good bad-weather options. See page 707.

▲▲**North Face Trail** Easy, view-filled hike from the top of Allmendhubel funicular to the villages of Mürren and Gimmelwald, passing farms with food service, mountain huts, and meadows. See page 709.

▲▲**Birg to Gimmelwald via Bryndli** High, scenic, difficult hike from Birg cable-car station below Schilthorn summit down to Gimmelwald. Trail winds past knobby summit of Bryndli, with nonstop views. See page 714.

▲▲**Schynige Platte to First** Demanding ridge walk from Schynige Platte train station to gondola station at First, with fabulous views of Jungfrau-area peaks and Lake Brienz. See page 714.

▲**Allmendhubel to Grütschalp** Fairly easy walk from Allmendhubel down to Grütschalp, with views of the Jungfrau (from Mürren, take the funicular to Allmendhubel, then hike to Grütschalp. See page 711.

More Sightseeing Options

▲▲**Ballenberg** Open-air folk museum near Interlaken, on Lake Brienz. See page 680.

▲**Trümmelbach Falls** Lauterbrunnen Valley's most powerful falls, accessed via elevator ride up into the mountain and dramatic walk through several wet caves. See page 688.

Berner Oberland

NOTE: THIS BIRD'S-EYE VIEW LOOKS **SOUTH**

JUNGFRAUJOCH
11,333'

Mönch
13,449'

Jungfrau
13,642'

Eiger
13,026'

Schilthorn
9,748'

TUNNEL

BIRG
8,784'

KLEINE
SCHEIDEGG   6,762'

GIMMEL-
WALD
4,593'

GREAT
HIKE   WENGERNALP   3,025'
STECHEL-
BERG   MÜRREN
5,381'

GRINDEL-
WALD
3,393'   MÄNNLICHEN
7,317'   LIFT
STN.   NICE
WALK

GRUND   GRÜTSCHALP
4,879'

To
First   WENGEN
4,180'   LAUTERBRUNNEN
2,612'

SCHYNIGE
Platte
6,454'   ZWEILÜTSCHINEN

WILDERSWIL
1,916'

To
Luzern   ISELTWALD   OST
STN.   To Bern

SPIEZ

BRIENZ   WEST
STN.   Lake Thun

Lake Brienz   Aare River

BALLENBERG
OPEN-AIR MUSEUM   INTERLAKEN
1,860'   ST. BEATUS CAVES

Note: Elevations in feet

Notes:
Swiss Passes cover travel to Wengen and Schilthorn; Eurail/other int'l passes cover travel only to Interlaken. (Passes offer discounts beyond these points.)

Rick's Tip: On Sundays and holidays, *hotels are open and lifts and trains run, but* **many stores are closed.** *At higher altitudes many hotels, restaurants, and shops close off-season: from late April until late May, and again from mid-October to early December.*

Sights

▲▲SWISS OPEN-AIR MUSEUM AT BALLENBERG

At the far end of Lake Brienz from Interlaken, the Ballenberg open-air museum is a rich collection of more than 100 traditional and historic buildings brought here from every region of the country. All the houses are carefully furnished, and many feature traditional craftspeople at work. The sprawling 50-acre park, laid out roughly as a huge Swiss map (Italian Swiss in the south, Appenzell in the east, and so on), is a natural preserve providing a wonderful setting for this culture-on-a-lazy-Susan look at Switzerland.

Ballenberg has entrances at either end (east and west, about a mile apart, each served by the local bus). If you start in the east and go west, it's a generally downhill stroll. Pick up a daily craft demonstration schedule at the entry, and the free map/guide so you'll know where you are. There

Alpine Lifts in the Berner Oberland

Jungfrau

GIMMELWALD

MÜRREN

JUNGFRAUJOCH   STECHELBERG

Mönch

LIFT STATION

Schilt-
horn

Eiger

Hourly Bus (4 SF) →

50-20

Trümm. Falls

6-5   6-5

LAUTER-
BRUNNEN

9-3   ALLMENDHUBEL

KLEINE
SCHEIDEGG

64-50

9-6   GRÜTSCHALP

11-14
(Lauterbrunnen to Mürren
via Grütschalp)

24-30

7-15

31-35   23-10   WENGEN
30-30

MÄNNLICHEN

Interlaken Ost to Lauterbrunnen – 8-20
Interlaken Ost to Kl. Scheidegg – 41-75
Interlaken Ost to Jungfraujoch – 105-140

GRINDEL-
WALD

11-35
(Interlaken Ost to Grindelwald)

30-30

ZWEI-
LÜTSCHINEN

First

32-55   WILDERSWIL
1,916'

Schynige
Platte

OST
STATION   4-5   WEST
STATION   To Bern

ISELTWALD

INTER-
LAKEN

To
Brienz

To Thun

Lake Brienz   4-3   Lake Thun

To
Luzern

8-20

Interlaken Ost
to Brienz

Not to Scale

Code:
1st # = Approx. cost in CHF: 2nd class 1-way.
2nd # = Duration of trip in min.

Notes:
Confirm prices locally.
Round-trip fares can be cheaper.
Most lifts run twice hourly.

are daily events and demonstrations, hundreds of traditional farm animals (like very furry-legged roosters, near the merry-go-round in the center), and a chocolate shop (under the restaurant, just outside the park, on the east side).

There are more historic buildings than you can see in a single visit. Survey your map, note where the demonstrations are happening, and make a smart plan. Buildings I particularly enjoy are: #1361 (cheese upstairs, cow bells you can ring downstairs); #911 (a big Appenzell house); #611 (barbershop museum upstairs); #321 (sausages hanging from the ceiling); and #221 (a house and farm designed for hands-on fun).

There are several places to eat. Picnic tables and grills with free firewood are scattered throughout the park.

Cost and Hours: 24 CHF, covered by Swiss Travel Pass; houses open daily mid-April-Oct 10:00-17:00, grounds and restaurants 9:00-18:00; tel. 033-952-1030, www.ballenberg.ch.

The trip from Interlaken to Ballenberg takes about 20 minutes by car (pay parking at either entrance), 50 minutes by train and bus, or 1.75 hours by boat and bus. By public transport, you'll first go to Brienz by train or boat, then from Brienz to Ballenberg by local bus. Trains for Brienz leave from the Interlaken Ost

Interlaken

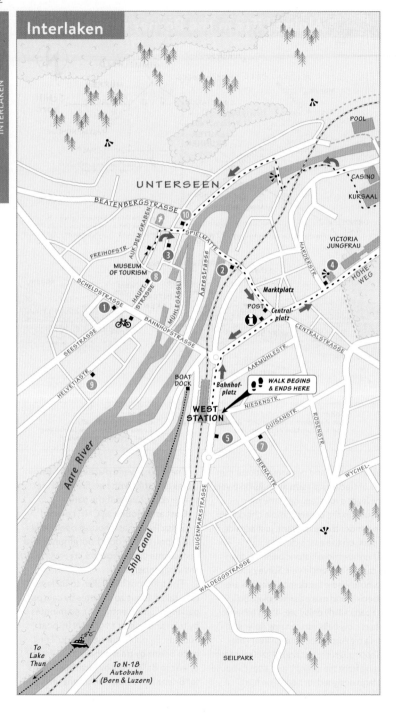

UNTERSEEN

POOL

CASINO

KURSAAL

VICTORIA JUNGFRAU

BEATENBERGSTRASSE

SPIELMATTE

HARDERSTR.

HOHE-WEG

FREIHOFSTR.

AUF DEM GRABEN

Aarestrasse

Marktplatz

POST

Central-platz

MUSEUM OF TOURISM

SCHELDSTRASSE

HAUPT-STRASSE

MÜHLEGÄSSLI

BAHNHOFSTRASSE

CENTRALSTRASSE

SEESTRASSE

AARMÜHLESTR.

HELVETIASTR.

BOAT DOCK

Bahnhof-platz

WALK BEGINS & ENDS HERE

WEST STATION

NIESENSTR.

GUISANSTR.

ROSENSTR.

BERNASTR.

WYCHEL-

Aare River

Ship Canal

RUGENPARKSTRASSE

WALDEGGSTRASSE

SEILPARK

To Lake Thun

To N-18 Autobahn (Bern & Luzern)

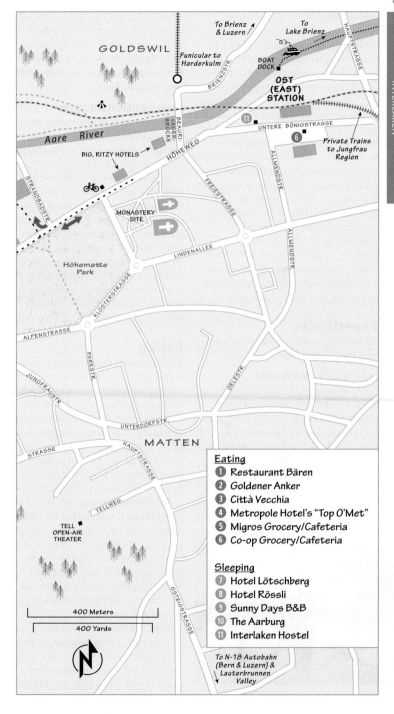

GOLDSWIL

To Brienz & Luzern

To Lake Brienz

Funicular to Harderkulm

BOAT DOCK

OST (EAST) STATION

Aare River

BRIENZSTR.

BEAURIVAGE-BRÜCKE

HAUPTSTRASSE

UNTERE BÖNIGSTRASSE

Private Trains to Jungfrau Region

BIG, RITZY HOTELS

HÖHEWEG

STRANDBADSTR.

FREIESTRASSE

ALLMENDSTR.

MONASTERY SITE

LINDENALLEE

Höhematte Park

KLOSTERSTRASSE

ALLMENDSTR.

ALPENSTRASSE

PARKSTR.

OELESTR.

JUNGFRAUSTR.

UNTERDORFSTR.

STRASSE

MATTEN

HAUPTSTRASSE

TELLWEG

TELL OPEN-AIR THEATER

GSTEIGSTRASSE

400 Meters

400 Yards

N

To N-18 Autobahn (Bern & Luzern) & Lauterbrunnen Valley

Eating
1. Restaurant Bären
2. Goldener Anker
3. Città Vecchia
4. Metropole Hotel's "Top O'Met"
5. Migros Grocery/Cafeteria
6. Co-op Grocery/Cafeteria

Sleeping
7. Hotel Lötschberg
8. Hotel Rössli
9. Sunny Days B&B
10. The Aarburg
11. Interlaken Hostel

train station (2/hour, 15-20 minutes). Boats to Brienz leave from a dock just behind the Ost train station (every 1-2 hours, first boat leaves Interlaken at 9:07, last return from Brienz usually at 17:40—at 15:40 early April-mid-May, 75 minutes, 30 CHF one-way, 51 CHF round-trip, free with Swiss Travel Pass, early April-late Oct only, tel. 058-327-4811, www.bls.ch). From the Brienz station or boat dock, catch local bus #151 to either museum entrance (hourly, 20 minutes). Use the online timetables at www.rail.ch to plan your trip, and check bus return times carefully—after 18:00, buses back to Brienz leave only from the park's west entrance. Without a rail pass, ask for the Ballenberg combo-ticket when buying your train or boat tickets: This covers your whole trip from Interlaken or beyond, and saves about 10 percent off your fare and park entry.

Experiences

For hikes and walks in the Berner Oberland, see "Hiking," later.

BIKE TOURS AND RENTAL

Flying Wheels offers bike tours of varying length and difficulty, including a three-hour Interlaken-only tour (79 CHF) and a tour of the Lauterbrunnen Valley (189 CHF, 6 hours, includes picnic and Trümmelbach Falls visit). A short walk from the Ost train station, this hip, well-organized, family-friendly outfit also rents bikes (electric, too). Its English-speaking staff give tips on where to go and can help you pick the right bike (bikes-35 CHF/half-day, 40 CHF/day;

electric bikes-45 CHF/half-day, 55 CHF/day; includes helmet, daily May-Sept 9:30-20:00, shorter hours off-season, across street from northeast corner of Höhematte Park at Höheweg 133, tel. 033-557-8838, www.flyingwheels.ch).

HIGH-ADRENALINE TRIPS

For the thrill-seeker with money, several companies offer trips such as rafting, canyoning (rappelling down watery gorges), bungee jumping, and paragliding. Costs range from roughly 150 CHF to 200 CHF—higher for skydiving and hot-air balloon rides. Interlaken's two dominant companies are **Alpin Raft** (tel. 033-823-4100, www.alpinraft.ch) and **Outdoor Interlaken** (tel. 033-826-7719, www.outdoor-interlaken.ch). Other companies are generally just booking agents for these two outfits. For an overview of your options, study the racks of brochures at most TIs and hotels.

Eating

$$$ Restaurant Bären is across the river in Unterseen, in a classic low-ceilinged building with cozy indoor and fine outdoor seating. It's a great value for *Rösti,* fondue, raclette, fish, traditional sausage, and salads (Tue-Thu 16:30-23:30, Fri-Sun 10:00-23:30 or later, closed Mon; from the West train station, turn left on Bahnhofstrasse, cross the river, and go a few blocks to Seestrasse 2; tel. 033-822-7526).

$$$ Goldener Anker, with its "melody rock and blues" ambience, is the local hangout. The big, flexible menu seems designed to make a good hot meal affordable to travelers, with 15-CHF "backpacker specials" that include a main dish and salad (takeout available, Mon-Sat from 16:00, closed Sun, Marktgasse 57, tel. 033-822-1672).

$$$ Città Vecchia serves decent Italian with seating indoors or out, on a leafy square (lunch specials, Thu-Mon 10:30-14:00 & 18:30-23:00, Tue-Wed 18:30-23:00, Untere Gasse 5, tel. 033-822-1754).

$$$ Metropole Hotel's "Top O'Met," capping Interlaken's 18-story aesthetic nightmare, is a good café/restaurant serving traditional and modern food at down-to-earth prices, with no gouging on drinks (daily lunch deals include two courses plus water and coffee, 50-CHF fondue for two; daily 8:00-23:00, Oct-May 10:00-22:00; hot food served 11:30-14:00 & 18:00-21:30, Höheweg 37, just step into the Metropole Hotel and go up the elevator as far as you can, tel. 033-828-6666).

Supermarkets: Interlaken's two big supermarkets sell picnic supplies and also have reasonable self-service restaurants. **Migros** is across the street from the West train station (Mon-Thu 8:00-19:00, Fri until 21:00, Sat until 18:00, closed Sun), with a ground-floor **$$** cafeteria (same hours plus Sun mid-July-mid-Aug 10:00-17:00, Rugenparkstrasse 1). The **Co-op** supermarket is across the square from the Ost train station and also has a good cafeteria (supermarket hours similar to Migros, cafeteria closes 30-60 minutes before store and open Sun 9:00-17:00, Untere Bönigstrasse 10). Smaller supermarkets in both train stations are open daily until 21:00.

Rick's Tip: *Hotels issue* **free Visitor Cards** *(Gästekarten) that include small discounts on some sights (paid for by your room tax).*

Sleeping

Interlaken is not the Alps. I'd sleep in Gimmelwald, or at least Lauterbrunnen (20 minutes away by train or car). In ski season, however, prices go down in Interlaken, while they shoot up at most mountain hotels.

$$$ Hotel Lötschberg, with a sun terrace, 24 rooms, and four apartments for longer stays, is run with lots of thoughtful touches by the English-speaking owners. Three of the cheaper rooms are in the building next door (closed Nov-mid-April, free self-service laundry, free loaner bikes; lounge with microwave, fridge, and free tea and coffee; 3-minute walk from the West train station: turn right from the station, after Migros at the circle go left to General-Guisan-Strasse 31; tel. 033-822-2545, www.lotschberg.ch, hotel@lotschberg.ch).

$$$ Hotel Rössli, across the river from the West train station, is nicely located, if a bit dated. Besides standard rooms, they offer "economy" rooms with a private bath down the hall and "budget" rooms with shared facilities (reserve on hotel website for best rates, closed Dec-mid-Jan, lots of stairs, comfy lounge, Hauptstrasse 10, tel. 033-822-7816, www.roessli-interlaken.ch, info@roessli-interlaken.ch).

$$ Sunny Days B&B is a homey, nine-room place in a quiet residential neighborhood (pay laundry, patio; from West train station, exit left and take first bridge to your left, after crossing two bridges turn left on Helvetiastrasse and go 3 blocks to #29; mobile 077-456-2338, www.sunnydays.ch, mail@sunnydays.ch).

$$ The Aarburg offers nine plain, peaceful rooms over a restaurant in a traditional-looking building, a 10-minute walk from the West train station (2 doors from launderette at Beatenbergstrasse 1, tel. 033-822-2615, www.theaarburg.ch).

¢ Interlaken Hostel is very convenient—right next to the Ost train station in a big, sterile modern building with 220 beds, including some private rooms (sheets and breakfast included, four-course dinner available, bike rental-25 CHF/day, pay laundry, lockers, no curfew, check-in 15:00-24:00, Untere Bönigstrasse 3, tel. 033-826-1090, www.youthhostel.ch/interlaken, interlaken@youthhostel.ch).

Transportation
By Train

Interlaken has two train stations: Ost (East) and West. Interlaken Ost is the name you'll see most often on train schedules, and it's the transfer point for narrow-gauge trains to the high mountains (to Lauterbrunnen,

Gimmelwald, etc.) and to Luzern. Use this station if you're headed to those destinations or staying at the recommended Interlaken Hostel (next door). Interlaken Ost has free WCs, lockers, ticket counters (daily 6:00-19:30), and a summer-only branch TI.

If you're staying elsewhere in Interlaken, get off at Interlaken West, which is closer to my listed hotels and downtown shopping and services. All trains from western Switzerland—Bern, the Golden Pass, Basel—stop at Interlaken West, and then continue to Interlaken Ost. Interlaken West has free WCs, lockers (by track 1), and ticket counters (daily 6:40-19:00).

It's a pleasant 20-minute walk between the West and Ost train stations; an easy 3-minute trip by train (2-3/hour, 3.60 CHF); or a 10-minute trip on any of several local buses (3.60 CHF; #21, #102, #103, or #104).

TRAIN CONNECTIONS

Interlaken, Bern, Basel, and Frankfurt are linked by an express train, but for most other destinations you'll change in Bern. Train info: Toll tel. 0900-300-300 or www. rail.ch.

From Interlaken Ost by Train to: **Lauterbrunnen** (1-2/hour, 20 minutes), **Bern** (1-2/hour, 1 hour), **Zürich** (2/hour, 2 hours, change in Bern, but 3-hour trip with change in Luzern is more scenic), **Zürich Airport** (2/hour, 2.5 hours, change in Bern), **Luzern** (hourly direct, 2 hours), **Zermatt** (1-2/hour, 2 hours, change in Spiez and Visp).

By Car

You can **drive** to Lauterbrunnen or Stechelberg, but not to Gimmelwald (park at the cable-car station near Stechelberg and ride up on the lift (explained later) or to Mürren, Wengen, or Kleine Scheidegg (park in Lauterbrunnen and take the cable car to Mürren or the train to Wengen or Kleine Scheidegg).

LAUTERBRUNNEN

Lauterbrunnen is the valley's commercial center and transportation hub. Sitting under sheer cliffs at the base of the valley, with its signature waterfall spurting mightily out from the cliff (floodlit at night), Lauterbrunnen (rated ▲) is a fine springboard for Jungfrau and Schilthorn adventures. But for spending the night, I still prefer Gimmelwald or Mürren, perched on the ledge above the valley.

Orientation

In addition to its train station and cable car, the one-street town is just big enough to have all the essential services (grocery, bank, post office, bike rental, launderette, and so on)—plus several hotels and hostels. It's idyllic, in spite of the busy road that slices it in two.

Tourist Information: Stop by the friendly TI to check the weather forecast, find out about guided walks and events, and buy hiking maps or regional train or lift tickets (June-Sept daily 8:30-12:00 & 14:00-18:30; Oct-May Tue-Sat 9:00-12:00 & 13:30-17:00, closed Sun-Mon; on the main street a few houses up from the train station, tel. 033-856-8568, www. mylauterbrunnen.com).

Arrival in Lauterbrunnen: The small, modern train station has a ticket office (daily 6:00-19:30), a few small lockers (check larger bags at the ticket office), and free WCs, and is across the main street from the cable-car station. Go left as you exit the station to find the TI. Drivers can pay to park in the large multistory lot behind the station.

Medical Help: Dr. Bruno Durrer has a clinic (with pharmacy) near the Jungfrau Hotel (look for *Arzt* sign). He and his associate both speak English (tel. 033-856-2626, answered 24/7).

Money: Several ATMs are along the main street, including one immediately across from the train station.

Laundry: The **Valley Hostel** has

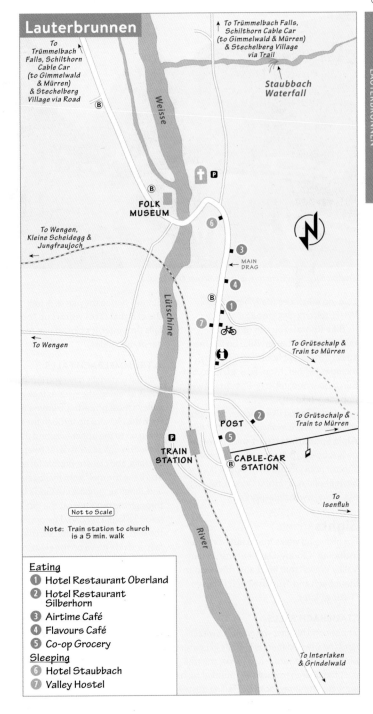

Lauterbrunnen

To Trümmelbach Falls, Schilthorn Cable Car (to Gimmelwald & Mürren) & Stechelberg Village via Road

↑ To Trümmelbach Falls, Schilthorn Cable Car (to Gimmelwald & Mürren) & Stechelberg Village via Trail

Staubbach Waterfall

Weisse

FOLK MUSEUM

To Wengen, Kleine Scheidegg & Jungfraujoch

← MAIN DRAG

Lütschine

← To Wengen

To Grütschalp & Train to Mürren

POST

To Grütschalp & Train to Mürren

TRAIN STATION

CABLE-CAR STATION

To Isenfluh

Not to Scale

Note: Train station to church is a 5 min. walk

River

To Interlaken & Grindelwald

Eating
1. Hotel Restaurant Oberland
2. Hotel Restaurant Silberhorn
3. Airtime Café
4. Flavours Café
5. Co-op Grocery

Sleeping
6. Hotel Staubbach
7. Valley Hostel

Traditional cow culture thrives in the Berner Oberland.

coin-op machines (daily 9:00-21:00, Wi-Fi, tel. 033-855-2008).

Bike Rental: You can rent mountain bikes at **Imboden Bike** on the main street (30 CHF/4 hours, 40 CHF/day, includes helmet, Mon-Fri 8:30-18:30, Sat-Sun 9:00-17:00, tel. 033-855-2114, www. imboden-bike.ch).

Sports Gear: Hiking boots, skis, and snowboards are available to rent at the **Alpia Sports/Intersport** shop (winter daily 8:00-12:30 & 13:30-18:30, slightly shorter hours in summer, closed during Easter holiday, at Hotel Crystal, tel. 033-855-3292, www.alpiasport.ch).

Sights

For hikes and walks from Lauterbrunnen, including "Cloudy-Day Lauterbrunnen Valley Walks" that link Lauterbrunnen to Staubbach and Trümmelbach falls, see "Hiking," later.

STAUBBACH FALLS

The second highest waterfall in Switzerland (nearly 900 feet) is literally in Lauterbrunnen's backyard—just follow the trail past the church toward the sound of rushing water. Its spray looks like falling dust—

Staub—hence the name. A trail is cut into the cliff that takes visitors up "behind" the falls (in winter, it's closed due to the danger of rock slides).

▲TRÜMMELBACH FALLS

If all the waterfalls have you intrigued, sneak a behind-the-scenes look at the valley's most powerful, Trümmelbach Falls. Ride the elevator up through the mountain, climb up to the upper falls, and then hike down through several caves (wet, with lots of stairs, and claustrophobic for some). You'll see the melt from the Eiger, Mönch, and Jungfrau grinding like God's band saw through the mountain at the rate of up to 5,200 gallons a second. The upper area is the best; if your legs ache, skip the lower falls and ride down on the elevator. A café (with WC) is directly across from the bus stop. The falls ticket kiosk is a three-minute walk beyond the café.

Cost and Hours: 11 CHF, daily July-Aug 8:30-18:00, early April-June and Sept-Oct 9:00-17:00, closed Nov-early April, opening date varies with ice conditions, tel. 033-855-3232, www.truemmelbachfaelle.ch.

Getting There: The falls are about halfway between Lauterbrunnen and the

Schilthornbahn cable-car station; from either, it's a short ride on the PostBus or a 45-minute walk. Or combine a visit to Trümmelbach with a walk on the valley floor (described later, under "Hiking").

LAUTERBRUNNEN VALLEY FOLK MUSEUM

This interesting museum shows off the region's folk culture and two centuries of mountaineering from all the towns of this valley. You'll see lots of lace, old tools, exhibits on cheese and woodworking, cowbells, and classic old photos.

Cost and Hours: 5 CHF, free with hotel Visitor Card, June-mid-Oct Tue and Thu-Sun 14:00-17:30, off-season by appointment, closed Mon and Wed year-round, English handout, just over bridge and below church at the far end of Lauterbrunnen town, tel. 033-855-3586, www.talmuseumlauterbrunnen.ch.

Eating

$$$ Hotel Restaurant Oberland serves tasty, good-value meals from a fun menu, including traditional Swiss dishes. It's a high-energy place with lots of tourists and a huge front porch good for lingering (pizzas, raclette, main courses, daily 11:30-21:00, tel. 033-855-1241).

$$$ Hotel Restaurant Silberhorn, with an elegant dining room, is the local choice for a fancy dinner out. Prices are reasonable, and they have all of the Swiss standards. Call to reserve a view table (lunch specials, daily 12:00-14:00 & 18:00-21:00,

classy indoor and outdoor seating, above the cable-car station, tel. 033-856-2210).

$$ Airtime Café feels like an alpine Starbucks with hot drinks, homemade treats, breakfast, simple lunches, and light early dinners. They can help you book adventure-sport activities such as tandem paragliding (daily 8:30-18:00, closed Nov, tel. 033-855-1515).

$$ Flavours, a café without a hint of yodeling or cowbells, serves up full breakfasts, burgers, focaccia sandwiches, and gelato (takeaway available, daily 9:00-18:00, shorter hours off-season, closed Nov-April, tel. 033-855-3652).

Supermarket: The small but well-stocked **Co-op** is on the main street across from the station (Mon-Fri 8:00-18:30, Sat until 17:00, closed Sun).

Sleeping

The price ratings listed are typical for high summer (July-Aug). Expect lower prices in winter (though many hotels close). Free parking is easy to find. For more peace, choose Gimmelwald or Mürren.

$$$ Hotel Silberhorn is a family-run, formal, 35-room hotel. It's in a very convenient location—a hundred yards uphill from the train station on a quiet side street. Almost every double room comes with a fine view and balcony (closed late Oct-mid-Dec, lots of stairs, dinner available, tel. 033-856-2210, www.silberhorn.com, info@silberhorn.com).

$$ Hotel Staubbach is one of the oldest hotels in the valley (1890). It has the

Lauterbrunnen Valley Folk Museum

Staubbach Falls is in Lauterbrunnen's backyard.

casual feel of a national park lodge, with 33 simple and comfortable rooms. It's family-friendly and has a kids' play area. Rooms that face up the valley have fabulous views (closed mid-Nov-March, airy breakfast room with great views, elevator, 10-minute walk up from station on the left, tel. 033-855-5454, www.staubbach.com, hotel@staubbach.com).

$$ **Hotel Oberland** is cheerfully located in the center of town, with 28 tidy, bright rooms, most with balconies and views of the Staubbach waterfall or Jungfrau (closed mid-Oct-mid-Dec, family rooms and apartments available, 5 rooms in nearby Crystal Hotel annex, popular with my tour groups, 5-minute walk up from station on the right, free parking, tel. 033-855-1241, www.hoteloberland.ch, info@hoteloberland.ch).

¢ **Valley Hostel** is practical and comfortable, offering 92 inexpensive beds for quieter travelers of all ages, with a pleasant garden. This is a manageable budget option for families (private rooms available, breakfast extra, kitchen, pay laundry, reception open 8:00-12:00 & 15:00-22:00—shorter hours off-season, 5-minute walk up from train station, tel. 033-855-2008, www.valleyhostel.ch,

info@valleyhostel.ch, Abegglen family: Martha, Alfred, Stefan, and Fränzi).

Transportation

The valley-floor towns of Lauterbrunnen and Stechelberg have connections by mountain train, bus, and cable car to the traffic-free villages, peaks, and hikes high above. Prices and trip durations given are one-way and per leg unless otherwise noted.

From Lauterbrunnen

By Train to: Interlaken Ost (1-2/hour, 20 minutes, 7.60 CHF), **Wengen** (2/hour, 15 minutes, 6.80 CHF), **Kleine Scheidegg** (2/hour, 45 minutes, 30.80 CHF), **Jungfraujoch** (2/hour, 1.5 hours, 94.80 CHF one-way, change in Kleine Scheidegg; **Männlichen** (for hike to Kleine Scheidegg—take train to Wengen and change to cable car).

By Cable Car to: Grütschalp (2-4/hour, 6 minutes), where the train waits to take you to **Mürren** (another 15 minutes); total trip time 20 minutes, total one-way cost 11.40 CHF, www.jungfrau.ch.

By PostBus to: Schilthornbahn cable-car station (buses timed to depart a few minutes after trains arrive in Lauterbrunnen, 15-minute ride, 4.40 CHF, covered by Swiss Travel Pass), continues to the hamlet of **Stechelberg.**

By Car to: Schilthornbahn cable-car station (10-minute drive, pay parking lot).

From Schilthornbahn Cable-Car Station near Stechelberg

By Cable Car to: Gimmelwald (2/hour, 5 minutes, 6.20 CHF); **Mürren** (2/hour, 10 minutes, 11.40 CHF, change in Gimmelwald); and the **Schilthorn** (2/hour, 22 minutes, 105 CHF round-trip, change in Gimmelwald, Mürren, and Birg). Cable cars run up from the valley station—and down from Mürren—at :25 and :55 past the hour (5:55-19:55; then only once an hour until 23:45 Sun-Thu, until 24:55 Fri-Sat). From Gimmelwald to both Mürren and the valley station, the cable car runs at :00 and :30 (6:00-20:00; after 20:00 runs only once an hour).

GIMMELWALD

Saved from developers by its "avalanche zone" classification, Gimmelwald was (before modern tourism) one of the poorest places in Switzerland. Its traditional economy was stuck in the hay, and its farmers—unable to make it in their disadvantaged trade—survived only on a trickle of visitors and Swiss government subsidies (and working the ski lifts in winter). Although the village's population dropped in the last century from 300 to about 120 residents, traditions survive. Raising hay in this rugged terrain is labor-intensive. Tough and proud, local families harvest enough to feed only about 15 cows each. But they'd have it no other way. Don't confuse Gimmelwald (rated ▲▲▲) and touristy Grindelwald—they couldn't be more different.

Take a walk through the town. The huge, sheer cliff face that dominates your mountain views is the Schwarzmönch ("Black Monk"). The three peaks above (or behind) it are, left to right, the Eiger, Mönch, and Jungfrau.

For some travelers, there's little to see in the village. Others (like me) enjoy a fascinating day sitting on a bench and learning why they say, "If heaven isn't what it's cracked up to be, send me back to Gimmelwald."

Gimmelwald's farmers raise just enough hay for their cows.

Rick's Tip: Gimmelwald has a helpful website *(www.gimmelwald.ch) where you can check out photos, get directions for the best hikes, and see the latest on activities and rooms for rent. Also, consider downloading the free* **Schilthorn Explore App,** *which includes a Gimmelwald Audio Village Tour (after downloading app via Apple's App Store or Google Play, look for "Trip Suggestion" to find the Gimmelwald tour).*

◉ Gimmelwald Walk

Gimmelwald, though tiny, with one zigzag street, offers a fine look at a traditional Swiss mountain community.

• *Start this quick self-guided walk at the...*

Cable-Car Station: When the lift came in the 1960s, the village's back end became its front door. As you walk out of the station, pause at the big Infopoint map to orient yourself. Then turn right (uphill).

Gimmelwald was, and still is, a farm village. As you start up the street, you'll see a sweet little hut on the right. Set on stilts to keep out mice, the hut was used for storing cheese (the rocks on the rooftop here and throughout the town are not decorative—they keep the shingles on through wild storms). Behind the cheese hut stands the former village schoolhouse, long the largest structure in town (in Catholic Swiss towns, the biggest building is the church; in Protestant towns, it's the school). Gimmelwald's students now go to school in Lauterbrunnen, and the building is used as a chapel when the Protestant pastor makes his monthly visit. The little gray tower-like structure on the roof is the town fire siren. Now turn around: On the other side of the street, next to the little playground, is a bench with a nice view, and just beyond it is the recommended Mountain Hostel.

• *Walk up the lane 50 yards, past the town's Dalí-esque art gallery (who's showing in the phone booth?), to Gimmelwald's...*

Swiss Cow Culture

Traditional Swiss cow farmers produce enough cheese to break even—they support their families on government subsidies of about $5,000 per cow. (Throughout the Alps, various governments support traditional farming as much for the tourism as for the cheese.) But these farmers have made a lifestyle choice to keep tradition alive and live high in the mountains.

The cows' grazing ground can range in elevation by as much as 5,000 feet throughout the year. In the summer (usually mid-June), the farmer straps elaborate ceremonial bells on his cows and takes them up to a hut at high elevation. The big bells weigh upward of 10 pounds and can cost more than 2,000 CHF apiece—a proud investment for a humble farmer. When the cows arrive at their summer home, the bells are hung under the eaves.

These high-elevation summer stables are called "alps." The cows stay at the alps for about 100 days (roughly from June 10 to September 21). The farmers hire a team of cheesemakers to work at each alp—mostly hippies, students, and city slickers eager to spend three summer months in mountainous solitude. Each morning, the hired hands get up at 5:00 to milk the cows; take them to pasture; and make the cheese, milking the cows again when they come home in the evening. In the summer, all the milk is turned into alp cheese (it's too difficult to get it down to the market in liquid form). In the winter, with the cows at lower altitudes, the fresh milk is sold as milk.

Meanwhile, the farmers, free of their bovine responsibilities in summer, turn their attention to making hay. The average farmer has a few huts at various altitudes, each surrounded by small hay fields. The farmer follows the seasons up into the mountains, making hay and storing it above the huts. In the fall, the cows come down from the alps and spend the winter moving from hut to hut, eating the hay the farmer spent the summer preparing for them.

Throughout the year you'll see farmers moving their herds to various elevations. If snow is in the way, farmers sometimes use tourist cable cars to move their cows.

"Times Square": The yellow alpine "street sign" shows where you are, the altitude (1,370 meters, or 4,470 feet), how many hours (*Std.*) and minutes it takes to walk to nearby points, and which tracks are serious hiking paths (marked with red and white, and further indicated along the way with red and white patches of paint on stones). You're surrounded by buildings that were built as duplexes, divided vertically right down the middle to house two separate families. Look for the Honesty Shop at Pension Gimmelwald, which features local crafts and little edibles for sale (summer only).

Behind the sign, the lettering high up on the post office building is a folksy blessing: "Summer brings green, winter

Gimmelwald

To Gimmeln & Mürren

To Sprutz Waterfall, Spielbodenalp, Bryndli, Rotstockhütte & Schilthorn

To Mürren (30-min. Uphill Hike)

WALTER'S HOTEL MITTAGHORN

PAVED ROAD

BENCHES

FIRE STN.

BENCHES

To Sefinen Valley

FORMER SCHOOL

VIA FERRATA SUSPENSION BRIDGE

To Mürren (5 min) & on to Schilthorn (30 min) via lift

CABLE-CAR STATION

Cliffs

Cliffs

Not to Scale

Note: Cable-car station to Walter's = 10-min. walk

To Stechelberg (1 Hour Hike)

To Schilthornbahn Valley Station, Bus Stop & Car Park

Eating & Sleeping
1. Olle & Maria's B&B
2. Esther's Guest House
3. Pension Gimmelwald & Honesty Shop
4. Hotel Mittaghorn
5. Mountain Hostel
6. Cheese Hut

brings snow. The sun greets the day, the stars greet the night. This house will protect you from rain, cold, and wind. May God give us his blessings." Small as Gimmelwald is, it still has daily mail service. The postman comes down from Mürren each day (by golf cart in summer, sled in winter) to deliver and pick up mail. The date on this building indicates when it was built or rebuilt (1911). Gimmelwald has a strict building code: For instance, shutters can only be painted certain colors.

• From this tiny intersection, walk away from the cable-car station and follow the town's...

Main Street: Walk up the road past the garden-gnome greeting committee on the right. On the left, notice the announcement board: one side for tourist news, the other for local news (such as deals on chain-saw sharpening and upcoming shooting competitions). Cross the street

and admire the big barn, dated 1995. At one front corner is a cow-scratcher. Swiss cows have legal rights (for example, in the winter they must be taken out for exercise at least three times a week). This big barn is built in a modern style. Traditionally, barns were small (like those on the hillside high above) and closer to the hay. But

"Main Street" in Gimmelwald

with trucks and paved roads, hay can be moved more easily, and farm businesses need more cows to be viable. Still, even a well-run big farm hopes just to break even. The industry survives only with government subsidies (see sidebar). As you wander, you'll also see private garden patches. Until recently, most locals grew their own vegetables—often enough to provide most of their family's needs.

• Go just beyond the next barn. On your right is a...

Water Fountain/Trough: This is the site of the town's historic water supply—still perfectly drinkable. Village kids love to bathe and wage water wars here when the cows aren't drinking from it.

• Detour left down a gravel path (along a wooden fence). First you'll pass the lovingly tended pea-patch gardens of the woman with the best green thumb in the village (on your left). Continue along the path, which ends after 50 yards at another water trough in front of a house called...

Husmättli: This is the oldest building in town, from 1658. (There are more 17th-century buildings on the road that zigzags down from Gimmelwald into the Sefinen Valley.) Study the log-cabin construction. Many old houses were built without nails. The wood was logged up the valley and cut on the water-powered village mill (also in the Sefinen Valley). Gimmelwald heats with wood, and since the wood needs to age a couple of years to burn well, it's stacked everywhere.

• Return to the main paved road and continue onward.

Twenty yards along, on the left, look for the house with the *Self Service* sign. Open the door and you'll find a refrigerator with local cheese sold on the honor system by the Rubin family. Just outside the door, in the summer months, you may see a bunch of scythes hanging above a sharpening stone. Farmers pound, rather than grind, the blade to get it razor-sharp for efficient mowing on slopes too rocky or steep for machines or grazing animals. Feel a blade...carefully.

A few steps farther, notice the cute **cheese hut** on the right. This is where the cheese you saw on sale is produced. The hut's front wall is an alpine art gallery with

Gimmelwald offers a fine look at traditional Swiss mountain life.

nail-shoes used as flower pots. Nail shoes grip the steep, wet fields—this is critical for a farmer's safety, especially when carrying a sharp scythe. Even today, farmers buy metal tacks and fasten them to boots. The hut is full of strong cheese—up to three years old.

Look up. In the summer, a few goats are kept here behind the hut (rather than at a high alp) to provide families with fresh milk (about a half-gallon per day per goat). The farmers fence the goats in so they eat only this difficult-to-harvest grass.

On the left (at the *B&B* sign) is Olle and Maria's home. They ran the local school until it closed in 2010. Now they both commute to teach at schools in other villages.
• *Fifty yards farther along on the right is the house called...*

Alpenrose: This is the old village school building, in use from about 1810 to 1930. Now it's a family home. You might see big ceremonial cowbells hanging under the eaves on the uphill side. These swing from the necks of cows during the procession from town to the high Alps (mid-June) and back down (mid-Sept).
• *At the end of town, pause where a lane branches off to the left, leading into the dramatic...*

Sefinen Valley: At the bottom of this wild valley is a stream that rushes down toward Stechelberg. All the old homes in town are made from wood cut from the left-hand side of this valley (shady side, slow-growing, better timber) and milled on the valley floor.
• *A few steps ahead, the road switches back at the...*

Gimmelwald Fire Station (Feuerwehrmagazin): Peer through the windows in the door at the tractor-like engines. Then walk up around the hairpin bend to the notice board on the side of the building. The *Föhnwacht Reglement* sheet explains rules to keep the village from burning down during the Föhn season, a period of fierce dry winds. During this time, there's a 24-hour fire watch, and even smoking cigarettes outdoors is forbidden.

Check out the other posted notices. This year's Swiss Army calendar tells reservists when and where to go (in all four official Swiss languages). Every Swiss male does a 22-week stint in the military, then serves three weeks a year in the reserves until age 34. The *Schiessübungen* poster details the shooting exercises required this year.
• *Unless you're really pooped, continue uphill along the road.*

High Road to Hotel Mittaghorn: The resort town of Mürren hovers in the distance. And high on the left, notice the hay field with terraces. These are from WWII days, when Switzerland, wanting self-sufficiency, required all farmers to grow potatoes. Today, this field is a festival of alpine flowers in season (best at this altitude in May and June).
• *In a couple of minutes, you'll reach a peaceful set of benches, just off the lane on the downhill side, which let you savor the view. Just beyond is Hotel Mittaghorn and steps downhill, which bring you quickly back to Gimmelwald's "Times Square." Up for more? For hikes from Gimmelwald, see "Hiking," later.*

Eating and Sleeping

Gimmelwald is my home base in the Berner Oberland. Poor and pleasantly stuck in the past, the village has only one restaurant and a few accommodation options—all of them quirky and memorable. Prices don't include breakfast (except for the hostel) but do include the local tax, which gives you free entry to the public swimming pool in nearby Mürren (at the Sportzentrum).

$$$ Pension Gimmelwald Restaurant has a good, simple menu served in a rustic indoor dining room or on a jaw-dropping view terrace (reservations required by phone if not staying overnight, daily mid-June-Sept and late Dec-mid-April 12:00-15:00 & 18:00-21:00, bar open until 23:00, closed off-season, tel. 033-855-1730, www.hotel-pensiongimmelwald.ch). The attached **$$ Pension Gimmelwald** has

10 simple shared-bath rooms, two rooms with private bath, a restaurant, and a cozy bar, plus a six-bed dorm that attracts more mature guests than a typical youth hostel (RS% with 2-night stay if you book direct, family room available, breakfast extra, dinner available, open June-mid-Oct and late Dec-mid-April, 2-minute walk up from cable-car station, tel. 033-855-1730, www.pensiongimmelwald.com, pensiongimmelwald@gmail.com).

Rick's Tip: *Consider packing in a* **picnic meal from Lauterbrunnen or Mürren,** *which have grocery stores and cafés selling sandwiches to go.*

$$$ At **Olle and Maria's B&B,** the Eggimanns rent three rooms—Gimmelwald's most comfortable and expensive—in their alpine-sleek house. Two rooms with shared bath are upstairs, while the "double" with private bath is a ground-level studio apartment with a kitchenette and a private entrance (family room available, breakfast extra, 3-night minimum, cash or PayPal only, nonrefundable 50 percent deposit via PayPal required, pay laundry service; from cable car, continue straight for 200 yards along the town's only road, look for B&B sign on left; tel. 033-855-3575, www.olleandmarias.ch, oeggimann@bluewin.ch).

$$ **Esther's Guest House,** overlooking the village's main intersection, rents seven clean, basic, and comfortable rooms with a two-night minimum. Three rooms have private bathrooms, and all share a generous lounge and kitchen (family rooms available—one sleeps up to 5, breakfast extra, sack lunches available, low ceilings, tel. 033-855-5488, www.esthersguesthouse.ch, info@esthersguesthouse.ch). Urs and Dana also rent two five-person **apartments** with kitchenettes next door (3-night minimum, see website for details).

$ **Hotel Mittaghorn** is a classic, thin-walled, alpine-style place with superb

views. It's run by Walter Mittler, an elderly Swiss gentleman, with help from trusty Tim. The hotel has three rooms with private showers and four rooms that share a coin-operated shower (2-night minimum, cash only, open mid-May-Oct, a 5-minute climb up the path from the village center, tel. 033-855-1658, www.mittaghorn.com, mittaghorn@gmail.com; reserve by e-mail—generally answered April-Oct only). If no one's there when you check in, look for a card in the hallway directing you to your room.

¢ **Mountain Hostel** is a beehive of activity, as clean as its guests, cheap, respectable, and friendly. The 50-bed hostel has low ceilings, a self-service kitchen, bar, pool table, and healthy plumbing. It's mostly a college-age crowd; families and older travelers will probably feel more comfortable elsewhere (sheets and breakfast included, pay showers, pay laundry, closed Nov, from the lift station it's 20 yards up the path to the left, tel. 033-855-1704, www.mountainhostel.com, info@mountainhostel.com).

Transportation

To get from Lauterbrunnen to Gimmelwald, you have two options:

1. Schilthornbahn Cable Car: The faster, easier way—best in bad weather or at the end of a long day with lots of luggage—is by road and then cable car. The cable-car station, near Stechelberg, is a 10-minute drive or 15-minute bus ride from Lauterbrunnen. Drivers can park at a pay lot at the cable-car station; otherwise, ride the PostBus from Lauterbrunnen (buses depart with the arrival of trains in Lauterbrunnen). The cable car whisks you in five thrilling minutes up to Gimmelwald.

Note that the Schilthornbahn cable car is closed for servicing for a week in late April or early May and for a month from early November through early December. If you're here during this time, you'll ride the cargo cable car from the valley floor directly up to Mürren, where a small bus shuttles you down to Gimmelwald.

2. Grütschalp Cable Car and Mürren Train: This is the more scenic route. Catch the cable car from Lauterbrunnen to Grütschalp. At Grütschalp, a special vintage train will roll you along the incredibly scenic cliffside to Mürren (the total trip takes 20 minutes). From there, either walk to the middle of Mürren and take a left down a moderately steep paved path 30 minutes to Gimmelwald, or walk 10 minutes across Mürren to catch the Schilthornbahn cable car down to Gimmelwald.

MÜRREN

Pleasant as an alpine resort can be, Mürren is traffic-free and filled with cafés, souvenirs, old-timers with walking sticks, employees enjoying incentive trips, and snap-happy tourists. Its chalets are pre-fab-rustic. With help from a cliffside train, a funicular, and a cable car, hiking options are endless from Mürren (rated ▲▲). Sitting on a ledge more than 2,000 feet above the Lauterbrunnen Valley, surrounded by a fortissimo chorus of mountains, the town has all the comforts of home (for a price) without the pretentiousness of more famous resorts.

Mürren dates from 1384, but its historic character has been overwhelmed by development (unlike Gimmelwald). Still, it's a peaceful town, with 400 permanent residents. Depending on the time of year, Mürren is either lively (winter and summer, when the population swells to 4,000) or completely dead (spring and fall).

Orientation

Mürren perches high on a ledge, overlooking the Lauterbrunnen Valley. You can walk from one end of town to the other in about 10 minutes.

Tourist Information: Mürren's TI, in the town sports complex, can help you find a room and gives hiking advice (daily 8:30-18:45, Dec-April until 20:00; May and Nov 8:00-12:00 & 13:00-17:00; above the village, follow signs to *Sportzentrum*, tel. 033-856-8686, www.mymuerren.ch).

Money: An ATM is at the cable-car station.

Laundry: Hotel Bellevue has a little self-service launderette in a shed on the side of the hotel (open 24/7 even when hotel is closed).

Bike Rental: You can rent mountain bikes at **Stäger Sport**—ask about returning the bike in Lauterbrunnen for an extra fee (30 CHF/half-day, 40 CHF/day, includes helmet, daily 9:00-12:00 & 13:00-17:00, closed late Oct-mid-May, in middle of town, tel. 033-855-2355, www.staegersport. ch). There's a bigger bike-rental place in Lauterbrunnen (Imboden Bike).

R & R: The slick **Sportzentrum** (sports center) that houses the TI is a world of indoor activities, including a sauna, hot tub, and steam bath. The café offers a reasonably priced, basic menu, with indoor and outdoor seating (daily 10:00-18:00). The pool is 10 CHF with the Visitor Card given out by hotels and hostels (otherwise 12 CHF, daily 13:00-20:00, Dec-March until 21:00, April-May until 18:00, closed Nov, tel. 033-856-8686, www. sportzentrum-muerren.ch). In season, they offer minigolf, table tennis, and a fitness room. In July and August, you can enjoy occasional folkloric evenings (some Wednesdays, at Sportzentrum).

Skiing and Snowboarding: The Mürren-Schilthorn ski area is the Berner Oberland's best place for experts, especially those eager to tackle the famous, nearly 10-mile-long Inferno run. The runs on top, especially the Kanonenrohr, are quite steep and have

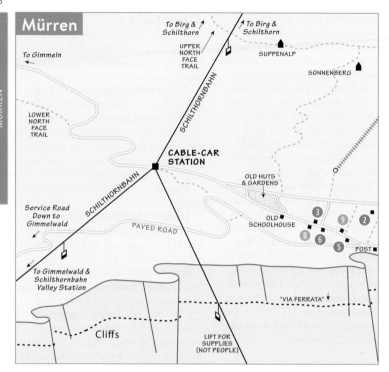

Mürren

To Birg & Schilthorn
To Birg & Schilthorn
To Gimmeln
UPPER NORTH FACE TRAIL
SUPPENALP
SONNENBERG
SCHILTHORNBAHN
LOWER NORTH FACE TRAIL
CABLE-CAR STATION
OLD HUTS & GARDENS
SCHILTHORNBAHN
Service Road Down to Gimmelwald
PAVED ROAD
OLD SCHOOLHOUSE
3
9
2
8
6
5
POST
To Gimmelwald & Schilthornbahn Valley Station
"VIA FERRATA"
Cliffs
LIFT FOR SUPPLIES (NOT PEOPLE)

predictably good snow; lower areas cater to all levels, but can be icier. For rental gear, try the friendly, convenient **Ed Abegglen** shop (best prices, next to recommended Chalet Fontana, tel. 033-855-1245), **Alfred's Sporthaus** (good selection and decent prices, between ski school and Sportzentrum, tel. 033-855-3030), or **Stäger Sport** (one shop in Sportzentrum and another in the town center, tel. 033-855-2330).

➲ Mürren Walk

Mürren has long been a top ski resort, but a walk across town offers a glimpse into a time before ski lifts. This stroll takes you through town on the main drag, from the train station (where you'll arrive if coming from Lauterbrunnen) to the cable-car station, then back up to the Allmendhubel funicular station.
• *Start at the...*

Train Station: The first trains pulled into Mürren in 1891. (A circa 1911 car is permanently parked at Grütschalp's station.) A display case inside the station displays an original car from the narrow-gauge, horse-powered line that rolled fancy visitors from here into town. The current station, built in 1964, comes with impressive engineering for heavy cargo.
• *Wander into town along the main road (take the lower, left fork) for a stroll under the...*

Alpin Palace Hotel: This towering place was the "Grand Palace Hotel" until it burned in 1928. Today it's closed, and no one knows its future. The small wooden platform on the left is the place where snow-removal trucks dump their loads over the cliff in the winter. Look back at the meadow below the station: This is a favorite grazing spot for chamois. Ahead, at Hotel Edelweiss, step to the far corner of the restaurant terrace for a breathtaking view stretching from the big three (Eiger, Mönch, and Jungfrau) on

Eating
1. Restaurant Edelweiss/Hotel
2. Restaurant Bellevue/Hotel
3. Restaurant Blumental/Hotel
4. Eiger Guesthouse Restaurant & Hotel Eiger
5. Stägerstübli Restaurant
6. Co-op Grocery

Sleeping
7. Hotel Jungfrau
8. Hotel Regina
9. Chalet Fontana

To Birg & Schilthorn

ALLMENDHUBEL

To Grütschalp

FUNICULAR

SPORT-ZENTRUM

To Grütschalp & Lift Down to Lauterbrunnen →

TENNIS COURTS

TRAIN STATION

Cliffs

Note:
Cable-car station to train station = 10-min. walk

Not to Scale

the left, past waterfalls gushing from the cliffsides (especially after a good rain), to the lonely cattle farm in the high alp on the right. Then look down.

• Continue toward an empty lot with a grand view.

Viewpoints: There are plans for a big apartment-hotel to be built here, but the project is waiting for investment money.

You'll have many hiking options from Mürren.

Detour from the main street around the cliff-hanging tennis court. Stop at one of the little romantic shelters built into the far wall. Directly below, at the base of the modern wall, is the start of a 1.5-mile *via ferrata*, a "trail" with a steel-cable guide that mountaineers use to venture safely along the cliff all the way to Gimmelwald. You can see the Gimmelwald lift station in the distance.

• Return to the main street and continue to...

"Downtown" Mürren: This main intersection (where the small service road leads down to Gimmelwald) has the only grocery store in town (the Co-op). A bit farther on, the tiny fire barn (labeled *Feuerwehr*) has a list showing the leaders of the volunteer force and their responsibilities.

About 65 feet beyond the fire barn (across the street from the old schoolhouse—Altes Schulhaus), detour right uphill a few steps into the oldest part of town. Explore the windy little lanes, admiring the ancient woodwork on the houses and the cute little pea patches.

• *Back on the main drag, continue to the far end of Mürren, where you come to the...*

Cable-Car Station: The larger cars that dock in the back of the station take hikers and skiers up to the Schilthorn and run down to the valley via Gimmelwald. The smaller cable car out front goes directly (and very steeply) to the valley floor. This was the main route down to Stechelberg until 1987, but today it is only for cargo, garbage, and backup passenger service in spring and fall when the newer cars are closed for maintenance.

• *Hiking back into town along the high road, you'll enter...*

Upper Mürren: You'll pass Mürren's two churches, the Allmendhubel funicular station, and the Sportzentrum (with swimming pool and TI).

• *Our walk is finished. Enjoy the town and the views.*

Experiences

During ski season and the height of summer, the Mürren area offers plenty of activities for those willing to seek them out. In spring and fall, Mürren is pretty quiet. For hikes from Mürren and Allmendhubel, see "Hiking," later.

ALLMENDHUBEL FUNICULAR (ALLMENDHUBELBAHN)

A surprisingly rewarding funicular (built in 1912, renovated in 1999) carries nature lovers from Mürren up to Allmendhubel, a perch offering a Jungfrau view that, though much lower, rivals the Schilthorn. At the station, notice the 1920s bobsled. Consider mixing a mountain lift, grand views, and a hike with your meal by eating at the restaurant on Allmendhubel (good chef, open daily until 17:00).

Allmendhubel is particularly good for families. The entertaining children's Adventure trail—with rough and thrilling kid-friendly alpine rides along the way—starts from here. This is also the departure point for the North Face hike and walks to Grütschalp. While at Allmendhubel, consider its Flower trail, a 20-minute loop with nice mountain views and (from June through Sept) a chance to see more than 150 different alpine flowers blooming.

Mürren's cute town center

Cost and Hours: 8.80 CHF one-way, 14 CHF round-trip, half-price with Swiss Travel Pass, early June-mid-Oct daily 9:00-17:00, runs every 20 minutes, tel. 033-855-2042 or 033-856-2141, www.schilthorn.ch.

TANDEM PARAGLIDING

If you've ever wondered what it's like to soar like an eagle, a tandem paragliding flight will give you a pretty good idea. **Airtime Paragliding** offers a guided flight called "The Wall," which takes off near the Mürren cable car station and ends near the Stechelberg cable car station (flights last around 15 to 20 minutes, depending on conditions). After your pilot rigs you in the tandem harness and gives you a few brief instructions, he'll take you on a short run downhill and then you're both up, up, and away—flying gracefully over the Lauterbrunnen Valley, along cliff faces, past waterfalls, and over treetops.

Cost: 170 CHF for Mürren-Stechelberg flight, transport to Mürren not included; various other flight options available, no experience necessary, based at recommended Airtime Café in Lauterbrunnen, tel. 079-247-8463, www.airtime-paragliding.ch.

Eating

Outside of summer and ski season, only a few places are open.

$$$ Hotel Edelweiss offers lunch and dinner with the most cliff-hanging dining in town—the views are incredible, and the prices are good, too (Swiss specialties, burgers, and salads; daily specials, family-friendly, tel. 033-856-5600).

$$$ Eiger Guesthouse Restaurant, a busy local hangout with a relaxed pub atmosphere, has long hours and a mostly Italian menu. They also do fondue, raclette, and *Rösti* (daily 8:00-22:00, closed Nov, tel. 033-856-5460).

$$$ Stägerstübli, in the town center, is in a 1902 building that was once a tearoom for rich tourists. Sitting on its terrace, you know just who's out and about in town

(*Rösti,* meat dishes, big portions, daily 11:30-20:30, closes for a week in early Sept, tel. 033-855-1316).

$$$ Hotel Blumental's restaurant (called La Grotte) specializes in typical Swiss cuisine, but also serves fish, international, and vegetarian dishes in a stony and woody dining area. It's one of Mürren's most elegant, romantic settings (fondue served for one or more, pastas, daily from 14:00, tel. 033-855-1826).

$$$$ Hotel Bellevue's restaurant is atmospheric, with three dining zones: a spectacular view terrace, a sophisticated indoor area, and the Jägerstübli—a cozy, well-antlered hunters' room (lamb and game, fondue, burgers, nonmeat dishes available, daily 11:30-14:00 & 18:00-21:00, tel. 033-855-1401).

Supermarket: The **Co-op** is the only grocery store in town, with good picnic fixings and sandwiches (Mon-Fri 8:00-12:00 & 13:45-18:30, Sat until 17:00, closed Sun, closed Tue-Thu afternoons in spring and fall). Given restaurant prices, this place is a godsend for those on a tight budget.

Sleeping

Except where noted, all of the hotels and restaurants listed here close in spring (anywhere from Easter to early June) and again in fall (sometime between mid-Oct and mid-Dec). Half-board, if available, is a good idea in Mürren.

$$$$ Hotel Eiger, a four-star hotel dramatically and conveniently situated just across from the tiny train station, is a good but expensive bet. It offers all the services you'd expect in a big-city hotel (plush lounge, elegant dining rooms, indoor swimming pool, exercise room, and saunas) while maintaining an Old World, woody elegance in its 50 rooms. Their family suites, while pricey, can be a good value for groups of four or five (grand breakfast, discounts for stays of 3 nights or more, email for best deals, elevator, tel. 033-856-5454, www.hoteleiger.com, info@hoteleiger.com).

At **$$$ Hotel Edelweiss,** it's all about the location—convenient and literally hanging on the cliff with devastating views. It's a big, modern building with 30 basic rooms (some with balconies) and a busy, recommended restaurant (closed Nov-mid-Dec, half-board available, elevator, piano in lounge, self-serve pay laundry, tel. 033-856-5600, www.edelweiss-muerren.ch, info@edelweiss-muerren.ch).

$$$ Hotel Bellevue has a homey lounge, solid woodsy furniture, a great view terrace, the hunter-themed Jäger-stübli restaurant, and 19 great rooms at fair rates—most with balconies and views (discount if staying 2 nights or more in early June or Sept-Oct, self-serve pay laundry, tel. 033-855-1401, www.bellevuemuerren.ch, bellevue@muerren.ch, Ruth and Othmar Suter).

$$$ Hotel Jungfrau offers 29 modern and comfortable rooms, and two apartments for up to six people (email for best deals, elevator, pay laundry service, pay Wi-Fi in rooms—free in common area, close to TI/Sportzentrum, tel. 033-856-6464, www.hoteljungfrau.ch, mail@hoteljungfrau.ch, Martin and Connie).

$$ Hotel Blumental has 16 rooms with woody accents and down comforters, a recommended restaurant in the main building, plus six modern rooms of equal quality in the chalet out back (RS%, half-board available, tel. 033-855-1826, www.hotel-blumental.com, blumental@muerren.ch; Ralph and Heidi von Allmen are fourth-generation owners).

$$ Eiger Guesthouse offers 12 good, small budget rooms across from the train station in a simply furnished, renovated older building with an easygoing ground-floor pub. Four of the rooms share two sets of bathroom facilities (RS%, closed Nov, lots of stairs, game room, view terrace, tel. 033-856-5460, www.eigerguesthouse.com, info@eigerguesthouse.com).

$$ Hotel Regina has 52 basic rooms (most with shared toilets and showers) and is conveniently located near the cable-car station. For solo travelers, the single rooms are a decent value (family deals, tel. 033-855-4242, www.reginamuerren.ch, info@reginamuerren.ch).

$ Chalet Fontana, run by charming Englishwoman Denise Fussell, is a fine budget option, with five simple, crispy-clean, and comfortable rooms (cash only, closed late Oct-April, fridge in common kitchen, across street from Stäger-stübli restaurant in town center, mobile 078-642-3485, www.chaletfontana.ch, chaletfontana@gmail.com). Denise also rents two family apartments with kitchen, bathroom, and breakfast (one in a separate building with a mountain view).

Transportation

There are two ways to get to Mürren: via the **Grütschalp cable car and train** from near Lauterbrunnen (the cable car connects to the train from Grütschalp; 20 minutes total) or on the **Schilthornbahn cable car** from near Stechelberg (10 minutes). The train and cable-car stations (which have lockers and free WCs) are at opposite ends of town. For several weeks in spring and fall, one (but never both) of these routes closes down for maintenance.

EXPLORING THE ALPS

Scenic Lifts and Trains

Many people enjoy a high-altitude thrill ride to one of the scenic viewpoints

described here, but they're quite expensive. You can also enjoy the mountains on foot with the help of more modestly priced lifts (see "Hiking," later).

▲▲▲SCHILTHORNBAHN

The Schilthornbahn cable car carries skiers, hikers, and sightseers effortlessly to the nearly 10,000-foot summit of the Schilthorn, where the Piz Gloria cable-car station awaits, with its solar-powered revolving restaurant, shop, and panorama terrace. At the top, you have a spectacular panoramic view of the Eiger, Mönch, and Jungfrau mountains, lined up on the horizon.

Times and Prices: You can ride to the Schilthorn and back from several points—the cable-car station near Stechelberg on the valley floor (105 CHF), cliff-hanging Gimmelwald (92.60 CHF), or the higher Mürren (82.20 CHF). If you have a Swiss Travel Pass, the ride to the summit is free. If you have a Eurail pass, you'll get 25 percent off the whole trip. You'll encounter fewer crowds at the summit if you go early or late (leaving Stechelberg 7:25-8:55 and 15:25-16:25; if going late confirm last descent—generally 17:55) and in spring and fall (roughly May and Oct). If you're going for breakfast (hearty 33-CHF

The Schilthornbahn cable car leaves the Gimmelwald station.

buffet), add it to your lift ticket to save a bit of money. If you're staying a few days in Mürren or Gimmelwald and planning to go up, the Schilthornbahn's Holiday Pass starts to make sense (free travel on all routes between Lauterbrunnen and the peak, 140 CHF/4 days or 160 CHF/6 days, available May-Oct only).

Lifts go twice hourly, and the ride from Gimmelwald (including two transfers) to the Schilthorn takes 30 minutes. Lifts run all year, except during maintenance closures (a week in April and four weeks in Nov-Dec). Drivers can leave their cars at the pay lot at the valley station near Stechelberg. For more information, including current weather conditions, see www.schilthorn.ch or call 033-826-0007.

Ascending the Schilthorn: As the cable car floats between Gimmelwald and Mürren you'll see the metal bridge that marks the end of the *via ferrata*. You'll also see fields of wooden tripods, which serve two purposes: They stop avalanches and shelter newly planted trees. From Mürren to Birg, keep an eye on the altitude meter. You can pause at Birg, where there's a café (not always open), the breezy Skyline Walk viewing platform that juts out

over the cliff face, and the Thrill Walk—a 600-foot-long catwalk bolted to the cliffside. If walking the see-through metal catwalk seems tame to you, there are also opportunities to tightrope across a cable bridge (there's a net below), cross a section of glass flooring, or crawl through a chain-link tube—all with airy views to the valley far below.

At the Top: Head up two escalators to the Skyline View Platform. Outside, information boards identify the peaks, and directional signs point hikers toward some seriously steep downhill climbs. Watch paragliders set up, psych up, take off, and fly with the birds. Walk along the ridge out back and step onto the Piz Gloria view platform at the end of the fenced area. This is a great place for a photo of the mountain-climber you. Youth hostelers—not realizing that rocks may hide just under the snow—scream down the ice fields on plastic-bag sleds from the mountaintop. (There's an English-speaking doctor in Lauterbrunnen).

Back inside, peek in the Skyline Top Shop for souvenirs or head down the stairs and follow the maze that leads to the Bond World 007 exhibit and cinema.

Viewing platform at the top of the Schilthorn

This interactive exhibit, well-signed in English, is worth a few minutes for even non-Bond fans. It takes you behind the scenes of the 1969 James Bond movie, *On Her Majesty's Secret Service,* which used the Schilthorn as one of its major locations (and financed the complex's completion). Step into the role of James Bond and try your hand at flying a helicopter to Piz Gloria or bobsledding down the Alps in the simulators. Don't miss the opportunity to morph your face onto one of several Bond stars (pictures available in the gift shop for a fee, of course). Even the WCs are Bond-themed—a sign in the men's room urged me to "Aim Like James."

At the end of the exhibit, the Bond World 007 cinema shows a 20-minute video of the natural wonders of the area, highlights a few activities (including racing down the famous Inferno ski run), briefly shares the story of the Schilthornbahn lift itself, and shows a substantial clip from *On Her Majesty's Secret Service.* If you haven't had enough Bond yet, peruse the 007 Walk of Fame, where cast and crew members from the film have left their handprints and personal messages (on the ridge to the Piz Gloria view platform).

You can hike down from the Schilthorn, but it's tough. (Hiking *up* from Gimmelwald or Mürren is easier on your knees... if you don't mind a 5,000-foot altitude gain.) For information on **hikes** from lift stations along the Schilthorn cable-car line, see "Hiking," later. My favorite "hike" from the Schilthorn is simply along the ridge out back, to get away from the station and be all alone on top of an Alp.

Summit-High Breakfast: The generous 33-CHF "007 Breakfast Buffet" is served starting at 8:00 on the top floor of the Piz Gloria. Save a few francs by adding the breakfast buffet to your lift ticket before heading up. The restaurant also serves salads, soups, and main dishes all day at prices that don't rise with the altitude.

▲▲▲JUNGFRAUBAHN

The literal high point of any trip to the Swiss Alps is a train ride through the Eiger mountain to the Jungfraujoch (the saddle between the Mönch and Jungfrau mountains). At 11,333 feet, it's Europe's highest train station. (If you have a heart or lung condition, you may want to check with your doctor before making this ascent.) Keep in mind that you can enjoy the Berner Oberland without taking this trip—it's long, slow, expensive, crowded, and cold. But if the weather's good and you have a spare day and spare cash, the views are exhilarating and it's fun to be up on a snowy glacier in midsummer.

Planning Your Trip: Visiting the Jungfraujoch takes most of a day. The trip up from Lauterbrunnen takes a little under two hours each way, with a change of trains halfway at Kleine Scheidegg. If you're coming from Interlaken, Gimmelwald, or Mürren, add another half-hour. You'll want at least 1.5 hours at the top—more if you eat, hike, or sled. Expect outdoor temperatures to be around freezing in summer—so if you plan to go outside, bring a hat and gloves, as well as shoes with good traction, sunglasses, and sunscreen. Even if you stay inside, the train is chilly, and you'll need a jacket. It's smart to buy tickets the day before (they can sell out in peak season). Check the weather forecast at www.jungfrau.ch before committing. If it's cloudy, skip the trip.

Times and Prices: The train runs about twice hourly year-round. Round-trip fares are 211 CHF from Interlaken Ost, 190 CHF from Lauterbrunnen, 176 CHF from Wengen, and 128 CHF from Kleine Scheidegg. At peak periods (especially July-Aug), trains are standing room-only, and you shouldn't expect to get a seat. You can guarantee a seat (above Kleine Scheidegg only) for 5 CHF extra when you make your reservation.

From May to late October, a "Good Morning Ticket" saves you 25 percent on the 6:35/7:05 departures from Interlaken

Enjoy a sky-high breakfast at the top of the Schilthorn.

Ride the Jungfraubahn to Europe's highest train station.

Ost, the 7:07/7:37 departures from Lauterbrunnen, and the 8:00/8:30 departures from Kleine Scheidegg. To get the discount you must leave the top by 13:00. Eurail pass holders get 25 percent off and can't combine discounts, so they should go whenever they want. The same goes for Swiss Travel Pass holders, who travel free as far as Wengen and pay only from there (also 25 percent off). For more information, visit www.jungfrau.ch or call 033-828-7233.

The **Jungfrau Travel Pass** (3-6 days, 180-255 CHF) offers discounted tickets to the Jungfraujoch as well as free rides on most other area trains and lifts (but not to Gimmelwald or up the Schilthorn). Buying this pass is a gamble on the weather, and it's usually hard to make it pay off unless you travel like mad.

Ascending the Jungfraujoch: The final 35 minutes of the trip—from Kleine Scheidegg—is mostly in a tunnel. On the ascent, the train makes two five-minute stops at two "stations"—one actually halfway up the notorious North Face of the Eiger. You have time to look out windows and marvel at how people could climb the Eiger—and how the Swiss built this train track more than a hundred years ago. Newer train cars run multilingual videos about the history of the train line.

At the Top: Once you reach the top, breathe deep, take it easy, and move slowly—you're way high up and your body isn't used to such altitudes. Study the map

to see your options. The main building has a reasonably priced self-service restaurant with expensive beverages, pricier restaurants with table service, luggage lockers, and touristy shops. A roped-in, snowy lookout plateau affords amazing views both north and south. Slip-slide along the corridors of the ice palace, which has some modest carvings. The "Alpine Sensation" is a cute, cheesy diorama with moving model trains.

You'll walk through a short tunnel to reach the most interesting parts of the complex. Take the elevator up to the Sphinx observation deck at 11,700 feet. (The Jungfrau Panorama is a 360-degree video that's pleasantly distracting while you wait in line for the elevator.) Here the views are truly astounding—deep below to the north are Kleine Scheidegg, Gimmelwald, and in the distance, Interlaken; to the south spreads the Aletsch Glacier—Europe's longest, at nearly 11 miles. The Sphinx has a tiny snack stand and a few benches where you can sit to munch a sandwich. There's a scientific measurement station here, and back downstairs by the elevator are some posters with interesting statistics on recent climate warming and the recovery of the ozone layer.

Just outside, a "Snow Fun Park" set up on the Aletsch Glacier offers skiing and snowboarding (35 CHF), sledding (20 CHF), and a zip line (20 CHF—prices include equipment; 45 CHF for all three

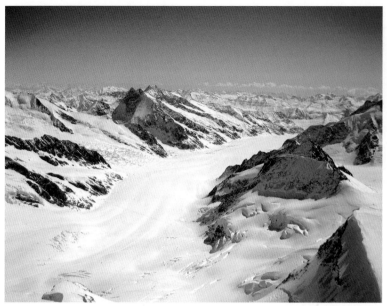

Jungfraujoch overlooks the longest glacial flow in the Alps.

activities, mid-May–mid-Oct). To get away from the Jungfraujoch crowds, you can hike an hour across the ice to Mönchsjochhütte (a mountain hut with a small restaurant).

You can combine your trip up to the Jungfraujoch with one of the best hikes in the region—from Männlichen to Kleine Scheidegg (see "Hiking").

HIKING

This area offers days of possible hikes. Many are a fun combination of trails, mountain trains, and cable-car rides. The information below can help you decide which hike to tackle, but isn't intended as a turn-by-turn guide. Good hiking maps and more detailed trail descriptions than what I've provided here are essential and available from area TIs and hotels. Before setting out on any hike, check locally to be sure you've made the best match between your skills, gear, and trail conditions (snow can persist on trails even into summer).

Rick's Tip: Hikers—if it rains, don't despair. *Clouds can roll out just as quickly. With good rain gear and the right choice of trail, you can still enjoy a hike, with surprise views as the clouds break. Some good* **bad-weather hikes** *are the North Face trail, the walk from Mürren/Allmendhubel to Grütschalp, and the Lauterbrunnen Valley walks, including a visit to Trümmelbach Falls.*

Easier Hikes

▲▲CLOUDY-DAY LAUTERBRUNNEN VALLEY WALKS

Try the easy trails along the floor of the Lauterbrunnen Valley. You don't ever need to (and shouldn't) walk along the main road, which parallels the river. A fine, paved, mostly vehicle-free farm lane (great for bikers) goes all the way along the valley on the opposite side of the river from the main road. Small bridges let you cross from the lane to the main road

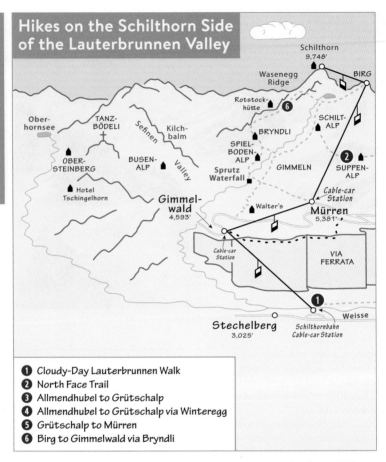

Hikes on the Schilthorn Side of the Lauterbrunnen Valley

Schilthorn 9,748'

Wasenegg Ridge

BIRG

Rotstock-hütte ❻

SCHILT-ALP

Ober-hornsee

TANZ-BÖDELI

Sefinen

Kilch-balm

BRYNDLI

SPIEL-BODEN-ALP

❷ SUPPEN-ALP

BUSEN-ALP

Valley

Sprutz Waterfall

GIMMELN

OBER-STEINBERG

Cable-car Station

Hotel Tschingelhorn

Gimmel-wald 4,593'

Walter's

Mürren 5,381'

Cable-car Station

VIA FERRATA

❶

Weisse

Stechelberg 3,025'

Schilthornbahn Cable-car Station

❶ Cloudy-Day Lauterbrunnen Walk
❷ North Face Trail
❸ Allmendhubel to Grütschalp
❹ Allmendhubel to Grütschalp via Winteregg
❺ Grütschalp to Mürren
❻ Birg to Gimmelwald via Bryndli

at various points. Near Lauterbrunnen, there's also a path right next to the river.

From Lauterbrunnen: For a smell-the-cows-and-flowers lowland walk—ideal for a cloudy day, weary body, or tight budget—try this three-mile, basically level ramble: Take the PostBus from Lauterbrunnen town to the Schilthornbahn cable-car station and follow the river back to Staubbach Falls, near the town church (you can reverse the route, but it's a very gradual uphill to Stechelberg).

As you amble back toward Lauterbrunnen, you can detour to Trümmelbach Falls (figure 45 minutes from the Schilthornbahn station to

Trümmelbach Falls

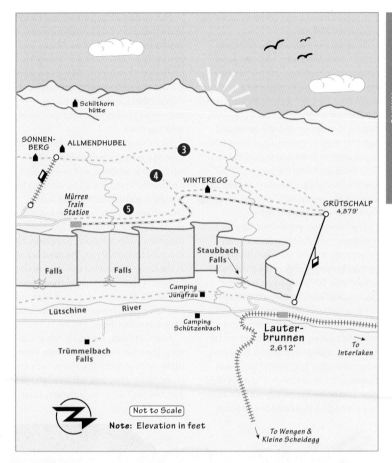

the falls, and another 45 minutes to Lauterbrunnen). For a shorter walk back, ride the bus only as far as Trümmelbach and start from there.

Along the way between Trümmelbach Falls and Lauterbrunnen, look up to see BASE jumpers—parachutists who leap from cliffs.

From Gimmelwald: If you're staying in Gimmelwald, try this plan: Take the Schilthornbahn lift down to the station near Stechelberg (5 minutes), then walk 1.5 hours along the river to Lauterbrunnen (side-tripping to Trümmelbach Falls after 45 minutes). To return to Gimmelwald from Lauterbrunnen, take the cable car up to Grütschalp (10 minutes), then either

walk to Gimmelwald (1.5 hours) or take the train to Mürren (10 minutes). From Mürren, it's a downhill walk (30 minutes) to Gimmelwald. (This loop trip can be reversed or started at any point along the way—such as Lauterbrunnen or Mürren.)

▲▲NORTH FACE TRAIL (FROM MÜRREN)

For a pleasant, fairly easy 2.5-hour hike, head out along this four-mile trail, starting at 6,385 feet and finishing at 5,375 feet (some stretches can be challenging if you're not in shape). As with any trail described here, before starting out, get a trail map from the Mürren TI or the cable-car station and confirm the route.

The signed route loops counterclockwise around to Mürren.

To reach the trail, ride the Allmendhubel funicular up from Mürren (good restaurant at top). Leaving the funicular, look for the children's play area and a blue *North Face Trail* sign. Follow the path uphill, skirting to the right around the play area, passing through small cattle gates, and past the chairlift station. From here, follow the blue signs down into the valley toward Sonnenberg. (Along the way, you'll see yellow directional signs pointing toward *Sonnenberg, Suppenalp, and Schiltalp,* as well as the blue *North Face Trail* signs.)

The hike offers great views, flowery meadows, mountain huts, and a dozen information boards, describing the fascinating climbing history of the great peaks around you. You'll also pass four farms (technically "alps," as they are only open in the summer) that serve meals and drinks. Sonnenberg was allowed to break the all-wood building code with concrete for protection against avalanches. Suppenalp is quainter. Lean against the house with a salad, soup, or sandwich, and enjoy the view. Just below Suppenalp is a little adventure park with a short zip line and a slide.

Notice how older huts are built into the protected side of rocks and outcrops, in anticipation of avalanches. Above Suppenalp, Blumental ("Flower Valley") is hopping with marmots. Because hunters are not allowed near lifts, animals have learned that these are safe places to hang out—giving tourists a better chance of spotting them.

From Suppenalp, the trail leads up and over to a group of huts called Schiltalp (good food, drink, and service, and a romantic farm setting). In some spots along the way, where the path is not clearly defined, look for white and red stripes painted on rocks. At Schiltalp, if the poles under the eaves have bells, the cows are up here. If not, the cows are still at the lower farms. Half the cows in Gimmelwald (about 100) spend their summers here. In July, August, and September, you can watch cheese being made and have a snack or drink.

From Schiltalp, the trail winds gracefully down toward Spielbodenalp. From there, you can finish the North Face trail (continuing down and left through meadows and the hamlet of Gimmeln, then back to Mürren).

The family-friendly North Face trail takes you past flowery meadows and mountain huts.

Hiking in the Berner Oberland

To do any serious hiking, invest in a good hiking map at any TI, and ask about current weather and trail conditions. For easy hikes, it's usually enough to use the 3-D maps in the free brochures (called *Wandern/Hiking*) published by the Schilthornbahn (for the west side of the valley) and the Jungfraubahn (for the east side); they're available at stations, hotels, and TIs. These overview maps of the mountainsides also make attractive souvenirs.

Don't forget a water bottle and some munchies. In addition to a good map, for serious hikes it's wise to carry sun protection, an extra layer of clothing, and basic first-aid supplies. Know when the last lifts run in the afternoon. Trails are well-marked, with yellow signs listing destinations and the estimated time it'll take you to walk there.

Weather Concerns: Snow can curtail your hiking plans, even in July. The high trails (Männlichen to Kleine Scheidegg, Schynige Platte to First, and anything from Schilthorn or Birg) are typically passable only from June into October.

Locals always seem to know the weather report (as much of their income depends on it). Clouds can roll in anytime, but on warm summer days, skies are usually clearest in the morning. All over the region, TV sets are tuned to the local weather station, with real-time views from all the famous peaks. You can also check weather reports and view live webcams at www.jungfrau.ch and www.schilthorn.ch. For more detailed weather reports in English, visit www.meteoswiss.admin.ch.

▲ALLMENDHUBEL TO GRÜTSCHALP (A.K.A. MOUNTAIN VIEW TRAIL)

For a not-too-tough two-hour walk with great Jungfrau views, ride the funicular from Mürren to Allmendhubel and walk to Grütschalp (a drop of about 1,500 feet), where you can catch the train back to Mürren. You'll see this route called the "Mountain View trail" on maps and brochures. An easier version goes from Allmendhubel to Grütschalp via Winteregg and its cheese farm.

▲GRÜTSCHALP TO MÜRREN

For a family-friendly, super-easy panorama stroll with grand views, walk either direction between Mürren (5,381 feet) and Grütschalp (4,879 feet)—roughly following the scenic train line between the same points. The trail from the tiny station at Grütschalp to Winteregg (5,177 feet) is a 30-minute scenic walk mostly on a gravelly lane. The trail between Winteregg and Mürren mostly parallels the train track—also scenic and gravelly, but less interesting. The highlight, along with the dramatic views of the Eiger, Mönch, and Jungfrau, is the wonderful restaurant/playground/cheese farm midway at Winteregg. (The Grütschalp-Mürren train also stops here.) The Alpkäserei Staubbach offers windows to peer into the cheese-making action, and they sell fresh yogurt and cheese. The Winteregg Restaurant has a dramatic view terrace and an extensive alp-happy playground.

Cow bells on a herder's hut

Easy trail between Mürren and Grütschalp

▲▲▲MÄNNLICHEN-KLEINE SCHEIDEGG HIKE (FROM LAUTERBRUNNEN OR WENGEN)

This is my favorite easy alpine hike (2.5 miles, 1-1.5 hours, 900-foot altitude drop to Kleine Scheidegg). It's entertaining all the way, with glorious mountain views. If you missed the plot, it's the Young Maiden (Jungfrau), being protected from the Ogre (Eiger) by the Monk (Mönch). The trail usually opens sometime in June and closes due to snow in October. Ask about conditions and get a map at the lift stations or at TIs; there are also useful webcams at www.maennlichen.ch and www.jungfrau.ch.

If the weather's good, start off bright and early. From the Lauterbrunnen train station, take the little mountain train up to Wengen. Sit on the right side of the train for great valley and waterfall views. In Wengen, buy a picnic at the Co-op grocery across the square from the station (daily 8:00-18:30 in summer), walk across town, and catch the lift to Männlichen, located on top of the ridge high above you (23 CHF one-way, half-price with Swiss Travel Pass, 3/hour, 2-minute trip, mid-May-mid-Oct first ascent at 8:30, at 8:10 July-mid-Sept, somewhat shorter hours off-season, tel. 033-855-2933, www.maennlichen.ch). The lift can be open even if the trail is closed; if the weather is questionable, confirm that the Männlichen-Kleine Scheidegg trail is open before ascending. Don't waste time in Wengen if it's sunny—you can linger back here after your hike.

Riding the gondola from Wengen to Männlichen, you'll go over the old lift station (inundated by a 1978 avalanche that buried a good part of Wengen—notice there's no development in the "red zone" above the tennis courts). Farms are built with earthen ramps on the uphill side in anticipation of the next slide. The forest of avalanche fences near the top was built after that 1978 avalanche.

When you get to the station at the top of the Wengen-Männlichen lift, see if they have any free "king for a day" envelopes by the ticket window; these fun souvenirs open up to make a panoramic crown that names the mountains you're seeing.

For a detour that'll give you an easy king- or queen-of-the-day feeling, turn left from the lift station, and hike uphill 10 minutes to the little peak (Männlichen Gipfel, 7,500 feet) topped with a crown-shaped viewpoint.

Then go back to the lift station (which has a great kids' area) and enjoy the walk—facing spectacular alpine panorama views—to Kleine Scheidegg for a picnic or restaurant lunch. To start the hike, leave the Wengen-Männlichen lift station to the right. Walk past the second Männlichen lift station (this one leads to Grindelwald, the touristy town in the valley to your left). Ahead of you in the distance, left to right, are the north faces of the Eiger, Mönch, and Jungfrau; in the foreground is the Tschuggen peak, and just behind it, the Lauberhorn. This hike takes you around

Hiking from Männlichen to Kleine Scheidegg: Wow!

the left (east) side of this ridge. Simply follow the signs for Kleine Scheidegg, and you'll be there in about an hour—a little more for gawkers, picnickers, and photographers. You might have to tiptoe through streams of melted snow—or some small snow banks, even well into the summer—but the path is well-marked, well-maintained, and mostly level all the way to Kleine Scheidegg.

About 35 minutes into the hike, you'll reach a bunch of benches and a shelter with incredible unobstructed views of all three peaks—the perfect picnic spot. Fifteen minutes later, on the left, you'll see the first sign of civilization: Restaurant Grindelwaldblick (the best lunch stop up here, open daily, closed Nov and May). Hike to the restaurant's fun mountain lookout to survey the Eiger and look down on the Kleine Scheidegg (rated ▲▲ for its spectacular panoramic mountain view). After 10 more minutes, you'll be at the Kleine Scheidegg train station, with plenty of lesser lunch options.

Optional Add-Ons: From Kleine Scheidegg, you can catch the train up to "the top of Europe" (see Jungfraujoch listing), take the train back down to Wengen, or hike downhill (gorgeous 30-minute hike to the Wengernalp station, a little farther to the Allmend stop; 60 more steep minutes from there into Wengen—not dangerous, but requires a good set of knees). The alpine views might be accompanied by the valley-filling mellow sound of cow bells, alphorns, and distant avalanches. If the weather turns bad or you run out of steam, catch the train at any of the stations along the way. The boring final descent from Wengen to Lauterbrunnen is knee-killer steep— catch the train instead.

More Difficult Hikes

Several tough trails lead down from the Schilthorn (there's a reason that virtually all visitors take the cable car down). Only a serious, experienced hiker should consider walking all or part of the way back into Gimmelwald. Proper shoes and clothing (weather can change quickly) and good knees are required. Don't attempt to hike down unless the trail is clear of snow.

While it's possible to make the steep descent directly from the top of the Schilthorn, I prefer the less strenuous (but still challenging) hike from the intermediate cable-car station at Birg.

▲▲BIRG TO GIMMELWALD VIA BRYNDLI (FROM THE SCHILTHORN)

You can combine this difficult downhill hike from the Birg cable-car station with a visit to the Schilthorn by buying the round-trip excursion early-bird fare (it's cheaper than the Gimmelwald-Schilthorn-Birg ticket). Visit the summit first, then descend to Birg to hike down.

The most interesting trail from Birg to Gimmelwald is the high one via Grauseeli lake and Wasenegg Ridge to Bryndli, then down to Spielbodenalp and the Sprutz Waterfall. Warning: This trail drops 4,500 feet, is quite steep and slippery in places, and can take four hours. Locals take their kindergarteners on this hike, but Americans unused to alpine hikes shouldn't attempt it.

From the Birg lift station, hike toward the Schilthorn, taking your first left down and passing along the left side of the little Grauseeli lake. From the lake, a gravelly trail leads down rough switchbacks (including a stretch where the path narrows and you can hang onto a guide cable against the cliff face) until it levels out. When you see a rock painted with arrows pointing to Mürren and Rotstockhütte, follow the path to Rotstockhütte (traditional old farm with light meals and drinks), traversing the cow-grazed mountainside.

The safer, well-signposted approach to Bryndli is to drop down to Rotstockhütte, then climb back up to Bryndli. Thrill-seekers instead follow Wasenegg Ridge. It's more scary than dangerous if you're sure-footed and can handle the 50-foot-long "tightrope-with-handrail" section along an extremely narrow ledge with a thousand-foot drop. This trail gets you to Bryndli with the least altitude change. A barbed-wire fence leads you to Bryndli's

knobby little summit, where you'll enjoy an incredible 360-degree view and a chance to sign your name on the register stored in the little wooden box.

From Bryndli, a steep trail winds directly down toward Gimmelwald and soon hits a bigger, easier trail. The trail bends right (just before the farm/restaurant at Spielbodenalp), leading to Sprutz. Walk under the Sprutz Waterfall, then follow a steep, wooded trail that deposits you in a meadow of flowers at the top side of Gimmelwald.

▲▲SCHYNIGE PLATTE TO FIRST (ABOVE INTERLAKEN)

The best day I've had hiking in the Berner Oberland was when I made this demanding six-hour ridge walk, with Lake Brienz on one side and all that Jungfrau beauty on the other. Start at the Wilderswil train station (just outside Interlaken), and catch the little train up to Schynige Platte (6,454 feet; 32 CHF one-way, goes every 40 minutes and takes about an hour, runs late May-late Oct). The high point on the trail is Faulhorn (8,790 feet, with a famous mountaintop hotel). From here, hike on to First (7,110 feet), where you ride a small gondola down to Grindelwald (30 CHF; runs continuously—until at least 17:00 in summer) and catch a train back via Zweilutschinen to wherever you're staying. Or, if you have a regional lift pass (or endless money), you could finish the day by riding the lifts and trains from Grindelwald up to Kleine Scheidegg or Männlichen, then back down to Lauterbrunnen.

You can also do this hike in reverse, which means less climbing, from First (7,113 feet) to Schynige Platte (last train down at 17:53). The TI produces a great Schynige Platte map/guide narrating the train ride up and describing various hiking options from there (available at Wilderswil train station).

Easier Options at Schynige Platte: For a shorter (3-hour) ridge walk, consider the well-signposted Panoramaweg, a loop from Schynige Platte to Daub Peak.

The alpine flower park at the Schynige Platte station offers a delightful stroll through several hundred alpine flowers (free, late May-late Oct daily 8:30-18:00, www.alpengarten.ch), including a chance to see edelweiss growing in the wild.

OTHER ALPINE RETREATS

I'd sleep in Gimmelwald, Mürren, or Lauterbrunnen, but you could also consider overnighting in the following places.

Sleeping in Wengen

Wengen—a bigger, fancier Mürren on the east side of the valley—has plenty of grand hotels, restaurants, shops, diversions, and terrific views. This traffic-free resort is an easy train ride above Lauterbrunnen and halfway up to Kleine Scheidegg and Männlichen. From Wengen, you can catch the Männlichen lift (www.maennlichen.ch) up to the ridge and take the rewarding, view-filled, nearly downhill ▲▲▲ Männlichen-Kleine Scheidegg hike.

Wengen's **TI** has info on hiking and sells trail maps (daily 9:00-18:00, closes for lunch Sat-Sun off-season, on Dorfstrasse, tel. 033-856-8585, www.wengen.ch).

The good-sized **Co-op grocery** is across the square from the train station (daily 8:00-18:30; closed Sun off-season).

For accommodations, consider **$$$$ Hotel Berghaus** with 19 rooms above a fine restaurant (open June-Sept and mid-Dec-early April, tel. 033-855-2151, www.berghaus-wengen.ch, info@berghaus-wengen.ch); **$$$$ Romantik Hotel Schönegg,** with 20 rooms with balconies and great views (half-board in good restaurant with big terrace available, tel. 033-855-3422, www.hotel-schoenegg.ch, mail@hotel-schoenegg.ch); or **$$$$ Bären Hotel,** with 17 tidy rooms and half-board included in the rates (**$$ lunch specials;** discount if you go without half-board; family rooms, closed mid-Oct-mid-Dec, tel. 033-855-1419, www.baeren-wengen.ch, info@baeren-wengen.ch).

Sleeping and Eating at or near Kleine Scheidegg

This high settlement above the timberline (6,762 feet) is as close as you can stay to the Jungfraujoch. All of these places serve

Wengen village

meals and let you sleep face-to-face with the Eiger. Confirm prices and availability before ascending. Note that the last train down to Lauterbrunnen leaves Kleine Scheidegg at 18:30.

Options include **$$$$ Hotel Bellevue des Alpes,** a classic old 60-room alpine hotel (breakfast and sumptuous four-course dinner included, closed mid-April–mid-June and mid-Sept–mid-Dec, tel. 033-855-1212, www.scheidegg-hotels.ch, welcome@scheidegg-hotels.ch); **¢–$$ Restaurant Bahnhof,** a handy hostel in the train-station building (some private rooms with shared bath; breakfast included, dinner extra; open year-round, tel. 033-828-7828, www.bahnhof-scheidegg.ch, info@bahnhof-scheidegg.ch); and **¢–$$ Restaurant Grindelwald-blick,** a 10-minute hike up along the path toward Männlichen, with 90 beds (sheets and breakfast included, closed Nov and May, tel. 033-855-1374, www.grindelwaldblick.ch, grindelwaldblick@grindelwald.ch); their **$$$ restaurant,** with a great sun terrace and a cozy interior, sells good three-course lunches and dinners.

Sleeping in Stechelberg

Stechelberg is the hamlet at the end of the road up the Lauterbrunnen Valley; it's about a mile beyond the Schilthornbahn lift that goes up to Gimmelwald, Mürren, and the Schilthorn. From the lift station, it's a five-minute ride on the same Post-Bus that comes from Lauterbrunnen (1-2/hour) or a 20-minute walk.

Choose between **$$ Hotel Stechelberg,** with 16 quiet rooms—half in a functional old building, half in a concrete, no-character new building (hotel closed in Dec, restaurant closed Mon-Tue off-season, tel. 033-855-2921, www.hotel-stechelberg.ch, hotel@stechelberg.ch), or the basic **¢ Alpenhof,** filling a former "Nature Friends' Hut" with 44 cheap beds (each group gets a private room, open nearly year-round, kitchen, tel. 033-855-1202, www.alpenhof-stechelberg.ch, alpenhof@stechelberg.ch).

TRANSPORTATION
Getting Around the Berner Oberland

For more than a century, this region has been the target of nature-worshiping pilgrims. And Swiss engineers and visionaries have made the most exciting alpine perches accessible.

By Lifts and Trains

Part of the fun here—and most of the expense—is riding the many mountain trains and lifts (gondolas and cable cars).

Trains connect Interlaken to Wilderswil, Lauterbrunnen, Wengen, Kleine Scheidegg, the Jungfraujoch, and also Grindelwald. Lifts connect Wengen to Männlichen and Grund (near Grindelwald); Grindelwald to First; Lauterbrunnen to Grütschalp (where a train connects to Mürren); and the cable-car station near Stechelberg to Gimmelwald, Mürren, and the Schilthorn.

For an overview of your many options, study the "Alpine Lifts in the Berner Oberland" map and the "Berner Oberland at a Glance" sidebar in this chapter. Lifts generally go at least twice hourly, from about 7:00 until about 20:00 (sneak preview: www.jungfrau.ch or www.schilthorn.ch).

Beyond Interlaken, trains and lifts into the Jungfrau region are 25 percent off with a **Eurail pass** (doesn't require a flexi-day); with the **Swiss Travel Pass,** they're covered up to Wengen (above Wengen, passholders get 25-50 percent off) and all the way to the top of the Schilthorn. Ask about discounts for early-morning and late-afternoon trips, youths, seniors, families, groups (assemble a party of 10 and you'll save about 25 percent), and those staying awhile. Generally, round-trips are double the one-way cost, though some high-up trains and lifts are 10-20 percent cheaper. It's possible to buy a package covering all of your lifts at once, but then you don't have the flexibility to change with the weather.

A gondola makes its way to Männlichen above Grindelwald.

The **Junior Travelcard,** valid across Switzerland for families traveling with children, lets kids under 16 travel free with at least one parent (children under 5 already travel free). It's a great deal that pays for itself within the first hour of travel on trains and lifts (30 CHF/one child, 60 CHF/two or more children, buy at Swiss train stations).

By Car

Interlaken, Lauterbrunnen, and Stechelberg are accessible by car. You can't drive to Gimmelwald, Mürren, Wengen, or Kleine Scheidegg, but don't let that stop you from staying up in the mountains: Park the car and zip up on a lift. To catch the lift to Gimmelwald, Mürren, and the Schilthorn, park at the cable-car station near Stechelberg (4 CHF/2 hours, 10 CHF/day). To catch the train to Wengen or Kleine Scheidegg, park at the train station in Lauterbrunnen (2.50 CHF/2 hours, 11 CHF/9-24 hours).

By Bus

A convenient local bus, called the Post-Bus, connects points along the valley and includes a stop at the Schilthornbahn cable-car station (www.postauto.ch).

Germany

ermany (Deutschland) is energetic and organized. The European Union's most populous country and biggest economy, Germany is home to 82 million people—one-third Catholic and one-third Protestant. It's 138,000 square miles (about half the size of Texas) and bordered by nine countries. Germany is young compared with most of its European neighbors ("born" in 1871) but was a founding member of the EU.

Germany offers travelers an intriguing mix: rollicking Munich, the little medieval-walled town of Rothenburg, the sleepy villages lining the mighty Rhine, and the surprising city of Berlin, with monuments that embody the country's past turbulence and modern resurgence.

CUISINE SCENE AT A GLANCE

Germanic food is filling, meaty, and—by European standards—inexpensive. Each region has its specialties, which are often good values. Be adventurous.

Traditional **restaurants** go by many names. At a beer hall (*Brauhaus*) or a beer garden (*Biergarten*), you can get big, basic, stick-to-the-ribs meals and huge liter beers (called *ein Mass* in German, or *"ein* pitcher" in English). Many beer halls have a cafeteria system; the food is usually *selbstdienst* (self-service). Any real beer garden will keep a few tables (those without tablecloths) available for customers who buy only beer and bring their own food.

Gasthaus, Gasthof, and *Gaststube* all loosely describe an informal, inn-type eatery. A *Kneipe* is a bar, and a *Keller* (or *Ratskeller*) is a restaurant or tavern located in a cellar. A *Weinstube* serves wine and usually traditional (that is, meaty) food as well.

Most eateries have menus tacked onto their front doors, with an English menu inside. Some restaurants offer inexpensive €6-9 weekday hot-lunch specials that aren't listed on the regular menu (look for the *Tageskarte* or *Tagesangebot,* or just ask—may be offered at dinner, too). For smaller portions, order from the *kleine Hunger* (small hunger) section of the menu. Vegetarians can opt for big dinner-size salads.

At any restaurant, a *Stammtisch* sign hanging over or on a table means that it's reserved for regulars.

Tipping: If you order your food at a counter, don't tip. At restaurants that have table service, a gratuity is included in your bill, so you don't need to tip further, but it's nice to round up your bill about 10 percent for great service.

Rather than leaving coins behind on the table (considered slightly rude), Germans usually pay directly: When the server comes by with the bill, simply hand over paper money, stating the total you'd like to pay. For example, if paying for a €10 meal with a €20 bill, while handing your money to the server, say "Eleven, please" (or *"Elf, bitte"* if you've got your German numbers down). The server will keep a €1 tip and give you €9 in change.

Lately, some restaurants in well-touristed areas have added a "Tip is not included" line, in English, at the bottom of the bill. This is misleading, as the prices on any menu in Germany *do* include service. I would not tip one cent more at a restaurant that includes this note on the bill.

Budget Options: It's easy to get a meal in Germany for €10 or less. Bakeries sell cheap sandwiches and often have tables. Department-stores usually have self-service cafeterias. A *Schnellimbiss* is a small fast-food takeaway stand that sells bratwurst and other grilled sausage. Some stands and shops sell Turkish-style *döner kebab* (gyro-like, pita-wrapped rotisserie meat).

Munich

Munich ("München" in German) is one of Germany's most historic, artistic, and entertaining cities. Until 1871, it was the capital of an independent Bavaria. Its imperial palaces and grand boulevards constantly remind visitors that Munich has long been a political and cultural powerhouse.

Walking through Munich, you'll understand why it is consistently voted one of Germany's most livable cities. It's safe, clean, cultured, built on a human scale, and close to the beauties of nature. Though Munich is a major metropolis, its low-key atmosphere has led Germans to dub it "Millionendorf"—the "village of a million people."

Orient yourself in Munich's old center, with its colorful pedestrian zones. Immerse yourself in the city's art and history—crown jewels, Baroque theater, royal palaces, great paintings, and beautiful parks. Spend time in a frothy beer hall or outdoor *Biergarten,* prying big pretzels from no-nonsense beer maids amidst an oompah atmosphere.

MUNICH IN 3 DAYS

Day 1: Follow the "Munich City Walk" laid out in this chapter, visiting sights along the way. After lunch, tour the Residenz.

On any evening: Try a beer hall one night and a beer garden on another. Stroll through Marienplatz and the core pedestrian streets. Have a dinner picnic at the English Garden.

Day 2: Visit the Dachau Memorial in the morning. Later, if the weather's fine, rent a bike to enjoy the English Garden. Or tour the top art museum, the Alte Pinakothek.

Day 3: Take your pick of these fine sights: Egyptian Museum, Deutsches Museum, Neue Pinakothek, Munich City Museum, and—away from the center—the Nymphenburg Palace and BMW-Welt and Museum.

With extra time: Day-trip options include a day-long bus tour to see "Mad" King Ludwig's Castles (covered in the Bavaria chapter) or even a visit to Salzburg (1.5 hours one-way by train).

ORIENTATION

The tourist's Munich is circled by a ring road (site of the Old Town wall) marked by four old gates: Karlstor (near the main train station—the Hauptbahnhof), Sendlinger Tor, Isartor (near the river), and Odeonsplatz (no surviving gate, near the palace). Marienplatz marks the city's center. A great pedestrian-only zone (Kaufingerstrasse and Neuhauser Strasse) cuts this circle in half, running neatly from the Karlstor and the train station through Marienplatz to the Isartor. Orient yourself along this east-west axis. Ninety percent of the sights and hotels I recommend are within a 20-minute walk of Marienplatz and each other.

Tourist Information

Munich has two helpful city-run TIs (www.muenchen.de). One is in front of the **main train station** (Mon-Sat 9:00-20:00, Sun 10:00-18:00, with your back to the tracks, walk through the central hall, step outside, and turn right). The other TI is on Munich's main square, **Marienplatz,** below the glockenspiel (Mon-Fri 9:00-19:00, Sat 9:00-16:00, Sun 10:00-14:00).

Private Munich Ticket offices inside the TIs sell concert and event tickets (www.muenchenticket.de). The free magazine *In München* lists all movies and entertainment in town (in German, organized by date).

At counter #1 in the train station's main *Reisezentrum* (travel center, opposite track 21), the hardworking, eager-to-help **EurAide desk** is a godsend for Eurailers and budget travelers. Paid by the German rail company to help you design your train travels (including day trips), EurAide makes reservations and sells train tickets, *couchettes,* and sleepers for the same price you'd pay at the other counters (open May-Oct Mon-Fri 8:30-20:00, Sat 8:30-14:00, closed Sun; off-season Mon-Fri 10:00-19:00, closed Sat-Sun and Jan-Feb, www.euraide.com). As EurAide helps about 500 visitors per day in the summer, a line can build up; do your homework and have a list of questions ready.

Tours

Munich's two largest tour companies, Radius Tours and Munich Walk, run comparable tours in Munich as well as day trips to Dachau, Neuschwanstein Castle, and other places. Both offer discounts to Rick Steves readers.

Munich Walk uses Marienplatz as its meeting point (tel. 089/2423-1767, www.munichwalktours.de). Consider a walking tour (€12-15, daily year-round, 2-2.5 hours), "Beer and Brewery" tour (€28, May-mid-Sept on Mon, Wed, and Fri-Sat at 18:15, fewer tours off-season, 3.5 hours), Bavarian food-tasting tour with lunch at Viktualienmarkt (€24 includes food), or bike tour (€25, April-Oct Sat-Sun only).

Radius Tours has a convenient office and meeting point in the main train station, in front of track 32 (tel. 089/543-487-7730, www.radiustours.com). Consider a walking tour (€13-15, daily at 10:00, 2-2.5 hours), "Bavarian Beer and Food" tour with samples and a visit to the Beer and Oktoberfest Museum (€30, April-mid-Oct Mon-Sat 18:00, 3.5 hours, reserve well in advance), or a 3.5-hour bike tour (€25, April-mid-Oct daily at 10:00).

Gray Line Tours has hop-on, hop-off city bus tours that leave from in front of the Karstadt department store at Bahnhofplatz, directly across from the train station (buses run 9:40-18:00). Choose the basic, 1-hour "Express Circle," or the more extensive 2.5-hour "Grand Circle," which includes Nymphenburg Palace and BMW-Welt and Museum and is an efficient way to see both. Just show up and pay the driver (€17 Express tour—valid all day, €22 Grand tour—valid 24 hours, daily in season, tel. 089/5490-7560, www.sightseeing-munich.com).

Rick's Tip: *If you're interested in a* **Gray Line bus tour** *of the city or to nearby castles,* **get discounted tickets at EurAide** *(cash only). They also sell* **Munich Walk** *tour tickets.*

While you can do many **day trips from Munich** on your own by train, going as part of an organized group can be convenient. All-day tours to **Neuschwanstein** are offered by **Radius,** using **public transit** (€42, €35 with rail pass, does not include castle admission; daily April-Dec;

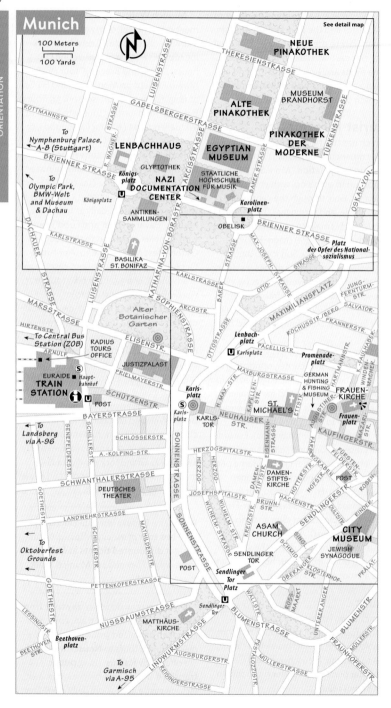

Munich

See detail map

100 Meters
100 Yards

NEUE PINAKOTHEK

THERESIENSTRASSE

MUSEUM BRANDHORST

ALTE PINAKOTHEK

PINAKOTHEK DER MODERNE

ROTTMANNSTR.

GABELSBERGERSTRASSE

To Nymphenburg Palace,
A-8 (Stuttgart)

LENBACHHAUS

EGYPTIAN MUSEUM

R. WAGNER STRASSE

BRIENNER STRASSE

GLYPTOTHEK

Königs-platz

STAATLICHE HOCHSCHULE FÜR MUSIK

To Olympic Park,
BMW-Welt
and Museum
& Dachau

NAZI DOCUMENTATION CENTER

Königsplatz

ANTIKEN-SAMMLUNGEN

Karolinen-platz

OBELISK

BRIENNER STRASSE

Platz der Opfer des National-sozialismus

KARLSTRASSE

BASILIKA ST. BONIFAZ

KATHARINA-VON-BORA-STR.

ARCOSTR.

KARLSTRASSE

MAX-JOSEPH-STRASSE

MARSSTRASSE

SOPHIENSTRASSE

Alter Botanischer Garten

MAXIMILIANSPLATZ

JUNG-FERNTURM-STR.

SALVATOR-STR.

HIRTENSTR.

To Central Bus Station (ZOB)

ELISENSTR.

RADIUS TOURS OFFICE

Lenbach-platz

PACELLISTR.

Promenade-platz

GERMAN HUNTING & FISHING MUSEUM

FRAUEN-KIRCHE

ARNULF

JUSTIZPALAST

Karlsplatz

MAXBURGSTR.

EURAIDE
TRAIN STATION

Haupt-bahnhof

PRIELMAYERSTR.

Karls-platz

H. MAX-STR.

KAPELLEN-STR.

ST. MICHAEL'S

Frauen-platz

POST

SCHÜTZENSTR.

Karls-platz

KARLS-TOR

NEUHAUSER-STR.

KAUFINGERSTR.

BAYERSTRASSE

SCHLOSSERSTR.

EISENMANN-STRASSE

FÜRSTEN-FELDER-STR.

To Landsberg via A-96

A.-KOLPING-STR.

HERZOGSPITALSTR.

FARBERGRABEN

POST

SCHWANTHALERSTRASSE

DEUTSCHES THEATER

JOSEPHSPITALSTR.

DAMEN-STIFTS-KIRCHE

HACKENSTR.

HOFSTR.

LANDWEHRSTRASSE

BRUNN-STR.

SENDLINGERSTR.

CITY MUSEUM

To Oktoberfest Grounds

ASAM CHURCH

JEWISH SYNAGOGUE

PETTENKOFERSTRASSE

SENDLINGER TOR

POST

Sendlinger Tor Platz

KLOSTERHOF

LESSINGSTR.

NUSSBAUMSTRASSE

Sendlinger Tor

BLUMENSTRASSE

Beethoven-platz

MATTHÄUS-KIRCHE

LINDWURMSTRASSE

AUGSBURGERSTR.

To Garmisch via A-95

REISINGERSTRASSE

MUNICH AT A GLANCE

In the Center

▲▲**Marienplatz** Munich's main square, at the heart of a lively pedestrian zone, watched over by New Town Hall and its glockenspiel show. **Hours:** Always open; glockenspiel jousts daily at 11:00 and 12:00, plus 17:00 May-Oct. See page 728.

▲▲**Viktualienmarkt** Munich's "small-town" open-air market, perfect for a quick snack or meal. **Hours:** Closed Sun; beer garden open daily 10:00-22:00 (weather permitting). See page 733.

▲▲**Hofbräuhaus** World-famous beer hall, worth a visit even if you're not chugging. **Hours:** Daily 9:00-23:30. See page 741.

▲▲**Residenz Complex** Elegant palace awash in Bavarian opulence. Complex includes the Residenz Museum (private apartments), Residenz Treasury (housing royal crowns and knickknacks), and the impressive, heavily restored Cuvilliés Theater. **Hours:** Museum and treasury—daily April-mid-Oct 9:00-18:00, mid-Oct-March 10:00-17:00; theater keeps shorter hours. See page 744.

▲▲**Alte Pinakothek** Bavaria's best painting gallery, with a wonderful collection of European masters from the 14th through 19th century. **Hours:** Tue 10:00-20:00, Wed-Sun 10:00-18:00, closed Mon. See page 754.

▲▲**Egyptian Museum** Easy-to-enjoy collection of ancient Egyptian treasures. **Hours:** Tue 10:00-20:00, Wed-Sun 10:00-18:00, closed Mon. See page 758.

▲**Asam Church** Small church dripping with Baroque. **Hours:** Sat-Thu 9:00-18:00, Fri 13:00-18:00. See page 737.

▲**Munich City Museum** The city's history in five floors. **Hours:** Tue-Sun 10:00-18:00, closed Mon. See page 752.

▲**Neue Pinakothek** The Alte's twin sister, with paintings from 1800 to 1920. **Hours:** Wed 10:00-20:00, Thu-Mon 10:00-18:00, closed Tue. See page 757.

▲**English Garden** The largest city park on the Continent, packed with locals, tourists, surfers, and nude sunbathers. (On a bike, I'd rate this ▲▲.) **Hours:** Always open. See page 758.

▲**Deutsches Museum** Germany's version of our Smithsonian Institution, with 10 miles of science and technology exhibits. **Hours:** Daily 9:00-17:00. See page 760.

Outside the City Center

▲▲**Nymphenburg Palace Complex** Impressive summer palace, featuring a hunting lodge, coach museum, fine royal porcelain collection, and vast park. **Hours:** Park—daily 6:00-dusk, palace buildings—daily April-mid-Oct 9:00-18:00, mid-Oct-March 10:00-16:00. See page 761.

▲▲**BMW-Welt and Museum** The carmaker's futuristic museum and floating-cloud showroom, highlighting BMW past, present, and future. **Hours:** BMW-Welt building—exhibits daily 9:00-18:00; museum—Tue-Sun 10:00-18:00, closed Mon. See page 766.

▲▲**Dachau Memorial** Notorious Nazi concentration camp, now a powerful museum and memorial. **Hours:** Daily 9:00-17:00. See page 786.

Jan-March tours run Mon, Wed, and Fri-Sun; reserve ahead, www.radiustours.com), and by **Gray Line Tours** via **private bus** (€51, does not include castle admission, daily all year, www.sightseeing-munich.com). Although they're a little more expensive, I prefer the guided private bus tours because you're guaranteed a seat (public transportation in summer is routinely standing-room only).

For organized tours to **Dachau,** see page 786.

Six people splitting the cost can make a **private guide** affordable. I've had great days with **Georg Reichlmayr** (€165/3 hours, tel. 08131/86800, mobile 0170-341-6384, www.muenchen-stadtfuehrung.de, info@muenchen-stadtfuehrung.de) and **Monika Hank** (€120/2 hours, €140/3 hours, tel. 089/311-4819, mobile 0172-547-8123, monika.hank@web.de).

Rick's Tip: *Supposedly* **"free"** **walking tours are advertised all over town.** *Tipping is expected, and the guides actually have to pay the company for each person who takes the tour—so unless you tip more than they owe the company, they don't make a penny. Expect a sales pitch for the company's other, paid tours.*

Helpful Hints

Museum Tips: Museums closed on Monday include the Alte Pinakothek, Munich City Museum, the BMW Museum, and the Beer and Oktoberfest Museum (also closed Sun). The Neue Pinakothek closes on Tuesday. The art museums are generally open late one night a week.

Taxi: Call 089/21610.

Private Driver: Johann Fayoumi is reliable and speaks English (€70/hour, mobile 0174-183-8473, www.firstclasslimousines.de).

Car Rental: Several car-rental agencies are located upstairs at the train station, opposite track 21 (open daily, hours vary).

MUNICH CITY WALK

With its pedestrian-friendly historic core, big, modern Munich feels like an easy-going Bavarian town. On this self-guided walk, rated ▲▲▲, we'll start in the central square, see its famous glockenspiel, stroll through a thriving open-air market, and visit historic churches with lavish Baroque decor. We'll sample chocolates and take a spin through the world's most famous beer hall.

Length of This Tour: It takes two or three hours to walk through a thousand years of Munich's history; allow extra time if you want to take a break to tour the museums (details under "Sights").

🎧 Download my free Munich City Walk audio tour.

❷ Self-Guided Walk

• *Begin at the heart of the old city, with a stroll through...*

❶ *Marienplatz*

Riding the escalator out of the subway into sunlit Marienplatz (mah-REE-en-platz, "Mary's Square," rated ▲▲) gives you a fine first look at the glory of Munich: great buildings, outdoor cafés, and people bustling and lingering like the birds and breeze with which they share this square.

The square is both old and new: For a thousand years, it's been the center of Munich. It was the town's marketplace and public forum, standing at a crossroads along the Salt Road, which ran between Salzburg and Augsburg.

Lining one entire side of the square is the impressive facade of the **New Town Hall** (Neues Rathaus), with its soaring 280-foot spire. The structure looks medieval, but it was actually built in the late 1800s (1867-1908). The style is "Neo"-Gothic—pointed arches over the doorways and a roofline bristling with prickly spires. The 40 statues look like medieval saints, but they're from around 1900, depicting more recent Bavarian kings and nobles. This medieval-looking style was all the rage in the 19th century as Germans were rediscovering their historical roots and uniting as a modern nation.

The New Town Hall is famous for its **glockenspiel.** A carillon in the tower chimes a tune while colorful figurines come out on the balcony to spin and dance. It happens daily at 11:00 and 12:00 all year (also at 17:00 May-Oct). The *Spiel* of the glockenspiel tells the story of a noble wedding that actually took place on the market square in 1568. You see the wedding procession and the friendly joust of knights on horseback. The duke and his bride watch the action as the groom's family (in Bavarian white and blue) joyfully jousts with the bride's French family (in red and white). Below, the barrel-makers—famous for being the first to dance in the streets after a deadly plague lifted—do their popular jig. Finally, the solitary cock crows.

At the very top of the New Town Hall is a statue of a child with outstretched arms, dressed in monk's garb and holding a book in its left hand. This is the **Münchner Kindl,** the symbol of Munich. The town got its name from the people who

first settled here: the monks *(Mönchen)*. You'll spot this mini monk all over town, on everything from the city's coat of arms to souvenir shot glasses to ad campaigns (often holding not a book, but maybe a beer or a smartphone). The city symbol was originally depicted as a grown man, wearing a gold-lined black cloak and red shoes. By the 19th century, artists were representing him as a young boy, then a gender-neutral child, and, more recently, a young girl. These days, a teenage girl dressed as the *Kindl* kicks off the annual Oktoberfest by leading the opening parade on horseback, and then serves as the mascot throughout the festivities.

For great **views** of the city, you can ride an elevator to the top of the New Town Hall tower (€2.50, May-Sept daily 10:00-19:00; Oct-April Mon-Fri 10:00-17:00, closed Sat-Sun, elevator located under glockenspiel).

The **golden statue** at the top of the column in the center of Marienplatz honors the square's namesake, the Virgin Mary. Sculpted in 1590, it was a rallying point in the religious wars of the Reformation. Back then, Munich was a bastion of southern-German Catholicism against the heresies of Martin Luther to the north.

New Town Hall

Glockenspiel

NAZI
DOCUMENTATION
CENTER

To Alte Pinakothek
& other Museums

Karolinen-
platz

■ OBELISK

O-V-MÜLLER-RING

Platz
der Opfer des
National-
sozialismus

BRIENNER

19

100 Meters
100 Yards

KARLSTRASSE

JUNGFERNTURMSTR.

MAXIMILIANSPLATZ

MAX-JOSEPH-STRASSE

OTTOSTRASSE

BARER STRASSE

SALVATORSTR.

ARCOSTRASSE

KOCHUSSTR. IBERG

PRANNERSTRASSE

TÜRKENSTRASSE

SOPHIEN-

STR.

Alter
Botanischer
Garten

Lenbach-
platz

PACELLISTRASSE

HOTEL
BAYERISCHER
HOF

K. FAULHABERSTRASSE

OTTOSTRASSE

U Karlsplatz

Promenade-
platz

10

LODEN-FREY
DEP'T STORE

JUSTIZ-
PALAST

MAXBURGSTRASSE

HARTMANNSTR.

AUFHAUSER
PASSAGE

WINDEN-
MACHER

SCHÄFF.

Karls-
platz
S

Karls-
platz

KARLS-
TOR

KAPELLEN-
STRASSE

H.-MAX-STRASSE

ST.
MICHAEL'S

8

ETTSTRASSE

GERMAN
HUNTING &
FISHING
MUSEUM

AUGUSTINERSTR.

9

FRAUEN-
KIRCHE

To
Train
Station

SONNENSTRASSE

OBLETTER
TOYS

NEUHAUSER
STRASSE

KAUFINGERSTR.

MAZARI-
STRASSE

7

HERZOGSPITALSTRASSE

EISENMANNSTR.

FÄRBERGRABEN

FÜRSTEN-
FELDERSTRASSE

ROSENSTR.

HERZOG-

DAMEN-
STIFTS-
KIRCHE

DAMENSTIFTSTR.

HOTTERSTRASSE

HOFSTR.

POST

JOSEPHSPITALSTRASSE

BRUNNSTR.

HACKENSTRASSE

RINDERMARKT

ROSENTAL

WILHELM-STRASSE

KREUZSTRASSE

ASAM
CHURCH

6

DULTSTR.

SINGL.

CITY
MUSEUM

5

CAFÉ
FRISCHUT

Sebastians
Platz

4

POST

SENDLINGER
TOR

SCHMID.

OHEL JAKOB
SYNAGOGUE

PRALAT-ZISTL

Sendlinger
Tor
Platz

WALLSTR.

OBERANGER

KLOSTERHOF

UNTERERANGER

BLUMENSTRASSE

ROSS-
MAARKT

U Sendlinger
Tor

Munich City Walk

1 Marienplatz
2 St. Peter's Church
3 Viktualienmarkt
4 Ohel Jakob Synagogue
5 Munich City Museum
6 Asam Church
7 Kaufingerstrasse
8 St. Michael's Church
9 Frauenkirche
10 Michael Jackson Memorial

11 Marienhof
12 Dallmayr Delicatessen
13 Platzl
14 Hofbräuhaus
15 Maximilianstrasse
16 Max-Joseph-Platz
17 Viscardigasse
18 Odeonsplatz
19 Brienner Strasse
20 Hofgarten

Notice how, at the four corners of the statue, cherubs fight the four great biblical enemies of civilization: the dragon of war, the lion of hunger, the rooster-headed monster of plague and disease, and the serpent. The serpent represents heresy —namely, Protestants. Bavaria is still Catholic country, and Protestants weren't allowed to worship openly here until about 1800.

To the right of the New Town Hall, the gray pointy building with the green spires is the **Old Town Hall** (Altes Rathaus). On its adjoining bell tower, find the city seal. It has the Münchner Kindl (symbolizing the first monks), a castle (representing the first fortifications), and a lion (representing the first ruler—Henry the Lion, who built them).

As you look around, keep in mind that the Allies bombed Marienplatz and much of Munich during World War II. Most of the buildings had to be rebuilt. The Old Town Hall looks newer now because it was completely destroyed by bombs and had to be rebuilt after the war. The New Town Hall survived the bombs, and it served as the US military headquarters after the Americans occupied Munich in 1945.

Before moving on, face the New Town Hall one more time and get oriented. Straight ahead is north. To the left is the pedestrian shopping street called Kaufingerstrasse, which leads to the old gate called Karlstor and the train station. To the right, the street leads to the Isartor gate and the Deutsches Museum. This east-west axis cuts through the historic core of Munich.

• *Turn around to the right to find Rindermarkt, the street leading from the southeast corner of Marienplatz. Head to St. Peter's Church, just beyond the square, with its steeple poking up above a row of buildings.*

❷ St. Peter's Church

The oldest church in town, St. Peter's stands on the hill where Munich's original monks probably settled—perhaps as far back as the ninth century (though the city marks its official birthday as 1158). Today's church (from 1368) replaced the original monastery church.

St. Peter's ("Old Peter" to locals) is part of the soul of the city. There's even a popular song about it that goes, "Munich is not Munich without St. Peter's."

Cost and Hours: Church-free, tower-€2, Mon-Fri 9:00-18:30, Sat-Sun 10:00-

Old Town Hall

Climb the tower of St. Peter's Church for great views.

18:30, off-season until 17:30.

Visiting the Church: On the outside of the church, notice the 16th- and 17th-century tombstones plastered onto the wall. Originally, people were buried in the holy ground around the church. But in the Napoleonic age, the cemeteries were dug up and relocated outside the city walls for hygienic and space reasons. They kept a few tombstones here as a reminder.

Step inside. (If there's a Mass in progress, visitors are welcome, but stay in the back. If there's no Mass, feel free to explore.) Typical of so many Bavarian churches, it's whitewashed and light-filled, with highlights in pastel pinks and blues framed by gold curlicues. The ceiling painting opens up to the heavens, where Peter is crucified upside down.

Some photos (on a pillar near the entrance) show how St. Peter's was badly damaged in World War II—the roof caved in, and the altar was damaged. But the beloved church was rebuilt and restored, thanks to donations—half from the Augustiner brewery, the rest from private donors. The accuracy of the restoration was possible thanks to Nazi catalog photos. For decades after World War II, the bells played a popular tune that stopped before the last note, reminding locals that the church still needed money to rebuild.

Explore further. The nave is lined with bronze statues of the apostles, and the altar shows a statue of St. Peter being adored by four church fathers. The finely crafted, gray iron fences that line the nave were donated after World War II by the local blacksmiths of the national railway. The precious and fragile sandstone Gothic chapel altar (to the left of the main altar) survived the war only because it was buried in sandbags.

Find the second chapel on the left side. Now there's something you don't see every day: a skeleton in a box. As the red Latin inscription says, this is St. Munditia. In the fourth century, she was beheaded by the Romans for her Christian faith.

Munich has more relics of saints than any city outside Rome. That's because it was the Pope's Catholic bastion against the rising tide of Protestantism in northern Europe during the Reformation. In 1675, St. Munditia's remains were given to Munich by the Pope as thanks for the city's devoted service. It was also a vivid reminder to the faithful that those who die for the cause of the Roman Church go directly to heaven without waiting for Judgment Day.

It's a long climb to the top of the **spire** (306 steps, no elevator)—much of it with two-way traffic on a one-lane staircase—but the view is dynamite. Try to be two flights from the top when the bells ring at the top of the hour. Then, when your friends back home ask you about your trip, you'll say, "What?"

• *Just beyond St. Peter's, join the busy commotion of the...*

❸ *Viktualienmarkt*

The market (rated ▲▲, closed Sun) is a lively world of produce stands and budget eateries. Browse your way through

Viktualienmarkt

The History of Munich

Born from Salt and Beer (1100-1500)
Munich began in the 12th century, when Henry the Lion (Heinrich der Löwe) established a lucrative salt trade near a monastery of "monks"—München. After Henry's death, an ambitious merchant family, the Wittelsbachs, took over. By the 1400s, Munich's market bustled with trade in salt and beer, the twin-domed Frauenkirche drew pilgrims, and the Wittelsbachs made their home in the Residenz. When the various regions of Bavaria united in 1506, Munich became the capital.

Religious Wars, Plagues, Decline (1500-1800)
While Martin Luther and the Protestant Reformation raged in northern Germany, Munich became the Catholic heart of the Counter-Reformation, decorated in the ornate Baroque and Rococo style of its Italian allies. Religious wars and periodic plagues left the city weakened. While the rest of Europe modernized, Munich remained behind the times.

The Golden Age of Kings (1806-1886)
When Napoleon invaded, the Wittelsbach duke surrendered and was rewarded with a grander title: King of Bavaria. Munich boomed. **Maximilian I** (r. 1806-1825), a.k.a. Max Joseph, rebuilt in Neoclassical style—grand columned buildings connected by broad boulevards. **Ludwig I** (r. 1825-1848) turned Munich into a modern railroad hub and budding industrial city. His son **Maximilian II** (r. 1848-1864) continued the modernization program. **Ludwig II** (r. 1864-1886) didn't much like Munich, preferring to build castles in the Bavarian countryside .

the stalls and pavilions, as you make your way to the market's main landmark, the blue-and-white striped maypole. Early in the morning, you can still feel small-town Munich here. Remember, Munich has been a market town since its earliest days as a stop on the salt-trade crossroads. By the 1400s, the market bustled, most likely beneath a traditional maypole, just like you see today.

Besides salt, Munich gained a reputation for beer. By the 15th century, more than 30 breweries pumped out the golden liquid, brewed by monks who were licensed to sell it. They stored their beer in cellars under courtyards kept cool by the shade of bushy chestnut trees—a tradition Munich's breweries still honor.

The market's centerpiece seems to be its **beer garden** (daily 10:00-22:00, weather permitting). Its picnic tables are filled with hungry and thirsty locals, all in the shade of the traditional chestnut trees. Shoppers pause here for a late-morning snack of *Weisswurst*—white sausage—served with mustard, a pretzel, and a beer. Here, you can order just a half-liter—unlike at other *Biergartens* that only sell by the full liter. As is the tradition at all of the city's beer gardens, some tables (those without tablecloths) are set aside for patrons who bring their own

End of the Wittelsbachs (1886-1918)

When Bavaria became part of the newly united Germany, Berlin overtook Munich as Germany's power center. Then World War I devastated Munich. After the war, mobs of poor, angry Münchners roamed the streets. In 1918, they drove out the last Bavarian king, ending 700 years of Wittelsbach rule.

Nazis and World War II (1918-1945)

In the power vacuum, a fringe group emerged—the Nazi party, headed by Adolf Hitler. Hitler rallied the Nazis in a Munich beer hall, leading a failed coup d'état known as the Beer Hall Putsch (1923). When the Nazis eventually took power in Berlin, they remembered their roots, dubbing Munich "Capital of the Movement." In World War II, nearly half the city was leveled by Allied air raids.

Munich Rebuilds (1945-Present)

After the war, with generous American aid, Münchners rebuilt. Nazi authorities had created a photographic archive of historic sights, which now came in handy. Munich chose to preserve its low-rise, medieval feel, but with a modern infrastructure. For the 1972 Olympic Games, they built a futuristic stadium, a sleek new subway system, and one of Europe's first pedestrian-only zones—Kaufingerstrasse. In 1990, when Germany reunited, Berlin once again became the country's focal point, relegating Munich to a backseat role.

Today's Munich is home to more banks and financial firms than any German city besides Frankfurt. With a population of 1.5 million, Munich is Germany's third-largest city, after Berlin and Hamburg. A center for book publishing, Munich also hosts universities, two TV networks, the electronics giant Siemens, the German branch of Microsoft, and BMW, maker of world-famous cars ("Bayerische Motoren Werke"—Bavarian Motor Works). Safe, clean, cultured, and productive, Munich is a success story.

food; they're welcome here as long as they buy a drink. The Viktualienmarkt is ideal for a light meal (see page 733).

Now make your way to the towering **maypole.** Throughout Bavaria, colorfully ornamented maypoles decorate town squares. Many are painted, like this one, in Bavaria's colors, white and blue. The decorations are festively replaced every year on the first of May. Traditionally, rival communities try to steal each other's maypole. Locals guard their new pole day and night as May Day approaches. Stolen poles are ransomed only with lots of beer for the clever thieves.

The decorations that line each side of the pole explain which merchants are doing business in the market. Munich's maypole gives prominence (on the

The market's maypole

bottom level) to a horse-drawn wagon bringing in beer barrels. And you can't have a kegger without coopers—find the merry barrelmakers, the four cute guys dancing. Today, traditional barrel-making is enjoying a comeback as top breweries like to have real wooden kegs.

The bottom of the pole celebrates the world's oldest food law. The German Beer Purity Law *(Reinheitsgebot)* of 1487 actually originated here in Bavaria. It stipulated that beer could consist only of three ingredients: barley, hops, and water. (Later they realized that a fourth ingredient, yeast, is always present in fermentation.) Why was beer so treasured? Back in the Middle Ages, it was considered liquid food.

From the maypole, take in the bustling scene around you. The market was modernized in the 1800s as the city grew. Old buildings were torn down, replaced with stalls and modern market halls. Now, in the 21st century, it's a wonder such a traditional place survives—especially because it sits on the most expensive real estate in town. But locals love their market, so the city protects these old-time shops, charging them only a small percentage of their gross income, enabling them to carry on.

• *At the bottom end of the Viktualienmarkt, spot* **Café Frischhut,** *with its colorful old-time sign hanging out front (at Prälat-Zistl-Strasse 8). This is Munich's favorite place to stop for a fresh Schmalznudel—a traditional fried-dough treat (best enjoyed warm with a sprinkling of sugar).*

Across the street, you'll pass the Pschorr beer hall. Continue just past it to a modern glass-and-iron building, the **Schrannen-halle.** *This 1800s grain exchange has been renovated into a high-end mall of deli shops. Chocoholics could detour downstairs here into* **Milka Coco World** *for tasty samples (and a good WC).*

When you're ready to move on, exit the Schrannenhalle midway down on the right-hand side (or if it's closed, walk around the top of the building to Prälat-Zistl-Strasse

and turn left). You'll spill out into Sebas-tiansplatz, a small square lined with healthy eateries. Continue through Sebastiansplatz and veer left, where you'll see a cube-shaped building, the...

❹ *Ohel Jakob Synagogue*

This modern synagogue anchors a revitalized Jewish quarter. In the 1930s, about 10,000 Jews lived in Munich, and the main synagogue stood near here. Then, in 1938, Hitler demanded that the synagogue be torn down. By the end of World War II, Munich's Jewish community was gone. But thanks to Germany's acceptance of religious refugees from former Soviet states, the Jewish population has now reached its prewar size. The new synagogue was built in 2006. There's also a kindergarten and day school, playground, fine kosher restaurant (at #18), and bookstore. Standing in the middle of the square, notice the low-key but efficient security.

While the synagogue is shut tight to nonworshippers, its architecture is striking from the outside. Lower stones of travertine evoke the Wailing Wall in Jerusalem, while an upper section represents the tent that held important religious wares during the 40 years of wandering through the desert. The synagogue's door features the first 10 letters of the Hebrew alphabet, symbolizing the Ten Commandments.

The cube-shaped **Jewish History Museum** (behind the cube-shaped synagogue) is stark and windowless. The

Ohel Jakob Synagogue

museum's small permanent collection focuses on Munich's Jewish history; good temporary exhibits might justify the entry fee (€6, ticket gets you half-price admission to Munich City Museum, Tue-Sun 10:00-18:00, closed Mon, St.-Jakobs-Platz 16, tel. 089/2339-6096, www.juedisches-museum-muenchen.de).

• *Facing the synagogue, on the same square, is the...*

❺ Munich City Museum (Münchner Stadtmuseum)

The highs and lows of Munich's history are covered in this surprisingly honest municipal museum (rated ▲). It covers the cultural upheavals of the early 1900s, Munich's role as the birthplace of the Nazis, and the city's renaissance during Germany's postwar "economic miracle." There's scant information posted in English, but an included audioguide can fill in the gaps.

• *You can stop and tour the museum now (see page 752). Otherwise, continue through the synagogue's square, past the fountain, across the street, and one block farther to the pedestrianized Sendlinger Strasse. Down the street 100 yards to the left, the fancy facade (at #62) marks the...*

❻ Asam Church (Asamkirche)

This tiny church (rated ▲) is a slice of heaven on earth—a gooey, drippy Baroque masterpiece by Bavaria's top two Rococonuts—the Asam brothers. Just 30 feet wide, it was built in 1740 to

Asam Church

fit within this row of homes. Originally, it was a private chapel where these two brother-architects could show off their work (on their own land, next to their home and business headquarters—to the left), but it's now a public place of worship.

Cost and Hours: Free, Sat-Thu 9:00-18:00, Fri 13:00-18:00, tel. 089/2368-7989. The church is small, so visitors are asked not to enter during Mass (held Tue and Thu-Fri 17:00-18:00, Wed 8:30-9:30, and Sun 10:00-11:00).

Visiting the Church: This place of worship served as a promotional brochure to woo clients, and is packed with every architectural trick in the book. Imagine approaching the church not as a worshipper, but as a shopper representing your church's building committee. First stand outside: Hmmm, the look of those foundation stones really packs a punch. And the legs hanging over the portico... nice effect. Those starbursts on the door would be a hit back home, too.

Then step inside: I'll take a set of those over-the-top golden capitals, please. We'd also like to order the gilded garlands draping the church in jubilation, and the twin cupids capping the confessional. And how about some fancy stucco work, too? (Molded-and-painted plaster was clearly an Asam brothers specialty.) Check out the illusion of a dome painted on the flat ceiling—that'll save us lots of money. The yellow glass above the altar has the effect of the thin-sliced alabaster at St. Peter's in Rome, but it's within our budget! And, tapping the "marble" pilasters to determine that they are just painted fakes, we decide to take that, too. Crammed between two buildings, light inside this narrow church is limited, so there's a big, clear window in the back for maximum illumination—we'll order one to cut back on our electricity bill.

On the way out, say good-bye to the gilded grim reaper in the narthex (left side as you're leaving) as he cuts the thread of life—reminding all who visit of our mortality...and, by the way, that shrouds have no pockets.

• Leaving the church, look to your right, noticing the Sendlinger Tor at the end of the street—part of the fortified town wall that circled Munich in the 14th century. Then turn left and walk straight up Sendlinger Strasse. Walk toward the Münchner Kindl, still capping the spire of the New Town Hall in the distance, and then up (pedestrian-only) Rosenstrasse, until you hit Marienplatz and the big, busy...

❼ Kaufingerstrasse

This car-free street leads you through a great shopping district, past cheap department stores, carnivals of street entertainers, and good old-fashioned slicers and dicers. As far back as the 12th century, this was the town's main commercial street. Traders from Salzburg and Augsburg would enter the town through the fortified Karlstor. This street led past the Augustiner beer hall (opposite St. Michael's Church to this day), right to the main square and cathedral.

Up until the 1970s, the street was jammed with car traffic. Then, for the 1972 Olympics, it was turned into one of Europe's first pedestrian zones. At first, shopkeepers were afraid that would ruin business. Now it's Munich's living room. Nearly 9,000 shoppers pass through it each hour. Merchants nearby are begging for their streets to become traffic-free, too.

The 1972 Olympics transformed this part of Munich—the whole area around Marienplatz was pedestrianized and the transit system expanded. Since then, Munich has become one of the globe's greenest cities. Skyscrapers have been banished to the suburbs, and the nearby Frauenkirche is still the tallest building in the center.

• Stroll a few blocks away from Marienplatz toward the Karlstor, until you arrive at the big church on the right.

❽ St. Michael's Church (Michaelskirche)

This is one of the first great Renaissance buildings north of the Alps. The ornate facade, with its sloped roofline, was inspired by the Gesù Church in Rome—home of the Jesuit order. Jesuits saw themselves as the intellectual defenders of Catholicism. St. Michael's was built in the late 1500s—at the height of the Protestant Reformation—to serve as the northern outpost of the Jesuits. Appropriately, the facade features a statue of Michael fighting a Protestant demon.

Cost and Hours: Church—free, open daily generally 8:00-19:00, stays open later on Sun and summer evenings; crypt—€2, Mon-Fri 9:30-16:30, Sat until 14:30, closed Sun; frequent concerts—check the schedule outside; tel. 089/231-7060.

Visiting the Church: Inside, admire the ornate Baroque interior, topped with a barrel vault, the largest of its day. Stroll up the nave to the ornate pulpit, where Jesuit priests would hammer away at Reformation heresy. The church's acoustics are spectacular, and the choir—famous in

St. Michael's Church

Munich—sounds heavenly singing from the organ loft high in the rear.

The **crypt** (*Fürstengruft*, down the stairs by the altar) contains 40 stark, somewhat forlorn tombs of Bavaria's ruling family, the Wittelsbachs. There's the tomb of Wilhelm V, who built this church, and Maximilian I, who saved Munich from Swedish invaders during the Thirty Years' War. Finally, there's Otto, who went insane and was deposed in 1916, virtually bringing the Wittelsbachs' seven-century reign to an end.

The most ornate tomb holds the illustrious Ludwig II, known for his fairy-tale castle at Neuschwanstein. Ludwig didn't care much for Munich. He escaped to the Bavarian countryside, where he spent his days building castles, listening to music, and dreaming about knights of old. His excesses earned him the nickname "Mad" King Ludwig. But of all the Wittelsbachs, it's his tomb that's decorated with flowers—placed here by romantics still mad about their "mad" king.

• *Our next stop, the Frauenkirche, is a few hundred yards away. Backtrack a couple of blocks up Kaufingerstrasse to the wild boar statue, which marks the* **German Hunting and Fishing Museum**. *This place has outdoorsy regalia, kid-friendly exhibits, and the infamous Wolpertinger—a German "jackalope" invented by creative local taxidermists. At the boar statue, turn left on Augustinerstrasse, which leads to Munich's towering, twin-domed cathedral, the...*

❾ *Frauenkirche*

These twin onion domes are the symbol of the city. They're unusual in that most Gothic churches have either pointed steeples or square towers. Some say Crusaders, inspired by the Dome of the Rock in Jerusalem, brought home the idea. Or it may be that, due to money problems, the towers weren't completed until Renaissance times, when domes were popular. Whatever the reason, the Frauenkirche's domes may be the inspiration for the characteristic domed church spires that mark villages all over Bavaria.

Cost and Hours: Free, open daily generally 7:00-19:00, tel. 089/290-0820.

Rick's Tip: If the **Frauenkirche** *towers are closed for renovation during your visit, you can enjoy great* **city views** *from* **New Town Hall** *(elevator) or the towers of* **St. Peter's Church** *(stairs only).*

Visiting the Church: The church was built in just 22 years, from 1466 to 1488. It's made of brick—easy to make locally, and cheaper and faster to build with than stone. Construction was partly funded by the sale of indulgences (which let sinners bypass purgatory on the way to heaven). It's dedicated to the Virgin—Our Lady (*Frau*)—and has been the city's cathedral since 1821.

Step inside, and remember that much of this church was destroyed during World War II. The towers survived, and the rest was rebuilt essentially from scratch.

Near the entrance is a big, black, ornate monument honoring Ludwig IV the Bavarian (1282-1347), who was elected Holy Roman Emperor—a big deal. The

Frauenkirche

Frauenkirche was built a century later with the express purpose of honoring his memory. His monument was originally situated in front at the high altar, right near Christ. Those Wittelsbachs—always trying to be associated with God. This alliance was instilled in people through the prayers they were forced to recite: "Virgin Mary, mother of our duke, please protect us."

Nearby, a relief (over the back pew on the left) honors one of Munich's more recent citizens. Joseph Ratzinger was born in Bavaria in 1927, became archbishop of the Frauenkirche (1977-1982), then moved to the Vatican, where he later served as Pope Benedict XVI (2005-2013).

Now walk slowly up the main aisle, enjoying stained glass right and left. This glass is obviously modern, having replaced the original glass that was shattered in World War II. Ahead is the high altar, under a huge hanging crucifix. Find the throne—the ceremonial seat of the local bishop. From here, look up to the tops of the columns, and notice the tiny painted portraits. They're the craftsmen from five centuries ago who helped build the church.

Now walk behind the altar to the apse, where there are three tall windows. These still have their original 15th-century glass. To survive the bombs of 1944, each pane had to be lovingly removed and stored safely away.

• *Our next stop is at Promenadeplatz, about 400 yards north of here. Facing the altar, take the left side exit and walk straight 50 yards until you see a tiny but well-signed passageway (to the left) called the Aufhauser Passage. Follow it through a modern building, where you'll emerge at a park (surrounded by concrete) called Promenadeplatz. Detour a few steps left into the park, where you'll find a colorful modern memorial.*

⑩ Michael Jackson Memorial

When Michael Jackson was in town, he'd stay at the Hotel Bayerischer Hof, like many VIPs. Fans would gather in the park waiting for him to appear at his window. He'd sometimes oblige (but his infamous baby-dangling incident happened in Berlin, not here). When he died in 2009, devotees created this memorial by taking over a statue of Renaissance composer Orlando di Lasso. They still visit daily, leave a memento, and keep it tidy.

• *Now backtrack and turn left, up Kardinal-Faulhaber-Strasse. The street is lined with former 18th-century mansions that have since become offices and bank buildings. At #11, turn right and enter a modern shopping mall called the **Fünf Höfe Passage**. The place tries to take your basic shopping mall and give it more class. It's divided into five connecting courtyards (the "fünf Höfe"), spruced up with bubbling fountains, exotic plants, and a hanging garden.*

Emerging on a busy pedestrian street, turn right, and head down the street (noticing the Münchner Kindl again high above), to a big green square: Marienhof, with the most aristocratic grocery store in all of Germany.

⑪ Marienhof

This square, tucked behind the New Town Hall, was left as a green island after the wartime bombings. If you find that the square's all dug up, it's because Munich has finally started building an additional subway tunnel here. With virtually the entire underground system converging on nearby Marienplatz, this new tunnel will provide a huge relief to the city's con-

Marienhof

gested subterranean infrastructure.

On the far side of Marienhof is ⓬ **Dallmayr Delicatessen.** When the king called out for dinner, he called Alois Dallmayr. This place became famous for its exotic and luxurious food items: tropical fruits, seafood, chocolates, fine wines, and coffee (there are meat and cheese counters, too). As you enter, read the black plaque with the royal seal by the door: *Königlich Bayerischer Hof-Lieferant* ("Deliverer for the King of Bavaria and his Court"). Catering to royal and aristocratic tastes (and budgets), it's still the choice of Munich's old rich (closed Sun, www.dallmayr.com).

• *Leaving Dallmayr, turn right and then right again to continue along Hofgraben. Walk three blocks gently downhill to Platzl—"small square." (If you get turned around, just ask any local to point you toward the Hofbräuhaus.)*

⓭ *Platzl*

As you stand here—admiring classic facades in the heart of medieval Munich—recall that everything around you was flattened in World War II. Here on Platzl, the reconstruction happened in stages: From 1945 to 1950, they removed 12 million tons of bricks and replaced roofs to make buildings weather-tight. From 1950 to 1972, they redid the exteriors. From 1972 to 2000, they refurbished the interiors. Today, the rebuilt Platzl sports new—but old-looking—facades.

Officials estimate that hundreds of unexploded bombs still lie buried under Munich. As recently as 2012, they found a 550-pound bomb in Schwabing, a neighborhood just north of the old city center. They had to evacuate the neighborhood and detonate the bomb.

Today's Platzl hosts a lively mix of places to eat and drink—pop-culture chains like Starbucks and Hard Rock Café alongside top-end restaurants like the recommended Wirtshaus Ayingers and Schuhbecks (Schuhbecks Eis is a favorite for ice cream; Pfisterstrasse 9-11).

• *At the bottom of the square (#   experience the venerable...*

⓮ *Hofbräuhaus*

The world's most famous beer hall (rated ▲▲) is a trip. Whether or not you slide your lederhosen on its polished benches, it's a great experience just to walk through the place in all its rowdy glory (with its own gift shop).

Before going in, check out the huge arches at the entrance and the crown logo. The original brewery was built here in 1583. As the crown suggests, it was the Wittelsbachs' personal brewery to make the "court brew" (*Hof Brau*). In 1880, the brewery moved out, and this 5,000-seat food-and-beer palace was built in its place. After being bombed in World War II, the Hofbräuhaus was one of the first places to be rebuilt (German priorities).

Now, take a deep breath and go on in. Dive headlong into the sudsy Hofbräu mosh pit. Don't be shy. Everyone's drunk anyway. The atmosphere is thick with the sounds of oompah music, played here every night of the year.

You'll see locals stuffed into lederhosen and dirndls, giant gingerbread cookies that sport romantic messages, and kiosks selling postcards of the German (and apparently beer-drinking) ex-pope. Notice the quirky 1950s-style painted ceiling, with Bavarian colors, grapes, chestnuts, and fun "eat, drink, and be merry" themes. You'll see signs on some tables reading

Hofbräuhaus

lammtisch, meaning they're reserved for regulars, and their racks of old beer steins made of pottery and pewter. Beer halls like the Hofbräuhaus sell beer only by the liter mug, called a *Mass* (mahs). You can get it light (*helles*) or dark (*dunkles*). A slogan on the ceiling above the band reads, *Durst ist schlimmer als Heimweh*—"Thirst is worse than homesickness" (daily 9:00-23:30, live oompah music during lunch and dinner; for details on eating here, see page 770).

• *Leaving the Hofbräuhaus, turn right and walk two blocks, then turn left when you reach the street called...*

⑮ Maximilianstrasse

This broad east-west boulevard, lined with grand buildings and exclusive shops, introduces us to Munich's Golden Age of the 1800s. In that period, Bavaria was ruled by three important kings: Max Joseph, Ludwig I, and Ludwig II. They transformed Munich from a cluster of medieval lanes to a modern city of spacious squares, Neoclassical monuments, and wide boulevards. At the east end of this boulevard is the palatial home of the Bavarian parliament.

The street was purposely designed for people and for shopping, not military parades. And to this day, Maximilianstrasse is busy with shoppers browsing Munich's most exclusive shops.

• *Maximilianstrasse leads to a big square—Max-Joseph-Platz.*

⑯ Max-Joseph-Platz

The square is fronted by two big buildings: the National Theater (with its columns) and the Residenz (with its intimidating stone facade).

The **Residenz,** the former "residence" of the royal Wittelsbach family, started as a crude castle (c. 1385). Over the centuries, it evolved into one of Europe's most opulent palaces (see page 744).

The centerpiece of the square is a grand statue of **Maximilian I**—a.k.a. Max

Joseph. In 1806, Max was serving in the long tradition of his Wittelsbach family as the city's duke...until Napoleon invaded and deposed him. But then Napoleon—eager to marry into the aristocracy—agreed to reinstate Max, with one condition: that his daughter marry Napoleon's stepson. Max Joseph agreed, and was quickly crowned not duke but king of Bavaria.

Max Joseph and his heirs ruled as constitutional monarchs. Now a king, Max Joseph was popular; he emancipated Protestants and Jews, revamped the Viktualienmarkt, and graced Munich with grand buildings like the **National Theater.** This Neoclassical building, opened in 1818, celebrated Bavaria's strong culture, deep roots, and legitimacy as a nation; four of Richard Wagner's operas were first performed here. It's now where the Bavarian State Opera and the Bavarian State Orchestra perform. (The Roman numerals MCMLXIII in the frieze mark the year the theater reopened after the WWII bombing restoration—1963.)

• *Leave Max-Joseph-Platz opposite where you entered, walking alongside the Residenz on Residenzstrasse for about 100 yards to the next grand square. But before you get to Odeonsplatz, pause at the first corner on the left and look down Viscardigasse at the gold-cobbled swoosh in the pavement.*

⑰ Viscardigasse

The cobbles in Viscardigasse recall one of Munich's most dramatic moments: It

Max-Joseph-Platz

was 1923, and Munich was in chaos. World War I had left Germany in shambles. Angry mobs roamed the streets. Out of the fury rose a new and frightening movement—Adolf Hitler and the Nazi Party. On November 8, Hitler launched a coup, later known as the Beer Hall Putsch, to try to topple the German government. It started with a fiery speech by Hitler in a beer hall a few blocks from here (which no longer exists). The next day, Hitler and his mob of 3,000 Nazis marched up Residenzstrasse. A block ahead, where Residenzstrasse spills into Odeonsplatz, stood a hundred government police waiting for the Nazi mob. Shots were fired. Hitler was injured, and 16 Nazis were killed, along with four policemen. The coup was put down, and Hitler was sent to a prison outside Munich. During his nine months there, he wrote down his twisted ideas in his book *Mein Kampf*.

Ten years later, when Hitler finally came to power, he made a memorial at Odeonsplatz to honor the "first martyrs of the Third Reich." Germans were required to raise their arms in a *Sieg Heil* salute as they entered the square. The only way to avoid the indignity of saluting Nazism was to turn left down Viscardigasse instead. That stream of shiny cobbles marks the detour taken by those brave dissenters.

• *But now that Hitler's odious memorial is long gone, you can continue to...*

⓲ *Odeonsplatz*

This square links Munich's illustrious past with the Munich of today. It was laid out by the Wittelsbach kings in the 1800s. They incorporated the much older (yellow) church that was already on the square, the Theatinerkirche. This church contains about half of the Wittelsbach tombs. The church's twin towers and 230-foot-high dome are classic Italian Baroque, reflecting Munich's strong Catholic bent in the 1600s.

Nearby, overlooking the square from the south, is an arcaded loggia filled with statues. In the 1800s, the Wittelsbachs commissioned this Hall of Heroes to honor Bavarian generals. It was modeled after the famous Renaissance loggia in Florence. Odeonsplatz was part of the Wittelsbachs' grand vision of modern urban planning.

At the far end of the square, several wide boulevards lead away from here.

Odeonsplatz and Theatinerkirche

First, face west (left) down **⑲ Brienner Strasse** (watch out for bikes). In the distance, and just out of sight, a black obelisk commemorates the 30,000 Bavarians who marched with Napoleon to Moscow and never returned. Beyond the obelisk is the grand Königsplatz, or "King's Square," with its Neoclassical buildings. Back in the 1930s, Königsplatz was the center of the Nazi party. Remember, Munich was the cradle of Nazism. Today, the Nazi shadow has largely lifted from that square (only two buildings from that era remain) and Königsplatz is home to Munich's cluster of great art museums. A few miles beyond Königsplatz is the Wittelsbachs' impressive summer home, Nymphenburg Palace.

Now turn your attention 90 degrees to the right. The boulevard heading north from Odeonsplatz is Ludwigstrasse. It stretches a full mile, flanked by an impressive line of uniform 60-foot-tall buildings in the Neo-Gothic style. In the far distance is the city's Triumphal Arch, capped with a figure of Bavaria, a goddess riding a lion-drawn chariot. The street is named for the great Wittelsbach builder-king, Ludwig I, who truly made Munich into a grand capital. ("I won't rest," he famously swore, "until Munich looks like Athens.") Ludwigstrasse was used for big parades and processions, as it leads to that Roman-style arch.

Beyond the arch—and beyond what you can see—lie the suburbs of modern Munich, including the city's modern skyscrapers and the famous BMW headquarters. Yes, Munich is a major metropolis, but you'd hardly know it by walking through its pleasant streets and parks.

• *We'll finish our walk in the enjoyable Hofgarten. Its formal gate is to your right as you're facing up Ludwigstrasse. Step through the gate and enter the...*

⑳ Hofgarten

This elegant "garden of the royal court" is a delight. Built by the Wittelsbachs as their own private backyard to the Residenz palace, it's now open to everyone. Just inside the gate is an arcade decorated with murals commissioned by Ludwig I in the early 1800s. While faded, they still tell the glorious story of Bavaria from 1155 until 1688. The garden's 400-year-old centerpiece is a Renaissance-style temple with great acoustics. (There's often a musician performing here for tips.) It's decorated with the same shell decor as was popular inside the Residenz.

Take some time to enjoy the garden as the royals did. If you're ready to eat, you have several choices, including Café Luitpold (best for coffee and cake) and the elegant Spatenhaus beer hall, both nearby.

• *This walk is done. Where to go next? You're near the English Garden (just a few blocks away—see the map; people surf in the rapids created as the small river tumbles underground beneath the bridge east of Haus der Kunst), the Residenz complex, and the Odeonsplatz U-Bahn stop for points elsewhere.*

SIGHTS

Most of the top sights in the city center are covered on my self-guided walk. But there's much more to see in this city.

***

Rick's Tip: *If you're unsure about which of Munich's top two palaces to visit, the* **Residenz** *is more central and has the best interior, while* **Nymphenburg** *has the finest garden and outdoor views.*

***

▲▲Residenz Complex

For 500 years, this was the palatial "residence" and seat of power of the ruling Wittelsbach family. It began (1385) as a crude castle with a moat around it. The main building was built from 1550 to 1650, and decorated in Rococo style during the 18th century. The final touch was the grand south facade modeled after Florence's Pitti Palace. In March 1944, Allied air raids left the Residenz in shambles, so much of what we see today is reconstructed.

The vast Residenz complex is divided into three sections, each with its own admission ticket: The **Residenz Museum** is a long hike through 90 lavishly decorated rooms. The **Residenz Treasury** shows off the Wittelsbach crown jewels. The **Cuvilliés Theater** is an ornate Rococo opera house. You can see the three sights individually or get a combo-ticket to see them all. I consider the museum and treasury to be the essential Residenz visit, with the Cuvilliés Theater as extra credit.

Rick's Tip: *The Bavarian Palace Department offers a* **14-day ticket** *(called the* **Mehrtagesticket***) that covers admission to Munich's Residenz and Nymphenburg Palace complexes, as well as the Neuschwanstein and Linderhof castles in Bavaria. If you're planning to visit at least three of these sights within a two-week period, the pass will likely pay for itself (€24, €44 family/partner pass, purchase at participating sights or online at www.schloesser.bayern.de).*

Planning Your Time: Start your visit with the Residenz Treasury because it's small and you can easily manage your time there. Then visit the sprawling Residenz Museum, where you can wander until you say "Enough." The Cuvilliés Theater doesn't take long to see and is easy to fit in at the start or end. If you run out of time or energy, you can reenter on the same ticket to visit anything you missed. The entrances on Max-Joseph-Platz and Residenzstrasse both lead to the ticket office, gift shop, and start of the treasury and museum tours.

Cost and Hours: Residenz Museum-€7, Residenz Treasury-€7 (both include audioguides), Cuvilliés Theater-€3.50; €11 combo-ticket covers museum and treasury; €13 version covers all three; treasury and museum open daily April-mid-Oct 9:00-18:00, mid-Oct-March 10:00-17:00; theater open April-mid-Sept Mon-Sat 14:00-18:00, Sun 9:00-18:00; mid-Sept-March Mon-Sat 14:00-17:00, Sun 10:00-17:00; for all three sights, last entry is one hour before closing, tel. 089/290-671, www.residenz-muenchen.de.

The Residenz—the "residence" of Bavaria's rulers

RESIDENZ TREASURY (SCHATZKAMMER)

The treasury shows off a thousand years of Wittelsbach crowns and knickknacks. You'll see the regalia used in Bavaria's coronation ceremonies, valuable liturgical objects and relics, and miscellaneous wonders that dazzled the Wittelsbachs' European relatives. It's the best treasury in Bavaria, with fine 13th- and 14th-century crowns and delicately carved ivory and glass.

⊙ **Self-Guided Tour:** In **Room 1,** the oldest jewels are 200 years older than Munich itself. The gem-studded 11th-century Crown of Kunigunde (on the left) is associated with the saintly Bavarian queen, who was crowned Holy Roman Empress in 1014 in St. Peter's Basilica in Rome. The pearl-studded prayer book of Charles the Bald (Charlemagne's grandson) allowed the book's owner to claim royal roots dating all the way back to that first Holy Roman Emperor crowned in 800. The spiky Crown of an English Queen (c. 1370) is actually England's oldest crown, brought to Munich by an English princess who married a Wittelsbach duke. The lily-shaped Crown of Henry II (c. 1270-1280) dates from Munich's roots, when the town was emerging as a regional capital.

Along the right side of the room are religious objects such as reliquaries and portable altars. The tiny mobile altar allowed a Carolingian king to pack light in 890—and still have a little Mass while on the road. Many of the precious objects in this room were confiscated from the collections of various prince-bishops when their realms came under Bavarian rule in the Napoleonic era (c. 1800).

Room 3: Study the reliquary with St. George killing the dragon—sparkling with more than 2,000 precious stones. Get up close (it's OK to walk around the rope posts)...you can almost hear the dragon hissing. A gold-armored St. George, seated atop a ruby-studded ivory horse, tramples an emerald-green dragon. The golden box below contained the supposed relics of St. George, who was the patron saint of the Wittelsbachs. If you could lift the minuscule visor, you'd see that the carved ivory face of St. George is actually the Wittelsbach Duke Wilhelm V—the great champion of the Catholic Counter-Reformation—slaying the dragon of Protestantism.

Room 4: The incredibly realistic carved ivory crucifixes from 1630 were done by local artist Georg Petel. Look at the flesh of Jesus' wrist pulling around the nails. In the center of the room is the intricate portable altarpiece (1573-74) of Duke Albrecht V, the Wittelsbach ruler who (as we'll see in the Residenz Museum) made a big mark on the Residenz.

Room 5: The freestanding glass case (#245) holds the impressive royal regalia of the 19th-century Wittelsbach kings—the crown, scepter, orb, and sword that were given to the king during the cor-

Crown of Henry II

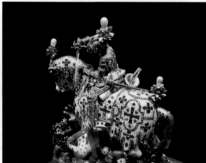

St. George reliquary

onation ceremony. (The smaller pearl crown was for the queen.) They date from the early 1800s when Bavaria had been conquered by Napoleon. The Wittelsbachs struck a deal that allowed them to stay in power under the elevated title of "king" (not just "duke" or "elector" or "prince-archbishop"). These objects were made in France by the same craftsmen who created Napoleon's crown.

Rooms 6-10: The rest of the treasury has objects that are more beautiful than historic. Admire the dinnerware made of rock crystal (Room 6), stone (Room 7), and gold and enamel (Room 8). Room 9 has a silver-gilt-and-marble replica of Trajan's Column. Finally, explore the "Exotica" of Room 10, including a green Olmec figure, knives from Turkey, and a Chinese rhino-horn bowl with a teeny-tiny Neptune inside.

• *From the micro-detail of the treasury, it's time to visit the expansive Residenz Museum. Cross the hall, exchange your treasury audioguide for the museum audioguide, and enter the...*

RESIDENZ MUSEUM (RESIDENZMUSEUM)

Though called a "museum," what's really on display here are the 90 rooms of the Residenz itself: the palace's spectacular banquet and reception halls, and the Wittelsbachs' lavish private apartments. The rooms are decorated with period (but generally not original) furniture: chandeliers, canopied beds, Louis XIV-style chairs, old clocks, tapestries, and dinnerware of porcelain and silver. It's the best place to glimpse the opulent lifestyle of Bavaria's late, great royal family. (Whatever happened to the Wittelsbachs, the longest continuously ruling family in European history? They're still around, but they're no longer royalty, so most of them have real jobs now—you may well have just passed one on the street.)

➏ **Self-Guided Tour:** The place is big. Follow the museum's prescribed route, using this section to hit the highlights and supplement it with the audioguide. Grab a free museum floor plan to help locate room numbers mentioned here. The route can vary because rooms are occasionally closed off.

• *One of the first "rooms" you encounter (it's actually part of an outdoor courtyard) is the...*

➊ **Shell Grotto** (Room 6): This artificial grotto is made of volcanic tuff and covered completely in Bavarian freshwater shells. In its day, it was an exercise in man controlling nature—a celebration of the Renaissance humanism that flourished in the 1550s. Mercury—the pre-Christian god of trade and business—oversees the action. Check out the statue in the courtyard—in the Wittelsbachs' heyday, red wine would have flowed from the mermaid's breasts and dripped from Medusa's severed head.

• *Before moving on, note the door marked OO, leading to handy WCs. Now continue into the next room, the...*

➋ **Antiquarium** (Room 7): This low, arched hall stretches 220 feet end to end. It's the oldest room in the Residenz, built around 1550. The room was, and still is, a festival banquet hall. The ruler presided from the raised dais at the near end (warmed by the fireplace). Two hundred dignitaries can dine here, surrounded by allegories of the goodness of just rule on the ceiling.

The hall is lined with busts of Roman emperors. In the mid-16th century, Europe's royal families (such as the Wittelsbachs) collected and displayed such busts, implying a connection between themselves and the enlightened ancient Roman rulers. There was such huge demand for these classical statues in the courts of Europe that many of the "ancient busts" were fakes cranked out by crooked Romans. Still, a third of the statuary you see here is original.

The small paintings around the room show 120 Bavarian villages as they looked in 1550. Even today, when a Bavarian historian wants a record of how his village once looked, he comes here. Notice the town of Dachau in 1550 (in the archway closest to the entrance door).

• *Keep going through a few more rooms, then up a stairway to the upper floor. Pause in the* **Black Hall** *(Room 13) to admire the head-spinning trompe l'oeil ceiling, which makes the nearly flat roof appear to be a much grander arched vault. From here, the prescribed route winds through a number of rooms surrounding a large courtyard.*

❸ **Upper Floor Apartments** (Rooms 14-45): In this series of rooms we get the first glimpse of the Residenz Museum's forte: chandeliered rooms decorated with ceiling paintings, stucco work, tapestries, parquet floors, and period furniture.

Rooms to the left of the Black Hall are the **Electoral Apartments** (Rooms 22-31), the private apartments of the monarch and his consort.

In the long **All Saints Corridor** (Room 32), you can glance into the adjoining All Saints' Chapel. This early-19th-century chapel, commissioned by Ludwig I, was severely damaged in World War II, didn't reopen until 2003, and is still being refurbished.

From the All Saints Corridor you can reach the **Charlotte Chambers/ Court-Garden Rooms,** a long row of impressive rooms across the courtyard from the Electoral Apartments, first used to house visiting rulers. Some of them later served as the private rooms of Princess Charlotte, Max Joseph's daughter.

• *Your visit eventually reaches a hallway—* ❹ *Room 45—where you have a choice: to the left is the "short" route that heads directly to the stunning Ornate Rooms (described later). But we'll take the "long" route to the right (starting in Room 47) that adds a dozen-plus rooms to your visit.*

❺ **The "Long" Route:** Use your Residenz-issued map to find some of the following highlights. The large **Imperial Hall** is in Room 111; the **Stone Rooms** (104-109) are so-called for their colorful marble—both real and fake. Then come several small rooms, where the centerpiece painting on the ceiling is just blank black, as no copy of the original survived World War II.

The **Reliquary Room** (Room 95) harbors a collection of gruesome Christian relics (bones, skulls, and even several mummified hands) in ornate golden cases.

The Antiquarium, the palace's banquet hall

Residenz Tour

Ground Floor

Odeonplatz

To Odeonsplatz [U]

100 Meters
100 Yards

Imperial Courtyard

Apothecary Courtyard

ACCESS TO CUVILLIÉS THEATER

RESIDENZ STRASSE

Chapel Courtyard

CUVILLIÉS THEATER ENTRANCE

CUVILLIÉS THEATER

COURT-CHAPEL

TOUR BEGINS

Grotto Courtyard

Fountain Courtyard

STAIRS FROM FIRST FLOOR

❶

❼

MUSEUM ENTRANCE

❷

COURT CHURCH OF ALL SAINTS

ACCESS TO MUSEUM & TREASURY

RESIDENZ MUSEUM*

TOUR ENDS

TICKETS

ACCESS TO MUSEUM & TREASURY

TREASURY ENTRANCE

TREASURY

STAIRS UP TO FIRST FLOOR

Max-Joseph-Platz

To Marienplatz

*Note: Residenz Museum is on two floors & extends over much of Residenz complex

---

First Floor

IMPERIAL HALL (ROOM 111)

RESIDENZ STRASSE

STONE ROOMS (ROOMS 104-109)

LONG ROUTE

Imperial Courtyard

Apothecary Courtyard

At this point go right to Long Route or left to Short Route (Direct to Ornate Rooms)

COURT CHAPEL (ROOMS 96 & 89)

❺

❹

CUVILLIÉS THEATER

MAX.I PRIVATE CHAPEL (ROOM 98)

Fountain Courtyard

RELIQUARY ROOM (ROOM 95)

❻

STAIRS DOWN TO GROUND FLOOR & EXIT

COURT CHURCH OF ALL SAINTS

HALLS OF THE NIBELUNGEN (CLOSED)

TREASURY

❸

STAIRS FROM GROUND FLOOR

---

❶ Shell Grotto
❷ Antiquarium
❸ Upper Floor Apartments
❹ Room 45

❺ The "Long" Route
❻ Ornate Rooms
❼ Porcelain Cabinet & Ancestral Gallery

• *A few more steps brings you to the balcony of the...*

Court Chapel (Rooms 96/89): Dedicated to Mary, this late-Renaissance/early-Baroque gem was the site of "Mad" King Ludwig's funeral after his mysterious murder—or suicide—in 1886. (He's buried in St. Michael's Church, described on page 738.) About 75 years earlier, in 1810, his grandfather and namesake (Ludwig I) was married here. After the wedding ceremony, carriages rolled his guests to a rollicking reception, which turned out to be such a hit that it became an annual tradition—Oktoberfest.

A couple of rooms ahead is the **Private Chapel of Maximilian I** (Room 98). Duke Maximilian I, the dominant Bavarian figure in the Thirty Years' War, built one of the most precious rooms in the palace. The miniature pipe organ (from about 1600) still works. The room is sumptuous, from the gold leaf and the fancy hinges to the miniature dome and the walls made of stucco "marble." Note the post-Renaissance perspective tricks decorating the walls; they were popular in the 17th century.

• *Whichever route you take—long or short—you'll eventually reach a set of rooms known as the...*

❻ Ornate Rooms (Rooms 55-62): As the name implies, these are some of the richest rooms in the palace. The Wittelsbachs were always trying to keep up with the Habsburgs, and these ceremonial rooms—used for official business—were designed to impress. The decor and furniture are Rococo—over-the-top Baroque. The family art collection, now in the Alte Pinakothek, once decorated these walls.

The rooms were designed in the 1730s by François de Cuvilliés, a Belgian who first attracted notice as the clever court dwarf for the Bavarian ruler. He was sent to Paris to study art and returned to become the court architect. Besides the Residenz, he designed the Cuvilliés Theater and the Amalienburg lodge at Nymphenburg Palace. Cuvilliés' style, featuring incredibly intricate stucco tracery twisted into unusual shapes, defined Bavarian Rococo. As you glide through this section of the palace, be sure to appreciate the gilded stucco ceilings above you.

Each room is unique. The **Green Gallery** (Room 58)—named for its green silk

Every Residenz room is unique and ornate.

damask wallpaper—was the ballroom. Imagine the parties they had here—aristocrats in powdered wigs, a string quartet playing Baroque tunes, a card game going on, while everyone admired the paintings on the walls or themselves reflected in the mirrors. The **State Bedroom** (Room 60), though furnished with a canopy bed, wasn't an actual bedroom—it was just for show. Rulers invited their subjects to come at morning and evening to stand at the railing and watch their boss ceremonially rise from his slumber to symbolically start and end the working day.

Perhaps the most ornate of these Ornate Rooms is the **Cabinet of Mirrors** (Room 61) and the adjoining **Cabinet of Miniatures** (Room 62) from 1740. In the Cabinet of Mirrors, notice the fun visual effects of the mirrors around you—the corner mirrors make things go on forever. Then peek inside the coral red room (the most royal of colors in Germany) and imagine visiting the duke and having him take you here to ogle miniature copies of the most famous paintings of the day, composed with one-haired brushes.

• *After exploring the Ornate Rooms (and the many, many other elaborate rooms here on the upper floor), find the staircase (near Room 65) that heads back downstairs. On the ground floor, you emerge in the long Ancestral Gallery (Room 4). Before walking down it, detour to the right, into Room 5.*

❼ **Porcelain Cabinet** (Room 5) and **Ancestral Gallery** (Room 4): In the 18th century, the royal family bolstered their status with an in-house porcelain works. See how the mirrors enhance the porcelain vases, creating the effect of infinite pedestals. If this inspires you to acquire some pieces of your own, head to the Nymphenburg Porcelain Store at Odeonsplatz (see page 769).

The Ancestral Gallery (Room 4) was built in the 1740s to display portraits of the Wittelsbachs. All official guests had to pass through here to meet the duke (and his 100 Wittelsbach relatives). The room's symbolism reinforced the Wittelsbachs' claims to being as powerful as the Habsburgs of Vienna.

Midway down the hall, find the family tree labeled (in Latin) "genealogy of an imperial family." The tree is shown being planted by Hercules to boost their royal street cred. Opposite the tree are two notable portraits: Charlemagne, the first Holy Roman Emperor, and to his right, Louis IV (wearing the same crown), the first Wittelsbach H.R.E., crowned in 1328. For the next 500 years, this lineage was used to substantiate the family's claim to power as they competed with the Habsburgs. (After failing to sort out their differences through strategic weddings, the two families eventually went to war.)

Allied bombs took their toll on this hall. The central ceiling painting has been restored, but since there were no photos documenting the other two ceiling paintings, those spots remain empty. Looking carefully at the walls, you can see how each painting was hastily cut from its frame. That's because—though most of Munich's museums were closed during World War II to prevent damage—the Residenz remained open to instill confidence in local people. It wasn't until 1944, when bombs were imminent, that the last-minute order was given to hide the paintings away.

• *Your Residenz Museum tour is over. The doorway at the end of the hall leads back to the museum entrance. If you're visiting the Cuvilliés Theater, from the exit walk straight through the courtyard to Residenzstrasse. Take a right and pass by the two green lions standing guard just ahead. Walk to the far end of the lane until you reach a fountain. Just above a doorway to the left you'll see a nondescript sign that says* Cuvilliés Theater.

CUVILLIÉS THEATER

In 1751, this was Germany's ultimate Rococo theater. Mozart conducted here several times. Designed by the same brilliant architect who designed the Ornate Rooms in the palace, this theater is dazzling enough to send you back to the days of divine monarchs.

It's an intimate, horseshoe-shaped performance venue, seating fewer than 400. The four tiers of box seats were for the four classes of society: city burghers on bottom, royalty next up (in the most elaborate seats), and lesser courtiers in the two highest tiers. The ruler occupied the large royal box directly opposite the stage. "Mad" King Ludwig II occasionally bought out the entire theater to watch performances here by himself.

François Cuvilliés' interior is exquisite. Red, white, and gold hues dominate. Most of the decoration is painted wood, even parts that look like marble. Even the proscenium above the stage—seemingly draped with a red-velvet "curtain"—is actually made of carved wood. Also above the stage is an elaborate Wittelsbach coat of arms. The balconies seem to be supported by statues of the four seasons and are adorned with gold garlands. Cuvilliés achieved the Rococo ideal of giving theater-goers a multimedia experience—uniting the beauty of his creation with the

beautiful performance on stage. It's still a working theater.

WWII bombs completely obliterated the old Cuvilliés Theater, which originally stood at a different location a short distance from here. Fortunately, much of the carved wooden interior had been removed from the walls and stored away for safekeeping. After the war, they built this entirely new building near the ruins of the old theater and paneled it with the original decor.

Near the Residenz
▲MUNICH CITY MUSEUM (MÜNCHNER STADTMUSEUM)

The museum's permanent exhibit on Munich's history is interesting, but it's exhaustive, and there's no posted English information. I'd use the following mini tour for an overview, then supplement it with the audioguide and English booklet.

Cost and Hours: €4 includes good audioguide, more for special (skippable) exhibits, Tue-Sun 10:00-18:00, closed Mon, ticket gets you half-price admission to Jewish History Museum, St.-Jakobs-Platz 1, tel. 089/2332-2370, www.muenchner-stadtmuseum.de. The

Cuvilliés Theater

humorous Servus Heimat souvenir shop in the courtyard is worth a stop.

Eating: The museum's recommended Stadt Café is handy for a good meal (see page 773).

Visiting the Museum: Start in the ticketing hall with the wooden model showing Munich today. Find the Frauenkirche, Isar River, New Town Hall, Residenz...and no skyscrapers. The city looks remarkably similar in scale to the model (in the next room) from 1570.

Ground Floor—Medieval: A big gray statue of Henry the Lion introduces us to the city's 12th-century founder. The eight statues of Morris dancers (1480) became a symbol of the vibrant market town (and the tradition continued with the New Town Hall glockenspiel's dancing coopers). On the rest of the ground floor, paintings, armor, and swords capture more medieval ambience.

First Floor—1800s: The "New Munich" was created when the city was expanded beyond the old medieval walls (see the illuminated view of the city from 1761 in the "Canaletto-Blick," opposite the top of the stairs). The city was prosperous, as evidenced by the furniture and paintings on display. In the center of the room, find big paintings ("Effigies") of the century's magnificent kings— Maximilian I, Maximilian II, and Ludwig I.

Second Floor—Munich 1900: As Munich approached its 700th birthday, it was becoming aware of itself as a major capital. The Münchner Kindl logo

was born. It was a city of artists (Wagner operas, Lenbach portraits, Von Stuck soirées), *Jugendstil* furniture, beer, and a cosmopolitan outlook (see the "emperor panorama," the big barrel-shaped 3-D peep show of African/Asian peoples). But after the destruction of World War I, Munich became a hotbed of discontent. The "revue" room shows the city's clash of ideas: communists, capitalists, Nazis, and the anarchic theater of comedian Karl Valentin and early works by playwright Bertolt Brecht. A nearby display gives some background on Munich's role as the birthplace of Nazism (much more thoroughly covered in the museum's National Socialism wing).

From here, you can detour upstairs to the **third floor puppet theater** to see an extensive collection of marionettes, Punch-and-Judy hand puppets, and paper cutouts of this unique Bavarian art form with a long cabaret tradition.

Back on the second floor, finish with a kaleidoscope of images capturing the contemporary Munich scene—rock music, World Cup triumphs, beer gardens, and other things that are..."typically Munich."

National Socialism Wing: This small but worthwhile exhibit of photos and uniforms takes you chronologically through the Nazi years, focused on Munich: the post-WWI struggles, Hitler's 1923 Beer Hall Putsch, his writing of *Mein Kampf*, the mass rallies in Königsplatz and Odeonsplatz, establishment of the Dachau concentration camp, and the destruction rained on Munich in World War II.

Museum Quarter (Kunstareal)

This quarter's cluster of blockbuster museums displays art spanning from 3000 B.C. right up to the present. Of the seven museums in the quarter, we'll focus on the top three: Egyptian Museum, Alte Pinakothek, and Neue Pinakothek. Most people don't come to Munich for the art,

Munich City Museum

Museum Quarter

but this group makes a case for the city's world-class status.

Getting There: Handy tram #27 whisks you right to the Pinakothek stop from Karlsplatz (between the train station and Marienplatz). You can also take bus #100 from the train station, or walk 10 minutes from the Theresienstrasse or Königsplatz stops on the U-2 line.

▲▲ALTE PINAKOTHEK

Bavaria's best painting gallery (the "Old Art Gallery," pronounced ALL-teh pee-nah-koh-TEHK) shows off a world-class collection of European masterpieces from the 14th to 19th century, starring the two tumultuous centuries (1450-1650) when Europe went from medieval to modern. See paintings from the Italian Renaissance (Raphael, Leonardo, Botticelli, Titian) and the German Renaissance it inspired (Albrecht Dürer). The Reformation of Martin Luther eventually split Europe into two subcultures—Protestants and Catholics—with their two distinct art styles

(exemplified by Rembrandt and Rubens, respectively). Because of a major renovation project, expect some galleries to be closed when you visit.

Cost and Hours: €4 during renovation (otherwise €7), €1 on Sun, open Tue 10:00-20:00, Wed-Sun until 18:00, closed Mon, free and excellent audioguide (€4.50 on Sun), pleasant Café Klenze; U-2: Theresienstrasse, tram #27, or bus #100; Barer Strasse 27, tel. 089/2380-5216, www.pinakothek.de/alte-pinakothek.

➲ **Self-Guided Tour:** All the paintings we'll see are on the upper floor, which is laid out like a barbell. This tour starts at one fat end and works its way through the "handle" to the other end. From the ticket counter, head up the stairway to the left to reach the first rooms.

German Renaissance (Room II): Albrecht Altdorfer's *The Battle of Issus (Schlacht bei Issus)* shows a world at war. Masses of soldiers are swept along in the currents and tides of a battle completely

Alte Pinakothek

To Neue Pinakothek

To Tram #27 Stop

ENTRANCE
(ON GROUND FLOOR)

SPANISH XIII							III N O R T H E R N
ITALIAN XII	17th C. DUTCH					ELEVATOR ⊠	**TOUR BEGINS**
	ITALIAN BAROQUE X	REMBRANDT IX	FLEMISH VIII	RUBENS ROOM VII	FLEMISH VI	VENETIAN PAINTING V	ITALIAN REN. IV	II
⊠ ← ELEVATOR						ELEVATOR → ⊠	A R T I
FRENCH XI	STAIRS DOWN TO ENTRANCE LOBBY (SHOP, CAFÉ & WC)			STAIRS UP FROM ENTRANCE LOBBY			EARLY DUTCH

BARER STRASSE

Grassy Lawn

To Königsplatz, Main Train Station & Egyptian Museum

50 Meters

50 Yards

To Pinakothek der Moderne

To Karlsplatz

---

beyond their control, their confused motion reflected in the swirling sky. Though the painting depicts Alexander the Great's history-changing victory over the Persians (find the Persian king Darius turning and fleeing), it could as easily have been Germany in the 1520s. Christians were fighting Muslims, peasants battled masters, and Catholics and Protestants were squaring off for a century of conflict. The armies melt into a huge landscape, leaving the impression that

Dürer, Self-Portrait in Fur Coat

the battle goes on forever.

Albrecht Dürer's larger-than-life *Four Apostles* (*Johannes und Petrus* and *Paulus und Marcus*) are saints of a radical new religion: Martin Luther's Protestantism. Just as Luther challenged Church authority, Dürer—a friend of Luther's—strips these saints of any rich clothes, halos, or trappings of power and gives them down-to-earth human features: receding hairlines, wrinkles, and suspicious eyes. The inscription warns German rulers to follow the Bible rather than Catholic Church leaders. The figure of Mark—a Bible in one hand and a sword in the other—is a fitting symbol of the dangerous times.

Dürer's *Self-Portrait in Fur Coat* (*Selbstbildnis im Pelzrock*) looks like Jesus Christ but is actually 28-year-old Dürer himself, gazing out, with his right hand solemnly giving a blessing. This is the ultimate image of humanism: the artist as an instrument of God's continued creation.

Italian Renaissance (Room IV): With the Italian Renaissance—the "rebirth" of interest in the art and learning of ancient Greece and Rome—artists captured the realism, three-dimensionality, and symmetry found in classical statues. Twenty-one-year-old Leonardo da Vinci's *Virgin*

Ⓐ *Leonardo da Vinci,* Virgin and Child
Ⓑ *Raphael,* Canigiani Holy Family
Ⓒ *Rubens,* Rubens and Isabella Brant

and Child (Maria mit dem Kinde) need no halos—they radiate purity. Mary is a solid pyramid of maternal love, flanked by Renaissance-arch windows that look out on the hazy distance. Baby Jesus reaches out to play innocently with a carnation, the blood-colored symbol of his eventual death.

Raphael's *Canigiani Holy Family (Die hl. Familie aus dem Hause Canigiani)* takes Leonardo's pyramid form and runs with it. Father Joseph forms the peak, with his staff as the strong central axis. Mary and Jesus (on the right) form a pyramid-within-the-pyramid, as do Elizabeth and baby John the Baptist on the left.

In Botticelli's *Lamentation over Christ (Die Beweinung Christi),* the Renaissance "pyramid" implodes, as the weight of the dead Christ drags everyone down, and the tomb grins darkly behind them.

Venetian Painting (Room V): In Titian's *Christ Crowned with Thorns (Die Dornenkrönung),* a powerfully built Christ sits, silently enduring torture by prison guards. The painting is by Venice's greatest Renaissance painter, but there's no symmetry, no pyramid form, and the brushwork is intentionally messy and Impressionistic. By the way, this is the first painting we've seen that is done on canvas rather than wood, as artists experimented with vegetable-oil-based paints.

Rubens and Baroque (Room VII): Europe's religious wars split the Continent in two—Protestants in the northern countries, Catholics in the south. (Germany itself was divided, with Bavaria remaining Catholic.) The Baroque style, popular in Catholic countries, featured large canvases, bright colors, lots of flesh, rippling motion, wild emotions, grand themes... and pudgy winged babies, the sure sign of Baroque. This room holds several canvases by the great Flemish painter Peter Paul Rubens.

In Rubens' 300-square-foot *Great Last Judgment (Das Grosse Jüngste Gericht),* Christ raises the righteous up to heaven (left side) and damns the sinners to hell (on the right). This swirling cycle of nudes was considered risqué and kept under wraps by the very monks who'd commissioned it.

Rubens and Isabella Brant shows the artist with his first wife, both of them the picture of health, wealth, and success. They lean together unconsciously, as people in love will do, with their hands clasped in mutual affection. When his first wife died, 53-year-old Rubens found a replacement—16-year-old Hélène Fourment, shown in an adjacent painting (just to the left) in her wedding dress. You may recognize Hélène's face in other Rubens paintings.

The Rape of the Daughters of Leucippus (*Der Raub der Töchter des Leukippos*) has many of Rubens' most typical elements—fleshy, emotional, rippling motion; bright colors; and a classical subject. The legendary twins Castor and Pollux crash a wedding and steal the brides as their own. The chaos of flailing limbs and rearing horses is all held together in a subtle X-shaped composition. Like the weaving counterpoint in a Baroque fugue, Rubens balances opposites.

Rembrandt and Dutch (Room IX): From Holland, Rembrandt van Rijn's *Six Paintings from the Life of Christ* are a down-to-earth look at supernatural events. The *Adoration (Die Anbetung der Hirten)* of Baby Jesus takes place in a 17th-century Dutch barn with ordinary folk as models. The canvases are dark brown, lit by strong light. The Adoration's light source is the Baby Jesus himself—literally the "light of the world." In the *Deposition (Kreuzabnahme)*, the light bounces off Christ's pale body onto his mother, Mary, who has fainted in the shadows, showing how his death also hurts her. The drama is underplayed, with subdued emotions. In the *Raising of the Cross (Kreuzaufrichtung)*, a man dressed in blue is looking on—a self-portrait of Rembrandt.

▲NEUE PINAKOTHEK

The Alte Pinakothek's younger sister is an easy-to-like collection located just across the street, showing paintings from 1800 to 1920. Breeze through a smattering of Romantics on your way to the museum's highlight: some world-class Impressionist paintings, and one of Van Gogh's *Sunflowers*.

Cost and Hours: €7, €1 on Sun, open Wed 10:00-20:00, Thu-Mon until 18:00, closed Tue, well-done audioguide is usually free but €4.50 on Sun, classy Café Hunsinger in basement spills into park; U-2: Theresienstrasse, tram #27, or bus #100; Barer Strasse 29, but enter on Theresienstrasse, tel. 089/2380-5195, www. pinakothek.de/neue-pinakothek.

Visiting the Museum: Pick up the audioguide and floor plan, and follow their prescribed route. Along the way, be sure to hit these highlights.

Rooms 1-3: In Room 1, Jacques-Louis David's curly-haired *Comtesse de Sorcy* shows the French noblewoman dressed in the ancient-Greek-style fashions popular during the Revolution. Room 3 features English painters—Turner's stormy seascapes and Gainsborough's contemplative *Mrs. Thomas Hibbert*. Nearby, you'll see other less-famous works by other major European artists.

Rooms 4-18: These rooms—the bulk of the museum—feature colorful, pretty, realistic (and mostly forgettable) paintings

Stieler, King Ludwig I in Coronation Robes *(detail)*

by German Romantics. In the remarkable *King Ludwig I in Coronation Robes* (Room 8), the young playboy king is both regal and rakish. (You can learn more on the king, the artist, and their Gallery of Beauties at Nymphenburg Palace; see page 764.) Caspar David Friedrich (Room 9) is Germany's best-known chronicler of the awe-inspiring power of nature (though these small canvases aren't his best). Carl Spitzweg's tiny *The Poor Poet* (Room 12) is often reproduced. Room 13 has huge (hard-to-miss) canvases: *The Destruction of Jerusalem by Titus* and the nationalist-themed *Thusnelda Led in Germanicus' Triumph*, showing a German noblewoman and her son, captured by the Romans, being paraded before the emperor.

Rooms 19-22: In these rooms, you'll find classic examples of all the Impressionist and Post-Impressionist masters: Degas' snapshots of women at work, Monet's sunny landscapes and water lilies, Manet's bourgeois Realism, Cézanne's still lifes, and Gauguin's languid Tahitian ladies. Van Gogh's *Sunflowers* is one of 11 such canvases he did.

In the final rooms, see works by Gustav Klimt and Munich's answer to Klimt, Franz von Stuck.

▲▲EGYPTIAN MUSEUM (STAATLICHES MUSEUM ÄGYPTISCHER KUNST)

To enjoy this museum, you don't need a strong interest in ancient Egypt (but you may have one by the time you leave). This new space was custom-made to evoke the feeling of being deep in an ancient tomb, from the wide staircase outside that descends to the narrow entry, to the twisty interior rooms that grow narrower and more catacomb-like as you progress. The museum's clever design creates a low-stress visit—just follow the one-way route marked by brass arrows in the floor.

Cost and Hours: €12, €6 on Sun, open Tue 10:00-20:00, Wed-Sun until 18:00, closed Mon; U-2 or U-8 to Königsplatz, tram #27 to Karolinenplatz, or bus #100 to Pinakothek stop; 10-minute walk from main train station, Gabelsbergerstrasse 35, tel. 089/2892-7630, www.smaek.de.

Near the River
▲ENGLISH GARDEN (ENGLISCHER GARTEN)

Munich's "Central Park," the largest urban park on the Continent, was laid out in 1789 by an American, Benjamin Thompson (who left New England when the American Revolution broke out). More than 100,000 locals commune with nature here on sunny summer days. The park stretches three miles from the center, past the university and the trendy Schwabing quarter. For the best quick visit, take bus #100 or tram #18 to the Nationalmuseum/Haus der Kunst stop. Under the bridge, you may see surfers. Follow the path, to the right of the surfing spot, downstream until you reach the big lawn. The Chinese Tower beer garden is just beyond the tree-covered hill to the right. Follow the oompah music and walk to the hilltop temple, with a postcard view of the city on your way. Afterward, instead of

Chinese Tower beer garden

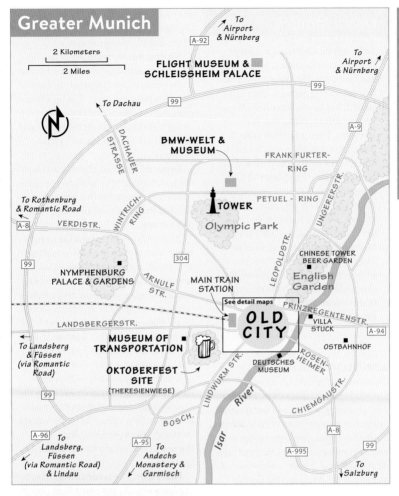

Greater Munich

To Airport & Nürnberg
A-92

FLIGHT MUSEUM & SCHLEISSHEIM PALACE

2 Kilometers
2 Miles

To Airport & Nürnberg

99

To Dachau

99

A-9

BMW-WELT & MUSEUM

FRANK FURTER-RING

DACHAUER STRASSE

To Rothenburg & Romantic Road
A-8

PETUEL - RING

TOWER
Olympic Park

WINTRICH-RING

VERDISTR.

UNGERERSTR.

LEOPOLDSTR.

99

NYMPHENBURG PALACE & GARDENS

304

ARNULF STR.

MAIN TRAIN STATION

CHINESE TOWER BEER GARDEN

English Garden

See detail maps
OLD CITY

PRINZREGENTENSTR.

VILLA STUCK

A-94

LANDSBERGERSTR.

To Landsberg & Füssen (via Romantic Road)

MUSEUM OF TRANSPORTATION

OKTOBERFEST SITE
(THERESIENWIESE)

LINDWURM STR.

ROSEN-HEIMER

OSTBAHNHOF

DEUTSCHES MUSEUM

99

BOSCH.

Isar River

CHIEMGAUSTR.

A-8

A-96 To Landsberg, Füssen (via Romantic Road) & Lindau

A-95 To Andechs Monastery & Garmisch

A-995

99

To Salzburg

English Garden

retracing your steps, you can walk (or take bus #54 a couple of stops) to the Giselastrasse U-Bahn station and return to town on the U-3 or U-6.

A rewarding respite from the city, the park is especially fun—and worth ▲▲—on a bike under the summer sun and on warm evenings (to rent some wheels, see page 784). Caution: While local law requires sun worshippers to wear clothes on the tram, the park is sprinkled with buck-naked sunbathers—quite a shock to prudish Americans (they're the ones riding their bikes into the river and trees).

Green Munich

Although the capital of a conservative part of Germany, Munich has long been a liberal stronghold. For nearly two decades, the city council has been controlled by a Social Democrat/Green Party coalition. The city policies are pedestrian-friendly—you'll find much of the town center closed to normal traffic, with plenty of bike lanes and green spaces. As you talk softly and hear birds rather than motors, it's easy to forget you're in the center of a big city. On summer Mondays, the peace and quiet make way for "blade Monday"—when streets in the center are closed to cars and as many as 30,000 inline skaters swarm around town in a giant rolling party.

▲ DEUTSCHES MUSEUM

Enjoy wandering through rooms of historic airplanes, spaceships, mining, the harnessing of wind and water power, hydraulics, musical instruments, printing, chemistry, computers, astronomy, and nanotechnology...it's the Louvre of technical know-how. The museum is dated, and not all the displays have English descriptions—but major renovations are under way. About a third of the collection will likely be closed during your visit, but with 11 acres of floor space and 10 miles of exhibits, even those on roller skates will still need to be selective. Use my mini tour to get oriented, then study the floor plan and choose which departments interest you.

Cost and Hours: €11, daily 9:00-17:00, worthwhile €7 English guidebook, tel. 089/21791, www.deutsches-museum.de.

Getting There: Take tram #16 to the Deutsches Museum stop. Alternatively, take the S-Bahn or tram #18 to Isartor,

then walk 300 yards over the river, following signs. (The entrance is near the far end of the building along the river.)

Visiting the Museum: After buying your ticket, ask about the day's schedule of demonstrations (for example, electric power or glass-blowing). Pick up a floor plan, then continue past the ticket taker, straight ahead, into a vast high-ceilinged room (Room 10) dominated by a tall-masted ship.

Ground Floor: Get oriented and locate the handy elevator behind you—it's one of the few elevators in this labyrinthine building that goes to all six floors. Now, let's explore.

Room 10's exhibit on **marine navigation** is anchored by the 60-foot sailing ship *Maria*. Take the staircase down, where you can look inside her cut-away hull and imagine life below decks. Before heading back upstairs, find the bisected U1 submarine (on the wall farthest from the entrance)—the first German *U-Boot* (undersea boat), dating from 1906.

Now make your way to several new technology exhibits—DNA and nano-technology. Children will enjoy the "Kinderreich" (downstairs in Room 24) and the exciting twice-daily high-voltage demonstrations (Room 9) showing the noisy creation of a five-foot bolt of lightning.

First Floor: The **aeronautics** collection occupies virtually the entire floor (Room 33). You'll see early attempts at flight—gliders, hot-air balloons, and a model of the airship pioneered by Germany's Count Zeppelin. The highlight is a Wright Brothers double-decker airplane from 1909—six years after their famous first flight, when they began to manufacture multiple copies of their prototype. By World War I, airplanes were becoming a formidable force. The Fokker tri-plane was made famous by Germany's war ace the Red Baron (Manfred von Richthofen, whose exploits, I've heard, prompted enemies to drop the f-bomb). The exhibit continues into WWII-era Junkers and Messer-schmitts and postwar passenger planes.

Second Floor: Gathered together near the main elevator, you'll find a replica of prehistoric **cave paintings** (Room 39) and daily **glass-blowing** demonstrations (Room 40).

Third Floor: The third floor traces the **history of measurement,** including time (from a 16th-century sundial and an 18th-century clock to a scary Black Forest wall clock complete with grim reaper), weights, and geodesy (surveying and mapping). In the computer section (Rooms 52-53), you go from the ancient abacus to a 1956 Univac computer—as big as a room, with a million components, costing a million dollars, and with less computing power than your smartphone.

Floors 4-6: If you have trouble finding your way to these floors, there's always that main elevator. The focus here is on **astronomy.** A light-show exhibit (Room 62) traces the evolution of the universe. The recently renovated planetarium (Room 63) requires a €2 extra ticket (purchase at the info desk beforehand)—but the lecture is in German. Finally, you emerge on the museum rooftop—the "sundial garden" (Room 64)—with great views. On a clear day, you can see the Alps.

▲▲Nymphenburg Palace Complex

For 200 years, this oasis of palaces and gardens just outside Munich was the Wittelsbach rulers' summer vacation home, a getaway from the sniping politics of court life in the city. Their kids could play, picnic, ride horses, and frolic in the ponds and gardens, while the adults played cards, listened to music, and sipped coffee on the veranda. It was at Nymphenburg that a 7-year-old Mozart gave a widely heralded concert, 60-year-old Ludwig I courted the femme fatale Lola Montez, and "Mad" King Ludwig II (Ludwig I's grandson) was born and baptized.

Today, Nymphenburg Palace and the surrounding one-square-mile park are a great place for a royal stroll or discreet picnic. Indoors, you can tour the Bavarian royal family's summer quarters and visit the Royal Stables Museum (carriages, sleighs, and porcelain). If you have time, check out playful extras, such as a hunting lodge (Amalienburg), bathhouse (Badenburg), pagoda (Pagodenburg), and fake ruins (Magdalenenklause). The complex also houses a humble natural history museum and Baroque chapel. Allow at least three hours (including travel time) to see the palace complex at a leisurely pace.

Cost and Hours: Palace–€6; combo-ticket–€11.50 (€8.50 off-season) covers the palace, Royal Stables Museum, and outlying sights open in summer. All of these sights are open daily April-mid-Oct 9:00-18:00, mid-Oct-March 10:00-16:00—except for Amalienburg and the other small palaces in the park, which are closed mid-Oct-March. The park is open daily 6:00-dusk and free to enter. Tel. 089/179-080, www.schloss-nymphenburg.de.

Getting There: The palace is three miles northwest of central Munich. Take tram #17 (direction: Amalienburgstrasse) from the north side of the train station (or catch it at Karlsplatz). In 15 minutes you reach the Schloss Nymphenburg stop. From the bridge by the tram stop, you'll see the palace—a 10-minute walk away. The palace is a pleasant 30-minute bike ride from the main train station (either follow Arnulfstrasse all the way to Nymphenburg, or turn up Landshuter Allee—at Donersburgerbrücke—then follow Nymphenburger Strasse until you hit the canal that stretches to the palace). Biking in the palace grounds is not permitted.

Eating: A café serves lunches in the former palm house, behind and to the right of the palace (open year-round). More eating options are near the tram stop.

NYMPHENBURG PALACE

In 1662, after 10 years of trying, the Bavarian ruler Ferdinand Maria and his wife, Henriette Adelaide of Savoy, finally had a son, Max Emanuel. In gratitude for a male heir, Ferdinand gave this land to his Italian wife, who proceeded to build an Italian-style Baroque palace. Their son expanded the palace to today's size. (Today's Wittelsbachs, who still refer to themselves as "princes" or "dukes," live in one wing of the palace.)

The palace interior, while interesting, is much less extensive than Munich's Residenz—you can visit only 16 rooms. The place is stingy on free information; you'll need the serviceable audioguide if you'd like more info than what I've provided below.

◐ **Self-Guided Tour:** Your visit starts in the **Great Hall** (a.k.a. **Stone Hall**). As the central room of the palace, this light and airy space was the dining hall, site of big Wittelsbach family festivals. One of the grandest and best-preserved Rococo rooms in Bavaria (from about 1758), it sports elaborate stucco work and a ceiling fresco by Johann Baptist Zimmermann (of Wieskirche fame).

Zimmerman's fresco opens a sunroof to the heavens, where Greek gods cavort. In the sunny center, Apollo drives his chariot to bring the dawn, while bearded Zeus (astride an eagle) and peacock-carrying Juno look on. The rainbow symbolizes the peace brought by the enlightened Wittelsbachs. Around the borders of the painting, notice the fun optical illusions: For example, a painted dog holds a stucco bird in its mouth. The painting's natural setting and joie de vivre reflect the pastoral pleasures enjoyed here at the Wittelsbachs' summer home. At one end of the fresco (away from the windows) lounges a lovely maiden with flowers in her hair: it's Flora, the eponymous nymph who inspired this "nymph's castle"—Nymphenburg.

From here, two wings stretch to the left and right. They're mirror images of one another: antechamber, audience chamber, bedchamber, and private living quarters. Guests would arrive here in the Great Hall for an awe-inspiring first impression, then make their way through a series of (also-impressive) waiting rooms for their date with the Wittelsbach nobility.

Nymphenburg Palace

Nymphenburg

200 Meters
200 Yards

CASCADE

WALL

TEMPLE

Badenburg
Lake

PAGODENBURG

Pagodenburg
Lake

BADENBURG

Nymphenburg
Park

← Canals

MAGDALENEN-
KLAUSE

Botanic
Garden

LARGE
PARTERRE

AMALIEN-
BURG

WALL

CAFÉ

MAIN
PALACE

QUEEN'S
WING

KING'S
WING

ROYAL STABLES
MUSEUM
(MARSTALLMUSEUM)

ENTRANCE,
TICKETS &
GREAT HALL

To Autobahn A-8
(Augsburg)

MUSEUM
OF MAN
& NATURE

MARIA-WARD-STR.

To Autobahn A-96
(Landsberg)

Pond

PORCELAIN
WORKS

WINTRICH-
RING

To
Olympiapark

WOTANSTR.

ROMANSTR.

AUFFAHRTSALLEE

AUFFAHRTSALLEE

SÜDLICHE

NÖRDLICHE

Romanplatz

Tram #17
to Munich

NOTBURGSTR.

Tram #17
from Munich

MENZINGERSTRASSE

ARNULFSTR.

← To Central Munich

• *The tour continues to the left (as you look out the big windows).*

North Wing (Rooms 2-9): Breeze quickly through this less interesting wing, filled with tapestries and Wittelsbach portraits (including curly-haired Max Emanuel, who built this wing). Pause in the long corridor lined with paintings of various Wittelsbach palaces. The ones of Nymphenburg show the place around 1720, back when there was nothing but countryside between it and downtown (and gondolas plied the canals). Imagine the logistics when the royal family—with their entourage of 200—decided to move out to the summer palace.

• *Return to the Great Hall and enter the other wing.*

South Wing (Rooms 10-20): Pass through the gold-and-white Room 10 and turn right into the red-walled Audience Chamber. The room calls up the exuberant time of Nymphenburg's founding couple, Ferdinand and Henriette. A portrait on the wall shows them posing together in their rich courtly dress. Another painting depicts them in a Greek myth: Henriette (as the moon-goddess Diana) leads little Max Emanuel by the hand, while Ferdinand (as her mortal lover Endymion)

receives the gift of a sword. The ceiling painting (of the earth goddess Cybele) and the inlaid table also date from the time of Nymphenburg's first family.

After admiring the Queen's Bedroom and Chinese lacquer cabinet, head down the long hall to **King Ludwig I's Gallery of Beauties.** The room is decorated top to bottom with portraits of 36 beautiful women (all of them painted by Joseph Stieler between 1827 and 1850). Ludwig I was a consummate girl-watcher.

Ludwig prided himself on his ability to appreciate beauty regardless of social rank. He enjoyed picking out the prettiest women from the general public and, with one of the most effective pickup lines of all time, inviting them to the palace for a portrait. Who could refuse? The portraits were on public display in the Residenz, and catapulted their subjects to stardom. The women range from commoners to princesses, but notice that they share one physical trait—Ludwig obviously preferred brunettes. The portraits are done in the modest and slightly sentimental Biedermeier style popular in central Europe, as opposed to the more flamboyant Romanticism (so beloved of Ludwig's "mad" grandson) also thriving at that time.

The Great Hall has remained unchanged since 1758.

Most of these portraits have rich stories behind them, none more than the portrait of Lola Montez, the king's most notorious mistress. The portrait shows her the year she met Ludwig (she was 29, he was 60), wearing the black-lace mantilla and red flowers of a Spanish dancer. (And where in the "gallery of beauties" is the portrait of Ludwig's wife, Queen Therese? She's not here...you'll have to duck into the elegant, green Queen's Study to see her portrait.)

Pass through the blue Audience Room (with elaborate curtain rods and mahogany furniture in the French-inspired Empire style) and into the (other) **Queen's Bedroom.** The room has much the same furniture it had on August 25, 1845, when Princess Marie gave birth to the future King Ludwig II. Little Ludwig (see his bust, next to brother Otto's) was greatly inspired by Nymphenburg—riding horses in summer, taking sleigh rides in winter, reading poetry at Amalienburg. The love of nature and solitude he absorbed at Nymphenburg eventually led Ludwig to abandon Munich for his castles in the remote Bavarian countryside. By the way, note the mirror in this bedroom. Royal births were carefully witnessed, and the mirror allowed for a better view. While

Stieler, Lola Montez *(detail)*

Ludwig's birth was well-documented, his death was shrouded in mystery.

PALACE GROUNDS

The wooded grounds extend far back beyond the formal gardens and are popular with joggers and walkers (biking is not allowed). Find a bench for a low-profile picnic. The park is laced with canals and small lakes, where court guests once rode on Venetian-style gondolas.

ROYAL STABLES MUSEUM (MARSTALLMUSEUM)

These former stables (to the left of the main palace as you approach the complex) are full of gilded coaches that will make you think of Cinderella's journey to the king's ball. Upstairs, a porcelain exhibit shows off some of the famous Nymphenburg finery. If you don't want to visit the main palace, you can buy a €4.50 ticket just for this museum (no audioguide available).

Visiting the Museum: Wandering through the collection, you can trace the evolution of **300 years of coaches**— getting lighter and with better suspension as they were harnessed to faster horses. In the big entrance hall is a golden carriage drawn by eight fake white horses. In 1742, it carried Karl Albrecht Wittelsbach to Frankfurt to be crowned Holy Roman Emperor. As emperor, he got eight horses—kings got only six. The event is depicted in a frieze on the museum wall; Karl's carriage is #159.

Other objects bear witness to the good times of the relaxed Nymphenburg lifestyle. You'll see the sleigh of Max Emanuel, decorated with a carved Hercules. The carousel (not always on display) was for the royal kids.

Next up are things owned by Ludwig II—several sleighs, golden carriages, and (in the glass cases) harnesses. Ludwig's over-the-top coaches were Baroque. But this was 1870. The coaches, like the king, were in the wrong century.

Head upstairs to a collection of

Nymphenburg porcelain. Historically, royal families such as the Wittelsbachs liked to have their own porcelain factories to make fit-for-a-king plates, vases, and so on. The Nymphenburg Palace porcelain works is still in operation (their factory store on Odeonsplatz is happy to see you). Find the large room with copies of 17th-century Old Masters' paintings from the Wittelsbach art collection (now at the Alte Pinakothek). Ludwig I had these paintings copied onto porcelain for safekeeping into the distant future. Take a close look—they're exquisite.

AMALIENBURG

Three hundred yards from Nymphenburg Palace, hiding in the park (head into the sculpted garden and veer to the left, following signs), you'll find a fine little Rococo hunting lodge, which takes just a few minutes to tour. In 1734, Elector Karl Albrecht had it built for his wife, Maria Amalia. Amalienburg was designed by François de Cuvilliés (of Residenz fame) and decorated by Johann Baptist Zimmermann. It's the most worthwhile of the four small "extra" palaces buried in the park that are included on the combo-ticket. The others are the Pagodenburg, a Chinese-inspired pavilion; Badenburg, an opulent bathing house and banquet hall; and the Magdalenenklause, a mini palace that looks like a ruin from the outside but has an elaborate altar and woody apartments inside.

Visiting Amalienburg: As you

approach, circle to the front and notice the facade. Above the pink-and-white grand entryway, Diana, goddess of the chase, is surrounded by themes of the hunt and flanked by busts of satyrs. The queen would shoot from the perch atop the roof. Behind a wall in the garden, dogs would scare nonflying pheasants. When they jumped up in the air above the wall, the sporting queen—as if shooting skeet—would pick the birds off.

Tourists now enter this tiny getaway through the back door. Doghouses under gun cupboards fill the first room. In the fine yellow-and-silver bedroom, the bed is flanked by portraits of Karl Albrecht and Maria Amalia—decked out in hunting attire. She liked her dogs. The door under the portrait leads to stairs to the rooftop pheasant-shooting perch.

The mini Hall of Mirrors is a blue-and-silver commotion of Rococo nymphs designed by Cuvilliés. In the next room, paintings depict court festivities, formal hunting parties, and no-contest kills (where the animal is put at an impossible disadvantage—like shooting fish in a barrel). Finally, the kitchen is decorated with Chinese-style drawings on Dutch tile.

Outside the Center

▲▲BMW-WELT AND MUSEUM

At the headquarters of BMW ("beh-em-VEH" to Germans), Beamer dreamers can visit two space-age buildings to learn more about this brand's storied heritage.

Royal Stables Museum

Amalienburg

The renowned *Autos* and *Motorräder* are beautifully displayed (perhaps even fetishized), but visitors who aren't car enthusiasts might find them less impressive. This vast complex—built on the site of Munich's first airstrip and home to the BMW factory since 1920—has four components: the headquarters (in the building nicknamed "the Four Cylinders"—not open to the public), the factory (tourable with advance reservations), the showroom (called BMW-Welt—"BMW World"), and the BMW Museum.

Cost and Hours: Museum—€10, Tue-Sun 10:00-18:00, closed Mon; BMW-Welt showroom—free, daily 9:00-18:00, tel. 089/125-016-001, www.bmw-welt.com/en.

Tours: English tours are offered of both the museum (€13, 1.5 hours, call ahead for times) and BMW-Welt (€7, daily at 14:00, 80 minutes). Factory tours must be booked at least two months in advance (€8, 2.5 hours, Mon-Fri only, ages 7 and up, book by calling 089/125-016-001, more info at www.bmw-werk-muenchen.de; ask at the BMW-Welt building about can-cellations—open spots are released to the public 15 minutes before each tour).

Getting There: It's easy: Ride the U-3 to Olympia-Zentrum; the stop faces the BMW-Welt entry. To reach the museum, walk through BMW-Welt and over the swoopy bridge. This area also makes for a pleasant destination by bike, and is easily reached, and well-signed, from the English Garden.

Visiting the BMW-Welt: The futuristic, bowl-shaped **BMW Museum** encloses a world of floating walkways linking exhibits highlighting BMW motorcycle and car design and technology through the years. The museum traces the Bavarian Motor Works' history since 1917, when the company began making airplane engines. Motorcycles came next, followed by the first BMW sedan in 1929. You'll see how design was celebrated here from the start. Exhibits showcase motorsports, roadsters, and luxury cars. Stand on an *E* for English to hear the chief designer talk about his favorite cars in the "treasury." And the 1956 BMW 507 is enough to rev almost anyone's engine.

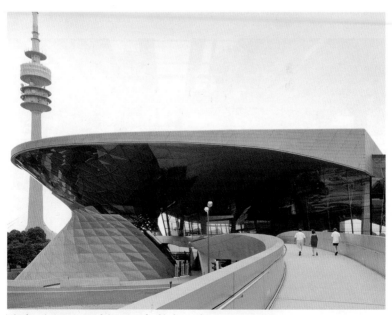

The futuristic BMW-Welt is a one-of-a-kind auto showroom.

The **BMW-Welt** building itself—a cloud-shaped, glass-and-steel architectural masterpiece—is reason enough to visit. It's free and filled with exhibits designed to enthuse car lovers so they'll find a way to afford a Beamer. While the adjacent museum reviews the BMW past, BMW-Welt shows you the present and gives you a breathtaking look at the future. This is where customers come to pick up their new Beamers (stand on the sky bridge to watch in envy), and where hopeful customers-to-be come to nurture their automotive dreams.

EXPERIENCES

Oktoberfest

A carnival of beer, pretzels, and wurst that draws visitors from all over the globe, Oktoberfest lasts just over two weeks, usually starting on the third Saturday in September and ending on the first Sunday in October (www.oktoberfest.de). It's held at the Theresienwiese fairground south of the main train station, in a meadow known as the "Wies'n" (VEE-zen), where about 15 huge tents can each seat several thousand beer drinkers. The festivities kick off with an opening parade, followed by a two-week frenzy of drinking, dancing, music, and food. A million gallons of beer later, they roast the last ox.

If you'll be here during the festivities, reserve a room early. During the fair, the city functions even better than normal, but is admittedly more expensive and crowded. It's a good time to sightsee, even if beer-hall rowdiness isn't your cup of tea.

The enormous beer tents are often full, especially on weekends—if possible, avoid going on a Friday or Saturday night. For some cultural background, hire a local guide (see page 728) or go with a group (Radius Tours, for example, offers a €110 tour that includes two beers, half a chicken, and guaranteed seating, Sun-Fri at 10:00, no tours on Sat, reserve ahead, www.radiustours.com; Size Matters Beer Tour runs one for €120, includes breakfast, lunch, four beers, and reserved seating, www.sizemattersbeertour.de).

In the city center, the humble **Beer and Oktoberfest Museum** (Bier- und Oktoberfestmuseum), offers exhibits and artifacts on the origins of the celebration and the centuries-old quest for the perfect beer (apparently achieved in Munich). The oldest house in the city center, the museum's home is noteworthy in itself (€4, Tue-Sat 13:00-18:00, closed Sun-Mon, between the Isartor and Viktualienmarkt at Sterneckerstrasse 2, tel. 089/2423-1607, www.bier-und-oktoberfestmuseum.de).

Rick's Tip: *The Theresienwiese fairground also hosts a* **Spring Festival** *(Frühlingsfestival, two weeks in late April-early May, www.fruehlingsfest-muenchen.de), and* **Tollwood,** *an artsy, multicultural event held twice a year—once in summer (late June-July) and in winter (alternative Christmas market, late Nov-Dec, www.tollwood.de).*

Shopping

The most glamorous shopping area is around Marienplatz. It's fun to window shop, even if you have no plans to buy.

The upscale **Ludwig Beck** department store, with six floors of designer clothing, has been a local institution since 1861 (Mon-Sat 9:30-20:00, closed Sun, Marienplatz).

The third floor of department store **Loden-Frey Verkaufshaus** is dedicated to classic Bavarian wear (*Trachten*) for

men and women (Mon-Sat 10:00-20:00, closed Sun, a block west of Marienplatz at Maffeistrasse 7, tel. 089/210-390, www.loden-frey.com).

The **Nymphenburg Porcelain Store** carries contemporary and classic dinnerware and figurines (Mon-Sat 10:00-18:00, closed Sun, Odeonsplatz 1, tel. 089/282-428, www.nymphenburg.com).

The **Hugendubel bookstore** on Karlsplatz has some English offerings (Mon-Sat 10:00-20:00, closed Sun, Karlsplatz 12, tel. 089-3075-7575, www.hugendubel.de).

Nightlife

Here are a few nightlife alternatives to the beer hall scene. Ballet and opera fans can check the schedule at the **Bayerisch Staatsoper,** centrally located next door to the Residenz. Book at least two months ahead—seats range from €13 to pricey (Max-Joseph-Platz 2, tel. 089/2185-1920, www.bayerische.staatsoper.de). The **Hotel Bayerischerhof's** posh nightclub hosts major jazz acts plus pop/soul/disco (Promenadeplatz 2, tel. 089/212-0994, www.bayerischerhof.de). For Broadway-style musicals (most in German), try the **Deutsches Theatre,** located near the train station (Schwanthalerstrasse 13, tel. 089/5523-4444, www.deutsches-theater.de).

EATING

Munich's cuisine is traditionally seasoned with beer. In beer halls, beer gardens, or at the Viktualienmarkt, try the most typical meal in town: *Weisswurst* (white-colored veal sausage—peel off the skin before eating, often available only until noon) with *süsser Senf* (sweet mustard), a salty *Brezel* (pretzel), and *Weissbier* ("white" wheat beer). Another traditional favorite is *Obatzda* (a.k.a. *Obatzter*), a mix of soft cheeses, butter, paprika, and often garlic or onions that's spread on bread. *Brotzeit*, literally "bread time," gets you a wooden platter of cold cuts,

770

MUNICH EATING

cheese, and pickles and is a good option for a light dinner.

Beer Halls and Gardens

For those in search of the boisterous, cli-chéd image of the beer hall, nothing beats the Hofbräuhaus (the only beer hall in town where you'll find oompah music). Locals prefer the innumerable beer gardens. On a warm day, when you're looking for the authentic outdoor beer-garden experience, your best options are the Augustiner (near the train station), the small beer garden at the Viktualienmarkt (near Marienplatz), or the sea of tables in the English Garden.

Rick's Tip: *By law,* **any place serving beer** *must admit the public (whether or not they're customers) to* **use the bathrooms.**

Near Marienplatz

The **$$ Hofbräuhaus** (HOAF-broy-howz) is the world's most famous beer hall. While it's grotesquely touristy, it's a Munich must. Drop by anytime for a large or light meal or just for a drink. Choose

from four zones: the rowdy main hall on the ground floor, a quieter courtyard under the stars, a dainty restaurant with mellow music one floor up, or the giant festival hall under a big barrel vault on the top floor. They sell beer by the *Mass* (one-liter mug, €8)—and they claim to sell 10,000 of these liters every day. Live oompah music plays at lunch and dinner (daily 9:00-23:30, 5-minute walk from Marienplatz at Platzl 9, tel. 089/2901-3610, www.hofbraeuhaus.de).

$$$ Wirtshaus Ayingers, just across the street from the Hofbräuhaus, is less chaotic. It serves quality Bavarian food—especially the schnitzels—and beer from Aying, a village south of Munich. There's lively outside seating on the cobbles facing the tourist chaos or a simple woody interior (€14-18 main courses, daily 11:00-24:00, Platzl 1a, tel. 089/2370-3666, www.ayingers.de).

$$ Andechser am Dom, at the rear of the twin-domed Frauenkirche on a breezy square, is a local staple serving Andechs beer and great food to appreciative regulars. Münchners favor the dark beer (ask for *dunkles*), but I love the light (*helles*). The *Gourmetteller* is a great sampler of

Munich's Beer Scene

In Munich's beer halls (*Brauhäuser*) and beer gardens (*Biergartens*), meals are inexpensive, white radishes are salted and cut in delicate spirals, and surly beer maids pull mustard packets from their cleavage. Beer is truly a people's drink— and the best is in Munich. The big question among connoisseurs is "Which brew today?"

Huge liter beers (*ein Mass* or "*ein* pitcher") cost about €8. You can order your beer *helles* (light), *dunkles* (dark), or ask for a *Weiss* or *Weizen* ("white" or wheat-based beer—cloudy and sweet) or a *Radler* (half lemon soda, half beer).

Beer-hall food is usually *selbstdienst* (self-service)—a sign may say *Bitte bedienen Sie sich selbst* (please serve yourself). If two prices are listed, *Schank* is for self-service, while *Bedienung* is for table service. At a large *Biergarten*, assemble your dream feast by visiting various counters, marked by type of food (*Bier* or *Bierschänke* for beer, *Bratwürste* for sausages, *Brotzeiten* for lighter fare served cold, and so on). Look for these specialties:

Fleischpfanzerl (or *Fleischklösse* or *Frikadellen*): Meatballs
Grosse Brez'n: Gigantic pretzel
Hendl (or *Brathähnchen*): Roasted chicken
Radi: Radish thinly spiral-cut and salted
Schweinrollbraten: Pork belly
Schweinshax'n (or *Hax'n*): Pork knuckle
Spareribs: Spareribs
Steckerlfisch: A whole fish (usually mackerel) herbed and grilled on a stick

their specialties, but you can't go wrong with *Rostbratwurst* with kraut (€8-20 main courses, daily 10:00-24:00, Weinstrasse 7a, reserve during peak times, tel. 089/2429-2920, www.andechser-am-dom.de).

$$ Nürnberger Bratwurst Glöckl am Dom, around the corner from Andechser am Dom, offers a more traditional, fiercely Bavarian evening. Dine outside under the trees or in the dark, medieval interior. Enjoy the tasty little *Nürnberger* sausages with kraut (€10-20 main courses, daily 10:00-24:00, Frauenplatz 9, tel. 089/291-9450, www.bratwurst-gloeckl.de).

$$$ Altes Hackerhaus serves its traditional Bavarian fare with a slightly fancier feel in one of the oldest buildings in town. It offers a small courtyard and a fun forest of characteristic nooks. This place is greatly appreciated for its Hacker-Pschorr beer (€8-10 wurst dishes, €9-25 main courses,

daily 10:30-24:00, Sendlinger Strasse 14, tel. 089/260-5026, www.hackerhaus.de).

Munich's **$$$ Ratskeller** fills the City Hall's vast cellar and also has some tables in the courtyard with 360-degree views. While it's hectic and touristy, locals still enjoy the timeless atmosphere (€14-24 main courses, daily 10:00-24:00, Marienplatz 8, tel. 089/219-9890, www.ratskeller.com).

$$$ Der Pschorr, an upscale beer hall occupying a former slaughterhouse, has a terrace overlooking the Viktualienmarkt and serves what many consider Munich's finest beer. With organic "slow food" and chilled glasses, this place mixes modern with classic dishes. The sound of the hammer tapping wooden kegs every few minutes lets patrons know their beer is good and fresh (€15-25 main courses, daily 10:00-24:00, Viktualienmarkt 15, at end of Schrannenhalle, tel. 089/442-383-940, www.der-pschorr.de).

The small **$ beer garden** at the center of the Viktualienmarkt has just about the best budget eating in town; it's just steps from Marienplatz. There's table service wherever you see a tablecloth; to picnic, choose a table without one—but you must buy a drink from the counter (daily 10:00-22:00). Countless stalls surround the beer garden and sell wurst, sandwiches, and produce.

Rick's Tip: *Most beer gardens have a €1* **deposit (Pfand) for their big glass steins.** *When you're finished drinking, take the mug and your deposit token (Pfandmarke) to the return man (Pfandrückgabe) for your refund. If you buy a bottled beer, pour it into the glass before you check out; otherwise you'll pay two deposits (one for the glass, the other for the bottle).*

$$$ Spatenhaus has served elegant food in a woody setting since 1896—maybe it's not even right to call its almost refined restaurant a "beer hall." You can also eat outside, on the square facing the opera and palace. It's pricey, but you won't find better Bavarian cuisine. The upstairs restaurant is a more formal dining room—reservations are advised (€15-30 main courses, daily 9:30-24:00, on Max-Joseph-Platz opposite opera, Residenzstrasse 12, tel. 089/290-7050, www.spatenhaus.de).

Near the Train Station

$$ Augustiner Beer Garden, a true under-the-leaves beer garden packed with Münchners, is a delight. In fact, most Münchners consider Augustiner the best beer garden in town—which may be why it has 5,000 seats. There's no music, it's away from the tourist hordes, and it serves up great beer, good traditional food, huge portions, reasonable prices, and perfect conviviality. The outdoor self-service ambience is best, making this place ideal on a nice summer evening (figure €15

for a main course and a drink). Parents with kids can sit at tables adjoining a sizable playground. There's also indoor and outdoor seating at a more expensive restaurant with table service (daily 11:00-24:00, Arnulfstrasse 52, 3 looooong blocks from station going away from the center—or take tram #16/#17 one stop to Hopfenstrasse, tel. 089/594-393, www.augustinerkeller.de).

$$ Park Café is a nice hideaway, tucked inside the Alter Botanischer Garden, just north of the train station. When it's hot, the prime spot is the beer garden out back, where you can also order Bavarian food from self-service counters or classy cocktails and cuisine from an international menu (€9-20 main courses). The indoor section is modern and cozy and features DJs or live music in the late evening (daily 10:00-24:00, beer garden opens at 11:30, Sophienstrasse 7, tel. 089/5161-7980, www.parkcafe089.de).

In the English Garden

For outdoor ambience and a cheap meal, spend an evening at **$$ Chinese Tower beer garden** (*Chinesischer Turm Biergarten*). You're welcome to B.Y.O. food and grab one of the 6,000 seats, or buy from the food stalls. This is a fine opportunity to try a *Steckerlfisch*, sold at a separate kiosk (daily, long hours in good weather, usually live music, playground, tel. 089/383-8730, www.chinaturm.de; take tram #18 from main train station or Sendlinger Tor to Tivolistrasse, or U-3 or U-6 to Giselastrasse and then bus #54 or #154 two stops).

Restaurants

Man does not live by beer alone. Well, maybe some do. But here are some alternatives for the rest of us.

On and near Marienplatz

$$$ Glockenspiel Café is good for a coffee or a meal with a bird's-eye view down on the Marienplatz action—I'd come for the view more than the food (€12-24 main courses, Mon-Sat 9:00-24:00, Sun 10:00-19:00, ride elevator from Rosenstrasse entrance, opposite glockenspiel at Marienplatz 28, tel. 089/264-256).

$$ Blatt Salate is a self-serve salad bar on a side street between the Frauenkirche and the New Town Hall; it's a great little hideaway for a healthy, quick lunch (€12-14 vegetarian and meat salads and soups, Mon-Fri 11:00-21:30, Sat until 18:00, closed Sun, Schäfflerstrasse 7, tel. 089/2102-0281).

Around the Viktualienmarkt

$$ Restaurant Opatija, in the Viktualienmarkt passage a few steps from Marienplatz, is homey and efficient, with an eclectic mix of Italian, Balkan, and German favorites. Choose between the comfortable indoor section and the outdoor seating in a quiet courtyard. It's family-friendly, and they offer takeout (good €7-8 pizzas, €8-13 main courses, daily 11:30-21:30, enter the passage at Viktualienmarkt 6 or Rindermarkt 2, tel. 089/2323-1995).

$ Die Münchner Suppenküche ("Munich Soup Kitchen"), a self-service soup joint at the Viktualienmarkt, is fine for a small, cozy sit-down lunch at picnic tables under a closed-in awning. The maroon chalkboard lists the soups

of the day—I go for the goulash or the carrot soup (€4-6 soup meals, Mon-Sat 10:00-18:00, closed Sun, near corner of Reichenbachstrasse and Frauenstrasse, tel. 089/260-9599).

Stadt Café is a lively café serving healthy fare with an inventive mix of Italian, German, vegetarian, salads, and a big selection of cakes by the slice. This no-frills restaurant draws newspaper readers, stroller moms, and locals meeting for a drink. Dine in the quiet cobbled courtyard, inside, or outside facing the new synagogue (daily specials for €7-12, daily 10:00-24:00, in same building as Munich City Museum, St.-Jakobs-Platz 1, tel. 089/266-949).

$$$ Prinz Myshkin Vegetarian Restaurant is an upscale vegetarian eatery in the old center. The seasonal menu is clever and appetizing, the arched ceilings are cool, and the outside seating is on a quiet street. They also have vegetarian sushi, pastas, Indian dishes, and their own baker, so they're proud of their sweets (€14-20 main courses, daily 11:00-23:00, Hackenstrasse 2, tel. 089/265-596).

Sebastiansplatz is a long, pedestrianized square between the Viktualienmarkt and the synagogue, lined with **$$ bistros** handy for a quick lunch. All serve €10 main courses on the busy cobbled square or inside—just survey the scene and choose. The **Schrannenhalle,** the former grain exchange overlooking the square, is busy with creative, modern eateries and gourmet delis (Mon-Sat 10:00-20:00, closed Sun).

Near Odeonsplatz

Café Luitpold is where Munich's high society comes to sip its coffee and nibble on exquisite cakes. The café is proudly home to the original *Luitpoldtorte*—sponge cake with layers of marzipan and buttercream, covered in dark chocolate (Tue-Sat 8:00-23:00, Sun-Mon 9:00-19:00, Brienner Strasse 11, tel. 089/242-8750).

Munich Restaurants

100 Meters

100 Yards

NEUE PINAKOTHEK

THERESIENSTRASSE

ALTE PINAKOTHEK

MUSEUM BRANDHORST

GABELSBERGERSTRASSE

ROTTMANNSTR.

LENBACHHAUS

GLYPTOTHEK

EGYPTIAN MUSEUM

PINAKOTHEK DER MODERNE

BRIENNER STRASSE

To Olympic Park, BMW-Welt and Museum & Dachau

Königs-platz

Königsplatz

ANTIKEN-SAMMLUNGEN

Karolinen-platz

OBELISK

BRIENNER STRASSE

Platz der Opfer des National-sozialismus

KARLSTRASSE

NAZI DOCUMENTATION CENTER

20

BASILIKA ST. BONIFAZ

KARLSTRASSE

MARSSTRASSE

11

Alter Botanischer Garten

MAXIMILIANSPLATZ

HIRTENSTR.

To Central Bus Station (ZOB) &

10

ELISENSTR.

Lenbach-platz

Karlsplatz

Promenade-platz

RADIUS TOURS OFFICE

Haupt-bahnhof

JUSTIZPALAST

PRIELMAYERSTR.

MAXBURGSTRASSE

FRAUEN-KIRCHE

3

EURAIDE

TRAIN STATION

Karls-platz

ST MICHAEL'S

Frauen-platz

4

SCHÜTZENSTR.

POST

Karls-platz

KARLS-TOR

NEUHAUSER STR.

KAUFINGERST.

BAYERSTRASSE

To Landsberg via A-96

SCHLOSSERSTR.

A.-KOLPING-STR.

HERZOGSPITALSTR.

POST

SCHWANTHALERSTRASSE

DEUTSCHES THEATER

LANDWEHRSTRASSE

22

DAMEN-STIFTS-KIRCHE

JOSEPHSPITALSTR.

5

HACKEN

17

ASAM CHURCH

16

CITY MUSEUM

21

POST

SONNENSTRASSE

SENDLINGER TOR

JEWISH SYNAGOGUE & HISTORY MUSEUM

PETTENKOFERSTRASSE

Sendlinger Tor Platz

NUSSBAUMSTRASSE

MATTHÄUS-KIRCHE

Sendlinger Tor

BLUMENSTRASSE

Beethoven-platz

To Garmisch via A-95

LINDWURMSTRASSE

AUGSBURGERSTR.

REISINGERSTR.

1 Hofbräuhaus Beer Hall

2 Wirtshaus Ayingers

3 Andechser am Dom

4 Nürnberger Bratwurst Glöckl am Dom

5 Altes Hackerhaus

6 Ratskeller

7 Der Pschorr Beer Hall

8 Viktualienmarkt Beer Garden & Die Münchner Suppenküche

9 Spatenhaus Beer Hall

10 To Augustiner Beer Garden

11 Park Café

12 To Chinese Tower Beer Garden

13 Glockenspiel Café

14 Blatt Salate

15 Restaurant Opatija

16 Stadt Café

17 Prinz Myshkin Veggie Rest.

18 Sebastiansplatz

19 Schrannenhalle

20 Café Luitpold

21 La Vecchia Masseria

22 Altin Dilim

23 Dallmayr's

Near the Train Station

$$ La Vecchia Masseria, between Sendlinger Tor and the train station hotels, serves Italian food inside amid cozy Tuscan farmhouse decor, or outside in a beautiful flowery courtyard (€6-8 pizza or pasta, €14-16 main courses, daily 11:30-23:30, reservations smart, Mathildenstrasse 3, tel. 089/550-9090).

$$ Altin Dilim, a cafeteria-style Turkish restaurant, is a standout among the many hole-in-the-wall Middle Eastern places near the station. A handy pictorial menu helps you order (€5 *döner kebab*, €8-13 main courses, daily 10:00-24:00, Goethestrasse 17, tel. 089/9734-0869).

Picnics

The crown in **Dallmayr's** emblem reflects that even the royal family assembled its picnics at this historic delicatessen. Assemble a royal (pricey) spread to munch in the nearby Hofgarten or visit the classy cafés that serve light meals on the ground and first floors (Mon-Sat 9:30-19:00, closed Sun, behind New Town Hall, Dienerstrasse 13-15, tel. 089/213-5110).

The **supermarkets** that hide in the basements of department stores are on the upscale side, such as the **Galeria Kaufhof** stores at Marienplatz and Karlsplatz, and the **Karstadt** across from the train station. Cheaper options include the **REWE** in the basement at Fünf Höfe (entrance is in Viscardihof) or the **Lidl** at Schwantaler Strasse 31, near the train-station hotels. They're generally open daily (until 20:00) except closed on Sunday.

SLEEPING

I've listed accommodations in two neighborhoods: within a few blocks of the central train station (Hauptbahnhof), and in the old center, between Marienplatz and Sendlinger Tor. Although I give the approximate price for a double room, hotels also have singles (which can be double rooms offered at a lower price), triples, and sometimes quads (which I term "family rooms" in listings). During major conventions and events, prices can increase 20 to 300 percent (worst at Oktoberfest; reserve well in advance).

Near the Train Station

Good-value hotels cluster in the multicultural area immediately south of the station. Some find it colorful; for others it feels seedy after dark (with erotic cinemas and men loitering in the shadows). It's sketchy only for those in search of trouble.

$$$ Marc München—polished, modern, and with 80 newly renovated rooms—is a good option if you need more luxury than the other listings here. It's just a half-block from the station on a relatively tame street, and has a nice lobby and classy breakfast spread. The cheaper "superior king" rooms are the best value (Db-€147-221, ask about Rick Steves discount, pay parking, air-con, Senefelderstrasse 12, tel. 089/559-820, www.hotelmarc.de, info@hotel-marc.de).

$$ Hotel Monaco is a delightful hideaway, tucked inside the fifth floor of a giant, nondescript building two blocks from the station (D-€75, Db-€79-99, family rooms, breakfast-€9, cash preferred, Schillerstrasse 9, entrance on Adolf-Kolping-Strasse, tel. 089/545-9940, www.hotel-monaco.de, info@hotel-monaco.de).

$$ Hotel Uhland is a stately mansion that rents 29 rooms with modern bathrooms in a genteel, residential neighborhood a slightly longer walk from the station (toward the Theresienwiese

Oktoberfest grounds). It's been in the Hauzenberger and Reim families for 60 years (small Db-€95, big Db-€105-118, family rooms, limited free parking, Uhlandstrasse 1, tel. 089/543-350, www.hotel-uhland.de, info@hotel-uhland.de). From the station, take bus #58 (direction: Silberhornstrasse) to Georg-Hirth-Platz, or walk 15 minutes: Out the station's south exit, cross Bayerstrasse, take Paul-Heyse-Strasse three blocks to Georg-Hirth-Platz, then take a soft right on Uhlandstrasse.

$$ Hotel Belle Blue, three blocks from the station, has 30 rooms and is a great value if you are looking for modern furnishings and air-conditioning (Db-€96, Schillerstrasse 21, tel. 089/550-6260, www.hotel-belleblue.de, info@hotel-belleblue.com, Irmgard). Their two apartments are perfect for families (7-night minimum in summer).

$$ Hotel Bristol is efficient, with 57 business-like rooms. It's located across the street from the Sendlinger Tor U-Bahn station (Db-€97, breakfast-€9.50, air-con in lobby, pay parking, Pettenkoferstrasse 2, tel. 089/5434-8880, www.bristol-munich.de, info@bristol-munich.de).

$$ Hotel Deutsches Theater, filled with brass and marble, has 27 three-star rooms. The back rooms face the courtyard of a neighboring theater, so there can be some noise (Db-€90-100, family rooms, pricier suites, breakfast-€9, Landwehrstrasse 18, tel. 089/545-8525, www.hoteldeutschestheater.de, info@hoteldeutschestheater.de).

$$ Hotel Europäischer Hof, across the street from the station, is a huge, impersonal hotel with 150 decent rooms. During cool weather, when you can keep the windows shut, the street-facing rooms are an acceptable option. Courtyard-facing rooms are quieter—and more expensive, except for a few cheap rooms with shared bath (streetside Db-€100; courtyard D with head-to-toe twin beds-€60; ask about Rick Steves discount, pay parking,

Bayerstrasse 31, tel. 089/551-510, www.heh.de, info@heh.de).

$ Hotel Royal is one of the best values in the neighborhood (as long as you can look past the strip joints flanking the entry). While institutional, it's clean and plenty comfortable. Most important, it's energetically run by Pasha and Christiane. Each of its 40 rooms is fresh and bright (Db-€74-94, family rooms, comfort rooms on quiet side cost €10 extra—worth it in summer when you'll want the window open, ask about Rick Steves discount, Schillerstrasse 11a, tel. 089/5998-8160, www.hotel-royal.de, info@hotel-royal.de).

$ Litty's Hotel is a basic hotel offering 37 small rooms with little personality (D-€72-€78, Db-€88, Wi-Fi at reception reaches lower floors, near Schillerstrasse at Landwehrstrasse 32c, tel. 089/5434-4211, www.littyshotel.de, info@littys hotel.de).

¢ The **CVJM (YMCA),** open to all ages, rents 85 beds in clean, slightly worn rooms with sinks in the rooms and showers and toilets down the hall. Doubles are head-to-head; triples are like doubles with a bunk over one of the beds (D-€64; only €10/night more per person during Oktoberfest—reserve 6-12 months ahead;

1 Hotel Marc München
2 Hotel Monaco
3 To Hotel Uhland
4 Hotel Belle Blue
5 Hotel Bristol
6 Hotel Deutsches Theater
7 Hotel Europäischer Hof
8 Hotel Royal
9 Litty's Hotel
10 CVJM (YMCA)
11 Wombat's Hostel, Euro Youth Hotel & Jaeger's Hostel
12 Hotel Blauer Bock
13 Derag Livinghotel
14 Mercure München Altstadt Hotel
15 Hotel am Viktualienmarkt
16 Hotel am Markt
17 Pension Lindner
18 Motel One Sendlinger Tor

includes linens and breakfast but no lockers; cheap Wi-Fi by reception, Landwehrstrasse 13, tel. 089/552-1410, www.cvjm-muenchen.org/hotel/jugendhotel, hotel@cvjm-muenchen.org).

"Hostel Row"

All three of the following hostels on Senefelderstrasse are casual and well-run, with friendly management, and all cater to the needs of young beer-drinking backpackers enjoying Munich on a shoestring. With 900 cheap dorm beds, this is a spirited street. There's no curfew, and each place has a lively bar that rages until the wee hours. All have 24-hour receptions, Wi-Fi, laundry facilities, lockers, and included linens. None has a kitchen, but each offers a buffet breakfast. Sleep cheap in big dorms, or spend more for a 2- to 4-bed room.

¢ **Wombat's Hostel,** perhaps the most hip and colorful, rents cheap doubles and dorm beds with lockers. The dorms are fresh and modern, and there's a relaxing and peaceful winter garden (dorm bed-€23-32, Db-€84, Senefelderstrasse 1, tel. 089/5998-9180, www.wombats.eu, office@wombats-munich.de).

¢ **Euro Youth Hotel** fills a rare pre-WWII building (dorm bed-€22-33, D-€70-85, includes breakfast for private rooms, Senefelderstrasse 5, tel. 089/5990-8811, www.euro-youth-hotel.de, info@euro-youth-hotel.de).

¢ **Jaeger's Hostel,** with 300 cheap beds, has fun and efficiency—plus the only air-conditioning on the street. This seems to be the quietest hostel of the group (dorm bed-€19-32, hotel-quality Db-€79-84, Senefelderstrasse 3, tel. 089/555-281, www.jaegershostel.de, office@jaegershostel.de).

In the Old Center

A few good deals remain in the area south of Marienplatz, going toward the Sendlinger Tor. This neighborhood is more genteel and is convenient for sightseeing.

$$$ **Hotel Blauer Bock,** formerly a dormitory for Benedictine monks, has been on the same corner near the Munich City Museum since 1841. Its 70 remodeled rooms are classy, if spartan for the price, but the location is great (D-€70-100, Db-€135-165, premium Db-€190-220, pay parking, Sebastiansplatz 9, tel. 089/231-780, www.hotelblauerbock.de, info@hotelblauerbock.de).

$$$$ **Derag Livinghotel**'s 83 sleek, tech-savvy rooms are located right off the Viktualienmarkt. Half the rooms are less modern and have kitchenette suites. If you can nab a double room for less than €180, it's a good deal (Db-€165-250 though official rates much higher, breakfast-€19.50, air-con, pay parking, Frauenstrasse 4, tel. 089/885-6560, www.deraghotels.de, vitualienmarkt@derag.de).

$$$$ **Mercure München Altstadt Hotel** is reliable, with all the modern comforts in its 75 business-class rooms, and is located on a quiet street close to the Marienplatz action. A few newer but less expensive rooms are available on the first floor (Db-€186, air-con, block south of the pedestrian zone at Hotterstrasse 4, tel. 089/232-590, www.mercure-muenchen-altstadt.de, h3709@accor.com).

$$$ At **Hotel am Viktualienmarkt,** everything about this 27-room hotel is small but well-designed, including the elevator and three good-value, tiny single rooms. It's on a small side street a couple of blocks from the Viktualienmarkt (Db-€135, family rooms, Utzschneiderstrasse 14, tel. 089/231-1090, www.hotel-am-viktualienmarkt.de, reservierung@hotel-am-viktualienmarkt.de).

$$ **Hotel am Markt,** right next to the Viktualienmarkt, has 32 decent rooms; it's a better deal if you skip the expensive breakfast (Db-€112-124, breakfast-€12, Heiliggeiststrasse 6, tel. 089/225-014, www.hotel-am-markt.eu, service@hotel-am-markt.eu).

$$ **Pension Lindner** is clean and quiet, with nine pleasant, pastel-bouquet rooms

off a bare stairway. Frau Sinzinger offers a warm welcome and good buffet breakfasts, but she rarely has room for last-minute bookings (D-€75, Db-€100, cash discount on doubles and triples, Dult-strasse 1, tel. 089/263-413, www.pension-lindner.com, info@pension-lindner.com, Marion Sinzinger).

$$ **Motel One Sendlinger Tor** is a busy, inexpensive, 241-room chain hotel with rushed-but-pleasant staff in a fine location around the corner from the Sendlinger Tor tram and U-Bahn stop. The stylish, modern rooms are fairly tight but are a good value—and sell out a few weeks in advance. Streetside rooms on upper floors have great views. When booking on their website, make sure to choose the Sendlinger Tor location—they have six other hotels in Munich (Db-€94, breakfast-€9.50, air-con, pay parking, Herzog-Wilhelm-Strasse 28, tel. 089/5177-7250, www.motel-one.com, muenchen-sendlingertor@motel-one.com).

TRANSPORTATION

Getting Around Munich

Much of Munich is walkable. But given that the city is laced by many trams, buses, and subways, it's worth learning the system and considering getting a day pass. Public transit also makes it super-easy to access sights outside the historic core, such as Dachau or Nymphenburg Palace. Cabbies are honest and professional, but taxis are expensive (about €12 between the Hauptbahnhof and Marienplatz) and generally unnecessary.

By Subway, Tram, and Bus

Subways are called U-Bahns and S-Bahns. (S-Bahns are actually commuter railways that run underground through the city and are covered by rail passes—but it's smarter to save your limited number of pass days for long-distance trips.) These transit lines are numbered (for example, S-3 or U-5). The U-Bahn lines mainly run north-south, while the S-Bahn lines are generally east-west. For more info, visit the transit customer-service center underground at the main train station or Marienplatz (closed Sun), call 0800-344-226-600 (Mon-Fri only), or visit www.mvv-muenchen.de.

TICKETS

The entire transit system (subway/bus/tram) works on the same tickets. There are four concentric zones—white, green, yellow, and orange. Almost everything described in this chapter is within the white/inner zone, except for Dachau (green zone) and the airport (orange zone).

Transit tickets are sold at booths in the subway and at ticket machines with the MVV logo. Machines take coins and €5-50 bills; newer ones take PIN-enabled credit cards, too. Start the transaction by choosing "English," then press "Transit Association-MVV," which displays the array of tickets and passes available.

A one-zone **regular ticket** (*Einzelfahrkarte*, €2.70) is good for three hours in one direction, including changes and stops. For short rides (four stops max, only two of which can be on the subway lines), buy the **short-stretch ticket** (*Kurzstrecke*, €1.40). The **all-day pass** (*Single-Tageskarte*, €6.20) for the white/inner zone is a great deal for a single traveler.

All-day small-group passes (*Partner-Tageskarte*) are an even better deal—they cover all public transportation for up to five adults (two kids count as one adult, so two adults and six kids can travel with this ticket). A *Partner-Tageskarte* for the white/inner zone costs €11.70 (the €14.80 *XXL* version includes Dachau; the €22.30 *Gesamtnetz* version includes the airport). These partner tickets are a real steal—the only catch is that you've got to stay together.

Munich Transportation

To Airport

S-1

U-2

Feldmoching Ⓢ Ⓤ

Olympia-zentrum Ⓤ   U-3   Peteul-ring Ⓤ   Scheidplatz Ⓤ   U-3

Olympic Park

BMW-WELT & MUSEUM   Ⓤ Hohenzollernplatz

U-2

● Amalienburgstrasse

CONCENTRATION CAMP

#726

Ⓢ Dachau

NYMPHENBURG PALACE

S-1

#17

● Romanplatz

S-2

NEUE PINAKOTHEK

ALTE PINAKOTHEK

#100

#100

#16, #17

LENBACH-HAUS ■

Königs-platz

MUSEUM QUARTER

U-4, U-5

#100

#27

CENTRAL BUS STN. (ZOB) ■

Karls-platz Ⓢ Ⓤ

Pasing Ⓢ   Ⓢ   Ⓢ   Ⓢ   Ⓢ Ⓤ   U-4, U-5   S-1 through S-8

Laim   Donnersberger-brücke   Hacker-brücke   #16, #17, #18

S-8

Hauptbahnhof
MAIN TRAIN STN.

To Herrsching (Bus #951 to Andechs Monastery)

U-4, U-5

Laimer Platz Ⓤ   Schwanthaler-höhe Ⓤ   Ⓤ Theresienwiese   #16, #17, #18, #27

TRANSPORTATION MUSEUM   🍺 **OKTOBERFEST GROUNDS**   U-1, U-2

Legend

—Ⓢ—   **S-BAHN**

—Ⓢ—   **S-BAHN "SPINE"**
MOST S-BAHN LINES FOLLOW THIS ROUTE, THEN BRANCH OFF

—Ⓤ—   **U-BAHN**

+++   **TRAM**

- - -   **BUS**

Not all lines & stations are shown

Not to Scale

U-6

Ⓤ
Klinikum Grosshadern   Fürstenried West Ⓤ

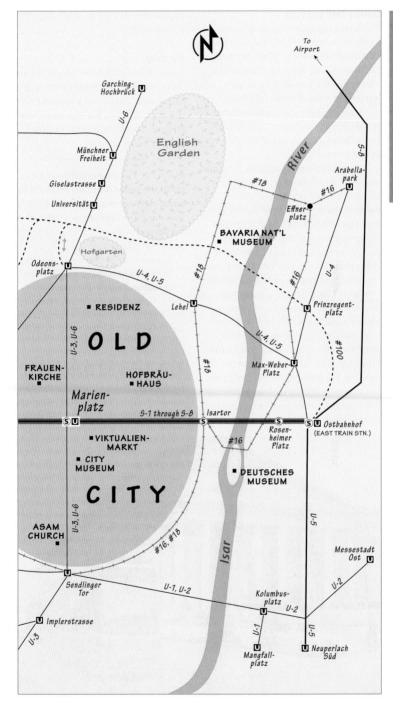

USING THE SYSTEM

To find the right platform, look for the name of the last station in the direction (*Richtung*) you want to travel. For example, a sign saying *Richtung: Marienplatz* means that the subway, bus, or tram is traveling in the direction of Marienplatz. Know where you're going relative to Marienplatz, the Hauptbahnhof, and Ostbahnhof, as these are often referred to as end points.

You must stamp tickets prior to using them (for an all-day or multiday pass, stamp it only the first time you use it). For the subway, punch your ticket in the blue machine *before* going down to the platform. For buses and trams, stamp your ticket once on board. Plainclothes ticket checkers enforce this honor system, rewarding freeloaders with stiff €60 fines.

Handy Lines: Several subway lines, trams, and buses are especially convenient for tourists. All the main S-Bahn lines (S-1 through S-8) run east-west along the main tourist axis between the Hauptbahnhof, Marienplatz, and the Ostbahnhof. For travel within the city center, just find the platform for lines S-1 through S-8. One track (*Gleis*) will be headed east to the Ostbahnhof, the other west to the Hauptbahnhof. Hop on any train going your direction.

By Bike

Level, compact, and with plenty of bike paths, Munich feels made for those on two wheels. You can take your bike on the subway, but not during rush hour (Mon-Fri 6:00-9:00 & 16:00-18:00) and only if you buy a bike day pass.

Rick's Tip: *The* **strip of pathway closest to the street is usually reserved for bikes.** *Signs painted on the sidewalk or blue-and-white street signs show which part of the sidewalk is designated for pedestrians and which is for cyclists.*

You can **rent bikes** quickly and easily from **Radius Tours** in the train station in front of track 32 (daily April-Oct 8:30-19:00, May-Aug until 20:00; closed Nov-March, tel. 089/543-487-7730, www.radiustours.com).

Arriving and Departing

By Plane

Munich's airport (code: MUC) is an easy 40-minute ride on the S-1 or S-8 **subway**

(every 20 minutes from 4:00 in the morning until almost 2:00 in the morning). The S-8 is a bit quicker and easier; the S-1 line has two branches and some trains split—if you ride the S-1 to the airport, be certain your train is going to the *Flughafen* (airport). The Munich *Gesamtnetz* day pass ("Airport-City-Day-Ticket") is worth getting if you'll be making even one more public transport trip that day. The trip is free with a validated and dated rail pass.

The **Lufthansa airport bus** links the airport with the main train station (€10.50, €17 round-trip, 3/hour, 45 minutes, buses depart train station 5:15-19:55, buy tickets on bus; from inside the station, exit near track 26 and look for yellow *Airport Bus* signs; www.airportbus-muenchen.de). Avoid taking a **taxi** from the airport—it's a long, expensive drive (roughly €65). Airport info: tel. 089/97500, www.munich-airport.de.

By Train

For quick help at the main train station (München Hauptbahnhof), stop by the service counter in front of track 18. For better English and more patience, drop by the EurAide desk at counter #1 in the *Reisezentrum* (see page 723). Train info: toll tel. 0180-699-6633, www.bahn.com.

You'll find a city-run **TI** (out front of station and to the right) and **lockers** (opposite track 26). Up the stairs opposite track 21 are **car-rental agencies** (overlooking track 22).

Subway lines, trams, and buses connect the station to the rest of the city (though some of my recommended hotels are within walking distance of the station). If you get lost in the underground maze of subway corridors while you're trying to get to the train station, follow the signs for *DB* (Deutsche Bahn) to surface successfully. Watch out for the hallways with blue ticket-stamping machines in the middle—these lead to the subway, where you could be fined if nabbed without a validated ticket.

From Munich by Train to: Füssen (hourly, 2 hours), **Oberammergau** (nearly hourly, 2 hours, change in Murnau), **Salzburg,** Austria (2/hour, 1.5 hours on fast trains, 2 hours on slower trains eligible for regional day ticket), **Cologne** (2/hour, 4.5 hours, some with 1 change), **Würzburg** (1-2/hour, 2 hours), **Rothenburg** (hourly, 2.5-4 hours, 2-3 changes), **Frankfurt** (hourly, 3.5 hours), **Dresden** (every 2 hours, 6 hours, change in Leipzig or Nürnberg), **Hamburg** (hourly direct, 6.5 hours), **Berlin** (1-2/hour, 6.5 hours).

By Bus

Munich's central bus station (ZOB) is by the Hackerbrücke S-Bahn station (from the train station, it's one S-Bahn stop; www.muenchen-zob.de). The Romantic Road bus leaves from here (see page 818).

NEAR MUNICH

DACHAU MEMORIAL

Established in 1933, Dachau was the first Nazi concentration camp. In its 12 dismal years of operation, more than 200,000 prisoners from across Europe were incarcerated here—and at least 41,500 died, many of them murdered. The memorial on the grounds today, rated ▲▲, is an effective voice from our modern but grisly past, pleading "Never again."

Planning Your Time: Allow about five hours, giving you at least 2.5 hours at the camp, and including round-trip travel from central Munich.

Cost and Hours: Free, daily 9:00-17:00. Note that the museum discourages parents from bringing children under age 12.

Getting There on Your Own: The camp is a 45-minute trip from downtown Munich. The **Munich XXL day pass** covers the entire journey, both ways (€8.30/person, €14.80/partner ticket for up to 5 adults).

Take the S-2 (direction: Petershausen) from any of the central S-Bahn stops in Munich to Dachau (3/hour, 20-minute trip from Hauptbahnhof). Then, at Dachau station, go down the stairs and follow the crowds out to the bus platforms; find the one marked *KZ-Gedenkstätte-Concentration Camp Memorial Sight*. Here, catch bus #726 and ride it seven minutes to the KZ-Gedenkstätte stop (3/hour). Before you leave this bus stop, be sure to note the return times back to the station.

Drivers follow Dachauer Strasse from downtown Munich to Dachau-Ost, then follow *KZ-Gedenkstätte* signs.

Getting There by Guided Tour: Two companies offer good-value tours to Dachau from Munich for about the same price (€24, includes public transportation, €2 Rick Steves discount). It's smart to reserve the day before, especially for morning tours. Choose between **Radius** (April-mid-Oct daily at 9:15 and 12:15, mid-Oct-March daily at 10:00, tel. 089/543-487-7730, www.radiustours.

Dachau today

com) and **Munich Walk** (April-Oct daily at 10:15 and 13:15, Nov-March daily at 10:15, tel. 089/2423-1767, www. munichwalktours.de).

Visitors Center: The visitors center, outside the camp wall, lacks exhibits, but has a bookstore with English-language books on Holocaust themes, a small cafeteria, and a WC (more WCs inside the camp).

At the center's information desk, you can rent an audioguide or sign up for a tour. The €3.50 **audioguide** covers the grounds and museum in 1.5 hours. **Guided walks** in English start from the visitors center (€3, daily at 11:00 and 13:00, 2.5 hours, limited to 30 people, so show up early—especially in summer, tel. 08131/669-970, www.kz-gedenkstaette-dachau.de).

◆ Self-Guided Tour

You enter the camp, like the prisoners did, through the infamous **iron gate** that held the taunting slogan *Arbeit macht*

frei ("Work makes you free"). Inside are these key stops: the museum, the bunker behind the museum, the restored barracks, and a pensive walk across the huge but now-empty camp to the memorials and crematorium at the far end.

Museum: Before touring the rooms, check show times for the museum's powerful 22-minute documentary film, a sobering, graphic, and sometimes grisly account of the rise of Hitler and the atrocities committed at the camp (usually shown 5 times/day in English). The

Iron gate with "Work makes you free" slogan

Dachau

To Dachauer Strasse & Munich →

ALTE RÖMERSTRASSE

GUARD TOWER ↗

RELIGIOUS MEMORIALS

FORMER

BARRACKS

RECONSTRUCTED BARRACKS

CARMELITE CONVENT

MUSEUM EXIT →

CINEMA

SCULPTURE ■

MUSEUM

"THE BUNKER"

PATER-ROTH-STRASSE

P

ENTRANCE ↗
"ARBEIT MACHT FREI" GATE

PERIMETER FENCE

CREMATORIUM & GAS CHAMBER

Memorial Garden

100 Meters

100 Yards

VISITORS CENTER

To Dachau Town Center & S-Bahn Station ↓

Ⓑ Bus #726 (To/From S-Bahn Station)

museum is organized chronologically, everything is thoughtfully described in English, and computer touch-screens let you watch early newsreels.

Rooms 1-2 cover the founding of the camp and give an overview of the Nazi camp system. Some were concentration camps, like Dachau, and others were extermination camps, built with the express purpose of executing people on a mass scale. Photos and posters chronicle the rise of Hitler in the 1920s.

Rooms 3-7 are devoted to the early years of the camp. Besides political activists, prisoners included homosexuals,

The Bunker (camp prison)

Jehovah's Witnesses, Roma, and Jews. The camp was run by the SS (Schutzstaffel), the organization charged with Germany's internal security. Dachau was a strictly regimented work camp: a wake-up call at 4:00, an 11-hour workday, roll call at 5:15 and 19:00, lights out at 21:00. The labor was hard, whether quarrying or hauling loads or constructing the very buildings you see today. The rations were meager, rule-breakers were punished severely, and all manner of torture took place here.

Rooms 8-15 document the war years and their immediate aftermath. After Germany invaded Poland on September 1, 1939, conditions at Dachau deteriorated. The original camp had been designed to hold just under 3,000 inmates. In 1937 and 1938, the camp was expanded, with barracks intended to hold 6,000 prisoners. During the war, the prisoner population swelled, and the Nazis found other purposes for the camp. It was less a concentration camp for German dissidents and more a dumping ground for foreigners and POWs. It was used as a special prison for 2,000 Catholic priests. From Dachau, Jewish prisoners were sent east to the gas chambers. Inmates were put to use as slave labor for the German war machine—many were shipped to nearby camps to make armaments. Prisoners were used as human guinea pigs for war-related medical experiments of human tolerance for air pressure, hypothermia, and biological agents like malaria.

As the Allies closed in on both fronts, Dachau was bursting with more than 30,000 prisoners jammed into its 34 barracks. Disease broke out, and food ran short in the winter of 1944-1945. With coal for the crematorium running low, the corpses of those who died were buried in mass graves outside the camp site. The Allies arrived on April 29. After 12 years of existence, Dachau was finally liberated.

Bunker: This was a cellblock for prominent "special prisoners," such as failed Hitler assassins, German religious leaders, and politicians who challenged Nazism. Exhibits profile the inmates and the SS guards who worked at Dachau, and allow you to listen to some inmates' testimonies. Cell #2 was the interrogation room. Cell #9 was a "standing cell"—inmates were tortured here by being forced to stay on their feet for days at a time.

Barracks: Take a look inside to get an idea of what sleeping and living conditions were like in the terribly overcrowded camp. When the camp was at its fullest, there was only about one square yard of living space per inmate.

Religious Remembrance Sights: At the far end of the camp, in space that once housed the camp vegetable garden, there are now several places of meditation and worship (Jewish to your right, Catholic straight ahead, and Protestant to your left). Beyond them, just outside the camp, is a Carmelite convent. In the garden near the crematoria is a Russian Orthodox shrine.

Camp Crematoria: These facilities were used to dispose of the bodies of prisoners. The larger concrete crematorium was built to replace the smaller wooden one. One of its rooms is a gas chamber, which worked on the same principles as the much larger one at Auschwitz, and was originally disguised as a shower room (the fittings are gone now). It was never put to use at Dachau for mass murder, but some historians suspect that a few people were killed in it experimentally. The memorial garden that now surrounds the crematoria is the main place of remembrance at Dachau.

Memorials throughout Dachau remind visitors: Never Again.

Rothenburg
and the
Romantic Road

The Romantic Road through Bavaria's medieval heartland is strewn with picturesque villages, farmhouses, onion-domed churches, Baroque palaces, and walled cities. The route, which runs from Würzburg to Füssen, is the most scenic way to connect Frankfurt with Munich. No trains run along the full length of the Romantic Road, but Rothenburg (ROH-tehn-burg), the most interesting town along the way, is easy to reach by rail. Drivers can either zero in on Rothenburg or take some extra time to meander from town to town on the way. For nondrivers, a tour bus travels the Romantic Road once daily in each direction.

Countless travelers have searched for the elusive "untouristy Rothenburg." There are many contenders (such as Michelstadt, Miltenberg, Bamberg, Bad Windsheim, and Dinkelsbühl), but none holds a candle to the king of medieval German cuteness. Even with crowds, overpriced souvenirs—and, yes, even the over-promoted, dry *Schneeballen* pastries—Rothenburg is the best. Save time and mileage and be satisfied with the winner.

ROTHENBURG AND THE ROMANTIC ROAD IN 2 DAYS

I'd spend one full day in Rothenburg this way: Start with my self-guided town walk, including a visit to St. Jakob's Church (for the carved altarpiece) and the Imperial City Museum (historic artifacts). Spend the afternoon visiting the Medieval Crime and Punishment Museum and taking my "Schmiedgasse-Spitalgasse Shopping Stroll," followed by a walk on the wall (from Spitaltor to Klingentor).

Cap your day with the entertaining Night Watchman's Tour at 20:00. Locals love *"Die blaue Stunde"* (the blue hour)—

the time just before dark when city lamps and the sky hold hands. Be sure to be out enjoying the magic of the city at this time.

Other evening options include beer-garden fun (at Gasthof Rödertor) if the weather's good, or the English Conversation Club (at Altfränkische Weinstube am Klosterhof) if it's Wednesday.

With extra time in Rothenburg, spread out your sightseeing and add the Old Town Historic Walk (offered by the TI), the Town Hall Tower climb, and the German Christmas Museum.

If you're driving, take in the top Romantic Road highlights en route, devoting a half-day to the sights on your way to Rothenburg and another half-day after leaving it.

ROTHENBURG OB DER TAUBER

In the Middle Ages, when Berlin and Munich were just wide spots on the road, Rothenburg ob der Tauber was a "free imperial city" beholden only to the Holy Roman Emperor. From 1150 to 1400, because of its strategic location on trade routes and the abundant resources of its surrounding farmlands, Rothenburg thrived, with a whopping population of 6,000. But the Thirty Years' War and a plague that followed did the town in. With no money to fix up its antiquated buildings, Rothenburg languished. Today, it's the country's best-preserved medieval walled town, enjoying tremendous popularity without losing its charm.

Rick's Tip: *Germany has several towns named Rothenburg.* **Make sure you're going to Rothenburg ob der Tauber** *(not "ob der" any other river). People really do sometimes drive or ride the train to the wrong Rothenburg by accident.*

Two-thirds of the 2,000 people who live within Rothenburg's walls are employed to serve tourists. Rothenburg is at its best in spring and fall, crowded in summer (but still fun), and dead in winter except for December (when its Christmas Market bustles).

While roughly 2 million people visit each year, most come only on day trips. Rothenburg is yours after dark, when the groups vacate and the town's floodlit cobbles seem made for romance.

Orientation

Think of the town map as a human head. Its nose—the castle garden—sticks out to the left, and the skinny lower part forms a neck, with the youth hostel and a recommended hotel being the Adam's apple. The town is a delight on foot. No sights or hotels are more than a 15-minute walk from the train station or each other.

Rick's Tip: *A* **fun pictorial town map,** *which also helpfully indicates some walking paths in the countryside beyond the town walls, is available for free with this book at the* **Friese shop** *(see page 812).*

Most of the buildings you'll see were in place by 1400. The city was born around

Picturesque Rothenburg ob der Tauber

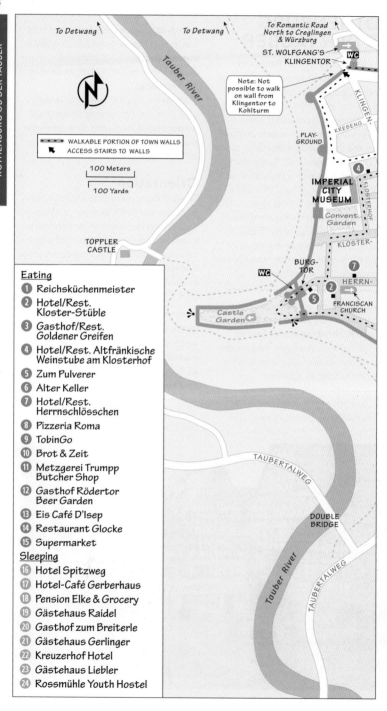

To Detwang

To Detwang

To Romantic Road
North to Creglingen
& Würzburg

ST. WOLFGANG'S
KLINGENTOR

WC

Tauber River

Note: Not
possible to walk
on wall from
Klingentor to
Kohlturm

KLINGEN-

KREBENG-

PLAY-
GROUND

IMPERIAL
CITY
MUSEUM

KLOSTERHOF

Convent
Garden

KLOSTER-

- - - - WALKABLE PORTION OF TOWN WALLS
↖ ACCESS STAIRS TO WALLS

100 Meters

100 Yards

TOPPLER
CASTLE

BURG-
TOR

WC

HERRN-

Castle
Garden

FRANCISCAN
CHURCH

Eating

1 Reichsküchenmeister
2 Hotel/Rest. Kloster-Stüble
3 Gasthof/Rest. Goldener Greifen
4 Hotel/Rest. Altfränkische Weinstube am Klosterhof
5 Zum Pulverer
6 Alter Keller
7 Hotel/Rest. Herrnschlösschen
8 Pizzeria Roma
9 TobinGo
10 Brot & Zeit
11 Metzgerei Trumpp Butcher Shop
12 Gasthof Rödertor Beer Garden
13 Eis Café D'Isep
14 Restaurant Glocke
15 Supermarket

Sleeping

16 Hotel Spitzweg
17 Hotel-Café Gerberhaus
18 Pension Elke & Grocery
19 Gästehaus Raidel
20 Gasthof zum Breiterle
21 Gästehaus Gerlinger
22 Kreuzerhof Hotel
23 Gästehaus Liebler
24 Rossmühle Youth Hostel

TAUBERTALWEG

DOUBLE
BRIDGE

Tauber River

TAUBERTALWEG

Rothenburg

ROTHENBURG AND THE ROMANTIC ROAD AT A GLANCE

Rothenburg

▲▲▲**Rothenburg Town Walk** A self-guided loop, starting and ending on Market Square, covering the town's top sights. See page 800.

▲▲**Night Watchman's Tour** Germany's best hour of medieval wonder, led by an amusing, medieval-garbed guide. **Hours:** Mid-March-Dec nightly at 20:00. See page 798.

▲▲**St. Jakob's Church** Home to Tilman Riemenschneider's breath-taking, wood-carved Altar of the Holy Blood. **Hours:** Daily April-Oct 9:00-17:15, Dec 10:00-16:45, Nov and Christmas-March 10:00-12:00 & 14:00-16:00, on Sun wait to enter until services end at 10:45. See page 802.

▲▲**Imperial City Museum** An artifact-filled sweep through Rothen-burg's history. **Hours:** Daily April-Oct 9:30-17:30, Nov-March 13:00-16:00. See page 805.

▲▲**Schmiedgasse-Spitalgasse Shopping Stroll** A fun look at crafts and family-run shops, on a (mostly) picturesque street running between Market Square and the town's most impressive tower, Spitaltor. See page 807.

▲▲**Walk the Wall** A strollable wall encircling the town, providing great views and a good orientation to Rothenburg. **Hours:** Always open and walkable. See page 809.

▲▲**Medieval Crime and Punishment Museum** Specializing in every-thing connected to medieval justice, this exhibit is a cut above the tacky torture museums around Europe. **Hours:** Daily April 11:00-17:00, May-Oct 10:00-18:00, Nov and Jan-Feb 14:00-16:00, Dec and March 13:00-16:00. See page 810.

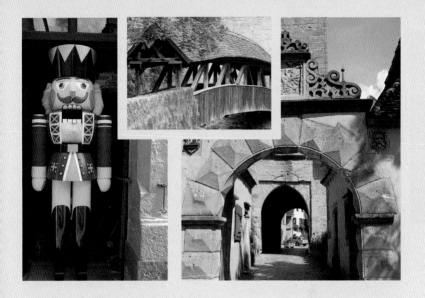

▲**Old Town Historic Walk** Covers the serious side of Rothenburg's history and the town's architecture. **Hours:** Easter-Oct and Dec daily at 14:00. See page 798.

▲**Historical Town Hall Vaults** An insightful look at Rothenburg during the Catholics-vs.-Protestants Thirty Years' War. **Hours:** Daily May-Oct 9:30-17:30, shorter hours off-season, closed Jan-Feb. See page 802.

▲**Town Hall Tower** Rothenburg's tallest perch, with a commanding view. **Hours:** Daily in season 9:00-12:30 & 13:00-17:00. See page 810.

▲**German Christmas Museum** Tells the interesting history of Christmas decorations. **Hours:** April-Dec daily 10:00-17:30, shorter and irregular hours Jan-March. See page 811.

Along the Romantic Road

▲▲**Wieskirche** Lovely Baroque-Rococo church set in a meadow. **Hours:** Daily April-Oct 8:00-20:00, Nov-March 8:00-17:00; interior closed to sightseers during services: Sun 8:00-13:00; Tue, Wed, and Sat 10:00-12:00; and Fri 17:00-20:00. See page 819.

▲**Nördlingen** Workaday town with one of the best walls in Germany and a crater left by an ancient meteor. See page 819.

▲**Dinkelsbühl** A town like Rothenburg's little sister, cute enough to merit a short stop. See page 820.

▲**Creglingen's Herrgottskirche** Church featuring Riemenschneider's greatest carved altarpiece. See page 821.

▲**Weikersheim** Picturesque town with an impressive palace, Baroque gardens, and a quaint town square. See page 821.

its long-gone castle fortress—built in 1142, destroyed in 1356—which was located where the castle garden is now. You can see the shadow of the first town wall, which defines the oldest part of Rothenburg, in its contemporary street plan. Two gates from this wall still survive: the Markus Tower and the White Tower. The richest and biggest houses were in this central part. The commoners built higgledy-piggledy houses farther from the center, but still inside the present walls.

Although Rothenburg is technically in Bavaria, the region around the town strongly identifies itself as "Franken," one of Germany's many medieval dukedoms ("Franconia" in English).

Tourist Information: The TI is on Market Square (May-Oct and Dec Mon-Fri 9:00-18:00, Sat-Sun 10:00-17:00; off-season Mon-Fri 9:00-17:00, Sat 10:00-13:00, closed Sun; Marktplatz 2, tel. 09861/404-800, www.tourismus.rothenburg.de, run by Jörg Christöphler). The free city map comes with a walking guide, and the *Events* booklet covers the basics in English. The TI has one free public computer with Internet access (15-minute maximum).

Bike Rental: Rad & Tat rents bikes for €14 for a 24-hour day (otherwise €10/6 hours, also has electric bikes; Mon-Fri 9:00-18:00, Sat until 13:00, closed Sun; Bensenstrasse 17, tel. 09861/87984, www.mietraeder.de). To reach it, leave the old town heading toward the train station, take a right on Erlbacher Strasse, cross the tracks, and look across the street from the Lidl supermarket.

Taxi: For a taxi, call 09861/2000 or 09861/7227.

Tours

▲▲NIGHT WATCHMAN'S TOUR

This tour is flat-out the most entertaining hour of medieval wonder anywhere in Germany. The Night Watchman (a.k.a. Hans-Georg Baumgartner) jokes like a medieval John Cleese as he lights his lamp and takes tourists on his rounds, telling slice-of-gritty-life tales of medieval Rothenburg. This is the best evening activity in town (€8, teens-€5, free for kids 12 and under, mid-March-Dec nightly at 20:00, in English, meet at Market Square, www.nightwatchman.de).

▲OLD TOWN HISTORIC WALK

The TI offers 1.5-hour guided walking tours in English. Just show up and pay the guide directly—there's always room. Take this tour for the serious side of Rothenburg's history, and to make sense of the town's architecture; you won't get as much of that on the fun—and completely different—Night Watchman's Tour. It would be a shame not to take advantage of this informative tour just because you took the other (€7, Easter-Oct and Dec daily at 14:00, no English tours off-season, departs from Market Square).

PRIVATE GUIDES

A local historian can really bring the ramparts alive. Reserve a guide by emailing the TI (€75/1.5 hours, €95/2 hours, info@rothenburg.de, more info at www.tourismus.rothenburg.de—look under "Tourism Service," then "Guided Tours"). I've had good experiences with **Martin Kamphans,** who also works as a potter (tel. 09861/7941, www.stadtfuehrungen-rothenburg.de, kamphans@posteo.de), and **Daniel Weber** (mobile 0795-8311, www.toot-tours.com, mail@toot-tours.com).

Rothenburg's Night Watchman

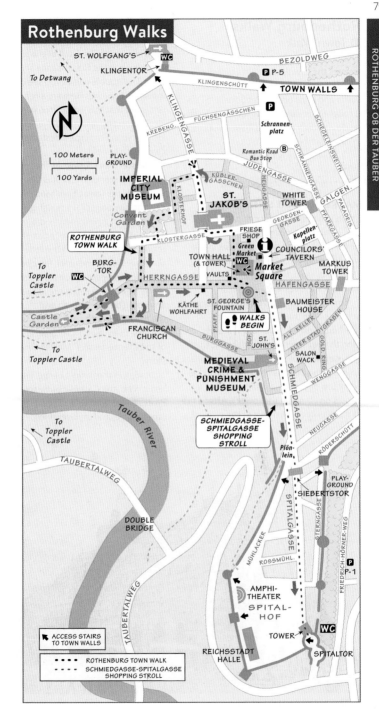

Rothenburg Walks

ST. WOLFGANG'S
WC
To Detwang
KLINGENTOR
BEZOLDWEG
P-5
KLINGENSCHÜTT
TOWN WALLS
P
KLINGENTORGASSE
FÜCHSENGÄSSCHEN
Schrannen-platz
KREBENG.
Romantic Road
Bus Stop
B
N
SCHRANNENGASSE
SCHEGELEINSWETH
JUDENGASSE
100 Meters
PLAY-GROUND
IMPERIAL CITY MUSEUM
KÜBLER GÄSSCHEN
HEUGASSE
100 Yards
KLOSTERHOF
ST. JAKOB'S
WHITE TOWER
GALGEN.
Convent Garden
GEORGEN-GASSE
PFARRGASSE
PARADEIS
ROTHENBURG TOWN WALK
KLOSTERGASSE
FRIESE SHOP
Kapellen-platz
BURG-TOR
To Toppler Castle
WC
TOWN HALL (& TOWER)
Green Market
WC
COUNCILORS' TAVERN
MARKUS TOWER
HERRNGASSE
VAULTS
Market Square
HAFENGASSE
KÄTHE WOHLFAHRT
ST. GEORGE'S FOUNTAIN
BAUMEISTER HOUSE
Castle Garden
FRANCISCAN CHURCH
WALKS BEGIN
ALT. KELLER
ALTER STADTGRABEN
GOLD RING
To Toppler Castle
BURGGASSE
ST. JOHN'S
SALON WACK
WENGGASSE
MEDIEVAL CRIME & PUNISHMENT MUSEUM
SCHMIEDGASSE
Tauber River
SCHMIEDGASSE-SPITALGASSE SHOPPING STROLL
NEUGASSE
To Toppler Castle
Plön-lein
RÖDERSCHÜTT
TAUBERTALWEG
PLAY-GROUND
SIEBERTSTOR
SPITALGASSE
STERNGASSE
FRIEDRICH-HÖRNER-WEG
DOUBLE BRIDGE
P-1
MÜHLACKER
ROSSMÜHL.
TAUBERTALWEG
AMPHI-THEATER
SPITAL-HOF
WC
TOWER
ACCESS STAIRS TO TOWN WALLS
REICHSSTADT HALLE
SPITALTOR
•••• ROTHENBURG TOWN WALK
---- SCHMIEDGASSE-SPITALGASSE SHOPPING STROLL

Rothenburg Walks
⊙ *Town Walk*

This self-guided loop, worth ▲▲▲, weaves the town's top sights together, takes about an hour without stops, and starts and ends on Market Square. (This is roughly the same route followed by city guides on their daily Old Town Historic Walk, described earlier.)

🎧 Download my free Rothenburg Town Walk audio tour.

• *Start the walk on Market Square.*

MARKET SQUARE SPIN-TOUR

Stand in front of the fountain at the bottom of Market Square (watch for occasional cars) and spin 360 degrees clockwise, starting with the Town Hall tower. Now do it again, this time more slowly to take in some details:

Town Hall and Tower: Rothenburg's tallest spire is the Town Hall tower *(Rathausturm)*. At 200 feet, it stands atop the old Town Hall, a white, Gothic, 13th-century building. Notice the tourists enjoying the best view in town from the black top of the tower (see page 810 for details on climbing the tower). After a fire in 1501 burned down part of the original

building, a new Town Hall was built alongside what survived of the old one (fronting the square). This half of the rebuilt complex is in the Renaissance style from 1570. The double eagles you see decorating many buildings here are a repeated reminder that this was a "free imperial city" belonging directly to the (Habsburg) Holy Roman Emperor, a designation that came with benefits.

Meistertrunk Show: At the top of Market Square stands the proud Councilors' Tavern (clock tower from 1466). In its day, the city council—the rich guys who ran the town government—drank here. Today, it's the **TI** and the focus of most tourists' attention when the little doors on either side of the clock flip open and the wooden figures (from 1910) do their thing. Be on Market Square at the top of any hour (between 10:00 and 22:00) for the ritual gathering of the tourists to see the less-than-breathtaking re-enactment of the Meistertrunk ("Master Draught") story:

In 1631, in the middle of the Thirty Years' War, the Catholic army took this Protestant town and was about to do its rape, pillage, and plunder thing. As was

Rothenburg's Town Hall and Tower

the etiquette, the mayor had to give the conquering general a welcoming drink. The general enjoyed a huge tankard of local wine. Feeling really good, he told the mayor, "Hey, if you can drink this entire three-liter tankard of wine in one gulp, I'll spare your town." The mayor amazed everyone by drinking the entire thing, and Rothenburg was saved. (While this is a nice story, it was dreamed up in the late 1800s for a theatrical play designed—effectively—to promote a romantic image of the town. In actuality, if Rothenburg was spared, it had likely bribed its way out of the jam.) The city was occupied and ransacked several times in the Thirty Years' War, and it never recovered—which is why it's such a well-preserved time capsule today.

For the best show, don't watch the clock; watch the open-mouthed tourists gasp as the old windows flip open. At the late shows, the square flickers with camera flashes.

Bottom of Market Square: As this was the most-prestigious address in town, it's ringed by big homes with big carriage gates. One of the finest is just downhill from the bottom end of the square—the **Baumeister** ("master builder") **Haus,** where the man who designed and built the Town Hall lived. It features a famous Renaissance facade with statues of the seven virtues and the seven vices. The statues are copies; the originals are in the Imperial City Museum (described later on this walk).

Behind you, take in the big 17th-century **St. George's fountain.** Its long metal gutters could slide to deposit the water into villagers' buckets. It's part of Rothenburg's ingenious water system: Built on a rock, the town had one real source above the town, which was plumbed to serve a series of fountains; water flowed from high to low through Rothenburg. Its many fountains had practical functions beyond providing drinking water—some were stocked with fish on market days

and during times of siege, and their water was useful for fighting fire. Because of its plentiful water supply—and its policy of requiring relatively wide lanes as fire breaks—the town never burned entirely, as so many neighboring villages did.

Two fine half-timbered buildings behind the fountain show the old-time lofts with warehouse doors and pulleys on top for hoisting. All over town, lofts like these were filled with grain. A year's supply was required by the city so they could survive any siege. The building behind the fountain is an art gallery showing off work by members of the local artists' association. To the right is Marien Apotheke, an old-time pharmacy mixing old and new in typical Rothenburg style.

The broad street running under the Town Hall tower is **Herrngasse.** The town originated with its castle fortress (built in 1142 but now long gone; a lovely garden now fills that space). Herrngasse connected the castle to Market Square. The last leg of this circular walking tour will take you from the castle garden up Herrngasse and back here.

For now, walk a few steps down Herrngasse and stop by the arch under the Town Hall tower (between the new and old Town Halls). On the wall to the left of the gate are the town's measuring rods—a reminder that medieval Germany was made of 300 independent little countries, many with their own weights and measures. Merchants and shoppers knew that these were the local standards: the

Herrngasse

rod (4.3 yards), the *Schuh* ("shoe," roughly a foot), and the *Ell* (from elbow to finger-tip—four inches longer than mine...climb up and try it). The protruding cornerstone you're standing on is one of many all over town—originally to protect buildings from careening horse carts. In German, going recklessly fast is called "scratching the cornerstone."

• *Careen around that stone and under the arch to find the...*

▲HISTORICAL TOWN HALL VAULTS (HISTORIENGEWÖLBE)

The vaults house an eclectic and grade-schoolish little museum that gives a waxy but interesting look at Rothenburg during the Catholics-vs.-Protestants Thirty Years' War. Popping in here can help prep your imagination to filter out the tourists and picture ye olde Rothenburg along the rest of this walk. With helpful English descriptions, it offers a look at "the fateful year 1631," a replica of the mythical Meistertrunk tankard, an alchemist's workshop, and a dungeon complete with three dank cells and some torture lore.

Cost and Hours: €3, daily May-Oct 9:30-17:30, shorter hours off-season, closed Jan-Feb, tel. 09861/86751.

• *Leaving the museum, turn left (past a venerable and much-sketched-and-photographed door) and find a posted copy of a centuries-old map showing the territory of Rothenburg.*

MAP OF ROTHENBURG CITY TERRITORY

In 1537 Rothenburg actually ruled a little country—one of about 300 petty dukedoms like this that made up what is today's Germany. The territory spanned a 12-by-12-mile area (about 400 square kilometers), encompassing 180 villages—a good example of the fragmentation of feudal Germany. While not to scale (Rothenburg is actually less than a mile wide), the map is fun to study. In the 1380s, Mayor Toppler purchased much

of this territory. In 1562, the city sold off some of its land to neighboring dukes, which gave it the money for all the fine Renaissance buildings that embellish the town to this day.

• *Continue through the courtyard and into a square called...*

GREEN MARKET (GRÜNER MARKT)

Once a produce market, this parking lot fills with Christmas stands during December. Notice the clay-tile roofs. These "beaver tail" tiles became standard after thatched roofs were outlawed to prevent fires. Today, all of the town's roofs are made of these. The little fences stop heaps of snow from falling off the roof and onto people below. A free public WC is on your left, and the recommended Friese gift shop is on your right.

• *Continue straight ahead to St. Jakob's Church. Study the exterior first, then pay to go inside.*

▲▲ST. JAKOB'S CHURCH (ST. JAKOBSKIRCHE)

Rothenburg's main church is home to Tilman Riemenschneider's exquisitely rendered, wood-carved *Altar of the Holy Blood*.

Cost and Hours: €2.50, daily April-Oct 9:00-17:15, Dec 10:00-16:45, Nov and Christmas-March 10:00-12:00 & 14:00-16:00, on Sun wait to enter until services end at 10:45.

Tours and Information: A free, helpful English info sheet is available. Concerts

Map of Old Rothenburg

and a tour schedule are posted on the door. Guided tours in English run on Sat at 15:30 (April-Oct) for no extra charge. The worthwhile audioguide (€2, 45 minutes) lets you tailor your education, offering a dual commentary—historical and theological—for a handful of important stops in the church.

Visiting the Church: Start by viewing the exterior of the church. Next, enter the church, where you'll see the main nave first, then climb above the pipe organ (in the back) to finish with the famous carved altar.

Exterior: Outside the church, under the little roof at the base of the tower, you'll see 14th-century statues (mostly original) showing Jesus praying at Gethsemane, a common feature of Gothic churches. The sculptor is anonymous—in the Gothic age (pre-Albrecht Dürer), artists were just nameless craftspeople working only for the glory of God. Five yards to the left (on the wall), notice the nub of a sandstone statue—a rare original, looking pretty bad after 500 years of weather and, more recently, pollution. Most original statues are now in the city museum. The better-preserved statues you see on the church are copies.

Before entering, notice how the church was extended to the west and actually built over the street. The newer chapel was built to accommodate pilgrims and to contain the sumptuous Riemenschneider carved altarpiece.

If it's your wedding day, take the first entrance—marked by a very fertile Eve and, around the corner, Adam showing off an impressive six-pack. Otherwise, head toward the church's second (downhill) door. Before going inside, notice the modern statue at the base of the stairs. This is **St. James** (a.k.a. Sankt Jakob in German, Santiago in Spanish, and Saint-Jacques in French). You can tell this important saint by his big, floppy hat, his walking stick, the gourd on his hip (used by pilgrims to carry water), and—most importantly—the scallop shell in his hand. St. James' remains are entombed in the grand cathedral of Santiago de Compostela, in the northwestern corner of Spain. The medieval pilgrimage route called the Camino de Santiago (recently back in vogue) passed through here on its way to that distant corner of Europe. Pilgrims would wear the scallop shell as a symbol of their destination (where that type of marine life was abundant). To this day, the word for "scallop" in many languages carries the name of this saint: *Jakobsmuschel* in German, *coquille Saint-Jacques* in French, and so on.

Inside the Church: Built in the 14th century, this church has been Lutheran since 1544. The interior was "purified" by Romantics in the 19th century—cleaned of everything Baroque or not original and refitted in the Neo-Gothic style. (For example, the baptismal font in the middle of the choir and the pulpit above the second pew *look* Gothic, but are actually Neo-Gothic.) The stained-glass windows behind the altar, which are most colorful in the morning light, are originals from the 1330s. Admiring this church, consider what it says about the priorities of a town of just a few thousand people who decided to use their collective wealth to build such a place. The size of a church is a good indication of the town's wealth when it was built. Medallions and portraits of Rothenburg's leading families and church leaders line the walls above the choir in the front of the church.

St. Jakob's Church

The **main altar,** from 1466, is by Friedrich Herlin. Below Christ are statues of six saints—including St. James (a.k.a. Jakob), with the telltale shell on his floppy hat. Study the painted panels—ever see Peter with spectacles (below the carved saints)? Go around the back of the altarpiece to look at the doors. In the upper left, you'll see a painting of Rothenburg's Market Square in the 15th century, looking much like it does today, with the exception of the full-Gothic Town Hall (as it was before the big fire of 1501). Notice Christ's face on the white "veil of Veronica" (center of back side, bottom edge). It follows you as you walk from side to side—this must have given the faithful the religious heebie-jeebies four centuries ago.

The **Tabernacle of the Holy Eucharist** (just left of the main altar—on your right as you walk back around) is a century older. It stored the wine and bread used for Holy Communion. Before the Reformation, this was a Roman Catholic church, which meant that the bread and wine were considered to be the actual body and blood of Jesus (and therefore needed a worthy repository). Notice the unusual Trinity: The Father and Son are bridged by a dove, which represents the Holy Spirit. Stepping back, you can see that Jesus is standing on a skull—clearly "overcoming death."

Now, as pilgrims did centuries ago, climb the stairs at the back of the church that lead up behind the pipe organ to a loft-like chapel. Here you'll find the artistic highlight of Rothenburg and perhaps the most wonderful wood carving in all of Germany: the glorious 500-year-old, 35-foot-high ***Altar of the Holy Blood.*** Tilman Riemenschneider, the Michelangelo of German woodcarvers, carved this from 1499 to 1504 (at the same time Michelangelo was working on his own masterpieces). The altarpiece was designed to hold a rock-crystal capsule—set in the cross you see high above—that contains a precious scrap of tablecloth stained in the shape of a cross by a drop of communion wine.

The altar is a realistic commotion, showing that Riemenschneider—a High Gothic artist—was ahead of his time. Below, in the scene of the Last Supper, Jesus gives Judas a piece of bread, marking him as the traitor, while John lays his head on Christ's lap. Judas, with his big bag of cash, could be removed from the scene (illustrated by photos on the wall nearby), as was the tradition for the four days leading up to Easter.

Everything is portrayed exactly as described in the Bible. In the relief panel on the left, Jesus enters the walled city of Jerusalem. Notice the exacting attention to detail—down to the nails on the horseshoe. In the relief panel on the right, Jesus prays in the Garden of Gethsemane.

Before continuing on, take a moment to simply linger over the lovingly executed details: the curly locks of the apostles' hair and beards, and the folds of their garments; the delicate vines intertwining above their heads; Jesus' expression, at once tender and accusing.

• *After leaving the church, walk around the corner to the right and under the chapel (built over the road). Go two blocks down Klingengasse and stop at the corner of the street called Klosterhof. Looking farther ahead of you down Klingengasse, you see the...*

Altar of the Holy Blood

KLINGENTOR

This cliff tower was Rothenburg's water reservoir. From 1595 until 1910, a 900-liter (240-gallon) copper tank high in the tower provided clean spring water—pumped up by river power—to the privileged. To the right of the Klingentor is a good stretch of wall rampart to walk. To the left, the wall is low and simple, lacking a rampart because it guards only a cliff.

Now find the shell decorating a building on the street corner next to you. That's once again the symbol of St. James, indicating that this building is associated with the church.

• Turn left down Klosterhof, passing the shell and, on your right, the colorful, recommended Altfränkische Weinstube am Klosterhof pub. As you approach the next stop, notice the lazy Susan embedded in the wall (to the right of the museum door), which allowed cloistered nuns to give food to the poor without being seen.

▲▲IMPERIAL CITY MUSEUM (REICHSSTADT-MUSEUM)

You'll get a vivid and artifact-filled sweep through Rothenburg's history at this excellent museum, housed in a former Dominican convent.

Cost and Hours: €4.50, €3 more to take photos (not worth it for most), daily April-Oct 9:30-17:30, Nov-March 13:00-16:00, pick up English info sheet at entrance, additional English descriptions posted, Klosterhof 5, tel. 09861/939-043, www.reichsstadtmuseum.rothenburg.de.

Visiting the Museum: As you follow the *Rundgang/Tour* signs to the left, watch for the following highlights:

Immediately inside the entry, a glass case shows off the 1616 Prince Elector's colorful glass tankard (which inspired the famous legend of the Meistertrunk, created in 1881 to drive tourism) and a set of golden Rothenburg coins. Down the hall, find a modern city model and trace the city's growth, its walls expanding like rings on a big tree. Around the corner (before going upstairs), you'll see medieval and Renaissance sculptures, including original sandstone statues from St. Jakob's Church and original statues that once decorated the Baumeister Haus near Market Square. Upstairs in the nuns' dormitory are craftsmen's signs that once hung outside shops (see if you can guess the craft before reading the museum's label), ornate locks, tools for various professions, and a valuable collection of armor and weapons. You'll then see old furniture and the Baroque statues that decorated the organ loft in St. Jakob's Church from 1669 until the 19th century, when they were cleared out to achieve "Gothic purity." Take time to enjoy the several rooms and shop fronts outfitted as they would have been centuries ago.

The painting gallery is lined with Romantic paintings of Rothenburg, which served as the first tourist promotion, and give visitors today a chance to envision the city as it appeared in centuries past. Look for the large, gloomy work by Englishman Arthur Wasse (labeled *"Es spukt"*)—does that door look familiar?

Back downstairs, circle around the cloister to see a 14th-century convent kitchen (*Klosterküche*) with a working model of the lazy Susan (give it a swing) and a massive chimney (step inside and look up); an exhibit of Jewish culture in Rothenburg through the ages (*Judaika*); and the grand finale (in the *Konventsaal*), the *Rothenburger Passion*. This 12-panel series of paintings showing scenes leading

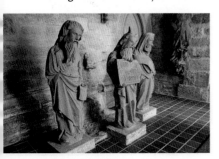

Imperial City Museum

up to Christ's Crucifixion—originally intended for the town's Franciscan church (which we'll pass later)—dates from 1492.

• *Leaving the museum, go around to the right and into the Convent Garden (when locked at night, continue straight to the T-intersection and turn right).*

CONVENT GARDEN

This spot is a peaceful place to work on your tan...or mix a poisoned potion. Monks and nuns—who were responsible for concocting herbal cures in the olden days, finding disinfectants, and coming up with ways to disguise the taste of rotten food—often tended herb gardens. Smell (but don't pick) the *Pfefferminze* (peppermint), *Heidewacholder* (juniper/gin), *Rosmarin* (rosemary), *Lavandel* (lavender), and the tallest plant, *Hopfen* (hops... monks were the great medieval brewers). Don't smell the plants that are poisonous (potency indicated by the number of crosses, like stars indicating spiciness on a restaurant menu). Appreciate the setting, taking in the fine architecture and expansive garden—all within the city walls, where land was at such a premium. It's a reminder of the power of the pre-Reformation Church.

• *Exit opposite from where you entered, angling left through the nuns' garden, leaving via an arch along the far wall. Then turn right and go downhill to the...*

TOWN WALL

This part of the wall takes advantage of the natural fortification provided by the cliff (view through bars, look to far right), and is therefore much shorter than the ramparts.

• *Angle left along the wall. Cross the big street (Herrngasse, with the Burgtor tower on your right—which we'll enter from outside momentarily) and continue downhill on Burggasse until you hit the town wall. Turn right, go through a small tower gate, and park yourself at the town's finest viewpoint.*

CASTLE GARDEN VIEWPOINT

From here, enjoy a fine view of fortified Rothenburg. You're looking at the Spitaltor end of town (with the most interesting gate and the former hospital). After this walk, you can continue with my "Schmiedgasse-Spitalgasse Shopping Stroll," which leads from Market Square down to this end of town, and then enter the city walls and walk the ramparts 180 degrees to the Klingentor tower (which we saw earlier on our walk, in the distance just after St. Jakob's Church). The droopy-eyed building at the far end of town (today's youth hostel) was the horse mill—which provided grinding power when the water mill in the valley below was not working (during drought or siege). Stretching below you is the fine parklike land around the Tauber River, nicknamed the "Tauber Riviera."

• *Now explore deeper into the park.*

CASTLE GARDEN (BURGGARTEN) AND THE BURGTOR GATE

The park before you was a castle fortress until it was destroyed in the 14th century.

Convent Garden

Burgtor Gate

The chapel (50 yards straight into the park, on the left) is the only surviving bit of the original castle. In front of the chapel is a memorial to local Jews killed in a 1298 slaughter. A few steps beyond that is a flowery trellis that provides a fine picnic spot. If you walk all the way out to the garden's far end, you'll find another great viewpoint (well past the tourists, and considered by local teenagers the best place to make out).

When you're ready to leave the park, approach the Burgtor, the ornate fortified gate flanked by twin stubby towers, and imagine being locked out in the year 1400. (There's a WC on the left.) The tall tower behind the gate was accessed by a wooden drawbridge—see the chain slits above the inner gate, and between them the "pitch" mask with holes designed to allow defenders to pour boiling Nutella on attackers. High above is the town coat of arms: a red (roten) castle (Burg).

Go through the gate and study the big wooden door with the tiny "eye of the needle" door cut into it. If trying to enter town after curfew, you could bribe the guard to let you through this door, which was small enough to keep out any fully armed attackers. Note also the square-shaped hole on the right and imagine the massive timber that once barricaded the gate.

• Now, climb up the big street, Herrngasse, as you return to your starting point.

HERRNGASSE

Many towns have a Herrngasse, where the richest patricians and merchants (the Herren) lived. Predictably, it's your best chance to see the town's finest old mansions. Strolling back to Market Square, you'll pass, on the right, the **Franciscan Church** (from 1285—the oldest in town). Across the street, the mint-green house at #18 is the biggest patrician house on this main drag. The front door was big enough to allow a carriage to drive through it; a human-sized door cut into it was used by those on foot. The family,

which has lived here for three centuries, has disconnected the four tempting old-time doorbells. The gift shop at #11 (on the right) offers a chance to poke into one of these big landowners' homes and appreciate their structure: living quarters in front above carriage-size doors, courtyard out back functioning as a garage, stables, warehouse, servants' quarters, and a private well.

Farther up, also on the right, is Hotel Eisenhut, Rothenburg's fanciest hotel and worth a peek inside. Finally, passing the Käthe Wohlfahrt Christmas headquarters/shop (described under "Shopping," later) you'll be back at Market Square, where you started this walk.

• From here, you can continue walking by following my "Schmiedgasse-Spitalgasse Shopping Stroll," next. This stroll ends at the city gate called Spitaltor, a good access point for a walk on the town walls.

❍ Schmiedgasse-Spitalgasse Shopping Stroll

After doing the town walk and visiting the town's three essential interior sights (Imperial City Museum, Medieval Crime and Punishment Museum, and St. Jakob's Church), your next priority might be Rothenburg's shops and its town wall.

I'd propose this fun walk, worth ▲▲, which goes from Market Square in a straight line south (past the best selection of characteristic family-run shops) to the city's most impressive fortification (Spitaltor). From Spitaltor you can access the town wall and walk the ramparts 180 degrees around the city to the Klingentor tower.

Standing on Market Square, with your back to the TI, you'll see a street sloping downward toward the south end of town. That's where you're headed. This street changes names as you walk, from **Obere Schmiedgasse** (upper blacksmith street) to **Spitalgasse** (hospital street), and runs directly to the **Spitaltor** tower and gate.

As you stroll down this delightful lane,

feel welcome to pop in and explore any shop along this cultural and historical scavenger hunt. I've provided the street number and "left" or "right" to indicate the side of the street.

Start on Market Square. The facade of the fine Renaissance **Baumeister Haus** at #3 (left) celebrates a secular (rather than religious) morality, with statues representing the seven virtues and the seven vices. Which ones do you recognize?

At #5 (left) **Gasthof Goldener Greifen** was once the home of the illustrious Mayor Toppler (d. 1408). By the looks of its door (right of the main entrance), the mayor must have had an impressive wine cellar. Note the fine hanging sign of a gilded griffin. Business signs in a mostly illiterate medieval world needed to be easy for all to read. The entire street is ornamented with fun signs like this one. Nearby, a pretzel marks the bakery, and the crossed swords advertise the weapon maker.

Shops on both sides of the street at #7 display examples of *Schneeballen* gone wild. These "snowballs," once a humble way to bake extra flour into a simple treat, are now iced and dolled up a million ways. Long ago, locals used a fork to pierce the middle, but today's tourists eat them like an apple. Watch them crumble.

Waffenkammer, at #9 (left), is "the weapons chamber," where Johannes Wittmann works hard to make a wonderland in which young-at-heart tourists can

shop for (and try out) medieval weapons, armor, and clothing. Fun photo ops abound, especially downstairs—where you can try on a set of chain mail and pose with a knight in shining armor.

At #18 (right), **Metzgerei Trumpp,** a top-end butcher, is a carnivores' heaven. Check out the endless wurst offerings in the window—a reminder that in the unrefrigerated Middle Ages meat needed to be smoked or salted.

At the next corner, with **Burggasse,** find the Catholic St. John's Church. The Medieval Crime and Punishment Museum (just down the lane to the right) marks the site of Rothenburg's first town wall. Below the church (on the right) is an old fountain. Behind and below that find a cute little doggie park complete with a doggie WC.

The **Jutta Korn** shop, on the right at #4, showcases the work of an artisan who has designed jewelry here for 30 years. At #6 (right), **Leyk** sells "lighthouses" made in town, many modeled after local buildings. The **Kleiderey,** an offbeat clothing store at #7 (left), is run by Tina, the Night Watchman's wife. The clothing is inspired by their Southeast Asian travels.

At #13 (left), look opposite to find a narrow lane **(Ander Eich)** that leads to a little viewpoint in the town wall, overlooking the "Tauber Riviera."

Continuing along, at #17 (left), the **Lebe Gesund Vegetarian** shop is all about healthy living. This charming little place seems designed to offer forgiveness to those who loved the butcher's shop but are ready to repent.

The **Käthe Wohlfahrt** shop at #19 (left) is just another of the KW shops around town, all selling German clichés with gusto. Also on the left, at #21, the **An Ra** Shop is where Annett Rafoth designs and sells her flowery clothes. You can pop in to see the actual work in the back. (There's more of An Ra across the street at #26.)

At #29 (left), **Glocke Weinladen am Plönlein** is an inviting shop of wine glasses and related accessories. The **Gasthof Glocke,** next door, with its wine-barrel-sized cellar door just waiting for some action, is a respected restaurant and home to the town's last vintner—a wonderful place to try local wines, as they serve flights of five tiny glasses.

The next corner, on the right, is dubbed **Plönlein** and is famously picturesque. If this scene brings you back to your childhood, that's because Rothenburg was the inspiration for the village in the 1940 Disney animated film *Pinocchio.*

Walk a few more yards and look far up the lane **(Neugasse)** to the left. You'll see some cute pastel buildings with uniform windows and rooflines—clues that the buildings were rebuilt after WWII bombings hit that part of town. Straight ahead, the **Siebertstor Tower** marks the next layer of expansion to the town wall. Continue through the tower. The former tannery is now a pub featuring **Landwehr Bräu,** the local brew.

Farther along, at #14 (right), **Antiq & Trödel,** which smells like an antique shop should, is fun to browse through.

Still farther down, on the left, at #25, **Hotel-Café Gerberhaus** is a fine stop for coffee and cake, with a delicate dining room and a peaceful courtyard hiding out back under the town wall.

The remaining few (boring) blocks take you to **Spitaltor,** the tall tower with a gate marking the end of town, and a good place to begin a ramparts ramble

(going counterclockwise), if you're up for it.

Walk through the gate (taking note of the stairs to the right—that's where you could begin your wall walk—described next). Standing outside the wall, ponder this sight as if approaching the city 400 years ago. The wealth of a city was shown by its walls and towers. (Stone was costly—in fact, the German saying for "filthy rich" is "stone rich.") Circle around to the right. Look up at the formidable tower. The guardhouse atop it, one of several in the wall, was manned continuously during medieval times. Above the entry gate, notice the emblem: Angels bless the double eagle of the Holy Roman Emperor, which blesses the town, symbolized by the two red towers.

❺ Walk the Wall

Just longer than a mile and a half around, providing superb views and a fine orientation, this walk, worth ▲▲, can be done by those under six feet tall in less than an hour. The hike requires no special sense of balance. Much of the walk is covered and is a great option in the rain. Photographers will stay very busy, especially before breakfast or at sunset when the lighting is best and the crowds are gone. You can enter or exit the ramparts at nearly every tower.

While the ramparts circle the city, some stretches aren't walkable per se: Along much of the western side of town, you can't walk atop the wall, but you can walk

The city ramparts

right alongside it and peek over or through it for great views outward from street level. Refer to the map on page 799 to see which portions of the walls are walkable.

If you want to make a full town circuit, Spitaltor—at the south end of town, with the best fortifications—makes a good starting place. From here, it's a counter-clockwise walk along the eastern and northern ramparts. After exiting at Klingentor, you can still follow the wall for a bit, but you'll have to cut inland, away from the wall, when you hit the Imperial City Museum, and again near the Medieval Crime and Punishment Museum. At the Kohlturm tower, back at the southern end of town, you can climb the stairs and walk atop the remaining short stretch of wall to the Spitalhof quarter, where you'll need to exit again. Spitaltor, where you started, is just a *Schneeball*'s toss away.

The TI has installed a helpful series of English-language plaques at about 20 stops along the route. The names you see along the way belong to people who donated money to rebuild the wall after World War II, and those who've more recently donated €1,000 per meter for the maintenance of Rothenburg's heritage.

Sights

Note that a number of sights (including St. Jakob's Church and the Imperial City Museum) have already been covered on the Rothenburg Town Walk.

On and Near Market Square
▲TOWN HALL TOWER
From Market Square you can see tourists on the crow's nest capping the Town Hall's tower. For a commanding view from the town's tallest perch, climb the steps of the tower. It's a rigorous but interesting 214-step climb that gets narrow and steep near the top—watch your head.

Cost and Hours: €2, pay at top, daily in season 9:00-12:30 & 13:00-17:00, enter from the grand steps overlooking Market Square.

▲▲MEDIEVAL CRIME AND PUNISHMENT MUSEUM (MITTELALTERLICHES KRIMINALMUSEUM)
Specializing in everything connected to medieval criminal justice, this exhibit (well-described in English) is a cut above all the tacky and popular torture museums around Europe. In addition to ogling spiked chairs, thumbscrews, and shame masks—nearly everything on display here is an actual medieval artifact—you'll learn about medieval police and criminal law. The museum is more eclectic than its name, and includes exhibits on general history, superstition, biblical art, and so on.

Cost and Hours: €5, daily April 11:00-17:00, May-Oct 10:00-18:00, Nov and Jan-Feb 14:00-16:00, Dec and March 13:00-16:00, last entry 45 minutes before closing, fun cards and posters, Burggasse 3-5, tel. 09861/5359, www.kriminalmuseum.rothenburg.de.

Visiting the Museum: It's a one-way route. Just follow the yellow arrows and you'll see it all. Keep an eye out for several well-done interactive media stations that provide extra background on the museum's highlights.

From the entrance, head downstairs to the **cellar** to see some enhanced-interrogation devices. Torture was common in the Middle Ages—not to punish, but to extract a confession (medieval "justice" required a confession). Just the sight of these tools was often enough to make an innocent man confess. You'll see the rack, "stretching ladder," thumb screws, spiked leg screws, and other items that would make Dick Cheney proud. Medieval torturers also employed a waterboarding-like technique—but here, the special ingredient was holy water.

Upstairs, on the **first and second floors,** the walls are lined with various legal documents of the age, while the dusty glass cases show off law-enforcement tools—many of them quite creative. Shame was a big tool back then; wrongdoers would be creatively shamed before their neighbors. The town could publicly humiliate those who ran afoul of the law by tying them to a pillory in the main square and covering their faces in an iron mask of shame. The mask's fanciful decorations indicated the crime: Chicken feathers meant promiscuity, horns indicated that a man's wife slept around (i.e., cuckold), and a snout suggested that the person had acted piggishly. A gossip might wear a mask with giant ears (heard everything), eyeglasses (saw everything), and a giant, wagging tongue (couldn't keep her mouth shut). The infamous "iron maiden" started out as more of a "shame barrel"; the internal spikes were added to play up popular lore when it went on display for 18th-century tourists. For more serious offenses, criminals were branded—so that even if they left town, they'd take that shame with them for the rest of their lives. When all else failed, those in charge could always turn to the executioner's sword.

To safely capture potential witches, lawmen used a device resembling a metal collar—with spikes pointing in—that was easy to get into, but nearly impossible to get out of. A neck violin—like a portable version of a stock—kept the accused under control. (The double neck violin could be used to lock together a quarrelsome couple to force them to work things out.) The chastity belts were used to ensure a wife's loyalty (giving her traveling husband peace of mind) and/or to protect women from attack at a time when rape was far more commonplace. The exit routes you through a courtyard garden to a **last building** with temporary exhibits (included in your admission and often interesting) and a café. (If you must buy a *Schneeball*, consider doing it here—where they are small, inexpensive, and fairly edible—and help support the museum.)

▲**GERMAN CHRISTMAS MUSEUM (DEUTSCHES WEIHNACHTSMUSEUM)**

This excellent museum, in a Disney-esque space upstairs in the giant Käthe Wohlfahrt Christmas Village shop, tells the history of Christmas decorations. There's a unique and thoughtfully described collection of tree stands, mini-trees sent in boxes to WWI soldiers at the front, early Advent calendars, old-time Christmas cards, Christmas pyramids, and a look at the evolution of Father Christmas, as well as tree decorations through the ages—including the Nazi era and when you were a kid. The museum is not just a ploy to get shoppers to spend more money, but a serious collection managed by professional curator Felicitas Höptner.

Cost and Hours: €4 most of the year, open April-Dec daily 10:00-17:30, shorter and irregular hours Jan-March, Herrngasse 1, tel. 09861/409-365, www.christmasmuseum.com.

Experiences
Shopping

Be warned...Rothenburg is one of Germany's best shopping towns. Do it here and be done with it. Lovely prints, carvings, wine glasses, Christmas-tree ornaments, and beer steins are popular. Rödergasse is the old town's everyday shopping street. Also try my Shopping Stroll on page 807. There's also a modern shopping center across the street from the train station.

KÄTHE WOHLFAHRT CHRISTMAS HEADQUARTERS

Rothenburg is the headquarters of the **Käthe Wohlfahrt** Christmas trinkets empire, which has spread across the half-timbered reaches of Europe. Rothenburg has six or eight Wohlfahrts (all stores open Mon-Sat 9:00-18:30, May-Dec also most Sun 10:00-18:00). Tourists flock to the two biggest, just below Market Square. Start with the **Christmas Village** (Weihnachtsdorf) at Herrngasse 1. This Christmas wonderland is filled with enough twinkling lights (196,000—mostly LEDs) to require a special electrical hookup. You're greeted by instant Christmas mood music (best appreciated on a hot day in July) and tourists hungrily filling little woven shopping baskets with goodies to hang on their trees. Let the spinning, flocked tree whisk you in, and pause at the wall of Steiff stuffed animals, jerking uncontrollably and mesmerizing kids. Then head downstairs to find the vast and sprawling "made in Germany" section, surrounding a slowly spinning 15-foot tree decorated with a thousand glass balls. (Items handmade in Germany are the most expensive.) They often offer a discount on all official KW products to my readers—ask. The fascinating **Christmas Museum** upstairs is described earlier, under "Sights." The smaller shop (across the street at Herrngasse 2) specializes in finely crafted wooden ornaments. Käthe opened her first storefront here in Rothenburg in 1977. The company is now run by her son Harald, who lives in town.

Rick's Tip: *To* **mail your goodies home,** *you can get handy yellow €2.50 boxes at the old town* **post office** *(Mon-Tue and Thu-Fri 9:00-13:00 & 14:00-17:30, Wed 9:00-13:00, Sat 9:00-12:00, closed Sun, inside photo shop at Rödergasse 11). The main post office is in the shopping center across from the train station.*

FRIESE SHOP

Cuckoo with friendliness, trinkets, and reasonably priced souvenirs, the Friese shop has been open for more than 50 years. Shoppers with this book receive tremendous service: a 10 percent discount and a free pictorial map (normally €1.50). Anneliese Friese, who runs the place with her son Bernie and granddaughter Dolores (a.k.a. "Mousy"), charges only her cost for shipping and lets tired travelers leave their bags in her back room for free (Mon-Sat 9:00-18:00, Sun 10:00-18:00, 20 steps off Market Square at Grüner Markt 8—around the corner from TI and across from free public WC, tel. 09861/7166).

Festivals

For one weekend each spring (during Pentecost), *Biergartens* spill out into the street and Rothenburgers dress up in medieval costumes to celebrate Mayor Nusch's **Meistertrunk** victory (www.meistertrunk. de). The **Reichsstadt festival** every September celebrates Rothenburg's history, and the town's **Weindorf festival** celebrates its wine (mid-Aug). For more info, check the TI website: www.tourismus. rothenburg.de.

In winter, Rothenburg is quiet except for its **Christmas Market** in December, when the entire town cranks up the medieval cuteness with concerts and costumes, shops with schnapps, stalls filling squares, hot spiced wine, giddy nutcrackers, and mobs of ear-muffed Germans. Try to avoid Saturdays and Sundays, when big-city day-trippers really clog the grog.

Eating

My recommendations are all within a five-minute walk of Market Square. While all survive on tourism, many still feel like local hangouts. Your choices are typical German or ethnic. You'll see regional Franconian (*fränkische*) specialties advertised, such as the German ravioli called *Maultaschen* and Franconian bratwurst (similar to other brats, but more coarsely ground, with less fat, and liberally seasoned with marjoram). Many restaurants take a midafternoon break, stop serving lunch at 14:00, and end dinner service as early as 20:00.

Traditional German Restaurants

Reichsküchenmeister's interior is like any big-hotel restaurant's, but on a balmy evening, its pleasant, tree-shaded terrace overlooking St. Jakob's Church and reliably good dishes are hard to beat (€10-25 main courses, €7-10 *Flammkuchen*— southern German flatbread, steaks, vegetarian options, daily 11:30-21:30, Kirchplatz 8, tel. 09861/9700).

$$ **Hotel Restaurant Kloster-Stüble,** on a small street off Herrngasse near the castle garden, is a classy place for delicious traditional cuisine, including homemade *Maultaschen*. Choose from their shaded terrace, sleek and modern dining room, or woody and traditional dining room (€10-20 main courses, Thu-Mon 18:00-21:00, Sat-Sun also 11:00-14:00, closed Tue-Wed, Heringsbronnengasse 5, tel. 09861/938-890).

$$ **Gasthof Goldener Greifen,** in a historic building with a peaceful garden out back, is just off the main square. The Klingler family serves quality Franconian food at a good price...and with a smile. The ambience is practical rather than posh (€8-17 main courses, €12-15 three-course daily specials, affordable kids'

meals, daily 11:30-21:00 except closed Sun in winter, Obere Schmiedgasse 5, tel. 09861/2281).

Rick's Tip: *For a rare chance to* **meet the locals,** *bring your favorite slang and tongue-twisters to the* **English Conversation Club** *at* **Altfränkische Weinstube am Klosterhof.** *Hermann the German and his sidekick Wolfgang are regulars. A big table is reserved from 18:30 on Wednesday evenings. Consider arriving early for dinner, or after 21:00, when the beer starts to sink in and everyone speaks that second language more easily.*

$ **Altfränkische Weinstube am Klosterhof,** classically candlelit in a 600-year-old building, seems designed for gnomes to celebrate their anniversaries with gourmet pub grub. It's a clear favorite with locals for an atmospheric drink or late meal. When every other place is asleep, you're likely to find good food, drink, and energy here (€7-15 main courses, hot food served Wed-Mon 18:00-21:30, closed Tue, off Klingengasse at Klosterhof 7, tel. 09861/6404).

$ **Zum Pulverer** ("The Powderer") is a

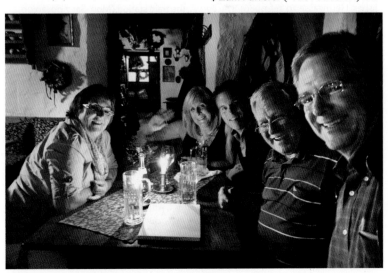

English Conversation Club

traditional wine bar just inside the Burg-tor gate that serves a menu of affordable regional fare, sometimes with modern flourishes. The interior is a cozy wood-hewn place that oozes history, with chairs carved in the shape of past senators of Rothenburg (€6-14 dishes, Wed-Fri and Mon 17:00-22:00, Sat-Sun 12:00-22:00, closed Tue, Herrengasse 31, tel. 09861/976-182, Bastian).

$ **Alter Keller** is a modest, tourist-friendly restaurant with a characteristic interior and outdoor tables on a peaceful square just a couple blocks off Market Square. The menu has German classics at reasonable prices (€8-14 main dishes, Wed-Sun 11:30-15:00 & 17:30-21:00, closed Mon-Tue, Alter Keller 8, tel. 09861/2268, Markus and Miriam).

A Non-Franconian Splurge

$$$$ **Hotel Restaurant Herrnschlöss-chen** is the local favorite fare, with a small menu of international and seasonal dishes. There's always a serious vegetarian option and a €50 fixed-price meal with matching wine. Sit in the classy dining hall or in the shaded Baroque garden out back. Reservations are a must (€20-30 main dishes, Herrngasse 20, tel. 09861/873-890, www.hotel-rothenburg.de).

Breaks from Pork and Potatoes

$$ **Pizzeria Roma** is the local favorite for pizza and pastas, with good Italian wine. The Magrini family moved here from Tuscany in 1970 and they've been serving pasta ever since (Thu-Tue 11:30-23:00, closed Wed and mid-Aug-mid-Sept, Galgengasse 19, tel. 09861/4540).

$ **TobinGo,** just off Market Square, serves cheap and tasty Turkish food to eat in or take away. Their *döner kebabs* must be the best €3.70 hot meal in Rothenburg. For about €1 more, try a less-bready *Dürüm Döner*—same ingredients but in a warm tortilla (daily 10:00-22:00, Hafengasse 2).

Sandwiches and Snacks

$ **Brot & Zeit** (a pun on *Brotzeit*, "bread time," the German term for snacking), conveniently located a block off Market Square, is like a German bakery dressed up as a Starbucks. Just inside the picturesque Markus Tower gate, they sell takeaway coffee, inexpensive sandwiches, and a few hot dishes (Mon-Sat 6:00-18:30, Sun 7:30-18:00, Hafengasse 24, tel. 09861/936-8701).

While any bakery in town can sell you a sandwich for a couple of euros, I like to pop into **Metzgerei Trumpp,** a high-quality butcher shop serving up cheap and tasty sausages on a bun with kraut to go (Mon-Fri 7:30-18:00, Sat until 16:00, usually closed Sun, a block off Market Square at Schmiedgasse 18).

A small **grocery store** is in the center of town (Mon-Fri 7:30-19:00, Sat-Sun until 18:00 except closed Sun off-season, Rödergasse 6). Larger supermarkets are outside the wall: Exit the town through the Rödertor, turn left through the cobbled gate, and cross the parking lot to reach the **Edeka supermarket** (Mon-Fri 8:00-20:00, Sat until 18:00, closed Sun); or head to the even bigger **Kaufland** across from the train station (Mon-Sat 7:00-20:00, closed Sun).

Beer Garden (Biergarten)

$ **Gasthof Rödertor,** just outside the wall through the Rödertor, runs a popular backyard *Biergarten,* where a rowdy crowd enjoys classic fare, pizza, and good beer. Their passion is potatoes (May-Sept daily 17:30-23:00 in good weather, table service only—no ordering at counter, Ansbacher Strasse 7, look for wooden gate, tel. 09861/2022). The *Biergarten* is open only in balmy weather, but their indoor restaurant, with a more extensive menu, is open year-round and also offers a good value (€8-13 main courses, Tue-Sun 11:30-14:00 & 17:30-21:30, closed Mon).

Dessert

Eis Café D'Isep has been making gelato in Rothenburg since 1960, using family recipes that span four generations. Their sidewalk tables are great for lazy people-watching (daily 10:00-22:00, closed early Oct-mid-Feb, one block off Market Square at Hafengasse 17, run by Paolo and Paola D'Isep and son Enrico).

Rothenburg's **bakeries** (*Bäckereien*) offer succulent pastries, pies, and cakes... but skip the bad-tasting *Rothenburger Schneeballen* promoted all over town: bland pie crusts crumpled into a ball and dusted with powdered sugar or frosted with sticky-sweet glop. Instead of wasting your appetite on a *Schneeball*, enjoy a curvy *Mandelhörnchen* (almond crescent cookie), a triangular *Nussecke* ("nut corner"), a round *Florentiner* cookie, a couple of fresh *Krapfen* (like jelly doughnuts), or a soft, warm German pretzel. But if the curiosity is too much to bear, try a fresh, handmade *Schneeball* from a smaller bakery (*frisch* is fresh; *handgemacht* is handmade), and avoid the slick places on the busy tourist avenues.

Wine-Drinking in the Old Center

$$ Restaurant Glocke, a wine bar with a full menu, is run by Rothenburg's oldest and only surviving winemakers, the Thürauf family. The very extensive wine list is in German only because the friendly staff wants to explain your options in person. Their special €5 wine flight lets you sample five Franconian white wines; other flights of reds and dessert wines are offered as well (€8-18 main courses, Mon-Sat 11:00-23:00, food until 22:00, closed Sun, Plönlein 1, tel. 09861/958-990).

Sleeping

Rothenburg is crowded with visitors, but most are day-trippers. Except for the rare Saturday night and during festivals (see page 812), finding a room is easy. If you want to splurge, you'll snare the best value by paying extra for the biggest and best rooms at the hotels I recommend. In the off-season (Nov and Jan-March), hoteliers may be willing to discount.

Train travelers save steps by staying in the Rödertor area (east end of town). Hotels and guesthouses will sometimes pick up tired heavy-packers at the station. If you're driving, call ahead to get directions and parking tips. Save some energy to climb the stairs: No hotels listed here have elevators.

Keep your key when out late. As Rothenburg's hotels are small and mostly family-run, they often lock up early (at about 22:00) and take one day a week off, so you'll need to let yourself in at those times.

In the Old Town

$$$ Hotel Herrnschlösschen prides itself on being the smallest (8 rooms) and most exclusive hotel in Rothenburg. If you're looking for a splurge, this is your best bet. This 1,000-year-old building has a beautiful Baroque garden and every amenity you'd ever want (including a sauna), but you'll pay for them (deluxe Db-€210, pricier suites, see website for seasonal discounts, Wi-Fi, Herrngasse 20, tel. 09861/873890, www.herrnschloesschen. de, info@herrnschloesschen.de).

$$ Hotel Kloster-Stüble, deep in the Old Town near the castle garden, is one of my classiest listings. Twenty-one rooms, each with its own special touches, fill two medieval buildings, connected by a modern atrium (traditional Db-€88-108, bigger and modern Db-€140-150, suites and family rooms, kids 5 and under free, just off Herrngasse at Heringsbronnengasse 5, tel. 09861/938-890, www.klosterstueble. de, hotel@klosterstueble.de).

$$$ Hotel Spitzweg is a rustic yet elegant 1536 mansion with 10 big rooms, open beams, antique furniture, and new bathrooms. It's run by gentle Herr Hocher, whom I suspect is the former Wizard of Oz—now retired and in a very good mood (Db-€90-100, family rooms and an apartment, nonsmoking, inviting old-fashioned breakfast room, free parking, Wi-Fi at son-in-law's nearby hotel, Paradeisgasse 2, tel. 09861/94290, www.hotel-spitzweg.de, info@hotel-spitzweg.de).

$$$ Gasthof Goldener Greifen is a traditional, 600-year-old place with 14 spacious rooms and all the comforts. It's run by a helpful family that also runs a good restaurant, serving meals in the back garden or dining room (small Db-€75, big Db-€85-104, family rooms, 10 percent less for 3-night stays, nonsmoking, full-service laundry-€8, free loaner bikes for guests, free and easy parking, half a block downhill from Market Square at Obere Schmiedgasse 5, tel. 09861/2281, www.gasthof-greifen-rothenburg.de, info@gasthof-greifen-rothenburg.de).

$$ Hotel Gerberhaus has 20 bright and airy rooms that mix modern amenities with half-timbered elegance. Enjoy the pleasant garden in back and the delightful breakfast buffet (Db-€89-130, family rooms and an apartment, €10 off second and subsequent nights and a *Schneeball* if you book direct and pay cash, nonsmoking, 4 rooms have canopied 4-poster *Himmel* beds, laundry-€10, limited free parking, close to P-1 parking lot, Spitalgasse 25, tel. 09861/94900, www.gerberhaus.rothenburg.de, gerberhaus@t-online.de).

$ Hotel Altfränkische Weinstube am Klosterhof is *the* place for well-heeled bohemians, with seven cozy rooms above the locals' favorite pub. The 600-year-old building has an upscale *Lord of the Rings* atmosphere, with open-beam ceilings, some canopied four-poster beds, and modern plumbing (Db-€69, bigger Db-€82, Db suite-€118, off Klingengasse at Klosterhof 7, tel. 09861/6404, www.altfraenkische.de, altfraenkische-weinstube@web.de).

$ Pension Elke rents 12 comfy rooms above a family grocery store (D-€57, Db-€65-69, cash only, request Rick Steves discount with this book if you stay at least 2 nights; reception in grocery store until 19:00, otherwise go around back and ring bell at top of stairs; near Markus Tower at Rödergasse 6, tel. 09861/2331, www.pension-elke-rothenburg.de, info@pension-elke-rothenburg.de).

$ Gästehaus Raidel rents eight rooms in a 500-year-old house with charming, ramshackle ambience. The beds and furniture are handmade by Norry Raidel himself. He also plays in a Dixieland band, has invented a fascinating hybrid saxophone/trombone called the Norryphone... and loves to jam (Db-€69, family rooms, cash only, pleasant terrace, Wenggasse 3, tel. 09861/3115, Norry asks you to use the reservations form at www.romanticroad.com/raidel).

$ Gasthof zum Breiterle offers 19 comfortable rooms with wooden accents above their restaurant near the Rödertor. Because it sits on a busy street, light sleepers may want to request a room not facing Wenggasse (Db-€78-88, apartment available, reception in restaurant, pay parking, Rödergasse 30, tel. 09861/6730, www.breiterle.de, info@breiterle.de).

$ Gästehaus Gerlinger, a fine value, has five comfortable rooms in a pretty 16th-century house with a small terrace for guests (Db-€62, an apartment, cash only, nonsmoking, easy parking, Schlegeleinsweth 10, tel. 09861/87979, mobile 0171-690-0752, www.pension-gerlinger.de, info@pension-gerlinger.de).

$ Kreuzerhof Hotel offers 11 decent rooms surrounding a courtyard on a quiet side street near the Rödertor (Db-€75-79, large Db-€92, family deals and rooms—including one for six people, nonsmoking, laundry-€7, parking in courtyard-€4/day, Millergasse 2-6, tel. 09861/3424, www.kreuzerhof.eu, info@kreuzerhof.eu).

$ Gästehaus Liebler rents two large, modern, ground-floor rooms with kitchenettes—great for real privacy close to the action. On the top floor is an attractive two-bedroom apartment (Db-€50, cash only, Rick Steves discount for 2 or more nights with this book, no breakfast but café nearby, nonsmoking, laundry-€5, behind Christmas shop at Pfäffleinsgässchen 10, tel. 09861/709-215, www.gaestehaus-liebler.de, info@gaestehaus-liebler.de).

¢ Rossmühle Youth Hostel rents 186 beds in two institutional yet charming buildings. Reception is in the huge building with droopy dormer windows—formerly a horse-powered mill. While most beds are in dorms, there are also 11 doubles (dorm bed-€25, bunk-bed Db-€61; guests over 26 pay €3.50 extra unless traveling with a family, nonmembers pay €4 extra, includes breakfast and sheets, dinner-€7, self-serve laundry with soap-€5, close to P-1 parking lot, entrance on Rossmühlgasse, tel. 09861/94160, www.rothenburg.jugendherberge.de, rothenburg@jugendherberge.de).

Transportation
Arriving and Departing
BY TRAIN

Arriving in Rothenburg: It's a 10-minute walk from the station to Rothenburg's Market Square (following the brown *Altstadt* signs, exit left from station, walk a block down Bahnhofstrasse, turn right on Ansbacher Strasse, and head straight into the Middle Ages). Taxis wait at the station (€6 to any hotel). Day-trippers can leave luggage in station lockers on the platform. Free WCs are behind the Speedy snack bar on track 1.

The station has a touch-screen terminal for fare and schedule information and ticket sales. If you need extra help, visit the combined ticket office/travel agency in the station building (€1-3 surcharge for most tickets, €0.50 charge for questions without ticket purchase, Mon-Fri 10:00-18:00, Sat 9:00-13:00, closed Sun, tel. 09861/7711, train info toll tel. 0180-699-6633, www.bahn.com).

Getting to/from Rothenburg via Steinach: If you take the train to or from Rothenburg, you'll transfer at Steinach. A tiny branch train line shuttles back and forth hourly between the two towns (14 minutes, generally departs Steinach at :35 and Rothenburg at :06). Train connections in Steinach are usually quick and efficient (trains to/from Rothenburg generally use track 5; use the conveyor belts to haul your bags smartly up and down the stairs). Steinach's station is unstaffed but has touch-screen ticket machines (though any ticket to or from Rothenburg will automatically include your transfer).

Note that the last train from Steinach to Rothenburg departs at about 22:30. But all is not lost if you arrive in Steinach after the last train: There's a subsidized taxi service to Rothenburg (cheaper for the government than running an almost-empty train). To use this handy service, called AST (*Anrufsammeltaxi*), make an appointment with a participating taxi service (call 09861/2000 or 09861/7227) at least an hour in advance (2 hours ahead is better), and they'll drive you from Steinach to Rothenburg for the cheap train fare (€4.60/person) rather than the regular €30 taxi fare.

From Rothenburg (via Steinach) by Train to: **Würzburg** (hourly, 70 minutes), **Nürnberg** (hourly, 1.5 hours, change in Ansbach), **Munich** (hourly, 2.5-4 hours, 2-3 changes), **Füssen** (hourly, 5 hours, often with changes in Treuchtlingen and Augsburg), **Frankfurt** (hourly, 2.5-3 hours, change in Würzburg), **Frankfurt Airport** (hourly, 3-3.5 hours, change in Würzburg), **Berlin** (hourly, 5.5 hours, 3 changes).

BY CAR

Driving and parking rules in Rothenburg change constantly—ask your hotelier for advice. In general, you're allowed to drive into the old town to get to your hotel. Otherwise, driving within the old walled center is discouraged. Some hotels offer private parking (either free or pay). To keep things simple, park in one of the lots—numbered P-1 through P-5—that line the outside of the town walls (€5/day, buy ticket from *Parkscheinautomat* machines and display, 5- to 10-minute walk to Market Square).

Driving from Frankfurt Airport: Even a jet-lagged zombie can handle the three-hour autobahn drive from the airport to Rothenburg. It's a 75-mile straight shot to Würzburg on the A-3 autobahn; just follow the blue autobahn signs toward *Würzburg*. Then turn south on A-7 and take the *Rothenburg o.d.T.* exit (#108).

NEAR ROTHENBURG

THE ROMANTIC ROAD

Along the Romantic Road, half-timbered towns are ringed by walls and towers, while flowers spill over the windowsills of the well-kept houses. Glockenspiels dance from Town Halls. Many travelers bypass these small towns by fast train or autobahn. But consider an extra day or two to take in the slow pace of life. I've included an overview of key sights on the route.

By Car

Wander through quaint hills and rolling villages along the scenic 220-mile driving route called the Romantic Road (*Romantische Strasse*, www.romantischestrasse. de). Stop wherever the cows look friendly or a town fountain beckons. If your goal is to meander and explore, don't use GPS—get a good map and follow the brown *Romantische Strasse* signs along two-lane roads. If you use GPS, you'll usually be routed to the nearest fast highway or autobahn, which isn't romantic at all.

If you're driving south of Rothenburg (whether heading toward it or leaving it), you could stop at the Wieskirche and the towns of Nördlingen and Dinkelsbühl.

If you're driving north of Rothenburg, good stops are Creglingen and Weikersheim.

By Bus

The Romantic Road bus runs daily from mid-April to late October. Every day, one bus goes north to south (Frankfurt to Munich to Füssen), and another goes south to north (Füssen to Munich to Frankfurt). You can begin or end your journey at any of the stops—including Rothenburg—along the way. Check the full timetable and prices at www. romantischestrasse.de.

South of Rothenburg

If you're driving from Füssen to Rothenburg, you'll encounter these three sights in this order:

The Romantic Road

Legend:
- ══ Romantic Road Bus Route
- ‑‑‑ Other Buses

Note: Not all rail lines are shown

▲▲Wieskirche

Germany's most glorious Baroque-Rococo church is beautifully restored and set in a sweet meadow. Bright and bursting with beauty, the church is worth the pilgrimage (see hours on page 797).

▲Nördlingen

Nördlingen is a real workaday town that has one of the best medieval walls in Germany, not to mention a surprising geologic history. For centuries, Nördlingen's residents puzzled over the local terrain, a flattish plain called the Ries, which rises to a low circular ridge that surrounds the town in the distance. In the 1960s, geologists figured out that Nördlingen lies in the middle of an impact crater blasted out 15 million years ago by a meteor.

Head into the center of town by zeroing in on the tower of **St. Georg's Church.** Climb the church tower for sweeping views of the town walls and crater. With more time, walk all the way around on the top of the **town wall,** which is even better preserved than Rothenburg's or Dinkelsbühl's. The town started building the wall in 1327 and financed it with a tax on wine and beer; it's more than a mile and a half long, has 16 towers and five gates, and offers great views of backyards and garden furniture.

Sleeping in Nördlingen: Several small hotels surrounding St. Georg's Church offer mediocre but reasonably priced rooms. Try **$$ Hotel Altreuter,** over an inviting bakery/café (Marktplatz 11, www. hotel-altreuter.de).

▲ Dinkelsbühl

A moat, towers, gates, and a beautifully preserved medieval wall all surround this pretty town. It's a delight to simply stroll here for an hour or two. Park at one of the free lots outside the town walls, which are well signed from the main road.

To orient yourself, head for the tower of **St. Georg's Cathedral,** at the center of town. This 15th-century church has a surprisingly light, airy interior and fine carved altarpieces. On good-weather summer weekends, you can climb to the top of the tower.

Outside the church, follow signs around the corner to the **TI,** which offers a free "Tour of the Town" brochure with a map and short walking tour (www. dinkelsbuehl.de).

Sleeping in Dinkelsbühl: Dinkelsbühl has a good selection of hotels, many of them lining the main drag in front of the church (though more choices and lower prices are available in Rothenburg and Nördlingen). Options include: **$$$ Hezelhof Hotel,** with modern rooms in an old shell (Segringer Strasse 7, www.hezelhof. com); **$$$ Weisses Ross,** attached to a historic restaurant (Steingasse 12, www. hotel-weisses-ross.de); and the town's unique **$ youth hostel,** in a medieval granary (Koppengasse 10, www.dinkelsbuehl. jugendherberge.de).

St. Georg's Church dominates Nördlingen.

Dinkelsbühl

North of Rothenburg
Creglingen

While Creglingen itself isn't worth much fuss, two quick and rewarding sights sit across the road from each other a mile south of town.

The peaceful 14th-century **Herrgottskirche Church,** worth ▲, is graced with Tilman Riemenschneider's greatest carved altarpiece, completed sometime between 1505 and 1510. The church's other colorful altars are also worth a peek (open daily in summer, afternoons only and closed Mon off-season, www.herrgottskirche.de).

The **Fingerhut Museum,** showing off thimbles (literally, "finger hats"), is far more interesting than it sounds. You'll step from case to case to squint at the collection, which numbers about 4,000 (but still fits in a single room) and comes from all over the world; some pieces are centuries old. Owner Thorvald Greif got a head start from his father, who owned a thimble factory (closed Mon and Jan-Feb, www.fingerhutmuseum.de).

▲Weikersheim

This picturesquely set town, nestled between hills, has a charming little main square offering easy access to a fine park and an impressive palace.

Weikersheim's **palace** (Schloss Weikersheim), across a moat-turned-park from the main square, was built in the late 16th century as the Renaissance country estate of a local count. With its bucolic location and glowing sandstone texture, it gives off a *Downton Abbey* vibe. It's viewable only by a guided tour in German; skip the tour and instead focus on exploring the palace's fine Baroque **gardens** (small entry fee, English audioguide www.schloss-weikersheim.de).

If you have time after your garden visit, Weikersheim's pleasant **town square** and cobbled old town are worth exploring. The **city park** (*Stadtpark*) makes a nice, free picnic spot, and from it you can peer over the hedge into the palace gardens.

The palace at Weikersheim has fine gardens.

Rhine Valley

The Rhine Valley is storybook Germany, a world of robber baron castles and fairy-tale legends. Cruise through the most turret-studded stretch of the romantic Rhine, listening for the song of the treacherous Loreley. Get hands-on thrills exploring the Rhineland's greatest castle, Rheinfels. Connoisseurs will also enjoy the fine interior of Marksburg Castle near Koblenz. Farther afield is Burg Eltz (a remarkable castle on the Mosel) and Cologne (with its incredible cathedral).

Spend your nights in a castle-crowned Rhine village, either delightful Bacharach or practical St. Goar. They're 10 miles apart, connected by milk-run trains, riverboats, and a riverside bike path. Bacharach is a more interesting town, but St. Goar has the famous Rheinfels Castle.

Marvel at the Rhine's ever-changing parade. Ever since Roman times, when this was the empire's northern boundary, the Rhine has been one of the world's busiest shipping rivers. Traveling along the river today, you'll see a steady flow of barges with 1,000- to 2,000-ton loads. Cars, buses, and trains rush along highways and tracks lining both banks, making it easy to get around.

If possible, visit the Rhine between April and October, when it's at its touristic best. In winter, some sights close, along with some hotels and restaurants, and only one riverboat runs.

THE RHINE VALLEY IN 1 OR 2 DAYS

With one day and two nights, stay in Bacharach. Cruise the best and most scenic stretch of the river (the hour from Bacharach to St. Goar), and tour Rheinfels Castle. Enjoy dinner in Bacharach, and maybe a wine tasting, too.

For a busier day, take a longer cruise, following all or part of my Rhine Blitz Tour. For example, you could cruise from Bacharach to Braubach (to tour Marksburg Castle), before returning by train to Bacharach.

With a second day, visit Burg Eltz on the Mosel as a day trip. Or bike or hike along the Rhine. This is a fun place to relax and explore.

If you're traveling by car, park it at your hotel, cruise the Rhine by boat, and visit Burg Eltz and/or Cologne on your drive in or out.

If a Rhine festival coincides with your

RHINE VALLEY AT A GLANCE

On the Rhine

▲▲▲**Rhine Blitz Tour** One of Europe's great joys—touring the Rhine River by boat, train, bike, or car. See page 826.

▲▲▲**Rheinfels Castle** The best opportunity to explore a ruined castle on the river. **Hours:** Mid-March-Oct daily 9:00-18:00, Nov-mid-March possibly Sat-Sun only 11:00-17:00 (call ahead). See page 846.

▲▲**Marksburg Castle in Braubach** The best-preserved medieval castle on the Rhine. **Hours:** Daily April-Oct 10:00-17:00, Nov-March 11:00-16:00. See page 854.

Near the Rhine Valley

▲▲▲**Burg Eltz, on the Mosel** My favorite castle in Europe, set deep in a forest, with a rare furnished interior—take the required guided tour. **Hours:** April-Oct daily from 9:30, last tour departs at 17:30, closed Nov-March. See page 857.

Rhine Overview

Düsseldorf•

Rhine

Cologne •

← UNROMANTIC RHINE

•Aachen

Bonn•

GERMANY
Berlin •

Remagen•

BEST OF
THE RHINE
See detail map

BELG.

BURG
ELTZ

• Koblenz

Frankfurt

Cochem•

St.
Goar•

Wies-
baden

Main R.

Beilstein •

Oberwesel

• Bingen

Mainz   Frankfurt

Mosel R.

Bacharach

LUX.

Trier

Hahn

Neckar R.

Lux.
City

GERMANY

Heidelberg

Rhine

50 Kilometers

50 Miles

FRANCE

---

visit, book your room well in advance; study ahead.

Rick's Tip: *Rhine Valley* **guesthouses and hotels often have similar names.** *When reserving, double-check that you're contacting the one in your planned destination.*

RHINE BLITZ TOUR

One of Europe's top thrills is traveling along the Rhine River, enjoying this tour, worth ▲▲▲. For short distances, cruising is best because it's slower. A cruise going upstream (heading south, toward Bingen) takes longer than the same cruise going downstream (north, toward Koblenz). If you want to draw out a short cruise, go upstream (for instance, from St. Goar to Bacharach).

To cover long distances (e.g., Koblenz to Bingen), consider the train. Or take the boat one way and the train back. See page 834 for specifics on traveling the Rhine.

● Self-Guided Tour

This easy tour (you can cut in anywhere) skips most of the syrupy myths filling normal Rhine guides. Follow along on a boat, train, bike, or car. By train, sit on the left (river) side going south from Koblenz; most of the castles listed are viewed from this side.

Castles of the Rhine

Many of the castles of the Rhine were "robber-baron" castles, put there by petty rulers (there were 300 independent little countries in medieval Germany) to levy tolls on passing river traffic. A robber baron would put his castle on, or even in, the river. Then, often with the help of chains and a tower on the opposite bank, he'd stop each ship and get his toll. There were 10 customs stops in the 60-mile stretch between Mainz and Koblenz alone.

Some castles were built to control and protect settlements, and others were the residences of kings. As times changed, so did the lifestyles of the rich and feudal. Many castles were abandoned for more comfortable mansions in the towns.

Most Rhine castles date from the 11th, 12th, and 13th centuries. When the pope successfully asserted his power over the German emperor in 1076, local princes ran wild over the rule of their emperor. The castles saw military action in the 1300s and 1400s, as emperors began reasserting their control over Germany's kingdoms.

The castles were also involved in the Reformation wars, in which Europe's Catholic and Protestant dynasties used a fragmented Germany as their battleground. The Thirty Years' War (1618-1648) devastated Germany. The outcome: Each ruler got the freedom to decide if his people would be Catholic or Protestant, and one-third of Germans died. (Production of Gummi Bears ceased entirely.)

The French—who feared a strong Germany and felt the Rhine was the logical border between the two countries—destroyed most of the castles as a preventive measure (Louis XIV in the 1680s, the Revolutionary army in the 1790s, and Napoleon in 1806). Many were rebuilt in the Neo-Gothic style in the Romantic Age—the late 1800s—and today are enjoyed as restaurants, hotels, hostels, and museums.

We're tackling 36 miles (58 km) of the 820-mile-long (1,320-km) Rhine. This tour starts at **Koblenz** and heads upstream to **Bingen**. If you're going the other direction, it still works. Just hold the book upside-down. With limited time, cruise just the best stretch: from St. Goar to Bacharach.

This tour is synched with the large black-and-white kilometer markers you'll see along the riverbank. I erected these years ago to make this tour easier to follow. They tell the distance from the Rhine Falls, where the Rhine leaves Switzerland and becomes navigable. Today, river-barge pilots also use these markers to navigate.

🎧 Download my free Best of the Rhine audio tour—it works in either direction.

Little Bacharach's dock and boat ramp

The Best of the Rhine

To Bonn & Cologne

DEUTSCHES ECK

EHRENBREITSTEIN

Koblenz **590**

416

49

Mosel

Lahn River

To Cochem & Burg Eltz

LAHNECK **586**

STOLZENFELS

Braubach

MARKSBURG **580**

Rhine

9

42

Boppard **570**

River

STERRENBERG **567**

LIEBENSTEIN

49

A-61

EXIT #42

MAUS **559**

9

E-31

St. Goarshausen

RHEINFELS **557**

KATZ **556**

St. Goar

LORELEY **554**

Emmels-hausen

EXIT #43

42

327

Oberwesel **550**

Kaub

To Hahn Airport

SCHÖNBURG

GUTENFELS **546**

PFALZ

EXIT #44

Bacharach **543**

STAHLECK

Rhine

Lorch **541**

9

River

EXIT #45

SOONECK **538**

REICHENSTEIN **534**

EHRENFELS **530**

RHEINSTEIN **533**

NIEDERWALD MONUMENT

42

Assmannshausen

MÄUSETURM

Rüdesheim

A-61

Bingen

E-31

To Mainz & Frankfurt

9

A-60

To Mannheim

NOTE:
590 Bold numbers refer to riverside signs indicating kilometers north of the Rhine Falls (Switzerland)

······ Car Ferries

42 Road Numbers

3 Kilometers

3 Miles

GERMANY

Munich

From Koblenz to St. Goar

Km 590—Koblenz: This Rhine blitz starts with historic Rhine fanfare, at Koblenz. Koblenz isn't terribly attractive (after being hit hard in World War II), but its place at the historic Deutsches Eck ("German Corner")—the tip of land where the Mosel River joins the Rhine—gives it a certain patriotic charm. A cable car links the Deutsches Eck with the yellow Ehrenbreitstein Fortress across the river.

Km 586—Lahneck Castle: Above the modern autobahn bridge over the Lahn River, this castle (*Burg*) was built in 1240 to defend local silver mines. The castle was ruined by the French in 1688 and rebuilt in the 1850s in Neo-Gothic style.

Km 580—Marksburg Castle: This castle stands bold and white—restored to look like most Rhine castles once did, with their slate stonework covered with stucco to look as if made from a richer stone. You'll spot Marksburg with the three modern chimneys behind it, just before the town of Spay. This is the best-looking of all the Rhine castles and the only surviving medieval castle on the Rhine. Because of its commanding position, it was never attacked in the Middle Ages (though it was captured by the US Army in March of 1945). It's now open as a museum (see page 854 for details).

Km 570—Boppard: Once a Roman town, Boppard has some impressive remains of fourth-century walls. Look for the Roman towers and the substantial chunk of Roman wall near the train station, just above the main square.

If you visit Boppard, head to the fascinating Church of St. Severus below the main square. Find the carved Romanesque crazies at the doorway. Inside, to the right of the entrance, you'll see Christian symbols from Roman times. Also notice the painted arches and vaults (originally, most Romanesque churches were painted this way). Down by the river, look for the high-water (*Hochwasser*) marks on the arches from various flood years. (You'll find these flood marks throughout the Rhine Valley.)

Km 567—Sterrenberg Castle and Liebenstein Castle: These are known as the "Hostile Brothers" castles, across from Bad Salzig. Take the wall between the castles (actually designed to improve the defenses of both castles), add two greedy and jealous brothers and a fair maiden, and create your own legend. Burg Liebenstein is now a fun, friendly, and affordable family-run hotel (Db-€140-150, 9 rooms, suites and family rooms, easy parking, tel. 06773/308, www.castle-liebenstein.com, info@burg-liebenstein.de).

Km 559—Maus Castle: The Maus (mouse) got its name because the next castle was owned by the Katzenelnbogen family. (*Katz* means "cat.") In the 1300s, it was considered a state-of-the-art fortification...until 1806, when Napoleon had it blown up with then-state-of-the-art explosives. It was rebuilt true to its original plans in about 1900. Today, Burg Maus is open for concerts, weddings, and guided

Boppard

Maus Castle

tours in German (weekends only, reservations required, 20-minute walk up, tel. 06771/91011, www.burg-maus.de).

St. Goar to Bacharach: The Best of the Rhine

Km 557—St. Goar and Rheinfels Castle: The pleasant town of St. Goar was named for a sixth-century hometown monk. It originated in Celtic times as a place where sailors would stop, catch their breath, send home a postcard, and give thanks after surviving the seductive and treacherous Loreley crossing. St. Goar is worth a stop to explore its mighty Rheinfels Castle. (For more on St. Goar, see page 845; for a self-guided castle tour, see page 848.)

Km 556—Katz Castle: Burg Katz (Katzenelnbogen) faces St. Goar from across the river. Together, Burg Katz (built in 1371) and Rheinfels Castle had a clear view up and down the river, effectively controlling traffic (there was absolutely no duty-free shopping on the medieval Rhine). Katz got Napoleoned in 1806 and rebuilt in about 1900.

About Km 555: A statue of the Loreley, the beautiful-but-deadly nymph (see next listing for legend), combs her hair at the end of a long spit—built to give barges protection from vicious ice floes that until recent years raged down the river in the winter. The actual Loreley, a cliff (marked by the flags), is just ahead.

Km 554—The Loreley: Steep a big slate rock in centuries of legend and it becomes a tourist attraction—the ultimate Rhinestone. The Loreley (flags on top, name painted near shoreline), rising 450 feet over the narrowest and deepest point of the Rhine, has long been important. It was a holy site in pre-Roman days. The fine echoes here—thought to be ghostly voices—fertilized legend-tellers' imaginations.

Because of the reefs just upstream (at km 552), many ships never made it to St. Goar. Sailors (after days on the river) blamed their misfortune on a *wunderbares Fräulein*, whose long, blond hair almost covered her body. Heinrich Heine's *Song of Loreley* (the CliffsNotes version is on local postcards) tells the story of a count sending his men to kill or capture this siren after she distracted his horny son, who forgot to watch where he was sailing and drowned. When the soldiers cornered the nymph in her cave, she called her father (Father Rhine) for help. Huge waves, the likes of which you'll never see today, rose from the river and carried Loreley to safety. And she has never been seen since.

But alas, when the moon shines brightly and the tour buses are parked, a

The scenic cliffs of the Rhine, steeped in history

The Rhine River Trade

Watch the river barges along the Rhine. There's a constant parade of action, and each boat is different. The flag of the boat's home country flies in the stern (Dutch—horizontal red, white, and blue; Belgian—vertical black, yellow, and red; Swiss—white cross on a red field; German—horizontal black, red, and yellow; French—vertical red, white, and blue).

Barge workers have their own subculture. Many own their own ships. The captain lives in the stern, with his family. The family car is often parked on the stern. Workers live in the bow.

Logically, imports (Japanese cars, coal, and oil) go upstream, and exports (German cars, chemicals, and pharmaceuticals) go downstream. A clever captain manages to ship goods in each direction. Recently, giant Dutch container ships (which transport five times the cargo) have been driving many of the traditional barges out of business, presenting the German economy with another challenge.

Going downstream, tugs can push a floating train of up to five barges at once, but upstream, as the slope gets steeper (and the stream gradient gets higher), they can push only one at a time. Before modern shipping, horses dragged boats upstream (the faint remains of towpaths survive at points along the river). From 1873 to 1900, workers laid a chain from Bonn to Bingen, and boats with cogwheels and steam engines hoisted themselves upstream. Today, 265 million tons travel each year along the 530 miles from Basel on the German-Swiss border to the Dutch city of Rotterdam on the Atlantic.

Riverside navigational aids are vital. Boats pass on the right unless they clearly signal otherwise with a large blue sign. Since ships heading downstream can't stop or maneuver as freely, boats heading upstream are expected to do the tricky maneuvering. Cameras monitor traffic and relay warnings of oncoming ships by posting large triangular signals before narrow and troublesome bends in the river. There may be two or three triangles per signpost, depending upon how many "sectors," or segments, of the river are covered. The lowest triangle indicates the nearest stretch of river. Each triangle tells whether there's a ship in that sector. When the bottom side of a triangle is lit, that sector is empty. When the left side is lit, an oncoming ship is in that sector.

The **Signal and River Pilots Museum** (Wahrschauer- und Lotsenmuseum), located at the signal triangles at the upstream edge of St. Goar, explains how barges are safer, cleaner, and more fuel-efficient than trains or trucks (free, May-Sept, Wed and Sat 14:00-17:00, outdoor exhibits always open).

soft, playful Rhine whine can still be heard from the Loreley. As you pass, listen carefully ("Sailors...sailors...over my bounding mane").

Km 552—The Seven Maidens: Killer reefs, marked by red-and-green buoys, are called the "Seven Maidens." OK, one more goofy legend: The prince of Schön-

burg Castle (*über* Oberwesel—described next) had seven spoiled daughters who always dumped men because of their shortcomings. Fed up, he invited seven of his knights to the castle and demanded that his daughters each choose one to marry. But they complained that each man had too big a nose, was too fat, too stupid, and so on. The rude and teasing girls escaped into a riverboat. Just downstream, God turned them into the seven rocks that form this reef. While this story probably isn't entirely true, there was a lesson in it for medieval children: Don't be hard-hearted.

Km 550—Oberwesel: The town of Oberwesel, topped by the commanding Schönburg Castle (now a hotel), boasts some of the best medieval wall and tower remains on the Rhine.

Notice how many of the train tunnels along here have entrances designed like medieval turrets—they were actually built in the Romantic 19th century. OK, back to the riverside.

Km 546—Gutenfels Castle and Pfalz Castle, the Classic Rhine View: Burg Gutenfels (now a privately owned hotel) and the shipshape Pfalz Castle (built in the river in the 1300s) worked very effectively to tax medieval river traffic. The town of Kaub grew rich as Pfalz raised its chains when boats came, and lowered them only when the merchants had paid their duty. Those who didn't pay spent time touring its prison, on a raft at the bottom of its well. In 1504, a pope called for the destruction of Pfalz, but the locals withstood a six-week siege, and the castle still stands. Notice the overhanging outhouse (tiny white room between two wooden ones). Pfalz (also known as Pfalzgrafenstein) is tourable but bare and

Festivals on the Rhine

During the annual **Rhine in Flames festival** (Rhein in Flammen), spectacular displays of fireworks take place along the Rhine's most scenic stretches, while beautifully illuminated ships ply the river, offering up-close views of the fireworks above. Held on five separate days (roughly one day per month) between May and September, the festival rotates between several Rhine towns. Traditional wine festivals and other local celebrations are often timed to coincide with the fireworks (www.rhein-in-flammen.com).

In September and October, some Rhine villages host **wine-fests** on weekends. Check town websites and book your room ahead for these popular times (www.bacharach.de, www.rhein-nahe-touristik.de, www.st-goar.de).

dull, accessible by ferry from Kaub (€3 entry, April-Oct Tue-Sun 10:00-18:00, closed Mon; closes at 17:00 off-season including March, Nov and Jan-Feb Sat-Sun only, closed Dec, mobile 0172-262-2800, www.burg-pfalzgrafenstein.de).

In Kaub, on the riverfront directly below the castles, a green statue (near the waving flags) honors the German general Gebhard von Blücher. He was Napoleon's

Pfalz Castle (left) and Gutenfels Castle (on hillside)

Stahleck Castle

nemesis. In 1813, as Napoleon fought his way back to Paris after his disastrous Russian campaign, he stopped at Mainz—hoping to fend off the Germans and Russians pursuing him by controlling that strategic bridge. Blücher tricked Napoleon. By building the first major pontoon bridge of its kind here at the Pfalz Castle, he crossed the Rhine and outflanked the French. Two years later, Blücher and Wellington teamed up to defeat Napoleon once and for all at Waterloo.

Immediately opposite Kaub (where the ferry lands, marked by blue roadside flags) is a gaping hole in the mountainside. This marks the last working slate mine on the Rhine.

Km 544—"The Raft Busters": Just before Bacharach, at the top of the island, buoys mark a gang of rocks notorious for busting up rafts. The Black Forest, upstream from here, was once poor, and wood was its best export. Black Foresters would ride log booms down the Rhine to the Ruhr (where their timber fortified coal-mine shafts) or to Holland (where logs were sold to shipbuilders). If they could navigate the sweeping bend just before Bacharach and then survive these "raft busters," they'd come home reckless and horny—the German folkloric equivalent of American cowboys after payday.

Km 543—Bacharach and Stahleck Castle: The town of Bacharach is a great stop (described on page 836). Some of the Rhine's best wine is from this town, whose name likely derives from "altar to Bacchus." Local vintners brag that the medieval Pope Pius II ordered Bacharach wine by the cartload. Perched above the town, the 13th-century Burg Stahleck is now a hostel.

From Bacharach to Bingen

Km 541—Lorch: This stub of a castle is barely visible from the road. Check out the hillside vineyards. Rhine wine is particularly good because the local slate absorbs the heat of the sun and stays warm all night, resulting in sweeter grapes. Wine from the steep side of the Rhine gorge—where grapes are harder to grow and harvest—is tastier and more expensive. Vineyards once blanketed four times as much of the valley as they do today, but modern economics have driven most of them out of business. The vineyards that do survive require government subsidies.

Notice the small car ferry, one of several along the bridgeless stretch between Mainz and Koblenz.

Km 538—Sooneck Castle: Built in the 11th century, this castle was twice destroyed by people sick and tired of robber barons.

Km 534—Reichenstein Castle and **Km 533—Rheinstein Castle:** Both are privately owned, tourable, and connected by a pleasant trail.

Km 530—Ehrenfels Castle: Opposite Bingerbrück and the Bingen station, you'll see the ghostly Ehrenfels Castle, which was clobbered by the Swedes in 1636 and by the French in 1689. Since it had no view of the river traffic to the north, the owner built the cute little *Mäuseturm* (mouse

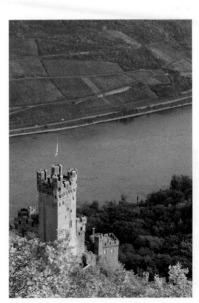

Sooneck Castle

tower) on an island (the yellow tower you'll see near the train station today). Rebuilt in the 1800s in Neo-Gothic style, it's now used as a Rhine navigation signal station.

Km 528—Niederwald Monument: Across from the Bingen station on a hilltop is the 120-foot-high Niederwald monument, a memorial built with 32 tons of bronze in 1877 to commemorate "the re-establishment of the German Empire." A lift takes tourists to this statue from the famous and extremely touristy wine town of Rüdesheim.

From here, the romantic Rhine becomes the industrial Rhine, and our tour is over.

Getting Around the Rhine

The Rhine flows from Switzerland north to the Netherlands, but the scenic stretch from Mainz to Koblenz hoards all the touristic charm. Studded with the crenellated cream of Germany's castles, it bustles with boats, trains, and highway traffic. Have fun exploring with a mix of big steamers, tiny ferries (*Fähre*), trains, and bikes.

By Boat

While you can do the whole Mainz-Koblenz trip by boat (5.5 hours downstream, 8.5 hours up), I'd focus on the most scenic hour—from St. Goar to Bacharach. Sit on the boat's top deck with your handy Rhine map-guide (or the

Ehrenfels Castle, with its little "mouse tower" on the river

kilometer-keyed tour in this chapter) and enjoy the parade of castles, towns, boats, and vineyards.

Two boat companies take travelers along this stretch of the Rhine. Boats run daily in both directions from early April through October, with only one boat running off-season.

Most travelers sail on the bigger, more expensive, and romantic **Köln-Düsseldorfer (K-D) Line** (recommended Bacharach-St. Goar trip: €12.80 one-way, €15.40 round-trip, bikes-€2.80/day, €2 extra if paying with credit card; discounts: up to 30 percent if over 60, 20 percent if you present a connecting train ticket or rail pass; tel. 06741/1634 in St. Goar, tel. 06743/1322 in Bacharach, www.k-d.com).

Complete, up-to-date schedules are posted at any Rhineland station, hotel, TI, and www.k-d.com. Confirm times at your hotel the night before. Purchase tickets at the dock up to five minutes before departure. The boat is never full. Romantics will enjoy the old-time paddle-wheeler *Goethe,* which sails each direction once a day (noted on schedule, confirm time locally).

The smaller **Bingen-Rüdesheimer Line** is slightly cheaper than the K-D, doesn't offer any rail pass deals, and makes three trips in each direction daily from early April through October (buy tickets at ticket booth or on boat, ticket booth only open just before boat departs, 30 percent discount if over 60; departs Bacharach at 10:10, 12:00, and 15:00; departs St. Goar at 11:00, 14:10, and 16:10; tel. 06721/14140, www.bingen-ruedesheimer.de).

By Car

Drivers have these options: 1) skip the boat; 2) take a round-trip cruise from St. Goar or Bacharach; 3) draw pretzels and let the loser drive, prepare the picnic, and meet the boat; 4) rent a bike, bring it on the boat, and bike back; or 5) take the boat one-way and return to your car by

K-D Line Rhine Cruise Schedule

Boats run from early April through October (usually 5/day, but 3-4/day in early April and most of Oct). From November through March, one boat runs daily for groups, but you can tag along if they know you're coming—call the boat directly (tel. 0172/1360-335) or the main office in Cologne (tel. 0221/2088-318) to confirm. Check www.k-d.com for the latest complete schedule; only a few stops are shown below.

Koblenz	Boppard	St. Goar	Bacharach
—	9:00	10:20	11:30
9:00*	11:00*	12:20*	13:30*
—	13:00	14:20	15:30
—	14:00	15:20	16:30
14:00	16:00	17:20	18:30
13:10	11:50	10:55	10:15
—	12:50	11:55	11:15
—	13:50	12:55	12:15
18:10	16:50	15:55	15:15
20:10*	18:50*	17:55*	17:15*

*These sailings are on the 1913 paddle-wheeler Goethe.

train. When exploring by car, don't hesitate to pop onto one of the many little ferries that shuttle across the river.

By Ferry (Across the Rhine)

As there are no bridges between Koblenz and Mainz, you'll see car-and-passenger ferries (usually family-run for generations) about every three miles. Some of the most useful routes are Bingen-Rüdesheim, Lorch-Niederheimbach, Engelsburg-Kaub, and St. Goar-St. Goarshausen (times vary; St. Goar-St. Goarshausen ferry departs each side every 15-20 minutes daily until 24:00, less frequently on Sun; one-way fares: adult-€1.70, car and driver-€4, pay on boat; www.faehre-loreley.de). For a fun little jaunt, take a quick round-trip (by car or bike) with some time to explore the other side.

By Bike

You can bike on either side of the Rhine, but for a designated bike path, stay on the west side, where a 35-mile path runs between Koblenz and Bingen. The six-mile stretch between St. Goar and Bacharach is smooth and scenic, but it's mostly along the highway. The bit from Bacharach south to Bingen hugs the riverside and is car-free. Either way, biking is a great way to explore the valley (though headwinds can slow you down). Many hotels provide free or cheap bikes to guests; some also rent to the public (including Hotel Hillen in Bacharach and Hotel an der Fähre in St. Goar).

Consider biking one-way and taking the bike back on the riverboat, or designing a circular trip using the fun and frequent shuttle ferries. A good target might be Kaub (where a tiny boat shuttles sightseers to the better-from-a-distance castle on the island).

By Train

Hourly milk-run trains hit every town along the Rhine (Bacharach-St. Goar in both directions about :20 after the hour, 10 minutes; Mainz-Bacharach, 40 minutes; Mainz-Koblenz, 1 hour). Tiny stations are not staffed—buy tickets at machines. Though generally user-friendly, the ticket machines are not all created equal. Some claim to only take exact change; others may not accept US credit cards. When buying a ticket, select "English" and follow the instructions carefully. For example, the ticket machine may give you the choice of validating your ticket for that day or a day in the near future—but only for some destinations (when you're not given this option, your ticket will automatically be validated for the day of purchase).

The **Rheinland-Pfalz-Ticket** day pass covers travel on milk-run trains to many destinations in this chapter, including Koblenz. It can save heaps of money, particularly on longer day trips or if there's more than one in your party (1 person-€24, up to 4 additional people-€4/ each, buy from station ticket-machines, good after 9:00 Mon-Fri and all day Sat-Sun, valid on trains labeled *RB*, *RE*, and *MRB*). For a day trip from Bacharach to Burg Eltz (normally €32 round-trip), even one person saves with a Rheinland-Pfalz-Ticket, and a group of five adults saves €120—look for travel partners at breakfast.

BACHARACH

Once prosperous from the wine and wood trade, charming Bacharach (BAHKH-ah-rahkh, with a guttural *kh* sound) is now just a pleasant half-timbered village of 2,000 people working hard to keep its tourists happy. Businesses that have been "in the family" for eons are dealing with succession challenges, as the allure of big-city jobs and a more cosmopolitan life lures away the town's younger generation. But Bacharach retains its time-capsule quaintness.

Orientation

Bacharach cuddles, long and narrow, along the Rhine. The village is easily strollable—you can walk from one end of town to the other along its main drag, Oberstrasse, in about 10 minutes. Bacha-

Riesling wine grapes blanket the Rhine's hillsides.

rach widens at its stream, where more houses trickle up its small valley (along Blücherstrasse) away from the Rhine. The hillsides above town are occupied by vineyards, scant remains of the former town walls, and a castle-turned-youth hostel.

Tourist Information: The TI, on the main street a block-and-a-half from the train station, will store bags for day-trippers (April-Oct Mon-Fri 9:00-17:00, Sat-Sun 10:00-15:00; Nov-March Mon-Fri 9:00-13:00, closed Sat-Sun; from train station, exit right and walk down main street with castle high on your left, TI will be on your right at Oberstrasse 10; tel. 06743/919-303, www.bacharach.de or www.rhein-nahe-touristik.de). They also book 1.5-hour tours in English (€70/group).

Bike Rental: While many hotels loan bikes to guests, the only real bike-rental business in the town center is run by Erich at **Hotel Hillen** (€12/day, daily 9:00-19:00, Langstrasse 18, tel. 06743/1287).

Parking: It's simple to park along the highway next to the train tracks or, better, in the big inexpensive lot by the boat dock (pay with coins at *Parkscheinautomat* and put ticket on dashboard, free overnight).

Private Guides: Thomas Gundlach happily gives 1.5-hour town walks to individuals or small groups for €35 (as well as 4- to 10-hour hiking tours for the more ambitious). He can also drive up to three people around the region in his car (€80/6 hours, mobile 0179-353-6004, thomas_gundlach@gmx.de). **Birgit Wessels** is also good (€45/1.5-hour walk, tel. 06743/937-514, wessels.birgit@t-online.de).

➲ Bacharach Town Walk

• *Start at the Köln-Düsseldorfer ferry dock (next to a fine picnic park).*

Riverfront: View the town from the parking lot—a modern landfill. The Rhine used to lap against Bacharach's town wall, just over the present-day highway. Every few years, the river floods, covering the highway with several feet of water. Flat land like this is rare in the Rhine Valley, where towns are often shaped like the letter "T," stretching thin along the riverfront and up a crease in the hills beyond.

Reefs farther upstream forced boats to

Classic and quaint Bacharach

unload upriver and reload here. Consequently, in the Middle Ages, Bacharach was the biggest wine-trading town on the Rhine. A riverfront crane hoisted huge kegs of prestigious "Bacharach" wine (which, in practice, was from anywhere in the region). Today, the economy is based on tourism.

Look above town. The **castle** on the hill is now a youth hostel. Two of the town's original 16 towers are visible from here (up to 5 if you look really hard). The bluff on the right, with the yellow flag, is the **Heinrich Heine Viewpoint** (the end-point of a popular hike). Old-timers remember when, rather than the flag marking the town as a World Heritage site, a swastika sculpture 30 feet wide and tall stood there. Realizing that it could be an enticing target for Allied planes in the last months of the war, locals tore it down even before Hitler fell.

Nearby, a stele in the park describes the Bingen to Koblenz stretch of the Rhine gorge.

• *Before entering the town, walk upstream through the...*

Riverside Park: New elements of the park are designed to bring people to the riverside and combat flooding. The park was originally laid out in 1910 in the English style: Notice how the trees were planted to frame fine town views, highlighting the most picturesque bits of architecture. The dark, sad-looking monument—its "eternal" flame long snuffed out—is a **war memorial.** The German psyche is permanently scarred by war memories. Today, many Germans would rather avoid monuments like this, which revisit the dark periods before Germany became a nation of pacifists. Take a close look at the monument. Each panel honors sons of Bacharach who died for the Kaiser: in 1864 against Denmark, in 1866 against Austria, in 1870 against France, in 1914 during World War I. The military Maltese cross—flanked by classic German helmets—has a "W" at its center, for Kaiser

Wilhelm. Review the family names on the opposite side of the monument: You may later recognize them on today's restaurants and hotels.

• *Look (but don't go now) upstream from here to see the...*

Trailer Park and Campground: In Germany, trailer vacationers and campers are two distinct subcultures. Folks who travel in motorhomes, like many retirees in the US, are a nomadic bunch, cruising around the countryside and paying a few euros a night to park. Campers, on the other hand, tend to set up camp in one place—complete with comfortable lounge chairs and TVs—and stay put for weeks, even months. They often come back to the same spot year after year, treating it like their own private estate. These camping devotees have made a science out of relaxing. Tourists are welcome to pop in for a drink or meal at the Sonnenstrand campground's terrace café (daily 13:00-21:00; it's a 10-minute walk).

High-water marks indicate the heights reached by floodwaters.

• *Continue to where the park meets the playground, and then cross the highway to the fortified riverside wall of the Catholic church, decorated with...*

High-Water Marks: These recall various floods. Before the 1910 reclamation project, the river extended out to here, and boats would use the rings in this wall to tie up.

• *From the church, go under the 1858 train tracks (and past more high-water marks) and hook right past the yellow floodwater yardstick and up the stairs onto the town wall. Atop the wall, turn left and walk under the long arcade. After 30 yards, on your left, notice a...*

Well: Rebuilt as it appeared in the 17th century, this is one of seven such wells that brought water to the townsfolk until 1900. Each neighborhood's well also provided a social gathering place and the communal laundry. Walk 50 yards past the well along the wall to an alcove in the medieval tower with a view of the

A facsimile of a 17th-century well

war memorial in the park. You're under the crane tower (*Kranenturm*). After barrels of wine were moved overland from Bingen past dangerous stretches of river, the precious cargo could be lowered by cranes from here into ships to continue more safely down the river. The Rhine has long been a major shipping route through Germany. In modern times, it's a bottleneck in Germany's train system. The train company gives hotels and residents along the tracks money for soundproof windows (hotels along here routinely have quadruple-pane windows...and earplugs on the nightstand).

• *Continue walking along the town wall. Pass the recommended Rhein Hotel just before the...*

Markt Tower: This marks one of the town's 15 original 14th-century gates and is a reminder that in that century there was a big wine market here.

• *Descend the stairs closest to the Rhein Hotel, pass another well, and follow Marktstrasse away from the river toward the town center, the two-tone church, and the town's...*

Main Intersection: From here, Bacharach's main street (Oberstrasse) goes right to the half-timbered red-and-white Altes Haus (which we'll visit later) and left 400 yards to the train station. Spin around to enjoy the higgledy-piggledy building styles. The town has a case of the doldrums: The younger generation is moving to the big cities and many long-established family businesses have no one to take over for their aging owners. In the winter the town is particularly dead.

• *To the left (south) of the church, a golden horn hangs over the old...*

Posthof: Throughout Europe, the postal horn is the symbol of the postal service. In olden days, when the postman blew this, traffic stopped and the mail sped through. This post station dates from 1724, when stagecoaches ran from Cologne to Frankfurt and would change horses here, Pony Express-style. As you enter, notice the cornerstones at the Posthof entrance, protecting the venerable building from reckless carriage wheels. Inside the old oak doors (on the left) is the actual door to the post office that served Bacharach for 200 years. Find the mark on the wall labeled *Rheinhöhe 3/1-4/2 1850*. This recalls a historic flood caused by an ice jam at the Loreley just downstream. Notice also the fascist eagle in the alcove on the right (from 1936; a swastika once filled its center).

Step into the courtyard—once a carriage house and inn that accommodated Bacharach's first VIP visitors, and now home to the recommended Posthof Bacharach restaurant, with a fine view of the church and a ruined chapel above.

Two hundred years ago, Bacharach's main drag was the only road along the Rhine. Napoleon widened it to fit his cannon wagons. The steps alongside the church lead to the castle.

• *Return to the church, passing the recommended Italian ice-cream café* **(Eis Café Italia),** *where friendly Mimo serves his special invention: Riesling wine-flavored gelato.*

Protestant Church: Inside the church (daily May-Sept 10:00-18:00, April and Oct until 17:00, closed Nov-March, English info on a stand near door), you'll find Grotesque capitals, brightly painted in medieval style, and a mix of round Romanesque and pointed Gothic arches. The church was fancier before the Reformation wars, when it (and the region) was Catholic. Bacharach lies on the religious

border of Germany and, like the country as a whole, is split between Catholics and Protestants. To the left of the altar, some medieval (pre-Reformation) frescoes survive where an older Romanesque arch was cut by a pointed Gothic one.

If you're considering bombing the town, take note: A blue-and-white plaque just outside the church's door warns that, according to the Hague Convention, this historic building shouldn't be targeted in times of war.

• *Continue down Oberstrasse to the...*

Altes Haus: Dating from 1368, this is the oldest house in town. Notice the 14th-century building style—the first floor is made of stone, while upper floors are half-timbered (in the ornate style common in the Rhine Valley). Some of its windows still look medieval, with small, flattened circles as panes (small because that's all that the glass-blowing technology of the time would allow), pieced together with molten lead (like medieval stained glass in churches). Frau Weber welcomes visitors to enjoy the fascinating ground floor of the recommended Altes Haus restaurant, with its evocative old photos and etchings (consider eating here later).

• *Keep going down Oberstrasse to the...*

Old Mint (Münze): The old mint is marked by a crude coin in its sign. As a practicality, any great trading town needed coinage, and since 1356, Bacharach minted theirs here. Across from the mint, the recommended **Bastian** family's wine garden is a lively place after dark. Above you in the vineyards stands a lonely white-and-red tower—your final destination.

• *At the next street, look right and see the mint tower, painted in the medieval style, and then turn left. Wander 30 yards up Rosenstrasse to the* **well.** *Notice the sundial and the wall painting of 1632 Bacharach with its walls intact. Study the fine slate roof over the well: The town's roof tiles were quarried and split right here in the Rhineland.*

Continue another 30 yards up Rosenstrasse to find the tiny-stepped lane behind the well up into the vineyard and to the...

Tall Tower: The slate steps lead to a small path through the vineyard that deposits you at a viewpoint atop the stubby remains of the medieval wall and a tower. The town's towers jutted out from the wall and had only three sides, with the "open" side facing the town. Towers were covered with stucco to make them look more impressive, as if they were made of a finer white stone. If this tower's open, hike up to climb the stairs for the best view. (The top floor has been closed to give nesting falcons some privacy.)

Romantic Rhine View: A grand medieval town spreads before you. For 300 years (1300-1600), Bacharach was big (population 4,000), rich, and politically powerful.

From this perch, you can see the chapel ruins and six surviving **city towers.** Visually trace the wall to the castle. The castle was actually the capital of Germany for a couple of years in the 1200s. When Holy Roman Emperor Frederick Barbarossa went away to fight the Crusades, he left his brother (who lived here) in charge of his vast realm. Bacharach was home to one of the seven electors who voted for the Holy Roman Emperor in 1275. To protect their own power, these prince electors did their best to choose the weakest guy on the ballot. The elector from Bacharach helped select a two-bit prince named Rudolf von Habsburg (from a no-name castle in Switzerland). However, the underestimated Rudolf brutally silenced the robber barons along the Rhine and established the mightiest dynasty in European history. His family line, the Habsburgs, ruled much of Central and Eastern Europe from Vienna until 1918.

Plagues, fires, and the Thirty Years' War (1618-1648) finally did in Bacharach. The town has slumbered for several centuries. Today, the castle houses commoners—40,000 overnights annually by youth hostelers.

In the mid-19th century, painters such as J. M. W. Turner and writers such as Victor Hugo were charmed by the Rhine-

Altes Haus is the oldest dwelling (1368) in Bacharach.

land's romantic mix of past glory, present poverty, and rich legend. They put this part of the Rhine on the old Grand Tour map as the "Romantic Rhine." Victor Hugo pondered the ruined 15th-century chapel that you see under the castle. In his 1842 travel book, *Excursions Along the Banks of the Rhine*, he wrote, "No doors, no roof or windows, a magnificent skeleton puts its silhouette against the sky. Above it, the ivy-covered castle ruins provide a fitting crown. This is Bacharach, land of fairy tales, covered with legends and sagas." If you're enjoying the Romantic Rhine, thank Victor Hugo and company.

• *Our walk is done. To get back into town, just retrace your steps. Or, to extend this walk, take the level path away from the river that leads along the once-mighty wall up the valley to the next tower, the...*

Wood Market Tower: Timber was gathered here in Bacharach and lashed together into vast log booms known as "Holland rafts" (as big as a soccer field) that were floated downstream. Two weeks later the lumber would reach Amsterdam, where it was in high demand as foundation posts for buildings and for the great Dutch shipbuilders. Notice the four stones above the arch on the uphill side of the tower—these guided the gate as it was hoisted up and down.

• *From here, cross the street and go downhill into the parking lot. Pass the recommended Pension im Malerwinkel on your right, being careful not to damage the old arch with your head. Follow the creek past a delightful little series of half-timbered homes and cheery gardens known as "Painters' Corner" (Malerwinkel). Resist looking into some pervert's peep show (on the right) and continue downhill back to the village center.*

Experiences
Wine Tasting
Bacharach is proud of its wine. Two places in town offer an inexpensive tasting alongside light plates of food.

Bastian's Weingut zum Grüner Baum is rowdy and rustic. Groups of 2-6 people pay €22.50 for a wine carousel of 15 glasses—14 different white wines and 1 lonely red—and a basket of bread. Spin the lazy Susan, share a common cup, and discuss the taste. The Bastian family insists: "After each wine, you must talk to each other." Along with their characteristic interior, they have two nice terraces (daily 12:00-22:00, closed in winter, just past Altes Haus, tel. 06743/1208).

Weingut Karl Heidrich is a fun wine shop and *Stube* in the town center, where Markus and daughters Magdalena and Katharina share their family's centuries-old wine tradition. They offer a variety of carousels with six wines, English descriptions, and bread (€12)—ideal for the more sophisticated wine taster—plus light meals and a €10.50 meat-and-cheese plate (Thu-Tue 11:00-22:00, closed Wed and Nov-mid-April, will ship to US, Oberstrasse 16, tel. 06743/93060).

Rick's Tip: *Bacharach goes to bed early, so if you're looking for* **nightlife,** *head to one of the* **wine-tasting places** *or* **Restaurant Zeus,** *which has long hours and outdoor seating that adds a spark to the town center after dark (daily 17:30-24:00, Koblenzer Strasse 11, tel. 06743/909-7171). The hilltop youth hostel,* **Jugendherberge Stahleck,** *serves cheap wine with priceless views until late in summer.*

Shopping
The **Jost** German gift store, across the main square from the church, carries most everything a souvenir shopper could want—from beer steins to cuckoo clocks—and can ship purchases to the US (March-Oct Mon-Fri 9:00-18:00, Sat-Sun 10:00-18:00, shorter hours in winter, closed Jan-Feb; Blücherstrasse 4, tel. 06743/909-7214). They offer discounts to my readers with a €10 minimum purchase: 10 percent with cash, 5 percent with credit card.

Eating
Restaurants

Bacharach has no shortage of reasonably priced, atmospheric restaurants offering fine indoor and outdoor dining.

The Rhein Hotel's **$$$ Stüber Restaurant** is Bacharach's best top-end choice. Andreas Stüber, his family's sixth-generation chef, creates regional plates prepared with a slow-food ethic. The menu changes with the season and is served at river- and track-side seating or indoors with a spacious wood-and-white-tablecloth elegance. Their Posten Riesling is well worth the splurge (€18-25 main courses, €35 fixed-price meals, always good vegetarian and vegan options, daily 17:00-21:15 plus Sat-Sun 11:30-14:15, closed mid-Dec-Feb, call to reserve on weekends or for an outdoor table, facing the K-D boat dock below town center, Langstrasse 50, tel. 06743/1243).

$$ Altes Haus serves classic German dishes within Bacharach's most romantic atmosphere—inside the oldest building in town. Find the cozy little dining room with photos of the opera singer who sang about Bacharach, adding to its fame (€10-20 main courses, Thu-Tue 12:00-15:00 & 18:00-21:30, longer hours on weekends, closed Wed and Dec-Easter, dead center by the Protestant church, tel. 06743/1209).

Casual Options

The **$ Posthof Bacharach** restaurant and café has nice outdoor seating and a medieval feel, with a view of the ruined chapel above (€8-12 main courses, daily Easter-Oct 12:00-21:00, closed Nov-Easter, Oberstrasse 45-49, tel. 06743/947-1830).

$ Kleines Brauhaus Rheinterrasse is a funky, family-friendly microbrewery serving meals, fresh-baked bread, and homemade beer under a 1958 circus carousel that overlooks the town and river (Tue-Sun 13:00-22:00, closed Mon, at the downstream end of town, Koblenzer Strasse 14, tel. 06743/919-179).

$ Bacharacher Pizza and Kebap Haus, on the main drag in the town center, is the town favorite for €4-6 *döner kebabs,* cheap pizzas, and salads (daily 10:00-22:00, Oberstrasse 43, tel. 06743/3127).

Eis Café Italia, on the main street, is known for its refreshing, Riesling-flavored gelato (daily April-mid-Oct 13:00-19:00, closed mid-Oct-March, Oberstrasse 48).

Pick up **picnic supplies** at **Nahkauf,** a basic grocery store (Mon-Fri 8:00-12:00 & 14:00-18:00, Sat 8:30-12:30, closed Sun, Koblenzer Strasse 2). For a gourmet picnic, call the **Rhein Hotel** to reserve a "picnic bag" complete with wine, cheese, small dishes, and a hiking map (€13/person, arrange a day in advance, tel. 06743/1243).

Sleeping

None of the hotels listed here have elevators. The only listings with parking are Pension im Malerwinkel, Pension Winzerhaus, and the youth hostel. At the others, drive in to unload your bags and then park in the public lot. If you'll arrive after 20:00, let your hotel know in advance (none have 24-hour reception desks).

$$ Rhein Hotel, overlooking the river with 14 spacious and comfortable rooms, is classy, well-run, and decorated with modern flair. Since it's right on the train tracks, its river- and train-side rooms come with quadruple-paned windows and air-conditioning (Db-€96, family rooms, cheaper for longer stays and off-season, free loaner bikes, directly inland from the K-D boat dock at Langstrasse 50, tel. 06743/1243, www.rhein-hotel-bacharach.de, info@rhein-hotel-bacharach.de). Their Stüber Restaurant is considered the best in town.

$ Hotel zur Post, clean and quiet, is conveniently located right in the town center with no train noise. Its 12 rooms are a good value, offering more solid comfort than old-fashioned character (Db-€71-76, family rooms, Oberstrasse 38, tel. 06743/1277, www.hotel-zur-post-bacharach.de, h.zurpost@t-online.de).

$ **Hotel Kranenturm,** offering castle ambience without the climb, combines hotel comfort with delightful *Privatzimmer* funkiness right downtown. This 16-room hotel is part of the medieval town wall. The rooms in the tower have the best views. While just 15 feet from the train tracks, a combination of medieval sturdiness, triple-paned windows, and included earplugs makes the riverside rooms sleepable (Db-€70, Db in tower room with views-€82, family rooms, cheaper for 3-night stay, cash preferred, €2 extra with credit card, showers can be temperamental, good breakfast, Langstrasse 30, tel. 06743/1308, www.kranenturm.com, hotel-kranenturm@t-online.de).

$ **Pension im Malerwinkel** sits like a grand gingerbread house that straddles the town wall in a quiet little neighborhood. The quiet place has 20 rooms, a picturesque garden, views of the vineyards, and easy parking—all a short stroll from the town center (Db-€69, cheaper for 2- to 3-day stays, family rooms, cash only, no train noise, bike rental-€6/day, parking; from Oberstrasse, turn left at the church, walkers can follow the path to the left just before the town gate but drivers must pass through the gate to find the hotel parking lot, Blücherstrasse 41;

tel. 06743/1239, www.im-malerwinkel.de, pension@im-malerwinkel.de).

$ **Hotel Hillen,** a block south of Hotel Kranenturm, has the train noise and the same ultra-thick windows. It offers five spacious rooms and good hospitality (D with shower-€50, Db-€60, family rooms, 10 percent discount for stays of 2 nights or longer, cash only, closed mid-Nov-Easter, Langstrasse 18, tel. 06743/1287, hotel-hillen@web.de).

$ **Pension Winzerhaus** has 10 rooms just outside the town walls, directly under the vineyards. The rooms are simple, clean, and modern, and parking is a breeze (Db-€55, family rooms, prices do not include €0.50/person per day tourist tax, cash only, laundry service for fee, free loaner bikes for guests, Blücherstrasse 60, tel. 06743/1294, www.pension-winzerhaus.de, winzerhaus@gmx.de).

¢ **Irmgard Orth B&B** rents three bright rooms, two of which share a bathroom on the hall. Charming Irmgard speaks almost no English, but is exuberant and serves homemade honey with breakfast (D-€40, Db-€42, cash only, Spurgasse 2, tel. 06743/1553—speak slowly, orth.irmgard@gmail.com).

¢ **Jugendherberge Stahleck** hostel is in the 12th-century castle on the hilltop—350 steps above Bacharach—with a royal Rhine view. Open to travelers of any age, this is a gem with 168 beds and a private modern shower and WC in most rooms. The hostel offers hearty all-you-can-eat buffet dinners (18:00-19:30 nightly), and in summer, its pub serves cheap local wine and snacks all day until late. From the train station, it's a €10 taxi ride to the hostel—call 06743/1653 (dorm beds-€21.50, Db-€54, nonmembers pay extra, includes breakfast and sheets, laundry-€6; reception open 7:30-20:00, call if arriving later and check in at bar until 21:30; curfew at 22:00, tel. 06743/1266, www.diejugendherbergen.de, bacharach@diejugendherbergen.de). If driving, don't go in the driveway; park on the street and walk 200 yards.

Transportation
Arriving and Departing
BY TRAIN

Milk-run trains stop at Rhine towns each hour starting as early as 6:00, connecting at Mainz and Koblenz to trains farther afield. Trains between St. Goar and Bacharach depart at about :20 after the hour in each direction (€3.60, buy tickets from the machine in the unstaffed stations, carry cash since some machines won't accept US credit cards).

The durations listed below are calculated from Bacharach; for St. Goar, the difference is only 10 minutes. From Bacharach (or St. Goar), to go anywhere distant, you'll need to change trains in Koblenz for points north, or in Mainz for points south. Milk-run connections to these towns depart hourly, at about :20 past the hour for northbound trains, and at about :30 past the hour for southbound trains. Train info: toll tel. 0180-699-6633, www.bahn.com.

From Bacharach by Train to: St. Goar (hourly, 10 minutes), **Moselkern** near Burg Eltz (hourly, 1.5 hours, change in Koblenz), **Cologne** (hourly, 1.5-2 hours with change in Koblenz, 2.5 hours direct), **Frankfurt Airport** (hourly, 1 hour, change in Mainz or Bingen), **Frankfurt** (hourly, 1.5 hours, change in Mainz or Bingen), **Rothenburg ob der Tauber** (every 2 hours, 4.5 hours, 3-4 changes), **Munich** (hourly, 5 hours, 2 changes), **Berlin** (hourly, 7 hours, 1-3 changes).

BY CAR

Bacharach and St. Goar are near Frankfurt and its airport, just an hour's drive away. Some travelers find that the Rhine Valley, with its small towns, makes a pleasant first (or last) stop in Germany.

If you're following my two-week itinerary, and you're driving north from Rothenburg to Bacharach, allow 3 hours, or figure on a 3.5-hour drive if you route your trip through Creglingen and Weikersheim (to visit Romantic Road sights mentioned on page 818). When leaving the Rhine, you could drive to Cologne or Frankfurt, drop off the car, and take the train to Berlin (or elsewhere).

ST. GOAR

St. Goar (sahnkt gwahr) is a classic Rhine tourist town. Its hulk of a castle overlooks a half-timbered shopping street and leafy riverside park, busy with sightseeing ships and contented strollers. Rheinfels Castle, once the mightiest on the river, is the single best Rhineland ruin to explore. While the town of St. Goar itself is less interesting than Bacharach, be sure to explore beyond the shops: Thoughtful little placards (in English) offer facts about each street, lane, and square. St. Goar also makes a good base for hiking or biking the region. A tiny car ferry will shuttle you back and forth across the busy Rhine from here.

Orientation

St. Goar is dominated by its mighty castle, Rheinfels. The village—basically a wide spot in the road at the foot of Rheinfels' hill—isn't much more than a few hotels and restaurants. From the riverboat docks, the main drag—a dull pedestrian mall without history—cuts through town before ending at the road up to the castle.

Tourist Information: The helpful TI, which books rooms and stores bags for free, is on the pedestrian street, three blocks from the K-D boat dock and train station (May-Sept Mon-Fri 9:00-18:00, Sat 10:00-13:00, closed Sun; shorter hours and closed Sat-Sun in off-season; from train station, go downhill around church and turn left, Heerstrasse 86, tel. 06741/383, www.st-goar.de).

Bike Rental: Hotel an der Fähre rents bikes for a fair price, but you need to call ahead to reserve (€10/day, pickup after 10:00, Heerstrasse 47, tel. 06741/980-577).

Parking: A free lot is at the downstream (north) end of town, by the harbor. For on-street parking by the K-D boat dock and recommended hotels, get a ticket from the machine (*Parkscheinautomat*) and put it on the dashboard (€4/day, daily 9:00-18:00, coins only, free overnight). Make sure you press the button for a day ticket.

Sights

▲▲▲RHEINFELS CASTLE (BURG RHEINFELS)

Sitting like a dead pit bull above St. Goar, this once mightiest of Rhine castles rumbles with ghosts from its hard-fought past. This hollow but interesting shell offers the best ruined-castle experience on the river. Impressive and evocative, it's but a shadow of its former self. Some areas may be inaccessible due to renovation.

Cost and Hours: €5, family card–€10, mid-March-Oct daily 9:00-18:00, Nov-mid-March possibly Sat-Sun only 11:00-17:00 (call ahead), last entry one hour before closing—weather permitting.

Information: The free castle map is helpful, but the €0.50 English booklet is of no real value, except to real history buffs. If it's damp, be careful of slippery stones. Tel. 06741/7753; in winter, tel. 06741/383, www.st-goar.de.

Services: A handy WC is immediately across from the ticket booth (check out the guillotine urinals—stand back when you pull to flush).

Rick's Tip: *To explore* **the castle tunnels at Rheinfels, bring a flashlight**—*or buy one at the ticket office. For real medieval atmosphere, they also sell candles with matches.*

Getting to the Castle: A **taxi** up from town costs €5 (tel. 06741/7011). Or take the kitschy "tschu-tschu" **tourist train** (€3 one-way, €4 round-trip, 8 minutes to the top, hours vary but generally April-Oct daily 9:30-16:30, departs from town at :15 and :45, from castle at :00 and :30, some narration, mobile 0171-445-1525). The train usually waits between the train station and the K-D dock, or at the Catholic Church just past the top end of the pedestrian street. **Parking** at the castle costs €1/hour (cash only).

To **hike** up to the castle, you can simply follow the main road up through the railroad underpass at the top end of the pedestrian street. But it's more fun to take the nature trail: Start at the St. Goar train station. Take the underpass under the tracks at the north end of the station, climb the steep stairs uphill, turn right (following *Burg Rheinfels* signs), and keep straight along the path just above the

St. Goar on the Rhine

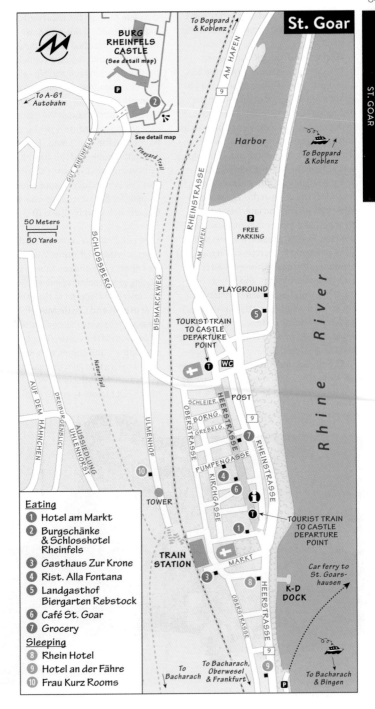

St. Goar

BURG
RHEINFELS
CASTLE
(See detail map)

See detail map

To A-61
Autobahn

To Boppard
& Koblenz

AM HAFEN

9

Harbor

To Boppard
& Koblenz

GUT RHEINFELS

Vineyard Trail

SCHLOSSBERG

RHEINSTRASSE

AM HAFEN

50 Meters
50 Yards

P FREE
PARKING

BISMARCKWEG

Nature Trail

PLAYGROUND

5

Rhine River

TOURIST TRAIN
TO CASTLE
DEPARTURE
POINT

T WC

AUF DEM HÄHNCHEN

DREIBURGENBLICK

AUSSEDLUNG
UHLENHORST

ULMENHOF

SCHLEIER

HEERSTRASSE

POST

BORNG

9

OBERSTRASSE

GREBELG.

7

PUMPENGASSE

RHEINSTRASSE

10

TOWER

4

KIRCHGASSE

6

i

T

1

TOURIST TRAIN
TO CASTLE
DEPARTURE
POINT

Eating
1 Hotel am Markt
2 Burgschänke
  & Schlosshotel
  Rheinfels
3 Gasthaus Zur Krone
4 Rist. Alla Fontana
5 Landgasthof
  Biergarten Rebstock
6 Café St. Goar
7 Grocery
Sleeping
8 Rhein Hotel
9 Hotel an der Fähre
10 Frau Kurz Rooms

TRAIN
STATION

MARKT

3

8

OBERSTRASSE

HEERSTRASSE

K-D
DOCK

Car ferry to
St. Goars-
hausen

To Bacharach,
Oberwesel
& Frankfurt

To
Bacharach

9

9

P

To Bacharach
& Bingen

old city wall. Small red-and-white signs show the way, taking you to the castle in 15 minutes.

Background: Burg Rheinfels *was* huge—for five centuries, it was the biggest castle on the Rhine. Built in 1245 to guard a toll station, it soon earned the nickname "the unconquerable fortress." In the 1400s, the castle was thickened to withstand cannon fire. Rheinfels became a thriving cultural center and, in the 1520s, was visited by the artist Albrecht Dürer and the religious reformer Ulrich Zwingli. It saw lots of action in the Thirty Years' War (1618-1648), and later became the strongest and most modern fortress in the Holy Roman Empire. It withstood a siege of 28,000 French troops in 1692. But eventually the castle surrendered to the French without a fight, and in 1797, the French Revolutionary army destroyed it. For years, the ruined castle was used as a source of building stone, and today— while still mighty—it's only a small fraction of its original size.

⊙ **Self-Guided Tour:** Rather than wander aimlessly, visit the castle by following this tour. We'll start at the museum, then circulate through the courtyards, up to the highest lookout point, and down around through the fortified ramparts, with an option to go into the dark tunnels. We'll finish in the dungeon and big cellar.

Pick up the free map and use its commentary to navigate from red signpost to red signpost through the castle. My self-guided tour route is similar to the one marked on the castle map. That map, the one in this book, and this tour all use the same numbering system. (You'll notice that I've skipped a few stops—just walk on by signs for ❷ *Darmstädter Bau,* ❺ *Stables,* ⓫ *Fuchsloch* (foxhole), and ⓭ *Gunsmiths' Tower.*)

• *The ticket office is under the castle's clock tower, labeled* ❶ Uhrturm. *Walk through the entranceway and continue straight, passing several points of interest (which we'll visit later), until you get to the* ❸ *museum.*

Museum and Castle Model: The pleasant museum, located in the only finished room of the castle, has good English descriptions and comes with Romantic Age etchings that give a sense of the place as it was in the 19th century (daily mid-March-Oct 10:00-12:30 & 13:00-17:30;

Rheinfels' inner courtyard

St. Goar's Rheinfels Castle

20 Meters
20 Yards

Cliffs
Cliffs
Cliffs

STAIRS
MUSEUM
SMALL MINE TUNNELS
WELL
CATAPULT BALLS
POSTS
BIG CELLAR
MOAT
2 ARCHES
WALK ENDS
WALK BEGINS
WC
PARKING LOT (SHUTTLE STOPS HERE)
ROAD
BRIDGE
BRIDGE
ROAD
To A-61 Autobahn
HOTEL/ RESTAURANT
Downhill to St. Goar
RHINE RIVER

········ Walking Tour Route
— — — Route From Parking Lot to Tickets

1 Ticket Office & Entry
2 Darmstädter Bau
3 Museum & Castle Model
4 Inner Courtyard
5 Stables
6 Well
7 High Battery
8 Clock Tower Lookout
9 Stairs to Battlements
10 Corner of Castle & Crossbow Slits
11 Foxhole & Mine Tunnel
12 Halsgraben ("Neck Ditch")
13 Gunsmiths' Tower
14 Dungeon
15 Slaughterhouse
16 Big Cellar

closed Nov–mid-March).

The seven-foot-tall carved stone immediately inside the door (marked *Flammensäule*)—a tombstone from a nearby Celtic grave—is from 400 years before Christ. There were people here long before the Romans...and this castle.

The sweeping castle history exhibit in the center of the room is well-described in English. The massive fortification was the only Rhineland castle to withstand Louis XIV's assault during the 17th century. At the far end of the room is a model reconstruction of the castle, showing how much bigger it was before French Revolutionary troops destroyed it in the 18th century. Study this. Find where you are. (Hint: Look for the tall tower.) This was the living quarters of the original castle, which was only the smallest ring of buildings around the tiny central courtyard (13th century). The ramparts were added in the 14th century. By 1650, the fortress was largely complete. Since its destruction by the French in the late 18th century, it's had no military value. While no WWII bombs were wasted on this ruin, it served St. Goar as a stone quarry for generations. The basement of the museum shows the castle pharmacy and an exhibit of Rhine-region odds and ends, including tools, an 1830 loom, and photos of icebreaking on the Rhine. While once routine, icebreaking hasn't been necessary here since 1963.

• *Exit the museum and walk 30 yards directly out, slightly uphill into the castle courtyard, where you'll see a sign for the inner courtyard (❹ Innenhof).*

Medieval Castle Courtyard: Five hundred years ago, the entire castle encircled this courtyard. The place was self-sufficient and ready for a siege, with a bakery, pharmacy, herb garden, brewery, well (top of yard), and livestock. During peacetime, 300 to 600 people lived here; during a siege, there would be as many as 4,000. The walls were plastered and painted white. Bits of the original 13th-century plaster survive.

• *Continue through the courtyard under the Erste Schildmauer (first shield wall) sign, turn left, and walk straight to the two old wooden upright posts. Find the pyramid of stone catapult balls on your left.*

Castle Garden: Catapult balls like these were too expensive not to recycle—they'd be retrieved after any battle. Across from the balls is a well (❻ *Brunnen*)—essential for any castle during the age of sieges. Look in. Thirsty? The old posts are for the ceremonial baptizing of new members of the local trading league. While this guild goes back centuries, it's now a social club that fills this court with a huge wine party every year on the third weekend of September.

• *Climb uphill to the castle's highest point by walking along the cobbled path (look for the To the Tower sign) up past the high battery (❼ Hohe Batterie) to the castle's best viewpoint—up where the German flag waves (signed ❽ Uhrturm).*

Highest Castle Tower Lookout: Enjoy a great view of the river, the castle, and the forest. Remember, the fortress once covered five times the land it does today. Notice how the other castles (across the river) don't poke above the top of the Rhine canyon. That would make them easy for invading armies to see.

From this perch, survey the Rhine Valley, cut out of slate over millions of years by the river. The slate absorbs the heat of the sun, making the grapes grown here well-suited for wine. Today, the slate is mined to provide roofing. Imagine St. Goar himself settling here 1,500 years ago, establishing a place where sailors—thankful to have survived the dangerous Loreley—would stop and pray. Imagine the frozen river of years past, when the ice would break up and boats would huddle in man-made harbors like the one below for protection. Consider the history of trade on this busy river—from the days when castles levied tolls on ships, to the days when boats would be hauled upstream with the help of riverside towpaths, to the

21st century when 300 ships a day move their cargo past St. Goar. And imagine this castle before the French destroyed it... when it was the mightiest structure on the river, filled with people and inspiring awe among all who passed.

• *Return to the catapult balls, walk downhill and through the tunnel, and veer left through the arch marked* **❾** *zu den Wehrgängen ("to the Battlements"). Pause here, just before the stairs, to look up and see the original 13th-century core of the castle. Now go down two flights of stairs. Turn left and step into the dark, covered passageway. From here, we'll begin a rectangular walk, taking us completely around (counterclockwise) the perimeter of the castle.*

Covered Defense Galleries with "Minutemen" Holes: Soldiers—the castle's "minutemen"—had a short commute: defensive positions on the outside, home in the holes below on the left. Even though these living quarters were padded with straw, life was unpleasant.

• *Continue straight through the dark gallery, up the stairs, and to the corner of the castle, where you'll see a red signpost with the number* **❿**. *Stand with your back to the corner of the wall.*

Corner of Castle: Gape up. That's the original castle tower. A three-story, half-timbered building originally rose beyond the tower's stone fortification. The two stone tongues near the top, just around the corner (to the right), supported the toilet. (Insert your own joke here.) Turn around and face the wall. The three crossbow slits were once steeper. The bigger hole on the riverside was for hot pitch.

• *Continue out along the back side of the castle. At the corner, turn left.*

Thoop...You're Dead: Look ahead at the smartly placed crossbow slit. While you're lying there, notice the stonework. The little round holes were for the scaffolds they used as they built up, which indicate that this stonework is original. Notice also the fine stonework on the

chutes. More boiling pitch...now you're toast, too.

• *Pick yourself up and keep going along the castle perimeter. Pass under the first of three arches and pause at the gray railing to enjoy the view. Look up the valley and uphill where the sprawling fort stretched (as far as the tiny farm on the ridge, a half-mile away). Below, just outside the wall, is land where invaders would gather. The mine tunnels are under there, waiting to blow up any attackers.*

Now continue under two more arches, jog left, go down five steps and into an open field, and walk toward the wooden bridge. The "old" wooden bridge is actually modern.

Dark Tunnel Detour: For a short detour through a castle tunnel—possible only if you have a light—turn your back to the main castle (with the modern bridge to your left) and face the stone dry-moat labeled **⓬** *Halsgraben "Neck Ditch."* (You'll exit in a few minutes at the high railing above the red #12 sign.) Go 20 yards down the path to the right, and enter the tunnel at the bottom of the wall, following the red *Hoher Minengang* sign. At the end of the short, big tunnel, take two steps up and walk eight level steps, turn left, and follow the long uphill ramp (this is where it's pitch-black, and adults will need to watch their heads). At the end, a spiral staircase takes you up to the high-railing opening you saw earlier, and then back to the courtyard.

• *When ready to leave this courtyard, angle left (under the* zum Verlies/Dungeon *sign, before the bridge) through two arches and through the rough entry to the* ⓮ Verlies *(dungeon) on the left.*

Dungeon: This is one of six dungeons. You just walked through an entrance prisoners only dreamed of 400 years ago. They came and went through the little square hole in the ceiling. The holes in the walls supported timbers that thoughtfully gave as many as 15 residents something to sit on to keep them out of the filthy slop that gathered on the floor. Twice a day, they were given bread and water. Some prisoners actually survived longer than two years in here. While the town could torture and execute, the castle had permission only to imprison criminals in these dungeons. Consider this: According to town records, the two men who spent the most time down here—2.5 years each—died within three weeks of regaining their freedom. Perhaps after a diet of bread and water, feasting on meat and wine was simply too much.

• *Continue through the next arch, under the white arrow, then turn left and walk 30 yards to the* ⓯ Schlachthaus.

Slaughterhouse: Any proper castle was prepared to survive a six-month siege. With 4,000 people, that's a lot of provisions. The cattle that lived within the walls were slaughtered in this room. The castle's mortar was congealed here (by packing all the organic waste from the kitchen into kegs and sealing it). Notice the drainage gutters. "Running water" came through from drains built into the walls (to keep the mortar dry and therefore strong...and less smelly).

• *Back outside, climb the modern stairs to the left (look for the* Zum Ausgang *sign). A skinny, dark passage leads you into the...*

Big Cellar: This ⓰ *Grosser Keller* was a big pantry. When the castle was smaller, this was the original moat—you can see the rough lower parts of the wall. The original floor was 13 feet deeper. The drawbridge rested upon the stone nubs on the left. When the castle expanded, the moat became this cellar. Halfway up the walls on the entrance side of the room, square holes mark spots where timbers made a storage loft, perhaps filled with grain. In the back, an arch leads to the wine cellar (sometimes blocked off) where finer wine was kept. Part of a soldier's pay was wine... table wine. This wine was kept in a single 180,000-liter stone barrel (that's 47,550 gallons), which generally lasted about 18 months.

The count owned the surrounding farmland. Farmers got to keep 20 percent of their production. Later, in more liberal feudal times, the nobility let them keep 40 percent. Today, the German government leaves the workers with 60 percent...and provides a few more services.

• *You're free. Climb out, turn right, and leave. For coffee on a terrace with a great view, visit Schlosshotel Rheinfels, opposite the entrance.*

Shopping

The Montag family runs two shops (one specializes in steins and the other in cuckoo clocks), both at the base of the castle hill road. The stein shop under **Hotel Montag** has Rhine guides and fine steins. The other shop, kitty-corner from the stein shop, boasts "the largest free-hanging cuckoo clock in the world" (both open daily 8:30-18:00, shorter hours Nov-April). They'll ship your souvenirs home—or give you a VAT form to claim your tax refund at the airport if you're carrying your items with you. A couple of other souvenir shops are across from the K-D boat dock.

Eating

$ Hotel am Markt serves tasty traditional meals with plenty of game and fish at fair prices, with good atmosphere and service. Specialties include marinated roast beef and homemade cheesecake. Choose cozy indoor seating, or dine outside with a river and castle view (€9-15 main courses, daily 8:00-21:00, closed Nov-Feb, Markt 1, tel. 06741/1689).

$$ Burgschänke offers the only reasonably priced lunches up at Rheinfels Castle. It's easy to miss on the ground floor of Schlosshotel Rheinfels (the hotel across from the castle ticket office—enter through the souvenir shop). Its fabulous outdoor terrace has a Rhine view (€8-10 pastas and *Flammkuchen*, €17-19 regional dishes, Sun-Thu 11:00-19:00, Fri-Sat until 21:30, tel. 06741/802-806).

$$$ Schlosshotel Rheinfels' dining room is your Rhine splurge, with an incredible indoor view terrace in an elegant, dressy setting. Call to reserve or arrive early if you're coming for breakfast or want a window table (€16 buffet breakfast, €19-28 main courses, also offers multicourse fixed-price meals, daily 7:00-11:00, 12:00-14:00 & 18:30-21:00, tel. 06741/8020).

$ Gasthaus Zur Krone, off the main drag, is the local choice for traditional German food. It's cozy and offers some outdoor seating, but no river view (€7-16 main courses, Thu-Tue 11:00-14:30 & 18:00-21:00, closed Wed, next to train station and church at Oberstrasse 38, tel. 06741/1515).

$ Ristorante Alla Fontana, tucked away on a back lane, serves the best Italian food in town at great prices in a lovely dining room or on a leafy patio (€6-9 pizzas and pasta, Tue-Sun 11:30-14:00 & 17:30-22:00, closed Mon, reservations smart, Pumpengasse 5, tel. 06741/96117).

$ Landgasthof Biergarten Rebstock is hidden on the far end of town on the banks of the Rhine. They serve schnitzel, beer, and wine. A nice playground nearby keeps the kids busy (April-Oct long hours daily—weather permitting, Am Hafen 1, tel. 06741/980-0337).

$ Café St. Goar is the perfect spot for a quick lunch or the German tradition of coffee and *kuchen*. Grab something for a picnic or enjoy the seating on the pedestrian-only street out front (Mon-Sat 7:00-18:00, Sun 10:00-18:00, Heerstrasse 95, tel. 06741/1635).

You can also buy picnic fixings on the pedestrian street at the tiny **St. Goarer Stadtladen** grocery store (Tue-Fri 8:00-18:00, Sat 8:00-13:00, closed Sun-Mon, Heerstrasse 106). The benches at St. Goar's waterfront park are great for a scenic picnic.

Sleeping

$$ Hotel am Markt features 17 rustic rooms in the main building (think antlers with a pastel flair), plus 10 classier rooms right next door, and a good restaurant. It's a decent value with all the modern comforts, just a stone's throw from the boat dock and train station (standard Db-€65, bigger Db with view-€80, closed Nov-Feb, pay parking, Markt 1, tel. 06741/1689, www. hotelammarkt1.de, hotel.am.markt@t-online.de).

$$$ Rhein Hotel, two doors down from Hotel am Markt, has 10 quality rooms—most with views and balconies—in a spacious building (Db-€90, larger Db-€100, family rooms, higher prices on Fri-Sat nights, laundry service for fee, closed mid-Nov-Feb, Heerstrasse 71, tel. 06741/981-240, www.rheinhotel-st-goar.de, info@rheinhotel-st-goar.de).

$ Hotel an der Fähre is a simple place on the busy road at the end of town, immediately across from the ferry dock. It rents 12 cheap but decent rooms (D-€45, Db-€55-60, cash only, street noise but double-glazed windows, closed Nov-Feb, Heerstrasse 47, tel. 06741/980-577, www.hotel-stgoar.de, hotel_anderfaehre@web.de).

$ Frau Kurz offers St. Goar's best B&B, renting three delightful rooms (sharing 2.5 bathrooms) with bathrobes, a breakfast terrace with castle views, a garden, and homemade marmalade (D-€56, 2-night minimum, D-€52 with stay of 4 nights or more, cash only, free and easy parking, no Internet access, bike rental for guests, Ulmenhof 11, tel. 06741/459, www.gaestehaus-kurz.de, fewo-kurz@kabelmail.de). It's a steep five-minute hike from the train station: Exit left from the station, take an immediate left under the tracks, and go partway up the zigzag stairs, turning right through an archway onto Ulmenhof; #11 is just past the tower.

MARKSBURG CASTLE IN BRAUBACH

Medieval invaders decided to give Marksburg a miss thanks to its formidable defenses, leaving it the best-preserved castle on the Rhine today. Worth ▲▲, it can be visited only with a guide on a 50-minute tour. In summer, tours in English normally run daily at 13:00 and 16:00. Otherwise, you can join a German tour (3/hour in summer, hourly in winter) that's almost as good—there are no explanations in English in the castle itself, but your ticket includes an English handout. It's an awesome castle, and between the handout and my commentary below, you'll feel fully informed, so don't worry about being on time for the English tours.

Cost and Hours: €6, family card-€15, daily April-Oct 10:00-17:00, Nov-March 11:00-16:00, last tour departs one hour before closing, tel. 02627/206, www.marksburg.de.

Getting There: Marksburg caps a hill above the village of Braubach, on the east bank of the Rhine. By **train,** it's a 10-minute trip from Koblenz to Braubach (1-2/hour); from Bacharach or St. Goar, it takes 1.5-2 hours, depending on the length of the layover in Koblenz. The train is quicker than the **boat** (downstream from Bacharach to Braubach-2 hours, upstream return-3.5 hours). Consider taking the downstream boat to Braubach, and the train back. If traveling with luggage, store it in the convenient lockers in the underground passage at the Koblenz train station (Braubach has no enclosed station—just platforms—and no lockers). If you're coming by **car** from Bacharach or St. Goar, take the car ferry at St. Goar across the Rhine, and drive north to Braubach (parking lot at castle).

If you reach Braubach by train, **walk** into the old town (follow *Altstadt* signs—

Marksburg Castle was built originally as a fortress, not a royal residence.

coming out of tunnel from train platforms, it's to your right); then follow the *Zur Burg* signs to the path up to the castle. Allow 20-30 minutes for the climb up. Scarce **taxis** charge at least €10 from the train platforms to the castle. A green **tourist train** circles up to the castle, but there's no fixed schedule, so don't count on it (Easter-mid-Oct Tue-Sun, no trains Mon or off-season, leaves from Barbarastrasse, tel. 06773/587, www.ruckes-reisen.de).

❷ **Self-Guided Tour:** Start inside the castle's **first gate.** The dramatic castles lining the Rhine are generally Romantic rebuilds, but Marksburg is the real McCoy—nearly all original construction. It's littered with bits of its medieval past, like the big stone ball that was swung on a rope to be used as a battering ram. Ahead, notice how the inner gate—originally tall enough for knights on horseback to gallop through—was made smaller, and therefore safer from enemies on horseback. Climb the Knights' Stairway, carved out of slate, and pass under the murder hole— handy for pouring boiling pitch on invaders. (Germans still say someone with bad luck "has pitch on his head.")

Coats of Arms: Colorful coats of arms line the wall just inside the gate. These are from the noble families who have owned the castle since 1283. In that year, financial troubles drove the first family to sell to the powerful and wealthy Katzenelnbogen family (who made the castle into what you see today). When Napoleon took this region in 1803, an Austrian family who sided with the French got the keys. When Prussia took the region in 1866, control passed to a friend of the Prussians who had a passion for medieval things—typical of this Romantic period. Then it was sold to the German Castles Association in 1900. Its offices are in the main palace at the top of the stairs.

Romanesque Palace: White outlines mark where the larger original windows were located, before they were replaced by easier-to-defend smaller ones. On the far right, a bit of the original plaster survives. Slate, which is vulnerable to the elements, needs to be covered—in this case, by plaster. Because this is a protected historic building, restorers can use only the traditional plaster methods...but no one knows how to make plaster that works as well as these 800-year-old surviving bits.

Cannons: The oldest cannon here— from 1500—was back-loaded. This was advantageous because many cartridges could be pre-loaded. But since the seal was leaky, it wasn't very powerful. The bigger, more modern cannons—from 1640— were one piece and therefore airtight, but had to be front-loaded. They could easily hit targets across the river from here. Stone balls were rough, so they let the explosive force leak out. The best cannonballs were stones covered in smooth lead—airtight and therefore more powerful and more accurate.

Gothic Garden: Walking along an outer wall, you'll see 160 plants from the Middle Ages—used for cooking, medicine, and witchcraft. *Schierling* (hemlock, in the first corner) is the same poison that killed Socrates.

Inland Rampart: This most vulnerable part of the castle had a triangular construction to better deflect attacks. Notice the factory in the valley. In the 14th century, this was a lead, copper, and silver mine. Today's factory—Europe's largest car-battery recycling plant—uses the old mine shafts as vents (see the three modern smokestacks).

Wine Cellar: Since Roman times, wine has been the traditional Rhineland drink. Because castle water was impure, wine— less alcoholic than today's beer—was the way knights got their fluids. The pitchers on the wall were their daily allotment. The bellows were part of the barrel's filtering system. Stairs lead to the...

Gothic Hall: This hall is set up as a kitchen, with an oven designed to roast an ox whole. The arms holding the pots have notches to control the heat. To this day, when Germans want someone to hurry up, they say, "give it one tooth more." Medieval windows were made of thin sheets of translucent alabaster or animal skins. A nearby wall is peeled away to show the wattle-and-daub construction (sticks, straw, clay, mud, then plaster) of a castle's inner walls. The iron plate to the left of the next door enabled servants to stoke the heater without being seen by the noble family.

Bedroom: This was the only heated room in the castle. The canopy kept in heat and kept out critters. In medieval times, it was impolite for a lady to argue with her lord in public. She would wait for him in bed to give him what Germans still call "a curtain lecture." The deep window seat caught maximum light for needlework and reading. Women would sit here and chat (or "spin a yarn") while working the spinning wheel.

Hall of the Knights: This was the dining hall. The long table is an unattached plank. After each course, servants could replace it with another pre-set plank. Even today, when a meal is over and Germans are ready for the action to begin, they say, "Let's lift up the table." The action back then consisted of traveling minstrels who sang and told of news gleaned from their travels.

Notice the outhouse—made of wood—hanging over thin air. When not in use, its door was locked from the outside (the castle side) to prevent any invaders from entering this weak point in the castle's defenses.

Chapel: This chapel is still painted in Gothic style with the castle's namesake, St. Mark, and his lion. Even the chapel was designed with defense in mind. The small doorway kept out heavily armed attackers. The staircase spirals clockwise, favoring the sword-wielding defender (assuming he was right-handed).

Linen Room: About the year 1800, the castle—with diminished military value—housed disabled soldiers. They'd earn extra money working raw flax into linen.

Two Thousand Years of Armor: Follow the evolution of armor since Celtic times. Because helmets covered the entire head, soldiers identified themselves as friendly by tipping their visor up with their right hand. This evolved into the military salute that is still used around the world today. Armor and the close-range weapons along the back were made obsolete by the invention of the rifle. Armor was replaced with breastplates—pointed (like the castle itself) to deflect enemy fire. This design was used as late as the start of World War I. A medieval lady's armor hangs over the door. While popular fiction has men locking up their women before heading off to battle, chastity belts were actually used by women as protection against rape when traveling.

The Keep: This served as an observation tower, a dungeon (with a 22-square-foot cell in the bottom), and a place of last refuge. When all was nearly lost, the defenders would bundle into the keep and burn the wooden bridge, hoping to outwait their enemies.

Horse Stable: The stable shows off bits of medieval crime and punishment. Cheaters were attached to stones or pillories. Shame masks punished gossipmongers. A mask with a heavy ball had its victim crawling around with his nose in the mud. The handcuffs with a neck hole were for the transport of prisoners. The pictures on the wall show various medieval capital punishments. Many times, the accused was simply taken into a torture dungeon to see all these tools, and, guilty or not, confessions spilled out of him. On that cheery note, your tour is over.

NEAR THE RHINE VALLEY

While you're in the region, another stop worth considering is Burg Eltz, a beautiful castle on the Mosel River. Many of Europe's castles are unfurnished shells, but Burg Eltz has a lived-in feel. If you're using public transit, Burg Eltz is easy to reach from the Rhine. It works better as a day trip than an overnight, since no accommodations are nearby.

BURG ELTZ

My favorite castle in all of Europe—worth ▲▲▲—lurks in a mysterious forest. It's been left intact for 700 years and is decorated and furnished throughout much as it was 500 years ago. Thanks to smart diplomacy, clever marriages, and lots of luck, Burg Eltz (pronounced "boorg elts") was never destroyed. It even survived one five-year siege. It's been in the Eltz family for 850 years.

Getting There

The castle is a pleasant 1.5-hour **walk** from the nearest train station, in the little village of Moselkern—the walk is not only easy, it's the most fun and scenic way to visit the castle.

Hiking to the Castle from Moselkern: You can hike between the Moselkern train station and Burg Eltz in 70 minutes at a steady clip, but allow an extra 20 minutes or so to enjoy the scenery (see map on page 858). The elevation gain is less than 400 feet. (You can reach Moselkern via train from towns on the Rhine—including Bacharach and Cologne—with a change at Koblenz.)

To find the **path up to the castle,** turn right from the Moselkern station along Oberstrasse and continue to the village church. Just past the church, as the street ends, turn right through the underpass. You'll follow the Elzbach stream all the way up to the castle. Just before a stone bridge crosses the stream, take either the foot-path or the bridge—they join up again later.

When the road ends at the parking lot of Hotel Ringelsteiner Mühle, stay to the right of the hotel and continue upstream along the easy-to-follow trail—from here, it's another 45 minutes through the forest to the castle.

By Bus from Treis-Karden: From May through October on Saturdays and Sundays only, bus #330 runs to Burg Eltz from the railway station in the town of Treis-Karden (4/day, 30 minutes; confirm times with bus operator at tel. 02671/8976 or at www.vrminfo.de).

By Taxi: You can taxi to the castle from the nearby towns of **Moselkern** (€28 one-way, taxi tel. 02672/1407) or **Karden** (€30 one-way, taxi tel. 02672/1407). If you're planning to taxi from Moselkern, call ahead and ask the taxi to meet your train at Moselkern station. Consider taxiing up to Burg Eltz and then enjoying the hike downhill back to the train station in Moselkern.

By Car: Cars (and taxis) park in a lot near, but not quite at, Burg Eltz. From the lot, hike 15 minutes downhill to the castle or wait (10 minutes at most) for the red castle shuttle bus.

Drive/Hike Combo: If you're traveling by car but would enjoy walking part of the path up to the castle, drive to Moselkern, follow the *Burg Eltz* signs up the Elz Valley, park at Hotel Ringelsteiner Mühle (buy ticket from machine), and hike about 45 minutes up the trail to the castle.

Orientation

Cost and Hours: €9 castle entry includes required 45-minute guided tour and treasury, April-Oct daily from 9:30, last tour departs at 17:30, closed Nov-March, tel. 02672/950-500, www.burg-eltz.de.

Eating at Burg Eltz: The **castle café** serves lunch, with soups and bratwurst-and-fries cuisine (April-Oct daily, cash only).

Rick's Tip: Bring cash! *The castle (including the parking lot and café) doesn't accept credit cards, and there's no ATM.*

Visiting the Castle

The first record of a *Burg* (castle) on the Elz is from 1157. (Elz is the name of a stream that runs past the castle through a deep valley before emptying into the Mosel.) By about 1490, the castle looked like it does today, with the homes of three big landlord families gathered around a tiny courtyard within one formidable fortification. Today, the excellent tour winds you through two of those homes, while the third is still the residence of the castellan (the man who maintains the castle). This is where members of the Eltz family stay when they're not at one of their other feudal holdings. The elderly countess of Eltz—whose family goes back 33 generations here (you'll see a photo of her family)—enjoys flowers. Each week for 40 years, she's had grand arrangements adorn the public castle rooms.

It was a comfortable castle for its day: 80 rooms made cozy by 40 fireplaces and wall-hanging tapestries. Many of its 20 toilets were automatically flushed by a rain drain. The delightful **chapel** is on a lower floor. Even though "no one should live above God," this chapel's placement was acceptable because it filled a bay window, which flooded the delicate Gothic space with light. The three families met—working out common problems as if sharing a condo complex—in the large "conference room." A carved jester and a

Burg Eltz

rose look down on the big table, reminding those who gathered that they were free to discuss anything ("fool's freedom"—jesters could say anything to the king), but nothing discussed could leave the room (the "rose of silence"). In the **bedroom,** have fun with the suggestive decor: the jousting relief carved into the canopy, and the fertile and phallic figures hiding in the lusty green wall paintings.

Near the exit, the **treasury** fills the four higgledy-piggledy floors of a cellar with the precious, eccentric, and historic mementos of this family that once helped elect the Holy Roman Emperor.

Berlin

Over the last two decades, Berlin has been a construction zone. Standing on ripped-up tracks and under a canopy of cranes, visitors have witnessed the rebirth of a great European capital: lively, fun-loving, and captivating.

Berlin is still largely defined by its tumultuous 20th century. The city was Hitler's capital during World War II, and in the postwar years, it became the front line of the Cold War between Soviet-style communism and American-style capitalism. The East-West division was set in stone in 1961 with the Berlin Wall, which would stand for 28 years. In 1990, after the Wall fell, the two Germanys—and the two Berlins—officially became one.

Urban planners seized on the city's reunification and the return of the national government to make Berlin a great capital once again. Today, the old "East Berlin" is where you feel the vibrant pulse of the city, while the old "West Berlin" feels like a chic, classy suburb.

But even as the city busily builds itself into the 21st century, Berlin acknowledges and remembers its past. Thought-provoking memorials confront Germany's difficult history. Lacing these sights into your sightseeing intensifies your understanding of the city. As you walk over what was the Wall and through the well-patched Brandenburg Gate, it's clear that history is not contained in books; it's an evolving story in which we play a part.

BERLIN IN 3 DAYS

Day 1: Begin your day getting oriented to this huge city. For a quick and relaxing once-over-lightly tour, jump on one of the many hop-on, hop-off buses (such as BEX Sightseeing Berlin) that make orientation loops through the city.

Then take Part 1 of my self-guided "Best of Berlin Walk," starting at the Reichstag (reservations required to climb its dome), going through the Brandenburg Gate, and down the boulevard, Unter den Linden. Visit the charming Gendarmenmarkt square. Then tour the German History Museum.

On any evening: Any of these neighborhoods (all near each other) are worth exploring: Hackescher Markt, Oranienburger Strasse, and Prenzlauer Berg. Take in live music or cabaret. Linger at a beer garden, or stroll the banks of the Spree River. Or even continue your sightseeing—a number of sights stay open late, including the Reichstag and its view dome.

Day 2: Start your morning at Bebelplatz with Part 2 of my "Best of Berlin Walk." Along the walk, visit any museum that interests you on Museum Island or nearby: Pergamon, Neues, or the DDR.

In the afternoon, catch a boat tour (or pedal a rented bike) along the parklike banks of the Spree River from Museum Island to the Chancellery. Explore the Hackescher Markt's shops and museums (and stay into the evening).

Day 3: Tour the sights of the Third Reich and Cold War: the Topography of Terror exhibit and Museum of the Wall at Checkpoint Charlie. The Jewish Museum Berlin is also nearby.

In the afternoon, visit the Gemäldegalerie art museum.

Head to Prenzlauer Berg to visit the Berlin Wall Memorial, then stay for the café and nightlife scene.

ORIENTATION

Berlin is huge, with 3.4 million people. The city is spread out and its sights numerous, so you'll need to be well-organized to experience it all. The tourist's Berlin can be broken into several digestible chunks:

Near the landmark **Brandenburg Gate,** you'll find the Reichstag building, Pariser Platz, and memorials to Hitler's victims.

From the Brandenburg Gate, the famous **Unter den Linden boulevard** runs eastward, passing the German History Museum and Museum Island (Pergamon Museum, Neues Museum, and Berlin Cathedral) on the way to Alexanderplatz (TV Tower).

South of Unter den Linden are the delightful Gendarmenmarkt square, noteworthy Nazi sites (including the Topography of Terror), good Wall-related sights (Museum of the Wall at Checkpoint Charlie), and the Jewish Museum.

Across the Spree River are the neighborhoods of Hackescher Markt, Oranienburger Strasse, and Prenzlauer Berg (lively restaurant/nightlife zone). The Berlin Wall Memorial is at the west edge of Prenzlauer Berg.

The Brandenburg Gate—historic and grand

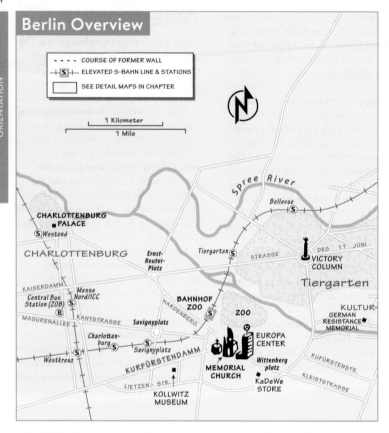

Berlin Overview

- - - - COURSE OF FORMER WALL
─**S**─ ELEVATED S-BAHN LINE & STATIONS
SEE DETAIL MAPS IN CHAPTER

1 Kilometer
1 Mile

Rick's Tip: *What Americans called* **"East Germany"** *was technically the German Democratic Republic—the Deutsche Demokratische Republik, or* **DDR** *(pronounced day-day-AIR). You'll still see those initials around what was once East Germany. The name for what was* **"West Germany"**—*the Federal Republic of Germany (Bundesrepublik Deutschland, or* **BRD**)—*is now the name shared by all of Germany.*

Central Berlin is dominated by the giant **Tiergarten park,** with its angel-topped Victory Column. South of the park are Potsdamer Platz (the Times Square of Berlin, and a transportation hub) and the Kulturforum museum complex, whose highlight is the **Gemäldegalerie,** a trea-

sure chest of European painting. To the north is the huge Hauptbahnhof (the city's main train station).

Western Berlin has the feel of a chic, classy suburb. It focuses on the **Bahnhof Zoo train station** (often marked "Zoologischer Garten" on transit maps) and the grand **Kurfürstendamm boulevard,** nicknamed "Ku'damm" (transportation hub and shopping). Even though the east side of the city is all the rage, big-name stores (like KaDeWe) and restaurants keep the west side buzzing.

Tourist Information

With any luck, you won't have to use Berlin's TIs. Appropriately called "info-stores," they are unlikely to have the information you need (tel. 030/250-025, www.

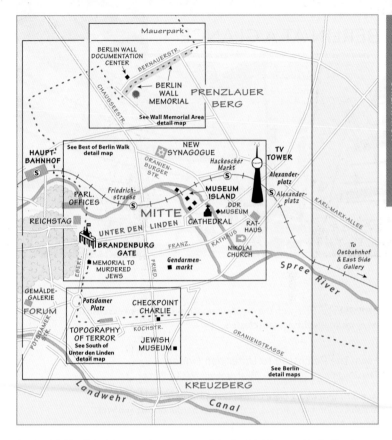

visitberlin.de). You'll find them at the **Hauptbahnhof** train station (daily 8:00-22:00, by main entrance on Europaplatz), at the **Brandenburg Gate** (daily 9:30-19:00, until 18:00 Nov-March), and at the **TV Tower** (daily 10:00-18:00, until 16:00 Nov-March, Panoramastrasse 1a).

Sightseeing Passes

The three-day, €24 **Museum Pass Berlin** is a great value and pays for itself in a hurry. It gets you into more than 50 museums, including the national museums and most of the recommended biggies (though not the German History Museum), on three consecutive days. Sights covered by the pass include the Museum Island museums (including Neues and Pergamon), Gemäldegalerie,

and the Jewish Museum Berlin. Buy it at the TI or any participating museum. The pass generally lets you skip the line and go directly into the museum.

The €18 **Museum Island Pass** (Bereichskarte Museumsinsel) covers all the venues on Museum Island and is a fine value—but for just €6 more, the three-day Museum Pass Berlin gives you triple the days and many more entries.

TIs sell the **WelcomeCard,** a transportation pass that includes discounts for many sights; it's a good value if you'll be using public transit frequently (see page 920).

Helpful Hints

Addresses: Many Berlin streets are numbered with odd and even numbers on

BERLIN AT A GLANCE

Berlin is huge. Even with the excellent transit system, it makes sense to organize your sightseeing in clusters.

From the Reichstag to Unter den Linden
These sights are part of my "Best of Berlin Walk," Part 1.

▲▲▲**Brandenburg Gate** One of Berlin's most famous landmarks, a massive columned gateway, at the former border of East and West. **Hours:** Always open. See page 875.

▲▲▲**Reichstag** Germany's historic parliament building, topped with a striking modern dome you can climb (reservations required). **Hours:** Daily 8:00-24:00, last entry at 22:00. See page 886.

▲▲**Memorial to the Murdered Jews of Europe** Holocaust memorial with almost 3,000 symbolic pillars, plus an exhibition about Hitler's Jewish victims. **Hours:** Memorial always open; information center open Tue-Sun 10:00-20:00, Oct-March until 19:00, closed Mon. See page 876.

▲▲**Unter den Linden** Leafy boulevard through the heart of former East Berlin, lined with some of the city's top sights. **Hours:** Always open. See page 878.

Museum Island and Nearby
You'll stop at Museum Island on my "Best of Berlin Walk," Part 2.

▲▲▲**Pergamon Museum** World-class museum of classical antiquities on Museum Island, partially closed through 2025 (including its famous Pergamon Altar). **Hours:** Daily 10:00-18:00, Thu until 20:00. See page 890.

▲▲▲**German History Museum** The ultimate swing through Germany's tumultuous story, located just west of Museum Island. **Hours:** Daily 10:00-18:00. See page 893.

▲▲**Neues Museum** Egyptian antiquities collection on Museum Island and proud home of the exquisite 3,000-year-old bust of Queen Nefertiti. **Hours:** Daily 10:00-18:00, Thu until 20:00. See page 891.

▲▲**DDR Museum** Quirky collection of communist-era artifacts, located just east of Museum Island. **Hours:** Daily 10:00-20:00, Sat until 22:00. See page 894.

South of Unter den Linden

▲▲**Gendarmenmarkt** Inviting square bounded by twin churches (one with a fine German history exhibit), a chocolate shop, and a concert hall. **Hours:** Always open. See page 894.

▲▲**Topography of Terror** Chilling exhibit documenting the Nazi perpetrators, built on the site of the former Gestapo/SS headquarters. **Hours:** Daily 10:00-20:00. See page 895.

▲▲**Museum of the Wall at Checkpoint Charlie** Kitschy but moving museum with stories of brave Cold War escapes, near the former site of the famous East-West border checkpoint; the surrounding street scene is almost as interesting. **Hours:** Daily 9:00-22:00. See page 897.

▲▲**Jewish Museum Berlin** Engaging, accessible museum celebrating Jewish culture, in a highly conceptual building. **Hours:** Daily 10:00-20:00, Mon until 22:00. See page 899.

Kulturforum Complex

▲▲**Gemäldegalerie** Germany's top collection of 13th- through 18th-century European paintings, featuring Holbein, Dürer, Cranach, Van der Weyden, Rubens, Hals, Rembrandt, Vermeer, Velázquez, and Raphael, located off Tiergarten park. **Hours:** Tue-Fri 10:00-18:00, Thu until 20:00, Sat-Sun 11:00-18:00, closed Mon. See page 901.

Across the Spree River

▲▲▲**Prenzlauer Berg** Lively, colorful neighborhood with hip cafés, restaurants, boutiques, and street life. **Hours:** Always open. See page 905.

▲▲▲**Berlin Wall Memorial** A "docu-center" with videos and displays, several outdoor exhibits, and the lone surviving stretch of an intact Wall section. **Hours:** Visitor Center Tue-Sun 10:00-18:00, closed Mon; outdoor areas accessible 24 hours daily. See page 906.

▲**New Synagogue** Largest prewar synagogue in Berlin. **Hours:** April-Oct Mon-Fri 10:00-18:00, Sun until 19:00; Nov-March exhibit only Sun-Thu 10:00-18:00, Fri until 15:00; closed Sat year-round. See page 905.

City Bus #100 Tour

For a cheap alternative to a hop-on, hop-off bus tour, you could follow this self-guided tour via **City Bus #100** instead. Running from the Bahnhof Zoo train station in western Berlin to Alexanderplatz in eastern Berlin, City Bus #100 laces together the major sights. A basic, single bus ticket is good for two hours of travel in one direction and buses leave every few minutes, so hopping on and off works great (see page 920 for ticketing details).

Here's a quick review of what you'll see: Leaving from Bahnhof Zoo, spot the bombed-out hulk of the **Kaiser Wilhelm Memorial Church,** with its jagged spire and postwar sister church. Then, on the left, the elephant gates mark the entrance to the much-loved **Berlin Zoo.** After a left turn, you cross the canal and pass Berlin's **embassy row.**

The bus then enters the vast 400-acre **Tiergarten** city park, once a royal hunting ground and now packed with cycling paths, joggers, and—on hot days—nude sunbathers. Straight ahead, the **Victory Column** (with the gilded angel) towers above. A block beyond the Victory Column (on the left) is the 18th-century late-Rococo **Bellevue Palace,** the residence of the federal president (if the flag's out, he's in).

Driving along the Spree River (on the left), you'll see several striking **national government** buildings. A metal Henry Moore sculpture entitled *Butterfly* floats in front of the slope-roofed House of World Cultures. Through the trees on the left is the **Chancellery**—Germany's "White House." The big open space is the **Platz der Republik,** where the Victory Column (which you passed earlier) stood until Hitler moved it. The Hauptbahnhof (Berlin's vast main train station, marked by its tall tower with the *DB* sign) is across the field between the Chancellery and the **Reichstag** (Germany's parliament—the old building with the new dome).

Hop off at the next stop (Reichstag/Bundestag) if you'd like to follow my "Best of Berlin Walk." But if you stay on the bus, you'll zip by the next string of sights, in this order:

Unter den Linden, the main east-west thoroughfare, stretches from the **Brandenburg Gate** through Berlin's historic core to the TV Tower in the distance. You'll pass the **Russian Embassy** and the Aeroflot airline office (right). Crossing **Friedrichstrasse,** look right for a Fifth Avenue-style conga line of big, glitzy department stores. Later, on the left, are the **German History Museum, Museum Island,** and the **Berlin Cathedral;** across from these (on the right) is the construction site of the **Humboldt-Forum Berliner Schloss** (with the Humboldt Box visitors center). You'll rumble to a final stop at the transit hub of **Alexanderplatz.**

the same side of the street, often with no connection to the other side (for example, Ku'damm #212 can be across the street from #14). To save steps, check the white street signs on curb corners; many list the street numbers covered on that side of the block.

City Overview: If you don't ascend the Reichstag's dome, try **Panoramapunkt,** which offers a speedy elevator and sky-scraping rooftop views (€6.50, €10.50 for VIP line-skipping ticket, daily 10:00-20:00, until 18:00 in winter, in red-brick building on Potsdamer Platz, S-Bahn and U-Bahn: Potsdamer Platz, tel. 030/2593-7080, www.panoramapunkt.de).

Rick's Tip: *There are still enough idiots on the street to keep the* **con men with their shell games** *in business. Don't be foolish enough to engage with any gambling on the street.*

Medical Help: The US Embassy has a list of local English-speaking doctors (tel. 030/83050, http://germany.usembassy. gov).

Tours

▲▲▲HOP-ON, HOP-OFF BUSES

Several companies offer a circuit of the city with unlimited hop-on, hop-off privileges all day for about €20 (about 15 stops at the city's major tourist spots—Museum Island, Brandenburg Gate, and so on). Go with a live guide rather than the recorded spiel (buses generally run April-Oct daily 10:00-18:00, departures every 10 minutes, last bus leaves all stops at around 16:00, 2-hour loop; Nov-March 2/hour and last departure at 15:00). Try BEX Sightseeing Berlin (www.berlinerstadtrundfahrten.de) or look for brochures in your hotel lobby or at the TI.

▲▲▲WALKING TOURS

Berlin's complex history can be challenging to appreciate on your own, so walking tours are worthwhile. Germany has no regulations controlling who can give city tours, so guides can be hit-or-miss. To land a great guide, use one of the companies I recommend. They all run tours daily. Most in-city tours cost about €12-15 and last about 3 to 4 hours.

Brewer's Berlin Tours specializes in in-depth walks that can flex with your interests. Their Best of Berlin introductory tour, billed at 6 hours, can last for 8; they also do a shorter 3.5-hour tour (free, tip expected). All tours depart from Bandy Brooks ice-cream shop at the Friedrichstrasse S-Bahn station (mobile 0177-388-1537, www.brewersberlintours.com).

Insider Tour runs the full gamut of itineraries, including pub crawls and a day trip to Dresden. Their tours meet at the McDonald's across from the Bahnhof Zoo train station, and at the AM to PM Bar at the Hackescher Markt S-Bahn station (tel. 030/692-3149, www.insidertour.com).

Original Berlin Walks gives a good overview in four hours (daily year-round). They also offer a Third Reich walking tour and other themes. Tours depart from opposite the Hackescher Markt S-Bahn station (tour info: tel. 030/301-9194, www. berlinwalks.de).

Rick's Tip: *Supposedly* **"free" tours are advertised all over town.** *English-speaking students deliver a memorized script and expect to be tipped (€5 minimum per person is encouraged). While the guides can be highly entertaining, when it comes to walking tours, you get what you pay for.*

PRIVATE GUIDES

Guides charge roughly the same for private tours (€50-60/hour or €200-300/day, confirm when booking). Consider **Nick Jackson,** an archaeologist and historian who makes museums come to life (mobile 0171-537-8768, www. jacksonsberlintours.com), or **Bernhard Schlegelmilch,** an enthusiastic historian who grew up behind the Wall (mobile 0176-6422-9119, www.steubentoursberlin. com).

BOAT TOURS

Several boat companies offer relaxing one-hour trips up and down the Spree River. Boats leave from various docks that cluster near the bridge at the Berlin Cathedral (just off Unter den Linden). For better views, choose a two-story boat with open-deck seating. I enjoy the Historical Sightseeing Cruise from **Stern und Kreisschiffahrt** (€14, mid-March-Nov daily 10:00-19:00, leaves from Nikolaiviertel Dock—cross bridge from Berlin Cathedral toward Alexanderplatz and look right, tel. 030/536-3600, www.sternundkreis. de). Confirm that the boat you choose comes with English commentary.

BEST OF BERLIN WALK

This two-mile self-guided walk, worth ▲▲▲, starts in front of the Reichstag, takes you under the Brandenburg Gate and down Unter den Linden, and finishes on Alexanderplatz. If you have just one day in Berlin, or want a good orientation to the city, simply follow this walk (allowing 2-3 hours at a brisk pace, not counting museum visits). By the end, you'll have seen the core of Berlin and its most important sights.

If you have more time and want to use this walk as a spine for your sightseeing, entering sights and museums as you go, consider doing Part 1 and Part 2 on different days. Part 1 goes from the Reichstag and takes you partway down Unter den Linden, with stops at the Brandenburg Gate, Memorial to the Murdered Jews of Europe, and Friedrichstrasse, the glitzy shopping street. Part 2 continues down Unter den Linden, from Bebelplatz to Alexanderplatz, and features Museum Island and the Spree River, Berlin Cathedral, and iconic TV Tower.

🎧 Download my free Best of Berlin Walk audio tour, which narrates the route.

⊙ Self-Guided Walk
Part 1: From the Reichstag to Unter den Linden

During the Cold War, the Reichstag stood just inside the West Berlin side of the Wall. Even though it's been more than 25 years since the Wall came down, you may still feel a slight tingle down your spine as you walk across the former death strip, through the once *verboten* Brandenburg Gate, and into the former communist east.

• *Start your walk directly in front of the Reichstag building, at the big, grassy park called...*

❶ PLATZ DER REPUBLIK

Stand about 100 yards in front of the grand Reichstag building and spin left to survey your surroundings. At the **Reichstag U-Bahn stop** is a big federal building overlooking the Spree River. The huge **main train station** (Hauptbahnhof) is in the distance (see the tower marked *DB*, for Deutsche Bahn—the German rail company). Farther left is the mammoth white concrete-and-glass **Chancellery,** nicknamed the "washing machine" by Berliners for its hygienic, spin-cycle appearance. It's the office of Germany's most powerful person, the chancellor (currently Angela Merkel). To remind the chancellor for whom he or she works, Germany's Reichstag (housing the parliament) is about six feet taller than the Chancellery.

Beyond the Chancellery is the Spree

River. When kings ruled Prussia, government buildings crowded right up to its banks. But today, the riverscape is a people-friendly zone (we'll see it later on this walk).

• Dominating the Platz der Republik is a giant domed building, the...

❷ REICHSTAG

The parliament building—the heart of German democracy and worth ▲▲▲—has a short but complicated and emotional history. When it was inaugurated in the 1890s, the last emperor, Kaiser Wilhelm II, disdainfully called it the "chatting home for monkeys" (Reichsaffenhaus). It was placed outside the city's old walls—far from the center of real power, the imperial palace. But it was from the Reichstag that the German Republic was proclaimed in 1918. Look above the door, surrounded by stone patches from WWII bomb damage, to see the motto and promise: Dem Deutschen Volke ("To the German People").

In 1933, this symbol of democracy nearly burned down. The Nazis—whose influence on the German political scene was on the rise—blamed a communist plot. A Dutch communist, Marinus van der Lubbe, was eventually convicted and guillotined for the crime. Others believed that Hitler himself planned the fire, using it as a handy excuse to frame the communists and grab power.

The Reichstag was hardly used from 1933 to 1999. Despite the fact that the building had lost its symbolic value, Stalin ordered his troops to take the Reichstag from the Nazis no later than May 1, 1945 (the date of the workers' May Day parade in Moscow). More than 1,500 Nazi soldiers made their last stand here—extending World War II by two days. On April 30, after fierce fighting on its rooftop, the Reichstag fell to the Red Army.

For the building's 101st birthday in 1995, the artist-partners Christo and Jeanne-Claude wrapped the entire thing in silvery gold cloth. It was then wrapped again—in scaffolding—and rebuilt by British architect Lord Norman Foster into the new

The Reichstag is the symbolic heart of German democracy.

Best of Berlin Walk

1. Platz der Republik
2. Reichstag
3. Memorial to Politicians Who Opposed Hitler
4. Berlin Wall Victims Memorial
5. Monument to the Murdered Sinti & Roma of Europe
6. Brandenburg Gate
7. Pariser Platz
8. US Embassy
9. Memorial to the Murdered Jews of Europe
10. Site of Hitler's Bunker
11. Unter den Linden
12. Russian Embassy
13. Intersection of Unter den Linden & Friedrichstrasse

parliamentary home of the Bundestag (Germany's lower house, similar to the US House of Representatives). In 1999, the German parliament convened here for the first time in 66 years. To many Germans, the proud resurrection of the Reichstag symbolizes the end of a terrible chapter in their country's history.

The **glass cupola** rises 155 feet above the ground. Its two sloped ramps spiral 755 feet to the top for a grand view.

Inside the dome, a cone of 360 mirrors reflects natural light into the legislative chamber below. Illuminated from inside after dark, this gives Berlin a memorable nightlight. The environmentally friendly cone—with an opening at the top—also helps with air circulation, expelling stale air from the legislative chamber (no joke) and pulling in fresh, cool air.

Visitors with advance reservations can climb the spiral ramp up into the cupola. If

14 Bebelplatz
15 Humboldt University
16 German State Opera
17 Neue Wache
18 German History Museum
19 Museum Island
20 Lustgarten
21 Berlin Cathedral

22 Humboldt-Forum Berliner Schloss
23 Spree River Cruises
24 DDR Museum
25 Marien Church
26 Women's Protest Memorial
27 TV Tower
28 Alexanderplatz

you haven't booked a slot, cross the street to the white booth to check available entry times (for details on making reservations and visiting the interior, including a self-guided dome tour, see page 886).

• *Face the Reichstag and walk to the right. Near the road in front of the building, enmeshed in all the security apparatus and crowds, is a memorial of slate stones embedded vertically in the ground.*

❸ MEMORIAL TO POLITICIANS WHO OPPOSED HITLER

This row of slabs, which looks like a fancy slate bicycle rack, is a memorial to the 96 members of the Reichstag who were persecuted and murdered because their politics didn't agree with Chancellor Hitler's. They were part of the Weimar Republic, the weak and ill-fated attempt at post-WWI democracy in Germany. These were the people who could have stopped

Hitler...so they became his first victims. Each slate slab memorializes one man—his name, party (mostly KPD—Communists, and SPD—Social Democrats), and the date and location of his death—generally in a concentration camp (indicated by *KZ* on the slabs). They are honored here, in front of the building in which they worked.

• *Walk along the side of the Reichstag, on busy Scheidemannstrasse, toward the rear of the building. At the intersection with Ebertstrasse, cross to the right (toward the park). Along a railing is a small memorial of white crosses. This is the...*

❹ BERLIN WALL VICTIMS MEMORIAL

This monument commemorates some of the East Berliners who died trying to cross the Wall. Many of them perished within months of the Wall's construction on August 13, 1961. Most died trying to swim the Spree River to freedom. This monument used to stand right on the Berlin Wall behind the Reichstag. The last person killed while trying to escape was 20-year-old Chris Gueffroy, who was shot through the heart in no-man's land nine months before the Wall fell in 1989. (To read more about the Wall, see the sidebar on page 898.)

• *Continue along Ebertstrasse for a few more steps before turning right on a peaceful leafy lane. Within a short distance, on your right, is the...*

❺ MONUMENT TO THE MURDERED SINTI AND ROMA OF EUROPE

Unveiled in 2012, this memorial remembers the roughly 500,000 Sinti and Roma victims of the Holocaust. "Sinti" and "Roma" (the main tribes and correct terms for those more commonly called "Gypsies") were as persecuted by the Nazis as were the Jews. And they lost the same percentage of their population to Hitler. The opaque glass wall, with a timeline in English and German, traces the Nazi abuse and atrocities.

Enter through the rusty steel portal. On the other side is a circular reflecting pool surrounded by stone slabs, some containing the names of the death camps where hundreds of thousands of Sinti and Roma perished. In the water along the rim of the pool is the wrenching poem "Auschwitz," by composer and writer Santino Spinelli, an Italian Roma. Dissonant music evoking the tragedy of the Sinti and Roma genocide adds to the atmosphere.

• *Retrace your steps to Ebertstrasse and continue right, toward the busy intersection dominated by the imposing Brandenburg Gate.*

Take this chance to get oriented. Behind you, as you face the Brandenburg Gate, is **Tiergarten park,** *its center marked by the landmark Victory Column. Now face the gate: It stands at one end of Unter den Linden, the Champs-Elysées of Berlin. In the distance, the red-and-white spire of the TV Tower marks the end of this walk.*

As you cross the street toward the gate,

Memorial to Politicans Who Opposed Hitler

Berlin Wall Victims Memorial

notice the double row of cobblestones beneath your feet—it goes about 25 miles around the city, marking where the Wall used to stand. Now walk under the gate that, for a sad generation, was part of a wall that divided this city.

❻ BRANDENBURG GATE

The historic Brandenburg Gate, rated ▲▲▲, is the last survivor of 14 gates in Berlin's old city wall. This one, dating from 1791, was the grandest and led to the neighboring city of Brandenburg. The gate was the symbol of Prussian Berlin—and later the symbol of a divided Berlin. It's crowned by a majestic four-horse chariot, with the Goddess of Peace at the reins. Napoleon took this statue to the Louvre in Paris in 1806. After the Prussians defeated Napoleon and got it back (1813), she was renamed the Goddess of Victory.

The gate sat unused, part of a sad circle dance called the Berlin Wall, for more than 25 years. Now postcards all over town show the ecstatic day—November 9, 1989—when the world rejoiced at the sight of happy Berliners jamming the gate like flowers on a parade float. Pause a minute and think about struggles for freedom—past and present. There's actually a special room built into the gate for this purpose (see the sidebar). A TI is also within the gate. Around the gate, information boards show how this area changed throughout the 20th century.

The gate sits on a major boulevard running east to west through Berlin. The

The Brandenburg Gate, Arch of Peace

More than 200 years ago, the Brandenburg Gate was designed as an arch of peace, crowned by the Goddess of Peace and showing Mars sheathing his sword. The Nazis misused it as a gate of triumph and aggression. Today a Room of Silence, built into the gate, is dedicated to the peaceful message of the original Brandenburg Gate. As you consider the history of Berlin in this silent and empty room, you may be inspired to read the prayer of the United Nations:

"Oh Lord, our planet Earth is only a small star in space. It is our duty to transform it into a planet whose creatures are no longer tormented by war, hunger, and fear, no longer senselessly divided by race, color, and ideology. Give us courage and strength to begin this task today so that our children and our children's children shall one day carry the name of man with pride."

western segment, called Strasse des 17 Juni (named for a workers' uprising against the DDR government on June 17, 1953), stretches for four miles from the Brandenburg Gate, through the Tiergarten, past the Victory Column, to the Olympic Stadium. But we'll follow this city axis in the opposite direction—east, along Unter den Linden into the core of old imperial Berlin, and past the site where the palace of the Hohenzollern family, rulers of Prussia and then Germany, once stood. The royal palace is a phantom sight, long gone, but its occupants were responsible for just about all you'll see.

• *Pass through the gate and stand in the middle of...*

Brandenburg Gate

❼ PARISER PLATZ

"Parisian Square," so named after the Prussians who defeated Napoleon in 1813, was once filled with important government buildings—all bombed to smithereens in World War II. For decades, it was an unrecognizable, deserted no-man's-land—cut off from the rest of the city by the Wall. Banks, hotels, and embassies have now reclaimed their original places on the square—with a few additions, including a palace of coffee: Starbucks. The winners of World War II enjoy this prime real estate: The American, French, British, and Russian embassies are all on or near this square.

As you face the gate, to your right is the French Embassy, and to your left is the ❽ **US Embassy,** which reopened in its historic pre-WWII location in 2008. For safety's sake, Uncle Sam wanted more of a security zone around the building, but the Germans wanted to keep Pariser Platz a welcoming people zone. The compromise: Extra security was built into the structure. Easy-on-the-eyes barriers keep potential car bombs at a distance, and the front door is on the side farthest from the Brandenburg Gate.

Turn your back to the gate. On the right, jutting into the square, is the ritzy **Hotel Adlon,** long called home by visiting stars and VIPs. In its heyday, it hosted such notables as Charlie Chaplin, Albert Einstein, and Greta Garbo. It was the setting for Garbo's most famous line, "I vant to be alone," uttered in the film *Grand Hotel.* Damaged by the Russians just after World War II, the original hotel was closed when the Wall went up in 1961 and later demolished. Today's grand Adlon was rebuilt in 1997. It was here that Michael Jackson shocked millions by dangling his infant son over a balcony railing.

• *Between the hotel and the US Embassy are two buildings worth a quick visit: the DZ Bank building and the Academy of Arts. We'll enter both.*

DZ Bank Building: This building's architect, Frank Gehry, is famous for Bilbao's Guggenheim Museum, Prague's Dancing House, Seattle's Experience Music Project, Chicago's Pritzker Pavilion, and Los Angeles' Walt Disney Concert Hall. Gehry fans might be surprised at the bank building's low profile. Structures on Pariser Platz are designed so as not to draw attention away from the Brandenburg Gate. But to get your fix of wild and colorful Gehry, step into the lobby. Built as an office complex and conference center, its undulating interior is like a big, slithery fish. Gehry explained, "The form of the fish is the best example of movement. I try to capture this movement in my buildings."

• *Leaving the DZ Bank, turn right and head into the next building, the...*

Academy of Arts (Akademie der Künste): Inside the glassy arcade, just past the café, is the office where Albert Speer, Hitler's architect, planned the rebuilding of postwar Berlin into "Welthauptstadt Germania"—the grandiose "world capital" of Nazi Europe. Pass through the glass door to see Speer's favorite statue, *Prometheus Bound* (c. 1900). This is the kind of art that turned Hitler on: a strong, soldierly, vital man, enduring hardship for a greater cause. Anticipating the bombing of Berlin, Speer had the statue bricked up in the basement here, where it lay undiscovered until 1995.

• *Exit the building out the back. Across the street, to the right, stretches the vast...*

❾ MEMORIAL TO THE MURDERED JEWS OF EUROPE

Completed in 2005, this Holocaust memorial, rated ▲▲, consists of 2,711 gravestone-like pillars. Designed by Jewish-American architect Peter Eisenman, it was Germany's first formal, government-sponsored Holocaust memorial. Using the word "murdered" in the title was intentional and a big deal. Germany, as a nation, was officially admitting to a crime.

Cost and Hours: The memorial is free and always open. The information center is open Tue-Sun 10:00-20:00, Oct-March until 19:00, closed Mon year-round; last entry 45 minutes before closing, S-Bahn: Brandenburger Tor or Potsdamer Platz, tel. 030/2639-4336, www.stiftung-denkmal.de. A €4 audioguide augments the experience.

Visiting the Memorial: The pillars, made of hollow concrete, stand in a gently sunken area, which can be entered from any side. The number of pillars isn't symbolic of anything; it's simply how many fit on the provided land. The pillars are all about the same size, but of differing heights.

Once you enter the memorial, notice that people seem to appear and disappear between the columns, and that no matter where you are, the exit always seems to be up. The memorial is lit and guarded at night.

The monument was criticized for focusing on just one of the groups targeted by the Nazis, but the German government has now erected memorials to other victims—such as the Roma/Sinti memorial we just visited, and a memorial to the regime's homosexual victims, also nearby. It's also been criticized because there's nothing intrinsically Jewish about it. Some were struck that there's no central gathering point or place for a ceremony. Like death, you enter it alone.

There is no one intended interpretation. Is it a symbolic cemetery, or an intentionally disorienting labyrinth? It's up to the visitor to derive the meaning, while pondering this horrible chapter in human history.

Memorial Information Center: The pondering takes place under the sky. For the learning, go under the field of concrete pillars to the state-of-the-art information center. Inside, excellent and thought-provoking installations study the Nazi system of extermination and personalize the plight of victims; there's also space for silent reflection. Exhibits trace the historical context of the Nazi and WWII era, present case studies of how the Holocaust affected 15 Jewish families from around Europe, and document

Memorial to the Murdered Jews of Europe

the different places of genocide. You'll also find exhibits about other Holocaust monuments and memorials, a searchable database of victims, and a video archive of interviews with survivors.

• *Wander through the gray pillars, but eventually emerge on the corner with the Information Center. Cross Hannah-Arendt-Strasse and go a half-block farther. Walk alongside the unpaved parking lot on the left to the info plaque over the...*

⑩ SITE OF HITLER'S BUNKER

You're standing atop the buried remains of the *Führerbunker*. In early 1945, as Allied armies advanced on Berlin, and Nazi Germany lay in ruins, Hitler and his staff retreated to a bunker complex behind the former Reich Chancellery. He stayed there for two months. It was here, as the Soviet army tightened its noose on the capital, that Hitler and Eva Braun, his wife of less than 48 hours, committed suicide on April 30, 1945. A week later, the war in Europe was over. The info board presents a detailed cutaway illustrating the bunker complex plus a timeline tracing its history and ultimate fate (the roof was removed and the bunker filled with dirt, then covered over).

• *From here, you can visit the important but stark Memorial to the Homosexuals Persecuted Under the National Socialist Regime, or you can continue the walk. To do either, first head back to Hannah-Arendt-Strasse.*

*It's a detour to see the **memorial**: go left one block at Hannah-Arendt-Strasse, cross the street, and head down a path into Tiergarten park. There, look for a large, dark gray concrete box. Through a small window you can watch a film loop of same-sex couples kissing—a reminder that life and love are precious.*

*To rejoin the **walk**, turn right on Hannah-Arendt-Strasse, go one block, then head left up Wilhelmstrasse. Because Wilhelmstrasse was a main street of the German government during World War II, it was obliterated by bombs, and all its buildings are new today.*

Imagining Hitler in the 21st Century

Germans tread lightly on their past. It took 65 years for the German History Museum to organize its first exhibit on the life of Hitler. No version of *Mein Kampf*, Hitler's political manifesto, was allowed printed in Germany until 2016, when the publication of a new version (annotated by historians) was greeted with controversy. It's a balancing act, and Germans are still in the process of figuring out how to confront their painful history.

Many visitors to Berlin are curious about Hitler sites, but not much survives from that dark period. The bunker where Hitler killed himself lies hidden underneath a parking lot, marked only by a small information board. The best way to learn about Hitler sites is to take a walking tour focused on the Third Reich (see page 869) or to visit the Topography of Terror (see page 895).

Back on Unter den Linden, head to the median, in front of Hotel Adlon, and take a long look down...

⑪ UNTER DEN LINDEN

In the good old days, this street, rated ▲▲, was one of Europe's grand boulevards. In the 15th century, it was a carriageway leading from the palace to the

Unter den Linden

hunting grounds (today's big Tiergarten). In the 17th century, Hohenzollern princes and princesses moved in and built their palaces here so they could be near the Prussian king. It is divided, roughly at Friedrichstrasse, into a business section, which stretches toward the Brandenburg Gate, and a cultural section, which spreads out toward Alexanderplatz. Frederick the Great wanted to have culture, mainly the opera and the university, closer to his palace and to keep business (read: banks) farther away, near the city walls.

Named centuries ago for its many linden trees, this was the most elegant street of Prussian Berlin before Hitler's time, and the main drag of East Berlin after his reign. Hitler replaced the venerable trees—many 250 years old—with Nazi flags. Popular discontent drove him to replant the trees. Later, Unter den Linden deteriorated into a depressing Cold War cul-de-sac, but it has long since regained its strolling café ambience.

• *In front of Hotel Adlon is the Brandenburger Tor S-Bahn station. Cover a bit of Unter den Linden underground by climbing down its steps and walking along the platform.*

Ghost Subway Station: The Brandenburger Tor S-Bahn station is one of Berlin's former ghost subway stations. It's a time warp, looking much as it did when built in 1936, with dreary old green tiles and original signage. During the Cold War, most underground train tunnels were simply sealed at the border between East and West Berlin. But a few Western lines looped through the East and then back into the West. To make hard Western cash, the Eastern government rented the use of these tracks to the West. For 28 years, as Western trains passed through otherwise blocked-off stations, passengers saw only East German guards and lots of cobwebs. Within days of the fall of the Wall, these stations reopened (one woman who'd left her purse behind in 1961 got a call from the lost-and-found office—it was still there).

• *Walk along the track and exit on the other side, to the right. You'll pop out at the Russian Embassy's front yard.*

⓬ Russian Embassy: This was the first big postwar building project in East Berlin. It's in the powerful, simplified Neoclassical style that Stalin liked. While not as important now as it was a few years ago, it's as immense as ever. It flies the Russian white, blue, and red. Find the hammer-and-sickle motif decorating the window frames—a reminder of the days when Russia was the USSR.

• *Keep walking down the boulevard for two blocks. You'll pass blocks of dull banks, tacky trinket shops, and a few high-end boutiques, eventually reaching cultural buildings—Humboldt University, the Berlin State Opera, and so on. That's intentional: The Prussian kings wanted to have culture closer to their palace. Pause when you reach the...*

⓭ Intersection of Unter den Linden and Friedrichstrasse: This is perhaps the most central crossroads in Berlin. And for several years more, it will be a mess as Berlin builds a new connection in its already extensive subway system. All over Berlin, you'll see big, colorful **water pipes** running aboveground. Wherever there are large construction projects, streets are laced with these drainage pipes. Berlin's high water table means that any new basement comes with lots of pumping out.

Brandenburger Tor ghost subway station

Looking at the jaunty DDR-style pedestrian "walk/don't walk" signals at this intersection is a reminder that a little of the old East survives. All along Unter den Linden (and throughout much of the former East Berlin), you'll see the perky red and green men—called **Ampelmännchen.** They were recently threatened with replacement by ordinary signs, but, after a 10-year court battle, the wildly popular DDR signals were kept after all (note the Ampelmann souvenir store across the street).

Before continuing down Unter den Linden, look farther down **Friedrichstrasse.** Before the war, this zone was the heart of Berlin. In the 1920s, Berlin was famous for its anything-goes love of life. This was the cabaret drag, a springboard to stardom for young and vampy entertainers like Marlene Dietrich. Now Friedrichstrasse is lined with department stores and big-time hotels. Consider detouring to the megastore **Galeries Lafayette** (closed Sun); check out the vertical garden on its front wall, have lunch in its basement food court, or, if the weather's nice, pick up some classy munchies here for a picnic. The short walk here provides some of Berlin's most jarring old-versus-new architectural contrasts—be sure to look up as you stroll.

• *We've reached the end of Part 1 of this walk. This is a good place to take a break, if you wish. The charming Gendarmenmarkt, with shops and eateries, is just a couple of blocks away (see page 894). Or, if you continue south down Friedrichstrasse, you'll wind up at Checkpoint Charlie in about 10 minutes (see page 897).*

But if you'd rather tackle Part 2 of this walk now, head down Unter den Linden a few more blocks, past the large equestrian statue of Frederick the Great, then turn right into Bebelplatz.

Part 2: From Bebelplatz to Alexanderplatz

• *Starting at Bebelplatz, head to the center of the square, and find the glass window in the*

Frederick the Great

Berlin was a humble, marshy burg until prince electors from the Hohenzollern dynasty made it their capital in the mid-15th century. Gradually their territory spread and strengthened, becoming the powerful Kingdom of Prussia, which dominated the northern Germanic world—both militarily and culturally.

The only Hohenzollern ruler worth remembering is **Frederick the Great** (1712-1786). This enlightened despot was both a ruthless military tactician and a culture lover. "Old Fritz," as he was called, played the flute, spoke six languages, and counted Voltaire among his friends. Practical and cosmopolitan, Frederick cleverly invited to Prussia Protestants who were being persecuted—including French Huguenots and Dutch traders. Prussia became the beneficiary of these groups' substantial wealth and know-how. Frederick left Berlin a far more modern and enlightened place than he found it. Thanks largely to him, Prussia was well-positioned to become a magnet of sorts for the German unification movement in the 19th century. When Germany first unified, in 1871, Berlin was its natural capital.

pavement. We'll begin with some history and a spin tour.

⑭ BEBELPLATZ

For centuries, up until the early 1700s, Prussia had been likened to a modern-day Sparta—it was all about its military. Voltaire famously said, "Whereas some states have an army, the Prussian army has a state." But Frederick the Great—who ruled from 1740 to 1786—established Prussia not just as a military power, but also as a cultural and intellectual heavyweight. This square was the center of the cultural capital that Frederick envisioned. His grand palace was just down the street.

Imagine that it's 1760. Pan around the square to see Frederick's contributions to Prussian culture. Everything is draped with Greek-inspired Prussian pomp. Sure, Prussia was a militaristic power. But Frederick also built an "Athens on the Spree"— an enlightened and cultured society.

To visually survey the square, start with the university across the street and spin counterclockwise:

🚺 **Humboldt University,** across Unter den Linden, is one of Europe's greatest. Marx and Lenin (not the brothers or the sisters) studied here, as did the Grimms (both brothers) and more than two dozen Nobel Prize winners. Einstein, who was Jewish, taught here until taking a spot at Princeton in 1932 (smart guy).

Turn 90 degrees to the left to face the former **state library** (labeled *Juristische Fakultät*). Bombed in World War II, the library was rebuilt by the East German government in the original style only because Vladimir Lenin studied law here during much of his exile from Russia. (On the ground floor is Tim's Espressobar, a great little café with light food, student

prices, and garden seating.)

The round, Catholic **St. Hedwig's Church,** nicknamed the "upside-down teacup," is a statement of religious and cultural tolerance. The pragmatic Frederick the Great wanted to encourage the integration of Catholic Silesians after his empire annexed their region in 1742, and so the first Catholic church since the Reformation was built in Berlin and dedicated to St. Hedwig, the patron saint of Silesia. Like all Catholic churches in Berlin, St. Hedwig's is not on the street, but stuck in a kind of back lot—indicating inferiority to Protestant churches.

The 🚹 **German State Opera** (Staatsoper) was bombed in 1941, rebuilt in 1943, and bombed again in 1945. It's currently undergoing an extensive renovation.

Now look down through the glass you're standing on: The room of empty bookshelves is a memorial repudiating a notorious Nazi **book burning** on this square. In 1933, staff and students from the university threw 20,000 newly forbidden books (authored by Einstein, Hemingway, Freud, and T. S. Eliot, among others) into a huge bonfire on the orders of the Nazi propaganda minister, Joseph

A plaque and memorial on Bebelplatz mark the site of a Nazi book burning.

Goebbels. Hitler chose this square to thoroughly squash the ideals of culture and enlightenment that characterized the Prussian heritage of Frederick the Great. Instead, he was establishing a new age of intolerance, where Germanness was correct and diversity was evil.

A plaque nearby reminds us of the prophetic quote by the German poet Heinrich Heine. In 1820, he wrote, "Where they burn books, in the end they will also burn people." A century later, his books were among those that went up in flames on this spot.

This monument reminds us of that chilling event in 1933, while also inspiring vigilance against the anti-intellectual scaremongers of today, who would burn the thoughts of people they fear to defend their culture from diversity.

• *Cross Unter den Linden to the university side and head toward the Greek-temple-like building set in the small chestnut-tree-filled park. This is the...*

⑰ NEW GUARDHOUSE

The emperor's former guardhouse (Neue Wache) now holds the nation's main memorial to all "victims of war and tyranny." Look inside, where a replica of the Käthe Kollwitz statue, *Mother with Her Dead Son*, is enshrined in silence. It marks the tombs of Germany's unknown soldier and an unknown concentration camp victim. Read the powerful statement (left of entrance). The memorial, open to the sky,

incorporates the elements—sunshine, rain, snow—falling on this modern-day pietà.
• *Next to the Neue Wache is Berlin's pink yet formidable Zeughaus (arsenal). Dating from 1695, it's considered the oldest building on the boulevard, and now houses the excellent* ⑱ *German History Museum—well worth a visit, and described in detail on page 893.*

Continue across a bridge to reach ⑲ *Museum Island (Museumsinsel), whose imposing Neoclassical buildings house some of Berlin's most impressive museums (including the Pergamon Museum); for details, see page 890.*

For now, we'll check out a few other landmarks on the island. First is the big, inviting park called the...

⑳ LUSTGARTEN

For 300 years, Museum Island's big central square has flip-flopped between being a military parade ground and a people-friendly park, depending upon the political tenor of the time. During the revolutions of 1848, the Kaiser's troops dispersed a protesting crowd that had assembled here, sending demonstrators onto footpaths. Karl Marx later commented, "It is impossible to have a revolution in a country where people stay off the grass."

Hitler enjoyed giving speeches from the top of the museum steps overlooking this square. In fact, he had the square landscaped to fit his symmetrical tastes and propaganda needs.

In 1999, the Lustgarten was made into a park (read the history posted in the corner opposite the church). On a sunny day, it's packed with people relaxing and is one of Berlin's most enjoyable public spaces.
• *The huge church next to the park is the...*

㉑ BERLIN CATHEDRAL

The century-old Berlin Cathedral (Berliner Dom) wears its bombastic Wilhelmian architecture as a Protestant assertion of strength. It seems to proclaim, "A mighty fortress is our God." The years of Kaiser Wilhelm's rule, from 1888 to 1918,

Memorial at the New Guardhouse

were a busy age of building. Germany had recently been united (1871), and the emperor wanted to give his capital stature and legitimacy. Wilhelm's buildings are over-the-top statements: Neoclassical, Neo-Baroque, and Neo-Renaissance, with stucco and gold-tiled mosaics. This Protestant cathedral is as ornate as if it were Catholic. With the emperor's lead, this sumptuous style came into vogue, and anyone who wanted to be associated with the royal class built this way. (The other big example of Wilhelmian architecture in Berlin is the Reichstag, which we saw earlier.) The church is most impressive from the outside (and there's no way to even peek inside without a pricey ticket).

Inside, the great reformers (Luther, Calvin, and company) stand around the brilliantly restored dome like stern saints guarding their theology. Frederick I (Frederick the Great's gramps) rests in an ornate tomb (right transept, near entrance to dome). The 270-step climb to the outdoor dome gallery is tough but offers pleasant, breezy views of the city at the finish line. The crypt downstairs is not worth a look.

Cost and Hours: €7 includes access to dome gallery, audioguide-€3, Mon-Sat 9:00-20:00, Sun 12:00-20:00, until 19:00 Oct-March, www.berliner-dom.de.

• *Kitty-corner across the main street from the Berlin Cathedral is a huge construction site, known as the...*

㉒ HUMBOLDT-FORUM BERLINER SCHLOSS

For centuries, this was the site of the Baroque palace of the Hohenzollern dynasty of Brandenburg and Prussia. Much of that palace actually survived World War II but was replaced by the communists with a blocky, Soviet-style "Palace" of the Republic—East Berlin's parliament building/entertainment complex and a showy symbol of the communist days. The landmark building fell into disrepair after reunification, and by 2009 had been dismantled.

After much debate about how to use this prime real estate, the German parliament decided to construct the Humboldt-Forum Berliner Schloss, a huge public venue filled with museums, shops, galleries, and concert halls behind a facade constructed in imitation of the

The elegant Berlin Cathedral (flanked by the DDR-era TV Tower)

original Hohenzollern palace. With a €600 million price tag, many Berliners consider the reconstruction plan a complete waste of money. The latest news is that it should be finished by 2019.

In the meantime, the temporary, bright blue **Humboldt-Box** provides info and a viewing platform from which to survey the construction (until it gets in the way and also has to be demolished). Consider popping in for a look at the beautiful model, on the first floor up, showing this area as it was in 1900 (free, daily 10:00-19:00).

• *Head to the bridge just beyond the Berlin Cathedral, with views of the riverbank. Consider...*

STROLLING AND CRUISING THE SPREE RIVER

This river was once a symbol of division—the East German regime put nets underwater to stymie those desperate enough for freedom to swim to the West. With the reunification of Berlin, however, the Spree River has become people-friendly and welcoming. A parklike trail leads from the Berlin Cathedral to the Hauptbahnhof, with impromptu "beachside" beer gardens with imported sand, BBQs in pocket parks, and lots of locals walking their dogs, taking a lazy bike ride, or jogging.

You may notice "don't drop anchor" signs. There are still unexploded WWII bombs in Berlin, and many are in this river. Every month, several bombs are found at construction sites. Their triggers were set for the hard ground of Scottish testing grounds, and because Berlin sits upon soft soil, an estimated one of every ten bombs didn't explode.

The recommended ㉓ **Spree River cruises** depart from the riverbank near the bridge by the Berlin Cathedral (for details, see page 882). Across the river from the cathedral is the interesting ㉔ **DDR Museum** (see page 894).

• *Leaving the bridge, continue walking straight toward the TV Tower, down the big boulevard, which here changes its name to...*

KARL-LIEBKNECHT-STRASSE

The first big building on the left after the bridge is the **Radisson Blu Hotel** and shopping center, with a huge aquarium in the center. The elevator goes right through the middle of a deep-sea world. (You can see it from the unforgettable Radisson hotel lobby—tuck in your shirt and walk past the guards with the confidence of a guest who's sleeping there.) Here in the center of the old communist capital, it seems that capitalism has settled in with a spirited vengeance.

In the park immediately across the street (a big jaywalk from the Radisson) are grandfatherly statues of **Marx** and **Engels** (nicknamed the "old pensioners"). Surrounding them are stainless-steel monoliths with evocative photos illustrating the struggles of the workers of the world.

Farther along, where Karl-Liebknecht-Strasse intersects with Spandauer Strasse, look right to see the red-brick **City Hall**. It was built after the revolutions of 1848 and was arguably the first democratic building in the city.

Continue toward ㉕ **Marien Church** (from 1270), with its spire mirroring the TV Tower. Inside, an artist's rendering helps you follow the interesting but faded old "Dance of Death" mural that wraps around the narthex inside the door.

• *Immediately across the street from the church, detour a half-block down little Rosenstrasse to find a beautiful memorial set in a park.*

Spree River sightseeing boats

㉖ Women's Protest Memorial: This sculpture is a reminder of a successful and courageous protest against Nazi policies. In 1943, when "privileged Jews" (men married to Gentile women) were arrested, their wives demonstrated en masse on this street, where the men were being held in a Jewish community building. They actually won the freedom of their spouses.

• *Back on Karl-Liebknecht-Strasse, look up at the 1,200-foot-tall...*

㉗ TV Tower (Fernsehturm): Built (with Swedish know-how) in 1969 for the 20th anniversary of the communist government, the tower was meant to show the power of the atheistic state at a time when DDR leaders were having the crosses removed from church domes and spires. But when the sun hit the tower—the greatest spire in East Berlin—a huge cross was reflected on the mirrored ball. Cynics called it "God's Revenge." East Berliners dubbed the tower the "Tele-Asparagus." They joked that if it fell over, they'd have an elevator to the West.

The tower has a fine view from halfway up, offering a handy city orientation and an interesting look at the flat, red-roofed sprawl of Berlin—including a peek inside the city's many courtyards (€13 timed-entry tickets, daily until 24:00). Consider a kitschy trip to the observation deck for the view and lunch in its revolving restaurant (mediocre food, reservations smart for dinner, tel. 030/242-3333, www.tv-turm.de).

• *Walk four more minutes down the boulevard past the TV Tower and toward the big railway overpass. Just before the bridge, on the left, is the half-price ticket booth called* **Hekticket**—*stop in to see what's on (for details, see page 909).*

Walk under the train bridge and continue for a long half-block (passing the Galeria Kaufhof mall). Turn right onto a broad pedestrian street, and go through the low tunnel into the big square where blue U-Bahn station signs mark...

㉘ ALEXANDERPLATZ

This square was the commercial pride and joy of East Berlin. The Kaufhof department store was the ultimate shopping mecca for Easterners. It, along with the two big surviving 1920s "functionalist" buildings, defined the square. Alexanderplatz is still a landmark, with a major U-Bahn/S-Bahn station. The once-futuristic, now-retro "World Time Clock," installed in 1969, is a nostalgic favorite and remains a popular meeting point.

Stop in the square for a coffee and to people-watch. You may see the dueling human hot-dog hawkers, who wear ingenious harnesses that let them cook and sell tasty, cheap German sausages on the fly. While the square can get a little rough at night, it's generally a great scene.

• *Our orientation stroll is finished. From here, you can hike back to catch the riverboat tour, visit Museum Island or the German History Museum, or take in the sights south of Unter den Linden.*

The TV Tower punctuates the skyline.

SIGHTS

The Reichstag and Nearby

Many of Berlin's top sights and landmarks are in this area, and are described in detail in the self-guided walk above, including the **Brandenburg Gate** (page 875), the **Memorial to the Murdered Jews of Europe** (page 876), and **Unter den Linden** (page 878).

▲▲▲REICHSTAG

Germany's historic parliament building—completed in 1894, burned in 1933, sad and lonely in a no-man's land throughout the Cold War, and finally rebuilt and topped with a glittering glass cupola in 1999—is a symbol of a proudly reunited nation. It's fascinating to climb up the twin ramps that spiral through its dome. Getting in requires a reservation. For more on the building's exterior and its history, see page 871 of the "Best of Berlin Walk."

Cost and Hours: Free, but reservations required—see below, daily 8:00-24:00, last entry at 22:00, no big luggage allowed, Platz der Republik 1; S- or U-Bahn: Friedrichstrasse, Brandenburger Tor, or Bundestag; tel. 030/2273-2152, www.bundestag.de.

Reservations: To visit the dome, you'll need to **reserve online;** spots often book up several days in advance. Go to www.bundestag.de, and from the "Visit the Bundestag" menu, select "Online registration" (be sure to have the names and birthdates of everyone in your party). You must print and bring your reservation with you.

If you're in Berlin without a reservation, try dropping by the tiny visitors center on the Tiergarten side of Scheidemann-strasse, across from Platz der Republik, to see if any tickets are available (open daily 8:00-20:00, until 18:00 Nov-March; go early to avoid lines; you must book no less than 2 hours and no more than 2 days out; your whole party must be present and ID is required).

Another option for visiting the dome, though pricey, is to make lunch or dinner reservations for the rooftop restaurant, Käfer Dachgarten (daily 9:00-16:30 & 18:30-24:00, last access at 22:00, reserve well in advance at tel. 030/2262-9933 or www.feinkost-kaefer.de/berlin).

Getting In: Report a few minutes before your appointed time to the temporary-looking entrance facility in front of the Reichstag, and be ready to show ID and your reservation printout.

Tours: The free **audioguide** (available after you exit the elevator at the base of the dome) explains the building and narrates the view as you wind up the spiral ramp to the top of the dome; the commentary starts automatically as you step onto the bottom of the ramp.

◆ Self-Guided Tour: The open, airy lobby towers 100 feet high, with 65-foot-tall colors of the German flag. See-through glass doors show the **central legislative chamber.** The message: There will be no secrets in this government. Look inside. Spreading his wings behind the podium is a stylized German eagle, the *Bundestagsadler* (a.k.a. the "fat hen"), representing the Bundestag (each branch of government has its own symbolic eagle). Notice the doors marked *Ja* (Yes), *Nein* (No), and *Enthalten* (Abstain)...an homage to the Bundestag's traditional "sheep jump" way of counting votes by exiting the chamber through the corresponding door (for critical votes, however, all 631 members vote with electronic cards).

The Reichstag's original facade

Ride the elevator to the base of the glass **dome.** Pick up the free audioguide and take some time to study the photos and read the circle of captions (around the base of the central funnel) for an excellent exhibit telling the Reichstag story. Then study the surrounding architecture: a broken collage of new on old, torn between antiquity and modernity, like Germany's history. Notice the dome's giant and unobtrusive sunscreen that moves as necessary with the sun. Peer down through the skylight to look over the shoulders of the elected representatives at work. For Germans, the best view from here is down—keeping a close eye on their government.

Start at the ramp nearest the elevator and wind up to the top of the **double ramp.** Take a 360-degree survey of the city as you hike: The big park is the **Tiergarten,** the "green lungs of Berlin." Beyond that is the **Teufelsberg** ("Devil's Hill"). Built of rubble from the destroyed city in the late 1940s, it was famous during the Cold War as a powerful ear of the West—notice the telecommunications tower on top.

Find the **Victory Column** (Siegessäule), glimmering in the middle of the park. Hitler moved it in the 1930s from in front of the Reichstag to its present position in the Tiergarten as part of his grandiose vision for postwar Berlin. Next, scenes of the new Berlin spiral into view— **Potsdamer Platz,** marked by the conical glass tower that houses Sony's European headquarters. Continue circling left, and find the green chariot atop the **Brandenburg Gate.** Just to its left is the curving fish-like roof of the **DZ Bank** building, designed by the unconventional American architect Frank Gehry. The **Memorial to the Murdered Jews of Europe** stretches south of the Brandenburg Gate. Next, you'll see **former East Berlin** and the city's next huge construction zone, with a forest of 300-foot-tall skyscrapers in the works. Notice the **TV Tower,** the **Berlin** Cathedral's massive dome, and the golden dome of the **New Synagogue.**

Follow the train tracks in the distance to the left toward Berlin's huge main train station, the **Hauptbahnhof.** Complete your spin-tour with the blocky, postmodern **Chancellery,** the federal government's headquarters. Continue spiraling up. You'll come across all the same sights again, twice, from a higher vantage point.

Inside the Reichstag's glass dome

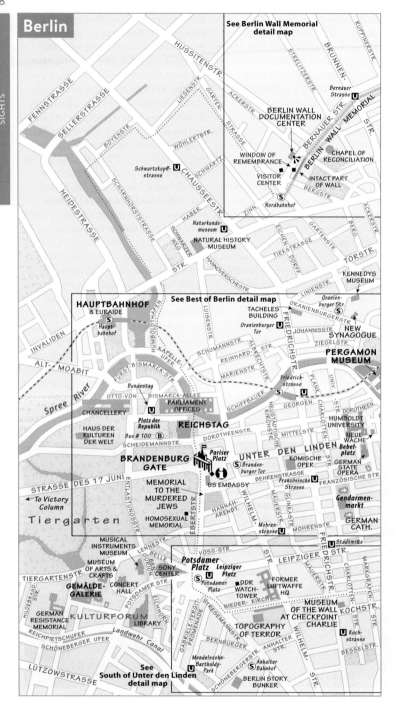

BERLIN SIGHTS

Berlin

See Berlin Wall Memorial detail map

FENNSTRASSE
SELLERSTRASSE
HEIDESTRASSE
SCHARNHORSTSTRASSE
INVALIDEN
ALT-MOABIT
HUSSITENSTR.
LIESENSTR.
GARTEN-STRASSE
ACKERSTR.
BOYENSTR.
WÖHLERTSTR.
SCHWARTZ
HABER
Schwartzkopff-strasse Ⓤ
CHAUSSEESTR.
SCHWARZER WEG
STR.
HANNOVERSCHESTR.

BERLIN WALL DOCUMENTATION CENTER
WINDOW OF REMEMBRANCE
VISITOR CENTER Ⓢ
Nordbahnhof Ⓢ
BERLIN WALL MEMORIAL
Bernauer Strasse Ⓤ
BERNAUER STR.
RUPPINERSTR.
STRELITZERSTR.
BRUNNEN-STR.
CHAPEL OF RECONCILIATION
INTACT PART OF WALL
BERGSTR.
ZINN
EICHEN
ACKERSTR.
BERG-STR.

Naturkunde-museum Ⓤ
NATURAL HISTORY MUSEUM
TIEKSTRASSE
GARTENSTR.
DORFE
TORSTR.
KENNEDYS MUSEUM

See Best of Berlin detail map

HAUPTBAHNHOF & EURAIDE
Haupt-bahnhof
HUMBOLDTHAFEN
KAPELLE UFER
LUISENSTR.
SCHUMANNSTR.
REINHARD-STR.
MARIENSTR.
ALBRECHTSTR.
TACHELES BUILDING
Oranienburger Tor Ⓤ
Oranienburger Str. Ⓢ
ORANIENBURGERSTR.
FRIEDRICHSTR.
JOHANNISSTR.
ZIEGELSTR.
LINIENSTR.
NEW SYNAGOGUE
PERGAMON MUSEUM
UNIV. STR.

Spree River
FÜRST-BISMARCK-STR.
Bundestag
OTTO-VON- Ⓤ BISMARCK-ALLEE
CHANCELLERY
Platz der Republik
HAUS DER KULTUREN DER WELT
Bus # 100 Ⓑ
SCHEIDEMANNSTR.
PARLIAMENT OFFICES
REICHSTAG
DOROTHEENSTR.
SCHIFFBAUER
GEORGEN
PLANCK
CHARLOTTEN-
DOROTHEEN-STR.
HUMBOLDT UNIVERSITY
NEUE WACHE
Friedrich-strasse Ⓢ Ⓤ
NEUSTÄDTISCHE KIRCHSTR.
MITTELSTR.
Bebel-platz

STRASSE DES 17 JUNI
← To Victory Column
ENTLASTUNGSSTR.
BRANDENBURG GATE
Pariser Platz
Brandenburger Tor Ⓢ
UNTER DEN LINDEN
KOMISCHE OPER
Behrenstr.
Französische Strasse Ⓤ
GERMAN STATE OPERA
Gendarmen-markt
FRANZÖSISCHE STR.

Tiergarten
MEMORIAL TO THE MURDERED JEWS
US EMBASSY
HANNAH-ARENDT-STR.
HOMOSEXUAL MEMORIAL
EBERTSTR.
WILHELM-STR.
GLINKASTR.
MAUERSTR.
Mohrenstr. Ⓤ
MOHRENSTR.
GERMAN CATH.

MUSICAL INSTRUMENTS MUSEUM
LENNESTR.
BELLE
GÖHREN
MUSEUM OF ARTS & CRAFTS
TIERGARTENSTR.
SONY CENTER
GEMÄLDE-GALERIE
CONCERT HALL
POTSDAMER STR.
EICHHORN-
VOSS-STR.
Potsdamer Platz Ⓤ Leipziger Platz
Potsdamer Platz Ⓢ
LEIPZIGER STR.
DDR WATCH-TOWER
FORMER LUFTWAFFE HQ
Städtmitte Ⓤ
FRIEDRICHSTR.
CHARLOTTEN-
MARKGRAFEN-
KOCHSTR.
MUSEUM OF THE WALL AT CHECKPOINT CHARLIE

HILDEBRAND-STR.
GERMAN RESISTANCE MEMORIAL
KULTURFORUM
LIBRARY
Landwehr Canal
REICHPIETSCHUFER
SCHÖNEBERGER UFER
GABRIEL-TEGEL-PROMENADE
STRESEMANNSTR.
NIEDER-KIRCH-STR.
BERNBURGER
TOPOGRAPHY OF TERROR
ANHALTER STR.
WILHELM-STR.
KOCHSTR.
Koch-strasse Ⓤ
BESSELSTR.

LÜTZOWSTRASSE
Mendelssohn-Bartholdy-Park Ⓤ
SCHÖNEBERGERSTR.
Anhalter Bahnhof
BERLIN STORY BUNKER
See South of Unter den Linden detail map

Former Course of the Wall

500 Meters
500 Yards

N

Sportpark
STADIUM

Mauer-
park

PRENZLAUER

BERG

Eberswalder
Strasse

LYCHENER

DUNCKERSTR.

DANZIGER STRASSE

DANZIGER STR.

EBERSWALDER STRASSE

ODERBERGER STRASSE

SREDZKI-
STRASSE

CHODOWIECKISTRASSE

RHEINSBERGER STR.

KREMM.

ANKLAMER-

ZIONS-

FEHR-

VETERANEN-
STR.

WÖLLINER STR.

SCHWEDTER

CHORINER STR.

BERG

STRASSE

KASTANIENALLEE

KIRCHSTR.

BELLINERSTR.

WEINBERGSWEG

←Kollwitz-
platz

KNAACKSTRASSE

KOLLWITZ-

BELFORTER STR.

METZER

PRENZLAUER ALLEE

CHRISTBURGERSTR.

MARIEN-STRASSE

WINSSTRASSE

IMMANUEL-
KIRCH

RAABESTR.

SCHÖNHAUSER ALLEE

Senefelder-
platz

DANZIGER STR.

BURGER

GREIFSWALDER STRASSE

PASTEURSTR.

HUFELANDSTR.

KÄTHE-
NIEDERKIRCHNER

Volkspark
am
Weinberg

Rosenthaler
Platz

ROSENTHALER STR.

LOTTUMSTR.

STRASSBURGER

PRENZLAUER

BERG

AM FRIEDRICHSHAIN

Volkspark
Friedrichshain

LINIEN-STR.

GORMANNSTR.

TORSTRASSE

ROSA-LUXEMBURG-STR.

Rosa-
Luxemburg-
platz

MOLL-

STRASSE

OTTO-BRAUN-STRASSE

GEORGEN-
KIRCHSTR.

BARNIMSTR.

BUSCHINGSTR.

WEINSTR.

FRIEDENSTRASSE

AUGUSTSTR.

GIPSSTR.

SOPHIENSTR.

HAMBURGER STR.

MÜNZSTR.

Wein-
meister-
strasse

MAX-BEER-STR.

BERLINGSTR.

Schilling-
strasse

KARL-

WEYDEMEYER STR.

LICHTENBERGER STRASSE

To Stasi
Museum

NEUE WEBERSTR.

HACKESCHE
HÖFE

Hackescher
Markt

DIRCKSEN-

ROCHSTR.

SPANDAUER STR.

LIEBKNECHT-

TV TOWER

Alexander-
platz

Alexander-
platz

STRASSE

JACOBYSTRASSE

MARX-

NEUE BLUMENSTR.

MAGAZIN.

ALLEE

Strauss-
berger
Platz

NEUES
MUSEUM

Museum
Island

GERMAN
HISTORY
MUSEUM

KARL-

DDR
MUSEUM

MARIEN
CHURCH

MITTE

STUDEN-

GRUNER-

KLOSTER-STR.

ALEXANDERSTR.

SCHILLINGSTR.

SINGERSTRASSE

BERLIN
CATHEDRAL

RATHAUS

CITY
HALL

NIKOLAI-
VIERTEL

Kloster-
strasse

NIKOLAI
CHURCH

MÖLLEN-
MARKT

STRALAUER STR.

Jannowitz-
brücke

KRAUTSTR.

WERDER-

BREITE STR.

GERTRAUDEN-STR.

FISCHER-

INSEL-

ROLANDUFER

Spree River

STR.

HOLZMARKTSTRASSE

STRALAUER

PLATZ

To East Side
Gallery→

Hausvogtei-
platz

KURSTR.

NIEDERWALL-R.

KRONEN-
STR.

WALL-STR.

Märkisches
Museum

INGELSTR.

BRÜCKEN-
STRASSE

OHMSTR.

KIRCHSTR.

KÖPENICKER STRASSE

Spittelmarkt

Heinrich-
Heine-
Strasse

ZIMMER-

KOMMAND-

SEYDELSTR.

JAKOBSTR.

ALTE

STALLSCHREIBERSTR.

ANNEN-

HEINRICH-HEINE-STR.

DRESDENER

SCHMIDSTR.

LEGIENDAMM

MICHAEL

ADALBERTSTR.

MELCHIORSTR.

ENGELDAMM

BETHANIENDAMM

MANTEUFFELSTR.

LINIENSTRASSE

ORANIENSTRASSE

RITTERSTRASSE

ALEXANDRINEN

ALTE

SEBASTIAN-

LÖBECKSTR.

PRINZENSTR.

Moritz-
platz

LEUSCHNERDAMM

ADALBERTSTR.

ENGELDAMM

WALDEMARSTR.

MARIANNENPLATZ

JEWISH
MUSEUM

KREUZBERG

ORANIEN-

Museum Island and Nearby

The Museum Island complex began taking shape in the 1840s under King Friedrich Wilhelm IV, who envisioned the island as an oasis of culture and learning. A formidable renovation now under way is transforming the island into one of the grandest museum zones in Europe. In the meantime, pardon their dust. I highlight the top two museums: Pergamon and Neues. Also, two recommended museums flank the island: the German History Museum across the river to the west, and the DDR Museum across the river to the east.

Note that three Museum Island landmarks—the **Lustgarten, Berlin Cathedral,** and the **Humboldt-Box**—are described earlier, in my "Best of Berlin Walk"; see page 870.

Getting There: The nearest S-Bahn station to Museum Island is Hackescher Markt, about a 10-minute walk away. From Prenzlauer Berg, ride tram #M-1 to the end of the line, and you're right at the Pergamon Museum.

▲▲▲PERGAMON MUSEUM (PERGAMONMUSEUM)

The star attraction of this world-class museum, part of Berlin's Collection of Classical Antiquities (Antikensammlung), is the fantastic and gigantic Pergamon Altar...but it—and all Hellenistic artworks in the collection—are off-limits to visitors until 2025, as the museum undergoes a major renovation. But there's much more to see here, including the Babylonian Ishtar Gate (slathered with glazed blue tiles from the sixth century B.C.) and ancient Mesopotamian, Roman, and early Islamic treasures.

Cost and Hours: €12, special exhibits extra, daily 10:00-18:00, until 20:00 on Thu, tel. 030/266-424-242, www.smb.museum.

When to Go: Mornings are busiest, and you're likely to find long lines any time of day on Saturday or Sunday. The least-crowded time is Thursday evening.

Crowd-Beating Tips: Avoid lines for the Pergamon by purchasing a timed ticket online, or book a free timed-entry reservation if you have a Museum Pass Berlin or a Museum Island Pass (www.smb.museum).

Visting the Museum: Make ample use of the superb audioguide (included with admission).

From the entry hall, head up the stairs and all the way back to 575 B.C., to the Fertile Crescent—Mesopotamia (today's Iraq). The Assyrian ruler Nebuchadnezzar II, who amassed a vast empire and enormous wealth, wanted to build a suitably impressive processional entryway to his capital city, Babylon, to honor the goddess Ishtar. His creation, the blue **Ishtar Gate,** inspired awe and obedience in anyone who came to his city. This is a reconstruction, using some original components. The gate itself is embellished with two animals: a bull and a mythical dragon-like combination of lion, cobra, eagle, and scorpion. The long hall leading to the main gate—designed for a huge processional

Ishtar Gate   *Market Gate of Miletus*

Museum Island

of deities to celebrate the new year—is decorated with a chain of blue and yellow glazed tiles with 120 strolling lions (representing the goddess Ishtar). To get the big picture, find the model of the original site in the center of the hall.

Pass through the gate, and flash-forward 700 years to the ancient Roman city of Miletus. Dominating this room is the 95-foot-wide, 55-foot-high **Market Gate of Miletus,** an ancient Anatolian city destroyed by an earthquake centuries ago and now painstakingly reconstructed here in Berlin. The exquisite mosaic floor from a Roman villa in Miletus has two parts: In the square panel, the musician Orpheus strokes his lyre to charm the animals; in

stark contrast, in the nearby rectangular mosaic (from an adjacent room), hunters pursue wild animals.

These main exhibits are surrounded by smaller galleries. Upstairs is the **Museum of Islamic Art.** It contains fine carpets, tile work, the Aleppo Room (with ornately painted wooden walls from an early 17th-century home in today's Syria), and the Mshatta Facade (walls and towers from one of the early eighth-century Umayyad "desert castles," from today's Jordan).

▲▲NEUES (NEW) MUSEUM

Oddly, Museum Island's so-called "new" museum features the oldest stuff around. There are three collections here: the Egyptian Collection (with the famous bust of Queen Nefertiti), the Museum of Pre-history and Early History, and some items from the Collection of Classical Antiquities (artifacts from Cyprus and ancient Troy—famously excavated by German adventurer Heinrich Schliemann).

After being damaged in World War II and sitting in ruins for some 40 years, the Neues Museum has been gorgeously rebuilt. Posted information and the fine audioguide offer fascinating insights into workaday Egyptian life as they describe the vivid papyrus collection, slice-of-life artifacts, and dreamy wax portraits decorating mummy cases.

Cost and Hours: €12, special exhibits extra, daily 10:00-18:00, until 20:00 on Thu, tel. 030/266-424-242, www.neues-museum.de, www.smb.museum.

Visiting the Museum: Pick up a floor plan showing the suggested route, then head up the central staircase.

The top draw here is the Egyptian art—clearly one of the world's best collections. But let's face it: The main reason to visit is to enjoy one of the great thrills in art appreciation—gazing into the still young and beautiful face of Queen Nefertiti. If you're in a pinch for time, make a beeline to her (floor 2, far corner of Egyptian Collection in Room 210).

To tour the whole collection, start at the top (floor 3), which is where you'll find the **prehistory section.** The entire floor is filled with Stone Age, Ice Age, and Bronze Age items. You'll see early human remains, tools, spearheads, and pottery.

The most interesting item on this floor (in corner Room 305) is the tall, cone-head-like **Golden Hat,** made of paper-thin hammered gold leaf. Created by an early Celtic civilization in Central Europe, it's particularly exquisite for something so old (from the Bronze Age, around 1000 B.C.). The circles on the hat represent the sun, moon, and other celestial bodies—leading archaeologists to believe that this headwear could double as a calendar, showing how the sun and moon sync up every 19 years.

Down on floor 2, you'll find **early history** exhibits on migrations, barbarians, and ancient Rome, as well as a fascinating look at the Dark Ages after the fall of Rome.

Still on floor 2, cross to the other side of the building for the **Egyptian** section. On the way, you'll pass through the impressive Papyrus Collection—a large room of seemingly empty glass cases. Press a button to watch a 3,000-year-old piece of primitive "paper" (made of aquatic reeds), imprinted with primitive text, trundle out of its protective home.

Then, finally, in a room all her own, is the 3,000-year-old bust of **Queen Nefertiti** (the wife of King Akhenaton, c. 1340 B.C.)—the most famous piece of Egyptian art in Europe. (She's had it with the paparazzi—photos of her are strictly *verboten*.) Called "Berlin's most beautiful woman," Nefertiti has all the right beauty marks: long neck, symmetrical face, and the perfect amount of makeup. And yet,

Neues Museum

Queen Nefertiti

she's not completely idealized. Notice the fine wrinkles that show she's human (though these only enhance her beauty). Like a movie star discreetly sipping a glass of wine at a sidewalk café, Nefertiti seems somehow more dignified in person. The bust never left its studio, but served as a master model for all other portraits of the queen. (That's probably why the left eye was never inlaid.) Stare at her long enough, and you may get the sensation that she's winking at you. Hey, beautiful!

▲▲▲GERMAN HISTORY MUSEUM (DEUTSCHES HISTORISCHES MUSEUM)

This fantastic museum, which sits across the river west of Museum Island, is a two-part affair: the pink former Prussian arsenal building and the I. M. Pei-designed annex. The main building (fronting Unter den Linden) houses the permanent collection, offering the best look at German history under one roof, anywhere. The modern annex features good temporary exhibits surrounded by the work of a great contemporary architect. This thoughtfully presented museum—with more than 8,000 artifacts telling not just the story of Berlin, but of all Germany—is clearly the top history museum in town. If you need a break during your visit, there's a restful café with terrace seating in season.

Cost and Hours: €8, excellent €3 audioguide, daily 10:00-18:00, Unter den Linden 2, tel. 030/2030-4751, www.dhm.de.

Getting In: If the ticket-buying line is long at the main entrance, try circling around the back to the Pei annex (to reach it, head down the street to the left of the museum—called Hinter dem Giesshaus), where entry lines are usually shorter (but audioguides for the permanent exhibit are available only at the main desk).

Visiting the Museum: The permanent collection packs two huge rectangular floors of the old arsenal building with historical objects, photographs, and models. From the lobby, head upstairs to the **first floor** and work your way chronologically down. This floor traces German history from A.D. 500 to 1918, with exhibits on early cultures, the Middle Ages, Reformation, Thirty Years' War, German Empire, and World War I. You'll see lots of models of higgledy-piggledy medieval towns and castles, tapestries, suits of armor, busts of great Germans, a Turkish tent from the Ottoman siege of Vienna (1683), flags from German unification in 1871 (the first time "Germany" existed as a nation), exhibits on everyday life in the tenements of the Industrial Revolution, and much more.

History marches on through the 20th century on the **ground floor,** including the Weimar Republic, Nazism, World War II, Allied occupation, and a divided Germany. Propaganda posters trumpet Germany's would-be post-WWI savior, Adolf Hitler. Look for the model of the impossibly huge, 950-foot-high, 180,000-capacity domed hall Hitler wanted to erect in

Exhibits at the German History Museum are comprehensive and thought-provoking.

the heart of Berlin, which he planned to re-envision as Welthauptstadt Germania, the "world capital" of his far-reaching Third Reich. Another model shows the nauseating reality of Hitler's grandiosity: a crematorium at Auschwitz-Birkenau concentration camp in occupied Poland. The exhibit wraps up with chunks of the Berlin Wall, reunification, and a quick look at Germany today.

For architecture buffs, the big attraction is the **Pei annex** behind the history museum, which complements the permanent collection with temporary exhibits. From the old building, cross through the courtyard (with the Pei glass canopy overhead) to reach the annex. A striking glassed-in spiral staircase unites four floors with surprising views and lots of light. It's here that you'll experience why Pei—famous for his glass pyramid at Paris' Louvre—is called the "perfector of classical modernism," "master of light," and a magician at uniting historical buildings with new ones.

▲▲DDR MUSEUM

The exhibits offer an interesting look at life in the former East Germany without the negative spin most museums give. It's well-stocked with kitschy everyday items from the communist period, plus photos, video clips, and concise English explanations. The exhibits are interactive—you're encouraged to pick up and handle anything that isn't behind glass. The reconstructed communist-era home lets you tour the kitchen, living room, and bedrooms. You'll crawl through a Trabant car (East German's answer to the West's popular VW Beetle) and pick up some DDR-era black humor ("East Germany had 39 newspapers, four radio stations, two TV channels...and one opinion").

Cost and Hours: €7, daily 10:00-20:00, Sat until 22:00, just across the Spree from Museum Island at Karl-Liebknecht-Strasse 1, tel. 030/847-123-731, www.ddr-museum.de.

South of Unter den Linden

▲▲GENDARMENMARKT

This delightful, historic square is bounded by twin churches, a tasty chocolate shop, and the Berlin Symphony's concert hall. In summer, it hosts a few outdoor cafés, Biergartens, and sometimes concerts. Wonderfully symmetrical, the square is considered by Berliners to be the finest in town (U6: Französische Strasse; U2 or U6: Stadtmitte; for nearby eateries, see page 911).

The name of the square, which is part French and part German (after the *Gens d'Armes*, Frederick the Great's royal guard, who were headquartered here), reminds us that in the 17th century, a fifth of all Berliners were French émigrés—Protestant Huguenots fleeing Catholic France. Back then, Frederick the Great's tolerant Prussia was a magnet for the persecuted (and their money). These émigrés vitalized Berlin with new ideas, practical knowledge, and their deep pockets.

The church on the south end of the square (left of the concert hall) is the **German Cathedral** (Deutscher Dom). This cathedral was bombed flat in the war and rebuilt only in the 1980s. It houses the thought-provoking "Milestones, Setbacks, Sidetracks" (*Wege, Irrwege, Umwege*) exhibit, which traces the history of the German parliamentary system—worth ▲. While light on actual historical artifacts, the well-done exhibit takes you quickly from the revolutionary days of 1848 to the

Gendarmenmarkt

South of Unter den Linden

SONY CENTER · Potsdamer Platz · Leipziger Platz · SOCIALIST REALISM MURAL · DDR WATCH-TOWER · Potsdamer Platz · POTSDAMER PLATZ TRAIN STN. · GERMAN FINANCE MINISTRY · MARTIN-GROPIUS BAU · TOPOGRAPHY OF TERROR · MENDELSSOHN-BARTHOLDY-PARK · Anhalter Bahnhof · BERLIN STORY BUNKER · To Brandenburg Gate · Mohren-strasse · QUARTIER 206 · Gendarmen-markt · GERMAN CATHEDRAL · Stadtmitte · MUSEUM OF THE WALL AT CHECKPOINT CHARLIE · Koch-strasse · JEWISH MUSEUM

······ Former Course of the Wall

500 Meters
500 Yards

1920s, and then more deeply through the tumultuous 20th century (free, Tue-Sun 10:00-19:00, Oct-April until 18:00, closed Mon year-round).

The **French Cathedral** (Französischer Dom), at the north end of the square, offers a viewpoint from the dome up top (€3, daily 10:00-18:00, until 17:30 in Nov-March, 244 steps, enter through door facing square, tel. 030/203-060, www.franzoesischer-dom.de).

Fun fact: Neither church is a true cathedral, as they never contained a bishop's throne; their German titles of *Dom* (cathedral) are actually a mistranslation from the French word *dôme* (cupola).

Fassbender & Rausch, on the corner near the German Cathedral, claims to be Europe's biggest chocolate store. After 150 years of chocolate-making, this family-owned business proudly displays its sweet delights—250 different kinds—on a 55-foot-long buffet. The window displays feature giant chocolate models of Berlin landmarks—Reichstag, Brandenburg Gate, a chunk of the Wall, and so on. If all this isn't enough to entice you, I have three words: erupting chocolate volcano. Upstairs is an elegant hot-chocolate café with fine views (Mon-Sat 10:00-20:00, Sun from 11:00, corner of Mohrenstrasse at Charlottenstrasse 60, tel. 030/757-882-440).

▲▲**TOPOGRAPHY OF TERROR (TOPOGRAPHIE DES TERRORS)**

This patch of land was once the nerve center for the Gestapo and the SS, the most despicable elements of the Nazi government. It's chilling to see just how seamlessly and bureaucratically the Nazi institutions and state structures merged to become a well-oiled terror machine. There are few actual artifacts here; it's mostly written explanations and photos, like reading a good textbook standing up. And, while you could read this story anywhere, to take this in atop the Gestapo headquarters is a powerful experience. The exhibits, sited indoors and out, are dense, but WWII historians (even armchair ones) will find it fascinating.

Cost and Hours: Free, includes audioguide for outdoor exhibit, daily 10:00-20:00, outdoor exhibit closes at dusk and in winter, Niederkirchnerstrasse 8, U-Bahn: Potsdamer Platz or Kochstrasse, S-Bahn: Anhalter Bahnhof or Potsdamer Platz, tel. 030/254-5090, www.topographie.de.

Background: This location marks what was once the most feared address in Berlin: the headquarters of the Reich Main Security Office (*Reichssicherheitshauptamt*). These offices served as the engine room of the Nazi dictatorship, as well as the command center of the SS (*Schutzstaffel*, whose members began as Hitler's personal bodyguards), the Gestapo (*Geheime Staatspolizei*, secret state police), and the SD (*Sicherheitsdienst*, the Nazi intelligence agency). This trio (and others) were ultimately consolidated under Heinrich Himmler to become a state-within-a-state, with talons in every corner of German society.

It was from these headquarters that the Nazis administered concentration camps, firmed up plans for their genocide of Jews, and organized the domestic surveillance of anyone opposed to the regime. The building was also equipped with dungeons, where the Gestapo detained and tortured thousands of prisoners.

Visiting the Museum: Start your visit inside, with the extensive **Topography of Terror** exhibit, which walks you through the evolution of Hitler's regime: the Nazi takeover; institutions of terror (Himmler's "SS State"); terror, persecution, and extermination; atrocities in Nazi-occupied countries; and the war's end and postwar. Some images here are indelible, such as photos of SS soldiers stationed at Auschwitz gleefully yukking it up on a retreat in the countryside (as their helpless prisoners were being gassed and burned a few miles away). The exhibit profiles specific members of the various reprehensible SS branches, as well as the groups they targeted: Jews; Roma and Sinti (Gypsies); the unemployed or homeless; homosexuals; and the physically and mentally ill (considered "useless eaters" who consumed resources without contributing work).

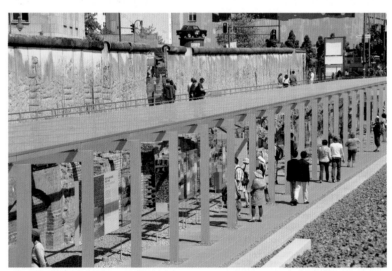

Some exhibits at the Topography of Terror are incorporated into a surviving stretch of the Berlin Wall.

Outside, you'll find the exhibit **Berlin 1933-1945: Between Propaganda and Terror** (ask at the information desk inside for the accompanying audioguide). The chronological survey begins with the post-WWI Weimar Republic and continues through the ragged days just after World War II. One display explains how Nazis invented holidays (or injected new Aryan meaning into existing ones) as a means of winning over the public. Other exhibits cover the "Aryanization" of Jewish businesses (they were simply taken over by the state and handed over to new Aryan owners); Hitler's plans for converting Berlin into a gigantic "Welthauptstadt (World Capital) Germania"; and the postwar Berlin Airlift, which brought provisions to some 2.2 million West Berliners whose supply lines were cut off by East Berlin.

Surviving stretches of the Wall are rare in downtown Berlin, but you'll find an **original fragment** of it here (also visible from Niederkirchnerstrasse).

▲CHECKPOINT CHARLIE

This famous Cold War checkpoint was not named for a person, but for its checkpoint number—as in Alpha (#1, at the East-West German border, 100 miles west of here), Bravo (#2, as you enter Berlin proper), and Charlie (#3, the best known because most foreigners passed through here). While the actual checkpoint has long since been dismantled, its former location is home to a fine museum and a mock-up of the original border crossing. The area has become a Cold War freak show and—as if celebrating the final victory of crass capitalism—is one of Berlin's worst tourist traps. A McDonald's stands defiantly overlooking the former haunt of East German border guards. (For a more sober and intellectually redeeming look at the Wall's history, head for the Berlin Wall Memorial at Bernauer Strasse, described on page 906.)

The rebuilt **guard station** now hosts two actors playing American guards who pose for photos. Notice the larger-than-life **posters** of a young American soldier facing east and a young Soviet soldier facing west. (Look carefully at the "Soviet" soldier. He was photographed in 1999, a decade after there were Soviet soldiers stationed here. He's a Dutch model. His uniform is a nonsensical pile of pins and ribbons with a Russian flag on his shoulder.)

A few yards away (on Zimmerstrasse), a **glass panel** describes the former checkpoint. From there, another double row of **cobbles** in Zimmerstrasse shows the former path of the Wall. A **photo exhibit** stretches up and down Zimmerstrasse, telling the story of the Wall.

Warning: Here and in other places, hustlers charge an exorbitant €10 for a full set of Cold War-era stamps in your passport. Don't be tempted. Technically, this invalidates your passport—which has caused some tourists big problems.

Cost and Hours: Free and always open, Friedrichstrasse 43, near the intersection with Zimmerstrasse, U-Bahn: Kochstrasse or Stadtmitte.

▲▲MUSEUM OF THE WALL AT CHECKPOINT CHARLIE (MAUERMUSEUM HAUS AM CHECKPOINT CHARLIE)

While the famous border checkpoint between the American and Soviet sectors is long gone, its memory is preserved by one of Europe's most cluttered museums. During the Cold War, the House at Checkpoint Charlie stood defiantly—within spitting distance of the border

Checkpoint Charlie

The Berlin Wall (and Its Fall)

The East German government erected the 96-mile-long Wall almost overnight in 1961. It was intended to stop the outward flow of people from the communist East to the capitalist West: Three million souls had leaked out between 1949 and 1961.

The Wall (*Mauer*) was actually two walls, with a no-man's-land in-between. During the 28 years it stood, there were 5,043 documented successful escapes (565 of these were East German guards). At least 138 people died or were killed at the Wall while trying to escape.

As a tangible symbol for the Cold War, the Berlin Wall got a lot of attention from politicians. Two of the 20th century's most repeated presidential quotes were uttered within earshot of the Wall. In 1963, President John F. Kennedy professed American solidarity with the struggling people of Berlin: "*Ich bin ein Berliner.*" In 1987, with the winds of change already blowing westward from Moscow, President Ronald Reagan issued an ultimatum to his Soviet counterpart: "Mr. Gorbachev, tear down this wall."

The actual fall of the Wall had less to do with presidential proclamations than with the obvious failings of the Soviet system, a general thawing in Moscow, the brave civil disobedience of ordinary citizens behind the Wall—and a bureaucratic snafu.

By November 1989, change was in the air. Hungary had already opened its borders to the West that summer, making it impossible for East German authorities to keep people in. Anti-regime protests swept nearby Leipzig, attracting hundreds of thousands of supporters. A rally in East Berlin's Alexanderplatz on November 4—with a half-million protesters chanting, "*Wir wollen raus!*" (We want out!)—persuaded the East German politburo to begin gradually relaxing travel restrictions.

The DDR intended to crack the door to the West, but an unknowing spokesman inadvertently threw it wide open. In back-room meetings early on November 9, officials decided they would allow a few more Easterners to cross into the West. The politburo members then left town for a long weekend. The announcement of the decision was left to Günter Schabowski, who knew only what was on a piece of paper handed to him moments before a routine press conference. At 18:54, Schabowski read the statement on live TV, with little emotion: "exit via border crossings...possible for every citizen." Reporters, unable to believe what they were hearing, prodded him about when the borders would open. Schabowski shrugged and offered his best guess: "*Ab sofort, unverzüglich.*" ("Immediately, without delay.")

Schabowski's words spread like wildfire. East Berliners showed up at Wall checkpoints, demanding that border guards let them pass. Finally, around 23:30, a border guard at the Bornholmer Strasse crossing decided to open the gates. Easterners flooded into the West, embracing their long-separated cousins, unable to believe their good fortune. Once open, the Wall could never be closed again. After that wild night, Berlin faced a fitful transition to reunification. Two cities—and countries—became one at a staggering pace.

guards—showing off all the clever escapes over, under, and through the Wall. Today, while the drama is over and hunks of the Wall stand like trophies at its door, the museum survives as a living artifact of the Cold War days. The yellowed descriptions, which have scarcely changed since that time, tinge the museum with nostalgia. It's dusty, disorganized, and overpriced, with lots of reading involved, but all that just adds to this museum's borderline-kitschy charm. If you're pressed for time, visit after dinner, when most other museums are closed.

Cost and Hours: €12.50, €3.50 audioguide, daily 9:00-22:00, U6 to Kochstrasse or U2 to Stadtmitte, Friedrichstrasse 43, tel. 030/253-7250, www.mauermuseum.de.

Visiting the Museum: Exhibits narrate a gripping history of the Wall, with a focus on the many ingenious **escape attempts** (the early years—with a cruder wall—saw more escapes). You'll see the actual items used to smuggle would-be escapees: a VW bug whose trunk hid a man, two side-by-side suitcases into which a woman

squeezed, a makeshift zip line for crossing over the border, a hot-air balloon in which two families floated to safety, an inflatable boat that puttered across the dangerous Baltic Sea, primitive homemade aircraft, two surfboards hollowed out to create just enough space for a refugee, and more. One chilling exhibit lists some 43,000 people who died in "Internal Affairs" internment camps during the transition to communism (1945-1950). Profiles personalize various escapees and their helpers, including John P. Ireland, an American who posed as an eccentric antiques collector so he could transport 10 refugees to safety in his modified Cadillac.

▲▲JEWISH MUSEUM BERLIN (JÜDISCHES MUSEUM BERLIN)

This museum surveys the rich and complicated history of Jews in Germany. The highly conceptual building is a sight in itself, and the museum inside is excellent, particularly if you take advantage of the informative and engaging audioguide. Rather than just reading dry texts, you'll feel this museum as fresh and alive—an exuberant celebration of the Jewish experience that's accessible to all.

Cost and Hours: €8, recommended €3 audioguide, daily 10:00-20:00, Mon until 22:00, last entry one hour before closing, closed on Jewish holidays, Lindenstrasse 9, tel. 030/2599-3300, www.jmberlin.de.

Getting There: Take the U-Bahn to Hallesches Tor, find the exit marked *Jüdisches Museum*, exit straight ahead, then turn right on Franz-Klühs-Strasse. The museum is a five-minute walk ahead on your left.

Eating: The museum's restaurant, Café Schmus, offers good meals in a pleasant setting.

Visiting the Museum: Designed by American architect Daniel Libeskind (the master planner for the redeveloped World Trade Center in New York), the zinc-walled building has a zigzag shape pierced by voids symbolic of the irreplaceable cultural loss caused by the Holocaust.

Museum of the Wall at Checkpoint Charlie

Enter the 18th-century Baroque building next door, then go through an underground tunnel to reach the museum interior.

Before you reach the exhibit, your visit starts with three **memorial spaces.** Follow the Axis of Exile to a disorienting slanted garden with 49 pillars (evocative of the Memorial to the Murdered Jews of Europe, across town). Next, the Axis of Holocaust, lined with artifacts from Jews imprisoned and murdered by the Nazis, leads to an eerily empty tower shut off from the outside world. The Axis of Continuity takes you to stairs and the main exhibit. A detour partway up the long stairway leads to the Memory Void, a compelling space of "fallen leaves": heavy metal faces that you walk on, making unhuman noises with each step.

Finish climbing the stairs to the top of the museum, and stroll chronologically through the 2,000-year **story of Judaism** in Germany. The exhibit, on two floors, is engaging, with lots of actual artifacts. Interactive bits (you can, for example, spell your name in Hebrew, or write a prayer and hang it from a tree) make it lively for kids.

The top floor focuses on everyday life in **Ashkenaz** (medieval German-Jewish lands). On the middle floor, exhibits detail the rising tide of anti-Semitism in Germany through the 19th century—at a time when many Jews were so secularized that they celebrated Christmas right along with Hanukkah. The exhibit segues into the **dark days** of Hitler—the collapse of the relatively tolerant Weimar Republic, the rise of the Nazis, and the horrific night of November 9, 1938, when, throughout Germany, hateful mobs destroyed Jewish-owned businesses, homes, synagogues, and even entire villages—called "Crystal Night" (Kristallnacht) for the broken glass that glittered in the streets.

The display brings us to the present day, with the question: How do you keep going after six million of your people have been murdered? You'll see how German society reacted to the two largest Nazi trials, complete with historical film clips of the perpetrators. In the last segment, devoted to Jewish life today, German Jews describe their experiences growing up in the postwar years.

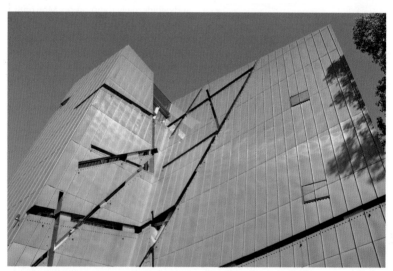

The Jewish Museum's fractured facade suggests the dislocation of the Holocaust.

Kulturforum Complex

The Kulturforum, off the southeast corner of Tiergarten park, hosts Berlin's concert hall and several sprawling museums, but only the Gemäldegalerie is a must for art lovers.

▲▲GEMÄLDEGALERIE

Literally the "Painting Gallery," the Gemäldegalerie is Germany's top collection of medieval and Renaissance European paintings (more than 1,400 canvases). They're beautifully displayed in a building that's a work of art in itself. If you're short on time or stamina, start in the North Wing galleries holding Northern European masterworks by Cranach, Dürer, Van Eyck, Brueghel, Rubens, Van Dyck, Hals, and Vermeer (to name just a few). You'll also encounter an impressive stash of Rembrandts. The South Wing is saved for the Italians—Giotto, Botticelli, Titian, Raphael, and Caravaggio.

Cost and Hours: €10, Tue-Fri 10:00-18:00, Thu until 20:00, Sat-Sun 11:00-18:00, closed Mon, audioguide included with entry, great salad bar in cafeteria upstairs, Matthäikirchplatz 4, tel. 030/266-424-242, www.smb.museum.

Getting There: Ride the S-Bahn or U-Bahn to Potsdamer Platz, then walk along Potsdamer Platz.

◑ **Self-Guided Tour:** I'll point out a few highlights, focusing on Northern European artists (German, Dutch, and Flemish), with a few Spaniards and Italians thrown in. To go beyond my selections, make ample use of the excellent audioguide.

The collection spreads out on one vast floor surrounding a central hall. Inner rooms have Roman numerals (I, II, III), while adjacent outer rooms are numbered (1, 2, 3).

Rooms I-III/1-4 kick things off with early German paintings (13th-16th century). In Room 1, look for the 1532 portrait of wealthy Hanseatic cloth merchant Georg Gisze by **Hans Holbein the Younger** (1497-1543). Gisze's name appears on several of the notes stuck to the wall behind him. And, typical of detail-rich Northern European art, the canvas is bursting with highly symbolic tidbits. Items scattered on the tabletop and on the shelves behind the merchant represent his lofty status and aspects of his life story. In the vase, the carnation represents his recent engagement, and the herbs symbolize his virtue. And yet, the celebratory flowers have already begun to fade and the scales behind him are unbalanced, reminders of the fleetingness of happiness and wealth.

In Room 2 are fine portraits by the remarkably talented **Albrecht Dürer** (1471-1528), who traveled to Italy during the burgeoning days of the early Renaissance and melded the artistic harmony and classical grandeur he discovered there with a Northern European attention to detail. In his *Portrait of Hieronymus Holzschuher* (1526), Dürer skillfully captured the personality of a friend from Nürnberg, right down to the sly twinkle in his sidelong glance. Technically, the portrait is perfection: Look closely and see each individual hair of the man's beard and fur coat, and even the reflection of the studio's windows in his eyes. Also notice

Holbein the Younger, The Merchant Georg Gisze

Dürer's little pyramid-shaped, D-inside-A signature. Signing one's work was a revolutionary assertion of Dürer's renown at a time when German artists were considered anonymous craftsmen.

Lucas Cranach the Elder (1472-1553), whose works are in Room III, was a court painter for the prince electors of Saxony and a close friend of Martin Luther (and his unofficial portraitist). But *The Fountain of Youth* (1546) is a far cry from Cranach's solemn portrayals of the reformer. Old women helped to the fountain (on the left) emerge as young ladies on the right. Newly nubile, the women go into a tent to dress up, snog with noblemen in the bushes (right foreground), dance merrily beneath the trees, and dine grandly beneath a landscape of phallic mountains and towers. This work is flanked by Cranach's Venus nudes. I sense a pattern here.

Dutch painters (Rooms IV-VI/4-7) were early adopters of oil paint (as opposed to older egg tempera)—its relative ease of handling allowed them to brush the fine details for which they became famous. **Rogier van der Weyden** (Room IV) was a virtuoso of the new medium. In *Portrait of a Woman* (c. 1400-1464), the subject wears a typical winged bonnet, addressing the viewer directly with her fetching blue eyes. In the same room is a remarkable, rare trio of three-panel altarpieces by Van der Weyden: The Marienaltar shows the life of the Virgin Mary; the Johannesaltar narrates the life of John the Baptist—his birth, baptizing Christ (with God and the Holy Spirit hovering overhead), and his gruesome death by decapitation; and the Middelburger Altar tells the story of the Nativity. Savor the fine details in each panel of these altarpieces.

Flash forward a few hundred years to the 17th century and Flemish (Belgian) painting (Rooms VII-VIII/9-10), and it's apparent how much the Protestant Reformation—and resulting Counter-Reformation—changed the tenor of Northern European art. In works by **Peter Paul Rubens** (1577-1640)—including *Jesus Giving Peter the Keys to Heaven*—calm, carefully studied, detail-oriented seriousness gives way to an exuberant Baroque trumpeting of the greatness of the Catholic Church. In the Counter-Reformation world, the Catholic Church had serious competition for the hearts and minds of its congregants. Exciting art like this became a way to keep people in the pews. In the next rooms (VIII and 9) are more Rubens, including the mythological *Perseus Freeing Andromeda* and *The Martyrdom of St. Sebastian by Arrows* (loosely based on a more famous rendition by Andrea Mantegna).

Dutch painting from the 17th century (Rooms IX-XI/10-19) is dominated by the convivial portraits by **Frans Hals** (c. 1582-1666). His 1620 portrait of Catharina Hooft (far corner, Room 13) presents a startlingly self-possessed baby (the newest member of a wealthy merchant family) dressed with all the finery of a queen, adorned with lace and jewels, and clutching a golden rattle. The smiling nurse supporting the tyke offers her a piece of fruit, whose blush of red perfectly matches the nanny's apple-fresh cheeks.

But the ultimate Dutch master is **Rembrandt van Rijn** (1606-1669), whose powers of perception and invention propelled him to fame in his lifetime. Displayed here are several storytelling scenes (Room 16), mostly from classical mythology or biblical stories, all employing Rembrandt's trademark chiaroscuro technique (with a strong contrast between light and dark). In *The Rape of Persephone,* Pluto grabs Persephone from his chariot and races toward the underworld, while other goddesses cling to her robe, trying to save her. In the nearby *Samson and Delilah* (1628), Delilah cradles Samson's head in her lap while silently signaling to a goon to shear Samson's hair, the secret to his strength. A self-portrait (Room X) of a 28-year-old

Rembrandt wearing a beret is paired with the come-hither 1637 *Portrait of Hendrickje Stoffels* (the two were romantically linked). *Samson Threatens His Father-in-Law* (1635) captures the moment just after the mighty Samson (with his flowing hair, elegant robes, and shaking fist) has been told by his wife's father to take a hike. I wouldn't want to cross this guy.

Although **Johannes Vermeer** (1632-1675) is today just as admired as Rembrandt, he was little known in his day, probably because he painted relatively few works for a small circle of Delft collectors. Vermeer was a master at conveying a complicated story through a deceptively simple scene with a few poignant details—whether it's a woman reading a letter at a window, a milkmaid pouring milk from a pitcher into a bowl, or (as in *The Glass of Wine*, Room 18) a young man offering a drink to a young lady. The young man had been playing her some music on his lute (which now sits, discarded, on a chair) and is hoping to seal the deal with some alcohol. The woman is finishing one glass of wine, and her would-be suitor stands ready—almost *too* ready—to pour her another. Vermeer has perfectly captured the exact moment of "Will she or won't she?"

Shift south to Italian, French, and Spanish painting of the 17th and 18th centuries (Rooms XII-XIV/23-28). Venetian cityscapes by Canaletto (who also painted Dresden) and lots of bombastic Baroque art hang in Room XII. Room XIII features big-name Spanish artists Murillo, Zurbarán, and the great **Diego Velázquez** (1599-1660). He gave the best of his talents to his portraits, capturing warts-and-all likenesses that are effortlessly real. His 1630 *Portrait of a Lady* conveys the subject's subtle, sly Mona Lisa smile. Her figure and face (against a dull gray background) are filtered through a pleasant natural light.

From here, the collection itself takes a step backwards—into Italian paintings

Ⓐ *Van der Weyden,* Portrait of a Woman
Ⓑ *Rubens,* Jesus Giving Peter the Keys to Heaven
Ⓒ *Rembrandt,* Self-Portrait with a Velvet Beret
Ⓓ *Vermeer,* The Glass of Wine

of the 13th-16th century (Rooms XV-XVIII/29-41). This section includes some lesser-known works by great Italian Renaissance painters, including Raphael (Rooms XVII and 29, with five different Madonnas, among them the *Terranuova Madonna,* in a round frame) and Sandro Botticelli (Room XVIII).

Across the Spree River

Several interesting, lively neighborhoods lie in a cluster across the river, just north of Museum Island (and easily accessed by the island's bridges and public transit): Hackescher Markt (with fun shops and fine little museums), Oranienburger Strasse (New Synagogue, eateries, and nightlife), and Prenzlauer Berg (Berlin Wall Memorial, eateries, accommodations, and more nightlife).

As you wander through the neighborhoods, you might notice small brass plaques in the sidewalk called *Stolpersteine,* marking the former homes of Jewish and other WWII victims of the Nazis.

Hackescher Markt

On a sunny day, a stroll (or tram ride) through this bursting-with-life area can be as engaging as any museum in town. Located in front of the S-Bahn station of the same name, this is a great people scene day and night. The brick trestle supporting the train track is a classic example of the city's Brandenburg Neo-Gothic brickwork. Most of the brick archways are now filled with hip shops. Within 100 yards of the S-Bahn station, you'll find Turkish and Bavarian restaurants, walking-tour and pub-crawl departure points, and tram #M1 to Prenzlauer Berg. Also nearby are two great examples of Berlin's traditional courtyards *(Höfe)*—one trendy and modern, the other retro-cool, with two fascinating museums.

HACKESCHE HÖFE

A block from the Hackescher Markt S-Bahn station (at Rosenthaler Strasse 40) is a series of eight courtyards bunny-hopping through a wonderfully restored 1907 *Jugendstil* (German Art Nouveau) building. Berlin's apartments are organized like this—courtyard after courtyard leading off the main road. This complex is full of artsy designer shops, popular restaurants, theaters, and cinemas. Courtyard #5 is particularly charming, with a children's park, and an Ampelmann store (see page 909). This courtyard system is a wonderful example of how to make huge city blocks livable. Two decades after the Cold War, this area has reached the final evolution of East Berlin's urban restoration: total gentrification. These courtyards also offer a useful lesson for visitors: Much of Berlin's charm hides off the street front.

HAUS SCHWARZENBERG

Next door (at Rosenthaler Strasse 39), this courtyard has a totally different feel. Owned by an artists' collective, it comes with a bar, cinema, open-air art space, and the basement-level "Dead Chickens" gallery (with far-out hydro-powered art). And within this amazing little zone you'll find two inspirational museums. The **Museum of Otto Weidt's Workshop for the Blind** (Museum Blindenwerkstatt Otto Weidt) vividly tells the amazing story of a Berliner heroically protecting blind and deaf Jews during World War II (free, daily 10:00-20:00). Otto Weidt employed them to produce brooms and brushes, and because that was useful for the Nazi war machine, he managed to

New Synagogue

finagle a special status for his workers. You can see the actual brushmaking factory with pedal-powered machines still lined up. The **Silent Heroes Memorial Center** (Gedenkstätte Stille Helden) is a well-presented exhibit celebrating the quietly courageous individuals who resisted the persecution of the Jews from 1933 to 1945 (free, daily 10:00-20:00).

Oranienburger Strasse

Oranienburger Strasse, a few blocks west of Hackescher Markt, is anchored by an important and somber sight, the New Synagogue. But the rest of this zone (roughly between the synagogue and Torstrasse) is colorful and quirky—especially after dark. The streets behind Grosse Hamburger Strasse flicker with atmospheric cafés, *Kneipen* (pubs), and art galleries.

▲NEW SYNAGOGUE (NEUE SYNAGOGUE)

A shiny gilded dome marks the New Synagogue, now a museum and cultural center. Consecrated in 1866, this was once the biggest and finest synagogue in Germany, with seating for 3,200 worshippers and a sumptuous Moorish-style interior modeled after the Alhambra in Granada, Spain. It was desecrated by Nazis on Crystal Night (Kristallnacht) in 1938, bombed in 1943, and partially rebuilt in 1990. Only the dome and facade have been restored—a window overlooks the vacant field marking what used to be the synagogue. On its facade, a small plaque—added by East Berlin Jews in 1966—reads "Never forget" (*Vergesst es nie*). Inside, past tight security, the small but moving permanent exhibit called Open Ye the Gates describes the Berlin Jewish community through the centuries. Skip the dome climb for an extra fee; the views are ho-hum.

Cost and Hours: April-Oct Mon-Fri 10:00-18:00, Sun until 19:00; Nov-March exhibit only Sun-Thu 10:00-18:00, Fri until 15:00; closed Sat year-round; audio-guide-€3, Oranienburger Strasse 28/30, enter through the low-profile door in the modern building just right of the domed synagogue facade, S-Bahn: Oranienburger Strasse, www.cjudaicum.de.

Prenzlauer Berg and Nearby
▲▲▲PRENZLAUER BERG

This is one of Berlin's most colorful neighborhoods. The heart of this area, with a dense array of hip cafés, restaurants, boutiques, and street life, is roughly between Helmholtzplatz and Kollwitzplatz and along Kastanienallee (U2: Senefelderplatz and Eberswalder Strasse; or take the S-Bahn to Hackescher Markt and catch tram #M1 north).

"Prenzl'berg," as Berliners call it, was largely untouched during World War II, but its buildings slowly rotted away under the communists. Then, after the Wall fell, it was overrun first with artists and anarchists, then with laid-back hipsters, energetic young families, and clever entrepreneurs who breathed life back into its classic old apartment blocks, deserted factories, and long-forgotten breweries.

Years of rent control kept things affordable for its bohemian residents. But now landlords are free to charge what the market will bear, and the vibe is changing. This is ground zero for Berlin's baby boom: Tattooed and pierced young moms and dads, who've joined the modern rat race without giving up their alternative flair, push their youngsters in designer strollers

Relaxing in Prenzlauer Berg

past trendy boutiques and restaurants.

Aside from the **Berlin Wall Memorial** at its western edge (see next) and the **Mauerpark** (Wall Park, once part of the Wall's death strip, today a Prenzlauer Berg green space), the area has few real sights—it's just a lively, laid-back neighborhood ignoring its wonderful late-19th-century architecture high overhead.

▲▲▲BERLIN WALL MEMORIAL (GEDENKSTÄTTE BERLINER MAUER)

While tourists flock to Checkpoint Charlie, this memorial is Berlin's most substantial attraction relating to its gone-but-not-forgotten Wall. Exhibits line up along several blocks of Bernauer Strasse, stretching northeast from the Nordbahnhof S-Bahn station. You can enter two different museums plus various open-air exhibits and memorials, see several fragments of the Wall, and peer from an observation tower down into a preserved, complete stretch of the Wall system (as it was during the Cold War). To brush up on the basics before your visit, read the sidebar on page 898.

The Berlin Wall, which was erected virtually overnight in 1961, ran right along Bernauer Strasse. People were suddenly separated from their neighbors across the street. This stretch was particularly notorious because existing apartment buildings were incorporated into the structure of the Wall itself. Film footage and photographs from the era show Berliners worriedly watching workmen seal off these buildings from the West, brick by brick. Some people attempted to leap to freedom from upper-story windows, with mixed results. One of the unfortunate ones was Ida Siekmann, who fell to her death from her third-floor apartment on August 22, 1961, and is considered the first casualty of the Berlin Wall.

Cost and Hours: Free; Visitor Center and Documentation Center open Tue-Sun 10:00-18:00, closed Mon, outdoor areas accessible 24 hours daily, memorial chapel closes at 17:00; Bernauer Strasse 111, tel. 030/4679-86666, www.berliner-mauer-gedenkstaette.de.

Getting There: Take the S-Bahn (line S-1, S-2, or S-25—all handy from Potsdamer Platz, Brandenburger Tor, Friedrichstrasse, Oranienburger Strasse, or Hackescher Markt) to the Nordbahnhof. Exit by following signs for *Bernauer Strasse*.

Fragments of the Berlin Wall in the memorial area

Berlin Wall Memorial Area

Berlin Wall Memorial
····· Former Course of the Wall

500 Meters
500 Yards

STADIUM

STAGE

Mauer-park Sportpark

Eberswalder Strasse

EBERSWALDER STR.

DANZIGER

PRENZLAUER

BERG

SREDZKISTR.

KNAACK

Kollwitz-platz

Jewish Cem.

BRUNNEN-

RUPPINERSTR.

FLEA MARKET (SUN.)

STRELITZERSTR.

Bernauer Strasse

BERNAUER STRASSE

KREMM.

ODERBERGER STR.

SCHWEDTER

SCHÖNEHAUSER

LYCHENER

HUSSITENSTR.

ACKERSTR.

BERLIN WALL DOCUMENTATION CENTER

WINDOW OF REMEMBRANCE

VISITOR CENTER

INTACT PART OF WALL

CHAPEL OF RECONCILIATION

RHEINS

ANKLAMER

ZIONS-

FEHR-

BERGSTR.

Nordbahnhof

ZINN-

INVALIDEN-STR.

GARTENSTR.

BERG.

ACKERSTR.

WOLLINER STR.

KASTANIENALLEE

CHORINER STR.

STRASSE

KIRCHSTR.

SCHÖNEHAUSER ALLEE

Senefelder-platz

Volkspark am Weinberg

VETERANEN-STR.

WEINBERGSWEG

BELLINERSTR.

ZEHDENICKER

LOTTUMSTR.

Rosenthaler Platz

KOLLWITZ-STRASSE

SAAR-BRÜCK

STRASSBURGER STR.

❸ **Self-Guided Tour:** Here's an overview of the route you'll take. From the Nordbahnhof station (which has some interesting Wall history in itself), head to the Visitor Center to get your bearings, then explore the assorted Wall fragments and other sights in the park across the street. Work your way up Bernauer Strasse to the Documentation Center, Wall System, memorial chapel, and remaining signposts (look for the escape-tunnel paths marked in the grass), until you reach the Bernauer Strasse U-Bahn station (or continue beyond the U-Bahn stop to see all the outdoor exhibits, which stretch up to the Mauerpark).

Nordbahnhof: This S-Bahn station was one of the "ghost stations" of Cold War Berlin. It was built in 1926, closed in 1961, and opened again in 1989. As it was a dogleg of the East mostly surrounded by the West, Western subway trains had permission to use the underground tracks to zip through this station (without stop-ping, of course) en route between stops in the West. East German border guards, who were stationed here to ensure that nobody got on or off those trains, were locked into their surveillance rooms to prevent them from escaping. (But one subway employee and his family used the tunnels to walk to the West and freedom.)

Follow signs down a long yellow hall to the Bernauer Strasse exit. Climbing the stairs up to the street, ponder that the doorway at the top (marked by the *Sperrmauer 1961–1989* plaque) was a bricked-off no-man's-land until 1989. Stepping outside, you'll see a park full of outdoor exhibits (directly across the street) and the Visitor Center (in a low rust-colored building kitty-corner across the street).

Visitor Center (Bezucherzentrum): This small complex has a helpful information desk, and two good movies that provide context for a visit (they run in English at :30 after the hour, about 30 minutes for the whole spiel): *The Berlin Wall* offers a great 15-minute overview of its history. That's followed by *Walled In!,* an animated 12-minute film illustrating the Wall as it functioned here at Bernauer Strasse. Before leaving, pick up the helpful brochures explaining the outdoor exhibits.

Wall Fragments and Other Sights: Across the street from the Visitor Center is a long stretch of Wall. The park behind it is scattered with a few more Wall chunks as well as monuments and memorials honoring its victims. To get your bearings, find the small model of the entire area when the Wall still stood (just across the street from the Nordbahnhof). The rusty "Window of Remembrance" monument honors slain would-be escapees. Before it was the no-man's-land between the walls, this area was the parish graveyard for a nearby church; ironically, DDR officials had to move a thousand graves from here to create a "death strip."

Berlin Wall Documentation Center (Dokumentationszentrum Berliner Mauer): The center's excellent **exhibit** is geared to a new generation of Berliners who can hardly imagine their hometown split so brutally in two. The ground floor details the logistics of the city's division and its effects on Berliners. Have a seat and listen to the riveting personal accounts of escapees—and of the border guards armed with machine guns and tasked with stopping them. The next floor up gives the historical and political context behind the Wall's construction and eventual destruction. Photos let you track the progression of changes at this exact site from 1965 to 1990.

Leaving the exhibit, climb the open-air staircase to an observation deck that gives you a bird's-eye view of the last remaining stretch of the complete Wall system—guard tower, barbed wire, and all.

Stretch of Intact Wall System: This is the last surviving intact bit of the complete Wall system (with both sides of its Wall—capped by the round pipe that made it tougher for escapees to get a grip—and its no-man's-land death strip). The guard tower came from a different part of the Wall; it was actually purchased on that great capitalist invention, eBay (somewhere, Stalin spins in his grave). View it from the observation deck, then visit it from ground level, where wall panels explain each part of the system. Plaques along the sidewalk mark the locations of escapes or deaths.

Chapel of Reconciliation (Kapelle der Versöhnung): Just beyond the Wall section (to the left), this chapel marks the spot of the late-19th-century Church of Reconciliation, which survived WWII bombs—but not the communists. Notice the larger footprint of the original church in the field around the chapel. When the Wall was built, the church wound up right in the middle of the death strip. It was torn down in 1985, supposedly because it got in the way of the border guards' sight lines. Inside the church, the carved wooden altarpiece was saved from the original structure. The chapel

Intact part of the Wall

Chapel of Reconciliation

hosts daily prayer services for the victims of the Wall.

Outdoor Exhibits: The memorial also includes a string of open-air exhibits along Bernauer Strasse that stretch all the way from the Nordbahnhof to the intersection with Schwedter Strasse and Oderberger Strasse, near the Mauerpark, at the heart of Prenzlauer Berg. Video and audio clips, photos, and huge photographic murals let you in on more stories of the Wall—many of which took place right where you're standing.

EXPERIENCES

Shopping

Shops all over town stock the typical array of souvenirs (T-shirts, posters, bottle openers, etc.) emblazoned with icons of Berlin: Brandenburg Gate, TV Tower, Berlin Wall, bears (the namesake and official mascot of "Bear-lin"), and so on.

If you're taken with the city's unofficial mascot, the Ampelmännchen (traffic-light man), you'll find a world of souvenirs slathered with his iconic red and green image at **Ampelmann Shops** (several locations, including along Unter den Linden at #35, near Gendarmenmarkt at Markgrafenstrasse 37, near Museum Island inside the DomAquarée mall, and in the Hackesche Höfe).

Fun and funky **designer shops** fill the **Hackesche Höfe** and are easy to find throughout Prenzlauer Berg, particularly along Kastanienallee and Oderberger Strasse.

Flea markets abound on weekends; virtually every neighborhood hosts one on a regular basis. The most central is along **Am Kupfergraben,** just across the canal from the Pergamon Museum, with lots of books, music, and art (Sat-Sun 10:00-17:00). One of the biggest is right next to the **Tiergarten park** on Strasse des 17 Juni, with great antiques, more than 200 stalls, and fun fast-food stands (Sat-Sun 6:00-16:00, S-Bahn: Tiergarten). The rummage market in Prenzlauer Berg's **Mauerpark** comes with lots of inventive snack stalls—and on Sunday afternoons, karaoke (Sat-Sun 7:00-17:00, U-Bahn: Eberswalder Strasse).

On the opposite end of the price spectrum are the swanky shopping centers clustered around **Gendarmenmarkt.** Find the corner of Jägerstrasse and Friedrichstrasse and wander through the **Quartier 206** department store. The adjacent, middlebrow Quartier 205 has more affordable prices.

In western Berlin, it's fun to browse through **Kaufhaus des Westens** (everyone calls it **KaDeWe**), one of Europe's fanciest department stores, with a good selection of souvenirs...and just about anything else you can think of. The top floor holds the Winter Garden Buffet view **cafeteria.** A **deli/food department** is on the sixth floor, along with a **ticket office** that sells music and theater tickets for all events (18 percent fee but access to all tickets; daily 10:00-20:00, Fri until 21:00, closed Sun, S-Bahn: Zoologischer Garten or U-Bahn: Wittenbergplatz, www.kadewe.de).

Nightlife

Berlin is a happening place for nightlife—whether it's clubs, pubs, jazz, cabaret, concerts, or even sightseeing.

Berlin Programm lists a nonstop parade of events (www.berlinprogramm.de); *Exberliner Magazine* doesn't have as much hard information, but is colorfully written in English (sold at kiosks, www.exberliner.com).

Hekticket, Berlin's ticket clearinghouse, offers tickets in advance and **same-day half-price tickets.** Drop by or call after 14:00 to see what's on the push list for this evening (Mon-Fri 12:00-18:00, closed Sat-Sun, half-price sales start at 14:00, near Alexanderplatz at Karl-Liebknecht-Strasse 13, tel. 030/230-9930, www.hekticket.de). **KaDeWe** also sells tickets for events (see listing above in "Shopping").

Rick's Tip: *Stretch your sightseeing day into the night. These museums are* **open late every day:** **Reichstag** *(last entry at 22:00),* **Museum of the Wall at Checkpoint Charlie** *(until 22:00),* **Topography of error** *(until 20:00), and* **Jewish Museum Berlin** *(Tue-Sun until 20:00, 22:00 on Mon). The* **Museum Island***'s museums are open until 20:00 on Thursdays. Outdoor monuments such as the* **Berlin Wall Memorial** *and the* **Memorial to the Murdered Jews of Europe** *are safe and well-lit late into the night, even though their visitor centers close earlier.*

Jazz

B-Flat Acoustic Music and Jazz Club, in the heart of eastern Berlin, has live music nightly—and shares a courtyard with a tranquil tea house (shows vary from free to €10-13 cover, open Sun-Thu from 20:00 with shows starting at 21:00, Fri-Sat from 21:00 with shows at 22:00, a block from Rosenthaler Platz U-Bahn stop at

Rosenthaler Strasse 13, tel. 030/283-3123, www.b-flat-berlin.de).

Rock and Roll

Berlin has a vibrant rock and pop scene, with popular venues at the Spandau Citadel, Olympic Stadium, and the outdoor Waldbühne ("Forest Stage"). Check out what's playing on posters in the U-Bahn, on the *Zitty* website (www.zitty.de), or at any ticket agency.

Cabaret

Bar Jeder Vernunft offers modern-day cabaret in western Berlin. This variety show—under a classic old tent perched atop the modern parking lot of the Berliner Festspiele theater—is a hit with German speakers, and can be fun for those who don't speak the language (as some of the music shows are in a sort of *Deutsch*-English hybrid). Some Americans even perform here periodically. Shows change regularly (about €22-30, performances generally Tue-Sat at 20:00, Sun at 19:00, seating can be cramped, south of

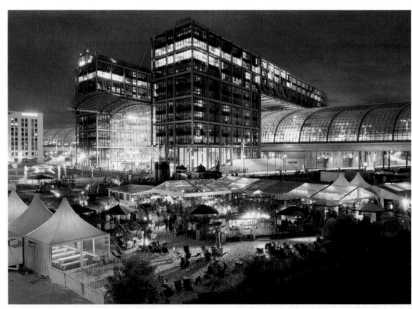

Festivals keep Berlin lively year-round.

Ku'damm at Schaperstrasse 24, U3 or U9: Spichernstrasse, tel. 030/883-1582, www. bar-jeder-vernunft.de).

Nightclubs and Pubs

Oranienburger Strasse is a trendy scene, with bars and restaurants spilling out onto sidewalks filled with people strolling. Nearby, the hip **Prenzlauer Berg** neighborhood is packed with everything from smoky pubs to small art bars and dance clubs (best scene is around Helmholtzplatz, U2: Eberswalder Strasse).

EATING

Near Unter den Linden

Georgenstrasse, a block behind the Pergamon Museum and under the S-Bahn tracks, is lined with fun eateries filling the arcade of the train trestle. **$$ Deponie3** is a reliable Berlin *Kneipe* (bar) usually filled with students from nearby Humboldt University. Garden seating in the back is nice if you don't mind the noise of the S-Bahn directly above you. The interior is a cozy, wooden wonderland. They serve basic salads, traditional Berlin dishes, and hearty daily specials (daily from 10:00, under S-Bahn arch #187 at Georgenstrasse 5, tel. 030/2016-5740).

$ Käse König am Alex has been serving traditional sauerkraut-type dishes since 1933. It's fast, the photo menu makes ordering fun, and prices are great (daily, Panoramastrasse 1 under the TV Tower, tel. 030/8561-5220). Nearby, **$ Brauhaus Mitte** is a fun, DDR-era beer hall that makes its own beer and offers a menu of Berliner specialties and Bavarian dishes (daily 11:00-24:00, across from the TV Tower at Karl-Liebknecht-Strasse 13, tel. 030/3087-8989).

Near Gendarmenmarkt

The twin churches of Gendarmenmarkt are surrounded by upscale restaurants serving lunch and dinner to local professionals. If in need of a quick-yet-classy lunch, stroll around the square and along Charlottenstrasse. For a quick bite, head to the cheap *Currywurst* stand behind the German Cathedral.

$$$ Lutter & Wegner Restaurant is well-known for its Austrian cuisine (schnitzel and sauerbraten), with fun sidewalk seating or a dark and elegant interior (€9-18 starters, €16-24 main dishes, daily 11:00-24:00, Charlottenstrasse 56, tel. 030/202-9540).

$$ Augustiner am Gendarmenmarkt, next door to Lutter & Wegner, has a classic beer-hall atmosphere, offers good beer and Bavarian cuisine (€6-12 light meals, €10-20 bigger meals, daily 10:00-24:00, Charlottenstrasse 55, tel. 030/2045-4020).

Galeries Lafayette Food Circus is a festival of eateries in the basement of the landmark department store. You'll find a good deli and prepared-food stands (most options €10-15, cheaper €5-10 sandwiches and savory crêpes, Mon-Sat 10:00-20:00, closed Sun, Friedrichstrasse 76-78, U-Bahn: Französische Strasse, tel. 030/209-480).

Hackescher Markt and Nearby

$$ Weihenstephaner Bavarian Restaurant serves upmarket traditional cuisine for around €10-15 a plate and excellent beer in the atmospheric cellar, the inner courtyard, and on the streetside terrace (daily 11:00-23:00, Neue Promenade 5 at Hackescher Markt, tel. 030/8471-0760).

Restaurants on Oranienburger Strasse, a few blocks west of Hackescher Markt, come with happy hours and lots of cocktails. **$$ Aufsturz,** a lively pub, serves pub grub and a huge selection of beer and whisky to a young crowd (Oranienburger Strasse 67). **$ Amrit Lounge** serves Indian food outdoors with an umbrella-drink Caribbean ambience (€10-14 meals, long hours daily, Oranienburger Strasse 45). Next door is **$$ QBA,** a fun Cuban bar and restaurant.

$ Schwarzwaldstuben, between Oranienburger Strasse and Rosenthaler Platz, is a Black Forest-themed pub—which explains the antlers and cuckoo clocks. It's friendly, with good service, food, and prices. If they're full, you can eat at the long bar or at one of the sidewalk tables (€7-16 meals, daily 9:00-23:00, Tucholskystrasse 48, tel. 030/2809-8084).

$$ Gipsy Restaurant serves good, reasonably priced German and Italian dishes in a bohemian-chic atmosphere (daily 12:30-23:00, at Clärchens Ballhaus, Auguststrasse 24, tel. 030/282-9295).

Near Rosenthaler Platz

Surrounding the U8: Rosenthaler Platz station, a short stroll or tram ride from the Hackescher Markt S-Bahn station, and an easy walk from the Oranienburger Strasse action, this busy neighborhood has several enticing options.

$ My Smart Break is a great spot to pick up a freshly made deli sandwich, hummus plate, salad, or other healthy snack. Linger in the interior, grab one of the sidewalk tables, or get it to go (€5-8 sandwiches, daily 8:00-23:00, Rosenthaler Strasse 67, tel. 030/2390-0303).

$ Transit is a stylish Thai/Indonesian/pan-Asian restaurant with a creative menu of €3 small plates and €8 big plates. Two people can make a filling meal out of three or four dishes (daily 11:00-24:00, cash only, Rosenthaler Strasse 68, tel. 030/2478-1645).

$ Restaurant Simon dishes up tasty Italian and German specialties—enjoy them in the restaurant's simple yet atmospheric interior, or opt for parkside seating across the street (€8-15 main dishes, Mon-Sat 17:00-23:00, closed Sun, cash only, Auguststrasse 53, at intersection with Kleine Auguststrasse, tel. 030/2789-0300).

In Prenzlauer Berg

The area surrounding the elevated Eberswalder Strasse U-Bahn station is the

Berliner Street Fare

In Berlin, it's easy to eat cheap, with a glut of *Imbiss* snack stands, bakeries (for sandwiches), and falafel/kebab counters. Train stations have grocery stores, as well as bright and modern fruit-and-sandwich bars.

Sausage stands are everywhere. Most specialize in **Currywurst,** a grilled pork sausage smothered with curry sauce. It was created in Berlin after World War II, when a cook got her hands on some curry and Worcestershire sauce from British troops stationed here. *Currywurst* comes either **mit Darm** (with casing) or **ohne Darm** (without casing). **Berliner Art**—"Berlin-style"—means that the sausage is boiled *ohne Darm*, then grilled. Either way, the grilled sausage is then chopped into small pieces or cut in half and topped with sauce. While some places simply use ketchup and sprinkle on some curry powder, real *Currywurst* joints use tomato paste, Worcestershire sauce, and curry. With your wurst comes either a toothpick or small wooden fork; you'll usually get a plate of fries as well.

Other good street foods to consider are **Döner Kebab** (Turkish-style skewered meat slow-roasted and served in a sandwich) and **Frikadelle** (like a hamburger patty; often called **Bulette** in Berlin).

Two companies, Grillwalker and Grillrunner, outfit their cooks in clever harnesses that let them grill and sell hot dogs from under an umbrella. For something quick, cheap, and tasty, find one of these portable human hot-dog stands.

epicenter of Prenzlauer Berg. It's worth the 10- to 15-minute walk from most of my recommended hotels.

$ Prater Biergarten offers both a rustic indoor restaurant and Berlin's oldest beer garden (with a family-friendly playground), each proudly offering its own microbrew. In the beer garden, step up to the counter and order (daily in good weather 12:00-24:00). The restaurant serves serious *Biergarten* cuisine and good salads (€10-20 plates, Mon-Sat 18:00-24:00, Sun from 12:00, cash only, Kastanienallee 7, tel. 030/448-5688).

$ Zum Schusterjungen Speisegaststätte ("The Cobbler's Apprentice") is a classic eatery that retains its circa-1986 DDR decor. Famous for its filling €9-13 meals (including schnitzel and Berlin classics such as pork knuckle), it has a strong local following (daily 12:00-24:00, corner of Lychener Strasse and Danziger Strasse 9, tel. 030/442-7654).

$$ La Bodeguita del Medio Cuban Bar Restaurant is pure fun, with an ambience that makes you want to dance. The main dishes are big enough to split and you can even puff a Cuban cigar at the sidewalk tables. Come early to eat or late to drink (€4-10 tapas, Cuban ribs and salad, Tue-Sun 18:00-24:00, closed Mon, cash only, a block from U2: Eberswalder Strasse at Lychener Strasse 6, tel. 030/4050-0601).

$ Konnopke's Imbiss has been cooking up the city's best *Currywurst* for more than 70 years. Located beneath the U2 viaduct, the stand was demolished in 2010 during roadwork. Berliners rioted, and Konnopke's was rebuilt in a slick glass-and-steel hut. Don't confuse this with the nearby Currystation—look for the real Konnopke's (Mon-Fri 9:00-20:00, Sat from 11:30, closed Sun; Kastanienallee dead-ends at the elevated train tracks, and under them you'll find Konnopke's at Schönhauser Allee 44A, tel. 030/442-7765).

$$ Restaurant Die Schule is a modern, no-frills place to sample traditional German dishes tapas-style (good indoor and outdoor seating, daily 11:00-22:00, Kastanienallee 82, tel. 030/780-089-550).

Funky pubs and nightspots fill the area around Helmholtzplatz (and elsewhere in Prenzlauer Berg). Oderberger Strasse is a fun zone to explore. For dessert, **Kauf Dich Glücklich** serves an enticing array of sweet Belgian waffles and ice cream in a candy-sprinkled, bohemian lounge (Mon-Fri 11:00-24:00, Sat-Sun from 10:00, indoor and outdoor seating—or get your dessert to go, Oderberger Strasse 44, tel. 030/4862-3292).

Berlin Eateries & Nightlife

1. Deponie3 Pub
2. Käse König am Alex
3. Brauhaus Mitte & Hekticket Half-Price Tix
4. Lutter & Wegner Rest.; Augustiner am Gendarmenmarkt
5. Galeries Lafayette Food Circus
6. Weihenstephaner Bavarian Restaurant
7. Oranienburger Strasse Eateries
8. Schwarzwaldstuben Pub
9. Gipsy Restaurant at Clärchens Ballhaus
10. My Smart Break & Transit Restaurant
11. Restaurant Simon
12. Prater Biergarten

..... Former Course of the Wall

500 Meters
500 Yards

⑬ Zum Schusterjungen
   Speisegaststätte
⑭ La Bodeguita del Medio
   Cuban Bar Restaurant
⑮ Konnopke's Imbiss
⑯ Restaurant Die Schule
⑰ Kauf Dich Glücklich
⑱ B-Flat Acoustic
   Music & Jazz Club

SLEEPING

Prenzlauer Berg

Gentrification has enlivened this colorful and gritty district with fun shops and eateries, happening nightlife—and great hotels. Think of the graffiti as some people's way of saying they care.

The closest U-Bahn stops are U2: Senefelderplatz at the south end of the neighborhood, U8: Rosenthaler Platz in the middle, or U2: Eberswalder Strasse at the north end. Or, for less walking, take the S-Bahn to Hackescher Markt, then catch tram #M1 north.

$$$ Myer's Hotel rents 60 lush rooms decorated in rich colors with classy furnishings. The gorgeous public spaces, including an art-filled patio and garden, host frequent cultural events. This peaceful hub is off a quiet garden courtyard and tree-lined street (Db-€108-235, air-con, elevator, sauna, bike rental, Metzer Strasse 26, 5-minute walk to Kollwitzplatz or U2: Senefelderplatz, tel. 030/440-140, www.myershotel.de, info@myershotel.de).

$$$ Hotel Jurine is a pleasant 53-room business-style hotel whose friendly staff aims to please. In good weather, enjoy the breakfast buffet on the peaceful backyard patio and garden (Db-€130-160, air-con only on upper floor, elevator, garage parking if you reserve ahead, Schwedter Strasse 15, 10-minute walk to U2: Senefelderplatz, tel. 030/443-2990, www.hotel-jurine.de, mail@hotel-jurine.de).

$$$ Hotel Kastanienhof, which offers helpful service, feels like a traditional small-town German hotel, even though it has 50 rooms. It's well-located on the Kastanienallee #M1 tram line, with easy access to the Prenzlauer Berg bustle (Db-€100-180, some rooms with air-con and/or balcony—request when you book, breakfast-€9, pay parking, 20 yards from #M1 Zionskirche tram stop at Kastanienallee 65, tel. 030/443-050, www.kastanienhof.biz, info@kastanienhof.biz).

$$ The Circus Hotel, with 60 colorful rooms, is fun, comfortable, and an excellent value. It overlooks a noisy intersection, so ask for a back room (Db-€95-€105, breakfast-€9, elevator, loaner iPads in rooms, mellow ground-floor restaurant, Rosenthaler Strasse 1, directly at U8: Rosenthaler Platz, tel. 030/2000-3939, www.circus-berlin.de, info@circus-berlin.de). The Circus also offers a range of spacious, modern **apartments** both within the hotel and two blocks away on Choriner Strasse.

$ Karlito Apartmenthaus has 12 comfortable, modern apartments above a hip café on a tranquil side street near Hackescher Markt. All the sleek, Ikea-esque units have miniature balconies (Db-€80-95, in-room breakfast-€10, elevator, bike rental, Linienstrasse 60—check in at Café Lois around the corner on Gormannstrasse, U8: Rosenthaler Platz, or 350 yards from S-Bahn: Hackescher Markt, mobile 0179-704-9041, www.karlito-apartments.de, info@karlito-apartments.de).

$ EasyHotel Berlin Hackescher Markt is part of an unapologetically cheap chain where you pay for exactly what you use—nothing more, nothing less. The hotel has inexpensive base rates (Db-€35-65), then charges separate fees for optional extras like Wi-Fi and TV. The 125 rooms are small and basic, but if you skip the extras, the price is right, and the location at Hackescher Markt is wonderful (elevator, request quieter back room, Rosenthaler Strasse 69, tel. 030/4000-6550, www.easyhotel.com).

$$$ Hotel Augustinenhof is on a side street near all the Oranienburger Strasse action. It's a clean hotel with 66 spacious rooms, nice woody floors, and some of the most comfortable beds in Berlin. Rooms in front overlook the courtyard of the old Imperial Post Office, rooms in back are quieter, and some rooms have older, thin windows (Db-€100-150, elevator, Auguststrasse 82, 50 yards from S-Bahn: Oranienburger Strasse, tel. 030/3088-6710, www.hotel-augustinenhof.de, augustinenhof@albrechtshof-hotels.de).

Farther East, in Friedrichshain

$ Michelberger Hotel, in the heart of gritty but gentrifying Friedrichshain, is so self-consciously hip that it'd be just too much...if it weren't for its helpful, friendly staff. Its 113 bright rooms are reasonably priced, and its common spaces—a bar/lounge and a breezy courtyard restaurant—are genuinely welcoming (Db-€80-90, bigger "loft" doubles and suites available, breakfast extra, elevator, bike rental; from atop Warschauer Strasse S-Bahn station turn left to cross the bridge—it's across from the U-Bahn station and #M10 tram stop at Warschauer Strasse 39; tel. 030/2977-8590, www.michelbergerhotel.com, reservations@michelbergerhotel.com).

$ Ostel is a fun, retro-1970s apartment building that re-creates the DDR lifestyle and interior design. All the furniture and room decorations have been meticulously collected and restored to their former socialist glory—only the psychedelic wallpaper is a replica (Db-€59, also 4-person apartments; no breakfast but supermarket next door, 24-hour reception, Wi-Fi in lobby, bike rental, free parking, free use of the community barbeque, right behind Ostbahnhof station on the corner of Strasse der Pariser Kommune at Wriezener Karree 5, tel. 030/2576-8660, www.ostel.eu, contact@ostel.eu).

Hotelesque Hostels

¢ Meininger is a budget-hotel chain with several locations in Berlin. With sleek, nicely decorated rooms, these can be a great value, even for nonhostelers. They have three particularly appealing branches: in Prenzlauer Berg (Schönhauser Allee 19 on Senefelderplatz), at Oranienburger Strasse 67 (next to the Aufsturz pub), and near the Hauptbahnhof, at Ella-Traebe-Strasse 9 (dorm bed-€20-40, Db-€70-120, all locations: breakfast extra, elevator, 24-hour reception, guest kitchen, bike rental, pay parking, tel. 030/666-36100, www.meininger-hostels.com, welcome@meininger-hostels.com).

¢ The Circus Hostel is a brightly colored, well-run place with 230 beds, a trendy lounge, and a bar downstairs. It has typical hostel dorms as well as some private rooms; for a few big steps up in comfort, see the listing for the Circus Hotel (dorm bed-€23-31, Db-€85, also apartments, breakfast extra, no curfew, elevator, guest iPads, bike rental, Weinbergsweg 1A, U8: Rosenthaler Platz, tel. 030/2000-3939, www.circus-berlin.de, info@circus-berlin.de).

¢ EastSeven Hostel rents the best cheap beds in Prenzlauer Berg. It's sleek and modern, with all the hostel services and more: 60 beds, inviting lounge, guest kitchen, lockers, quiet backyard terrace, and bike rental. Children are welcome. Easygoing people of any age are comfortable here (dorm bed-€15-25, D-€54-60, breakfast extra, laundry, no curfew, 100 yards from U2: Senefelderplatz at Schwedter Strasse 7, tel. 030/9362-2240, www.eastseven.de, info@eastseven.de).

¢ Hotel Transit Loft, actually more of a hostel, is located in a refurbished factory. Its 81 stark, high-ceilinged rooms and wide-open lobby have an industrial touch.

Berlin Hotels

1. Myer's Hotel
2. Hotel Jurine
3. Hotel Kastanienhof
4. The Circus Hotel
5. Karlito Apartmenthaus
6. EasyHotel Berlin Hackescher Markt
7. Hotel Augustinenhof
8. To Michelberger Hotel & Ostel
9. Meininger Hotels (3)
10. The Circus Hostel
11. EastSeven Hostel
12. Hotel Transit Loft
13. Motel One (3)

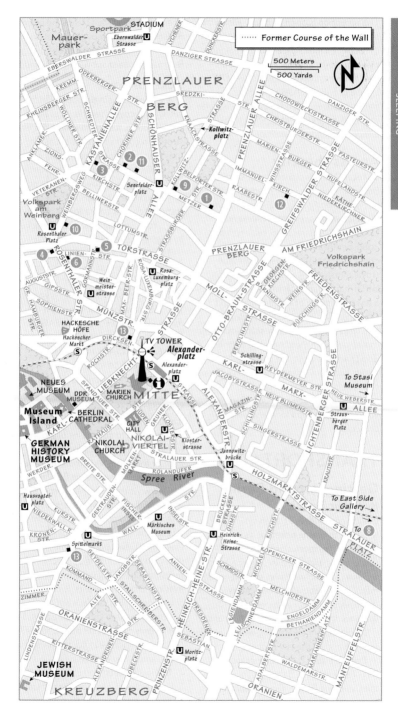

The reception is open 24 hours, with a bar serving drinks all night long (Db-€73, family rooms, includes sheets and breakfast, elevator, down alley facing inner courtyard at Immanuelkirchstrasse 14A; U2/U5/U8 or S-Bahn: Alexanderplatz, then tram #M4 to Hufelandstrasse and walk 50 yards; tel. 030/4849-3773, www.transit-loft.de, loft@hotel-transit.de).

Across the City

$ Motel One has eight locations across Berlin; all have the same posh-feeling-but-small rooms. The four most convenient locations are right on Alexanderplatz (Dircksenstrasse 36, tel. 030/2005-4080, berlin-alexanderplatz@motel-one.com); just behind the Hauptbahnhof (Invalidenstrasse 54, tel. 030/3641-0050, berlin-hauptbahnhof@motel-one.com); a few blocks east of Gendarmenmarkt (Leipziger Strasse 50, U2: Spittelmarkt, tel. 030/2014-3630, berlin-spittelmarkt@motel-one.com); and near the Bahnhof Zoo (Kantstrasse 10, tel. 030/3151-7360, berlin-kudamm@motel-one.com). They tend to charge the same prices (Db-€84, breakfast extra, air-con, guest iPads, elevator, limited pay parking, www.motel-one.com).

TRANSPORTATION

Getting Around Berlin
By Public Transit

Berlin's consolidated transit system uses the same ticket for its many modes of transportation: U-Bahn (*Untergrund-Bahn*, Berlin's subway), S-Bahn (*Stadtschnellbahn*, or "fast urban train," mostly aboveground), *Strassenbahn* (tram), and bus. For all types of transit, there are three lettered zones (A, B, and C). Most of your sightseeing will be in zones A and B (the city proper).

Berlin's public transit is operated by BVG (except the S-Bahn, which is run by the Deutsche Bahn). Timetables and the latest prices are available on the helpful BVG website (www.bvg.de). Get and use the excellent *Discover Berlin by Train and Bus* map-guide at subway ticket windows.

TICKET OPTIONS

The €2.70 **basic single** ticket (*Einzelfahrschein*) covers two hours of travel in one direction. It's easy to make this ticket stretch to cover several rides...as long as they're in the same direction.

The €1.60 **short-ride** ticket (*Kurzstrecke Fahrschein*) covers a single ride of up to six bus/tram stops or three subway stations (one transfer allowed on subway). You can save on short-ride tickets by buying them in groups of four.

The €9 **four-trip** ticket (*4-Fahrten-Karte*) is the same as four basic single tickets at a small discount.

The **day pass** (*Tageskarte*) is good until 3:00 the morning after you buy it (€6.90 for zones AB, €7.40 for zones ABC). For longer stays, consider a seven-day pass (*Sieben-Tage-Karte*; €29.50 for zones AB, €36.50 for zones ABC), or the WelcomeCard (described below). The *Kleingruppenkarte* lets groups of up to five travel all day (€16.90 for zones AB, €17.40 for zones ABC).

If you plan to cover a lot of ground using public transportation during a two- or three-day visit, the **WelcomeCard** is usually the best deal (available at TIs; www.visitberlin.de/welcomecard). It covers all public transportation and gives you up to 50 percent discounts on lots of minor and a few major museums (including Checkpoint Charlie), sightseeing tours (including 25 percent off the recommended Original Berlin Walks), and music and theater events. It's especially smart for families, as each adult card also covers up to three kids under age 15. The Berlin-only card covers transit zones AB (€19.50/48 hours, €27.50/72 hours, also 4-, 5-, and 6-day options).

Buying Tickets: You can buy U-Bahn/S-Bahn tickets from machines at stations. (They are also sold at BVG pavilions at

Stadtmitte U-Bahn underground station sign

train stations and at the TI, from machines onboard trams, and on buses from drivers, who'll give change.) *Erwachsener* means "adult"—anyone age 14 or older. Don't be afraid of the automated machines: First select the type of ticket you want, then load the coins or paper bills. (Coins work better, so keep some handy.)

Boarding Transit: As you board the bus or tram, or enter the subway, punch your ticket in a clock machine to validate it (or risk a €60 fine; stamp passes only the first time you ride). Be sure to travel with a valid ticket. Tickets are checked frequently, often by plainclothes inspectors. You may be asked to show your ticket when boarding the bus (technically that's required), though most drivers skip this.

By Taxi

Cabs are easy to flag down, and taxi stands are common. A typical ride within town costs €8-10, and a crosstown trip will run about €15. Tariff 1 is for a *Kurzstrecke* ticket (see later). All other rides are tariff 2 (€3.40 drop plus €1.80/km for the first 7 kilometers, then €1.28/km after that). If possible, use cash—paying with a credit card comes with a hefty surcharge (about €4, regardless of the fare).

Money-Saving Taxi Tip: For any ride of less than two kilometers (about a mile), you can save several euros if you take advantage of the *Kurzstrecke* (short-stretch) rate. To get this rate, it's important that you flag the cab down on the street—not at or even near a taxi stand. You must ask for the *Kurzstrecke* rate as soon as you hop in: Confidently say *"Kurzstrecke, bitte"* (KOORTS-shtreh-keh, BIT-teh), and your driver will grumble and flip the meter to a fixed €4 rate (for a ride that would otherwise cost €7).

By Bike

Flat Berlin is a bike-friendly city, but be careful—Berlin's motorists don't brake for bicyclists (and bicyclists don't brake for pedestrians). Fortunately, some roads and sidewalks have special red-painted bike lanes. Don't ride on the regular sidewalk—it's *verboten* (though locals do it all the time). Bike shops can suggest a specific route.

Fat Tire Bikes rents good bikes at two locations, east—at the base of the TV Tower near Alexanderplatz—and west, at Bahnhof Zoo (leaving the station onto Hardenbergplatz, turn left and walk 100 yards to the big bike sign). Both locations have the same hours and rates (€14/day, cheaper for two or more days, daily May-Aug 9:30-20:00, March-April and Sept-Oct 9:30-18:00, shorter hours or by appointment only Nov-Feb, tel. 030/2404-7991, www.berlinbikerental.com).

In eastern Berlin, **Take a Bike**—near the Friedrichstrasse S-Bahn station—is owned by a lovely Dutch-German couple who know a lot about bikes and have a huge inventory (3-gear bikes: €12.50/day, cheaper for longer rentals, more for better bikes, includes helmets, daily 9:30-19:00, Neustädtische Kirchstrasse 8, tel. 030/2065-4730, www.takeabike.de). To find it, leave the S-Bahn station via the Friedrichstrasse exit, turn right, go through a triangle-shaped square, and hang a left on Neustädtische Kirchstrasse.

All around town, simple **Rent a Bike** stands are outside countless shops, restaurants, and hotels. Most charge €10-12 a day, and are convenient, given their ubiquitous availability—but these bikes don't come with the reliable quality, advice, helmets, or maps commonly offered by full-service rental shops.

Arriving and Departing
By Train

Berlin's grandest train station is Berlin Hauptbahnhof (a.k.a. "der Bahnhof," abbreviated Hbf). All long-distance trains arrive here. This is also a "transfer station," where the national train system meets the city's S-Bahn trains.

Services: On the main floor, you'll find the **TI** and a Deutsche Bahn information center/ticket office; up one level are a 24-hour **pharmacy** and **lockers** (directly under track 14).

Rick's Tip: **EurAide** *is an American-run* **information desk** *with answers to your questions about train travel around Europe. It's located at counter 12 inside the Deutsche Bahn information center on the Hauptbahnhof's first upper level. This is a good place to make fast-train and couchette reservations (closed Jan-Feb and Sat-Sun year-round; www.euraide.com).*

Getting into Town: Taxis and buses wait outside the station, but the S-Bahn is

Berlin Hauptbahnhof train station

probably the best means of connecting to your destination within Berlin. It's simple: All S-Bahn trains are on tracks 15 and 16 at the top of the station. All trains on track 15 go east, stopping at Friedrichstrasse, Hackescher Markt (with connections to Prenzlauer Berg), Alexanderplatz, and Ostbahnhof; trains on track 16 go west, toward Bahnhof Zoo.

To reach most recommended hotels in the Prenzlauer Berg neighborhood, it's fastest to take any train on track 15 two stops to Hackescher Markt, exit to Spandauer Strasse, go left, and cross the tracks to the tram stop. Here you'll catch tram #M1 north (direction: Schillerstrasse).

From Berlin by Train to: Dresden (every 2 hours, 2.5 hours), **Hamburg** (1-2/hour direct, 2 hours), **Frankfurt** (hourly, 4 hours), **Bacharach** (hourly, 7 hours, 1-3 changes), **Würzburg** (hourly, 4 hours, 1 change), **Rothenburg** (hourly, 5.5 hours, 3 changes), **Nürnberg** (hourly, 4.5 hours), **Munich** (1-2/hour, 6.5 hours, night train possible), **Cologne** (hourly, 4.5 hours, night train possible).

By Bus

The city's bus station, **ZOB** (Zentraler Omnibusbahnhof), is on the western edge of Berlin, in Charlottenburg (Masurenallee 4-6, U2: Kaiserdamm). **MeinFernBus, Flix, Berlin Linien,** and **Eurolines** all operate from here to locations around Germany and Europe.

By Plane

Berlin is trying to finish construction of its new airport, **Willy Brandt Berlin-Brandenburg International,** located about 13 miles from central Berlin (airport code: BER), but the project has been perennially delayed. You'll most likely use **Tegel Airport,** which is four miles from the center (airport code: TXL). **Bus** #TXL goes between the airport, the Hauptbahnhof (stops by Washingtonplatz entrance), and Alexanderplatz. A **taxi** from Tegel Airport costs about €30 to Alexanderplatz.

Most flights from the east and discount airlines arrive at **Schönefeld Airport** (12.5 miles from center). From the old Schönefeld arrivals hall, it's a three-minute walk to the train station, where you can catch a regional express train into the city. Airport Express RE and RB trains go directly to Ostbahnhof, Alexanderplatz, Friedrichstrasse, and Hauptbahnhof (€3.30, 2/hour, direction: Nauen or Dessau, rail pass valid). A taxi to the city center costs about €35.

The Netherlands

The Netherlands—sometimes referred to by its nickname, "Holland"—is one of Europe's most densely populated, wealthiest, and best-organized countries. Occupying a delta near the mouth of three large rivers, the Netherlands ("low lands") has battled the sea for centuries, reclaiming low-lying land and converting it into fertile farmland.

The Netherlands has 16.8 million people: 80 percent are Dutch, and half have no religious affiliation. Despite its small size (16,000 square miles—about twice the size of New Jersey), the Netherlands boasts the planet's 23rd-largest economy. It also has one of Europe's lowest unemployment rates, relying heavily on foreign trade through its port at Rotterdam, Europe's largest.

Amsterdam, laced with grand canals and crisscrossed by bikes, has the powerhouse sights, while the nearby town of Haarlem is wonderfully *gezellig*—this much-prized Dutch virtue means having an atmosphere of relaxed coziness.

Treat yourself to new taste experiences in the Netherlands: Try pickled herring at an outdoor stand, enjoy a sweet "syrup waffle" *(stroopwafel)*, and sip an old *jenever* with a new friend. It's *gezellig*.

CUISINE SCENE AT A GLANCE

Traditional Dutch food is basic and hearty, with lots of bread, soup, fish, and meat. Lunch and dinner are served at typical American times (roughly 12:00-14:00 and 18:00-21:00). For the Dutch, dinner is the biggest meal of the day, consisting of meat or seafood with boiled potatoes, cooked vegetables, and a salad. Popular drinks are light, pilsner-type beer and gin (*jenever*).

The tastiest "Dutch" cuisine comes from the former colony of Indonesia. Seek out an *Indisch* restaurant to experience a rijsttafel ("rice table"). The spread usually includes many dishes, ranging from small sides to entrée-sized plates (some are spicy) and a big bowl of rice. A rijsttafel can be split (when restaurants allow it) and still fill two hungry tourists. Vegetarian versions are always available. For a smaller version, order *nasi rames* (several portions on one plate). Or try *bami goreng* (stir-fried noodles) or *nasi goreng* (fried rice), served with rijsttafel items.

A *café* or *eetcafé* serves simple fare in a generally comfortable but no-nonsense setting.

Pancake restaurants serve sweet and savory pancakes (*pannenkoeken*) all day. Dutch pancakes are halfway between a fluffy American-style pancake and a thin French crêpe.

Bruin cafés ("brown cafés") are named for their nicotine-stained walls, though smoking was banned indoors in 2008. They serve drinks and Dutch food in a dimly lit bar-like setting.

A *salon de thé* serves tea, coffee, sandwiches, and pastries. In contrast, a "coffeeshop" is the code word for an establishment where marijuana is sold and consumed, though most offer drinks and munchies, too.

Tipping: At restaurants, tipping is not necessary (15 percent service is usually included in the menu price), but a tip of about 5-10 percent is a nice reward for good service. In bars, rounding up to the next euro ("keep the change") is appropriate if you get table service, rather than ordering at the bar.

Budget Options: Takeout places serve fast food and sandwiches (*broodjes*). Small stands sell *friets* (french fries, served with mayonnaise), pickled herring, falafels (fried chickpea balls in pita bread), *shoarmas* (lamb in pita bread), or *döner kebabs* (a Turkish version of a *shoarma*). And it's easy to forage for picnic fare at delis and groceries.

Amsterdam

In Amsterdam, you'll enjoy good living, cozy cafés, street-corner jazz, great art, stately history, and a spirit of live and let live. The city still looks much like it did in the 1600s—the Dutch Golden Age—when it was the cradle of capitalism. Wealthy, democratic burghers built a wonderland of canals lined with trees and townhouses topped with fancy gables. Immigrants, outcasts, and political rebels were drawn here by its open-minded atmosphere, while painters such as young Rembrandt captured that atmosphere on canvas.

For centuries, the city has advocated tolerance for things other places try to forbid. Its international sea-trading port has always attracted sailors and businessmen, so it was profitable to allow them to have a little fun. In the 1960s, Amsterdam became a magnet for Europe's hippies. Since then, it's become a world capital of alternative lifestyles. This bold experiment in freedom may box your Puritan ears. Prostitution is allowed in the Red Light District, while "smartshops" sell psychedelic drugs, and marijuana is openly sold and smoked in "coffeeshops."

Take in all of the city's charms, then pause to watch the clouds blow past its stately old gables—and see the Golden Age reflected in its quiet canals.

AMSTERDAM IN 2 DAYS

Day 1: In the morning, follow my self-guided Amsterdam City Walk, leading from the train station to Leidseplein, via the Amsterdam Museum (which you could tour now) and the flower market. Stop for lunch along the walk.

From Leidseplein, take a one-hour canal boat tour (unless you'd rather save it for an evening activity).

Later in the day, tour the Anne Frank House. Reserve online (or waste an hour or two standing in line).

On any evening: Have an Indonesian rijsttafel dinner, wander through Vondelpark (rent a bike?), or stroll the eye-opening Red Light District (but not after 22:30, when it's sketchy). Visit late-night sights: The Van Gogh Museum is open late on Fridays and some Saturdays (until 21:00), and the Anne Frank Museum is open until 22:00 on many nights. Nurse a drink at a traditional "brown" café or take a canal boat ride. Get high at a coffeeshop if you want; it's legal!

Day 2: Visit these top museums—Rijksmuseum and Van Gogh—next to each other on Museumplein (it's smart

Amsterdam Neighborhoods

NORTH AMSTERDAM

EYE FILM INSTITUTE

IJ Channel

CRUISE TERMINAL

CENTRAAL STATION

WEST AMSTERDAM

Singelgracht

JORDAAN

Damrak

SEX

RED LIGHT DISTRICT

NORTHEAST AMSTERDAM

ANNE FRANK HOUSE

Dam Square

Singel

CENTRAL AMSTERDAM

MARITIME MUSEUM

Rokin

MINT TOWER

WATERLOO-PLEIN

JEWISH QUARTER

LEIDSE-PLEIN

Heren-gracht

Keizers-gracht

Prinsen-gracht

REMBRANDT-PLEIN

SOUTHEAST AMSTERDAM

ARTIS ZOO

SOUTHERN CANAL BELT

Amstel

Singelgracht

Vondelpark

VAN GOGH MUSEUM

RIJKSMUSEUM

River

SOUTHWEST AMSTERDAM

500 Meters

500 Yards

to reserve both museums online in advance). If you want to minimize crowds (which are heaviest at midday), start with the Van Gogh Museum when it opens at 9:00. Visit the Rijksmuseum after lunch (crowds begin to subside after 14:00). In between visiting these two major museums, have lunch (cafés are at the museums and nearby), hang out at lively Museumplein, tour the Stedelijk (modern art), or visit Vondelpark.

With extra time: You could easily spend another day or two in Amsterdam, visiting anything else that appeals: the Dutch Resistance Museum, Amstelkring (hidden church), Hermitage Amsterdam, the Netherlands Maritime Museum, or the street markets (Albert Cuyp and Waterlooplein, closed Sun). And you can day-trip to the cozy town of Haarlem.

ORIENTATION

Amsterdam's Centraal Station, on the north edge of the city, is your starting point, with the TI, bike rental, and trams branching out to all points. Damrak is the main north-south axis, connecting Centraal Station with Dam Square (people-watching and hangout center) and its Royal Palace. From this main street, the city spreads out like a fan, with 90 islands, hundreds of bridges, and a series of concentric canals that were laid out in the 17th century, Holland's Golden Age. Amsterdam's major sights are all within walking distance of Dam Square.

To the east of Damrak is the oldest part of the city (today's Red Light District), and to the west is the newer part, where you'll find the Anne Frank House and

AMSTERDAM AT A GLANCE

▲▲▲**Rijksmuseum** Best collection anywhere of the Dutch Masters—Rembrandt, Hals, Vermeer, and Steen—in a spectacular setting. **Hours:** Daily 9:00-17:00. See page 949.

▲▲▲**Van Gogh Museum** More than 200 paintings by the angst-ridden artist. **Hours:** Daily April-Aug 9:00-19:00, Fri until 21:00, Sat until 18:00 (April-June) and 21:00 (July-Aug); Sept-Oct 9:00-18:00, Fri until 21:00; Nov-March 9:00-17:00, Fri until 21:00. See page 954.

▲▲▲**Anne Frank House** Young Anne's hideaway during the Nazi occupation. **Hours:** Daily 9:00-22:00; Nov-March Mon-Fri 9:00-20:00, Sat until 22:00, Sun until 19:00. See page 958.

▲▲**Stedelijk Museum** The Netherlands' top modern-art museum. **Hours:** Daily 10:00-18:00, Fri until 22:00. See page 957.

▲▲**Vondelpark** City park and concert venue. See page 958.

▲▲**Amsterdam Museum** City's growth from fishing village to trading capital to today, including some Rembrandts and a playable carillon. **Hours:** Daily 10:00-17:00. See page 961.

▲▲**Amstelkring Museum** Catholic church hidden in the attic of a 17th-century merchant's house. **Hours:** Mon-Sat 10:00-17:00, Sun 13:00-17:00. See page 961.

▲▲**Red Light District** Women of the world's oldest profession on the job. See page 962.

▲▲**Netherlands Maritime Museum** Rich seafaring story of the Netherlands, told with vivid artifacts. **Hours:** Daily 9:00-17:00. See page 962.

▲▲**Hermitage Amsterdam** Russia's Czarist treasures, on loan from St. Petersburg. **Hours:** Daily 10:00-17:00. See page 963.

▲▲**Dutch Resistance Museum** History of the Dutch struggle against the Nazis. **Hours:** Tue-Fri 10:00-17:00, Sat-Mon 11:00-17:00. See page 963.

▲**Leidseplein** Lively square with cafés and street musicians, best on sunny afternoons. See page 948.

▲**Museumplein** Square with art museums, street musicians, and crafts. See page 948.

▲**Hash, Marijuana, and Hemp Museum** All the dope, from history and science to memorabilia. **Hours:** Daily 10:00-22:00. See page 962.

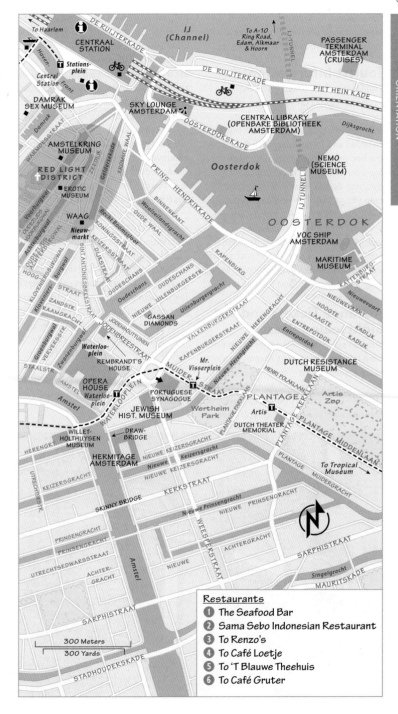

To Haarlem

DE RUIJTERKADE

CENTRAAL STATION

IJ (Channel)

To A-10 Ring Road, Edam, Alkmaar & Hoorn

IJTUNNEL

PASSENGER TERMINAL AMSTERDAM (CRUISES)

Stationsplein

Central Station Front

Haven

DE RUIJTERKADE

PIET HEIN KADE

DAMRAK SEX MUSEUM

Damrak

SKY LOUNGE AMSTERDAM

OOSTERDOKSKADE

CENTRAL LIBRARY (OPENBARE BIBLIOTHEEK AMSTERDAM)

Dijksgracht

WARMOESSTRAAT

AMSTELKRING MUSEUM

ZEEDIJK

KROMME WAAL

PRINS HENDRIKKADE

Oosterdok

NEMO (SCIENCE MUSEUM)

RED LIGHT DISTRICT

EROTIC MUSEUM

GELDERSKADE

Voorburgwal

OUDEZIJDS ACHTERBURGWAL

BINNENKANT

Waalseilandsgracht

OUDE WAAL

IJTUNNEL

WAAG

Recht Boomssloot

Nieuwmarkt

KONINGSSTRAAT

KEIZERSTRAAT

DIJKSTRAAT

OUDESCHANS

OUDESCHANS

OUDESCHANS

O O S T E R D O K

VOC SHIP AMSTERDAM

KATTENBURGSTRAAT

MARITIME MUSEUM

RAPENBURG

NIEUWE UILENBURGERSTR.

Uilenburgergracht

Uilenburgerstraat

NIEUWEVAART

HOOG-

SINT ANTONIESBREESTRAAT

KLOVENIERSBURGWAL

KLOVENIERS STRAAT

ZANDSTR.

RAAMGRACHT

HOOGTE

NIEUWEWEGVAART

LAAGTE

KADIJK

KADIJK

ENTREPOTDOK

Entrepotdok

GASSAN DIAMONDS

JODENHOUTTUINEN

VALKENBURGERSTRAAT

NIEUWE HERENGRACHT

HERENGRACHT

Groenburgwal

VERVERSSTR.

Zwanenburgwal

JODENBREESTRAAT

Waterlooplein

RAPENBURGERSTRAAT

NIEUWE HERENGRACHT

DUTCH RESISTANCE MUSEUM

STAALSTR.

AMSTEL

REMBRANDT'S HOUSE

MUIDERSTRAAT

Mr. Visserplein

HENRI POLAKLAAN

Artis Zoo

PLANTAGE KERKLAAN

OPERA HOUSE

Waterlooplein

WATERLOOPLEIN

PORTUGUESE SYNAGOGUE

Nieuwe Herengracht

PLANTAGE

Artis

PLANTAGE

JEWISH HIST. MUSEUM

Wertheim Park

PLANTAGEPARKLAAN

PLANTAGE MIDDENLAAN

DUTCH THEATER MEMORIAL

HERENGR.

WILLET-HOLTHUYSEN MUSEUM

DRAW-BRIDGE

PLANTAGE MUIDERGRACHT

To Tropical Museum

UTRECHTSESTRAAT

HERMITAGE AMSTERDAM

NIEUWE KEIZERSGRACHT

Nieuwe KEIZERSGRACHT

NIEUWE KEIZERSGRACHT

KEIZERSGRACHT

KERKSTRAAT

Nieuwe Prinsengracht

NIEUWE PRINSENGRACHT

SKINNY BRIDGE

WEESPERSTRAAT

PRINSENGRACHT

PRINSENGRACHT

Amstel

NIEUWE

ACHTERGRACHT

SARPHISTRAAT

UTRECHTSEDWARSSTRAAT

ACHTER-GRACHT

NIEUWE

WEESPERSTRAAT

Singelgracht

MAURITSKADE

SARPHISTRAAT

300 Meters

300 Yards

STADHOUDERSKADE

Restaurants

1. The Seafood Bar
2. Sama Sebo Indonesian Restaurant
3. To Renzo's
4. To Café Loetje
5. To 'T Blauwe Theehuis
6. To Café Gruter

the peaceful Jordaan neighborhood. Museums and Leidseplein nightlife cluster at the southern edge of the city center.

Tourist Information

The Dutch name for a TI is "VVV," pronounced "fay fay fay." The city's main TI, located across the street from Centraal Station, is centrally located, but it's crowded and sometimes inefficient, and the free maps are poor quality (Mon-Sat 9:00-17:00, Sun 10:00-16:00, tel. 020/702-6000). The TI sells a good city map (€2.50) and the *A-Mag* entertainment guide (€3.50). A second Centraal Station TI is in the section on the north side. While it's labeled the "I Amsterdam Store," it really is an official TI and is much less crowded (Mon-Sat 8:00-19:00 except Thu-Sat until 20:00, Sun 9:00-18:00).

Advance Tickets and Sightseeing Passes

You can avoid long ticket lines (common from late March-Oct) at Amsterdam's most popular sights—the Rijksmuseum, Van Gogh Museum, and Anne Frank House—by booking tickets in advance or getting a sightseeing pass. (If you're vis-

iting off-season, these strategies are less important, especially if you use my other crowd-beating tips.)

Advance Tickets: It's smart to buy tickets online for the three major museums through each museum's website, generally with no extra booking fee. For the Anne Frank House, online timed-entry tickets go on sale two months in advance and are released gradually over the two-month window; keep checking back. Print your ticket and bring it to the ticket-holders' line. You can also buy advance tickets at TIs (though availability isn't guaranteed).

Sightseeing Passes: For a brief visit, I'd skip all the passes (and make individual reservations at the sights instead). But if you'll be visiting many museums, a pass can save you money (and time in line).

The €60 **Museumkaart** pass covers any five museums (out of many country-wide) in 31 days, including the Rijksmuseum, Van Gogh Museum, Anne Frank House, and Amsterdam Museum. You'll save a bit, and sometimes get to bypass lines. Foreigners can only buy it in person at a covered sight, even though the confusing Dutch-only website doesn't mention this option (www.museumkaart.nl).

The widely advertised **I Amsterdam City Card** covers the Rijksmuseum, Van Gogh Museum, and Stedelijk (but not the Anne Frank House), a canal boat ride, and public transportation—and lets you skip the line at the Van Gogh Museum if you book a time slot (€59/24 hours, €74/48 hours, €87/72 hours, www.iamsterdamcard.com). The Holland Pass is not worth it.

Without Advance Tickets or a Pass: If you visit the Anne Frank House without a reservation, show up late in the day; this works better in early spring and fall than in busy summer. The Van Gogh sometimes requires timed-entry tickets for entry (check www.vangoghmuseum.com for the latest), but if they don't, go late (it's open until 21:00 Fri and summer Sat).

Rick's Tip: *For a brief visit,* **skip all the sightseeing passes and buy advance tickets online** *instead.*

Helpful Hints

Theft Alert: Tourists are considered green and rich, and the city has more than its share of hungry thieves—especially in the train station, on trams, in and near crowded museums, at places of drunkenness, and at the many hostels. Wear your money belt.

Street Smarts: When you're on foot, be extremely vigilant for silent but potentially painful bikes, electric mopeds, trams, and crotch-high bollards. Don't walk on tram tracks or pink/maroon bicycle paths. Before you step off a sidewalk, do a double- or triple-check in both directions to make sure all's clear.

Maps: Given the city's maze of streets and canals, I'd definitely get a good city map (€2.50 at Centraal Station TI). I like the *Carto Studio Centrumkaart Amsterdam* map. Amsterdam Anything's virtual "Go Where the Locals Go" city map is also worth checking out, especially if you have mobile Internet access (www.amsterdamanything.nl).

Laundry: Try **Clean Brothers Wasserij** in the Jordaan (€7 self-service, daily 8:00-20:00; €9 drop-off, ready in an hour, Mon-Fri 9:00-17:00, Sat 9:00-18:00, no drop-off Sun; Westerstraat 26, one block from Prinsengracht, tel. 020/627-9888) or **Powders,** near Leidseplein (daily 8:00-22:00, €6-10 self-service, €13 drop-off available Mon-Fri 8:00-17:00, Sat 9:00-15:00, no drop-off Sun, Kerkstraat 56, one block south of Leidsestraat, mobile 06-5741-2403).

Tours

🎧 To sightsee on your own, download my free Rick Steves Audio Europe app with **audio tours** that illuminate some of Amsterdam's top neighborhoods, including my Amsterdam City Walk (see sidebar on page 938 for details).

By Boat

▲▲TRADITIONAL CANAL BOAT TOURS

Long, low, tourist-laden boats leave continually from several docks around town for a relaxing, if uninspiring, one-hour introduction to the city (with recorded headphone commentary). Select a tour based on your convenience: your proximity to its starting point, or whether it's included with your I Amsterdam City Card.

Rick's Tip: *Canal boats leave only when full, so* **jump on a full boat to avoid waiting at the dock.**

Rederij P. Kooij is cheapest (€11, 3/hour in summer 10:00-22:00, 2/hour in winter 10:00-17:00, boats dock opposite Centraal Station, tel. 020/623-3810, www.rederijkooij.nl).

Blue Boat Company's boats depart from near Leidseplein (€18, €16 if you book online; runs daily 10:00-18:00, every half-hour March-Oct, hourly Nov-Feb 10:00-18:00; 1.25 hours, Stadhouderskade 30, tel. 020/679-1370, www.blueboat.nl). Their evening cruise includes the Red Light District (€21, €19 online, nightly at

Central Amsterdam

20:00, 1.5 hours, March–Oct also at 21:00 and 22:00, reservations required).

Gray Line offers a standard one-hour trip and a variety of longer tours from the docks opposite Centraal Station (€18, €15 if you book online; 1-hour "100 Highlights" tour, daily 2–4/hour 9:00–22:00; Prins Hendrikkade 33a, tel. 020/217-0500, www.canal.nl).

On Foot
RED LIGHT DISTRICT TOURS
If you'd be more comfortable exploring Amsterdam's most infamous neighborhood with a group, **Randy Roy's Red Light Tours** gives fun, casual, yet informative 1.5-hour walks through this fascinating and eye-popping district. Call or email to reserve (€15 includes a drink in a colorful bar at the end, nightly at 20:00, Fri and Sat also at 22:00, no tours Dec–Feb, tours meet in front of Victoria Hotel—in front of Centraal Station, mobile 06-4185-3288, www.randyroysredlighttours.com, kimberley@randyroysredlighttours.com).

WALKING TOURS
Amsterdam has many competing food tours. I enjoyed the **Eating Amsterdam** tour, which takes 6-12 people on an eight-stop, four-hour food tour of the Jordaan neighborhood. You'll sample cheese, cider, pancakes, *bitterballen,* herring, apple pie, and more. They also offer a tour that includes a short boat ride (Jordaan tour-€77, Tue–Sat at 11:00; food tour with canal boat-€101, March–Dec Tue–Sat at 10:30; managed by Thijs van Royen, tel. 020/808-3099, www.eatingamsterdamours.com).

FREE CITY WALK
New Europe Tours "employs" native, English-speaking students to give irreverent and entertaining three-hour walks. While most guides lack a local's deep understanding of Dutch culture, not to mention professional training, they're certainly high energy. This long walk covers a lot of the city with an enthusiasm for the contemporary pot-and-prostitu-

tion scene (free but tips expected, 5/day, www.neweuropetours.eu). They also offer paid tours (Red Light District-€14, daily at 19:00; coffeeshop scene-€14, daily at 15:00; Amsterdam by bike-€20, includes bike, daily at 12:00). All tours leave from the National Monument on Dam Square.

PRIVATE GUIDES
Larae Malooly, an American expat who's now thoroughly local, gives lively cultural and historic tours with a fun twist (€150/3-4 hour tour for up to 4 people, tel. 06-2516-1727, www.amsterdamsel.com, info@amsterdamsel.com).

Albert Walet is a knowledgeable local guide who enjoys personalizing tours for Americans interested in knowing his city (€70/2 hours, €120/4 hours, up to 4 people, on foot or by bike, mobile 06-2069-7882, abwalet@yahoo.com). Al also takes travelers to nearby towns, including Haarlem, Leiden, and Delft.

By Bike
GUIDED BIKE TOURS
Yellow Bike Guided Tours offers city bike tours of either two hours (€22.50, daily at 10:30, in winter at 13:30) or three hours (€27.50, daily at 13:30), which both include a 20-minute break. All tours leave from Nieuwezijds Kolk 29, three blocks

Amsterdam City Walk

from Centraal Station (reservations smart, tel. 020/620-6940, www.yellowbike.nl).

Joy Ride Bike Tours pedal through the pastoral polder land in 4.5 hours (€33, April-Sept Sat, Mon, and Thu; meet at 10:15 and depart precisely at 10:30, no kids under 13). They also offer private tours (tours offered April-Nov, €225/4 people plus €25/person after that). Helmets, rain gear, and saddlebags are provided. Private tours must be booked in advance; tours meet behind the Rijksmuseum next to the Cobra Café (mobile 06-4361-1798, www.joyridetours.nl).

AMSTERDAM CITY WALK

Take a Dutch sampler walk from one end of the old center to the other, tasting all that Amsterdam has to offer along the way: quintessentially Dutch scenes, hid-

1. Centraal Station
2. Damrak
3. Stock Exchange
4. Dam Square
5. Royal Palace
6. New Church
7. Kalverstraat
8. De Papegaai Hidden Church
9. Amsterdam Museum & Amsterdam Gallery
10. Begijnhof
11. Spui Square
12. Mint Tower
13. Flower Market
14. Koningsplein
15. Leidsestraat Canals
16. Shops
17. Leidseplein

den churches, surprising shops, thriving happy-hour hangouts, and eight centuries of history. This three-mile walk starts at Centraal Station and ends at Leidseplein, near the Rijksmuseum. Allow three hours.

❶ Centraal Station

Centraal Station sits on reclaimed land at what was once the harbor mouth. With red brick and prickly spires, the station is the first of several Neo-Gothic buildings

we'll see from the late 19th century, the era of Amsterdam's economic revival. One of the station's towers has a clock dial; the other tower's dial is a weather vane.

Let's get oriented: *nord, zuid, ost,* and *vest.* Facing the station, you're looking north. On the other side of the station is the IJ (pronounced "eye"), the body of water that gives Amsterdam access to the open sea.

Now turn your back to the station and face the city, looking south. The city

The Neo-Gothic central train station borders the Old Town.

spreads out before you like a fan, in a series of concentric canals. Ahead of you stretches the street called Damrak, which leads—like a red carpet for guests entering Amsterdam—to Dam Square a half-mile away. That's where we're headed.

To the left of Damrak is the city's old (*oude*) town. More recently, that historic neighborhood has become the Red Light District. Towering above the old part of town is St. Nicholas Church. It was built in the 1880s, when Catholics—after about three centuries of oppression—were finally free to worship in public. To your far left is the DoubleTree by Hilton Hotel, with the city's best viewpoint.

Rick's Tip: Although sea-level Amsterdam is notoriously horizontal, you can get the big picture at the rooftop Sky Lounge Amsterdam, on the 11th floor of the DoubleTree by Hilton Hotel (daily until very late, 5-minute walk east of train station).

To the right of Damrak is the new (*nieuwe*) part of town, where you'll find the Anne Frank House and the peaceful Jordaan neighborhood.

On your far right, in front of Ibis Hotel, is a huge, multistory parking garage— for bikes only. Biking in Holland is the way to go—the land is flat, distances are short, and there are designated bike paths everywhere. The bike parking garage is completely free, courtesy of the government, and intended to encourage this green and ultra-efficient mode of transportation.

• *With your back to the station, walk to the head of Damrak. Be careful crossing the street—be aware of trams, bikes, and cars. Keep going south straight along the right side of the street, following the crowds on...*

❷ Damrak

This street was once a riverbed. It's where the Amstel River flowed north into the IJ, which led to a vast inlet of the North Sea called the Zuiderzee. It's this unique geography that turned Amsterdam into a center of trade. Boats could sail up the Amstel into the interior of Europe, or out to the North Sea, to reach the rest of the world.

As you stroll along Damrak, look left. There's a marina, lined with old brick buildings. Though they aren't terribly

Souvenir Scene

Stock Exchange

historic, the scene still captures a bit of Golden Age Amsterdam. Think of it: Back in the 1600s, this area was the harbor, and those buildings warehoused exotic goods from all over the world.

Today you'll pass a veritable gauntlet of touristy shops. These seem to cover every Dutch cliché. You'll see wooden shoes, which the Dutch used to wear to get around easily in the marshy soil, and all manner of tulips; the real ones come from Holland's famed fresh-flower industry. Heineken fridge magnets advertise one of the world's most popular pilsner beers. There are wheels of cheese, marijuana-leaf hats, team jerseys for the Ajax football (soccer) club, and memorabilia with the city's "XXX" logo. You'll likely hear a hand-cranked barrel organ and see windmill-shaped saltshakers. And everything seems to be available in bright orange—the official color of the Dutch royal family.

At the **Damrak Sex Museum** at Damrak 18, you'll find the city's most notorious commodity on display. As a port town catering to sailors and businessmen away from home, Amsterdam has always accommodated the sex trade.

Continue up Damrak (noting the **canal boats** on your right) for more touristy delectables. You'll also pass places selling the popular local fast food, *Vlaamse frites* (Flemish fries). The stand at Damrak 41 is a favorite, where plenty of locals stop to dip their fries in mayonnaise (not ketchup). As you pass Damrak's

many restaurants, you'll see many offering international cuisine. Rijsttafel, a sampler of assorted Indonesian dishes, is especially popular, thanks to the days when the Dutch East Indies were a colony.
• *The long brick building with the square clock tower, along the left side of Damrak, is the...*

❸ Stock Exchange (Beurs van Berlage)

This impressive structure, a symbol of the city's long tradition as a trading town, was built with nine million bricks. Like so many buildings in this once-marshy city, it was constructed on a foundation of pilings—some 5,000 tree trunks hammered vertically into the soil. When the Beurs opened in 1903, it was one of the world's first modernist buildings, with a geometric, minimal, no-frills style. Emphasizing function over looks, it helped set the architectural tone for many 20th-century buildings.

Make your way to the end of the long, century-old building. Amsterdammers have gathered in this neighborhood to trade since medieval times. Back then, "trading stock" meant buying and selling any kind of goods that could be loaded and unloaded onto a boat—goats, chickens, or kegs of beer. Over time, they began exchanging slips of paper, or "futures," rather than actual goods. Traders needed moneychangers, who needed bankers, who made money by lending money. By the 1600s, Amsterdam had become one of the world's first great capitalist cities, loaning money to free-spending kings, dukes, and bishops.

• *Continue south along the busy boulevard until it opens into Dam Square. Make your way—carefully—across the street to the cobblestone pavement. Stand in the middle of the square and take it all in.*

❹ Dam Square

The city got its start right here in about the year 1250, when fishermen in this marshy delta settled along the built-up banks of the Amstel River. They built a *damme,* blocking the Amstel River, and creating a small village called "Amstel-damme." To the north was the *damrak* (meaning "outer harbor"), a waterway that eventually led to the sea. That's the street we just walked. To the south was the *rokin* ("inner harbor"), for river traffic—and nowadays also a main street. With access to the sea, fishermen were soon trading with German riverboats traveling downstream and with seafaring boats from Stockholm, Hamburg, and London. Land trade routes converged here as well, and a customs house stood in this spot. Dam Square was the center of it all.

Today, Dam Square is still the center of Dutch life, at least symbolically. The Royal Palace and major department stores face the square. Mimes, jugglers, and human statues mingle with locals and tourists. As Holland's most recognizable place, Dam Square is where political demonstrations begin and end.

Pan the square clockwise, starting with the Royal Palace—the large domed building on the west side. To its right stands the New Church (Nieuwe Kerk); it's located on the pedestrian-only shopping street called Nieuwendijk, which runs parallel to Damrak and stretches all the way to Centraal Station. Panning past Damrak, see the proud old De Bijenkorf ("The Beehive") department store.

Farther right, the Grand Hotel Krasnapolsky has a lovely circa-1900 glass-roofed "winter garden." The white obelisk is the National Monument, honoring WWII casualties. A few blocks behind the hotel is the edge of the Red Light District. To the right of the hotel stretches the street called the Nes, lined with some of Amsterdam's edgy live-theater venues. Panning farther right, find Rokin street—Damrak's southern counterpart, continuing past the square. Next, just to the right of the touristy Madame Tussauds, is Kalverstraat, a busy pedestrian-only shoppers mall (look for *Rabobank* sign).

Dam Square is the historic heart of Amsterdam.

❺ Royal Palace (Koninklijk Huis)

Despite the name, this is really the former City Hall—and Amsterdam is one of the cradles of modern democracy. In medieval times, this was where the city council and mayor met. In about 1650, the old medieval Town Hall was replaced with this one. Its style is appropriately Classical, recalling the democratic Greeks. The triangular pediment features denizens of the sea cavorting with Neptune and his gilded copper trident—all appropriate imagery for sea-trading Amsterdam. The small balcony (just above the entry doors) is where city leaders have long appeared for major speeches, pronouncements, executions, and (these days) for newly married royalty to blow kisses to the crowds. Today, the palace remains one of the four official residences of King Willem-Alexander.

• *A few paces away, to the right as you're facing the Royal Palace, is the...*

❻ New Church (Nieuwe Kerk)

Though called the "New" Church, this building is actually 600 years old—a mere 100 years newer than the "Old" Church in the Red Light District. The sundial above the entrance once served as the city's official timepiece. While it's pricey to enter the church (which offers little besides the temporary exhibits), cheapskates can see much of it for free. Enter through the "Museumshop" door to the left of the main entrance, then climb the stairs to a balcony with a small free museum and great views of the nave.

Take in the church's main highlights. At the far left end is an organ from 1655, still played for midday concerts. Opposite the entrance, a stained-glass window shows Count William IV giving the city its "XXX" coat of arms. And the window over the entrance portrays the inauguration of Queen Wilhelmina (1880-1962), who became the steadfast center of the Dutch resistance during World War II. The choir, once used by the monks, was, after the Reformation, turned into a mausoleum for a great Dutch admiral.

Leave the shop via the main church entrance. Back outside, look at the **monument** standing tall in the middle of Dam Square, built in 1956 as a WWII memorial. The Nazis occupied Holland from 1940 to 1945; in those years they deported some 60,000 Jewish Amsterdammers, driving many—including young Anne Frank and her family—into hiding. Near the end of the war, the "Hunger Winter" of 1944-1945 killed thousands of Dutch and forced many to survive on little more than

The Royal Palace got its start as Amsterdam's City Hall.

tulip bulbs. The national monument both remembers the suffering of that grim time and offers hope for peace.

• *From Dam Square, head south (at the Rabobank sign) on* ❼ **Kalverstraat.** *This strictly pedestrian-only strip has been a traditional shopping street for centuries. But today it's notorious among locals as a noisy, soulless string of chain stores.*

*For smaller and more elegant stores, try the adjacent district called De Negen Straatjes (**"The Nine Little Streets"**). About four blocks west of Kalverstraat, it's where 200 or so shops and cafés mingle along tranquil canals.*

About 100 yards along, keep a sharp eye out for the next sight: It's on the right, just before and across from the McDonald's, at #58. Now pop into...

❽ *De Papegaai Hidden Church* (Petrus en Paulus Kerk)

This Catholic church—with a simple white interior, carved wood, and Stations of the Cross paintings—is an oasis of peace amid crass 21st-century commercialism. It's not exactly a hidden church

(after all, you've found it), but it keeps a low profile. That's because it dates from an era when Catholics in Amsterdam were forced to worship in secret. While technically illegal, Catholics could worship so long as they practiced in humble, unadvertised places, like this church. The church gets its nickname from a parrot (*papegaai*) carved over the entrance of the house that formerly stood on this site. Now, a stuffed parrot hangs in the nave to remember that original *papegaai*.

• *Return to Kalverstraat and continue south for about 100 yards. At #92, where Kalverstraat crosses Wijde Kapel Steeg, look to the right at an archway that leads to the entrance and courtyard of the Amsterdam Museum.*

❾ *Amsterdam Museum and Amsterdam Gallery*

Pause at the entrance to the museum complex to view the archway. On the slumping arch is Amsterdam's coat of arms—a red shield with three Xs and a crown. The X-shaped crosses represent the crucifixion of St. Andrew, the patron saint of fishermen. They also represent the

New Church

WWII obelisk-memorial on Dam Square

three virtues of heroism, determination, and mercy—symbolism that was declared by the queen after the Dutch experience in World War II. (Before that, they likely symbolized the three great medieval threats: fire, flood, and plague.) The crown dates from 1489, when Maximilian I—a Habsburg emperor—also ruled the Low Countries. He paid off a big loan with help from Amsterdam's city bankers and, as thanks for the cash, gave the city permission to use his prestigious trademark, the Habsburg crown, atop its shield.

The courtyard leads to the best city history museum in town, the **Amsterdam Museum** (described in "Sights in Amsterdam," later). Next to the museum's entrance is a free, glassed-in passageway lined with paintings. If it's closed, you'll need to backtrack to Kalverstraat to continue our walk (continue south, then turn right on Begijnensteeg, then look for the gate leading to the Begijnhof). Otherwise, step into the **Amsterdam Gallery** (Schuttersgalerij).

This hall features group portraits of Amsterdam's citizens from the Golden Age to modern times. Giant statues of Goliath and a knee-high David (from 1650) watch over the whole thing. Civic Guard paintings from the 1600s (featuring men and their weapons) established a tradition of group portraits that continues today. Stroll around and gaze into the eyes of the hardworking men and women who made tiny Holland so prosperous and powerful.

Don't miss the colorful patchwork carpet. Dutch society has long been a melting pot society and this—with a patch representing each country from where Dutch immigrants originated—celebrates today's multicultural reality. (A chart locates the various countries.)

• *The gallery offers a shortcut to our next stop, a hidden and peaceful little courtyard. To get there, exit out the far end of the Amsterdam Gallery. Once in the light of day, continue ahead one block farther south and find the humble gate on the right, which leads to the...*

❿ *Begijnhof*

This quiet courtyard, lined with houses around a church, has sheltered women since 1346 (and is worth ▲). For centuries this was the home of a community of Beguines—pious and simple women who removed themselves from the world at large to dedicate their lives to God. When it was first established, it literally was a "woman's island"—a circle of houses facing a peaceful courtyard, surrounded by water. As you enter, keep in mind that this spot isn't just a tourist attraction; it's also a place where people live. Be considerate.

Begin your visit at the **statue** of one of these charitable sisters, just beyond the church. The Beguines' ranks swelled during the Crusades, when so many men took off, never to return, leaving society with an abundance of single women. Later, women widowed by the hazards of overseas trade lived out their days as

Kalverstraat

Dove relief at the Amsterdam Museum

Begijnhof courtyard

Mint Tower

Beguines. They spent their days deep in prayer and busy with daily tasks—spinning wool, making lace, teaching, and caring for the sick.

Now turn to the brick-faced **English Reformed church** (Engelse Kerk). The church was built in 1420 to serve the Beguine community. But then, in 1578, Catholicism was outlawed, and the Dutch Reformed Church took over many Catholic monasteries. Still, the Begijnhof survived; in 1607, this church became Anglican. The church served as a refuge for English traders and religious separatists fleeing persecution in England, including the Pilgrims, who prayed here before boarding the Mayflower.

A **Catholic church** faces the English Reformed Church. Because Catholics were being persecuted when it was built, this had to be a low-profile, "hidden" church—notice the painted-out windows on the second and third floors. This church served Amsterdam's oppressed 17th-century Catholics, who refused to worship as Protestants.

The last Beguine died in 1971, but this Begijnhof still thrives, providing subsidized housing to about 100 single women (mostly Catholic seniors). The statue of the Beguine faces a black **wooden house,** at #34. This structure dates from 1528, and is the city's oldest. Originally, the whole city consisted of wooden houses like this one. They were eventually replaced with brick houses, to minimize the fire danger of so many homes packed together.

• *Near the wooden house, find a little corridor leading you back into the modern world. Head up a few steps to emerge into the lively...*

⑪ *Spui Square*

Lined with cafés and bars, this square is one of the city's more popular spots for nightlife and sunny afternoon people-watching. Its name, Spui (rhymes with "now" and means "spew"), recalls the days when water was moved over dikes to keep the place dry. Head two blocks to the left, crossing busy Kalverstraat, to the bustling street called the **Rokin.** A small black statue of Queen Wilhelmina on the Rokin shows her daintily riding sidesaddle. Remember that in real life, she was the iron-willed inspiration for the Dutch resistance against the Nazis.

Continue south on Kalverstraat. Just before the end of this shopping boulevard, on the right, you'll see modern **Kalvertoren** shopping mall.

Rick's Tip: For a **city view** *(rare in flat Amsterdam), enter the Kalvertoren mall and take the slanting glass elevator to the recommended top-floor* **Blue Amsterdam Restaurant** *for a coffee or light lunch.*

• *At the center of the next square stands the...*

⑫ Mint Tower (Munttoren)

This tower marked the limit of the medieval walled city and served as one of its original gates. In the Middle Ages, the city walls were girdled by a moat—the Singel canal. Until about 1500, the area beyond here was nothing but marshy fields and a few farms on reclaimed land. The Mint Tower's steeple was added later—in the year 1620, as you can see written below the clock face. Today, the tower is a favorite within Amsterdam's marijuana culture. Stoners love to take a photo of the clock and its 1620 sign at exactly 4:20 p.m.—the traditional time to quit work and light one up. (On the 24-hour clock, 4:20 p.m. is 16:20...Du-u-u-ude!)

• *Continue past the Mint Tower, first walking a few yards south along busy Vijzelstraat (keep an eye out for trams). Then turn right and walk west along the south bank of the Singel canal. It's lined with the greenhouse shops of the...*

⑬ Flower Market (Bloemenmarkt)

Browse your way along while heading for the end of the block. The Netherlands is by far the largest flower exporter in Europe, and a major flower power worldwide. If you're looking for a souvenir, note that certain seeds are marked as OK to bring back through customs into the US (the marijuana starter-kit-in-a-can is probably...not).

• *The long Flower Market ends at the next bridge, where you'll see a square named...*

Flower Market

⑭ Koningsplein

This pleasant square, with a popular outdoor *heringhandel* (herring shop), is a great place to choke down a raw herring—a fish that has a special place in every Dutch heart. After all, herring was the commodity that first put Amsterdam on the trading map. Locals eat it chopped up with onions and pickles, using the Dutch-flag toothpick as a utensil.

• *Turn left, heading straight south to Leidseplein along Koningsplein, which changes its name to Leidsestraat.*

⑮ Leidsestraat Canals and ⑯ Shops

As you walk along, you'll reach Herengracht, the first of several grand canals. Look left down Herengracht to see the so-called **Golden Curve** of the canal. It's lined with townhouses sporting especially nice gables. Amsterdam has many different types of gable—bell-shaped, step-shaped, and so on. This stretch is best known for its "cornice" gables (straight across); these topped the Classical-looking facades belonging to rich merchants—the *heren*.

Cross over the next canal (Keizersgracht) and find the little **smartshop** on the right-hand corner (at Keisersgracht 508). While "smartshops" like this one are all just as above-board as any other in the city, they sell drugs—some of them quite strong, most of them illegal back home, and not all of them harmless. But since all these products are found in nature, the Dutch government considers them legal. Check out the window displays, or go on in and browse.

Just over the next bridge, where Leidsestraat crosses Prinsengracht, you'll find the **Delft Blue Shop** (to the right, at Prinsengracht 440), which sells the distinctive ceramics known as Delftware. In the early 1600s, Dutch traders brought home blue-and-white porcelain from China, which became so popular that Dutch potters scrambled to come up with their own version.

Leidseplein bustles with action day and night.

Bulldog Café and Coffeeshop

• *Follow Leidsestraat down to the big, busy square, called...*

⑰ Leidseplein

This is Amsterdam's liveliest square, worth ▲, filled with outdoor tables under trees; ringed with cafés, theaters, and nightclubs; bustling with tourists, diners, trams, mimes, and fire eaters. Leidseplein's south side is bordered by a gray Neoclassical building that houses a huge Apple Store. Nearby is the city's main serious theater, the **Stadsschouwburg.** The theater company dates back to the 17th-century Golden Age, and the present building is from 1890. Does the building look familiar, with its red brick and fanciful turrets? This building, Centraal Station, and the Rijksmuseum were all built by the same architect, Pierre Cuypers, during the city's late-19th-century revival.

The neighborhood beyond Burger King is Amsterdam's **"Restaurant Row,"** featuring countless Thai, Brazilian, Indian, Italian, Indonesian—and even a few Dutch—eateries. Next, on the east end of Leidseplein, is the flagship **Bulldog Café and Coffeeshop.** (Notice the sign above the door: It once housed the police bureau.) A small green-and-white decal on the window indicates that it's a city-licensed "coffeeshop," where marijuana is sold and smoked legally.

• *Our walk is over. Vondelpark, the Rijksmuseum, and the Van Gogh Museum are one*

stop away on tram #2 or #5. To return to Centraal Station (or to nearly anyplace along this walk), catch tram #1, #2, or #5 from Leidseplein.

SIGHTS

One of Amsterdam's delights is that it has perhaps more small specialty museums than any other city its size. From houseboats to sex, from marijuana to Old Masters, you can find a museum to suit your interests.

For tips on how to save time otherwise spent in the long ticket-buying lines of the big three museums—the Anne Frank House, Van Gogh Museum, and Rijksmuseum—see "Advance Tickets and Sightseeing Passes" on page 934. The following sights are arranged by neighborhood for handy sightseeing.

Museumplein
▲MUSEUMPLEIN

Bordered by the Rijks, Van Gogh, and Stedelijk museums, and the Concertgebouw (classical music hall), this park like square is interesting even to art haters. Amsterdam's best acoustics are found underneath the Rijksmuseum, where street musicians perform everything from chamber music to Mongolian throat singing. Mimes, human statues, and crafts booths dot the square. Skateboarders careen across a concrete tube, while locals enjoy a park bench or a coffee at the Cobra Café (playground nearby). In the gardens (tuinen) by the Rijksmuseum, kids frolic through a mysterious fountain that lets them emerge without getting wet. And the city's marketing brilliant—and climbable—"I Amsterdam" letters await the world's selfies.

▲▲▲RIJKSMUSEUM

Built to house the nation's great art, the Rijksmuseum (RIKES-moo-zay-oom, "Rijks" rhymes with "bikes") owns several thousand paintings, including an incom-parable collection of 17th-century Dutch Masters: Rembrandt, Vermeer, Hals, and Steen. Its vast collection also includes interesting artifacts—such as furniture—that help bring the Golden Age to life.

The 17th century saw the Netherlands at the pinnacle of its power. The Dutch had won their independence from Spain, trade and shipping boomed, wealth poured in, the people were understandably proud, and the arts flourished. This era was later dubbed the Dutch Golden Age. With no church

The Rijksmuseum's collections pay homage to Dutch art and history.

bigwigs or royalty around to commission big canvases in the Protestant Dutch Republic, artists had to find different patrons—and they discovered the upper-middle-class businessmen who fueled Holland's capitalist economy. Artists painted their portraits and decorated their homes with pretty still lifes and unpreachy, slice-of-life art.

This delightful museum—recently much improved after a long renovation—offers one of the most exciting and enjoyable art experiences in Europe. As if in homage to Dutch art and history, the Rijksmuseum lets you linger over a vast array of objects and paintings, appreciating the beauty of everyday things.

Cost and Hours: €17.50; daily 9:00-17:00, tram #2 or #5 from Centraal Station to Rijksmuseum stop. The entrance is off the passageway that tunnels right through the center of the building.

Avoiding Crowds/Lines: The museum is most crowded on weekends and holidays, and there's always a midday crush between 11:00 and 14:00. Plan your visit for either first thing in the morning or later in the day (it's least crowded after 15:00). With a Museumkaart or advance ticket, use the separate entrance; with an I Amsterdam City Card, join the queue.

Information: The helpful information desk in the lower-level Atrium has free maps. Info tel. 020/674-7047, www.rijksmuseum.nl.

Tours: Guided tours are often offered at 11:00, 13:00, and 15:00 (€5). A multimedia videoguide (€5) offers both a 45-minute highlights tour and a more in-depth tour. Use this chapter to hit the highlights, then (if you choose) explore the rest of the collection with the videoguide.

Eating: The Rijksmuseum Café, in the Atrium, is outside the ticket entry, so you don't need a museum ticket to eat here. On the south side of the building, there's a restaurant in the Philips Wing and a pleasant coffee-and-pastry café in the garden to the right. Nearby on Museumplein, you'll find the Cobra Café, a number of takeout stands, and (at the far end, near the Stedelijk Museum), an

Albert Heijn grocery. Museumplein and nearby Vondelpark are both perfect for a picnic.

⮕ SELF-GUIDED TOUR

Dutch art is meant to be enjoyed, not studied. It's straightforward, meat-and-potatoes art for the common man. The Dutch love the beauty of mundane things painted realistically and with exquisite detail. So set your cerebral cortex on "low" and let this art pass straight from the eyes to the heart, with minimal detours.

Follow the crowds up the stairway to the top (second) floor, where you emerge into the **Great Hall.** With its stained-glass windows, vaulted ceiling, and murals of Golden Age explorers, it feels like a cathedral to Holland's middle-class merchants. Gaze down the long adjoining hall to the far end, with the "altarpiece" of this cathedral—Rembrandt's *The Night Watch.*

• *Follow the flow of the crowds toward it, into the...*

Gallery of Honor: This grand space was purpose-built to hold the Greatest Hits of the Golden Age by the era's biggest rock stars: Hals, Vermeer, Steen, and Rembrandt.

• *In the first alcove to the left is the work of...*

Frans Hals (c. 1582-1666): Hals was the premier Golden Age portrait painter. Merchants hired him the way we'd hire a wedding photographer. With a few quick strokes, Hals captured not only the features, but also the personality. In *A Militiaman Holding a Berkemeyer,* a.k.a. *The Merry Drinker* (c. 1628-1630), you're greeted by a jovial man in a black hat, capturing the earthy, exuberant spirit of the Dutch Golden Age. Notice the details—the happy red face of the man offering us a berkemeyer drinking glass, the sparkle in his eyes, the lacy collar, the decorative belt buckle, and so on. He often painted common people, fishermen, and barflies such as this one. Hals used a stop-action technique, freezing the man in mid-gesture, with the rough brushwork

🅐 *Hals,* The Merry Drinker
🅑 *Vermeer,* The Milkmaid
🅒 *Steen,* The Merry Family

creating a blur that suggests the man is still moving.

• *A little farther along are the small-scale canvases of...*

Johannes Vermeer (1632-1675): Vermeer is the master of tranquility and stillness. He creates a clear and silent pool that is a world in itself. Most of his canvases show interiors of Dutch homes, where Dutch women engage in everyday activities, lit by a side window.

The Rijksmuseum has the best collection of Vermeers in the world—four of them. (There are only some 34 in captivity.) But each is a small jewel worth lingering over. Vermeer's *The Milkmaid* (c. 1660) brings out the beauty in everyday things. The subject is ordinary—a kitchen maid—but you could look for hours at the tiny details and rich color tones. These are everyday objects, but they glow in a diffused light: the crunchy crust, the hanging basket, even the rusty nail in the wall with its tiny shadow.

In paintings such as *Woman Reading a Letter* (c. 1663), notice how Vermeer's placid scenes often have an air of mystery. The woman is reading a letter. From a lover? A father on a two-year business trip to the East Indies? Not even taking time to sit down, she reads intently, with parted lips and a bowed head. It must be important. Again, Vermeer has framed a moment of everyday life. But within this small world are hints of a wider, wilder world—the light coming from the left is obviously from a large window, giving us a whiff of the life going on outside.

• *In an alcove nearby are some rollicking paintings by...*

Jan Steen (c. 1625-1679, pronounced "yahn stain"): Steen was the Norman Rockwell of his day, painting humorous scenes from the lives of the lower classes. As a tavern owner, he observed society firsthand.

Find the painting *The Merry Family* (1668). This family is eating, drinking, and singing like there's no tomorrow. The broken eggshells and scattered cookware

Rembrandt, The Night Watch

symbolize waste and extravagance. The neglected proverb tacked to the fireplace reminds us that children will follow in the footsteps of their parents. Dutch Golden Age families were notoriously lenient with their kids. Even today, the Dutch describe a rowdy family as a "Jan Steen household."

In *Adolf and Catharina Croeser*, a.k.a. *The Burgomaster of Delft and His Daughter* (1655), a well-dressed burgher sits on his front porch, when a poor woman and child approach to beg, putting him squarely between the horns of a moral dilemma. On the one hand, we see his rich home, well-dressed daughter, and a vase of flowers—a symbol that his money came from morally suspect capitalism. On the other hand, there are his poor fellow citizens and the church steeple, reminding him of his Christian duty.

• *You're getting closer to the iconic* Night Watch, *but first you'll find other works by...*

Rembrandt van Rijn (1606-1669): Rembrandt was the greatest of all Dutch painters. Whereas most painters specialized in one field—portraits, landscapes, still lifes—Rembrandt excelled in them all.

The son of a Leiden miller who owned a waterwheel on the Rhine ("van Rijn"), Rembrandt took Amsterdam by storm with his famous painting *The Anatomy Lesson of Dr. Nicolaes Tulp* (1632). Commissions poured in, and he was soon wealthy and married. Holland's war with England (1652-1654) devastated the art market, and Rembrandt's free-spending ways forced him to declare bankruptcy— the ultimate humiliation in success-oriented Amsterdam. His bitter losses added a new wisdom to his work. In his last years, his greatest works were his self-portraits, showing a tired, wrinkled man stoically enduring life's misfortunes. His death effectively marked the end of the Dutch Golden Age.

At the far end of the Gallery of Honor is the museum's star masterpiece—*The Night Watch*, a.k.a. *The Militia Company of Captain Frans Banninck Cocq* (1642). This is Rembrandt's most famous—though not necessarily greatest—painting. Created in 1642, when he was 36, it was one of his most important commissions: a group portrait of a company of Amsterdam's Civic Guards to hang in their meeting hall. It's an action shot. With flags waving and drums beating, the guardsmen (who, by the 1640s, were really only an honorary militia of rich bigwigs) spill onto the street from under an arch in the back. These guardsmen on the move epitomize the proud, independent, upwardly mobile Dutch.

Why is *The Night Watch* so famous? Compare it with group portraits nearby, where every face is visible and everyone is well-lit, flat, and flashbulb-perfect. By contrast, Rembrandt rousted the Civic Guards off their fat duffs. By adding movement and depth to an otherwise static scene, he took posers and turned them into warriors. He turned a simple portrait into great art.

Now backtrack a few steps to the Gallery of Honor's last alcove to find Rembrandt's *Self-Portrait as the Apostle Paul* (1661). Rembrandt's many self-portraits show us the evolution of a great painter's style, as well as the progress of a genius's life. For Rembrandt, the two

Rembrandt, Self-Portrait

were intertwined. With a lined forehead, a bulbous nose, and messy hair, he peers out from under several coats of glazing, holding old, wrinkled pages. His look is...skeptical? Weary? Resigned to life's misfortunes? Or amused?

This man has seen it all—success, love, money, fatherhood, loss, poverty, death. He took these experiences and wove them into his art. Rembrandt died poor and misunderstood, but he remained very much his own man to the end.

The Rest of the Rijks: The Rijks is dedicated to detailing Dutch history from 1200 until the present, with upward of 8,000 works on display. There's everything from an airplane (third floor, in the 20th-century exhibit) to women's fashion and Delftware (lower level). The Asian Art Pavilion shows off 365 objects from the East Indies—a former Dutch colony— as well as items from India, Japan, Korea, and China. (The bronze Dancing Shiva, in Room 1 of the pavilion, is considered one of the best in the world.)

You might want to seek out the **Van Gogh self-portrait** in Room 1.18 (from the stained-glass Great Hall, go back downstairs the way you came to floor 1 and turn left). The **Philips Wing** hosts temporary exhibits upstairs (with themes that complement the Rijksmuseum's strengths) and a rotating photography collection downstairs (admission covered by Rijksmuseum ticket).

▲▲▲VAN GOGH MUSEUM

Near the Rijksmuseum, this remarkable museum features works by the troubled Dutch artist whose art seemed to mirror his life. Vincent, who killed himself in 1890 at age 37, is best known for sunny, Impressionist canvases that vibrate and pulse with vitality. The museum's 200 paintings—which offer a virtual stroll through the artist's work and life—were owned by Theo, Vincent's younger, art-dealer brother. Highlights include *Sunflowers, The Bedroom, The Potato Eaters,* and many brooding self-portraits. The third floor

shows works that influenced Vincent, from Monet and Pissarro to Gauguin, Cézanne, and Toulouse-Lautrec. The worthwhile audioguide includes insightful commentaries and quotes from Vincent himself. Temporary exhibits fill the new wing, down the escalator from the ground-floor lobby.

Cost and Hours: €18; daily April-Aug 9:00-19:00, Fri until 21:00, and Sat until 18:00 (April-June) and 21:00 (July-Aug); Sept-Oct 9:00-18:00, Fri until 21:00; Nov-March 9:00-17:00, Fri until 21:00; Paulus Potterstraat 7, tram #2 or #5 from Centraal Station to Van Baerlestraat or Rijksmuseum stop.

Avoiding Lines: Buy timed-entry tickets online at www.vangoghmuseum. com; tickets go on sale about four months in advance. At times, you can get in only with tickets reserved online; check their website for the latest. If you have a Museumkaart, you'll queue up at a short line. With an I Amsterdam City Card, you can skip the line if you book a time slot online in advance.

Information: Tel. 020/570-5200, www. vangoghmuseum.nl.

Tours: The €5 multimedia guide gives insightful commentaries about Van Gogh's paintings and his technique, along with related quotations from Vincent himself. There's also a kids' audioguide (€3).

Cuisine Art: Try the on-site cafeteria.

◗ SELF-GUIDED TOUR

The collection is laid out roughly chronologically, through the changes in Vincent van Gogh's life (1853-1890). But you'll need to be flexible—the paintings are spread over three floors, and every few months there's a different array of paintings from the museum's large collection. On level 0, self-portraits introduce you to the artist. Level 1 has his early paintings; level 2 focuses on the man and his contemporaries; and level 3 has his final works. The paintings span five periods of Van Gogh's life—spent in the Netherlands, Paris, Arles, St-Rémy, and Auvers-sur-Oise.

You could see Vincent van Gogh's canvases as a series of suicide notes—or as the record of a life full of beauty... perhaps too full of beauty. He attacked life with a passion, experiencing highs and lows more intensely than the average person. The beauty of the world overwhelmed him; its ugliness struck him as only another dimension of beauty. He tried to absorb the full spectrum of experience, good and bad, and channel it onto a canvas. The frustration of this overwhelming task drove him to madness. If all this is a bit overstated—and I guess it is—it's an attempt to show the emotional impact that Van Gogh's works have had on many people, me included.

• *Pass through security and the ticket booth into the glass-pavilion reception hall. Here you'll find an info desk (pick up a free floor plan), bag check, multimedia-guide rental, and WCs. There's also a bookstore (with several good, basic "Vincent" guidebooks and lots of posters with mailing tubes) and an excellent temporary exhibit gallery (generally free).*

Ascend to level 1. Work clockwise around the floor and follow the stages of Vincent's life.

The Netherlands (1880-1885): Start with his stark, dark early work. These dark, gray canvases show us the hard, plain existence of the people and town of Nuenen, in the rural southern Netherlands. The style is crude—Van Gogh couldn't draw very well and would never become a great technician. The paint is laid on thick, as though painted with Nuenen mud. The main subject is almost always dead center, with little or no background, so there's a claustrophobic feeling. We are unable to see anything but the immediate surroundings. For example, *The Potato Eaters* (1885), is set in a dark, cramped room lit only by a dim lamp, where poor workers help themselves to a steaming plate of potatoes. They've earned it. Their hands are gnarly, their faces kind. Vincent deliberately wanted the canvas to be potato-colored.

• *Continue to the room with work he did in...*

Paris (March 1886-Feb 1888): After his father's death, Vincent moved from rural, religious, poor Holland to the City of Light. There his younger brother Theo, an art dealer, provided the financial and emotional support that allowed Vincent to spend the rest of his short life painting.

The sun begins to break through, lighting up everything he paints. His canvases are more colorful and the landscapes more spacious, with plenty of open sky, giving a feeling of exhilaration after the closed, dark world of Nuenen. In the cafés and bars of Paris' bohemian Montmartre district, Vincent met the revolutionary Impressionists. First, Vincent copied from the Impressionist masters. He painted garden scenes like Claude Monet, café snapshots like Edgar Degas, "block prints" like the Japanese masters, and self-portraits like...nobody else.

In his *Self-Portrait as a Painter* (1887-1888), the budding young artist proudly displays his new palette full of bright new

Van Gogh Museum

Van Gogh, The Potato Eaters

colors, trying his hand at the Impressionist technique of building a scene using dabs of different-colored paint. In *Red Cabbages and Onions* (1887), Vincent quickly developed his own style: thicker paint; broad, swirling brushstrokes; and brighter, clashing colors that make even inanimate objects seem to pulsate with life. Despite his new sociability, Vincent never quite fit in with his Impressionist friends. He wanted peace and quiet, a place where he could throw himself into his work completely. He headed for the sunny south of France.

• *Travel to the next room to reach...*

Arles (Feb 1888-May 1889): After the dreary Paris winter, the colors of springtime overwhelmed Vincent. The blossoming trees and colorful fields inspired him to paint canvas after canvas, drenched in sunlight. One fine example is *The Yellow House,* a.k.a. *The Street* (1888). Vincent rented this house with the green shutters. (He ate at the pink café next door.) Look at that blue sky! He painted in a frenzy, working feverishly to try and take it all in. His unique style evolved beyond Impressionism—thicker paint, stronger outlines, brighter colors (often applied right from the paint tube), and swirling brushwork that makes inanimate objects pulse and vibrate with life.

He invited his friend Paul Gauguin to join him, envisioning a sort of artists' colony in Arles. He spent months preparing a room upstairs for Gauguin's arrival. He painted *Sunflowers* (1889) to brighten up the place. At first, Gauguin and Vincent got along great. But then things went sour. They clashed over art, life, and their prickly personalities. On Christmas Eve 1888, Vincent went ballistic. Enraged during an alcohol-fueled argument, he pulled out a razor and waved it in Gauguin's face. Gauguin took the hint and quickly left town. Vincent was horrified at himself. In a fit of remorse and madness, he mutilated his own ear and presented it to a prostitute.

The people of Arles realized they had a madman on their hands. A doctor diagnosed "acute mania with hallucinations," and the local vicar talked Vincent into admitting himself to a mental hospital.

• *Ascend to level 2, where you may see displays about Van Gogh's contemporaries—Gauguin, his brother Theo—as well as more Van Gogh paintings. The visit concludes on level 3, with Vincent's final paintings.*

St-Remy (May 1889-May 1890): In the mental hospital, Vincent continued to paint whenever he was well enough. At St-Remy, we see a change from bright, happy landscapes to more introspective subjects. The colors are less bright and more surreal, the brushwork even more furious. The strong outlines of figures are twisted and tortured, such as in *The Garden of Saint Paul's Hospital,* a.k.a. *Leaf Fall,* (1889). A solitary figure (Vincent?) winds along a narrow, snaky path as the wind blows leaves on him. The colors are

Van Gogh, Red Cabbages and Onions

Van Gogh, The Yellow House

Van Gogh, Wheat Field with Crows

surreal—blue, green, and red tree trunks with heavy black outlines. A road runs away from us, heading nowhere.

Vincent moved north to Auvers-sur-Oise (May-July 1890), a small town near Paris where he could stay under a doctor-friend's supervision. *Wheat Field with Crows* (1890) is one of the last paintings Vincent finished. We can try to search the wreckage of his life for the black box explaining what happened, but there's not much there. His life was sad and tragic, but the record he left is one not of sadness, but of beauty—intense beauty.

The windblown wheat field is a nest of restless energy. Scenes like this must have overwhelmed Vincent with their incredible beauty—too much, too fast, with no release. The sky is stormy and dark blue, almost nighttime, barely lit by two suns boiling through the deep ocean of blue. The road starts nowhere, leads nowhere, disappearing into the burning wheat field. Above all of this swirling beauty fly the crows, the dark ghosts that had hovered over his life since Nuenen. On July 27, 1890, Vincent left his room, walked out to a nearby field, and put a bullet through his chest. He stumbled back to his room, where he died two days later, with Theo by his side.

Art Beyond Van Gogh: Scattered throughout the museum are works by those who influenced Van Gogh and those who were influenced by him: Academy painters and their smooth-surfaced canvases, Impressionists Claude Monet and Camille Pissarro, and fellow Post-Impressionists Paul Gauguin, Paul Cézanne, and Henri de Toulouse-Lautrec.

Also on Museumplein
▲▲STEDELIJK MUSEUM

The Netherlands' top modern-art museum, the Stedelijk (STAYD-eh-lik), is filled with a fun, far-out, and refreshing collection of 20th-century classics as well as cutting-edge works by Picasso, Chagall, and many more. Before entering, notice the architecture of the modern entrance—aptly nicknamed "the bathtub." Once inside, pick up the current map and envision the museum's four main sections: the permanent collection 1850-1950 (ground floor, right half), Dutch design (ground floor, left half), permanent collection 1950-present (first floor), and various temporary exhibits (scattered about, usually some on each floor). Each room comes with thoughtful English descriptions. (And if you're into marijuana, I can't think of a better space than the Stedelijk in which to enjoy its effects.)

Cost and Hours: €15, daily 10:00-18:00, Fri until 22:00, top-notch gift shop, Paulus Potterstraat 13, tram #2 or #5 from Centraal Station to Van Baerlestraat, tel. 020/573-2911, www.stedelijk.nl. The fine

Modern art fills the Stedelijk Museum.

Vondelpark

€5 audioguide covers both permanent and temporary exhibits.

▲▲VONDELPARK

This huge, lively city park is popular with the Dutch—families with little kids, romantic couples, strolling seniors, and hipsters sharing blankets and beers. It's a favored venue for free summer concerts. On a sunny afternoon, it's a hedonistic scene that seems to say, "Parents...relax." The park's 'T Blauwe Theehuis ("The Blue Tea House") is a delightful spot to nurse a drink and take in the scene.

Rick's Tip: **Vondelpark** *is a joy to* **explore by bike.** *MacBike has a rental shop nearby at Leidseplein (listed under "Transportation," later).*

West Amsterdam
Jordaan District

By the 1600s—Amsterdam's Golden Age—residents needed more land and developed the Jordaan neighborhood. The **Singel canal** was the original moat running around the old walled city. It was served by a new church to the west—the **Westerkerk.** The area still looks much as it might have during the Dutch Golden Age of the 1600s, with houses shoulder-to-shoulder, leaning this way and that.

For me, the bridge over the Egelantiersgracht canal and its surroundings capture the essence of the Jordaan. Take it all

in: the bookstores, art galleries, working artists' studios, and small cafés full of rickety tables. The quiet canal is lined with trees and old, narrow buildings with gables—classic Amsterdam. The street called Tweede Egelantiersdwarsstraat is the laid-back Jordaan neighborhood's main shopping-and-people street, where you'll find boutiques, galleries, antique stores, hair salons, and an enticing array of restaurants.

▲▲▲ANNE FRANK HOUSE

A pilgrimage for many, this house offers a fascinating look at the hideaway of young Anne during the Nazi occupation of the Netherlands. Anne, her parents, an older sister, and four others spent a little more than two years in a "Secret Annex" behind her father's business. While in hiding, 13-year-old Anne kept a diary chronicling her extraordinary experience. The thoughtfully designed exhibit offers thorough coverage of the Frank family, the diary, the stories of others who hid, and the Holocaust.

Cost and Hours: €9, €9.50 online, daily 9:00-22:00; Nov-March Mon-Fri 9:00-20:00, Sat until 22:00, Sun until 19:00; best to reserve online up to two months in advance—only advance-ticket holders are admitted 9:00-15:30, same-day tickets sold only after 15:30; no baggage check, no large bags allowed inside, Prinsengracht 267, near Westerkerk, tel. 020/556-7100, www.annefrank.org.

Anne Frank House

The secret bookcase

Advance Reservations: Online timed-entry tickets go on sale exactly two months in advance (for example, to visit on Aug 15, tickets are available June 15). Tickets are released gradually over the two-month window between on-sale and visit dates. Museumkaart holders get in free but must reserve an entry time online for €0.50. You can make this reservation even if you haven't purchased a card yet—but be sure to buy the pass at another sight before your Anne Frank House visit.

Visiting the Museum: Watch the important five-minute **video,** then peruse several rooms of background information. Head up to the **first floor offices,** where Otto Frank ran a successful business called Opekta, selling spices and pectin for making jelly. See the photos and displays (typewriters, balance sheets). When the Frank family hid in the back of the building during the Nazi occupation, Otto's colleagues kept his business going and secretly brought supplies to the Franks. Upstairs in the **second floor storeroom,** models show the two floors where Anne, her family, and four others lived. All told, eight people lived in the tiny apartment.

In July 1942, the family and four fellow Jews went into hiding. Otto handed over the keys to the business to his "Aryan" colleagues, sent a final postcard to relatives, gave the family cat to a neighbor, spread rumors that they were fleeing to Switzerland, and prepared his family to "dive under" (*onderduik,* as it was called).

At the back of the second floor storeroom is the clever hidden passageway into the **Secret Annex.** Though not exactly a secret (since it's hard to hide an entire building), the annex was a typical back-house *(achterhuis),* a common feature in Amsterdam buildings, and the Nazis had no reason to suspect anything on the premises of the legitimate Opekta business. Pass through the bookcase entrance into **Otto, Edith, and Margot's Room.** The room is very small, even without the furniture. Imagine yourself and two fellow tourists confined here for two years. Pencil lines on the wall track Margot's and Anne's heights, marking the point at which these growing lives were cut short.

Next is **Anne Frank's Room.** Pan the room clockwise to see some of the young girl's idols in photos and clippings she pasted there herself. Photos of flowers and landscapes gave Anne a window on the outside world she was forbidden to see. Out the window (which had to be blacked out) is the back courtyard, which had a chestnut tree and a few buildings. These things, along with the Westerkerk bell chiming every 15 minutes, represented the borders of Anne's "outside world." Imagine Anne sitting here at a small desk, writing in her diary.

Ascend the steep staircase—silently—to the **Common Living Room.** This was the kitchen (note the remains of the stove and sink) and dining room. Otto Frank

Anne Frank House: Secret Annex

2nd FLOOR

SWINGING BOOKCASE

FRONT HOUSE

LANDING

BOOKCASE ENTRANCE

STAIRS (UP)

DOORS

BATH-ROOM

Not to Scale

BED

OTTO, EDITH & MARGOT'S ROOM

BED

BED

ANNE'S ROOM

SOFA

BACK COURTYARD

3rd FLOOR

FRONT HOUSE

FLAT ROOF

STAIRS (DOWN)

BED

MURPHY BED

PETER'S ROOM

DRESSER

STAIRS (UP)

TABLE

LIVING ROOM
(ALSO KITCHEN, DINING ROOM & BEDROOM FOR HERMANN & AUGUSTE)

BACK COURTYARD

Note: Furniture shown is approximately where it was during the Secret Annex years.

was well off, and early on, the annex was well-stocked with food. Later, as war and German restrictions plunged Holland into poverty and famine, they survived on canned foods and dried kidney beans. The inhabitants spent their days reading and studying in this room. At night, it became sleeping quarters for Hermann and Auguste van Pels.

The next space is **Peter van Pels' Room.** Initially, Anne was cool toward Peter, but after two years together, a courtship developed, and their flirtation

culminated in a kiss. The **staircase** (no visitor access) leads up to where the inhabitants stored their food. Anne loved to steal away here for a bit of privacy. At night they'd open a hatch to let in fresh air. From here we leave the Secret Annex, returning to the Opekta storeroom and offices in the front house.

On August 4, 1944, a German policeman accompanied by three Dutch Nazis pulled up in a car, politely entered the Opekta office, and went straight to the bookcase entrance. No one knows

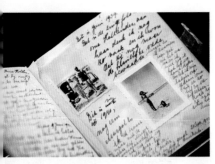

who tipped them off. The Franks were sent to Auschwitz, a Nazi extermination camp in Poland. On the platform at Auschwitz, they were "forcibly separated from each other" (as Otto later reported) and sent to different camps. Anne and Margot were sent to Bergen-Belsen. They both died of typhus in March 1945, only weeks before the camp was liberated. The other Secret Annex residents—except Otto—were gassed or died of disease.

The Rest of the Museum: The Otto Frank Room has a 1967 **video** in which Anne's father talks about his reaction as he read the diaries. Downstairs you can see Anne's **diaries.** (You may see one, two, or all three of them, as well as individual pages.) Other exhibits display **memorabilia** of the Franks and their friends.

It was Otto Frank's dream that visitors come away from the Anne Frank House with hope for a better world. He wrote: "The task that Anne entrusted to me continually gives me new strength to strive for reconciliation and for human rights all over the world."

Central Amsterdam, near Dam Square
▲▲AMSTERDAM MUSEUM
Housed in a 500-year-old former orphanage, this creative museum traces the city's growth from fishing village to world trade center to hippie haven. The museum does a good job of making it engaging and fun. Try not to get lost somewhere in the 17th century as you navigate the meandering maze of rooms.

Start with the easy-to-follow "DNA" section, which hits the historic highlights from 1000-2000. In the first (long) room, you learn how the city was built atop pilings in marshy soil (the museum stands only four feet above sea level). By 1500, they'd built a ring of canals and established the sea trade. As you pass into the next room, the Golden Age (1600s) comes alive in fine paintings of citizens—sometimes even featuring a portrait or two by Rembrandt. Cross the skybridge into rooms covering the last two centuries. The 1800s brought modernization and new technologies like the bicycle. Then, after the gloom of World War II, Amsterdam emerged to become the "Capital of Freedom." The museum's free pedestrian corridor—lined with old-time group portraits—is a powerful teaser.

Cost and Hours: €12.50, includes audioguide, daily 10:00-17:00, pleasant restaurant, next to Begijnhof at Kalverstraat 92, tel. 020/523-1822, www.ahm.nl. This museum is a fine place to buy the Museumkaart.

Red Light District
▲▲▲AMSTELKRING MUSEUM
Although Amsterdam has long been known for its tolerant attitudes, 16th-century politics forced Dutch Catholics to worship discreetly for a few hundred years. At this museum near Centraal Station, you'll find an intriguing hidden Catholic church, filling the attic of three 17th-century merchants' houses. For two centuries (1578-1795), Catholicism in Amsterdam was illegal but tolerated (similar to marijuana in our generation). When hard-line Protestants took power, Catholic churches were vandalized and shut down, priests and monks were rounded up and kicked out of town, and Catholic kids were razzed on their way to school. The city's Catholics were forbidden to worship openly, so they gathered secretly to say Mass in homes and offices. In 1663, a wealthy merchant built Our Lord in the

Amsterdam Museum

Amstelkring Museum

Attic (Ons' Lieve Heer op Solder), one of a handful of places in Amsterdam that served as a secret parish church until Catholics were once again allowed to worship in public.

This one-of-a-kind church provides a rare glimpse inside a historic Amsterdam home straight out of a Vermeer painting. Don't miss the silver collection and other exhibits of daily life from 300 years ago.

Cost and Hours: €10, includes audioguide, Mon-Sat 10:00-17:00, Sun 13:00-17:00, Oudezijds Voorburgwal 38, tel. 020/624-6604, www.opsolder.nl.

▲▲RED LIGHT DISTRICT

Europe's most popular ladies of the night tease and tempt here, as they have for centuries, in several hundred display-case windows around Oudezijds Achterburgwal and Oudezijds Voorburgwal, surrounding the Old Church. Drunks and druggies make the streets uncomfortable late at night after the gawking tour groups leave (about 22:30), but it's a fascinating walk earlier in the evening.

The neighborhood, one of Amsterdam's oldest, has hosted prostitutes since 1200. Prostitution is entirely legal here, and the prostitutes are generally entrepreneurs, renting space and running their own businesses, as well as filling out tax returns and even paying union dues. Popular prostitutes net about €500 a day (for what's called "S&F" in its abbreviated, printable form, charging €30-50 per customer).

MARIJUANA SIGHTS

Three related establishments cluster together along a canal in the Red Light District. The **Hash, Marijuana, and Hemp Museum,** worth ▲, is the most worthwhile of the three; it shares a ticket with the less substantial **Hemp Gallery.** Right nearby is **Cannabis College,** a free nonprofit center that's "dedicated to ending the global war against the cannabis plant through public education."

Cost and Hours: Museum and gallery—€9, daily 10:00-22:00, Oudezijds Achterburgwal 148, tel. 020/624-8926, www.hashmuseum.com. College entry free, daily 11:00-19:00, Oudezijds Achterburgwal 124, tel. 020/423-4420, www.cannabiscollege.com.

Northeast Amsterdam

▲▲NETHERLANDS MARITIME MUSEUM (NEDERLANDS SCHEEPVAARTMUSEUM)

This huge, kid-friendly collection of model ships, maps, and sea-battle paintings fills the 300-year-old Dutch Navy Arsenal (cleverly located a little ways from the city center, as this was where they stored the gunpowder). The Paintings rooms illustrate how ships changed from sail to steam, and how painting styles changed from realistic battle scenes to Romantic seascapes to Impressionism and Cubism.

Red Light District

The Navigational Instruments section has quadrants (a wedge-shaped tool you could line up with the horizon and the stars to determine your location), compasses, and plumb lines. In Ornamentation, admire the busty gals that adorned the prows of ships, and learn of their symbolic meaning for superstitious sailors.

Downstairs on the first floor, see yacht models through the ages, from early warships to today's luxury vessels. The section on atlases shows how human consciousness expanded as knowledge of the earth grew. The finale is a chance to explore below the decks of a replica of the *Amsterdam,* an 18th-century tall-masted cargo ship.

Cost and Hours: €15, includes audioguide, daily 9:00-17:00, bus #22 or #48 from Centraal Station to Kattenburgerplein 1, tel. 020/523-2222, www.scheepvaartmuseum.nl.

Southeast Amsterdam

The following sights are close enough to link by tram, bike, or even on foot. From Centraal Station, take tram #9 or #14 to Waterlooplein. On foot from the Mint Tower, it's a 10-minute stroll along the pleasant shopping street called Staalstraat.

▲▲HERMITAGE AMSTERDAM

The famous Hermitage Museum in St. Petersburg, Russia loans art to Amsterdam for a series of rotating, and often exquisitely beautiful, special exhibits in the Amstelhof, a 17th-century former nursing home that takes up a whole city block along the Amstel River.

Cost and Hours: Generally €15, price varies with exhibit; daily 10:00-17:00, come later in the day to avoid crowds, audioguide-€4, mandatory free bag check, café, Nieuwe Herengracht 14, tram #9 from the train station, recorded info tel. 020/530-7488, www.hermitage.nl.

▲▲DUTCH RESISTANCE MUSEUM (VERZETSMUSEUM)

This is an impressive look at how the Dutch resisted (or collaborated with) their Nazi occupiers from 1940 to 1945. You'll see propaganda movie clips, study forged ID cards under a magnifying glass, and read about ingenious and courageous efforts—big and small—to hide local Jews from

Netherlands Maritime Museum

Dutch Resistance Museum

the Germans and undermine the Nazi regime. This museum presents a timeless moral dilemma: Is it better to collaborate with a wicked system to effect small-scale change—or to resist outright, even if your efforts are doomed to fail? You'll learn why some parts of Dutch society opted for the former, and others for the latter.

Cost and Hours: €10, includes audioguide; Tue-Fri 10:00-17:00, Sat-Mon 11:00-17:00, English descriptions, mandatory and free bag check, tram #9 from station or #14 from Dam Square, Plantage Kerklaan 61, tel. 020/620-2535, www.verzetsmuseum.org.

EXPERIENCES

Smoking

For tourists from lands where you can do hard time for lighting up, the open use of marijuana here can feel either somewhat disturbing, or exhilaratingly liberating... or maybe just refreshingly sane. Several decades after being decriminalized in the Netherlands, marijuana causes about as much excitement here as a bottle of beer. Throughout Amsterdam, you'll see "coffeeshops"—cafés selling marijuana, with display cases showing various joints or baggies for sale.

Rules and Regulations: The retail sale of marijuana is strictly regulated, and proceeds are taxed. The minimum age for purchase is 18, and coffeeshops can sell up to five grams of marijuana per person per day. It's illegal to advertise marijuana; in fact, in many places you must ask to see the menu.

Shops sell marijuana and hashish both in prerolled joints and in little baggies. Joints are generally sold individually (€4-5, depending on whether it's hash with tobacco, marijuana with tobacco, or pure marijuana), though some places sell only small packs of three or four joints. Baggies generally contain a gram and go for €8-15. The better pot, though costlier, can actually be a better value, as it takes less to get high—and it's a better high. But if you want to take it easy, as a general rule, cheaper is milder.

Smoking Tips: Shops have loaner bongs and inhalers, and dispense rolling papers like toothpicks. While it's good style to ask first, if you're a paying customer (e.g., you buy a cup of coffee), you can generally pop into any coffeeshop and light up, even if you didn't buy your pot there.

Tourists who haven't smoked pot since their college days are famous for overindulging in Amsterdam. Coffeeshop baristas nickname tourists about to pass out "Whitey"—the color their faces turn just before they hit the floor. They warn Americans (who aren't used to the strength of the local stuff) to try a lighter leaf. If you do overdo it, the key is to eat or drink something sweet to avoid getting sick. Cola is a good fast fix, and coffeeshop

Window-shopping

At a marijuana coffeeshop

staff keep sugar tablets handy. They also recommend trying to walk it off.

Don't ever buy pot on the street in Amsterdam. Well-established coffeeshops are considered much safer, and coffeeshop owners have an interest in keeping their trade safe and healthy. They're also generally very patient in explaining the varieties available.

Coffeeshops

Most of downtown Amsterdam's coffeeshops feel grungy and foreboding to American travelers who aren't part of the youth-hostel crowd. I've listed a few places with a more pub-like ambience for Americans wanting to go local, but within reason.

Paradox is the most cozy coffeeshop—a mellow, graceful place. The managers, Ludo and Wiljan, and their staff are happy to walk you through all your options. This is a rare coffeeshop that serves light meals (daily 10:00-20:00, loaner bongs, games, Wi-Fi, two blocks from Anne Frank House at Eerste Bloemdwarsstraat 2, tel. 020/623-5639).

The Grey Area—a hole-in-the-wall with three tiny tables—is a cool, welcoming, and smoky place appreciated among local aficionados as a perennial winner at Amsterdam's Cannabis Cup Awards. You're welcome to just nurse a bottomless cup of coffee (daily 12:00-20:00, between Dam Square and Anne Frank House at Oude Leliestraat 2, tel. 020/420-4301).

Siberië Coffeeshop is a short walk from Centraal Station, but feels cozy, with a friendly canalside ambience. Clean, big, and bright, this place has the vibe of a mellow Starbucks, hosts the occasional astrology reading, and is proud that all their pot is "lab tested" (daily 10:00-23:00, Fri-Sat until 24:00, Wi-Fi for customers, helpful staff, English menu, Brouwersgracht 11, tel. 020/623-5909).

The Bulldog Café is the high-profile, leading touristy chain of coffeeshops. These establishments are young but welcoming, with reliable selections. They're comfortable for green tourists wanting to just hang out for a while. The flagship branch, in a former police station right on Leidseplein, is very handy, offering alcohol upstairs, pot downstairs, and fun outdoor seating on a heated patio (daily 10:00-24:00, later on weekends, Leidseplein 17, tel. 020/625-6278). Their original café still sits on the canal near the Old Church in the Red Light District.

"Brown" Cafés

Be sure to experience the Dutch institution of the *bruin* café (brown café)—so called for the typically hardwood decor and nicotine-stained walls. (While smoking was banned several years ago—making these places even more inviting to nonsmokers—the prior pigmentation persists.) Exemplifying the *gezellig* (cozy) quality that the Dutch hold dear, these are convivial hangouts.

In the Jordaan: $ Café 't Papeneiland has Delft tiles, an evocative old stove, and a stay-awhile perch overlooking a canal with welcoming benches (daily 10:00-24:00, drinks but almost no food—cheese or liverwurst sandwiches, overlooking northwest end of Prinsengracht at #2, tel. 020/624-1989).

$ Café 't Smalle serves simple meals of soups, salads, and sandwiches from 11:00 to 17:30 (plenty of fine Belgian beers on tap, interesting wines by the glass; at Egelantiersgracht 12—where it hits Prinsengracht, tel. 020/623-9617); **$$ Café de Prins** is a fine spot for *poffertjes*—those beloved tiny Dutch pancakes—as well as bar food, steaks, and fries (daily 10:00-late, Prinsengracht 124, tel. 020/624-9382).

Between Centraal Station and the Jordaan: $ Proeflokaal Arendsnest displays the day's 52 Dutch beers on a big chalkboard. The only food is Dutch bar snacks—local meats and cheeses with crackers—but the place is inviting, with seating inside and on the canal (daily 12:00-24:00, Herengracht 90, tel. 020/421-2057).

$ Café De II Prinsen, dating from 1910, feels more local. It's relaxed and convivial, with a few outdoor tables facing a particularly pretty canal and a lively shopping street (Dutch beers on tap, daily 12:00-24:00, Prinsenstraat 27, tel. 020/428-4488).

Near Rokin: With a lovely secluded back room and peaceful canalside seating, **$$ Café 't Gasthuys** cranks out light lunches, sandwiches, and reasonably priced basic dinners (cheeseburgers are a favorite, daily 12:00-16:30 & 17:30-22:00, Grimburgwal 7—from the Rondvaart Kooij boat dock, head down Langebrugsteeg, and it's one block down on the left, tel. 020/624-8230).

On Spui Square: $ Café Hoppe is a classic drinking bar. "Hoppe" is their house brew, but there are many beers on tap and a good selection of traditional drinks, sandwiches at lunch, very simple bar food, a packed interior, and fun stools outside to oversee the action on Spui (Mon-Thu 14:00-24:00, Fri-Sun 12:00-24:00, Spui 18, tel. 020/420-4420).

Nightlife

On summer evenings, people flock to the main squares for drinks at outdoor tables. Leidseplein is the liveliest square, surrounded by theaters, restaurants, and nightclubs. The slightly quieter Rembrandtplein (with adjoining Thorbeckeplein and nearby Reguliersdwarsstraat) is the center of gay clubs and nightlife. Spui features a full city block of bars.

The Red Light District (particularly Oudezijds Achterburgwal) is less sleazy in the early evening, and almost carnival-like as the neon lights come on and the streets fill with tour groups. But it starts to feel scuzzy after about 22:30.

The brown cafés recommended earlier are ideal after-hours hangouts. Peruse those listings for pre- or post-dinner drink ideas.

For entertainment and nightlife information, the TI's website, www.iamsterdam.com, has good English listings for upcoming events (select "What to do," then "What's on"). Newsstands sell the **A-Mag** entertainment guide and Dutch newspapers (Thu editions generally list events).

Shopping

Pick up the TI's *Shopping in Amsterdam* brochure. Street markets (generally 9:30-17:00, closed Sun) include **Waterlooplein** (the flea market), the huge **Albert Cuyp** street market (southeast of the Rijksmuseum), and various flower markets (such as the Singel canal **Flower Market** near the Mint Tower).

Most shops in the center are open 10:00-18:00 (later on Thu—typically until 20:00 or 21:00); many shopkeepers take Sundays and Monday mornings off. Supermarkets are generally open Monday-Saturday 8:00-20:00, with shorter hours on Sunday; Albert Heijn grocery stores are open until 22:00 every day.

Handy stores include **Hema** (at Kalverstraat 212, in the Kalvertoren shopping mall and at Centraal Station) and the **De Bijenkorf** department store, towering high above Dam Square, with a ritzy cafeteria.

Rick's Tip: *The* **fancy self-service cafeteria** *in the Bijenkorf department store has a fine* **rooftop terrace** *(daily 10:00-20:00, fifth floor).*

The **gift shops at the major art museums**—Rijks and Van Gogh—sell frameable prints (plus mailing tubes to protect them), totes, cups, scarves, and many clever items.

A fun shopping zone is **The Nine Little Streets (De Negen Straatjes),** between Dam Square and the Jordaan, home to diverse shops and trendy cafés. Walking west from the Amsterdam Museum/Spui Square or south from the Anne Frank House puts you in the thick of things. For a preview, see www.theninestreets.com.

EATING

Amsterdam has a thriving and ever-changing restaurant scene. While I've listed options, one good strategy is simply to pick an area and wander. Note that many of my listings are lunch-only (usually termed "café" rather than "restaurant")—good for a handy bite near major sights. Similarly, many top restaurants serve only dinner. Before trekking across town to any of my listings, check the hours.

Central Amsterdam

You'll likely have lunch at some point in the city's core (perhaps at a place listed here), but you'll find a better range of more satisfying choices in the Jordaan area of West Amsterdam (described later).

On and near Spui

$$$ Restaurant Kantjil en de Tijger is a lively, modern place serving Indonesian food; the waiters are happy to explain your many enticing options. Their four rijsttafels (traditional "rice tables" with about a dozen small courses) are designed for two, but three people can make a meal by getting a rijsttafel for two plus a soup or light dish (daily 12:00–23:00, reservations smart, mostly indoor with a little outdoor seating, Spuistraat 291, tel. 020/620-0994, www.kantjil.nl).

$ Kantjil To Go is a tiny Indonesian takeout bar. Their printed menu explains the mix-and-match plan (daily 12:00–21:00, a half-block off Spui Square at Nieuwezijds Voorburgwal 342, behind the restaurant listed above, tel. 020/620-3074). Split a large box, grab a bench on the charming Spui Square around the corner, and you've got perhaps the best cheap, hot meal in town.

$$$$ Restaurant d'Vijff Vlieghen has a candlelit interior right out of a Rembrandt painting. It's a huge, dressy, and romantic place offering Dutch and international cuisine, professional service, and a multicourse tasting menu with wines (nightly 18:00–22:00, Spuistraat 294, tel. 020/530-4060).

$ Singel 404 Lunch Café, just across the Singel canal from Spui and near the Nine Little Streets, is popular for sandwiches (daily 10:30–18:00, Singel 404, tel. 020/428-0154).

$$$ The Seafood Bar focuses on fresh and fishy, and is understandably popular—reserve ahead for lunch or dinner (daily 12:00–22:00, Spui 15, tel. 020/233-7452 www.theseafoodbar.nl). Another branch is near the Rijksmuseum (listed later).

Near the Mint Tower

De Jaren Café ("The Years") is chic yet inviting, and clearly a favorite with locals. Upstairs is a minimalist **$$$ restaurant** with a top-notch salad bar and canal-view deck (dinners after 17:30, meals include salad bar). Downstairs is a modern **$$ café,** great for light lunches (soups, salads, and sandwiches served all day and evening). On a sunny day, the café's canalside patio is a fine spot to savor a drink (daily 9:30–24:00, a long block up from Muntplein at Nieuwe Doelenstraat 20, tel. 020/625-5771).

$$ Blue Amsterdam Restaurant, high above the Kalvertoren shopping mall on Kalverstraat, serves light lunches with one of the best views in town (just ride up the slanted elevator, free Wi-Fi, daily 11:00–18:30, tel. 020/427-3901).

Fries: While Amsterdam has no shortage of Vlaamse friets ("Flemish fries") stands, locals and in-the-know visitors head for **$ Vlemnickx,** an unpretentious hole-in-the-wall friets counter hiding just off the main Kalverstraat shopping street. They sell only fries, with a wide variety of sauces—they call themselves "de sausmeesters" (daily 12:00–19:00, Thu until 20:00, Voetboogstraat 31).

West Amsterdam, in the Jordaan District

$$$$ Restaurant Daalder is all about quality, fun, and the chef's surprise.

A traditional rijsttafel ("rice table")

There's no menu. Your waiter will discuss with you your interests and then you must sit back, relax, and dine on a multicourse meal. The dishes are French/Italian/Asian/Dutch and playful, and reservations are a must (options range from €45/4 courses to €68/7 courses, daily 12:00-14:00 & 18:00-22:00, Lindengracht 90, tel. 020/624-8864, http://daalderamsterdam.nl).

$$$ Café Restaurant de Reiger must serve up the best cooking of any *eetcafé* in the Jordaan. Famous for its fresh ingredients, ribs, good beer on tap, and delightful bistro ambience, it's part of the classic Jordaan scene. They're proud of their fresh fish and French-Dutch cuisine. The café, which is crowded late and on weekends, takes no reservations. Come early and have a drink at the bar while you wait (daily 17:00-24:00, Nieuwe Leliestraat 34, tel. 020/624-7426).

$$$ Ristorante Toscanini is an upmarket Italian place that's always packed. With a lively, spacious ambience and great Italian cuisine, this place is a treat—if you can get a seat. Reservations are essentially required (Mon-Sat 18:00-22:30, closed Sun, deep in the Jordaan at Lindengracht 75, tel. 020/623-2813, http://restauranttoscanini.nl).

Jordaan's "Restaurant Row" is located along the Jordaan's trendiest street. Tweede ("2nd") Egelantiersdwarsstraat is home to a variety of tempting places to eat. This is a youthful and exuberant scene, with high-energy eateries that spill out into lively brick-sidewalk seating. Stroll its length from Egelantiers Canal to Westerstraat to survey your options; consider reserving a spot for a return dinner visit. My favorites include **$ Urker Viswinkel,** a classic fish-and-chips joint (at #13); the lively **$$ La Perla** for wood-fired pizza (at #14, with a few humble tables, great sidewalk tables, and a more formal dining room across the street); and the fun **$$$ Ristorante Hostaria,** a tight, steamy Italian place

with an open kitchen (at #9).

Dessert: A popular neighborhood joint, **Monte Pelmo Ice Cream** has delightful ice cream and a helpful staff. It's not surprising there's always a line (daily 13:00-22:00, closes earlier in winter, Tweede Anjeliersdwarsstraat 17).

Southwest Amsterdam

While a few eateries are within just a few steps of the big museums, my less-touristy picks are generally within a 10-minute walk and have better food and service—but none is worth going out of your way for.

$$$ The Seafood Bar—modern, slick, and extremely popular—features a tasty array of seafood. The decor is white-subway-tile trendy, and the food focuses on fresh and sustainable dishes with a Burgundian flair. You can try dropping by, but it's best to reserve during mealtimes (daily 12:00-22:00, Van Baerlestraat 5, between the Rijksmuseum and Vondelpark, tel. 020/670-8355, www.theseafoodbar.nl).

$$$ Sama Sebo Indonesian Restaurant is considered one of the best Indonesian

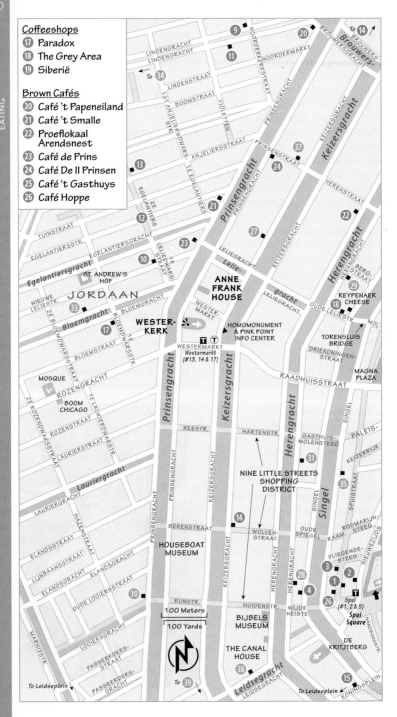

Coffeeshops
17 Paradox
18 The Grey Area
19 Siberië

Brown Cafés
20 Café 't Papeneiland
21 Café 't Smalle
22 Proeflokaal Arendsnest
23 Café de Prins
24 Café De II Prinsen
25 Café 't Gasthuys
26 Café Hoppe

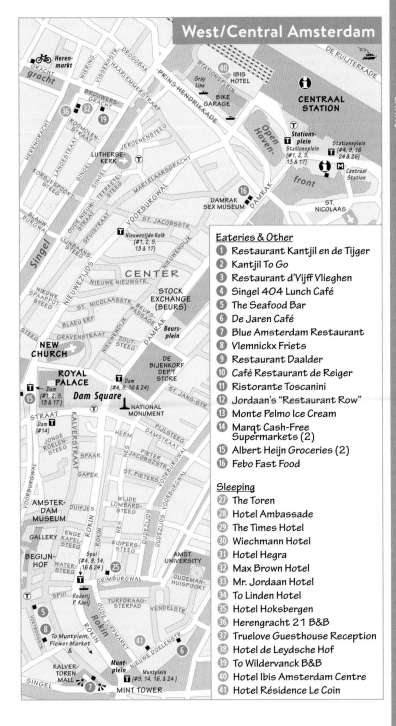

West/Central Amsterdam

Eateries & Other

1. Restaurant Kantjil en de Tijger
2. Kantjil To Go
3. Restaurant d'Vijff Vlieghen
4. Singel 404 Lunch Café
5. The Seafood Bar
6. De Jaren Café
7. Blue Amsterdam Restaurant
8. Vlemnickx Friets
9. Restaurant Daalder
10. Café Restaurant de Reiger
11. Ristorante Toscanini
12. Jordaan's "Restaurant Row"
13. Monte Pelmo Ice Cream
14. Marqt Cash-Free Supermarkets (2)
15. Albert Heijn Groceries (2)
16. Febo Fast Food

Sleeping

27. The Toren
28. Hotel Ambassade
29. The Times Hotel
30. Wiechmann Hotel
31. Hotel Hegra
32. Max Brown Hotel
33. Mr. Jordaan Hotel
34. To Linden Hotel
35. Hotel Hoksbergen
36. Herengracht 21 B&B
37. Truelove Guesthouse Reception
38. Hotel de Leydsche Hof
39. To Wildervanck B&B
40. Hotel Ibis Amsterdam Centre
41. Hotel Résidence Le Coin

restaurants in town. It's a venerable local favorite for rijsttafel. I prefer the energy in the casual "bodega" to the more formal restaurant (and only in the bodega will they serve the smaller lunch plate for dinner). Their 17-dish, classic rijsttafel spread is as good as any. At lunch the bami goreng or nasi goreng (fried noodles or rice) is a feast of its own (Mon-Sat 12:00-15:00 & 17:00-22:00, closed Sun, reservations smart for dinner, P. C. Hooftstraat 27, between the Rijksmuseum and Vondelpark, tel. 020/662-81460, www.samasebo.nl).

$ Renzo's is a tempting Italian delicatessen where you can buy good sandwiches or prepared pasta dishes and *antipasti* (priced by weight, can be heated up). Get your food to go, or pay a bit more to sit at one of the tables in the tiny interior, with more seating upstairs (house wine by the glass, or buy a bottle for the takeaway price to enjoy with your meal, daily 11:00-21:00, Van Baerlestraat 67, tel. 020/763-1673).

$$ Café Loetje has a rollicking neighborhood-beer-hall feel. Of the three dining zones, the interior is least interesting; head instead for the glassed-in winter garden (in bad weather) or the sprawling outdoor tables (in good weather). In addition to beer, they slam out good, affordable pub grub (daily 11:00 until late, Johannes Vermeerstraat 52, several blocks southeast of Museumplein, tel. 020/662-8173).

In and Near Vondelpark: $$ 'T Blauwe Theehuis ("The Blue Tea House") is a venerable meeting point where, since the 1930s, all generations have come for drinks and light meals. The setting, deep in Vondelpark, is like a Monet painting. Sandwiches are served at tables outside, inside, and on the rooftop from 11:00 to 16:00, drinks and apple pie are served all day, and pot smoking—while discreet—is as natural here as falling leaves (daily 9:00-22:00 in summer, Vondelpark 5, tel. 020/662-0254).

$$ Café Gruter is just outside Vondelpark. With a classic brown café interior and great seating on a little square, it's a neighborhood hangout—away from the center's tourism in a ritzy residential zone with fashion boutiques and leafy squares (lunch daily 11:00-16:00, also serves dinner, open very late, Willemsparkweg 73, tel. 020/679-6252). Ride tram #2 to the Jacob Obrechtstraat stop—one tram stop beyond the Van Gogh Museum—near a gateway to Vondelpark.

Cheap and Fast Eats

To dine cheaply yet memorably alongside the big spenders, grab a meal to go, then find a bench on a lively neighborhood square or along a canal. Sandwiches (*broodjes*) of delicious cheese on fresh bread are cheap at snack bars, delis, and *broodje* shops. Ethnic restaurants—many of them Indonesian or Surinamese, and seemingly all named with varying puns on "Wok"—serve inexpensive, splittable carryout meals. Middle Eastern fast-food stands and diners abound, offering a variety of meats wrapped in pita bread.

Supermarkets: Marqt Cash-Free Supermarket (credit cards only) is the picnicking hipster's dream, with the freshest organic produce and plenty of prepared foods. **Albert Heijn** grocery stores are more traditional, cheaper, take cash, and have great deli sections with picnic-perfect takeaway salads and sandwiches. None of their stores accept US credit cards: Bring cash, and don't get in the checkout lines marked *PIN alleen.*

Dutch Fried Fast Food: $ Febo caters mainly to late-night drinkers looking for greasy fried foods to soak up the booze. A wall of self-service, coin-op windows provides piping-hot fried cheese, burgers, croquettes, and so on (change machine on wall). You'll find branches all over town, including Leidsestraat 94, just north of Leidseplein.

SLEEPING

Canalside Hotels

$$$$ The Toren is a smartly renovated, chandeliered mansion with a pleasant canalside setting and a peaceful garden for guests out back. Run by the Toren family, this super-romantic hotel is classy yet friendly, with 38 rooms in a great location on a quiet street two blocks northeast of the Anne Frank House. The capable staff is a good source of local advice. The gilt-frame, velvet-curtained rooms are an opulent splurge (RS%, breakfast extra, air-con, elevator, Keizersgracht 164, tel. 020/622-6033, www.thetoren.nl, info@thetoren.nl).

$$$$ Hotel Ambassade is elegant and fresh, lacing together 57 rooms in a maze of connected houses sitting aristocratically on Herengracht. The staff is top-notch, and the public areas (including a library and a breakfast room) are palatial, with antique furnishings and modern art (RS%, breakfast extra, air-con, elevator, Herengracht 341, tel. 020/555-0222, www.ambassade-hotel.nl, info@ambassade-hotel.nl).

$$$ The Times Hotel is a business-comfort hotel in a scenic canal setting. The 34 modern rooms are tight, but most have a real bathtub instead of just a shower. Each room features a wall mural of a Dutch masterpiece—if you majored in art history, you might love a blown-up version of Vermeer—or you might hate it (breakfast extra, air-con, elevator, Herengracht 135, tel. 020/330-6030, www.thetimeshotel.com, info@thetimeshotel.com, entertaining Sherman at the front desk).

$$$ Wiechmann Hotel's 37 pricey rooms are sparsely furnished with just the dark-wood essentials, but they're spacious, and the *gezellig* (cozy) public areas are chock-full of Old World charm. Expect lots of stairs and no elevator in this historic building (some canal views, back rooms are quiet, nicely located at Prinsengracht 328, tel. 020/626-3321, www.hotelwiechmann.nl, info@hotelwiechmann.nl, John and Taz the welcome dog).

$$$ Hotel Hegra is cozy, with nine rooms filling a 17th-century merchant's house overlooking the canal. While some rooms are small, everything is clean, modern, and functional (some rooms with canal view, breakfast extra, just north of Wolvenstraat at Herengracht 269, tel. 020/623-7877, www.hotelhegra.nl, info@hotelhegra.nl, Robert).

$$$ Max Brown Hotel, the flagship hotel of a boutique-style chain, has a trendy urban design geared toward a hipster clientele. Located in a quiet neighborhood near Centraal station, it offers 34 modern rooms and public areas with funky-chic details. Rooms with canal views are pricier and breezier (continental breakfast, tangled floor plan connecting three canalside buildings, Herengracht 13, tel. 020/522-2345, www.maxbrownhotels.com, hello@maxbrownamsterdam.com). They have another location near Vondelpark and the Rijksmuseum.

$$$ Mr. Jordaan Hotel, in the heart of this Greenwich Village-like neighborhood, offers 34 newly renovated rooms with funky-but-stylish touches—Twin Peaks meets Brooklyn Heights. Some are very tight, but they warn you in advance it's a "cozy" double. Hotel manager Eko will charm you as he shares neighborhood secrets (family rooms available, breakfast extra, elevator, Bloemgracht 102, tel. 020/626 5801, www.mrjordaan.nl, stay@mrjordaan.nl).

$$$ Linden Hotel is Mr. Jordaan's sister hotel—similar in decoration, with tight rooms and friendly staff, and at a slightly cheaper rate. While it is on the edge of the Jordaan neighborhood, some of its 25 rooms have canal views (RS% use "enjoy-linden" when booking, family rooms, fans, breakfast extra, Lindengracht 251, 020/622-1460, www.lindenhotel.nl, info@lindenhotel.nl).

$$ Hotel Hoksbergen is your budget option for a canalside setting, so expect cramped rooms, a decidedly lived-in feel, and lots of steep stairs. The new owners are updating the 14 rooms, but avoid Room 4, which is sold as a double but should be a single (ask about apartments, fans, all day coffee and tea in the common room, Singel 301, tel. 020/626-6043, www.hotelhoksbergen.com, info@hotelhoksbergen.nl).

B&Bs and Private Rooms

$$$ **Herengracht 21 B&B** has two stylish, intimate rooms in a canal house filled with art and run by lovely Loes Olden (air-con, Herengracht 21, tel. 020/625-6305, mobile 06-2812-0962, www.herengracht21.nl, loes@herengracht21.nl).

$$$ **B&B Helmers,** a few blocks from Vondelpark, has two comfortably equipped rooms, lots of stairs, and a rooftop terrace, ideal for enjoying breakfast (minimum stay 3 nights, rooftop access only in the morning, Eerste Constantijn Huygensstraat 59, tram lines #1, #3, #12, mobile 06-2487-2223, www.bedandbreakfasthelmers.com, info@bedandbreakfasthelmers.com, warm Odette).

$$ With **Truelove Guesthouse,** a room-rental service, you'll feel like you're staying at your Dutch friends' house while they're out of town. René and Ingrid—whose jewelry store and bike-rental shop on Prinsenstraat doubles as the reception desk for their rental service—have 11 rooms and apartments in houses sprinkled throughout the northern end of the Jordaan neighborhood. The apartments are stylish and come with kitchens and pull-out beds (2-night minimum on weekends, no breakfast, pick up keys in store at Prinsenstraat 4, mobile 06-5334-0866, info@trueloveguesthouse.com).

$$$ **Hotel de Leydsche Hof,** a hidden gem located on a canal, doesn't charge extra for its views. Its four large rooms are a symphony in white—some overlooking a tree-filled backyard, others a canal—but be prepared for lots of stairs. Frits and Loes give their big, elegant, old building a

stylish air. Breakfast is served in the grand canal-front room (cash only, 2-night minimum, Leidsegracht 14, tel. 020/638-2327, mobile 06-3099-2744, www.freewebs.com/leydschehof, loespiller@planet.nl).

$$$ **Wildervanck B&B,** run by Helene and Sjoerd Wildervanck with the help of their three kids, offers two tastefully decorated rooms in an elegant 17th-century canal house. If you want to meet a friendly Dutch family, this is the place (2-night minimum, cash only, breakfast in their pleasant dining room, just west of Leidsestraat at Keizersgracht 498, tel. 020/623-3846, www.wildervanck.com, info@wildervanck.com).

Southwest Amsterdam, near Vondelpark and Museumplein

These options cluster around Vondelpark in a safe neighborhood. Though they don't have a hint of Old Dutch or romantic canalside flavor, they're reasonable values and only a short walk from the action. Unless noted, these places have elevators. Many are in a pleasant nook between rollicking Leidseplein and the park, and most are a 5- to 15-minute walk to the Rijks and Van Gogh museums. They are easily connected with Centraal station by tram #2 or #5.

$$$ **Hotel Piet Hein** offers 81 stylishly sleek yet comfortable rooms as well as a swanky lounge, good breakfast, and a peaceful garden, all on a quiet street. Be aware that the "economy double" is so tight, you'll have to climb over your partner to get to the other side of the bed (breakfast extra, air-con in some rooms, Vossiusstraat 51, tel. 020/662-7205, www.hotelpiethein.nl, info@hotelpiethein.nl).

$$$ **Hotel Fita** has 20 bright rooms in a great location—100 yards from the Van Gogh Museum, an even shorter hop from the tram stop, and on a pleasant corner. The style is modern yet rustic, with nice extras, including espresso machines in every room. It's well-run by Roel, who offers a friendly welcome and generous

advice (air-con on upper floors, elevator, free laundry service, Jan Luijkenstraat 37, tel. 020/679-0976, www.fita.nl, info@fita.nl).

$$ Hotel Alexander is a modern, newly renovated 34-room hotel on a quiet street. Some of the rooms overlook the garden patio out back. If you're looking for a smart, clean, relaxed place, this is it (breakfast extra, tel. 020/589-4020, Vondelstraat 44, www.hotelalexander.nl, info@hotelalexander.nl).

¢ Stayokay Vondelpark (IYHF), is one of Amsterdam's top hostels for the under-25 set—but over-25s will feel comfortable here too (family rooms, lots of school groups, bike rental, right on Vondelpark at Zandpad 5, tel. 020/589-8996, www.stayokay.com, vondelpark@stayokay.com).

No-Nonsense Central Hotels

You won't get a warm welcome, but if you're looking for a hotel that's convenient to plenty of tram lines, these fit the bill.

Near the Train Station: $$$ Hotel Ibis Amsterdam Centre is a modern, efficient, 363-room place. It offers a central location, comfort, and good value, without a hint of charm (book long in advance—especially for Sept-Oct, air-con, elevators, facing Centraal Station, go left toward multistory bicycle garage to Stationsplein 49; tel. 020/721-9172, www.ibishotel.com, h1556@accor.com).

Near the Flower Market: $$$ Hotel Résidence Le Coin has 42 larger-than-average rooms complete with small kitchenettes. The bathrooms have been updated, while the rooms have a slightly dated look. Located near the Mint Tower, this hotel is a two-minute walk to the Flower Market and a five-minute walk to Rembrandtplein (breakfast extra, elevator, Nieuwe Doelenstraat 5, tel. 020/524-6800, www.lecoin.nl, hotel@lecoin.nl).

TRANSPORTATION

Getting Around Amsterdam

Amsterdam is big, and you'll find the trams handy. The longest walk a tourist would make is an hour from Centraal Station to the Rijksmuseum.

By Tram, Bus, and Metro

Amsterdam's public transit system includes trams, buses, and an underground Metro. Of these, trams are most useful for most tourists.

Tickets and Day Passes: I find a pass to be the simplest option when staying in Amsterdam for a few days. **Passes** good for unlimited transportation are available for 24 hours (€7.50), 48 hours (€12.50), 72 hours (€17.50), and 96 hours (€22.50). Some passes include the train ride to Schiphol Airport. Given how expensive single tickets are, think about buying a pass before you buy that first ticket.

Within Amsterdam, a **single transit ticket** costs €2.90 and is good for one hour on the tram, bus, and Metro, including transfers. Public buses and trams do not accept cash onboard (use a credit card with a PIN code, or buy tickets in advance). The full range of tickets and passes are available at Metro-station vending machines, at GVB public-transit offices, at TIs, and at some souvenir shops; for these options you can pay with cash or credit card.

Amsterdam's Public Transportation

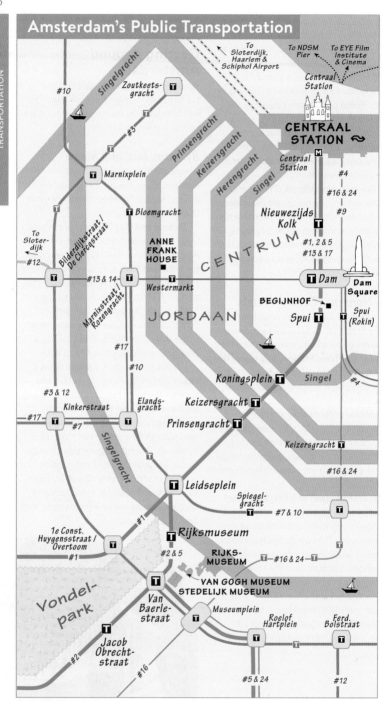

To Sloterdijk, Haarlem & Schiphol Airport

To NDSM Pier

To EYE Film Institute & Cinema

Centraal Station

CENTRAAL STATION ≈

#10

Zoutkeetsgracht

Singelgracht

Prinsengracht

Keizersgracht

Herengracht

Singel

#3

Marnixplein

Centraal Station

#4

#16 & 24

#9

Nieuwezijds Kolk

Bloemgracht

ANNE FRANK HOUSE

To Sloterdijk

Bilderdijkstraat / De Clercqstraat

#12

#1, 2 & 5

#13 & 17

CENTRUM

#13 & 14

Westermarkt

Dam

Dam Square

Marnixstraat / Rozengracht

JORDAAN

BEGIJNHOF

Spui

Spui (Rokin)

#17

#10

Koningsplein

Singel

#4

#3 & 12

Kinkerstraat

Elandsgracht

Keizersgracht

Singelgracht

#17

#7

Prinsengracht

Keizersgracht

#16 & 24

Leidseplein

Spiegelgracht

#7 & 10

1e Const. Huygensstraat / Overtoom

#1

Rijksmuseum

#2 & 5

RIJKS-MUSEUM

#16 & 24

VAN GOGH MUSEUM
STEDELIJK MUSEUM

Vondel-park

Van Baerlestraat

Museumplein

Roelof Hartplein

Ferd. Bolstraat

Jacob Obrecht-straat

#2

#16

#5 & 24

#12

To IJplein

IJ (Channel)

CRUISE TERMINAL

Muziekgebouw / Bimhuis

#26

Azart-plein

Kattenburger-straat

Centraal Station

Nieuwe

#22 & 48

MARITIME MUSEUM

#48

Nieuwmarkt

RED LIGHT DISTRICT

Herengracht

#22

#26

Rietlandpark

N
Not to Scale

Not all stations shown on map

#51

#53

#54

#10

#22

Rembrandt-plein

REMBRANDT'S HOUSE

JEWISH HISTORY MUSEUM

#14

#9

Waterlooplein

#4

Mr. Visserplein

DUTCH THEATER

Artis / Pln. Kerklaan

ARTIS ZOO

Herengracht

Keizersgracht

Keizersgracht

Prinsengracht

Prinsengracht

#9

Pln. Badlaan

#14

Alexanderplein

Frederiks-plein

#7 & 10

Weesperplein

#7

Stadhouders-kade

Amstel

#4

Van Woustraat

#3

Wibautstraat

#3

#4

River

	Tram #1, 2 & 5
	Tram #4, 16 & 24, 9
	Tram #13, 14 & 17
	Tram #7 & 10, 3 & 12, 26
	Metro #51, 53 & 54
	Bus #22 & 48

If you're staying longer than three or four days or plan to use Dutch trains as well as trams and buses, consider the **TripKey card** (€3.50 initial fee, rides are charged to your credit card; register in advance from home, then pick it up at the Hertz car rental desk at Schipol Airport or at the Amsterdam Ticket Shop at Kerkstraat 155a in Amsterdam; see www.tripkey.nl).

Information: For more on riding public transit and a free transit map, visit the helpful GVB public-transit information office in front of Centraal Station (Mon-Fri 7:00-21:00, Sat-Sun from 8:00, www.gvb.nl).

Riding Trams: Board the tram at any entrance that's not marked with a red/white "do not enter" sticker. If you need a ticket or pass, pay the conductor (in a booth at the back, payment by credit card with PIN code only); if there's no conductor, pay the driver in front. You must always "check in" as you board by scanning your ticket or pass at the pink-and-gray scanner, and "check out" by scanning it again when you get off. The scanner will beep and flash a green light after a successful scan. Be careful not to accidentally scan your ticket or pass twice while boarding, or it becomes invalid. Occasionally controllers fine people who don't check in and out. To open the rear door when you reach your stop, press a button on one of the poles near the exit. Don't try to exit through the front door—it's not allowed.

Note that some trams may be renumbered and rerouted (for the latest, see https://en.gvb.nl and select "Travel").

Trams #1, #2, and #5 travel **north-south from** Centraal Station, the Jordaan, and many recommended hotels to Leidseplein. Trams #2 and #5 (but not #1) continue to the Rijksmuseum, Van Gogh Museum, and Vondelpark. At Centraal Station, catch trams on the west side of the plaza (with station behind you, on your right).

To go **west-east,** use tram #14, which connects Westermarkt near the Anne Frank House and Jordaan neighborhood with Rembrandtplein, Waterlooplein, and Alexanderplein.

If you get lost in Amsterdam, remember that most of the city's trams eventually take you back to Centraal Station, and nearly all drivers speak English.

Buses and Metro: Tickets and passes work on buses and the Metro just as they do on the trams—scan your ticket or pass as you enter and again when you leave.

By Bike

Everyone uses this mode of transport. It's by far the smartest way to travel in a city where 40 percent of all traffic rolls on two wheels. You'll get around town by bike faster than you can by taxi. One-speed bikes, with *"brrringing"* bells, rent for about €10 per day.

Rental Shops: Star Bikes Rental has cheap rates, long hours, and inconspicuous black bikes (€5/3 hours, €7/day, €9/24 hours, €12/2 days, €17/3 days, Mon-Fri 8:00-19:00, Sat-Sun 9:00-19:00, shorter hours in winter, requires ID but no monetary deposit, 5-minute walk from east end of Centraal Station—walk underneath tracks near DoubleTree by Hilton Hotel and then turn right, De Ruyterkade 143, tel. 020/620-3215, www.starbikesrental.com).

MacBike, with thousands of bikes, is the city's bike-rental powerhouse—you'll see their bright-red bikes all over town. It has a huge and efficient outlet at Centraal Station (€7.50/3 hours, €9.75/24 hours, €6/extra day, more for 3 gears and optional insurance, leave €50 deposit plus a copy of your passport, or provide credit-card number; free helmets, also rents electric bikes, daily 9:00-17:45; at east end of station—on the left as you're leaving; tel. 020/624-8391, www.macbike.nl). They have a smaller satellite at Leidseplein (Weteringschans 2). Return your bike to the station where you rented it. MacBike sells several €1-2 pamphlets outlining bike tours with a variety of themes in and around Amsterdam.

Lock Your Bike: Bike thieves are bold

and brazen. Bikes come with two locks and stern instructions to use both. The wimpy ones go through the spokes, whereas the industrial-strength chains are meant to be wrapped around the actual body of the bike and through the front wheel, and connected to something stronger than any human. (Note the steel bike-hitching racks sticking up all around town, called "staples.") Follow your rental agency's locking directions diligently. If you're sloppy, it's an expensive mistake and one that any "included" theft insurance won't cover.

Biking Tips: As the Dutch believe in fashion over safety, no one here wears a helmet. They do, however, ride cautiously, and so should you: Use arm signals, follow the bike-only traffic signals, stay in the obvious and omnipresent bike lanes, and yield to traffic on the right. Fear oncoming trams and tram tracks. Carefully cross tram tracks at a perpendicular angle to avoid catching your tire in the rut. Warning: Police ticket cyclists just as they do drivers. Obey all traffic signals, and walk your bike through pedestrian zones.

Fines for biking through pedestrian zones are reportedly €30-50. A handy bicycle route-planner can be found at www. routecraft.com (select "bikeplanner," then click British flag for English).

By Boat

While the city is great on foot, bike, or tram, you can also get around Amsterdam by hop-on, hop-off boat. **Lovers** boats shuttle tourists on two routes covering different combinations of the city's top sights. Their Green Line, for example, stops near the Hermitage, Rijksmuseum/ Van Gogh Museum, and Centraal Station (€25, runs about every 20 minutes, 2 hours). Sales booths in front of Centraal Station (and the boats) offer free brochures listing museum hours and admission prices. Most routes come with recorded narration (departures daily 9:30-18:15, tel. 020/530-1090, www.lovers.nl).

The similar **Canal Bus** is another hop-on, hop-off boat, offering nine stops on two different boat routes (€24/24-hour pass, online discounts, departures daily 9:30-19:00, until 20:00 July-Aug, leaves near Centraal Station at the Gray Line dock, tel. 020/217-0500, www.canal.nl).

If you're simply looking for a floating, nonstop tour, the regular canal tour boats (without the stops) give more information, cover more ground, and cost less (see "Tours," earlier).

For do-it-yourself canal tours and lots of exercise, Canal Bus also rents "canal bikes" (a.k.a. paddleboats) at several locations: near the Anne Frank House, near the Rijksmuseum, near Leidseplein, and where Leidsestraat meets Keizersgracht (€8/1 hour, €11/1.5 hours, €14/2 hours, prices are per person, daily July-Aug 10:00-21:00, Sept-June 10:00-18:00).

By Taxi and Uber

For short rides, Amsterdam is a bad town for taxis. The city's taxis have a high drop charge (about €7) for the first two kilometers (e.g., from Centraal Station to the Mint Tower), after which it's €2.12 per kilometer. You can wave them down, find a rare taxi stand, or call one (tel. 020/777-7777). All taxis are required to have meters. Uber works in Amsterdam like in the US (€28 from the airport into downtown).

You'll also see **bike taxis,** particularly near Dam Square and Leidseplein. Negotiate a rate for the trip before you board (no meter, estimate €1/3 minutes, no surcharge for baggage or extra weight, sample fare from Leidseplein to Anne Frank House: about €6).

Arriving and Departing

The Netherlands is so small, level, and well-covered by trains and buses that transportation is a snap. Bus stations and bike-rental shops cluster around train stations. The easy-to-navigate airport is well-connected to Amsterdam and other destinations by bus and train. Use the comprehensive transit website www.9292.nl to plan connections inside the Netherlands by train, bus, or both.

By Train

Amsterdam is the country's hub, but all major cities are linked by speedy trains that come and go every 15 minutes or so. Dutch rail schedules are online at www.ns.nl (domestic) and www.nshispeed.nl (international).

The portal connecting Amsterdam to the world is its aptly named Amsterdam Centraal. The station's train-information center can require a long wait. Save lots of time by getting international train tickets and information at a small-town station (such as Haarlem), the airport upon arrival, or online.

If you have a rail pass, it's quicker to validate it when you arrive at Schiphol Airport than in Amsterdam's Centraal station, but keep in mind that you don't need to start using your rail pass that day; you could buy an inexpensive point-to-point ticket into Amsterdam, and save your rail-pass travel days for a longer journey.

Thalys has a monopoly on direct trains between Amsterdam and Paris. For pass-holders, Thalys trains require you to book a seat reservation (which can sell out quite early).

TRAIN CONNECTIONS

From Amsterdam to: Schiphol Airport (4-6/hour, 15 minutes, buy from a machine to avoid lines), **Haarlem** (8/hour, 20 minutes), **London** (6/day, 4 hours, transfer in Brussels; Eurostar discounted with rail pass, www.eurostar.com), **Bacharach/St. Goar** (roughly every 2 hours, 5.5

hours), **Frankfurt** (every 2 hours, 4 hours direct), **Berlin** (5/day, 6.25 hours), **Munich** (roughly hourly, 8 hours with 2 transfers; one direct night train, 10.5 hours), **Paris** (nearly hourly, 3.25 hours direct on fast Thalys train or 4.75 hours with change to Thalys train in Brussels, www.thalys.com). When booking Thalys trains, even rail-pass holders need to buy a seat reservation.

By Bus

If you don't have a rail pass, the cheapest way to get to **Paris** is by Eurolines bus (about 6/day, 8 hours, about €46 one-way, €80 round-trip; price depends on demand—nonrefundable, advance-purchase one-way tickets as cheap as €17 and round-trip as cheap as €28, check online for deals, Julianaplein 5, Amstel station, five stops by Metro from Centraal station, tel. 020/560-8788, www.eurolines.com).

By Plane

Schiphol (SKIP-pol) Airport is located about 10 miles southwest of Amsterdam's city center (code: AMS, www.schiphol.nl). Though Schiphol officially has four terminals, it's really just one big building. All terminals have ATMs, banks, shops, bars, and free Wi-Fi.

Baggage-claim areas for all terminals empty into the same arrival zone, officially called Schiphol Plaza but generally signed simply *Arrivals Hall*. Here you'll find a busy **TI** (near Terminal 2, daily 7:00-22:00), a train station, and bus stops for getting into the city.

To get train information or buy a ticket, take advantage of the **"Train Tickets and Services" counter** (Schiphol Plaza ground level, just past Burger King). They have an easy info desk and generally short lines.

GETTING FROM THE AIRPORT TO AMSTERDAM

Direct **trains** to Amsterdam's Centraal Station run frequently from Schiphol Plaza (4-6/hour, 20 minutes, €5.40).

The Connexxion **shuttle bus** departs from lane A7 in front of the airport and takes you directly to most hotels. There are three different routes, so ask the attendant which one works best for you (2/hour, 20 minutes to the first hotel, up to 45 minutes to the last, €17 one-way, pay driver cash, pay inside at Connexxion desk with credit card, or book online, tel. 088-339-4741, www.airporthotelshuttle.nl).

Public bus #397 (departing from lane B9 in front of the airport) is handy for those going to the Leidseplein district (€5, buy ticket from driver or online, www.connexxion.nl).

By **taxi,** allow about €50 to downtown Amsterdam. Uber serves the airport for about €28.

NEAR AMSTERDAM

HAARLEM

A Golden Age kind of town, cute and cozy Haarlem is quintessentially Dutch. With small-town warmth and easy access to Amsterdam or Schiphol Airport (20 minutes by train), Haarlem makes a good day trip or even a home base.

The Gothic Grote Kerk, or Great Church, towers over the market square (Grote Markt). Enjoy the market on Monday (clothing) or Saturday (general), when the atmospheric square bustles like a Brueghel painting, with cheese, fish, flowers, and families.

Haarlem's top museum features the work of its most famous son, portrait artist Frans Hals. The Corrie ten Boom House relates the inspirational story of a family that courageously hid Jews from the Nazis. If it's a sunny day and you need a beach, head to nearby Zandvoort.

Orientation

Getting There: Direct trains run frequently from Amsterdam Central Station (8/hour, 20 minutes). From Schiphol Airport, your best option is the **bus** (4-10/hour, 40 minutes, €5—buy ticket from driver, bus #300).

Arrival in Haarlem: If you arrive at the train station, you'll see that two parallel streets flank the station (Kruisweg and Jansweg). Head up either street, and you'll reach the town square and church within 10 minutes. Buses from Schiphol Airport stop both in the center (Centrum/Verwulft stop, a short walk from Grote Markt) and at the train station. By taxi, the drop charge of €7.50 gets you a little over a mile.

Tourist Information: Haarlem's TI (VVV), in the Town Hall building on Grote Markt, is friendlier, more helpful, and less crowded than Amsterdam's, so you

Haarlem has a small-town feel.

could ask your Amsterdam questions here (April-Sept Mon-Fri 9:30-17:30, Sat until 17:00, Sun 12:00-16:00; Oct-March Mon 13:00-17:30, Tue-Fri from 9:30, Sat 10:00-17:00, closed Sun; tel. 023/531-7325, www. haarlem.nl, info@vvvhaarlem.nl).

Bike Rental: You can rent bikes from **Pieters Fietsverhuur** inside the train station (fixed-gear bike-€6.50/day, 3-speed bike-€10/day, €50 deposit and passport number required, Mon-Sat 6:00-24:00, Sun from 7:30-24:00, Stationsplein 1, tel. 023/531-7066, www.rijwielshoppieters. nl). They often run out of bikes by mid-morning—especially when the weather's good. **Rent a Bike Haarlem** charges more, but is friendly and efficient, and carries plenty of new, good-quality bikes (fixed-gear bike-€10/day, 3-speed bike-€13.50/day, mountain and electric bikes available, leave ID or €150 cash deposit; April-Sept daily 9:00-18:30; Oct-March Mon-Sat 10:00-17:00, closed Sun; near station at Lange Herenstraat 36, tel. 023/542-1195, www.rentabikehaarlem.nl).

Canal Cruises: Making a scenic 50-minute loop through and around Haarlem with a live guide who speaks Dutch and sometimes English, **Smidtje Cruise**'s little trips are more relaxing than informative (€12.50; April-Oct departs daily at the top of the hour 12:00-16:00; reservations smart; also evening cruises, across canal from Teylers Museum at Spaarne 11a, tel. 023/535-7723, www. smidtjecanalcruises.nl).

Haarlem Canal Tours runs similar but longer tours, and uses an open boat. You'll find them farther down Spaarne, across from #17 (€13.50, online reservations smart, 70 minutes, runs every 1.5 hours daily 10:00-19:00, may not run in bad weather and off-season, www. haarlemcanaltours.com).

Sights
▲▲GROTE MARKT (MARKET SQUARE)
Haarlem's Grote Markt, where 10 streets converge, is the town's delightful centerpiece...as it has been for 700 years. Enjoy a coffee or beer here, simmering in Dutch

Haarlem's main square is perfect for people-watching.

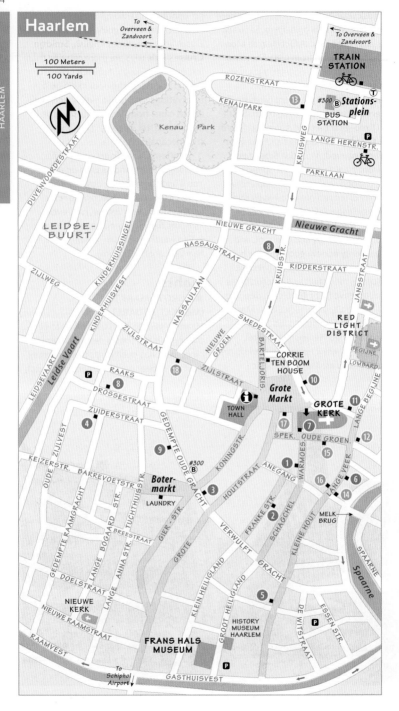

Haarlem

To Overveen & Zandvoort

To Overveen & Zandvoort

TRAIN STATION

100 Meters
100 Yards

ROZENSTRAAT

KENAUPARK

Kenau Park

13

#300 Stations-plein
B BUS STATION

DUYVENVOORDESTRAAT

KRUISWEG

LANGE HERENSTR.

PARKLAAN

LEIDSE-BUURT

NIEUWE GRACHT

Nieuwe Gracht

KINDERHUISSINGEL

NASSAUSTRAAT

8

KRUISSTR.

RIDDERSTRAAT

JANSSTRAAT

ZIJLWEG

NASSAULAAN

SMEDESTRAAT

RED LIGHT DISTRICT

LEIDSEVAART

Leidse Vaart

ZIJLSTRAAT

NIEUWE GROEN.

BARTELJORIS.

BEGIJNE

LOMBARD

RAAKS

8

DROSSESTRAAT

ZIJLSTRAAT

18

CORRIE TEN BOOM HOUSE

10

GROTE KERK

11

ZUIDERSTRAAT

4

i TOWN HALL

Grote Markt

17

7

LANGE BEGIJNE

OUDE ZIJLVEST

KEIZERSTR.

BARREVOETESTR.

GEDEMPTE OUDE GRACHT

SPEK.

OUDE GROEN.

15

12

LANGE VEER

9

#300 B

Boter-markt

3

KONINGSTR.

HOUTSTRAAT

ANEGANG

WARMOES

1

16

6

14

LANGE VEER

GIER - STR.

LAUNDRY

FRANKE STR.

2

SCHAGCHEL

KLEINE HOUT

MELK BRUG

GEDEMPTE RAAMGRACHT

LANGE BOGARD STR.

TUCHTHUISSTR.

BREESTRAAT

LANGE ANNA STR.

GROTE

VERWULFT

GRACHT

SPAARNE

Spaarne

DOELSTRAAT

NIEUWE KERK

NIEUWE RAAMSTRAAT

KLEIN HEILIGLAND

GROOT HEILIGLAND

5

HISTORY MUSEUM HAARLEM

DE WITSTRAAT

ESSEN STR.

P

RAAMVEST

To Schiphol Airport

FRANS HALS MUSEUM

GASTHUISVEST

P

One-Way Streets →
Traffic Barriers

Eating & Nightlife
1. Jacobus Pieck Eetlokaal
2. De Lachende Javaan Rest.
3. Pizzeria-Rist. Venezia
4. Jopenkerk
5. Restaurant ML
6. Lange Veerstraat Eateries & High Times Coffeehouse
7. Gelateria Bartoli
8. Albert Heijn Supermarkets (3)
9. DekaMarkt
10. Café Studio
11. In Den Uiver

Sleeping
12. Hotel ML
13. Hotel Lion D'Or
14. Brass Haarlem & Haarlem Hotelsuites
15. Ambassador City Centre Hotel
16. Hotel Joops
17. Hotel Amadeus
18. Hotel Malts

good living. Observe. Sit and gaze at the church, appreciating essentially the same scene that Dutch artists captured centuries ago in oil paintings that now hang in museums. Until the 1990s, trolleys ran through the square, and cars were parked everywhere. But now it's a pedestrian zone, with market stalls filling the square on Mondays and Saturdays, and café tables dominating on other days.

▲GROTE KERK (CHURCH)

This 15th-century Gothic church (now Protestant) is worth a look, if only to see Holland's greatest pipe organ (from 1738, 100 feet high). Its more than 5,000 pipes impressed both Handel and Mozart. Note how the organ, which fills the west end, seems to steal the show from the altar. Quirky highlights of the church include a replica of Foucault's pendulum, the "Dog-Whipper's Chapel," and a 400-year-old cannonball.

Cost and Hours: €2.50, not covered by Museumkaart; Mon-Sat 10:00-17:00, closed Sun to tourists, Sun service at 10:00 (May-Oct) and 19:00 (June-Sept); tours offered Sat by request (€5); Grote Markt 22, tel. 023/553-2040, www.bavo.nl. Nice WCs are inside, just after the ticket desk.

Concerts: Consider attending even just part of a concert to hear Holland's greatest pipe organ (regular free concerts Tue at 20:15 mid-May-mid-Oct, additional concerts Thu at 16:00 July-Aug; bring a sweater—the church isn't heated; enter through south transept, around the back).

Rick's Tip: *The local favorite for* **ice cream** *is* **Gelateria Bartoli,** *on the south side of the church (daily, closed Jan-Feb).*

▲▲FRANS HALS MUSEUM (FRANS HALSMUSEUM)

Haarlem is the hometown of Frans Hals (c. 1582-1666), the foremost Dutch portrait painter of the 17th-century Golden Age. This bold humanist painted everyday people in their warts-and-all glory. He was a forerunner of Impressionist brushwork, a master of composition, and an articulate visual spokesman for his generation.

This refreshing museum displays many of Hals' greatest paintings. You'll stand eye-to-eye with life-size, lifelike portraits of Haarlem's citizens—brewers, preachers, workers, bureaucrats, and housewives. Take a close look at the people who built the Dutch Golden Age, and then watched it start to fade.

Cost: €12.50, includes audioguide, €17.50 combo-ticket with Teylers

Haarlem's Red Light District

Museum (purchase at TI), sometimes more with special exhibits; Tue-Sat 11:00-17:00, Sun 12:00-17:00, closed Mon; a five-minute walk from Grote Markt at Groot Heiligland 62, tel. 023/511-5775, www.franshalsmuseum.nl.

▲▲CORRIE TEN BOOM HOUSE

Haarlem was home to the Ten Boom family, who, from this house, created a safe haven for Jews during World War II. This museum gives the other half of the Anne Frank story—the point of view of those who risked their lives to hide Dutch Jews during the Nazi occupation. The family's story was popularized by Corrie ten Boom's inspirational 1971 book (and 1975 movie), The Hiding Place.

Access to the Ten Boom House is by tour only—check the sign on the door for the next start time. The gentle and loving one-hour tours come with a little evangelizing that some may find objectionable.

Cost and Hours: Free, but donations accepted; April-Oct Tue-Sat first English tour at 10:00, last at 15:00; Nov-March Tue-Sat first English tour at 11:00, last at 14:30; closed Sun-Mon year-round; 50 yards north of Grote Markt at Barteljorisstraat 19; the clock-shop people get all wound up if you go inside—wait in the little side street at the door, where tour times are posted; tel. 023/531-0823, www.corrietenboom.com.

Reservations: Tours are limited to 20 people and often fill up in high season. You can reserve a spot only on morning tours—sign up at least 10 days in advance on their website or via email at tours@corrietenboom.com. A donation of €2.50/person is requested if you reserve in advance. Without a reservation in high season, check the sign on the door for openings, and line up at least 20 minutes before the tour begins.

▲RED LIGHT DISTRICT

Wander through a little Red Light District that's as precious as a Barbie doll—and

Ⓐ *Grote Kerk nave*
Ⓑ *Pew decoration, Grote Kerk*
Ⓒ *Frans Hals Museum*
Ⓓ *Corrie Ten Boom House*

The beach at Zandvoort

legal since the 1980s (2 blocks northeast of Grote Markt, off Lange Begijnestraat, no senior or student discounts). Don't miss the mall on Begijnesteeg marked by the red neon sign reading 't Steegje ("free"). Just beyond that, the nearby 't Poortje ("office park") costs €6 to enter. Jog to the right to pop into the much more inviting "Red Lantern" (window-shopping welcome, at Korte Begijnestraat 27). As you wander through this area, remember that the people here don't condone prostitution any more than your own community back home probably does; they just find it practical not to criminalize it and drive it underground, but instead to regulate it and keep the practice as safe as possible.

▲DE ADRIAAN WINDMILL

Haarlem's old-time windmill, located just a 10-minute walk from the station, welcomes visitors with a short video, a little museum, and fine town views. The windmill may look old, but it's a replica from 2002 (the original windmill burned down in 1932). Be prepared for steep stairs that are more like ladders—if you get vertigo, skip it.

Cost and Hours: €3.50, not covered by Museumkaart; March-Nov Mon and Wed-Fri 13:00-17:00, Sat-Sun 10:30-17:00, closed Tue; Dec-Feb Fri-Mon 13:00-16:30, closed Tue-Thu; Papentorenvest 1, tel. 023/545-0259, www.molenadriaan.nl.

NEAR HAARLEM: ZANDVOORT

For a quick and easy look at the windy coastline in a shell lover's Shangri-la, visit the beach burg of Zandvoort, just 10 minutes away from Haarlem. This pretty, manicured resort has plenty of cafés, ice-cream parlors, *Vlaamse* friet stands, restaurants, and boutiques. Just beyond the town is the vast and sandy beach, lined with cafés and rentable chairs. Above it all is a pedestrian promenade and a line of high-rise hotels. South of the main beach, sunbathers work on all-over tans.

Tourist Information: The helpful TI is on Bakkerstraat 2 (Mon-Fri 9:00-17:00, Sat 10:00-17:00, closed Sun, tel. 023/571-7947, www.vvvzandvoort.nl).

Getting There: It's easy to reach by **train** (4/hour from Haarlem in summer, 10 minutes; 2/hour, 30 minutes from Amsterdam). By **bike,** it's a breezy 45-minute ride from Haarlem, heading west and

Grote Markt

following road signs for *Bloemendaal,* then *Zandvoort.*

Smoking

Haarlem is a laid-back place for observing the Dutch approach to recreational marijuana. The town is dotted with about a dozen coffeeshops, where pot is sold and smoked by relaxed, noncriminal types. These easygoing coffeeshops are more welcoming than they may initially seem—bartenders understand that Yankee travelers might feel a bit out of their element and are happy to answer questions.

If you don't like the smell of pot, avoid places sporting wildly painted walls, plants in the windows, or Rastafarian yellow, red, and green colors. **High Times,** with a living-room ambience and loaner bongs, is inviting and particularly friendly to American visitors. Smokers choose from 14 varieties of joints in racks behind the bar (neatly prepacked in trademarked "Joint Packs," €2-5, Mon-Fri 8:00-23:00, Sat from 9:00 until late, Sun from 11:00 until late, Lange Veerstraat 47, www.coffeeshophightimes.nl).

Nightlife

Grote Markt is lined with trendy bars that seem made for nursing a drink—**Café Studio** is generally the hot spot for a drink here (at Grote Markt 25); I'd also duck into the dark interior of In Den Uiver (near the Grote Kerk entry at Riviervischmarkt 13, live jazz on Tue twice a month). Lange Veerstraat (behind the Grote Kerk) is colorful and bordered with lively spots. Botermarkt (connected to Grote Markt by Koningstraat street) is more convivial and local, as it's less central and away from the tourists—or try the nearby Jopenkerk brewpub (described in "Eating").

Eating

$$ Jacobus Pieck Eetlokaal is popular with locals for its fine-value "global cuisine," good salads, and unpretentious flair. Sit in the peaceful garden courtyard, at a sidewalk table, or in the romantically cozy interior. The Oriental Peak Salad is a perennial favorite, and the dish of the day (dagschotel, €12.50) always sells out (great sandwiches at lunch, Tue-Sat 11:00-16:00 & 17:00-22:00, closed Sun-

Tranquil winter scene in Haarlem

Mon, cash only, Warmoesstraat 18, behind church, tel. 023/532-6144).

$$$$ De Lachende Javaan ("The Laughing Javanese") is a long-established Indonesian place serving a memorable rijsttafel that can be ordered for single diners—a rare option in the Netherlands (Tue-Sun 17:00-22:00, closed Mon, Frankestraat 27, tel. 023/532-8792).

$$ Pizzeria-Ristorante Venezia, run for 25 years by the same Italian family from Bari, is Haarlem's default place for pizza or pasta (daily 13:00-23:00, Verwulft 7, tel. 023/531-7753). Sit outdoors for quality people-watching, or indoors at a well-worn table.

Trendy Brew Pub: Jopenkerk, with 18 brews on tap, including a Hoppenbier from a 1501 recipe, is a beer lover's mecca. Budget pub grub—burgers, salads, and quiche—is served on the **$** ground floor, or try the upstairs **$$$$** restaurant for more elegant fare (brewpub daily 10:00-24:00; restaurant Tue-Sat 17:30-22:00, closed Sun-Mon; Gedempte Voldersgracht 2, tel. 023/533-4114).

Dressy Splurge: At **$$$$ Restaurant ML,** expert chef Mark Gratama serves chichi French-fusion cuisine in an elegant 17th-century dining room. This Michelin-rated restaurant offers four- to seven-course tasting menus starting at about €68 (reservations necessary, Tue-Sat 18:00-22:00, closed Sun-Mon, enter through nondescript door at Kleine Houtstraat 70, tel. 023/534-5343, www. restaurant-ml.nl).

Restaurant Row: If you don't know what you want to eat, stroll the delightful Lange Veerstraat behind the church and survey a fun range of restaurants (from cheap falafels to Cuban, and much more).

Supermarkets: Albert Heijn has three convenient locations; all are cash only and open daily. One is in the train station, another is at Kruisstraat 10, and their largest store is near the river and recommended Jopenkerk pub at Drossestraat 11. The **DekaMarkt** is a few blocks west of Grote Markt (daily, Gedempte Oudegracht 54, near V&D department store).

Sleeping

$$$ Hotel ML, modern yet elegant, is located in a renovated 300-year-old building with a grand staircase. With bare floors, comfy high-quality beds, and minimalist touches in its 17 rooms, what it lacks in warmth it makes up for in style and value. Many rooms have church views and the double-paned windows help keep down the noise. It's just a block east of Grote Markt, with a bustling brasserie and bar downstairs (suites available, breakfast extra, elevator, Klokhuisplein 9, tel. 023/512-3910, www.mlinhaarlem. nl, welkom@mlinhaarlem.nl).

$$$ Hotel Lion D'Or, across from the train station, is a classy 43-room business hotel with all the professional comforts and pleasingly posh decor. Its new owners are pouring money into upgrading the rooms—expect more amenities and higher prices (RS%, air-con, elevator, Kruisweg 34, tel. 023/532-1750, www.hotelliondor.nl, reservations@ hotelliondor.nl, friendly Dirk Pauw).

$$$ Brasss Haarlem rents 10 upscale suites in a turn-of-the-century building once home to Haarlem's first department store. Each cushy room is named after a fish and has an open-floor plan with a see-through bathroom (in-room espresso machine, air-con, Korte Veerstraat 40, tel. 023/542-7804, www.brassshaarlem. nl, info@brassshaarlem.nl). They also run the nearby **$$$ Haarlem Hotelsuites,** offering 14 cozy apartment-style units with kitchens (check-in at Brasss Haarlem, www.haarlem-hotelsuites.nl, haarlemhotelsuites@gmail.com).

$$ Ambassador City Centre Hotel, with 99 comfortable if tight rooms in a big plain hotel, is located just behind the Grote Kerk. If you're willing to trade some street noise for amazing church views, ask for a room in the front (breakfast buffet extra, Oude Groenmarkt 20, tel. 023/512-5300, www.acc-hotel.nl, info@acc-hotel. nl). They also run **$$ Hotel Joops,** with 32 rooms, a block away (studios and apartments with kitchenettes, breakfast extra).

$$ Hotel Amadeus, on Grote Markt, is charming and has 15 small, bright, and basic rooms. Front rooms with views of the square are noisy, while the back rooms are relatively quiet. Breakfast is served in a trendy restaurant overlooking the main square—a great place to watch the town greet a new day. Mike and Inez take good care of their guests (RS%, Grote Markt 10— from the square it's a steep climb to the lounge, check-in at ground-floor restaurant where there's an elevator accessible during open hours, otherwise expect lots of stairs, tel. 023/532-4530, www.amadeus-hotel.com, info@amadeus-hotel.com).

$$ Hotel Malts rents 14 modern, bright, and fresh rooms in a central location for a good price. Owners Henk and Annemarie have a wealth of Haarlem knowledge and sit with each guest over coffee to share the town's secrets (honor bar, no elevator and steep stairs, Zijlstraat 58, tel. 023/551-2385, www.maltshotel.nl, info@ maltshotel.nl).

Practicalities

HELP!

Emergency and Medical Help

In any of the countries covered in this book, **dial 112** for any emergency service—ambulance, police, or fire. You can also ask at your hotel for help—they'll know the nearest medical and emergency services. If you get a minor ailment, do as the locals do and go to a pharmacist for advice.

Theft or Loss

To replace a passport, you'll need to go in person to an embassy (listed later). If your credit and debit cards disappear, cancel and replace them. If your things are lost or stolen, file a police report, either on the spot or within a day or two; you'll need it to submit an insurance claim for lost or stolen rail passes or travel gear, and it can help with replacing your passport or credit and debit cards. For more information, see RickSteves.com/help.

Damage Control for Lost Cards

If you lose your credit, debit, or ATM card, report the loss immediately to your card company. Visa's and MasterCard's websites list European toll-free numbers by country. If you report your loss within two days, you typically won't be responsible for any unauthorized transactions on your account, although many banks charge a liability fee of $50. You can generally receive a temporary replacement card within two or three business days in Europe.

US Embassies and Consulates

ENGLAND

In London: Tel. 020/7499-9000 (all services), no walk-in passport services, 24 Grosvenor Square, http://uk.usembassy.gov/

FRANCE

In Paris: Tel. 01 43 12 22 22, 2 Avenue Gabriel, http://fr.usembassy.gov

Avoiding Theft

Pickpockets are common in crowded, touristy places, but fortunately, violent crime is rare. Thieves don't want to hurt you; they just want your money and gadgets.

My recommendations: Stay alert and wear a money belt (tucked under your clothes) to keep your cash, debit card, credit card, and passport secure; carry only the money you need for the day in your front pocket.

Treat any disturbance (e.g., a stranger bumps into you, spills something on you, or tries to get your attention for an odd reason) as a smoke screen for theft. Be on guard waiting in line at sights, at train stations, and while boarding and leaving crowded buses and subways. Thieves target tourists overloaded with bags or distracted with smartphones.

When paying for something, be aware of how much cash you're handing over (state the denomination of the bill when paying a cabbie) and count your change.

GERMANY

In Berlin: Tel. 030/83050, by appointment only, closed Sat-Sun and last Thu of month, Clayallee 170; http://de.usembassy.gov

ITALY

In Rome: 24-hour emergency tel. 06-46741, nonemergency tel. 06-4674-2420, Via Vittorio Veneto 121, http://it.usembassy.gov
In Florence: Tel. 055-266-951, Lungarno Vespucci 38, http://it.usembassy.gov

NETHERLANDS

In Amsterdam: Tel. 020/575-5309, after-hours emergency tel. 070/310-2209, Museumplein 19, services by appointment only, http://nl.usconsulate.gov.

SPAIN

In Barcelona: Tel. 932-802-227, after-hours emergency tel. 915-872-200, Paseo Reina Elisenda de Montcada 23, http://es.usconsulate.gov

SWITZERLAND

In Bern: Tel. 031-357-7011, after-hours tel. 031-357-7777, Sulgeneckstrasse 19, services by appointment only, closed Sat-Sun, http://ch.usembassy.gov

MONEY

Here's my basic strategy for using money in Europe:

• Upon arrival, head for a cash machine (ATM) at the airport and withdraw some local currency, using a debit card with low international transaction fees.

• Pay for most purchases with a credit card with low (or no) international fees.

• Use cash for small purchases, tips, and transit fares.

• Keep your cards and cash safe in a money belt.

What to Bring

I pack the following and keep it all safe in my money belt.

Debit Card: Use at ATMs to withdraw local cash.

Credit Card: Use to pay for most items (at hotels, larger shops and restaurants, travel agencies, car-rental agencies, and so on).

Backup Card: Some travelers carry a third card (debit or credit; ideally from a different bank), in case one gets lost, demagnetized, eaten by a temperamental machine, or simply doesn't work.

US Dollars: I carry $100-200 US as a backup. While you won't use it for day-to-day purchases, American cash in your money belt comes in handy for emergencies, such as if your ATM card stops working.

What NOT to Bring: Resist the urge to buy the local currency before your trip or you'll pay the price in bad stateside exchange rates. Wait until you arrive to withdraw money.

Before You Go

Report your travel dates. Let your bank know that you'll be using your debit and credit cards in Europe, and when and where you're headed.

Know your PIN. Make sure you know the numeric, four-digit PIN for each of your cards, both debit and credit. Request it if you don't have one and allow time to receive the information by mail.

Adjust your ATM withdrawal limit. Find out how much you can take out daily and ask for a higher daily withdrawal limit if you want to get more cash at once. Note that European ATMs will withdraw funds only from checking accounts; you're unlikely to have access to your savings account.

Ask about fees. For any purchase or withdrawal made with a card, you may be charged a currency conversion fee (1-3 percent) and a Visa or MasterCard international transaction fee (1 percent).

In Europe

Using Cash Machines: European cash machines work just like they do at home—except they spit out local currency instead of dollars, calculated at the day's standard bank-to-bank rate. In most places, ATMs are easy to locate. When possible, withdraw cash from a bank-run ATM located just outside that bank.

If your debit card doesn't work, try a lower amount—your request may have exceeded your withdrawal limit or the ATM's limit. If you still have a problem, try a different ATM or come back later—your bank's network may be temporarily down.

Avoid "independent" ATMs, such as Travelex, Euronet, Moneybox, Cardpoint, and Cashzone. These have high fees, can be less secure than a bank ATM, and may try to trick users with "dynamic currency conversion" (see later).

Exchange Rates

1 euro (€1) = about $1.20. To convert prices in euros to dollars, add 20 percent: €20 is about $24.

1 British pound (£1) = about $1.40. To convert prices in pounds to dollars, add 40 percent: £20 = about $28.

1 Swiss franc (1 CHF) = about $1.

Check Oanda.com for the latest exchange rates.

Exchanging Cash: Avoid exchanging money in Europe; it's a big rip-off. In a pinch you can always find exchange desks at major train stations or airports—convenient but with crummy rates.

Using Credit Cards: Although US cards no longer require a signature for verification, don't be surprised if a European card reader generates a receipt for you to sign. If a cashier is present, you should have no problems. Some card readers will accept your card as is; others will prompt you to enter your PIN (so it's important to know the code for each of your cards).

At self-service payment machines (transit-ticket kiosks, parking, etc.), results are mixed, as US cards may not work in unattended transactions. If your card won't work, look for a cashier who can process your card manually—or pay in cash.

Drivers Beware: Be aware of potential problems using a credit card to fill up at an unattended gas station, enter a parking garage, or exit a toll road. Carry cash and be prepared to move on to the next gas station if necessary. When approaching a toll plaza, use the "cash" lane.

Dynamic Currency Conversion: Some European merchants and hoteliers cheerfully charge you for converting your purchase price into dollars. If it's offered, refuse this "service." You'll pay extra for the expensive convenience of seeing your charge in dollars.

Restaurant Code

Eateries in this book are categorized (using dollar signs) according to the average cost of a typical main course. Drinks, desserts, and splurge items can raise the price considerably.

Code	England	France	Spain, Italy, Germany & Netherlands	Switzerland
$$$$ Splurge	Over £20	Over €25	Over €20	Over 30 CHF
$$$ Pricier	£15-20	€20-25	€15-20	20-30 CHF
$$ Moderate	£10-15	€15-20	€10-15	10-20 CHF
$ Budget	Under £10	Under €15	Under €10	Under 10 CHF

Tipping

Tipping in Europe isn't as automatic and generous as it is in the US. For special service, tips are appreciated, but not expected. As in the US, the right amount depends on your resources and the circumstances, but some general guidelines apply.

Restaurants: You don't need to tip if you order your food at a counter. At restaurants, check the menu to see if service is included; if it isn't, generally a tip of 5-10 percent is normal. France is the exception, where tipping isn't necessary.

Taxis: Round up your fare a bit (for instance, if your fare is €13, pay €14). If the cabbie hauls your bags and zips you to the airport to help you catch your flight, you might want to toss in a little more. But if you feel like you're being driven in circles or otherwise ripped off, skip the tip.

Services: In general, if someone in the service industry does a super job for you, a small tip of a euro or two is appropriate...but not required. If you're not sure whether (or how much) to tip for a service, ask a local for advice.

EATING

Each country has its own cuisine, specialties, deals, and unique quirks. See the "Cuisine Scene at a Glance" sidebars at the beginning of every country section for my best advice.

In any country, you'll find that the most authentic eateries are family-run and located in lower-rent spots a few blocks off the main square. A posted menu in the native language is a good tip-off they have a loyal, local following.

As you travel, make it a point to try regional specialties. Enjoy *salade niçoise* in Nice, paella in Barcelona, and the best *Wurst* in Germany.

I like to order family-style so I can eat my way through more of the menu. Sometimes, rather than getting two main courses, my travel partner and I share a little buffet of appetizers or first courses—they're filling, less expensive, and more typically local than main courses. These small plates go by different names throughout Europe: tapas in Spain and *antipasti* in Italy.

To save money, mix picnics and quick, budget eats with atmospheric restaurant meals. If you splurge one day, go cheap the next; you can find a satisfying dinner for the equivalent of $20 or less anywhere in Europe. If you have more money, of course, it's delightful to spend it dining well.

SLEEPING

I've categorized my recommended accommodations using a Sleep Code (see sidebar). The price ranges are based on one-night stays in peak season, and

Sleep Code

Hotels in this book are categorized (using dollar signs) according to the average price of a standard double room in high season:

Code	England	France	Spain, Italy, Germany & Netherlands	Switzerland
$$$$ Splurge	Over £160	Over €250	Over €170	Over 220 CHF
$$$ Pricier	£120-160	€190-250	€130-170	180-220 CHF
$$ Moderate	£80-120	€130-190	€90-130	120-180 CHF
$ Budget	£40-80	€70-130	€50-90	80-120 CHF
¢ Backpacker	Under £40	Under €70	Under €50	Under 80 CHF

For the best deal, *book directly with the hotel*. Ask for a discount if paying in cash; if my listing includes **RS%,** request a Rick Steves discount.

Note that the French have a simple hotel rating system based on amenities and rated by stars, indicated in this book by asterisks, from basic hotels (*) up to the most luxurious (*****).

Unless otherwise noted, credit cards are accepted, hotel staff speak basic English, and free Wi-Fi is available. For the best prices, always book directly with the hotel.

Some cities require hoteliers to charge a **tourist tax** (about €1-5/person, per night, often payable only in cash).

assume you're reserving directly with the hotel, not through a booking website or TI. For tips on making reservations, see the next page.

If you're on a budget, it's smart to email several hotels to ask for their best price. Comparison-shop and make your choice. In general, prices can soften if you do any of the following: offer to pay cash, stay at least three nights, or mention this book.

Types of Accommodations
Hotels

In this book, the price for a double room in a hotel ranges from €60 (very basic) to €200-plus (maximum plumbing and the works). You'll pay more for accommodations in bigger cities. While I favor family-run hotels, I also recommend some chain hotels when they're a good value.

If you arrive at your hotel in the morning, your room probably won't be ready.

Check your bag safely at the hotel and dive right into sightseeing.

Hoteliers can be a great help and source of advice. Most know their city well, and can assist you with everything from public transit and airport connections to finding a good restaurant, the nearest launderette, or a late-night pharmacy.

Even at the best places, mechanical breakdowns occur: Sinks leak, hot water turns cold, toilets may gurgle or smell, the Wi-Fi goes out, or the air-conditioning dies when you need it most. Report your concerns clearly and calmly at the front desk. For more complicated issues, don't expect instant results.

To guard against theft in your room, keep valuables out of sight. Some rooms come with a safe, and other hotels have safes at the front desk. I've never bothered using one.

Making Hotel Reservations

Requesting a Reservation: For family-run hotels, it's generally cheaper to book your room directly via email or a phone call. For business-class hotels, or if you'd rather book online, reserve directly through the hotel's official website (not a booking agency's site). For complicated requests, send an email.

Here's what the hotelier wants to know:
- type(s) of rooms and size of your party
- number of nights you'll stay
- your arrival and departure dates, written European-style as day/month/year
- special requests (such as en suite bathroom vs. down the hall, cheapest room, twin beds vs. double bed, quiet room)
- applicable discounts (such as a Rick Steves reader discount, cash discount, or promotional rate)

Confirming a Reservation: Most places will request a credit-card number to hold your room. If you're using an online reservation form, look for the *https* or a lock icon at the top of your browser. If you book direct, you can email, call, or fax this information.

Canceling a Reservation: If you must cancel, it's courteous—and smart—to do so with as much notice as possible, especially for smaller family-run places. Cancellation policies can be strict; read the fine print or ask about these before you book. Many discount deals require prepayment, with no cancellation refunds.

Reconfirming a Reservation: Always call or email to reconfirm your room reservation a few days in advance. For B&Bs or very small hotels, I call again on my day of arrival to tell my host what time to expect me (especially important if arriving late—after 18:00).

Phoning: For tips on calling hotels overseas, see page 1000.

From: rick@ricksteves.com
Sent: Today
To: info@hotelcentral.com
Subject: Reservation request for 19-22 July

Dear Hotel Central,
I would like to reserve a room for 2 people for 3 nights, arriving 19 July and departing 22 July. If possible, I would like a quiet room with a double bed and private bathroom inside the room.

Please let me know if you have a room available and the price.

Thank you!
Rick Steves

Using Online Reviews

User-generated review sites and apps such as Yelp, Booking.com, and TripAdvisor can give you a consensus of opinions about everything from hotels and restaurants to sights and nightlife. If you scan reviews of a hotel and see several complaints about noise or a rotten location, it tells you something important that you'd never learn from the hotel's own website.

But as a guidebook writer, my sense is that there is a big difference between the uncurated information on a review site and the vetted listings in a guidebook. A user-generated review is based on the limited experience of one person, who stayed at just one hotel in a given city and ate at a few restaurants there. A guidebook is the work of a trained researcher who forms a well-developed basis for comparison by visiting many hotels and restaurants year after year.

Both types of information have their place, and in many ways, they're complementary. If something is well reviewed in a guidebook and it also gets good online reviews, it's likely a winner.

While it's customary to pay for your room upon departure, it can be a good idea to settle your bill the day before, when you're not in a hurry and while the manager's there. That way you'll have time to discuss and address any points of contention.

Above all, keep a positive attitude. Remember, you're on vacation. If your hotel is a disappointment, spend more time out enjoying the city you came to see.

Hostels

A hostel provides cheap dorm beds and sometimes has a few double rooms and family rooms. Travelers of any age are welcome. Most hostels offer kitchen facilities, guest computers, Wi-Fi, and a self-service laundry.

There are two kinds of hostels: **Independent hostels** tend to be easygoing, colorful, and informal (no membership required); try Hostelworld.com, Hostelz.com, or Hostels.com. **Official hostels** are part of Hostelling International (HI), share an online booking site (Hihostels.com), and typically require that you either have a membership card or pay extra per night.

Other Accommodation Options

Renting an apartment can be a fun and cost-effective way to go local. Websites such as Booking.com, Airbnb, VRBO, and FlipKey let you browse properties and correspond directly with European property owners or managers. Airbnb also lists rooms in private homes. Beds range from air-mattress-in-living-room basic to plush-B&B-suite posh. If you want a place to sleep that's free, try Couchsurfing.com.

STAYING CONNECTED

One of the most common questions I hear from travelers is, "How can I stay connected in Europe?" The short answer is: more easily and cheaply than you might think.

The simplest solution is to bring your own device—mobile phone, tablet, or laptop—and use it just as you would at home (following the tips below, such as connecting to free Wi-Fi whenever possible). Another option is to buy a European SIM card for your mobile phone—either your US phone or one you buy in Europe. Or you can use European landlines and computers to connect. Each of these options

Tips on Internet Security

Make sure that your device is running the latest versions of its operating system, security software, and apps. Next, ensure that your device and key programs (like email) are password- or passcode-protected. On the road, use only secure, password-protected Wi-Fi hotspots. Ask the hotel or café staff for the specific name of their Wi-Fi network, and make sure you log on to that exact one.

If you must access your financial info online, use a banking app rather than accessing your account via a browser. A cellular connection is more secure than Wi-Fi. Avoid logging onto personal finance sites on a public computer.

Never share your credit-card number (or any other sensitive information) online unless you know that the site is secure. A secure site displays a little padlock icon, and the URL begins with *https* (instead of the usual *http*).

is described next, and more details are at www.ricksteves.com/phoning. For a very practical one-hour talk covering tech issues for travelers, see www.ricksteves.com/mobile-travel-skills.

Using a Mobile Phone in Europe

Here are some budget tips and options.

Sign up for an international plan. Using your cellular network in Europe on a pay-as-you-go basis can add up. To stay connected at a lower cost, sign up for an international service plan through your carrier. Most providers offer a simple bundle that includes calling, messaging, and data. Your normal plan may already include international coverage (T-Mobile's does).

Before your trip, call your provider or check online to confirm that your phone will work in Europe, and research your provider's international rates. Activate the plan a day or two before you leave, then remember to cancel it when your trip's over.

Use free Wi-Fi whenever possible. Unless you have an unlimited-data plan, you're best off saving most of your online tasks for Wi-Fi. You can access the Internet, send texts, and even make voice calls over Wi-Fi.

Most accommodations in Europe offer free Wi-Fi, but some—especially expensive hotels—charge a fee. Many cafés (including Starbucks and McDonald's) have free hotspots for customers; look for signs offering it and ask for the Wi-Fi password when you buy something. You'll also often find Wi-Fi at TIs, city squares, major museums, public-transit hubs, airports, and aboard trains and buses.

Minimize the use of your cellular network. Even with an international data plan, wait until you're on Wi-Fi to Skype, download apps, stream videos, or do other megabyte-greedy tasks. Using a navigation app such as Google Maps over a cellular network can take lots of data, so do this sparingly or use it offline.

Limit automatic updates. By default, your device constantly checks for a data connection and updates apps. It's smart to disable these features so your apps will only update when you're on Wi-Fi.

Use Wi-Fi calling and messaging apps. Skype, WhatsApp, FaceTime, and Google+ Hangouts are great for free or low-cost calls and texts over Wi-Fi. With an app installed on your phone, tablet, or laptop, you can log on to a Wi-Fi network and contact friends or family members who use the same service. If you buy credit in advance, with some of these services you can call or send a text anywhere for just pennies per minute.

How to Dial

Here's how to make an international call. For the dialing instructions below, use the complete phone number, including the area code (if there is one).* I've used the telephone number of one of my recommended Paris hotels as an example (tel. 01 45 51 63 02).

From a Mobile Phone

It's easy to dial with a mobile phone. Whether calling from the US to Europe, country to country within Europe, or from Europe to the US—it's all the same.

Press zero until you get a + sign, enter the country code (33 for France), then dial the phone number.

→ To call the Paris hotel from any location, dial +33 1 45 51 63 02.

From a US Landline to Europe

Dial 011 (US/Canada access code), country code (33 for France), and phone number.

→ To call the Paris hotel from home, dial 011 33 1 45 51 63 02.

From a European Landline to the US or Europe

Dial 00 (Europe access code), country code (1 for the US, 33 for France), and phone number.

→ To call my US office from France, dial 00 1 425 771 8303.

→ To call the Paris hotel from Germany, dial 00 33 1 45 51 63 02.

For more phoning help, see www.howtocallabroad.com.

Drop an initial zero, if present, when dialing a European phone number—except when calling Italy.

Time Zones: When calling from the US to Europe, keep Europe's time zones in mind, especially if you're trying to hit business hours. The countries covered in this book are six/nine hours ahead of the East/West Coasts of the US, except for England. England, which is one hour earlier than most of continental Europe, is five/eight hours ahead of the East/West Coasts of the US. For an online converter, see Timeanddate.com/worldclock.

Country	Country Code	Country	Country Code
Austria	43	Hungary	36
Belgium	32	Ireland/N Ireland	353/44
Croatia	385	Italy	39
Czech Republic	420	Netherlands	31
Denmark	45	Norway	47
England	44	Portugal	351
France	33	Scotland	44
Germany	49	Spain	34
Greece	30	Switzerland	41

Using a European SIM Card

With a European SIM card, you get a European mobile number and access to cheaper rates than you'll get through your US carrier. This option works well for those who want to make a lot of voice calls or need faster connection speeds than their US carrier provides. Fit the SIM card into a cheap phone you buy in Europe, or swap out the SIM card in an "unlocked" US phone.

SIM cards are sold at mobile-phone shops, department-store electronics counters, some newsstands, and vending machines. Costing about $5-10, they usually include prepaid calling/messaging credit, with no contract and no commitment. Expect to pay $20-40 more for a SIM card with a gigabyte of data. If you travel with this card to other countries in Europe, there may be extra roaming fees.

Without a Mobile Phone

Most **hotels** charge a fee for placing calls—ask for rates before you dial. You can use a prepaid international phone card (usually available at post offices, newsstands, tobacco shops, and train stations) to call out from your hotel.

You'll only see **public pay phones** in a few post offices and train stations. Most don't take coins but instead require insertable phone cards, which you can buy at a newsstand, convenience store, or post office. Except for emergencies, they're not worth the hassle.

Most hotels have **public computers** in their lobbies for guests to use; otherwise you may find them at public libraries (ask your hotelier or at the TI).

TRANSPORTATION

This section covers the basics on trains, buses, rental cars, and flights.

Trains

Considering the efficiency of Europe's trains (and buses), you'd never need to use a car. You can buy point-to-point tickets (either in advance or as you travel) or buy a rail pass.

High-speed, long-distance, international, and overnight trains are more likely to require **reservations.** If so, you automatically get reservations when you buy point-to-point tickets, but if you're using a rail pass, you'll need to make any required reservations yourself. You can reserve the more critical journeys from home (through RickSteves.com/rail); otherwise you can make them all at one time at any staffed station in Europe.

To check **train schedules** online, see Bahn.com (Germany's excellent Europe-wide timetable).

Tickets

Point-to-point tickets are just that: tickets bought individually to get you from Point A to Point B.

First Class vs. Second Class: On most trains in most countries, tickets in second class cost about a third less than those in first class. First-class cars are more spacious and less crowded than second class, but riding in second class gets you there at the same time, and with the same scenery.

Discount Fares: If you reserve a ticket on a fast train in advance and are comfortable committing to particular departure times, you can usually enjoy substantial savings over full-fare tickets. Discounted fares go on sale several months in advance and remain available until one day before departure—unless all the cheap seats sell out early (which often happens). Rules vary per country.

Savings on Slow Trains: You can save money on point-to-point tickets if you're willing to limit yourself to regional trains.

Buying Tickets: You can buy tickets directly at a **train station** at the counter or from machines. If lines are long at the station, it can be quicker to buy tickets from a **travel agency in town** (at a small fee, but less of a language barrier). Or you can buy tickets **online** in advance from the train

Point-to-Point Train Tickets: Cost & Time

First number between cities = Approximate cost in $US for a one-way, second-class ticket (for first-class fare, add 50 percent).

Second number = Number of hours the trip takes.

Important: Times and fares are for express trains where applicable.

company's website (Nationalrail.co.uk for Britain, Eurostar.com for the Chunnel linking England and France, Sncf.com for France, Bahn.com for Germany, Trenitalia.com for Italy, Ns.nl for the Netherlands, Sbb.ch for Switzerland, and hard-to-use Renfe.com for Spain).

If you must board a train without a ticket, find the **conductor** before he finds you (or he'll fine you) and ask to buy a ticket (you'll pay extra for this service).

Rail Passes

A rail pass covers train travel in one or more countries for a certain number of days (either a continuous span of days or a number of days spread over a wider window of time). Depending on how many trips you take, passes can offer a savings over regular point-to-point tickets.

Pass prices vary depending on the number of days and type of pass you choose, and discounts are offered for two or more people traveling together.

For a multicountry trip, a Eurail pass generally offers the best deal. For instance, the **Select Pass** covers travel in two, three, or four adjacent countries (e.g., Italy, Switzerland, France, and Germany) on four to 10 travel days within two months. The pricier **Global Pass** covers most of Europe (but not Great Britain), and allows for travel on five to 15 travel days spread out (5 or 7 days within one month, 10 or 15 days within two months), or for continuous periods lasting between 15 days and three months.

If you're taking just a couple of train rides, look into buying individual point-to-point tickets instead, which may save you money over a pass, particularly if you get an advance-purchase discount.

Rick Steves' GUIDE TO
Eurail Passes

How to choose and use the rail pass that
best fits your trip—and your budget

January
2018
Edition

Use the "Point-to-Point Train Tickets: Cost & Time" map in this chapter to add up approximate fares for your itinerary, and compare the total to the price of a rail pass. For prices, download my free guide to Eurail Passes (RickSteves.com/rail-guide). For advice on figuring out the smartest options for your train trip, visit RickSteves.com/rail. Rail passes are generally sold only outside Europe (through travel agents or Rick Steves' Europe).

Long-Distance Buses

While buses don't offer as extensive a network as trains, they do cover the most popular cities for travelers, quite often with direct connections. Bus tickets are sold on the spot (on board and/or at kiosks at some bus terminals), but because the cheapest fares often sell out, it's best to book online as soon as you're sure of your plans (at a minimum, book a few days ahead to nab the best prices).

Renting a Car

Research car rentals before you go. It's cheapest to arrange most car rentals from the US. Consider several companies to compare rates. Most of the major US rental agencies (including Avis, Budget, Enterprise, Hertz, and Thrifty) have

offices throughout Europe. The two major Europe-based agencies are Europcar and Sixt, and consolidators include Auto Europe/Kemwel (AutoEurope.com).

Always read the fine print carefully for add-on charges—such as one-way drop-off fees, airport surcharges, or mandatory insurance policies—that aren't included in the "total price."

For the best deal, rent by the week with unlimited mileage (though for longer trips, see "Leasing," later). I normally rent the smallest, least expensive model with a stick shift (generally cheaper than an automatic). If you need an automatic, request one in advance; be aware that these cars are usually larger models.

Figure on paying roughly $250 for a one-week rental for a basic compact car. Allow extra for supplemental insurance, fuel, tolls, and parking.

If you want to rent a car for only a couple of days to explore a region, you could work directly with a local rental company, reserving in advance by email or phone.

Picking Up Your Car: Compare pickup costs (downtown can be less expensive than the airport) and explore drop-off options. Always check the hours of the location you choose: Many rental offices close from midday Saturday until Monday morning and, in smaller towns, at lunchtime.

When you pick up the car, check it thoroughly. Rental agencies in Europe are very strict when it comes to charging for even minor damage, so make sure any damage is noted on your rental agreement. Before driving off, find out how your car's gearshift, lights, turn signals, wipers, radio, and fuel cap function, and know what kind of fuel the car takes (diesel vs. unleaded). When you return the car, make sure the agent verifies its condition with you. Some drivers take pictures of the returned vehicle as proof of its condition.

Car Insurance Options

When you rent a car, you are liable for a very high deductible, sometimes equal to the entire value of the car. Limit your financial risk with one of these three options:

• Buy Collision Damage Waiver (CDW) coverage with a low or zero deductible from the car-rental company.

• Get coverage through your credit card, which is free if your card automatically includes zero-deductible coverage. But in case of damage, it can be time-consuming to resolve the charges with your credit-card company. Before you decide on this option, quiz your credit-card company on how it works.

• Get collision insurance as part of a larger travel-insurance policy. If you're already purchasing a policy for your trip, adding collision coverage can be economical. Travel Guard is one of the companies that offers this add-on.

For **more on car-rental insurance,** see RickSteves.com/cdw.

Leasing

For trips of three weeks or more, consider leasing, which automatically includes zero-deductible collision and theft insurance. Leasing provides you a new car with unlimited mileage and a 24-hour emergency assistance program. You can lease for as little as 21 days to as long as 5.5 months. Cars can most easily be picked up and returned in France, but you can pick up or drop off in neighboring countries for a fee. Car leases must be arranged from the US. One of several companies offering affordable leasing is Auto Europe.

Driving

Be aware of typical European road rules; for example, some countries require headlights to be turned on at all times, and nearly all forbid handheld mobile-phone use. Seat belts are mandatory for all, and two beers under those belts are enough to land you in jail. You're required to use low-beam headlights if it's overcast, raining, or snowing. In Europe, you're not allowed to turn right on a red light, unless

a sign or signal specifically authorizes it, and on expressways it's illegal to pass drivers on the right.

Be warned that driving is restricted in many Italian city centers. If you drive in an area marked *Zona Traffico Limitato* (ZTL, often shown above a red circle), your license plate can be photographed and a hefty (€80-plus) fine mailed to your home without you ever being stopped by a cop.

You'll pay to use tollways in Italy, France, and Spain, and will need to buy a toll sticker if you enter Switzerland.

At self-service gas pumps and automated parking garages, your US credit and debit cards might not work. Carry cash to fuel your trip.

If you have questions about road rules, ask your car-rental company or check the US State Department website (Travel. State.gov, search for your country in the "Country Information" box, then click on "Travel & Transportation").

Flights

The best comparison search engine for both international and intra-European flights is Kayak.com. An alternative is Google Flights, which has an easy-to-use system to track prices. For inexpensive flights within Europe, try Skyscanner.com.

Flying to Europe: Start looking for international flights at least four to six months before your trip, especially for peak-season travel. Depending on your itinerary, it can be efficient to fly into one city and out of another.

Flying within Europe: If you're considering a train ride that's more than five hours long, a flight may save you both time and money. When comparing your options, factor in the time it takes to get to the airport and how early you'll need to arrive to check in.

These days you can fly within Europe on major airlines affordably for around $100 a flight. If you're using a budget carrier, be aware of the potential draw-

Resources from Rick Steves

My mobile-friendly **website** is *the* place to explore Europe. You'll find thousands of fun articles, videos, photos, and radio interviews; a wealth of money-saving tips for planning your dream trip; my travel talks and blog; and guidebook updates (RickSteves.com/update).

Our **Travel Forum** is an immense collection of message boards where our travel-savvy community answers questions and shares personal travel experiences—and our well-traveled staff chimes in when they can help.

Our **online Travel Store** offers bags and accessories designed to help you travel smarter and lighter. These include my popular bags (which I live out of four months a year), money belts, totes, toiletries kits, adapters, guidebooks, planning maps, and more.

Choosing the right **rail pass** for your trip can drive you nutty. Our website will help you find the perfect fit for your itinerary and your budget: We offer easy, one-stop shopping for rail passes, seat reservations, and point-to-point tickets.

Guidebooks, Shows, Audio Europe, and Tours

Books: *Rick Steves Best of Europe* is just one of many books in my series on European travel, which includes country and city guidebooks, Snapshot guides (excerpted chapters from my country guides), Pocket Guides (full-color little books on big cities), and my budget-travel skills handbook, *Rick Steves Europe Through the Back Door.* My phrase books are practical and budget-oriented. A more complete list of my titles appears near the end of this book.

TV Shows: My public television series, *Rick Steves' Europe,* covers Europe from top to bottom with over 100 half-hour episodes. To watch full episodes online for free, see RickSteves.com/tv. Or to raise your travel I.Q. with video versions of our popular **classes** (including my talks on travel skills, packing smart, most European countries, and European art), see RickSteves.com/travel-talks.

Audio: My weekly public radio show, *Travel with Rick Steves,* features interviews with travel experts from around the world. A complete archive is available at RickSteves.com/radio, and much of this audio content is available for free, along with my audio tours of Europe's top sights, through my **Rick Steves Audio Europe** app (see page 17).

Small-Group Tours: Want to travel with greater efficiency and less stress? We organize tours with more than three dozen itineraries reaching the best destinations in this book...and beyond. You'll enjoy great guides and a fun but small group of travel partners. For all the details, and to get our tour catalog, visit RickSteves.com or call us at 425/608-4217.

backs and restrictions: nonrefundable and nonchangeable tickets, minimal or nonexistent customer service, pricey and time-consuming treks to secondary airports, and stingy baggage allowances with steep overage fees. To avoid unpleasant surprises, read the small print before you book.

CONVERSIONS

Numbers and Stumblers

- Europeans write a few of their numbers differently than we do: 1 = 1, 4 = 4, 7 = 7.
- In Europe, dates appear as day/month/year; Christmas is 25/12.
- Commas are decimal points and decimals are commas. A dollar and a half is $1,50. One thousand is 1.000.
- When counting with fingers, start with your thumb. If you hold up your first finger to request one item, you'll probably get two.
- What Americans call the second floor of a building is the first floor in Europe.
- On escalators and moving sidewalks, Europeans keep the left "lane" open for passing. Keep to the right.

Clothing and Shoe Sizes

Shoppers can use these US-to-European comparisons as general guidelines, but note that no conversion is perfect.

Women: For clothing or shoe sizes, add 30-32 (US shirt size 10 = European size 40 or 42, depending on the country; US shoe size 8 = European size 38-39).

Men: For shirts, multiply by 2 and add about 8 (US size 15 = European size 38). For jackets and suits, add 10. For shoes, add 32-34.

Children: Clothing is sized by height—in centimeters (2.5 inches = 1 cm), so a US size 8 roughly equates to 132-140. For shoes up to size 13, add 16-18, and for sizes 1 and up, add 30-32.

Metric Conversions

A **kilogram** equals 1,000 grams and about 2.2 pounds. One hundred **grams** (a common unit at markets) is about a quarter-pound.

One **liter** is about a quart, or almost four to a gallon.

A **kilometer** is six-tenths of a mile. To convert kilometers to miles, cut the kilometers in half and add back 10 percent of the original (120 km: 60 + 12 = 72 miles). One **meter** is 39 inches—just over a yard.

Using the **Celsius** scale, 0°C equals 32°F. To roughly convert Celsius to Fahrenheit, double the number and add 30. For weather, 28°C is 82°F—perfect. For health, 37°C is just right. At a launderette, 30°C is cold, 40°C is warm (default setting), and 60°C is hot.

Packing Checklist

Whether you're traveling for five days or five weeks, you won't need more than this. Pack light to enjoy the sweet freedom of true mobility.

Clothing

- ❑ 5 shirts: long- & short-sleeve
- ❑ 2 pairs pants (or shirts/capris)
- ❑ 1 pair shorts
- ❑ 5 pairs underwear & socks
- ❑ 1 pair walking shoes
- ❑ Sweater or warm layer
- ❑ Rainproof jacket with hood
- ❑ Tie, scarf, belt, and/or hat
- ❑ Swimsuit
- ❑ Sleepwear/loungewear

Money

- ❑ Debit card(s)
- ❑ Credit card(s)
- ❑ Hard cash (US $100-200)
- ❑ Money belt

Documents & Travel Info

- ❑ Passport
- ❑ Ticket & confirmations: flights, hotels, trains, rail pass, car rental, sight entries
- ❑ Driver's license
- ❑ Student ID, hostel card, etc.
- ❑ Photocopies of important documents
- ❑ Insurance details
- ❑ Guidebooks & maps

Toiletries Kit

- ❑ Basics: soap, shampoo, toothbrush, toothpaste, floss, deodorant, sunscreen, brush/comb, etc.
- ❑ Medicines & vitamins
- ❑ First-aid kit
- ❑ Glasses/contacts/sunglasses (with prescriptions)
- ❑ Sewing kit

- ❑ Packet of tissues (for WC)
- ❑ Earplugs

Electronics

- ❑ Mobile phone
- ❑ Camera & related gear
- ❑ Tablet/ebook reader/laptop
- ❑ Headphones/earbuds
- ❑ Chargers & batteries
- ❑ Phone car charger & mount (or GPS device)
- ❑ Plug adapters

Miscellaneous

- ❑ Daypack
- ❑ Sealable plastic baggies
- ❑ Laundry supplies: soap, laundry bag, clothesline, spot remover
- ❑ Small umbrella
- ❑ Travel alarm/watch
- ❑ Notepad & pen
- ❑ Journal

Optional Extras

- ❑ Second pair of shoes (flip-flops, sandals, tennis shoes, boots)
- ❑ Travel hairdryer
- ❑ Picnic supplies
- ❑ Water bottle
- ❑ Fold-up tote bag
- ❑ Small flashlight
- ❑ Mini binoculars
- ❑ Small towel or washcloth
- ❑ Inflatable pillow/neck rest
- ❑ Tiny lock
- ❑ Address list (to mail postcards)
- ❑ Extra passport photos

French Survival Phrases

When using the phonetics, try to nasalize the n sound.

English	French	Pronunciation
Good day.	Bonjour.	bohn-zhoor
Mrs. / Mr.	Madame / Monsieur	mah-dahm / muhs-yur
Do you speak English?	Parlez-vous anglais?	par-lay-voo ahn-glay
Yes. / No.	Oui. / Non.	wee / nohn
I understand.	Je comprends.	zhuh kohn-prahn
I don't understand.	Je ne comprends pas.	zhuh nuh kohn-prahn pah
Please.	S'il vous plaît.	see voo play
Thank you.	Merci.	mehr-see
I'm sorry.	Désolé.	day-zoh-lay
Excuse me.	Pardon.	par-dohn
(No) problem.	(Pas de) problème.	(pah duh) proh-blehm
It's good.	C'est bon.	say bohn
Goodbye.	Au revoir.	oh vwahr
one / two	un / deux	uhn / duh
three / four	trois / quatre	twah / kah-truh
five / six	cinq / six	sank / sees
seven / eight	sept / huit	seht / weet
nine / ten	neuf / dix	nuhf / dees
How much is it?	Combien?	kohn-bee-an
Write it?	Ecrivez?	ay-kree-vay
Is it free?	C'est gratuit?	say grah-twee
Included?	Inclus?	an-klew
Where can I buy / find...?	Où puis-je acheter / trouver...?	oo pwee-zhuh ah-shuh-tay / troo-vay
I'd like / We'd like...	Je voudrais / Nous voudrions...	zhuh voo-dray / noo voo-dree-ohn
...a room.	...une chambre.	ewn shahn-bruh
...a ticket to ____.	...un billet pour ____.	uhn bee-yay poor ____
Is it possible?	C'est possible?	say poh-see-bluh
Where is...?	Où est...?	oo ay
...the train station	...la gare	lah gar
...the bus station	...la gare routière	lah gar root-yehr
...tourist information	...l'office du tourisme	loh-fees dew too-reez-muh
Where are the toilets?	Où sont les toilettes?	oo sohn lay twah-leht
men	hommes	ohm
women	dames	dahm
left / right	à gauche / à droite	ah gohsh / ah dwaht
straight	tout droit	too dwah
When does this open / close?	Ça ouvre / ferme à quelle heure?	sah oo-vruh / fehrm ah kehl ur
At what time?	À quelle heure?	ah kehl ur
Just a moment.	Un moment.	uhn moh-mahn
now / soon / later	maintenant / bientôt / plus tard	man-tuh-nahn / bee-an-toh / plew tar
today / tomorrow	aujourd'hui / demain	oh-zhoor-dwee / duh-man

For more user-friendly French phrases, check out *Rick Steves' French Phrase Book and Dictionary* or *Rick Steves' French, Italian & German Phrase Book*.

In a French Restaurant

English	French	Pronunciation
I'd like / We'd like...	Je voudrais / Nous voudrions...	zhuh voo-dray / noo voo-dree-oh<u>n</u>
...to reserve...	...réserver...	ray-zehr-vay
...a table for one / two.	...une table pour un / deux.	ewn tah-bluh poor uh<u>n</u> / duh
Is this seat free?	C'est libre?	say lee-bruh
The menu (in English), please.	La carte (en anglais), s'il vous plaît.	lah kart (ah<u>n</u> ah<u>n</u>-glay) see voo play
service (not) included	service (non) compris	sehr-vees (noh<u>n</u>) koh<u>n</u>-pree
to go	à emporter	ah ah<u>n</u>-por-tay
with / without	avec / sans	ah-vehk / sah<u>n</u>
and / or	et / ou	ay / oo
special of the day	plat du jour	plah dew zhoor
specialty of the house	spécialité de la maison	spay-see-ah-lee-tay duh lah may-zoh<u>n</u>
appetizers	hors d'oeuvre	or duh-vruh
first course (soup, salad)	entrée	ah<u>n</u>-tray
main course (meat, fish)	plat principal	plah pra<u>n</u>-see-pahl
bread	pain	pa<u>n</u>
cheese	fromage	froh-mahzh
sandwich	sandwich	sah<u>n</u>d-weech
soup	soupe	soop
salad	salade	sah-lahd
meat	viande	vee-ah<u>n</u>d
chicken	poulet	poo-lay
fish	poisson	pwah-soh<u>n</u>
seafood	fruits de mer	frwee duh mehr
fruit	fruit	frwee
vegetables	légumes	lay-gewm
dessert	dessert	day-sehr
mineral water	eau minérale	oh mee-nay-rahl
tap water	l'eau du robinet	loh dew roh-bee-nay
milk	lait	lay
(orange) juice	jus (d'orange)	zhew (doh-rah<u>n</u>zh)
coffee / tea	café / thé	kah-fay / tay
wine	vin	va<u>n</u>
red / white	rouge / blanc	roozh / blah<u>n</u>
glass / bottle	verre / bouteille	vehr / boo-tay
beer	bière	bee-ehr
Cheers!	Santé!	sah<u>n</u>-tay
More. / Another.	Plus. / Un autre.	plew / uh<u>n</u> oh-truh
The same.	La même chose.	lah mehm shohz
The bill, please.	L'addition, s'il vous plaît.	lah-dee-see-oh<u>n</u> see voo play
Do you accept credit cards?	Vous prenez les cartes?	voo pruh-nay lay kart
tip	pourboire	poor-bwahr
Delicious!	Délicieux!	day-lee-see-uh

Spanish Survival Phrases

Spanish has a guttural sound similar to the J in Baja California. In the phonetics, the symbol for this clearing-your-throat sound is the italicized h.

English	Spanish	Pronunciation
Good day.	Buenos días.	**bway**-nohs **dee**-ahs
Do you speak English?	¿Habla Usted inglés?	**ah**-blah oo-**stehd** een-**glays**
Yes. / No.	Sí. / No.	see / noh
I (don't) understand.	(No) comprendo.	(noh) kohm-**prehn**-doh
Please.	Por favor.	por fah-**bor**
Thank you.	Gracias.	**grah**-thee-ahs
I'm sorry.	Lo siento.	loh see-**ehn**-toh
Excuse me.	Perdóneme.	pehr-**doh**-nay-may
(No) problem.	(No) problema.	(noh) proh-**blay**-mah
Good.	Bueno.	**bway**-noh
Goodbye.	Adiós.	ah-dee-**ohs**
one / two	uno / dos	**oo**-noh / dohs
three / four	tres / cuatro	trays / **kwah**-troh
five / six	cinco / seis	**theen**-koh / says
seven / eight	siete / ocho	see-**eh**-tay / **oh**-choh
nine / ten	nueve / diez	**nway**-bay / dee-**ayth**
How much is it?	¿Cuánto cuesta?	**kwahn**-toh **kway**-stah
Write it?	¿Me lo escribe?	may loh ay-**skree**-bay
Is it free?	¿Es gratis?	ays **grah**-tees
Is it included?	¿Está incluido?	ay-**stah** een-kloo-**ee**-doh
Where can I buy / find...?	¿Dónde puedo comprar / encontrar...?	**dohn**-day **pway**-doh kohm-**prar** / ayn-kohn-**trar**
I'd like / We'd like...	Quiero / Queremos...	kee-**ehr**-oh / kehr-**ay**-mohs
...a room.	...una habitación.	**oo**-nah ah-bee-tah-thee-**ohn**
...a ticket to _____.	...un billete para _____.	oon bee-**yeh**-tay **pah**-rah _____
Is it possible?	¿Es posible?	ays poh-**see**-blay
Where is...?	¿Dónde está...?	**dohn**-day ay-**stah**
...the train station	...la estación de trenes	lah ay-stah-thee-**ohn** day **tray**-nays
...the bus station	...la estación de autobuses	lah ay-stah-thee-**ohn** day ow-toh-**boo**-says
...the tourist information office	...la oficina de turismo	lah oh-fee-**thee**-nah day too-**rees**-moh
Where are the toilets?	¿Dónde están los servicios?	**dohn**-day ay-**stahn** lohs sehr-**bee**-thee-ohs
men	hombres, caballeros	**ohm**-brays, kah-bah-**yay**-rohs
women	mujeres, damas	moo-**heh**-rays, **dah**-mahs
left / right	izquierda / derecha	eeth-kee-**ehr**-dah / day-**ray**-chah
straight	derecho	day-**ray**-choh
When do you open / close?	¿A qué hora abren / cierran?	ah kay **oh**-rah **ah**-brehn / thee-**ay**-rahn
At what time?	¿A qué hora?	ah kay **oh**-rah
Just a moment.	Un momento.	oon moh-**mehn**-toh
now / soon / later	ahora / pronto / más tarde	ah-**oh**-rah / **prohn**-toh / mahs **tar**-day
today / tomorrow	hoy / mañana	oy / mahn-**yah**-nah

In a Spanish Restaurant

English	Spanish	Pronunciation
I'd like / We'd like...	Quiero / Queremos...	kee-**ehr**-oh / kehr-**ay**-mohs
...to reserve...	...reservar...	ray-sehr-**bar**
...a table for one / two.	...una mesa para uno / dos.	**oo**-nah **may**-sah **pah**-rah **oo**-noh / dohs
Nonsmoking.	No fumador.	noh foo-mah-**dohr**
Is this table free?	¿Está esta mesa libre?	ay-**stah** ay-stah **may**-sah **lee**-bray
The menu (in English), please.	La carta (en inglés), por favor.	lah **kar**-tah (ayn een-**glays**) por fah-**bor**
service (not) included	servicio (no) incluido	sehr-**bee**-thee-oh (noh) een-kloo-**ee**-doh
cover charge	precio de entrada	**pray**-thee-oh day ayn-**trah**-dah
to go	para llevar	**pah**-rah yay-**bar**
with / without	con / sin	kohn / seen
and / or	y / o	ee / oh
menu (of the day)	menú (del día)	may-**noo** (dayl **dee**-ah)
specialty of the house	especialidad de la casa	ay-spay-thee-ah-lee-**dahd** day lah **kah**-sah
tourist menu	menú turístico	meh-**noo** too-**ree**-stee-koh
combination plate	plato combinado	**plah**-toh kohm-bee-**nah**-doh
appetizers	tapas	**tah**-pahs
bread	pan	pahn
cheese	queso	**kay**-soh
sandwich	bocadillo	boh-kah-**dee**-yoh
soup	sopa	**soh**-pah
salad	ensalada	ayn-sah-**lah**-dah
meat	carne	**kar**-nay
poultry	aves	**ah**-bays
fish	pescado	pay-**skah**-doh
seafood	marisco	mah-**ree**-skoh
fruit	fruta	**froo**-tah
vegetables	verduras	behr-**doo**-rahs
dessert	postres	**poh**-strays
tap water	agua del grifo	**ah**-gwah dayl **gree**-foh
mineral water	agua mineral	**ah**-gwah mee-nay-**rahl**
milk	leche	**lay**-chay
(orange) juice	zumo (de naranja)	**thoo**-moh (day nah-**rahn**-hah)
coffee	café	kah-**feh**
tea	té	tay
wine	vino	**bee**-noh
red / white	tinto / blanco	**teen**-toh / **blahn**-koh
glass / bottle	vaso / botella	**bah**-soh / boh-**tay**-yah
beer	cerveza	thehr-**bay**-thah
Cheers!	¡Salud!	sah-**lood**
More. / Another.	Más. / Otro.	mahs / **oh**-troh
The same.	El mismo.	ehl **mees**-moh
The bill, please.	La cuenta, por favor.	lah **kwayn**-tah por fah-**bor**
tip	propina	proh-**pee**-nah
Delicious!	¡Delicioso!	day-lee-thee-**oh**-soh

Italian Survival Phrases

English	Italian	Pronunciation
Good day.	Buon giorno.	bwohn **jor**-noh
Do you speak English?	Parla inglese?	**par**-lah een-**gleh**-zay
Yes. / No.	Sì. / No.	see / noh
I (don't) understand.	(Non) capisco.	(nohn) kah-**pees**-koh
Please.	Per favore.	pehr fah-**voh**-ray
Thank you.	Grazie.	**graht**-see-ay
You're welcome.	Prego.	**preh**-go
I'm sorry.	Mi dispiace.	mee dee-spee-**ah**-chay
Excuse me.	Mi scusi.	mee **skoo**-zee
(No) problem.	(Non) c'è un problema.	(nohn) cheh oon proh-**bleh**-mah
Good.	Va bene.	vah **beh**-nay
Goodbye.	Arrivederci.	ah-ree-veh-**dehr**-chee
one / two	uno / due	**oo**-noh / **doo**-ay
three / four	tre / quattro	tray / **kwah**-troh
five / six	cinque / sei	**cheeng**-kway / **seh**-ee
seven / eight	sette / otto	**seh**-tay / **oh**-toh
nine / ten	nove / dieci	**noh**-vay / dee-**ay**-chee
How much is it?	Quanto costa?	**kwahn**-toh **koh**-stah
Write it?	Me lo scrive?	may loh **skree**-vay
Is it free?	È gratis?	eh **grah**-tees
Is it included?	È incluso?	eh een-**kloo**-zoh
Where can I buy / find...?	Dove posso comprare / trovare...?	**doh**-vay **poh**-soh kohm-**prah**-ray / troh-**vah**-ray
I'd like / We'd like...	Vorrei / Vorremmo...	voh-**reh**-ee / voh-**reh**-moh
...a room.	...una camera.	**oo**-nah **kah**-meh-rah
...a ticket to _____.	...un biglietto per _____.	oon beel-**yeh**-toh pehr _____
Is it possible?	È possibile?	eh poh-**see**-bee-lay
Where is...?	Dov'è...?	doh-**veh**
...the train station	...la stazione	lah staht-see-**oh**-nay
...the bus station	...la stazione degli autobus	lah staht-see-**oh**-nay **dehl**-yee **ow**-toh-boos
...tourist information	...informazioni per turisti	een-for-maht-see-**oh**-nee pehr too-**ree**-stee
...the toilet	...la toilette	lah twah-**leh**-tay
men	uomini / signori	**woh**-mee-nee / seen-**yoh**-ree
women	donne / signore	**doh**-nay / seen-**yoh**-ray
left / right	sinistra / destra	see-**nee**-strah / **deh**-strah
straight	sempre dritto	**sehm**-pray **dree**-toh
What time does this open / close?	A che ora apre / chiude?	ah kay **oh**-rah ah-**pray** / kee-**oo**-day
At what time?	A che ora?	ah kay **oh**-rah
Just a moment.	Un momento.	oon moh-**mehn**-toh
now / soon / later	adesso / presto / tardi	ah-**deh**-soh / **preh**-stoh / **tar**-dee
today / tomorrow	oggi / domani	**oh**-jee / doh-**mah**-nee

In an Italian Restaurant

English	Italian	Pronunciation
I'd like...	Vorrei...	voh-**reh**-ee
We'd like...	Vorremmo...	vor-**reh**-moh
...to reserve...	...prenotare...	preh-noh-**tah**-ray
...a table for one / two.	...un tavolo per uno / due.	oon **tah**-voh-loh pehr **oo**-noh / **doo**-ay
Is this seat free?	È libero questo posto?	eh **lee**-beh-roh **kweh**-stoh **poh**-stoh
The menu (in English), please.	Il menù (in inglese), per favore.	eel meh-**noo** (een een-**gleh**-zay) pehr fah-**voh**-ray
service (not) included	servizio (non) incluso	sehr-**veet**-see-oh (nohn) een-**kloo**-zoh
cover charge	pane e coperto	**pah**-nay ay koh-**pehr**-toh
to go	da portar via	dah **por**-tar **vee**-ah
with / without	con / senza	kohn / **sehnt**-sah
and / or	e / o	ay / oh
menu (of the day)	menù (del giorno)	meh-**noo** (dehl **jor**-noh)
specialty of the house	specialità della casa	speh-chah-lee-**tah deh**-lah **kah**-zah
first course (pasta, soup)	primo piatto	**pree**-moh pee-**ah**-toh
main course (meat, fish)	secondo piatto	seh-**kohn**-doh pee-**ah**-toh
side dishes	contorni	kohn-**tor**-nee
bread	pane	**pah**-nay
cheese	formaggio	for-**mah**-joh
sandwich	panino	pah-**nee**-noh
soup	zuppa	**tsoo**-pah
salad	insalata	een-sah-**lah**-tah
meat	carne	**kar**-nay
chicken	pollo	**poh**-loh
fish	pesce	**peh**-shay
seafood	frutti di mare	**froo**-tee dee **mah**-ray
fruit / vegetables	frutta / legumi	**froo**-tah / lay-**goo**-mee
dessert	dolce	**dohl**-chay
tap water	acqua del rubinetto	**ah**-kwah dehl roo-bee-**neh**-toh
mineral water	acqua minerale	**ah**-kwah mee-neh-**rah**-lay
milk	latte	**lah**-tay
(orange) juice	succo (d'arancia)	**soo**-koh (dah-**rahn**-chah)
coffee / tea	caffè / tè	kah-**feh** / teh
wine	vino	**vee**-noh
red / white	rosso / bianco	**roh**-soh / bee-**ahn**-koh
glass / bottle	bicchiere / bottiglia	bee-kee-**eh**-ray / boh-**teel**-yah
beer	birra	**bee**-rah
Cheers!	Cin cin!	cheen cheen
More. / Another.	Di più. / Un altro.	dee pew / oon **ahl**-troh
The same.	Lo stesso.	loh **steh**-soh
The bill, please.	Il conto, per favore.	eel **kohn**-toh pehr fah-**voh**-ray
Do you accept credit cards?	Accettate carte di credito?	ah-cheh-**tah**-tay **kar**-tay dee **kreh**-dee-toh
tip	mancia	**mahn**-chah
Delicious!	Delizioso!	day-leet-see-**oh**-zoh

For more user-friendly Italian phrases, check out *Rick Steves' Italian Phrase Book & Dictionary* or *Rick Steves' French, Italian, and German Phrase Book*.

German Survival Phrases

When using the phonetics, pronounce ī like the long *i* in "light." Bolded syllables are stressed.

English	German	Pronunciation
Good day.	Guten Tag.	**goo**-tehn tahg
Do you speak English?	Sprechen Sie Englisch?	**shprehkh**-ehn zee **ehgn**-lish
Yes. / No.	Ja. / Nein.	yah / nīn
I (don't) understand.	Ich verstehe (nicht).	ikh fehr-**shtay**-heh (nikht)
Please.	Bitte.	**bit**-teh
Thank you.	Danke.	**dahng**-keh
I'm sorry.	Es tut mir leid.	ehs toot meer līt
Excuse me.	Entschuldigung.	ehnt-**shool**-dig-oong
(No) problem.	(Kein) Problem.	(kīn) proh-**blaym**
(Very) good.	(Sehr) gut.	(zehr) goot
Goodbye.	Auf Wiedersehen.	owf **vee**-der-zayn
one / two	eins / zwei	īns / tsvī
three / four	drei / vier	drī / feer
five / six	fünf / sechs	fewnf / zehkhs
seven / eight	sieben / acht	**zee**-behn / ahkht
nine / ten	neun / zehn	noyn / tsayn
How much is it?	Wieviel kostet das?	**vee**-feel **kohs**-teht dahs
Write it?	Schreiben?	**shrī**-behn
Is it free?	Ist es umsonst?	ist ehs oom-**zohnst**
Included?	Inklusive?	in-kloo-**zee**-veh
Where can I buy / find...?	Wo kann ich kaufen / finden...?	voh kahn ikh **kow**-fehn / **fin**-dehn
I'd like / We'd like...	Ich hätte gern / Wir hätten gern...	ikh **heh**-teh gehrn / veer **heh**-tehn gehrn
...a room.	...ein Zimmer.	īn **tsim**-mer
...a ticket to _____.	...eine Fahrkarte nach _____.	**ī**-neh **far**-kar-teh nahkh
Is it possible?	Ist es möglich?	ist ehs **mur**-glikh
Where is...?	Wo ist...?	voh ist
...the train station	...der Bahnhof	dehr **bahn**-hohf
...the bus station	...der Busbahnhof	dehr **boos**-bahn-hohf
...the tourist information office	...das Touristen-informations-büro	dahs too-**ris**-tehn-in-for-maht-see-**ohns**-**bew**-roh
...the toilet	...die Toilette	dee toh-**leh**-teh
men	Herren	**hehr**-rehn
women	Damen	**dah**-mehn
left / right	links / rechts	links / rehkhts
straight	geradeaus	geh-**rah**-deh-**ows**
What time does this open / close?	Um wieviel Uhr wird hier geöffnet / geschlossen?	oom **vee**-feel oor veerd heer geh-**urf**-neht / geh-**shloh**-sehn
At what time?	Um wieviel Uhr?	oom **vee**-feel oor
Just a moment.	Moment.	moh-**mehnt**
now / soon / later	jetzt / bald / später	yehtst / bahld / **shpay**-ter
today / tomorrow	heute / morgen	**hoy**-teh / **mor**-gehn

In a German Restaurant

English	German	Pronunciation
I'd like / We'd like...	Ich hätte gern / Wir hätten gern...	ikh **heh**-teh gehrn / veer **heh**-tehn gehrn
...a reservation for...	...eine Reservierung für...	**ī**-neh reh-zer-**feer**-oong fewr
...a table for one / two.	...einen Tisch für eine Person / zwei Personen.	**ī**-nehn tish fewr **ī**-neh pehr-zohn / tsvī pehr-**zoh**-nehn
Nonsmoking.	Nichtraucher.	**nikht**-rowkh-er
Is this seat free?	Ist hier frei?	ist heer frī
Menu (in English), please.	Speisekarte (auf Englisch), bitte.	**shpī**-zeh-kar-teh (owf **ehng**-lish) **bit**-teh
service (not) included	Trinkgeld (nicht) inklusive	**trink**-gehlt (nikht) in-kloo-**zee**-veh
cover charge	Eintritt	**īn**-trit
to go	zum Mitnehmen	tsoom **mit**-nay-mehn
with / without	mit / ohne	mit / **oh**-neh
and / or	und / oder	oont / **oh**-der
menu (of the day)	(Tages-) Karte	(**tah**-gehs-) **kar**-teh
set meal for tourists	Touristenmenü	too-**ris**-tehn-meh-**new**
specialty of the house	Spezialität des Hauses	**shpayt**-see-ah-lee-**tayt** dehs **how**-zehs
appetizers	Vorspeise	**for**-shpī-zeh
bread / cheese	Brot / Käse	broht / **kay**-zeh
sandwich	Sandwich	**zahnd**-vich
soup	Suppe	**zup**-peh
salad	Salat	zah-**laht**
meat	Fleisch	flīsh
poultry	Geflügel	geh-**flew**-gehl
fish	Fisch	fish
seafood	Meeresfrüchte	**meh**-rehs-**frewkh**-teh
fruit	Obst	ohpst
vegetables	Gemüse	geh-**mew**-zeh
dessert	Nachspeise	**nahkh**-shpī-zeh
mineral water	Mineralwasser	min-eh-**rahl**-vah-ser
tap water	Leitungswasser	**lī**-toongs-vah-ser
milk	Milch	milkh
(orange) juice	(Orangen-) Saft	(oh-**rahn**-zhehn-) zahft
coffee / tea	Kaffee / Tee	kah-**fay** / tay
wine	Wein	vīn
red / white	rot / weiß	roht / vīs
glass / bottle	Glas / Flasche	glahs / **flah**-sheh
beer	Bier	beer
Cheers!	Prost!	prohst
More. / Another.	Mehr. / Noch eins.	mehr / nohkh īns
The same.	Das gleiche.	dahs **glīkh**-eh
Bill, please.	Rechnung, bitte.	**rehkh**-noong **bit**-teh
tip	Trinkgeld	**trink**-gehlt
Delicious!	Lecker!	**lehk**-er

For more user-friendly German phrases, check out *Rick Steves' German Phrase Book and Dictionary* or *Rick Steves' French, Italian & German Phrase Book*.

Dutch Survival Phrases

Most people speak English, but if you learn the pleasantries and key phrases, you'll connect better with the locals. To pronounce the guttural Dutch "g" (indicated in phonetics by *h*), make a clear-your-throat sound, similar to the "ch" in the Scottish word "loch."

English	Dutch	Pronunciation
Hello.	*Hallo.*	**hah**-loh
Good day.	*Dag.*	dah
Good morning.	*Goedemorgen.*	**hoo**-deh-mor-hehn
Good afternoon.	*Goedemiddag.*	**hoo**-deh-mid-dah
Good evening.	*Goedenavond.*	**hoo**-dehn-ah-fohnd
Do you speak English?	*Spreekt u Engels?*	shpraykt oo **eng**-ehls
Yes. / No.	*Ja. / Nee.*	yah / nay
I (don't) understand.	*Ik begrijp (het niet).*	ik beh-**hripe** (heht neet)
Please. (can also mean "You're welcome")	*Alstublieft.*	**ahl**-stoo-bleeft
Thank you.	*Dank u wel.*	dahnk oo vehl
I'm sorry.	*Het spijt me.*	heht spite meh
Excuse me.	*Pardon.*	**par**-dohn
(No) problem.	*(Geen) probleem.*	(hayn) **proh**-blaym
Good.	*Goede.*	**hoo**-deh
Goodbye.	*Tot ziens.*	toht zeens
one / two	*een / twee*	ayn / t'vay
three / four	*drie / vier*	dree / feer
five / six	*vijf / zes*	fife / zehs
seven / eight	*zeven / acht*	**zay**-fehn / aht
nine / ten	*negen / tien*	**nay**-hehn / teen
What does it cost?	*Wat kost het?*	vaht kohst heht
Is it free?	*Is het vrij?*	is heht fry
Is it included?	*Is het inclusief?*	is heht in-**kloo**-seev
Can you please help me?	*Kunt u alstublieft helpen?*	koont oo **ahl**-stoo-bleeft **hehl**-pehn
Where can I buy / find...?	*Waar kan ik kopen / vinden...?*	var kahn ik **koh**-pehn / **fin**-dehn
I'd like / We'd like...	*Ik wil graag / Wij willen graag...*	ik vil hrah / vy **vil**-lehn hrah
...a room.	*...een kamer.*	ayn **kah**-mer
...a train / bus ticket to	*...een trein / bus kaartje naar*	ayn trayn / boos **kart**-yeh nar
...to rent a bike.	*...een fiets huren.*	ayn feets **hoo**-rehn
Where is...?	*Waar is...?*	var is
...the train / bus station	*...het trein / bus station*	heht trayn / boos **staht**-see-ohn
...the tourist info office	*...de VVV*	deh fay fay fay
...the toilet	*...het toilet*	heht **twah**-leht
men / women	*mannen / vrouwen*	**mah**-nehn / **frow**-ehn
left / right	*links / rechts*	links / rehts
straight ahead	*rechtdoor*	**reht**-dor
What time does it open / close?	*Hoe laat gaat het open / dicht?*	hoo laht haht heht **oh**-pehn / diht
now / soon / later	*nu / straks / later*	noo / strahks / **lah**-ter
today / tomorrow	*vandaag / morgen*	**fahn**-dah / **mor**-hehn

In a Dutch Restaurant

The all-purpose Dutch word *alstublieft* (ahl-stoo-bleeft) means "please," but it can also mean "here you are" (when the server hands you something), "thanks" (when taking payment from you), or "you're welcome" (when handing you change). Here are other words that might come in handy at restaurants:

English	Dutch	Pronunciation
I'd like / We'd like...	*Ik wil graag / Wij willen graag...*	ik vil *hrah* / vy **vil**-lehn *hrah*
...a table for one / two.	*...een tafel voor een / twee.*	ayn **tah**-fehl for ayn / t'vay
...to reserve a table.	*...een tafel reserveren.*	ayn **tah**-fehl ray-zehr-feh-rehn
...the menu (in English).	*...het menu (in het Engels).*	heht meh-**noo** (in heht **eng**-ehls)
Is this table free?	*Is deze tafel vrij?*	is **day**-zeh **tah**-fehl fry
to go	*om mee te nemen*	ohm may teh **nay**-mehn
with / without	*met / zonder*	meht / **zohn**-der
and / or	*en / of*	ehn / of
special of the day	*dagschotel*	**dahs**-hoh-tehl
specialty of the house	*huisspecialiteit*	**hows**-shpeh-shah-lee-tite
breakfast	*ontbijt*	**ohnt**-bite
lunch	*middagmaal*	**mid**-dah-mahl
dinner	*avondmaal*	**ah**-fohnd-mahl
appetizers	*hapjes*	**hahp**-yehs
main courses	*hoofdgerechten*	**hohfd**-heh-reh-tehn
side dishes	*bijgerechten*	**bye**-heh-reh-tehn
bread / cheese	*brood / kaas*	brohd / kahs
sandwich	*sandwich*	**sand**-vich
soup / salad	*soep / sla*	soop / slah
meat / chicken / fish	*vlees / kip / vis*	flays / kip / fis
fruit / vegetables	*vrucht / groenten*	fruht / **hroon**-tehn
dessert / pastries	*gebak*	heh-**bahk**
I am vegetarian.	*Ik ben vegetarisch.*	ik behn vay-heh-**tah**-rish
mineral water / tap water	*mineraalwater / kraanwater*	min-eh-rahl-**vah**-ter / **krahn**-vah-ter
milk / (orange) juice	*melk / (sinaasappel) sap*	mehlk / **see**-nahs-ah-pehl (sahp)
coffee / tea	*koffie / thee*	**koh**-fee / tay
wine / beer	*wijn / bier*	vine / beer
red / white	*rode / witte*	**roh**-deh / **vit**-teh
glass / bottle	*glas / fles*	hlahs / flehs
Cheers!	*Proost!*	prohst
More. / Another.	*Meer. / Nog een.*	mayr / noh ayn
The same.	*Het zelfde.*	heht **zehlf**-deh
The bill, please.	*De rekening, alstublieft.*	deh **ray**-keh-neeng **ahl**-stoo-bleeft
Do you accept credit cards?	*Accepteert u kredietkaarten?*	**ahk**-shehp-tayrt oo kray-deet-**kar**-tehn
Is service included?	*Is bediening inbegrepen?*	is beh-**dee**-neeng in-beh-**hray**-pehn
tip	*fooi*	foy
Tasty.	*Lekker.*	**leh**-ker
Enjoy!	*Smakelijk!*	**smah**-keh-like

INDEX

INDEX

MAP INDEX

Our website enhances this book and turns

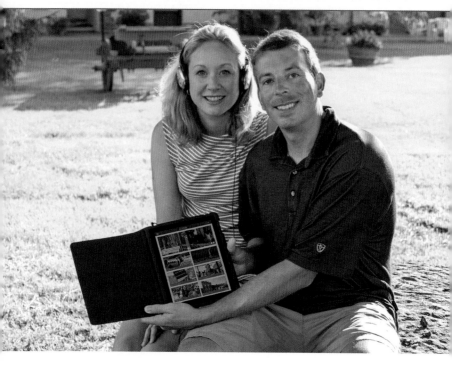

Explore Europe

At ricksteves.com you can browse through thousands of articles, videos, photos and radio interviews, plus find a wealth of money-saving travel tips for planning your dream trip. And with our mobile-friendly website, you can easily access all this great travel information anywhere you go.

TV Shows

Preview the places you'll visit by watching entire half-hour episodes of Rick Steves' Europe (choose from all 100 shows) on-demand, for free.

ricksteves.com

your travel dreams into affordable reality

Radio Interviews

Enjoy ready access to Rick's vast library of radio interviews covering travel tips and cultural insights that relate specifically to your Europe travel plans.

Travel Forums

Learn, ask, share! Our online community of savvy travelers is a great resource for first-time travelers to Europe, as well as seasoned pros. You'll find forums on each country, plus travel tips and restaurant/hotel reviews. You can even ask one of our well-traveled staff to chime in with an opinion.

Travel News

Subscribe to our free Travel News e-newsletter, and get monthly updates from Rick on what's happening in Europe.

Audio Europe™

Rick's Free Travel App

Get your FREE Rick Steves Audio Europe™ app to enjoy…

- Dozens of self-guided tours of Europe's top museums, sights and historic walks
- Hundreds of tracks filled with cultural insights and sightseeing tips from Rick's radio interviews
- All organized into handy geographic playlists
- For Apple and Android

With Rick whispering in your ear, Europe gets even better.

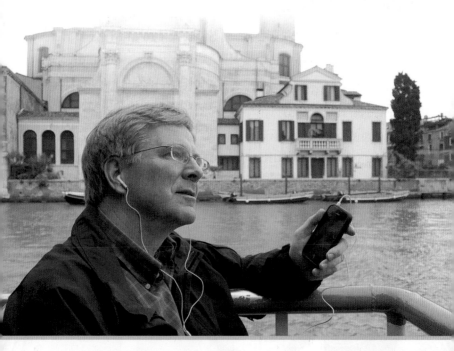

Find out more at ricksteves.com

Pack Light and Right

Gear up for your next adventure at ricksteves.com

Light Luggage

Pack light and right with Rick Steves' affordable, custom-designed rolling carry-on bags, backpacks, day packs and shoulder bags.

Accessories

From packing cubes to moneybelts and beyond, Rick has personally selected the travel goodies that will help your trip go smoother.

Shop at ricksteves.com

Rick Steves has

Experience maximum Europe

Save time and energy

This guidebook is your independent-travel toolkit. But for all it delivers, it's still up to you to devote the time and energy it takes to manage the preparation and logistics that are essential for a happy trip. If that's a hassle, there's a solution.

Rick Steves Tours

A Rick Steves tour takes you to Europe's most

great tours, too!

with minimum stress

interesting places with great guides and small groups of 28 or less. We follow Rick's favorite itineraries, ride in comfy buses, stay in family-run hotels, and bring you intimately close to the Europe you've traveled so far to see. Most importantly, we take away the logistical headaches so you can focus on the fun.

travelers—nearly half of them repeat customers— along with us on four dozen different itineraries, from Ireland to Italy to Athens.

Is a Rick Steves tour the right fit for your travel dreams? Find out at ricksteves.com, where you can also request Rick's latest tour catalog.

Join the fun

This year we'll take thousands of free-spirited

Europe is best experienced with happy travel partners. We hope you can join us.

See our itineraries at ricksteves.com

A Guide for Every Trip

BEST OF GUIDES

Full-color easy-to-scan format, focusing on Europe's most popular destinations and sights.

Best of England
Best of Europe
Best of France
Best of Germany
Best of Ireland
Best of Italy
Best of Spain

COMPREHENSIVE GUIDES

City, country, and regional guides with detailed coverage for a multi-week trip exploring the most iconic sights and venturing off the beaten track.

Amsterdam & the Netherlands
Barcelona
Belgium: Bruges, Brussels, Antwerp & Ghent
Berlin
Budapest
Croatia & Slovenia
Eastern Europe
England
Florence & Tuscany
France
Germany
Great Britain
Greece: Athens & the Peloponnese
Iceland
Ireland
Istanbul
Italy
London
Paris
Portugal
Prague & the Czech Republic
Provence & the French Riviera
Rome
Scandinavia
Scotland
Spain
Switzerland
Venice
Vienna, Salzburg & Tirol

THE BEST OF ROME

Rome, Italy's capital, is studded with Roman remnants and floodlit-fountain squares. From the Vatican to the Colosseum, with crazy traffic in between, Rome is wonderful, huge, and exhausting. The crowds, the heat, and the weighty history of the Eternal City where Caesars walked can make tourists wilt. Recharge by taking siestas, gelato breaks, and after-dark walks, strolling from one atmospheric square to another in the refreshing evening air.

...mired **Pantheon**—which ...rgest dome until the ...early 2,000 years old ...a day over 1,500).

...ol of Athens in the **Vat-**...bodies the humanistic ...sance.

...u, gladiators fought ...e another, entertaining ...0.

...his Rome **ristorante.**
...rds at **St. Peter's**
...k serious...

Rick Steves guidebooks are published by Avalon Travel, an imprint of Perseus Books, a Hachette Book Group company.

POCKET GUIDES

Compact, full-color city guides with the essentials for shorter trips.

Amsterdam
Athens
Barcelona
Florence
Italy's Cinque Terre
London

Munich & Salzburg
Paris
Prague
Rome
Venice
Vienna

SNAPSHOT GUIDES

Focused single-destination coverage.

Basque Country: Spain & France
Copenhagen & the Best of Denmark
Dublin
Dubrovnik
Edinburgh
Hill Towns of Central Italy
Krakow, Warsaw & Gdansk
Lisbon
Loire Valley
Madrid & Toledo
Milan & the Italian Lakes District
Naples & the Amalfi Coast
Normandy
Northern Ireland
Norway
Reykjavik
Sevilla, Granada & Southern Spain
St. Petersburg, Helsinki & Tallinn
Stockholm

Rick Steves books are available
from your favorite bookseller.
Many guides are available as ebooks.

CRUISE PORTS GUIDES

Reference for cruise ports of call.

Mediterranean Cruise Ports
Scandinavian & Northern European
Cruise Ports

Complete your library with...

TRAVEL SKILLS & CULTURE

Study up on travel skills before visiting "Europe through the back door" or gain insight on European history and culture.

Europe 101
European Christmas
European Easter
European Festivals
Europe Through the Back Door
Postcards from Europe
Travel as a Political Act

PHRASE BOOKS & DICTIONARIES

French
French, Italian & German
German
Italian
Portuguese
Spanish

PLANNING MAPS

Britain, Ireland & London
Europe
France & Paris
Germany, Austria & Switzerland
Ireland
Italy
Spain & Portugal

Be creative! You...
"Two, please,"
"Please, wher...
any language, espec...
want, such as the b...
please).

HELLOS
Pleasantrie...
Hello.
Do you speak
English?
Yes. / No.
I don't speak
French.
I'm sorry.
Please.
Thank you
much).
Excuse n
attentio
Excuse
OK?
OK. (It'
say it)
Good

PHOTO CREDITS

Avalon Travel
Hachette Book Group
1700 Fourth Street
Berkeley, CA 94710

Text © 2018 by Rick Steves' Europe, Inc. All rights reserved.
Maps © 2018 by Rick Steves' Europe, Inc. All rights reserved.
Paris Métro: Printed with permission from Agency Cartographique, property of the RATP.
London Underground: Printed with permission from Transport for London via Pulse Creative
Limited.

Printed in China by RR Donnelley, Shenzhen
First printing November 2018

ISBN 978-1-63121-803-3
Second Edition

For the latest on Rick's talks, guidebooks, Europe tours, public radio show, free audio tours, and
public television series, contact Rick Steves' Europe, 130 Fourth Avenue North, Edmonds, WA
98020, 425/771-8303, www.ricksteves.com, rick@ricksteves.com.

RICK STEVES' EUROPE
Special Publications Manager: Risa Laib
Managing Editor: Jennifer Madison Davis
Project Editor: Suzanne Kotz
Editorial & Production Assistant: Jessica Shaw
Graphic Content Director: Sandra Hundacker
Maps & Graphics: David C. Hoerlein, Mary Rostad

AVALON TRAVEL
Editorial Director: Kevin McLain
Senior Editor and Series Manager: Madhu Prasher
Editors: Jamie Andrade, Sierra Machado
Copy Editor: Maggie Ryan
Proofreader: Kelly Lydick
Indexer: Stephen Callahan
Interior Design: McGuire Barber Design
Interior Layout and Production: Tabitha Lahr
Cover Design: Kimberly Glyder Design
Maps & Graphics: Kat Bennett

COVER PHOTOS
Front Cover Photos: Top, from left: © Janoka82 | Dreamstime.com, © ruigsantos | Dreamstime.
com; © Douglas_freer | Dreamstime.com; Bottom: © Rudi1976 | Dreamstime.com
Back Cover Photos: from left: © Masterlu | Dreamstime.com; © Marinomarini | Dreamstime.
com; Tomas IIII © Dreamstime.com

Let's Keep on Travelin'

Your trip doesn't need to end.

Follow Rick on social media!